Contemporary
Literary Criticism

Guide to Gale Literary Criticism Series

When you need to review criticism of literary works, these are the Gale series to use:

If the author's death date is:	You should turn to:
After Dec. 31, 1959 (or author is still living)	**CONTEMPORARY LITERARY CRITICISM** for example: Jorge Luis Borges, Anthony Burgess, William Faulkner, Mary Gordon, Ernest Hemingway, Iris Murdoch
1900 through 1959	**TWENTIETH-CENTURY LITERARY CRITICISM** for example: Willa Cather, F. Scott Fitzgerald, Henry James, Mark Twain, Virginia Woolf
1800 through 1899	**NINETEENTH-CENTURY LITERATURE CRITICISM** for example: Fedor Dostoevski, Nathaniel Hawthorne, George Sand, William Wordsworth
1400 through 1799	**LITERATURE CRITICISM FROM 1400 TO 1800** *(excluding Shakespeare)* for example: Anne Bradstreet, Daniel Defoe, Alexander Pope, François Rabelais, Jonathan Swift, Phillis Wheatley **SHAKESPEAREAN CRITICISM** Shakespeare's plays and poetry
Antiquity through 1399	**CLASSICAL AND MEDIEVAL LITERATURE CRITICISM** for example: Dante, Homer, Plato, Sophocles, Vergil, the Beowulf Poet

---

Gale also publishes related criticism series:

CHILDREN'S LITERATURE REVIEW

This series covers authors of all eras who have written for the preschool through high school audience.

SHORT STORY CRITICISM

This series covers the major short fiction writers of all nationalities and periods of literary history.

ISSN 0091-3421

Volume 58

Contemporary Literary Criticism

Excerpts from Criticism of the
Works of Today's Novelists, Poets,
Playwrights, Short Story Writers, Scriptwriters,
and Other Creative Writers

Roger Matuz
EDITOR

Cathy Falk
Sean R. Pollock
David Segal
Bridget Travers
Robyn V. Young
ASSOCIATE EDITORS

 *Gale Research Inc.* • *DETROIT* • *NEW YORK*
WASHINGTON, D.C. • *CHICAGO* • *LONDON*

STAFF

Roger Matuz, *Editor*

Cathy Falk, Sean R. Pollock, David Segal, Bridget Travers, Robyn V. Young, *Associate Editors*

Mary K. Gillis, Susanne Skubik, *Assistant Editors*

Jeanne A. Gough, *Production & Permissions Manager*
Linda M. Pugliese, *Production Supervisor*
Jennifer Gale, David G. Oblender, Suzanne Powers, Maureen A. Puhl, Linda M. Ross, *Editorial Associates*
Donna Craft, *Editorial Assistant*

Victoria B. Cariappa, *Research Supervisor*
H. Nelson Fields, Judy L. Gale, Karen D. Kaus, Eric Priehs,
Maureen Richards, Mary D. Wise, *Editorial Associates*
Jill M. Ohorodnik, *Editorial Assistant*

Sandra C. Davis, *Permissions Supervisor (Text)*
Josephine M. Keene, Kimberly F. Smilay, *Permissions Associates*
Maria L. Franklin, Michele Lonoconus, Camille P. Robinson,
Shalice Shah, Denise M. Singleton, *Permissions Assistants*

Patricia A. Seefelt, *Permissions Supervisor (Pictures)*
Margaret A. Chamberlain, *Permissions Associate*
Pamela A. Hayes, Lillian Quickley, *Permissions Assistants*

Mary Beth Trimper, *Production Manager*
Marilyn Jackman, *External Production Assistant*

Art Chartow, *Art Director*
C. J. Jonik, *Keyliner*

Laura Bryant, *Production Supervisor*
Louise Gagné, *Internal Production Associate*

Copyright © 1990
Gale Research Inc.
835 Penobscot Bldg.
Detroit, MI 48226-4094

Library of Congress Catalog Card Number 76-38938
ISBN 0-8103-4432-7
ISSN 0091-3421

Printed in the United States of America

Published simultaneously in the United Kingdom
by Gale Research International Limited
(An affiliated company of Gale Research Inc.)

Contents

Preface   vii

Acknowledgments   xi

Authors Forthcoming in *CLC*   xvii

Preface

Literary criticism is, by definition, "the art of evaluating or analyzing with knowledge and propriety works of literature." The complexity and variety of contemporary literature makes the function of the critic especially important to today's reader. The critic assists the reader in identifying significant new writers, recognizing trends, understanding the importance and implications of particular works, and mastering new terminology. Until the publication of the first volume of *Contemporary Literary Criticism (CLC)* in 1973, there existed no ongoing digest monitoring scholarly and popular sources of critical opinion and explication. *CLC,* therefore, has fulfilled an essential need.

Scope of the Work

CLC presents significant passages from published criticism of works by today's creative writers. Each volume of *CLC* includes excerpted criticism on about thirty authors who are now living or who died after December 31, 1959. More than 2,000 authors have been included since the series began publication. Since many of the writers covered by *CLC* inspire continual critical commentary, authors frequently appear in more than one volume. There is, of course, no duplication of reprinted criticism.

Authors are selected for inclusion for a variety of reasons, among them the publication or dramatic production of a critically acclaimed new work, the reception of a major literary award, revival of interest in past writings, or the dramatization of a literary work as a film or television screenplay. For example, the present volume includes Alice Walker and Maxine Hong Kingston, whose recent novels, *The Temple of My Familiar* and *Tripmaster Monkey*, respectively, received much attention from critics and whose works are frequently discussed in Women's Studies courses; Harold Pinter, a major contemporary dramatist whose recent plays, *One for the Road* and *Mountain Language*, represent his deeper concern for political themes; and Václav Havel, a leading Czechoslovakian dramatist and dissident who endured years of harrassment and imprisonment by Communist officials before being elected President of his native land in 1989. Perhaps most importantly, works that frequently appear on the syllabuses of high school and college literature classes are represented by individual entries in *CLC; Lord of the Flies,* by William Golding, and *In Cold Blood,* by Truman Capote, are examples of works of this stature covered in the present volume. Attention is also given to several other groups of writers—authors of considerable public interest—about whose work criticism is often difficult to locate. These include mystery and science fiction writers, literary and social critics, foreign writers, and authors who represent particular ethnic groups in the United States.

Format of the Book

Altogether there are about 500 individual excerpts in each volume—with approximately seventeen excerpts per author—taken from hundreds of book review periodicals, general magazines, scholarly journals, monographs, and books. Entries include critical evaluations spanning from the beginning of an author's career to the most current commentary. Interviews, feature articles, and other published writings that offer insight into the author's works are also presented. Students, teachers, librarians, and researchers will find that the generous excerpts and supplementary material provided by *CLC* supply them with vital information needed to write a term paper, analyze a poem, or lead a book discussion group. In addition, complete bibliographical citations facilitate the location of the original source and provide all of the information necessary for a term paper footnote or bibliography.

A *CLC* author entry consists of the following elements:

- The **author heading** cites the form under which the author has most commonly published, followed by birth date, and death date when applicable. Uncertainty as to a birth or death date is indicated by a question mark.

- A **portrait** of the author is included when available.

- A brief **biographical and critical introduction** to the author and his or her work precedes the excerpted criticism. The first line of the introduction provides the author's full name, pseudonyms (if applicable), nationality, and a listing of genres in which the author has written. Since *CLC* is not intended to be a definitive biographical source, *cross-references* have been included to direct readers to these useful sources published by Gale Research: *Short Story Criticism,* which provides excerpts of criticism on the works of short story writers; *Contemporary Authors,* which includes detailed biographical and bibliographical sketches of nearly 95,000 authors; *Children's Literature Review,* which presents excerpted criticism on the works of authors of children's books; *Something about the Author,* which contains heavily illustrated biographical sketches of writers and illustrators who create books for children and young adults; *Dictionary of Literary Biography,* which provides original evaluations and detailed biographies of authors important to literary history; *Contemporary Authors Autobiography Series,* which offers autobiographical essays by prominent writers; and *Something about the Author Autobiography Series,* which presents autobiographical essays by authors of interest to young readers. Previous volumes of *CLC* in which the author has been featured are also listed in the introduction.

• The **excerpted criticism** represents various kinds of critical writing, ranging in form from the brief review to the scholarly exegesis. Essays are selected by the editors to reflect the spectrum of opinion about a specific work or about an author's literary career in general. The excerpts are presented chronologically, adding a useful perspective to the entry. All titles by the author featured in the entry are printed in boldface type, which enables the reader to easily identify the works being discussed. Publication information (such as publisher names and book prices) and parenthetical numerical references (such as footnotes or page and line references to specific editions of a work) have been deleted at the editors' discretion to provide smoother reading of the text.

• A complete **bibliographical citation** designed to help the user find the original essay or book follows each excerpt.

Other Features

• A list of **Authors Forthcoming in *CLC*** previews the authors to be researched for future volumes.

• An **Acknowledgments** section lists the copyright holders who have granted permission to reprint material in this volume of *CLC*. It does not, however, list every book or periodical reprinted or consulted during the preparation of the volume.

• A **Cumulative Author Index** lists all the authors who have appeared in *CLC, Twentieth-Century Literary Criticism, Nineteenth-Century Literature Criticism, Literature Criticism from 1400 to 1800, Classical and Medieval Literature Criticism,* and *Short Story Criticism,* with cross-references to these Gale series: *Children's Literature Review, Contemporary Authors, Contemporary Authors Autobiography Series, Contemporary Authors Bibliographical Series, Dictionary of Literary Biography, Something about the Author, Something about the Author Autobiography Series, Yesterday's Authors of Books for Children,* and *Authors & Artists for Young Adults.* Readers will welcome this cumulated author index as a useful tool for locating an author within the various series. The index, which lists birth and death dates when available, will be particularly valuable for those authors who are identified with a certain period but whose death date causes them to be placed in another, or for those authors whose careers span two periods. For example, Ernest Hemingway is found in *CLC,* yet a writer often associated with him, F. Scott Fitzgerald, is found in *Twentieth-Century Literary Criticism.*

• A **Cumulative Nationality Index** alphabetically lists all authors featured in *CLC* by nationality, followed by numbers corresponding to the volumes in which they appear.

• A **Title Index** alphabetically lists all titles reviewed in the current volume of *CLC*. Listings are followed by the author's name and the corresponding page numbers where the titles are discussed. English translations of foreign titles and variations of titles are cross-referenced to the title under which a work was originally published. Titles of novels, novellas, dramas, films, record albums, and poetry, short story, and essay collections are printed in italics, while all individual poems, short stories, essays, and songs are printed in roman type within quotation marks; when published separately (e.g., T.S. Eliot's poem *The Waste Land*), the title will also be printed in italics.

• In response to numerous suggestions from librarians, Gale has also produced a **special paperbound edition** of the *CLC* title index. This annual cumulation, which alphabetically lists all titles reviewed in the series, is available to all customers and will be published with the first volume of *CLC* issued in each calendar year. Additional copies of the index are available upon request. Librarians and patrons will welcome this separate index: it saves shelf space, is easy to use, and is disposable upon receipt of the following year's cumulation.

A Note to the Reader

When writing papers, students who quote directly from any volume in the Literary Criticism Series may use the following general forms to footnote reprinted criticism. The first example pertains to material drawn from periodicals, the second to material reprinted from books:

[1]Anne Tyler, "Manic Monologue," *The New Republic* 200 (April 17, 1989), 44-6; excerpted and reprinted in *Contemporary Literary Criticism,* Vol. 58, ed. Roger Matuz (Detroit: Gale Research, 1990), p. 278.

[2]Patrick Reilly, *The Literature of Guilt: From 'Gulliver' to Golding* (University of Iowa Press, 1988); excerpted and reprinted in *Contemporary Literary Criticism,* Vol. 58, ed. Roger Matuz (Detroit: Gale Research, 1990), pp. 153-60.

Suggestions Are Welcome

The editors welcome the comments and suggestions of readers to expand the coverage and enhance the usefulness of the series. Please feel free to contact us by letter or by calling our toll-free number: 1-800-347-GALE.

Acknowledgments

The editors wish to thank the copyright holders of the excerpted criticism included in this volume, the permissions managers of many book and magazine publishing companies for assisting us in securing reprint rights, and Anthony Bogucki for assistance with copyright research. We are also grateful to the staffs of the Detroit Public Library, the Library of Congress, the University of Detroit Library, Wayne State University Purdy/Kresge Library Complex, and University of Michigan Libraries for making their resources available to us. Following is a list of the copyright holders who have granted us permission to reprint material in this volume of *CLC*. Every effort has been made to trace copyright, but if omissions have been made, please let us know.

COPYRIGHTED EXCERPTS IN *CLC*, VOLUME 58, WERE REPRINTED FROM THE FOLLOWING PERIODI-CALS:

America, v. 154, May 10, 1986 for "Two Fables" by Richard A. Blake; v. 161, August 12-19, 1989 for a review of "The Temple of My Familiar" by Christopher Zinn. © 1986, 1989. All rights reserved. Both reprinted by permission of the respective authors.—*The American Book Review,* v. 5, July-August, 1983; v. 8, November-December, 1986. © 1983, 1986 by *The American Book Review.* Both reprinted by permission of the publisher.—*American Film,* v. XIV, March, 1989 for "Dennis Potter" by Graham Fuller. Copyright 1989 by *American Film.* Reprinted by permission of the author.—*The American Poetry Review,* v. 14, January-February, 1985 for "Territorial Voices" by Frederick Garber. Copyright © 1985 by World Poetry, Inc. Reprinted by permission of the author.—*The American Scholar,* v. 40, Summer, 1971. Copyright © 1971. Reprinted by permission of the publishers.—*The Antioch Review,* v. XXX, Spring, 1970. Copyright © 1970 by the Antioch Review Inc. Reprinted by permission of the Editors.—*Ariel: A Review of International English Literature,* v. 17, January, 1986 for "The Impact of Pinter's Work" by Daniel Salem. Copyright © 1986 The Board of Governors, The University of Calgary. Reprinted by permission of the publisher.—*Australian Literary Studies,* v. 12, May, 1986 for "Lawler's Demythologizing of the 'Doll: Kid Stakes' and 'Other Times' " by Joy Hooton. Reprinted by permission of the author.—*Best Sellers,* v. 33, June 1, 1973. Copyright 1973, by the University of Scranton. Reprinted by permission of the publisher./ v. 40, May, 1980. Copyright © 1980 Helen Dwight Reid Educational Foundation. Reprinted by permission of the publisher.—*Book World—World Journal Tribune,* November 13, 1966. © 1966, *The Washington Post.* Reprinted by permission of the publisher.—*Book World—The Washington Post,* November 15, 1970. © 1970 Postrib Corp. Reprinted by courtesy of the *Chicago Tribune* and *The Washington Post.*/ June 7, 1981; March 21, 1982; December 23, 1984; July 14, 1985; April 10, 1988; May 7, 1989; May 14, 1989. © 1981, 1982, 1984, 1985, 1988, 1989, *The Washington Post.* All reprinted by permission of the publisher.—*Books,* London, n. 2, May, 1987. © Gradegate Ltd. 1987. Reprinted by permission of the publisher.—*Books in Canada,* v. 13, October, 1984 for "A Star Reborn" by Judith Fitzgerald; v. 16, January-February, 1987 for "Starting Over" by David Helwig; v. 17, August-September, 1988 for "Prison Mail" by Cary Fagan. All reprinted by permission of the respective authors.—*Brick: A Journal of Reviews,* n. 27, Spring, 1986. Reprinted by permission of the publisher.—*British Book News,* August, 1983; June, 1984; November, 1985. © *British Book News,* 1983, 1984, 1985. All courtesy of *British Book News.*—*Canadian Drama/L'Art dramatique canadien,* v. 2, Fall, 1976; v. 11, Spring, 1985. Copyright © 1976, 1985 *Canadian Drama/L'Art dramatique canadien.* Both reprinted by permission of the publisher.—*The Canadian Forum,* v. LXVII, August-September, 1987 for a review of "The Late Great Human Road Show" by Judith Carson. Reprinted by permission of the author.—*Canadian Literature,* n. 85, Summer, 1980 for "On the Edge: Michael Cook's Newfoundland Trilogy" by Brian Parker; n. 106, Fall, 1985 for "Intelligent Anger" by David O'Rourke; n. 116, Spring, 1988 for "Island & Road" by Paul Jacob. All reprinted by permission of the respective authors.—*Canadian Poetry: Studies, Documents, Reviews,* n. 20, Spring-Summer, 1987. Reprinted by permission of the publisher.—*Chicago Tribune—Books,* April 16, 1989 for "Painting with Words" by Anne Tyler. Copyrighted © 1989 by Anne Tyler. All rights reserved. Reprinted by permission of Russell & Volkening, Inc., as agents for the author./ April 16, 1989 for "Far-Out West" by Herbert Gold. © copyrighted 1989, Chicago Tribune Company. All rights reserved. Reprint by permission of the author./ December 25, 1988. © copyrighted 1988, Chicago Tribune Company. All rights reserved. Used with permission.—*The Christian Science Monitor,* April 21, 1989 for "An Updated, High-Tech 'Faust' " by John Beaufort. © 1989 The Christian Science Publishing Society. All rights reserved. Reprinted by permission of the author./ January 21, 1960. © 1960 The Christian Science Publishing Society. All rights reserved. Reprinted by permission from *The Christian Science Monitor.*—*CM: Canadian Materials for Schools and Libraries,* v. XII, November, 1984 for "Celestial Navigation: Poems" by donalee Moulton-Barrett. Copyright 1984 The Canadian Library Association. Reprinted by permission of the publisher and the author.—*The Commonweal,* v. LXVII, February 21, 1958. Copyright © 1958 Commonweal Publishing Co., Inc. Reprinted by permission of Commonweal Foundation.—*Contemporary Literature,* v. 23, Fall, 1982; v. 27, Spring, 1986. © 1982, 1986 by the Board of Regents of the University of Wisconsin System. Both reprinted by permission of The University of Wisconsin Press.—*Critical Quarterly,* v. 2, Summer, 1960 for a review of "Lord of the Flies" by C. B. Cox. Reprinted by permission of the author.—*Daily Mail,* October 5, 1988. Reprinted by permission of the publisher.—*Daily News,* New York, November

Authors Forthcoming in *CLC*

Contemporary Literary Criticism, Vol. 59: Yearbook 1989 will be devoted to an examination of the outstanding achievements and trends in literature during 1989. Along with entries on major new writers, prizewinners, and notable authors who died during the year, *CLC-59* will feature commentary on literary events and issues that generated extensive public interest and media coverage. Volumes 60 and 61 will contain a number of authors not previously covered as well as criticism on newer works by authors included in earlier volumes.

To Be Included in Volume 60

Douglas Adams (English novelist)—In his popular series of satirical novels beginning with *The Hitchhiker's Guide to the Galaxy,* Adams uses the devices of science fiction to lampoon modern culture. Adams blends slapstick and fantasy in his recent novels, *Dirk Gently's Holistic Detective Agency* and *The Long Dark Tea Time of the Soul,* to portray the unusual adventures of a private investigator.

Erskine Caldwell (American novelist and short story writer)—The author of such controversial Depression-era novels as *Tobacco Road* and *God's Little Acre,* Caldwell blended realism and comic pathos in his work to portray the desperate existence of poor Southerners.

Annie Dillard (American essayist and poet)—Dillard is best known for *Pilgrim at Tinker Creek,* her Pulitzer Prize-winning meditation on nature that critics have compared to Henry David Thoreau's *Walden.* She has also earned praise for her works of literary criticism, poetry, and autobiography.

Umberto Eco (Italian novelist and semiotician)—Acclaimed for his international best-seller *The Name of the Rose,* Eco has generated widespread interest with his recent mystery novel, *Foucault's Pendulum.* Spanning several centuries and exploring the nature of language and words, this work combines intrigue, autobiography, political commentary, and esoteric motifs.

Carlos Fuentes (Mexican novelist and essayist)—In his internationally acclaimed works, Fuentes often employs myth, legend, and history to examine Mexico's past and contemporary social and cultural issues. This entry will focus on his recent novel, *Christopher Unborn,* and *Myself with Others: Selected Essays.*

Shirley Jackson (American novelist and short story writer)—A prolific author, Jackson is generally known for such Gothic horror tales as "The Lottery" and *The Haunting of Hill House.* In lucid prose juxtaposing humor with intense psychological states and an atmosphere of foreboding, Jackson explores the dark side of human nature.

Harper Lee (American novelist)—Lee's Pulitzer Prize-winning novel *To Kill a Mockingbird,* which examines racial attitudes in the Deep South through the experiences of a young girl in a small Alabama town, will be the focus of this entry.

Anaïs Nin (French-born American diarist, novelist, and short story writer)—Nin is best known for the erotic pieces she wrote during the 1930s and 1940s and for her numerous books containing excerpts from her diaries. This entry will emphasize recent analyses of her work.

Molly Peacock (American poet)—In such collections as *Raw Heaven* and *Take Heart,* Peacock uses humor, unusual rhyme schemes, and contemplative tones to examine family bonds, love, and sexuality.

Kurt Vonnegut (American novelist and short story writer)—Widely regarded as a masterful contemporary writer, Vonnegut uses satire, irony, and iconoclastic humor to explore social values and the meaning of life. This entry will focus on *Slaughterhouse-Five; or, The Children's Crusade,* Vonnegut's absurdist novel about his experiences as a prisoner of war during the firebombing of Dresden, Germany, in World War II.

Nicholson Baker (American novelist)—Baker has received critical praise for his debut novel, *The Mezzanine,* a contemplative, detail-oriented work in which an escalator ride inspires revelations on the unexamined, seemingly trivial aspects of daily life.

Malcolm Bradbury (English novelist and critic)—A prolific author, Bradbury writes satirical novels about British and American university life in which he examines themes of social dislocation and liberalism.

Gillian Clarke (Welsh poet)—Considered an important new voice in contemporary Welsh poetry, Clarke utilizes traditional Celtic metrics that resonate throughout her primarily meditative verse. Clarke often employs these subtle sound and rhythmic patterns to explore the nature of female experience.

Maria Irene Fornés (Cuban-born American dramatist)—Winner of six Obie awards, Fornés is a leading off-Broadway dramatist. Although unconventional, her humorous, intelligent plays reflect such traditional concerns as human relationships and social and political corruption.

Larry Gelbart (American scriptwriter and dramatist)—Chief writer for the first five years of the television series "M*A*S*H," Gelbart has recently garnered praise for his comic plays *Mastergate*, a satire on the Iran-Contra scandal, and *City of Angels*, a parody of 1940s detective films.

Ernest Hemingway (American novelist and short story writer)—Recognized as one of the preeminent American authors of the twentieth century, Hemingway wrote powerful, terse narratives of disillusionment, personal loss, and stoic resolve in the face of an apparently meaningless world. Critical commentary in Hemingway's entry will focus upon his acclaimed novel, *The Sun Also Rises*.

Zora Neale Hurston (American novelist and short story writer)—Regarded as an important writer of the Harlem Renaissance, Hurston is respected for works that provide insights into black culture and the human condition. Hurston's entry will focus on her novel *Their Eyes Were Watching God*, which is enjoying renewed popularity through Women's Studies courses.

Jack Kerouac (American novelist)—Kerouac was a key figure in the artistic and cultural phenomenon known as the Beat Movement. This entry will focus on his novel *On the Road*, considered a quintessential work of Beat literature for its experimental form and its portrayal of a rebellious, hedonistic lifestyle.

Stephen King (American novelist and short story writer)—King is a prolific and popular author of horror fiction. Non-supernatural in emphasis, King's recent novels include *Misery*, in which a best-selling writer is held captive by a psychotic nurse, and *The Dark Half*, about a pseudonymous author attempting to shed his false persona who finds that his submerged alter-ego seeks revenge.

George F. Walker (Canadian dramatist)—Closely associated with the Factory Theatre, a group that promotes alternative drama in Toronto, Walker writes social satires in which he employs black humor and a variety of unconventional theatrical devices. His recent play, *Nothing Sacred*, for which Walker received his second Governor General's Award, was popular in regional theaters in the United States and Canada.

Fernando Arrabal

1932-

(Born Fernando Arrabal Terán) Moroccan-born Spanish dramatist, novelist, scriptwriter, and poet.

A controversial Spanish playwright whose works are primarily produced in French, Arrabal is often associated with the Theatre of the Absurd, an experimental dramatic movement typified by black humor and often surreal portraits of the human condition. Preoccupied with memories of personal and political upheavals experienced during the Spanish Civil War, Arrabal attacks governmental, religious, and psychological restrictions upon freedom. His nightmarish dramas, which abound with violent, scatological and sadomasochistic images, have been variously condemned as obscene, blasphemous, and misogynic. Nevertheless, Arrabal has garnered critical accolades for his meticulously realized, highly original vision of morality in a dehumanized, technological age. Allen Thiher observed: "Arrabal's obsessive fantasies have given rise to a body of work that is among the most promising of the New Theater. With the modernity of a happening and the courage to face the delirium of our times, it may well come to be among the most significant in this second half of the twentieth century."

Arrabal was born in Spanish Morocco to a highly conservative Catholic mother and a politically liberal father. In 1936, Arrabal's father, an army officer, was arrested and sentenced to prison for thirty years after refusing to join the forces of Generalissimo Francisco Franco in the Spanish Civil War. Eight years later, after allegedly becoming insane, he escaped from the prison's psychiatric ward and disappeared. Humiliated by her husband's actions at the time of his arrest, Arrabal's mother informed her children that their father had died, then attempted to eradicate all memories of him by burning his papers and excising his image from photographs. However, at seventeen, Arrabal became aware of his mother's deception after discovering a trunk containing letters and documents belonging to his father. Commentators contend that this traumatic event coupled with his disturbing experiences as a strictly disciplined Jesuit school student in fascist Spain fostered in the playwright the rebelliousness and sadomasochistic sensuality that permeate his work. In his first novel, *Baal Babylone* (1959), later adapted for the screen as *Viva la muerte* (1970), Arrabal recreates his early experiences. The protagonist, a child during the Spanish Civil War, relies on memories of his absent father to escape his oppressive mother, whom he believes denounced her husband to authorities.

Arrabal's early plays feature adults whose childish innocence is frequently compared to Charlie Chaplin's tragicomic characters. These amoral individuals, according to Martin Esslin, "are often cruel because they have failed to understand, or even to notice, the existence of a moral law; and, like children, they suffer the cruelty of the world as a meaningless affliction." In Arrabal's first play, *Los soldados* (1952; *Pique-nique en Campagne*), the parents of a naive soldier travel to a battlefield for a picnic. However, after cordially inviting a captured enemy soldier to join them, the entire party is abruptly killed by machine-gun fire. Like most of Arrabal's dramatic works, this play is best known in its French transla-

tion. In the opening scene of *Fando et Lis* (1955), Fando pushes his paralyzed lover Lis in a baby carriage on the road to the mythical city of Tar. While Fando displays his love for Lis by playing for her on his drum, he also torments her: he undresses her before four "gentlemen," then leaves her exposed on the road throughout the night. The next morning, after being placed in chains by Fando, Lis accidentally breaks her lover's drum. Enraged, Fando beats Lis to death, then continues to Tar with the four gentlemen. *Le Cimetiére des Voitures* (1957) recreates the passion of Jesus Christ in a squalid automobile graveyard populated by vagrants and prostitutes. In the play, Emanou, a trumpet-playing Christ-figure, desires to be virtuous, but has only memorized a rote creed concerning goodness. After illegally performing for the other junkyard inhabitants, Emanou is betrayed with a kiss by his friend Topé, then crucified on the handlebars of a bicycle by two policemen.

In other dramas, Arrabal associates the arbitrary cruelty of the state as portrayed in *Los soldados, Le Cimetiére des Voitures,* and *Guernica* (1959), a later play, with the exercise of familial authority through the image of a sadistic mother. In *Le Deux Bourreaux* (1956), for example, a woman conspires with her eldest son to win the support of his rebellious younger brother after betraying their father to the authorities.

While presenting herself as a long–suffering martyr, the woman also delights in her husband's torture and death. As the play progresses, the younger son's resolve to defend his father weakens and he ultimately asks his mother's forgiveness. Janet Winecoff Diaz concluded that *Le Deux Bourreaux* "presents a travesty of justice, showing authority as inherently cruel, insensitive, inhuman, sadistic and nearly blind— capable only of seeing that which condemns, never the evidence to the contrary. . . . The title [*The Two Executioners*] has a double application, to the literal executioners who take the father's life, and figuratively to the mother and the elder son, who kill the integrity, innocence and youth of the younger boy."

After having settled in France in the mid-1950s, Arrabal formed the "Panic Group" with Mexican director Alexandro Jodorowsky and French painter Roland Topor. Drawing upon the theories of the avant-garde French dramatist Antonin Artaud, the Panic Group characterized their doctrine not as a theatrical or artistic movement, but as " 'a manner of being,' controlled by confusion, humor, terror, chance, and euphoria." Rejecting conventional Christian society, which, they argued, suppressed this fundamental reality, Arrabal and his associates took as their aesthetic symbol the hedonistic Greek god Pan. Arrabal, who experimented with wordless drama in *Orchéstration Théatrale* (1959), regards language and sequential plot as restrictive and he created the "panic ceremony" based upon the ritualistic origins of drama. Arrabal's work during this period presents a kaleidoscopic union of opposites—tragedy and farce, poetry and vulgarity, romantic love and sadistic eroticism—intended to elicit a profusion of emotions, or "panic," within the audience. In the play *La Communion solennelle* (1963), for example, Arrabal evokes both repulsion and fascination as he juxtaposes religious ritual with deviant sexuality. The play opens as a grandmother dresses her young granddaughter for her first communion beside a coffin containing the body of a dead woman. As she advises the girl on how to lead a Christian life, a necrophiliac enters, undresses, and climbs into the coffin. Unperturbed, the grandmother and the child leave, but the granddaughter soon returns in full communicant dress, brandishing a knife. Approaching the coffin, she thrusts the knife into the necrophiliac and, as blood sprays her white clothing, red balloons rise from the coffin, symbolizing the dead man's release from repressed existence.

In the opening scene of *L'Architecte et l'Empereur d'Assyrie* (1965), Arrabal's best known play of the panic movement, a Western businessman, the only survivor of a plane crash, introduces himself as the Emperor of Assyria to the lone inhabitant of a remote island. The following action then occurs two years later, when the Emperor has educated the "noble savage" in the ways of the scientific, civilized world and has named him the "Architect of Assyria." Their relationship, which now involves ritualistic role playing, lampoons repressive attitudes and actions in its scatological and sadomasochistic content. These games culminate in a trial of the Emperor, who accuses himself of murdering his mother. After the witnesses, all played by the Emperor, testify, he confesses to the act and demands to be killed and eaten by the Architect. In a parody of the Holy Communion, the protogé consumes the Emperor then metamorphosizes into his master. Peter. L. Podol asserted: "*The Architect and the Emperor of Assyria* is a complex, virtuoso demonstration of the full range of dramatic possibilities of Panic. Structurally and ideologically, it develops to its absolute limit the idea of the repeating cycle,

elevating this concept to a metaphysical plane reminiscent of the Argentine writer Jorge Luis Borges. Language, structure, and ritual lend a lyrical quality to this two character play which surpasses all of Arrabal's previous efforts toward creation of poetic theater."

In 1967, Arrabal was arrested in Spain for writing a seditious dedication in a copy of his novel *Fêtes et Rites de la Confusion* (1974). He spent a month in prison until several authors, including Samuel Beckett and Eugéne Ionesco, successfully petitioned for his release. This ordeal fostered in Arrabal a heightened awareness of the suffering endured by his father and all prisoners of conscience. His resulting dramas, often referred to as "Guerrilla Theatre," utilize techniques of the panic movement to convey the barbarity of totalitarianism. *Et ils passèrent des menottes aux fleurs* (1969), for example, draws upon Arrabal's conversations with fellow inmates as it surrealistically presents the memories and immediate experiences of four political prisoners dehumanized during their prolonged incarceration. So that members of the audience might fully appreciate such terror, Arrabal directs that they be separated from their companions, verbally and physically abused by the actors, and encouraged to intervene directly in the action on stage. The drama *Sur le Fil ou la ballade du train fantome: piece melancolque* (1975), which Arrabal also produced under the titles of *Sur le Fil* and *La Ballade du train fantome,* addresses the playwright's anxieties concerning his separation from Spain. In the work, Tharsis, an exiled artist, arrives in the abandoned town of Madrid, New Mexico with the Duke of Gaza, who is held hostage by Tharsis at his own behest. They are soon joined by another Spanish expatriate, the aerialist Macchabeus Wichita, who teaches Tharsis to walk the high wire, an exploit the artist longs to perform above the well-known Spanish square, Puerta del Sol. During the play, the pair discuss returning to their homeland, but conclude that its repressive atmosphere would prove unbearable. However, when Wichita commits suicide, Tharsis and the Duke return to Puerta del Sol where, amid government machine-gun fire, Tharsis triumphantly walks the wire. Thomas John Donahue observed that in this play, Arrabal "has objectivized and placed some distance between his anguish and that of the new Spain emerging after four decades of oppression. He himself can never be free of the cultural ties that join him to Spain, but his creative talents are not totally dependent on it. He is the high-wire artist of his own drama."

In addition to his plays, Arrabal has also produced several novels. These include *L'Eterrement de la sardine* (1960), a surrealistic work based upon the Francisco Goya painting of the same title; *The Compass Stone* (1985), in which a young woman records her sadistic sexual encounters with men lured to her father's mansion; and *The Tower Struck by Lightning* (1988), which features a chess match between two disturbed geniuses.

(See also *CLC,* Vols. 2, 9, 18; *Contemporary Authors,* Vols. 9-12. rev. ed.; and *Contemporary Authors New Revision Series,* Vol. 15.)

MARTIN ESSLIN

Arrabal's world derives its absurdity not . . . from the despair of the philosopher trying to probe the secrets of being, but from the fact that his characters see the human situation with uncomprehending eyes of childlike simplicity. Like children, they are often cruel because they have failed to understand, or even to notice, the existence of a moral law; and, like children, they suffer the cruelty of the world as a meaningless affliction.

Arrabal's first play, **Pique-nique en Campagne** (the title is a cruel pun—it might be taken to mean "picnic in the country," but actually stands for "picnic on the battlefield"), already clearly shows this approach. He wrote the play at the age of twenty, under the influence of the news from the Korean War. This short one-act play shows a soldier, Zapo, isolated in the front line of the fighting. His father and mother, who are too simple to grasp the ferocity of modern war, arrive to visit him, so that they can have a Sunday picnic together. When an enemy soldier, Zepo, turns up, Zapo takes him prisoner, but later invites him to join the picnic. As the party gaily proceeds, a burst of machine-gun fire wipes out all the participants.

This is Chaplinesque comedy without the redeeming happy end; it already contains the highly disturbing mixture of innocence and cruelty so characteristic of Arrabal. This is also the atmosphere of **Oraison,** a *drame mystique* in one act, which opens the volume of Arrabal's *Théâtre,* published in 1958. A man and a woman, Fidio and Lilbé (notice the baby talk of the names), sit by a child's coffin discussing ways and means of being good—from today. Lilbé cannot grasp what it means to be good:

> LILBÉ: Shall we not be able to go and have fun, as before, in the cemetery?
> FIDIO: Why not?
> LILBÉ: And tear the eyes out of the corpses, as before?
> FIDIO: No, not that.
> LILBÉ: And kill people?
> FIDIO: No.
> LILBÉ: So we'll let them live?
> FIDIO: Obviously.
> LILBÉ: So much the worse for them.

As this discussion on the nature of goodness proceeds, it is gradually revealed that Fidio and Lilbé are sitting by the coffin of their own child, whom they have killed. Naïvely they discuss the example of Jesus, and come to the conclusion that they will have a try at being good, although Lilbé foresees the likelihood that they will get tired of it.

In **Les Deux Bourreaux** (**The Two Executioners**), we are faced with an analogous situation, but here conventional morality is more directly attacked as self-contradictory. A woman, Françoise, comes with her two sons, Benoît and Maurice, to denounce her husband to the two executioners of the title. He is guilty of some unspecified crime. Françoise, who hates him, wants to witness his being tortured in the next room. She rejoices in his sufferings, and even rushes into the torture chamber to put salt and vinegar on his wounds. Benoît, who is a dutiful son of his mother, accepts her behavior, but Maurice protests. Maurice is thus a bad son, who disobeys his mother and hurts her. When the father finally dies of his tortures, Maurice persists in accusing his mother of having caused his death, yet finally he is persuaded into the path of duty. He asks to be forgiven for his insubordination, and as the curtain falls the mother and her sons embrace.

In **Fando et Lis,** a play in five scenes, Fando is pushing his beloved, Lis, who is paralyzed, in a wheelchair. They are on the road to Tar. Fando loves Lis dearly, and yet, at the same time, he resents her as a burden. Nevertheless he tries to amuse her by playing her the only thing he knows on his drum, the Song of the Feather. They meet three gentlemen with umbrellas, who are also on the way to Tar, a place that they, like Fando and Lis, find it almost impossible to reach. Instead of getting to Tar, they always arrive back in the same place. Fando proudly displays Lis's beauty to the three gentlemen, raising her skirt to show off her thighs, and inviting them to kiss her. Fando loves Lis, but he cannot resist the temptation to be cruel to her. In Scene 4, we learn that, to show her off to the gentlemen, he left her lying naked in the open all night. Now she is even more ill than before. Fando has her in chains, and puts handcuffs on her, just to see whether she can drag herself along with them. He beats her. Falling down, she breaks his little drum. He is so furious that he beats her unconscious. When the three gentlemen arrive, she is dead. The last scene shows the three gentlemen with umbrellas confusedly discussing what has happened. Fando appears with a flower and a dog—he promised Lis that when she died he would visit her grave with a flower and a dog. The three gentlemen decide to accompany him to the cemetery. After that the four of them can try to make their way to Tar.

In its strange mixture of *commedia dell'arte* and Grand Guignol, **Fando et Lis** is a poetic evocation of the ambivalence of love, the love a child might have for a dog, which is cuddled and tormented in turn. By projecting the emotions of childhood into an adult world, Arrabal achieves an effect that is both tragicomic and profound, because it reveals the truth hidden behind a good deal of adult emotion as well.

Arrabal's most ambitious play to date is **Le Cimetière des Voitures (The Automobile Graveyard),** a play in two acts, which attempts no less than a reconstruction of the passion of Christ seen through Arrabal's childlike eyes and placed in a grotesque landscape of squalor. The scene is a derelict graveyard of old motorcars, which is, however, run on the lines of a luxury hotel. A valet, Milos, provides the service—breakfast in bed and a kiss from Dila, the prostitute, for every gentleman before he falls asleep. The hero, Emanou (i.e., Emanuel), a trumpet player, is the leader of a group of three musicians: his companions are Topé, the clarinetist, and Fodère, the saxophone player, a mute modeled on Harpo Marx. Emanou, like Fidio in *Oraison* wants to be good. This desire expresses itself in his providing music for dancing to the inmates of the automobile graveyard every night, although the playing of musical instruments is strictly forbidden by the police. Throughout the play, two indefatigable athletes, a man, Tiossido, and an elderly woman, Lasca, cross the scene in a grotesque show of sportsmanship. In the second act, these two are revealed as police agents who are after Emanou. They pay Topé to betray his master for money—he will identify him by a kiss. When this happens, the mute Fodère denies him by vigorously shaking his head as he is asked whether he knows Emanou. Emanou is savagely beaten and taken away, dying, his arms tied to the handle bars of a bicycle. The grotesque high life of the automobile graveyard continues.

Emanou's desire to be good is shown as a vague wish rather than a rational conviction. He recites his creed of goodness mechanically: "When one is good, one feels a great interior joy, born from the peace of the spirit that one knows when one sees oneself similar to the ideal image of man," but by the end of the play he seems to have forgotten this text and gets into a complete muddle when trying to recite it. At the same time, he earnestly discusses with his disciples whether it would not be more profitable to take up another profession—such as stealing or murder—and decides against these occupations merely on the ground that they are too difficult. (pp. 186-89)

Although the parallels between Emanou and Christ are made so obvious as to border on the blasphemous (he was born in a stable, his father was a carpenter, he left home at the age of thirty to play the trumpet), the play achieves an impression of innocence—the search for goodness pursued with total dedication in a universe that is both squalid and devoid of meaning. In such a world there cannot be any understandable ethical standards and the pursuit of goodness becomes an enterprise tragic in its absurdity, as absurd as the strenuous running of the police spies in the pursuit of sportsmanship.

Arrabal's preoccupation with the problem of goodness—the relationship between love and cruelty, his questioning of all accepted ethical standards from the standpoint of an innocent who would be only too eager to accept them if only he could understand them—is reminiscent of the attitude of Beckett's tramps in *Waiting for Godot*. Arrabal, who insists that his writing is the expression of his personal dreams and emotions, acknowledges his deep admiration for Beckett. (p. 189)

Arrabal's published plays are intensely human. Yet he is also greatly interested in developing an abstract theatre that would eliminate any human content altogether. In his *Orchéstration Théâtrale* . . . , he has tried to create a dramatic spectacle consisting entirely of the movements of abstract three-dimensional shapes, some of which were mechanical devices, while others were moved by dancers. The formal world of this strange spectacle was based on the inventions of Klee, Mondrian, Delauney, and the mobiles of Alexander Calder. Arrabal is convinced that the incongruities of mechanical movement are a potential source of highly comic effects. The script of *Orchéstration Théâtrale,* which contains no dialogue whatever, resembles the notation of a gigantic game of chess (Arrabal is a passionate chess player) and is illustrated by fascinating colored diagrams. The difficulties of putting this daring conception on the stage . . . proved so formidable that the lack of public acclaim achieved by the experiment is by no means conclusive proof of the impossibility of an abstract mechanical theatre. (pp. 189-90)

Martin Esslin, "Parallels and Proselytes," in his The Theatre of the Absurd, *Anchor Books, 1961, pp. 168-228.*

JACQUES GUICHARNAUD

Beckett, Ionesco, Adamov (first period), Charlie Chaplin, the Marx Brothers (especially Harpo), Kafka—such influences or possible associations make it clear that Arrabal is a modern playwright. With the help of Goya and Hieronymus Bosch (the acknowledged spirits behind Arrabal's novel *L'Enterrement de la sardine*), his modernism is strongly colored by the most nightmarish aspects of a certain brand of surrealism. The whole thing is deeply rooted in the history of our times, by the very fact of the writer's personal life (see his novel *Baal Babylone*), strongly marked by the Franco regime in Spain and a formidable mother image.

If Arrabal ever really makes the grade, literary historians will

have no difficulty in showing how much the trio of musicians (*Le Cimetière des Voitures*), one of whom is mute, owes not only to the Gospels but to the Marx Brothers; how much the mother who hands her husband over to executioners (*Les Deux Bourreaux*) owes to the playwright's personal experience; how much the aged couple who are prisoners in the ruins of their own house (*Guernica*) have in common with the couple in Ionesco's *Les Chaises* or the couples that haunt Beckett's works; how much the themes of *Fando et Lis,* and the useless attempts and sterile repetitions throughout Arrabal's works are again reminiscent of Beckett; how *La Bicyclette du condamné,* with its tortures and shifting of roles, recalls Adamov; and how most of his heroes echo Charlie Chaplin, as Geneviève Serreau has already pointed out. Like the "tramp," they are gentle and innocent; they do their best within their poverty and their clumsy love affairs. Proud of their meager successes, they soon lose any benefit they might have derived from them. They love and betray what they love with the same innocence. They are often cowards, but have spurts of dignity. They are always bewildered by the world, sometimes manage to cheat it, but instead of happily or doubtfully going off into the sunset, they end by being crushed in some frightful way.

Yet Arrabal's works are not merely a reflection of influences or a reminder of illustrious predecessors. First of all, most of his gentle heroes are murderers or accomplices in murder and physical torture. (pp. 116-17)

Crime in Arrabal, whether committed by the heroes or inflicted upon them, is spectacular. But the spectacle is horrifying or sordid. When Bruno is foresaken by Etienne, he hangs himself with a toilet chain; as the curtain goes up on Act II of *Le Tricycle,* we see Apal peacefully asleep on a blood-stained bench; bicycles are used to pull coffins or transport corpses; throughout all of *Les Deux Bourreaux* we hear the father scream as he is being tortured, and his corpse is carried away on a stick, like an animal killed in the hunt. In a world, whether Franco's Spain or any other, in which torture has been re-established in the name of order, Arrabal's fantasies permit him to escape from the lie of clean and dignified execution, and to bring out the reality.

The real atrocity of torture and murder, as well as the presence (or threatening absence) of the policeman-executioner, have already been strikingly expressed by Adamov's scenic metaphors in *Tous contre tous* and *La Grande et la Petite Manœuvre,* for example. But the combination of that horror with Chaplinesque tenderness and an element only suggested in Adamov's dreamlike world, a basic childishness of the characters, gives Arrabal his originality. His world of clownery and blood is seen with the eye of a child, and embodied in men-children and in the scenic presentation of their phantasms.

The characters are all adolescents or adults: they prove it by their sexual capacities. But they have the mentality of children. When they try to make conversation and proudly show off their intelligence, they talk in platitudes or meaningless phrases, either going into raptures over what the other says or rejecting it with the innocent bad faith of a child who makes no distinction between reality and play. They live in a world in which urinating is extraordinarily interesting—at any rate, of prime importance, as well as the places and privileged objects such an obsession implies. Basically, they are exhibitionists or voyeurs, often both; at the same time, they can be unexpectedly prudish. Although murderers who, once they commit a crime, lose all interest in it, or who from the depths of their innocence judge that it is good, they can show great consideration and spontaneous tenderness for others, and forget it just as quickly.

Above all, and because of the innocence with which they judge themselves, they act like guilty children—that is, when someone in authority appears or when they are caught. At such times, they would willingly have someone else die for them or would die in the place of someone else. They kill as children secretly smoke in the john—and the image of the policeman who lies in wait for them is not far from that of the headmaster. For them torture and punishment—even when they hand it out—come from on high, from some higher Terror, which they acknowledge, but which, in a certain sense, is not their concern. The tragedy is that they inevitably become the victims of it.

The childish fear of the police—which requires the simultaneous presence of child and policeman, two complementary yet incompatible figures—is, after all, a perfectly clear, valid, and dramatic symbol of the situation of man in any more or less police state, under any regime in which the guilt imposed from the outside, from on high (either politically or religiously), does not coincide with freely chosen responsibility. And of course, by definition, they never can coincide. On another level, how can one be both innocent and guilty? Behind Arrabal's fantasies, which directly call to mind social and political injustice, hovers the intolerable injustice of God's judgment. Arrabal makes no secret of it when he invokes Kafka and throws his hero into the hands of Justin, the Father, and of a judge who is a slave to the father (*Le Labyrinthe*), any more than he does in a kind of juvenile delinquency drama like *Le Tricycle.*

The ambiguity of the metaphor of childhood sometimes comes off rather well. The "automobile graveyard," in the play of that name, successfully and synthetically represents both the junkyards in which children play and the projection of such games in the universe of adult sexuality. In other plays, anger—childish to begin with—smoothly leads to its necessary conclusion: the adult gesture of murder. Because of the characters' childish oscillation, innocence and goodness are like the dead evoked by Ulysses: we see them clearly, but when we want to grasp them they disappear. A lost paradise? Rather, a missing paradise.

But conscious childishness *can* become downright silly. And perverse evangelism in an atmosphere of torture can become as sticky as sanctimonious evangelism among the sheep. Too much complacency with regard to the incoherency of the soul's simplicity and the comic possibilities therein leads to a kind of drivel in which all real tension disappears. Of course, over all the babble, such as that between Climando and Mita in *Le Tricycle* . . . , hangs the face of death (we know that Climando, in this instance, will be sentenced to die)—but there is an obvious lack of proportion. Children often delight us by the alternation of their innocent remarks and their perversity, but they can manage to wear us out by talking too much, and when—along with us—they are in danger of death, we rather feel like doing something else. All things considered, innocents *aux mains brisées* are in many cases hardly more satisfying than innocents *aux mains pleines.* With Arrabal we often lose sight of the man-child symbol, submerged as we are in the drivel of plainly backward individuals. It takes a Beckett to create, in a convincing-

ly symbolic and human way, the vagabond who is at once childish, feminine, and lethargic, such as Estragon in *Godot.*

Arrabal is perhaps more a visionary than a dramatist. He has the merit of being faithful to what he sees: his anonymous language—correct but without style, very similar to Adamov's—makes it impossible for him to cheat. He has seen the automobile graveyard, its characters, their gestures and their shapes; but when he bludgeons us with the Emanou-Christ symbolism, the effect is destroyed. In almost all his plays the curtain goes up on a valid universe, with a familiar object in an unfamiliar situation (sheets hung out to dry, a piano, a carrier-tricycle arriving on stage, a john, etc.) and then the play itself gets lost in a lot of avant-garde chatter or in a nightmare that is repeated to exhaustion, adding nothing to the initial shock. Apart from *Les Deux Bourreaux,* in which the predominant and formidable mother image is the inexorable instrument of the hero's tragic submission, with a rigor that recalls Dürrenmatt, we are left with no more than tableaux: a family picnicking on a battlefield, for example, or corpses being transported across the stage.

And indeed that is perhaps the direction Arrabal should take: the creation of a series of ever-moving tableaux. Beckett's static quality is clearly not for him. Once the image is given and immediately exhausted, there must be another. Arrabal is an extraordinary witness, an extraordinary voyeur, if not a *voyant,* but he does not move on fast enough. His novels, particularly *L'Enterrement de la sardine,* show that he has an essentially kaleidoscopic imagination—which does not exclude recurrent images; on the contrary. But by going round in circles, the fascinating child—innocent and condemned—is in danger of becoming a mechanical doll who concerns us no longer. (pp. 117-19)

Jaques Guicharnaud, "Forbidden Games: Arrabal," in Yale French Studies, *No. 29, Spring-Summer, 1962, pp. 116-20.*

JANET WINECOFF DÍAZ

Arrabal's theater is, until now, unique in Spain, with its most immediate probable antecedent being the *esperpentos* of Valle-Inclán. His plays differ considerably from the conventional postwar dramatic groupings of *teatro de la victoria, teatro de consumo* and *teatro de evasión,* on the one hand, with their conservative tendencies, pro-regime propaganda and light entertainment with little or no transcendent literary value. Neither do the works of Arrabal coincide, on the other hand, with the counter-currents of *teatro comprometido* and *teatro social.* In these latter, similar but not identical groupings, art is conceived as a means of changing society, tending to a variety of thesis play. Arrabal's work, while in some ways related to the *teatro comprometido,* is more universal and less specifically Spanish, lacking the explicit political, economic and ideological content.

His writings, of a more human, subjective and less sociological tone, come very close to the theater of the absurd, with some of his plays falling entirely within that category. This, too, is unique, for with the exception of the Catalán dramatist, Manuel de Pedrolo, Arrabal is the only Spaniard to achieve any distinction in this particular area of the theater. Arrabal has disclaimed any prior knowledge of the theater of the absurd, even stating that when he first heard his work compared to Beckett's, he thought the reference was to Bécquer. Critics of Arrabal have compared him favorably with Ionesco and Beckett, even considering him superior in certain respects.

A great many sources of possible influence have been suggested; in fact, the number and variety of comparisons is almost bewildering. Resemblances have been noted between Arrabal and Strindberg, Kafka, Jarry, Vitrac, Buñuel, Baudelaire and Sade. In addition, the *teatro pánico* movement launched in Paris by Arrabal and the Mexican Alejandro Jodorowsky has been seen as deriving from surrealism and Dada. Arrabal has not helped to simplify matters, for he has at one and the same time proclaimed himself the successor of Góngora, Cervantes, Goya and Gómez de la Serna. . . . The above list is by no means complete, for in another interview, Arrabal stated that his teachers included Gracián and Gaudí, and has several times mentioned *The Castle* of Kafka and Lewis Carroll's *Alice in Wonderland* as his favorite readings. He has repeatedly called Kafka and Carroll his most important models among foreign authors, and the reading of several Arrabal works will yield much evidence in support of this statement.

There are undoubtedly additional influences, conscious or unconscious, not mentioned either by Arrabal or his critics to date, including the Gothic novel, with its atmosphere of magic, mystery and horror; Cocteau, with the use of mirrors as access to the other world, the idea of the artist's obligation to descend into the unexplored depths of the unconscious, thence to dredge up fragments of the "inner night," and the tenet that as the artistic process creates the unfamiliar, disturbing the reader in his innermost being, literary creation must be scandal. Cocteau anticipates one tenet of the *movimiento pánico* with his statement that "everything is a hazard." Another antecedent of this movement, in all probability, is Apollinaire with his paradoxical faith in "the ordering force of chance," expressed in his work. Arrabal has stated that the themes and sources of the *hombre pánico* include allegory, symbols, sex, humor, sordidness, the use of all postulates, philosophies and moral systems, "y claro está, sobre todo: Azar, Memoria, Confusión." ["and, of course, above everything: Chance, Memory, Confusion"].

Unnoticed heretofore is the considerable philosophical substratum of Arrabal's work, wherein much importance is given to epistemology, the inquiry into the nature of knowledge, wrestling with the unknown, the absurd, the limits of human understanding, and a special emphasis on memory. There is, as in the theater of the absurd in general, a predominance of existentialist themes, while other preoccupations of Arrabal are particularly suggestive of Bergson, either directly or through his Spanish disciple, Antonio Machado. Intuition, the problem of time, duration in relation to human consciousness, the issue of mechanism versus life (automatic behavior, clichés, convention), the distrust of reason—all occur insistently in these three writers, while the symbolic use of labyrinths and mirrors, related to philosophical and epistemological implications is frequent in both Machado and Arrabal. The threat posed to the individual by the technological state is a persistent theme which Arrabal shares with Machado and Ortega (*The Revolt of the Masses*). At the risk of misleading the reader, however, it should be noted that the philosophical in its overt manifestations is often overshadowed in Arrabal's work by other considerations, and tends to appear more in his narratives than in his theatrical works.

Despite his frequently serious intellectual preoccupations, Arrabal's bizarre, eccentric, picturesque behavior and dress have prompted some to question whether any of his work can be taken seriously. He frequently exhibits a real or feigned megalomania and Narcissism, and has had himself portrayed in many paintings suggesting or exemplifying complexes. A favorite theme is self-dismemberment; the pictorial versions of a mutilated Arrabal seem to be second only to those showing him as a supernatural or mythological being. He is often shown before a mirror, or playing chess; in one case, playing chess with another Arrabal, using chess pieces with Arrabal faces. This has an importance beyond the merely personal or biographic, inasmuch as analogies with chess, or certain of its moves, apparently hold a key to interpretation of parts of his work. Arrabal is more than just an *aficionado;* chess for him is a serious activity, and he recently won an international championship in Paris. (pp. 143-45)

Certain aspects of Arrabal's life help to clarify his works. His having grown up under a military dictatorship, witnessing the abrogation of individual liberties, Church repression, police terrorism, corruption in high places, boredom, monotony, poverty and the "farce" of the Generalísimo, all constitute possible sources for the Kafkaesque atmosphere of **Los dos verdugos, El laberinto, La bicicleta del condenado,** and several episodes in the narrative volume, **Arrabal celebrando la ceremonia de la confusión. Baal Babylon,** his first novel (with a typically high autobiographic content), shows the boy as half crushed beneath family and social prohibitions, bigotry, inhibition, restriction, and repressed hates, over-protected and simultaneously exploited by his protectors. This cluster of emotions goes a long way to explaining Arrabal's obsession with the hyper-possessive, domineering, pseudo-martyr, self-justifying mother figure, as well as the ambivalence of many of his characters toward their mothers—a combination of explosive, contained hate with latent or active incest, often coupled with the absence of the father. Deviation is also an obsession with Arrabal, who has treated a wide range of its forms, including sadism, masochism, whipping, chaining, various tortures, lesbianism, male homosexuality, necrophilia, sex murders, and other various and assorted psychic and sexual abnormalities. Critical invocations of Sade are obviously amply justified. Arrabal is also interested in the probing of many other complexes, minor and major, which are not so extreme as to constitute overt abnormality, but which have an unquestioned importance in the lives of his characters.

This author's works have been seen as a reaction against crushing family and social restriction, a self-defense with laughter as the weapon. (p. 146)

In order of publication, Arrabal's books observe a strict alternation between theatrical and narrative. If this pattern is maintained—inasmuch as the latest volume was a collection of theater—the next will be narrative. This is probably no accident, since Arrabal also uses an alternating pattern in **El entierro de la sardina,** telling one narrative (present tense) in odd-numbered chapters, and another, separate but related (past tense), in the even-numbered. Likewise, there is a mathematical basis to the constructive of his next narrative collection, **Arrabal celebrando la ceremonia de la confusión.** The first two chapters each have nine "laberintos," followed by an intermission third chapter; then there follow two more chapters subdivided in nine, with the sixth corresponding to the third.

The theatrical works, too, show careful and deliberate construction, not so obviously mathematical, but with frequent repetitions, either identical or with slight variations, and at least one case of a work which ends exactly with the situation with which it began. The cyclical pattern, with slight modification, is used with increasing frequency in Arrabal's more recent works. The attention to "architecture" may clarify Arrabal's assertion that Benavente was one of his masters, for the latter was an expert in structure and composition. The use of characters also reflects the mathematical or "theme and variations" principles of construction: there are frequent uses of pairs, opposites, role reversal, metamorphosis, and even an incident in which one character *becomes* the other, not only assuming his behavioral and physical characteristics, but devouring and thereby incorporating the body of the other. In this work, *The Architect and the Emperor of Assyria,* the two characters play an unbelievable number of roles, symbolically representing all the relationships of man, all social prototypes, and psychological archetypes, and simultaneously revealing their complexes, secrets, guilt and dreams. At the same time, they manage to slaughter every imaginable sacred cow, past and present, social, political, religious, philosophical, moral and cultural.

In *Oración,* a man and woman appear seated on a coffin, later revealed to contain the body of their child, whom they have killed, not from hate or malice but as a result of a childlike delight in torture, curiosity and boredom. The work is one of considerable moral ambivalence, for these characters at the same time express a sincere, ingenuous desire to be conventionally good, to go through the motions expected of them, even while anticipating that this, too, will be boring. They discuss moral and religious themes, unaware of what is good and evil, repeating things they have heard but not assimilated, uncomprehending and utterly spontaneous. As with most Arrabal characters, their language and mentality are infantile, their ages indefinite, their ideas over-simplified.

Los dos verdugos incorporates the typical Kafka atmosphere of trial and condemnation for a mysterious, unknown, possibly non-existent offense, with subsequent torture, suffering and death. The author presents a travesty of justice, showing authority as inherently cruel, insensitive, inhuman, sadistic and nearly blind—capable only of seeing that which condemns, never the evidence to the contrary. As occurs in the work of Kafka (and later in *El laberinto*), the very innocence of the accused or those defending him—their righteous indignation and protest—contributes to condemn. The central situation recalls *Baal Babylon,* whose young protagonist has dim, disturbing memories of his father, a Jewish anarchist arrested and convicted on the basis of his wife's testimony. This ignorant, self-righteous woman indulges in continual auto-justification, pictures herself as a martyr, and endeavors to erase all memory of her husband from her son's mind. Frequent in Arrabal's works, this mother figure could perhaps be a symbolic representation of the church, but its human and emotional content seem excessive for a symbol. In *Los dos verdugos,* this mother-type, supported by her traditionalistic elder son, defends her denunciation of the husband to the younger son, and the two succeed in confusing his values to a point where he finally accepts their "truth" and begs his mother's pardon, though still suspecting in his heart that his father has been sacrificed for the mother's secret revenge. The title has a double application, to the literal executioners who take the father's life, and figuratively to the mother and elder son, who kill the integrity, innocence and youth of the younger boy. Strong Freudian elements in addition to the mother syndrome include repression and aggression.

Elements typical of the theater of the absurd are more numerous in *Fando y Lis,* which recalls particularly *Waiting for Godot.* Its situation is absurd in that it cannot be resolved— all characters are on the road to Tar, an impossible goal, or at least, one which no one yet has managed to reach. As in *El laberinto,* no matter how far the characters travel, they always arrive at the same point. It is interesting to remember here a similar situation in *Through the Looking Glass:* The Red Queen has to run as fast as her legs will carry her if she wants to stay in the same spot. And just as Lewis Carroll relates adventures in which all participants except Alice are animated chess pieces, there is a part of *La ceremonia de la confusión* wherein Arrabal describes, obliquely and without mentioning the name of the game, a chess situation. Lewis Carroll taught mathematics, sometimes reflected in the construction of his literary works, suggesting another area of possible influence on Arrabal. Still another, and obviously important similarity is the use by both of nonsense syllables and the writing of nonsense verse, which Arrabal uses repeatedly in *La ceremonia de la confusión.* (pp. 147-49)

As usual in Arrabal, psychology and speech are childlike, and the protagonists display an unrealistic, ingenuous optimism. Their relationship is a complex mixture of love and cruelty, with possessiveness carried to the extreme of chaining and torturing the beloved, which contrasts with an almost simultaneous generosity, kindness and willingness to "share"—to the extent that Fando invites strangers to admire Lis, to touch and embrace her, and forces her to spend the night naked on the road so that others may enjoy her beauty. The work is thoroughly existentialist in its expression of the need for the Other, the absurdity of life and human activity, and the radical solitude and incommunication of the individual.

In the end, one character tells another a story, whose plot and details are identical to those just presented in the play, a story of a man who was carrying a paralyzed woman in a wheelbarrow on the road to Tar. (The wheelbarrow motif reappears; a variation of the same is the use of a baby carriage for the transportation of adults, and in another case, a sort of cage on a bicycle.) The conclusion of *Fando y Lis* mentions plot material from other Arrabal works, and the "story-telling" motif is used also in *Guernica* or *Ciugrena,* in which one character offers to amuse another by telling a story wherein the central situation is identical to their own. Arrabal's characters are never aware that the supposedly fictitious situation has any relation to their own existence. There is a related use by Arrabal of the situations from other of his works, in which occasionally a "story" is told which is recognizable as the germ of a previous or future Arrabal writing. However, he does not seem to be creating his own interrelated literary world as did Balzac or Galdós, nor are his characters aware as with Cervantes or Unamuno, of their existence as "entes de ficción."

One of the most complex of Arrabal's early works is *El cementerio de automóviles.* Its original situation, with various characters living in an automobile graveyard as though in a luxury hotel, is absurd, but could conceivably be seen as an ironic commentary on the critical housing shortage existing in Spain when it was written. As in most of Arrabal's works, attitudes toward sex are unconventional, and related ironically to morality in general. The female lead is defined as good because she will let anybody sleep with her. In other works, characters may be murderers who have broken nearly every rule, but these tend to be puritanically virginal and intolerant of those who are not, because "eso es malo."

A particularly important aspect of *El cementerio de automóviles* is its evident parody of the Crucifixion in modern times—a crucifixion perhaps by society, or more concretely, by the mechanisms of authority, represented by the police, or perhaps by machines—the theme of loss of individuality in the technological state enunciated by Ortega in *La rebelión de las masas* and subsequently the preoccupation of many existentialist writers. This suggests an explanation for Arrabal's use of a bicycle upon which the protagonist, Manu (Immanuel), is quite literally crucified. Because of the numerous surrealistic elements in Arrabal—interest in the subconscious, Freudian themes, the use of dreams, and nightmarish creatures and atmosphere—it may be pertinent here that Apollinaire has also represented the crucifixion by means of a machine (an airplane). The context of crucifixion is inevitably suggested by elements such as the name of Manu, his sense of mission, his relation to his "disciples," and the "Magdalena"; even his ultimate betrayal by one of his followers.

Pic-nic en campaña deals with the absurdity of war; "enemies" distinguish each other only by the color of their uniforms. Individual soldiers have no idea of the reasons underlying the conflict, bear each other individually no animosity, and want only to return home. Bored, between bombings, one makes paper flowers in the trenches, while his enemy knits (symbolic of the innately gentle, constructive nature of both). Emphasis is placed on their similarities; even their names are nearly identical. Zapo's prisoner, Zepo, is as naive and polite as his captor, his exact reflection in a different colored uniform. Ironies abound: their observances of polite niceties in the midst of war; Zapo's reaction (typical of the stereotyped tourist) in wanting his picture taken with his foot on the prisoner's chest; the fact that captor and captive alike are annihilated by bombs in a moment of peaceful, joyous camaraderie. In this powerful, pacifistic miniature, Arrabal implies that wars are forced on peace-loving men by their governments.

Mita, in *El triciclo* is another character essentially typical of Arrabal, childlike, naive, with a sort of primeval innocence, but at the same time prematurely corrupt, promiscuous, with the soul and possibly other attributes of a prostitute. This female type is even more frequently encountered than the "evil" mother. Mita and her friends decide to kill a rich man in order to pay the rent on the *triciclo* and buy anchovy sandwiches, a crime decided upon without hesitation, although Climando demurs that it seems an unnecessarily complicated form of robbery. As usually happens after crimes in this dramatist's work, the murder is forgotten immediately, and the criminals return to childlike innocence, naive optimism, and impossible plans for the future. They are interrupted by the arrival of the police, who are equally absurd; they speak a language all their own, bureaucratic, incomprehensible, and personify that authority against which resistance is futile and whose punishment is certain. Absurd, pathetic fear and infantile attempts to ingratiate themselves are to no avail for the prisoners, nor are their idiotic ruses. Their final despair is lost on those who remain and inherit the *triciclo,* and thus have neither time nor inclination to mourn the departed.

In *El laberinto* guilt is again the central motif, recalling Kafka even in the quotation at the beginning, as well as in the underlying sentiment of a pursuing, persecuting "justice" which inevitably condemns and kills. There is a pervading feeling of the incomprehensibility, inescapability, absurdity

and mystery of bureaucratic mechanisms. Like *Ciugrena,* this play takes place inside or in the immediate environs of a latrine, symptomatic of increasing scatological preoccupations in the author. The labyrinth is immense, of unknown extent and design, with an absurd purpose. . . . The labyrinth is a trap—all its exits are false. There may be religious symbolism in the myth of the "father" who has constructed this private world, who disposes all, knows all, judges and punishes.

Ciugrena seems to suggest the absurdity of all touched by war, not merely caricaturing the aggressors, or those who profit by the conflict (represented by the journalist who expects fame from "immortalizing" the heroic inhabitants of the massacred village), but also the victims themselves. As represented by the old man and woman, the Basque population of Guernica has been caught in a most absurd, ridiculous moment: the bombs have trapped Lira in the water closet, in a fashion reminiscent of Cela's combinations of the supposedly sublime with the all too ludicrously human. . . . Absurd, too, is [Fanchou's] gift of a blue balloon when he is unable to help Lira escape. The blue balloon as a present to one denied liberty (effectively condemned to death) occurs also with special insistence in *La bicicleta del condenado.* The characteristic puerile innocence and ignorance of proper procedure, combined with the situationally absurd desire to act according to the best etiquette appears when Lira asserts that she is dying. After an incredulous moment, Fanchou inquires, "¿Quieres que prevenga a la familia?" It immediately develops that they have no family, and in any case, communication with the outside world has been impossible, but Fanchou peevishly insists that notifying the family is what is done in case of death.

Guilt once more forms the central motif in *La bicicleta del condenado.* As in *El cementerio de automóviles,* the use of the bicycle is related to torture and death. Again, the victim is something of a musician, possibly recalling the Orpheus myth. Even the construction suggests a musical composition, with repetition of themes and a counterpoint technique. Pantomime acquires a new prominence, a tendency accelerated in Arrabal's more recent works. The atmosphere of *La bicicleta . . .* is Kafkaesque, inquisitorial—the protagonist is an unwilling participant in a mysterious game of life and death. In contrast to the awareness of his counterpart in *El laberinto,* however, Viloro is unaware that he is the one condemned and being taken to execution. Again, Arrabal uses two executioners. As in *Laberinto,* he employs the child's train (or playing train), a motif which seems to associate the inquisitorial or judicial process with children's games. This would also seem to be the implication of the happy infantile laughter heard at the end of *La bicicleta . . .* when Viloro is taken off to execution. Children do, in fact, play at death and execution, and—as with Arrabal characters—their actions may also be unconsciously, innocently erotic. This use of the childlike personality is also closely associated with moral ambivalence, and the general incomprehension of all forms of authority characteristic of Arrabal works, but it never seems to add up to constructive implications or suggestions.

Like other absurdist playwrights, Arrabal appears to believe that human existence is absurd because we are born without asking to be born, and die without seeking death, we live between birth and death trapped within our bodies and the limits of our reason, in a complex of self-defeating paradoxes, a check and balance of power and impotence, knowledge and ignorance, attunement and alienation. Like modern absurdists, also, Arrabal resists the traditional separation of farce and tragedy, and in his *teatro pánico* goes beyond this to reject the most fundamental traditional concepts of the theater (the use of a stage, separation between performers and the audience, etc.). Many absurdists have discarded psychology as a control of action; Arrabal perhaps has not discarded it, but it is largely abnormal or irrational psychology which interests him.

As with most absurdists, Arrabal plays often appear to be utterly illogical until one realizes that the logic is not directly expressed, but symbolically embodied in the action. The use of symbolism and allegory is more frequent in the theater of the absurd than perhaps at any time since the Baroque era, and Arrabal is no exception to this. The absurdist playwright in general tends to distrust language, which is linked to the existentialist distrust of reason and negation of communication. Their concern with the gulf of misunderstanding existing, for example, between our expression of self and its apprehension by others, is a frequent absurdist theme, which some express by forcing language to nonsense, of which there are examples in Arrabal. A prime concern with the theater of the absurd is the depiction of monotony, a symbolic representation of absurdity, an assessment of the value of all action as transitory, illusory, imperfect, absurd. This implies a monotony of value, or moral ambivalence—frequent in Arrabal—and monotony is conveyed by the repetition of speeches, scenes, personalities, names, and even plots.

The underlying message of the absurdist is negative or nihilistic, insofar as in most cases it is limited to a statement of the existence of absurdity, with perhaps some sadistic pleasure in portraying man's agonizing struggle. Seldom do they portray man's coming to grips with the problem of absurdity, or his successful existential action with respect to it. Arrabal's later narratives suggest that he is searching for some way out of this personal labyrinth; should he succeed (in finding it), it could open new areas of dramatic activity. (pp. 149-54)

> *Janet Winecoff Díaz, "Theater and Theories of Fernando Arrabal," in* Kentucky Romance Quarterly, *Vol. XVI, No. 2, 1969, pp. 143-54.*

ALLEN THIHER

One of the newest names among the dramatists of the New Theater is that of Fernando Arrabal, a young, enigmatic Spaniard who writes in French and who is today well known by the Parisian theater public. Though he was reared in Spain during the Civil War, he has escaped his background and joined the ranks of those European playwrights who have come to look upon the stage as a place where mere "literature" is no longer to be tolerated. It is in this light that we should read the following manifesto by Arrabal:

> I dream of a theater where humour and poetry, panic and love would be only one. Theatrical rites would then change themselves into an "opera mundi" like Don Quijote's dreams, Alice's nightmares, K.'s delirium, indeed, the humanoid dreams which might haunt the nights of an IBM machine.

And rejecting any label, Arrabal goes on to say:

> The theater we are now elaborating, which is neither modern nor avant-garde, neither new nor absurd, aspires only to be infinitely freer and better.

Theater, in all its splendor, is the richest mirror of images that art can offer us today, it is the extension and sublimation of all the arts. (From **"Le théâtre comme cérémonie panique,"** *Théâtre* **IV**)

Arrabal's new theater is to be a "panic," a manifestation that brings terror as Pan supposedly did when he appeared to men. It is clear that Arrabal, perhaps consciously influenced by Antonin Artaud's theories, intends to create panic by means of a "total spectacle" in which absurd ritual and demented violence are the stuff plays are made of. Moreover, Arrabal's efforts to create a "freer theater" mean that the theater is to become the privileged locus where his private fantasies and obsessions can be transformed into ritual.

Before turning to Arrabal's plays, we might well consider his first novel, **Baal Babylone.** This novel serves as a good introduction to Arrabal's later work, for it is a semi-autobiographical narrative that gives many insights into the dramatist's not too secret traumas. Writing in a deceptively simple, childlike language, Arrabal sets forth the portrait of a Spanish child at a period perhaps immediately after the Civil War. The child's father is gone, but his presence remains vivid for the boy. The child must cling to his father's memory as a means to escape from his odious, oppressive surroundings. It seems that the boy's mother, a domineering woman possessed with her own martyrdom, has denounced the father to the police "for his own good." The mother is thus the prototype for the gallery of sadistic figures who, in Arrabal's theater, cruelly but joyously destroy what they profess to love. In **Baal Babylone** the child refuses to surrender to his mother and her voracious demands. The father's memory thus becomes a symbol of deliverance in the smothering atmosphere where a devouring maternal love is sanctified by the duties the state church would impose upon the child. The boy's silent revolt is made manifest when he exposes himself and urinates before a convent grill. Arrabal's theater, in which exhibitionism, chamber pots, and urination are frequent images, continues this scatological form of revolt, though in a less symbolic manner. For in his theater, Arrabal's revolt becomes a ritual of assault that attacks with unmediated directness.

Guilt, oppression, sadism, childish revolt, erotic fantasies, matricide, all of these fit together to form a surprisingly coherent dramatic world, whatever may be the excesses that Arrabal gives into at times. And since Arrabal published his first play some ten years ago, his work has undergone an evolution that points to a greater understanding of the theater. He began with short plays, such as **Orison, Fando et Lis,** and **Guernica,** in which the influences of such writers as Ionesco and Adamov are quite evident. His work has evolved toward more complex spectacles in which ritual and ceremony are used to give more stylized expression to his obsessions. Plays such as **Le Grand Cérémonial** and **Concert dans un oeuf** should be viewed as erotic ballets or celebrations into which the spectator should enter for purposes of communion and exorcism. Arrabal has also experimented with "pure" spectacles where a kinetic *mise en scène,* using motifs from Klee, Mondrian, and Delaunay, becomes an abstract drama. In both his ritual and his abstract works, Arrabal again calls to mind Artaud and his call for a total spectacle. . . . In 1967, this search for a freer theater culminated in **L'Architecte et l'Empereur d'Assyrie.** In this play Arrabal attained a synthesis between abstract mime and poetical fantasy, a synthesis which marks his mastery of the stage and perhaps of his personal anxieties. This latest work is certainly Arrabal's finest play, though his work's evolution is such that it is often difficult to compare individual plays. Bearing this in mind, we can now examine the recurrent obsessions that make up Arrabal's dramatic universe.

Baal Babylone's mother-child relation, which might be likened to an inverted Oedipal relationship, is savagely exploited in one of Arrabal's earliest plays, *Les Deux Bourreaux* (translated as *The Executioners*). In this work of patent sadism, the mother-martyr not only turns the father over to the police, but she happily watches as he is tortured by two anonymous executioners. . . . In *Les Deux Bourreaux* the mother has two sons, one of whom is a model of filial loyalty toward her. His example points up the rebellion of the ungrateful son who resists his mother's carnivorous affection. Yet the mother is too powerful and convinces the rebel to beg her forgiveness for the unnatural act of turning against maternal love. The father thus disposed of, the mother can retire to enjoy her son's exclusive love.

It would thus appear that an ambivalent Oedipal relationship, although directly portrayed in a relatively limited number of plays, is central to an understanding of Arrabal's fantasies. Two of his later, more developed plays cast more light on the mother-son relation and are worth examining in this respect. The first play, *Le Grand Cérémonial,* is a bizarre "ceremonial" in which a hunchbacked lover, appropriately named Cavanosa, plays the rôle of the doting yet rebellious son. Cavanosa, a seemingly emasculated lover, first claims to have murdered his mother and then claims to have murdered each night a girl whom he has loved. In fact, it seems that he has been reduced to making love to a collection of life-sized dolls that he beats and fondles with equal relish. Yet if Cavanosa is capable of transferring the erotic relationship he has with his mother, his only gesture of love can be to kill the woman he has taken to bed—the bed being the altar on which he sacrifices to the demands of maternal love. The suggested pattern of homicidal coitus is broken by Sil, a lover who, against her will, escapes death. She is offered to the mother as a slave to be tortured at the mother's pleasure. Such is the price of love in Arrabal's theater, where no amorous affair can be complete without whips and chains, or at least the confining prison of a baby carriage. And a more striking portrayal of a repressed Oedipal development, displaced as it may be, can hardly be imagined.

In *L'Architecte et l'Empereur d'Assyrie,* the second later play centering largely on the mother-son relation, Arrabal offers a slightly different view of filial affection. This brilliant comedy turns into a burlesque trial in which the Emperor, an Everyman figure much in the same manner as the King in Ionesco's *Exit the King,* must defend himself against the charge of having murdered his mother. Playing the rôles of all the witnesses in the imaginary trial, the accused accuser reveals his crime—he fed his mother to his pet dog—and condemns himself to be eaten by the Architect. The Architect must wear the mother's clothes while carrying out the act of expiation and ritual incorporation. This ferocious comedy of incest turns back upon itself, for the Architect, through stage sleight of hand as well as through transubstantiation, becomes the Emperor himself. The play ends (or begins again) with the Emperor returning as the Architect. The rôles are reversed, and the ritual begins anew to celebrate the eternally necessary crime of matricide.

For Arrabal, then, love, as derived from the mother-son symbiosis, is either a form of bondage or a homicidal activity.

Slavery and murder form the two poles of love's dialectic. So it is hardly surprising that sadism, a mediator that reconciles both bondage and destruction, is love's principal manifestation in this theater of violent fantasy. Cavanosa, the surrealist Don Juan of *Le Grand Cérémonial,* gives the most concise definition of love when he tells Sil:

> If someone had really loved you, he would have tied you to the bars of a bed and he would have whipped you until your body was just a sore. (*Théâtre* III)

Such a concept of love and its representation on the stage places Arrabal with those other European dramatists who are to be ranged under the aegis of Artaud. Arrabal's theater of sadism seems to be a direct reply to Artaud's cry for "a new idea of eroticism and cruelty" in the theater. And Arrabal, going far beyond what Artaud had meant by a "theater of cruelty," would certainly agree with Artaud's assertion:

> Without an element of cruelty as the basis for any spectacle, theater is not possible. In the state of degeneracy where we are, it is through the skin (par la peau) that metaphysics will be driven into minds. (*Le Théâtre et son double,* Collection Idées)

The metaphysics of cruelty is at the heart of Arrabal's theater. Metaphysics, as Artaud used the term in its original sense, means a world beyond the world that naturalistic and even lyrical theater had tried to incorporate as stage reality. Theatrical metaphysics is, to recall the language of Arrabal's manifesto, the sublimation of the theater, the "raising up" and the creation of new fantasies that can be celebrated only on the autonomous stage. Thus the theater, seen in this light, seems to be the most natural outlet for Arrabal's obsessions with eroticism and cruelty, obsessions that have led him to the creation of ritual forms that present, in Artaud's sense, a metaphysics of sadism. (pp. 174-78)

Arrabal's repertoire of sadistic, murderous acts encompasses a wide number of variations which, through the force of surprise, are designed to drive "metaphysics" into the most hardened skins. Take, for example, the short play, *La Communion solennelle.* A young girl dresses for her first communion while her grandmother gives her advice on how to conduct—in reality on how to suffocate in cleanliness—her eventual marriage. At the same time Arrabal sets forth a scene of necrophilia which ends when the girl knifes the necrophiliac in a coffin. This image of "communion" is a startling, morbid enactment of love as death and death-bringing, of grotesque eroticism that falls victim to cruel, homicidal purity.

A more traditional portrayal of sadism is to be found in *Fando et Lis.* These two infantile lovers are hopelessly traveling to Tar, an enigmatic land possessing the same degree of reality as Kafka's castle. Lis, a paralytic, rides in a baby carriage pushed by Fando. Fando feels a continual compulsion to put chains on his captive inamorata, and when she complains, he finally beats her to death in a fit of childish rage. . . . The dramatic force of *Fando et Lis* is not in its neo-Kafka statement of absurdity nor in its assault upon the banalities of language and pseudo-logic. Beckett and Ionesco are certainly more convincing than Arrabal in conveying a drama of existential anguish or in conjuring the destructive powers of words. Rather it is in the creation of a closed world of childish sadism and erotic bondage that Arrabal is an original and forceful playwright. The infantile mentality of most of Arrabal's non-heroes allows him to exploit his themes of sadism and violence with a comic sense that would be denied to a theater of more mature protagonists. His retarded characters play at "forbidden games" which mix horror and tenderness in dreamlike proportions. Yet his characters, ideal partners for the Oedipal relationship in this respect, are endowed with very adult sexual powers and lusts.

In spite of their homicidal fury, most of Arrabal's protagonists, as children, retain their innocence, or at least the innocence that *non compos mentis* confers. The police powers are nonetheless ready to punish them for crimes either they did not commit, or, more usually, they do not understand. . . .

Arrabal's characters often play at being criminals, but, their childish innocence notwithstanding, they are subject to bloody reprisals they cannot hope to grasp.

The obsessive quest for goodness that Arrabal's infantile heroes undertake serves as a counter-motif to their sadism and lusty criminality. Arrabal's retarded lovers feel remotely the need to be good, to stop killing or fornicating, although their search for goodness is usually as senseless a whim as their casual murders. For example, Emanou, the jazz playing Jesus in *La Cimetière des voitures* (*The Automobile Graveyard* or *The Car Cemetery*), admits to having "killed a few," but he has ready for all occasions a definition of goodness that he has memorized with the conscientiousness of a well behaved child:

> . . . when you are good, you experience a great, internal joy that is born of the peace of mind that you feel when you know yourself to be like the ideal image of man. (*Théâtre* I)

The pointlessness of the definition—and of goodness—is clear at the play's end when Emanou can only stammer helplessly, racking his brains to find the now forgotten definition, until he is given over to the police to be tortured and crucified.

The torturers as well as the tortured can also feel a compulsive need to be good. In Arrabal's first play, *Orison,* his recurrent couple, Fidio and Lilbé, stands beside a murdered infant's coffin and, in a moment of boredom, resolves henceforth to lead a good life. Goodness will not only alleviate their childish ennui, but it will also gain them heaven and God's good favor. But after a minute's thought, the prospect of sexual abstinence and refraining from "putting out dead people's eyes" is too bleak, and Lilbé unenthusiastically concludes, "That's going to be boring." . . . The desire for goodness in Arrabal's plays is a negative motif that, by its comic futility, points up the blatant cruelty that his characters decidedly prefer. One can also see that the manic quest for goodness in its most puerile form is a part of the obsession with childishness and, hence, a part of the child-parent fantasy that pervades Arrabal's theater. Goodness as a negation is largely equated with repressing erotic desires, which, in turn, must be viewed in light of the infantile fear of sexuality that runs throughout the plays.

For another aspect of Arrabal's dialectic of goodness and sadism is his obsessive fear of the sexual act. In an interview Arrabal stated that he must forego all sexual activity, except masturbation, or risk losing his poetical powers. If one can take this interview seriously, and it reads like one of Arrabal's most demented plays, it seems obvious that the eroticism implicit in the mother-son relation carries with it a fear of defilement that counterbalances his sexual fantasies. Defilement

must lead to destruction, as in *Le Couronnement* (*The Coronation*), where loss of virginity causes death. . . . [in *Concert dans un oeuf*], goodness means to avoid indulgence, for impurity, as a child sees it, can only lead to being a "sex maniac." A similar theme is central to *Cérémonie pour un noir assassiné.* In this "ceremony" the two actor-heroes offer the Negro as a lover to a fatherless girl and then knife him to death. They stab him not only because of the "ugly things" that ensue, but because they fear losing the chance to torture the girl for her crime of sexuality. Sadism in Arrabal can quickly become a form of anti-eroticism, however enthusiastically his characters may fornicate in chains. This anti-eroticism is undoubtedly infantile, as are his characters' sadistic antics; it is nonetheless a strong motif in Arrabal's creation of a dramatic tension founded on lustful bondage and sterile destruction. An anti-eroticism grounded in fear establishes one limit to Arrabal's fantasy world.

Just as in *Baal Babylone* the child's father was an absent presence that weighed upon the child, in Arrabal's theater it is God the Father whose absence is felt everywhere. In *Baal Babylone* the father represented a source of deliverance. In the theater an inversion occurs, perhaps illustrating another aspect of the ambivalent mother-son relation and, more especially, showing that God the Father, being identified with the mother, becomes the figure against whom it is necessary to revolt. For in the theater God is a stifling force that must be exorcized by various forms of blasphemy. Arrabal's blasphemy is peculiarly Catholic and Spanish, similar in kind, say, to the mock Last Supper in Buñuel's *Viridiaña*. *Le Couronnement,* for example, presents a mock coronation of the Virgin in which the erotico-religious themes intertwine to suggest both a willed defilement of the Virgin and a fear of death that the loss of virginity entails. *L'Architecte et l'Empereur d'Assyrie* is animated by more comic forms of blasphemy. The Emperor tells at length how he tried once to prove God's existence with a pinball machine—if he reached a thousand points, God existed. But a drunk made the machine tilt with only ten more certain points to score, thus leaving the Emperor plunged in cosmic doubt. His doubt notwithstanding, he teaches the Architect to blaspheme and declares that he uses his daily excretion to write insults to God. The Emperor's scatological sacrilege is a way of asserting what he vehemently denies. . . . Arrabal's characters often have a personal hatred of God; yet, their anger with Him is often a result of His refusal to exist. It is difficult to revolt against the absent Father.

While considering the religious motif, special commentary should be given to *La Cimetière des voitures.* This play has received the most criticism and has been dismissed, on the one hand, for its contrived cleverness and, on the other hand, for the degrading image it presents. The play takes place in a sordid dump yard where people live in junked cars in a way that recalls the organization of a hotel or a housing project. The play's hero, Emanou, is a jazz musician who plays for the poor and is finally crucified on a bicycle. . . . The play does set forth an image of total degradation, but it should also be seen as a mock passion play—one with sociological overtones perhaps. This passion play is another aspect of Arrabal's rebellious parody of religion, but it also seems to be an attempt to portray a religious vision for our time. *La Cimetière des voitures* is ambiguous, since it is both blasphemous buffoonery and a celebration honoring the dead Father's vestigial presence in the presence of his crucified son.

A final important motif in Arrabal's theater is that of the police state and its arbitrary powers of oppression and torture. Arrabal's experience during the Spanish Civil War is sufficient to explain his obsession with this nightmarish fantasy. In *Les Deux Bourreaux,* as shown previously, the mother is associated with the executioners in this theater where pointless cruelty receives the sanction of a nameless, omnipotent state. Indeed, for Arrabal the state is defined through its capacity to inflict torture. . . . *Le Labyrinthe,* shows that Kafka's influence is as much at the heart of Arrabal's vision of universal guilt and condemnation as is Franco's Spain. Resembling a dramatized version of *The Trial,* **Le Labyrinthe** is set in a forest of blankets from which a traveler, Etienne, cannot escape. The forest's owner, a father figure possessing absolute power over his domain, chains Etienne to a urinal. In breaking his chains Etienne is brutal to a fellow prisoner who, though nearly paralyzed, hangs himself. Etienne is tried for murder and commits a series of errors that inexorably bring about his condemnation. The play is remarkable for its creation of an atmosphere where innocence, or near innocence, is forced to impeach itself by the relentless logic of arbitrary power. In a comparable fashion, *Guernica,* a play inspired by Picasso's painting, also depicts a universe founded upon guilt. A nameless officer's stare and the sight of his handcuffs are enough to implicate in guilt those who are helplessly caught in the war's anonymous destruction. Authority, whatever form it may take in Arrabal, is synonymous with gratuitous persecution. The absent father, the possessive mother, and the anonymous state all share this feature.

Arrabal's obsessive fantasies have given rise to a body of work that is among the most promising of the New Theater. With the modernity of a happening and the courage to face the delirium of our times, it may well come to be among the most significant in this second half of the twentieth century. (pp. 178-83)

> Allen Thiher, "Fernando Arrabal and the New Theater of Obsession," in Modern Drama, *Vol. XIII, No. 2, September, 1970, pp. 174-83.*

FERNANDO ARRABAL AND OTHERS

[*In the interview excerpted below, Arrabal speaks with a group of students and faculty members in a conversation which originally took place at Cornell University in April 1974.*]

[Interviewer]: *A common opinion among those inclined to be critical of culture and wines produced south of the Pyrenees is that Spanish literature is always derivative of something. Specifically, I have heard it said that your theater is half Goya, half Beckett. What is your reaction?*

[Arrabal]: Of Goya there is a great deal in my work. But at the time I was writing my first plays, I was living in a small, primitive village in Spain, oblivious to the very existence of Beckett. I wrote those plays in perfect innocence, and when I showed them to some bright friends of mine, they said: "But that's very much like Beckett!" "Who is Beckett?" I asked. And they told me: "He's a writer." I read his work, and indeed there were points of contact between us—a very understandable phenomenon, since we are both witnesses to our time and were traveling at that moment along the same path. Starting with my second volume of plays, my theater has very little connection with Beckett's. In the period when Ionesco and Beckett were beginning to write, the playwright was faced with a very important problem: the search for reality.

Reality was to be seized by figures such as Ionesco, Beckett, Adamov—the so-called dramatists of the absurd. Their literature, which they considered realistic, was called absurd and avant-garde, even though it was the very opposite, a literature that reflected reality to perfection. That was the problem facing men who are now between sixty and seventy years old, and we only happened on the scene *after* that. Their whole theater is a theater of communication through the Word, ruled by His Majesty the Word. Then we came with our theater, which said that no longer was the Word exclusive ruler; rather, His Majesty was image, gesture, body, movement. We created a theater of movement, gesture. (p. 54)

You talk about the "Word," but you do exactly the opposite of what earlier dramatists did. You seem to destroy words, debase language. We might ask ourselves if the theater can survive if it destroys its own medium.

I believe (and I speak for us all) that we are not attempting to annihilate the word, but to enrich the theater with something it was in danger of losing, that is, movement and imagery. That should make it obvious that we are not out to crush the theater. My theater is very modest; I do not mean to place myself on a level with my colleagues, but I do believe that, thanks to our work and that of the groups I mentioned earlier, we are at the moment witnessing a rebirth of the theater.

What sort of reaction do you look for in your spectators or readers? Is it a negative one, since there is so much that is shocking and repulsive in your plays? In **And They Put Handcuffs on the Flowers,** *for example, one leaves the theater completely horrified, disgusted, and with the feeling of having lost contact with everything. If the spectator loses contact with the play, the dramatist fails. Is that the response you expect, or is there something positive to be gleaned from your work?*

You are playing the Devil's Advocate, and you don't want to see what it's all about. One shouldn't spit into a mirror. I am the mirror and witness of society. In some productions of the play I would ask the actors to exhibit a certain degree of violence toward the audience. I don't know if you felt this. It was necessary because I wanted the audience to be party to the condition of a Spanish political prisoner. You say that the play is disgusting, horrible. Well, I wanted it to be exactly that—every bit as atrocious as reality is. Only a few weeks ago, in Barcelona, some young boys—one a Spaniard, the other a Czech—were executed by the same method described in my play, the garrote.. . . . We cannot hide our heads in the sand; we must look reality in the face, as witnesses to it. That may shock you. I would like to shock you more deeply yet, to the point of getting you to cry out against this horror and keep it from happening again.

One does indeed emerge from the play with a feeling of horror, and of course one feels compassion for the prisoners. But all those frightful scenes destroy everything, even the positive emotions that might be aroused.

No, I think that most of the critics who wrote about *And They Put Handcuffs on the Flowers* understood that it is a play filled with tenderness. I was constantly saying to the actors performing it in New York (I express myself badly in English): "Big emotion!" That was the main thing, to display much emotion, to be very nostalgic, very sentimental. But even if you were left shocked and shattered, I know people just like you, who are shocked and shattered but nevertheless spend their summers in Madrid peacefully under the protection of the fascist police. While you and I are talking, there are people who have spent over twenty years in a Madrid prison cell. That, to me, is much more shocking. (pp. 54–5)

Do you write your plays in Spanish or French?

Forgive me for saying so, but that is the classic question put by fascists who then end up by reproaching me for not writing in Spanish. If I do not publish in Spanish, it is because the Franco censorship prevents me from doing so. I write in Spanish, and with my wife I translate my work into French.

How has the handling of a language that is not your own affected your work?

Some critics who have studied my theater, my novels, and my poems mention my style. I think that an important aspect of my style is the fact that I speak French badly, and in so doing I enrich the language. But I am not unique in this. The contemporary French theater (the most important in the world) is made up in large part of foreigners: Beckett, Ionesco, Adamov. . . .

Then that gives you an advantage?

Yes, of course, since it is so difficult for us, who are foreigners and half-breeds, to master a foreign language. We enjoy the battle, and in the end, it serves our purpose.

Do you believe that there are other systems of communication aside from violence, at least after that one has been exhausted?

I have forty plays and there are all sorts of voices in them. It would seem that nothing but violence is seen in them (our Devil's Advocate said so). My theater, my films, my novels are works of tenderness. I am always surprised to see a shocked and irritated audience. My theater overflows with love. (p. 56)

René Girard, in his book La Violence et le sacré, *speaks of the sacrificial ceremony as a means utilized by society to destroy the violence in its midst, and he writes that the act of choosing a victim resembles violence but is not actual violence. Thus, when you mentioned the ceremony that the Spanish police performed in destroying an individual, it seemed to me that what the police did was to recreate this violence. However, in your theater, since this violence is unreal, in the sense that one is playing at violence, the reaction provoked is not exactly nonviolent.*

I think that you have read my plays differently from me. In my plays, no one pretends anything. My theater is direct: what is said is said. As to the question of violence, we have arrived at a society in which there is almost no domestic violence, no violence of daily habit. There are sudden explosions, like Vietnam and Chile, because there is no violence in private, conjugal relationships. It is a pity that relationships between couples are not more intense, as they were, for example, in Spain, where a husband would beat his wife because she had looked out of the window during his absence. The couples were always united by very powerful bonds, and next day the husband would go back to his work, while the wife, in the patio, would tell us everything that had happened because she was proud of it. That's a thing of the past.

But you have said that your theater is a reaction against the brutality of events in Spain.

Brutality in the intimacy of love relationships does not distress me at all. On the contrary, I approve of it heartily. What disturbs me is institutionalized brutality. After the reign of Catholic Kings, Spain submitted to the inquisition and to intolerance: that disturbs me.

Does your theater reach the audience for which you create it?

Unfortunately, we are shut out from society. We work with all our might, but that does not prevent you, who are among the elite of society, and all the other madmen like you, who rule the world and don't give a penny for the arts, from thumbing your noses at us. The only thing left for us is to pour out our feelings with as much sincerity as we can muster. When I was in prison, Beckett wrote to the Spanish judge to say that Arrabal should be freed, and he used a sentence applicable to writers in general, not only to me in particular: "The writer should not be kept in prison because we must not add to his suffering." I think Beckett is right. The writer is a man who suffers; he reveals his pain in his art; and unfortunately the world around us, the body powerful, doesn't give a royal damn. . . . The Spanish *petite bourgeoisie* joined forces with liberty and fought for it. But once they had lost the war, there was nothing for them, nothing to lose, nothing to gain. Which is why for us, who belong to this *petitie bourgeoisie,* the only refuge is a kind of ceremony, something wordless that can be expressed only through humor or exile. (pp. 56-7)

Your mention of ceremony brings to mind the type of theater called "ceremonial." How did the theater develop in this direction? What theater existed in the Spain of the nineteen-fifties? How did you begin to write?

It so happens that I was the first to speak of ceremony. Why? It is not a question of esthetic options but of a deliberate choice. What is a ceremony? It is a spiritual vehicle through which a group may communicate with someone whose language is unknown. For example, a group of Protestants meet in a church or temple, and in order to communicate with God, they create a ceremony. Or another example: we, my social class, the *petite bourgeoisie,* were shattered by the Civil War. I am in Spain, trying to speak to my neighbor, whose language is incomprehensible to me, and for that reason I create this ceremony. That is why from its very origins my theater has encompassed ceremony as well as blasphemy and eroticism. Their meaning in this context is diametrically opposed to their usual connotations. Today, when a writer creates an erotic or pornographic work, he may do it for a variety of reasons. In my case, I hoped to liberate my body and soul, to purge myself, to free my spirit. to break the chains of fascism and Catholicism. When Breton published the only play ever to appear in the surrealist review, *La Brèche,* it was one of mine . . . , although he felt that "theater is an obscenity that leads to crime." In point of fact, I believe that Breton did not find this vileness in my work and was impelled to commit a surrealist crime: publish a play by Arrabal, simply because my text was a poetic expression.

Can one say that your theater, rather than a challenge to modern society, is an effort to carry the dramatic art back to its roots and convert it into a primitive rite?

I would prefer it to be a ceremony in favor of liberty and tolerance.

What relationship do you see between pantomime and drama? Can you explain your idea of an abstract mechanical theater that you raised in connection with **Orchestration théâtrale?**

I am not interested in pantomime. **Orchestration** reflects a period (1960) of abstract pictorial fanaticism.

Could you specify what you mean by "Panic theater" and in what way it differs from that of Michel de Ghelderode, for example?

Panic theater and Ghelderode, my God! Alexandro Jodorowsky, Topor, and I formed part of the surrealist movement, and one fine day we were shocked to discover that the surrealist group was dictatorial and dogmatic. We were troubled by this dogmatism, and that is why we created the Panic theater in 1963. Shortly thereafter it was completely forgotten, but now it is gathering momentum . . . : there are quite a few people who proclaim themselves its partisans, and in the 1973 exhibition at the *Grand Palais,* the painters of the Panic movement were out in front. But it is a child that has grown up too fast, and as such we reject it.

One critic has said that your contribution to the theater is that of having initiated a comic style. Is that true? If so, what kind of humor do you see in your work?

Geneviève Lemeau wrote that in 1959. But although I received the Black Humor prize, I do not believe that humor is a principal element in my theater. (pp. 57-8)

Why have you written a book about chess?

I find chess very interesting because the game has a great deal in common with the theater.. . . . For me a game of chess is an act in which chance plays a large part and which is like a battle, a boxing match. One cannot have a single, fixed plan, even though in theory this is essential. It can't be so because everything depends on what the opponent does. The opponent can play extremely well or extremely badly, and with each move one must create a plan that counteracts the preceding one—just as in life, as in the theater.

Insofar as all your earlier work derives its strength from its position vis-à-vis a certain social reality, it seems to me that this obsession with chess represents an abandonment of that direction.

Not at all! I am the opposite of what you take me for; I consider myself an esthete of the minority, unfortunately for me.

I am thinking of another one of your old colleagues, Topor, who also formed part of the Panic theater in 1963 and who produced a deplorable film called La Planète magique.

It is not deplorable and it is not called *magique* but *La Planète sauvage.* He did not make the film, only the drawings.

Without Topor, there would have been no film. I agree that his drawings are sensational. Nevertheless, the film is fanciful and has absolutely nothing to do with any sort of social reality . . .

We are too shocked by social reality to have the idiotic nerve to speak of it directly. Topor lived in Poland, he sufferd to the very marrow because of his Jewish parents, he suffered terribly. We too, in Spain, have suffered. But we dare not to do what the majority does and parade that suffering openly.

You mean to say that **Viva la muerte** *is the synthesis of a private experience, of personal suffering?*

Yes. **Viva la muerte** has as its sole aim the portrayal of a child who witnesses the arrival of fascism and crime. It is very simple. Take a book that describes a situation in general terms, let's say the Spanish Civil War. You can't really form an im-

pression of it, but if you talk to me about it, you can, because I can tell you about the food, about what one saw every day, and in that way you can understand what happened. Our mission is to be witnesses to our time and to shock the bourgeois, without meaning to, something which is frowned upon nowadays. The artist's mission is to be original, to explore the future, to explore confusion. It is a most exalting human activity.

You speak a great deal about confusion. How can you be a lover of chess and at the same time a preacher of confusion?

I am passionate and fanatical about chess and about mathematics, and this leads me to believe ever increasingly in confusion. I believe that one can construct a dialectic about history out of the past. Once an event has occurred, we can analyze it. But the future acts as a bolt from the blue; we cannot anticipate what will happen tomorrow. I call that confusion. It is better to admit that than to try, as Marxist analysts would, to imagine that everything is ordered, that one can know in advance how life is to unfold. It would be sheer fantasy to discover the laws of confusion and the rules governing Utopia.

Then we might say that you are guided by an esthetic of confusion. Yet in almost all your works, especially in one like **The Architect and the Emperor of Assyria** *we can see a perfect structure. Doesn't this play represent a negation of confusion, and isn't the very act of writing a triumph over confusion?*

No, no. Obviously I can create a perfectly structured theater, but the more perfect the structure, the greater the confusion of what is said.

Do you see your theater as based on a social conscience, or does it have a poetic foundation? I ask you this because you often speak as a theoretician of the theater.

A poetic foundation. I would prefer to be a poet in the theater.

One thing troubles me. You say that you have never written anything of a social nature and that it is purely by accident that you are prohibited in Spain. I wonder to what extent you believe your work to have a subversive content?

It is subversive in Spain. It is forbidden because my plays are not pieces of political propaganda. The Franco government readily accepts propaganda, whatever its nature, but I do not write propaganda, and that is why I am feared. In my work there is something that escapes the authorities, something dangerous. They cannot tolerate my activities. Were I to proclaim myself Communist or Socialist or Democrat, they would know exactly the limits to which I would go.

What exactly is the difference between a propaganda play and those that you write?

In propaganda, spontaneity is crushed by the need to say something. No theater of propaganda has ever been successful propaganda. I experimented with the theater of propaganda only once. In Paris, at the *Théâtre National Populaire* (a very large hall with four thousand seats), we created a play together with the actors. . . . We had a great deal of money and everything going for us, but it was a catastrophe. It was a propaganda piece, and no one believed in it. The images were drowned out by the plan as a whole. There were some good things, especially a bullfight, but the play fell flat because it was propaganda. I was no longer a witness; I was ful-filling an obligation.

You say you are a witness to your era. That means that you place yourself into an historical perspective and that you must have a vision of the future. Do you see how the theater could influence the future? When you give your testimony, is it for the moment at hand, is it to present a new concept of the world, or for some other purpose?

The demands I make are perfectly innocent: freedom, toler-ance, etc. But it would be too pretentious to imagine that my theater could bring about all that. When World War II ex-ploded in Paris, very few people resisted the Nazis. Jean-Paul Sartre and Simone de Beauvoir do not join the Resistance; they put on plays in 1943-44. German officers are seen in the theaters. At the same time, there is a man, Samuel Beckett, who, the moment the war breaks out, forms part of a resis-tance network and fights. That, I think, is admirable. When times are difficult, it is Beckett—by no means a political indi-vidual—who fights with the Resistance, while Sartre presents plays for the Nazis to see. The situation in Spain is similar. Who is killed at the outset of the Civil War? The only Spanish poet who was not political: García Lorca. (pp. 58-60)

Normally a playwright expects applause from his audience. Do you?

These days everybody applauds and spoils the occasion. What was done in Spain in my youth was better: some people would applaud and some would hiss and boo. That's not done anymore. In New York a play is put on. It is badly received by the critics and the audience; but nevertheless, on the day of the dress rehearsal and at the opening performance, the public applauds. There are plays in which I did everything possible to have the spectators in passionate opposition and disinclined to applaud, for example in **And They Put Hand-cuffs on the Flowers.** But convention rules the theater, and the audience always applauds at the end. (p. 60)

Fernando Arrabal and others, in a conversation in Diacritics, *Vol. 5, No. 2, Summer, 1975, pp. 54-60.*

THOMAS JOHN DONAHUE

Born of passion, pain, fire, the memories of his childhood and the Spanish Civil War, Arrabal's theater represents a special moment in the development of the avant-garde theater in this century. Once shunted aside as a minor element of the so-called Theater of the Absurd, in sheer size his theater has grown to fourteen published volumes, developed an interna-tional reputation that touches all the continents, and causes an uproar as a succès de scandale whenever a major produc-tion of one of his plays is mounted. This does not, however, prevent his theater from sometimes being wrongheaded, banal, boring, and muddled in its outlook. Interesting ideas sometimes become entangled in the wreckage of their own rhetoric or sufficiently blurred by Arrabal's wanton use of the banally pornographic to leave even the most hardy fan of his brand of theater somewhat jaded. But his theater can no lon-ger be ignored. He has brought life to an art that seems at times to have been left untouched by the extraordinary devel-opments in the arts in the twentieth century.

Arrabal's theater, even when it is closest to the absurdist tra-dition, possesses marked characteristics. It has the obtrusive odor of sulfur about it; it is blasphemous, obscene, bawdy,

and outrageous; and yet it has an unmistakable charm of its own. Arrabal was able to brew this mixture of charm and blasphemy thanks to the creation of the adult children such as Fando and Lis, Emanou and Dila, Fidio and Lilbé. These characters, sometimes capable of a demented cruelty that is difficult to find elsewhere in the avant-garde theater, are also the givers and receivers of a guileless, tender love. As they wander through the marginal areas of society looking for some type of fulfillment or satisfaction that children are wont to hope for, the realities of an adult world—of the forces of order and oppression—are frequently all they find. Although reminiscent of Beckett's couples, Didi and Gogo, Clov and Hamm, their resemblance to Buñuel's street urchins and to Pablo Picasso's *saltimbanques* becomes apparent as they play their delightful games that soon turn to murderous forays into a baroque and macabre world of juvenile crime and pas-sion.

The erotic cruelty; the mad tenderness; and the games of in-nocence, guilt, and pardon within a metaphoric framework give way in his Panic Theater to a series of rituals that lead his adolescent characters to the knowledge of love and panic. His plays become fast-moving, kaleidoscopic visions that create the chaos and confusion that stand at the center of his panic theories. His characters become interchangeable; they are subject to rapid transformations; and, like the Emperor and the Architect, they occasionally exchange personae. The entire panoply of secondary effects, of lighting, slide projec-tions, film clips, helps to create an atmosphere of a world gone wild. The Panic Theater is a visual feast that tends to-ward the spectacle and, perhaps more important, brings to the theater a technique of scenic juxtaposition that used to be the sole reserve of the cinema.

Yet for all its richness from a theatrical point of view, the Panic Theater can be singularly void of any substantive ideas. What human being, for example, would not want to be both omniscient and free of any fetters on sexual and social behav-ior, as is Giafar at the conclusion of **The Lay of Barabbas.** One may be amused by the sheer spectacle presented here, but the poverty of language eventually takes its toll on our attention and concentration. One longs for the charm and in-nocence of Arrabal's children of paradise. Yet when the Panic Theater succeeds, as it most certainly does in **The Ar-chitect and the Emperor of Assyria,** the effect is a profoundly meaningful metaphor about the human condition, its joys and its pains.

While maintaining the ceremonial aspect of his Panic Theater and its transformations, in his Guerrilla Theater Arrabal ex-plores some of the more pressing social problems of the con-temporary world, and especially of Spain during the regime of Francisco Franco. He presents a stinging indictment of prison systems, tyranny, and oppression. He tries to create a theater that is a means of mobilizing public opinion, a con-sciousness-raising act, a prod to action for or against some as-pect of the social or political status quo. Whenever his own fantasies do not set the picture awry, he succeeds remarkably well in emotionally involving us in the lives of the oppressed and of those hungry for freedom.

The importance Arrabal gives to ceremony in both his Panic Theater and his Guerrilla Theater makes him part of the ef-forts of many playwrights and directors who attempt to make the theater return to its roots and away from the storytelling dramatic literature that is of more recent vintage. Jerzy Gro-towski, Jodorowsky, García, Lavelli, Savary, Peter Brook, and Richard Schechner as directors and leaders of troupes have contributed their talents to this movement toward a ritualistic and communal theater. Their success can be measured in the number of plays even in the naturalistic mold that use the ritual and ceremony as an underlying structure.

But we cannot overlook the role the writings of Antonin Artaud have played in this movement. . . . Arrabal fortunately has benefited from the freedom to experiment with all the various elements of the theater that Artaud's works have instilled in the contemporary scene. If he himself has not gone to that source of imaginative and poetic thought on the theater, he has surely felt its impact. The best productions of his works are staged by directors who are in debt to Artaud, since Arrabal, like Artaud, wants to create a world of chaotic illusion and confusion, of gesture and cacophony, of dreams, nightmares, and poetry that would lead to a communal theatrical experience. (pp. 138-41)

For his production of **Automobile Graveyard** in Dijon in 1966, the Argentine director Victor García created a playing space with U-shaped walkway, a multilevel stage, and old automobile carcasses hanging from the ceiling. When it was restaged in Paris at the Théâtre des Arts in December 1967, some of the public was seated on swivel chairs that permitted them to follow the fast-paced action that took place about them. They were treated to a spectacle that included strident screams and an almost continual clanging of metal—a spectacle that Gabriel Marcel called "a degrading technique."

García, whose French at the time was minimal, cared little for the text per se: he interposed within its action both **Orison** and **First Holy Communion.** Although he changed not a word of the original text, he was obviously more interested in its structure, which could be re-formed to fit his scenic demands and needs. Like Arrabal, García seems more intrigued by the structure of a work, its theatricality, and its scenic vision rather than by its linguistic thrust. He is one of the directors who can easily synthesize Arrabal's conceptions with his own; and this he does, thanks to the freedom that Artaud, through the influence of his writings, has wrought in the contemporary theater.

Similarly, Arrabal, in his own production of **and they put handcuffs on the flowers** experimented with the theatrical environment. A darkened room provided an entrance into the playing space proper. There the actors led the audience one by one, separating them from the real world of their friends and their work and into the "real" world of Arrabal's prisoners. The spectators then were shown to their places on a scaffolding set up around the playing space.

Arrabal's direction, not surprisingly, emphasized the performance rather than the text. Movement that becomes dance, dance that becomes ritual, language that becomes poetry, poetry that becomes music and incantation—these are what he strives for. Some forms of theatrical experimentation discard the text entirely, but for Arrabal it remains the starting point of a process in which directors and actors seek out various ways of "doing a play." As we have seen, Arrabal's emphasis on a particular type of surrealistic, poetic language prevents him from abandoning the text completely.

Arrabal's experimentation has also led to an attempt to alter the relationship between the audience and the performer, especially in the plays of his Guerrilla Theater. He tries to include the audience in the theatrical event by giving its members an opportunity to speak and to share their dreams and fantasies with the group. By doing so he has also changed the relationship among the spectators and has tried to move them away from their normally passive posture.

In effect, Arrabal has experimented with most of the permutations that the theater "game" allows: he treats the text as a *pre*text for theater; he attempts to alter the relationship between the actor and the theatrical environment, between the spectator and the theatrical environment, between the actor and the spectator, and among the spectators themselves. Of course he has not done this in any one play, but his willingness to experiment has been part of his theater almost from its inception.

In many cases, Arrabal has tried to return to the origins of the theater in his search for new patterns. These patterns, uncommon in our traditional theater in which sequential logic and organic development of plot and character have been touchstones, rely more on a subjective and aesthetic logic than on a linear dramatic organization. The result is a theater in which randomness, disorder, and anarchy reign supreme, in which baroque excess and the grotesque frequently constitute the salient characteristics.

Given the fact that Arrabal tries to create a scenic metaphor and relies less on language than the playwrights of the traditional theater, he can be placed among the absurdists of the post World War II period. Yet there are distinguishing characteristics in his theater that cannot be overlooked. Arrabal's characters to a man remain true to a type of psychic innocence even in face of their obvious guilt, which is, of course, imposed upon them by the morality of a society that lies beyond their comprehension. Instead of the world-weary, worldwise, and jaded characters of the absurdists, one encounters either adult children living in a world of their own devising or juveniles about to be initiated into the fantasy world of love and panic. Even the prisoners of **and they put handcuffs on the flowers,** despite dozens of years in the hell hole of a prison, do not lose a certain innocence, a sense of the marvelous, a childlike wonder. Too, the characters of the **Théâtre bouffe** go on their zany way, ignoring the perils of the technological world they live in. This attitude of Arrabal's characters in face of a grim world of reality, in conjunction with the emphatically grotesque and erotic elements and the ritualistic structure, give him at least a special niche in the pantheon of the absurdists, if not a theatrical chapel all his own.

Although Arrabal has lived in Paris for more than twenty years and has a following that is international, it would be an error to entirely discount the influences of his Spanish background on his theater. The Spanish government even in the post-Franco period continued to place him among the most troublesome of political enemies until 1977. Even now he refuses to return to Spain until all political prisoners have been released. Arrabal has not forgotten that he is Spanish, despite his international fame, although he does admit to speaking a Spanish that is less than contemporary. The political situation in Spain under Franco plays an obvious and important role in at least three plays: **The Two Executioners,** in which Françoise betrays her husband to the Fascist authorities; **Guernica,** which depicts an elderly couple, Fachou and Lira, immediately after the firebombing of that Basque village; and finally, **and they put handcuffs on the flowers,** set in a Spanish prison. The Spanish state, one of the principal preoccupations of most Spaniards, according to George Wellwarth, shows its totalitarian head most explicitly in these plays. But like most of his fellow Spanish writers, Arrabal has a strong taste for allegory behind which he may hide a critique of the Spanish regime. Thus, it could be argued that the figure of the police in such plays as *The Tricycle* and *Ceremony for a Murdered Black* also represents the oppression of the police state in Spain. Similarly, *The Labyrinth,* in which a godlike figure named Justin turns out to be a tyrant in his universe of blankets and bedclothes, could be meant to represent a tyrant of Franco's ilk. Arrabal, like many modern playwrights, writes of his personal universe, but he does not ignore the lack of freedom imposed by the governmental system in his homeland. His password is freedom, and he denounces all tyrannies, both political and spiritual.

In more recent years, his attacks on the tyranny of the state, church, or any other authority have become more insistent. *Heaven and Crap* and *The Twentieth Century Revue* leave no doubt as to the target of Arrabal's barbs, be they in Spain or elsewhere. Hitler, Truman, and Our Lady of Fatima are openly caricaturized in these grotesque comic strips for the theater. Moreover, post-Franco Spain, as it enters into the capitalistic mainstream and perforce leaves some of the old Spanish traditions behind, receives a panicky warning from Arrabal in *The Tower of Babel.* Nowhere is Arrabal more touching in his expression of feelings toward his mother country than in *On the High Wire,* where the Duke, Tharsis, and Wichita represent the Arrabal caught between the freedom necessary for his art that he has found in Paris and the desire to see Spain revere its artists and respect their freedom.

Dependent as he is on his memories for inspiration, Arrabal cannot sublimate his Catholic education in a country that remains the stepchild of the Inquisition. A cursory view of his plays easily uncovers the Christ figures: Emanou in *Automobile Graveyard,* Tosan in *and they put handcuffs on the flowers,* and Chester in *Today's Young Barbarians.* The simplistic carrot-and-stick morality of Arrabal's adult children; the pervasive ideas of guilt, innocence, and pardon; and the harsh and unjust superiors show Arrabal's debt to his early education in the strict tradition of Spanish Catholicism. The macabre but comic action of *First Holy Communion* underscores Arrabal's fascination with the grotesque distortion of Catholic beliefs. In *The Garden of Earthly Delights,* we see a portrait of Catholic convent schools as prisons, or mother superiors as wicked wardens, and of students as oppressed victims of a system that provides no mercy for young individualists. *The Architect and the Emperor of Assyria* contains some typically scurrilous attacks on the concept of confession. . . . *And they put handcuffs on the flowers* portrays the church in collusion with the state, priests as toadies to be castrated, visions of Our Lady of Fatima as distortions of erotic and scatological dreams.

Although repressed sexuality is by no means a uniquely Spanish phenomenon, the resultant display of a bloody, baroque violence seems to be very Spanish. Here again the puritanical views of the Spanish church come into direct conflict with the openly erotic aspects of the Spanish character. Bataille's thesis that eroticism is generated only by the dialectic of interdict and transgression could not find a more pertinent proof than in the Iberian Peninsula. Neither can one find a more insistent example in the contemporary avant-garde theater than in the sadomasochistic games of Cavanosa in *The Grand Ceremonial* or in the ever-increasing violence of *The Condemned Man's Bicycle.* Where in the theater is love pictured as a wild but tender gorilla as it is in *The Garden of Earthly*

Delights? Such florid images are not to be found elsewhere in the theater today, nor shall we find a playwright of major international stature who brings so much of his ethnic character to bear on his works as does Arrabal.

Much of the originality of Arrabal's theater derives from his rich repertory of images, fantasies, and illusions. His theater is indeed a personal insight on the verities of the human condition. Yet it is at this point that conflict arises, for if Arrabal is to be successful he must translate the personal, even intimate vision into terms that can be understood by the general public. It is clear that he frequently succeeds in this task; it is equally clear that he sometimes fails. In comparision with a Beckett or an Ionesco, his works appear unkempt and untidy—far from the jewel-like precision that those two masters display in their craft. But Arrabal's more elaborate vision requires more attention to the details that will permit his genius to show. The spontaneity of his metaphors must not be sacrificed to technique and to a studied posture, as frequently happens in the Panic Theater, but must be preserved and nurtured in a careful elaboration of his vision. When he is successful in finding the appropriate theatrical framework, Arrabal touches our deepest emotions, he brings life to the liveliest of the arts, and he teaches us what it means to be human. Arrabal's theater is a unique adventure. (pp. 141-46)

> *Thomas John Donahue, in his* The Theater of Fernando Arrabal: A Garden of Earthly Delights, *New York University Press, 1980, 153 p.*

PETER NORRISH

An investigation of the personally experienced, psychological symbolism within Arrabal's ritual reveals . . . some interesting affinities in terms of genre and expression. On the surface, Arrabal's theatre is alternately light and dark; underneath, it is usually consistently sombre. With this composition, it has a place in new developments in France in the field of tragic farce, more so because of the juxtaposition or fusion of moods than because of content, which may be less "absurdist" in Arrabal's case than is sometimes supposed. Much of Arrabal's writing has some superficial resemblances to traditional types of farce, and it also fits, to a much greater degree, into the very different modern frameworks of farce as redefined by the avant-garde movement of the 1950's and 1960's. This is an aspect of his work that has been neglected. Most of the well-known innovations were achieved by Beckett, and especially by Ionesco, in the first of the two decades. It was in the sixties that Arrabal (born in 1932) joined them in their success, his particular contribution consisting of a combination of farce and ritual.

Farce and ritual are terms that are sometimes loosely applied. It may be helpful to recall in the first place that traditional farce has been defined as "broad, physical, visual comedy, whose effects are pre-eminently theatrical and intended solely to entertain; comedy which is slapstick, if you like, in a more or less coherently funny narrative. . . . " Ionesco and Beckett brought farce much closer to tragedy, mingling lightness and darkness to such an extent that farce became something of a hybrid. . . . As for ritual, it is described by anthropologists as a special kind of behaviour, having a clear shape or pattern that may be repeated in a series of closely similar performances; this patterned behaviour is also of a kind that leads itself usually to symbolic interpretation. By adding ritual to his farce . . . Arrabal gives it a dramatic pattern with ceremonial emphasis, an emphasis that is also symbolic of deeply disturbed psychological experience. At the same time, in using both farce and ritual, he seems to have a dual purpose: to attack the people who controlled his childhood and youth, and to liberate himself from them. Not only personal distresses, but also personal revolt and attempted release are involved, as Arrabal turns memories and nightmares (themselves repetitive, like rituals) into organized patterns.

More so perhaps than either Ionesco or Beckett, Arrabal presents the more conventionally farcical aspects of his plays within a framework that the French would call *burlesque:* that is, he relies to some extent on grotesque exaggeration, the grotesque element being atypical of "normal" human behaviour and quite often ugly. Parody, and more especially visual and verbal fantasy, built into Arrabal's burlesque, as well as the conventionally farcical boasting, caricature, disguises, falling down, running away, and similar antics. Grotesque exaggeration combined with would-be limitless fantasy sometimes overflows from Arrabal's burlesque into the darker, more desperate areas of drama, and one is reminded of the imagination of the Marquis de Sade, or his disciple Georges Bataille, as religion, sex, and the scatological are stirred together to concoct a brew potent enough that the partaker may transcend the known confines of reality. The more sombre aspects of Arrabal's drama are largely bound up with his use of ritual, as will be shown, but they are also linked to some extent with his use of farce.

An important part of Arrabal's technique is his habit of switching suddenly from the serene to the sinister. For example, in **Le Labyrinthe** . . . we are indeed greatly surprised and amused at first, but increasingly alarmed later, to find characters imprisoned in a weird maze of blankets fixed to clothes-lines, on the edge of which a man soon tries to hang himself on a lavatory chain. If this is farce, then it is surely what Ionesco calls tragic farce: in fact, the very setting—which implies a vast area of smothering proliferation well beyond the lines which cross in all directions over the whole stage—is similar to the ones Ionesco uses in *Les Chaises* and *Le Nouveau Locataire* (1957). The tragic/farcical note is reinforced when Bruno, having apparently succeeded in hanging himself on the chain and having had his corpse disposed of, turns up again at the end with enough life left in him to go on tormenting the poor hero, Étienne, who has already been tried (in a trial as unreal as the rest of this nightmare) for murder.

Earlier productions of Arrabal plays featured other wildly absurd situations, with bizarre dialogue to match. . . . A number of these early plays, such as **Fando et Lis** (1955/6), have ambivalent characters whose way of talking and acting is both childish and adolescent at the same time, and who are naïvely, erotically tender or cruel in turn, according to their unpredictable changes of mood. The more recent plays are on the whole less farcical and more earnest and politically inclined; but they also include the familiar blend. **Bestialité érotique** (1968), for example, although considerably more restrained than its title suggests, does indulge in an extreme parody of love relationships, again involving both tenderness and cruelty. And the plays of **Théâtre Bouffe,** which appear as volume XII of the Christian Bourgois edition (1978), and comprise **Vole-moi un petit milliard** (first produced in 1977), **Le Pastaga des loufs ou Ouverture orang-outan,** and **Punk et Punk et Colégram,** have farcical situations with multiple mistaken identities, disguises galore, extreme caricature, un-

subtle jokes, and other acknowledged borrowings from boulevard plays, bedroom scenes and all. (pp. 320-23)

The best illustration of Arrabal's type of farce occurs in the outstanding play already mentioned, **L'Architecte et l'Empereur d'Assyrie**. . . . (p. 323)

[Farcical] episodes abound [in this play]. In one of the most outrageous, the Emperor gives birth to a baby girl whose face is the "spit and image" of the face of the cathedral clock. There are also funny parodies of war and religion; insulting names that might have come from Jarry's pen and are hurled at the poor Architect-pupil by his absurdly tyrannical master; references to such things as the erotic novel *Histoire d'O* and artificial phalluses; much play with masks and other disguises; and, of course, constant clowning, which culminates in the "miracle" (which would have been known in the *commedia dell' arte* as a *burla,* that is, a practical joke) of turning a glass of water into *Eau de Javel,* instead of the whisky or wine that had been requested. All in all, the play is, at the surface level, a series of crazy, fast-moving, and highly imaginative games played by two grown men who sometimes also *talk* like children.

Yet this apparently delirious, farcical creation may also be seen as a sinister fable, the transposition of a kind of dream ending in a nightmare. When **L'Architecte et L'Empereur d'Assyrie** was first produced, Professor Charles V. Aubrun of the Sorbonne described it in the programme as "cette farce tragique," and also as "une psycho-farce." . . . The play does indeed present us with a blend of farce and tragedy. Before seeing how this comes about, we may consider how the farce is affected by the use of ritual, not only in this case but also in Arrabal's work as a whole.

Many of Arrabal's plays may be described as ritualistic in the sense that their partly circular action suggests repetition, while their plots are like games—some having religious connotations, some not—that seem to be repeat performances. Sometimes, as in ritual, their dialogues have obsessive refrains. Any doubt that ritual or ceremony is essential to their performance . . . should have been dispelled in some cases by their very titles. One thinks in particular of **Oraison, Le Grand Cérémonial, Cérémonie pour un noir assassiné,** and **La Communion solennelle.** In all cases where ritualized action occurs, in these and many other plays, it has some meaning beneath the surface: even when it is pushed to farcical extremes, though the degree of symbolism involved varies greatly. We have seen how farcical situations merge into dark, potentially tragic ones. Generally speaking, ritual has the effect of turning farce into something still closer to tragedy, because it uncovers obsessions that are sombre in the extreme.

Nearly always the ritual in Arrabal is anti-conventional and highly provocative. For instance, **La Communion solennelle,** billed as a "Cérémonie panique," superimposes the dressing of a little girl by her grandmother, in preparation for her first Holy Communion, onto another scene in which a necrophile slowly undresses in preparation for *his* preferred form of rite. Clearly, in cases like this, Arrabal is using ritual as a form of revolt. The blatant sacrilege recurs in [**Le Ciel et la merde**]. . . . After acquaintance with these and similar plays, it is surprising to find some critics who claim that Arrabal is, in spite of appearances to the contrary, reaching out to a higher order, a kind of mystical reality, or that his theatre may be construed as *"profoundly religious."* Rather, Arrabal seems to use ritual in reinforcing his expressions of distress and revolt, thus giving a new dimension to his farce.

Arrabal was brought up in the Catholic faith, and he says it stamped him for life. . . . [In the late sixties], he was trying to free himself from the negative aspects of his religious up-bringing by his mother with its constant threats of a punishing God, hell-fire and torture. In the early seventies, he told another interviewer that he felt very hostile towards Catholicism, blaming it to a great extent for having made his life such an excruciatingly unhappy one. The agonizing fear of punishment for sin was still giving him frequent nightmares. "I try to rationalize," he said, "to tell myself that these things are really impossible, a figment of the imagination; and yet these fearful ideas return time and time again to haunt me." But he made it clear to both interviewers that the intense faith of his youth, which he had since abandoned, had its residue in what he described as both attraction to the Christ myth and "moments of deist nostalgia." He also professed not to understand why people found him blasphemous and provocative.

However, blasphemous and provocative Arrabal undoubtedly is, though these qualities must be seen in the context of his unhappy memories. One now well-known and particularly traumatic experience stands out: at the age of seventeen, he discovered by chance some letters and photographs which proved that his father had not died thirteen years earlier in Spanish Morocco, where they then lived, as his mother had led him to believe. Instead, his father had been taken to prison by Franco's police because of his left-wing beliefs at the time of the *coup d'état.* Perhaps the worst part of the grim story is that Arrabal suspected his mother at first of having encouraged his father's arrest; he came to feel later that she might not have betrayed him, but that she had done little or nothing to help him. In addition, apparently from the time of his arrest and invented death, no mention of his father was allowed at home. This was because of his mother's conservative convictions, the belief in order, religion and the fatherland which she had inherited from her family of middle-class tradespeople. There can be no doubt that the memory of this particular series of events, as well as the transformation they caused in the boy's mind and heart from intensely jealous love of his mother to bitter hatred for her (mingled with habitual affection), and from deep religious faith to a loathing of Catholicism (mingled with nostalgia), has since dominated Arrabal's life and writing. One of the outlets for his anger and distress has been blasphemy and sacrilege.

We may now see how Arrabal uses ritualized farce with both light and, more particularly, sombre effects in his key play, *L'Architecte et l'Empereur d'Assyrie.* The ritual here consists basically of a circular movement in the playing of roles, a process which includes role-inversion. At the end of the action, then, the Architect becomes the Emperor, having literally absorbed him in a grotesque communion rite; and the "exchange" Architect appears, in a way equally miraculous, to confront him in exactly the same manner and circumstances that opened the play. Obviously, the couple have not advanced. Like Fando and Lis in Arrabal's earlier play of that name, they have simply gone round to the point where they began. Other aspects of ritual in *L'Architecte* include built-in refrains, a variety of games that lend themselves to frequent repetition, and movement towards a sacrificial climax which intensifies in the second act.

Religion assumes a blasphemous and sacrilegious character in almost all instances where it features in this play. It is part of the ritual, and it is also characteristic of Arrabal's burlesque farce. In Act I, the audience is warned not to take too seriously either the Emperor's condemnation of the poor native Architect for his want of a baptism, or his promises of eternal roasting and other unmentionable forms of torture. After the exciting recollection of a wager on the existence of God—a wager made by playing a pin-ball machine and lost through ironical bad luck when a drunk causes the machine to tilt just as the game is almost won—there are pieces of sado-masochistic eroticism with sacrilegious connotations, followed by a blasphemous quotation from André Breton, which the Emperor playfully attributes to his own invention. Act II consists largely of the mock trial of the Emperor, with rest intervals from time to time (for light relief also, no doubt) between the various stages of this lawcourt game. These intervals, and parts of the trial itself, allow further disrespectful references to the Almighty. The first is harmless enough, as the two characters, asking themselves whether the Creator went mad before or after the Creation, play at looking for Him in a hole in the earth with the help of binoculars. The second contains a parody of the *Dies Irae* from the Requiem Mass, which is hummed by the Emperor in the prurient context of a boy's perversion of his younger brother. In another rest period, the Emperor and the Architect decide to entertain themselves with a farcical performance of blasphemy which they consider setting to music, choosing the kind of music "qui emmerde le plus Dieu." However, once the game gets underway, humour is succeeded by scatological insult and overt defiance. Finally, in an incident referred to above, when the Architect devours the dead Emperor, and requests that the latter perform a miracle by turning a glass of water into whisky or wine, the Emperor obliges to the extent of turning it into *Eau de Javel.* If that farcical action proves that there is another life, as the Architect observes musingly when he has recovered from his disgust, it does little to honour the Biblical story of the first miracle in Cana. With regard to religion in the play, the most one might say positively is that the Architect demonstrates his gift of supernatural powers by controlling the forces of Nature, and that Domingos Semedo is probably right in suggesting that Arrabal provokes God because he wants to find Him. . . . (pp. 324-27)

L'Architecte was written in the same year (1966) as Arrabal's most important article on his celebrated "panic," which appears in the same (fifth) volume of his collected plays. The essay is entitled **"Le Théâtre comme cérémonie 'panique' "**; and *L'Architecte* is a good illustration of "panic theatre" as presented in Arrabal's introduction to this volume, or as anticipated in a talk he gave in August 1963 at the University of Sydney, where his early play *Fando et Lis* was being performed. In the introduction, he defines "panic theatre" as ceremonial or ritualistic theatre which mingles genres, moods, and tastes, pushing them to extremes . . . to the ritualization of what he calls *"the sordid and the sublime"* in *"this feast, this 'panic' ceremony."* *L'Architecte* not only lives up to all of these expectations, but also offers in its main character, the Emperor, a good example of "un homme panique," in the literal sense of a man who takes fright.

The Emperor is in a seemingly relaxed and even cheerful frame of mind at the start of the play, but he becomes more frightened as it proceeds, until panic leads him to virtual suicide. His fear seems to go much deeper than that of the Architect, whose panic in the opening scene has, then at least, the appearance of pure farce. The Emperor's panic, which is partly due to his consternation at being discovered as the weak, unimportant man he really is, has other roots that are more hidden. His eventual confession of having murdered his mother is less significant psychologically than the extremely bizarre fact that he wants the Architect to eat him, as equivalent and just punishment for his crime, *wearing his mother's clothes.* Thus, apart from seeking identification with his friend, he also wants to return to the womb, his murderous instinct fused with the sentiment of nostalgic love and the need for protection. In earlier parts of the play, he had revealed his habit of turning to his "mother," whose part was acted obligingly by the Architect whenever needed, every time his companion required sympathy. Despite all the games and jokes he shares with the Architect, the Emperor is a pathetic figure who makes a very poor job of coping with his situation. Through him, Arrabal portrays a syndrome of mercurial moods ranging from despair, emotional flatness and irritableness to joy, cheeky exuberance and friendly affection. The negative aspects of this syndrome are well known to psychologists who have studied the effects of isolation from society for long periods. On a more symbolic and technical level, the Emperor's alternating periods of elation and depression, together with delusions both of grandeur and of persecution, suggest a deep affective personality disorder which probably involves an element of paranoia. Only the symptom of worry about physical abnormality (which was, however, very much present in earlier plays) is missing from the characteristic list. The Emperor is also inclined, like other of Arrabal's characters, to seek satisfaction in particular from being chained up, and in general, as I have pointed out, from sado-masochistic eroticism with a sacrilegious flavour. Doubtless, then, other affective disorders are involved, falling clinically within the region of psychoses.

In terms of the symbolism of the ritualistic games played by the two men, the Architect is at first sight simpler to comprehend. He seems to be in most respects merely a kind of foil who benefits the Emperor in the games they play where the Emperor is usually the dominant figure. In this role, the Architect's usefulness extends from being a simple playmate to being a substitute mother. He has at least one other role, however, and possibly two. An autonomous person, he is half man, half supernatural being. As a man, he is susceptible, vulnerable, and subject to metaphysical yearnings. In his greater than human qualities, he causes the Emperor some understandable amazement and jealousy, not only because of his great age combined with everlasting youthfulness, but because of his magic power to command Nature by transmission of thought. He may be perceived as a representative of primitive times, *le bon sauvage,* a contrast to the Emperor, who is helpless by comparison and may represent the obviously sham progress of civilization. At the same time, the Architect may stand for another side of the Emperor's personality. Seen from the latter angle, the Architect is not just pretending to be the Emperor's mother: he becomes an extremely powerful mother-image. . . . (pp. 327-28)

Just as the very mention of his mother early in the play throws the Emperor back to his dreams and a mingling of terror and delight, so the Architect's experience is partly contained in a dream-world, sometimes tender and poetic, but sometimes nightmarish. For even farce, which is funny as a spectacle, may be frightening for those who experience it, first in reality, then in dreams. . . . Is reality for Arrabal inseparable, in the end, from this feeling of panic? Is it a farcical but frightening dream that, ritual-like, keeps starting all over again? At all events, Arrabal's writing is extremely personal and peculiar to him. His stress is finally less on *l'absurde,* or on metaphysics of any kind, than on the acting out of fantasy based on individual experience, most of it unpleasant. (pp. 328-29)

Peter Norrish, "Farce and Ritual: Arrabal's Contribution to Modern Tragic Farce," in Modern Drama, *Vol. XXVI, No. 3, September, 1983, pp. 320-30.*

FRANCIS DONAHUE

The child is often the father of the playwright. Many a dramatist excels when he draws on painful experiences rooted in his early years. Eugene O'Neill in *Long Day's Journey into Night* reopens psychological wounds inflicted by verbal cross-fires over the family dining room table. Tennessee Williams in *Glass Menagerie* revives guilt-laden scenes from his early years with Mother and Sister.

In this tradition of the organic playwright—one who creates out of his own inner compulsions, often to exorcize his obsessions—stands Fernando Arrabal, in his fifties, the most famous contemporary Spanish playwright, who has long been in antagonistic exile from family and country alike. A Paris resident since 1954, Arrabal writes in Spanish, with his French-born wife Luce turning his works into French, in which language they originally reach the stage. To his credit are more than 45 plays, translated to some 20 languages, and performed widely throughout the world. These plays often touch off sharp controversies due to the garland of dramatic taboos which Arrabal cultivates: sadism, masochism, matricide, necrophilia, transvestism, cannibalism, blasphemy, sexuality, scatology, perversion, and stage nudity.

During the Franco Era (1939-1976) Arrabal saw only one of his works performed in Madrid. Since 1976 a few of his plays have been staged in Spain with indifferent success. His themes do not appeal to the still-conservative Spanish playgoers, nor does his dramatic format, which is avantguardist. Arrabal's reputation rests on his triumphs on the international theater circuit. . . . (pp. 187-88)

Through the years, Arrabal has cultivated a personal image as a flamboyant artist, provocative and controversial, temperamental and myth-like. . . . Lurking in his psychological background are recurring self-doubts and insecurities, as well as fearful memories of his childhood, especially of his mother. The latter reared her son in a family atmosphere marked by strict adherence to dogmatic Catholic practices. When he was "naughty," she used to tie thongs around his thighs. Arrabal has long suspected that his mother denounced his father to the Franco forces at the outset of the Spanish Civil War. His parents differed radically on the political issues then at stake. The father was jailed for his liberal beliefs and subsequently disappeared in a political prison hospital, never to be seen again. Thereafter, the mother forbad Arrabal and his sister and brother to speak of their father. . . . With corrosive bitterness Arrabal recalls the "Fascist Catholic" schools in which he was enrolled, where the slightest mention of sex or the human body was forbidden, and where students were subjected to corporal punishment. He was traumatized by the Franco dictatorship, with its sternly repressive police and military guardians. Memories of these early years have scarred the Arrabal psyche and have served regularly as source material for his plays. (p. 188)

As an organic playwright, Arrabal writes plays which serve to salve his psychic wounds through the interplay of four themes arising out of his personal experience: his obsession with the "evil" mother and with family treachery; his alienation from an unjust and incomprehensible life style in Franco Spain; his attempt to win victories over God and His agent, the Catholic Church, as well as to assuage a troubled conscience; and his striking out at repression (by the family, the military, or the police) of personal, political, and artistic freedoms.

In his plays the protagonist is normally a dramatic surrogate for Arrabal himself, who reportedly believes that "half crushed under the yoke of familial and social prohibitions, the solitary 'little man,' ever endowed with an incredible desire for hope, attempts by laughter to purge himself of fear. On this basis a work is born."

During the first phase of his career (1958-1962) Arrabal was working in the absurdist mode, albeit he did not know the works of Samuel Beckett at the time he wrote his first plays. Influencing his production was his own subjective world of hidden fears and repressed aggressions, as well as the surrealist films of the Marx Brothers, the novels of Franz Kafka and Feodor Dostoevski, together with the works of Lewis Carroll (*Through the Looking Glass*), who is often considered a forerunner of Surrealism.

The early Arrabal writes short plays which are not fixed in time or space, and which blend grotesque and farcical elements. These plays have the consistency of dream fantasies, neglecting plot and character development to concentrate on a poetry of mood. They constitute gentle excursions into the modern adult world as seen through the eyes of guileless children. Yet, those eyes don't belong to children but to characters like Charlie Chaplin or Pozzo and Lucky (Beckett's *Waiting for Godot*). These characters regularly mouth platitudes and meaningless phrases and engage in playful word games. They set off in search of goodness in life, yet are bereft of any notion of what it means to be good. They are often sadistic for they lack the ability to project themselves into the role of another. For them, no moral law exists. Hence there is violence without passion and crime without remorse.

In *The Automobile Graveyard* (1958) Arrabal offers a blasphemous parody of the Passion of Christ, featuring three jazz musicians patterned on the Marx Brothers: Emanou, a trumpeter and a flawed Christ figure who admits to criminal acts; Fodere (Peter), a mute saxophonist (the Harpo figure); and Tope (Judas), a clarinetist. The three live in a rusting graveyard of abandoned cars—a metaphor for the human wreckage of our age—where the "director" provides breakfast in (auto) bed for each "guest." A bedtime kiss is supplied to each by the resident prostitute, whom Emanou terms good since she will let anybody sleep with her.

Emanou—who was born in a stable and who, at age 30, left home—volunteers to play music for dancing, one of the many ways he devises to do good. Still, he has only a memorized understanding of what goodness is. . . . He is soon discussing with fellow musicians whether they should get into another occupation, such as stealing or murder, but decides against those occupations as too dangerous. After Emanou is betrayed by a kiss from Tope, two police agents seize him and wheel him across the stage, his arms lashed to the handlebars of a bicycle—a mime of the Crucifixion. Trailing him wanly is a woman carrying a cloth to wipe Emanou's face. What it all adds up to is a dramatic statement of the futility of goodness and Christian charity in the human graveyard which is today's world.

With *The Two Executioners* (1958) Arrabal offers his most autobiographical play, one set in a Kafkaesque atmosphere of trial and condemnation for an unnamed offense. It is a one-act melodrama theatricalizing the denunciation of Arrabal's father by his mother. Francisca (Mrs. Arrabal) continuously recalls how she has sacrificed for her husband and family. Maurice (Arrabal) is the rebellious, "unnatural" son, who stoutly opposes his mother, whereas Benoit (Arrabal's brother Julio), the "dutiful" son, supports her even as she goes to the torture chamber. . . . After the father succumbs, two guards bear him out on a pole, like an animal. Comments Francisca, "When your father compromised the future of his children and his wife because. . . . " She never explains what he did. Benoit, at his mother's behest, now convinces Maurice to return to the path of "duty" by approving the mother's actions and asking forgiveness for his insubordination.

The "two executioners" of the title refer to the Mother and Brother who insidiously strip Maurice of his sense of personal integrity and loyalty toward his father.

In examining his own pschological state as a young man, Arrabal produces *Fando y Lis* (1958), a tragi-comedy in which the protagonist Fando (Fernando) is pushing his paralyzed girl friend Lis (Luce) in a pram toward Tar (which, with the letters rearranged—ART—may symbolize Utopia or artistic self-realization). Between the two protagonists is an unexplained tension, due perhaps to Fando's inability to perform sexually because of a physical or psychological impediment. Toward Lis he displays a disturbing mixture of love and sadism. . . . When she makes an awkward move and breaks his little drum, an irate Fando strikes her, then turns to fix his drum, oblivious to the fact that Lis is dying nearby. In the final scene, three men in the Marx Brothers mold huddle together under an umbrella as they observe Fando who, with a dog and a flower, goes to visit Lis's grave. A Jungian interpretation of this play sees Fando projecting on Lis an "anima" or inner personality representative of his mother, thereby rekindling a latent desire to kill his mother because of the feelings of self-doubt and inadequacy which she had instilled in him.

To indict a hostile society based on power, money and a baffling system of justice is Arrabal's purpose in *The Tricycle* (1961), which depicts the timeless existence of two amiable bums, who, like the Marx Brothers, defy social and moral restrictions with humor and wide-eyed innocence. As their only possession they treasure a rented tricycle, which they rent to children in the park. After verbal romps in which the playwright scores the importance given to reason in bourgeois thinking, the bums are faced with the need to pay the rent. Almost by accident they stumble on a solution: simply murder the Man with the Banknotes. This they do with plentiful blood, yet without rancor. They mean no harm. . . . Soon a gendarme is haranguing them in a gibberish neither can understand. Clearly, no real communication is possible, particularly on significant occasions. Finally, the two bums are marched off, and their tricycle, with the rent now paid, is ridden off happily by friends.

In his second phase as a Neosurrealist—a phase initiated in 1962 and continuing with modifications until today—Arrabal evolves a synthetic praxis leading to the production of ritual-laden plays of a ceremonial nature. This praxis—to which the playwright originally gave the name "Panic Theater"—draws on a wide range of avant-garde techniques, the most prominent of which are surrealist. From the theoretician of Surrealist Theater, Antonin Artaud (*The Theater and Its Double*) Arrabal derives his predilection for "total theater," casting aside narrative and psychological realism and relegating dialogue to an intermediate role. Artaud has also influenced Arrabal toward emphasizing visual and tonal shock images, as well as the affective use of costuming, mime, and multimedia effects. From a "Theory of Confusion" espoused by Spanish surrealist painter Salvador Dali comes Arrabal's interest in the union of opposites: poetry and vulgarity, tragedy and the Punch and Judy Show, the sacred and the sacrilegious, impotence and eroticism, routine and chaos, bad taste and aesthetic refinement, the sordid and the sublime.

To these formal techniques Arrabal contributes his own polymorphic characters, his recurrent sadomasochism, together with his use of masks, games, and ritual acts, the most significant of which are the mimed killing of a mother or a woman, and the violent attack on the name, image, or role of God or Jesus Christ. Enveloping the stage action is an oneiric quality, the result of a bizarre reality raised to the level of dreams or nightmares, which supply Arrabal with a measure of wish-fulfillment.

For Arrabal, the term "Panic" draws on the original meaning of the Greek word "Pan": a pastoral god sporting horns and a beard, with a penchant for shouting. Pan was feared by travelers whom he loved to throw in a "panic," that is, into a type of fear or frenzy. The Spanish playwright, with his "coups de théâtre," hopes to touch off "panic" in his audiences through a black sanctification of the evil that lives in all men. To this end, he strives to transform acts of torture, cannibalism, and necrophilia, into "panic" rituals.

Representative of this Neosurrealist phase is *First Communion* (1967), a play which evokes a "panic" mood, mingling horror, repulsion, and violence, with a profanation of Catholic ritual linked to a pathological sexuality. A Grandmother is engaged in dressing a Little Girl for her First Communion. Facing them are a coffin occupied by a woman, an iron cross, and two candelabra. It is never clear who has died. Just as the Necrophiliac enters, two men praying nearby, horrified, pick up the coffin and carry it out of the room. All the while, Grandmother is giving the Little Girl a low-keyed homily on the virtues of being a good wife in the future. (pp. 189-95)

After the coffin is returned, the Necrophiliac hurries back to contemplate the dead woman longingly, then begins to undress in a manner suggesting ritual. He penetrates the coffin to the bemused curiosity of Grandmother and Little Girl. Grandmother explains that the man is sleeping with the dead lady, adding that God will soon descend into the Little Girl's heart and remove all her faults.

With the footlights dimming, Little Girl returns in full communicant dress, fingering a knife. She thrusts the knife into the coffin and through the body of the Necrophiliac. Spurting blood stains her communicant dress, red balloons rise heaven-ward from the coffin, and Little Girl laughs merrily.

During the performance the audience experiences a mixture of rapt attraction, revulsion, perhaps even personal guilt for being swept up emotionally in this "panic" confluence of the erotic (Necrophiliac), the religious (First Communion) and the mundane (advice to a future housewife).

With *The Architect and the Emperor of Assyria* (1967) Arrabal spins a fascinating-repelling fantasy in dramatic short-hand. This two-act work deals with the sole survivor of a plane crash, a civilized man, who encounters a type of noble savage, the sole inhabitant of an isolated island. Actually, the survivor is a conventional business executive. . . . He has long dreamed of being a great Emperor. Accordingly, on the island he passes himself off as the Emperor of Assyria. (pp. 195-96)

The noble savage, as the natural man, controls the forces of nature. He can bring night or day into existence at will. Uncontaminated by civilization, he is a ready foil for the games and role-playing of the Emperor. The latter gradually introduces the noble savage—called the Architect, since he is to be trained as such—into the wonders of civilization: a perishable world of science and philosophy, war and masturbation, eloquence and automobiles, satellites and homosexuality, sonnets and hypocritical justice, demagogy and miles of thought.

The play evolves into a series of rapidly shifting scenes in which the two characters don masks to enact different roles. The scenes shape up, wax engagingly for a few moments, then wane as one character or another rips off his mask in anger or disagreement.

Evident is an interplay between Comico-Land and Serio-Land. In the former the two characters buffoonly act out roles miming the effects of an atomic blast or the pattern of a birth scene. Less than a sentence's distance away lies Serio-Land, where the spectator is brought up short—"panicked"—by the rapier-like attacks on such windmills of conformity as mother love, Catholicism, traditional morality, group-think and group-do.

A highly personal note comes into focus through a revealing statement which Arrabal puts in the mouth of the Emperor:

> I will build myself a cage of wood and I'll shut myself inside it. From here I will pardon humanity for all the hate that it has always shown toward me. And I'll pardon my father and my mother for the day when their bellies united to beget me. And I'll pardon my city and my friends and my neighbors who have always underestimated my worth.

The cage is, assuredly, the play into which Arrabal has shut himself up, and from which he hopes to work out long-standing psychological compulsions. The Emperor is Arrabal himself, and the play comes across as a surrogate for a Psycho Drama allowing a troubled playwright to attempt to exorcise his mother complex and his conscience-feud with God and the Church.

The entire Second Act—which assumes the form of a mock trial designed to shed light on the Emperor's life and the offenses with which he is charged—constitutes Arrabal's transmutation of private experiences and feelings into artistic pawns on stage. Unmistakable is the Emperor's ambivalent relationship with his Mother, whom he "hated like a devil and loved like an angel." . . . After trying to punish her unnaturally because of the hatred he feels toward her, he plots to kill her, which he does with a hammer.

In pursuing his private war with God, the playwright conveys a humorous stamp of approval to homosexuality, transvestism, masturbation, cannibalism, and sadism. The Emperor imagines God as peacefully embedded in the center of the earth, "like a worm, happy, completely mad, and thinking He's a transistor." (pp. 196-97)

Later, as the mock trial draws to a close, the Emperor insists on being sentenced to death for his misspent life. He directs the Architect to kill him and eat him, while dressed like the Emperor's Mother. Dutifully, the Architect carries out the Emperor's orders.

As a result of [his] 1967 encounter with political and police repression in a Franco jail, Arrabal experienced a quickening of his political conscience. And he resolved to write plays arising out of his observations and conversations with Spanish political prisoners. He continues to structure his works along Neosurrealist lines, and regularly includes assaults on his favorite targets: the "evil" mother and God and the Church.

His major political play, ***And They Put Handcuffs on the Flowers*** (1969), is a scathing attack on prison conditions in Franco Spain. The playwright covers a gamut of favorite taboos: scatology, castration, pornography, coprophilia, and desecration of Catholic rituals.

With kaleidoscopic effect the play recreates the torture, anguish, memories, and fantasies—erotic, sadistic, and blasphemous—of four prisoners who have been animalized by their long years in prison. The plot unfolds on two levels: actual prison life, and the dreams and memories of the prisoners acted out. (p. 198)

During the stage action Arrabal subjects the audience to blinking searchlights and the clanging of prison doors, all designed to give them a visceral taste of what it is to be a victim of ruthless police methods.

The Ballad of the Ghost Train (1975) reflects Arrabal's growing concern for his plight as a writer-in-exile, as well as his mounting fear that he will never be able to return to Spain to live. The story-line follows the efforts of Tharsis, a surrogate for Arrabal . . . , who has abducted a Spanish Duke, for whom he hopes to exact ransom from Spanish authorities. No ransom is forthcoming. The two men are in Madrid, New Mexico, a ghost town, "as is Madrid, Spain," due to the exodus of famous artists like Pablo Picasso and Pablo Casals and the stifling of free expression in all fields. In New Mexico Tharsis meets a former tightrope walker who offers to teach him to perform on the high wire. In due time Tharsis returns to the Spanish capital to walk a high wire strung across the Puerta del Sol, Madrid's most famous square. For this feat, and for defying the Franco helicopter sent to bring him down, Tharsis is acclaimed by people in Madrid as a harbinger of long-awaited freedom.

This plot once again allows Arrabal to continue his soul-searching on stage. Through Tharsis, the playwright reveals his pique at the lack of Spanish recognition for his works:

> It is forbidden to speak of me in Spain . . . to show what I write . . . one can speak only if it is to slander me or to revile me . . . they have recently written that I should be castrated so that I'll not produce children in my own image.

On the personal side, Tharsis says:

> I am so small, so humble, so weak, so inferior to others. . . . To see myself in the mirror is painful. . . . When I go strolling I avoid the large

store windows with huge mirrors which return my reflection.

The Duke likewise serves to prick Tharsis's conscience, scoring him for being too obsessed with his own sexual feelings, for engaging in sadomasochistic activities and for torturing women whose only crime is being taller and prettier than himself.

Today, Arrabal, heartened by his international success, continues at his Neosurrealist workbench in Paris. Of his future one thing is certain: subsequent works by this organic playwright will be shaped by his current and future life experiences, laced with a generous amount of holdover obsessions and taboos. (pp. 199-200)

> *Francis Donahue, "Arrabal: Organic Playwright,"
> in* The Midwest Quarterly, *Vol. XXV, No. 2, Winter, 1984, pp. 187-200.*

DANIEL ODIER

The setting [of Arrabal's novel ***The Tower Struck by Lightning***] is the 25th world chess championship at the Beaubourg Center in Paris. The adversaries are named Marc Amary and Elias Tarsis. There is an element of East and West in this; indeed, Amary and Tarsis are compared with the Soviet chess master Anatoly Karpov and the American Bobby Fischer. But the dimension here is cosmic. What if ***The Tower Struck by Lightning*** were Karpovfischerian in the highest degree, what if each chess piece and each square on the board were mingled black and white in a Taoist way and what if Fernando Arrabal had achieved perfection through "serenity in disorder," as the great Taoist Chuang-tzu wrote?

This book can be seen as an opera, a film, a philosophical tale, an adventure novel. At first we might take it to be a novel about chess and politics, a supremely clever, diabolical, comical and vitriolic intellectual game—until, among the observers of the game whom Mr. Arrabal refers to without really describing them, we discover not some crimson Dadaist but the ghost of Jorge Luis Borges. Which means that this novel is far from a baroque medley.

In a foreword, Anthony Kerrigan, the excellent translator, tells a story that nicely conjures up Mr. Arrabal, the Spanish playwright, novelist, artist and film maker. Mr. Kerrigan had hoped to meet him in Spain, only to discover that Mr. Arrabal had left the country and the Franco regime would not let him return. But Mr. Kerrigan did find, plastered on walls in Madrid streets, large posters, photographs of Mr. Arrabal nude. They displayed a writer whose stature may be small, but one part of him definitely is not. "This *cartel,* this *affiche*," Mr. Kerrigan says, "was apparently his most artistic, his most bohemian, reply in the circumstances. He could thereby cry *Presente!,* in the Hispanic ritual of both Left and Right. And: 'The Style is the Man'; and style may be physiological."

In ***The Tower Struck by Lightning*** (the title is taken, of course, from a tarot card), Tarsis and Amary are inescapably linked to each other not only by the game, which relegates the world to the state of a fantasy, but also by their pasts, which intersect between moves on the chessboard. It might be said, if such divisions were not a little simplistic, that Tarsis is creativity, intuition, eternity, the right hemisphere of the brain, playing against Amary, who is analysis, science, time, the left hemisphere.

Tarsis is Spanish and knows that all disorder arises from immanent order. What is at stake lies more in the way of playing than in victory, but that does not prevent him from wanting to crush his opponent's ideology by beating him. At the beginning of the game, goaded by his certainty that Amary is a murderer, he even wonders if he should not kill him immediately. Amary is Swiss, a physicist and a likely candidate for a Nobel Prize. He flees from freedom, the mother of chaos, by means of "maniacal ceremonies," "the rites of a castrated eunuch." But he is also working on the grand unification theory to explain all the forces of the universe—and that may seem paradoxical.

We learn between games that when he was in school Tarsis reduced a fellow student to slavery and locked him in a toilet where he inflicted humiliation and torture on him, and that Tarsis "was overcome with an infinite desire to cry, in the knowledge that he was alone and abandoned." . . .

Amary's childhood was a little different. His insane mother was confined in a psychiatric clinic. His father, a diplomat, was always absent. He shared a luxurious apartment with a brother in Geneva, a place with a "forbidden" bedroom where secret creatures waited for him. . . . He stole, he swallowed his mother's pearl necklaces, he named himself The Master in passages of a laconic diary, he got excellent grades in school by inventing quotations and authors and referring to imaginary scientific theories. And he conceived the paranoid dream of solving the overall enigma of the universe. He also killed his mother by infecting her with lovingly cultivated tetanus germs and justified himself by quoting Chairman Mao: "Some terror is always necessary."

In the novel the chess players reduce the world's wars to a war of their own and become indifferent to external combat. . . . Amary is the ultimate revolutionary, and his terrorist dream—he is suspected of having abducted a member of the Soviet Politburo to demonstrate that revolution could come from parallel Marxisms—makes the world whirl around the motionless chessboard. Tarsis feels cannibalistic joy when he chews up Amary's chess pieces. Tarsis is "a rational artist," Amary "an irrational scientist." Between them is destiny, a key piece in the game—in the person of the scientist Christophe de Kerguelen, Amary's political comrade but also a jealous colleague who will drastically affect the outcome of the combat.

Diagrams of the chessboard are scattered through the book, enabling us to follow the game. Between moves we witness a mystical crisis in Tarsis' life. After being a jeweler's apprentice and then a pimp in Barcelona, "a place where he suffered pleasure," he became a faithful servant of the Society of Jesus. . . . Like Amary torturing the kidnapped Politburo member, Tarsis became an inquisitor, racking his mistress, Nuria, with interrogations. After confession, Tarsis was told by his spiritual father, "You will be a fine Jesuit," maybe even "a minor saint." Just then, in one of the linkages Mr. Arrabal is so good at making, Tarsis takes Amary's bishop.

Tarsis fled Barcelona and in Valencia came under the spell of one Soledad Galdós, a mystical shepherdess who held together the trio she formed with Tarsis and Nuria, who had followed his trail to his place of exile. Nuria's breakdown, the love and compassion of Soledad, the hermaphroditic union of the three characters—all this has magical power.

But chess was invented to settle cosmic disputes. Tarsis and Amary are indissolubly bound together by a discovery made by Kerguelen. And the denouement seals that bond.

The Tower Struck by Lightning is cut like an emerald. Underlying it are an admirably controlled lyricism and an inventiveness that contrast sharply with the rosy naturalism creeping into the novel more and more these days.

Daniel Odier, "The Cosmic Chessboard," translated by Lowell Bair, in The New York Times Book Review, September 25, 1988, p. 22.

PETER L. PODOL

Fernando Arrabal's first works for the theater were written in his native Spain. Life in that country soon proved to be intolerable for the young dramatist, and he sought political and artistic liberation in France. When he left Spain in 1955, at the age of twenty-three, the very forces that provided the impetus for his self-imposed exile were frequently incorporated into the themes and aesthetic of his dramas. Black humor, a penchant for the grotesque, and a predilection for ritual based on the Catholic mass were combined with his intense feelings about oppression in Spain to produce plays like *Los dos verdugos* (*The Two Executioners*), 1956, *El cementerio de automóviles* (*The Car Cemetery*), 1957, and *Guernica*, 1959. In these works, Arrabal's affinity for the tragically grotesque and the religiously erotic strongly affirms his Spanish temperament.

Within a matter of a few short years, Arrabal managed to penetrate the inner circle of the avant-garde in Paris. His contact with other writers and artists had a considerable impact on his work. By the mid-1960s, it was evident that the dramatist's recourse to his Spanish roots was no longer apparent in either the artistic conception or the thematic focus of his work. If fate had not intervened, Arrabal might well have expurgated all manifestations of his temperament, aesthetic, and concept of theater that could be identified as Spanish.

Fate did intervene, however, in the form of the much celebrated incident resulting in Arrabal's arrest and incarceration in Spain in 1967; the cause was a blasphemous dedication he wrote in a copy of one of his novels that he was publicly distributing. Although the end result of his experience was a more definitive exile from his native land, Arrabal left Spain with a renewed, expanded commitment to combat political oppression and Francoism as well as a revitalized, intensified identification with his father and concomitantly with his Spanish roots. (p. 131)

Arrabal's theater abounds in cycles, patterns, recurring motifs, and the repetition of specific historical and autobiographical incidents. The most significant constant that occurs throughout his work, however, is thematic. From his very first play through his most recent endeavors, the quest for liberation is asseverated on a political and a personal level. Geneviève Serreau's observation about Arrabal's early theater, written in 1960, is as valid now as it was then: "Arrabal's theater is a theater of deliverance, resolutely oriented—not by virtue of an explicit ideological choice, but by a simple reaction of self-defense—toward a liberation of man." (pp. 131-32)

Certain technical terms and concepts will be utilized in this study as a direct result of its emphasis on the *modus operandi* of the playwright's dramas as works to be staged in the theater. "Praxis" refers essentially to the action of the characters on stage, to what they actually do during the play; and "poesis" focuses on the actors and on what they do in the process of portraying those characters. "Theoria" alludes to the activity of the audience, to its participation in the theater experience; this experience consists of a conscious effort to shape the action, to interact with all of the components of the drama in production, including characters, actors and staging. Finally, the "spine" of the play is, in Stanislavskian terms, the principal "doing," the action that best identifies the central thrust of the work as a whole.

Among the features of Arrabal's early theater that are most frequently identified by critics are the child-like nature of his characters, their fascination with games and with bodily functions, their amorality and ingenuousness, all of which often clash, generating some vivid grotesque images. There is also a strong autobiographical note, as evidenced by the dramatist's identification with many of his protagonists. The entire *corpus* of Arrabal's first period appears to have as its function, in a manner akin to Strindberg, the examination and resolution of intense psychological traumas. A central figure throughout many of these works authored before 1960 is the mother. José Polo de Bernabé states: "The mother represents for Arrabal the prolonging of the intrautcrinc pcriod (symbolized in his theater by the scenic images of the prison, the egg, the garden of delights) which protects the man-child from his own inadequacies so that he may confront the dangers of the outside world."

The most concrete, direct example of the importance of the Mother both as a character and as a force that influences the dramatist's sense of stage space is the play **The Two Executioners.** In that work, Arrabal dramatizes a recurring nightmare inspired by his anguished childhood: the mother's denunciation of her husband to the authorities and subsequent participation in his torture and death. Arrabal's horrifying depiction of his father's fate at the outbreak of Spain's Civil War and of the successful efforts of his mother and brother to win over the frightened and outraged young boy finds much of its impact in the equation of the home and the prison. By superimposing those two spaces on stage, he succeeds in portraying the mother as the incarnation of the most onerous aspects of Church and State. (pp. 132-33)

The mother's self-martyring attitude and religious fervor are quintessentially Spanish in character, as is the grotesque scene in which her sadistic rubbing of salt and vinegar into the wounds of her suffering husband produces sexual climax for her and uncomfortable laughter in the audience. There is little hope in this painfully vivid portrayal of psychic capitulation; its unremitting horror is balanced only by the defense mechanism of involuntary laughter, producing a grotesque that is reminiscent in nature of that of the Spanish artist, Francisco Goya.

The Car Cemetery is generally considered to be the finest achievement of Arrabal's early theater. A far more complex work than **The Two Executioners,** it lends itself well to an Artaudian approach. The play proved to be instrumental in solidifying Arrabal's reputation as an important innovative voice among avant-garde dramatists; that success was due, to a large extent, to the production of the work mounted initially in Dijon, France, by the Argentine director Víctor García. (p. 133)

The Car Cemetery explores the concepts of good and evil, values or ideas deprived of all meaning in the context of a fascist environment. Arrabal's Spanish roots are reflected both in his choice of the Christ story as the basis for his work and in the unique manner in which he adapts that story to reflect his vision of contemporary life. Ritual, inspired by his childhood immersion into the world of Spanish Catholicism and recognized instinctively by him as the basis for all theater, proved to be central to his conception of this drama. García conceived his production with a view toward underscoring that dimension of the play. Emanou, who is the play's protagonist, is the Christ figure who performs miracles and entertains the poor by playing music for them. However he also kills them at times in order to spare them the miseries of living. He has memorized a trite formula which defines "goodness"; his definition allows him to judge his girlfriend Dila as "good" because she willingly seeks to satisfy all men sexually. The central visual image that gives shape to the microcosmos in which these characters struggle to cope with the senselessness of life on a day to day basis is the graveyard itself, filled with wrecked cars, a symbol of the destructive nature of modern civilization.

García, finding his inspiration in Artaud's *The Theater and Its Double,* furnished the spectators with swivel chairs and hung wrcckcd automobiles from the ceiling, providing them with an active, enveloping production that aggressively assaulted their senses. . . . A U-shaped runway was constructed paralleling the three walls of the theater in Dijon. The runway was utilized primarily by Lasca and Tiossido, trainer and athlete respectively, who repeatedly traversed that route in their quest for a new world record. Toward the end of the work, they metamorphose into police who, with the aid of Emanou's friend and fellow musician, Tope (Judas), identify, arrest, flagellate, and crucify Arrabal's Christ figure. At the conclusion of the piece, they reverse roles and continue their quest for the record, Lasca now assuming the part of the athlete. The circularity of their route, which is underscored by the bicycle on which Emanou is crucified, reinforces the idea of the claustrophobic nature of existence. The runway functions to transform the entire theater into a closed-in space, to force the audience to experience with the actors the suffocating cycle that is life. The spine of **The Car Cemetery,** in light of its visual emphasis on confinement, might be stated as follows: to entrap and destroy all overtures toward liberty and charity in the individual. The idea of the circle thus functions to underscore the hopelessness that permeates existence; destructiveness seems destined to be repeated endlessly, both in Spain and in the modern world at large.

The circle is a favorite motif of Arrabal's, but its significance is by no means constant and unvarying. *Guernica,* a pivotal work of his first period—which is firmly rooted in Spanish history and tradition—utilizes another circular object, the balloon, in a manner that is largely optimistic. In this work, Arrabal's Spanish sense of Black Humor is especially evident. Lira's entrapment in the toilet during the bombing of the Basque spiritual capital in 1937 creates the sort of tension between the horrifying and the comic that characterizes the grotesque. Her dialogue with her husband Fanchou, which alludes to his sexual insufficiency and reveals their mutual selfishness and lack of true empathy, indicts them without diminishing the horror of their plight and of the air attack itself. The villains of the work are the novelist and reporter, who demonstrate no concern for their country and its people and who seek to exploit the situation for their own professional gain. Arrabal's indictment of the Spanish press is anything but subtle.

The feeling of entrapment noted in the two earlier plays is certainly present again; but, at the very end, encapsulation and pessimism are countered by the symbol of the balloons which cannot be shot down by the soldiers who have just killed Fanchou and Lira. The latters' spirits, in the form of those playful spheres, survive intact. Visually, Arrabal utilizes vertical movement for the purpose of affirming hope and liberation; this affirmation is further supported by the chorus of voices celebrating the survival of the tree of Guernica at the play's conclusion.

The theme of liberty takes many forms throughout Arrabal's theater. Emanou's refusal to capitulate to the system and cease entertaining the poor led to his destruction in *The Car Cemetery.* But freedom as art, despite the protagonist's death, could not be suppressed in *La bicicleta del condenado* (*The Condemned Man's Bicycle*), 1959; in that play Paso's scales on the piano are heard louder than ever after his murder; and, again, balloons are utilized to affirm the triumph of his art and his spirit. Viewed as an entity, Arrabal's early plays are characterized by a *praxis* in which the characters seek to hide from, and to deny, the existence of an oppressive, unyielding macrocosmos. They generally fail; and their failure—in light of a *poesis* characterized by the direct, simple and ingenuous expression of basic needs and desires—produces a most disquieting *theoria.* Hints of a more optimistic dramatic vision can be identified, however, and, in *Guernica,* the role of vertical space in that vision is clearly established.

In the 1960s Arrabal immersed himself in the "Panic" movement that he founded in conjunction with Alejandro Jodorowsky and Roland Topor. During that period of time, his contact with André Breton and the Surrealists, his collaboration with leading avant-garde directors, and his growing sophistication as an influential French playwright with his own following in Paris all served to distance him from his Spanish roots. Although there were continued references to autobiographical events and although some of the elements of his technique and aesthetic clearly reflected his Spanish sensibility, Arrabal's image of himself was one that emphasized the cosmopolitan Parisian. His arrest and incarceration in Spain as well as his subsequent participation in the student rebellion in Paris in 1968 radically changed both that self-image and the fundamental direction of his work. A heightened political awareness and a renewed identification with his father and with the oppressed peoples of the world served to revive his interest in Spain and to strengthen the element of protest in his theater. That need to protest also caused him to develop more fully his Goyesque sense of Black Humor and of the grotesque and to explore the possibilities of applying some of the Surrealist techniques developed during the 1960s to a somewhat different end. This new attitude resulted most immediately in a major work of guerilla theater: *Y pondrán esposas a las flores* (*And They Put Handcuffs on the Flowers*), 1969.

The possibilities for an Artaudian approach to *The Car Cemetery* . . . are explicitly mandated by Arrabal in his stage directions for *Handcuffs.* At the beginning of that work, the playwright specified that the audience was to be accosted by members of the cast in a dark room outside the principal theater space, separated from their companions, and addressed in a cryptic, threatening manner—techniques aimed

at the obliteration of all audience-actor separation. . . . Violence becomes the central theme and technique of this dramatic event. Flashes of light, abrupt transpositions of time and space, and the juxtaposition of harsh reality with erotic dreams and horrifying nightmares all underscore the aggressive nature of the work.

The central dialectic of the play, which recurs rhythmically throughout, is effected by the telling juxtaposition of the claustrophobic horror of Spanish prisons with the motif of space exploration. The structure of *Handcuffs* results from several different elements in the play. On the level of plot, the episodic nature of the work, reinforced by the abrupt transitions from present reality to the dream sequences, ultimately provides a central focus through the saga of the arrest and eventual execution of Tosan. Based on the case of Julián Grimau, the last political prisoner to be executed in Spain as a consequence of his participation in the Civil War twenty-five years earlier, the play moves rapidly and inexorably to its conclusion once Tosan appears. Church, State, and the wealthy oligarchy are all indicted for their role in disavowing all possibility for clemency and kindness in Franco's Spain. The striking visual prop of a bloodstained flag (stretched above the heads of the audience), which representatives of those three segments of Spanish society utilize to wipe their bloody hands after refusing to heed Tosan's wife's pleas for mercy, constitutes one telling example of the visceral impact effected by a staged production of the play.

Arrabal's dark sense of humor, indulgence in blasphemy, and savage grotesqueries reveal his Spanish temperament at work in this aggressive condemnation of man's inhumanity to man. That idea is further supported by the utilization of the same actors to portray both the prisoners and their tormentors. The extreme visuality of some of the work's most grotesque moments is evidenced by their incorporation into Arrabal's first film, *Viva la muerte* (*Long Live Death*), 1970. . . . A number of the violent grotesqueries of [*And They Put Handcuffs on the Flowers*] are generated by historical occurrences. One especially poignant example is Arrabal's depiction of the execution of Federico García Lorca, whose verses provided the image utilized in the title of the play. The juxtaposition of handcuffs and flowers echoes the clash between the subterranean depths of the prison and the wonderment caused by men walking on the moon. Arrabal seems to be suggesting that the greatest achievements are debased by repeatedly being deprived of true meaning through the irrationality and perverseness of other actions.

In *Handcuffs,* Arrabal's strong need to return to the horror of his own childhood experiences in strife-torn Spain is affirmed through his incorporation of the key nightmare dramatized in *The Two Executioners.* In *Handcuffs,* however, a note of hope is interjected into what was the unrelenting pessimism of the earlier drama. That hope takes the form of a fellow prisoner's words of consolation spoken to reassure the suffering father: "Your children . . . when they grow up, then you'll see. You'll be their idol. And the more hatefully she treated you—she and her friends and family—the more devoted they'll be to you. Look, you're a painter. Your children will be artists. They'll immortalize your name."

Arrabal appears to be struggling to reconcile the optimism he has begun to find in his artistic liberation and his new found commitment to a socio-political cause with the depressing reality of his direct confrontation with totalitarian oppression in Spain and France (the student rebellion of

1968). This struggle is reflected in the difficulty he experienced deciding upon a suitable ending for **Handcuffs.** In its original version, published in French, Tosan urinates out of fear while being garrotted. A celestial chorus is then heard as the urine changes into blood and as Tosan's wife, Falidia, washes her hands and face in the liquid. This "miracle" allows the drama to conclude on an optimistic note. That positive ending has sometimes been deleted by the author, most notably in a production that he directed in New York.

The multiple roles played by the actors produce a radically different *poesis* than in earlier works. The mutability of existence and the fine line between nightmare and waking reality both challenge the cast to avoid projecting a fixed, well-defined identity on stage. Communicative images, gestures, movement, and physical action become the ingredients which the actor must combine to express the broad range of emotions that arise during the course of a performance. At the end of the play, most productions of **Handcuffs** called for the spectators to share fears and anxieties with the cast and with one another. The *theoria,* therefore, has been expanded in time and scope; total involvement in the theatrical experience was directly sought and encouraged by the work in production. Regardless of which ending is utilized, the spine of the play is: to imprison. Arrabal is unquestionably guilty of some pornographic excesses in this drama; the critical polemic inspired by its first New York production alone underscores the controversial nature of the work. Excesses like the act of fellatio performed on the body of Christ seem gratuitous to this critic, but the impact of Arrabal's "shout of protest" is undeniable. **Handcuffs** is certainly not Arrabal's finest piece of dramatic literature, but it is an overwhelming theatrical *tour de force* that served his ends perfectly at that point in his artistic and personal life. It is clearly a work that supports Michael Goldman's observation that "aggression, complexly projected but intimately and immediately received by the audience is the stuff of drama."

Just as Arrabal's incarceration in Spain directly inspired **Handcuffs,** another chance event provided the inspiration for his drama **En la cuerda floja (On the Wire),** 1974. While traveling through New Mexico in April 1974, Arrabal spotted a road sign for the town of Madrid. Curiosity prompted him to abandon his itinerary and investigate that unexpected reminder of his native country in the southwestern United States. When he discovered that Madrid, New Mexico, was a ghost town, a whole series of images and metaphors was generated. They formed the basis for **On the Wire,** his most important and interesting work for the theater since **Handcuffs.** Uniting the theme of exile with a consideration of the role of the artist in ameliorating social conditions, Arrabal again demonstrated in this drama that his most intriguing and successful plays are those in which his personal feelings, obsessions, and dreams provide the central focus and imagery for his work.

As in **Handcuffs,** a central dialectic, both visual and thematic, is constructed around a vertical axis. The depths of the abandoned mine in Madrid, New Mexico—which come to represent both political and social oppression—constitute one end of that axis. It is there that the phantom train (the play's other title is: **The Ballad of the Phantom Train**) delivers the remains of the town's former inhabitants to the "company," which then utilizes the corpses to manufacture dog food. That metaphoric representation of the state's degradation of the individual is revealed to the play's protagonist,

Tharsis, shortly before his climactic tightrope walk across the Puerta del Sol in Madrid, Spain, an act intended to assert the freedom and power of the creative artist. Tharsis' daring, uplifting and ultimately triumphant feat occurs high above the heads of the spectators at the other extreme of Arrabal's vertical axis. The vertical dialectic is paralleled by a telling horizontal juxtaposition—the equation of Spain's capital with a ghost town. The dramatist's imagery, utilized to link those two Madrids in a manner that captures all of his anguish resulting from the political state of his native land, is reminiscent of the nihilistic vision of such great Spanish writers of the past as Francisco Quevedo (*Los sueños—The Dreams*) or Mariano José de Larra ("El día de los difuntos"—"The Day of the Dead"). However, Arrabal's concluding image interjects a strong note of optimism into his dream. Vertical space serves to support the theme of the artist's power to combat successfully the restraints of the totalitarian state. Tharsis struggles with his art, failing in his initial attempts to implement the advice of the old master, Wichita, who has taught him the techniques of tightrope walking. Like Paso in **The Condemned Man's Bicycle,** his greatest success as an artist results from his direct resistance of the system's efforts to suppress totally his creative spirit.

Arrabal's identification with Tharsis is as complete and as anguished as was his identification with the bewildered and ingenuous protagonists of his early dramas. Through Tharsis he expresses the feelings of pain caused by his own alienation and exile from his native land. . . . Throughout **On the Wire,** Arrabal wrestles with his own decision to go into exile. His bout with tuberculosis is equated with the miners' black lung disease in New Mexico. Moreover the final melodramatic triumph of Tharsis on the wire (Franco's forces try but fail to shoot him down) serves as an affirmation of the writer's own life and art, as well as a call for freedom. It is accompanied by a chorus of voices chanting "Liberty" and by the sound of a "Hallelujah."

On the Wire creates and projects a magical, oneiric ambience. Its central dialectic, which derives from the juxtaposition of the mines and the train with the high wire, is infused with an intensity generated by the playwright's personal concerns. The melodramatic conclusion is compensated for by the power and daring of that final visual image, which requires that the actor playing the role of Tharsis actually be a tightrope artist. . . . The play's *theoria* produces a feeling of euphoria in the audience, a feeling that relates directly to the spine of the work. That spine may be stated as follows: to free oneself of all constraints and perform with total abandonment. At the center of this quest for artistic freedom and affirmation of art lies the dramatist and his relationship to his native country. **On the Wire** establishes traditional Spain and her history as a vital source of inspiration for Arrabal, a source that will form the basis for his most successful and intriguing works for the theater in the years to follow.

It is by no means surprising that **Oye, patria, mi aflicción (Hear, My Country, My Affliction),** 1975, proved to be the dramatist's first work to truly succeed in performance in post-Franco Spain. In this play, Arrabal unites his expanding repertoire of visual, cinematographic effects with his highly subjective, grotesque vision of a number of prominent literary and historical figures culled from Spain's past. The result is a strong affirmation of the vitality of his Spanish sensibility, reflected in both his choice of themes and his dramatic technique. There is a definite resonance between the dramatist's affliction, or pain, and his country's. The play's protagonist is Latidia, the Duchess of Teran (Teran being the name of the author's mother). The fanciful and the grotesque figures and events that constitute the heart of the play may then be viewed as subjective projections of the dreams and obsessions of that protagonist.

Arrabal had previously translated the nightmares that dominated the inner world of his protagonist into a dazzling array of images in his film *Long Live Death.* That work in the medium of film served him particularly well in *Hear, My Country, My Affliction.* The fourth scene of the play, in which Latidia passes in review before the mummies of the greats of Spanish history while wearing a gas mask to avoid their rank odor, constitutes a quintessential grotesque image strongly suggestive of the world of cinema. The great Spanish filmmaker, Luis Buñuel, and his masterpiece, *Viridiana,* are directly evoked in another scene in which three beggars, having assumed the identities of El Cid, Che Guevara and Don Juan, participate in a grotesque banquet. Arrabal's sense of irony and sarcasm has never been stronger than in this evocation of the decadence that has consumed Spain and undermined and distorted the highest achievements of her past great figures.

The central episode of *Hear, My Country, My Affliction* concerns Latidia's efforts to retain her castle, which has been sold to the Count and Countess d'Ecija. Her determination to remain there is linked to such disparate events in Spanish history as the defense of the city of Numancia against the Romans and La Pasionaria's (Communist leader, known for her oratory in support of the Republic during the Civil War) famous slogan, used during Spain's Civil War, "No pasarán" ("They shall not pass"). Arrabal ironically undermines Latidia's heroic struggle to hold on to the past, however, through the repeated motif of the termites which gradually destroy the castle from within. Images of putrefaction recur throughout the work and serve to make a powerful statement about the dramatist's view of the state of his native land. Arrabal seems to be calling for a total regeneration of modern Spain. Past traditions are ruthlessly mocked in scenes where Saint Theresa, Cervantes, El Cid and his wife, Jimena, and other historical notables engage in sado-masochistic acts. These violent aberrations prompted the critic Enrique Llovera to link Arrabal's vision of Spanish myths with Valle-Inclán's *esperpentos,* which distort an already grotesque reality by viewing it as reflected in a concave mirror. Latidia's and Spain's hope for salvation seems to lie in the realm of imagination; the Martian Ass that Latidia flies away with at the end of the work appears only when she is on stage and comes to represent her inspiration, her subconscious effort to find hope for personal and national vitality through the magical realm of artistic creativity.

As in *On the Wire,* vertical stage space is utilized to affirm Arrabal's sense of hope for the possible regeneration of Spain. In the final scenes of *Hear, My Country, My Affliction,* Latidia and the Martian Ass, now metamorphosed into a Pilgrim, descend ladders together in search of the lost plans for the Tower of Babel. Each rung of the ladder represents an earlier period of Spain's history. As they go back in time, the destructive work of the termites reaches a rapid conclusion. The collapse of the Castle is quickly followed by the rise of the Tower of Babel which now symbolizes harmony and renewal. Latidia and the Martian Pilgrim ascend to the top of the tower and fly off together in seeming triumph as a "Mag-

nificat" is played. The resultant feeling of exhilaration is enhanced by this dramatic opening up of theater space. Much like the zooms that climax his films *Long Live Death* and *Guernica* (1975), the mature Arrabal seems to have found genuine optimism through the palliative powers of the artist's creative energies. A possible spine for *Hear, My Country, My Affliction* then would be: to destroy in order to create.

The utilization of an oxymoron to summarize the central action of an Arrabal play is significant in that it captures the essential role of dualities, contradictions, and telling juxtapositions in his theater. Those features of his work have never been more in evidence than in his drama *Inquisition,* 1980. In that piece, the site of the home of the protagonist, Nínive, proves to be the same as the locations where María Sulamita was tortured and burned by the Spanish Inquisition, where the Marquis de Sade carried out his depraved acts designed to link eroticism and pain, and where Tubal played music to alleviate the horrors of a concentration camp. Nínive is a noted scholar specializing in the history of the Inquisition. Her intense personal identification with María Sulamita structures Arrabal's utilization of time. Like the two Madrids in *On the Wire,* Nínive and her historical counterpart are evoked in a series of telling parallels and juxtapositions which help to establish the multiplicity of the term "inquisition."

The rapid oscillations between past and present, between the Spanish Inquisition in the sixteenth century and other more contemporary manifestations of the formalized suppression of freedom and individuality, climax in the theatrical scene in which Nínive, assuming the role of María Sulamita, addresses the Inquisitors. She slips in and out of character, lamenting the monotony of her present life in comparison with the heroic acts of María. Her dissatisfaction with her existence reaches its climax at the end of this scene when she sets herself on fire, the supreme gesture aimed at finalizing her identification with her historical alter-ego.

As in many of Arrabal's works, sexual perversions, especially those of a sado-masochistic nature, are frequently practiced and discussed. These function to heighten dramatic tension while concomitantly evincing the playwright's call for freedom in a sexual, as well as socio-political, sense. In *Inquisition,* Nínive's fascination with the tortures of the Inquisition and with De Sade as well as her own relationship with her former lover, Galgala—in which she assumed the role of dominatrix—function to generate a note of irony in the context of the drama's theme: the condemnation of the Spanish Inquisition and all of its more recent permutations. Arrabal's sensitivity to his Spanish roots is quite evident here in his evocation of the Spanish cult of the martyrs. . . . This theme, which has intrigued the playwright since his earliest works, acquires an additional dimension when incorporated into a play that focuses on the significance of Spain's Inquisition. The idea of torture used to suppress freedom resonates with the suppression of a form of sexuality in which pain and pleasure are linked. Oxymoron as a rhetorical device has been extended here to an ideological plane; the plays on ideas evoke Quevedo's baroque conceits in their intricacy and their recourse to black humor.

Much of the play's structure derives from the periodic appearances of the airplane that delivers songs of freedom to the characters below. When these songs arrive, they are then sung by Nínive and her current lover, Carioth, who serves as a mediator between her inner world and external reality. The plane itself acquires additional meaning near the end of the work when it is revealed that its pilot is Galgala, Nínive's former lover. Visually, its appearances link the concept of freedom with vertical space, continuing the tradition that Arrabal established in earlier works. A note of dialectical tension is also generated by the aircraft because of its dual role as the destroyer of Nínive's research (which it firebombs) and the inspiration for renewed protest through the songs that it furnishes at key moments throughout *Inquisition*. (pp. 133-43)

Arrabal's growing optimism, which is accompanied by an upward expansion of theater space, is closely linked with his revitalized sensitivity to his Spanish roots. His own interpretation of *Inquisition* reflects his conscious awareness of a diverse range of associations that are inextricably linked to his native land. In explicating the relationship between Carioth and Nínive, Arrabal proposed a role reversal paralleling that of Don Quixote and Sancho Panza at the end of Cervantes' novel. Carioth may be equated with Sancho, the realist, who maintains contact with the outside world throughout the work, only to embrace Nínive's ideal at the conclusion. And Nínive, like Don Quixote, renounces her highly subjective dream world in order to return to the reality of the surrounding macrocosmos. Arrabal's analysis of his own characters in terms of the quintessential work of Spanish literature suggests quite strongly that his dramatic vision and his aesthetic are, and will continue to be, closely tied to his native Spain. In conjunction with his penchant for dark humor and his predilection for dramatic ceremonies that reflect (and often parody) Spanish Catholicism, he clearly belongs to the line of Spanish writers, artists and filmmakers highlighted by such names as Cervantes, Quevedo, Goya, Valle-Inclán and Buñuel.

Significantly, *Inquisition* became Arrabal's first play since the 1950s to premiere in Spain. The horrors of Spain's history receive their maximum expression in this play as well as in his other works of the 1970s in which he deals with his native country. The collective spine of these works is, nevertheless, to free oneself from the horrors of the past and present and to *ascend* to a nobler existence. There is a clear evolution in the playwright's utilization of theater space; early works communicate visually a sense of closure and entrapment that is steadily countered later by the vertical expansion of his dramatic vision. Arrabal's search for artistic, political, and existential freedom reverberates throughout his entire dramatic production. As he moves closer to the realization of his quest, his utilization of stage space expands in a manner that is entirely consonant with his growing optimism. Concomitantly, he has repeatedly and strikingly demonstrated the central role of his Spanish roots in shaping both the subject matter and the aesthetic of his theater in production. (pp. 143-44)

Peter L. Podol, "Spain: A Recurring Theme in the Theater of Fernando Arrabal," in The Contemporary Spanish Theater: A Collection of Critical Essays, *edited by Martha T. Halsey and Phyllis Zatlin, University Press of America, 1988, pp. 131-45.*

Patricia Beer

1919?-

English poet, novelist, nonfiction writer, autobiographer, and editor.

Written in a subdued, lyrical style, Beer's poems often reveal a fascination with death, theology, and the uncertainties of everyday existence. Beer's life and verse are profoundly influenced by her austere upbringing in the Plymouth Brethren, a fundamentalist religious sect that stresses personal salvation through faith, respectability, and morality. Although sometimes faulting her limited subject matter, critics praise Beer's economical phrasing, candor, and ironic observations. Carol Rumens commented: "She is that rare phenomenon, a religious poet stripped of the blurring consolations of religion. She is certainly a treasurably astringent and rather quirky voice in the Babel of modern English poetry." Beer's first work, *The Loss of the Magyar and Other Poems* (1959), discusses the death motif that frequently dominates art, literature, and legend. In "The Loss of the Magyar," for example, Beer ruminates on the nautical disaster that killed her grandfather. Literary and fabled figures appear throughout *The Survivors* (1963), which is generally considered a more intimate collection. Critics noted in "Epitaph in a Country Churchyard" the emergence of a more intense, skilled lyricism. In *Just Like the Resurrection* (1967), Beer shifts her thematic focus from death to an exploration of relationships between the deceased and the living, often addressing the subject with subtle wit, as in "Concert at Long Melford Church," where she visualizes concert-goers milling about a chapel graveyard as the resurrected dead.

In her next collection, *The Estuary* (1971), Beer reminisces on her rural childhood in Devon, England. While reviewers applauded such pieces as "Happy Ending," a sardonic study of humanity's ambivalence towards life, and "The Estuary," in which a river represents the end of childhood and a passage to the future, the majority of the poems are restrained chronicles of minor events that disappointed critics who believe Beer's best work to be symbolic and ironic. *Driving West* (1975) was more roundly praised. In this volume Beer continues to reflect upon her youth, but avoids the impediments of *The Estuary* by combining vibrant nature imagery with a strong sense of Elizabethan history. Beer also approaches the topic of death from a new perspective, that of a middle-aged woman, and corresponds the theme to changing seasons in a British landscape. Douglas Dunn asserted: "Observations are presented with a balance struck between the concrete and the intangibles of feeling. Things and feelings interact in the ways of the best nature poetry." The chronological arrangement of *Selected Poems* (1979) led reviewers to notice Beer's steadily narrowing thematic range and stricter syntax. *The Lie of the Land* (1983) is a departure from Beer's usual concerns. Linked by a focus on the controlling influence of time, the poems in this volume concentrate on the simultaneous existence of love and death and the momentary illuminations which occur in life. "The Spinsters and the Knitters in the Sun," for example, is a subtle contemplation of mortality. Several critics likened Beer to Emily Dickinson in her ability to describe events in exact yet enigmatic terms, and others

noticed influences of Shakespearean comedy throughout *The Lie of the Land.*

In addition to writing poetry, Beer has also published a highly acclaimed autobiography, *Mrs. Beer's House* (1968), which concentrates on her childhood and the powerful influence of the Plymouth Brethren on her and her sister. With relatives employed as coffin-makers and tombstone-carvers, the children were surrounded by the concept of death at a very early age. Beer ends the work with the untimely death of her mother, which was poorly explained to the girls by their father. *Mrs. Beer's House* was reissued in 1978 to coincide with the publication of *Moon's Ottery,* a novel that begins with the death of a young girl's mother. Set in 1588, the story chronicles the neuroses and concerns of the citizens of Moon's Ottery, a tiny English village. Rich in period detail, the novel vividly presents the town's scandals against the threatening advances of the Spanish Armada. Related chiefly from the point of view of Rosalind, an imaginative adolescent, the novel illustrates humanity's prevailing pettiness throughout history.

(See also *Contemporary Authors,* Vols. 61-64, rev. ed.; *Contemporary Authors New Revision Series,* Vol. 13; and *Dictionary of Literary Biography,* Vol. 40.)

MARTIN DODSWORTH

Humanity is the quality lacking in *Just Like the Resurrection.* Miss Beer is an extremely accomplished and gifted poet, getting better and better in each successive book. She is original; she is clever. She is very sure of what she is doing and how she will do it; and she does it. But there is no sense of the dyer's hand: what she works in is subdued to Miss Beer, rather than *vice versa.* Her poems tend to finish on a note of surprise, but the surprise, so regularly used, comes to be forced and predictable. We cease to be moved; the poem's efficiency in saying what it has to say so memorably drives off our emotions, and we are not involved, ultimately not held by it.

There is, too, a hint of unconscious smugness in the delicacy with which Miss Beer leaves the point of so many poems so carefully unstated, as though she were to say to the reader: 'You and I understand, of course, but poor benighted humanity—those people I write about . . .' Her poem about herself as a child looking at a picture of Curtius leaping into the gulf has this air of conspiracy and repugnant certainty about it:

> I simply stood there, well-grown for my age.
> Bandaged and blindfolded and gagged,
> Near a gulf, too, very far from leaping.
> I would as soon have answered my mother back.

It is very good—acute and subtle; but this irony at her own expense strikes me as numbing and sad, as though denying all continuity to existence. (p. 720)

> *Martin Dodsworth, "The Human Note," in* The Listener, *Vol. 78, No. 2018, November 30, 1967, pp. 720, 722.*

ALAN BROWNJOHN

Patricia Beer, in *The Estuary,* lacks nothing of her usual craft and care, or her customary sallies of descriptive ingenuity and freshness. There is still, though, a curious kind of contentment with the minor, whimsical theme while the sinister or alarming, or simply the more challenging, ideas seem to get gently edged aside. The title-poem [**"The Estuary"**] is pleasant, but lacks the emotional force she hopes for; **"Happy Ending"** has glimpses of alarm and irony, but could surely be more astringent? This prosaic treatment of themes—and, too often, prosaic, unambitious diction—is a pity in a poet who is best when she is most explicit, or suddenly catches things from another angle. **"The Underground Garage"** starts a genuine chill, the slant is original and the language tauter:

> With twenty yards to go before
> The night, our lamps' beam confronts
> A column of dead leaves advancing
> Down the tunnel towards us.
>
> Dead, curled, colourless, stiff,
> They march away from their trees, and spread
>
> A sort of thin plausible life
> Over the concrete. Dead, thrusting.
>
> (p. 792)

> *Alan Brownjohn, "Time & Change," in* New Statesman, *Vol. 82, No. 2124, December 3, 1971, pp. 791-92.*

CHRISTOPHER RICKS

Patricia Beer's last book of poems [*Just Like the Resurrection*] took its title from the final line of her poem **"Concert at Long Melford Church"**:

> They spread all over the churchyard. They scan
> The crowd, recognise, smile and shake hands.
> By each tombstone a well-dressed person stands.
>
> It looks just like the Resurrection.

The laconic finality, as of a last judgment, is delicately caught in a limbo between overstatement and understatement: overstatement in the demure presumption of 'just like', understatement in that 'Resurrection' isn't a true rhyme and moreover won't scan (the rhyme-word 'scan' admonishes us) unless we give it that archaic extra syllable, as archaic as the Resurrection itself. These earlier poems, as the blurb said, explored 'the reciprocal relations between the living and the dead'. Her new book, *The Estuary,* considers a bleaker possibility, and considers it with an augmented humour and gravity: that the only place from which those reciprocal relations would be visible is an aloof limbo.

Almost all of the 28 poems occupy, and are preoccupied by, some limbo, some moment or place or phenomenon which is poised, abstracted but anxious. **"The Estuary"** wonders what is river, what sea, and what estuary; it gazes upon the opposing banks, but to do so it has to contemplate the unrealisable wish to locate itself for good in that odd no-man's-sea. Its coolness is unearthly or Olympian—as is the coolness of Troilus in the next poem, **"Looking Back"**. Back, or down? For Troilus, rapt at last into the spheres of heaven, has only a brief moment before earth's painful but fertile continuance impinges on him again; his limbo is not a limbo of fools. . . . **"Happy Ending"** tries to think whether hope—and not gullibility—is even envisagable in all those cases where a loved one wishes neither to survive nor be survived. **"The Eyes of the World"** faces the fact that mostly we die unregarded. **"The Faithful Wife"** exhibits a pained candour at the 'non-affair' which 'a career woman at a conference' conducts, a limbo of nursing unacted desires. (pp. 811-12)

In the world of these poems, it is not surprising that 'nothing' proffers itself as possessing a travesty of perilous vitality:

> We walk towards it.
> But we reach nothing.

Or:

> The level-crossing gates
> Guard passers-by from nothing
> Now.

What is suspended is animation, possessing—like the column of wind-blown leaves—'a sort of thin plausible life', where the rhetorical 'a sort of . . .' is understood as itself possessing only a thin plausible life. The life of **"The Branch Line"**:

> If the particular fast
> Bright dragon of childhood
> Is null, I feel the same,
> Extinct; not obsolete
> Nor dead, but lightweight.
> The line has left no ghost
> Even, but is as void
> As my discarded name.

The necessary risk, obviously, is that the words themselves

will be lightweight and void: but what enforces and compre-hends Miss Beer's poetic concerns is her sense of such sus-pended animation in phrasing. She is at her most assured when her half-rhymes temper her rhymes' assurance. She has, too, a particular way with dead metaphors and clichés, neither leaving them for dead nor animating them with the pun of life: phrases like 'come to grief', or 'keep in close touch', are deliberately given a thin plausible life—she needs to suspend them, neither dead nor alive. . . .

The movement of the poems entails a falling away of adjec-tives, similes and metaphors (all of which seem sometimes to offer the wrong poetic consolations), and an arrival at a taut frayed last-ditch ordinariness. They are good poems to quote but hard to quote from, just because it is their whole move-ment which makes manifest their significant suspending. But the end of **"Arms"** should give the feel of their tentative con-clusiveness, their shedding of the epithets of reassurance. She has dreamed of the drowned world and its drowned animals:

> These limbs were not immortal
> And, perishing, they woke me
> As in a story I heard:
> When my grandfather went down
>
> With his brig in the North Sea
> On a calm clear evening
> There was no wireless to send
> Last love on. He put his arms
> Round his son and there he stood,
> Protector, up to his knees
> In death, and that was the last
> That anyone saw of him.

Without ever degenerating into a trick or a mannerism, such a sequence of feeling repeatedly braces the poems. As T. S. Eliot said, such an 'interest in "technique" is something much more comprehensive than an interest in the skilful dis-position of words for their own sake: it is a recognition of the truth that not our feelings, but the pattern which we may make of our feelings, is the centre of value.' (p. 812)

Christopher Ricks, "Patricia Beer," in The Listener, *Vol. 86, No. 2228, December 9, 1971, pp. 811-12.*

THE TIMES LITERARY SUPPLEMENT

[Patricia Beer's new collection of poems, **The Estuary,** con-tains] restrained, unshowy pieces which avoid the pitfalls of confessional rhetoric or emotional exhibitionism at the cost of an imaginative thinness. Their unruffled steadiness of tone results, at best, in some effectively suggestive understate-ments; at worst it leads to an excessively level-headed, unin-spired sort of reportage which has the advantages neither of detailed observation nor of metaphorical resonance:

> The platform is now old
> And empty, but still shows
> The act of waiting.
> Beyond it the meadows,
> Where once the toy shadows
> Of funnel and smoke bowled,
> Are pure green, and no echoes
> Squeeze into the cutting.

In the title-poem ["The Estuary"], metaphor *is* effectively ex-ploited, as a means of relating the physically observed and emotionally felt; otherwise, in the tactics of a particular poem, it is kept to a spare minimum, so that the language

seems at once tautly controlled and sensuously impoverished. Emotional complexities of a kind are suggested, but made to hover beneath a poem's surface, strictly subdued by the clipped evenness of tone and syntax; and since several of the poems are about childhood this has the effect of intensifying their air of remoteness from an urgent actual experience.

"Everything under Control," in The Times Literary Supplement, *No. 3646, January 14, 1972, p. 32.*

DOUGLAS DUNN

Patricia Beer lives in the suburbs . . . and she remembers a rural childhood. [In **The Estuary** the] situation is standard and middle-class, and to write about it poetically demands honesty and a talent for irony. Mrs Beer has both qualities. For example, she is not unaware of the irony in **"Self-help"** that a girl brought up on "notions of self-help / Not that it was so-called and none of us / Had read or heard of Samuel Smiles," should be sitting in Hampstead Village on a Geor-gian sofa "reading Samuel Smiles / *In paperback with* after-word and foreword." The poem is particularly about women "Practising lawful self-advancement"; but the idea is not at-tractive, to her and most other people. The poem ends by spreading out into the wide-open scale of death that only Philip Larkin can pull off convincingly:

> and through
> The white comfortable mist a wind blows holes
> Lays bare the quagmire reaching for us all
> Whispers how soon we could be shouting "Help."

In **"The Coming of the Cat"** she is seen to accept the limita-tions of the suburb at the same time as she notices the false-ness of its gentility and repression:

> We have been taught to take
> Our dreaming like medicine.
>
> Night ticks on. Here in Hampstead
> No owls hoot and the church clock
> In the "village" is throttled
> Till seven tomorrow morning.

She regrets and approves. In other poems, suburban morality is endorsed (**"Safe Lives"**, **"The Faithful Wife"**). There is nothing wrong with this; but it's very plain, and what is safe in life is unfortunately often dull in poetry. (p. 76)

Douglas Dunn, "A Bridge in Minneapolis," in En-counter, *Vol. XXXVIII, No. 5, May, 1972, pp. 73-8.*

RUSSELL DAVIES

Patricia Beer's book [**Driving West**] is so neat and friendly . . . that one could almost mistake it for a house-wifely volume, especially if one opened it at the poem **"Home"**:

> Out of the window
> I see the opposite roofs
> Fitting well like ours.
>
> This house is as warm
> And secure as bathwater.
> Yet very often
>
> Through the double glazing
> I imagine people crying,

Somewhere out there.

The end of the poem goes on to shake the bathwater up somewhat, but not quite enough to justify the foregoing; one fears the worst. But very little else in this collection, fortunately, is perceived through the double glazing, unless you experience irony as an insulation. The book is full of sensible griefs, and an awareness that everything might have been otherwise. Even a commonplace might-have-been poem like **"Middle Age"** offers up its real alternatives in the end:

> Everywhere I look it is the same,
> The churchyard or the other side of the bed.
> The one who is not lying there
> Could have been.

Obedient to the urging of her title-poem [**"Driving West"**], Miss Beer moves steadily into the West Country towards the end of the book, and you can feel her relax with a little too much relief into the world of the seasons, the churchyard, the Water Diviner ('All we can do is dig / a well and prove him right') and the Healer, whose only failure was with his wife's migraine. But the last line of all, as she watches the village festival ('It is years later than you think. Oh, be careful.') suggests that Miss Beer's return to Devon will produce more dramatic material. (p. 726)

> *Russell Davies, "Mug Shots," in* New Statesman, *Vol. 90, No. 2333, December 5, 1975, pp. 725-26.*

D. A. N. JONES

Patricia Beer must be well aware that her title poem [in **Driving West**] will make readers think of John Donne's poem, "Good Friday 1613: Riding Westward". She has written a book, **An Introduction to the Metaphysical Poets,** about Donne and his contemporaries, in which she traces a resemblance between this 17th-century work and the poems of her own contemporaries. She suggests that the poets of the 17th and 20th centuries differ from the poets of the two centuries between, because of their immediacy and spontaneity: they 'seem to be thinking as they write . . . We have come to demand and enjoy the experience of hearing a poet exploring his own mind and heart, seeming to work out the sum as he goes along, not just giving us the answer'.

Comparing "Riding Westward" with **"Driving West"**, we can see that both poets are working something out as they travel; but the difference between their concerns is so large that the resemblance seems trivial. Donne claims to feel that he ought to be riding eastwards, on this day, travelling towards Christ, and he works out an argument that, nevertheless, there is a sense in which it is appropriate for him to ride in the opposite direction. He begins:

> Let mans Soule be a Spheare, and then, in this,
> The intelligence that moves, devotion is.

Miss Beer's poem begins with more immediacy:

> New car. One of the great
> Roads of the west country
> That Fielding remembered,
> Dying abroad . . .

What is Henry (presumably) Fielding doing here? He does not reappear in this short poem. I suppose he might make one think of *Tom Jones* and picaresque novels and (in this context) of a yearning for a happier past. If so, Miss Beer's next

point in the poem follows on naturally enough. The ride and the weather make her

> feel sane and rich,
> An eighteenth-century
> Monseigneur in his coach.

The best-known 'Monseigneur in his coach' is the man in *A Tale of Two Cities,* who runs down pedestrians; and that is what Miss Beer is thinking about, it seems. The Monseigneur in her poem feels sane and rich because of the 'vulnerable' sparrows and the 'crushable' dog which cross his path, so that he 'suddenly' thinks of the poor, and 'for once' pities the mad.

The poet's drive makes her think of power and status and guilt: she does not put herself in a good light. Donne thinks of his direction, proudly associating it with his journey towards his Saviour—while acknowledging his sins, his 'rust and deformity'. The difference in spirit between the Metaphysical poets and Miss Beer . . . is enormous.

> *D. A. N. Jones, "Westward Ho!" in* The Listener, *Vol. 95, No. 2449, March 18, 1976, p. 350.*

DOUGLAS DUNN

Rhymes in Patricia Beer's **Driving West** are often of the "half-" or "near-" variety. Her almost obtrusively lyrical intentions probably insist on some form of music to support them. Occasionally the result is a music that can hardly be heard, if at all. "Before" and "law", for instance, are not, in my accent, rhymes: they hardly even associate to form assonance. "Eyes" and "buzz" is another example. More poets are passing this off as rhyme than is really decent. There is something academic or half-hearted about accepting so approximate a music as in some way part of a legal craftsmanship, as fulfilling the unwritten laws of contemporary metrics.

When Ms Beer's rhymes are kept close to an idea of music you can actually hear (some poets would rhyme "idea" and hear", but I can't), the result is more than acceptable. Technically, Ms Beer is perhaps more scrupulous than fussy, which goes some way towards compensating for what to my taste is a lack of doctrinal excitement. In that lack I do see—self-effacingly—the virtue of her poems being directed at the imaginary reader but not wanting to change or flatter social or imaginative orders. The remark may seem a strange one. But for all the local disturbances of her lyricism her poems are not, in the context of contemporary poetry, in the merest way disturbing. To question death or love is not disturbing in poetry, where such questions are familiar; unless the questions are new or surprising. Her poems have charm—a more serious literary concept than is usually admitted; few poets are as content with it as they should be. An example:

> A heavy frost last night,
> The longest night of the year,
> Makes the land at first light
> Look spruced up for death,
> Incurably white. . . .
>
> Not far behind, a track
> Of frost is following
> That the sun cannot lick
> Completely green in time,
> Before night rolls back.

Her writing is native. Observations are presented with a balance struck between the concrete and the intangibles of feeling. Things and feelings interact in the ways of the best nature poetry. Again, it is minor writing; but it pleases immensely. (pp. 79-80)

Douglas Dunn, " 'Make It Old!' " in Encounter, *Vol. XLVI, No. 5, May, 1976, pp. 75-81.*

RONALD BLYTHE

Great events cast their irritations in Patricia Beer's first novel [*Moon's Ottery*], about rural Devon in Armada days. Like most villages, Moon's Ottery is chronically introverted, but it notes such matters as Sir Francis's knighthood, the queen's majesty, the execution of Mary (briskly unlamented, a sort of tidying-up of Catholic loose ends), the Armada itself (a bore, like fire-watching) and the Reformation (what will they think of next?). But what really turns the whole place on is any variation of its own toil, pastimes and scandal. The story swivels on the sensible basis of there being no such thing as a village secret, only varying notions of the facts. Drama is created by manipulating common knowledge in an interesting manner. The entire community is in cahoots, of course, on the make and self-sufficient. Patricia Beer uses it to deflate history and prick its bombast. Time itself is cut down to size—how fundamentally different are we after 400 years?

The vicar, who has wearily adorned himself in vestments for one sovereign and stripped them off for another, leads the field in giving Xavier the stranger the benefit of the doubt—'Why, we was all papists once.' But Xavier, who courts Farmer Mutter's daughter, is a Spanish spy. Nice Mr Suckbitch, Gent., finds this out, and thus allows the tale to end in the classic standard historical fiction manner of bliss after a bloodletting. The latter includes the miscarriage of the Spaniard's baby—another sensible tying-up of Catholic loose ends. . . .

Patricia Beer's method is either to inject our Elizabeth I ancestors with some mid-Elizabeth II liberation, or to suppose that society doesn't alter all that much and that there was plenty of it in them anyway. It makes her story pleasantly tart and gives it originality. The class system, with the squire's wife no more than some queen bee . . . in a ruff, and with copyholder, labourer and yeoman showing no sign at all that they intend to keep their place, reveals an uppertiness in the nation which hasn't improved with the years. As for the permissive, when the handsome young Pulman brothers are discovered to be lovers, nobody dreams of reporting them to the Bawdy Court. Incestuous gaiety is bad, certainly, but the village seems to think that there are worse things, possibly sheep.

Mrs Clapp flourishes among her stinking simples as the proto-district nurse and Henry Suckbitch is all a country scholar should be: learned, mildly ambivalent and in touch with the town. He is the type of Elizabethan one finds immortalised in a footnote by Dr A. L. Rowse. There is also much period detail, effectively distributed, and some acute asides which penetrate through to the real Tudor Devon.

These are knowing bucolics and they contain some excellent writing, but they do not wholly convey the one essential of the historical novelist proper—even a comic one—which is the overriding, infectious conviction that history is romance.

Ronald Blythe, "Upperty Ottery," in The Listener, *Vol. 99, No. 2561, May 25, 1978, p. 681.*

SUSANNAH CLAPP

In a television interview several years ago Patricia Beer was asked why she started to write poetry. She gave a plain reply: "I was good at words: I knew I couldn't write novels or plays because I couldn't write dialogue, and I had no ability at all at imagining I was someone else. And so—poetry." Her first novel, *Moon's Ottery,* is not noticeably impeded by these obstacles. The way they were overcome is illuminated by the simultaneous reissue of the author's excellent autobiographical study, *Mrs Beer's House,* which not merely expands her fiction but overlaps with it and seems to propel it.

Mrs Beer's House was first published in 1968. It is unusual in being the story of a good child, one who grows up in Devon with a more luscious-looking sister, a strong-minded mother and an ineffectual, mostly excluded father. It is also, informatively, the story of growing up among the Plymouth Brethren, who, with their insistence on "stout, infinitely concealing" underclothes, on the "weird and desperate gymnastics of trusting", on the perils of roundabouts, cinemas and bobbed hair, built up an effective barrier between a subscribing family and an outside world threatening Popishness and prurience. The village of Ottery St Mary features briefly, like a benign version of Larkin's Coventry, as a place where the Beer children were taken to see blazing tar-barrels rolled down a hill, and missed them—a venture to be ranked alongside outings to hear nightingales which never sang and eclipses which were misted over. The volume ends with the death of Patricia Beer's mother.

Moon's Ottery begins with the death of the heroine's mother. The heroine is the plainer and more intellectual of two sisters whose father, like Miss Beer's own father, is notable for his capacity to "carry objects and people, literally though not metaphorically". Like the young Miss Beer, the heroine is fluent at parody and skinny; like Miss Beer's own sister, the heroine's better-endowed sister is nicknamed "Venus". Most interestingly, however, *Moon's Ottery* is set in an enclosed community which is threatened—more realistically, though the news is taken more calmly—by a Popish invasion. The time is 1588. . . .

Moon's Ottery glimmers with romantic settings and situations precisely expressed. Rosalind and Alice Mutter, farmer's daughters, move, neat-handed and sharp-tongued, from dairy to cobbled courtyard to village green and church. Alice falls in love and sits by the hall fire holding hands with her suitor; Rosalind is thwarted in love and applies to the local white witch for an aphrodisiac potion; they listen to news of Marlowe and Lord Burghley, they star in an Accession Day pageant; they are present at the lighting of the village beacon which warns of the Armada's approach; Rosalind watches the crescent of ships from the top of mustard-covered slopes. They have a brush with murder and a spy. Both marry satisfactorily.

Rosalind's is the predominant voice, and it is an imaginative and logical one—quick to point out to a father maudlin about their mother's empty chair that their mother always sat on a stool, eager to tease out the implications of wordy philosophies and evasive asides. The same qualities invigorate the novel's prose. The inescapable quaintness produced by references to covered baskets, rosewater and elderflower wine is balanced by a lack of self-conscious charm in the dialogue; although some of the Devonian turns of speech have a rather too cultivated rustic ring, there is no intriguing antique, no fustian, and characters can say "bullshit" without sounding as if they have escaped from a novel by Joseph Heller. Sweetness is also held at bay by a batch of uncompromisingly vigorous surnames: Pook, Bash, Clapp and Suckbitch all figure centrally, though, encouragingly, no one is damned by being so titled.

More centrally, the style of acuteness which the characters are allowed is altogether different from the retrospective knowingness and self-importance which marks the more hectic type of historical novel. It is always difficult to mention actual historical figures without seeming to be nudging initiated modern readers, and some references to John Dee or Francis Walsingham do not escape this awkwardness. But on the whole things and people are wryly or admiringly regarded not for what hindsight has revealed them to be, but for the manner in which they go about their lives: the white witch Clapp is mocked not for witchiness but for her own, euphemism-studded brand of ineffective witchery.

The novel is peopled by stock village characters—bailiff, vicar, local gentry, labourers—and these are not without their expected characteristics. But the suggestion that the rural round confers homogeneous good-heartedness is avoided, not only by the introduction of unusual antics—such as the incestuous homosexuality of two stalwart brothers—but by a coolness which questions the virtues displayed. Simple kindliness is rightly shown to entail disadvantages: Farmer Mutter, proving, like Miss Beer's own father, incapable of responsibility, weeps as he carries his sick daughter off to care in another household. The collective impression of the villagers, who are given ample opportunity to display themselves collectively, is an unrosy if amiable one: at the wedding of a deaf and dumb couple, they gawp and nudge, creating an atmosphere "too good-humoured to be cruel but it was certainly heartless".

The same understanding aloofness characterizes the necessarily recurrent descriptions of frosts, dusks, greennesses and wetnesses. In *Mrs Beer's House* Patricia Beer talks of her adolescent pleasure in Gray's poetry, and of how she enjoyed in much the same spirit talk of the "thorny bed of pain" and of "new-born flocks, in rustic dance", liking such floridities not because they chimed with her own experience as a country-bred girl but because they were so systematically alien to it: "Although I dumbly and inarticulately loved the meadows and the trees of my home, this feeling lay beneath conscious observation: I did not really notice the seasons, for example, until I was grown up." The progress from genial acceptance to thoughtful observing stands her in good stead in *Moon's Ottery.* Farming life and the shifting of seasons are made more vivid by lack of lauding or belabouring: whatever the sickness of heart, there will always be some task to execute. The dominant images of the book—the mists by the river and the beacon on the hill—are to the point of the plot: they are not badgered for the mysticism which they might seem to suggest but perceived as important individual occurrences. A central feature of Miss Beer's poetry has been the demonstration that a sense of strangeness does not preclude strong-mindedness and plain speaking. Her novel shares this.

> Susannah Clapp, "Threats of Invasion," in The Times Literary Supplement, No. 3973, May 26, 1978, p. 573.

MARY HOPE

Moon's Ottery is a strange, quiet, likeable book which sets small dramas against great ones: domestic and parochial concerns against a moving backdrop of the events leading up to the Spanish Armada. Indeed, that great fleet actually puts in an appearance. The story is basically girls's magazine material: two sisters, Rosalind and Alice, witty, lively, earthy if inexperienced, lose their mother, go to live with an aunt, have unhappy love affairs (one requited, one unrequited) with an undesirable dark stranger, and finally marry the Messrs Right. Their village has its share of 'characters'; but these are far removed from the cosy world of token Elizabethan Archers: a white witch, whose potions never quite work, but whose diagnostic indelicacy is remarkable for its prurient circumlocutions; homosexual incestuous brothers whose chief peculiarity is always to object 'I do' whenever just cause or impediment is called for at weddings where they fancy the groom; a deaf and dumb couple whose wedding is watched as a theatrical treat by the whole of the village. These and others are so distinct and detailed, so intensely quirky and idiosyncratic that they must surely be drawn from life.

The strangeness and attraction of the book is in the matter-of-factness of modern psychological detail, set in what often threatens to become historical flummery. A handy character, for instance, puts in many useful man-hours, pounding up to London and returning with News from Court—knowing nudges for the modern readers; simples, possets *et al* are also made much use of. Yet, surely, earthy though much of the language is, it is also un-Elizabethan. It is this blithe intermingling of ingenuousness and psychological sophistication which, though not making a classic historical novel gives a kind of out-of-kilter charm.

> Mary Hope, in a review of "Moon's Ottery," in The Spectator, Vol. 240, No. 7822, June 3, 1978, p. 25.

IAN STEWART

For a historical novel Patricia Beer's *Moon's Ottery* has an agreeably cavalier way with anachronisms such as the "own goal" metaphor when the Spaniards blow up one of their Armada ships, and the reference to a young man with a penthouse-style moustache. What is equally agreeable is the way the picture of life in Elizabethan Devon emerges so vividly without any obvious effort at establishing period atmosphere. Winters are harsh in Moon's Ottery, but in spring we find yeoman farmer Mutter and his men at Sparkhayes Farm out all day spreading dung, picking up stones and sowing the last crops. The valley of the Otter is enveloped by a sinister evening mist while nearer the sea the hedges are luxuriant with foxgloves and wild roses and on the Sidmouth cliffs are great clumps of mustard. May Day is celebrated with wrestling and a pageant, there are the exigencies of harvest time, and the parson collects his tithe of corn. The author displays a disarming boldness rather than simplicity in the handling of the action. Not only is there the drama in the life of the Mutter family and the loves of the two Mutter girls but the village is caught up in the events of a larger drama, the threatened Spanish invasion of 1588, and these are vividly and entertainingly narrated.

> Ian Stewart, in a review of "Moon's Ottery," in The Illustrated London News, Vol. 266, No. 6961, August, 1978, p. 50.

ANDREW MOTION

As one might expect in a *Selected Poems,* Patricia Beer offers . . . variety. Her book draws on five previous collections—the first published 21 years ago—as well as including some recent work. In the early days, she used a predictably large number of poeticisms and spent a good deal of time worrying about the comparative ease of her life. Her solution was a familiar one, to turn the absence of danger into a threat. In **"On the Cobb at Lyme Regis"**, for instance: 'this safety is different. I know / From my teachers what is impossible. / I am in no danger, the sea cannot rise, / Which is the most frightening thing of all'.

By her third book [*Just Like the Resurrection*], this guilty anxiety about living in a post-war, post-mythological world had undergone a transformation. And what it became has remained one of her greatest strengths, as well as the potential constrainer of her talent: a fascination with the curious and uncanny. On one hand it satisfied her wish to escape an entirely sanitised, predictable universe, and on the other it forced her to realise that she didn't want to live anywhere *too* unpredictable. Hence the usual tone of voice adopted in her middle years—she is an inexhaustible guide to oddities, but her unflappable rhythms and no-nonsense syntax tend to dissipate the mystery she seeks to preserve:

> This is a strange museum. In one square yard see
> A mummified ibis and a postilion's boot.
> Grey litter fills the house. For years every dead Man
> Had some cast-off curious object to donate.

Beer's main difficulty, and her most considerable achievement, has been to alter and excite this manner. She admits to having been 'a child who dared not seem / Gloomy', but over the years she has become increasingly prepared to say what she feels. The fear of death and the lack of absolute religious security have proved more than a match for her instinct to explain and placate:

> I have not seen your writing
> For ages, nor have been fretting
> To see it. As once, darling.
>
> This letter will certainly be
> About some book, written by you or by me.
> You turned to other ghosts. So did I.
>
> It stopped raining long ago
> But drops caught up in the bough
> Fall murderously on me now.

As Patricia Beer gets sadder she gets more attentive to the world around her.

Andrew Motion, "Running on the Spot," in New Statesman, *Vol. 100, No. 2572, July 4, 1980, p. 24.*

CAROL RUMENS

As readers of her childhood autobiography know, Patricia Beer grew up in the bosom (pronounced *boosom*) of the apocalyptic Plymouth Brethren. Their doomy pronouncements—"I know not when my Lord will come, I know not how or where"—left her, she says, feeling helpless, with only "the weird and desperate gymnastics of trusting" as a defence. Illness and death were not concealed from her, save the one death she needed to be in touch with—that of her mother. So we find in the mature poet an obsessive practising for death,

spritely, trim and almost common-sensical though the performance is. She is that rare phenomenon, a religious poet stripped of the blurring consolations of religion. She is certainly a treasurably astringent and rather quirky voice in the Babel of modern English poetry. . . .

[*Selected Poems*] brings together poems from all five of her published collections, plus a satisfying sneak preview of what one hopes will be her sixth. The first two [*The Loss of the Magyar* and *The Survivors*] are sparsely represented, the rest reprinted almost complete. It makes for a certain uniformity, which it would be churlish to complain at, since with a few minor exceptions it is a uniformity of excellence.

Ms Beer has developed by narrowing rather than extending her range. In retrospect, much of her early work seems a rather florid, over-literary encircling of what are finally to be her true concerns. The title sequence of her first book, **"The Loss of the Magyar"**, omitted here, is a case in point. By her standards now it looks over-written. In the fourth book, *The Estuary* (1971), the mature writer is able to treat this ancestral shipwreck in a far more oblique and telling way. All the emotional intensity that ran unchecked in those early stanzas is distilled into nine perfectly measured lines:

Nevertheless, a few babies have been cast out with the bathwater. **"The Witch"**, for example, with her "black, pointed heart" and menacing determination for the rights of the subconscious to prevail, surely deserved to make these selected poems—a brighter candidate, perhaps, than the Vampire, who takes four stanzas to say what is obvious to any self-respecting post-Freudian. (That lovely image of the moth-brown ship pinned in its harbour was his passport, perhaps.)

Among the earliest poems in which Patricia Beer discovers her own voice is **"Epitaph in a Country Churchyard"** from *The Survivors.* "I picked on myself", she says, "to come through the smell of nettles to the smooth spade." Thus begins an artful, tough-minded, English brand of extremism which owes little to Sexton, Hughes or Plath. By her third book *Just like the Resurrection,* she is in full spate with such splendid pieces as **"Concert at Long Melford Church"** [and] **"Lion Hunt."** . . . [In *The Estuary,* Beer's next collection], the estuary is a symbol of childhood's end, the split between what is safely familiar and what is unknown and frightening; it is echoed in poems haunted by the move from the country to the city. These are painful subjects, handled with an increasingly adventurous technique. Not all the adventurers succeed: Ms Beer's syllabic writing, though it works well in **"Arms,"** lures her away from her usual economy of means in **"A Birthday Card"** and **"The Eyes of the World."** She seems essentially to be a rhythmic poet. . . .

If parts of *The Estuary* represent a slight trough in the poet's achievement, she is back on form in *Driving West,* particularly in the title poem, as well as **"John Milton and My Father"**, **"Festival"** and the extraordinary **"Prochorus Thompson"**, its tight-lipped vacillation between pity and cynicism and rage contained by a most terse and economical language. The recent poems also seem to me among her best, with their strong, dark, medieval flavour. Ms Beer's view of death seems inexhaustibly productive; what is most impressive, though, is how well she succeeds in not writing the same poem over and over again. There is always a new slant to surprise or to shock or even, in **"Telling Them"** finally to raise a wry smile. Blackness—to reverse the words of Parson Hawker—has been a friend to this poet.

It is difficult, however, to know where she could go from here. Perhaps a piece of brightly enamelled, almost imagistic free verse like **"Spanish Balcony"** is the clue to how she might broaden a poetry that is as neat and harsh and tightly carpentered as the final box that shadows it. Patricia Beer is so brilliantly accomplished that one feels she could now afford to take the sort of risks from which she learnt so well in those discarded early poems. But perhaps there is no reason why she should.

> Carol Rumens, *"The Friendly Blackness," in* The Times Literary Supplement, *No. 4041, September 12, 1980, p. 990.*

PETER PORTER

For years now Miss Beer has been refining her talent until perception of feeling and a sense of inward illumination require of her very few words. For her, economy of utterance is a certain sign of poetry's being present. Her spare and well-shaped stanzas stay quiet: it is the events they muster which expand in the mind.

In **"Lookalikes"** [from *The Lie of the Land*], she begins with an odd sight seen from a train, two men walking away from a dead horse, 'his expensive coat still on.' Then in horror everything begins to look like the left-behind horse, until a living horse lifts the curse from her:—

> And as the train slowed down
> At last a living horse,
> Prostrate but flicking up
> Tail or a leg by choice,
>
> Seemed to be in the grip
> Of a strong inshore breeze:
> Seaweed after a storm
> And several dry days.

It isn't the horse's living self which provides the balm, but a second benign image purging her mind of the deathly first one.

"Midsummer in Town" is a poem of equal subtlety. She notices how dark houses can become in the bright season when abundant foliage outside blocks their light. . . . Although 'Under this elegant town roof / Midsummer darkness is a spoof,' the message which comes through is terminal:—

> The magic of a trumped-up storm
> That gives an out-of-kilter charm
> To the precision of the pit
> Waiting beneath the oubliette.

Miss Beer is much obsessed by death, but never ghoulishly or rhetorically. Death is a familiar of her countryside and townscape, not the trigger of the literary man's biggest gun. *The Lie of the Land* has fewer words than any book of poems since the heyday of the Minimalists. Paradoxically, it is full of human presences.

> Peter Porter, *"The Still Small Voice," in* The Observer, *March 20, 1983, p. 33.*

JOHN MOLE

Patricia Beer's poems [in *The Lie of the Land*] are full of ghosts. They move fleetingly across her miniature canvases like figures in a pageant to the tolling of a passing bell. She is preoccupied with time, and her work has the monitory elegance of a collection of hourglasses in which the light is continually catching the sifting sand. To take a phrase from **"The Spinsters and The Knitters in the Sun"**, one of the finest poems in her new collection, she works in a "spotlit darkness", contemplating her own mortality as part of the shadow-play of history. She is attuned to intimation and rumour ("At the top of the lane / Wars went by", "Somewhere a horse galloped"), and this gives an edge to the precise, domestic observation which is one of her great strengths:

> I watch the shadows of the house climbing
> Slantwise and high up the back field.
> The east chimney puffs out a black ghost.

That "slantwise" is tell-tale, an accurate perception both visually and as an indication of Patricia Beer's method. Like Emily Dickinson she knows how to tell it slant, so that nothing is ever quite what it seems although it is defined with great exactitude. The lie of the land is deceptive—and the pun in the book's title is surely intended. Patricia Beer's poems are full of images, and the cleverness is absorbed into the landscapes they serve to depict, giving it an idiosyncratic character and perspective: she risks whimsy and turns the slightest effect to advantage—"The trees are parsley magnified" or "Today / Impromptu meres, whiskery / In fields, raise half / A fence for an eyebrow." A quizzical look, and Patricia Beer's eyebrow is raised back, a match for it.

My favourite poem in *The Lie of the Land* is **"Bereavement."** It has a pained beauty, an oddly hymn-like stately simplicity in which Blake meets with the Ancient and Modern Victorians. Its rhythms and rhymes . . . are haunting in their contrived blend of knowingness and naivety: the Lamb of God is a lost child, fierce in its sense of betrayal:

> I was too young. I had to watch
> My heavy mother lie on her back to scratch.
> They never touched ground again, those brittle feet.
>
> I cannot eat what all the others eat.
>
> Foolish mother, rolling to death, how long
> Shall the deserted bare an aching tongue
> To call for what is drying up inside you
> As the afternoon trees begin to shade you?
>
> Soon he will come, the farmer, and haul away
> And hide that sheep, who treacherously
> Lay down, where I can never find her
> Nor go into the slaughter-house behind her.
>
> The sharp May grass sings under my nose
> And soon the farmer will hear a new voice
> That lost the day wailing about hunger
> But towards nightfall turns to anger.

Nightfall, again, as in so many of the poems, and time running out. "The clock on the night storage heating / Ticks like a taxi waiting." (pp. 70-1)

> John Mole, *"Everyday Worlds," in* Encounter, *Vol. LX, No. 6, June, 1983, pp. 68-74.*

DICK DAVIS

In her new collection [*The Lie of the Land*], Patricia Beer has a poem called **"The Spinsters and the Knitters in the Sun"**; we are in Illyria—

Mark it, Cesario; it is old and plain,
The spinsters and the knitters in the sun
And the free maids that weave their thread with bones
Do use to chant it. It is silly sooth,
And dallies with the innocence of love
Like the old age.

Orsino's speech from *Twelfth Night* is an admirable guide to
the prevailing tone of this book, concerned as it largely is with
idylls glimpsed and lost, lives summed up by brief epiphanies
in sunlight, a sense of nostalgia and sweetness modified—but
not cancelled—by the knowledge that 'it is silly sooth'. Many
of the poems are very close in feeling to Shakespearian comedy; it is remarkable how often they are about high summer,
the mind dazed with sensations of beneficent richness, evil
and good temporarily reconciled (this last is touchingly presented in **"Saint George and the Dragon: from an Elizabethan
Pageant"** in which the two agree not to fight). Even a poem
on the battle of Waterloo ends with a note of pastoral quiet
that remains curiously undistorted by the images of carnage
that precede it:

Sky and a kind of joy came back together,
Almost too late to show a lost and glorious
Summer day, the sun about to set.

Not that the writing is self-deceiving: in **"The Simple Life"**,
which invokes *As You Like It,* the Arts and Crafts idyll is
shown to be an enervating sideshow to normal existence. The
poem that for me sums up the book's atmosphere is **"Some
Sunny Day"** (on the Vera Lynn song) in which the desire to
believe in the song's lachrymose promise is balanced by the
knowledge that

Nobody
Now could underwrite a pledge so costly,
Assure two people they will meet again
With enduring earth to walk on, in the sun.

Promise and knowledge are poignantly balanced in the closing stanza, 'Now fear shakes / The apple-trees of Eden'. Not
all the poems in *The Lie of the Land* are about this tension,
but almost all are at least ghosted by it and the ones that deal
with it explicitly are the most successful. The only poems that
do not, I think, quite come off are a few of those that attempt
empathy with figures from the past, in particular **"Lament
for the Duke of Medina Sidonia"** and **"Coriolanus Leaves
Home"**. But in the main the language is beautifully limpid
and considered without ever fussily drawing attention to itself; the finest pieces gathered here are certainly among the
best that Patricia Beer has published.

Dick Davis, "Apple-Trees of Eden," in The Listener,
Vol. 110, No. 2819, July 28, 1983, p. 23.

PETER READING

Patricia Beer's verse may have become a bit more casual and
comprehensible with each volume, but the noticeable thing
about the thirty years' work presented in her *Collected
Poems* is an unchanging quality. This is not only because the
poems have consistently addressed themselves to those
themes (death, love, nature, religious mystery, momentary illumination) popularly regarded as immutable—for those,
after all, are the props of all decent art—but also because the
approach has remained tenaciously modest in its metrics,
small-scale, often domestic and, above all, whimsical.

The *Collected Poems* assembles, in chronological order, the
pared-down contents of Beer's seven collections . . . and finishes with a section of pieces the latest of which were written
"just before the book went to press". *Loss of the Magyar*
(1959) and *The Survivors* (1963) are lumped together as
"Early Poems". The earliest of these, **"The Fifth Sense"**, is
uncharacteristically direct. A first-person monologue, motivated by a sense of outrage at a news item, describes the
shooting by security forces of a Greek Cypriot (subsequently
found to be deaf) who, in the troubles of 1957, had failed to
respond to their challenge—"For I may never touch, smell,
taste or see / Again, because I could not hear." Elsewhere,
though, are to be found some of the ingredients which typify
the later work. There are poems about Italy (where Beer had
taught from 1946 to 53), about the Devon of her birth and
upbringing, about her Plymouth Brethren ancestors, about
literature, landscape and the deaths of her parents, "When
the clock strikes / The latest hour there is".

Alarm clocks like this keep going off all over the place (indeed, one poem, from *Just Like the Resurrection,* 1967, is entitled **"The Clock"**): "Obviously / Death cannot come each
time / The clock stops. It may be / Good practice to think
so". . . .

Reading Patricia Beer, one is not reminded of many other
writers. Her prosodic range encompasses iambic pentame-
ters, the occasional flaccid sonnet, the odd flirtation with syl-
labics including a one-off haiku almanac: nothing *outré*. The
preferred metre is one of rhythmic, fluid informality, sometimes with irregular or loose rhyme, which enables the poet
to introduce her frequent twists and surprises with maximum
effect. It's this element of quirky, child-like or sham-naive unexpectedness, a little reminiscent of Stevie Smith with whom
"There had been friendship, not close, coming late in the
day", that establishes Beer's individuality, as is evident in
"Mating Calls" from *Driving West* (1975):

It is not so much the song
Of the hump-backed whale, reaching
Through a hundred miles of sea
To his love that strikes us. We
Can be heard farther than he . . .

or in **"Four Spells"** from *Poems* (1979):

Two angels came from the East.
The one said "Gorge", the other said "Fast".
Out Lent! In locust!
In the name of water-into-wine and the marriage feast.

There is something of a painter's observation and vision here,
too. Certain caught moments could almost be those of Stanley Spencer: **"Looking Sideways"** produces (as well as dreary
metaphor) some striking optical distortions; at Long Melford
church, well-dressed concert-goers, taking a breather in the
graveyard during the interval, look just like a Resurrection;
a drunk in the dark "Comes tacking up the road / In a white
macintosh / Charming as a yacht"; a crowd in a dark square
is pictured playing with illuminated yo-yos. Elsewhere, the
moon is "White and rumpled like a vaccination mark", and
there's a splendidly Martian snapshot of a funeral, where
"Down the path shuffled the sad six-legged turtle / One huge
wreath alone on its carapace".

The poems in this omnium gatherum, then, have a predominantly Hesperian orientation. **"Driving West"**, going west,
"Called Home"; we are all to gather at the river in the sweet
by-and-by, as the poet's early experiences with the Plymouth
Brethren informed her. Lemmings do it, birds do it, our

mothers and fathers do it, "The dance goes on straight and forever". Most forcefully, perhaps, little Prochorus Thompson, who had "Three months of life two hundred years ago", did it, in **Driving West** (1975). Here, the smallest bones in the churchyard attract the attention of tourists; the corpses of all those men and women who lived once for fifty or sixty years, worked hard and then dropped dead, are neglected:

> The balance of the churchyard must be righted.
> May the full-grown dead seem interesting. May all
> Children live longer than Prochorus Thompson.
> Strangle the church tower and the passing bell.

> *Peter Reading, "Stepping Westward," in* The Times Literary Supplement, No. 4477, January 20-26, 1989, p. 59.

Yves Bonnefoy

1923-

French poet, essayist, translator, and editor.

Bonnefoy is widely regarded as one of the most important French poets to emerge after World War II. Critics note in his work affinities with both the Metaphysical poets of the seventeenth century and the Surrealists of the twentieth century for his investigation of spiritual and philosophical matters and his preference for exploring the subconscious rather than material reality and conscious perceptions. Much of Bonnefoy's poetry is preoccupied with loss and death, and the transience of all earthly things is emphasized as a paradoxical compensation for the loss of hope for immortality. Some critics view his work as a quest for what Bonnefoy himself terms "le vrai lieu" (the true place), a location in time or space, or a state of mind wherein the fundamental unity of all things is perceived. Bonnefoy's insistence on the importance of accepting the presence of death in everyday life has prompted many commentators to regard him as the first existentialist poet. Jean Starobinski commented: "The work of Bonnefoy offers us today one of the most committed and deeply pondered examples of [the] modern vocation of poetry. His writings as poet and essayist, in which the personal accent is so clear, and in which the *I* of subjective assertion is manifested with force and simplicity, have for object a relation to the world, not an internal reflection on the self. This *oeuvre* is one of the least narcissistic there is."

Bonnefoy was born in Tours, France, and earned a degree in philosophy from the University of Paris. His study of the influential German philosopher Georg Friedrich Wilhelm Hegel is evident throughout his work. Hegel's theory of the dialectical nature of existence posits that each entity supposes its own opposite, each "thesis" its own "antithesis," in Hegel's terminology. This theory operates both thematically and structurally in Bonnefoy's poetry, allying his work with Surrealism. Jean Paris commented: "[Bonnefoy] developed an essentially dialectical poetry where hope and despair, darkness and light are presented as two faces of the same mirror. While seeking life, this poetry has therefore to assume death, and then Bonnefoy's writings are basically founded on ambiguity."

Bonnefoy's first three volumes of verse, *Du mouvement et de l'immobilité de Douve* (1953; *On the Motion and Immobility of Douve*), *Hier régnant désert* (1959), and *Pierre écrite* (1965; *Words in Stone*), are often considered a poetic cycle. Each volume is composed of short, interrelated poems that expand or resolve themes present in the others. Bonnefoy's reputation as a serious poet was established with the publication of *On the Motion and Immobility of Douve*. Critics have variously interpreted Douve as the speaker's beloved, a mythological symbol for all women, a river or moat, a forest, the poetic principle, and as the poem itself. Against a surreal and stark landscape in which wind, stone, and fire are discernible elements, Douve repeatedly dies, decomposes, and comes back to life. Michael Bishop remarked: "Death, despite its 'frightful', 'silly' orchestrations is felt, throughout these intense poems, to be doubly positive. It is the one phenomenon that,

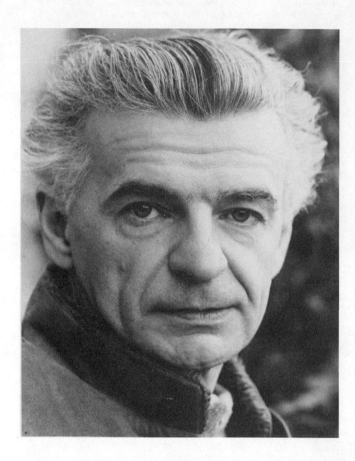

for Bonnefoy, flings us back towards our existence, our leaking yet potentially full being-in-the-world."

Hier régnant désert explores the significance of death and its presence in daily life. Although Bonnefoy employed a more optimistic tone and less violent imagery in this collection, the poems are generally considered more difficult and have garnered the least critical attention of the three volumes in the cycle. In an essay that presents *Hier régnant désert* as a continuation of the journey begun in *On the Motion and Immobility of Douve* and completed in *Words in Stone,* Marc Hofstadter wrote: "Beginning in despair of the validity of the search or of the self's ability to pursue it . . . *Hier régnant désert* takes the poet and us through a journey that ends, after all, in an opening up towards presence." *Words in Stone* emphasizes presence in the here-and-now and maintains the optimism which concluded *Hier régnant désert* by praising the present moment as not only all there is but all that the speaker desires.

The poems in *Dans le leurre du seuil* (1975) continue the discussion of Plato's theory of Ideas that Bonnefoy originally addressed in *Anti-Platon* (1962). Plato's according the highest degree of reality to ideas, of which all material "reality" is a mere reflection, is analogous, according to Bonnefoy, to the modern individual's experience of the world without a deity. Throughout his career, Bonnefoy has espoused the importance of appraising the material world in all its imperfection and mortality as the only means for peace in a godless universe. The poems in *Dans le leurre du seuil* celebrate the physical world.

Bonnefoy's nonfiction works include *L'improbable* (1959), *Un rêve qui fait à Mantoue* (1967), *L'arrière-pays* (1972), and *Le nuage rouge* (1977). Critics often refer to Bonnefoy's essays on art, literature, and architecture for a more straightforward explication of his concepts than in his verse. "Les tombeaux de Ravenne" (1953) and "L'acte et le lieu de la poesie" (1958), both from *L'improbable,* are most frequently utilized. In the first essay, Bonnefoy's perception of the baroque tombs in Ravenna provides an example of the paradoxical ability of art to portray the immediacy of death. "L'acte et le lieu de la poesie" applies this concern to the poetry of Stéphane Mallarmé, Arthur Rimbaud, Charles Baudelaire, and others.

(See also *CLC,* Vols. 9, 15 and *Contemporary Authors,* Vols. 85-88.)

MARIO MAURIN

Yves Bonnefoy's arresting title, ***Du mouvement et de l'immobilité de Douve,*** may at first glance have puzzled critics, accustomed to more laconic labels; it did not deter them from expressing their enthusiasm. In the field of contemporary poetry, where landmarks were few and already weatherbeaten, no work had arisen in recent years that was more immediately rewarding and seemed better prepared to wear the patina of time. To be able at least to praise unconditionally was delightful, and critics were pleased with themselves as much as with the poet. (p. 16)

It was a welcome relief, as it had been in 1917 with Valéry's *La Jeune Parque,* to find in 1953 a poet whose work effortlessly inserted itself in the body of French poetry and secured the backing of tradition without the least evidence of retrogression. The comparison is neither forced nor fortuitous. Just as one was led to think of Racine and Mallarmé without disparaging Valéry's dazzling creation, *Douve* gravely recapitulated, as it moved on its dark journey, the achievement of the past. If a characteristic adjective such as "infuse" confirmed the Scèvian resonance of this poetry, in its compact and emblematic secrecy, hints of flowing majestic litanies pointed to St. John Perse's use of language ("Il s'agissait d'un vent plus fort que nos mémoires"), only to harden immediately into Char's rock-crystal, Surrealist imagery or Michaux's ferocious matter-of-factness ("A présent se disloquent les menuiseries faciales. A présent l'on procède a l'arrachement de la vue"). . . . Even Péguy's obstinate plodding shuffles for a moment at the threshold of the volume's concluding segment. Most of these reminiscences occur, however, in the first part titled "Théâtre." This fact leads us to wonder whether, besides other areas of meaning later to be discussed, this review of poetic signatures in the glow of the footlights, as it were, is not intended to strike the balance of the process in its historical unfolding, to pay homage to its outstanding realizations by consciously appropriating them, but in so doing to destroy and transcend them. That this is the very

motion of the work under consideration, these remarks, however spotty and inadequate, will endeavor to make plain.

The familiarity of the poems is delusive, therefore, but nonetheless operates on the reader. He feels on safer ground than usual. If respect means looking back, he is confronted with an essentially respectful poet. Bonnefoy's backward glance, however, is also Orpheus' glance: inspired by impatience and love, it destroys what it brings to the light. What appears to be the gravitational pull of traditional prosody may be interpreted as a centrifugal force. To use the author's own image . . . a wound is reopened in classic meters, less blandly than by Baudelaire, more blatantly than by Mallarmé.

The main asset of ***Du mouvement et de l'immobilité de Douve,*** however, is its unity. This is no agglomeration of disconnected poems, but a tightly-knit sequence that relates or, more accurately, undergoes an experience which we are called upon to share. This experience takes the mythical form of the journey, of the metamorphosis. Before attempting to assess its implications, a few superficial observations on ***Douve's*** structure may be in order. The volume is divided into five parts: "Théâtre," "Derniers Gestes," "Douve parle," "L'Orangerie," "Vrai lieu." The first part, a series of nineteen untitled poems, is the longest. The last one, on the other hand, is the shortest and with seven poems is roughly three times briefer than "Théâtre." The central panels form a triptych of fourteen poems each: whether by sheer coincidence, I cannot say, though I am inclined to doubt it. Some will probably lament that the first part was not made up of 21 poems, as may well have been the author's original intention. This would have clinched the position of 7 as the key to the whole structure. As it is, the work avoids mathematical rigidity while adhering to firmly organized patterns, and the final movement, "Vrai lieu," appears more intense and compressed than any of the preceding parts. This configuration is, on the whole, repeated within the movement itself by the growing predominance of short lines over the initial alexandrines. The last poem of the book is a mere quatrain that hurls its question into silence. And just as "Théâtre" formally looked back on the past to carry on its own forward movement, throughout ***Douve*** recurrent secondary motifs act as echoes of the poems that preceded and confirm the coherence of the whole, already insured by the dominant themes. Each poem is grounded on its own past, no material is left dangling. However doubtful the sense may remain in each particular case, reiteration establishes significance. Such is the typical mode of operation of an important range of "symbolist" literature, where it is possible to discover meanings if one is willing to apply specific coordinates, but where what is actually being communicated is a certain structure of experience. Beckett's *Waiting for Godot* may be considered an admirable example of this type of work.

The central experience of ***Douve,*** as the complete title implies, is dialectical. It is a passage from life to death, from day to night and light to darkness, from Summer's warmth to cold, from motion to immobility, from white to black, from high to low; but a passage without end, for these polarizations exist only in function of each other. Who is Douve? What is Douve? The most frequent meaning of the word, in French, is that of "moat" or "trench filled with water.". . . . But at other times Douve is a flowing river, a forest, a stretch of low land, a woman. In all these impersonations, one common character is shared: the pull of gravity, a tendency to lie low or recline, a downward movement, a descent which is cosmically mirrored by the waning of Summer and the setting of the sun. (pp. 16-18)

[There is a] traditional connection between the imagery of descent and the theme of death. Indeed, the whole first part is occupied by Douve's acceptance of and submission to death. Her body is picked clean by insects, she merges with the landscape in a series of poems reminiscent of Lautréamont on the one hand, on the other of Arcimboldo's and Dalí's visual puns or double images. Is not this merging the return to substance which Bonnefoy, in an intricate article on the painter Balthus, indicated as the goal of the artist's quest? Her funeral journey willingly, ecstatically undertaken, Douve disappears like water absorbed by sand. But this disappearance is the necessary condition of her resurrection, and she is greeted by the names that cannot fail to suggest the ambiguity of her experience: salamander and phoenix. Both these emblematic animals survive the ordeal of the flame, they thrive in it, and an odd image like "les basses flammes de la mer" makes it plain that in Bonnefoy's order the waters of death and the fire of the spirit are but two aspects of a single inextricable element. We reach here the core of the poet's attempt, the key to the series of gestures "mimed" by the poems and gathered into what Bonnefoy proudly calls " . . . plus grand cri qu'être ait jamais tenté."

Douve is the Word, her death is the life of the spirit. One wonders whether the author has not been attracted by the linguistic and thematic proximity of the emblem of the Holy Ghost, the Dove. The suggestion, I think, is not entirely preposterous, since Bonnefoy knows English well enough to have translated Shakespeare's *Julius Caesar*. Douve is white as well as coal-black, she is winged as well as irreducible and low. Be that as it may, from the very start the reader is given an indication as to the significance of the journey he is about to undertake, for a quotation from Hegel ushers him into the poet's syncretic Hades: "Now the life of the spirit does not cringe in front of death nor keep itself pure from its ravage. It supports death and maintains itself in it." No references are given, but the passage is taken from the Preface to the *Phenomenology of the Spirit*. . . . If spirit is to retain its power, it must, says Hegel, sojourn with the Negative and look at it in the face. "This sojourn is the magic power which converts the negative into being." When Bonnefoy writes: "Et je t'ai vue te rompre et jouir d'être morte" or again: "Mourir est un pays que tu aimais," he merely concretizes or personalizes the Hegelian concept that man's death is an immanent or autonomous end, that is to say, a conscious and voluntary end, and emphasizes that willingness to die which is the only possible way of life for consciousness. Awareness of this self-activating process makes it easier to understand how, in "L'Orangerie," after a continuous thread of downward motion, the last line of the final poem can become: "Que faire d'une lampe, il pleut, le jour se lève," just as the last line of the preceding part was: "Quand la lumière enfin s'est faite vent et nuit." The dialectical conversation has taken place, the lamp of consciousness destroys itself but, in so doing, like the phoenix, insures its own rebirth. The same reversal is pointed at by another terminal poem, **"Art Poétique."** It also occurs in the experience of love, which is an essential facet of Douve's itinerary: the moment of "death" is that which gives life, and there is no need to insist on the traditional connection between the act of love and *knowing*, here explicitly stated: "Ayant vécu l'instant ou la chair la plus proche se mue en connaissance." *Douve* temporalizes an experience which is of course instantaneous and timeless, and so it ends by a

victory which, hollowed out and denied by Becoming, already begins to doubt itself:

> Le jour franchit le soir, il gagnera
> Sur la nuit quotidienne.
> O notre force et notre gloire, pourrez-vous
> Trouer la muraille des morts?

> The day strides over the evening, it will win
> Against quotidian night.
> Oh, our strength and our lustre, will you be able
> To pierce the rampart of the dead?

The journey is forever to be started all over again, the new beginning is but a continuation, the interrogation is raised in anxiety, the plural "the rampart of the dead" denounces this unending descent into Hell which is the life of the spirit and which opposes the perspective of its massive unalterability to our joy, and yet exerts this very joy by allowing it to be born and to die. The "Théâtre" of the first part has become the "Vrai Lieu" of the last.

The aridity of Bonnefoy's poetry is its wealth and its plenitude. As he would phrase it, it lives in opulence on the very scene of disaster. Through absence, presence is regained, and presence is salvation. If this be the authentic theme of our time, little wonder that critics found in *Douve* a work whose spell could not be shaken. (pp. 18-21)

Mario Maurin, "On Bonnefoy's Poetry," in Yale French Studies, *No. 21, Spring-Summer, 1958, pp. 16-22.*

JEAN PARIS

[*The essay excerpted below was originally published in French in a slightly different form in* The American Society French Legion of Honor Magazine, *1960.*]

[If] poetry is an avowal of death, it is also and fundamentally a quest for a new life. The rare merit of Yves Bonnefoy is to unite these two movements in the same profound drama. As a philosopher, Bonnefoy devoted much time to Hegel: he knows that every truth supposes its opposite. As a critic, he has written one of the best essays on Baudelaire, the first modern poet who mingled two contradictory notions in a single image (*Voici le soir charmant, ami du criminel . . . Here is the charming night, friend of the criminal . . .*). Combining these capacities, he developed an essentially dialectical poetry where hope and despair, darkness and light are presented as the two faces of the same mirror. While seeking life, this poetry has therefore to assume death, and then Bonnefoy's writings are basically founded on ambiguity. His first and most impressive book, *Du Mouvement et de l'Immobilité de Douve* (*On the Movement and Immobility of Douve*), joins in its own title these opposite realities and creates a language in which they constantly exchange their virtues.

As to the poetic entity that Bonnefoy called "Douve," he himself defined it as the relationship between consciousness and nothingness. From the outset, Douve seems to be provided with a twofold nature: she is referred to as death and, at the same time, as the awareness of our death, which is life. In a first section, written both in prose and verse, Bonnefoy describes the agony, death and burial of Douve; the rest of the book is an attempt to discover what may remain of her in the visible world. This pattern is highly symbolical, even mystical, as in Dante's *Inferno* and *Paradiso*, or Milton's *Par-*

adise Lost and *Paradise Regained,* or Proust's *Temps perdu* and *Temps retrouvé,* for poetry here confronts its own disappearance. In other words, death becomes the *vrai lieu,* the "real ground," of the poem, its vocation, its essence: Douve will be dismembered, she will return, like Ophelia, to her basic elements. But, at the same time, the ordeal will assert her nobility. A strange dignity will mark her departure *marching like suns in funeral spaces.* Dead in her flesh, she will be so alive in nature that the poet will hear her in the trees, in the wind. These two movements of death and resurrection form the central theme of Bonnefoy's poems. . . . (pp. 134-35)

> *Jean Paris, "The New French Poetry," in* On Contemporary Literature, *edited by Richard Kostelanetz, second edition, Avon Books, 1969, pp. 128-40.*

WALTER ALBERT

[In an essay on baroque architecture, Bonnefoy's] insistence upon transitory form, the vital and perhaps irregular dispersion of energy in the structure, and the pursuit of a more stable shape through the metamorphoses of architectural form, are equally applicable to his poetry. Like the architect of space, Bonnefoy is working with resistant materials as his poetry turns to images of rock and stone in its search for permanency and durability; and like the architect, capturing his subject in an unstable mold, Bonnefoy is, in spite of the imminent disintegration of his subject, concerned with the construction of a place in which the poetic identity can endure.

The three volumes of Bonnefoy's poetry are an attempt to build an edifice that will survive the dissolution of structural essentials experienced in the earliest of the texts, *Du mouvement et de l'immobilité de Douve.* . . . The total commitment to the building of this edifice makes of each succeeding volume not an independent structure, but a part of an evolving, cyclical concept. The entire cycle, prolonging the violence of *Douve* in *Hier régnant désert* and seeming to find a tonal and substantive reconciliation in *Pierre écrite,* is both an extension and a denial of the initial experience of the ecstasy of death. The discovery, a sudden, excited, even joyous revelation, will be torturously disassembled, analyzed and refashioned, as a continuing sensory awareness, paradoxically ignoring the finality of death, will give meaning to the taut, apparently irreconcilible frame upon which the poetry is built. This triumphant perception also prepares us for the larger contradiction of the cycle: the search for a permanent place to contain an unstable poetic identity, expressed in a poetic structure that, responding to the disintegration and refusing to admit the formal measures of classical verse as a controlling medium, is of itself a constantly dissolving and shifting body.

The poems, rarely surpassing in length the space restrictions of a single page, and often contracting to four and even two lines of sparse commentary, are so many terse notations that refuse to expand. . . . The line-lengths are also irregular, fixing most often on a line of eight or twelve syllables but capable of extension or contraction within the individual poem. There is also, in the first section of *Douve,* recourse to the prose poem which alternates rhythmically with a series of very free verse poems, suddenly and rather startlingly resolving into two quatrains, unrhymed, but using a strict Alexandrine. And taking advantage of this sudden "rest," the opening poem **"Aux Arbres,"** of the following section, maintains this meter, with only two lapses into a ten syllable line, throughout four quatrains, the longest regular succession in the early part of the poem.

This variation of the poetic line is no lax handling of formal structure. The classical line is dismembered, its regularity broken, even as Douve is disarticulated. The series of brief poetic statements, taking on by systematic accretion the dimensions of a larger poem, are in a real sense the reconciliation of Poe's dictum about the brevity essential to poetry and the poet's need to expand and develop his multiple perceptions of reality. The extended narrative sequence which the long poem utilizes to hold its members together is no longer necessary, the temporal progression so dependent upon the prosy nature of the sequence can be attacked and reordered, and the strain of maintaining the poetic voice for lengthy periods is minimized. The terseness of the statements whose links are implicit rather than explicit, the increase in density as horizontal progression is fragmented both intensifies the poetic quality and permits the poet a freedom of movement and reference that the more cohensive rhythms of the longer poem make immensely difficult. Bonnefoy, in his essay on baroque architecture, speaks of the breakdown in certain baroque structures of the preoccupation with the visible perfected form which had obsessed an artist like Michelangelo. Beauty, in the classical sense, is an impossible, torturous obsession that is antagonistic to the contemporary sensibility and to a newly awakened consciousness of the possibilities of art. In a poetic world in which the traditional forms of the sonnet, the ode, the more massive lines of the epic, are no longer useful to the poet, the very idea of this beauty is repugnant. (pp. 590-92)

Fragmentation is also evident in the landscape of Bonnefoy's poetry. Bonnefoy's landscape is a ruined, often desolate world in which death is the primary experience. The coordinates which situate the "being" spatially are, in the various volumes, a river, a shore, a room, a wood springing from Douve's disarticulated members, a garden, and on the distant horizon, a panoply of stars (in *Pierre écrite*) or a feeble, uncertain dawn (in *Hier régnant désert*). It might be argued that in a world in which death initially dominates, remnants of a more densely staged theatre where the living play their roles exist to heighten the separateness and isolation of death. Yet it is the momentary nature of the detachment that Bonnefoy insists upon and the movement initiated by this primal act is not toward complete dispersion and annihilation but toward reintegration and eventual reconciliation. The disintegration of Douve's body permits the growth of the wood in **"Aux Arbres"** and death is a transitional phase, a moment of ecstasy and pleasure in itself, that is a pretext for another kind of existence posited in terms of a rebuilding and a rebirth. There is, however, an uncertainty about the permanency of the rebirth, and the fragmentation corresponds to that uncertainty and difficulty of definition as the voice animating the poetry, diffuse and multiple, seems to come from all parts of the landscape. If this is a theatre, as *Douve* suggests, the characters that persist are illusory phantoms, bewildering in their diverse nature. The reader is struck in all three volumes by the headings "Une Voix," "Une Autre Voix," "Voix basses et phénix," "La même voix toujours," with the multiplicity of speakers (yet reducible to the same and the one) expressive of a more extensive disintegration attacking the poetic voice. The pronouns of reference are *je, tu, nous,* the other "characters" are Cassandra, Aglaure, the Salamander, the Phoenix, a stone, and although the distinctions may at times seem to be rigorously observed, they are always perilously close to chaos. In the section "Douve parle," there is a brief introduction in which the poetic "I" already notes the breakdown of the Douve-poet distinction.

Quelle parole a surgi près de moi,

. . . . .

Pourtant ce cri sur moi vient de moi,
Je suis muré dans mon extravagance.

A transitional section heightens the questioning, questing preoccupation of the poem but when Douve speaks, the temporal sequence is suddenly disrupted. The progression in the present is broken by the abrupt introduction of a past ("disais-tu"), so that Douve's speech which should logically have followed hard upon the preparatory verse, is rejected into a previous temporal sequence. Douve is apparently continuing or has made the same speech at some point or points in the past, and the reader, attempting to follow a coherent sequence in which Douve dies and disintegrates, and then, veiled in death, communicates her ecstasy, discovers that the entire sequence has already been consummated and is turning-back upon its own matter. The poet, waiting for the cry which is without and within him, possesses instinctively an already contained knowledge of what Douve will say (or has said) and finds within himself actuality, possibility and accomplishment.

We can see now a remarkable congruence in the breaking-up of the materials of the poem. The broken form, the ambiguous multiplicity of speakers and the out-of-sequence nature of the temporal order complement one another as the basic elements of structure, perspective and time are disordered. What was earlier acted as an apparent contradiction in the paradoxical concept of life in death is the propulsive genesis of the poem whose very incongruity enhances its vitality.

There is still the larger question of the coherence of the image in the architecture of this disordered poetic universe. Jean-Pierre Richard, in a penetrating essay on Bonnefoy, has attempted to clarify the idea of the poetry through an examination of a small complex of recurrent images. What he himself admits he has left untouched is the cohesiveness of the images and their relation to the total structure of the work. He has suggested a possible approach through what he calls the "dominante imaginaire" of each collection: " . . . pour *Douve* par exemple, la constellation vent-pierre-végétal, pour *Hier régnant désert* le paysage du port, de la rive, de l'eau." The difficulty with such a formulation is that by abstracting a dominant, it fails to qualify the minor modes which give the entire cycle (*Pierre écrite* was unpublished when Richard was working on his essay) a curious overlapping effect. The wind-stone-plant grouping of *Douve* thus becomes subordinate to the port-shore-water complex of *Hier régnant désert* which in turn is subordinated to the garden-stone-body sequence of *Pierre écrite.* The entire work is a complex polyphonic arrangement in which a verbal melody is explored, gradually overtaken by a secondary melody which becomes the principal line and, in its turn, is dominated by a newly developing line. These successive waves give a distinctive tonal coloration and it is this schematic pattern of the work I should like to consider in some detail.

The initial "fact" of the work is the death and disintegration of Douve. The event commences in ecstasy (" . . . toute / En quête de la mort sur les tambours exultants de tes gestes.")

and suddenly subsides into the perception and partial acknowledgement by the witness of Douve's "death." "Le vent te pénètre, Douve, lande résineuse endormie près de moi." Douve's collapse which seemed to resolve itself into the posture of a death-like sleep is broken by a series of slow, dance-like gestures, performed with the arms, which are in themselves a final slowing-down and increasingly evident submission to death. "Gestes de Douve, gestes déjà plus lents, gestes noirs." Yet the ecstasy with which Douve greets death, succeeded by a slower, more mechanical movement into death, is sharply opposed by a Douve who, at the extremities of life and death, hesitates. "Et la touche souillée des dernières étoiles / Rompre d'un cri l'horreur de veiller dans ta nuit." The final gestures are now accomplished, and once again the witness finds Douve, stretched out in the attitude of death, now being disjointed by an invasion of insects and the slow, inevitable corruption of the earth, yet still attentive and, in death, not overcome but merely waiting. (pp. 593-95)

This initiation of a sequence of ecstasy/death/corruption is prolonged and reconsidered in the second section, "Derniers gestes." The slow, inevitable dissolution of the form is suspended as the body, no longer prey to the attack of the earth and the insects, is tutored and perceived in flight. "Elle fuit vers les saules. . . ." In one of the most characteristic movements of Bonnefoy's poetry, the thing destroyed cannot be released, and the painful work of reconstitution has begun. As the distinction so precariously maintained between living and dead is lost, Douve, purified with the rites of death, is animated by the voice of her lover. "Douve, je parle en toi. . . ." And with the ventriloquist-like animation, there is increasingly evident an undercurrent of sexuality and sensuality ("Si brûlant soit le gel de notre intimité. . . .") that survives the retreat into death. Acceptance and refusal, movement and immobility, cold and heat, life and death, the relationships are compounded of exclusive demands that reconcile and enter into the building of the place and the jealous perserverance of the flesh. " . . . et je t'enserre/Dans l'acte de connaître et de nommer."

The flight of Douve, the descent into the earth, the crossing of the river of death, are basic gestures of flight and withdrawal that struggle against the hard fixity of the tomb. The movements are succeeded by a return to the site of the tomb, to the place where Douve, colored in a mockery of life, lies seemingly dead. The tomb, the chamber to which the dead body is brought, its final resting-place in this world, prefigures the *chambre* which will be the "true place" of Douve's regeneration. Tombs are constructed in memory of the dead, but the place to which Douve will come, although it will be tainted with the odor of blood, will house the living, not the dead. The two poles of the poem may be seen as movement from the place, and the "fact," of Douve's death, to the room in which Douve, reborn, will remain with the worshipping lover. Any progression in this restricted voyage is made haltingly and sparingly, underlining the poverty of the witnesses' certainty. The spareness of the vocabulary, the brevity of the individual poems, the insubstantial quality of the revelations, these are so many intensifiers of the total response of the poetry. It is seldom that one receives such an overwhelming sense of the travail that creation involves, of its defeats, of its minute victories. We are constantly reminded that an edifice has been destroyed, that its elements have been absorbed into the earth. The poet must dedicate himself to the building of a structure in which he can dwell and which will be the incorruptible, new form of the "other," whether she is Douve, the

Menade, the lover, or the tomb which is both the body and the presence of the dead one. "Je nommerai désert ce château que tu fus. . . ." "Cette pierre ouverte est-ce toit, ce logis dévasté, / Comment peut-on mourir?"

At the conclusion of the section "Douve parle," the narrator and the "other" abandon the place of death.

> Ainsi marcherons-nous sur les ruines d'un ciel immense,
> Le site au loin s'accomplira
> Comme un destin dans la vive lumière.

This is both a movement toward the destined place, the "vrai lieu" as Bonnefoy puts it, which will consummate this volume, and the initiation of a voyage that will extend into *Hier régnant désert.* The light in *Hier régnant désert* will be feeble and not bright, underlining the deceptive quality of the distant vision. The volumes may fit, as it were, but the joining involves a diminishing, as the accomplishments of the primary voyage, seen as bright and even resplendent in the first flush of discovery, become less certain. Indeed, the work ends not affirmatively, triumphantly, now that the edifice is built and Douve is established in her dwelling-place, but with a question. "O notre force et notre gloire, pourrezvous / Trouer la muraille des morts?" The *orangerie,* the temple built for Douve, is a place tainted with blood, a deceptive edifice that will not long contain the restless spirit. . . . The pavillon contains its own warning and reservation. Douve and her attendant come to it as to the true place, the transcendent dwelling which surmounts death and houses the shrived spirit. It would seem to be a place of refuge and, indeed, the opening lines of the last section of Douve, "Vrai lieu," suggest this promise. "Qu'une place soit faite à celui qui approache / Personnage ayant froid et privé de maison." But this is not a place of repose. The room, with the window, the door, the "nuit de janvier sur les delles," is itself a place in which violence must be done, and it becomes a waiting-place for the sacrifice. Douve's cycle of disintegration and apparent regeneration and repose is not closed but suspended. (pp. 595-97)

In *Douve,* violence was done to the person. In *Hier régnant désert,* violence is done to the place. The table becomes a true *tabula rasa* as the witness draws back before the double fire of their death. In *Douve,* there was a painful acceptance of death as the necessary mediation toward life; in *Hier régnant désert,* there is a flight from death. [In his essay, **"L'acte et le lieu de la poésie,"** Bonnefoy stated:] "Ils (les poètes nouveaux) ont fait une table rase, celle du geste assuré. Puis inventé à nouveau les quelques gestes élémentaires qui nous unissent aux choses, dans l'incessante aube froide d'une vie anxieuse d'absolu." These few words might serve as the epigraph of *Hier régnant désert,* for the first section ("Menaces du témoin") begins with the *table rase* and the last section ("Terre d'aube"), with the hesitant approach of the dawn, "fille des larmes." The space traversed is not great, for the narrator commands the dawn to reestablish "la chambre dans sa paix de chose grise." The pavillon of *Douve* persists, still open, and the place which was a tomb, which was the body of *Douve,* and finally the intended place of refuge, has been penetrated by the grey light of dawn. As the line in *Douve.* "Cette pierre ouverte est-ce toi, ce logis dévasté, / Comment peut-on mourir?" suggested the ravaged tomb, its stone rolled away, that was the sign of the risen Christ, so this ravaged room, finally admitting the light, announces the revival of life the following poem in *Hier régnant résert* celebrates so triumphantly.

> Ecoute-moi revivre dans ces forêts
> Sous les frondaisons de mémoire
> Où je passe verte,
> Sourire calciné d'anciennes plantes sur la terre,
> Race charbonneuse du jour.
> Ecoute-moi revivre, je te conduis
> Au jardin de présence,
> . . . . .

The room is now transcended in a single, resplendent movement, as it both houses memory and, like the opened tomb, leads into a new dwelling-place for the poet, the garden, freshly restored and inhabited. The agonizing sense of absence and loss revealed at the beginning of *Hier régnant désert* . . . is forgotten as the cycle seeks a new resolution. In a series of simple, moving statements which speak of "elementary gestures" there is described, in this grey place, the invasion of a new tonality. This tonality, suggestive of color, affirms movement and a slow, almost imperceptible restoration of time to fulfill the command of the poem **"L'Aube fille des larmes.":** "Colore peu à peu le temps recommencé." (pp. 598-99)

The opening poem of *Pierre écrite* prolongs the imagery of the concluding section of *Hier régnant désert. . . .* If, however, the garden, the ripe fruit, the new range of color and the lightening of the initial anguish of *Hier régnant désert* are all consistent with the final victories of that volume, there has been a loss. The angel is near, but the dawn is only imminent, not yet invading the night. What seemed finally, at the end of *Hier régnant désert,* the indissoluble presence of the light and day has retreated into the night. But in that resolution of contradictions which marks Bonnefoy's poetry, the grey dawn, the minute advance of the light against the night, has given way to a new night more splendid than the promise of the day. This sudden eruption of color, the green and orange of the ripe fruits, presaged by the entrance into the garden and the hint of color in "la rose d'ombres" of the earlier collection, brings a new range to the half-lighted world of Bonnefoy where stone and flaccid water were the dominating presences. The sacrificial fire of *Hier régnant désert* has become the burning of innumerable stars in the firmament and with the symbolic tearing of the flesh ("Mais ton épaule se déchite dans les arbres," *Pierre écrite,*), a red the color of blood and ochre is spilled onto the monochromatic canvas. . . . The irruption of color precedes the joining of flesh and where the relationship had once implied a subservience on the part of the attendant, the two figures now participate in the feverish act of love. (pp. 599-600)

This act of love is more than the union of two bodies. It is a song of celebration of the reconstruction of the castle of the spirit in the flesh and, ultimately, the revitalization of the poem and of its aesthetic. The final poem of *Pierre écrite* is an *art poétique* speaking of reconciliation and shriving, of the cleansing and purification of the body and the revival of the "voice" of poetry. In *Douve,* this cleansing of the body was the ritual act of the purification of the dead, painting the face to recall the colors of life. The color was forced upon the body and there was the suggestion that something that had been beautiful in life was being degraded. "Lisse-moi, farde-moi." And this desperate coloring of the body was accompanied by the feeling of the limitations of language and of the poem itself. "Oui, c'est bientôt périr de n'être que parole, / Et c'est tache fatale et vain couronnement." In *Hier régnant désert,* there was a refusal to see color or light until the final pages when the dawn gave the narrator the hope of repossessing joy. Now, in *Pierre écrite,* the poet is reconciled to death, color is rampant and both the body and the image have been revitalized. The ultimate purification has cleansed the suffering, restored the utility and sense of validity to the poetic act ("un éblouissement dans les mots anciens," and emphasized the primacy of the heart. " . . . On a dit au coeur / D'être le coeur."

These spare remarks on the general outline of the three published volumes of Bonnefoy's poetry can only suggest the complexity of the verse. It is a dense, terse poetry that, retracing the Surrealists' experience of the disintegrating landscape and personality, heavy with the weight of the indissoluble presence of numerous but sparsely ordered elements, instead of ultimately referring to the impossibility of assimilating and ordering this experience, is constantly attempting to pass beyond the destructive act of dissolution. Bonnefoy has said of Surrealism that it is "the only genuine poetic movement this century has had." Yet he has also said that he is repelled by the emptiness of the poetry, the expression of a "negative theology," and its inability to extend its discoveries. The disintegration of Bonnefoy's poetry is only an intermediate gesture which seeks to resolve itself in a light-bathed landscape. Here the elements of the body (a hand, a shoulder, a "mortal face"), annihilated as it were in death, rebuild not a dream landscape but a dwelling-place of stone and cold fire, more durable than the body it celebrates. The anguish and suffering are transitory displays and it is the joy and ecstasy of experience and discovery which illuminate this poetry. It is a poetry that honors the love of life, of death, of the body, of the minute, indissoluble things of this world. And like the poetry of the Renaissance which celebrated beauty in and beyond death, and the regeneration of beauty in line and verse, it is a feast of delight in the sensuous contours of the sparsely recreated body, present only in its most revelatory elements of line and gesture. (pp. 600-02)

It also extends a major preoccupation of 20th century poetry. Bonnefoy is the spiritual inheritor of the voyage ("La Quête de Bonnefoy," as [Jean-Pierre Attal] has labelled his poetry) of Claudel and Saint-John Perse, suggesting the Christian ethic of transcendence of the one and the dedication to the durable forms and shapes of the visible world of the other. "C'est de pierre aujourd'hui qu'il s'agit. . . ." It is no longer the breathless, crushing verset of the two older poets, suggestive of their belief in the incantatory powers of rhythm and of the poet's "mission." Bonnefoy's conscious contraction of their optimistic, impelling linear verse into a tight, compact line from which all extraneous elements have been filtered to achieve a rare condensation and beauty, is also the symbol of the poet's awareness of a more "real" world, in which faint echoes of a transcendent universe remain, but where the only reliable coordinates are hard, small and lasting, like the stone, or eternal and ageless, like the tree or the sea, now reduced to a still stream, or present only as a shore and a port.

Bonnefoy has penetrated to a depth at which total shapes compose themselves and where the poet, trusting in the stone and the image, and in its durability, perceives and constructs a new edifice in which he and his poetry can survive. And there, in this temple, the unexpected surges up again to betray the serenity and control of the poet's search. . . . The poetry itself becomes a sacrifice and the god's face, that rises up in *Pierre écrite,* is at the frontiers of the dream. "J'imagine souvent, au-dessus de moi, / Un visage sacrificiel, dont les rayons / Sont comme un champ de terre labourée." "Dieu qui n'es pas, pose ta main sur notre épaule, / Ebauche notre corps du poids de ton retour. . . ." The imminently returning God, "who is not," still exists and in this landscape where dream and reality are no longer opposites but companions in the temple, and handmaidens of the poet's search, what seems non-existent is as forceful as the phantoms of the real world. This poetry is the tangible evidence of the encounter of opposites that find themselves reconciling their differences and it is in this encounter and eventual birth of a poetry apparently exorcized of its demons that Bonnefoy's poetry endures. (pp. 602-03)

Walter Albert, "Yves Bonnefoy and the Architecture of Poetry," in MLN, *Vol. 82, No. 5, December, 1967, pp. 590-603.*

ALEX L. GORDON

Acclaimed by many critics as the best new French poet of the last twenty years, Yves Bonnefoy is an author of many interests. . . . All of [his] works display a remarkable gravity of tone and convey a uniform sense of spiritual quest. A true seeker, Yves Bonnefoy has been drawn down many paths, but always, it would seem, in the hope of finding his own particular grail.

Bonnefoy's gravity must at once attract the reader who asks the fundamental questions. Yet, although the poet's austerity may win our adherence in theory, in practice we are likely to find him a difficult and often enigmatic master. "Rayonnante et difficile," wrote Marc Alyn in a review of *Pierre écrite.* A new kind of poetry, explained an American critic, which was "intended to stretch the powers of French poetic language not only beyond its conceptual limits but perhaps beyond the evocative function of the image itself." Many other voices have joined this choir of puzzled admirers, and as is natural, bewilderment can lead in some to a kind of hostile scepticism. (pp. 55-6)

It would be idle to try and deny the obscurity of Bonnefoy's verse. No amount of exegesis can remove it entirely, for it is essential to the themes and must remain if Bonnefoy is to succeed in conveying to us his sense of ultimate mystery, the conviction so magnificently formulated by Mallarmé, that the universe will never yield to any probing its final irreducible *X*. We must therefore allow the poet his shadows and prepare to keep him company as best we can. (p. 56)

Probably the most striking aspect of a Bonnefoy poem is its strange anonymity, the absence of particularising references, the indistinction of the characters speaking. *Je, tu* and *elle* appear with practically no hint as to the identity of the people referred to. Many poems are simply entitled *Une voix,* and in *Pierre écrite* somewhat less mysteriously *Une pierre.* The identity of Douve in *Du Mouvement et de l'immobilité de Douve* is deliberately concealed and was the source of much nervous speculation on the part of reviewers. Paradoxically the obscurity of this generalness is sometimes matched by an obscurity due to the opposite cause of recondite specificness. The reader, wandering through a landscape of anonymous trees, streams and water, a location which is no place and every place, is suddenly confronted with a name, Trieste, which indicates one place and no other. Or again, among the faceless *je*'s and *elle*'s we discover an unprecedented but clearly delineated Aglaure, a minor figure from Greek mythology. Similar juxtaposing of named and unnamed leads to the appearance of the Brancacci Chapel in an architectural series which includes rooms, castles and chapels no more specific than the generalized names that point to them. Most astonishing of all is perhaps the naming of the voice of Kathleen Ferrier among the many unowned voices that declare themselves in *Hier régnant désert.* Clearly Bonnefoy is concerting a structured dialectic in which vagueness and clarity are complementary, but which by pushing to extreme limits the tendency to generalise and the opposite one to specify, can lead in both cases to tantalising obscurity.

A dialectical structure can imply a continuing process and doubtless some of Bonnefoy's obscurity stems from his refusal to pronounce a last word. Two points might be made in this respect. Firstly, all three Bonnefoy volumes are structured ensembles like the *Fleurs du Mal* and may not be treated in the same way as a haphazard collection of discrete compositions. No Bonnefoy poem can be seen in isolation or can yield its full resonance until the whole of which it is a part has been perceived. It is easy to understand the compounding of difficulty when we acknowledge that the obscurity of one poem will be somewhat diminished only when we have discovered the secret of fifty or so other obscure pieces. And we might add that the three volumes interlock just as the individual poems do. *Via tenebrarum.*

A second consequence of the dialectical principle is the need to destroy what has been constructed and to negate what has been affirmed, a process which must inevitably tease the mind of a reader who is bent on obtaining a clear statement. Bonnefoy's preference goes to all art which contains its own denial. His devotion is reserved for the badly lit trains of evening, for statues lying face downwards in the grass, for a door in the cathedral of Valledolid which had been walled up by bricks the colour of blood. No image could illustrate more clearly than the latter the defeat of an artistic and functional shape and yet within that defeat preserve for us the proof of the artist's original intention. The concern to reconcile opposites leads within the poetry to brilliant stylistic arrangements. Bonnefoy must demonstrate both form and non-form and so in a poem of careful alexandrines he may destroy the perfection of the emerging prosodic shape by including a line either too long or too short. As to the question of obscurity, it must be obvious from our remarks that Bonnefoy could never allow himself a categorical pronouncement. He may go so far along the road to clarity, but inevitably he will wish to add the shadows which set that clarity off and complete the impression of dynamic verisimilitude.

In sum, Bonnefoy's obscurity is of a type common to many avant-garde artists. The dissolution of the object and the elimination of any identifiable self have been with us for many years. The anonymous voices of Bonnefoy find a close parallel in the unassigned or cryptically numbered voices of some Beckett plays. In the visual arts analogies might be made with the schematic figures or geometric outlines of a Miro painting. Generally an illuminating comparison has been drawn by Bosquet between a Bonnefoy volume of poems and a mobile by Alexander Calder. One can distinguish the various parts, one can observe them move and interact but a final stable position is made impossible by the inherent nature of the structure. (pp. 56-8)

Du Mouvement et de l'immobilité de Douve explores in an elegiac, lyrical manner the theme of death. . . . Divided into five sections, its structure is strongly reminiscent of a classical tragedy with a downward curve through the first three movements and an upward sweep to resolution in the last two. Bonnefoy has entitled the first section "Théâtre," and it is consistent with his other views for him to emphasize action and metamorphosis rather than the immutable archetype. Death is presented at the outset as a physical reality which in the end cannot be conceived. Our human power to grasp is severely limited, not only in respect to others, but also in respect to ourselves. Thus Douve, the narrator's beloved, escapes him in the otherness of her body. "C'était jour de tes seins / Et tu régnais enfin absente de ma tête." But Douve's possession of herself is equally precarious. Her identity is threatened on every side by the destructive power of elemental forces—earth and water, flame and wind "plus fort que nos mémoires." Bonnefoy displays in vivid images how Douve's body finally crumbles before the onslaught of this cruel attack, "tu passais devant ces flammes / La tête quadrillée les mains fendues et toute / En quête de la mort . . .". Douve gradually succumbs, her body is silted over by sand and humus, her bones are picked clean by insect hordes, the feverish activity of the brain is burnt away. Death is viewed as a fact both obscure and manifest. On the one hand its insidious movement escapes all perception and not even an image can catch its split-second growth. On the other, its eventual triumph through time is indisputable and must be confronted as in this funeral poem where all personal identity is lost.

> Le ravin pénètre dans la bouche maintenant,
> Les cinq doigts se dispersent en hasards de forêt maintenant,
> La tête première coule entre les herbes maintenant,
> La gorge se farde de neige et de loups maintenant,
> Les yeux ventent sur quels passagers de la mort et c'est nous dans ce vent dans cette eau dans ce froid maintenant.

Clearly Bonnefoy has conveyed the sense of death's physical reality. His heroine's enemies are the elemental basis of the universe and her death is an event which overtakes her body and dissolves its unity in the shapeless multiplicity of grass and foliage or the non-form of earth, wind and snow. No concept protects the reader from the immediate horror of decomposition, but some hope is provided by a second theme which accompanies the main funereal line and depicts the strange happiness of the victim. Douve may betray her lover's mental image but she reigns in the privacy of her body; and when she is in turn betrayed by her own evanescent self, she confronts her nothingness with a singular absence of fear. "Parée pour une fête dans le vide / Et les dents découvertes comme pour l'amour," she pursues her death with an undeniable sensual relish. The reason for this enjoyment lies in the sense of participation experienced both by Douve and the narrator in the life and death sequence as the necessary basis of existence. (pp. 61-2)

The double reality of death and exultation is described in "Théâtre" in an impassive, neutral fashion. The sequence presents images with only a few hints as to their possible significance. Parts II and III, while giving further body to the double theme of the opening, clarify the attitudes of the hero and the heroine to the momentous events in which they are engaged. "Derniers gestes" depicts the last movements of the stricken Douve, but it is chiefly interesting for the light it sheds on the narrator's first accommodation with inevitable dying. This he achieves, first through lucid but lyrical acceptance of the antithetical nature of reality, and secondly by faith in the word of poetry not as an end, but as a bridge permitting the transition from the mystery of origin to that of night. . . . In "Théâtre" the world had been directed primarily by unconscious matter and almost speechless flesh. In "Derniers gestes" consciousness proclaims its right to bear witness to Douve's death and to pass articulate commentary. The narrator thus proceeds to identify bodily with his dead beloved and after a mystic marriage with her exposes in quasi-religious terms her "vrai nom" and her "vrai corps." Her true name is neither castle, voice nor face, but desert, night, and absence, the nothingness to which her being was irresistibly drawn. "Mourir est un pays que tu aimais." Douve's true body is a corpse washed and purified for the rite of interment, but so closely apprehended by the narrator that he can voice its condition. The conclusion of Section II thus establishes the union which had been destroyed in Section I, but on better grounded terms since the narrator no longer attempts to lock an evolving life in a mental prison but seeks now to speak freely for a creature truly dead. Whereas consciousness in the first instance had cramped and destroyed, it is called upon now to liberate and give life. It must discover in Douve the phoenix of resurrection.

Section III, "Douve parle," constitutes to some degree at least, a reply to the bold assertions of the narrator in Section II. Many voices mutter in this limbo-like sequence where consciousness is almost extinct and individual shapes are barely perceptible in the eery twilight. This is Douve's world of the almost dead and when she speaks three times in a clearly identifiable manner, it is to protect the integrity of its deadness from the fantasizing voice of the narrator who had offered to speak of it. . . . What Douve really fears is that the word of poetry will fail to keep pace with her funeral descent; perhaps it will become detached and abstract, unable to confirm its own validity in the subtly-moving living and dying, which is Douve's existence. . . . Douve intends to cherish hope; she wishes to rise again from her ashes, but she knows that this can be achieved truthfully only if all forms of death are acknowledged, not only the physical disintegration of "Théâtre" but also the dumbfounding of the word of poetry which had made such bold claims in Section II.

The last two movements of **Douve** represent a slow struggle upward from the nadir of total death. Redemption is sought first in the "Orangerie," a symbol for Bonnefoy of the luminous art of the seventeenth century. Open on all sides to the sun of being, the orangery is flooded with light, but by this very fact, it is a place of artifice whose total clarity suggests a darkness equally absolute. The hot-house structure recalls in many ways the sunlit world of radiant forms desired by Phèdre, but attainable only through her death. The orangery in short offers no habitation for the living. It is "ce moi vacant," an immaculate project for Racine's death-obsessed characters, but no real answer to their anguish since it can only obliterate their worldly presence.

Thus Douve halts, but does not stay in the "Orangerie." She is well aware of the dangers of an ideal light which floods the opaque realities of existence and robs them of their true character. Even the human heart loses its palpable mystery before the indiscretion of the sun. It is emptied of content, rendered transparent and lifeless as a ghost. This explains the repeated appeals of the narrator to the healing power of Douve's dead impenetrable presence.

> Lisse-moi, farde-moi. Colore mon absence.
> Désoeuvre ce regard qui méconnaît la nuit.
> Couche sur moi les plis d'un durable silence,
> Eteins avec la lampe une terre d'oubli.

In the end the solution offered by the "Orangerie" is seen not as a deliverance but as an unsatisfactory stasis; although a limpid perception of spiritual and bodily being has been achieved, the two remain separate, unvivified by the blood which must be spilt in any continuing life.

The "true place" discovered in the last poems resolves these problems by permitting the co-existence of inter-acting life and death, movement and immobility, light and dark. The salamander, which had appeared parenthetically in the "Orangerie," now emerges as the adequate emblem in which is concentrated every aspect of existence. It can merge with the dense otherness of stone and it can also live unscathed in the fire of the spirit. The inert mass of its body is an incontrovertible sign, but its heart continues to beat and it will move to victory after its breathless sojourn on the soil to which it clings. We should note however that, in keeping with Bonnefoy's concern for ongoing life, this victory is never definitively won. The salamander provides a model for action, but the whole volume ends with a question:

> O notre force et notre gloire, pourrez-vous
> Trouer la muraille des morts?

Du Mouvement et de l'immobilité de Douve attempted to integrate the reality of death into life. It worked out in poetic terms the phrase from Hegel quoted on the title page: "The life of the mind is not that life which shrinks from death and seeks to keep itself clear of all corruption, but rather the life which endures the process of death within itself and preserves itself alive within death." The accommodation with death was achieved chiefly through a heightened consciousness of death's reality both for the body and the soul, and the precarious final solution was born of anxiety. "Timor mortis conturbat me." Bonnefoy's second volume, **Hier régnant désert,** while it treats similar themes, starts not from a basis of anxiety but of indifference. Consciousness has been dulled and all spiritual energy exhausted. . . . To this dangerous apathy Bonnefoy opposes the vivifying power of poetry, the "dure parole" which can discover significance even in apparent platitude. The monotonous stillness of the opening poems is thus seen not as a sign of spiritual stagnation, but of a desire to embrace even more complete death. . . . The middle section of **Hier régnant désert** examines the poetic means which must be used to uncover the values implicit in the opening poems of abdication. Bonnefoy's poetry, we learn, has concentrated on death since the poet's childhood years. It is devoid of any aesthetic beauty; its goal is to discover the still more nocturnal shore. Essentially it is a poetry which, while seeking absolutes and supposing their virtual reality, invariably sees in them a threat to living process and hence wills their destruction. Beauty may clarify and bring into ordered focus the chaotic appearance of the world, but it must never be allowed a last say; it indicates being, but being can never be confined within its elegant forms. (pp. 62-6)

The imperfection sought by Bonnefoy is not of course a casual approximation, but should be understood as perfection with an open end. It characterizes all art that points compellingly to a higher reality, but remains itself modestly unobtrusive. It can be felt in the voice of Kathleen Ferrier "qui hésite aux lointains du chant qui s'est perdu" and whose pure beauty mediates another song, the only Absolute. Bonnefoy envisages in the gravest sense an inspirational art and chooses for poetry a goal similar to that selected by Saint-John Perse "pour mieux vivre, et plus loin." He is painfully conscious, however, of the fragile nature of poetry's epiphany, and many poems in the last pages of *Hier régnant désert* have as their subject the desolate time of non-significance and the need to maintain faith through this period. We are reminded that absence permits presence, that the phoenix must die in order to rise again, and that in a universe of opposites fire must wane and yield to night. Time effects the transition from one state of grace to the next. It is the enemy that destroys but it is also the agent of new life. Alternating phases are linked in such a way that one generates the other. "Oh, quel feu dans le pain rompu, quelle aube / Pure dans les étoiles affaiblies!" Thus the silent site of Delphi on the second day can be faced with equanimity; the stones will speak again and time will move through the cycle of life and death which was implicit even in the dialectical title—*Hier régnant désert.*

Bonnefoy's last volume of poetry, *Pierre écrite,* maintains the characteristic alternations of his first two, but in spite of the title which refers to the tombstones of the dead, it unfolds its progression in a much more radiant and confident landscape. Its main theme combines the integration of death as in *Douve* and the maintenance of hopeful vision as in *Hier régnant désert.* The annihilating power of death dominates the second section where we pass from epitaph to epitaph as in a graveyard. Death is for everyman, for Jean and Jeanne, the loving archetypal pair, whose simple names are mentioned once among the hordes of anonymous dead. Death is a universal rule but the rule is validated in concrete particulars.

The theme of vision opens the volume onto a garden which is Eden restored. The sky, leaves, and fruit, form a reassuring presence. . . . But permanence being foreign to human experience, the vision begins to lose its power; an insidious spiritual lethargy similar to that of *Hier* threatens a new nothingness, "Tout ce qui est bougeait comme un vaisseau qui tourne / Et glisse, et ne sait plus son âme dans la nuit." Above all the vision itself desires to be vivified and redefined by renewed contact with the dark energies of the earth. . . . All things, in sum, follow a universal pattern of life and death, victory and defeat; the vision must be recreated just as the living self of each instant is formed from the dead selves of previous time. (pp. 67-8)

The reconciliation of death and the vision of paradise, merely hinted at in the early poems, is worked out fully after death has proclaimed its implacable presence in the epitaph suite. Bonnefoy bolsters faith by emphasizing the continuing and indivisible nature of experience. Everything lives its destiny and can do nothing else. Reassuring presences, by the act of living their lives, create their own deaths—the tree ages in the tree, the bird flies through its song. But this dying life has fulfilled its function by mediating to the further shore of other life. . . . Furthermore, moments of apparent sterility should hold no terrors for those who have once experienced presence. They must be patient for the imminent day which time will bring, "Et tout ton sang voûté sous une main rêveuse, / O proche, ô tout mon jour." And they can hasten the arrival of a god, who is virtual but different from his predecessor because the light has changed, simply by cultivating the initiatory words of poetry and by asking questions. The sphinx does answer, as we recall in the epitaph, where her secrets were wrenched from her and presence was revealed in the evanescent foam of a real sea:

> Qu'aurai-je aimé? L'écume de la mer
> Au-dessus de Trieste, quand le gris
> De la mer de Trieste éblouissait
> Les yeux du sphinx déchirable des rives.

The intuition is held for a moment, and the condition of its birth may be forgotten in euphoria:

> Je suis l'heure simple
> Et l'eau non troublée.
> Ai-je su t'aimer,
> Ne sachant mourir;

but the quest is infinitely renewable; peace abundant, though simple and poor "comme ce cri d'insecte, irrégular, / Qu'un dieu pauvre faconne," may be sought again by returning to the proven effectiveness of the word of poetry:

> Tu vieilliras
> Et, te décolorant dans la couleur des arbres,
> Faisant ombre plus lente sur le mur,
> Etant, et d'âme enfin, la terre menacée,
> Tu reprendras le livre à la page laissée,
> Tu diras, C'étaient donc les derniers mots obscurs.

Pierre écrite concludes then on a note of conditional optimism. The flowers of death, asphodel and jasmine, strew our country and cast their fatal radiance even over the poet's sense of presence; but this sense puts up an equal fight and draws us into the future, like the "grandeur interne" of Valéry "sonnant dans l'âme un creux toujours futur" or magnetizing the horizon like "les hauts plateaux où je puis vivre" of Bonnefoy himself. True, Bonnefoy's goal remains implicit but it is confidently awaited. "Un feu va devant nous"; imperfection is still the summit for we can know only "le nom presque dit d'un dieu presque incarné," but a new confidence is accorded to the human heart. Body and soul are reconciled, assume their immortality and nourish each other's substance as in the Pietà of Tintoretto. (pp. 68-9)

Bonnefoy has been compared to many predecessors—to Scève and Sponde, to Baudelaire and Valéry, to Jouve and even to Géraldy. In tone and atmosphere, his works recall the paradox-ridden, death-bent verse of the Renaissance masters. His attention to the minute flickerings of the mind brings him close to Valéry. The very title of *Douve* evokes irresistibly the basic polarity of the *Cimetière marin* and the volume itself seems to harmonise the immobility and movement which in Valéry are forever sundered. Nearer to our time, the preoccupations of Bonnefoy do not seem too different perhaps from those of Camus, Sartre or Beckett. **"L'imperfection est la cime"** might be viewed as a lyrical version of Sisyphus; the stones and trees of Bonnefoy's landscape also provide a décor for Sartre; and the feeling of expectancy generated by every Bonnefoy poem suggests at once the anxiety experienced by Beckett's characters as they await their elusive god. Indeed the progressive reduction of configuration in the internal shape of *Oh! les beaux jours* or *Fin de partie* might serve as a diagram for the consciousness portrayed in Bonnefoy. Winnie describes every day an ever-reduced existence, and one day, as with Bonnefoy, her being, her dying and her consciousness will coincide.

In an interview granted to Georges Piroué, Bonnefoy declared that he turned to poetry because "c'est de ce côté-là qu'il me fallait chercher une solution aux problèmes de l'existence." It is legitimate to ask if he found the support he sought. Judging from the strained security of *Pierre écrite* we must answer yes. For us as readers Bonnefoy supplies a moving image of the vast labour of the spirit which, having recognised its mortal condition and that of its bodily home, strives nonetheless to approach the *vrai lieu* of presence. This it does by naming again and again, and as immediately as possible "les objets les plus vifs de cette terre—l'arbre, un visage, une pierre." Bulwarks of the true place, these fundamental realities are in Bonnefoy's eyes "un cortège du Graal qui passe." Named in his poetry with grave but passionate conviction they stir in the reader's heart a new feeling of sacred horror. (p. 70)

Alex L. Gordon, "Things Dying, Things New Born: The Poetry of Yves Bonnefoy," in Mosaic: A Journal for the Comparative Study of Literature and Ideas, Vol. VI, No. 2, Winter, 1973, pp. 55-70.

SARAH LAWALL

Yves Bonnefoy is one of the major poets to come into prominence in France after World War II, and is probably the major French lyric poet of this period. He writes a metaphysical poetry of modern times, whose clear, depersonalized voice gives aesthetic form to questions of being and nothingness, identity and communion, speech and silence—the ways of consciousness.

The Heideggerian themes of Bonnefoy's poetry are familiar to a general audience as part of existential literature in the post-war period, especially in the novels and plays of Sartre and Camus. As an existential poet, however, Bonnefoy does not seem influenced by his contemporaries so much as by earlier art and literature. Gothic murals, Piero della Francesca, Bernini and Rubens, Racine, Baudelaire, the Gnostics and Hegel, all exist in the background of Bonnefoy's poems. His style combines the allusive imagery, precision, and density of Symbolist poetry with the Surrealist's visionary self-consciousness and leaps of the imagination. The work of this first existentialist poet, as St. Aubyn has called him, is secured in a continuing aesthetic and philosophical tradition. (p. xi)

Bonnefoy writes difficult poetry in simple language. Individual images and scenes are beautiful in themselves, individual statements appear simple and clear; yet the total effect is often paradoxical, or tantalizingly open-ended. *Simplicity* is a word that recurs often in Bonnefoy's work, and it implies not superficiality but a basic rightness, a correspondence with *things as they are*. To achieve this simplicity, the poet must lead his readers into a closed, almost hermetic poetic world where each reality is completed by its opposite. Presence and absence, life and death, perfection and a fuller imperfection, concrete and abstract, are all so many levels of a total reality which the poet must reveal. (p. xii)

Christian metaphors play a great part in this poetry, although they do not indicate any hope of otherworldly salvation. Rather, Bonnefoy transposes the themes and images of Christian idealism to convey the burning wish for transcendence that pervades his purely humanistic philosophy. The ship and journey metaphors of **Words in Stone (Pierre écrite)**, the ambiguous flow and metamorphosis of **On the Motion and Immobility of Douve (Du mouvement et de l'immobilité de Douve)**, the passage between two shores of the underworld in **In the Illusion of the Threshold (Dans le lourre du seuil)** are all aspects of a central quest that leads to an earthly Grail. In modern French poetry, says Bonnefoy, there is a "procession of the Grail which passes, the most alive things of this earth—tree, face, stone—and they must be named." Bonnefoy turns the sense of the Grail legend in upon itself: where Parsifal was not bold enough to question the Grail carried before him, the poet will name what he sees; where Joseph of Arimathea's earthen cup was transmuted by the blood of Christ into a mystical chalice, Bonnefoy's Grail becomes an earthen vessel and vision of immanence.

In **Words in Stone,** Bonnefoy's quest for the Grail begins with an intuition of the return to Eden, and it is completed by encounters with death and materiality as elements that must be incorporated into a final vision. The voice of God does not appear through a burning bush, but the bush itself becomes a sign of the angel. "The angel, who is the earth, / Enters each bush, to appear there and burn, / I am the empty altar . . ." Communion on this empty altar and from this earthen cup does not invoke the presence of transcendent divinity. It symbolizes a relationship between human consciousness and what is outside; the typical existential awareness of Self and Other, clothed here in religious symbols. This otherness may be material: the hard surface of stone in which an artist inscribes traces of human will and desire, or it may be the stony grayness of words, in which the writer plunges the "red blade" of his experience. Bonnefoy is impelled to see himself in relation to the otherness outside his own human consciousness, and he adds aesthetic force to this philosophical impulse by comparing it with the mystical desire for another world. His poetry makes frequent references to an "other" day, an "other" summer, or an "other" world, using the imagery of traditional religious idealism to imply a fuller vision of this same earth. In naming the things of this earth, says Bonnefoy, modern poetry names its own procession of the Grail: establishes its own search for the equally elusive Grail of total understanding.

The quest for an earthen Grail leads Bonnefoy to see this world as a "true place," a "here and now" that must be recognized for itself and not as the threshold of things to come. Images of "place" and "threshold" reappear frequently in this poetry, and always with the feeling that the wished-for Eden is not just across the threshold, but is the threshold itself from which we intuit a possible transcendence.

Bonnefoy's task is to describe this "here and now" in "essentialized" terms that will let us grasp the abstract in the concrete. The blending of real and ideal occurs in a spare, almost mythological description which avoids long descriptive passages, chooses essentialized words, and works within the framework of a consciously limited vocabulary. Bonnefoy is quite specific in **"The Act and Place of Poetry"** about how he chooses essentialized rather than particularized words: "stone," for example, rather than "brick." Essentialized language is not an escape from reality into abstract idealism: Bonnefoy retains specific concrete details like the "foam at Trieste" to pin the poem down to a particular place on earth. However, his poetry aims at an impression of mythological clarity and precision by stripping the language bare of extended particularized description. Richness is obtained by the shifting of voice and of perspective inside a same horizon. Red is almost the only color used, and there is a characteristic landscape composed of a few essential elements: flat surfaces, light and darkness, foliage and germination, water, stone, and earth. Relationships change inside this landscape: the ship is earth, summer, or life; sky is an angel's shoulder; time "lies in pools of color." Mythological references join with Christian images to interpret the appearance of reality: the phoenix dies and rises from its ashes, and the salamander lives in its bed of flames. Angles of vision are displaced and different, and unnamed voices speak to one another and to the writer.

Inside a picture composed of a limited number of the most ordinary words, Bonnefoy employs unexpected associations, symbolic structures, and existential themes to let us see a complexly interwoven "beyond" immanent in the framework of everyday experience.

Art alone makes us aware of this complex experience. The grief of Tintoretto's *Pieta,* says Bonnefoy, is a cause of spiritual awakening because of its aesthetic "elegance." Emotion tears through the veil of the painted image, but only because of the image can that emotion appear. In the last poem of **Words in Stone, "Art of Poetry,"** Bonnefoy attributes to poetry the power of regeneration that creates a new Eden. Here, the poet's "look" or power to see has been dredged up from the depths of night, and a "bloody, disconsolate voice" has been "washed and called forth" to live again.

This resurrection of an artistic voice is not a secure and comfortable promise of immortality, the kind of doctrinaire salvation that Verlaine achieved towards the end of his career. Resurrection in Bonnefoy is an imperfect salvation, an imperfection that he has already called a "summit" above perfection itself. Any ideal of eternal, unchanging perfection is unacceptable to a poet of the *here and now,* who celebrates his perpetual awareness of an unfinished, unstable reality. Bonnefoy's poet must accept his own disappearance, yet find a way to describe it. He composes the poetry of being and nothingness in an unfinished "dialogue between anguish and desire"—between the desire for transcendence, and the anguished awareness of earth. The words in stone symbolize this harsh partnership between human will and inert materiality. Their inscribed stone marks the poet's decision to celebrate the existential consciousness in its earthly paradise. (pp. xiii-xvi)

> *Sarah Lawall, in an introduction to* Pierre Écrite/Words in Stone *by Yves Bonnefoy, translated by Susanna Lang, University of Massachusetts Press, 1976, pp. xi-xvi.*

MARC HOFSTADTER

Hier régnant désert is perhaps the most enigmatic of Yves Bonnefoy's works. Less well-known than *Du mouvement et de l'immobilité de Douve* and *Pierre écrite,* its predecessor and successor respectively, it also has been less read by literary critics. Writing of it himself in 1970, twelve years after its original appearance, Bonnefoy commented: "*Hier régnant désert* m'est maintenant obscur et, en quelques points, presque étranger." Yet this book, less striking than *Douve,* less serene than *Pierre ecrite,* less emphatic than *Dans le leurre du seuil,* has, as I will try to show, its own distinctive character and importance.

The critics have rarely examined *Hier régnant désert* with fullness or precision. Charles Duits' 1958 review in *Critique* is one of the few articles that has been entirely devoted to the book, but it avers itself at once puzzled and attracted by the poems' obscurity, and Duits asserts that their meaning is quite far beyond any signification that can be described in (other) words. By the very fact of its existence, my essay will be an attempt to show that this belief is exaggerated. . . . The most penetrating analytic studies of *Hier régnant désert* to date have been John Jackson's chapter in his book *Yves Bonnefoy* (the only full-length work on the poet) and the section in his recent work, *La question du moi: un aspect de la modernité poétique européenne.* For Jackson *Hier régnant désert* is dominated by duration, ordinary time—the time not of instantaneous ecstatic insight and closed-off form, as in *Douve,* but of on-going earthly existence—and by the opening of the word of poetry to the "imperfection" of this time. I take Jackson's perspective as the starting-point for this essay, as I intend to develop and expand his crucial (although not fully fleshed out) insights in relation to the book's place in Bonnefoy's life and total *oeuvre* and to its internal structure. For me, however, the embracing of the world of time, finitude and death in the book is not merely a "consenting" that constitutes a risk (as Jackson would have it) but an actual, perceived (so to speak) interpenetration of the desired and the actual. For Jackson the here and now is not to be loved but to be endured, and for that reason the act of accepting it is never complete but must forever be re-undertaken. For me, by the end of *Hier régnant désert* reality is felt as a fulfillment. In addition, Jackson regards *Hier régnant désert* as displaying an "inhibition de la puissance inventive," as being a work in which Bonnefoy's creative energy became less exuberant, less sure of itself. It will be part of the purpose of this essay to show that *Hier régnant désert* is not dominantly a work of indecision, vacillation or poverty but is a journey from an anguished alienation to full reconciliation.

Hier régnant désert is unlike Bonnefoy's other books in being situated more in the "grisaille" of ordinary time and existence, more remote from a dream of transcendence or a moment of vision. Whereas *Douve* is a violent attempt to penetrate, to live through, to *know* death and thereby attain to another degree of existence, and whereas *Pierre écrite* is an approach to an intermingling of death and life in a kind of transcendent peace, *Hier régnant désert* is a passage through time, a sometimes despairing, sometimes patient, usually difficult waiting for the coming of a fullness of being. In tone, language and very color it is more restrained than the other books, as Jackson points out. Consisting of poems of this earth, of finite things, of our present life, it could employ as epigraph these words from its fifth lyric: "Consens-tu de n'aimer que le fer d'une eau grise . . . ?"

This movement through duration, this rootedness in our earth are not only, though, the special characteristics of this book *Hier régnant désert.* They are the result and embodiment of what has been thus far the most crucial metamorphosis in Bonnefoy's *life,* a change that lies behind every word in the volume: the movement from the dream of a transcendent world (an "ailleurs," an "absolu," the "arrière-pays") to an attitude in which, still pursuing the eternal, Bonnefoy nevertheless embraces the earth, seeing in it *the only possible incarnation of the beyond.* There may seem to be a contradiction in the idea that the "elsewhere," the "eternal" can manifest itself in (and only in) the "here and now." But the world of dreams and our world need not be entirely apart, and all of Bonnefoy's work can be seen as an effort to resolve the seeming contradiction between them. The book called *L'Arrière-pays* is an account of Bonnefoy's slow and tortuous growth from a separation of the two realms to their fusion.

Bonnefoy writes in *L'Arrière-pays* that the first poems of *Hier régnant désert* came into existence during his "saisons les plus noires," when he was reproaching himself for forever dreaming of another world, for letting fall the torch of the effort to find an incarnate plenitude, for ignoring the inescapable realities of existential time and other people, for valuing too highly an art which closed itself off in a perfection unrelated to the world—the art, he thought, of *Douve.* Before these black months, Bonnefoy had for years imagined another place—the place the rejected path at a crossroads always seemed to lead to—that, while being much like our earth, possessed a fullness, a depth, a resonance that made our existence on earth seem but an exile. He had dreamed this dream on many of his voyages to Italy, to Greece, to Japan and elsewhere, in reading as a child the book *Dans les sables rouges,* in hearing of distant places such as Tibet and the Gobi Desert, in experiencing and remembering the idyllic childhood world of his family's summer home in Toirac, in studying Virgil and Latin literature, in misinterpreting (as he later came to believe) the images of Italian Quattrocento painting. Finally, at the time of the commencing of *Hier régnant désert,* he had concluded that this dream was an illusion, a negative refusal to accept time and finitude as they are. Life, he thought, was essentially limitation and mortality, and writing was practically a vain endeavor because, once opened to the nothingness running through existence, the closure of its form was undermined and it could only approach silence. There was a truth to these beliefs, he says in *L'Arrière-pays*—but it was not the complete truth. He had not yet seen how writing could express a fullness of *this* earth, a plenitude which, while imperfect and finite, realizes a union of existence and dream. He still had not gone "jusqu'au bout." An embracing of the mortality of life was not to become his whole theme.

By the time he had created the last poems in *Hier régnant désert,* however, Bonnefoy had approached a new understanding, begun a new "apprentissage" that transcended this earlier, incomplete realization. . . . Dreams of another world, he realized, though not really antagonistic to existential reality (as he had thought them to be when beginning *Hier régnant désert*), are only so *if* one recognizes them as dreams. For then they dissipate and the reality of the world approaches more and more fully. This reality is for a time mere limitation and mortality. But within it, sometimes, at special and unexpected moments, the "arrière-pays," having disappeared, "se reforme" in the here and now. At such times, made possible by our awakening from dreams, the earth is transformed. The momentary emptiness of the dreamless present fills and reality expands, taking on the resonance and depth of dream. Things in the world seem to intercommunicate and merge. People become open to one another, the hidden nature of the things of the earth is disclosed, divisions and separations are abolished and truth appears in shining incarnations everywhere. We realize that the earth is the *one place,* the locus of truth; it is "all rustling with unity." Life becomes now, at last, Rimbaud's "vraie vie," or what Bonnefoy sometimes calls "le vrai réel." And poetry is not a negative or vain activity undermined by nothingness; it can express this refound unity. Now "quelques mots pour finir brilleront peut-être, qui, bien que simples et transparents comme le rien du language, seront pourtant tout, et réels." A few simple words will express everything that needs to be said. The world will be full, and at peace, and words will be, not only not useless, but *real;* poetry will be the speech of reality. (pp. 333-37)

[Bonnefoy] believes that the world is essentially One, that all comes together in a wholeness transcending separation. . . . The One makes individual beings possible, it knits all things together and sanctifies everything. This is what we discover when we put away dreams and let the reality of things come to us. The One is not, Bonnefoy makes clear, God. Modern poetry is "la poésie sans les dieux." But modern poetry is a promise, a hope of salvation, of a life in touch with the oneness of things. Bonnefoy's poetry, in particular, is an attentive waiting for the revelation of a living unity.

Hier régnant désert is one step on the endless path towards a fullness of being, a revealed unity, and it is a new type of step for Bonnefoy. *Douve* was a first attempt at discovery, but incomplete because not sufficiently aware of the temptation to close words off in their own dream, apart from reality. Beginning in despair of the validity of the search or of the self's ability to pursue it (partly because of *Douve*'s very imperviousness), *Hier régnant désert* takes the poet and us through a journey that ends, after all, in an opening up towards presence. *Pierre écrite* realizes the full blossoming of the vision as it mixes death and life, darkness and light, earth and dream, infinity and concreteness in a scene in which "quelques mots" almost shine with a final shining. Let us look at the progression from book to book and within the books more closely.

Douve consists of an extreme, often violent attempt to transform reality in a single effort of intensity. Its words take us beyond ordinary life toward the uttermost limits—to utter death, to another world, to a joy beyond agony. . . . The voyage toward the limits is one of deprivation, of nothingness, of death. The woman-muse-nucleus of the book, Douve, is continually being ravished and blinded, is disintegrating and dying as she (and the poet, and we) approach, more and more, a last blackness. In the first section of the volume she is becoming one with the earth. This movement continues in the second part, but by the third she has reached a kind of beyond of death, night, suffering, cold. The fourth section, "L'Orangerie," begins to reveal a scene of painful transfiguration which, incomplete, becomes in the fifth and last part a hopeful waiting. *Douve* is the most ambiguous of Bonnefoy's books in that it is hardest to say, in it, to what one has attained at any point. The book is a series of overlapping, complex efforts to pierce through to an ultimate peace. Douve dies, dies again, is buried, is buried again, speaks the words of ultimate cold many times to try to reach the sought-for transformation. The book progresses, and yet does not substantially progress. At the end we are left still in cold, in privation, in waiting, though the violence of Douve's repeated deaths is, it is true, behind us. A sort of peace has perhaps been achieved, but the dominating mood is still one of prayer, waiting and questioning. . . . In *Douve* Bonnefoy attempted to reach a metamorphosis through the instant—an instant constantly repeated, intensified. His most dramatic book and his most famous, it did not however achieve a lasting peace, nor resolve the struggles inside him.

Pierre écrite, on the other hand, represents a resolution, as suffering leads into an expanding, full happiness. Bonnefoy decided on the epigraph to the book at the time of his discovery in Venice, the epigraph that consists of the quotation from *A Winter's Tale:* "Thou mettest with things dying; I with things new born." Bonnefoy glosses this in *L'Arrière-pays* by saying that it concerns "ce qui meurt, ce qui naît, et le passage de l'un à l'autre." *Pierre écrite* is the passage from a world dominated by death and time to one imbued with birth and fullness. . . . Beginning in illusion and despair, *Pierre écrite* achieves the culmination of a redemptive movement that began with *Douve.*

To understand this movement fully we must look at *Hier régnant désert,* which comes in between, deepening and rechanneling the earlier book and preparing the path for the later one. Lacking *Douve*'s extremes and also the lyric beauty of *Pierre écrite, Hier régnant désert* is a book of transition (as Jackson has said) but it gradually frees Bonnefoy of his illusions and isolation from time and other people, opening him toward reality and giving him faith in the ability of art to accomplish a new kind of synthesis.

We can see Bonnefoy's denunciation of his own illusions—a denunciation which is the initial subject of *Hier régnant désert*—in the very epigraph to the book, a free translation from Hölderlin's prose fiction *Hyperion:* " 'Tu veux un monde,' dit Diotima. 'Cest pourquoi tu as tout, et tu n'as rien.' " Like the idealistic dreamer Hyperion, Bonnefoy has wanted "a world"—a complete, unflawed, paradisical place untouched by time or commonness. The Bonnefoy of *Douve* believed that through poetic language he could create a beauty, a perfection that, as he writes in *L'Arrière-pays,* "assurait *tout* au poète; sauf qu'en se séparant de l'ouvert des jours, méconnaissant le temps, et autrui, il ne tendait à rien, et fait, que la solitude." Believing he had everything, he in fact had nothing, because his dream was a part from reality, from time, from others. He wanted a perfect sphere, but had now to come to face the fragmentary openness and inconclusion of the world.

In the poems of *Hier régnant désert* Bonnefoy begins by rejecting the negativism implicit in this wishful thinking, its denial of reality. "Que voulais-tu dresser sur cette table, / Sinon le double feu de notre mort?" What were you really establishing by your dreaming but death? These are the first words of the book. A long and radical transformation works itself out between these initial, despondent syllables and those of the end. *Hier régnant désert* is the record of what may be called a "dark night of the soul." Like the structure of that typical Bonnefoyian moment in which dreams, having been recognized as such, dissipate into an abyss of nothingness which is then replaced by the reformed "beyond" in a transformed, early incarnation, this work has the form of a descent followed by an ascent, a night succeeded by day. Having lost his dreams, the poet finds himself bereft of hope and passes through a painful night of suffering and self-questioning finally to attain to a dawn of reconciliation and acceptance. The images Bonnefoy uses—concrete yet generalized, particular yet essentialized and archetypal—are the prime means by which we experience this rite of passage. (pp. 338-42)

In the last poem of the volume, **"L'Oiseau des ruines,"** a bird flies toward the sun, source of day. Having begun in dark despondency, the book ends in a triumphant flight toward the light.

We can view this voyage through night from alienation to fulfillment more exactly by contemplating the images of fire the book contains. A fire, flame or burning of some sort appears explicitly in twenty-two of the fifty-six lyrics in the work, in addition to being suggested by cognate images (candles, a phoenix, the burning sun, lamps) in more than ten others. In fact, the basic "narrative" of the work (insofar as one can be discerned in a movement so complex, so full of hesitations, backtrackings and foreshadowings) is not only a progression from day through night to new day, but one involving a fire that seems to die at evening only to lie burning feebly during the night, and then to be renewed gradually and burst forth afresh with dawn's light. (This correspondence between the book's general atmosphere and one of its central images lends a feeling of interrelation and universality to the mythic journey we take by reading it.) (pp. 343-44)

[In the poem] **"Le Ravin,"** appear two other of the key figures of *Hier régnant désert:* the hero-knight and the bird. The knight exists in two other poems in the volume, **"L'Ordalie"** and **"Tu entendras . . . ,"** in both of which (as in **"Le Ravin"**) he extricates a sword from a massive stone in which it has been buried. Derived from the medieval *Queste del Saint-Graal,* of which Bonnefoy completed Albert Béguin's translation into modern French, this mythic tale suggests the heroic effort of poetry to open up the opacity of finitude and death to man that he may enter into and accept them. The image of the bird recurs frequently, typically connoting a magic appeal to a destiny that the poet (conflated with the hero) must take up. The mythic feat of the knight and the magic appeal of the bird draw us toward the "new shore" which is the earth finally known for itself, the dark but familiar place of our mortal "sojourn," where we must live and which we *have* loved in spite of alienation ("exil") or suffering. . . . In **"L'Oiseau des ruines"** the bird flies to the sun, that greatest of fires; "L'oiseau . . . se sépare de la mort," he attains "l'éternel." Now, finally having been accepted and taken into the self, death and existential time turn to—eternity. The flawed earth and the realm of dreams are no longer distinguishable. Only through an embracing of our earth—these poems are telling us—is the self able, in the end, to fly free. But such a liberation does not entail, even at its culmination, an abandonment of the actual. For here in the sun, where the bird builds his nest, we find "la pierre grise"— the gray, humble substance of earth. The eternal is not a realm transcending the finite, not an Ideal, not a separate "beyond"; it is existence itself, fulfilled. In the incarnation that concludes *Hier régnant désert* the separation of the real and the ideal is shown to be an illusion. The unity that is revealed is at once magical and of our mortal place and time. Things with which we are daily acquainted remain themselves, yet are utterly transformed from within, and shine. Truth exists not apart from things, but inside them, in their very cores. We have found "la vraie vie."

Not sufficiently heeded in the past by critics or readers, *Hier régnant désert,* as we have seen, embodies the struggle, crucial to Bonnefoy's work, to embrace reality as it is, and it ultimately achieves that end. With this work Bonnefoy became engaged in an effort to leave behind the element in Symbolism and Romanticism (movements that played great roles in his development) that sought to flee the world for the Ideal. Unlike Baudelaire or Mallarmé, Bonnefoy tries (like many poets of our century) to glimpse a unity beyond the divisions and yearnings of Romantic and post-Romantic poetry. The incarnate stone of reality, absorbing dreams, is more real to him than the moon of a detached imagination. And it is enough . . . We need not seek for anything beyond what is in front of our eyes and in ourselves. If we bring all our intensity to the world, we will discover in *it* the land we have been looking for. For Bonnefoy life is not a condition of inevitable separation but a realm where sleeping giants lie, ready to spring awake. The touch of poetry, he believes, calls them to a life that, though buried and unsuspected, is really there in the hours and events of our daily life. (pp. 346-48)

Marc Hofstadter, "From Alienation to Incarnation: Yves Bonnefoy's 'Hier régnant désert'," *in* The Romanic Review, *Vol. LXXII, No. 3, May, 1981, pp. 333-48.*

JEAN STAROBINSKI

[*The article excerpted below was originally published in French in 1982.*]

They looked as they had heard of a world ransomed, or one destroyed. This line from the last act of *The Winter's Tale,* the recognition scene (V, 2), appears as an epigraph to Yves Bonnefoy's **Dans le leurre du Seuil.**

The preceding volume, **Pierre écrite,** already had an epigraph from the same play (III, 3): *Thou mettest with things dying: I with things new-born.* Taken from a work Bonnefoy has translated admirably, and whose mythical substance is dear to him, these epigraphs do not merely imply the choice of a landmark in the great tradition of Western poetry; they are the voice of the past alerting us and pointing to what is at stake for us now; they indicate precisely, it seems to me, in an emblematic and seminal way, the double question that predominates in the poetry of Yves Bonnefoy. The word "world" tells us that it has to do with the world, or with *a* world; that is, with a coherent totality, and a set of *real* relations. But the very existence of this world is in suspense, in the alternation that opposes *ransomed* and *destroyed, things dying* and *things new-born.* The poetic work here points to its initial concern, the place it has sprung from: the moment of peril, where all hovers between life and death, between "redemption" and "perdition." The Shakespearean epigraphs, by the very force of their antitheses, speak of tornness, of uncertainty, but also of the élan of hope: the only sources—beyond any possessed assurance—that Bonnefoy assigns to his poetry. They are its *constants.* The epigraph borrowed from Hegel, at the head of Bonnefoy's first book, **Du mouvement et de l'immobilité de Douve** (1953), already evokes the confrontation of life and death: "But the life of the spirit is not frightened at death and does not keep itself pure of it. It endures death and maintains itself in it." The question of the *world,* in turn, was already pointed to, but critically, in the epigraph to the second book, **Hier régnant désert,** in a phrase taken from Hölderlin's *Hyperion:* "You want a world, said Diotima. That is why you have everything and yet have nothing." Here too the notion of the "world" is tied to an alternation, established in the great opposition of "all" and "nothing." For an artist so given to lucidity, the choice of epigraphs equals a declaration of intention, a guide to reading and comprehension, allowing us to see the new work in the light of past works, whose memory it has kept and to which it feels a need to respond. *The Winter's Tale* is a great myth of reconciliation. Behind the quotations from Hegel and Hölderlin we can discern the Neoplatonic themes of the One, of division, and of reintegration—questions whose urgency is renewed for Bonnefoy, beyond any guarantee assured by earlier art and thought. The passages he uses as epigraphs, words from the past, are an encouragement to consider the *present* situation of language as a moment when the human relation must be reborn, out of a state of dispersal. The quotation is a viaticum on the threshold of a journey that faces unexplored lands, the space of night, the places of disunion.

The *world* is in question: let us bear that in mind. And it is important for us to recall that the word *world,* especially in poetry, has acquired over the past two centuries a value that it did not have before. Earlier, it meant first the whole of creation within the order of nature; then, in the religious sense, it meant "this" world as opposed to "the other"; finally, in a looser sense, it signified a wide earthly space, a continent, "new" or "old." When Shakespeare speaks of a world "ransomed" or "destroyed," he takes the word in its religious sense, and, secondarily, in the last sense mentioned above, as a continent. . . . The triumph of physics and mathematical cosmology has brought with it the disappearance of religious representations tied to the ancient image of the cosmos: there no longer is any empyrean, any dwelling place of the angels or of God, beyond the planetary orbits. Nothing in the universe is different from this world; the profane world is the sole beneficiary of the application of scientific rationality. The sacred, if it is not to disappear, must take refuge in "inner" experience, join with the act of living, with communication, with shared love—and thus make its dwelling place the sensible, language, art.

This, it seems to me, is the paradoxical condition in which poetry has found itself, for not quite the past two centuries: a precarious condition, since it disposes of no such system of proofs as lends authority to scientific discourse, but at the same time a privileged condition in which poetry consciously assumes an ontological function—by which I mean at once an experience of being and a reflection on being—for which it did not have to bear the responsibility or the care in earlier centuries. Behind it there is a lost world, an order in which it was included, and which it knows cannot be revived. It carries within it the hope of a new order, a new meaning, whose establishment it must imagine. It brings everything to bear on the task of hastening the coming of the as yet unexpressed *world,* which is the ensemble of living relations in which we would find the fullness of a new presence. The world that poetry thus takes responsibility for is thought of as future, as the recompense for poetic labor. (pp. 181-84)

The work of Bonnefoy offers us today one of the most committed and deeply pondered examples of this modern vocation of poetry. His writings as poet and essayist, in which the personal accent is so clear, and in which the *I* of subjective assertion is manifested with force and simplicity, have for object a relation to the world, not an internal reflection on the self. This *oeuvre* is one of the least narcissistic there is. It is entirely turned toward the external object which is what matters for it, and whose singularity, whose unique character, always implies the possibility of sharing. Subjective assertion is thus only the first term of a relation whose developed form is the summons: the *you* that is addressed to another person (to reality outside the self), but equally the *you* in which the poet transcribes an appeal addressed to him, are at least as insistent as the *I* of personal affirmation. The self, one might say, is kept alert by its care for the world, to which it is accountable through its use of language. Turning to the vocabulary of ethics, Bonnefoy tells us that what is at stake is a common *good*—a *good* which must necessarily be realized and felt in individual experience, but not solely for the benefit of the separate individual. The subject, the self, so forcefully present in the act of expression, does not remain alone on stage in what it expresses: it leaves much room for the other, for what demands compassion, and accepts that individual consciousness, in the face of the world, must bend to the demands of a *truth* which it has no right to dispose of arbitrarily. The solipsism of much "poetic discourse" in the modern age draws the strongest objections from Bonnefoy. It is not the self but the world that must be "ransomed," or more precisely: the self cannot be "ransomed" unless the world is "ransomed" with it. About this point, too, the epigraph is entirely revealing. (pp. 184-85)

We should note here that the *world* whose emergence Bonnefoy seeks to assure takes its full meaning only from the opposition it maintains: it is the world won back from abstraction, the world freed from the nocturnal waters of dream; and this implies effort, work, journey. The world, even if we finally come to realize that it was *already there,* is at first absent, veiled, and must be recovered, by the eye and the word, from a situation of isolation and want. All of Bonnefoy's texts—poetry, prose, essays—include a sequence of moments, comparable to moments of passage, in which a desire keeps watch divided between memory and hope, between nocturnal cold and the warmth of a new fire, between denunciation of the "lure" and straightness of sight. They are situated, so to speak, between two worlds (in personal history as well as in collective history): there *was* a world, a fullness of meaning, but they have been lost, broken, scattered. (This affirmation is the starting point of gnostic doctrines—and the fact that he shares it with them makes Bonnefoy all the more careful to separate himself from them later on.) For him who does not let himself be taken in by chimeras, or by despair, there *will be* a world once more, a habitable place; and this place is not "elsewhere," or "yonder," it is "here"—in the place itself, found again like a new shore, in a new light. But this new shore is only foreshadowed, prefigured, discovered by hope. So that this space *between two worlds* may be considered the field in which Bonnefoy's work develops—a field necessarily open to images of movement and journeying, which sometimes calls for narration, with all the "adventures" that take place in stories of quest: wanderings, traps, false paths, the entering of ports and gardens. In fact, this spatial projection is only an image, an allegorical virtuality which Bonnefoy knows he must also defend himself against. Between two worlds: the trajectory is essentially one of life and thought, it is constituted by the change of relations with objects and beings, by the development of an experience of language.

Bonnefoy's extreme exactingness with regard to the *authenticity* of the second world he wishes to come to determines a series of warnings or means of nonacceptance with regard to what threatens to turn him from it or to take the place of it too completely. We must go so far as to say that, precisely because of its projection into the future, beyond the point reached by our investigation, the second world is defined less by its own character (which can be revealed only by its advent) than by the rejection of illusory or partial worlds that offer themselves in its place.

This dimension of future and hope is essential. However intense his feeling of a lost world, Bonnefoy does not let the backward glance or nostalgic thought prevail. Often, of course, he lets it be known that in the past of human cultures there was a sacred alliance with the earth, testimony of which has been gathered by the mythologies: but mythical utterance has ceased, and cannot be reborn in its old form. It only indicates the possibility of a fullness that human existence was capable of in a world prior to the schism that separated the language of science (of the concept) from that of poetry. Henceforth it is the task of poetry, or at least of a new practice of the word, to invent a new relation to the world—a relation which, charged with *memory* though it may be, will not be a *repetition* of the old alliance. If we glimpse fleetingly, in Bonnefoy, the light of a former unity, it never yields to restorative (or regressive) reveries, which would make do with a simulacrum of return: Bonnefoy limits himself to evoking, forcefully but without insistence, a first intimacy with natural innocence. For the break, or "fall," is too obvious to him for him to engage in any act of pure restoration: reveries of a gol-

den age, the lyricism of the idyll, are foreign to him. Such a "fixation of regret" is imaginable only for someone who hopes to avoid difficult confrontations, who can be content with an "image" in place of the missing "reality." No worship of the past, then, even though a certain past, difficult to pinpoint, appears privileged in relation to our present condition. The first world can no longer serve as our refuge. If Bonnefoy, in his essays, happens to use words, mainly verbs, marked by the prefix of repetition—to "reanimate" or "recenter" speech, to "recommence a dwelling place," to "recover presence"—we should know that he is not inviting the return of a former fullness, or attributing an unsurpassable authority to it: it is a matter of defining the second world as the place of a new life, another fullness, a different unity, through which the loss of the first world may in some sense be made good. Keeping his distance with regard to Christianity and Hegel, Bonnefoy remains attached nonetheless to a certain figure of progression, of the step forward, which hopes to find *in the end,* in a simplified and more intimately possessed truth, thanks to the work of mediation (which is trial and death), that which was lost or abandoned *in the beginning.* The backward look is certainly not impugned: poetic works, languages, myths call for hearing and meditation, but in order to nourish hope and to turn the mind toward what is still unknown.

To entrust the task to language, to poetry, is, for Bonnefoy, to posit in principle that the second world has its basis in the act of speech which names things and calls them into "being" in a living communication with the other person (our neighbor). In his texts on art and poetry, Bonnefoy defines this task mainly by way of negation, by exposing the peril attaching to the use of language, when it breaks with the world, and above all with the other person, and opts proudly for its own autonomous perfection. He often returns to this point, and his commentators, beginning with Maurice Blanchot, have paid sufficient attention to it, so that we need not set out here all the arguments with which Bonnefoy arms his warning against the seductions that would turn us from the quest for the "true place" and "entrap" us (the word expresses very well a final ill-fated immobilization) in a separate universe. This warning is not only theoretical; it is not only an article of aesthetic or anti-aesthetic doctrine promoting some sort of "death of art" as a condition of access to the second world. Reading *L'Arrière-pays* ("The Back-Country"), which testifies to Bonnefoy's personal development, we observe that for him it is a question of a peril intimately experienced in the gnostic temptation of an "elsewhere," in the fever induced by the call, "yonder," of a "true place" which is only the illusion of the true place, since it demands a desertion of the *here and now,* of the reality in which the poet finds himself uncentered, exiled. Separation is a sin: it is the sin committed by "speakers of words" when they abandon the "real" (or being) for their own notions; when the dream turns to the distance; when the image, in its glory, prevails over the humble presence of things; when the book or work isolates itself in its closed perfection, aloof, in the "abstract" purity of its structure. There is a deadly power in language—when it supplants reality by concealing it, by replacing it with an image, an insubstantial reflection. It must then be reduced to silence. But nothing can alter the fact that language is also the bearer of our "hope of presence." Thus the peril of the choice between a "world destroyed" or a "world ransomed" is lodged in writing itself. If there is somewhere a danger that threatens "being," Bonnefoy does not claim to be untouched by it, or lay the blame for it only on some evil force outside himself: the age, society, deceitful ideologies. He admits to seeing it in the signs his own hand traces, in objects whose beauty holds his attention, in the false "gnostic" way on which his own dream of salvation risks losing itself. There exists, then, for Bonnefoy, not only a first schism (for which, as we have seen, the "concept" bears its share of responsibility), but an increased loss in addition, when deliverance is sought in an "image-world," through what Bonnefoy again calls a "concept," but this time referring to purified words, verbal essences, dreamed forms. The image-world is the product of an aggravated sin, even if we must recognize at its source a genuine hope of unity, an impulse toward fullness: for the impulse becomes fixed in a "mask," and creates an obstacle that comes between our desire and its finality—real presence. Of course the image world, the mask-world, is the negation of the impoverished and "disassembled" world in which we live in a state of waiting; but these words, these essences, which are born of a sacrifice of the immediate, of a putting to death of the first principle of existence, do not give birth and life to the second world: they shine with the brightness of death. The exigency of which Bonnefoy makes himself the spokesman (an ethical, or rather an ontological exigency, far more than an aesthetic one) calls for a second negation, a second death, a negation of the negation: an "existential" negation of the "intellectual" negation which produced the work: the closed figure in which "Beauty" is isolated, the system (the verbal world) in which *language* or, better, the *work* as language, is imprisoned, must be broken, consumed, abused, shattered, so that out of this enduring of death *speech* may be born, the living act of communication. Let us immediately add one observation on this point: it is because conceptual organisms in their expansive pride, in their "cold" radiance and in their power of concealment take on the figure of the world, that this word is most often replaced by others when it is a question of designating what we have called the "second world:" Bonnefoy speaks more readily of a *second earth* (the title of an essay from *Le Nuage rouge* ["The Red Cloud"]), or *land;* he also speaks of a *true place.* For the word *world,* heavy with reminiscences from antiquity, when the stable character of *harmony* was attributed to the cosmos, does not say enough about finitude, mortality, time granted in passing moments, which are the lot of earthly life, to which we are asked to assent. And we see Bonnefoy regularly turning to the word *world* to denounce the *intelligible* worlds, or *languages,* enclosed in their own perfection.

The earth recovered, thanks to a living speech that would be able to reunite, to *reassemble.* This word, often used by Bonnefoy in his essays, and which appears at the end of *Dans le leurre du seuil,* belongs to that category we have already mentioned of words with the prefix of repetition, but meaning more than a simple return. To reassemble (conjugated most often in the conditional, the mode of a hope that clings to no certainty), is to realize the "co-presence" which the concept had promised but never truly achieved. It announced a simultaneous grasp: *con-cipere, be-greifen*—their etymological kinship makes them near equivalents of *reassemble.* But, if we listen to Bonnefoy, the concept universalizes thought about the object, but misses the object itself in its finite presence. The pride of this mental *grasp* avoids the pain of incarnation: using an emphatic term, Bonnefoy speaks in this connection of *excarnation.* On the contrary, to reassemble, as Bonnefoy defines it in some of his most striking texts, is to hold precarious existences together, in the light of the moment, sustained by meaning, attaining to being by grace of a speech that has

opened itself to them, preferring them to itself, in trust and compassion.

The earth, the place, the simple, have no need, then, to lay an entire world out before us: it is enough if the few needful precursory words announce it, bringing proof of its truth. The "second earth" is not to be reached through a proliferation of tangible species, in the bad infinity of the enumeration of things (unless, as in one of the qualities Bonnefoy admires in Saint-John Perse, each word, charged with memory of the real, can awaken those momentary divinities previously encountered in childhood, at the heart of the natural world). His fundamental intuition does not lead him to verbal luxuriance, great lexical floods, the polyphony of perceptions—even though he attributes to regenerated language the uplifting power of a wave (the "tide that uplifts," the "unlimited, unstinting wave"). The ark he builds is not one of exhaustiveness. Only those words should come to life in poetry which have, in the poet's conscience, gone through the test of meaning, which have been torn from coldness and inertia to be joined by a living bond. For Bonnefoy it is not the multiplicity of things named that matters, but the quality of the relation that brings them into reciprocal presence—a relation one might have called syntactical, if syntax did not exhaust itself in the order it sets up: it is a question, in Bonnefoy's hope, of a movement that establishes (or re-establishes) an order, which comes through and *opens*—the metaphor of opening is a suitable one for reconciling fidelity (the *recovery* of the world, or at least the *re*calling of it) and the inaugural function that devolves upon speech (beginning to live according to meaning). The ambition expressed many times by Bonnefoy is to "clarify" a few of the words "that help us live." An apparently limited pledge, but one that takes on a conquering élan in the image of dawn ("this gleam that appears in the east, out of densest night") or of a fire catching and beginning to glow. The task assigned to poetry is that of making "a few great reanimated words live together, opening on an infinite radiance." The infinity is in the radiance, not in the multiplicity of words. (pp. 186-91)

Dans le leurre du seuil begins at a moment of ebb: the reassembling (which already took place) is undone, meaning (which had shone) is scattered; we are back in the night again. To what has proved to be only a dream (which "failed of celebration"), a new dream succeeds. Negation appears once more, at the very beginning:

> But no, once again
> Unfolding the wing of the impossible
> You awaken, with a cry,
> From the place which is only a dream. . . .

External reality is perceived once again not in its incarnate presence, in its finitude, but merely as the reflection of a world located elsewhere. . . . (p. 194)

In the future, too, the "leap toward the impossible" will be repeated, a recent text tells us, though at the end of *Dans le leurre du seuil,* answering the second verse of the long poem (in which the "wing of the impossible" is unfolded), unity is promised among things brought back to presence—the "wing of the impossible, *folded back again.*" The step is never taken for good. One must start again from the dream, and again repudiate it.

Repudiate it? Perhaps, finally, Bonnefoy (the author of admirable dream-stories) comes to something like an armed truce with it. Perhaps, without losing his hope of the "true place," he comes to accept that the space of the act of speech should be between two worlds, even in a double sense: between the arid world of our exile and the image-world constructed by words, and then between this mirage and the "garden of presence." Perhaps he must consent to the image, to form, to the structures of language (which are a conceptual exile), in order to accede to presence, which is not a second transcendence but a willing return to the precarious truth of appearances. The image may bring us there, despite its "coldness," if we avoid solidifying it, if we are able to make it admit its own precariousness. At the end of *Dans le leurre du seuil,* the worlds (image-worlds, as I read them) re-form again after being scattered:

> Ash
> Of imaginary worlds dispelled,
>
> Dawn, even so,
> Where worlds linger near the summits,
> Breathing, huddled
> Against each other
> Like silent beasts,
> Stirring, in the cold.

The two times—of a refusal of the imaginary, then of a return to the imaginary, but pluralized, and "breathing" now—are marked here, to my mind, in the clearest way. It seems as if the imaginary, accused of having concealed reality, of having slandered appearances, of having set itself up as a separate world, is finally received as a legitimate part of a vaster, reconciled world. A text on Basho admirably indicates this same consent to what had been denounced as a concealing force (language as a stable structure, formal beauty), on condition that what produces the opening intervene immediately. Bonnefoy perceives the fine dividing line that marks, within a brief poem (a haiku), the divergence of two worlds:

> . . . Listening more intensely, you hear two sounds under this appearance of fixed stars, two sounds at once distinct and very close like the cry of the barnowl, and this union within difference is itself the dialectic of wandering and return. . . . Notions, yes, at first, that structure which tends to exist as soon as there are words in our mouths, and the lightning exchanges between them in the realm of the intelligible. . . . The moment of excarnation, always virtual in language as its native failing, is succeeded by the cry of incarnation. Which is sometimes as slight as the falling of a dry leaf, but what more is needed than a few ripples on the water for the idea of the instant to trouble the peace of essence?

The two times—and the divergence of two worlds—are here brought extremely close—initiating a "dialectic" held in a "brief duration." An attentive examination will show that this "dialectic" is at work every moment in the very issue of *Dans le leurre du seuil,* so that the between-two-worlds makes itself felt not only between the opening and the final lines of the poem, but everywhere, even in the closing verses:

> Words like the sky
> Today,
> Something that gathers, and scatters.
>
> Words like the sky,
> Infinite
> But all here suddenly in the brief pool.

The *double* element is everywhere: the image-world of words and the open space of the sky; the time of gathering, immediately followed by scattering; infinity, but captured in the "brief pool" (reflection and image legitimized, by very reason of their precariousness, their brevity); space above, where clouds pass, and the earthly soil, where water lies humbly in the pool. . . . In these simple words the conflict is appeased, but the threshold has not been crossed: the peace that comes allows the divergence of the two worlds to remain, the opposition without which unity would have no meaning. (pp. 195-97)

> Jean Starobinski, "Poetry between Two Worlds," in
> Poems: 1959-1975 by Yves Bonnefoy, translated by
> Richard Pevear, Random House, 1985, pp. 181-97.

MICHAEL BISHOP

> Les mots comme le ciel
> Infini
> Mais tout entier soudain dans la flaque brève

From the publication in 1953 of his first major collection of poetry, *Du mouvement et de l'immobilité de Douve,* Yves Bonnefoy has exercised a fascination and influence in the realm of French letters that, having steadily grown, may now be said to have reached their point of full blossoming. His importance in the history of modern French literature is quite assured and may well be deemed ultimately even greater than those responsible for the 1983 *colloque de Cerisy* devoted to his work clearly already think. Author of fine translations of Shakespeare, eloquent and profound writings on the history and nature of art and poetry, Bonnefoy has allowed his poetics, and his creativity to develop away from the strict confines of literary schools and even broad contemporary intellectual trends, and rather in loose, though intimate contact with powerful and solitary voices of both the past—Baudelaire, Rimbaud, Mallarmé, Jouve, for example—and his own time: Jacques Dupin, Philippe Jaccottet, André Frénaud, André du Bouchet and others. . . . My aim here is to map the principal features of a poetics that has guided him both in his criticism and his creative writing from his earliest poetic utterances of *Anti-Platon* and even the *Traité du pianiste,* down through *Du mouvement et de l'immobilité de Douve* and the determining *proses* of *L'Improbable* and *Un Rêve fait à Mantoue,* to the essays of *Le Nuage rouge* and the sweeping, slow majesty of *Dans le leurre du seuil.* Whilst a good deal of material cannot be touched upon, the general rigour and constancy of Bonnefoy's poetics will in this way come clearly into focus, as, it is hoped, will also the complexity and multifaceted nature of his thinking and approach. We shall thus have occasion to speak of aspects of Bonnefoy's poetics such as the distinction between presence and concept, the significance of death, ephemeralness and imperfection, hope and love, withdrawal and assent, language considered as problem and solution, and so on. Our final appreciation will reveal a poet working, both through the articulation of his poetics and his poetic praxis, at the intersection of the infinite and the briefest of illuminations.

The very early texts of *Anti-Platon,* dating back to 1947, still retain something of that air of enigma and obscurity that Bonnefoy himself is troubled to dispel in his reading, twenty years after their initial appearance, of the poems of *Hier régnant désert.* At the same time, however, they clearly mark out the principal obsessions and concerns that will be repeatedly elaborated and refined in his later work, both poetic and critical. The liminal poem of *Anti-Platon* stresses immediately the essential role that the particular, the specific, has to play in Bonnefoy's poetics, the inescapable importance—the importance we must not escape from—of the 'this-ness' of the world and our experience of it, set against the shimmering chimera of Idea. . . . What we need to assume . . . is the very fragility, the precariousness, of our condition, in short the death that lies attendant upon us all, that is a consequence of the 'this-ness' of our being and whose message, paradoxically of fullness rather than banal finality, is central to Bonnefoy's poetics in general and especially, as we shall now see in our analysis of **"Les Tombeaux de Ravenne"** and *Du mouvement et de l'immobilité de Douve,* the earlier expression of it.

The 1953 essay **"Les Tombeaux de Ravenne"** presents Bonnefoy's fundamental thinking with respect to our being-in-the-world, opposing as it does the simplicity of human salvation through our acts of presence, to the perverseness and sophistry of our dismaying tendency to 'conceptualize' the world and our being in it. In this perspective Bonnefoy moves to show that the concept always involves 'un profond refus de la mort'; it always entails evasion, *fuite,* a denial of human destiny, an effort to erase the ephemeralness and danger of existence and replace them with 'une demeure logique où les seuls principes qui vaillent sont de permanence et d'identité. Demeure faite de mots, mais éternelle'. Where lucidity in the face of the openness, imperfection and sheer *hasard* of existence should prevail, a drugged 'idealism' sidesteps the world in order to remake it, force it to cohere, systematize itself comfortably, reassuringly. . . . It is at this point that Bonnefoy evokes the Ravenna tombs. Initially impressed by their ornamentation, he is tempted to see in them, in this memorial locus of death, merely another, regrettably typical effort to refuse presence, here death, in an act of embellishment, abstraction, transcendence. Art in the face of death, would seem to flee the latter's 'truth'. And yet, Idea, embedding itself in stone, 'risks' itself, Bonnefoy soon realizes. The ornamentation of the tombs is denied evasion and transcendence by the truth, presence and particularness, 'this-ness', of an object that thus reaffirms passage, becoming, 'une liberté qui se lève', at the expense of (aesthetic) *angélisme.* Whereas conceptualization leads to an abandonment of what is, an abandonment that is 'ennui, angoisse, désespoir' in Bonnefoy's eyes, the Ravenna tombs provide an instance of insurrection of the world whereby 'comme par grâce tout le vif et le pur de l'être dans un instant est donné', and spirit and matter once more reach some precarious but joyous communion. In the place of the abstract generality of concept Bonnefoy offers us a 'universality' that always has its locus, its myriad loci, each depending upon our gaze, the use to which we put it, for the reciprocal exaltation and, as Reverdy would say, ontic 'consubstantiation' that self and world together can secure. In place of absence, we are given presence, which puts us, at least fleetingly, in contact with that Baudelairean 'unité profonde de tout'. And presence brings not the stupour of permanence and effete composure; it is on the contrary the epitome of fragmentation and dispersal—yet a fragmentation and a dispersal that *are.* Ontic depth, 'toute la profondeur de ce qui est', is not, then, to be found in the sterilized illusions and veiled, feeble 'divinity' of our conceptualization of the world, but rather is evidenced by breakage and wound, passingness and vulnerability. The 'immortality', the universality, the eternity that haunts Bonnefoy offers neither perfection nor any absolute, for they are steeped in time, marked by death: 'conjonction d'une immortalité impossible et d'une immortalité sentie', he argues, 'l'immortalité qu'il y a dans la présence du lierre est de l'éternel que l'on goûte, elle n'est pas

la guérison de la mort'. It is important to stress, however, that in all of this, caught as he is in this essay in the abstractions of philosophical discourse, Bonnefoy's argument is restricted to this minimum. His ambition, his 'devoir absolu', is uncluttered, unpretentious, though utterly crucial: the affirmation of our being through a naming, a saying of presence. Poetry's function in this is serious, morally bound, privileged, uplifting. 'Voici le monde sensible', he declares, 'il faut que la parole, ce sixième et ce plus haut sens, se porte à sa rencontre et en déchiffre les signes. Pour moi je n'ai de goût qu'en cette tâche, recherche du secret que Kierkegaard n'avait plus'. If there are obstacles in the path of such an ambition, as indeed there are in abundance, there is equally the buoying or at least conpensatory thought that it is only in following this path that our starkly beautiful salvation may be found. 'L'acte de présence est en chaque instant la tragédie du monde et son dénouement', Bonnefoy tells us. So, too, homologously, for *l'acte poétique.*

In the same year that **"Les Tombeaux de Ravenne"** appeared, Bonnefoy published his remarkable *Du mouvement et de l'immobilité de Douve* and it is to an examination, firstly, of this determining and influential volume of poetry and, secondly, of that obscure but flickeringly brilliant subsequent collection, *Hier régnant désert,* that we now turn in order to see what, in actual poetic context, in the very *acte poétique* itself, continue to be the central obsessions, the fundamentals, of his poetics. The opening poems of *Du mouvement et de l'immobilité de Douve* establish in effect immediately and forcefully the primacy of the imagination of death in this collection. Everywhere Bonnefoy is appalled by its 'breakage', filled with horror at its 'musique affreuse', yet oddly resistant to the apparent finality of burial, strangely enthused even by the bizarre chemistry of disintegration he so powerfully evokes:

> Le ravin pénètre dans la bouche maintenant,
> Les cinq doigts se dispersent en hasards de forêt maintenant,
> La tête première coule entre les herbes maintenant,
> La gorge se farde de neige et de loups maintenant,
> Les yeux ventent sur quels passagers de la mort et c'est nous
> dans ce vent dans cette eau dans ce froid maintenant.

Everywhere, then, Bonnefoy is summoned by what flees, by what lies dark or is torn asunder in death, by what he senses to be its problematic though centrally significant 'logic'. Bonnefoy's attitude to death is thus less confused, ambivalent, radically divided, than simply clear-eyed, lucidly aware of the essentially paradoxical nature of this logic. There are two related factors at play here. Death, despite its 'frightful', 'silly' orchestrations, is felt, throughout these intense poems, to be doubly positive. It is the one phenomenon that, for Bonnefoy, flings us back towards our existence, our leaking yet potentially full being-in-the-world. It provides that very point of anchorage, that totally irreversible attachment to the earth that, viewed falsely, inauthentically, evasively, death itself ironically has so often deprived us of. In short, it is the 'bottom line', the very fundament, of our life. Furthermore, so many texts of *Du mouvement et de l'immobilité de Douve* succeed in bringing out what might, in fact, be thought of as a metaphor for this conception of death, but what may be equally regarded as an extension, an intimately related elaboration of it, namely the notions of continuity and cyclicalness that cling to this conception, death's 'complicity' with life. Douve may thus be 'blessée confuse dans les feuilles', but she remains 'prise par le sang de pistes qui se perdent, / Complice encore du vivre'. (Douve's) being may be 'undone', but its undoneness is instantly reversed by an act of gathering initiated also by being this time construed as unconquerable. . . . Ravaged, insect-infested, caught in the dark process of earth's perpetuity, Douve thus still radiates joy, exults in her capacity for some stunning continuity and gritty illumination. Her precise, exact and still emanating presence is what strikes Bonnefoy, finally. Conveyor of the 'cold secret' of death she is, indubitably, essentially, yet there is an oddly crucial way in which Bonnefoy, in no spirit of false, empty, blind transcendence, it should be emphasized, sees this 'dead presence' as 'vivante, de ce sang qui renaît et s'accroît où se déchire le poème'. 'Il te faudra franchir la mort pour que tu vives', he declares in a later poem of the same volume, 'la plus pure présence est un sang répandu'. Death in this perspective becomes the threshold of existence, our 'presence' being, reciprocally, paradoxically, most perfectly 'conveyed' by its dispersal, its act of loss. And, in consequence, a shimmering field of mirrored equivalences is set up between what appear to be mutually exclusive, contradictory, antagonistic phenomena: being and nothingness, presence and disappearance, disintegration and assembly. If death is, of necessity, still what it always has been, its meaning is not. For the poems of *Du mouvement et de l'immobilité de Douve* confirm, amongst other things I shall speak of later, not a frightened retreat from death but rather its firm, lucid embrace, its rooting of our being always in the movingness of existence, the rendering quasi-equivalent of the meaning of our true place of dwelling and the meaning of death's simultaneous 'ruination' and founding of this place.

Hier régnant désert appeared in 1958 and if certain of its poems inevitably echo the imaginative emphases of *Du mouvement et de l'immobilité de Douve,* other stresses emerge—albeit elliptically, bathed in a briefly flecked obscurity Bonnefoy himself is sensitive to—to which we shall give our attention here. As with the purely 'theoretical' text of **"L'Acte et le lieu de la poésie"** which was published in the same year . . ., what always underpins the enigmatic discourse of this new collection is the role of language, of speech, poetry, in our existence. In one of the early poems Bonnefoy succinctly states the problem of language, its misuse, its purposelessness, its tendency always to be besides the point, and at the same time evokes allusively the healing we may bring to it:

> Et pourquoi disons-nous d'aussi vaines paroles,
> Allant et comme si la nuit n'existait pas?
> Mieux vaut marcher plus près de la ligne d'écume
> Et nous aventurer au seuil d'un autre froid.

(The) language (of poetry), as Bonnefoy generally sees it, is thus characterized by loss, unhappy orientation, it is turned away from those phenomena of our human condition that, only, can restore its authenticity, its value, opting at once for an indifference and sterility in the face of the world's streaming rawness, and for a beauty that, whilst thought transcendent, is, rather, empty in the idealizing harmonies it procures. Such a beauty, 'celle qui ruine l'être', must be discredited, Bonnefoy unflinchingly, unremittingly argues, 'déshonorée, dite coupable, faite sang. / Et cri, et nuit, de toute joie dépossédée'. Moreover, it is within the framework of this destruction, this dismissal, that the 'inguérissable espoir' informing all of Bonnefoy' writing asserts itself. The 'torturing' of beauty, of the beauty of (the) language (of poetry), is not a wanton, gratuitous act; the 'blood' spilled, the 'scream'

echoing in the night air, are, precisely, of infinitely greater (in)significance than the hollow, ringing perfection of anything we may articulate for the sake of, in (oblivious) praise of, its mere 'beauty'. **"L'imperfection est la cime"**, as the title of one of the poems of *Hier régnant désert* unambiguously affirms. The problem of language finds its solution in an unlikely fashion, for, essentially, it has arisen through a progressive perversion of its relation to being, experience, both the quotidian and the marvellous. Indeed the problem of language, and thus its solution, are profoundly ontological. And, in consequence, so many of the poems of this volume stress what we have seen already and shall continue to see throughout Yves Bonnefoy's writings, poetic or critical, namely the necessary imbrication of the logics of language and death, the turning of poetry's language away from its cosmetic effects back to the vital urgency of its elementary and elemental concerns, back to the frozen, broken simplicity of a nettle. Language's healing thus depends upon the birth of a new or renewed vision of its relation to presence, upon a new perception of the world as 'une terre d'aube', when, finally, 'l'inquiète voix consent d'aimer / La pierre simple'. . . . In the face of continuing uncertainty the poet commits himself to an action that at least, risking all, meaning and world, 'risks' equally a seizing of something fundamentally human and crucial despite its otherness, its reclusion. Hiatus there no doubt is between being and language, but in the optic of Bonnefoy's poetics obstacle and setback are never held to be definitive. There dominates, rather, an atmosphere of possibility, accomplishment and reawakening. (pp. 117-24)

From the opening lines of **"L'Acte et le lieu de la poésie"**, Bonnefoy's desire to restore hope to poetry, to render them identical even, is transparent. Moreover, the absolute availability of this hope, this possibility that is poetry, is, for Bonnefoy, blatantly evident, if only we can understand what we truly want and need. 'Comment ne pas reconnaître', he asks, quite rhetorically, 'au delà de ses bergeries, le goût de la poésie pour quelque chose d'errant et de livide qui semble sous des arbres éternels le spectre de la limite que l'on voudrait oublier?' The 'new' hope that we must 'reinvent' does not thus float off into some thin, unbreathable ethereal atmosphere with its frozen crystalline forms; it anchors us, rather, in what may be thought of as the spirituality of our being-in-the-world, our limitless wandering among the leaden-hued limits of the earth. The poetry—the hope—that Bonnefoy proposes to us, offers us openness, future, movement, instead of congealment, past and sterility. Very nearly *'un réalisme initiatique'* in the sense that it is 'au point de connaître, dans son durable exil, ce que peut ouvrir la *présence*' poetry, the poetry of Bonnefoy, the poetry 'to come', may thus finally attain to grace, truth, even beauty, providing it remains rooted in this fusion of hope and lucidness that Bonnefoy calls 'cette ardente mélancolie'. Only within the bounds of this tensely interlocking relation can true poetry articulate itself. Only from the depths of his known poverty, his aware deprivation, can the crucial giving of a true poet come forth. Words themselves, as Bonnefoy argues Baudelaire came to understand, cannot constitute our salvation, which lies rather, as we saw in **Anti-Platon,** in our affirmation, and our love, of 'la seule réalité, irremplaçable, qui est telle chose ou tel être'. Upon the ruins of such mortality there then appears, for poetry, for humanity, a loving and loved possibility. But here again it must be understood that no end, no ultimate solution, is implied. Openness prevails once more; poetry is open-ended in that it can only be movement towards, approach, means. It can never, must never be what we want itself. It remains as search, never constituting in itself the object of our desire, 'la vérité de parole étant une proximité', as Bonnefoy puts it, a continuing quest we assume as our moral, and ontological, duty. (pp. 126-27)

[In passing] to an appraisal of the imaginative inspiration of *Dans le leurre du seuil* in the context of the poetics under consideration, we pass to what, undoubtedly, is not only Bonnefoy's finest poetic creation to date but perhaps the finest he will ever produce, for it ranks amongst the most magnificent pieces of sustained poetry of the twentieth century. It should be understood before proceeding to this necessarily compact account, that a number of other recent books and collections could equally well have merited and held our attention, especially given our present purposes: the somewhat earlier *Rome, 1630* (1970) or *L'Arrière-pays* (1972), the various essays of *Le Nuage rouge* and the *récits* of *Rue traversière,* both published in 1977, or the very recent *Entretiens sur la poésie* (1981) which gathers together material of the past fifteen years. In choosing to conclude with a discussion of the 1975 *Dans le leurre du seuil,* then, we have opted, over the pressing merits of powerfully eloquent critical essays and intense shorter poetic *proses,* for the continuity and coherence of a great poem. Such a choice will, it is hoped, also remind us that, if Bonnefoy has written so much, so obsessively, *about* poetry, what matters ultimately is its practice from which its function may then flow. Moreover, in the case of this poem, as with *Du mouvement et de l'immobilité de Douve,* Bonnefoy offers us a superbly delicate imbrication of praxis and poetics, a self-reflexive creation whose passion embraces, and precisely according to his conception of 'la fonction du poème' and the basic principles of his poetics, the interlocking, in a sense potentially equivalent, ontological natures of word and world.

The first part of *Dans le leurre du seuil,* entitled "Le Fleuve", offers us an awakening, a suddenness of speech; it tells of a looking that is intent and imperative, at things no longer caught in some fictitious 'forever', 'cet à-jamais de silencieuse / Respiration nocturne', but flowing before the self and still signalling a possibility clearly crucial to Bonnefoy's poetics. Everywhere there is paradox, tension, 'choice', as we may like to think of it. Meaning may appear coagulated, somehow disastrously lost, blackly enigmatic, and yet the signs are still there. There is a fullness, even, a kind of perfection of form and substance in the world. There is, in short, equally, an evidence, and a feeling of certainty and joy that oddly persist. Here, Boris de Schloezer's death is, surprisingly, suddenly evoked, the bliss and illumination upon his face contrasted with those 'eaux brûlées d'énigme' that he left behind. The moment seems somehow to symbolize for Bonnefoy the jarring confrontation of a poetics of possible intuition and one of flat submission to the kaleidoscopic unfolding of incomprehensible acts and events upon 'l'amère terre nocturne'. "Le Fleuve", however, is a poem of traversal, navigation and difficult continuity.

'Dans le leurre du seuil' is the title of the second part of Bonnefoy's long poem. Its tone, too, is imperative, one of unambiguous moral compulsion and unremitting forcefulness. 'Heurte, / Heurte à jamais', Bonnefoy begins, 'Dans le leurre du seuil. / A la porte, scellée. / A la phrase, vide. / Dans le fer, n'éveillant / Que ces mots, le fer. / Dans le langage, noir'. The striking is, must be, persistent, an act of dogged continuity addressing itself to everything before us, world and word, in a effort to salvage *le célébrable* within. Bonnefoy is aware

of the lateness of the gesture, certainly, but it is precisely this lateness that gives urgency to a gesture made against all the odds, often 'blindly' and in fatigue. It is important also to remain sensitive to the dual nature of the hammering, the 'striking' of the poet: it takes place in, upon, reality, primary experience, and in, upon, language, specific words. But, of course, these acts are essentially one and the same. Language may be holed, battered, devastated; the world's multiple 'faces tournées vers nous' may be plunged into silence. But, clearly, their separate healings are mutually dependent; the wholeness, the identity we have heard Bonnefoy speak of, can only come about through a therapeutic interaction or interpenetration whereby the sick and deprived heal one another. To achieve this cure, however, the necessity, the preciousness of the poet's / our continued listening and watching, Bonnefoy repeatedly writes, cannot be stressed enough. The empty noise of words, swept along in the wind, is, too, a constant anxiety in all of this. The time lived is not the time desired. It is still provisional, initiatory, transitional; a time, still, of hope and promise not yet—and indeed, Bonnefoy wonders, can it ever quite be?—beyond them. A time of striking 'dans le leurre du seuil'.

The following two sections of *Dans le leurre du seuil,* "Deux couleurs" and "Deux barques", continue to elaborate the fundamental themes at play in Bonnefoy's poetics, though, of course, there is no logical, systematic development of thought finely parcelled out into the illusory compartments of some overall thesis. What he initially affirms, in that style of shimmeringly coherent ellipses articulating themselves at the intersection of the unconscious and a sense of their *justesse,* is at once the difficulty of the (poetic/existential) gesture and a confidence that still clings firmly to it. The search Bonnefoy and the poem itself initiate, takes place so that 'la vie / De rien qu'un rêve' may be born. Their joint human and poetic intention would match being with ideal, existence with dream—an ideal and a dream that, whilst central, demanding a focussing of our entire attention, are, it is essential to underscore, in a sense also minimal, mere, *rien qu'un rêve,* a crucially significant goal oddly veined with the paradox of slightness and even a certain insignificance well known to poets such as Stéphane Mallarmé, André Frénaud or Michel Deguy. Despite a muddiness clouding our view of the threshold, the place of access, 'l'arbre d'étoiles' is glimpsed, definitely there, moving in the water; and the sense—and the need, both ethical and aesthetic—of a birth, a new life welling up within us is urgent and real. Despite, too, the 'mauvais désir de l'infini' that continues to make itself felt, Bonnefoy gives confidence to that impulse that bids him 'consent' to the mortality of the world, to go forth into 'l'été mortel', joining with it, erasing all dualities, dissipating, being dissipated, miraculously realizing 'tard, l'inespéré, soudain'. In that movement, simple, crucial, access to an elusive yet briefly available peace and illumination becomes possible:

> Paix, sur l'eau éclairée. On dirait qu'une barque
> Passe, chargée de fruits; et qu'une vague
> De suffisance, ou d'immobilité,
> Soulève notre lieu et cette vie
> Comme une barque à peine autre, liée encore.

Bonnefoy's intuition, fleeting in itself, is of a fleeting yet sure phenomenon that speaks of plenitude and gentle adequacy. It is a phenomenon offering that quiet, almost inconspicuous transmutation of our experience, a transmutation edging us towards a sense of some marvellous otherness while maintaining an essential and firm attachment to substance and 'evident' reality—an experience, in short, of immediacy and transmutation, simultaneously.

The section of *Dans le leurre du seuil* that follows is entitled "La Terre". It opens by picturing the poet shouting out his pressing, emotionally intense message to others, a message that urges them—all of us—to see the world, and the word, afresh, in the light of a simple though rich proximity that, rather than precluding an invisibility and a measure of eternity, on the contrary, and paradoxically, invites their collusion. In this new, or renewed, optic, 'rien n'a changé, / Ce sont les mêmes lieux et les mêmes choses, / Presque les mêmes mots, / Mais, vois, en toi, en moi / L'indivis, l'invisible se rassemblent'. What Bonnefoy calls the 'knotty', 'rent', 'forever earthy' side of the human condition thus embraces, and is in a sense simultaneous, synonymous with, 'la part impérissable de la vie', and he can henceforth speak with passion and conviction of 'l'à jamais de la fleur éphémère' without any sense of contradiction insinuating itself into his words. Life, the earth, is, then, once again seen as offering a conjunction, even a superimposition, of the forces of passing and consumption, and those of continuity and (re)incarnation. The earth itself—and of course the poet in his reading of its signs—is a place at once of dispersal and gathering, death and celebration of the dying. In its myriad fading and dying movements, the world leaps continually into incandescence, its insignificance suddenly—yet all the time—significant, 'toute une indifférence, illuminée'. And language, too, *parole*—that human, death-governed phenomenon—in passing, shines forth; in its brilliance, dies, but not without giving off its curiously persistent after-glow. The poet and the world—like all things and all people—in some freshly thought conformity with that *poétique de l'éclair* of René Char, thus conspire to be 'l'un pour l'autre comme la flamme / Quand elle se détache du flambeau, / La phrase de fumée un instant lisible / Avant de s'effacer dans l'air souverain'. What *already is,* then, may in this way be revealed anew, yet reaffirmed, as what we had never quite understood it to be. 'Oui', Bonnefoy goes on, 'toutes choses simples / Rétablies / Ici et là, sur leurs / Piliers de feu'. Everything, things and words, magnificently self-revealing at the moment of fiery farewell. What may be a source of anguish for others, the 'nothingness', as it were, of the being of world and word, thus remains a source of sober joy for Bonnefoy. His speech, his poetic utterance, may be a seemingly empty slobbering, 'la salive du rien', but, in the piercing purity of its articulation, it manages to bridge and heal and gladden.

"Les Nuées" is the name given to the penultimate section of this long poem, with its obsessively voiced and criss-crossing lines of sense. It stresses, in a particularly important passage, the need for faith and perseverance in the enterprise Bonnefoy proposes. Only if we show, despite all, what Sartre considered to be that clearly required faith in language, can meaning grow within our words and the earth be saved in that stunning process of birth and maturation whose reality and whose truth the poet dreams. Whilst, then, Bonnefoy never forgets 'la misère du sens', 'la tache noire dans l'image'—those elements that force his poetics to the brink of the tragic—he has still, and especially in *Dans le leurre du seuil,* that grittiness and air of suffused confidence that, though never seeking to abandon this sober perspective, see the world, and its language, as a kind of Mother Courage leading forth things and words in the midst of their evaporation, their 'woundedness', their imperfection. Consciously endeavouring to thrust aside 'la voix néante qui essaie de par-

ler à travers la mienne', the conceits and idle satisfactions the latter alluringly proposes, Bonnefoy's poetic act nevertheless builds itself upon ontological and linguistic defect and incompletion in a joyously impulsive movement towards the retention of this fleeting, maimed substance, in the lucid—and no longer simply 'childish'—hope of rendering, if not meaning itself, 'au moins l'idée du sens—à la lumière'. His poetics thus boldly, tragically and jubilantly, 'assumes' our insubstantialness, our cloud-like ephemeralness, our constant moving in and out of being / nothingness, in the intuition of a rock-bottom, minimal transcendence of the latter in that special place of conjuncture,

> Quand nous passons
> Déserts
> Dans la vitre embrasée de ce pays
> Qui ressemble au langage: illuminée
> Au loin, pierreux ici.

'L'Epars, l'indivisible', are the title words set before the closing pages of *Dans le leurre du seuil.* They speak, as do so many texts of Michel Deguy or, again, Perse's last poem, *Chant pour un équinoxe,* of a scattering and division that are matched, even in a sense equated, with a special mode of unity and coherence that depend upon them. The text proper begins with an outburst of renewed affirmations which soon becomes a thrilling, restless, all-embracing litany of assent to the endless phenomena that gather their teeming diversity around, in and through, us, to constitute our being. In conformity with his poetics of an ephemeralness and death that illuminate, Bonnefoy seeks everywhere to confirm his approval and acceptance less of phenomena that seem to speak blatantly of fullness and wholeness than, for example, of that sun, that fire that lights up the world in its passingness, in its gleamingly traced and erased path through a world constantly giving fruit, giving birth at the moment of a death. 'Oui, par ce feu', he declares, 'par son reflet de feu sur l'eau paisible, / Par notre lieu, qui va, / Par le chemin de feu sous le fruit mûr'. Being and nothingness are hence tied together, constantly jostling and leap-frogging each other, creating an energy, a warmth, a light that permit what can be to be in an act and time that simultaneously burst into life and die. And of course the language to which the poet aspires will mould itself to this conception of things. Nothing will be total, totalizing, systemic, symphonic, perfected either formally or notionally. What will remain will be 'ces quelques mots que j'ai sauvés / Pour une bouche enfante'. Assent will be given to language, but only in its incompleteness, its imperfection: 'Oui, par les mots, / Quelques mots', he affirms. The gesture of poetry is not an All, an Absolute; it is merely—though crucially—a partial gesture, caught in time, even though straining beyond, better through, its particularness, towards some renewable, potentially (ever-)reborn meaning. This meaning, however, Bonnefoy repeats here, cannot be located in the closed space of a structure or what he likes to think of as an 'image'. Such meaning is to be dashed upon the rocks to the benefit of a meaning in flux, open, holed and more recessed, one that must be preserved: 'Et d'une main, / Certes, lever le fouet, injurier le sens, / Précipiter / Tout le charroi d'images dans les pierres / —De l'autre, plus profonde, retenir'. Moreover, in the key passage of 'L'Epars, l'indivisible' that immediately follows, Bonnefoy stresses the dangers of the imaginary heterocosm, the substitute, 'other' structure of the mind, in which we may erroneously seek refuge. No 'building' can truly occur, in effect; we must maintain, in simplicity and compassion, and yet profundity, a sense of 'la dérive majeure de la nuée', the deeply significant ephemeralness and 'informality' of it all—world and word. Pursuing 'dans l'orgueil le néant de quelque forme' is not, finally, worthy of humanity. Better, infinitely, to 'atteindre à la terre brève' and to ponder the sober yet profound lessons of its (in)significance. None of this implies that beauty lacks meaning. Despite death, beauty can gather the things of the world, in time; the 'minimalness' of being can be edged towards a simple yet spectacular maximum, as with André Frénaud. But it is not the beauty of what Bonnefoy thinks of as formal 'repose', the echoing empty chamber of words as form; but rather, through the 'violence' of the written act, a beauty affording peace with the world, yet ragged, raw, dying. Language, poetry, and the beauty and happiness they can offer, are yet, in all their illuminated ephemeralness, powerfully caught up in a sense Bonnefoy never loses and cares even at the close of his vastly majestic poem to underscore, of the endless process of reincarnation and continuity that comple-

ments that of death. His poetic assent thus affirms itself of necessity 'par la vie sans fin / . . . / Par hier réincarné, ce soir, demain / Oui, ici, là, ici, là-bas encore'. The 'wave' that is at once life and language, thus obeys and mimes this logic, gathering itself, swelling into shape and fullness, spending itself, breaking and crumbling, in a continuous process of discontinuous being and becoming. 'Les mots comme le ciel, / Aujourd'hui', Bonnefoy quietly but intensely proclaims as he bids us farewell, 'quelque chose qui s'assemble, qui se disperse. / Les mots comme le ciel / Infini / Mais tout entier soudain dans la flaque brève'. Language, poetry, like the world: breathing, rhythmically pulsing, mortal. But a mortality, a flashing briefness that reach, through their endless becoming, now, beyond themselves, towards an infinity bathed in the light of passing immediacy. (pp. 130-36)

Michael Bishop, "Yves Bonnefoy," in his The Contemporary Poetry of France: Eight Studies, *Rodopi, 1985, pp. 117-36.*

Kay Boyle

1902-

American novelist, short story writer, poet, essayist, translator, and editor.

Boyle is best known for her intense psychological portraits of individuals searching for meaning and love in a chaotic, disordered world. Since the publication of her first major work of fiction, *Wedding Day and Other Stories,* in 1930, Boyle has been associated with the Lost Generation, a group of American expatriate writers in Paris whose works reflected the alienation and disillusionment experienced by many people following World War I. One of the most prolific writers of that period, Boyle experimented with fictional forms and explored the thoughts and feelings of disoriented characters, which are common features of Lost Generation fiction. Katherine Anne Porter considered Boyle one of most promising talents of her generation: "[She] sums up the salient qualities of [the Lost Generation]; a fighting spirit, freshness of feeling, curiosity, the courage of her own attitude and idiom, a violently dedicated search for the meanings and methods of art."

Born to affluent parents in St. Paul, Minnesota, Boyle was exposed to the arts at an early age. Her mother, an avid reader of fiction, often entertained her family by reading aloud passages from such classic novels as Jane Austen's *Pride and Prejudice* and Francis Hodgson Burnett's *Little Lord Fauntleroy.* From 1917 to 1919, Boyle studied architecture at the Ohio Mechanics Institute in Cincinnati. In 1922, she moved to New York City and later married Robert Brault, a French student she met while attending college. She gained employment as an assistant to Lola Ridge, editor of the literary journal *Broom,* and met such writers as Marianne Moore, John Dos Passos, and William Carlos Williams.

In the summer of 1923, Boyle travelled with her husband to northern France to visit his family. Although she intended to return to the United States, Boyle remained in Europe until 1941. While in Paris and later in England, Boyle published poetry and short stories in such magazines as *This Quarter, Forum,* and *Contact.* Boyle also met and established friendships with many of the Left Bank expatriate writers. In 1927, Boyle was asked to contribute stories to *transition,* a new avant-garde literary journal that encouraged experimental writing. Her review of William Carlos Williams's collection of essays, *In the American Grain,* and her short story, "Theme," appeared in the premiere issue of *transition.*

Boyle's early fiction is largely autobiographical, often set in France, and explores the subtle tensions between Americans and Europeans. For example, her first novel, *Plagued by the Nightingale* (1931), which is based on her interaction with her husband's family, concerns an American woman who marries a Frenchman and finds herself overwhelmed by his country's culture and customs. *Year Before Last* (1931) relates a complicated love affair between Martin, an Irish poet stricken with tuberculosis, and Hannah, a young American woman trapped in a loveless marriage. In *Gentlemen, I Address You Privately* (1933), Boyle stresses the importance of meaningful relationships, no matter how unconventional, by portraying love and betrayal between a former priest and a sailor who

deserted his post. *My Next Bride* (1934) is an expansion of Boyle's short story, "Art Colony." Loosely based on personal experience, the novel depicts a young American woman's involvement with a utopian artist colony located outside of Paris. Disdaining the commune's hypocrisy and its eccentric leader, the woman falls into a life of promiscuity until she is befriended by an American expatriate couple. This work was particularly noted for Boyle's graphic description of her heroine's back-alley abortion. Her next book, *Death of a Man* (1936), foreshadows her subsequent World War II novels in its tale of an American heiress's love for a brilliant Austrian doctor who is also a rising member of the Nazi party. *Monday Night* (1938) revolves around two men searching for a reclusive scientist, who is suspected of providing false testimony to convict innocent men.

Boyle and her family spent most of the late 1930s in flight from the threat of nazism. They lived precariously in Austria, Switzerland, France, and Spain, and witnessed the fall of France in 1940. *Primer for Combat* (1942), published a year after her return to the United States, is the first in a series of works relating to World War II. This book, which is written in diary form from the point of view of an American woman married to a French historian, explores how residents of a provincial French town cope with life under German occupation. In *Avalanche* (1944), which was first serialized in the *Saturday Evening Post,* Boyle documents the bravery of the French Resistance. The book concerns the efforts of American Fenton Ravel to find her lover, a Resistance fighter missing in action. Fenton joins the movement and helps capture a Gestapo agent. *A Frenchman Must Die* (1946), also serialized in the *Saturday Evening Post,* is set after the liberation of France in 1944 and details a former Resistance fighter's quest to bring a French aristocrat, who had collaborated with the Nazis, to justice. *1939* (1948) and *His Human Majesty* (1949) are based on the experiences of Boyle's third husband, Joseph von Franckenstein, an Austrian exile who became an American citizen and later served with the United States 87th Mountain Infantry and the Office of Strategic Services. *The Seagull on the Step* (1955) and *Generation without Farewell* (1960) document the difficulties endured by the French and Germans while rebuilding their war-torn nations. *The Underground Woman* (1975), Boyle's only novel published after 1960, is set in San Francisco and revolves around a middle-aged professor and social activist whose youngest daughter is recruited into a mysterious cult.

Boyle is also considered an accomplished poet, based on her seven collections of verse. Such early volumes as *Landscape for Wyn Henderson* (1931), *A Statement* (1932), and *A Glad Day* (1938) reveal Boyle's penchant for exploring new poetic forms as well as reflecting her mastery of more traditional verse. Her later poetry, collected in *Testament for My Students and Other Poems* (1970) and *This Is Not a Letter and Other Poems* (1985), delve into contemporary American social and political issues. Both volumes also contain personal remembrances and pieces exploring aging and death.

Boyle's short story collections share many of the thematic concerns found in her novels. The pieces in such early volumes as *Short Stories* (1929), *Wedding Day and Other Stories* (1930), and *The First Lover and Other Stories* (1933) reveal the influence of *transition*'s endorsement of such stylistic techniques as startling imagery and stream of consciousness narrative. *The White Horses of Vienna and Other Stories* (1936) and *The Smoking Mountain: Stories of Postwar Germany* (1951) complement Boyle's novels about World War II Europe. Boyle's recent collection of short fiction, *Life Being the Best and Other Stories* (1988), features individuals searching for love and meaning in their lives. In a review of this volume, Ann Hornaday summarized Boyle's accomplishments: "*Life Being the Best* gives breadth to the themes that have preoccupied Ms. Boyle throughout her career: the inviolate integrity of the human soul, the impact of external events on the most intimate of feelings, our fractured experience of love versus duty, self-respect versus hubris, social convention versus personal ethic. For 60 years, Kay Boyle's steady hand in rendering detail, authentic characterization and unequivocal moral vision has never faltered. She is still unquestionably modern."

(See also *CLC,* Vols. 1, 5, 19; *Short Story Criticism,* Vol. 5; *Contemporary Authors,* Vols. 13-16, rev. ed.; *Contemporary Authors Autobiography Series,* Vol. 1; and *Dictionary of Literary Biography,* Vols. 4, 9, 48.)

RICHARD C. CARPENTER

After twenty-five years of writing short stories and novels, Miss Boyle manages to bring to her work the same vividness, the freshness of style, the subtle insights, and the craftsmanship that marked her first writing. Several of the tales in her most recent book, **The Smoking Mountain,** are as taut and clean as those which appeared in **First Lover and Other Stories** twenty years ago and as intense in their emotional currents as her first novel, **Plagued by the Nightingale,** which was published in 1931. The stories that appear from time to time in the *New Yorker* show no diminution of ability, and the chances are that reading one will bring an absorbing experience.

Yet Kay Boyle is singularly little known. . . . Her some dozen novels and over a hundred short stories, while frequently praised and often reprinted, have not given her a wide reputation. Few people have encountered such fascinating tales as **Monday Night** or **The Bridegroom's Body,** both of them eminently worth reading. However, the fact remains that Miss Boyle has done much excellent work and should be better known.

Encouraged by her mother, she started to write early and had by the age of seventeen written "hundreds of poems, short stories, and a novel." . . . In 1931 she started a full-fledged career of writing and, following her first novel, **Plagued by the Nightingale,** brought out four novels and two collections of short stories in the next five years. **Year before Last, Gentlemen, I Address You Privately,** and **My Next Bride,** all of them concerned with the pathos of love lost through weakness or circumstance, proved that she was a very subtle analyst of personality and established (together with **First Lover and Other Stories** and **The White Horse of Vienna**) her reputation as a stylist—an exquisite manipulator of the nuances of phrase and a craftsman with image and metaphor. By 1938 it appeared that she had laid claim to this title, for the blurbs on her books announced it, and the critics in general followed suit. While they praised her stylistic ability, they did, however, regret that her situations were not more realistic and that her people lived too much in the pale light of another world. At the same time they noted her uncanny immediacy and impact, for these tales are without doubt weirdly fascinating.

That she was an expatriate, using European backgrounds and characters largely, and that she soon came to be engrossed with political and social themes also were noticed—to her irritation, for she feels that she is writing about people, not places or politics. Still, such novels as **Death of a Man,** with its sympathetic analysis of the ideas and feelings of an Austrian Nazi; **Avalanche** and **A Frenchman Must Die,** "elegant potboilers"; and the short stories of this period show a preoccupation with the effect of political turmoil and war on quite ordinary people. Probably her weakest book, **His Human Majesty** (1949), is the result of her attempt to write on such a problem, the lives and loves of ski-troops, a task eminently unsuited to her kind of fiction.

A selection from her stories of the last twenty years or so, **Thirty Stories** (1946) affords ample evidence, nevertheless, that she is more than either a stylist or a writer mesmerized by the confusions and alarums of our weary world. It becomes clear, on reading through these stories, that her twice winning the O. Henry Memorial Prize for the best short story of the year, her constant appearance in such magazines as the *New Yorker* and *Harper's Bazaar,* and the recent inclusion of her novella *The Crazy Hunter* in Ludwig and Perry's *Nine Short Novels* (in the company of James, Kafka, and Mann) have been no mere flukes and are due to more solid virtues than are comprised in style or political consciousness, good though those may be.

Of course, it is undeniable that she is an able manipulator of language. She enjoys the play of words; she has a keen eye for the striking image; and she can fascinate with the bold trenchancy of her metaphors: "Here then was April holding them up, stabbing their hearts with hawthorn, scalping them with a flexible blade of wind," or "The waves came in and out there, as indolent as ladies, gathered up their skirts in their hands, and with a murmur, came tiptoeing in across the velvet sand." Especially is it true that she can create amazingly sharp, vivid pictures: "Prince and Star were black as seals and here they stood in the white unmelting world, the two black horses steaming against the hard, bright, crusted snow. The white boughs of the trees were forked full in the woods around, and the twigs of the underbrush were tubed in glass the length of the frozen falls." (pp. 81-2)

Style is obviously integral to her work and makes it peculiarly her own; it undoubtedly helps heighten the intensity and immediacy which most readers recognize as the hallmark of Miss Boyle's writing. Dagger-sharp images and crackling metaphors do assist in raising the temperature of a story. Other qualities, however, seem to me to be more basic. First of all, a thorough acquaintance with the bulk of her work leads to an increasing appreciation of her mastery of her own kind of fictional technique. She has a most delicate touch in unfolding the lives of her characters, an exquisite sense of reticence and balance, all the while that the tale is trembling on the edge of pathos or sentimentality. Much of this effect she manages by carefully limiting the area of perception (something she may have learned from Chekhov or perhaps from Faulkner, whom she admires most highly), so that the reader becomes *aware* in the form of a gradual revelation, as do the principal characters. This contributes greatly to developing the "specification of reality," the sense of immediacy which James desired of fiction. When used, as Miss Boyle frequently does use it, with judicious foreshadowing, it creates a considerable current of tension without having much "happen" in the sense of the usual well-plotted story. We do not leisurely savor her stories but breathlessly turn pages, sure that these apparently innocuous events are somehow tremendously vital.

Beyond technique, Miss Boyle's basic themes are also productive of suspense and intensity. Her fiction world is not a happy one: she deals with disease, war, perversion, cowardice, frustration. Her people are complex souls undergoing a variety of torments, prevented either by their own weaknesses or by the devils of circumstance from living the rich and full lives which should be theirs. To make things worse, her people are not degraded but *potentially* fine and *potentially* happy. They are sensitive, courageous, artistic, profoundly emotional. We like them, usually, and would like to see them happy, but they are the beautiful and the damned. Miss Boyle achieves her characteristic force by showing us a vision of humanity in need of pity and understanding, a central idea that does not make for light reading but one which we inescapably feel as we read through her work. While probably not the end result of a reasoned philosophy, it is a telling and significant attitude toward life that makes of her writing much more than a pretty

toy or a tract. Miss Boyle is not simply *interested* in people; she is vitally *concerned* with people and profoundly moved to write about their struggles with themselves and with their dreams. She does not write just to tell a tale, to make money, to create a thing of beauty, even though these may sometimes be her motives; but, as she has said, she also writes "out of anger, out of compassion and grief . . . out of despair." (pp. 82-3)

From her earliest work we can see Miss Boyle working out this idea. *Plagued by the Nightingale* and *Year before Last* explore the relations between people whose happiness is shadowed by disease; *Gentlemen, I Address You Privately* is an analysis of perverted love. *Plagued by the Nightingale* is the story of an American girl who has married into a French family cursed with a hereditary disease which cripples the legs of the men. The conflict grows out of the insistence of the family, particularly Papa, that the young couple have a child, even though everyone knows the risk. A silent but bitter struggle, beneath the surface of an idyllic family life, is waged, with the family using the lever of promised money to weaken the son's resistance. The family loses, eventually, but the girl loses as well, for she leaves her husband, and her love, at the end. The novel is almost a parable, with Bridget and Nicholas—youth, beauty, and love—defeated by age and corruption, symbolized by the nature of the disease, a "rotting of the bone" as it is called. The corruption comes closer to home in her second novel, *Year before Last,* since Martin, the hero, is handsome, brave, sensitive, deeply in love, as well as tuberculous. He is, perhaps, a bit too much of these things and a trifle impossible, but he and his inamorata, Hannah, reiterate for us that the beautiful *are* often the damned. As we watch them flee across the south of France, with the hemorrhages becoming more frequent and deadly, we find our feeling of pity and our sense of irony steadily increasing until the inevitable death at the conclusion.

An interesting aspect of these novels is that they ought to be merely depressing instead of enthralling. However, through the poetic use of language and the method of implication and reticence, Miss Boyle lifts the story. Besides, because the reader creates the emotional tone for himself, as he gradually becomes aware of the situation, the essential tragedy is not sharply emphasized. The tale unfolds slowly, flower-like, so that we are almost able—almost, but not quite, like the characters themselves—to close our eyes on the worm i' the bud. The enervation of some of her later work is undoubtedly due to a partial abandonment of this method of implication for that of stream of consciousness and interior monologue where we are brought directly and explicitly into contact with the people's thoughts and emotions, usually in italics. In her weaker writing Miss Boyle tells us too much; in her better we float on a placid, shimmering current, all the time aware of the cold, black, rushing depths beneath.

Naturally, this method can be overdone, as it is in her third novel, *Gentlemen, I Address You Privately,* where we see everything through a glass most darkly, so much so that it is difficult to realize what the theme is. An analysis of the chiaroscuro, however, shows that all the characters are twisted in some way: the cast is composed of two homosexuals, two Lesbians, a prostitute, a fanatic, a sadist, and one fine woman starved for love. In general, love is perverted in this novel; the characters are lost souls, whirled through the darkness of their desires.

The tale comes to a flat and tasteless end, despite some tension in the last chapters, and its people are too much for us to swallow—possible perhaps, but hardly probable. Still, with all its frigidity and confusion, it somehow sticks in the mind, like a reflection in a distorting mirror, concentrating for us the pathos and irony of Miss Boyle's theme. (pp. 83-4)

Throughout Miss Boyle's writings prior to the war we can see the same techniques, the same quivering emotion held in tight leash, the concern with the interrelations of personality, the same bitter brew. Though the short stories naturally play many variations, they show the same fundamental theme, not difficult to recognize once it has been analyzed.

In some stories the problem is pride, as in **"Keep Your Pity,"** where the Wycherlys, impoverished Englishmen in the south of France, preserve appearances even beyond death. In others, such as **"The White Horses of Vienna,"** it is the pathos of prejudice and misunderstanding. The young Jewish student-doctor, who has been called in to assist the injured Austrian Nazi, ought to be able to be a friend—he and the Austrian are really much alike, the Austrian with his worship of power and the Jew with his nostalgic idealism, his memory of the royal white horses of Vienna, "the relics of pride, the still unbroken vestiges of beauty bending their knees to the empty loge of royalty where there was no royalty any more." But of course they cannot be friends.

Other stories are tales of initiation, in which an innocent or unknowing character learns evil—as in **"Black Boy,"** where a young white girl learns that she cannot have an innocent friendship with a black boy, at least not as far as her grandfather is concerned. . . . In **"Natives Don't Cry"** we see the beautifully low-keyed treatment of the real pathos in the old maid's life as the governess tries to pretend she is getting letters from her young man, when the mail was not delivered that day.

"Wedding Day," one of Miss Boyle's best, a light and delicate study of personal relations between brother and sister on her wedding day, does not force theme on our attention, but there is still the sense of loss, of youth left somewhere behind, forever. **"Count Lothar's Heart"** concerns itself with what has happened to a young man who has had a homosexual experience during the war and cannot get it out of his mind, his perversion symbolized by the swans of the Traunsee, emblems of passion. **"One of Ours"** studies through image and symbol the hidden feelings of a most proper Englishwoman who thinks a savage at an exposition is lusting after her—a projection of her desires, for he is really interested in the doll she is holding. The theme of distortion is carried out by her fascination with the savage's maleness as well as her fear of him.

It might be wondered whether or not Miss Boyle offers anything but utter blank and bitter pessimism with this constant iteration of the theme of a world out of joint. Indeed, it could be maintained that there is nothing else. A novel like *My Next Bride* (1934) leaves about as bad a taste in our mouths as anything we could find, with an American girl who deserves no evil falling into utter degradation through her love for another woman's husband. Perversely she becomes promiscuous rather than having her affair with Antony, making her pregnancy by some unknown especially fruitless. Probably the most unpleasant sequences Kay Boyle has ever written are to be found in the account of Victoria's attempts at abortion.

Yet the novel, *Monday Night* (1936), which has a protagonist who is repulsively dirty and possesses a nauseatingly mutilat-

ed ear, manages to distil something more positive from the flowers of evil. The contrast between the clean and the filthy, the innocent and the obscene, is implicit perhaps, but it is still there to provide a kind of counterpoint to the basic theme. In fact, this counterpoint may be seen running through many of her writings, indicating a corollary to the pessimism. A passage in **"Count Lothar's Heart"** symbolizes what this may be; speaking of the swans, she writes:

> Some of them had thrust the long stalks of their throats down into the deeper places before the falls and were seeking for refuse along the bottom. Nothing remained but the soft, flickering short peaks of their clean rumps and their leathery black elbows with the down blowing soft at the ebony bone. In such ecstasies of beauty were they seeking in the filth of lemon rinds and shells and garbage that had drifted down from the town, prodding the leaves and branches apart with their dark, lustful mouths.

Miss Boyle seems to be saying that the polarity between the beautiful and the ugly, the good and the bad, is central in our lives. Wilt, in *Monday Night,* disreputable and dirty, is yet a dreamer of beautiful dreams which he conveys to us in long monologues written in an incantatory style strongly reminiscent of Faulkner, who, Miss Boyle says, strongly influenced the book. Wilt ought to be a great writer, yet he is a seedy drunk. Miss Boyle is not telling us that he is going to triumph over himself; rather she is showing us that he cannot possibly do so: the fact that he and his friend never reach the goal they seek is the only logic that the underlying theme will permit the plot. Yet Wilt is somehow noble. He is giving himself to an ideal; the tale is almost an allegory, a *Pilgrim's Progress* of this modern world, where modern man fails of heaven as a goal but finds his soul in the quest itself. Here, as in other places, we can see Miss Boyle implying that devotion, integrity, and courage are the means by which we transcend our fate.

This implication is particularly evident in the tales since the war; dealing with social and political themes, they throw the contrast between what is and what ought to be into clearer light. In the backwash of a war-world, the need for undramatic devotion and integrity is particularly great. A number of tales since 1938 benefit from this larger context. There is less tendency toward attenuating the situation; the characters are often more believable, their suffering justified, their bravery less self-conscious, their defeat more real. It must be admitted that they transcend their fate but seldom. Many tales are vitiated by Miss Boyle's indiscriminate tenderness toward those who are the victims of war. Her best work in this type of writing is rather that which grows out of indignation, the failure of devotion and integrity. **"Defeat,"** which won the O. Henry Memorial Prize in 1941, shows this indignation combined effectively with tenderness, the indignation coming from the failure of the French girls to resist the German blandishments of food and dance music, the tenderness for the men who realize their country is defeated only when its women are defeated.

Her most recent book, *The Smoking Mountain,* rings the changes on Miss Boyle's preoccupation with the war: there are some good stories in it and some that strain after sentiment. She is trying to show us the atmosphere of an occupied land in which all the old hatreds still smolder under the ashes of defeat. Probably the most interesting part of the book is the long, nonfiction Introduction, the account of Germans against German in the trial of a former Gestapo brute, a new kind of venture for her and one that may lead to more significant writing. A new venture is needed; to this reader it does not seem that Miss Boyle has lost any of her ability to perceive and convey human feelings and relations, there is no slackening of her mastery of prose style, and she has certainly not turned into a shallow optimist. Yet it would be a pleasant change to see a tale not tied to particular "conditions and conflicts," as she calls them, as universal as, let us say, the novelle *The Crazy Hunter* and *The Bridegroom's Body,* tales rich in background and symbol, powerfully motivated from within the characters themselves, subtly reproducing the conflicts of personality. To my mind, these two short novels are the cream of her writing, together with such stories as **"The White Horses of Vienna," "Wedding Day,"** and **"Natives Don't Cry."** It is fortunate that [*The Crazy Hunter* has been reprinted], and it would be well if someone would do the same for *The Bridegroom's Body,* that eerie yet unforgettable re-creation of the swannery on the rain-drenched coast of England, with the magnificently vital yet tragically lonely Lady Glourie and the bitter irony of Miss Cafferty's love for her. Then more readers might be able to see that Miss Boyle not only can dazzle us with style but also can move us to a deeper understanding. (pp. 84-7)

Richard C. Carpenter, "Kay Boyle," in College English, *Vol. 15, No. 2, November, 1953, pp. 81-7.*

JAMES KELLY

If the mark of a literary style is its recognition quality then the poetic journalism of Kay Boyle must be stamped and passed. One thinks (naturally) of Rex Warner, Rumer Godden, and Katherine Anne Porter among her peers. Or of Miss Boyle's dozen novels, countless short stories, and sentient foreign dispatches for *The New Yorker* among exhibits submitted. Whether or not her new novel, *The Seagull on the Step,* comes off as planned, there is always this light-struck, beautifully articulated prose to weave a spell. Sometimes the action is without movement or excitement, like still shots from a very good camera. Sometimes the characters are more cerebral points of view than flesh and blood, partially obscured by anger or passion or message. But always, as in this novel which diagnoses the pains of postwar France through the cosmos of a tiny fishing village, the reader comes away with a sense of having been present where interesting things are going on. . . .

We pick up our story aboard a little bus racketing through the dusty roads of the vineyard country while the red-necked young driver shouts his grievances against monarchists, Europe-firsters, and American interlopers. It is a running, noisy argument involving all passengers except a teen-age American art student, Mary Farrant. She is running away from Paris and her wealthy fiancé, Peter Cornish. But her thoughts turn toward Michael Vaillant, an idealistic former *maquis* hero who has sent a plea for any representative American to come and see first hand " . . . the deeply enduring patience of France, so poorly rewarded, so heedlessly abused."

It is a crescendo of noise, cut off sharply when the bus brakes fail on a hill and nearly everybody dies except Mary and the aristocratic old widow Madame Marceau. Now the girl, separated from her past by amnesia, becomes absorbed in the life of the village. First as an object of hatred because she is identified as a rich American and suspected of causing the bus accident. And second because she becomes the center of a tug-of-war between Vaillant, representing Romance, and the horrible Dr. Angelo, representing Greed. In the smoldering background are bitter labor troubles between poverty-stricken fishermen and the crooked politicians.

Soon events begin to move even faster than the wayward bus on the hill. Michael is thrown into jail on the trumped-up charge that he had sabotaged the bus brakes. Mary falls into the hands of the evil Dr. Angelo when she rescues Marrakech, his Algerian mute, from a mauling by villagers. Saved at a Jack Dalton climax by intervention of the local curé, Mary manages to join ancient but resourceful Madame Marceau in exposing the real saboteur and murderer. But not without some eerie violence in the nearby caves and cliffs, another casualty or two, and display of dirty linen on all sides. At the end Peter Cornish and Michael engage in a friendly water joust, not for money or the tourist trade, but for Mary.

Most observers will agree that *The Seagull on the Step* does what its author intended: feelingly explain a complex situation behind the French façade and wrap it up in a presentable story. *Çela suffit.*

James Kelly, "Behind the Facade," in The Saturday Review, *New York, Vol. XXXVIII, No. 20, May 14, 1955, p. 16.*

PAUL ENGLE

This novel [*The Seagull on the Step*] differs from all others about contemporary France in that it offers a new way of lighting the bitter problem of French-American relations. For Michel Vaillant, schoolteacher of Abelin, has learned a great affection for Americans through helping American flyers to escape during the war, and has dedicated his life to diminishing the loathing so many of his countrymen feel toward the USA, and the ignorance so many of us have for France.

Everything Kay Boyle writes has fluency of prose and imaginativeness of conception. This has more of both those qualities than some others of her books. It is as if she had fired the story with all of her unique insight and devotion toward the country where she lived so long. The taste and smell and intonation of France are here, and along with them, a troubled concern for her own country. When Kay Boyle describes a harbor with the fishing boats going out, or a conversation on a bus along the Mediterranean, the cast of the net and the cast of the voice are French.

It's a wonderful story Kay Boyle tells. An American girl, studying art in Paris while keeping an eye on her boy friend in the diplomatic service, reads a letter in a newspaper. It is from a Frenchman on the south coast asking for the American flyer, with whom he walked the dangerous roads at night, to come to his village and see what he is trying to do. She cannot persuade her official friend to go, so she travels herself. The book opens with the bus taking her to the village. The driver is furiously anti-American and his steady attacks on the USA are warmly received by most of the passengers. Going down a steep hill the brakes will not work and the bus plunges over the edge.

The girl regains consciousness in a strange house with a woman who had also been on the bus. The balance of the book is the narrative of the girl's discovery of the village: of

67

Vaillant, who had written the letter; of the cripple Marrakech; of the doctor who treats her and turns out to be a poisoner; of the whole confusion and conflict between propertied and professional villagers on the one hand and fishing people on the other. Through her presence, all of the forces are activated and brought to crisis. (pp. 38-9)

Because she was on the bus at the time of its accident, the girl is blamed for it, on the ground of distracting the driver. The ultimate story of who actually did cut the brake tubes, and of the whole murderous life of the small community, is integrated with the revelation of the still powerful impacts of the war on the villagers and of the struggle for how to use American funds to aid the village. Through it, there is the gradual affection of Vaillant and the girl for each other, and the final scene in which Vaillant and Cornish act out the ancient ritual of the joust from boats, striving to knock each other into the water, in a struggle for the girl. . . .

There are two flaws. The girl is generalized "girl," a point of view toward action and others, and not an individual. And there is too much deliberate stating of abstractions, as when the girl says to Vaillant, when they meet on a cliff at night as she is escaping from the doctor, who has just shoved Marrakech over, to his death:

> This year, this moment, as you hold my shoulders,
> Vaillant, I believe that France is just beginning,
> that this is the new frontier, and everything to be
> won yet, to be discovered.

The author has put her own conviction too abruptly into the mouths of her characters.

But these are small concerns in a romantic, moving and yet immediate novel. Reading it, this reviewer wishes that the State Department, or the Fulbright authority, would send fewer respectable, uncreative, cautious professors to France, to reach a handful of academic people, and send more Kay Boyles. But that is absurd. There is only one Kay Boyle, whose elegant English, idiomatic French, imaginative energy and personal creativeness are a common glory shared by France and America. (p. 39)

> *Paul Engle, "Hope Out of France," in* The New Republic, *Vol. 132, No. 20, May 16, 1955, pp. 38-9.*

VIRGILIA PETERSON

Always a lyrical troubling writer, Kay Boyle has never written more poignantly, never come closer to absolute pitch than in this new novel, **Generation Without Farewell,** set in Germany during the American military occupation. Miss Boyle has drawn before, for a number of stories, upon her experience as foreign correspondent for *The New Yorker* in postwar Germany. In this latest book she has gone beyond the obvious ironies implicit in the attempt of the victor to establish a *modus vivendi* with the vanquished, beyond the frontiers of nationality, to probe the vulnerability of the modern soul. She does not soften or cheapen her tone by so much as a breath of sentimentality: her bitterness and her anger are as pure as her compassion. She weeps for man without condoning what he does, and in so doing, she has surpassed herself.

For some, however, **Generation Without Farewell** may not be acceptable. The villain of the tale—if Miss Boyle could create so simple a human artifact as a villain—is not a German but an arrogant American colonel. Those of us who look upon Americans as universally harmless are bound to resent and disbelieve him. With his huge shoulders, ruddy dewlaps, unquenchable thirst and instinctive menace to everything that is tentative and tender, Colonel Roberts, commander of all he surveys, is more of an enemy than any German in the book.

Miss Boyle is too truly an artist to force us to meet Colonel Roberts—or, for that matter, anyone on his staff or in his family—head on. We come to know them only through the young German newspaper reporter, called Jaeger, who is at once the narrator of the story and a participant in it, a self-constituted but all too fragile bridge between the occupied and the occupiers, between the Germans and the Americans, to neither of whom he feels he quite belongs. Two years in Colorado as prisoner of war had been enough for Jaeger to learn the American lingo, loosen the knots that regimentation and brutality had so tightly tied. Those two years had allowed buds of hope to swell for the first time; they had been enough to make him a stranger in his own land when he returned to it; but they had not been enough to make him an American.

So it is subjectively, through Jaeger's double vision, that we see the intolerably high-handed American colonel. Through him, we meet the colonel's breathtaking wife Catherine who enters Jaeger's heart like a spear; the colonel's inscrutable and impassioned 18-year-old daughter, Milly; the sycophantic lieutenant on whom the colonel has his eye as son-in-law. Through Jaeger, we evaluate a civilian man-of-good-will, Seth Honerkamp—who is the director of the local America House, dedicated to re-creating a German image for the Germans which not only they themselves but the whole world can respect. (p. 4)

Because of the darkness of the colonel's motives and those of his lieutenant and his intelligence officer, we are sometimes confused as to who shot at whom and how murderous their respective intents actually were. But we are never for a moment confused by the *leitmotif* itself, the age-old battle between principle and blood. To write about Americans and Germans in post-war Germany is still a perilous adventure—and Miss Boyle risks it unafraid. From this nettle, danger, she has plucked the flower of her truth. (p. 26)

> *Virgilia Peterson, "There Is No Armistice," in* The New York Times Book Review, *January 17, 1960, pp. 4, 26.*

MELVIN MADDOCKS

The curious thing about **Generation Without Farewell** is that it might have been a journalistic novel written in a simple, workmanlike style. Miss Boyle, who served as foreign correspondent for the *New Yorker* in Germany from 1946 to 1953, has what amounts to a report to make on a nation whose predicament she has become fascinated with, and her knowledge of her subject is visible on every page.

The strongest sense of milieu and historical perspective pervades the book. The story is set in a Bavarian town with houses in the solid burgher tradition, haunted by old Hausmeisters playing the ghost of prewar Germany. A medieval Schloss stands for an older Germany. In its stables live Lipizzaners, dainty white dancing horses that suggest all the inutilitarian graces of an extinct aristocracy, being superbly groomed at the expense of a rich businessman from Brooklyn.

Thus, through ironic scenes that are the novelist's equivalent of the journalist's anecdotes, Miss Boyle skillfully places her Germans into their topsy-turvy context—confused, dislocated people posed against a historic Protestant passion for order. A dozen planes of interplay are set up, between old Germany and new Germany, between Germans and Americans, between the American military and government department civilians.

The problems are all there, articulately and reasonably stated. But when Miss Boyle attempts to translate them into concrete dramatic terms, the novel falls apart. She has apparently been so anxious to bring feeling to her reportage that she has written in a quivering, overdecorated style. . . .

It is to Miss Boyle's credit that she has tried for more than the safety of journalism. But the particular excesses she has chosen make utterly artificial and unconvincing the platonic affair between the wife of an unfeeling American colonel and her young German tutor, which occupies the center of the stage, or the bizarre illicit love of her daughter for a horse trainer.

The colonel's obsessive hunt for a wild boar, a subplot in which Miss Boyle has amused herself with intricate symbolism, does little to give the mythic *Moby Dick* power to her story she evidently hoped for.

One cannot help feeling that an important novel has been spoiled by the kind of overwriting that runs away not only with sentences but with characters and action as well.

> *Melvin Maddocks, in a review of "Generation without Farewell," in* The Christian Science Monitor, *January 21, 1960, p. 11.*

DAVID RAY

The reader who opens Kay Boyle's [*Collected Poems*] will find a poem beginning:

> Now the time of year has come for the leaves to be burning.

And a few lines later, we have "the sumac turning," and we know that it's time to write a poem. Surely poems should leap into existence for more pressing reasons. But here we find only a projection of the poet as sentimental woods-walker, the poet as professor of friendships, as dedicator of deeply felt midnight greetings. . . .

My own preference is for poets who address beings smaller than History or America, and yet I do not doubt Miss Boyle's authority or importance (and I envy her certainty) when she addresses Carson McCullers:

> As statues take their height, their pure, unswerving
> gaze, their classic line from the chaotic clay.
>
> In days like these, when peoples in migration stage
> the allegory of racial flight,
>
> We have become articulate. When generations play
> the individual's tragedy
>
> And triumph out, then we are marvelously and
> faithfully portrayed. Shall we
>
> Despair that men we love move from the wings and
> take their part in history?

Such rhetoric moves at a level far above my head. Ironically, Miss Boyle has dedicated her book to William Carlos Williams—a poet who has moved most of his followers to admire metaphor rather than statement, the American idiom rather than an attempt at elevated rhetoric. Yet occasionally Miss Boyle achieves a lyric intensity, as in **"The Evening Grass,"** a poem about suicide. It is also true that her rhetoric justifies its claim to wisdom and finality in poems like **"The Artist Speaks."** My central objection is that her poems are largely impersonal, predictable poems about suitably poetic subjects. (p. 22)

> *David Ray, "Two Poets and Their Muses," in* The New Republic, *Vol. 147, No. 19, November 10, 1962, pp. 22-3.*

RICHARD HOWARD

Kay Boyle has added eighteen poems from the last ten years to her earlier work in verse that culminated in the long 1944 poem **"American Citizen;"** these *Collected Poems* are elusive but—as always in the poetry of a writer whose characteristic achievement is in prose—they offer a reliable thematic index to Miss Boyle's preoccupations over the years: she aspires to be, doubtless is, a good European, the kind of person who knows the right café to sit in front of, the interesting wine to order, a hard ski slope to descend, an easy man to love. Her landscapes, both American and European, are made into emblems of the wild heart, the behavior of her animals likened to the actions of men. It is not entirely fair, by the way, to refer to her "earlier work in verse", since so many of these difficult pieces are experiments in mixing verse with extended prose passages; indeed, however obscure it may be, such prose is always firmer and, if not more deeply felt, then more dramatically honed than the verse, which in even the very latest poems is without much spine or spring, though Miss Boyle has spirit and to spare. The best—and last—poem of this conjugated sort, **"A Winter Fable,"** is a startling success; following an evocation of Salzburg, the speaker switches to an anti-scene:

> . . . six old hags cast up against the wainscoting
> Of Grand Central's ladies' room . . .

These women are beguiled, as are we, by a Negro confidence-woman's cat, trained to select victims who will give money to its mistress. Here Miss Boyle's prose, with its finely-tuned dialogue and extravagant imagery, works cruelly against such matter-of-fact lines as these:

> The water ran into the basins
> The toilets flushed and
> Mrs. Morgan picked up
> The dripping mop and pushed it
> Across the floor.

I think that by such alternations, so carefully inflected, she has produced a really new form. Another poem I particularly like is the very last, **"The Evening Grass,"** a meditation on suicide that by its superb phrasing, its breathing, one might say, overcomes the lack of effective stress-pattern so noticeable in the other poems. When we hear her voice speaking just under her breath (or over it, as in certain impassioned political poems that are often more personal than her choked *intimeries*), Miss Boyle strikes the note which has sounded in her stories for so many years. Yet these poems do not define the arena of her concern distinctly enough to reveal what combats are being fought in it, and if it were not for Kay Boyle's novels and stories, I should be even more uncertain of her present focus. Yet knowing what we all know of Miss Boyle's fiction, we can readily find the values of her verse: despite the do-it-yourself punctuation, the slack and period rhythms, here is the true timbre of explicit agony, the kind of certainty-in-chaos Miss Boyle has already administered to enlarge the province of our prose. There is no odium in juxtaposing, to show the continuity of her effort, this passage from her 1938 novel *Monday Night* with one from her latest poem (1961):

> "You go to sleep now, Bernie" Wilt said half aloud, and lying here sleep the deep forgetful sleep of the child, the chasm between us as well as the claim we have on each other being that we have sought all night together the flesh of our libido, you the suckler seeking the breast, I the phantasy maker seeking through fabrication the substance of his unaltered childhood dream.

>   You ran
> The jagged staircase of your grief for all
> Who say tonight tonight tonight
> Yes LIFE tonight to liquid ears and no
> One hears it was for paintings out of frames that
> Lean on warehouse walls for all
> The lost engravings of the heart wild
> Cardiographs of lust you wept for flesh
> That did not lie upon his mouth . . .

Miss Boyle is a maker. (pp. 253-55)

> *Richard Howard, in a review of "Collected Poems,"*
> *in* Poetry, *Vol. CII, No. 4, July, 1963, pp. 253-55.*

MAXWELL GEISMAR

Kay Boyle has been one of the most elusive characters in contemporary American fiction. I say this with some feeling, because I have tried to categorize her work in every decade since the early 1930's, and each decade, it seems, I have been wrong. (p. 4)

Her major medium has always been the short story and the novelette. (And it is typical of this aristocrat, whose earlier work lay in the tradition of Edith Wharton and Henry James, not to use the fashionable word, novella.) But even here, she was in the early thirties, a writer of superior sensibility—or so I thought—using a foreign scene more successfully than her native one, and belonging, in essence, both to the expatriate line of James and Wharton and to that later "lost generation" of the 1920's.

What this new collection of Miss Boyle's short stories and novelettes [*Nothing Ever Breaks Except the Heart*] does prove is that while all of the speculation above is somewhat true, none of it is really true, or profoundly true. She has all these elements in this new collection of her mature work. But, as in the case of every first-rank writer, she rises above the disparate elements in her work or in her temperament, to become something else. What *Nothing Ever Breaks Except the Heart* proves, in short, is that Kay Boyle has at last become a major short-story writer, or a major writer in contemporary American fiction, after three decades of elusiveness, sometimes of anonymity, almost of literary "classlessness," while she has pursued and has finally discovered her true metier. It is a joy to discover such an event: not a new talent, which is rare enough, but an established and mature talent which

has developed and perfected itself—and particularly in an epoch when so many false talents are proclaimed every year.

Unlike her earlier collection of *Thirty Stories,* which was arranged chronologically—and that earlier volume is fascinating now to read over and to compare with the present one—*Nothing Ever Breaks Except the Heart* is arranged topically: "Peace," "War Years" and "Military Occupation." And perhaps one should add, in the selfish concern of pure art, that nothing better could have happened for Kay Boyle than World War II and the periods of military occupation, by the German and then the Allied forces. For even in the present volume, the first section, "Peace," is less effective than the remainder of the book—and still Kay Boyle is less effective about the American than she is about the European scene. When it comes to a story like **"Anschluss,"** dealing with a world-weary Parisian fashion-writer and a marvelously gay brother and sister in a dying Austria, she is superb. (pp. 4, 16)

In Miss Boyle's writing, there has always been a traditional sense of character—romantic, pagan at heart and best exemplified in her heroines rather than her heroes—but the European *Walpurgisnacht* of the late thirties gave her a dramatic social background that she could hardly afford to ignore. Thus, too, in her first novel, *Plagued by the Nightingale,* first published in 1931 and just recently reissued, the central theme was of an ingrown and diseased French bourgeois family, of an American heroine's struggle against this family. . . .

The style, too, of her first novel is more precious, studied and "literary" than her present, apparently more prosaic, and truly more beautiful style. As late as 1938, she could still turn out such a mediocre novel as *Monday Night,* a picaresque mystery, still about that "family romance" which any true novelist must have in his bones, but which, in itself, is never enough. Perhaps it was only with *Primer for Combat,* in 1942—which is curiously close to the place and theme of the **"Anschluss"** story—that the *larger* European scene of social and moral disintegration and corruption appeared so firmly and so incisively and so brilliantly. And it was in *Generation Without Farewell* (1960) that she added the American Occupation Forces to her Nazi conquerors, in order to prove that human debasement—the evil soul, the vicious soul, the lost soul—can be a matter of social circumstance rather than of national origins.

Indeed, in *Nothing Ever Breaks Except the Heart,* it is a toss-up as to who the true villains are, Germans or Americans or just plain Occupiers—while the heroes, to Miss Boyle, are those who have been conquered and occupied, those who have resisted, those who have put to the acid test their property, their career and their lives. To her earlier vision of sensibility, she has added what every first-rate writer must have, a standard of human morality—and the fact that human morality is usually, if not always, related to a specific social or historical context.

It is this familiar concept missing in so much current and "new" American fiction, that is embodied in the magnificent stories of her maturity. . . . ["**Nothing Ever Breaks Except the Heart**"] is another beauty: a Hemingway tale, so to speak, (about a pilot who is finished) but produced by an intensely feminine talent, and with an anti-Hemingway moral. (By this I mean anti-late-Hemingway, when all that remained in him was the killer pitted against a hostile, menacing universe.)

What is so remarkable in these late tales of Kay Boyle, by contrast, is the increased sense of sympathy in them for all the losers, all the defeated persons and peoples of contemporary history.

Here again, an earlier sense of nostalgia in her work has become an intense sense of compassion. I don't pretend to know the secrets of this fine craftsman, but I do realize how many of these stories leave you on the brink of tears. And a world in tears; since Kay Boyle has become the American writer to express the texture of European life after Chamberlain and Daladier and Munich.

There is still a final phase of writing in *Nothing Ever Breaks Except the Heart*, still another epoch of our modern history: the period of the Occupation, the black market and the reappearance of the same old people, asking for privilege and power and "deals" all over again, after the heroism, the gallantry, the selflessness of the liberation battle. No wonder that the last one of these stories describes an American State Department official returning to a McCarthyite America—ironic sequel to the war for European freedom. And no wonder that the last of these beautiful tales describes an American mother, who agrees with "a terrified race"—the French peasants of the atomic age. " 'I am American,' she said to that unseen presence of people in the silent room, 'and the wrong voices have spoken out for me, and spoken loudly, and I too, I too, am terribly afraid.' " (p. 16)

> Maxwell Geismar, "Aristocrat of the Short Story," in The New York Times Book Review, *July 10, 1966, pp. 4, 16.*

THEODORE L. GROSS

Kay Boyle reveals in [*Nothing Ever Breaks Except the Heart*] the wisdom and humility, the anger and the passion of a thoughtful woman who looks back upon this generation with something like tender discontent and discovers that in spite of all her chastening experiences she is, after all, an American sharing the fate of her own country.

The book's title suggests Miss Boyle's humanistic point of view; the contents—divided into rubrics of "Peace," "War Years," and "Military Occupation"—indicate her intention to measure historically the central issues of our time.

Set in the United States, the first group of stories deals with various kinds of victims—usually children but often people with childlike sensibilities. Confronting a bleak urban life that threatens to twist their innocence into bitter skepticism, their love into hatred, they survive only because of some other sensitive individual's response. In **"Seven Say You Can Hear Corn Grow"** the idealistic son of a tired waitress comes upon a drunken man lying like a dead child on Christopher Street in New York. Crouched beside the derelict, trying to pull him out of danger from the traffic, is a vagrant girl, who proves as cynical as the young man's mother. The author subtly suggests the need for belief, for pity, for hope in a time when these human attributes tend to be characterized as merely sentimental or quixotic.

The theme of the stories in the "Peace" section—the need for compassion—is always clear. The technique, however, is often intricate and indirect, symbolic and allusive, implying more than is stated. Miss Boyle informs her work with an air of calculated haste, as if peace is always being threatened—by

mechanistic forces, by impending war, by all that threatens to injure human love. . . .

In the second section—"War Years"—we see an American woman's romance wither because her Austrian lover has welcomed the rise of Hitler; we share the loneliness of a Frenchman as he learns of his country's defeat; we feel the awkward alliances that exist between a British colonel and distrustful Italian partisans. We are haunted by the portrait in [**"Nothing Ever Breaks Except the Heart"**] of frightened refugees, none of whom realizes that the ex–pilot who might take them to their destination suffers from shattered nerves, his heart broken despite his ostensible self-control. Miss Boyle, who always measures war in terms of its effect on the human sensibility, is extraordinarily deft in creating its macabre, neurasthenic ambience. . . .

The last story, **"Fire in the Vineyards,"** is a coda to the entire volume, for it glances at devastated postwar France and measures the prosperous Germans, the poor English, the Americans who are "not afraid of what may happen" to Europe and who read the signs "U.S. Go Home" or *"Les Américains en Amérique."* Miss Boyle is fully aware of and at times sympathetic to the anti-Americanism of the French; she too reviles the arrogance of the G.I. away from home who tells the French that "France never did nothing but sit on a corner holding a tin cup out, and we're sick of dropping the dollars in." But she realizes that to be an American is to suffer, in Henry James's words, "a complex fate."

Kay Boyle has created a large and impressive body of literature over a forty-year period. She has been a novelist and foreign correspondent, a poet and a translator, a lecturer, educator, and children's storyteller. But her real contribution to American letters is in the form of the short story. Unlike Hemingway or Faulkner, she has no unique vision. Nor is her technique so individual that she modifies the tradition of the short story that precedes her. Although most effective when she is least specific, Miss Boyle is at times unnecessarily opaque. And, more rarely, her intense emotion can sweeten into sentimentality. But her best work has undeniable authority; stories like **"Wedding Day," "The White Horses of Vienna,"** and **"White as Snow"** are already minor classics, artistic records of what life was like in the age of Hitler. This new collection demonstrates that she is one of the few living American artists who have seriously examined the effect of the Second World War upon Europeans and upon Americans in Europe.

Nothing Ever Breaks Except the Heart can only enhance Kay Boyle's reputation.

> Theodore L. Gross, "Where Have All the Children Gone?" in Saturday Review, *Vol. XLIX, No. 29, July 16, 1966, p. 35.*

ROBERTS W. FRENCH

Reading through [Kay Boyle's *Testament for My Students, 1968-1969, and Other Poems*], one learns of students beaten by police, of children burned in Vietnam, of Black Power, of the persecution of the Jews, of the murder of three civil rights workers in Mississippi. The earlier poems are not so topical but, like many of her colleagues, Miss Boyle has been drawn into the front ranks. Her sympathies are clear: she is with the students, the blacks, the suffering Vietnamese, "the outcast, the hungry, the condemned." It is with such as these that she talks in her poems, and for such that the poems were written. (pp. 695-96)

For Kay Boyle the dominant movement has been outward rather than inward. Seldom does she appear in isolation, for most of her poems reveal a speaker establishing a relationship with someone else. Significantly, seventeen of the twenty-eight poems in her book are poems either "to" or "for" someone, and most of them speak directly to another person:

> Each year you came jogging or loping down that
>   hall . . .
> You said it all, everything,
> A long time before anyone else knew
> How to say it.
> Your sentences cast print and paper to the
>   winds . . .
> I wish you triumphs that are yours already . . .
> I offer you a heart of red isinglass outlined in tinsel.

Characteristically, Kay Boyle's poems develop out of responses to the words or deeds of the person addressed, and one senses behind them the generating force of an urgent moral and emotional compulsion. (p. 696)

Although her book contains poems dating back to 1925, there is not a rhymed poem in it. In general, her poems are written in long, variable lines that threaten to break into prose, and sometimes do; but, as Eliot said in "East Coker," the poetry does not matter. Miss Boyle's title poem, for example, is aptly titled **"Testament for my Students"** rather than, say, "Poem for my Students," since the idea of a *testament*—a statement of belief—is more important than the idea of a *poem*. The point of the thing is praise, and the objects of praise are the students, "sweet emissaries from Arizona/Montana, Illinois, Mass.," beautiful, fragile, perched precariously upon the times:

> At your temples pools of blood always trembled
> And I would see them spill.

"You were not afraid of death," Miss Boyle tells her students, and she has seen them beaten down, gassed, clubbed.

And only they can answer her question:

> What good were the poets to you then, Baudelaire, Whit-
>   man
> Rimbaud, Poe? "All the good in the world!" you shouted
>   out
> Through the blood in your mouths. They were there be-
>   side you on
> The campus grass, Shakespeare, Rilke, Bronte, Radiguet
> Yeats, Apollinaire, their fingers on the pulse in your wrists
> Their young arms cradling your bones.
>   (pp. 696, 698)

[At] her best, she awakens us not to memory, but to realization of that which is before our eyes. (p. 698)

Roberts W. French, "'I' Poems and 'You' Poems," in The Nation, *New York, Vol. 210, No. 22, June 8, 1970, pp. 695-96, 698.*

CHAD WALSH

The one time I saw Kay Boyle was almost two years ago, in an overcrowded San Francisco church where a phalanx of Bay area poets had assembled to read their verse, commend the strike at San Francisco State, and denounce Dr. Hayakawa. Miss Boyle's new book [*Testament for My Students, 1968-1969, and Other Poems*] recaptures the heady mood of that occasion.

Miss Boyle writes out of a generous heart, with a total commitment to the young, the radical, the dark-skinned. The world of this book is divided into good guys and bad guys. It is a moving collection of poetry; only afterward does the reader wonder whether things were quite that clear-cut. Robert Frost's distinction also comes to mind. Griefs make good poetry; grievances are harder to transmute into enduring verse. Yeats's "Easter, 1916," renders grief eternal. Miss Boyle's book will age, as time sadly reveals other and different oppressions, and the inflated rhetoric of many lines becomes evident. But though it is not immortal poetry, *Testament for My Students* captures perhaps for all time the mood and moral tone of a significant moment in history, and will be quoted by researchers as they try to penetrate into the nuances of that desperate year, 1968.

Chad Walsh, "Generous Hopes, and Living without Illusion," in Book World—The Washington Post, *November 15, 1970, p. 6.*

KAY BOYLE [INTERVIEW WITH DAVID R. MESHER]

In a career which spans the last half-century, Kay Boyle has published more than thirty volumes of poetry, fiction, and non-fiction. Her writings and their author are known for uncompromising integrity and intensity. Boyle's life has often been lived against a background of headlines, literary and otherwise. She was one of the Americans in Paris in the 1920's and 1930's, and knew many of the expatriate writers. She lived in Austria before the Anschluss, in England from 1936 to 1937, and then in France during the German occupation. In 1941, Boyle returned to America for the first time since leaving in 1922. After the war, she lived in the U.S. zone of occupied Germany with her third husband, the Baron Joseph von Franckenstein. . . . Franckenstein's responsibilities as an American diplomat included working to ensure that no former Nazis regained professional positions in the new Federal Republic. With the purblind logic of McCarthyism, such anti-Nazism became translated into pro-Communism; even after an inquiry had cleared him, Franckenstein was blacklisted and lost his job. The couple spent nine years labouring to clear their names. After their "rehabilitation," Franckenstein was appointed cultural attaché at the U.S. Embassy in Teheran, where Boyle joined him briefly before his death in 1963. That same year, she began to teach at San Francisco State, remaining there for seventeen years until she retired in 1980, and taking a major part in movements and protests from the four months' picket line during S. I. Hayakawa's SFSU presidency, to the Indian occupation of Alcatraz and anti-war activities throughout the Vietnam era. (pp. 82-3)

[Mesher]: *Did you get to know many of the other American expatriates, like Hemingway and Fitzgerald?*

[Boyle]: For what may seem a very silly reason, I refused to meet Hemingway. Fitzgerald I never did meet (in Paris). I met him in New York when I was a teen-ager. When his first book came out and he was signing it at Columbia, and I was taking a course at Columbia. Then, in his last years when he was an editor at some publishing house, he wrote to me for manuscripts of young people in Paris. A very, very touching letter, making one realize he was a completely broken man. (pp. 89-90)

Did any of these expatriates have a great influence on your own writing? What were the influences you were most conscious of?

I know Faulkner influenced me, but that was long after the Paris days. I don't think I could ever have written *Monday Night* if I hadn't read *Pylon*. And D. H. Lawrence, of course, in several of my short stories. But certainly not Hemingway. But as I said, maybe to you but I've certainly said it elsewhere, there could never have been a Hemingway without Gertrude Stein and Sherwood Anderson. He took everything from them. And then he wrote *The Torrents of Spring*, an unforgivable betrayal of Anderson, who had done much to help him. He was a betrayer as well of Gertrude Stein.

In retrospect, then, you don't think the years in Paris were such a glorious period for the expatriates.

I feel very strongly about this myth that has grown up. I may have mentioned this to you before, but I think it's because people want to believe that sometime, somewhere, there was something that was really wonderful happening. But it wasn't: there were suicides, there was poverty, there was drunkenness. And all the writers really lived outside Paris, and came in now and then. Look at Hart Crane's life—my God! That led to suicide in the end.

I've got a wonderful lecture of Nelson Algren's which I use in my courses here [at Eastern Washington University], a lecture he gave in the last years of his life. In it he stresses the tragedy of so many of the famous American male writers. You know, French writers don't crack up. German writers don't crack up. But look at Fitzgerald, look at Hemingway, look at all of these gifted people who cracked up in one way or another. I don't know whether it's the pressures—Nelson puts it on the pressures of American life, the publishers' demands, and the public's demands. This demand to *know* the writer is so terrible. Is it because the European writers live a different kind of life? Or because American writers feel, they are persuaded, that they must play a public role?

Katherine Anne Porter was so unhappy writing *Ship of Fools*. She would write me a lot of desperate letters saying, "How did I get into this terrible thing? I can't bear it, I can't stand it." But she was pressured by the publishers. And I think that's what happens to our American writers. (pp. 90-1)

[Many] *of your early stories were published in* transition, *so I assume you subscribed then to one of the mottoes of that journal: "The writer expresses; he does not communicate." Do you still believe that?*

No. . . . I can see what I meant then, but I certainly don't mean it now. Rimbaud was my idol, and in many ways he still is—he was a revolutionary, a rebel, obviously, but doing it in his own way, not in any political way. No, I've changed. I don't think now that "the plain reader" should be "damned." I think I do write to communicate.

It's very different, as you undoubtedly know, in the context of the European approach to these things. I mean, every European writer is political. And not every American writer is. And I think we were saying that the writer does not communicate, at the same time realizing that politics played a great part in our lives and in our writing. . . . Everybody's on trial every minute of his life. I feel very strongly now that you've got to express your convictions *and* communicate them at the same time.

Do you think your writing has received the attention it merits? I ask this, in part, because of the cover that was used when **Monday Night** *(which I read somewhere you consider your best novel) was reprinted in 1977. The cover was a photograph of a letter to you from Dylan Thomas, where he says, among other things, "I realised that I'd been wanting to write to you for a long time, without knowing your address. Ever since you published* **Monday Night.** *I thought that was a very grand book, indeed, and I wrote a review of it—a meagre little one, it had to be—which I do hope you saw. This is a fan letter. You haven't got a greater admirer than me." It just seemed to me a bit of uncharacteristic self-promotion, the use of that letter.*

I did not know this letter was to be used until I received a copy of the book. This was the publisher's decision. I've never known a publisher who would allow an author to decide about the dust-jacket of his book. . . . I don't get seriously irritated, but I do get a little bit annoyed when people say (that I haven't received the attention I've deserved), as Margaret Atwood says in her introduction (to a new edition of **Three Short Novels**). It really makes me squirm. I've had all the attention that I like and want. I feel I have the respect of most of my contemporaries in the writing world, and that's the thing that matters. Now I did write one book that had a terrific sale. The U.S. Armed Forces bought 250,000 copies of **Avalanche.** I came back (to the United States during the war) and I was horrified to hear people say that France "had laid down on the job." I'd been there and I knew the Resistance was beginning. And (**Avalanche**) sold to the movies (though it was never produced). And I meet today, in the past ten years or so, Air Force pilots who had to read that book before they flew over France, so if they had to parachute or if they were shot down, they would know what the various political issues were. So I made a terrific amount of money out of that, and everyone thought I was going to be a very popular writer for the rest of my life. But (in **Avalanche**) I did compromise, in that I wrote the book in a more direct way because I wanted to get the message across. I wanted "the plain reader" to understand. I wanted the American public to realize what was going on in France. But I did not compromise to the extent of saying anything that I didn't believe.

Well, let me ask it another way. American women have often been recognized as great short story writers, but rarely as great novelists. You've written more than a dozen novels, as well as several volumes of poetry and non-fiction, yet you are most widely considered a short story writer. Do you think your novels have been slighted? And why do you think American women have received so much more attention for their stories than for their longer fiction?

Actually, I would prefer to be known as a poet, but I'm afraid it's a vain hope. . . . I can't talk about why other people's, other women's novels have been slighted, and I'm not sure it's true. But I know exactly why mine have been. I remedied that in *Monday Night.* That awful figure of the American woman does not appear in that book, and that's very good. I think that's what really condemned all my other novels. I don't like the first-person singular. I don't like to read it and I don't like to write it. Except for a very few exceptions. But I was more or less doing the first-person singular in all my novels, with this American woman who was always, I'm afraid, rather virtuous and always a very noble creature—and that's not good writing, not authentic writing. Now, in *Monday Night* I got away from that woman, and that's why I'm satisfied with it. . . . In the short stories I get away completely from that American woman. No first-person, I don't think there are any first-person stories, and that's all to the good. (pp. 91-3)

Kay Boyle and David R. Mesher, in an interview in
The Malahat Review, *No. 65, July, 1983, pp. 82-95.*

ROBERT W. SMITH

Few Americans have written so beautifully of the human condition with love and courage as Kay Boyle. [*Words That Must Somehow Be Said,* a] collection of 25 essays, reviews and memoirs spanning over 50 years wonderfully catches her career as a writer and social activist. . . .

She knew many of the world's important writers, a familiarity that produces evocative prose. She is exceptionally good on down-and-outers and misfits like E. Carnevali, dying bravely of life and sleeping sickness, killing the promise of a new literature that William Carlos Williams saw in him; Katherine Mansfield, unable to connect with the life outside; and Edward Dahlberg, author of the minor classic *Because I Was Flesh,* for whom a book is "a battle of the soul and not a war of words." . . .

These selections show a heart and head at work. Here is the preface to *The Smoking Mountain,* in which she writes of H. Baab, that small-time Eichmann, who is indicted in 1950 for indirect involvement in 56 murders. A brute who thought he'd beat the rap because of German resistance to the Allied denazification campaign after World War II, Baab is found guilty when his victims and their relatives and friends doom him in a Frankfurt courtroom. In other selections, she writes of trying to block cops from entering the San Francisco State campus during the 1968 disorders, telling them, "This campus belongs to the faculty and students, not to the police"; of spending 21 days in prison for sitting down in a doorway of the Oakland Induction Center; and of joining the American Indian encampment on Alcatraz in 1970. And she speaks out against the shah's imprisonment of 4,000 Iranian women (**"Sisters of the Princess"**) and surveys San Francisco morticians as they pretty up American corpses from Vietnam for the folks back home. (One tells her, "We feel we owe it to the boy's family that he goes home looking just as good as he did when he went away—and sometimes even better.")

In **"The Triumph of Principles,"** she gives us words to take away with us, words as contemporary as the weather report—and a good deal more important. Here, in dealing with the duty of the writer to speak out on current problems, she quotes George Kennan on ridding ourselves of nukes, Stuart Chase ("It is no longer a question of defending one's home by defending one's nation. Now it is only by defending all mankind that one can save his country"), and Chester Bowles ("the Bill of Rights might not be voted today because too few of us understand the need to protect the freedom of those with whom we disagree").

An old Irish prayer goes, "God says take what you want—but pay for what you take." Kay Boyle chose her portion of life fully aware of the cost. None of it, she'd say, was courageous—it was simply the thing one had to do at the time. Had she truckled to the establishment and not made waves, her literary reputation doubtless would have been enhanced. But this endearing writer will always be too busy to care about that.

Robert W. Smith, "Kay Boyle: From the Left Bank to the New Left," in Book World—The Washington Post, *July 14, 1985, p. 10.*

HUGH FORD

[*Words That Must Somehow Be Said*] brings together 25 essays, reviews and prefaces composed over six decades but mostly between the mid-1940's and the late 70's. Many appeared in *The Nation* and *The New Republic,* journals that accepted the writer's work when others didn't. As a supplement to her *Fifty Stories* (1980), *Words That Must Somehow Be Said* is invaluable. It is also a welcome confirmation of Miss Boyle's prolific and variegated career. . . .

Many of the essays in the present volume afford unfaded, disturbing glimpses into our country's traumatic past and Miss Boyle's impassioned concerns, from the McCarthyism epidemic to the Vietnam War protests and the Attica prison riots. There is much autobiography here too, and a portrait emerges of the author as a bold and articulate defender of civil liberties and humane treatment of the neglected and defenseless. . . .

In the first essay, **"The Family,"** we get a sense of the writer's ancestry. Affectionately described are a general in Washington's army, a frontier doctor, a Kansas schoolteacher, an aunt who drew cartoons for the National Woman's Party and the author's mother, a stalwart and independent woman who had a profound influence on her daughter. From them Miss Boyle claims her pioneering spirit and devotion to free inquiry. In some evocative passages, they are revealed as moral touchstones guiding her deliberations.

The essays under the heading "On Writers and Writing" include early reviews of works by William Carlos Williams and Hart Crane (both appeared in *transition* magazine in the late 1920's). She celebrates Williams's essays in *In the American Grain* as an authentic rendering of America, unencumbered by inheritance, an original depiction grounded in "chastity of fact." She dismisses Crane's poems in *White Buildings,* however, as empty and dull, lacking the raw substance of life. In Katherine Mansfield's stories she discerns an "inadequacy to see in any other terms the things she sensed so acutely," but in William Faulkner's 1938 novel, *The Unvanquished,* she finds consummate skill and vision to effect both a personal and national passage out of violence. . . .

Doubtless the imperatives she issued in **"A Declaration for 1955"** after she had borne the contumely of McCarthyism were reactions to the time, but her insistence that authors must not just speak their beliefs but also defend them, devoting themselves to altering society according to the "higher standards" of the individual, remains compelling. Among those who met the challenge to speak the "words that must somehow be said" she cites Dylan Thomas, Edward Dahlberg and James Baldwin.

In the book's final section, "On the Human Condition," Miss Boyle addresses the tragedy of this century: genocide. In a 1945 essay, she excoriates the beggarly conduct of André Gide, Sacha Guitry and Maurice Chevalier, who, during the Occupation, stood by while 11,000 Jews were incarcerated and deported. In 1949 she writes of two women traveling on the same train to Frankfurt. One is a civilian War Department employee who assuages her hatred of Germany ("a leper's colony") by spending weekends in Paris. The other is a German refugee, a Jew, who sustained herself in exile by remembering the words of Goethe: "freedom and life are deserved only by those who conquer them anew each day." . . .

Her account of the trial of Heinrich Baab, a former Gestapo official accused of participating in over 50 murders, offers harrowing testimony about the difficulties facing a nation of bewildered and divided people. When a German jury finds Baab guilty and a German judge sentences him to hard labor for life, a young court guard Miss Boyle had noticed during the trial turns toward the press bench, his face "as clear as light with vindicated pride." "Until there has been a national upheaval, a cleaning of our house by our own hands," a German friend told the author, "the twilight will remain." . . .

If Kay Boyle defines the human condition in terms of war and its aftermath—the suffering and extinction of multitudes, violations of human dignity by totalitarian and democratic nations and relentless preparations for conflict under the guise of security—it is not because she has lost faith that man can prevail but because she believes he will. With the abolitionist John Brown, she holds that "a minority convinced of its rights, based on moral principles will, under a republican government, sooner or later become the majority." As this collection impressively attests, Kay Boyle has spent a lifetime speaking for the voiceless and acting for the inactive in pursuit of that goal.

> *Hugh Ford, "60 Years of Passion and Compassion," in* The New York Times Book Review, *August 25, 1985, p. 20.*

women in Iran, written in 1976, should be followed by one on Vietnam written in 1967. Some items are thin and hardly worth including, such as a review (written in 1942) of four of Elizabeth Bowen's novels and *Bowen's Court* in which she reproves the writer for "restraint" and "unreality", or a sentimental glimpse of Dylan Thomas in a Fitzrovia pub, tenuously linking him to the cause of intellectual freedom in America in the 1950s. Both Boyle's sentiments and her prose can seem overheated.

Sometimes, however, the good causes coincide with good writing and the effect is exhilarating. Boyle's account of a spell in prison in 1968 (she was arrested during a protest against the Vietnam war) is excellent, as is an earlier report on the trial of a war criminal in a provincial town in Germany. Best of all is an ironic, simple and moving description of the arrival of refrigerated coffins from Saigon at Travis Air Force base near San Francisco. "We feel we owe it to the boy's family that he goes home looking just as good as he did when he went away—and sometimes even better," she was told by an embalming assistant.

Boyle, whose fiction is largely autobiographical, has perhaps always been more naturally gifted as a reporter than as a novelist. She will probably soon be established as a heroine by younger radicals and feminists. She deserves celebration, for her indomitable spirit and for the tradition she upholds: the radical intellectual streak in American culture, now unfashionable, which holds that dissent on grounds of conscience is not anti-American but essentially American.

> *Anne Chisholm, "Virtues of Dissent," in* The Times Literary Supplement, *No. 4304, September 27, 1985, p. 1076.*

ANNE CHISHOLM

The American novelist and reporter Kay Boyle, now in her eighties, has long held an exalted view of the writer's role in society. Since the 1920s she has produced over twenty books of fiction (including **The White Horses of Vienna, Avalanche,** and **Plagued By The Nightingale**) and together with Robert MacAlmon, a well-known book of memoirs, **Being Geniuses Together,** while simultaneously writing literary and social criticism, teaching and generally stirring up the American conscience. "It is always the writers", she announces in one of the pieces reprinted in this first collection of her non-fiction writings, [**Words That Must Somehow Be Said**], "who must bear the full weight of moral responsibility . . . we considered ourselves a portion of the contemporary conscience, and we had no pity on the compromiser or the poor in spirit of our time". Not for her what Orwell called the moral effort of objectivity.

This collection of her writings is both annoying and, in the end, impressive. The introduction, by the editor, Elizabeth Bell, is short on facts and too free with tributes. It is exaggerated to claim that Kay Boyle has been "in the forefront of this century's major cultural and political movements" and irritating to be assured that she had "an unswerving dedication to reflecting in her work life as she perceived it" (as opposed, no doubt, to how she did not). The selection and ordering of the pieces is confusing; the three main sections, **"On Writers and Writing", "On the Body Politic"** and **"On The Human Condition",** contain overlapping and repetitious material. It is hard to see, for example, why a piece on the plight of

DAVID DWYER

Through a long career, into this "age of specialization," Kay Boyle has paid the price for being too good at too many things. (p. 22)

[It] is safe to say that recent generations of American readers and writers are most likely to know her, if at all, as the coauthor of **Being Geniuses Together.**

This memoir of Paris in the '20s deserves its high repute. In the currently available edition, it is Boyle's 1968 revision of the story her late husband Robert McAlmon first told in 1938. As such, it provides an engrossing and much-needed counter-weight to the masculinist view of what was going on in English literature back then, the view enshrined in such works as Hemingway's *A Moveable Feast.*

But Boyle's other writing deserves to be far better known among those who love to hear words used, as Blake says, with "passion and imagination." The poems in **This Is Not A Letter,** written over the last twenty-some years, provide as good an introduction as we could hope for to her large and various body of work, and one of the best of them is brief enough to quote in full:

"Advice To the Old (including myself)"

> Do not speak of yourself (for God's sake) even
>   when asked.
> Do not dwell on other times as different from the
>   time

Whose air we breath; or recall books with broken
   spines
Whose titles died with the old dreams. Do not re-
   sort to
An alphabet of gnarled pain, but speak of the lark's
   wing
Unbroken, still fluent as the tongue. Call out the
   names of stars
Until their metal clangs in the enormous dark.
   Yodel your way
Through fields where the dew weeps, but not you,
   not you.
Have no communion with despair; and, at the end,
Take the old fury in your empty arms, sever its
   veins,
And bear it fiercely, fiercely to the wild beast's lair.

The sure-footed sprung hexameters of this fine poem, at once well-wrought and easy sounding, are typical of Boyle's verse. But it would be a disservice to her to suggest that this brief, more-or-less personal poem defines her range.

On the contrary, Kay Boyle has always been the kind of writer that used to be called *engagé,* writing (and marching) not just for good art but for social justice, concerned as much for the future as for the past. Much of the poetry in **This Is Not A Letter** concerns itself with such issues as contemporary Fascism (**"A Poem for the Students of Greece"**) and the forced relocation of American Indians (**"A Poem for the Teesto Diné of Arizona"**). Yet she never descends to mere rant, the curse of much well-intentioned literary protest; at its most political, Boyle's speech is nonetheless poetic. . . . (pp. 22-3)

Those fortunate enough to be familiar with her work will need no recommendation to seek out **This Is Not A Letter,** but I hope that this little book may win Kay Boyle some new readers, and that they will be led by it back to some of her earlier work. Either **Thirty Stories** or **Fifty Stories** would make a good next step. And, for a glimpse of her lighter side, I'd suggest a wartime thriller, **Avalanche.** It's not high art, but it's lots of fun—"a tale of danger and courage . . . a richly emotional love story," as the blurbs said. (p. 23)

> David Dwyer, " 'Take the Old Fury in Your Empty Arms . . .'," in The American Book Review, Vol. 8, No. 6, November-December, 1986, pp. 22-3.

RACHEL HADAS

The characteristic ploy throughout Kay Boyle's collection **This Is Not a Letter** is definition through denial. It's programmatic that her poems, through apparently often addressed to particular recipients, transcend the selfish decorum of the epistle. Boyle deftly weaves the voices, even apparently the exact words, of others into her lines without lapsing into privatism or obscurity. . . . (p. 220)

She can be imperious and obsessive, hammering home her negatives—until we remember that what she is negating is negation, and that an effective way to name something is to refuse repeatedly to name it. **"Excerpts from A Poem for Samuel Beckett"** is an extended refusal of this sort:

> I'll not discuss death with you by any name, however gently, soberly, you ask.
> When the spectacle of it comes downstage. . . .
>   [t]hen are we authorized to dance . . .
>   suffered to sing,

> But not with the voice of mourning dove in the tearful willow grieving,
> *"Seul, pas seul. Seul, pas seul,"* but between strophes preening, grooming,
> The few remaining feathers of our iridescence, lovely they were—but stop the music!
> No past tense permitted either here or there.

"Poets, remember your skeletons. In youth or dotage, / remain as light as ashes," admonishes Boyle in **"Poets"**; the soul *ought* to be as insubstantial as that tattered coat upon a stick, as long as it's also elegant and active. The sense of unencumbered bones, of burdens carried with all possible lightness, clearly informs Boyle's emotional style. The refusal to mourn comes down to a kind of etiquette everywhere in the book, but most pointedly in **"Advice to the Old (including myself)"**:

> Do not speak of yourself (for God's sake) even when asked.
> Do not dwell on other times as different from the time
> Whose air we breathe; or recall books with broken spines
> Whose titles died with the old dreams. Do not resort to
> An alphabet of gnarled pain, but speak of the lark's wing
> Unbroken, still fluent as the tongue.

There's no point in debating the moral value of such advice, intriguing as it might be to envision those lines framed on the wall of a nursing home. The question is, rather, whether Boyle's austerities, when followed through, enrich or impoverish her poems; and I find it's striking to what extent she manages to follow her own advice, to mourn or lament only by indirection.

Boyle fears flabbiness in her verse as one surmises she does in her person; and the book as a whole is both beautifully designed and bracingly lean. Despite the prevailing poetic (and perhaps intelligent editing), however, it has to be said that a certain single-mindedness—or, more unkindly, monotony—characterizes this collection. I imagine this limitation has less to do with Boyle's age (she is now eighty-five) than with the fact that she has always been primarily a prose writer and hence probably turns to poetry only for certain kinds of utterance. It is fortunate for her and for us that her talents as an elegist ("This is *not* an elegy," I can hear her interrupting) are blossoming now; we always need poems that face death. The following excerpt from the Beckett poem refers to Pueblo precepts; I was reminded as well of the Niobe passage in the last book of the *Iliad*. Whatever her sources, Boyle makes the material her own, with her characteristically long, loose lines and special blend of doughtiness and sublimity:

> The Pueblo knows harm is done when guests feast, drink and cry aloud at a funeral,
> For the priest warns of the hazards if the living mourn over long
> Or with excessive lamentation. "As the axe splinters the live tree," he says,
> "So the ritual of the hours is sundered by grief. To weep while fires
> Go unlit is to question the cycle of the seasons. It is blasphemous
> To ask winter to bear guilt for its failure to be spring. Long bewailing,"
> He says to the bereaved, "detains the spirits when they seek to go.
> Hasten now to sprinkle the road out of the village so that the dust
> Lies quiet under their departing feet.

. . . Clear the treachery of dusk
From your eyes so that you can distinguish east
    from west, north from south.
If you go weeping through the forest, how will you
    find the way? O,
Wrench the iron of sorrow from your throats so
    that your voices are discordant no longer.
Dwell instead on the courage of the dead. They
    enter a world where they will carry
The sun as a shield and learn to use their left in-
    stead of their right hands."
O, hearken!

When the time comes, this poem will be a good instruction manual on how not to mourn the death of Kay Boyle. (pp. 221-23)

> *Rachel Hadas, "Refusals to Mourn," in* Parnassus: Poetry in Review, *Vol. 14, No. 2, 1988, pp. 215-32.*

ANN HORNADAY

[*Life Being the Best and Other Stories*] celebrates the enduring artistic discipline of Kay Boyle, who, unlike some of her better-known peers, survived the halcyon days of Paris in the 1920's. Although Ms. Boyle is not as notorious as some of the other Moderns—those intrepid expatriate writers who set out to change language, mesh literature and social context and expose the dissonance of contemporary life—she evokes these tensions with a gossamer finesse. Her characters (wise, sad children; jilted ladies; demimondaines; women on the cusp of consciousness) are each preserved in fleeting, almost prosaic moments, each fraught with weakness and passion. Ms. Boyle animates their interior lives with unsentimental grace and acute prescience. . . . ["**Life Being the Best**"]—in which an alienated, dignified boy answers a hypothetical question with simple, terrible justice—provides the rest of the book with pitch and momentum. *Life Being the Best* gives breadth to the themes that have preoccupied Ms. Boyle throughout her career: the inviolate integrity of the human soul, the impact of external events on the most intimate of feelings, our fractured experience of love versus duty, self-respect versus hubris, social convention versus personal ethic. For 60 years, Kay Boyle's steady hand in rendering detail, authentic characterization and unequivocal moral vision has never faltered. She is still unquestionably modern.

> *Ann Hornaday, in a review of "Life Being the Best & Other Stories," in* The New York Times Book Review, *July 3, 1988, p. 12.*

DEBORAH DENENHOLZ MORSE

Kay Boyle's novel, *My Next Bride* (1934), concerns the moral development of its heroine, Victoria John, a young American artist who travels to Thirties Paris in search of Experience and Art, in retreat from American philistinism. The novel is thinly disguised autobiography. It details Boyle's own Left Bank experiences in Twenties Paris, experiences she recalled in the 1968 version of Robert McAlmon's 1938 memoirs, *Being Geniuses Together,* which Boyle edited, and in which chapters of her own recollections alternate with McAlmon's reminiscences. It is in this context that *My Next Bride* has received the contemporary critical appreciation of Boyle scholars like Sandra Spanier (Boyle's biographer) and writers such as Doris Grumbach, the author of the Afterword to the newly reissued . . . edition of the book.

While this historical and biographical context of Boyle's writings is central to an evaluation of the significance of her work, another important context for consideration of *My Next Bride* is as a female version of the *Künstlerroman,* the story of the artist's youthful apprenticeship. James Joyce, one of Boyle's companion expatriates in Paris, had written in 1916 what was to become the most famous modern *Künstlerroman* in the English language, *A Portrait of the Artist as a Young Man,* eighteen years before Boyle wrote her novel. (p. 334)

Many of the important portraits of the artist as a young woman that followed Joyce's book tell stories in which the heroine's need to be free of patriarchal dictates for women overshadows Stephen's need to escape institutional authority in order to create. The most galling confinement for the female artist, as defined by these texts, is the prison of gender. For example, two other books about a female artist written by British authors at precisely the same time as the American Boyle wrote *My Next Bride* are Antonia White's *Frost in May* (1933) and Vita Sackville-West's *All Passion Spent* (1931), novels that clearly illustrate this distinction between the male and female artist plot. The novels offer overtly contrasting versions of the female artist plot that in fact are informed by a similar feminist ideology. White's book, a portrait of the artist as a young girl, traces the evolution of the artist's rebellious consciousness in Nanda Grey, as she comes of age in the conventional world of a Catholic girls' school. In contrast, Sackville-West's novel begins when Lady Slane is eighty-eight, just after the death of her husband. The rest of the book is concerned with the heroine's memories of her youthful aspirations to be a painter, and hence includes long sections which paint a portrait of the artist as a young girl. . . . The feminist ideology underlying both texts emphasizes the repression of the female artist by cultural expectations of womanhood, and the necessity of rebellion against those expectations in order to forge the identity of the female artist.

Boyle's vision of the nature of the female artist's rebellion as a liberation from masculinist values is akin to that embodied in other female artist plots. Her portrayal of the means of enacting that rebellion in order to create art—like White's and Sackville-West's—thus is radically different than Joyce's in *Portrait.* Stephen Dedalus, Joyce's artist-hero, always feels isolated and alienated, and moves toward his expatriation from Ireland in order "to encounter for the millionth time the reality of experience and to forge in the smithy of my soul the uncreated conscience of my race." Victoria John, Boyle's artist-heroine, begins her experience in expatriation from America, and moves toward community rather than isolation, toward engagement rather than alienation. In her exploration of Victoria's moral development, Boyle opposes her sense of the female artistic vision as necessarily grounded in social concerns to Joyce's embodiment of the male artistic vision as private, unique, and necessarily isolated.

Like other stories of the female artist's formative years, Boyle's novel focuses on the protagonist's realization of how society limits her sex, but her portrait of Victoria John's accretive self-knowledge is much less overtly polemical than many texts of the female artist: Sackville-West's or White's, for instance. It is only when two formal structures of *My Next Bride* are foregrounded that one can perceive that the subtext of this female *Künstlerroman* is a critique not only of male cultural values, but also of the early Joycean vision of the artist as separate from community, necessarily divided from political concerns. The first of these formal structures is the tripartite division of *My Next Bride,* a division that marks the stages of Victoria's artistic apprenticeship. The second is the prominence of metaphors of ravishment and nurturance, metaphors that suggest Boyle's awareness of feminist concerns and her sense of a male/female cultural opposition. The import of Boyle's novel, and the cultural lessons that Victoria John learns, lead both the reader and Victoria to see the artist's vision—and her mission—as political. Boyle ultimately prophesies a new role *within* society for the artist.

In Victoria's story, her progress to emotional and artistic maturity is marked by three stages, each of which is represented by a section of the book titled with the name of the figure who most influences Victoria at that point in her development. Each of these figures is also an artist, and is thus identified with Victoria, serving both as mentor and as the embodiment of an alternative experience for her. The first, Sorrel, is the *avant-garde* patriarch of a Left Bank commune in its demise. Victoria's willingness to serve Sorrel, whose ideology of the Rousseauistic natural man obscures his true moral corruption, marks the first stage of her development, in which she is willing to play female muse to the male artist. Based on Boyle's real-life experiences in 1928 in Raymond Duncan's colony at Neuilly, the depiction of Sorrel's ravages on his people indicts Duncan's immoral artistic vision, which vindicates the abuse of others for the glory of the male artist.

Sorrel's colony is a cooperative, happy community only in theory; in reality it is an autocracy that oversees exploitation of its less favored or weak members—including its children. Sorrel's commune once prospered under the auspices of his wife, the dancer Ida (based on Isadora Duncan); however, it has become decadent under Sorrel, whose own egotism coupled with the rule of his sensual wife Mathilde—controller of the colony's pursestrings—has brought spiritual and material ruin. (pp. 334-36)

Victoria's realization of Sorrel's debased sense of values, demonstrated most painfully in his treatment of the commune's starving, ignored children, leads to her rejection of him and to her continued search for a more humane vision and a true community in which there is congruence between theory and practice. Instead of finding identity and purpose in the serene, natural communal life that well-heeled tourists come to revere, Victoria uncovers the greed and love of comfort behind Sorrel's rhetoric of the austere and the "natural." She finds him unwilling to accept moral responsibility even for his smallest acts of selfishness—implicitly asking permission to use communal money for treats, like a child, while the real children of the commune starve, eating "winter carrots and stewed turnips, cooked fast so that their hearts were hard and done to death in flour in the cold."

Victoria's longing to believe in Sorrel as spiritual and artistic mentor leads her into complicity with the hypocrisy of his colony. As she tells Antony Lister (the wealthy, sensitive American expatriate who will be her second mentor), "Like any woman, I belong to the thing I have undertaken." This longing, and her physical hunger, allow her to take Estelle's dish of ratatouille and "the hearts of things cooked delicate as a Chinese dish" in the face of the children's starvation; the same desire to believe in Sorrel impels the myth of the harmonious colony that she weaves for the wealthy American customer, Mrs. Brookbank, in hopes of getting her money for Sorrel.

In Boyle's view, Sorrel's colony becomes a metaphor of the ravishment of both the body and the spirit. Many things impose the truth about Sorrel's moral bankruptcy on Victoria, even before the final "exposure" scene in which she stands by while Peri, a colony member abused for years by Sorrel, rises up to accuse his oppressor after Sorrel spends Mrs. Brookbank's money not on a printing press, but on a fancy American car. The most important of these revelations is her love for Antony, and his relentless search for identity and intense passion for the poetic vision of D. H. Lawrence, of Emily Dickinson. Unlike the egocentric Sorrel, Antony loves other people. As he tells Victoria about life with Fontana, "We like people more than anything else in life." (pp. 337-38)

Victoria's experiences with the colony's children crystallize her discontent with Sorel and force her to see the evil consequences of his hypocrisy. In one devastating scene, Victoria takes the children to a park for the first time in their lives. These children, who bear classical names like Hippolytus and Prosperine, have in truth no connection to Nature and are terrified of grass. Clad in togas like ancient Greek children—in accordance with Sorrel's aesthetic—the children are totally uncared for. One child, Bishinka, is in pain because, as Boyle's narrator ironically comments, the "ties on his sandals had been badly sewn." Moreover, his "toenails had not been cut, had never been cut perhaps, and they were growing inward like great yellow sabres." The children are described as "four little overtures to death, their feet whispering over the mosses an invitation to the grave." In reaction to their plight, Victoria creates a story for them of the promised land, but the children in this colony supposedly dedicated to the creation of art are in truth so deprived that they have diminished imaginations; the sound of the story "was unfamiliar: they could not recognize their own faces unless they were Hippolytus, Athenia, Prosperine and Bishinka waiting in the common room for supper or lying down at night to sleep upon the floor."

The next stage of Victoria's apprenticeship leads her to Antony, with whom she has a romantic, unconsummated love affair. Antony (based on the real-life Harry Crosby) is a failed artist who has nearly given up his own painting; significantly, he offers his paints to Victoria. He also offers love and money—patronage—to her. Most importantly, Antony talks constantly of his wife, the sculptor Fontana—of their love of poetry and art; it is this talk, which brings Fontana (Caresse Crosby, to whom *My Next Bride* is dedicated) and Victoria together, that is his greatest legacy to both of these women. Although Antony is thus a mentor to Victoria, his vision is warped by his upbringing, which has been ruled by the values of the patriarchy. His father, Horace, insists that he quit painting, and reviles him for living on his wife's money while he pursues his art—although Fontana supports this unconventional situation. Significantly, it is only when Antony is alone with Fontana that he paints, while she sculpts. Together, they scrawl the words of D. H. Lawrence on the walls leading to their country house. But the conflicting claims of the materialistic patriarchy and of his own attraction to the spiritually redemptive beauty of art generate a destructive tension in Antony, an identity crisis that is ultimately consummated in suicide. (pp. 338-39)

Nowhere in *My Next Bride* is Antony's crisis of identity and purpose more vividly illustrated than in the brilliant scene in which a poor street violinist refuses to take Antony's suit as a gift. Here, Boyle sets up a visual opposition between the most impoverished of art's practitioners and Antony: Antony tries to assume the identity of a poor worker, in his corduroys and labouring jacket, while the violinist will not take on the identity of a wealthy businessman, embodied in Antony's suit. The image of Antony's discarded suit, stretched "long and empty across the pieces of thin white ice that roofed the cobbles in the gutter, the loose limbs of it curved in weariness and the arms fallen open, the white shirt laid in at the neck, the jacket buttons buttoned, as if the man who wore it had lain down there and wasted to nothingness within," is eerily prophetic of Antony's suicide, the end of his assertion to Victoria that "one cannot be nothing."

In his search for identity in relation to other human beings, Antony shares with Victoria and Fontana a longing to find social and spiritual values that will take precedence over material concerns. The reckless generosity with which Antony stuffs a great amount of money in Victoria's purse when he takes her home from a wild party, for instance, contrasts with the stingy grasping after money of Sorrel and Mathilde. The progress of this money through Victoria to the ones who need it most—the starving Russian noblewomen—serves as a kind of metaphor of the socialist beliefs of Boyle herself. And Victoria's gift of money, of freedom, to Miss Fira and Miss Grusha—who have been virtually imprisoned in one room for fifty years—continues a pattern of nurturing toward these two impoverished women that contradicts the alienation they have experienced since the Revolution. In the following scene, the images of release from pain are metaphors of a loosening of the specifically female strictures that have bound them to their place, to their outcast fate:

> She could not say put your hands down here on my knees, little women, let me take the pins out of your hair, let me draw the bones from your lace like taking splinters from your flesh. Whatever I do, I have enough left over, enough food, drink, love, time enough, enough to touch your hands and make you go to sleep quiet. You must believe in me for I am not afraid of anything the world can do.

It is this fearless effort toward assuaging pain that, in Boyle's view, is not only the artist's but the human being's responsibility.

Similarly, when Antony sends food to Victoria, she shares it with Miss Fira and Miss Grusha. Later, Victoria cannot enjoy her lavish meal with Antony until they send delicacies to the Russian sisters. Finally, the Archibald MacLeish quotation that Antony sends with his first gift of food to Victoria ("Ah how the throat of a girl and a girl's arms are Bright in the riding sun and the young sky And the green year of our lives where the willows are—") conjoins nurturance with both human love and with art.

For a time Victoria allows her frustrated love for Antony to lead her into despair, following his pattern of experiential exploration. She is led to an orgiastic party with him, but goes to bed with someone else—she's not sure who—and winds up pregnant. Antony takes her home and leaves her money—but after that she's on her own. He leaves on his ill-fated trip to America, which he had postponed in order to be with her. Victoria's life spirals into physical and moral degradation after this, until Fontana rescues her from the colony's store and takes her home with her. From here, Victoria is taken care of by Fontana, who arranges a safe abortion for her and—with immense generosity of spirit—comforts Victoria at Antony's death. (pp. 339-41)

Victoria expects the elegant Fontana to respond to her predicament with fastidious disapproval, to "pick up [her] skirts and go." Instead, Fontana leads Victoria out to the filthy privy behind the colony shop (itself a metaphor of the nastiness behind Sorrel's facade of purity), reassuring her: "I'll go with you . . . You might faint somewhere alone." Like the poor woman "with shaking hands and warts around her nose" who gives Victoria a clean handkerchief and five francs after she soils herself in public, the beautiful, rich Fontana responds to human misery with practical, unjudgmental succor.

The final stage of Victoria's apprenticeship begins with her recovery from despair under the care of Fontana. An integral part of this recovery is the inherently feminist realization that her frustrated desire to end an unwanted pregnancy safely and cheaply is a plight shared by many other women:

> All the girls who had ever come into the place, the chambermaids from cheap hotels, and the girls from the Bon Marché and the nougat-stands in the travelling fairs, and the girls who must dance at Bobino or the Empire for a living, cheaply painted and cheaply paid; and all the others, the nameless ones *sans domicile fixe* and *sans profession,* with their heels walked sideways, like Victoria's, and their faces walked long and bony like horses' faces, all of them came forbidden and unbidden out of the darkness of the corners and gathered there around them. . . . And there must be something better than this, said Fontana drawing back from the sight of them in the place, there must be something better. . . . They were out the door, they were on the landing, and behind them in the silence of the *sage-femme's* rooms they could hear the dripping, the endless dripping of the life-blood as it left the bodies of those others; the unceasing drip of the stream as it left the wide, bare table and fell, drop by drop, to the planks beneath it, dripping and dripping on for ever like a finger tapping quickly on the floor.

The long passage details Victoria's and Fontana's (and Boyle's) horrified reaction to the spectre of death faced by women undergoing abortion. While Stephen Dedalus's experiences lead him to affirm his own isolated, superior self, Victoria John's experiences lead her instead to an understanding of her identity with all womankind, of her body's kinship with those other female bodies. This realization of a commonality of experience is the basis of the nurturant social role Boyle envisions for the female artist. That Boyle is exploring the possibilities of this role is suggested by the fact that in *My Next Bride,* Victoria's pilgrimage to Paris is framed by the experiences of other female artists. Her inspiration as an artist comes from three women: her painting teacher, her mother, and her friend, the vaudeville performer, Mary de Lacey—who are themselves artists; she ends up in closest alliance with another female artist, the expatriate from wealthy New York society, Fontana, who is not only a devotee of literature and the arts, but is herself a talented sculptor. The book explores imagined possibilities for Victoria as artist—within Sorrel's colony, in love with Antony (who has abandoned his own painting), joined in mutual solace with Fontana after Antony's suicide.

In defining her artistic identity, Victoria learns from the experiences of these other artists, rejecting what is false (the hypocrisy of Sorrel), surviving the identity crises and the impulse to self-destruction that ended in suicide for Mary de

Lacey and Antony, and ultimately being nourished by what is true—learning to have the strength of her Midwest art teacher, the conviction of her mother, and the commitment to beauty of Ida, Sorrel's dead wife, "a woman of poetic vision." During her stay at the colony, Victoria is implicitly asked by Sorrel's sly, greedy mistress, Mathilde, to replace Ida as his muse, and while Victoria is under his influence, she paints the faces of old men, hoping that "perhaps something will happen to my own face." Her developing moral awareness results in a clearer sense of identity, and her ultimate alliance is, significantly, with a sister artist, Fontana, whose words are the last of the novel, her voice "picking it up and putting it together and going on with it forever." Victoria will be neither Sorrel's muse nor Antony's "next bride" but, by the end of the novel, a woman who has suffered and matured, and has formed a moral vision that she will embody in her art.

This focus on the role of the female artist is especially prominent in the second chapter of the book, which opens with Victoria establishing herself in the room of a once grand Parisian home turned boardinghouse in which she has taken a room. The first thing she unpacks are three photographs, "the faces of three women separately framed.". . . The first photograph is of Victoria's art teacher, a silent, reclusive woman, a "stranger" who nevertheless inspired Victoria to travel East on foot "looking for whatever there is." The second photograph is of Victoria's mother, a gentle woman with a "full, loving mouth," whose artistic efforts are beginnings that Victoria wants to complete in her own life. . . . (pp. 341-43)

The last photograph, from a newspaper article telling of her suicide, is of the "Australian songbird," Mary de Lacey. Riding the freight cars to Montreal with Lacey, Victoria learns of female comradeship. . . . From Lacey, who tells of her past experiences on the run from her abusive husband—three-year-old-son and ailing mother in tow—she also learns of female courage, pain, and victimization. When Lacey's mother dies, the police find cyanide pills that Lacey planned to use herself if her husband found her, and the authorities require an autopsy. The pain of having her mother's body carved up is dramatized by the horror of the corpse being fed to the sharks in the harbor—an image that confirms the prophetic vision Lacey sees in the ink of the palm of her hand, a picture of sharks jumping, "fighting like mad over something or other. . . ." The hungry, whirling sharks that tear a woman's body—like the image of the bleeding women's bodies at the *sage-femme's*—serve as a metaphor of ravishment defining a vision of human existence against which the female artist must create both her moral self and her art. (pp. 343-44)

The commitment to another human being, that intimate social and moral relation, is necessary to the artist's larger social and moral vision, the vision that will be embodied in her art. Amid all the human wreckage of the novel, it is Fontana's love and care that will not only ensure Victoria's psychic and physical survival, but will also validate that moral vision toward which Victoria has been moving during the novel. In her generosity to Miss Fira and Miss Grusha and in her care for the colony's children, Victoria has acted upon a belief in the redemptive power of human kindness in the face of cruelty and hypocrisy.

As a measure of Victoria's progress toward this vision, Boyle creates two comparable scenes of women together, one at the beginning of her novel and one at the end. In the first scene,

when Victoria and Lacey embrace in the boxcar, their intimacy is imperfect because neither woman can fully accept the other's need for nurturance. Victoria told Lacey, addressing her picture after her death, "I never said some things to you, I never said love because of the shy sound it had beside you." In the closing scene of the book, Boyle consciously echoes her previous words when she has Victoria say, " 'I like you,' . . . and she felt shy at saying anything so simply out." Lacey insists that "I don't need anyone, don't kid yourself. I don't need anyone at all." Fontana, in contrast, says, "You lie down, Victoria John, and I'll lie down beside you." Like the "sitting parent" who falls asleep with the little girl Felicia in her arms in the 1946 Boyle story, **"Winter Night,"** Fontana recognizes our need for one another in our pain, and responds compassionately. Victoria, who "never cried", is moved to weeping at Antony's death, crying for him, for all his lost possibilities. The women lying beside one another and the tears shed for another's pain are metaphors for a vision of life that contrasts absolutely with the terrifying vision of ravishment conjured by the starving children in Sorrel's colony, their toe-nails "growing inward like great yellow sabres," by Victoria's plundered body at the privy, by Lacey's mother's corpse mangled by sharks, and by the bleeding women at the *sage-femme's*.

The full measure of the final scene in **My Next Bride** can be appreciated only with the echo of a previous scene in the reader's mind: in that scene, Sorrel, justly excoriated by Peri, cries for himself, "alone, without anyone, in the dark." In company with Fontana, Victoria has moved beyond the concentration on self that precludes Sorrel from weeping for anyone else, from true care for others. In the compassionate response of Fontana and Victoria—in life and in art—Boyle identifies the only possibility for our moral salvation. With the strength and awareness Victoria has gained in her journey toward self-knowledge, she has finally learned to cry, going beyond Lacey's cynical outlook or Antony's despair toward a vision of compassion for a world in pain. In creating that vision, Boyle has helped to shape a new kind of female *Künstlerroman* in which the expatriate hero of Joyce's text would indeed find himself on foreign terrain. (pp. 344-45)

Deborah Denenholz Morse, " 'My Next Bride': Kay Boyle's Text of the Female Artist," in Twentieth Century Literature, *Vol. 34, No. 3, Fall, 1988, pp. 334-46.*

EDWARD M. UEHLING

In his famous introduction to the anthology *Men at War,* Hemingway observes that in combat "learning to suspend your imagination and live completely in the very second of the present minute with no before and no after is the greatest gift a soldier can acquire." That statement has become, at least implicitly, the measure for all war fiction because the central figures in modern war novels have been revealed to us as they succeed and, more interestingly, fail to maintain such a perspective. Paul Bäumer (*All Quiet on the Western Front*), Frederic Henry, Billy Pilgrim, Paul Berlin (*Going after Cacciato*), and other such figures take on dramatic, moral intensity as they struggle with physical and psychological brutalities of war. Yet there are many stories of war—Vietnam has reminded us of that—and Kay Boyle's short fiction of World War II makes equally compelling statements about war and its consequences.

Harold Krebs, the shell-shocked veteran of Hemingway's "Soldier's Home," longs for "a world without consequences"; in such a story as **"The Lost,"** Boyle captures what would terrify Krebs: a world of overwhelming consequences for "survivors" without homes to which they might return. It is Boyle's world of consequences that gives us the other side of the coin; however disquieting, it is one we must understand if we are to know the full cost of war. The social and political wisdom of Boyle's war fiction is all the more remarkable, though, for its skillful telling. Fiction written during or shortly after a war often struggles to find its moral and aesthetic center because the artist has not yet established sufficient distance. . . . The relative speed with which Boyle could write about World War II and her control of difficult materials invite our closest critical attention. (pp. 375-76)

Boyle exhibits a . . . fascination with the possibilities and failures of language as she examines the people—soldiers and civilians; men, women, and children—of World War II Europe. I want to discuss two stories, **"Army of Occupation"** and **"The Lost,"** although there are many others (**"Hotel Behind the Lines,"** for instance) which similarly deal with this issue of language and are more overtly political, as well. But these two, both describing the aftermath of war, look from several angles at the gap between private thought and public utterance. In each story, as language fails, we see and hear more than the failure of moral courage: we discover a failure of human understanding and sympathy that suggests complete spiritual sterility.

"Army of Occupation" begins in Paris as a troop train prepares to return with American soldiers to occupied Germany "after a furlough spent . . . in pursuit of love." The presence of American GIs so dominates the scene that there is no other sense of time or place: we are told, "it was not a French train," and the MPs and GI ticket men stand, passing judgment on the French girls who have come to say goodbye. Whatever values emerge must come from the American soldiers on that train and the unnamed American correspondent who travels to meet her husband.

The intense drama of this brief story unfolds in a frightening counterpoint of voices and levels of meaning. As the woman boards the train, ignoring gapes from the men on the platform, we hear a chorus of voices from within. Drunken and terrible, it is described as a "sad, wild longing outcry—no longer recognizable as singing." . . . We hear, but the woman is apart from this, perhaps by temperament: "the things that passed through her mind were different. She did not look toward the men, and she did not seem to hear them calling out." From the outset, Boyle underscores the difference in sensibilities between the woman, whose "look of modesty, of shyness and vulnerability" is reflected in the self-willed reality of her private thoughts, and the men, whose calls, whistles, and roaring are aggressively animalistic. The disparate voices of the story, motivated by fear, perverse longing, or disgust, are powerfully expressive but insular: no one hears or listens.

Stepping into one compartment of this soiled, discordant world, the woman faces three soldiers, each as distinctively ugly in speech as he is in physical presence and gesture. One, a sergeant, crudely waves and caresses a cognac bottle that hangs "between his spread knees." The second, a big red-haired man, is educated enough to refer to Lochinvar and Morpheus but joins the sergeant in trying to coax her to drink from their bottles. The third, described as a farm boy, isolates

himself and only occasionally blurts out contemptuous remarks about French war brides being no ladies. . . . From the moment she sets foot in the compartment, we witness a striking cluster of images that mock civilized, cultivated behavior. The sergeant's first "words" are not words at all but a baying wolf call. The big soldier apes polite conversation as he suggests that the woman is a commodity to be consumed: " 'Take a glance, gentlemen, at what they're passing around with coffee and leecures tonight.' " Indeed, throughout the confrontation of the story, he associates her with the bottle of cognac. Before the sergeant has grabbed the woman with encouragement from his big companion—" 'You take it first. I'll take what's left' "—she belies her assertion that she is not afraid.

As a signal of her growing fear, the narrator distinguishes what the woman does say from what she thinks by italicized passages that indicate her attempt to impose a sense of calm: for instance, *"in thirteen hours now, a little less than thirteen"*; or, *"They can't do anything, not a single thing. In a little while he'll walk down the platform, looking in every window for me."* Ironically, once inside the compartment, she does begin to hear the crude chorus, although it has grown less distinct, and even takes some comfort in the singing as she tries to think of her husband and not those with her.

At the same time, there are no instances of genuine communication as the two soldiers first attempt to seduce the terrified woman and then nearly succeed in forcing themselves on her. Their words, wholly artificial and perverse, distort the reality she internalizes and we would wish for. For instance, the sergeant attempts to evoke pity from the woman by showing her a certificate that verifies his attendance four days earlier at the funeral of his infant son by an English war bride. But as his comrade drunkenly observes, " 'Does it occur to you that the lady is bored with all this kind of talk?' " . . . By resorting to speaking about her as though she were not present, the two demonstrate their crude intention and the inadequacy of any response she might offer to halt its progress. At this moment, the third soldier, from whom one might hope for moral outrage, can muster only disgust for everyone unlike himself. . . . He issues another brief, unintentionally ironic condemnation of French war brides (and really all women); " 'I found out too much just in time. . . .' He looked at them in something like hesitation a moment, as if there were more to say and as if he were about to say it, and then turned back to the fleeting darkness. . . . 'Roll me over / In the clover,' came the faint, sad chorus of crying down the corridor."

Yet we have not experienced the utter failure of language until a blue-eyed corporal enters the compartment, ostensibly to offer his seat in another car to the woman, but really to make a childish bid for her favor. . . . Although we are told "his ears [were] deaf to everything except what she might say," she says nothing to him until the increasing threat of physical violence drives her to attempt to accept the offer of his seat. Instead, the corporal literally takes the woman's place, is essentially raped with the ubiquitous bottle in her place.

While the "farm boy [sleeps] in peace against the cold, dark window glass," the sergeant knocks the corporal senseless with a bottle. As he lies "as if in sleep," the sergeant prepares for another blow, when the woman cries out: " 'Don't touch him! Don't you dare to hit him again!' " The story closes with an ironic juxtaposition of inadequate voices and silences. The woman's own private voice fairly races in an effort to save from annihilation the actual flesh and bone of all that remained of decency. *"They're other people on this train, like people you know, like people you see in the street. . . . They're Wacs, and brothers, and sons, and husbands . . . they're people singing. . . . People who understand words, if I can get to them . . ."*

To the woman's final spoken words—"Get out of my way!"—the sergeant makes a noteworthy response: "And he did not speak, but, half smiling still as she flung by him, he lifted his hand and stroked her soft, dark hair." The story's final words suggest that what she runs from may be no worse than what she runs to—"toward the sound of the sad, sweet, distant voices in the rushing train." What is real? The loneliness of those voices, as well as the tenderness perversely evoked by their description? Or simply their message—"Roll me over / In the clover."

The paradox of Boyle relying on words for her art when developing this idea of failed language is perhaps even more pronounced in **"The Lost."** This is a story of children displaced by the war and the American woman who manages a Children's Center from which they may be officially relocated. As in **"Army of Occupation,"** setting reinforces a distorted pattern of historical connections. Once a massive baronial manor house in Bavaria, the Center conveys to the arriving America Relief Team "the chill of winter and silence and death that stood like a presence in its feudal halls." But that is only one past reality of the place: during the war, it served as a Selection Camp for genetic and racial losers who were dutifully recorded, photographed, and sent to labor or extermination. From their neatly alphabetized records, their pictures haunt us: "It was the eyes of these men and women, who were there no longer, which looked now at the Americans, and beyond them, upon some indescribable vista of hopelessness and pain." Against such a background, the American presence seems more orderly than useful—a source of food and playground equipment, but not of restored identity.

The story's most powerful representation of "hopelessness and pain" comes through its many voices. Three figures, called "boys" by the narrator, are addressed as "men" by the American woman. Orphans and mascots of various U.S. Infantry units, they are neither civilians nor children. How to name or understand them is more difficult still because of their speech and what it implies. The oldest, Janos, is fifteen, once was Czechoslovakian, calls himself Johnny Madden, and speaks with the accent of the black sergeant from Tennessee, Charlie Madden, by whom he hopes to be adopted. The other two are younger, perhaps fourteen and twelve, and remain unnamed. The fourteen-year-old, filled with cynicism, looks for an angle or a private deal and refuses to recross the threshold of the Center and the child's world it suggests. "His accent might have come straight from Brooklyn," we are told, "except that it had come from somewhere else before that, and, as he spoke, he folded his arms upon his breast, and spat casually." The youngest, whose grandfather is eventually located in Naples, is able at least superficially to rejoin the world of swings and sandboxes, but his voice parrots that of the GIs with whom he has lived.

During their initial interview, the woman discourages hope of adoption in the practiced litany of a middle-level bureaucrat:

> And probably when the G.I.s made you those

promises they thought they would be able to keep them. . . . I've talked to some of these men, I've had letters from them, and I know they believed they would be able to keep the promises. But there were other kinds too. There were some kinds who didn't care what happened to you men afterward. . . . They wanted you to learn how to drink and smoke and gamble and shoot crap and use the kind of language they used—

The twelve-year-old's reply betrays his misunderstanding: " 'I begin shooting crap in Naples,' the small boy said in his high, eager voice. 'I clean up seven bucks the first night there.' " For once her composure is punctured: " 'Look, kid . . . if Italy's your country, perhaps you ought to pack up and go back there.' " The play of language in this exchange is remarkable. Her irritation leads her to replace "men" with "kid," a term nearer to the truth but still without sympathy or even recognition of individuality. Moreover, both speakers' use of "crap" to describe the game of dice, "craps," suggests that neither the woman nor the child fits in this strange world of war; it further hints at the ineffectuality of such talk/"crap." The woman evokes a startling reply from the boy: " 'I ain't no Eyetie no more,' he said and he did not raise his eyes to her because of the tears that were standing in them. 'I'm American. I wanna go home where my outfit's gone.' " (pp. 376-80)

In fact, throughout **"The Lost,"** people rarely look at or hear each other. That failure develops most obviously through numerous images of dark and lightness. For instance, the second hayloft scene, in which Janos brings table scraps to the second boy, contains many plays on light and dark that underscore shifts in language and its ultimate inadequacy. Janos crosses the stable door "in the darkness" and finds the boy framed by the window through which there are "stars shining clearly . . . and Janos could hear his [the other's] voice speaking out across the hay-sweet dark." The words are even harder and more defensive now: " 'My God-damned lighter's gone dry as a witch's tit,' the boy said. 'I've got to get me to a PX and get me some lighter fluid.' " Perhaps for him there is already no other possibility of light than that of the now empty Zippo. His sweater, we are told, "showed dark against the starry square of night." It might be argued that his language makes him darker than the night; certainly the contrast of his fierce despair with Janos' insistent hope for a future sense of place rings clearly in Boyle's representation of their voices. Offering a nearly empty bottle of schnapps to his older companion, the outsider says, " 'Have a swig, kid,' " echoing the woman's retort. Then there is more tough talk: " 'I've got to get me to a man's-size town where there's a PX quick,' the boy was saying in the darkness." To Janos' innocuous reply, the other begins laughing and Boyle writes, "He lay . . . beyond Janos in the darkness."

For the sixth time in this scene darkness is mentioned as Janos recalls Sergeant Madden's instruction on the naming and placing of stars. Two qualities of his declaration are noteworthy. First, the reference to stars and thus to light and hope is linked to the one trustworthy figure in Janos' world. Although we do not hear his buddy's words, they obviously have remained with Janos as proof of the order represented by Madden. Equally revealing, Janos conveys all of this as though he is speaking to himself or at least without expecting that his words can become part of a real communication in the darkened loft. We discover that such words, with their implicit faith in happy endings, can elicit only the briefest acknowledgment of pain before the facade of the Brooklyn accent resurfaces: " 'Oh, Christ' " the other boy mutters as he curses a system where rank has privilege, a system that will always exclude him. Another spasm of ironic laughter jerks from him and he dismisses Janos' hope: " 'You listen, kid, . . . The cards is stacked against us.' "

Hearing these American dialects apart from the sources that should accompany them makes us wince, particularly because the topics addressed would be painful even to adults. All three children speak of their parents' deaths matter-of-factly; their voices would be utterly detached except that they are eager to prove that they may go "home to America" because their parents have not survived. The unconscious mimicry of their voices echoes their empty lives.

Finally only Janos remains, writing every night to Madden, who has taught him to fix things, and practicing the mechanical skills that he hopes to use in Madden's garage. But the final image of darkness, Charlie Madden's race, catches him. It is, as the woman explains, "the color question."

> Janos stood there listening to the words she said, and, as he listened, the woman again ceased being woman, ceased being human being even, and it was merely a voice in the shed that spoke quietly and bitterly of the separate lives that must be lived by people of different colors, as she had on that first day spoken of the hopes that might never come to anything at all.

Yet the final sorrow of this unresolved story is not that Janos cannot live with a black man in Tennessee. It is the manner in which he rejects even the compromise of living with another family in America. "Neatly and inaccurately" he composes the polite lie to Madden and disappears without a trace: "Yesstidy I talk to the US consil Charlie and what do ya think now? Seems my fammillys jus as good as they ever waz so Charlie I make up my mynd sudden to go back whar they waz waiting for me Im shure ya thinks its for the best Charlie so I says so long."

Earlier, Janos' writing every night might be regarded as a form of light in the darkness. But the effect of his final letter is quite different. Here its flawed form and substance underscore the displacement of meaningful language by an English that intends to protect both sender and recipient but does not connect; an English that is distorted, false, occupying yet lost. Either way, heads or tails, the world of Boyle's war stories is an unforgiving, lonely place. (pp. 381-82)

Edward M. Uehling, "Tails, You Lose: Kay Boyle's War Fiction," in Twentieth Century Literature, *Vol. 34, No. 3, Fall, 1988, pp. 375-83.*

Truman Capote

1924-1984

(Born Truman Steckfus Persons) American novelist, nonfiction writer, short story writer, essayist, dramatist, scriptwriter, and memoirist.

The following entry presents criticism on Capote's *In Cold Blood: An Account of a Multiple Murder and Its Consequences* (1965). For complete coverage of Capote's career, see *CLC*, Vols. 1, 3, 8, 13, 19, 34, 38.

An accomplished author of fiction in the Southern Gothic tradition, Capote is best remembered for his self-proclaimed "nonfiction novel," *In Cold Blood.* Originally serialized in *The New Yorker* and published in book form in 1965 following nearly six years of research and advance publicity, this book chronicles the murder of Kansas farmer Herbert W. Clutter and his family, who were bound, gagged, robbed, and shot by two ex-convicts for less than fifty dollars in November, 1959. In addition to garnering Capote an Edgar Award from the Mystery Writers of America, *In Cold Blood* became a bestseller and generated several million dollars in royalties and profits related to serialization, paperback, and film rights. Written in an objective and highly innovative prose style that combines the factual accuracy of journalism with the emotive impact of fiction, *In Cold Blood* is particularly noted for Capote's subtle insights into the ambiguities of the American legal system and of capital punishment.

Although known primarily as the author of such novels as *Other Voices, Other Rooms* (1948) and *Breakfast at Tiffany's* (1958), Capote completed several works of nonfiction prior to *In Cold Blood,* including *Local Color* (1950), a collection of essays recounting his impressions and experiences in Europe, and *The Muses Are Heard: An Account of the Porgy and Bess Tour to Leningrad* (1956). From these projects Capote developed the idea of creating a work that would combine fact and fiction. "It seemed to me," Capote stated, "that journalism, reportage, could be forced to yield a serious new art form: the 'nonfiction novel,' as I thought of it." In Capote's view, the nonfiction novel would require absolute adherence to fact and disallow authorial commentary. Chancing upon an article in the *New York Times* describing the apparently motiveless murder of a prosperous Kansan family, Capote judged the crime to be sufficiently universal to warrant consideration as a nonfiction novel. Arriving at the Clutter's hometown of Holcomb, Kansas, Capote gradually gained the confidence of residents as well as detectives and other professionals associated with the case. Nearly two years later, police apprehended two suspects following a tip from a convict at Kansas State Penitentiary who claimed to have told a fellow inmate about the Clutter's prosperous farm and a safe rumored to be hidden there. Over the next four years of their captivity, Capote conducted literally hundreds of interviews with Richard Eugene Hickock and Perry Edward Smith. Convicted of murder, both men were executed in April, 1965.

While admitting that *In Cold Blood* reflects his own viewpoint regarding which material would be included or excluded, Capote considered his own presence intrusive to the narrative, and so eliminated himself by developing an omni-

scient, objective style in which events are presented from the perspectives of many people. To avoid the reluctance and self-consciousness often associated with the use of a tape recorder or camera in interviewing subjects, Capote claimed to have trained himself to accurately memorize conversations which he later transcribed into notes. By comparing the accounts of friends and neighbors of the Clutters, as well as those of the two killers, who were separated during the first few months of their incarceration and thus unable to compare stories, Capote attempted to determine and report the most accurate account of the events leading up to and following the murders.

In Cold Blood begins cinematically, juxtaposing the domestic normality of the Clutter family with the fateful approach of the murderers. Most critics consider Herbert Clutter a symbol of the American work ethic and family man. Clutter's sternness and emotional rigidity may have resulted in feelings of unimportance for Bonnie, his neurotic wife. The Clutter children include Kenyon, a shy adolescent, and Nancy, the epitome of the "all-American" girl. As symbols of the American Dream attained, the Clutters contrast sharply with Smith and Hickock, who met in prison while serving sentences for petty theft. Smith and Hickock emerge in Capote's narrative as social dropouts with criminal mentalities, disillusioned romantics who are physically deformed by road accidents—Hickock with a battered head and a face that looks as though it was "composed of mismatching parts," and Smith with stunted legs so painful that he became addicted to aspirin. To delay the dramatic climax and build suspense, Capote next shifts to the Clutter home the following morning, focusing on police as they attempt to determine a motive for the murders. In subsequent chapters, Capote juxtaposes the progress of detectives in solving the case with the aimless wanderings of Smith and Hickock across North America—first to Miami, Florida, then to Acapulco, Mexico, back to Kansas, and finally to Las Vegas, Nevada, where they are apprehended. The remainder of *In Cold Blood* depicts the incarceration and interrogation of the killers. Although Smith initially stated to detectives that both he and Hickock had murdered the Clutters, Capote chose to recreate the murder scene from a confession Smith made to him during an interview, in which he insisted that he and Hickock had planned the crime but that he alone had committed the murders.

Upon publication, *In Cold Blood* elicited among the most extensive critical interest in publishing history. Although several commentators accused Capote of opportunism and of concealing his inability to produce imaginative fiction by working with ready-made material, most responded with overwhelmingly positive reviews. F. W. Dupee designated *In Cold Blood* "the best documentary account of an American crime ever written"; a reviewer from *Newsweek* called it "the product of one of the most astonishingly sustained acts of will and hard work in the life of any writer"; and Conrad Knickerbocker proclaimed the book "a masterpiece—agonizing, terrible, possessed, proof that the times, so surfeited with disasters, are still capable of tragedy." In Great Britain, Kenneth Tynan provoked a bitter debate in *The Observer* by judging as inadequate the defense of Joseph P. Jenkins, counsel for Hickock and Smith, and by proposing that Capote should have provided psychiatric testimony that might have saved the defendants from capital punishment. Speculating that without their deaths, *In Cold Blood* might not have been published, Tynan stated: "[It] seems to me that the blood in which his book is written is as cold as any in recent literature." Both Jenkins and Capote responded by accusing Tynan of opportunism and distortion. Tynan denied these allegations as well as Capote's charge that he had used falsified sources to draw personal conclusions that might have resulted in a libel case. Other critics also expressed moral reservations regarding the stark objectivity of *In Cold Blood*. Several suggested that Capote may have identified too closely with Smith, as both men experienced nomadic childhoods characterized by neglectful mothers and absent fathers. Despite the reproach of critics such as Diana Trilling, who accused Capote of "employing objectivity as a shield for evasion," most concurred with the opinion of Jenkins: "Capote helped Hickock and Smith more as an impartial observer and recorder than by actually becoming an advocate for them."

Many critics have placed *In Cold Blood* in the tradition of American quest literature exemplified by such novels as Mark Twain's *Huckleberry Finn,* Vladimir Nabokov's *Lolita,* Jack Kerouac's *On the Road,* and particularly, Theodore Dreiser's *An American Tragedy,* in which Dreiser commented upon an actual murder that he believed to symbolize the tragedy of his time. Although one faction of critics treated *In Cold Blood* as a work of nonfiction, most classified the book as a novel due to its dramatic urgency and tone. These reviewers perceived Capote's intent to be closer to the novel

form, the major purpose of which, according to William Wiegand, "is to 'suggest' and 'extend.' " Many praised his objective yet compassionate treatment of Hickock and Smith, whose biographies were compared to those of the grotesque social misfits and outcasts of Capote's fiction. Hickock is portrayed as an essentially petty criminal capable of planning murder but incapable of actually killing, while Smith emerges as the classic victim of a brutal childhood. Attempting to identify possible motives for the murders from biographical and psychiatric data, Capote implies that the prime cause stems from the killers' pursuit of the same force that ironically resulted in the Clutters' prosperity—the myth of the American Dream. Obsessed with this ideal of success and unlimited freedom, the two drifters collide with the embodiment of that myth, resulting in what Tony Tanner called "the terrible meeting of the cursed and the blessed."

Many commentators have placed *In Cold Blood* in the journalistic documentary tradition that includes John Hersey's *Hiroshima* and Lillian Ross's *Picture.* As truth seemed to be stranger than fiction to many following the events of second World War, numerous American critics forecast the demise of the novel, viewing nonfiction forms as more imaginative and more appropriate to the modern age than those of fiction. Although some critics faulted Capote's work as circumstantial and decried his lack of documentation, most concurred with the assessment of a reviewer for *The Times Literary Supplement*: "The form is not new or remarkable, but it is handled here with a narrative skill and delicate sensibility that make this re-telling of a gruesome murder story into a work of art." Robert Pearman, in an article for the *Kansas City Times,* and Phillip K. Tompkins, in a piece for *Esquire,* identified several inaccuracies and exaggerations after having returned to Kansas to search for verification of Capote's claims to factual accuracy. The most damaging evidence of distortion relates to Capote's romanticization of Smith, whom he depicts as apologetic for the Clutter murders prior to his execution despite eyewitness accounts by newspaper and radio reporters who stated that he had shown no remorse. William L. Nance remarked, however, that if Capote's work is to be judged as a nonfiction novel, "*In Cold Blood* is certainly one of the finest specimens of that 'impure genre' and quite possibly the best piece of artistic journalism ever written." Nance added: "Capote's deep sympathy for Perry [Smith] makes *In Cold Blood* a powerful work of art and a probing and admirable attempt to understand a human being. If it is less than completely successful, so are all such efforts."

(See also *Short Story Criticism,* Vol. 2; *Contemporary Authors,* Vols. 5-8, rev. ed., Vol. 113 [obituary]; *Contemporary Authors New Revision Series,* Vol. 18; *Dictionary of Literary Biography,* Vol. 2; *Dictionary of Literary Biography Yearbook: 1980, 1984,* and *Concise Dictionary of American Literary Biography, 1941-1968.*)

CONRAD KNICKERBOCKER

With the obsessiveness of a man demonstrating a profound new hypothesis, [Mr. Capote] spent more than five years unraveling and following to its end every thread in the killing of Herbert W. Clutter and his family. ***In Cold Blood,*** the resulting chronicle, is a masterpiece—agonizing, terrible, possessed, proof that the times, so surfeited with disasters, are still capable of tragedy.

The tragedy was existential. The murder was seemingly without motive. The killers, Perry Smith and Richard Hickock, almost parodied the literary anti-hero. Social dropouts filled with nausea, disillusioned romantics, they were the perfect loners. Their relationship, if not physical, was spiritually homosexual, similar to the exalted *Freundschaft,* bound in blood, of SS brothers. Smith, the archetypal underground exile, had the usual existential loathing of the body; he hated his crushed legs. Chewing aspirin and drinking root beer, he daydreamed in his crushed heart of a Mexican beach paradise with treasure under the sea. At night, sometimes afflicted with enuresis, he dreamed of a giant yellow bird that would lift him to salvation. Sometimes his captors saw in him the violence and power of a maimed jungle animal. Hickcock, on the other hand, was nothing, merely the kid next door gone totally wrong. He was only charming while unloading hot checks on clothing salesmen. One of his weaknesses was little girls, and to the end he loudly asserted he was "a normal."

The Clutters made especially poignant victims. It was not that they wanted killing, but their lives, like so many of their countrymen's, rigid, solidly reliant on the grace of affluence, denied the possibility of evil and thus were crucially diminished. Mr. Clutter tolerated no drinkers among those who worked on his farm. He ate apples in the morning and bought everything by check. The wax on the floors of his $40,000 house exuded a lemon scent. His daughter, Nancy, lovely and virginal, baked pies and attended 4-H Club meetings. Once, her father caught her kissing a boy, but she could never marry him because he was a Catholic. His son Kenyon made good things with his hands in the basement workshop. Mrs. Clutter, the pious Bonnie, afflicted with deathly cold shivers and fits of anxiety amid the sunny bounties of a Kansas farm, was the only discordant element in this American dream. Finally they knew terror, and the knowledge in Mr. Capote's words becomes heartbreaking.

The crime confronted the townsfolk of Holcomb with their own isolation. Neighborliness evaporated. The natural order seemed suspended. Chaos poised to rush in. They distrusted and came to suspect not terrible strangers, but themselves. At the trial, struck mostly silent, they gaped. A squadron of psychiatrists, about the best we can produce in the way of a tragic chorus, emphasized the banality and dehydration of the current articulations of motive. "Paranoid orientation," they said. "Schizophrenic reaction. Severe character disorder."

Perry Smith, on the other hand had mastered the true modern vocabulary. He spoke with the nightmare logic of all the socially and emotionally dispersed: "I thought he was a very nice gentleman. . . . I thought so right up to the moment I cut his throat."

There are two Truman Capotes. One is the artful charmer, prone to the gossamer and the exquisite, of *The Grass Harp* and Holly Golightly. The other, darker and stronger, is the discoverer of death. He began the latter exploration as a very young man in his first novel *Other Voices, Other Rooms* and in such stories as **"Master Misery," "The Headless Hawk"** and **"A Tree of Night."** He has traveled far from the misty, moss-hung, Southern-Gothic landscapes of his youth. He now broods with the austerity of a Greek or an Elizabethan.

As he says in his interview with George Plimpton [see following excerpt], he wrote **In Cold Blood** without mechanical

aids—tape recorder or shorthand book. . . . Yet it is difficult to imagine such a work appearing at a time other than the electronic age. The sound of the book creates the illusion of tape. Its taut cross-cutting is cinematic. Tape and film, documentaries, instant news, have sensitized us to the glare of surfaces and close-ups. He gratifies our electronically induced appetite for massive quantities of detail, but at the same time, like an ironic magician, he shows that appearances are nothing.

In Cold Blood also mocks many of the advances (on paper) of anti-realism. It presents the metaphysics of anti-realism through a total evocation of reality. Not the least of the book's merits is that it manages a major moral judgment without the author's appearance once on stage. At a time when the external happening has become largely meaningless and our reaction to it brutalized, when we shout "Jump!" to the man on the ledge, Mr. Capote has restored dignity to the event. His book is also a grieving testament of faith in what used to be called the soul. (pp. 1, 37)

> Conrad Knickerbocker, "One Night on a Kansas Farm," in The New York Times Book Review, January 16, 1966, pp. 1, 37.

TRUMAN CAPOTE [INTERVIEW WITH GEORGE PLIMPTON]

In Cold Blood is remarkable for its objectivity—nowhere, despite his involvement, does the author intrude. In the following interview, done a few weeks ago, Truman Capote, presents his own views on the case, its principals, and in particular he discusses the new literary art form which he calls the nonfiction novel . . .

[Plimpton]: *Why did you select the particular subject matter of murder; had you previously been interested in crime?*

[Capote]: Not really, no. During the last years I've learned a good deal about crime, and the origins of the homicidal mentality. Still, it is a layman's knowledge and I don't pretend to anything deeper. The motivating factor in my choice of material—that is, choosing to write a true account of an actual murder case—was altogether literary. The decision was based on a theory I've harbored since I first began to write professionally, which is well over 20 years ago. It seemed to me that journalism, reportage, could be forced to yield a serious new art form: the "nonfiction novel," as I thought of it. Several admirable reporters—Rebecca West for one, and Joseph Mitchell and Lillian Ross—have shown the possibilities of narrative reportage; and Miss Ross, in her brilliant *Picture,* achieved at least a nonfiction novella. Still, on the whole, journalism is the most underestimated, the least explored of literary mediums.

Why should that be so?

Because few first-class creative writers have ever bothered with journalism, except as a sideline, "hack-work," something to be done when the creative spirit is lacking, or as a means of making money quickly. Such writers say in effect: Why should we trouble with factual writing when we're able to invent our own stories, contrive our own characters and themes?—journalism is only literary photography, and unbecoming to the serious writer's artistic dignity.

Another deterrent—and not the smallest—is that the reporter, unlike the fantasist, has to deal with actual people who have real names. If they feel maligned, or just contrary, or greedy, they enrich lawyers (though rarely themselves) by instigating libel actions. This last is certainly a factor to consider, a most oppressive and repressive one. Because it's indeed difficult to portray, in any meaningful depth, another being, his appearance, speech, mentality, without to some degree, and often for quite trifling cause, offending him. The truth seems to be that no one likes to see himself described as he is, or cares to see exactly set down what he said and did. Well, even I can understand that—because I don't like it myself when I am the sitter and not the portraitist: the frailty of egos!—and the more accurate the strokes, the greater the resentment.

When I first formed my theories concerning the nonfiction novel, many people with whom I discussed the matter were unsympathetic. They felt that what I proposed, a narrative form that employed all the techniques of fictional art but was nevertheless immaculately factual, was little more than a literary solution for fatigued novelists suffering from "failure of imagination." Personally, I felt that this attitude represented a "failure of imagination" on their part.

Of course a properly done piece of narrative reporting requires imagination!—and a good deal of special technical equipment that is usually beyond the resources—and I don't doubt the interests—of most fictional writers: an ability to transcribe verbatim long conversations, and to do so without taking notes or using tape-recordings. Also, it is necessary to have a 20/20 eye for visual detail—in this sense, it is quite true that one must be a "literary photographer," though an exceedingly selective one. But, above all, the reporter must be able to empathize with personalities outside his usual imaginative range, mentalities unlike his own, kinds of people he would never have written about had he not been forced to by encountering them inside the journalistic situation. This last is what first attracted me to the notion of narrative reportage.

It seems to me that most contemporary novelists, especially the Americans and the French, are too subjective, mesmerized by private demons; they're enraptured by their navels, and confined by a view that ends with their own toes. If I were naming names, I'd name myself among others. At any rate, I did at one time feel an artistic need to escape my self-created world. I wanted to exchange it, creatively speaking, for the everyday objective world we all inhabit. Not that I'd never written nonfiction before—I kept journals, and had published a small truthful book of travel impressions: **Local Color.** But I had never attempted an ambitious piece of reportage until 1956, when I wrote **The Muses Are Heard,** an account of the first theatrical cultural exchange between the U.S.A. and the U.S.S.R.—that is, the *Porgy and Bess* tour of Russia. It was published in *The New Yorker,* the only magazine I know of that encourages the serious practitioners of this art form. Later, I contributed a few other reportorial finger-exercises to the same magazine. Finally, I felt equipped and ready to undertake a full-scale narrative—in other words, a "nonfiction novel."

How does John Hersey's Hiroshima *or Oscar Lewis's* Children of Sanchez *compare with "the nonfiction novel?"*

The Oscar Lewis book is a documentary, a job of editing from tapes, and however skillful and moving, it is not creative writing. *Hiroshima* is creative—in the sense that Hersey isn't taking something off a tape-recorder and editing it—but it still hasn't got anything to do with what I'm talking about. *Hiro-*

shima is a strict classical journalistic piece. What is closer is what Lillian Ross did with *Picture.* Or my own book, **The Muses Are Heard**—which uses the techniques of the comic short novel.

It was natural that I should progress from that experiment, and get myself in much deeper water. I read in the paper the other day that I had been quoted as saying that reporting is now more interesting than fiction. Now that's *not* what I said, and it's important to me to get this straight. What I think is that reporting can be made *as* interesting as fiction, and done *as* artistically—underlining those two "as"es. I don't mean to say that one is a superior form to the other. I feel that creative reportage has been neglected and has great relevance to 20th-century writing. And while it can be an artistic outlet for the creative writer, it has never been particularly explored.

What is your opinion of the so-called New Journalism—as it is practiced particularly at The Herald Tribune?

If you mean James Breslin and Tom Wolfe, and that crowd, they have nothing to do with creative journalism—in the sense that I use the term—because neither of them, nor any of that school of reporting, have the proper fictional technical equipment. It's useless for a writer whose talent is essentially journalistic to attempt creative reportage, because it simply won't work. A writer like Rebecca West—always a good reporter—has never really used the form of creative reportage because the form, by necessity, demands that the writer be completely in control of fictional techniques—which means that, to be a good creative reporter, you have to be a very good fiction writer.

Would it be fair to say, then, since many reporters use nonfiction techniques—Meyer Levin in Compulsion, *Walter Lord in* A Night to Remember *and so forth—that the nonfiction novel can be defined by the* degree *of the fiction skills involved, and the* extent *of the author's absorption with his subject?*

Compulsion is a fictional novel suggested by fact, but no way bound to it. I never read the other book. The nonfiction novel should not be confused with the documentary novel—a popular and interesting but impure genre, which allows all the latitude of the fiction writer, but usually contains neither the persuasiveness of fact nor the poetic altitude fiction is capable of reaching. The author lets his imagination run riot over the facts! If I sound querulous or arrogant about this, it's not only that I have to protect my child, but that I truly don't believe anything like it exists in the history of journalism.

What is the first step in producing a "nonfiction novel?"

The difficulty was to choose a promising subject. If you intend to spend three or four or five years with a book, as I planned to do, then you want to be reasonably certain that the material will not soon "date." The content of much journalism so swiftly does, which is another of the medium's deterrents. A number of ideas occurred, but one after the other, and for one reason or another, each was eventually discarded, often after I'd done considerable preliminary work. Then one morning in November, 1959, while flicking through *The New York Times,* I encountered, on a deep-inside page, this headline: Wealthy Farmer, 3 of Family Slain. (pp. 2-3)

[Why] did you decide it was the subject you had been looking for?

I didn't. Not immediately. But after reading the story it suddenly struck me that a crime, the study of one such, might provide the broad scope I needed to write the kind of book I wanted to write. Moreover, the human heart being what it is, murder was a theme not likely to darken and yellow with time.

I thought about it all that November day, and part of the next; and then I said to myself: Well, why not *this* crime? The Clutter case. Why not pack up and go to Kansas and see what happens? Of course it was a rather frightening thought!—to arrive alone in a small, strange town, a town in the grip of an unsolved mass murder. Still, the circumstances of the place being altogether unfamiliar, geographically and atmospherically, made it that much more tempting. Everything would seem freshly minted—the people, their accents and attitudes, the landscape, its contours, the weather. All this, it seemed to me, could only sharpen my eye and quicken my ear.

In the end, I did not go alone. I went with a lifelong friend, Harper Lee. . . .

We traveled by train to St. Louis, changed trains and went to Manhattan, Kan., where we got off to consult Dr. James McClain, president of Mr. Clutter's alma mater, Kansas State University. Dr. McClain, a gracious man, seemed a little nonplussed by our interest in the case; but he gave us letters of introduction to several people in western Kansas. We rented a car and drove some 400 miles to Garden City. It was twilight when we arrived. I remember the car-radio was playing, and we heard: "Police authorities, continuing their investigation of the tragic Clutter slayings, have requested that anyone with pertinent information please contact the Sheriff's office. . . . "

If I had realized then what the future held, I never would have stopped in Garden City. I would have driven straight on. Like a bat out of hell.

What was Harper Lee's contribution to your work?

She kept me company when I was based out there. I suppose she was with me about two months altogether. She went on a number of interviews; she typed her own notes, and I had these and could refer to them. She was extremely helpful in the beginning, when we weren't making much headway with the town's people, by making friends with the wives of the people I wanted to meet. She became friendly with all the churchgoers. A Kansas paper said the other day that everyone out there was so wonderfully cooperative because I was a famous writer. The fact of the matter is that not one single person in the town had ever heard of me. (p. 3)

How much research did you do other than through interviews with the principals in the case?

Oh, a great deal. I did months of comparative research on murder, murderers, the criminal mentality, and I interviewed quite a number of murderers—solely to give me a perspective on these two boys. And then crime. I didn't know anything about crime or criminals when I began to do the book. I certainly do now! I'd say 80 per cent of the research I did I have never used. But it gave me such a grounding that I never had any hesitation in my consideration of the subject.

What was the most singular interview you conducted?

I suppose the most startled interviewee was Mr. Bell, the meat-packing executive from Omaha. He was the man who picked up Perry and Dick when they were hitchhiking across Nebraska. They planned to murder him and then make off with his car. Quite unaware of all this, Bell was saved, as you'll remember, just as Perry was going to smash in his head from the seat behind, because he slowed down to pick up another hitchhiker, a Negro. The boys told me this story, and they had this man's business card. I decided to interview him. I wrote him a letter, but got no answer. Then I wrote a letter to the personnel manager of the meat-packing company in Omaha, asking if they had a Mr. Bell in their employ. I told them I wanted to talk to him about a pair of hitchhikers he'd picked up four months previously. The manager wrote back and said that they *did* have a Mr. Bell on their staff, but it was surely the *wrong* Mr. Bell since it was against company policy for employees to take hitchhikers in their cars. So I telephoned Mr. Bell and when he got on the phone he was very brusque: he said I didn't know what I was talking about.

The only thing to do was to go to Omaha personally. I went up there and walked in on Mr. Bell and put two photographs down on his desk. I asked him if he recognized the two men. He said, why? So I told him that the two were the hitchhikers he said he had never given a ride to, that they had planned to kill him and then bury him in the prairie—and how close they'd come to it. Well, he turned every conceivable kind of color. You can imagine. He recognized them all right. He was quite cooperative about telling me about the trip, but he asked me not to use his real name. There are only three people in the book whose names I've changed—his, the convict Perry admired so much (Willie-Jay he's called in the book), and also I changed Perry Smith's sister's name.

How long after you went to Kansas did you sense the form of the book? Were there many false starts?

I worked for a year on the notes before I ever wrote one line. And when I wrote the first word, I had done the entire book in outline, down to the finest detail. Except for the last part, the final dispensation of the case—that was an evolving matter. It began, of course, with interviews—with all the different characters of the book. Let me give you two examples of how I worked from these interviews. In the first part of the book—the part that's called "The Last to See Them Alive"—there's a long narration, word for word, given by the school teacher who went with the sheriff to the Clutter house and found the four bodies. Well, I simply set that into the book as a straight complete interview—though it was, in fact, done several times: each time there'd be some little thing which I'd add or change. But I hardly interfered at all. A slight editing job. The school teacher tells the whole story himself—exactly what happened from the moment they got to the house, and what they found there.

On the other hand, in that same first part, there's a scene between the postmistress and her mother when the mother reports that the ambulances have gone to the Clutter house. That's a straight dramatic scene—with quotes, dialogue, action, everything. But it evolved out of interviews just like the one with the school teacher. Except in this case I took what they had told me and transposed it into straight narrative terms. Of course, elsewhere in the book, very often it's direct observation, events I saw myself—the trial, the executions. (pp. 3, 38)

You've kept yourself out of the book entirely. Why was that—considering your own involvement in the case?

My feeling is that for the nonfiction-novel form to be entirely successful, the author should not appear in the work. Ideally. Once the narrator does appear, he has to appear throughout, all the way down the line, and the I-I-I intrudes when it really shouldn't. I think the single most difficult thing in my book, technically, was to write it without ever appearing myself, and yet, at the same time, create total credibility.

Being removed from the book, that is to say, keeping yourself out of it, do you find it difficult to present your own point of view? For example, your own view as to why Perry Smith committed the murders.

Of course it's by the selection of what you choose to tell. I believe Perry did what he did for the reasons he himself states—that his life was a constant accumulation of disillusionments and reverses and he suddenly found himself (in the Clutter house that night) in a psychological cul-de-sac. The Clutters were such a perfect set of symbols for every frustration in his life. As Perry himself said, "I didn't have anything against them, and they never did anything wrong to me—the way other people have all my life. Maybe they're just the ones who had to pay for it." Now in that particular section where Perry talks about the reason for the murders, I could have included other views. But Perry's happens to be the one I believe is the right one, and it's the one that Dr. Satten at the Menninger Clinic arrived at quite independently, never having done any interviews with Perry.

I could have added a lot of other opinions. But that would have confused the issue, and indeed the book. I had to make up my mind, and move towards that one view, always. You can say that the reportage is incomplete. But then it has to be. It's a question of selection, you wouldn't get anywhere if it wasn't for that. I've often thought of the book as being like something reduced to a seed. Instead of presenting the reader with a full plant, with all the foliage, a seed is planted in the soil of his mind. I've often thought of the book in that sense. I make my own comment by what I choose to tell and how I choose to tell it. It is true that an author is more in control of fictional characters because he can do anything he wants with them as long as they stay credible. But in the nonfiction novel one can also manipulate: if I put something in which I don't agree about I can always set it in a context of qualification without having to step into the story myself to set the reader straight.

When did you first see the murderers—Perry and Dick?

The first time I ever saw them was the day they were returned to Garden City. I had been waiting in the crowd in the square for nearly five hours, frozen to death. That was the first time. I tried to interview them the next day—both completely unsuccessful interviews. I saw Perry first, but he was so cornered and suspicious—and quite rightly so—and paranoid that he couldn't have been less communicative. It was always easier with Dick. He was like someone you meet on a train, immensely garrulous, who starts up a conversation and is only too obliged to tell you *everything*. Perry became easier after the third or fourth month, but it wasn't until the last five years of his life that he was totally and absolutely honest with me, and came to trust me. I came to have great rapport with him right up through his last day. For the first year and a half, though, he would come just so close, and then no closer. He'd retreat into the forest and leave me standing outside. I'd hear him laugh in the dark. Then gradually he would come back. In the end, he could not have been more complete and candid.

How did the two accept being used as subjects for a book?

They had no idea what I was going to do. Well, of course, at the end they did. Perry was always asking me: Why are you writing this book? What is it supposed to mean? I don't understand why you're doing it. Tell me in one sentence why you want to do it. So I would say that it didn't have anything to do with changing the readers' opinion about anything, nor did I have any moral reasons worthy of calling them such—it was just that I had a strictly aesthetic theory about creating a book which could result in a work of art.

"That's really the truth, Perry," I'd tell him, and Perry would say, "A work of art, a work of art," and then he'd laugh and say, "What an irony, what an irony." I'd ask what he meant, and he'd tell me that all he ever wanted to do in his life was to produce a work of art. "That's all I ever wanted in my whole life," he said. "And now, what has happened? An incredible situation where I kill four people and *you're* going to produce a work of art." Well, I'd have to agree with him. It was a pretty ironic situation.

Did you ever show sections of the book to witnesses as you went along?

I have done it, but I don't believe in it. It's a mistake because it's almost impossible to write about anybody objectively and have that person really like it. People simply do not like to see themselves put down on paper. They're like somebody who goes to see his portrait in a gallery. He doesn't like it unless it's overwhelmingly flattering—I mean the ordinary person, not someone with genuine creative perception. Showing the thing in progress usually frightens the person and there's nothing to be gained by it. I showed various sections to five people in the book, and without exception each of them found something that he desperately wanted to change. Of the whole bunch, I changed my text for one of them because, although it was a silly thing, the person genuinely believed his entire life was going to be ruined if I *didn't* make the change.

Did Dick and Perry see sections of the book?

They saw some sections of it. Perry wanted terribly much to see the book. I had to let him see it because it just would have been too unkind not to. Each only saw the manuscript in little pieces. Everything mailed to the prison went through the censor. I wasn't about to have my manuscript floating around between those censors—not with those Xerox machines going clickety-clack. So when I went to the prison to visit I would bring parts—some little thing for Perry to read. Perry's greatest objection was the title. He didn't like it because he said the crime wasn't committed in cold blood. I told him the title had a double meaning. What was the other meaning? he wanted to know. Well, that wasn't something I was going to tell him. Dick's reaction to the book was to start switching and changing his story . . . saying what I had written wasn't exactly true. He wasn't trying to flatter himself; he tried to change it to serve his purposes legally, to support the various appeals he was sending through the courts. He wanted the book to read as if it was a legal brief for presentation in his behalf before the Supreme Court. But you see I had a perfect control-agent—I could always tell when Dick or Perry wasn't telling the truth. During the first few months or so of interviewing them, they weren't allowed to speak to each other. They were in separate cells. So I would keep crossing their stories, and what correlated, what checked out identically, was the truth.

How did the two compare in their recounting of the events?

Dick had an absolutely fantastic memory—one of the greatest memories I have ever come across. The reason I know it's great is that I lived the entire trip the boys went on from the time of the murders up to the moment of their arrest in Las Vegas—thousands of miles, what the boys called "the long ride." I went everywhere the boys had gone, all the hotel rooms, every single place in the book, Mexico, Acapulco, all of it. In the hotel in Miami Beach I stayed for three days until the manager realized why I was there and asked me to leave, which I was only too glad to do. Well, Dick could give me the names and addresses of any hotel or place along the route where they'd spent maybe just half a night. He told me when I got to Miami to take a taxi to such-and-such a place and get out on the boardwalk and it would be southwest of there, number 232, and opposite I'd find two umbrellas in the sand which advertised "Tan with Coppertone." That was how exact he was. He was the one who remembered the little card in the Mexico City hotel room—in the corner of the mirror—that reads "Your day ends at 2 p.m." He was extraordinary. Perry, on the other hand, was very bad at details of that sort, though he was good at remembering conversations and moods. He was concerned altogether in the overtones of things. He was much better at describing a general sort of mood or atmosphere than Dick who, though very sensitive, was impervious to that sort of thing.

What turned them back to the Clutter house after they'd almost decided to give up on the job?

Oh, Dick was always quite frank about that. I mean after it was all over. When they set out for the house that night, Dick was determined, before he ever went, that if the girl, Nancy, was there he was going to rape her. It wouldn't have been an act of the moment—he had been thinking about it for weeks. He told me that was one of the main reasons he was so determined to go back after they thought, you know for a moment, they wouldn't go. Because he'd been thinking about raping this girl for weeks and weeks. He had no idea what she looked like—after all, Floyd Wells, the man in prison who told them about the Clutters, hadn't seen the girl in 10 years: it had to do with the fact that she was 15 or 16. He liked young girls, much younger than Nancy Clutter actually.

What do you think would have happened if Perry had faltered and not begun the killings? Do you think Dick would have done it?

No. There is such a thing as the ability to kill. Perry's particular psychosis had produced this ability. Dick was merely ambitious—he could *plan* murder, but not commit it.

What was the boys' reaction to the killing?

They both finally decided that they had thoroughly enjoyed it. Once they started going, it became an immense emotional release. And they thought it was funny. With the criminal mind—and both boys had criminal minds, believe me—what seems most extreme to us is very often, if it's the most expedient thing to do, the *easiest* thing for a criminal to do. Perry and Dick both used to say (a memorable phrase) that it was much easier to kill somebody than it was to cash a bad check. Passing a bad check requires a great deal of artistry and style, whereas just going in and killing somebody requires only that you pull a trigger.

There are some instances of this that aren't in the book. At one point, in Mexico, Perry and Dick had a terrific falling-out, and Perry said he was going to kill Dick. He said that he'd already killed five people—he was lying, adding one more than he should have (that was the Negro he kept telling Dick he'd killed years before in Las Vegas) and that one more murder wouldn't matter. It was simple enough. Perry's cliché about it was that if you've killed one person you can kill anybody. He'd look at Dick, as they drove along together, and he'd say to himself, Well, I really ought to kill him, it's a question of expediency.

They had two other murders planned that aren't mentioned in the book. Neither of them came off. One "victim" was a man who ran a restaurant in Mexico City—a Swiss. They had become friendly with him eating in his restaurant and when they were out of money they evolved this whole plan about robbing and murdering him. They went to his apartment in Mexico City and waited for him all night long. He never showed up. The other "victim" was a man they never even knew—like the Clutters. He was a banker in a small Kansas town. Dick kept telling Perry that sure, they might have failed with the Clutter score, but this Kansas banker job was absolutely for certain. They were going to kidnap him and ask for ransom, though the plan was, as you might imagine, to murder him right away.

When they went back to Kansas completely broke, that was the main plot they had in mind. What saved the banker was the ride the two boys took with Mr. Bell, yet another "victim" who was spared, as you remember, when he slowed down the car to pick up the Negro hitchhiker. Mr. Bell offered Dick a job in his meat-packing company. Dick took him up on it and spent two days there on the pickle line—putting pickles in ham sandwiches, I think it was—before he and Perry went back on the road again.

Do you think Perry and Dick were surprised by what they were doing when they began the killings?

Perry never meant to kill the Clutters at all. He had a brain explosion. I don't think Dick was surprised, although later on he pretended he was. He knew, even if Perry didn't, that Perry would do it, and he was right. It showed an awfully shrewd instinct on Dick's part. Perry was bothered by it to a certain extent because he'd actually done it. He was always trying to find out in his own mind why he did it. He was amazed he'd done it. Dick, on the other hand, *wasn't* amazed, *didn't* want to talk about it, and simply wanted to forget the whole thing: he wanted to get on with life.

Was there any sexual relationship, or such tendencies, between them?

No. None at all. Dick was agressively heterosexual and had great success. Women liked him. As for Perry, his love for Willie-Jay in the State Prison was profound—and it was reciprocated, but never consummated physically, though there was the opportunity. The relationship between Perry and Dick was quite another matter. What is misleading, perhaps, is that in comparing himself with Dick, Perry used to say how totally "virile" Dick was. But he was referring, I think, to the practical and pragmatic sides of Dick—admiring them because as a dreamer he had none of that toughness himself at all.

Perry's sexual interests were practically nil. When Dick went to the whorehouses, Perry sat in the cafes, waiting. There was only one occasion—that was their first night in Mexico when the two of them went to a bordello run by an "old queen," according to Dick. Ten dollars was the price—which they weren't *about* to pay, and they said so. Well, the old queen looked at them and said perhaps he could arrange something for less; he disappeared and came out with this female midget about 3 feet 2 inches tall. Dick was disgusted, but Perry was madly excited. That was the only instance. Perry was such a little moralist after all.

How long do you think the two would have stayed together had they not been picked up in Las Vegas? Was the odd bond that kept them together beginning to fray? One senses in the rashness of their acts and plans a subconscious urge to be captured.

Dick planned to ditch Perry in Las Vegas, and I think he would have done so. No, I certainly don't think this particular pair wanted to be caught—though this is a common criminal phenomenon.

How do you yourself equate the sort of petty punk that Detective Alvin Dewey feels Dick is with the extraordinary violence in him—to "see hair all over the walls."?

Dick's was definitely a small-scale criminal mind. These violent phrases were simply a form of bragging meant to impress Perry, who *was* impressed, for he liked to think of Dick as being "tough." Perry was too sensitive to be "tough." Sensitive. But himself able to kill.

Is it one of the artistic limitations of the nonfiction novel that the writer is placed at the whim of chance? Suppose, in the case of **In Cold Blood** *clemency had been granted? Or the two boys had been less interesting? Wouldn't the artistry of the book have suffered? Isn't luck involved?*

It is true that I was in the peculiar situation of being involved in a slowly developing situation. I never knew until the events were well along whether a book was going to be possible. There was always the choice, after all, of whether to stop or go on. The book could have ended with the trial, with just a coda at the end explaining what had finally happened. If the principals had been uninteresting or completely uncooperative, I could have stopped and looked elsewhere, perhaps not very far. A nonfiction novel would have been written about any of the other prisoners in Death Row. . . . (pp. 38-41)

With the nonfiction novel I suppose the temptation to fictionalize events, or a line of dialogue, for example, must at times be overwhelming. With **In Cold Blood** *was there any invention of this sort to speak of—I was thinking specifically of the dog you described trotting along the road at the end of a section on Perry and Dick, and then later you introduce the next section on the two with Dick swerving to hit the dog. Was there actually a dog at that exact point in the narrative, or were you using this habit of Dick's as a fiction device to bridge the two sections?*

No. There was a dog, and it was precisely as described. One doesn't spend almost six years on a book, the point of which is factual accuracy, and then give way to minor distortions. People are so suspicious. They ask, "How can you reconstruct the conversation of a dead girl, Nancy Clutter, without fictionalizing?" If they read the book carefully, they can see readily enough how it's done. It's a silly question. Each time Nancy appears in the narrative, there are witnesses to what she is saying and doing—phone calls, conversations, being overheard. When she walks the horse up from the river in the twilight, the hired man is a witness and talked to her then.

The last time we see her, in her bedroom, Perry and Dick themselves were the witnesses, and told me what she had said. What is reported of her, even in the narrative form, is as accurate as many hours of questioning, over and over again, can make it. All of it is reconstructed from the evidence of witnesses—which is implicit in the title of the first section of the book—"The Last to See Them Alive."

How conscious were you of film techniques in planning the book?

Consciously, not at all. Subconsciously, who knows?

After their conviction, you spent years corresponding and visiting with the prisoners. What was the relationship between the two of them?

When they were taken to Death Row, they were right next door to each other. But they didn't talk much. Perry was intensely secretive and wouldn't ever talk because he didn't want the other prisoners—York, Latham, and particularly Andrews, whom he despised—to hear anything that he had to say. He would write Dick notes on "kites" as he called them. He would reach out his hand and zip the "kite" into Dick's cell. Dick didn't much enjoy receiving these communications because they were always one form or another of recrimination—nothing to do with the Clutter crime, but just general dissatisfaction with things there in prison and . . . the people, very often Dick himself. Perry'd send Dick a note: "If I hear you tell another of those filthy jokes again I'll kill you when we go to the shower!" He was quite a little moralist, Perry, as I've said.

It was over a moral question that he and I had a tremendous falling-out once. It lasted for about two months. I used to send them things to read—both books and magazines. Dick only wanted girlie magazines—either those or magazines that had to do with cars and motors. I sent them both whatever they wanted. Well, Perry said to me one time: "How could a person like you go on contributing to the degeneracy of Dick's mind by sending him all this 'degenerate filthy' literature?" Weren't they all sick enough without this further contribution towards their total moral decay? He'd got very grand talking in terms that way. I tried to explain to him that I was neither his judge nor Dick's—and if that was what Dick wanted to read, that was *his* business. Perry felt that was entirely wrong—that people had to fulfill an obligation towards moral leadership. Very grand. Well, I agree with him up to a point, but in the case of Dick's reading matter it was absurd, of course, and so we got into such a really serious argument about it that afterwards, for two months, he wouldn't speak or even write to me.

How often did the two correspond with you?

Except for those occasional fallings-out, they'd write twice a week. I wrote them both twice a week all those years. One letter to the both of them didn't work. I had to write them both, and I had to be careful not to be repetitious, because they were very jealous of each other. Or rather, Perry was terribly jealous of Dick, and if Dick got one more letter than he did, that would create a great crisis. I wrote them about what I was doing, and where I was living, describing everything in the most careful detail. Perry was interested in my dog, and I would always write about him, and send along pictures. I often wrote them about their legal problems.

Do you think if the social positions of the two boys had been different that their personalities would have been markedly different?

Of course there wasn't anything peculiar about Dick's social position. He was a very ordinary boy who simply couldn't sustain any kind of normal relationship with anybody. If he had been given $10,000, perhaps he might have settled into some small business. But I don't think so. He had a very natural criminal instinct towards everything. He was oriented towards stealing from the beginning. On the other hand, I think Perry could have been an entirely different person. I really do. His life had been so incredibly abysmal that I don't see what chance he had as a little child except to steal and run wild.

Of course, you could say that his brother, with exactly the same background, went ahead and became the head of his class. What does it matter that he later killed himself. No, it's there—it's the fact that the brother *did* kill himself, in spite of his success, that shows how really awry the background of the Smiths' lives were. Terrifying. Perry had extraordinary qualities, but they just weren't channeled properly—to put it mildly. He was really a talented boy in a limited way—he had a genuine sensitivity—and, as I've said, when he talked about himself as an artist, he wasn't really joking at all.

You once said that emotionality made you lose writing control—that you had to exhaust emotion before you could get to work. Was there a problem with **In Cold Blood,** *considering your involvement with the case and its principals?*

Yes, it was a problem. Nevertheless, I felt in control throughout. However, I had great difficulty writing the last six or seven pages. This even took a physical form: hand paralysis. I finally used a typewriter—very awkward as I always write in longhand.

Your feeling about capital punishment is implicit in the title of the book. How do you feel the lot of Perry and Dick should have been resolved?

I feel that capital crimes should all be handled by Federal Courts, and that those convicted should be imprisoned in a special Federal prison where, conceivably, a life-sentence could mean, as it does not in state courts, just that.

Did you see the prisoners on their final day? Perry wrote you a 100-page letter that you received after the execution. Did he mention that he had written it?

Yes, I was with them the last hour before the execution. No, Perry did not mention the letter. He only kissed me on the cheek and said, "Adios, amigo."

What was the letter about?

It was a rambling letter, often intensely personal, often setting forth his various philosophies. He had been reading Santayana. Somewhere he had read *The Last Puritan,* and had been very impressed by it. What I really think impressed him about me was that I had once visited Santayana at the Convent of the Blue Nuns in Rome. He always wanted me to go into great detail about that visit, what Santayana had looked like, and the nuns, and all the physical details. Also, he had been reading Thoreau. Narratives didn't interest him at all. So in his letter he would write: "As Santayana says—" and then there'd be five pages of what Santayana *did* say. Or he'd write: "I agree with Thoreau about this. Do you?"—then

he'd write that he didn't care what I thought, and he'd add five or ten pages of what he agreed with Thoreau about.

The case must have left you with an extraordinary collection of memorabilia.

My files would almost fill a whole small room, right up to the ceiling. All my research. . . . I have some of the personal belongings—all of Perry's because he left me everything he owned; it was miserably little, his books, written in and annotated; the letters he received while in prison . . . not very many . . . his paintings and drawings. Rather a heartbreaking assemblage that arrived about a month after the execution. I simply couldn't bear to look at it for a long time. I finally sorted everything. Then, also, after the execution, that 100-page letter from Perry got to me. The last line of the letter—it's Thoreau, I think, a paraphrase, goes, "And suddenly I realize life is the father and death is the mother." The last line. Extraordinary.

What will you do with this collection?

I think I may burn it all. You think I'm kidding? I'm not. The book is what is important. It exists in its own right. The rest of the material is extraneous, and it's personal, what's more. I don't really want people poking around in the material of six years of work and research. The book is the end result of all that, and it's exactly what I wanted to do from it.

Detective Dewey told me that he felt the case and your stays in Garden City had changed you—even your style of dress . . . that you were more "conservative" now, and had given up detachable collars. . . .

Of course the case changed me! How could anyone live through such an experience without it profoundly affecting him? I've always been almost overly aware of the precipice we all walk along, the ridge and the abyss on either side; the last six years have increased this awareness to an almost all-pervading point. As for the rest—Mr. Dewey, a man for whom I have the utmost affection and respect, is perhaps confusing comparative youth (I was 35 when we first met) with the normal aging process. Six years ago I had four more teeth and considerably more hair than is now the case, and furthermore I lost 20 pounds. I dress to accommodate the physical situation. By the way, I have never worn a detachable collar. (pp. 41-3)

What has been the response of readers of **In Cold Blood** *to date?*

I've been staggered by the letters I've received—their quality of sensibility, their articulateness, the compassion of their authors. The letters are not fan letters. They're from people deeply concerned about what it is I've written about. About 70 per cent of the letters think of the book as a reflection on American life—this collision between the desperate, ruthless, wandering, savage part of American life, and the other, which is insular and safe, more or less. It has struck them because there is something so awfully inevitable about what is going to happen: the people in the book are completely beyond their own control. For example, Perry wasn't an evil person. If he'd had any chance in life, things would have been different. But every illusion he'd ever had, well, they all evaporated, so that on that night he was so full of self-hatred and self-pity that I think he would have killed *some*body—perhaps not that night, on the next, or the next. You can't go through life without ever getting anything you want, ever.

At the very end of the book you give Alvin Dewey a scene in the country cemetery, a chance meeting with Sue Kidwell, which seems to synthesize the whole experience for him. Is there such a moment in your own case?

I'm still very much haunted by the whole thing. I have finished the book, but in a sense I *haven't* finished it: it keeps churning around in my head. It particularizes itself now and then, but not in the sense that it brings about a total conclusion. It's like the echo of E. M. Forster's Marabar Caves, the echo that's meaningless and yet it's there: one keeps hearing it all the time. (p. 43)

George Plimpton, "The Story Behind a Nonfiction Novel," in The New York Times Book Review, January 16, 1966, pp. 2-3, 38-43.

STANLEY KAUFFMANN

[*In Cold Blood*] is a readable, generally interesting book about four murders in Kansas in 1959. If the author were John Doe, literary consideration could well end there. One might perhaps add that some of the writing is overripe, much of the detail is extraneous "color," some of the handling of material injudicious, and that a 343-page true-crime chronicle which does little more than recount a crime is inflated. Beyond that, however, the treatment, the style, the result would preclude extensive criticism. . . .

It is not flogging of the author with the publisher's blurb to quote: "*In Cold Blood* . . . represents the culmination of [Capote's] long-standing desire to make a contribution toward the establishment of a serious new literary form: the Non-fiction Novel." . . . The stated aim is worth discussion, but that Capote has accomplished it is untrue. When I reviewed his [*Selected Writings*] in this journal, I noted that he seemed to me an author in search of a character, that his affinity with non-fiction was evident, that his forthcoming book might provide the role as writer for which he has observably, if not consciously, been looking during all his professional life. *In Cold Blood* is not a happy conclusion to that search, if it is a conclusion. The role in which it puts Capote is less than one could have hoped for. The book has been executed without the finesse of which, at his best, he has been capable, and it is residually shallow. . . .

Capote's structural method can be called cinematic: he uses intercutting of different story strands, intense close-ups, flashbacks, traveling shots, background detail, all as if he were fleshing out a scenario. There is nothing intrinsically defective in the method (although it seems the most obvious choice); but its mechanisms creak here because the hand of the maker is always felt, pushing and pulling and arranging. The chief defect, or imbalance, in the structure is that by page 74 we know that four people have been butchered by two degenerates and we wonder what in the world is going to occupy the remaining 269 pages. Just a detective story? Some psychoanalytical delving? The account of the trial and appeals and execution? All of these are included, of course, but none of them is sufficiently interesting to justify the length accorded them. All of them are overdone, except the psychological inquiry, which is insufficient.

There are attractions in the book. The narrative has impetus, although it is diluted in the latter sections. Western Kansas—wide, flat, almost a separate sovereignty—is well established, a notch all its own in the Bible Belt. Some of the characters

are vivid, such as Nancy Clutter, the cheerful, scrubbed, healthy daughter. There are snatches of simon-pure flavorful dialogue. A lunchroom owner (a woman): "Some people say I'm a tough old bird, but the Clutter business sure took the fly out of me." (p. 19)

But it is ridiculous in judgment and debasing of all of us to call this book literature. Are we so bankrupt, so avid for novelty that, merely because a famous writer produces an amplified magazine crime-feature, the result is automatically elevated to serious literature just as Andy Warhol, by painting a soup-carton, has allegedly elevated it to art? (Already I regret writing that; some Capote partisan may take it as the book's pop *raíson d'être*, if this has not already been done.) Look first at the writing. Capote demonstrates on almost every page that he is the most outrageously overrated stylist of our time. There is the congenital inability to write straightforward English. The mail messenger seems "younger than her years, which amount to seventy-five." Why not "seems younger than her seventy-five years"? Another woman is "sparsely fleshed." Why not "gaunt" or "spare" or "thin"? There is continual strain for the unusual word, a sure sign of insecurity: "His apartment was not the ideal lair for a would-be author." Does Capote know what "lair" means? If so, will he explain why would-be authors need a different kind from other authors? There is much of the clumsy, crammed, *New Yorker*-type sentence: "Though as yet unpublished, young Hendricks, a he-mannish [*sic*] ex-sailor from Oklahoma who smokes a pipe and has a mustache and a crop of untamed black hair, at least looks literary. . . ." There is, inevitably, much "fine" writing: "Though mud abounded underfoot, the sun, so long shrouded by snow and cloud, seemed an object freshly made, and the trees . . . were lightly veiled in a haze of virginal green." Or the very last line: "Then, starting home, he walked toward the trees, and under them, leaving behind him the big sky, the whisper of wind voices in the wind-bent wheat." (Presumably he decided not to take the sky and the wind voices with him.) This is Reddiwip writing—goo that gushes out under the force of compressed air and that, unless one puts it to the test of taste, looks like the real thing. Capote has also made sure to include what is probably the oldest solecism in English: " . . . an old man who hissed at him: 'Killer! Killer!' "

Sometimes poor writing is separable from illumination. In non-fiction, particularly, the distinction between style and content is easier to make than in fiction and is more relevant. But Capote's illumination goes little further than supplying us with facts—and he has vastly oversupplied facts. Condensation by about a third would have improved the book threefold. He suffers from the current craze for fact-gathering and the inability to "waste" material once he has gathered it. On a television panel a few years ago he made the truthful comment about the Kerouac school of fiction: "That isn't writing, it's typing." One can say of this book—with sufficient truth to make it worth saying: "This isn't writing, it's research."

Thus we get: three pages about the brief friendship after the crime between the dead girl's boy friend and her close girl friend; five pages of biography about a man who merely happens to be a fellow-prisoner of Hickock and Smith in Death Row; extensive cute details of the home life of the detective who solved the case; and much, much more superfluous material.

We do get fairly clear pictures of the two murderers, but this is surely minimal in so long a book; and the portraits, though extended, are not deep. Some of the more penetrating comment comes from biographical statements that the two men prepared and from a long letter written to Smith by his married sister when he was in prison a year before the murders—this letter is the most interesting document in the book. Statements like these, from people not customarily given to writing, are often phrased pungently and contain perceptions that, probably snobbishly, we would not expect. There seems to be an impulse to biography, towards preservation of self on paper, which is buried in the normally unliterate and which is released by an occasion that forces them to write.

Nevertheless we do not know enough about these two men at the close to justify the time we have spent with them. It is possibly unjust to ask Capote to solve the mystery of criminal behavior when psychologists, penologists, sociologists are baffled, but if some reasonably satisfactory attempt is not made in this direction, then what *is* the justification for such a book? Mere accretion of grisly fact and the thrills therefrom?

Even the deployment of fact, as such, is wobbly. For example, a major point about Hickock—his sexual predilection for little girls—is not even mentioned until Page 201. Again, there is no comment on the odd relationship between the two criminals. Nothing homosexual occurs overtly, but Hickock constantly calls the other man "honey," there were strange feminine jealousies between them, and Smith was sometimes in the same room while Hickock had intercourse with a girl. No Freudian sage is needed to reveal the girl as a surrogate. Capote leaves unexplored this whole area of latent homosexuality.

In the *Life* interview about this book [see the January 7, 1966 issue], Capote says:

> My theory, you see, is that you can take *any* subject and make it into a nonfiction novel. By that I don't mean a historical or documentary novel—those are popular and interesting but impure genres, with neither the persuasiveness of fact nor the poetic altitude of fiction. . . . What I've done is much harder than a conventional novel. You have to get away from your own particular vision of the novel.

In itself the statement is ludicrous. (Presumably their "own particular vision" is what hamstrung Flaubert, Proust, and Joyce.) What it all amounts to is the puffery of an artistically unsuccessful writer of fiction pursuing his love of the Gothic (which he established in his first novel and his short stories) into life. Why poetize about mules hanging by their necks from balcony railings (as in *Other Voices, Other Rooms*), which is only manufactured grotesquerie, when you can write fancily about real events leading up to and including two real hangings of men? (pp. 20-1)

[What] lies under Capote's statement and the rest of the interview is the question currently much debated—the present pertinence of fiction; whether the writing of factual books is not more appropriate than fiction to talented writers today, whether the functions of the novel have been historically concluded, whether the context for fiction—social structure, community ideals, accepted cosmology—is lacking. It is my view that, in both old and new modes of fiction, much interesting work is being done today; but the question is valid, and anyone who predicted that the status and health of the novel will be no worse a century from now would be, to say the least, sanguine.

In Capote's book, however, there is no kind of answer to the question. There is little fusion of the insights of art with the powers of fact—not as much use of the novelist's eye as there was, for instance, in *The Muses Are Heard*. . . . The Nonfiction Novel is a term that, as such, may stand with "hardtop convertible" and "fresh-frozen food," but it is possibly a worthy ideal, an avenue for writers who feel that the anatomization and re-synthesis of experience is a doubtful process in a society without implicit guidelines. However, there is little in Capote's book to help clear that avenue. He says:

> I don't think that crime is all that interesting a subject. What could be more cut and dried, really, than two ex-convicts who set out to rob a family and end up killing them? The important thing is the depth you can plunge to and height you can reach.

Agreed. The depth in this book is no deeper than its mineshaft of factual detail; its height is rarely higher than that of good journalism and often falls below it.

The *Life* article settles one other point. While I was reading the book, I wondered at the absence of photographs. *Life* includes a number of photographs of the victims, the killers, some of the other principal persons and places, and indirectly explains why Capote was wise to leave them out. Any one of the pictures is worth several thousand of his words. (p. 23)

Stanley Kauffmann, "Capote in Kansas," in The New Republic, *Vol. 154, No. 4, January 22, 1966, pp. 19-21, 23.*

HILTON KRAMER

The belief, apparently widely held, that Truman Capote is a "master" of the art of fiction is not one that critical scrutiny can sustain. His early books were the work of a writer with a gift for surfaces—of language, of feeling, of life itself. To penetrate those carefully wrought surfaces was to find oneself, not in a credible world of the author's creation but in a very stylish void. Capote's sense of evil, so extravagantly praised, turned out to be mainly a sense of interior decoration. All those exquisite symbolic situations resembled nothing so much as beautifully decorated, elaborately wrapped boxes gotten up for display: Upon examination, they proved to be perfectly empty.

No, the author of *Other Voices, Other Rooms* and *A Tree of Night* was no master. But he was an interesting literary and publishing phenomenon. At a time when news of Faulkner and Henry James was just beginning to get through to a larger reading audience, he brought enough syntactical glitter, Gothic distortion, and simulated intellectual density to his work to make it seem somehow related to the accomplishments of these newly discovered figures. At the same time, Capote was careful not to tax his readers with anything like Faulkner's or James' moral complexities. His fiction gave one the sensation of reading something serious and artful while exacting very little in the way of cerebration or even involvement. But slight as it was, Capote's fiction enjoyed a considerable vogue. Its acclaim prompted a succession of imitations. For a time, the atmosphere was quite thick with a kind of literary wisteria, behind which one could just barely discern some evidence of the real world—mainly pederasty in various forms of decorative disguise. Capote's fiction was never as meretricious as Tennessee Williams', but, like Williams', its interest lay primarily in its being an episode in the history of taste.

If one feels compelled to underscore this point now, it is because the press campaign surrounding the publication of Capote's extraordinary new book, ***In Cold Blood,*** is so patently designed to suggest that a major novelist has succeeded in turning some kind of literary handspring. Through the miracle of modern publicity, we are invited to take a job of inspired reportage as a new and superior form of fiction. What nonsense! It is not enough, apparently, for this book to be very good; it must be thought great. It is not enough that it has something to tell us about our own time, but must be promoted as if it were a work for all time. As Capote's whole career has been, to a large extent, a product of the publishing industry's public relations machine, it would have been expecting too much to think his best book—actually rather modest in design, but powerful in its detail—could be launched with anything less than a campaign that might have been a little overdone for the emergence of a new political personality. Still, it is worth insisting that both Capote's real accomplishment in ***In Cold Blood*** and its limitations do not exactly correspond to the transcendent object described by this army of heady publicists for whom Capote himself . . . has served as both field commander and chief strategist.

The narrative is already too familiar to bear retelling here. The murder of the Clutter family by Dick Hickock and Perry Smith had about it more than the requisite horror for holding our interest—and not for holding it only, but for exciting and aggravating it, like an exposed nerve stretched taut. The crime itself had an almost folk-tale simplicity in its moral counterpoint. Capote exploits this counterpoint . . . for all it is worth; and he shows it to be worth, in terms of its power to haunt our minds, a great deal. We are made to feel that . . . it was a case of virgin blood being ruthlessly and senselessly shed: a slaughter of the innocents, American-style. Much of Capote's skill has gone into rendering this moral contrast of the victims and their executioners with exceptional pictorial vividness. Here is the world of a Norman Rockwell Thanksgiving Day poster invaded by two evil spirits out of Dostoevsky by way of Sherwood Anderson—the homely odor of clean linen and the savory smells of the country kitchen overcome by the stink of the lower depths.

Reading the story in installments in the *New Yorker,* alternately impressed and aghast, and certainly too pained and absorbed to question the subtleties and deceptions of craft involved, one accepted the awful tale on its own terms—or what then seemed, in the magazine, to be its own terms—and accepted them completely. The vignettes of minor characters were sharp and memorable, yet even their humor and surpassing corniness served to distend still further the shock one felt on first reading the bloody details. The reader's initial stunned response was kept raw and unresolved by its reflection and extension in the "real" response registered by these minor figures, whose actual lives—one had to remind oneself—had been so exacerbated by the real villainy.

There was shock of an altogether different, more delightful, more sheerly literary kind, too, in the wonderful talk of these figures. . . . Capote has filled his book with this talk . . . and not the least of one's pleasure in reading his dreadful narrative was the sense it gave one of what, after all the calculated artifice of recent fiction, that speech could mean again for the art of the novel.

Still, Capote has not written a novel, and it remains to be seen whether his brilliant journalistic use of this virtually rediscovered language will lead to anything significant in the fiction of the future. Capote himself, though he now writes a markedly less florid prose than formerly (the beneficent influence of the *New Yorker* perhaps?), still reaches for something fancy and elevated wherever circumstance permits—and succeeds, too, I think, in effecting a beautiful prose rhythm in this orchestration of plain and fancy styles. But it is, all the same, the prose rhythm of a superior reporter; it is not what the language of fiction, the medium of a significant art, always is: the refraction of a serious moral imagination.

Rereading the story now in book form, it is this last deficiency that stands out on every page, that not only renders Capote's claim to have created a new form of the novel mere highfalutin, but clarifies something central to his whole sensibility. It is not, of course, that one believes fiction alone to have the requisite moral specifications. A work like Henry James' *The American Scene* or, at a somewhat lower altitude, the reportage of Rebecca West or the essays of James Baldwin—these shed, not only on the subjects at hand but on experience at large, precisely the kind of light one finds missing from Capote's painstaking journalistic reconstruction. Such works have, first of all, a voice that never feigns innocence, that refuses to separate itself from the events passing before us, that openly acknowledges its own stake in the issues under scrutiny. And to the extent that the writer feels himself implicated, not as a mere observer but as a moral agent, so the reader too feels himself drawn into the moral vortex of the experience being portrayed.

Capote's craft is designed to have quite the opposite effect. It leaves one removed, distant, even a little cynical. Its detailed accounts of the lives of the murderers—the only lives we are given in any depth—are explanations in a void. The irony on which the book closes—the hapless murderers themselves murdered by judicial decree—is too pat, too easy, too abstract. So successful has the author been in keeping himself "out" of the tale that one closes the book mentally searching him out, suspecting at last that there is a far more revealing story to be told in his own involvement with the characters and events whose fate is so icily recounted. And until *that* story is revealed—a real novelist would, of course, have found in that connection his moral crux—everything else remains only brilliantly delineated evidence placed before a jury disabused of its pieties.

Admittedly, there is something ungrateful about these strictures. They are the observations of a reader who has been through the story twice. The first time around one was perfectly pleased to have the author out of sight; one gave oneself up to his shattering tale, and waited impatiently, week by week, for more. . . . I had never before appreciated the force of Miss I. Compton-Burnett's remark that "Real life seems to have no plots"; rereading ***In Cold Blood,*** the remark cuts deeper, for Capote has written a book that puts that observation to a crucial test, and ends by confirming its wisdom. (pp. 18-19)

Hilton Kramer, "Real Gardens with Real Toads," in The New Leader, *Vol. XLIX, No. 3, January 31, 1966, pp. 18-19.*

REBECCA WEST

It is to Mr. Capote's disadvantage that every book he writes turns into what our great grandmothers used to call "a pretty book." He knows that ours is a bloodstained planet but he knows also that it turns on its axis and moves round the sun with a dancer's grace, and his style defines the dancer as ballet-trained. For this reason Mr. Capote is often not taken as seriously as he should be, and it is possible that his new book, **In Cold Blood,** may be regarded simply as a literary *tour de force* instead of the formidable statement about reality which it is.

In six long years Mr. Capote crawled like an ant of genius over the landscape where, on a November night in 1959, a prosperous Kansas farmer, his wife, his daughter of sixteen, and his son of fifteen, were murdered. . . . That Mr. Capote has invented nothing and recorded with a true ear and utter honesty is proved by the conversations in the book. The inhabitants of Holcomb, Kansas, do not on any page engage in the subtle and economical dialogue Mr. Capote ascribes to the characters in his novels. They speak the words which reporters hear when they interview the participants in prodigious events, and listen to with embarrassed ears. The stuff is corny, yet not just corny. The corn is celestial. Even the cleverest writer who tries to invent it achieves an obvious fakery, which is quite absent from this book. (p. 108)

The two murderers were drawn to the Clutters' home because its beneficence had so impressed the twilit mind of a convict that he made a symbol for it in a wholly imaginary safe stuffed with dollars. He had babbled of this to Richard Hickock, whom he had known in prison, the younger of the two murderers, and the simpler character. . . . When [Hickock] was a boy a neighbor's son had come back from a holiday on the Gulf Coast with a collection of shells. These he had stolen, and hammered one by one into dust. "Envy," writes Mr. Capote, "was constantly with him; the Enemy was anyone who was someone he wanted to be or who had anything he wanted to have." As he appears in **In Cold Blood** he is the most complete study I can remember of the spite which makes a certain sort of criminal, such as the men whose entries in the card index of burglars of Scotland Yard are of a special color, because they make a practice, when they have neatly packed up their loot, of defecating on the best carpet on the premises.

The other murderer, Perry Smith, was worse because he was better. He was a physical oddity, with the torso of an athlete and stunted legs, so that he stood no taller than a twelve-year-old child. He had a hideous life, being born into a family disrupted by misfortune, and subjected during his childhood to institutional experiences which, whether they were as he recalled them, filled him with resentment. He spent some time in the merchant marine, and went with the Army to Korea and Japan, where he piled up a crime sheet, returned to the United States, and was injured in an automobile accident far worse than Hickock's, which seven years after left him with agonizing pains in his legs and made him an aspirin addict. . . .

He was half-Cherokee and had a dark charm; he was literate, read verse, was musical, loved his guitar, cultivated his sensitiveness, and bore himself according to the rumor of the romantic tradition which had reached him from far-off. And his woe was real. He had, Mr. Capote tells us, "the aura of an exiled animal, a creative walking wounded." He excites pity

as Hickock does not. Yet he was far more dreadful, as Mr. Capote admits with heroically honest detachment. If one asks why he was so dreadful, the answer seems to be that he was guilty of a sin which is the spiritual equivalent of usury. He exploited all his misfortunes to the full; he laid them out with cool prudence to bring in the heaviest possible yield of pity: he came to love pity too much. He coveted the precious substance more and more, he could not bear anyone else to get any, he wanted all there was in the world. He became infinitely cruel, as was shown in his relations with his father. (p. 110)

Perry's inhumanity was exhibited also in his relations with his one surviving sister, Barbara, who had burrowed her way out of the family hell and made a good life out of a modest marriage. She understood her brother well, and uttered a very competent analysis of one of his characteristics, the generalized sensitiveness of the romantic:

> He can seem so warmhearted and sympathetic. Gentle. He cries so easily. Sometimes music sets him off and when he was a little boy he used to cry because he thought a sunset was beautiful. Or the moon. Oh, he can fool you. He can make you feel so sorry for him.

She might have said worse, for he had committed a considerable offense against her. He had sent her a young girl, with a letter saying that this was his twenty-year-old wife, and asking that she be looked after as he was in trouble. After a day or two the girl (who was in fact fourteen and nobody's wife) departed with her hosts' suitcases, crammed with their clothes, their silver, and the kitchen clock. Nevertheless when Perry was in prison Barbara wrote him a long, clumsy, touching, unhappy, loving letter, asking him not to blame his father for his misfortunes and to get on with his life. He kept it only because of the "very sensitive" commentary on it which was written in pidgin psychologese by a fellow prisoner, an Irish tenor who had spent twenty years in prison for dismal little thefts, and thought nothing of Barbara. Perry loved jargon; he kept a little notebook, full of rare words, such as "thanatoid" and "amerce." Also he loved contempt. He was an inveterate moralizer. Almost any act committed by any person other than himself provoked him to sneering condemnation on high ethical grounds.

Perry was to exhibit this holier-than-thou attitude very strangely in the death house. To an Army buddy, a saintly young man, who visited him out of Christian charity, he explained he felt no remorse for murdering the Clutters:

> It's easy to kill—a lot easier than passing a bad check. Just remember, I only knew the Clutters maybe an hour. If I'd really known them, I guess I'd feel different. I don't think I could live with myself. But the way it was, it was like picking off targets in a shooting gallery.

But he had prefaced these blank and icy words by a brief exercise of his talent for moralizing on a subject which never ceased to shock him.

> Soldiers don't lose much sleep. They murder, and get medals for doing it. The good people of Kansas want to murder me—and some hangman will be glad to get the work.

He could not get over the disgusting barbarism which made the inhabitants of the State of Kansas retain capital punishment on their statute book and voluntarily incur the blood guilt of hanging him. Yet it was he who had killed all four

Clutters. Hickock had conspired with him to kill them, but Perry confessed that it was he who had cut Mr. Clutter's throat and shot the others. Before Perry got to the death house he had reason to know that he had not been attacked by a unique and unrepeated impulse. Twice after the murder he and Hickock had stood in the highway and thumbed a lift from prosperous drivers, meaning to rob and murder them. . . . Yet to the end Perry looked down on the citizens of Kansas because they found themselves capable of killing him. "I don't believe in capital punishment, morally or legally," he said on the gallows. What bourgeois today could achieve such a fine flower of hypocrisy? Tartuffe still lives, but has changed his address.

In Cold Blood leaves us asking whether the waste of these six lives could have been avoided by a society which had the wits and was willing to take the pains. Some elements in the tragedy are beyond our control. Nothing in Hickock's origin or upbringing explains his spite, and Perry Smith's situation explains his all too well. It is one of the few notable omissions in the book that Mr. Capote does not tell us if he found any material in the California child-welfare files, to throw any light on the degree to which Perry was helped or abandoned in his childhood. One can imagine that he would have been as hard to help as a trapped animal. For the rest, the trial of the two was consonant with the law. Hickock was hanged for murder which he had not committed, when he should have been sentenced to a term of imprisonment as an accessory, but this was his own fault. The truth could only be established if both he and Perry chose to give evidence, but this, for a reason Mr. Capote does not explain, they did not do. This curious abstinence is a proof of the irrelevance of capital punishment. The prospect of hanging could never have acted as a deterrent to these two men who were, to use a word from Perry Smith's little book, obstinately thanatoid. They were obsessed with death. (pp. 112-13)

It is within the knowledge of all of us that life is often hard to bear. But it has oddly happened that our society which is, if not perfect, at least more generally comfortable than any society has succeeded in being before, has produced a literature quite often taking as its basis the pretense that life is quite unbearable. This pretense is behind some good plays and novels and some bad ones. A work of art does not have to be completely valid either in its facts or in its philosophy, so it may share imperfection with books and plays which cannot be classed as works of art at all. This pretense is behind some good plays and novels and some bad ones. A work of art does not have to be completely valid either in its facts or in its philosophy, so it may share imperfection with books and plays which cannot be classed as works of art at all. This pretense that life is unbearable is not accepted as literally true by any but a minute number of readers or writers; very few people commit suicide. But it is widely adopted as an intellectual counter, not an opinion which one sincerely holds and would act upon, but which one uses as a substitute for opinion when talking or writing, like the chips one uses when gambling at casinos. It then passes into general currency, in films, on television, in chatter, and so it happens that one day a naïve person with stronger dramatic instincts than most, and less sense of self-preservation, comes to believe that sophisticated people believe life to be unbearable, and therefore it is not terrible to carry the belief to its logical conclusion and to deprive his fellowmen of their lives. When society shows its horror the murderer feels himself lifted into the distinction so difficult to attain in our vast societies: he is one of the few strong and

logical people in a community of weaklings afraid to act up to their beliefs.

What air do these people breathe not permeated with the culture we have made? Where else could they have caught this infection but from us? There is a hateful continuity between the world of literature and the world of Mr. Capote's criminals. Hickock bought an expensive gun on credit from the store beside his parents' home, took it with him to the Clutters' house, where it did its work, took it back to his parents' home, and abandoned it there. They, thinking he had used it only once on a pheasant shoot, tried to get the storekeeper to take it back, but he refused, and they had to pay for it. At all times they were poverty-stricken and his father was dying of cancer. It is depressing to recognize how easily this episode would find a home in fiction. It would work in nicely to a certain kind of Roman Catholic novel, in which God would find the ripe sinnerhood of Hickock far preferable to the insipid Pelagian virtue of his parents. It would be warmly welcomed in a violence cult novel, which would maintain that the murder of the Clutters would extend the experience of the murderers so far beyond ordinary limits, that they would rank as supermen, and the parents could be regarded as serfs justly paying tribute to their lords. It would also find a place in the physical-horror type of novel, which would revel in Hickock's father's cancer and Perry's habit of bed-wetting. Literature must go its own way, sometimes a blessing to its age, sometimes a curse; for no soothsayer can ever predict when it is going to be the one or the other. All the same there are occasions when it is comprehensible why Plato felt fear lest the poets corrupt the minds of the people. But at any rate nothing but blessing can flow from Mr. Capote's grave and reverend book. (p. 114)

Rebecca West, "A Grave and Reverend Book," in Harper's Magazine, *Vol. 232, No. 1389, February, 1966, pp. 108, 110, 112-14.*

F. W. DUPEE

In Cold Blood is the best documentary account of an American crime ever written, partly because the crime here in question is not yet a part of the heritage. Only in the region where it took place was the Clutter murder large-scale news. Generally ignored elsewhere (there have since been so many other virtually gratuitous rampages of blood and sex), the Clutter affair has been spared the attentions of the memorialists. Its horrors, its meanings, its supposed relation to the *Zeitgeist* have gone unexplored. For Mr. Capote the incident is pristine material; and the book he has written about it is appropriately and impressively fresh.

But if *In Cold Blood* deserves highest marks among American crime histories, it also raises certain questions. What, more or less, is the narrative intended to be; and in what spirit are we supposed to take it? While the book "reads" like excellent fiction, it purports to be strictly factual and thoroughly documented. But the documentation is, for the most part, suppressed in the text—presumably in order to supply the narrative with a surface of persuasive immediacy and impenetrable omniscience. Nor are the author's claims to veracity set forth in any detail elsewhere in the volume. They are merely asserted in a brief introductory paragraph wherein his indebtedness to several authorities ranging from the Kansas police to William Shawn, editor of *The New Yorker*, is acknowledged. With all respect to the author, how can anyone be sure that the book's numerous angles, including Mrs. Clutter's dream speed and the social portrait of Holcomb, are in any reasonable degree authentic? To ask such questions of a book that is otherwise so praiseworthy may be captious; but to praise without asking is foolish. For these are years not only of neurotic suspiciousness but of much that is really, and grossly, suspect, in art as in politics. As the present writer has at times felt obliged to remark in print, a lot of what passes for sociological observation is only private fantasy, the pulse not to the patient but of the hypochondriac healer at the bedside. "Parajournalism" is Dwight Macdonald's perhaps too glamorous-sounding term for this "creative" reportage or social criticism. And parajournalism is detestable because, to the many real crises that now lurk and loom, it adds another and quite unnecessary one, a crisis of literary truthfulness.

I am myself convinced that *In Cold Blood* is not parajournalism. Its general authenticity is established, for me, by what I hope to show is a species of internal evidence. I do nevertheless wish that Mr. Capote had gone to the trouble of taking us into his confidence—perhaps by way of an appendix explaining his procedures—instead of covering his tracks as an interviewer and researcher, and of generally seeming to declaim, with Walt Whitman in one of his seizures of mystical clairvoyance, "I am there . . . I witness the corpse with its dabbled hair, I note where the pistol has fallen." A journalist turned poet, Whitman went on to write what was unmistakably poetry, so far, at least, as its frankly visionary immersion in man's total experience was concerned. At present, all reportorial writing aspires to the condition of poetry, or of myth or—in the still more abused word—of "story." *In Cold Blood*'s similar aspirations are, as I say, largely justified by its unique excellence. Meanwhile, the questions have proliferated. . . . (p. 3)

Some of these questions had to do with documentation. Others were more intangible, "personal," and, as I now think, impertinent. Given, for example, the preoccupations of Capote's early fiction, its nostalgia for states of innocence together with its fascination with deformed or precocious or oddball types of human creepiness (that Miss Bobbitt in **"Children on Their Birthdays"**! That New York City dream collector in **"Master Misery"**!)—given, in short, Capote's repertory of fictional themes, to what extent did he impose it upon the actualities of the Clutter case, "identifying" with one or another of the figures in the case and distorting this or that situation? In their original form such speculations have, as I say, proved to be mostly irrelevant. But they were not without justification if one considers Capote's seeming possessiveness towards his subject, his determination to make the subject his *very* own, to the point of refusing to share with the public the means by which he has done so.

Perhaps his reportorial activities, which I understand were arduous and prolonged, are another story, to be made public later, like Gide's *Journal of "The Counterfeiters."* Meanwhile Mr. Capote, interviewed by a *New York Times* reporter, has suggested further reasons for his suppressing documentation. The book, he says, is an attempt at what is in effect a new genre, the "non-fiction novel." To this claim the only possible retort is a disbelieving grin. The book chills the blood and exercises the intelligence just because it reports, without much novelistic comment or simplification, what one is persuaded really and horribly *happened*. Nor do "genres" as such really matter; certain of anyone's favorite books—*A Sentimental Journey, Walden*—are *sui generis*. If anything, Capote has

perfected an old form of journalism and done so by virtue of qualities peculiar to his subject and to himself. Not the book's admirable essence but its glittering aureole of fame achieved and money made in heaps is what is likely to attract imitators.

Whatever its "genre," *In Cold Blood is* admirable: as harrowing as it is, ultimately, though implicitly, reflective in temper. Capote's possessiveness towards his subject is understandable in terms of the industry, intelligence, and passion he has brought to the book's making. One's belief in its merits deepens on re-reading *In Cold Blood* in its present form as a volume. Indeed the book has the special merit of *requiring*, and repaying, thoughtful attention even while it tempts one to devour its contents with uninterrupted excitement. Many of the original questions are effectively answered, and the speculations silenced, by re-reading the work in all its astonishing abundance of provocative detail.

This abundance flows chiefly from two circumstances: the character of the two criminals and the nature of Capote's participation in the proceedings. To speak first of the criminals: one of them, Richard Hickock, combined a high IQ and a gift of almost total recall with a marked deficiency of imagination and feeling. The other, Perry Smith, had imagination and feeling in fearful and wonderful plentitude. Smith was a disappointed *poète maudit*. Repeatedly he dreamed or daydreamed of vague paradises, of great winged creatures that did injury to others in return for the injuries done to him. (pp. 3-4)

Factually speaking, what Smith remembered about the crime itself and about their subsequent wanderings was less extensive than Hickock's memories. But the recollections of both were in substantial agreement. Naturally Smith's memories included things that escaped Hickock's less impressionable mind or that didn't concern him. Among them were the brutality and neglect to which Smith had been subjected as a child, the suicides of a sister, a brother, and the brother's wife. Among his memories, too, was the far-off presence of a second sister, Bobo, and her success, thus far, in eluding the family curse. Bobo had acquired a respectable husband, three children, a house and home. This good fortune on her part seems to have made Perry despise Bobo in proportion as he envied her. It made him express a strange wish concerning her, express it repeatedly and almost to the end—he and Hickock remained quite unrepentant during their trial and the long years they spent in the death house of the Kansas State Penitentiary until, in April of last year, their original sentence of death by hanging was finally carried out—Smith wished that his sister Bobo had been present that night in the Clutters' house. In his mind, obviously, her precarious respectability got connected with the manifest respectability of the Clutters. On first seeing their large farmhouse and extensive grounds by moonlight, he thought them "sort of *too* impressive"; and he almost succeeded in convincing Hickock and himself to abandon the "score," as Hickock called the felonious job they had undertaken.

No doubt Smith's voluble confessions to the police and, one gathers, his conversations with Capote, contributed much to the abundance of circumstantiality that characterizes *In Cold Blood.* Inevitably they also awoke in Capote, as surely they must in almost any reader, a kind of sick compassion and wonder. That so much suffering could be taken and given by a single youthful human creature is a fact that unsettles the intelligence and works with desperate confusion upon the emotions, especially when one comes to know the creature as intimately as one does Perry Smith in the pages of *In Cold Blood.* A half-breed and, virtually, an orphan like the fictional Joe Christmas of Faulkner's *Light in August,* Perry Smith has exactly what Faulkner's killer lacks, a personality.

Does, then, the author seem to identify himself with *this* particular specimen of human oddness, who is even short-legged like several of Capote's early characters? Beyond a point, definitely not. Any such sentimental conjunction of egos or alter-egos is precluded by what is gradually revealed about Perry Smith in and between the lines of the book. Smith's excess of imagination and feeling was his undoing and that of the Clutters. It was his blandishments, as contrasted with Dick's bullying, that reassured the Clutters as to the probable intentions of the two intruders, and caused the Clutters to go to their deaths without resistance, perilous as resistance must have been in any case. Perry's will to deceive—perhaps to deceive himself—was matched by the Clutters' will to believe, which in turn sprang from simple shock and fear. Moreover, it was Perry who, after thwarting Hickock's intention of raping Nancy, sat down at her bedside for a pleasant chat about horses, which she loved, and other innocent things. It was Perry who thought Mr. Clutter a nice gentleman at the very moment that he put the knife to Mr. Clutter's throat. Finally, it was Perry who pillowed his victims, tucked them in their beds, or otherwise made them as comfortable as possible, considering that he had also used his ex-seaman's skill to tie them up and that he was soon to slaughter them, one by one. That Pal Perry is no Pal Joey, and thus a projection of the author's fears or desires concerning himself, becomes certain, if only because the *facts,* again, make it impossible. Perry Smith is a heel to end all the heels in modern American fiction.

Not that the slaughter itself was a foregone conclusion. True, "no witnesses" had been Hickock's slogan from the start. But during their four-hundred mile drive to Holcomb, Smith had thought of avoiding detection by masking their faces with women's stockings—black ones. Their attempts to secure these unfashionable articles failed, and the whole stocking-hunt forms one of the more grotesque elements in the wonderful configuration of choices and chances, identities within differences, appearances and realities, which shows everywhere in Capote's narrative.

Between Hickock and Smith, tensions developed during their lengthy occupation of the Clutters' house. Besides keeping Hickock away from Nancy, Smith annoyed him by crediting Mr. Clutter's insistence that there really was no safe in the house. Dick, on the other hand, kept searching for the safe, his whole "score," and the self-esteem that went with it, being at stake for him. Except for these tensions, they might have left the Clutters tied up and unharmed, making their escape with the small portable radio, the pair of binoculars, and the fifty-odd dollars in cash they did find and take. But something, or everything together, awoke in Perry Smith an hallucinated state of mind. He took leave, not merely of his senses, but of his very self, amorphous as it was at best. He was suddenly someone else, the observer of a scene in which his other self was fated to act out its essential impulses. The cutting of Mr. Clutter's throat confirmed Perry's sense of his doubleness. By this act of gratuitous violence, this former petty thief, and, like Dick, parolee from the state prison, became what he had earlier dreamed about and bragged about being, a killer, the avenging bird.

Here, then, is some of the internal evidence (or my version of it) that persuades me *In Cold Blood* is to be read as *fact,* its author's claims to the contrary. Even the propriety of his including Bonnie Clutter's dream speech is thus established, apart from its great dramatic value. He got it, directly or indirectly, from the dreamer herself, an acquaintance of Mrs. Clutter's and the wife of the local police investigator whose involvement in the case was urgent throughout. Similarly with the portrait of Holcomb and its environs. This is as convincing as any such sociological panorama is ever likely to be, especially because of the presence in it of other, somewhat more worldly, "enclaves" beyond the Clutter circle, which is strictly Methodist, Republican, temperance, and 4-H Club. (p. 4)

As for Capote's part in the proceedings, these consisted in his making himself so thoroughly familiar with the circumstances and the surviving people involved that he was able to feel himself almost a participant and to make the reader feel a participant also. Thus the various possible clues and suspects are introduced, not with the mechanical trickery of a detective story, but as they might have been dreamed up by the natives or pursued by the police from day to day on the spot. Meanwhile, in alternating chapters, we are made aware of Hickock and Smith, parolees on the loose, meeting at distant Olanthe, Kansas, consuming their root beers and aspirins, or vodka orange blossoms, planning the job in their shrewd but half-baked way, and starting on the long drive to the isolated farmhouse which neither of them has ever seen, which only Hickock has heard about, from a former cellmate . . . whose account of the Clutter setup included a money-filled safe which isn't, and never was, there.

In short, Capote has it both ways, the mystification and the clarification. And the narrative evolves through a succession of firmly written scenes—scenes that are occasionally, I think, *too* slickly executed and that end with too obtrusive "curtains." These, unfortunately, embrace a concluding graveyard scene where the weather and the sentiment—Life Goes On—are unmitigated Hollywood.

But no known film maker could easily convey in his medium that elusive interplay of the gratuitous and the determinate which makes *In Cold Blood* at its best both artful and lifelike. True, Perry Smith, although thoroughly individualized, is also a clinically perfect type of the misfit turned psychopath and the psychopath turned killer. But his partner? Nothing in Hickock's antecedents accounts for his becoming a criminal on this scale of brutal inconsequence. In so far as the crime has a definable and possibly remedial cause, it lies in the nature of prisons, the kind of mentalities and associations apt to be fostered by prisons. For the rest the cause is something in the relationship of Smith and Hickock, a relationship so involuted and internal that it can be made believable, as Capote does make it, not through any of the usual formulas of partnership or palship, but solely in the shifting minutiae of their behavior from incident to incident. How, moreover, to represent in any medium less flexible than Capote's, other significant relationships? For example, that of Mrs. Clutter and her daughter, the mother who feels herself displaced and the daughter who, in all apparent humility and sweetness, has filled her place? Or that of the two principal fathers, Nancy Clutter's and Perry Smith's, who never of course meet but who are, each in his own place, Kansas and Alaska, and in his own way, embodiments of free enterprise and the pioneering spirit?

Until now, Truman Capote's literary record has been somewhat uneven. A series of well-written, never quite negligible, passes at literature has made it up. At last, in a small Kansas town disrupted by a peculiarly horrible and bewildering crime, he seems to have found, for a time, a sort of spiritual home, complete with a lovable police force. At least he discovered there a subject equal to his abilities. These appear to have required that he profess, and no doubt sincerely believe, that he was composing a non-fiction *novel*. In a way, Capote's claim is the more believable because it perpetuates, by inversion, an ancient literary impulse: the impulse of romancers to create a fiction within a fiction. The tale twice told of Cervantes or of Hawthorne, the story shaped within the consciousness of some imaginary observer (Henry James and others), are of this tradition. Capote's inversion of the tradition is itself a striking response to the present-day world and to the tendency noted earlier in this review; the tendency among writers to resort to subjective sociology, on the one hand, or to super-creative reportage, on the other. As Lionel Trilling once observed, it is no longer poetry but history, preposterous current history, which beggars the literary imagination and requires us to attempt a "willing suspension of disbelief." But it is surely to Capote's credit that one cannot quite suspend one's disbelief that *In Cold Blood* is a novel. (pp. 4-5)

> F. W. Dupee, "Truman Capote's Score," in The New York Review of Books, *Vol. VI, No. 1, February 3, 1966, pp. 3-5.*

KENNETH TYNAN

[*The essay excerpted below was originally published in* The Observer, *March 13, 1966.*]

One Saturday in November 1959 two young men drove 400 miles across the State of Kansas to an imposing white house in the lonely village of Holcomb. There they killed—at point-blank range, with a shotgun—four people whom, until that day, they had never seen. (p. 441)

[*In Cold Blood*] is certainly the most detailed and atmospheric account ever written of a contemporary crime. Sometimes, you suspect that Capote's vision of Kansas is over-sentimental (cf., too many phrases like 'the well-loved piece of prairie where he had always hoped to build a house'); often, that he bowdlerises out of deference to the *New Yorker*'s well-known primness. At one point Perry says 'shit': this is the only four-letter word used by any of the characters, criminal or law-abiding, and it was omitted from the *New Yorker* serialisation. (p. 442)

[How] can we verify events and statements that only the hanged men could corroborate? Driving towards Mexico, Dick deliberately swerves to run over a dog and says: 'Boy! We sure splattered him!' Capote adds that 'it was what he always said after running down a dog'. But did he get that from Dick, or is it Perry trying to make Dick look bad? We are given no clue, here or in many similar dilemmas.

Even so, the book is by any standards a monumental job of editing and a most seductive piece of writing: the first section, cutting back and forth between the unsuspecting Clutters and the approaching killers, is agonisingly well constructed. That said, we must pose the two central questions: Is it art? and is it morally defensible?

The first is easier to answer. Capote calls the book a 'non-fiction novel', by which he means a documentary tale handled with the psychological insight of a novelist. He believes that much of modern fiction is merely a device to evade the libel laws; thus, a breezy, adipose Londoner absurdly appears in print as a tight-lipped, skeletal Scot. If I remember him correctly (my median percentage of recall is in the high sixties), Capote feels that unless you are a Joyce or a Kafka, able to create a world of your own, you are likely to find your richest artistic opportunities in the world of fact. This will be news only to those who (perhaps like Capote himself) were brought up to despise journalism; or who never heard John Grierson's famous definition of documentary—'the creative treatment of actuality'. Like any other art, of course, creative journalism can be abused: witness *Time* magazine, that weekly anthology of nonfiction short stories.

The question of morality is tougher and (for me) more personal. Early in 1960, when I was in New York, upper-Bohemian dinner-guests were already full of 'Truman and his marvellous bit about Perry and Dick'. I attended one such party, which Capote regaled with a dazzling account of the crime and his friendship with the criminals. I said they seemed obviously insane, and he agreed they were 'nuts'. And what would happen to them? 'They'll swing, I guess,' he said.

When I asked whether he thought insane people should be hanged, he said I couldn't understand unless I had read Nancy Clutter's diary: Perry and Dick had destroyed 'such a lovely, intelligent girl'. 'You mean it would have mattered less if she'd been ugly and stupid?' I said.

I don't recall his answer to that, but I do remember several subsequent disputes—one in which I failed to persuade him that he (or the *New Yorker*) ought to provide Perry and Dick with the best available psychiatric testimony; and another in which I convinced him, much against his will, that if he was writing a book about death in cold blood he owed it to his readers to be present at a really cold-blooded killing—the legal strangulation of his friends.

Capote's references in the book to the mental state of the murderers are confused and ambiguous. Early on, we learn that, in Dick's opinion, Perry was 'that rarity, "a natural killer"—*absolutely sane* but conscienceless . . .' (my italics). Later, Capote cites the belief of Dr Joseph Satten, a veteran psychiatrist working at the Menninger Clinic in Kansas, that when Perry killed Mr Clutter (the first and hence the crucial murder, since the other three had the rational purpose of eliminating witnesses), he was 'under a mental eclipse, deep inside a schizophrenic darkness'. The phrase is Capote's and it has the same fanciful vagueness as something he afterwards said to an interviewer: 'Perry never meant to kill the Clutters at all. He had a brain explosion.'

In essence, the only explanation Capote offers for the gratuitous slaughter of Mr Clutter—the *raison d'être,* after all, of his book—is a single remark of Perry's: 'It wasn't because of anything the Clutters did. They never hurt me. . . . Like people have all my life. Maybe it's just that the Clutters were the ones who had to pay for it.' And maybe not: the woolliness is contagious. Nowhere does Capote commit himself to stating that the killers were technically insane, and therefore ought not to have been executed. Indeed, he goes out of his way to stress that Dick was a supporter of capital punishment: 'I'm not against it. Revenge is all it is, but what's wrong with revenge?' 'Essentially,' Capote told *Life* magazine, 'I'm on the side of the victim, not the murderer.'

The accused men received only the most perfunctory psychiatric examination: so much is brutally obvious. The day before the trial began a young psychiatrist named Mitchell Jones volunteered to interview them without payment. He asked them to write out autobiographical statements, which they did in the courtroom while the jury was being selected. And that was all.

In Dr Jones's view, Dick might have been suffering from 'organic brain damage', and Perry showed 'definite signs of severe mental illness'. But he was not allowed to say this in court. Kansas follows the ancient McNaghten Rules, whereby a man is held to be sane and legally responsible for his actions if he knows that what he is doing is wrong. Dr Jones testified that Dick *did* know, and, when asked about Perry, said he had no opinion. He was dismissed at once from the stand. Had he been a psychiatrist of national repute, more skilled in courtroom niceties, would his evidence have been heard? We shall never know.

What we do know, however, is that when the verdict was appealed, three Federal judges declared: 'There was no substantial evidence then, *and none has been produced since,* to substantiate a defence of insanity' (my italics). And they were right; none was produced; although Capote, who investigated so much else, had five years in which he might have unearthed it. He could surely have faced the expense. In cold cash, it has been estimated that *In Cold Blood* is likely to earn him between two and three million dollars.

Had Perry and Dick been reprieved, the book might have been rather different. George Plimpton, in an interview for the *New York Times Book Review* . . . [see excerpt above dated January 16, 1966], asked Capote whether his 'artistry' would have suffered if clemency had been granted: he hedged, and changed the subject. He also told Plimpton that neither Perry nor Dick saw the manuscript *in toto*; that Perry's 'greatest objection' was to the title; that Dick wanted changes made ('to serve his purposes legally') and expressed the opinion that 'what I had written wasn't exactly true'.

In the same interview Capote says that someone suggested the break-up of a marriage as a possible theme for a future 'non-fiction novel'; he rejected the idea because 'you'd have to find two people . . . who'd sign a release'. Perry and Dick did sign a release after reading 'three-quarters of the book' (Capote's words). This shows a remarkable degree of tolerance in them since in the course of the book Capote alleges (*a*) that Dick frequently tried to rape pubescent girls, (*b*) that he intended (but failed) to kill a fellow-prisoner in a Kansas jail, and (*c*) that he and Perry were prevented only by chance from carrying out the premeditated murder of a travelling salesman who gave them a lift. (In his chat with Plimpton, Capote adds: 'They had two other murders planned that aren't mentioned in the book.') There is no evidence to substantiate these charges outside the killers' graves, to which Capote contributed the cost of the headstones.

A prominent Manhattan lawyer has given me the following opinion: 'I would doubt whether the book would have been released prior to the decease of the accused.'

We are talking, in the long run, about responsibility; the debt that a writer arguably owes to those who provide him—down to the last autobiographical parenthesis—with his subject-matter and his livelihood. And we are not discussing a third-rate crime reporter or professional ghoul; one does not waste space on condemning trash. For the first time, an influential writer of the front rank has been placed in a position of privileged intimacy with criminals about to die, and—in my view—done less than he might have to save them.

The focus narrows sharply down on priorities: does the work come first or does life? An attempt to help (by supplying new psychiatric testimony) might easily have failed: what one misses is any sign that it was even contemplated. It is irrelevant to say that Capote writes with genuine pity of his dead friends, and gives them a fraternal quatrain from Villon by way of epigraph. Compassion is the least we expect of an obituarist.

In a recent letter to a former colleague, Dr Satten of the Menninger Clinic . . . agrees that Capote didn't try to help the condemned men, but sees nothing wrong in this: 'In the conversations I have had with Mr Capote over the years, I think he saw his task as that of an observer and recorder rather than that of an active participant.' By this reasoning, a writer who befriended Timothy Evans at the time of his conviction would have been under no obligation to tell society that it was executing a probably innocent half-wit. Where lives are threatened, observers and recorders who shrink from participation may be said to betray their species: no piece of prose, however deathless, is worth a human life.

The colleague to whom Dr Satten addressed his letter (and who showed it to me) is a woman psychiatrist who knows the Clutter case well. For professional reasons I will not divulge her name. She worked in Kansas, mainly with criminal patients, in 1963-64, and has no doubt that if the Clutter murderers could have been shown to be paranoid schizophrenics, they would have won their appeal. On their relationship with Capote she takes a firm and original line. In her view, he set himself up—consciously or not—as their analyst and confessor; not, however, to bring them comfort but to gain their trust and obtain information.

In a letter to me she reconstructs the situation. She writes: 'The same dependence and fascination that Dick once evoked in Perry is now expanded in both of them towards Capote. In a sense they are telling him what Perry told Dick: "I'm going to put myself in your power. I'm going to tell you something I never told anybody." We know what Dick did with this confidence: he used Perry to kill the people he had in mind. And what did Capote do with their trust?'

Perry, she hazards, came to identify Capote with his father, with whom he had spent many of his few contented days. And at the same time, Capote may have begun to see aspects of himself in Perry: the diminutive stature, perhaps, and the voice that Capote describes as 'both gentle and prim—a voice that, though soft, manufactured each word exactly, ejected it like a smoke ring issuing from a parson's mouth'.

She continues: 'The situation now becomes chaotic. Who's who? Who is the criminal? Who is the interviewer? . . . Is it possible that Capote was gaining satisfaction out of acting as "confessor" to the criminals because of an intense identification with them? At some time or other all of us feel like killing; but now Capote can avoid the real situation, since someone with whom he strongly identifies has done the killing instead.'

Whether Capote identified or not, it seems to me that the

blood in which his book is written is as cold as any in recent literature. (pp. 442-46)

Kenneth Tynan, "The Coldest of Blood," in his Tynan Right & Left: Plays, Films, People, Places, and Events, *Atheneum, 1967, pp. 441-46.*

TONY TANNER

Thoreau wrote: 'I would so state facts that they shall be significant, shall be myths or mythologic' and Capote is continuing an old American tradition when he tries to get at the 'mythic' significance of the facts by simply stating them [in his book *In Cold Blood*]. It is a tradition based on the belief that 'if men would steadily observe realities only' they would discover that 'reality is fabulous' (again the words are Thoreau's); a tradition which reaches back to Emerson and encompasses writers like Hemingway, Sherwood Anderson, and William Carlos Williams. Capote's contribution to this tradition, judging by the tremendous popularity of [*In Cold Blood*] in America, seems to have been to extract a black fable from contemporary reality which has a peculiar relevance for his society.

By juxtaposing and dovetailing the lives and values of the Clutters and those of the killers, Capote produces a stark image of the deep doubleness in American life. For here is a 'true' parable of the outlaw against the community; the roving life of random impulse cutting across the stable respectability of continuous ambition; the gangster versus the family man. It is many other things as well. Dangerous footloose dreamers intruding on sober industrious farmers; the maimed and lethal throw-outs of society pouncing, as from a black nowhere, on to the prosperous pillars of the community; the terrible meeting of the cursed and the blessed of America.

Perhaps most graphically it is a collision between the visible rewards and the suppressed horrors of American life which resulted in four people splattered all over their imposing 'lovely home' and two more hanging from the gallows. It is the American dream turning into an American nightmare. Clearly this feeling of the frightening double life of America goes very deep. Norman Mailer wrote in one of *The Presidential Papers:* 'Since the First World War Americans have been leading a double life, and our history has moved on two rivers, one visible, the other underground.' On one level is the life of the ordinary, respectable, money-making community—'concrete, factual, practical and unbelievably dull'; 'and there is a subterranean river of untapped, ferocious, lonely and romantic desires, that concentration of ecstasy and violence which is the dream life of the nation.' Capote's story corroborates this vision of the two rivers of American life.

Thus by constructing the last day in the life of the Clutters, Capote gives us a sort of shorthand summary of the respectable surface of American life in its most extreme form. Mr. Clutter ('eminent Republican and church leader'), rigidly abstemious and harshly intolerant of all users of tobacco and alcohol, surveys his land, helps a neighbour, takes out an insurance policy. . . .

The killers, by contrast, inhabit a different world even if it is on the same continent. A world, for a start, of endless travel and movement (they have both been smashed up in serious road accidents). We first see Perry Smith ('an incessant conceiver of voyages') hunched over a well-used map, and we follow both of them into Kansas, down to Mexico, out to California, back to Florida, on to Kansas where, incredibly, they returned, thence to Las Vegas where they were caught. (p. 331)

Perry is the most interesting character in the book. Capote of course has always had a feeling for the loner, the lost one, the unloved, the fatherless, and in Perry Smith he found someone with a life which made his powers of invention redundant (although his romantic feeling for the type emerges in the imagery he provides for Perry; in the court 'he looked as lonely and inappropriate as a seagull in a wheatfield'). . . . Most touching is [Perry's] personal treasure trove, his box of memorabilia which he carts around wherever he goes. It held not only his Korean War medal, but lyrics and songs, notebooks containing lists of 'beautiful' or 'useful' words, and a diary full of interesting facts and quotations. Sad tokens of hopeless, inchoate literary ambitions. His last words on the gallows apparently were: 'Maybe I had something to contribute, something. . . . ' He emerges as not only a pathetic, but a sympathetic figure, an unwanted crippled dreamer whose moment of appalling violence was somehow not of his own making. One might compare one's feelings in reading the factual report on Lee Oswald, another messed-up failure lashing out at the supreme symbol of American success. Horror, certainly—but also a sort of stunned compassion.

There is no doubt that Capote has written a remarkable book, a book which, casting its net wide, does draw together some terribly revealing facts about America. But a word about his technique is in order. He claims to have written a 'Non-Fiction Novel,' to have assembled only facts derived from observation, official records, and interviews. He does not comment, he presents; he does not analyse, he arranges. This means, for one thing, that he cannot approach the profound inquiring insights into the significance of the psychopath offered by, for example, Musil in his analytic study of Moosbrugger. However, since his material is 'true,' it has its own kind of powerful impact: the illusion is of art laying down its tools as helpless and irrelevant in front of the horrors and mysteries of life itself. But I find something just a shade suspicious in this maintained illusion of objective factual presentation. Certainly it is in the American grain—'pleads for itself the fact,' said Emerson. But facts do *not* 'sing themselves,' as Emerson maintained. Facts are silent, as Conrad said, and any singing they do depends on their orchestration by a human arranger.

As Goethe insisted, there is no such thing as pure objectivity. 'Looking at a thing gradually merges into contemplation, contemplation into thinking, thinking is establishing connections and thus it is possible to say that every attentive glance which we cast on the world is an act of theorising.' The way Capote 'establishes connections' reveals his subjective feeling about the world he presents, and this should not be overlooked. . . . It is Capote who provides some of the atmospheric detail. Thus when the police open up Perry's case: 'A cockroach emerged, and the landlady stepped on it, squashing it under the heel of her gold leather sandal.' It did? I wonder. Isn't it rather that behind the mask of the dispassionate reporter we can begin to make out the excited stare of the southern gothic novelist with his febrile delight in weird settings and lurid details (the red ball bouncing down the stairs in *Other Rooms, Other Voices*)? There are other such details, not the least dubious being the 'reminiscence' accredited to Detective Dewey as he watches Perry hang. This ends the book and, if this were a plain novel, it would be regarded as pretty cheap and sentimental. 'If ' is, of course, the point. Because 'if ' this were a novel one might be more liable to notice the lapses into bad and clichéd writing ('The detective's trained eye roamed the scrubbed and humble room') and a marked penchant, not wholly pleasing, for just that arrangement or schematisation of details which will make life appear at its most queasily macabre.

I am not saying that Capote has twisted the facts so that life appears as a Capote novel. But tampering there has been, and a subtle exploitation or highlighting of ghastly or pathetic effects which leaves me feeling a little uneasy about the enormous appeal of this book (rather as I am made uneasy by those 'art' films about concentration camps). Say what he will, Capote *has* manipulated the facts to produce a particular kind of *frisson*. The great novels about a criminal act—by Dostoievsky, Stendhal, etc.—may be initially provoked by an actual reported crime. But by making their works frankly 'fictions' they tacitly assumed that to explore the latent significance of the grim, silent facts, the most valuable aid is the human imagination. I cannot see that Capote goes anywhere near to proving them wrong. (pp. 331-32)

> *Tony Tanner, "Death in Kansas," in* The Spectator, *Vol. 216, No. 7186, March 18, 1966, pp. 331-32.*

TRUMAN CAPOTE

Ah, and so at last we know! Mr Kenneth Tynan's chief literary concern is the integrity and responsibility of the writer. But how very surprising—when one considers that these are the particular qualities most notably absent from his article about my book, **In Cold Blood** [see excerpt above dated March 27, 1966]. . . .

Without quoting the piece virtually word by word, I scarcely know how to disentangle this knotted cat's-cradle that Tynan's egocentric ignorance has created. My only choice is to indicate, before tackling the larger issues, a few of the distortions so general to the infested whole.

Certainly the following is typical of Tynan's lazy inaccuracy:

> . . . in the course of the book Capote alleges (a) that Dick frequently tried to rape pubescent girls, (b) that he intended (but failed) to kill a fellow prisoner in a Kansas jail, and (c) that he and Perry were prevented only by chance from carrying out the premeditated murder of a travelling salesman who gave them a lift. . . . There is no evidence to substantiate these charges outside the killers' graves, to which Capote contributed the cost of the headstones.

No evidence?

Clearly Tynan's reading of the book is as haphazard as his prose-style; otherwise he could not have failed to notice that Richard Hickock himself describes, in a statement for Dr W. Mitchell Jones, the defence psychiatrist, his sexual interest in pubescent girls, and how, on a number of past occasions, he had implemented that interest. The text of this statement is printed in Part Four. Moreover, is there any *question* that Hickock intended to rape Nancy Clutter? Not only is that a part of the trial record, not only did he never deny it, but he describes the matter at length in an article he himself wrote

and published in an American magazine (*Male,* November, 1961).

And now to items (b) and (c). In a brief preface to my book there appears this sentence: "All the material in this book not derived from my own observation is either taken from official records or is the result of interviews with the persons directly concerned. . . . " Perhaps Tynan thinks this a mere idle phrase. It is not. Almost all the substance of the book can be verified in one form or another, as Tynan would have soon discovered had he taken his work seriously. Yes, the stories involved in (b) and (c) were told to me by Smith and Hickock; but these particular anecdotes were *also* told at separate times to four different agents of the Kansas Bureau of Investigation (Clarence Duntz, Harold Nye, Alvin Dewey, and Roy Church—unlike Tynan, I name my sources), and are a part of the official Kansas Bureau dossier.

That's three factual errors in one paragraph; and as for the final reference to my having contributed to the cost of Hickock and Smith's gravestones, Tynan seems to be scornful of this action. Why? If I had not done it no one else would; I was their sole financial support during the entire time of their imprisonment.

Later on, when quoting a remark of mine made in an interview ("Essentially I'm on the side of the victim, not the murderer"), Tynan implies that it is morally wrong of me to have a greater sympathy for victims than criminals; and he *even,* heaven help us, tries to twist the statement into meaning that I am a devoted proponent of capital punishment! Again, in the same grotesquely censorious spirit, the gentleman chastises me for the fact that the book contains only one four-letter word—which only demonstrates how *derrière-garde* this fading hipster has become: doesn't he know that four-letter words are nowadays unrequired everywhere except on television?

Now, to approach the lower slopes of the major contention: that I did not do all I might have done to aid Smith and Hickock in their appeals against execution, and hints that the underlying reason for my (unproved) behaviour was that I could not have published the book as long as Hickock and Smith were alive.

He writes: "A prominent Manhattan lawyer has given me the following opinion: 'I would doubt whether the book would have been released prior to the decease of the accused.' " Mr Tynan is *so* fond of quoting anonymous persons; indeed, he is very like Senator McCarthy, and his whole piece, riddled with ghostly accusators, has the atmosphere of an old-time McCarthy hearing. And so may I say this: I don't believe Tynan ever consulted "a prominent Manhattan attorney" or obtained any such statement. And I will back my belief with the following offer: if the name and address of this person can be produced, along with a sworn affidavit that he expressed such an opinion to Tynan, I will hand over a cheque for $500 to Tynan's favourite charity (if so uncharitable a spirit *has* a favourite charity).

What I am about to tell illustrates perfectly the quantity, as well as the beyond-contempt quality, of the research the languorous Mr Tynan accomplished before sitting down to type his pious tirade. A few days before *The Observer* published this piece, the literary editor of the paper, Mr Terence Kilmartin, sent me a copy of the manuscript, then later telephoned to ask what I thought of it. I pointed out a major error in the article—which the editor duly corrected. But it's very important, this error: a good portion of Tynan's case depended on it. Because, in the original article, Tynan claimed I could not have published my book because I could never have obtained legal releases from the two murderers—that is, a release exonerating me from any possible libel action.

But what is the truth of the matter? This: I had legal releases, drawn by lawyers and signed before witnesses and notarised, from almost every person who appears in the book—*including Smith and Hickock*. Legally, there was nothing to have prevented me from publishing the book at any time.

The sole deterrent was that no one could judge with any certainty whether my book would help or hinder the case as it was being appealed through the Federal courts, and I was not willing to risk publishing anything that might have proved detrimental to Smith and Hickock's chances for a reversal, especially because both they and the man who was their chief defence counsel during the last three years, Mr Joseph P. Jenkins, were more than hopeful that a new trial would eventually be secured by way of reversal of a verdict in the Federal courts. This hope went undiminished until the very day of the execution, at which time Mr Jenkins still had an action before the Supreme Court. If Mr Tynan doubts that, then all he has to do is write to Mr Jenkins, a lawyer who *does* exist, and whose address is: The Huron Building, Kansas City, Kansas.

However, to move on (though certainly not upward) to the principal area of Tynan's uninformed criticism: "Nowhere does Capote commit himself to stating that the killers were technically insane, and therefore should not have been executed." Please remember that I was not writing a polemic but, as far as possible, an objective work of reportage. And, in the role of reporter, why on earth should I have committed myself to a view I feel to be quite untrue? I'm not at all sure that both Smith and Hickock were not a mite saner than Kenneth Tynan (that's not a joke; I mean it). The latter, by slyly alluding to Timothy Evans, seems to suggest that Smith and Hickock were (a) half-wits like Evans, and (b) perhaps even innocent, like Evans; the full implication is that I let two possibly innocent half-wits go to their death without stirring up a storm! Wow! It really takes one's breath away (as Mr Welch said to Senator McCarthy: "Have you *no* shame, sir?").

Okay, let's get down to brass tacks. Despite Tynan's entirely ludicrous claims to acquaintance with a third psychiatric expert on the Clutter case (this is another anonymous person who doesn't exist, at least not in the role of expert that Tynan assigns her), there are only *two* psychiatrists who know at first-hand anything about it whatever.

One of them is Dr Joseph E. Satten of the Menninger Clinic in Topeka, Kansas. . . . The other is Dr W. Mitchell Jones, a *protégé* of Dr Satten's and, at present, the director of the Prairie View Clinic in Newton, Kansas. Dr Jones, whom Tynan, arrogant and ill-informed as ever, attempts to discard as some inexperienced young incompetent, examined Smith and Hickock prior to their trial and remained in *continuous contact* with them throughout the five and a half years spent on Death Row.

Now, neither Dr Satten nor Dr Jones ever thought either Smith or Hickock was more than a severely pathological personality; neither they nor any other competent observer considered them "insane" in the sense Tynan means. On the contrary, both Smith and Hickock had unusually high intelligence quotients, were super-alert and possessed a wide range of information (see Dr Jones's Written Report: Part Four).

No one . . . *ever* thought that a successful appeal could be made in Kansas courts (which abide by the McNaghten Rule) on the basis of insanity or "diminished responsibility."

The unpardonable thing is that Tynan was well aware of this fact when he wrote his article. How so? Because Dr Satten himself had told him that I was correct, and that no appeal of this nature could have succeeded in a Kansas court. But Tynan ignores Dr Satten's opinion, he does not mention it at all, for had he done so it would have entirely demolished that little guillotine of an essay he was constructing. To suppress vital information that does not serve one's critical purposes—is *that* an act of integrity, the response of a responsible writer?

And while we're on the subject of ethics, here's a footnote to chew on: Dr Satten specifically told Tynan that he could not quote from any of his (Dr Satten's) letters without my expressed permission, and yet Tynan went right ahead and did it without a fare-you-well. A very scrupulous lad. Very.

But now the moment has come to turn to the matter of the Third Psychiatrist. If you have become bored, and are beginning to doze, please wake up because we are now going to discuss something of truly eerie interest.

The manner in which Tynan introduces this character, and his reasons for introducing her at all, are McCarthy-technique at its serpentine suavest. He tells us only, and of course without providing any name, that she is a woman psychiatrist who at one time worked in Kansas, and who, he assures us, "knows the Clutter case well." But why has Tynan suddenly led this veiled and mysterious lady stage-front, and how does he intend to use her? He means to use her the same way a ventriloquist uses a dummy. Why? Because Tynan is a bully; and, true to tradition, he is also a coward. There are some very rotten things he wants to say about me, but he hasn't the guts to come right out and say them himself.

And so, hiding behind the skirts of the female psychiatrist, this fair-fighting, very sporting fellow allows her to speak for him, lets her analyse and fancify on the relationship between me and the two condemned men (though she never knew any one of us), make accusations that range from the gravely unjust ("In her view, he [Capote] set himself up, consciously or not, as their analyst and confessor: not, however, to bring them comfort but to gain their trust and obtain information"), to frivolous libel ("Is it possible that Capote was gaining satisfaction out of acting as 'confessor' to the criminals because of an intense identification with them?") . . .

Even a man with the morals of a baboon and the guts of a butterfly could not do anything sneakier or more cowardly than that: it would bring a blush to the cheeks of Uriah Heep.

On the surface of it, the most plausible-seeming of Tynan's recriminations is that I did not help these men sufficiently in their legal struggle to avoid execution; in his opinion I should have hired an eminent psychiatrist to "unearth evidence" of their insanity; he tells us that his friend, the shadowy woman psychiatrist, has "no doubt that if the Clutter murderers could have been shown to be paranoid schizophrenics, they would have won their appeal."

Well, if the lady really believes that, then she must be every bit as ignorant of American jurisprudence, and particularly the laws of Kansas, as our chum Tynan (and, as Perry Smith used to often say, that is about as "ignorant as a day-old nigger"). Although this subject was treated in detail in my book.

I will spell it out once more for inattentive readers like Mr Tynan.

The courts of Kansas are under *no obligation* to admit psychiatric testimony, and very seldom do. If 50 world-famous psychiatrists had trooped into court prepared to swear that Smith and Hickock were "paranoid schizophrenics" (which they weren't, though apparently that point is irrelevant to Tynan), it still would not have done a damn bit of good, because Kansas courts abide by the McNaghten Rule and would not have allowed any testimony that deviated from its confines. In the final portion of the book, I described at length the case of Lowell Lee Andrews, a multiple murderer who was *definitely* schizophrenic, and for whom the staff of the Menninger Clinic, led by Dr Satten, conducted a famous crusade; yet Andrews was hanged, his defenders having been defeated for the reasons stated above.

One last point: supposing Tynan is right, supposing, as a friend of these two men. I ought to have sought out a renowned psychiatrist—where in the U.S. would I have found anyone more renowned or better qualified than Dr Satten, who was already right there on the scene and involved in the case from the start?

It is not for me to estimate how much I aided these pitiful friends of mine, or how much "comfort" I brought to them; but I feel confident in predicting that, if queried, those closest to the situation, honest and reputable men like Dr Jones and attorney Jenkins and the prison chaplain, James Post, would express opinions poles apart from Tynan's.

As they say around the courthouses, a man who acts as his own lawyer has a fool for a client. And perhaps the artist who defends himself against a critic has one, too. I don't believe in artists replying to criticism, and I have never done so myself, for I think it shows lack of pride and really serves small purpose. But this bullyboy chicanery concocted by Tynan is one over the odds.

> Truman Capote, *"The Guts of a Butterfly," in* The Observer, *March 27, 1966, p. 21.*

DIANA TRILLING

One can dispose quickly enough of the issue Truman Capote has himself made salient in discussion of his book—*In Cold Blood* is not a novel, as Mr. Capote would have us think; it is "only" a book, a work of journalism of an exceptionally compelling kind. Whatever else it may or may not be, the novel is a literary form in which the writer is free to make any use he wishes of material drawn from real life. It was Mr. Capote's decision to stay wholly with the facts of the Clutter murders; in their presentation he employs various strategies learned in his practice of fiction. This does not mean he has discovered a new fiction form nor—for that matter—a new form of nonfiction. Works of autobiography such as Isak Dinesen's *Out of Africa,* works of history such as Cecil Woodham Smith's *The Reason Why,* works of journalism like James Agee's *Let Us Now Praise Famous Men* are all at least as close to, or far from, proposing a new nonfiction form as Mr. Capote's *In Cold Blood.*

Indeed, a comparison of Truman Capote's report on the Clutter murders with James Agee's report on the condition of the sharecroppers during the Depression is useful in demonstrating some of the accomplishments, but more of the shortcomings, of *In Cold Blood* even as a work of nonfiction. That Mr. Capote's prose is flaccid, often downright inept, and that his narrative is overmanipulated in order to keep things at a constant high pitch of suspense: these are defects apparent without reference to Agee's uncommon talent. But it is in the difference in their approaches to the journalistic enterprise that comparison makes its sharp—but not simple—point.

Let Us Now Praise Famous Men was conceived not in loyalty to fact but in its author's loyalty to himself as an artist; which is to say, in the interplay between the actuality on which Agee had undertaken to report and his own sensibility. Just as Mr. Capote went West for *The New Yorker,* Agee had gone South on commission from *Fortune* magazine. But Agee's "assignment" had at once yielded in importance (perhaps perversely, but this is of only tangential, chiefly biographical, interest) before the imaginative possibilities of the material which presented itself to him. He comprehended only subjectively the world he had set out to describe—in splendid lyrical bursts, he castigated, and eventually celebrated, himself for being a well-fed man, a middle-class man, a writer (of all improbable human apparitions!) daring to spy upon lives this remote from his own. It turned out that this subjectivity was so intense that it largely dominated the object under investigation; *Let Us Now Praise Famous Men* implicates us much more with its author than with the sharecroppers. Its bias also distorted the social actuality on which Agee was supposed to be reporting—surely people are not, as *Let Us Now Praise Famous Men* would have it, innocent in proportion as they are miserable and poor, nor can one readily suppose that sharecroppers are the superlative instance of humankind that Agee, in his impulse to self-abasement before suffering, makes them out to be. Nevertheless, by licensing his consciousness to prevail over external fact, Agee was able to create an artistic reality, that of his own felt experience. His book intensified our capacity to feel acutely about something, if not about sharecroppers.

Truman Capote's method is exactly the opposite. It was Mr. Capote's decision to report the Clutter case wholly objectively, in as much as possible of its manifest social and personal complication, and to give us both the Clutter family and their murderers without permitting himself any partisanship to either of the extreme oppositions embodied in the two sets of characters. Now on first glance this seems an acceptable enough intention. But, not too surprisingly, it develops that in his submission to actuality, or factuality, and his abrogation of the artist's right to emphasize or even to suppress or distort reality for his own purposes, Mr. Capote prepared for himself an almost inevitable artistic defeat. The neutrality of his posture announces itself even in his prose, whose indistinctiveness is of a sort with which we are familiar in popular writing, where communication is believed to be impeded rather than created by an author's presence on his page. The social object of Mr. Capote's investigation remains intact. And the dramatic impact of his story is not diminished by the impersonality of his approach. On the contrary, it is reinforced, but this only makes for a sensationalism proportionate to the horror of the actual events which are being described. The overtones of *In Cold Blood*—if, in a book so lacking in literary resonance, we can call them that—are those of a socially—well-documented story of crime and detection, not of a work of the imagination.

Still, even as we admit the inadequacy of *In Cold Blood* as a work of literary art, it is hard for us to suppose that this alone would account for the large, odd, often unformulable, reservations which so many different kinds of readers have about it. These seem to me to be reservations of a moral, or "human," more than of an esthetic nature, and they derive, I think, from Mr. Capote's stance as the wholly neutral reporter of facts-from-life which, while themselves so highly charged, are presented to us by a mind which refuses to be adequate to their tortuous meanings or appropriate to their terror. By his unwillingness to be implicated in his story, whether by the way he disposes his emotions between the murderers and their victims or by the way he invests his narrative with the intensity and anxiety proper to an unresolvable moral dilemma, Mr. Capote is employing objectivity as a shield for evasion. This is what is resented.

Certain of Mr. Capote's readers would wish he had thrown his weight to the Smith-Hickock side of the moral equation; these, of course, are the readers who believe that psychopaths and criminals, because they live outside the social order, have a special call on our tenderness. There are other readers who, though immune to the particular appeal of psychopaths and criminals, feel that in his unquestioning acceptance of Kansas farmers, members of 4-H Clubs, even KBI agents, Mr. Capote by strong implication gives his assent to American society in terms long outmoded in serious writing. Still others accuse Mr. Capote of having been seduced by personal acquaintance with Smith and Hickock, of having let himself forget the hideousness of their crime and of portraying them *too* sympathetically. If this diversity of negative response requires some common denominator of disappointment, it must be found in the sense shared in some dim way by virtually all of Mr. Capote's audience of having been unfairly used in being made to take on the burden of personal involvement pridefully put aside by Mr. Capote himself. An unpleasant critical charge leveled against *In Cold Blood* is that it is itself written in cold blood, exploiting tragedy for personal gain. One does not have to concur in this harsh opinion (I do not); one can even recognize that if anyone is misused by Mr. Capote it is not the Clutters or their murderers but we, the public. . . . (pp. 252-54)

And yet Mr. Capote's book has virtues which are perhaps not to be detached from the objectivity of his method. It is full of well-reported social detail: here at least Mr. Capote handsomely takes over what was once, in a less subjective day, an important function of the novelist. And his book speaks to us with disquieting force on psychiatry and the law—Mr. Capote may not tell us to what end he delved so deep into the Clutter killings, but he thoroughly impresses upon us the small progress our society has made in solving the legal problems posed by criminals like Smith and Hickock. And certainly *In Cold Blood* has a healthily unsettling effect on some of our easier assumptions about social and human casualty.

What—Mr. Capote asks us—are we to do about our psychopathic murderers: kill them; put them in prison; put them in hospitals? Although little approval is now given to capital punishment for any class of criminal, it still exists in the majority of American states. But let us suppose—hopefully—that soon this form of punishment will everywhere be abolished, . . . what then do we do with our Smiths and Hickocks? Obviously they cannot be let free in society. Shall it then be prison or hospitalization? If prison, rehabilitation is hopeless. But so too, in the case of murderers like Smith and Hickock, is psychiatric cure virtually hopeless in our present state of therapeutic knowledge. What distinguishes

these cold-blooded killers, Smith, Hickock, the young Andrews who was with them in the death row, from at least some persons who commit crimes of passion is their incapacity to feel remorse for their crimes. (pp. 254-55)

But there are even knottier problems than this which Mr. Capote's book brings out of the professional parish where they usually stay hidden from general view. Not only has the law not discovered a proper disposition of the incurable criminal, it has not yet devised a reliable method for separating out the offender who is susceptible of cure from incurables like Smith and Hickock. The legal sanity of these two men was tested by the M'Naghten Rule which still obtains in most states, not only in Kansas. In accordance with this Rule, which asks but a single question, whether the defendant was able to distinguish right from wrong at the time of the crime, Smith and Hickock were clearly able to stand trial for the Clutter murders. True, they had been "driven" to commit these terrible killings by forces beyond their control, and they had none of the emotions appropriate to wrongdoing. Under psychiatric examination they exhibited a wide range of symptoms of severe mental disorder. But there is no doubt that they were intellectually capable of telling right from wrong, and knew they had done wrong in killing the Clutter family; the awareness of wrongdoing may in fact have given added zest to their criminal acts. None of this complicated pathology could of course be introduced into a court which abides by the M'Naghten Rule, or certainly not without clinical evasion or imprecision. (pp. 255-56)

By his equal emphasis upon the life stories of Smith and Hickock and of the family they killed, so that it is in the glaring immediate light of the *outcome* of the pathologies of the two murderers that we examine their personal histories, Mr. Capote gives an unusual stringency to the enterprise of sociopsychological understanding. The presence of the Clutters within the same pages as the men who so vagrantly murdered them denies us, or should, recourse to sentimentality; it restrains us, or should, from sliding too smoothly into the grooves prepared for us by our present-day preference for the deterministic view of society. Perry Smith, to be sure, has a life story so casebook as to be a cliché of the environmental explanation of mental disease and crime. So awful were the circumstances of his early life . . . that the question in our minds is not how did this man come to be as he was but, rather, how did his sister manage to salvage herself, if we can think it salvation, for her life of tortured respectability? But the Hickock story is different; Hickock is not at all the social victim, or at least not in the sense of being a product of gross want, mistreatment and neglect. While he was disadvantaged economically, it was in circumstances which according to old-time fable are supposed to make for the peculiar American heroism of success. His parents were industrious, honest, clean-living, loyal and loving. Even after their son had been caught in his crime, they never deserted him. A picture like this controverts our readiest notions about the genesis of the psychopathic criminal—until we look more closely and see that, shamed and anguished though they were by what their son had done, Hickock's parents felt no more actual revulsion (however mitigated by love) from their son's crime than the son did himself. The peculiarly awful nature of the Clutter killings reached them only as an idea—a social idea, so to speak—without an emotional affect appropriate to the act itself. One is led to conclude that well before Hickock had arrived on the family scene, the tragic outcome of his life had already been made emotionally possible for him.

Nor is this the only element in the Smith-Hickock story to upset our too-mechanical psychological assumptions. If the two men were unable to experience guilt for taking human life, this does not mean, as we might expect, that they were simply lacking in conscience, any kind of conscience. What someone else might feel about committing murder, Smith and Hickock would seem to have felt about being physically dirty: washing, shaving, showering, caring for their nails was a major occupation of their nonviolent hours. Even more demanding was their concern with language. For Smith, the more literate of the pair, it constituted a measurable and well-exercised superiority to Hickock that he could correct his friend's errors or infelicities of speech, and offer so many more and better words for communicating the complex life of feeling. Everywhere on his travels, as far as his last jail, Smith took with him lists of "beautiful" and "useful" words, obscure bits of information, poems and literary quotations he had anthologized in substitute for the education he had missed. He thought of himself as someone who might have been, who should have been, an artist, and it was from his sense of himself as an artist that he plumbed the depths of his "sensitivity" and nourished his spirit in self-pity. This was met, on Hickock's side, by a highly ambivalent respect for so gifted a friend, an envious admiration which could not but encourage at least his half of their (concealed) homosexual attachment. If we are to say of Smith and Hickock that they were emotionally incapable of our usual old-established moral valuations, we must in accuracy add that they were not without other valuations of a sort to which we are accustomed to give moral weight.

But it is not alone Smith and Hickock but the Clutters too, who, especially as we are shown them confronting their murderers, reveal a far more complicated personal and social principle than we are in the habit of ascribing to virtuous, substantial, Republican, churchgoing, civicminded citizens of the Middle West. At the head of the family stands Mr. Clutter—and was anyone ever more the head of his family, more the whole source and apex of its authority? Certainly there was never such a man of policy, in formulated control of every minute and act of his life, even—or so he would have hoped—of every secret terror. (pp. 256-58)

From Mr. Capote's detailed reconstruction of the night of the murders, Mr. Clutter was not only himself unable to meet the aggression directed against him by this invasion of his home, he would seem to have incapacitated his grown son and daughter for any self-defense, even by effective guile. Smith and Hickock were of course armed. But it was an hour between the time they arrived in the Clutter farmhouse and the killings. In this period, which included an interval when the family was locked, untied, in a bathroom and several intervals when the two intruders were separated from each other in different parts of the house, no one screamed, no one fought, no one tried to drop out of the bathroom window to run for help. It was apparently inconceivable to Mr. Clutter, and therefore to his obedient son and daughter, that the two men might do worse than rob them, harm them. Only the poor neurotic Mrs. Clutter was available to this kind of imagination. Her "fantasy" was quickly countered by Mr. Clutter's "realism"—it would, one can suppose, have been a familiar situation as between this husband and wife.

Indeed, for me, by far the most interesting aspect of Mr. Capote's book as an American story lies not in the gratuitous violence of the crime it describes—this is not an American

invention, though it is as ready to hand for us as if it were—nor in the dreary circumstances of the lives of Smith and Hickock—of this we already have some knowledge—but in the curiously ambiguous personality of Mr. Clutter. If Mr. Capote is at all a novelist in this book, it is, paradoxically enough, as an accident of his entirely literal reporting of this highly "masculine" character undone by his passivity and by—if you will—his lack of actual identity. One is reluctant (it seems like chic) to draw so exemplary a citizen, a successful teetotaling Republican devout progressive farmer, into the circle of self-alienated Americans. Yet manifestly this was a man without connection with his inner self, living by forced intention, by conscious design, programmatically, rather than by any happy disposition of natural impulse. His response to anger could not have been more contemporary in its "enlightened" propitiatoriness and in its lack of instinctual manliness. (pp. 258-59)

Diana Trilling, "Capote's Crime and Punishment," in Partisan Review, *Vol. XXXIII, No. 2, Spring, 1966, pp. 252-59.*

DWIGHT MacDONALD

Mr. Capote has constructed, with enormous pains and skill, an artifact that works efficiently in its own terms, appealing to the whole range of the mass audience, from the most to the least sophisticated. He invested six years of his life on the research and writing [of *In Cold Blood*] and he deserves his millions as much as John D. Rockefeller, Henry Luce, Somerset Maugham and other hard-working, hardheaded entrepreneurs deserved theirs. But let's not exaggerate. Mr. Capote talks grandly about "the nonfiction novel" as a breakthrough out of the impasse the novel has reached in our time—and indeed long before our time; the novel has been dying ever since it was invented; Jane Austen and Stendhal revived it from suffocation by the Defoe-Fielding-Richardson tradition, and a small case could also be made for Sir Walter Scott's romantic pulmotor; James and Joyce and Proust rescued it from inanition a century later; the French antinovelists in our time have smothered it with their efforts at resuscitation; and now Mr. Capote. But despite the dedication with which he collected his massive research, . . . and the cleverness with which he has deployed it for maximum effect, including such movie techniques as the Griffith cross-cutting in the first chapter between the Clutter family and the steadily approaching death car, the "establishing" long shots of the Kansas milieu, the psychological close-ups of the killers, the death-row prison background, with the other condemned killers playing bit grotesques counterpointed against the decent, normal home life of the chief detective and his wife—despite all this craftsmanship he has achieved not a breakthrough but rather a *tour de force* whose limitations are not apparent because it is *cosa nostra,* our thing. With the unerring touch of a bad dentist he hits and keeps hitting a sensitive nerve of our time, as is obvious from the response—instant best sellerdom, . . . The New York *Times* Sunday book section giving six pages to an interview with him by George Plimpton [see excerpt above dated January 16, 1966], an absorbing document because of the skill of the questions and the frankness of the answers, plus a less fascinating front-page review by Conrad Knickerbocker [see excerpt above dated January 16, 1966] which retells the story as reverently as if it were the siege of Troy, contains on close analysis no traces whatever of deleterious criticism, and ends not with a whimper but with a bang: "[Capote] broods with the austerity of a Greek or an Elizabethan. . . . *In Cold Blood* presents the metaphysics of anti-realism through a total evocation of reality." (Earlier he observed, "The tragedy was existential.") "Not the least of the book's merits is that it manages a major moral judgment without the author's appearance once on stage. . . . Mr. Capote has restored dignity to the event. His book is also a grieving testament of faith in what used to be called the soul."

Mr. Knickerbocker's "total evocation of reality" puzzles me because what seems most dubious to me about Capote's "nonfiction novel" is its claim to documentary truth. I don't doubt every fact in it can be found somewhere in that small room full of data, though I wish he had given some indications of where he got what, nor am I reassured by his remark to Plimpton: "I think I may burn it all. The book is what's important. It exists in its own right. . . . I don't really want people poking around in the material of six years' work and research." But facts can lie as much as the camera can: they are part of the truth but they are not the truth. It makes a difference which facts are chosen ("One must be a 'literary photographer,' though an exceedingly selective one"), and also how they are arranged: "In the nonfiction novel one can also manipulate: if I put something in which I don't agree about I can always set it in a context of qualification. . . ." The very qualities that make the book such a remarkable *tour de force*—the author's intelligence, his sense of form and the strength of his personality—play an ambiguous role. The answers he got to his questions, which constitute the bulk of his data, were to some extent shaped by the questions and by his relation to the respondents. In the case of Perry Smith, this was extremely close and lasted for years right up to the day Perry left him, with a kiss, to go out to be hanged. . . . [Might] Perry Smith, in that long intimacy with his fascinating and dominating literary friend, have become a Truman Capote character? Interviewing someone many times over a period of years—and Smith wasn't the only informant of which this was true—may set up a feedback, a ventriloquial effect. "He was a really talented boy, in a limited way," Capote told Plimpton, "he had a genuine sensitivity [and] when he talked about himself as an artist, he wasn't really joking at all." He added that when Perry asked him, "Why are you writing this book?", he said he had "no moral reasons worthy of calling them such, it was just that I had a strictly aesthetic theory about creating a book which could result in a work of art. . . . And Perry would . . . laugh and say, 'What an irony!' . . . And he'd tell me that all he ever wanted to do in his life was to produce a work of art. 'That's all I ever wanted in my whole life,' he said. 'And now what has happened? . . . I kill four people and *you*'re going to produce a work of art.' " Capote adds, with that detachment that is one of his most admirable traits, "Well, I'd have to agree with him. It was a pretty ironic situation." Admirable, but kind of creepy too. . . . (pp. 44, 46, 48)

The other puzzling thing about Mr. Knickerbocker's peroration is that "moral judgment," restoring "dignity to the event," and "a grieving testament of faith" in "the soul" are precisely what I don't find in the book. I agree with the author that he wrote it for artistic and not moral reasons—to such an extent that a serious artistic flaw is its failure to present any moral attitude, indeed any attitude, to the terrible events it so effectively narrates. The title cuts two ways, as I think the admirably frank author has noted somewhere. The kind of coldblooded detachment requisite to his concep-

tion of "the nonfiction novel" limits its artistic scope as may be seen by comparing *In Cold Blood* with two fictional novels about neurotically motivated murders: *Crime and Punishment* and *The Stranger.* Capote has just enough freedom of selection and manipulation to make the result not quite truthful, but not enough to make it a work of art. He is hobbled by his self-imposed limitation to "the facts" he can extract from other people ("My feeling is that for the nonfictional novel to be entirely successful, the author should not appear in the work"). At best his "nonfiction novel" is a virtuoso triumph like a chess master playing twenty opponents blindfolded or a fighter with one hand tied behind his back. . . . Since Dostoevsky and Camus could invent what they needed, they could express their ideas about the meaning of their fictions, could make their own moral judgments and give some human relevance, thus dignity, to "the event." The former created characters who talk much, and expressively, to his purpose—there are plenty of remarks as memorable as Perry Smith's in *Crime and Punishment.* The latter used a different method: a deliberate sparseness, almost banality, of description and dialogue that renders his sense of the hero's alienation and anomie better than any transcript, however shrewdly edited, of sloppy, garrulous contradictory reality.

Coming at last to the movies, I think *In Cold Blood* is a "natural" for filming today for the same reasons that it is an instant, one might say a pre-frozen, best seller. Namely, and roughly, (1) its subject is an atrocious crime which found the victims helpless, and (2) the motor of the action is abnormal psychology.

(1) It's become unfashionable to object to subject matter and with some reason when one remembers that *Madame Bovary, Ulysses* and *Sister Carrie* were once attacked as "sordid," "unpleasant," etc. But I think Capote's subject may be objected to on the same grounds that a cat playing with a mouse may be: that it is morally unedifying—prurient might be a more up-to-date term—and not interesting dramatically. It is a one-way business, no conflict: the Clutters didn't have a chance; their human qualities, the husband's strength (which might have prevailed) or the wife's weakness (which might have aroused pity) didn't and couldn't, given the circumstances and the psychology of the killers, make any difference. Although Capote takes pains to describe them as individuals, the Clutters were depersonalized by the event that overwhelmed them. This is not tragedy, where the conflict of character determines the catastrophe, but more like a traffic accident. Homer could make an epic of the bloody, barbarous Trojan war because there was enough equality in the opposing forces for their human qualities to make a difference; the gods intervened, but they had conflicting loyalties. An *Iliad* in which all the gods were on one side would have been like what happened to the Clutter family—not a very interesting *Iliad.* For the same reason, the Nazi death camps, or our atomization of Hiroshima and Nagasaki, are horrors beyond tragedy, unsuitable to art because the victims were helpless before a catastrophe that had no more relation to their characters, motives or actions than an earthquake.

(2) The depersonalization of the victims is matched by that of their executioners, who kill for reasons of abnormal psychology so removed from rationality as to be unpredictable and almost accidental. (The psychotic motives behind the Nazis' massacre of the Jews is obvious, but our government's decision to obliterate those two cities seems to me to also have its peculiar aspects.) These depersonalizations are in terms of

plot, of why what happens that does happen. Capote goes to much greater, and more successful, efforts to describe the contrasting personalities of the two murderers than he gives to their four victims—the material was, of course, much more extensive, also the actor is in general a more interesting subject than those he acts upon—and each of the six, killers and killed, does emerge as an individual. But this individuality, this humanity played no part in determining the fate of the Clutters and very little in deciding the actions of Perry Smith and Dick Hickock. The objection to introducing a mentally disturbed person into a drama, whether as criminal or as victim, is that he or she is by definition a "wild" card in the pack, unfair artistically, since anything can happen, and severely limiting the human or moral or general meaning, since madness is eccentric, in the literal sense of being outside the central human experience as well as being impenetrable to all but psychiatric specialists. Also, contrary to popular belief, the madder, the duller. The cat is no more edifying, or interesting, than the mouse. (pp. 48, 58)

Dwight MacDonald, *"Cosa Nostra,"* in Esquire, *Vol. LXV, No. 4, April, 1966, pp. 44, 46, 48, 58, 60, 62.*

KENNETH TYNAN

On the strength of his article last Sunday, Truman Capote seems to have invented yet another new art form: after the Non-Fiction Novel, the Semi-Documentary Tantrum. Ignoring the tone of the piece, let's look at the points he raises.

First, the minor ones. I wasn't suggesting that Dick Hickock never tried to rape pubescent girls; merely that Capote's allegations could not have been substantiated in court. A confidential statement to a psychiatrist is not evidence in the legal sense; and Nancy Clutter, aged 16, can hardly be called pubescent.

As to Capote's disclosure that Hickock and Smith had told the cops as well as himself about other murders they had contemplated: I took it for granted that if the police had possessed such damning information, the fact would somewhere be mentioned in the book. Here, as elsewhere, it's impossible to deduce from the text which statements are corroborated and which are not.

A couple of months ago I asked my friend Aaron Frosch, partner in the well-known Manhattan law firm of Weissberger and Frosch (120 East 56th Street, New York City), whether Capote's allegations—if based solely on unsupported hearsay—would have been actionable, had the killers lived to deny them. Founding his answer on this assumption, he said: "I would doubt whether the book would have been released prior to the decease of the accused." He continued: "References in the book to the personal habits of the deceased, unless these were part of the charges against him or were true or were reported in newspapers, would be a basis for action if the accused were still alive."

Mr Frosch, of course, is the "prominent Manhattan lawyer" whose existence Capote insultingly denies. His letter is on my desk, in lieu of "a sworn affidavit"; but unless Capote still believes that I am concocting fictitious quotes from a fictitious source, I shall expect his cheque for $500 within a few days. It should be made out to the Prisoners' Aid Society.

To get to more serious matters: the fact that Perry and Dick signed legal releases is quite irrelevant to my central point, which was (and is) that Capote could have done more than he did to save his friends by means of psychiatric evidence.

The day before the trial began, they were examined by Dr Mitchell Jones, a psychiatrist who volunteered his services to the defence lawyers. When asked in court whether Perry knew right from wrong at the time of the offence, he said he had no opinion. According to Dr Joseph Satten of the Menninger Clinic in Kansas, a psychiatrist highly esteemed by Capote: "This possibly was a tactical error or a misunderstanding on Mitchell Jones's part in the heat of testifying." (I must pause here to nail a wild misstatement on Capote's part—viz: "Dr Satten specifically told Tynan that he could not quote from any of his [Dr Satten's] letters without my expressed permission." I have never been told anything of the sort, nor have I ever written to Dr Satten or received a letter from him.)

Capote maintains that there were *"two* psychiatrists" who knew the case "at first-hand," the other being Dr Satten. But the truth is that Dr Satten never met either Perry or Dick. He merely discussed them with Mitchell Jones, *who was the only psychiatrist ever to interview the murderers.* I won't bother to refute Capote's naïve assumption that they must have been sane because they had high I.Q.s; but I must challenge his blithe assertion that neither was a paranoid schizophrenic. On page 245 we read of Perry: "His present personality structure is very nearly that of a paranoid schizophrenic." This opinion is expressed by Mitchell Jones and endorsed by Satten.

Capote speaks of my "entirely ludicrous claims to acquaintance with a third psychiatric expert on the Clutter case . . . another anonymous person who doesn't exist. . . . " The psychiatrist's name is Dr Estela D'Accurzio; a friend of Dr Satten's, she worked with criminal patients at the Topeka State Hospital and the Kansas Reception and Diagnostic Centre in 1963-64, and believes that the Clutter murderers could have won their appeal if psychiatric testimony had shown them to be paranoid schizophrenics. Capote, on the other hand, contends that "50 world-famous psychiatrists . . . would not have done a damn bit of good," because Kansas abides by the M'Naghten Rule.

He protests too much; and his plea is demonstrably frail. The M'Naghten Rule can be overthrown (and often has been) by any psychiatrist prepared to state that the accused did not know the nature of his act. . . .

[There are many] borderline cases in British law. American examples are just as numerous: consider the trial of Kenneth Chapin (Massachusetts, 1955), who murdered a 14-year-old girl, pleaded insanity and got the death penalty. It was commuted to life imprisonment after the intervention of a celebrated psychiatrist, who declared the condemned man a schizophrenic.

Where Capote is concerned, I see no reason to modify my original judgment: "An attempt to help (by supplying new psychiatric testimony) might easily have failed: what one misses is any sign that it was even contemplated." The three Federal judges who turned down the appeal rightly said that no evidence had been produced to substantiate a defence of insanity. But it might have been: in which case it is not inconceivable that one or both of Capote's confidants might now be alive.

In his preface to the book, Capote expresses his thanks to the people who helped him—such as the citizens of Finney County, the staff of the Kansas Bureau of Investigation, and many others. From this roll of honour, there are two notable absentees. I hope Capote will not object if I repair the omission by paying tribute, on his behalf, to Perry Smith and Dick Hickock, without whose co-operation, garrulity and trust *In Cold Blood* would never have been written.

> Kenneth Tynan, *"Tynan Replies,"* in The Observer, *April 3, 1966, p. 31.*

JOHN CROSBY

I would like to put in my two cents' worth about Mr Capote's book, *In Cold Blood.*

When I left the United States roughly four years ago, this book was already being acclaimed a masterpiece. . . . Time and again at parties I met people—usually girls—who would tell me this book was the greatest masterpiece of reporting since Thucydides; that the human heart was laid bare in a manner unknown since Shakespeare.

I would sit there hushed with admiration. "When did you read it?" I'd ask. Then I'd get a wounded look. "I haven't read it." "Why not?" I'd ask. "Well, it's not written. I mean Truman's still working on it."

Capote has many friends—rich, famous, beautiful and, above all, talkative people—and the fame of this then unwritten and unnamed book rose and rose until everyone was talking about how marvellous it was and what a breakthrough in literature. I got so fed up with this adulation that I once interjected into a conversation the firm opinion that not only did I *not* think it was a masterpiece, but that I also thought it was very badly written. And what's more, poorly structured.

There was a moment's appalled silence. Then someone—a girl, of course—said: "How *can* you say such a disgusting thing about a book you haven't even read?" That's how the game's played. You can't say things like that about a book you haven't read. You can say it's a masterpiece. You can't say it's lousy until you've read it. And by then it's too late, because it's already at the top of the best-seller list.

Four years ago, I thought that Capote had better leave well alone. He already had a masterpiece. Why spoil things by writing it? At one point, a film company—so help me—offered $250,000 for this unwritten book in its then unwritten condition. However, if the book got written, then the price went up to $400,000.

The book came out finally and it is . . . a superb job of police reporting, the best in my memory (although you can safely ignore all that malarkey about a new art form of fiction—non-fiction. It's old as history).

> John Crosby, *"The Cult of the Instant Legend,"* in The Observer, *April 3, 1966, p. 40.*

JOSEPH P. JENKINS

As one of the attorneys who represented and fought for Richard Eugene Hickok and Perry Edward Smith to the very end, I resent the literary tantrums indulged in by Mr Tynan, not only because his critique of Truman Capote's *In Cold Blood*

[see excerpt above dated March 13, 1966] was written without any apparent knowledge of the facts or the law, but also because, by innuendo and implication, he has cast an imputation of legal inadequacy upon the lawyers who were closest to the situation.

Mr Tynan says that the "central point" of his theme is that Capote could have done more than he did to save his friends by means of psychiatric evidence. As I understand Tynan, psychiatric evidence that Hickok and Smith were some sort of "paranoid schizophrenics" might have unlocked their cells on death row and saved them from the gallows. Hedging, however, Tynan then states that even if such testimony were unsuccessful, Capote was to be censured because he did not at least *try* to obtain such testimony.

In the first place, it was no concern of Mr Capote's. A writer has no business interfering with the orderly procedure and processes in a court of law. I happen to know, however, that Capote *did* feel an obligation to help, but after some rather bad experiences with the lawyers, he kept his distance. If the lawyers didn't want Capote's help, what was he to do?

But, back to the central point. We attorneys who worked without one cent of compensation or reimbursement of expenses for almost three years, and who are impeccably cognizant of every factual detail and legal point involved, did everything we could to reopen the case. A great number of legal points were raised, of which the insanity issue was only one. At the habeas corpus hearing in the federal court, which spanned a week including night sessions, *we did present top-notch psychiatric testimony.* Dr Herbert Modlin, a renowned Menninger Foundation neuropsychiatrist, testified at length on the inadequacy of the examination given Hickok and Smith prior to the State trial, and sought to establish either that they were mental defectives or at least that there was enough evidence to warrant a complete psychiatric examination, and that the lack of such examination was a denial of due process of law.

Tynan, however, indicates no knowledge of the procedural problems of using belated psychiatric testimony. . . . Where would we have integrated such testimony? There is no provision in our Federal Rules of Criminal Procedure permitting us to hire top psychiatrists for the purpose of conducting a lengthy psychoanalysis of Hickok and Smith and then eliciting such testimony from the witness stand.

Apparently Mr Tynan . . . [does] not know that the purpose of the federal habeas corpus proceeding in the United States is to determine if error of constitutional magnitude has been made. The federal judge is bound by what did or did not take place in the State court. . . . The federal judge who heard this case ignored Dr Modlin's testimony and fell back on the McNaghten Rules when he stated in his order: "A review of the trial record of this hearing and an observation of their actions during the hearing reveals that both petitioners demonstrate a complete comprehension of the issues and matters at stake before the court."

Tynan then points out that three Federal judges on appeal declared: "There was no substantial evidence then, *and none has been produced since,* to substantiate a defence of insanity" (Tynan's italics) The court did say this, but did not volunteer any method to get such testimony before it. But Tynan fails to add the next sentence, which clearly reflects this court's view: "The attempt to establish insanity as a defence because of serious injuries in accidents years before, and headaches and occasional fainting spells of Hickok, was like grasping at the proverbial straw."

What about a complete psychiatric examination at Garden City prior to trial? The original lawyers did try to obtain a court order directing such a psychiatric examination at the Larned State Hospital. The State, however, vigorously contested the application. The court was in complete agreement. Now, what could Capote have done that the lawyers could not do?

Mr Tynan relies heavily upon the professional opinion of Dr D'Accurzio. He points out that he had never written to Dr Joseph E. Satten, the renowned Menninger Foundation psychiatrist, nor had he ever received a letter from him. Why should he? Dr D'Accurzio wrote for him.

Dr Satten's reply to her is never mentioned by Tynan in his articles. Dr Satten in substance points out that Capote helped Hickock and Smith more as an impartial observer and recorder than by actually becoming an advocate for them. "I do not think anything more could have been done for these two men with regard to the issue of capital punishment, or with regard to the issue of mental illness. By being a neutral observer, I think Mr Capote helped as much as anyone could have helped under the circumstances that existed."

While this is not Mr Tynan's "central point," he is apparently of the opinion that the book would not have been published if we had been successful and had saved the pair from the gibbet. He even wrote to a Manhattan lawyer and quoted him thus: "I would doubt whether the book would have been released prior to the decease of the accused."

The implication is clear. Hickok and Smith had to die to insure publication. However, I would be interested in the Manhattan lawyer's answer if he had been told by Tynan that Capote had valid and legally binding releases from the pair. I personally know that Mr Capote did not want Hickok and Smith to die. The artistic purpose of his book had been accomplished—it would be published whether Hickok and Smith were alive or dead. But it would not be until the case had been appealed through the courts.

Truman was not impatient, as Tynan has charged. After he discovered I was friendly to him, he called me offering advice, as a layman familiar with the facts in Garden City and Topeka, the State capital. *His approach to me was aimed solely at clemency.* Furthermore, Dr Satten agrees with me that Capote didn't want them to die when he says in his letter to Dr D'Accurzio: "One satisfactory resolution 'would have been for the Supreme Court to commute sentence, and I'm sure that Mr Capote would have preferred that to the fact of their execution. Either would have ended the case satisfactorily from the point of view of publication of the book."

Lastly, Mr Tynan makes an incredible and certainly naïve statement in his reply (April 3) [see excerpt above], when he asserts that the McNaghten right or wrong test can be "overthrown (and often has been) by any psychiatrist prepared to state that the accused did not know the nature of his act." Surely, he doesn't mean that a psychiatrist should testify to such a state of facts unless they actually exist. If they do exist, then the expert is staying legally, morally and ethically within the McNaghten rule, and his oath. But if he cannot say that the accused was ignorant of the difference between right and wrong, *then he must not say it.* No psychiatrist can "overthrow" the rule unless the court goes along with him. In Kansas, as well as the great majority of American jurisdictions, the courts will not go along with him.

Joseph P. Jenkins, "Tynan Attacked by Lawyers," in The Observer, *April 24, 1966, p. 31.*

KENNETH TYNAN

[*The essay excerpted below was originally published in* The Observer, *May 1, 1966.*]

Before answering the questions raised last Sunday by Joseph P. Jenkins [see excerpt above dated April 3, 1966], I'd like to deplore the false and flashy heading that *The Observer* ran above his letter. 'Tynan attacked by lawyers,' it said across four columns, thus conveying the impression that I had been ambushed by a mob, whereas in fact Jenkins was my sole assailant.

Readers of **In Cold Blood** will recall that Jenkins's association with the Clutter case began in 1962—two years after the killers had been tried and convicted—when a Federal judge appointed him as unpaid attorney to the condemned men. I have no doubt at all that he and his colleagues fought for the lives of Perry Smith and Dick Hickock as hard as they knew how.

A longer version of Jenkins's letter appeared last week in the American press, lashing me with phrases like 'utter balderdash' and 'God help journalism!', which I patiently accept as part of the shrill and formalised ritual of American courtroom rhetoric. But since I'm accused of neglecting the facts, I might as well start by pointing out a couple of peripheral blunders on Jenkins's part. He triumphantly claims that I 'never mentioned' the letter written by Dr Joseph Satten of the Menninger Foundation to my psychiatrist friend, Dr D'Accurzio: in fact, there are quotations from it both in my original article and in my reply to Truman Capote. And it's a pity, considering Jenkins's concern for the defendants, that he manages to misspell Hickock's name throughout.

But to move towards matters of importance: Jenkins reveals a sadly tenuous knowledge of (and faith in) psychiatry when he scoffs at the value of evidence tending to prove that Hickock and Smith were 'some sort of "paranoid schizophrenics."' He says that among the legal points he brought up, 'the insanity issue was only one.' In the American text he adds, 'and a minor one at that.' But it was not minor; it was crucial; and this is where I part company with him and Capote, his clients' chronicler.

Let's look first at the pre-trial period, between January 7, 1959, when lawyers were assigned to the accused, and March 22, when court proceedings began. During those 10 weeks Capote could certainly have helped to provide the two men with more adequate psychiatric examination than the hasty two-hour session with Dr Mitchell Jones which they received the day before the trial opened. It's true, as Jenkins says, that the original lawyers failed to obtain a court order directing psychiatric examination in a State hospital; but there is no reason (except lack of funds) why the defendants should not have been examined at length inside the county jail.

Parenthetically, Jenkins remarks that 'even if such testimony were presented at the original trial, a jury would not have to believe it.' Of course; but does that mean that it should not have been proffered? As for the McNaghten Rule: I said that it could be overthrown by 'any psychiatrist prepared to state that the accused did not know the nature of his act.' By this I naturally meant an honest psychiatrist. Jenkins seems to imply that I was advocating perjury. I won't comment on this astonishing assumption.

Now for the post-trial period and the appeals, Jenkins initiated a habeas corpus hearing in the Federal court, at which an unpaid neuropsychiatrist named Dr Herbert Modlin (who never met either Smith or Hickock: from first to last, Mitchell Jones was the only psychiatrist to have that privilege) testified that the accused had not been given adequate psychiatric examination. His evidence cut no ice. 'There is no provision,' says Jenkins, 'in our Federal Rules of Criminal Procedure permitting us to hire top psychiatrists for the purpose of conducting a lengthy psycho-analysis of Hickok [*sic*] and Smith and then eliciting such testimony from the witness stand.' But if other psychiatrists had known what Capote knew about the private fantasies and psychotic drives of the two killers, and had taken the stand to support Dr Modlin, the judge could have ordered a full psychiatric examination.

According to Jenkins: 'The Federal judge is bound by what did or did not take place in the State court. He is not permitted to open new avenues.' This is simply untrue. To determine whether a constitutional error has been made, a Federal judge can (and frequently does) admit testimony adducing facts that were not raised at the trial. The Supreme Court ruled in 1963 (case of Townsend versus Sain) that where a constitutional point was involved in a habeas corpus hearing, a Federal judge might decide 'to hold evidentiary hearings— that is, to try issues of fact anew.' In other words, the question of sanity could have been reopened. And in any case, irrespective of whether Hickock and Smith were insane at the time of the murders or the trial, psychiatrists could have been hired to interview them in prison, in order to establish whether they were fit for execution. The hanging of insane men is clearly 'a cruel and unusual punishment,' and as such forbidden by the Constitution.

So much for the legal quibbles. We touch on the nerve of my complaint when Jenkins says, of the case in general, that: 'it was no concern of Mr Capote's. A writer has no business interfering with the orderly procedure and processes in a court of law.' Really? Had Zola no business interfering in the Dreyfus case? Was it wrong for the late Felix Frankfurter—then a law professor at Harvard—to influence public and legal opinion by writing a famous article in the *Atlantic Monthly* about the Sacco-Vanzetti case? Must we rebuke the many authors and polemicists who tried to prevent the execution of the Rosenbergs and Caryl Chessman? In matters of life and death, there are no interlopers.

One would feel less uneasy about Mr Capote's role in this sorry affair if he had said—even once, even in an interview— that he did not think his friends deserved to hang. 'I personally know,' says Jenkins, 'that Mr Capote did not want Hickok [*sic*] and Smith to die.' No doubt: but it was an opinion that Mr Capote never saw fit, in the course of five long years, to make public. (pp. 457-60)

Kenneth Tynan, in a letter to the editor, in his Right & Left: Plays, Films, People, Places and Events, *Atheneum, 1967, pp. 457-60.*

PHILLIP K. TOMPKINS

As every literate American must know by now, *In Cold Blood* is the "true account of a multiple murder and its consequences." . . . *In Cold Blood* is organized into four main parts and eighty-six unnumbered chapters which generally alternate between events in Kansas and the travels of the killers. Actually the chapters are more like short stories; many of them could stand by themselves with little or no additional context. All together they constitute the substance of Capote's claim that he has established a new literary form: the "nonfiction novel."

How does one evaluate a new literary form? Does it require a new method of criticism? Obviously one must begin by asking after the author's purpose. If the novel is defined as a "fictional prose narrative of substantial length," Capote's new form must be a self-contradiction: nonfiction fiction. He cannot have it both ways; and he seems not to want it both ways. . . . Capote's strongest statement on the authenticity of his book was made in *The New York Times Book Review:* "One doesn't spend almost six years on a book, the point of which is factual accuracy, and then give way to minor distortions." Mr. Capote asks us to believe his book is true, is without even "minor distortions."

It seems apparent that the criteria of conventional novelistic criticism cannot be brought to bear fully on this work. How can one be critical of the plot probabilities of true events? The only relevant criteria would seem to be those normally applied to journalism and history. In other words, is the work good reportage? If facts are basis for the plot, and if the artistic success of such a work must rest upon their accuracy, is the author's account of the events, by objective standards, true? (p. 125)

On February 4, 1966, a cold and snowy morning in Detroit, I left on a nine-day trip to Kansas to look for external evidence. My methods were those of conventional journalism: interviews with principals and a search for documentary confirmation. I had been anticipated in my search by another reporter with the same interests. In a lengthy Kansas City *Times* article of January 27, with numerous photographs, Robert Pearman suggested the possibility of several minor inaccuracies in the book by interviewing some of the principals in Garden City and Holcomb.

Bobby Rupp, the last person (other than the killers) to see the Clutters alive, told Pearman: "He [Capote] put things in there that to other people make good reading but the people who were actually involved know that he exaggerated a little bit. . . . He makes me out to be some kind of great athletic star and really I was just an average small-town basketball player." (This is not false modesty on Rupp's part; I talked to several people who had seen him play.) "And he has me always running back and forth to the Clutter place. I didn't do that."

And the conclusion of Pearman's article:

"There is one character in the book that Capote was dead wrong about—Nancy Clutter's riding horse Babe. Capote has the horse sold to a Mennonite farmer for a plow horse for $75." (pp. 125, 127)

" 'Hell, I couldn't even get a bid in until the mare got to $100,' says Seth Earnest, father of the postmaster, the man who actually bought Babe. Mr. Earnest is neither Mennonite by religion nor farmer by occupation.

" 'I gave $182.50 for Babe,' he said. 'I wanted her for a couple of reasons. One was sentimental and the other was that she was in foal to a registered quarter horse, Aggie Twist, and I wanted the colt.' . . .

The significant point about this rather minor interpolation is that it provides the flourish Capote needed to complete short story number seventy.

If the discrepancies in Capote's account were all as minor as these, one might easily dismiss them as quibbles. They lead, however, into questions of greater import—questions of how much license a purportedly objective reporter can be permitted in selecting and interpreting one set of facts as opposed to another equally or even more convincing set of facts. In life, truth is complicated and often ambiguous. The same is true of art. But the artist, to make his point, can eliminate certain awkward complications the better to suggest a larger truth. Because Capote has not chosen to make his stand in *In Cold Blood* on artistry alone, but claims literal truth, an awareness of Capote's method in rendering the climax of *In Cold Blood* is enlightening and disturbing. The climax is literally and ironically the moment of truth in the book; until that point the reader is unsure of just how, and by whom, the Clutter murders were committed. In the sixty-first chapter we learn that, although Hickock has made a statement in the Las Vegas City Jail blaming Smith for all four killings, Smith has admitted only the falsity of his alibi—nothing more. Capote wrote: "And though even (K.B.I. agent) Duntz had forfeited his composure—had shed, along with his tie and coat, his enigmatic drowsy dignity—the suspect seemed content and serene; he refused to budge. He'd never heard of the Clutters or Holcomb, or even Garden City."

In the sixty-third chapter . . . , K.B.I. agents Dewey and Duntz, along with Smith, are in the first of a two-car caravan headed for Garden City. Smith has still not budged. The agents try to goad Smith into confessing by repeating parts of Hickock's confession—with no success. Agent Dewey, without anticipating any unusual response from the accused, mentions an incident in which Smith had supposedly beaten a Negro to death some years earlier.

> To Dewey's surprise, the prisoner gasps. He twists around in his seat until he can see, through the rear window, the motorcade's second car, see inside it: "The tough boy!" Turning back, he stares at the dark streak of desert highway. "I thought it was a stunt. I didn't believe you. That Dick let fly. The tough boy! Oh, a real brass boy. Wouldn't harm the fleas on a dog. Just run over the dog." He spits. "I never killed any nigger. But *he* thought so. I always knew if we ever got caught, if Dick ever really let fly, dropped his guts all over the goddam floor—I knew he'd tell about the nigger." He spits again. "So Dick was afraid of me? That's amusing. I'm very amused. What he don't know is, I almost did shoot him."
>
> Dewey lights two cigarettes, one for himself, one for the prisoner. "Tell us about it, Perry."

And Perry Smith tells.

An alternative version exists in the office of the Clerk of the Supreme Court of Kansas, where there is on file the official transcript of case number 2322, District Court of Finney County, Kansas: "THE STATE OF KANSAS, Plaintiff, vs. RICHARD EUGENE HICKOCK and PERRY EDWARD SMITH, Defendants." . . . The following exchange, between Logan Green (assistant to the County Attorney) and K.B.I. agent Dewey, is taken verbatim from pages 231-233. Dewey is testifying as to the first time that Smith made a remark implicating himself in the crime.

Q: Where was that?

A: That was at the Police Department at Las Vegas.

Q: Did he give you any information concerning the crimes?

A: He did. I told Perry Smith that Hickock had given the other agents a statement and that Hickock had said that they had sold the radio, the portable radio, that they had taken from Kenyon Clutter's room, that they had sold it in Mexico City. I told Smith that . . . I wanted to know for sure that where Hickock said that radio was, that it was there. Present when I was talking to Perry Smith on this occasion was Mr. Duntz and Mr. Nye of the Kansas Bureau of Investigation. Mr. Nye told Perry Smith where Hickock had said that he sold the portable radio, and Smith said that was right.

Q: Did he give you any further information in connection with the crimes at that time?

A: No, sir.

Q: Subsequent to that did you have any other conversation with him?

A: Yes. I talked to Perry Smith later that same day, which was on the 4th of January, 1960. At that time I talked to him when we were in the car en route back to Garden City.

(p. 127)

Q: On the way back you say he gave you some additional information?

A: He did.

Q: I will ask you to tell the Court and jury what he said to you.

A: As we were leaving Las Vegas, before we were out of the city limits—Sheriff Robinson, Hickock and Mr. Church were in the lead car. Myself, Perry and Mr. Duntz were following, and Perry could see in the car ahead and Hickock was talking, and Perry said to us, he says, "Isn't he a tough guy?" meaning Hickock. He says, "Look at him talk." He said, "Hickock had told me that if we were ever caught that we weren't going to say a word but there he is, just talking his head off." He then asked me what Hickock said in regard to the killing of the Clutter family, who killed them. I told Perry that Hickock says that he killed all of the family. Perry told me that wasn't correct, but he said, "I killed two of them and Hickock killed two of them."

Several inferences can be drawn from this testimony. First, contrary to Capote's account, Perry had begun to crack in the Las Vegas City Jail. His remarks about Kenyon Clutter's radio implicated him in the crime. Second, contrary to Capote's account, Dewey, Duntz and Smith were not in the lead car; Smith would have seen nothing but a dark streak of desert highway had he turned around to see out the rear window at that moment. Third, contrary to Capote's account, Sheriff Robinson was in the lead car (Capote neither has Robinson on the trip to Las Vegas nor the return to Garden City).

Indeed, it was Robinson's car in the lead; the Garden City *Telegram*'s account of the trip chronicled a small crisis when Robinson's car suffered a burned-out wheel bearing in Lamar, Colorado, and Hickock had to be transferred twice to get him to Garden City. Fourth, contrary to Capote's account, it was not the "nigger" incident that precipitated the sudden confession from Smith. Rather, it was simply Smith's observation of Hickock's loquaciousness in the lead car.

At this point I began to wonder about the "nigger" incident. Had Dewey simply forgotten that by relating this story he had forced Smith to gasp and confess? The answer came later, in Duntz's testimony of the same events. After establishing that he, Duntz, had first become acquainted with Smith in the "forepart of March, 1956" (a coincidence unmentioned in the book), Duntz went on to mention the first time Smith had implicated himself in the Clutter case. The direct examination is by County Attorney Duane West:

> A: That was also at Police Headquarters and we were just making arrangements to leave and Agent Nye was making preparation to go to look for the radio that we had information had been taken. Perry was asked by Mr. Dewey if he cared to tell us where that was.
>
> Q: Did he do so?
>
> A: Yes, he did.
>
> (pp. 127, 166)
>
> Q: Mr. Duntz, what further conversation did you have with the defendant, if any?
>
> A: Very little. I can't recall any there at Police Headquarters after that.
>
> Q: Did you have conversation with the defendant after you left Las Vegas?
>
> A: Yes.
>
> Q: Would you relate to the jury where this conversation was and when it was?
>
> A: It was soon after we had left Las Vegas en route back to Kansas.
>
> Q: Would you tell the jury just exactly what happened, as you recall it?
>
> A: Perry Smith asked—do you mind if I clarify myself how we were riding?
>
> Q: Go ahead.
>
> A: I was riding in the car with Mr. Dewey and Perry Smith. They were riding in the front seat. I was in the back seat. The conversation was had between Perry Smith and Mr. Dewey. Perry asked Mr. Dewey if he could tell him what Dick had said about the murder and Mr. Dewey answered, "Yes, Dick said that you tied and killed all of them," and Perry said, "That isn't right." He said, "He killed two and I killed two."
>
> Q: Was there any further conversation at that time, Mr. Duntz?
>
> A: Well, at that time I told Perry of a conversation that I had had with Richard Hickock at Las Vegas . . . that pertained to an incident that was supposed to have happened previous to the time that Perry got in trouble—pardon me, in 1955—

and Richard Hickock told me if I would tell Perry Smith that Perry had told him that previous to that time he had killed a nigger by clubbing him to death, then Perry would know that he, Richard Hickock, had been talking to us and giving us a statement.

Several inferences can also be drawn from this testimony. First, it corroborates Dewey's testimony—establishing that Smith had begun to crack in the Las Vegas City Jail, establishing also that it was Dewey's answer to a question from Smith that preceded the confession. Second, contrary to Capote's account, the "nigger" incident was related by the agents to Smith *after* he admitted two of the slayings. Third, contrary to Capote's account, it was Duntz, not Dewey, who repeated the fictitious story to Smith.

We now have the word, given under oath, of two of the three principals to the climax of the story. We can presume that this pair of professionals did not perjure themselves; can we be so sure of what Smith may have told Capote? And if Capote favors Smith's version over the one given by Dewey and Duntz, is he not discrediting Dewey as a source? How then should we evaluate the remaining portions of the book in which we see events through Dewey's eyes?

So much for the manner of the confession. What of its contents? During the trial, Dewey was forced to testify as to the substance of Smith's confession because the statement was never signed by the defendant. Newspaper reports of Dewey's testimony at the trial . . . do not conform with Capote's version of the contents of the confession. Nevertheless, one might raise the possibility that Capote—by means of his intimacy with the principals—had been able to do a better job of reporting than these Kansas newspapermen who had to get their stories in the courtroom and hurriedly write copy for deadlines.

Here is Capote's account of Smith's confession to the murder of Mr. Clutter, the first victim: . . .

> After, see, after we'd taped them, Dick and I went off in a corner. To talk it over. Remember, now, there were hard feelings between us. Just then it made my stomach turn to think I'd ever admired him, lapped up all that brag. I said, "Well, Dick. Any qualms?" He didn't answer me. I said, "Leave them alive, and this won't be any small rap. Ten years the very least." He still didn't say anything. He was holding the knife. I asked him for it, and he gave it to me, and I said, "All right, Dick. Here goes." But I didn't mean it. I meant to call his bluff, make him argue me out of it, make him admit he was a phony and a coward. See, it was something between me and Dick. I knelt down beside Mr. Clutter, and the pain of kneeling—I thought of that goddam dollar. Silver dollar. The shame. Disgust. And *they'd* told me never to come back to Kansas. But I didn't realize what I'd done till I heard the sound. Like somebody drowning. Screaming under water. I handed the knife to Dick. I said, 'Finish him. You'll feel better.' Dick tried—or pretended to. But the man had the strength of ten men—he was half out of his ropes, his hands were free. Dick panicked. Dick wanted to get the hell out of there. But I wouldn't let him go. The man would have died anyway, I know that, but I couldn't leave him like he was. I told Dick to hold the flashlight, focus it. Then I aimed the gun.

(p. 166)

In contrast to this account, Dewey's testimony was as follows:

> . . . So they debated who was going to do what and who was going to start it, and finally Smith said, "Well," he says, "I'll do it," so he said Hickock had the shotgun and the flashlight at this time and that he, Smith, had the knife and he said he put this knife in his hand with the blade up along his arm so that Mr. Clutter couldn't see it and he walked over to where Mr. Clutter was laying on this mattress cover and he told him that he was going to tighten the cords on his hand, and he said he made a pretense to do that and then he cut Mr. Clutter's throat. Smith said that after doing that he got up and Hickock said to him, "Give me the knife," and he said about that time they heard a gurgling sound coming from Mr. Clutter and Smith said that Hickock walked over to where Mr. Clutter was just as Smith was walking off of this cardboard box, and he said he turned for just a second and then Dick plunged this—Hickock plunged this knife into Mr. Clutter's throat, either once or twice. He said he couldn't tell which, but he heard the slap of the knife go in, and he said that he thought it went in full length because he heard a sound that went something—as he described to me, something like this (indicating). He said that after Hickock stepped away from Mr. Clutter that Mr. Clutter jerked one arm loose, his left arm, I believe, and he put it to his throat to try to stop the bleeding, and he said after that Hickock ran over to where he was and he said, "Let's get the hell out of here," and Smith said that he could see that Mr. Clutter was suffering and told Hickock that that was a hell of a way to leave a guy, because he felt he was going to die anyway, so Smith said he said to Hickock, "Shall I shoot him?" and Hickock said, "Yes, go ahead," so Smith said that he shot Mr. Clutter in the head while Hickock held the flashlight. . . .

The two versions differ in many small details, but the most serious discrepancy concerns the mental state of Smith at the moment of the murder. Capote has Smith say, "But I didn't mean it." And, "But I didn't realize what I'd done till I heard the sound." (In The New York *Times* interview, Capote referred to Smith's mental state at that moment as a "brain explosion.") Dewey, on the other hand, has Smith committing the murder with *full consciousness and intent*. On Dewey's word, the act was premeditated to the degree that Smith announced his intention, took pains to conceal the knife from the victim and deceived Mr. Clutter into thinking he was going to tighten his bonds. He made that pretense—and then cut Mr. Clutter's throat. The two versions suggest different mental states.

I see three possible explanations that Capote might offer for these discrepancies: first, that the oral confession given during the automobile trip from Las Vegas was different from the statement Smith made upon arriving in Garden City (it was about the latter that Dewey was testifying); second, that Smith later told Capote of details that he did not reveal while confessing to Dewey; and third, that Smith's later recollections of the confession (as told to Capote) were more accurate than Dewey's recollections (as told to the Court).

We can dismiss the first explanation, that the confession in the car was different from the one dictated in the Sheriff's private office in Garden City. Capote describes, on page 255,

the second confession by saying it "recounted admissions already made to Alvin Dewey and Clarence Duntz." Furthermore, there is no indication in either the book or the transcript that the two confessions differed in any way.

The second possible explanation, that Smith told Capote details he had not revealed to Dewey, is undoubtedly true; Capote claims to have had more than two hundred interviews with the killers. But to include these remarks is not to report the confession as it took place. And I doubt, for reasons to be discussed later, that Smith could have truthfully given such radically different versions of the confession. (Wendle Meier, former Undersheriff of Finney County, told me that he had visited Smith at Lansing; that Smith told him that there would be inaccuracies in the book; that when he, Meier, asked what these would be, Smith would only say: Read it and see for yourself.)

The third possible explanation, that Smith's later recollections of the confession (as told to Capote) were more accurate than Dewey's testimony, is not difficult to refute. Duntz's testimony in the transcript corroborates Dewey's testimony in every way. More conclusive is the fact that Dewey gave an extremely accurate account of the contents of the confession. I know because I have examined it. It is now in the possession of former County Attorney West; like the transcript of the trial, it was taken down in shorthand and transcribed by Mrs. Valenzuela. This sample is relevant to the point at issue.

> . . . I think we was debating who was going to do what and who was going to start it, so I told him, "Well," I says, "I'll do it," so I walked over to Mr. Clutter and he couldn't hear us talk from where we was over at the door. We was kind of talking in a whisper. I walked over to Mr. Clutter and Dick come over close. He had the flashlight and had the shotgun in his hand and I would say he was standing, oh, about at Mr. Clutter's feet, and Mr. Clutter didn't see the knife. I had it with the handle in my hand and the blade up like this (indicating) and down about my side. I went up toward Mr. Clutter's head and I told him I was going to tie his hands a little tighter and he was laying on his right side and he was taped then. He didn't say anything or he didn't mumble and, well, as I made a pretense to tie his hands again I cut Mr. Clutter's throat. That's when I cut Mr. Clutter's throat, and he started to struggle and I got up right away and Dick says, "Give me that knife." I could see he was nervous and that's when the gurgling sound of Mr. Clutter was noticed. . . .

Here we have Smith's own words, taken verbatim from official records. There is hardly an implication of either "brain explosion," or "mental eclipse," or "schizophrenic darkness" at this critical moment.

After Hickock and Smith were returned to Garden City, they were housed in the County Jail. To separate them, Smith was kept in an isolated unit inside the Sheriff's residence; occupying the residence at that time were Undersheriff Meier and his wife. Smith's cell adjoined Mrs. Meier's kitchen; it is from her point of view that we learn of Smith's stay there. For example, the final paragraph of the sixty-fifth chapter is narrated by her; she is describing a discussion she and her husband had in bed shortly after Smith had been jailed. She remarks that Smith was not the worst young man she had met. Mr. Meier reprimands her for such thoughts.

While in Garden City, I talked to Mr. Meier about the incident; he was adamant that it had not taken place. On February 26, 1966, I placed a long-distance telephone call to Mrs. Meier (she had been out of town while I was in Garden City). She also insisted that this incident had never taken place—and that she had not told Capote any such thing. She explained that her husband—as did all the officers involved—worked day and night on the case. She rarely saw him during that period. When he did get a chance to get some sleep, the last thing he wanted to talk about was the case. In short, the only two principals to this event insist that it did not take place—and that they did not tell Capote any such story.

The finishing touch of the seventy-seventh chapter evokes considerable sympathy for Perry Smith. Mrs. Meier is quoted as saying:

> I heard him crying. I turned on the radio. Not to hear him. But I could. Crying like a child. He'd never broke down before, shown any sign of it. Well, I went to him. The door of his cell. He reached out his hand. He wanted me to hold his hand, and I did, I held his hand, and all he said was, "I'm embraced by shame."

During our telephone conversation, Mrs. Meier repeatedly told me that she *never* heard Perry cry; that on the day in question she was in her bedroom, not the kitchen; that she did not turn on the radio to drown out the sound of crying; that she did not hold Perry's hand; that she did not hear Perry say, "I'm embraced by shame." And finally—that she had never told such things to Capote. Mrs. Meier told me repeatedly and firmly, in her gentle way, that these things were not true.

Mrs. Meier said that she actually saw very little of Perry Smith. She had only occasional conversations with him while working in the kitchen. She said that she saw him the day after he received the death penalty and that he was rather bitter. But again, she never heard him cry. Perhaps Smith told Capote of these things, but it is inaccurate to put these words in Mrs. Meier's mouth—and even more inaccurate to have her participate in events that did not take place.

Now let us turn to another significant part of the book—the conclusion. In the final chapter of **In Cold Blood** we see the execution of the killers. Hickock was hanged first. Smith was brought into the warehouse and asked whether or not he wished to make a statement. Those last words, as quoted by Capote, are:

> "I think," he said, "it's a helluva thing to take a life in this manner. I don't believe in capital punishment, morally or legally. Maybe I had something to contribute, something—" His assurance faltered; shyness blurred his voice, lowered it to a just audible level. "It would be meaningless to apologize for what I did. Even inappropriate. But I do. I apologize."

Bill Brown, editor of the Garden City *Telegram,* represented the Kansas newspapers as a witness of the execution. He stood four feet from Smith when these words were spoken (Capote was unable to watch; he walked away, out of earshot). Brown took notes. He immediately compared his notes with those of the wire-service representatives standing on either side of him—they were identical. Here are Smith's last words as recorded and reported by Brown in the *Telegram* of April 14, 1965:

> Asked if he had anything to say before mounting

the gallows, Smith stated, "Yes, I would like to say a word or two.

> "I think it is a hell of a thing that a life has to be taken in this manner. I say this especially because there's a great deal I could have offered society. I certainly think capital punishment is legally and morally wrong.

> "Any apology for what I have done would be meaningless at this time. I don't have any animosities toward anyone involved in this matter. I think that is all."

Brown is today convinced that Smith did not apologize.

Tony Jewell of Garden City's radio station KIUL was the first radio newscaster to be invited to witness an execution in Kansas. Immediately after the execution, Jewell and Brown telephoned their reports from the prison to the radio station in Garden City; the remarks were recorded for later broadcasts. I have a tape recording of that broadcast; again, there was no apology from Smith. Furthermore, there is no indication of an apology in the Associated Press story filed that day.

Finally, in a telephone conversation with Alvin A. Dewey on February 5, I asked him how Capote had obtained Smith's last words (in the book it is through Dewey's eyes and ears that we see and hear these events). Mr. Dewey did not know. "Perhaps he overheard me talking about it later," he suggested. Had Perry apologized? Mr. Dewey could not recall Perry's exact words, but thought they were "something along that line." What is certain is that Capote did not hear Perry's words at firsthand. Dewey, the narrator of the event in the book, is now unsure of the words spoken by Smith and also unsure of how Capote gathered the information. Capote's reconstruction, then, conflicts with the report by two newsmen who made their notes on the spot—not sometime later, which is the method of recording Capote tells us he used. The best evidence supports the conclusion that Perry Smith did not apologize.

In addition to searching for documentation while in Kansas, I was curious about the legal question raised by Rebecca West in her *Harper's* review of **In Cold Blood** [see excerpt above dated February, 1966]:

> Hickock was hanged for murder which he had not committed, when he should have been sentenced to a term of imprisonment as an accessory, but this was his own fault. The truth could only be established if both he and Perry chose to give evidence, but this, for a reason Mr. Capote does not explain, they did not do.

Who would know the answer?

The newspaper files show that former County Attorney Duane West played a significant, if not the most significant, role in the case. . . . (In the book, however, West is made to appear somewhat lower in rank than a law clerk.)

Legally, as Attorney West told the jury (and me), it made no difference whether Hickock killed any or all of the Clutters. Under the Felony Murder Rule, which applies in Kansas and many other states, any party to a felony in which a life is taken can be prosecuted for murder. (pp. 166-68, 170)

West had decided to try Smith and Hickock together; when it became known that they might request separate trials, West moved to have their names added to the list of witnesses (which he could not do if they were to be tried together). "Our feeling was that Perry would testify against Dick. He was willing to take the blame for all four killings to make it easier for Hickock's mother, but he was not willing to take the blame for the idea and the plan."

West told me on two occasions that he believed Smith's confession to be true—that Hickock killed the two Clutter women. Another man intimate with the case from beginning to end, Bill Brown, agrees that Hickock did two of the killings. And so, apparently, did Alvin A. Dewey. When asked, during the trial, why he would not allow Smith to change his confession (to take the blame for all four murders), Dewey explained that Smith and Hickock had been able to shout back and forth from their respective cells and negotiate the changes. They knew that, regardless of the details of the confessions, they would both "swing." Smith was willing to make the changes to spare Hickock's family that much pain. The clear implication of the testimony is that Dewey did not believe Smith. The most we can say for Capote on this point is that it was poor reporting to lead such a careful reader as Rebecca West to the confident conclusion that Smith had committed all of the Clutter murders while the principals were less than unanimous.

Before offering my hypothesis for these discrepancies, let me state that Capote's awareness of the errors is not an issue. It is conceivable that they are completely unintentional. As Capote told Jane Howard of *Life,* within three hours of each interview he retreated to his motel, wrote up his notes and filed them. "Funnily enough," he said, "I seldom had to look at my notes after that: I had it all in my head." The transformation of facts may well have resulted from his failure to consult his notes more closely.

Capote himself has given us a broad, general hypothesis to explain the discrepancies. A nonfiction novel is more difficult than a conventional novel, he said to *Life,* because "you have to get away from your own particular vision of the world." But possibly Capote did not succeed in doing so; he presumably still needed that very conventional element of the novel as he knows it—a dramatic climax, a moment of truth. Thus, there followed a subtle but significant alteration of the facts to fit a preconception of the novelistic, transforming an unexciting confession into a theatrical catharsis.

But the occasion for transformation demands a more extended explanation, a closer inspection of the characterization of Perry Smith. Capote was drawn to him more than to Hickock. It is Perry Smith—not the victims, the investigators, the lawyers, not even the pair of killers—who dominates this book. When Smith stood up, wrote Capote, "he was no taller than a twelve-year-old child." The Avedon photographs of the two standing together reveal that Capote, if anything, is a "slippery spray" of hair shorter than Smith. Furthermore, Smith had a miserable childhood. Harper Lee, who has known Capote long and well, told *Newsweek,* "I think every time Truman looked at Perry he saw his own childhood."

But there the similarities—which may have attracted Capote to Smith—would appear to end. Smith, after all, lived in a world very different from Capote's, a world of violence. A measure of the emotional and cultural gap between them is that Perry invented a tale in which he had beaten a Negro to death. It was a boast, calculated to increase the esteem in which his friend Dick held him. Capote, on the other hand,

told the *Saturday Review:* "I am not interested in crime per se; I hate violence."

In his vision of the world, Capote found it difficult, if not impossible, to understand how a man could kill, and do so without feeling. He could understand, however, that an outcast and accursed poet might kill while under a "mental eclipse," while deep inside a "schizophrenic darkness"—a "brain explosion" if you will—and thus avenge the wrongs "they" had done him.

And so were the facts transformed. Perry Smith, who could hardly utter a grammatical sentence while dictating his confession, becomes *le poète maudit,* corrects the grammar in newspaper articles about him. To judge from his confession, Perry Smith was an obscene, semiliterate and cold-blooded killer. But, as Yuric correctly guessed in the *Nation,* we cannot rest with the Perry Smiths as they are: "Before we kill them we make sure they negate themselves by turning into literate, psychopathic heroes."

By having Smith say, "I didn't realize what I'd done," Capote projected his own vision of the world onto Smith at that moment. In so doing he created a hybrid of Capote-Smith predispositions and the real Smith becomes even less understandable. Should we believe he suffered a "brain explosion" when he poised the rock to open the head of the Omaha salesman? And again when he wished out loud that he could have killed his sister along with the Clutters? And when he planned with Hickock two other murders which Capote told The *Times* he chose to omit from the book? Capote appears to have fallen into the trap of believing that operational definition of insanity one frequently hears: "Anyone who can kill *has* to be insane."

Perry's values toward human life derived from a world in which men expect to kill and be killed. He explained these values quite succinctly (and demonstrated just how much shame he felt) to his friend, Donald Cullivan, on page 291 of the book. Perry insisted that he was not sorry for what he had done; he was only sorry that he could not walk out of the cell with his visitor. Cullivan, like Capote, could scarcely believe that Perry was so devoid of conscience and compassion.

Perry said, "Why? Soldiers don't lose much sleep. They murder, and get medals for doing it. The good people of Kansas want to murder me—and some hangman will be glad to get the work. It's easy to kill—a lot easier than passing a bad check."

For premeditated murder performed in cold blood, Capote substituted unpremeditated murder performed in a fit of insanity. Art triumphs over reality, fiction over nonfiction. By imparting conscience and compassion to Perry, Capote was able to convey qualities of inner sensitivity, poetry and a final posture of contrition in his hero. . . . It is a moving portrait but not, I submit, of the man who actually was Perry Smith— the man who, in real life, told his friend Cullivan he was *not* sorry, the same man who would not play the hypocrite with Cullivan or his old friend Willie-Jay.

In describing Perry, Capote wrote: "His own face enthralled him. Each angle of it induced a different impression. It was a changeling's face." In *Newsweek* Capote described himself: "If you looked at my face from both sides you'd see they were completely different. It's sort of a changeling face." And when Jane Howard of *Life* asked him whether or not he liked Perry and Dick, he said, "That's like saying, 'Do you like yourself?'" Capote's characterization of Smith clearly tells us more about the former than the latter.

As for Capote's unwillingness to deal completely with the question of Hickock's involvement in the actual killings, one plausible explanation is that it makes for a more simplified narrative in an already complex book to let readers assume that there was unanimity among the principals on the point. But, in addition, Capote's conception of the novel places high value on irony. His choice of title, for example, can only be read as irony; he wants us to believe the murders were emotional, spontaneous acts. (After examining the evidence, the title becomes a double irony.) And how much more ironic to present the true, the only, killer in the case as the more appealing figure of the two.

By applying his great artistry to the facts of the Clutter case, Capote has found the inspiration for a multitude of short, internal dramas with effective final curtains. He has achieved a theatrical climax in his confession scene. He has created a heroic, poetic villain—a villain capable of evoking considerable sympathy (as Hollywood was quick to realize). Perhaps we should not have expected anything different from Capote. (pp. 170-71)

Capote has, in short, achieved a work of art. He has told exceedingly well a tale of high terror in his own way. But, despite the brilliance of his self-publicizing efforts, he has made both a tactical and a moral error that will hurt him in the short run. By insisting that "every word" of his book is true he has made himself vulnerable to those readers who are prepared to examine seriously such a sweeping claim. (p. 171)

Phillip K. Tompkins, "In Cold Fact," in Esquire, *Vol. LXV, No. 6, June, 1966, pp. 125, 127, 166-68, 170-71.*

WILLIAM WIEGAND

By the time Truman Capote's book, ***In Cold Blood,*** gets waxed into paperback and moving pictures, . . . what remains of the integrity of the original work will probably be forgotten. Also forgotten may be Capote's notion that he had created something new in writing this book. ***In Cold Blood*** was not like a "documentary novel," or a "historical novel," Capote said. Least of all did it need a crime to make it work; its nature could only be described as a "non-fiction novel."

A "non-fiction novel" was a term the purists were not ready for, but rather than disturb the sleeping issue of the difference between literature and journalism which Hemingway had pretty well settled for this generation, Capote's claim was left as simple vanity. Surely this sort of thing had been done before even if, as most were ready to allow, seldom so well.

Still, if the book is good, one wants to know why, and Capote's term, ungainly as it is, serves to call attention to the high standards against which the book wants to be measured. "Non-fiction" implies a willingness to be held responsible for the data included as literally factual. The story actually happened. Newspapermen could "cover" it, and in the Clutter murder case newspapermen, of course, did.

Being covered though need not imply that the primary aim of the book is the same as journalism's aim. Ordinarily, journalism seeks to inform the reader about a particular event, or to "discuss" it. But the purpose of ***In Cold Blood*** is closer to that of the "novel," the chief aim of which is to "suggest" and "extend." The novel shares this chief aim with other art forms. What is therefore important in defining the novel, Capote would say, is not the imagined, or fictional, character of the material (compare the factual fidelity of many historical novels); but it is rather the suggesting and extending capacity all art forms share. (p. 243)

With experienced novelists, cross-fertilization between fiction and journalism produces some paradoxes. When, for example, John Hersey chooses as subject for a novel the uprising of the Warsaw ghetto in World War II, he elects to invent "documentation" for the story by employing journals, notebooks, and other records from the inhabitants of the ghetto, as though to imply that the best insurance for the novelist is to convince the reader that it actually happened.

But when Hersey decides in writing about Hiroshima not to fictionalize it, he now chooses fictional techniques in order to maximize the emotive impact of the dropping of the bomb. He preserves the dramatic fluency of each subject's account of the experience. Further, he multiplies the force of it by making the reader undergo five times the violence of the event. The effect of the extended intensity of a single point of view is exploited in a way that was unknown before certain developments in the technique of the novel took place. But for all that, *Hiroshima* is not a novel, and Hersey would be the last to claim that it was.

It is only with Capote that the growing obliteration of the lines that demark journalism from fiction seems virtually complete. He wages total war with journalism and its conventions by his conscious intention to keep the instinct to inform and discuss subordinated to the novelistic objective throughout. With this perspective the new form he seeks can evolve (and perhaps it is the way all forms evolve) because the intentions are no longer mixed.

Some of this can be seen by comparing Capote with the kind of writer who on the surface does the same sort of thing. Stanley Kauffman chooses John Bartlow Martin, a veteran true-crime man, whose work Kauffman finds sufficiently like Capote's to make him feel that ***In Cold Blood*** is no particular innovation. The apparent logic is that both Martin and Capote treat a criminal case at considerable length, with drama and with "depth" psychology, and both publish originally in installments in the most well-paying periodicals.

Beyond this, their assumptions are really quite different. Martin writes in the old *Police Gazette, American Weekly* tradition as it was sophisticated by the slick magazines in the Thirties and Forties. This sophistication was achieved chiefly by the infusion of sociological and psychiatric method into a narrative which still basically depended on the old Gothic evocation of the scene of the crime. Martin's one full-length, true-crime book, the story of an Ann Arbor, Michigan, murder committed by three teenagers, depends on these habits.

Martin begins with the "shadow-lined" streets on which the crime occurs and proceeds from there through the newsman's catalogue of names and places to a series of interviews with people who knew the principals in the case. He emphasizes the class levels of the three defendants in these interviews. The attitude of the community toward the principals is also examined. At last, he answers his question, *Why Did They Kill?,* which serves as the title of the book, almost entirely by means of the psychiatrist's reports, here a labeling process which discerns after the fact that criminals had criminal tendencies. (pp. 245-46)

It is odd that Capote has been criticized for "cold-bloodedness" on the grounds that he is acting "scientific" without the proper diploma. The business of crime-reporting would appear to Kenneth Tynan and Dwight MacDonald and some others properly to belong to the pro. The police reporter and the psychiatrist can dispose of the matter with what are evidently the only answers it is decent for us to have.

Actually, Capote handles the clinical matters almost with diffidence. Although the psychiatrist's report is included in the data pertinent to the case file on Smith and Hickock, by the time the reader reaches this report in the book, the medical diagnosis does not seem to mean very much. Its conclusions are intelligible in terms of the evidence Capote had previously presented. But the conclusions as such seem no more than a professional label fixed on a pair of consciousnesses that have been rendered more justly and more emphatically in the material that has preceded. The subject Capote chose has already been realized, and such realization transcends the functionalism of a clinical analysis. For by this point he has also realized the Clutter family, the small-town life of western Kansas, and the spirit of a certain time and place. None of the victims are made to seem mere integers, created for the purpose of being acted upon. They hold their space in existence for the short hour of their time; and what they stood for, unsentimentally, endures side by side with what is represented by their aimless and pathetic antagonists. Nor are the impulses of the Smiths and the Hickocks vanquished by an execution, even though the period is placed with stubborn impassivity at the end of this particular case.

The real strength of the Capote book is achieved by the way he exploits a whole battery of novelistic techniques which enforce the structure and hence the meaning of the Clutter case. First, in the opening section he builds the emphatic involvement of the reader by the familiar technique of cross-cutting. Scenes taking place in the Clutter home are alternated with scenes between Smith and Hickock preparing for their trip and en route to their destination. At first the two stories are made to seem completely independent. They take place hundreds of miles apart; the respective principals are strangers to the opposite party. In a machine age, antagonisms are impersonal; what you don't know is more likely to hurt you than what you do. The Clutters don't know, and neither do Smith and Hickock. They don't know the pot of gold at the end of the rainbow is nonexistent, but such uncertainty is of the order of things.

Within this section of the book, Capote also keys the identity of the two forces before they collide. Smith and Hickock are identified with the road and the automobile. They are introduced in a garage, subsequently they are seen in quick-stop cafes. The Clutters, on the other hand, are rigidly established on their homestead. Where they have settled seems not only the heart of their family, but the heart of the community. In

the scenes recorded on the final day of their lives, friends visit them at their home. . . . (pp. 247-48)

At the end of the first section of the book, with the last guest of the Clutters departing into the darkness of the night, the terrible collision between the two forces is about to take place. But Capote tells nothing about it here. On one hand, he is delaying the impact of it until later in the book where weight will be required and where its more immediate relevance to Smith and Hickock as independent psychologies can be apprehended. On the other hand, to dramatize it directly, as all the early sections of the book have been dramatized, will be too much for the reader. The crime needs the cushion of an interpolater; it needs to be recounted secondhand, as violence was on the Greek stage.

Also, more important to Capote at this early point is the shattering effect of the crime on the community. He takes up the story from its first felt moment within the house the following morning when the Clutters are discovered by friends who would pick them up on the way to church. The interdependence of the Clutters and the community has already been demonstrated in the first section. Now, as the news whirls into the larger vortex, Capote shows how self-doubt, and even doubt of the Clutters, produces a cacophony of discordant opinion. (p. 248)

Thus, it is not shock as much as it is a more dangerous force—disunity—which must be coped with in Holcomb and Garden City. At this point, Capote introduces his folk hero, Police Captain Dewey, who must restore the town to health. A thoroughly inconspicuous and unprepossessing man, Dewey must be carefully and subtly developed. He must be given space in the book where he is by himself, occupied not so much in thought as in solemn meditation. Accordingly, there are paragraphs in which Dewey contemplates nothing, except perhaps the land. For there is nothing to contemplate. The clue-hunting methods which might succeed in a rational universe are almost useless here. Dewey goes through the motions, but Capote never tempts us to feel that the little grey cells, as the detective story would have it, offer very much hope. Dewey is cast as the conscience of the community, a moral force. (p. 249)

In the meantime, the antagonists, Hickock and Smith, are shown like hurled pebbles still skipping across the water after their refracting impact on that half-yielding, half-impenetrable surface. Their flight is not presented as panicky. Instead, it is more like the dissipation of momentum. They are "on the road," reflexively, as they have always been. They experience neither hope nor fear. Their stops whether long or short afford encounters with other transients, and it is only their fantasies perhaps that give them any appearance of having a will, a plan.

In this part of the book Capote distinguishes Smith from Hickock. While earlier the spectacle of their combined force has received the emphasis, now the components of their individual mediocrities are separated out. Smith and Hickock derive from different native heritages. Hickock belongs to an exhausted bourgeois line of clock-watchers; his father is dying, his mother whines and clings, and refuses to believe. Smith, on the other hand, comes from an older frontier tradition, of medicine shows and Indian rodeo riders, of prospectors and extravagant aspiration. In a way, both of them are distorted shadows of their forbears, both of them are reflected as if in funhouse mirrors. But it is important to understand, or to try to understand, that an incompetent father or a clumsy mother is only part of the story, that that father had a father too. If it is fair to say that Hickock wanted too little in life and Smith wanted too much, it is worth knowing what contributed to the different aspirations.

Distinguishing them as Capote does during this section prepares the reader for an acceptance of the dramatic climax of the book, the account of the murders by Smith after the arrest. In order that the morbid and sensational aspects of the account may be softened, the question of "who?" has been allowed to become more central than "how?". The gory details of the crime, while they are not denied, are thus sublimated in the rather more pertinent psychological, and social, question as to which of these two forces—that represented by Smith or that represented by Hickock—is the more violent, the more ruthless, the more unstable. Wanting to know who pulled the trigger each of the four times may be beneath the law's notice (Smith and Hickock were both guilty "ten times over"); but Capote creates the curiosity in the reader. It is of more than passing interest to know who presses the button—the glib, initiating Hickock or the Christ-painting guilt-ridden Smith. Capote says that, four times over, it is Smith.

The last quarter of the book, a longer proportion than most writers would allot to this part of the case, shows Smith and Hickock in the community of the condemned, ironically the only community in which they have existed with such lingering permanence. Capote takes the trouble of describing the personalities and the crimes of some of the other inhabitants of death row in order to give definition to the community in which they spend their final years. The temper of this place gets contrasted, in alternate sections, with the temper of Garden City, which is seen in the last part of the book both during the murder trial and in the appeal. While Garden City, that solid reality earlier in the book, drifts off in the mists of the ephemeral words of some undistinguished attorneys, the drier reality of the prison and the inevitable execution scene replaces it. Capote includes the "last words": Hickock, like Willy Loman appreciating the good turnout at a funeral, and Smith, not unlike Raskolnikov, "apologizing."

There is a brief coda, a cemetery scene between Dewey and one of Nancy Clutter's girl friends. The scene restores consideration of the Clutters to the proper importance for the reader. Further, it turns again to the landscape, the concealing earth, and to Dewey, the hero of the narrative, who endures, untriumphant, with decency and luck. (pp. 249-50)

William Wiegand, "The 'Non-fiction' Novel," in New Mexico Quarterly, Vol. XXXVII, No. 3, Autumn, 1967, pp. 243-57.

ALFRED KAZIN

[The essay excerpted below is based partly on a lecture given by Kazin at the University of California, Los Angeles.]

When Truman Capote explained, on the publication of *In Cold Blood,* that the book was really a "nonfiction novel," it was natural to take his description of his meticulously factual and extraordinarily industrious record of research as the alibi of a novelist whose last novel, *Breakfast at Tiffany's,* had been slight, and who was just now evidently between novels. . . .

[What] struck me most in Capote's labeling of his own book

was his honoring the profession of *novelist.* Novels may be expendable, but *novelist* is still our great instance of original genius. What interested me most about [*In Cold Blood*] after two readings—first in *The New Yorker* and then as a book—was that though it *was* journalism and all its secrets were out on first reading, it had the ingenuity but not the total ambition of fiction, it *was* fiction except for its ambition to be documentary. . . .

In Cold Blood is ultimately a fiction in the *form* of fact. But how many great novels of crime and punishment are expressly based on fact! *The Possessed* is based on the Nechayev case, *An American Tragedy* on the Chester Gillette case. What, to leave other considerations aside for the moment, makes *In Cold Blood* formally a work of "record" rather than of "invention"? Because it says it is a documentary, external, with victims and murderers appearing under their own names, as their attested identities, in an actual or as we now say a "real" Kansas town.

Why, then, did Capote also attempt to honor his book as in some special sense a "novel"? Why bring up fiction at all? Because Capote depended on records but was not content to make a work of record. He wanted, wholly and exclusively, to make a work of art, he needed to do this because of a certain intimacy between himself and what the reader quickly sees as "his" characters. He wanted, ultimately, not the specificity of fiction, which must be content to be itself alone, but to make an emblematic human situation for our time that would relieve it of mere factuality. Through his feeling for both the Clutter family and their murderers, he was able to range them against each other in a way that would document the central theme in his own fiction—the loss of home and the fall of innocence.

Fiction, not fact, is Capote's natural aim as a writer; in *In Cold Blood* he practices it as a union of Art and Sympathy. His book, like other nonfiction novels in our day, is a resonantly sexy work, transparent in its affections to a degree that further explains why it could not have been a novel in any formal sense—abstractly loving to daughter Nancy Clutter, respectfully amazed by Father Clutter, helplessly sorry for always ailing Mother Clutter. None of these Capote knew, but he became extremely involved with the murderers, Perry Smith and Dick Hickock, whom he interviewed endlessly for his book and came to know only as we know people who fascinate us. (p. 26)

This personal relationship to characters whom Capote assiduously attended in jail, by the force of his attention symbolically protected when they were in the death house, whom he interviewed within an inch of *their* lives—literally so, up to the scaffold—is one of the many hypertrophied emotions on Capote's part that keeps the book "true" even when it most becomes a "novel." Capote also feels himself intensely related to Alvin Dewey of the Kansas Bureau of Investigation, who more than any other cop on the case brought the murderers in. He is always sympathetic to Nancy Clutter, who laid out her best dress for the morrow just before she got murdered.

Nancy is the fragile incarnation of all that might have been who gets our most facile sympathy. But despite his interest in Mr. Clutter's old-fashioned rigidity and his sense of Mrs. Clutter as in part the victim of the stiff-necked culture all around her, the actively passionate relationship, repelled because they *are* murderers, irresistible because they are such lonelies, is with "Perry and Dick." Almost to the end one feels that they might have been saved and their souls repaired—and this not only because Capote is always with them to write his book, but because of what he feels for them, which explains the success of his book.

This felt concern for actual persons makes the book too personal for fiction. The emotion pervading *In Cold Blood* is by no means all horror. There is an emotional keenness to stunted youth, to Perry's grotesquely dwarfish legs, to a subtler imbalance in Dick's outwardly normal masculinity—his mechanical destructiveness. Before he has seen them, on the way to "rob" the Clutters, Dick can already say—"Let's count on eight, or even twelve. The only *sure* thing is every one of them has got to go." . . . But despite the interest of this companionship, the crime retains its sufficient horror in our minds only because the crime, *this* crime, is central to our sense of life today.

We may all have passing dreams of killing, But here are two who killed, killed for the sake of killing, yet with an incestuous sentimentality in the last comforts they offered their victims that establishes their cringing viciousness. And the crime, like the great mass crimes of our time, is on record. The fascination of Capote's book, the seeming truthfulness of it all, is that it brings us close, very close, to the victims, to the murderers, to the crime itself. It all becomes a primal scene, reconstituted with all the suspense of a thriller and all the elegant selectivities of Capote's style. This he presents to us as a model we can hold, study, understand. The artfulness of the book gets us to realize and possess and dominate this murder as a case of the seemingly motiveless malignity behind so many crimes in our time. An ambition of the book is to give us this mental control over the greatest example in human nature of the uncontrolled. (pp. 26-7)

Capote's book raises many questions about its presumption as a whole, but many of the little scenes in it are as vivid as single shots in a movie can be—and that makes us wonder about the meaning of so much easy expert coverage. One of the best bits is when the jurors, looking at photographs of the torn bodies and tortured faces of the Clutters, for the first time come into possession of the horror, find themselves focusing on it in the very courtroom where the boyishness and diffidence of the defendants and the boringly longwinded protocol of a trial have in a sense kept up the jurors' distance from the crime.

There is indeed a continuing unreality about the murder of the four Clutters that Capote all through his book labored to eliminate by touch after touch of precious fact. But though he is understandably proud of every harrowing or grotesque detail he can dredge up, . . . the labor after so many facts emphasizes the unreality it is meant to abolish. But this a nonfiction novel must by its very nature preserve as a mystery of iniquity. The essence of the book lies in our being made witness to a crime we cannot and perhaps should not understand. There is in us, as well as in the townspeople, "a shallow horror sensation that cold springs of personal fear swiftly deepened."

The shallow horror is in the nature of the material. What *can* be reconstructed as fact from actual events may take the form of a cinematic "treatment" and easily use many shifts of time and place. But it makes our sympathies more narrow and helpless than a real novel does. The "shallow horror sensation" that is also Capote's aim will be induced by identifying

us with "real" people we think we know better than we do—victims and murderers both.

The reason for the nonfiction novel is that it points to events that cannot ever be discharged by a writer's imagination, assimilated by us as tragedy. Capote worked so long on this case because it cannot ever be "resolved," like Raskolnikov's murder of the old pawnbrokeress or Billy Budd's murder of Claggart. The crime is not "personal," as even Gatsby could have admitted about *his* murderer's mistake in killing him. The Clutters were there just for their murderers to murder them.

The event is inscrutable though in the public light, just one of many murders in our time by people who did not know their victims. As in so many political crimes against innocent strangers, many witnesses and documents are needed to reconstruct the facts. But the truth is missing, for there is no sense to the crime. In any good bourgeois novel, a single murderer has a single victim; the relationship between them can be intimate and intense. The resolution of the murderer's private guilt must in some way be morally expressible.

In the mass murders that have so deeply affected the imagination of our time, murderers and victims remain in every retrospect forever strange to each other. Auschwitz, Hiroshima, Dresden, the murder by policemen in a Detroit motel of three Negroes just because they have been found with white women, the killing of parents and children on a Kansas farm by two not abnormally rootless American boys, . . . the public confessions and executions of so-called enemies of the state in Russia and China—these are all horrors taking place in the public space that is now the domain of "our" reality. (p. 27)

Alfred Kazin, "The World as a Novel: From Capote to Mailer," in The New York Review of Books, *Vol. XVI, No. 6, April 8, 1971, pp. 26-30.*

JOHN J. McALEER

When Truman Capote's *In Cold Blood* was published in 1965 the *London Sunday Express* hailed it as "one of the stupendous books of the decade." The *New York Review of Books* agreed. Capote's book was "the best documentary of an American crime ever written" [see excerpt dated February 3, 1966]. And in *Harper's* Rebecca West wrote: "Nothing but blessings can flow from Mr. Capote's grave and reverend book" [see excerpt above dated February, 1966]. Yet the editor of the *Atlantic Monthly,* Edward Weeks, who might be supposed to know something about fact-based novels since Nordhoff and Hall wrote the Bounty trilogy at his behest, demurred: "In *In Cold Blood,*" he wrote, "Truman Capote is providing the readers with a high-minded, aesthetic excuse for reading about a mean, sordid crime." (p. 569)

While contending critics framed their avowals with matching ardor and indignation, only one, Granville Hicks, thought to praise *In Cold Blood* at the expense of another crime novel— Theodore Dreiser's *An American Tragedy*—which on its appearance forty years earlier likewise met a divided critical response. Applauding Capote's restraint in limiting "himself to ascertainable facts," Hicks told readers of the *Saturday Review:* "If Dreiser had done the same sort of thing with the Gillette-Brown case . . . *An American Tragedy* might have been a better book."

Although Dreiser, unlike Capote, unabashedly had fictionalized his source, critics berating *An American Tragedy* picked grounds similar to those Capote's detractors would occupy when they denounced *In Cold Blood.* Russell Blankenship, for example, had dismissed it as "simply a mammoth example of the reporter's art." No one suggested, however, that Dreiser had exploited a lurid situation for mere sensationalism. Unlike Capote, Dreiser had a thesis that went deeper than a demonstration of form. Critics could and did dispute Dreiser's thesis yet there could be no pretending that he lacked one.

To Joyce Cary *An American Tragedy* was "a great book," to H. G. Wells it was "one of the great novels of this century," to Joseph Wood Krutch, "the greatest American novel of our generation." Anderson, Lewis, Bennett, Fitzgerald, Agee, Dos Passos, Wright, Warren, Bellow, Mailer—to seek for commentary only among Dreiser's fellow novelists—also have lauded Dreiser's achievement. . . . If, then, *In Cold Blood* is a better book than *An American Tragedy,* Capote's success has been notable. To determine if it has been, let us see his book in overlay to Dreiser's. (pp. 569-70)

Capote's own account of why he wrote *In Cold Blood* centers on one fact—he wanted to give the nonfiction novel status as an art form. He had, he admits, "no natural attraction to the subject matter," choosing it on the theory that "Murder is a theme not likely to yellow with time." Even then he was ready to abandon this topic if he found another that suited his purpose better. Since Capote makes no declaration of intention in writing *In Cold Blood* beyond stating his desire to illustrate the feasibility of his form, we must wonder if his announced resolve really took him beyond the goal of achieving a dramatic ordering of facts, in felicitous prose, to serious consideration of how the potentials of his materials might be utilized to express a true, universalizing experience. Capote seems to have mistaken craft for art.

Dreiser did not write *An American Tragedy* to establish a literary method, nor was murder incidental to his purpose. Like Capote he did have trouble choosing his starting point, like Capote, it took him five years to complete his book once it was under way. But he had no doubts about the area in which he intended to work. He believed that murders such as the one Chester Gillette had committed were indigenous to America and his book was to be about the typicality of such a murder—murder carried out under the auspices of the American Dream. He researched "ten or fifteen" such murders and weighed their narrative potential before he chose the Gillette-Brown case (1906). He was not interested in the crime as a crime but in the social pressures which fostered it. (p. 571)

An American Tragedy, then, has a social direction. Its author wishes to identify and condemn a social evil which, under the pretext of opening the way to self-realization, lures men to ruin. This therapeutic aim does not mean that *An American Tragedy* is a tract; that is hardly better than calling it an expanded exercise in journalism. Art is not always vanquished by preachment, and in his ultimate handling of his subject Dreiser detaches himself from society and its failings to write with insight and power of problems of the human condition which transcend time and place. . . . (pp. 571-72)

Regardless of the reason each author gave to explain his choice of subject, any record of the parallels between *An American Tragedy* and *In Cold Blood* must begin with aware-ness of how each author quarried from his own past, episodes which let him identify with his protagonist and, through such identification, draw upon an inner store of psychic perceptions. Neither author was new to the practice. *The 'Genius'* (1915), with its near American Tragedy ending (its protagonist, Eugene Witla, actually wishes his wife, Angela, dead, so that he might marry a young girl with whom he is infatuated), fictionalized Dreiser's own unhappy life up till the age of forty. Capote admits that *Other Voices, Other Rooms* (1948) is "all about" himself.

Both Dreiser and Capote have insisted that, in childhood, they never were wanted enough. In his own early poverty and aspirations Dreiser found a pattern that paralleled the history of Chester Gillette, whom he fictionalized as Clyde Griffiths. [Robert Penn Warren] says of Dreiser's autobiographical volumes: "In *Dawn* and in the first twenty-two chapters of *A Book About Myself,* not only the basic personality and life pattern of Dreiser himself have been presented and analyzed, but the basic characters, situations, and issues of *An American Tragedy* have been projected." (p. 572)

Dreiser then refashioned his own experiences to give verisimilitude to portions of Clyde's history. Although fealty to facts would not allow Capote to interpolate such data into his novel, it could not keep him from seeing himself in one of his protagonists—Perry Smith. Novelist Harper Lee, who was at Capote's side during those months when he made a final assessment of the materials he had gathered for *In Cold Blood,* relates: "I think every time Truman looked at Perry he saw his own childhood." The early years of both Smith and Capote were nomadic. Both hungered to escape from poverty and obscurity. Both were estranged from their fathers, neglected by their mothers. Both had talents which went unrecognized and therefore unencouraged. Although these are riches that go unclaimed, there is fully as much of Truman Capote in Perry Smith as there is in the autobiographical child-protagonist of *Other Voices, Other Rooms*—Joel Knox. (pp. 572-73)

[Through] their protagonists, Clyde, Perry, and Perry's companion in crime, Dick Hickock, both Dreiser and Capote incorporate the reader into their lives at a level of compassion and sympathy which deplores not only the treatment which society dispenses but what Dreiser identifies as "the substance of the demands of life itself"—those circumstances which are the soil in which tragedy ripens toward its season of reaping. All three have experienced poverty, inequality, lack of success in satisfying basic needs, insecurity, frustration, and futility of quest. Clyde and Dick had godfearing parents. Perry's father, as well as his institutional keepers, tried to instill moral lessons. Yet both books insist that powerful moral influences are actual incentives to rebellious behavior when blind authority and emotionalism would try to enforce them.

Now consider how society deals with these protagonists as transgressors. Although in both books the crowds—society made visible—are amazed that such well-appearing boys could have committed the crimes they are charged with, no one thinks to investigate this paradox. We become aware, instead, of the morbid curiosity of a public which, despite its alleged Christian adherence, is titillated by the unfolding drama. A carnival atmosphere takes over as Roberta's letters are hawked in the street at Clyde's trial, along with peanuts, hotdogs, and popcorn. A local church sponsors a gala auction of the effects of the Clutter family. Hotdogs and soda pop are sold to the crowd gathered to see Dick and Perry arraigned. Though the defendants want a change of venue, their lawyers dissuade them on the theory that the community is religious-minded and will deal leniently with them. Yet, in each instance, the prosecution calls down Old Testamental wrath on their heads. Defense attorneys, in both books, ultimately ask the court if a fair trial is possible in a community so emotionally aroused. The limited mentality of the jurors is stressed. Farm people are the victims and farm people sit in judgment on the accused. In *In Cold Blood,* when the verdict is reached the judge himself has to be fetched from his farm. The governor, who refuses clemency, is, like the murdered man, a rich farmer. Both books disclose that forthcoming elections influence the conduct of the trials. For Orville Mason, in *An American Tragedy,* and Al Dewey, in *In Cold Blood,* stalwarts of the law, a verdict of guilty becomes an epic obsession. And in Kansas, as in New York, the aristocracy of the community holds aloof from the trial.

The post-trial phase of legal justice, in the reversal of public interest which occurs, becomes society's subtlest barbarism. Legal postponements in the death house are excruciating. Dreiser deplores the "unauthorized cruelty and stupidity and destructive torture" which these delays constitute. Capote finds that the state exacts a thousand other deaths besides the one which the sentence calls for. In *An American Tragedy* Dreiser relates that the dimming of the prison lights as a man is electrocuted, is a psychological ordeal for other occupants of the death house. In *In Cold Blood* Capote says that the sound of the floor dropping on the gallows constitutes mental torture for others, confined within earshot, who await hanging. (pp. 573-74)

Concerning the underlying causes of the crimes—what Dreiser speaks of as "the substance of the demands of life itself"—both books convey an "only in America" emphasis—a strong sense of America as the logical environment sponsoring these murders. As Margaret Mead has noted, the title itself records Dreiser's intent "to make it [*An American Tragedy*] universal, at least for the American scene." The Dream of Success is paramount. . . . The Clutter murders truly appall because the crime occurs within the premises of paradise. Clutter himself says: "an inch more of rain and this country would be paradise—Eden on earth." The mythic Garden of the World is violated. In this context, observe that a condition of happiness, an archetypal situation as ancient as Eden, is imposed. Clyde is told that he must, under no circumstances, fraternize with girls working in the Griffiths' factory. Perry and Dick are forbidden to fraternize with former convicts. In each case the tragedy becomes possible when this injunction is flouted. That Dreiser appreciates this fact is affirmed by Clyde's Adamic lamentation, after his condemnation, that his failure to heed the mandate had cost him paradise. For Capote, it is simply another fact, stored among an array of facts, and left unevaluated. It is, as we shall see, this misguided reluctance on Capote's part to make functional use of his facts, save at the most literal level, that causes the two books to cleave apart. (p. 575)

Although Capote, unlike Dreiser, makes an elaborate use of flashbacks to cover the early histories of Perry and Dick, thereby precipitating the reader at once into a gory drench, he pays a steep price for the dramatic appeal gained. Emphasis falls on effect rather than cause, a predictable consequence for an operational plan which gives to method precedence over matter. That Capote recognized an obligation to do

something more may be inferred from the several efforts he made to provide a context for the crime. Among his notations, a principal instigating cause for the murder of the Clutters leaps to prominence. But Capote himself does not see it. He tries to mask his bewilderment by offering a succession of probable causes, creating for the reader a veritable solve-it-yourself packet. And that, of course, gives head to chaos.

When the film version of *In Cold Blood* was made, the moviemakers proffered one of Capote's implied secondary causes—Perry's Oedipal frustrations—as chief cause of the murders. When Perry cut Mr. Clutter's throat, Hollywood suggested, he thought he was butchering his father. When he climbed the gallows he saw his father as hangman. These Freudian revelations do not appear in Capote's book. When, however, the evidence is evaluated as Capote ought to have evaluated it, but failed to do, the cause of the murders of the Clutters proves to be identical with the cause of Roberta Alden's death, that is, blind pursuit of the American Dream. That is the theme Capote gropes for throughout *In Cold Blood* and which, despite his floundering, he most nearly proved valid. (p. 576)

In truth, in his preoccupation with form, Capote did not give enough thought to what conclusions his materials would lead to. Perhaps he believed that if he kept serving up facts they would supply their own logic—make their own gravy—with no assistance from him. As fiction writer Dreiser was free to deal with the uncut gem in his possession in whatever way best served his aims so long as he took into full account its natural planes of cleavage. As documentary-novelist, Capote was shackled by commitments which permitted him neither to release fully the potentials of his materials nor to concentrate their power for maximum effectiveness.

Capote's topic of prime focus is, like Dreiser's, the destructive encroachments of the American Dream. Although preoccupation with his experiment in form caused him to look on this theme and other lesser themes as intrusive, it surfaces too often not to be recognized. We have his word for it. He assures us: "The arbitrary act of violence springs from the poverty of Perry's life. . . ." Perry's resentment of those making good is illustrated in his attitude toward his sister, Bobo: "One fine day he'd pay her back . . . spell out in detail the things he was capable of doing to people like her, respectable people, safe and snug people, exactly like Bobo." In striking down the Clutters, Perry is striking at the embodiment of the American Dream—not, however, because he disapproves of it, but because he cannot get in on it. In a revealing statement, Perry confesses: "They [the Clutters] never hurt me, maybe it's just that the Clutters were the ones who had to pay for it." Capote says that the key to Perry's personality is "self-pity."

Dick's thinking parallels Perry's. At the trial a psychiatrist explains: "He secretly feels inferior to others . . . and dissatisfaction with only the normal slow advancement he could expect from his job. . . . These feelings seem to be overcompensated for by dreams of being rich and powerful . . . spending sprees when he has money." The Christmas following the killings, Dick and Perry are in Miami. " 'Didn't I promise you we'd spend Christmas in Miami, just like millionaires?' " Dick asks Perry. But they are not millionaires and Dick soon shows the same kind of resentment that caused Perry to kill the Clutters. They see a shapely blonde masseuse hovering over a wealthy racketeer, at poolside at the Fontainebleau. We are told that Dick mused: "Big-shot bastards like that had better be careful or he might open them up and let a little of their luck spill on the floor." Capote sees the key to Dick's personality as "envy." Self-pity and envy—defects of character which Clyde Griffiths shares and which impel him in pursuit of the American Dream.

Consider the trip to Mexico, the dreams of sunken treasure, a hill of diamonds, of Cozumel, the island paradise. Contrast with these things the ignominy which Perry feels wriggling on his belly beneath Nancy Clutter's bed, in pursuit of a keepsake silver dollar. The disparity between his hopes and his gains, produces a rage and shame which leads directly to the killings. In prison, awaiting execution, Perry whimpers: " 'I was better than any of *them.*' " Why should the "haves" have while he has not? This thought makes a murderer of him.

Perry's last thoughts, at the foot of the gallows, are of his father and his father's "hopeless dreams." Here is the point about Perry's father which Capote must have wanted to implant in the reader's consciousness. The failure of the elder Smith to attain the American Dream, yet his relentless quest for that Dream, contributed much to Perry's discontent. Perry could and probably did hate his father for the false hopes he had engendered. Yet he could not rid himself of the habit of hoping which his father had implanted in him. He did not reject his father's goals, only his idealistic methods of pursuing them. When he killed Herbert Clutter he was not cutting his father's throat, he was splitting open a money bag.

When the Clutters were murdered their neighbors sensed at once that they had been killed because they emblemized the American Dream. . . . Capote himself has described the Clutters to an interviewer as "a perfect embodiment of the good, solid, landed American gentry." Their neighbors wonder, indeed, if a wealthier family, living near the Clutters, had not been the intended victims, since they were even more representative. Perry's and Dick's dreams of riches are, after all, the dreams of the community that judges them. That really is why it had admired the Clutters. Accordingly the community is outraged not so much by the murders as by the assault on the American Dream which the murders signify. The community hates the persons who have sullied that Dream and, by implication, challenged its validity. An ironic feature of the tragedy is that the Clutters were not that much to be envied. Imagine winning, as a prize, a weekend with the Clutter family! Clutter himself, perched in his chair, as on the night of the murders, reading *The Rover Boys,* trying to escape back into the untroubled days of his boyhood. The Clutter children, Nancy and Kenyon, restively testing their father's fundamentalist authoritarianism. Daft Mrs. Clutter shut away in her room, as she has been for years, her neuroticism a likely by-product of her husband's obsessive concern with piling up riches. To pursue the American Dream he had neglected her emotional needs. . . . Here, indeed, is a household the occupants of which are leading "lives of quiet desperation." Thus, both Perry and Clutter are double victims of the American Dream. Pursuing the Dream and persuading his son to pursue it, Perry's father had destroyed his home life. In pursuit of the Dream, Clutter, too, had destroyed his family life, and was slain, at last, by someone pursuing the Dream who envied him his apparent attainment of it. This game had no winners.

At the close of *In Cold Blood* a reporter opines that the only good that came of the Clutter case was that a lot of newspapers had been sold. The final irony: the Clutter murders had been good for business, good for someone's pursuit of the American Dream. Inevitably, critics would say that Truman Capote's dream had come true, also, when *In Cold Blood* brought him a fortune amounting to millions. Dreiser had known the same opprobrium, if not the same rewards.

A further dilemma faced Truman Capote as author of a nonfiction novel based on the Clutter case. He had dual protagonists. Now Chester Gillette had been the protégé of not one but two uncles. He had courted not one but three society girls. Not committed, as Capote was, to presenting facts without variance, Dreiser was able to merge the uncles into one, and to alloy the three belles. As co-protagonist, alleged instigator of the Clutter killings but not the actual killer, Dick Hickock is an incumbrance to Capote as storyteller. He "doesn't fit," as Capote himself has owned. Capote's narrative would have gone better if he could have dispensed with him entirely. His rapport was with Perry. It was Perry who wrote him a ten thousand word farewell letter and kissed him goodby before ascending the gallows. Capote lavished every attention on him. That is not surprising if, as Harper Lee surmises, Capote saw himself in Perry, just as Dreiser saw himself in Clyde. Dick's role, on the other hand, seems like something thrown in to strike the bargain. Since Dreiser sifted through at least ten American tragedies before he settled on Chester Gillette as the representative victim of the American Dream, it might be supposed that other victims of the same illusion, insofar as they approach typicalness, would resemble Clyde Griffiths. Dick does not. Perry does, in numerous particulars.

Dick's get-it-easy attitude and good looks remind us of Clyde. Otherwise he is nonrepresentative—an unwanted excrescence. Had Dreiser found such a personage bulking on the landscape of the Gillette-Brown case, he would have excised him without a pang, or telescoped his salvageable parts into a single characterization, just as he did with the dual uncles and triad of society girls. A good artist must have the surgical touch and apply it as needed. Capote's attempts to handle Hickock peripherally show that he realizes this. But he had to retain him because the scheme he had bound himself to demanded it. Hickock further illustrates, then, the quagmire the writer steps into who supposes that a work of art can be shaped from uninterpreted facts.

The parallels between Perry and Clyde, unlike those between Dick and Clyde, are both intimate and sustained:

> Neither has a father with whom he can identify.
>
> Both seek mother surrogates.
>
> Both are unable to establish lasting and meaningful relationships.
>
> Both despise religious rigorism.
>
> Both are rootless, nomadic, and in flight from failure.
>
> Both envy prosperous relatives.
>
> Both are quick to excuse the conduct of sisters who have shared in their hardships.
>
> Both are described as following a "mirage."
>
> Both dream of coming into possession of fabled riches—Aladdin's treasures; a hill of diamonds.
>
> Both have in their natures a strain of tenderness,

vivid but ephemeral—a by-product of their own hardships and disappointments.

(pp. 577-81)

Granting the reality of coincidence, we must none the less concede that many of these parallels go beyond chance. Certainly if an anthropologist turned up so many matching bones we would not hesitate to concede that they probably came from creatures of the same species. Yet even if we did not know that Capote was working from facts alone, it would be unwise to conclude that he had plundered *An American Tragedy* for confirming touches for his narrative. On the other hand, if Dreiser's fictionalization had postdated Capote's nonfiction novel, how many critics would have been ready to bring in an indictment against him, charging plagiarism! Actually, when two authors are mining the same vein such duplications are inevitable. What is unforgettable is the realization that much of what Capote dug from the bedrock in his role as documentarian, Dreiser, through a remarkable use of the creative faculty, was able to provide out of his own intuition. Dreiser's sense of the American Tragedy type of individual was so unerring, he was able to identify with such a personage so totally, that he summoned up, out of his own innate sense of what was probable about such a man, a wealth of details which find actual substantiation in Capote's true-life record of Perry Smith.

Dreiser met none of the principals involved in the Gillette-Brown murder case, but he rowed to Moon Cove on Big Moose Lake where the murder occurred and lingered there for two hours; he sat in a cell on Death Row with a man awaiting execution, he went to a shirt factory and studied the process of shirt manufacturing, all in preparation for writing *An American Tragedy*. And he went beyond these physical preparations, beyond a scrutiny of the trial record and newspaper accounts, to take on an actual sense of the identity of Chester Gillette. In doing that he created as honestly as Michelangelo did when he summoned David from his marmoreal cerements. Only a wraith of the Clyde Griffiths whom Dreiser created exists in the Chester Gillette of the trial record, yet in the truth of the characterization we are given an archetypal grasp of the American Tragedy type of protagonist, and of his dilemma, such as no dossier ever has been ample enough to hold. And all future portrayals of him, to the extent that they correspond to the facts, must resemble that archetype. (pp. 582-83)

By fictionalizing his material Dreiser gained vastly more in truth of nature than Capote did when he deployed his material without creative intervention. Capote's nonfiction novel format kept him from sorting out his major theme from secondary ones. It shackled him to petty data, kept him from soaring, from taking creative possession of his material. Lacking a viable artistic alternative, he let a debilitating morbidity, sponsored by his closeness both to the events and personages involved, and perhaps by his own narcissistic needs, inundate the resultant vacuum. The result is a work which avoids what Warren calls "the dreary factuality of an old newspaper account" solely by its dependency on an exalted style and on an emotionalism which combines Gothicism and sentiment in equal measure. (p. 583)

Not committed to rote delivery of hard facts, Dreiser is able to make the pace of his narrative less deliberate than Capote, to convey better a sense of Clyde's stumbling progress through life, with things falling out for him, as they do, by caprice rather than calculation. Against this pattern the pathos of his own petty scheming is better grasped and the reader prepared both for the ineptitude which characterizes his plan of murder, and the irony which lets chance make of it a foolproof vehicle for his destruction.

Dreiser is able to speak openly, too, of the inadequacies of the law. Capote, dealing with actual people, many of whom will be searching his narrative for grounds for libel, has to report on their shortcomings inferentially. Recognizing, also, that the appeal of his book is blunted by the absence of a love plot, Capote patches on an extraneous account of Nancy Clutter's lost love. Indeed, because Capote does not know how to tie together his facts, the whole final portion of *In Cold Blood* is fragmentary. He might have assured harmony, as Dreiser did, with the use of a relay character, like the Reverend Duncan McMillan, who could carry on the protagonists' quest and help them to order their thoughts on their ordeal. Dreiser was free to invent McMillan to serve this end and to invent little Russell whose role, at the close of the book, is to affirm that the action of the novel is about to unwind itself again, and will continue to do so, *ad infinitum,* until society itself alters. Wanting such characters, Capote loses his final chance to force an assessment of the true meaning of the Clutter murders. (pp. 584-85)

We have remarked that in *An American Tragedy,* Dreiser, without being on the scene as Capote was, or privy to confessional disclosures, again and again accurately intuited what was classic in such instances. The documentation which Capote provides on an American Dream sponsored murder in *In Cold Blood* confirms Dreiser's extraordinary instinct for the relevant in crimes of this specific kind. *In Cold Blood's* chief value then—the real blessing which flows from it—may well be its affirmation, as an accurate but uninventoried stockpile of American Tragedy details, of the soundness of Dreiser's intuitions and methods. It is striking proof of the timeless integrity of *An American Tragedy*. What Dreiser saw as true in 1925, is shown by Capote's documentation forty years after to be true still. Capote has reported on an event. Transcending time (and, indeed, as Mason Gross has observed, there is by design little in *An American Tragedy* to confine it to an era), Dreiser has reported on the truth of human nature. (p. 585)

Dreiser's achievement confirms the essential role of the creative faculty and its generosity in supplying authenticating detail when the author acts from an understanding of the human condition founded on genuine responsiveness to the universe. By its very amplitude, it affirms the pity of a creative faculty stifled by limiting forms, of which the nonfiction novel, at least in Capote's understanding of it, is a repelling example. Capote's facts adorn him like leg irons. He is, in turn, jailer to imprisoned archetypes, myths, and symbols, inherent in his material, but denied liberty. They stare out at us like bugs in amber. Through Dreiser's method they could gorgeously soar. Even when style approaches the luminosity of Holy Writ, and Capote's sometime does, that is not enough if the facts strain for release, without avail, against the membrane of words enclosing them. (p. 586)

John J. McAleer, " 'An American Tragedy' and 'In Cold Blood'," in THOUGHT, *Vol. XLVII, No. 187, Winter, 1972, pp. 569-86.*

TRUMAN CAPOTE [INTERVIEW WITH **DENIS BRIAN**]

[*Brian*]: *To produce* **In Cold Blood** *you trained your memory so you could recall accurately almost 95 percent of what you heard. Would you at the end of this interview be able to repeat something I'd said earlier on?*

[Capote]: I don't think I can today because I'm not in a very good mood. I'm not feeling so well. So don't let's try anything tricky . . . (Chuckles.)

All right. [*Regarding* **In Cold Blood**: *did*] *Perry Smith and Richard Hickock lie to you, or try to mislead you, in the early stages of your contact with them?*

I suppose so, inasmuch as Perry Smith had always told me that Dick killed the other two [of the four victims]. I mean, that's what he told me earlier on. Then later, he told me the truth.

What d'you think was his reason for cooperating with you?

Loneliness. There they were, the first year I knew them, and I knew them almost six years, in this little town in Kansas. Nobody talked to them. Nobody would do anything for them. Nobody had heard of them. Nobody had even heard of their case. You know, there was nothing. I was this person who was there doing this thing and I was very attentive to them. I was drawing them out: out of boredom and out of loneliness, if nothing else. Who else was paying any attention to them? They were very grateful to me, although they were both very suspicious about what I was doing.

Weren't psychiatrists showing any interest?

There was only one psychiatrist and I don't think he was interested in them until he found out that I was. And he only saw them once. (Sigh)

You say they were suspicious of why you were doing it. Did you ever tell them why?

Certainly, I told them the truth from the very beginning. But they couldn't understand. I mean, they didn't understand what I was doing. Well, why should they? None of my friends did, either. Nobody could understand what it was that I was doing. They couldn't understand what the end result of it was going to be.

Did your interviewing technique change over the years you were gathering material for **In Cold Blood**?

After a bit I wouldn't say it was interviewing in any real sense of the word: it was just talking. I was very, very friendly with them. In fact I was the only friend they had in the world.

How did you persuade the townspeople to talk about such a tragic and depressing subject?

It wasn't a matter of my just going in there bang, bang, bang, like some ordinary reporter. I went to that town and I moved into the town. And I began to cultivate people, you know. And on a very friendly basis, they'd introduce me to another person, who introduced me to another person. When I first lived there the case had only just happened. It was a couple of months before it was solved. Nobody had ever heard of Perry and Dick. I didn't know whether I'd have a book or not. I was just sort of experimenting with the whole thing. And so I just cultivated people and by the time the case broke, I was on such friendly terms with the detective in

charge of the case (Alvin Dewey), that I was the first person he told. (pp. 87-9)

You gave $50 apiece to Perry Smith and Hickock to get them to talk with you initially. Could you tell me the gist of your talk then, when you tried to get them to agree to be interviewed—after they'd accepted the money?

It was very brief, because they had their lawyers in the room and were terribly uptight. They'd only just been caught. This was maybe the day after they were returned to Garden City. They wanted $50. They wouldn't speak to any other reporter and I think that the only reason that the lawyers were able to arrange it was the money. If it hadn't been for that I would never have been able to have spoken, so the whole thing would never have started. I just wanted to establish a contact with them on which I could build. From that point on I supplied them with magazines and writing paper and all the little things that nobody else would think of doing, and they became very dependent on me, you see. (pp. 89-90)

Could you ever feel warmly toward Hickock, knowing that he delighted in killing dogs by hitting them with his car?

It isn't a question of feeling warmly, but when you get to know somebody as well as I got to know those two boys—I knew them better than they knew themselves—feelings don't enter, of like or dislike. It's some kind of extraordinary condition of knowledge takes place. I found that, of course, appalling and repulsive, you know. (The killing of dogs.) But there it is, it was part of his insensitivity and indifference to life in general.

Were you serious when you said of the **In Cold Blood** *interview that you could tell if people weren't being accurate, by their eyes shifting from right to left?*

I don't know if I said that, but I've often noticed it. When you get right down to hard ground with them, their eyes will start shifting. Shifty eyes (chuckles) is an old phrase.

Any other clues that indicated to you that people weren't telling the truth?

You know, all of that's so instinctual. After you get the feel of a person, can't you always tell more or less when somebody's really not leveling with you?

I think so, yes. The accuracy of **In Cold Blood** *was challenged by Phillip K. Tompkins in* Esquire *of June 1966 [see excerpt above]. According to him Mrs. Meier denied that she said she had seen worse men than Perry, denied that she ever heard him cry, denied that he ever held her hand and said: "I'm embraced by shame." And although you say that Perry Smith killed all the victims, Duane West (prosecuting attorney) and Alvin Dewey (chief detective) still believe that Dick Hickock killed the two women. Is this just a difference of opinion: you say it's true and they say it isn't?*

What I wrote in the book was true. It is absolutely accurate. Mrs. Meier, wife of the under sheriff at the jail, turned against me. And Duane West is one of my bitterest enemies. And they were sort of working tooth and tong. As for Alvin Dewey, I don't know why he believed that. He always has and I don't know why he does because it's absolutely untrue. And Mrs. Meier is just not telling the truth.

Malcolm Cowley said to me that although **In Cold Blood** *was meant to be a plea against capital punishment, he felt that it* *supported it, in that the execution of the two men was the only thing that gave their lives any stature, esthetically.*

Meaning what? Or does he mean in respect to the book? If the boys hadn't been then . . . that was one of Tynan's great things . . . if the boys hadn't been executed then I wouldn't have had an effective ending for the book.

Tynan's was a snide thing, wasn't it? He was implying that you would have wanted them to die. But Cowley doesn't imply that you wanted that. He says that men like them, who do gruesome things and lead "worthless" lives, can only achieve stature, either as characters in a book or as human beings, by being executed.

I don't see his point about it in terms of life. The fact of a person being executed—what has estheticism got to do with that? Estheticism is purely something in terms of art. (pp. 90-2)

What surprised me about **In Cold Blood** *was that there was no obscene language from either of the men.*

That's what *The New York Times* pointed out. They said: "If these things are absolutely accurate, why is the language so," you know . . . As a matter of fact Perry Smith was extraordinarily prissy in conversation. I make a great point of it.

Did you use any euphemisms for Hickock's language?

No, I really didn't. The only word that Dick used to say all the time was "shit." But Perry would never say that.

Was there anything remarkable or moving in the hundred-page farewell letter Perry wrote to you just before he was executed?

I don't know if I ever said it or not. It was about . . . it was about . . . Oh my God, I really shouldn't go into all this. It just upsets me so much anyway. (Sighs.) All the time they had been in prison, all those years, they were only allowed to have a certain amount of money. And I always gave them each whatever it was they were allowed to have. Anyway, the thing was that in the letter there was a check for the money. Perry had never spent a penny of it and he was, you know, giving it back to me. I don't know why, but that one thing upset me more than any other thing. It just tore me up. Because I mean . . . oh God . . . it was touching, as though that all along . . . I can't go into it . . . (pp. 92-3)

I told [William F. Buckley, Jr.] that the only thing that worried me was Smith's lack of memory for the crucial time. Particularly as he was supposed to be a man in control of his emotions. And Buckley said the same thing worried him. But don't you agree that the evidence against the other suspect seemed very strong?

You can make anything seem very strong. No, I think he did do it. I mean, I'm convinced that he did. (p. 93)

[Have you ever met] anyone absolutely evil?

Absolutely evil? Let me think. I think Kenneth Tynan is absolutely evil, I really do. He's evil because he's the ultimate in hypocrisy and duplicity.

You never settled the argument where he accused you of not making any effort to prevent Smith and Hickock from being executed?

Oh, we settled it. I wrote a piece about it in the *Observer* that went on and on for a month [see various excerpts above dated March-April, 1966]. To me it has everything to do with duplicity and what not because he was pretending to be such a friend of mine, and living in my house, and I was so generous to him in every way. And all the time, months before the book came out, he was plotting this attack on me, for no reason, except what he was going to get out of it. It was reprinted everywhere in the world and he made a lot of money out of it. To me, that's really evil.

And you think his motive was greed?

Greed and jealousy.

What makes you cry?

Oh lord, anything to do with cruelty to animals. Or cruelty in any event. Deliberate cruelty is the only thing I can't forgive.

What scares you?

I don't think I used to be scared of anything that I automatically saw, but after doing all the research for *In Cold Blood* and all the murderers that I interviewed, hundreds of them, the very sight of a hitchhiker gives me a shiver. I've driven back and forth across the country several times and the idea of running out of gas in one of those lonely Midwestern places creates a tremendous sense of anxiety in me. (pp. 97-8)

Would you be very surprised if Kenneth Tynan apologized to you?

If I ever see him I'm going to kill him. He'd better stay out of my path. (Laughs.)

I'll have to record that you laughed when you said that.

But I usually laugh when I mean it the most. (Chuckles.) (p. 98)

Do you agree that the First Amendment should be interpreted to mean that there should be no libel law and that one should be able to write or say anything about anyone else without fear of prosecution?

Yes, I agree with that. I personally don't care what anyone writes or says about me, so I'd just as soon (chuckles) that whole right was given to me. (p. 101)

After a Playboy *interviewer interviewed you, you said to Jerry Tallmer: "It's really fun. I'm probably going to have to leave the country." What had you said to the* Playboy *interviewer in 1968 that would cause you to leave the country?*

Undoubtedly it was a reference to things that were taken out of the interview. They took an awful lot of things out, on grounds of libel.

For example?

Capote: Some of the things I said about Kenneth Tynan were absolutely hair-raising and they took those out because Kenneth Tynan was a great buddy of the *Playboy* people, which I didn't know at that time, in fact, practically an editor (chuckles). (p. 103)

Truman Capote and Denis Brian in an interview in Murderers and Other Friendly People: The Public and Private Worlds of Interviewers *by Denis Brian, McGraw-Hill Book Company, 1973, pp. 85-116.*

MAS'UD ZAVARZADEH

An essentially right angle of reference is maintained between two zones of experience in Truman Capote's *In Cold Blood,* one of the achieved nonfiction novels written in the postwar years. The book evokes, through an exploration of the actual, the myths shaping contemporary consciousness. By mapping the visible surfaces, Capote sustains the tension between the factual and the fictional, and manages to capture in the modal ambiguity of the narrative the inherent complexity of contemporary reality. In Capote's book, the blurring of boundaries and its agonizing effects on communal consciousness in a small American town are formalized with such intensity and precision that the actual reverberates with and echoes the mythic. Holcomb, Kansas, is explored so thoroughly that the smallest details of everyday life begin to reveal their interior space and complexity until each sign becomes a symbol, and the usual distinction between the literal and the metaphorical, the happened and the imagined, the fact and fiction, vanishes. The town itself gradually loses its geographical solidity and becomes an emblem of quintessential America, where what happens is less a random murder than a collision between the forces and ideas which have shaped the American Dream and "a certain [amount of nothing]" in the "dream deferred." The narrative energy of the book is generated by that formative force which Capote thinks is "so awfully inevitable about what is going to happen: the people in the book are completely beyond their own control."

In Cold Blood opens with a graphic description of "out there"—a lonesome area on the high wheat plains of Kansas that forms the topography of the narrative. Although the area has a literal existence outside the book, it also becomes a metaphorical place where the facts of this bizarre event assume a universal resonance. Holcomb lies about seventy miles east of the Colorado border, home to people who are "quite content to exist inside ordinary life—to work, to hunt, to watch television, to attend school socials, choir practice, meetings of the 4-H club." The first part of the book, "The Last to See Them Alive," is, in essence, a testing of the thinness of the security and contentment of those who lack the inner resources to confront untamed reality.

An alien reality, symbolized by the two strangers who stealthily enter the village in the darkness of the night, shatters the life routine of the village and creates an almost communal psychosis. The rural innocence of the people, evoking the lost innocence of America, is violated by the urban experience of the two strangers who finally kill Mr. Clutter—the epitome of the values and attitudes of the community—and his entire family. The shotgun blasts echo the collision of "desperate, savage, violent America" with "sane, safe, insular, even smug America," of "people who have every chance" and "people who have none." The incident is so bizarre that, as Paul Levine observes, it seems to come straight out of the world of contemporary fiction. The trust, confidence, and assurance of the small community is so destroyed that "old neighbors" are now viewed as "strangers" and people cannot look at each other "without kind of wondering!" Fear paralyzes people's self-confidence and upsets their life pattern. In the village, at night, one now sees: "windows ablaze, almost every window in almost every house, and, in the brightly lit rooms, fully clothed people, even entire families, who had sat the whole night wide awake, watchful, listening." Holcomb has become a crisis city: a state of existence reflecting contemporary America, which, having failed to cope with emerging urban reality, is immersed in a total communal fear, estrangement, and paranoia.

The force of the collision and the subsequent emotional paralysis of the village are captured by the technique of "synchronic narration." After a short topographical description of Holcomb in the first section, the next sixteen sections of Part I focus alternately on the last day of the Clutters and on the progress of the killers toward their home. The intermingling of the two systems of actemes continues throughout the narrative and, consequently, sustains an inscriptional suspense. Moreover, the "synchronic narration" in *In Cold Blood,* as well as in other nonfiction novels, permits measurable, chronological clock time, not the dramatically heightened interior time of Modernist fiction, to be the main organizing device. In these early sections, Capote narrates the events in a chronological order. The intercutting of actemes—[Zavarzadeh defines *acteme* as "the result of the configuration of experiential events," replacing traditional notions of plot]—enacts the contingency of experience, the unsuspected collision of events. While the Clutters prepare for the Thanksgiving reunion and their daughter Beverly's approaching wedding, Perry Smith and Richard Hickock contemplate the type of rope and tape most suitable for tying and gagging them.

The last day in the life of the Clutters, a retrieving of events which actually took place on November 14, 1959, bears an uncanny resemblance to June 16, 1904, the day in *Ulysses* in which Joyce condensed a whole universe. In Joyce's narrative, the human condition is totalized through the invention of a fictive paradigm; in Capote's book, the actuality itself is registered, and the visible surface reveals the fictuality of a day's life. Details of the Clutter family life during this day are subjected to an exegesis, which reveals, without any intervention from the writer's inventive imagination, the symbolic resonance of each act. Nancy helps a little girl bake a cherry pie; Mrs. Clutter, during a conversation with the little girl, reveals her deeply troubled mind; Kenyon goes about his routine life of making things, and Mr. Clutter, among other things, provides for the family's future by purchasing "a forty-thousand-dollar policy that in the event of death by accidental means, paid double indemnity." These actions are typical of the family which, according to one town resident, "represented everything people hereabouts really value and respect." The annihilation of such a family creates a vacuum: "It's like being told there is no God," says one local observer. (pp. 115-18)

The happiness of the Clutters, as it turns out, is more a veneer than a deep, richly rooted, inner peace. Mrs. Clutter almost symbolically represents the sensitive soul estranged, unable to conform with the stiff-necked culture all around her. Her dissatisfaction with purely materialistic and pragmatic values is reflected in an inward rebellion which manifests itself in the form of what the Clutter family and their friends euphemistically refer to as "little nervous spells." Tellingly enough, the source of her difficulty in adjusting to the surrounding life is believed to be not in her "head" but in her "spine"—in the physical. However, in order to regain her "old self," she must undergo an "operation." Adjustment has brought her a social "maturity" which has "reduced her voice to a single tone, that of apology," and a personality now nothing but "a series of gestures blurred by the fear that she might give offense." Husband and wife have two different paths: his is "a public route, a march of satisfying conquests," but hers "a private one that eventually [winds] through hospital corridors." (pp. 118-19)

Mr. Clutter, who publicly stands for family life, is himself denied the private sharing of any nourishing emotional intimacy. The gnawing contraries of his seemingly fulfilled life surface when we learn that he does not share the same bedroom with his wife. There is some speculation that another woman might have been involved in his private life. His affection for his family is, one suspects, more a matter of public respect than felt personal attachment. (p. 119)

After the first part of *In Cold Blood* examines the lives of the Clutters, the remaining three parts register the lives and backgrounds of the actants, Perry Smith and Richard Hickock. The registration takes various forms: letters, confessions, autobiographical sketches, and interviews during which they talk about themselves to an "acquaintance" or a "journalist"—a device Capote uses to keep himself out of the main flow of the narrative.

The very values which have shaped the Clutter family life of public fulfillment and interior emptiness have also shaped the life-style of their killers. They are in a real sense the incarnation of the darker side of the Middle American psyche, the side inhibited and exiled from the consciousness which perceives and reacts to everyday reality. They represent the unacknowledged inner anxieties which, like canker, eat up the private life of the Clutters. The same cultural values which endow the Clutters with wealth and public security prevent the human development of the abilities of Perry and Richard, and deny them any personal fulfillment. The antagonism, if one may describe the relationship between the Clutters and their murderers as such, is quite impersonal, more the result of unresolved problems of a culture in its totality than a conscious effort by two outsiders to eliminate those who symbolize the oppressive forces. Perry perhaps refers to this impersonal clash of eruptive forces when, in a conversation with Donald Cullivan, his only visitor at the prison, he emphasizes that: "They [the Clutters] never hurt me. . . . Maybe it's just that the Clutters were the ones who had to pay for it." The collision is so tragically inevitable. . . . (p. 120)

Unlike Herb Clutter and his family, Perry Smith is marked with spontaneity, intuition, and an emotional response to life. The dream of freedom and escape activates his life, which is otherwise "an ugly and lonely progress toward one mirage and then another." He is "an incessant conceiver of voyages," a collector of maps of faraway lands, a man whose recurring dream is that of the journey back, "a dream of drifting downward through strange waters, of plunging toward a green sea-dusk, sliding past scaly, savage-eyed protectors—a drowned cargo of diamonds and pearls, heaping caskets of gold." He is the Knight of the Seas who is maimed. Despite his underwater reveries and much talk about skin-diving, he has never entered the water and cannot swim; his short legs were badly injured in a motorcycle accident. Perry is the man-child outsider; a half-breed Cherokee; a bed-wetter, with legs too short for his torso: "when he stood up he was no taller than a twelve year old child." He is arational in his reaction to outside reality and works his way through life by hunches and intuitions. (pp. 120-21)

Richard is Perry's anti-self. Perry is the poet, conceiving of the outside world in terms of a network of metaphors and dreams; Richard is "very literal-minded," having "no understanding of music or poetry." Richard's very pragmatism and literalness make him seem the authentically tough and "totally masculine" person to Perry. Richard likes to think of himself as a quite normal person looking for a " 'regular life' with a business of his own, a house, a horse to ride, a new car and 'plenty of blonde chicken.' " His preoccupation with normality creates fear and guilt that his sexual predilection for little girls may be found out. He is callous and also brutalized by his life experiences; he runs down dogs as a hobby. Both Perry and Richard are smashed in accidents on the road—roads which were supposed to take them "away, away from here." They are the refugees of the American Dream.

Perry's inner life, his background, and his attitude toward the external world are all conveyed in the narrative through a number of documents. Capote shuns internal analysis and such Modernist techniques as interior monologue. The method of informing the reader is similar to the way the reader as a real person in his or her own life gathers information about other people: external observations and statements made by the people themselves or their friends, relatives, and acquaintances. . . . The author refrains from any analysis himself; he merely acquires the appropriate documents and inserts them in the narrative. The same method is employed in discussing the life and ideas of the Clutter family and Richard. There are numerous interviews, testimonies, and statements in the book, but documentation in *In Cold Blood* is mostly covert in the text.

Through documentation and the insertion of such verifiable information as the names of persons, cities, hotels, or references to publications (the paper by Dr. Satten in *The American Journal of Psychiatry,* July 1960), Capote authenticates his narrative. The documents, which are the self-verifying apparatus of the narrative, form a pole of external reference in the book and point outside the narrative to the actual world. But what emerges from the registration of facts is a narrative charged with fictive resonance. The relationship between Perry, the dark-skinned half-Indian, and Richard, the white male devoid of any mature and sustained heterosexual love, the obsession of at least one of them with death, and the latent, innocent homosexuality embedded in their friendship echoes the archetypal pattern which Leslie Fiedler has discovered in American fiction. . . . The pattern of the killers' relationship in *In Cold Blood,* a transcription of an actual friendship between two persons, bears an unmistakable resemblance not only to the fictive patterning of relationships in such contemporary novels as Mailer's *Why Are We in Vietnam?* but also to such classic American fictions as *The Adventures of Huckleberry Finn.* In Capote's bi-referential narrative, the fictive and the factual are no longer valid categories. The mythos develops out of actemes and points to an area of experience which is metafictional, meta-factual.

The writer of a nonfiction novel, unlike the fictionist, does not "father" a fictional universe, but is merely the "midwife" of experiential reality: he or she attempts to find the appropriate technical means to assist the verbal birth of a segment of reality, However . . . the nature of man's perception of the outside world and the nonfiction novelist's need to use language, which is the depository of communal values, inevitably create in the nonfiction novel a view of reality. Such a view is "local" and is epistemologically different from the "global" *Weltanschauung* of the totalizing novel. Capote cannot transcribe everything which has happened; the necessities of his medium, which prevent durational realism, force him to select.

The type of distortions that the limitations of the medium impose on the nonfiction novel is illustrated by the ending of *In Cold Blood.* Part of the fault in the ending, of course, is Capote's. Faced with the necessity of bringing the narrative to an end, he falls back on his habits as a novelist. Tony Tanner has observed that the ending would have been "regarded as pretty cheap and sentimental" if the book were a "plain novel" [see excerpt dated March 18, 1966]. Vladimir Nabokov has also objected to the ending: "I like some of Truman Capote's stuff, particularly *In Cold Blood.* Except for that impossible ending, so sentimental, so false." My point is that the falseness of the ending of *In Cold Blood,* as of other nonfiction novels, including Norman Mailer's *The Armies of the Night,* goes beyond the clumsy handling of a technical problem by a particular author. It is more "ontological" than "compositional" and is connected to the all-important question of closure in the nonfiction novel. Any ending in such narratives will be to a certain degree "false," since an ending is an arbitrary and artificial but required imposition of a medium on the uninterruptable flow of life, whose movements the nonfiction novel follows. The closing of such unimagined narratives, in other words, works against the open-endedness which informs the body of the narrative and life itself.

One of the important elements of the "imaginal" component of Capote's nonfiction novel is its narrative point of view, which is largely responsible for the narrative's "architectonics." An examination of the narrative point of view in *In Cold Blood* will clarify the manner in which the nonfiction novelist transcribes reality without imposing a personal vision upon it, since point of view is basically a variable of the writer's relationship with reality in his narrative. The point of view in *In Cold Blood* corresponds to what is traditionally referred to as "omniscient." A contradiction seems to arise between the intention of the nonfiction novel and the point of view adopted in *In Cold Blood:* what is the legitimacy of the use of the seemingly totalizing omniscient point of view in a non-totalizing narrative? Early in the narrative, when Capote relates the events of the Clutters' last day, he quotes Mr. Clutter's talk with the pheasant hunters from Oklahoma who are offering him hunting fees. Mr. Clutter refuses the money: "I'm not as poor as I look. Go ahead, get all you can." Then we hear the voice of the omniscient narrator interrupting the flow of narrative to add: "Then touching the brim of his cap, he headed for home and the day's work, *unaware that it would be his last*" (emphasis added). When speaking of Nancy Clutter, Capote mentions in parentheses that the dress he is describing will later be the dress she is buried in. The question here is, of course, the question of authority: how does the nonfiction novelist, who records events as they unfold, know that a particular day is the last day in a person's life or that a certain dress will later be the burial dress? A Dickens knows such facts because he is the god of his universe. Though the point of view used in *In Cold Blood* resembles the omniscient point of view employed in *Our Mutual Friend, Middlemarch,* and many other fictive novels, the omniscience which informs a non-fiction novel is based on the writer's thorough research, rather than on his or her imaginative authority. In other words, the omniscient point of view of *In Cold Blood* is an "empirical omniscience." Truman Capote knows that Nancy Clutter will be buried in a particular dress, and so informs his reader, because he has learned it through his research

While the fictive novelist's authority for shaping and presenting his reality through his control of the point of view is his totalization of the experiential *donnée,* the authority of the nonfiction novelist is obtained through exegesis of his *données.* In using "empirical omniscience" in *In Cold Blood,* the all-knowing author substantiates his authority by weaving the narrative web from interviews, official documents, autobiographical sketches, and even the article in the learned journal.

Ironically enough, the source of concern for the reader of *In Cold Blood* is less the intrusive voice of the author than some of the events recorded in the book. Mr. Clutter, for example, buys an insurance policy with double indemnity on the day which proves to be his last. Perry and Richard are arrested just after withdrawing from the post office the box containing the boots that matched the footprints left at the Clutter house. Such events seem contrived, but life is the contriver; it hands the author coincidences no fictive novelists would dare invent today. Can one be critical of "plot" probabilities for true events? The very concept of "plot," as I have suggested earlier, will have to be replaced by the concept of "acteme."

The events of a nonfiction novel are known beforehand, so the nonfiction novelist has very little use for the conventional "situational suspense" which sustains a fictive novel. Instead of "situational suspense" (suspense based on unknown events and new turns of the story), the nonfiction novel offers "inscriptional suspense." To build such suspense, Capote does not invent new incidents but dwells on the details of the existing ones. The "irony" in *In Cold Blood* is also derived from the bizarre permutations of events and not from the writer's imagination. When, in recording the last day of Mr. Clutter, Capote mentions Clutter's conversation with Mr. Johnson, the insurance man, and quotes Johnson's remark, "Why, Herb, you're a *young* man. Forty-eight. And from the looks of you, from what the medical reports tell us, we're likely to have you around a couple of weeks more," he is recording such an empirical irony.

In Cold Blood uses a modally complex narrative to capture an event which is inherently ambiguous and so bizarre that it cannot be categorized as either factual or fictional by our current epistemological standards. The event has occurred and thus qualifies as factual, but the factual is enveloped by the atmosphere and ambiance of the fictional. The sense of wonder and puzzlement is clearly reflected in the behavior of the experienced chief detective, Alvin Dewey, who in many ways represents the common sense of the community. Having heard the confessions of Perry and Richard, he is disappointed because "the confessions failed to satisfy his sense of meaningful design."

A factual or a fictional solution would have distorted the event by simplifying it. The actemes can be revealed, not resolved. Capote has combined the power of art with the authority of facts to write an anti-illusionist narrative about what Norman Mailer in *The Presidential Papers* calls the double life of the Americans, "one visible, the other underground." On one level, the life is "concrete, factual, practical, and unbelievably dull." But also present is "a subterranean river of untapped, ferocious, lonely and romantic desire, that concentration of ecstasy and violence which is the dream life of the nation." Capote refuses a fictional logic, and forces the reader to confront these two zones of experience through his fictual narrative. (pp. 121-27)

Mas'ud Zavarzadeh, "The Stubborn Fact: The Exegetical Nonfiction Novel," in his The Mythopoeic

Reality: The Postwar American Nonfiction Novel,
University of Illinois Press, 1976, pp. 93-127.

JACK DE BELLIS

When Truman Capote serialized *In Cold Blood* in *The New Yorker* in autumn 1965, no òne imagined that his much-heralded "nonfiction novel" was an unpolished work. Yet a comparison of the magazine edition and publication by Random House ten weeks later reveals that Capote made nearly five-thousand changes, ranging from crucial matters of fact to the placement of a comma. Since Capote claimed that his new art form contained not only perfect factual accuracy, but "the poetic altitude fiction is capable of reaching," his own intentions did not seem precisely clear. However, few people questioned Capote's assertion of complete accuracy. No one, of course, suggested that Capote's style might be deficient. Yet careful analysis of *The New Yorker* and Random House editions reveals that a great many doubts lingered in the author's mind after he had committed his six-year work to print. Many of his changes seem so personal that they are incomprehensible. The impression persists that he could not resist re-examining his research and his style. And since many of the things changed in the Random House edition originally appeared in "official records" and numerous interviews conducted entirely without aid of recorders or pencils, it is all the more surprising that they might be subject to revision. (pp. 519-20)

The most interesting revisions in the "non-fiction novel" are those purporting to correct factual errors. Capote altered numerical counts, for example, changing the number of churches in Garden City from twenty-two to twenty-eight, and giving detective Dewey eighteen assistants rather than seventeen. Times, directions, and places were also altered. In *The New Yorker* Perry was paroled in the summer, but the time is spring in revision. The killers are east of Holcomb, not northeast. The site of a murder shifts from Tampa to Tallahassee, momentarily implicating the killers in another crime. Utah is subtracted from the list of states the fugitives crossed Capote changes product titles, offering "Miller High Life" for "Miller's High Life" and "The Topeka *Daily Capital*" for "The Topeka *Capital.*" . . . Naturally, such specificity gives *In Cold Blood* "persuasiveness of fact," but it also raises questions about the accuracy of the narrative, since *The New Yorker* version was ostensibly accurate to begin with.

Of more importance, perhaps, are changes contributing to characterization. Although Smith's brother originally "killed his wife one day and himself the next," Capote clears him of murder in the Random House version. In fact, Smith's sister-in-law had placed a shotgun to her head and triggered it with her big toe. Capote's comment that Myrtle Clare dresses like a man is deleted from Random House. Although Mrs. Helm was originally described as the family housekeeper and confidante of Bonnie Clutter, this was deleted. (pp. 522-23)

The richest character changes, however, are naturally those involving Smith and Hickock. When Hickock observes Smith staring in a mirror, he accuses him of looking at a "woman" originally, but a "piece of butt" in Random House. During his first interrogation Hickock refers to "Virgin Lane" but calls this "Cherry Row" in revision. Capote gives him queries not in the serialization when he has him ask a whore, "Is it good, baby? Is it good?" More extensive, though, are Capote's revisions of Smith. Originally he described Smith's reac-

tions to fellow-prisoner Lee Andrews this way: "Was it any wonder he never opened his mouth? Andrews meant well, but Perry couldn't stand him—yet for a long time he did not admit it." Revision changes the tone of Smith's reaction: "Better to keep your mouth shut than to risk one of the college kid's snotty lines, like: 'Don't say *dis*interested. When what you mean is *un*interested.' Andrews meant well, he was without malice, but Perry could have boiled him in oil—yet he never admitted it." Does "boiled him in oil" clarify the precise quality of Smith's feeling as he experienced it? Or is Capote attempting to vivify Smith's character by showing the close relation in Smith's mind between violence and his intellectual insecurity? As we shall see, revisions in the character of Smith offer clues about why Capote failed in his intention to write a "nonfiction novel."

Elsewhere, Capote diminishes characterization by deleting details, removing, for example, his depiction of Hickock as "pallid as a funeral lily." Although the magazine revealed Judge Tate's lips "curved downward, his eyes blazed," the Judge simply "scowls" in the Random House edition. Repeatedly, Capote removes all remarks which might draw attention to himself in order to provide more "objective" reporting. (pp. 523-24)

Simple substitution of single words often allowed Capote a more vivid characterizing detail. Hickock's lips do not "move" but "writhe" on revision when he spots Floyd Wells in court. Smith is coarsened by the simple addition, "Shit." On the other hand, Capote augments Smith "hurried on" to "Smith's pencil sped almost indecipherably." (p. 524)

Of course such interest in arriving at the *mot juste* touches all aspects of *In Cold Blood.* Apparently to create a less formal tone he changed "lugubrious" to "mournful"; "encompassed" to "included"; "festooned" to "trimmed"; and "not unbrave" to "no coward." Other changes are less comprehensible: "photographers" to "cameramen"; "engine" to "motor"; "roadworker" to "Highway employee"; and "khaki" to "suntans." . . . To say "alternative" rather than "alternate" jurors were selected is to import an error into the Random House version. But the view of the jurors retiring to "determine" rather than "discuss" the verdict corrects an original mistake.

Such attention to nuances of meaning enables Capote to defamiliarize his characters by referring, for example, to the killers as Smith and Hickock, rather than Perry and Dick, particularly after their capture. Likewise, Judge Tate becomes simply "the Judge," and the sarcasm of "specimens" is dispelled by the neutral "townsfolk." Perhaps the possibility of rhyme suggested the alteration from "crimes of violence" to "ill deeds," since Capote had written that country lawyer Fleming "was more happily at home with land deeds than ill deeds." Again, the result is distance. (p. 525)

In most revisions involving syntax changes, Capote, as expected, improves his work; yet a surprising amount of indecision surfaces concerning sentence fluidity and punctuation. Reducing simple awkwardness and redundancy, he changed "The young girls described certain observations they had made," to "the young girls described what they saw." Improving an effect by repetition, he alters "The state stopped him there, and it halted Cullivan too" to "The state stopped him there, and stopped Cullivan too." Capote tidies referents to improve syntactical relations: "the daughter of the subject" becomes "Mrs. Johnson." But syntax is contorted by the addition of a needless "as": "the journalist was as equally well acquainted with Smith as he was with Hickock." The first "as" had been added. Another revision creates more problems than it solves: "his intelligence, the formal quality of his college training" becomes "the formal quality of his college-trained intelligence." This suggests that "intelligence" can be "trained" and that this can be detected in some vague "formal quality," while assuming what is obscure, that a logical relation exists between "formal quality," "training," and "intelligence." . . . Although Norman Mailer has praised Capote for writing the best sentences "rhythm upon rhythm" among living authors, such peculiar errors in revision call into question Capote's sense of style.

Although he made few grammatical changes, some that he did make caused problems occasionally. Revisions of the conditional were frequent but inconsistent. He corrects a mistake in the use of "lay" and "lie" and alters the movement of tenses during Smith's confession from past to present. In one quoted passage his alteration of voice entirely changes the meaning: "Margaret Edna attracted him" became "was attracted to him," shifting the emphasis of admiration from Hickock to his wife. (pp. 525-26)

[Whether] or not a change is due simply to typographical error is difficult to establish clearly. . . . Certainly some of the changes which might be attributed to initial error are actually a result of Capote's editorial decisions. He has made changes in nineteen cases involving direct quotations. Therefore, these changes, some of which are obviously errors, create problems when we attempt to discover the special contribution he made toward a new art form in which every word would be true. . . . Because the evidence does not allow us to decide with certainty whether a change is made because of typographical error or because of editorial decision, we are precluded from establishing an authoritative text in these cases.

Turning now to Capote's handling of punctuation, we find his primary goal repeatedly realized: to increase formality. Hence, Capote prefers the colon to the comma before quotations, as well as the colon followed by the semi-colon after items in series, rather than dashes followed by commas. Dashes regularly become commas, semi-colons, colons, or even periods. Parentheses replace dashes, as do single quotes when sobriquets are indicated. Dashes, however, replace the sequence of dots to indicate deleted matter. Quotation marks are uniformly deleted in diary entries, letters, signs, and headlines. Movie and book titles formerly placed in quotes are now italicized. Quoted material is frequently paraphrased. His deletions of punctuation created a more rapidly-paced narrative. Commas are removed after introductory clauses, phrases, and words, as well as after final items in a series. He discontinues commas for appositions and interruptors. Sometimes their deletion creates comma splices or obscures meaning, as in: "And *that,* freedom apart [,] was what he most desired." Elsewhere, Capote deletes the comma for sentence rhythm: "Hickock consented to take the test [,] and so did Smith." Comma reduction helps improve sentence rhythms, as in: "Fleming, who was seventy-one, was a former mayor of Garden City, a short man who habitually enlivened an unsensational appearance with rather conspicuous neck-wear. He resisted the assignment." In the Random House edition this becomes: "Fleming, seventy one, a former may or of Garden City, a short man who enlivens an unsensational appearance with rather conspicuous neckwear, resisted the assign-

ment" (R: 257). The removal of an inert "to be" verb, the decision to change to past tense, to drop "habitually," and the suggestion of cause and effect between Fleming's age, height, and appearance with his resistance to the assignment are facilitated by the blending of ideas actuated by the comma before the final clause. (pp. 527-28)

Additions in punctuation almost entirely concern commas, especially when clarifying apposition. Otherwise, Capote corrects mistakes in the apostrophe, as in "counsels'." He even deletes an apostrophe in a letter from Smith's father, ending "All's well with me," which becomes "Alls." Since Capote tells us that Smith destroyed his father's note at once, one wonders how Capote was able to decide to delete the apostrophe. My assumption throughout, of course, has been that, because of Capote's celebrated method of interviewing, his interviewees gave him no notes in their own hand.

Capote's most consistent practice is the addition of the hyphen, particularly in "T-shirt." Though usually spelled "T shirt" in *The New Yorker,* Capote adds the hypen not only in his narration, but in Smith's police statement. Since Smith's statement was undoubtedly recorded orally and then transcribed by a court reporter, why should Capote have allowed such an interpolation to overrule his own professional stylistic sensitivity? Curiously, he adds a hyphen to "pre-emptory," which is not only incorrect but misspelled, as it had been in *The New Yorker.* Other minor additions include the employment of italics for store names, Latin phrases, and boat names and the use of quotes for slang words like "shiv."

Although many of Capote's revisions occur in unverifiable quoted sources, his changes in the punctuation and diction in a poem provide a case in which his fastidiousness can be tested. In *The New Yorker* the ninth stanza of Gray's "Elegy Written in a Country Churchyard" appears this way:

> The boast of heraldry, the pomp of pow'r
> And all that beauty, all that wealth e'er gave,
> Awaits alike the inevitable hour:
> The paths of glory lead but to the grave.

But the Random House edition contains two word changes: "boasts" replaces "boast"; and "await" supplants "awaits." The comma after "pow'r" was deleted from the book as well. However, in all three cases *The New Yorker* version agrees with the best sources. No edition of the "Elegy" uses "boasts." Did Capote decide to rely on his notes on revising his work, realizing that since the stanza had been given to Hickock by another prisoner its inaccuracies would not be his own responsibility? The reader, finally, cannot be sure which version represents a truthful rendering of what Capote observed. When a breach of trust is created with the reader over such confirmable matters, his doubts begin to gather about other matters of plot, characterization, symbolism, and theme of *In Cold Blood.* (pp. 528-29)

Interesting as these analyses of Capote's revisions may be in themselves, they become more important for the light they cast upon Capote's intentions to contribute to a new art form. Since the best available evidence suggests that five-thousand revisions were crammed into the ten weeks separating the serialization and the Random House publication, Capote's re-examination of his book appears to have been obsessive, perhaps stemming from a fear that his high ambitions were not being realized.

His major claim, of course, was that he had produced a "nonfiction novel." . . . In such a genre the subject is of no importance but is merely the "X" in the "quadratic equation" of a "stylistic problem." Capote's special contribution would be the removal of the narrator entirely to provide "vertical interior movement." This forced him to "empathize" with people he otherwise would not have written about. However, I suggest that a strain developed between Capote's intellectual strategy and the emotional reality he faced. And since "emotionality" made him "lose writing control" and his five-year "schizophrenic experience" forced him to live intimately with deliberate cruelty, "the only unforgivable thing," it is no wonder that he described the book as "written on the edge of my nerves." This is scarcely the condition in which to apply "fantastic concentration . . . right down to the very comma" in which "any distraction at all is fatal," especially when the ultimate aim is "to have it all perfectly." The strain he faced was most apparent in his handling of Perry Smith, for as Capote has said, "I did identify with him to a great degree. Never did deny it. It's also quite true that my portrait of him is absolutely one hundred per cent the way he was."

The more cautious reviewers of **In Cold Blood** suggested that verification was needed before Capote's claim to total accuracy could be accepted. F. W. Dupee asserted that "to praise without proof is foolish," and he wondered about Capote's decision to suppress his documentation in the text itself [see excerpt above dated February 3, 1966]. Other commentators wondered why Capote made so elaborate a pretense of holding to the facts and suggested that his sacrifice of the artist's vision was not worth the gain in objective reportage. I would like to pursue this two-pronged criticism, examining first the factual accuracy of the work and then the "distractions" which interfered with his ambitions.

Although Capote prided himself for possessing the equivalent of an auditory photographic memory, he nevertheless conceded that it was not foolproof but at best ninety-percent effective, "and who cares about the other ten percent." This alone would be sufficient to account for errors which even Capote's revisions would not catch. Many other ways can be adduced which import errors into his narrative, yet reliance upon the revisions already examined is sufficient to show that Capote's errors in revision weaken credibility in his method of gathering evidence. But without foundation, such doubt rests on speculative sands. Though one assumes that revisions represent corrections, verifiable evidence might reveal otherwise. And such is, in fact, the case with Capote's handling of the killers' tattoos. Although Capote indentified a snake tattoo on Smith's right arm in *The New Yorker* and deleted its position in the Random House edition, he placed it on Smith's left arm when later referring to it in the book. Nevertheless, his revision was inaccurate, for the photographs by Richard Avedon of Smith and Hickock show clearly that *The New Yorker* was right; Smith's snake is on his right arm. Furthermore, a cat design described as being on Hickock's right hand appears on his left hand in Avedon's photograph. Not only does this show that Capote incorrectly revised **In Cold Blood,** but it reveals that original errors transported from the serialization to the book which could have been corrected fairly easily were never changed. This suggests that Capote was simply unaware of mistakes which even a reader of *Life* or *Newsweek* might uncover with little difficulty.

Soon after the publication of the book two reporters sought to verify Capote's handling of facts and found discrepancies. Robert Pearman discovered that Capote erred in his presentation of the sale of Nancy Clutter's horse Babe, reaching for pathos rather than realism. Bobby Rupp told Pearman that Capote mischaracterized him, and Perry Smith confided to undersheriff Meier that the book would contain inaccuracies, saying, "read it and see for yourself." (pp. 530-32)

The first examiner to study Capote's sources extensively was Philip Tompkins, who uncovered four discrepancies [see excerpt above dated June, 1966]. The most serious involve Perry Smith. Although Capote recorded that the wife of undersheriff Meier heard Smith cry and say, "I am embraced by shame," Mrs. Meier absolutely denied this ever happened when Tompkins re-questioned her. She insisted that she never "told such things to Capote." Besides this disputed scene, witnesses at the execution offered different opinions about Smith's last words. None of the other reporters, editors, or wire-service representatives recorded that Smith said, as Capote indicated, "I apologize." Detective Dewey told Tompkins he was unsure what Smith had said. . . . Capote himself has said that during Smith's last speaking moments all he could hear was "the roar of blood in my ears." Later Capote stated that Smith was "upset that he *didn't* have any conscience"; elsewhere he noted that all multiple murderers he had ever interviewed admitted that "they couldn't care less."

Tompkins' discovery that Smith's pathetic plea for sympathy never occurred and Capote's virtual admission that Smith did not feel the apology he records in **In Cold Blood** suggests that the revisions concerning Perry Smith contain the "poetic altitude fiction is capable of reaching" rather than "the persuasiveness of fact." Perhaps Capote's personal involvement with Smith was the chief reason for his extraordinary number of alterations.

In Cold Blood's first reviewers detected how "uncannily" Smith fit into the pattern of Capote's other characters. Like them he was short-legged and thus grotesque, precocious and childlike, artistic, and irrational. He represented an eruption from the "nocturnal world" delineated in Capote's early stories. He is a dreamer, an androgynous father-seeker like Joel Knox of **Other Voices, Other Rooms.** Like Holly Golightly he seeks his own morality. Later commentators suggested other parallels. The practice seems reasonable since Capote has said "Perry was a character that was also in my imagination . . . [he] could absolutely . . . [have stepped] right out of one of my stories."

But various commentators have also asserted that Capote's own relation to Smith weakened his ability to restrain his personal vision. . . . Capote himself drew attention to their similarity of faces by using the same image, that of the "changeling's face," to describe himself and Smith. In a recurrent dream, Smith is characterized as avenging himself on his enemies in the guise of Perry O'Parsons. Capote's original name was Truman Persons. (pp. 532-34)

[Despite their similarities], Tompkins finds that Smith and Capote differ over the crucial matter of violence. But this leads Tompkins to suggest that Capote labored to shorten the emotional gap which he felt isolated him from Smith by insisting that Smith was only able to kill while in a "schizophrenic darkness." Thus, Smith, with whom Capote had come to have "great rapport," could be understood and forgiven. . . . Tompkins further suggests that Capote could not be true to his basic intention of getting away from his "own particular vision of the world." Capote had found an imaginary toad in his real Kansas garden and chose to convert his scheme so that he might produce an apparently real toad in an apparently real garden. This way he could give the density of reality to images from his nocturnal world. (pp. 534-35)

Yet there is more to the story than Perry Smith, and there may be more to Capote's envelopment, for he tended to conceive of Kansas as symbolic of his "daylight world" of "the good, solid, landed American gentry," "the world of safety." The collision of this world with the nocturnal world "representing the dangerous psychotic element, empty of compassion or conscience," would inevitably produce death. If one wished to speculate that Kansas represented the South in Capote's imagination and could accept the view of Smith as Capote's doppelgänger, *In Cold Blood* then becomes the author's revenge upon the section which gave him the dual vision of his fiction, daylight and nocturnal, and which prompted the extreme tactic of the "nonfiction novel" as a way of release from his psychological bondage to the South. The revenge would be depicted in such a way that the author bore no responsibility for his fantacizing. This fantasy contains an element of the child's imagined revenge upon his parents. But by recording the consequences for Smith and Hickock, Capote recognized society's right to self-protection from the dangerous visionaries it creates and then consciously or unwittingly destroys. Perhaps he saw in Smith's life and death a parable about the serious artist in America. Paradoxically, however, he had to purge himself of his own resentments of the "world of safety" in order to develop as an artist with greater conscious control and wider sympathies. The story called to him at rather deep levels.

Perhaps this is why he said of the Clutters, "They selected me." The "madness of art" had its own reasons, regardless of Capote's need to solve his stylistic quadratic equation. Little wonder he would admit, "I'm still very much haunted by the whole thing. I have finished the book, but in a sense I *haven't* finished it: it keeps churning around in my head. It particularizes itself now and then, but not in the sense that it brings about a total conclusion." What total conclusion could be possible? The meaning of the experience, like Smith's motives for murder and Capote's reasons for endless revision, may never fully disclose its secrets. If, however, he consciously deceived his public with *In Cold Blood,* his fate is clear, for Capote has stated, "Perry always said that if I told any lies about him he was going to come back from the grave and kill me." (pp. 535-36)

Jack De Bellis, "Visions and Revisions: Truman Capote's 'In Cold Blood'," in Journal of Modern Literature, *Vol. 7, No. 3, September, 1979, pp. 519-36.*

ERIC HEYNE

What do we mean when we contend that a nonfiction narrative is literary? This question has become increasingly important in light of excellent writing by Norman Mailer, Tom Wolfe, Michael Herr, and others, and in response to literary historians, such as Robert Scholes and David Lodge, who argue that our cultural aesthetic is demanding texts that define "reality" and "realism" in new ways. Critical attention to the New Journalism has succeeded in increasing our understanding and appreciation of particular works, but there remains a great deal of confusion about theoretical issues, such as the distinction between fact and fiction, the qualities

of literary status in nonfiction, and the responsibilities of the author in turning history into art. Much of the confusion comes from terms such as "nonfiction novel," grandiose assertions such as "there is no difference between fiction and nonfiction," and simple-minded definitions of artistic nonfiction based on the use of techniques common in fiction. In this essay I will argue that literary nonfiction and fiction are fundamentally different, despite their resemblances in structure or technique, and that this difference must be recognized by any theory that hopes to do justice to powerful nonfiction narratives.

In "The Logical Status of Fictional Discourse" John Searle points out that the distinction we commonly make between factual and fictional statements is based, not on any characteristic of the statements themselves, but on our perception of the kind of statement being intended. Suppose a friend tells an amazing anecdote. If we believe it to be a joke or an invention, we look for a punchline or narrative flourishes; if we think it is a true story, we may formulate questions in our minds, asking for supplementary information. The proper response is indicated by the type of story we think we are being told, and that decision in turn is influenced by factors such as our relationship with the storyteller, the social context, and the antecedent conversation, as well as by properties of the story itself. (pp. 479-80)

If Searle's distinction makes sense, it follows that the author is sole determinant of whether a text is fact or fiction, whereas the reader must decide for herself whether a work is good or bad fact. I will use the terms "factual status" and "factual adequacy" to distinguish between these two different kinds of truth. A fictional text has neither factual status nor factual adequacy; a nonfiction text has factual status, but readers would have to resolve individually or by debate the question of its factual adequacy. (pp. 480-81)

As a case study for this essay I will use Truman Capote's *In Cold Blood: A True Account of a Multiple Murder and Its Consequences.* In subtitle, Acknowledgements, and interviews Capote claimed that the book was "immaculately factual." There is little doubt that he wanted his book to have factual status, and most readers have taken *In Cold Blood* as nonfiction. However, there is a strong tendency among critics to talk about the book as a kind of novel. This tendency is based, oddly enough, on two very different evaluations of the book. Some critics argue that *In Cold Blood* is radically inaccurate, and so should be labeled "fiction," whereas others so admire its dramatic power that they want to grant it honorary status as a novel. Analyzing these two positions may help clarify the notions of factual status and factual adequacy and explain their usefulness in a theory of literary nonfiction.

Perhaps the most interesting reaction to the publication of *In Cold Blood* was Philip K. Tompkins' research into the events of the book [see excerpt above dated June, 1966]. His article, "In Cold Fact," details the discrepancies he found, places where Capote deliberately or accidentally departed from the actual events so far as Tompkins could determine them. Though he is willing to grant Capote the benefit of every doubt, Tompkins concludes that at the very least Capote put his own observations into the mouths and minds of other characters, and at the worst he created a mixed up, inaccurate portrait of the murderer Perry Smith. . . . If Capote did indeed "create" Perry Smith [as Tompkins asserts], that decision has important consequences for our evaluation of *In Cold Blood,* because critics have generally agreed that Smith is the protagonist of the book and that one of Capote's central aims is indicated by the intended irony of the title: it is Smith rather than the Clutter family who is killed "in cold blood."

If Capote's book were a novel, Tompkins' research would, of course, be impossible. Because it is nonfiction, however, competing accounts are relevant, perhaps even vital. How factually adequate is *In Cold Blood,* and how important is the answer to that question in deciding on the value of the book? Melvin J. Friedman believes that Capote "cheated" but that his doing so does not matter much: "Despite the convincing claims of unreliability . . . we must still believe in the essential authenticity and integrity of Capote's account." Unfortunately, Friedman does not go into detail about what constitutes "the essential authenticity and integrity" of the book, nor about how that may be preserved in the face of inaccuracies. If one believes, on the other hand, that Capote's "cheating" weakened his book (primarily through sentimentalizing his protagonist), what is the appropriate response? For Tompkins, it is to conclude that "art triumphs over reality, fiction over nonfiction."

In the terms of our analysis, Tompkins reasons from factual inadequacy to fictional status. Ignoring Capote's intentions, Tompkins decides to read all or part of *In Cold Blood* as fiction. This is the same move as labeling an exposed hoax, such as the "Hitler diaries," a fiction, in the common use of the word to describe anything false. But for the purposes of literary criticism do we really want a definition of fiction that includes discredited narratives of fact, such as lies, misguided histories, and unethical journalism? . . . Tompkins is doing a disservice to "art" by relegating to it whatever errors Capote may have made. If Capote seriously misrepresented the character of Perry Smith, the result is not a triumph of "fiction over nonfiction," but of lying over truth-telling, or blindness over insight.

There is more involved in Tompkins' position, however, than just a different use of the word "fiction." Undercutting the value of his own investigations, Tompkins concludes that *In Cold Blood* is a "work of art" that will be enjoyed "for its own sake" long after the "discrepancies of fact" have been forgotten. Unlike Friedman, Tompkins believes that the book's inaccuracies are central, but, like Friedman, Tompkins believes that the book is good enough to survive as literature, though metamorphosed into fiction. It may be easy to accept this claim, because *In Cold Blood* is a skillfully-constructed narrative, and very much like many novels in its structure, style, and effects. However, I believe there is another kind of confusion involved here: this time it is not between factual status and factual adequacy but between fictional status and literary merit.

In his study of literary nonfiction, *Fables of Fact,* John Hellmann argues that "the new journalist presents fact in fictional form, but it is fiction only in the more sophisticated and original sense of the word that has led Northrop Frye to apply it to 'any work of art in prose'." Frye's use of the term may have been "original," but he is now one of many critics who have suggested that traditional literary genres be conflated into a larger category, such as literary discourse. As Frye and Hellmann use "fiction," it becomes merely a synonym for literary prose and leaves us without a way to distinguish between fiction and nonfiction. To quote Searle again, "the concept of literature is a different concept from that of fiction. Thus, for example, 'the Bible as literature' indicates a theologically neutral attitude, but 'the Bible as fiction' is tendentious."

Hellmann is correct when he observes that "we think of the works of Capote, Mailer, Wolfe, Herr, Thompson, and other new journalists as members of a single genre, despite their being spread throughout the Library of Congress . . ." However, I would argue that part of the reason we would group them together would be to *separate* them from novels, as nonfiction narratives of such power and complexity that they deserve the attention of literary critics. (pp. 481-83)

In *The Mythopoeic Reality* Mas'ud Zavarzadeh has attacked the fact/fiction distinction from the more radical position that "the epistemological crisis of our 'age of suspicion' " has rendered the whole notion of fact versus fiction obsolete. According to Zavarzadeh, the "fictuality" of contemporary life has produced narratives that cannot be taken as either factual or fictional but only as somehow both simultaneously. Like Hellmann, Zavarzadeh employs a model of narrative based on "direction" inward or outward, toward the self-contained world of the narrative or the confusing, largely nonverbal world of real events. Where he differs is in his characterization of the "nonfiction novel" as a narrative balanced between the two directions, with no final allegiance to either the inner or the outer world. The appeal of his argument is that it seems to explain the difficulty people have making decisions about truth. Every narrative is a version, and there are not always firm principles for judging all versions, nor enough information available to make satisfying decisions about representational accuracy. The modern reader in search of narrative truth cannot trust newspapers, must weigh competing historical accounts, and often ends up deciding that a story is more or less true, rather than just true or false. Zavarzadeh suggests that we will have to abandon the fact/fiction distinction in the face of increasingly complex modes of telling applied to an increasing amount of information. This is an interesting piece of advice, but it certainly is not a description of what people do. We commonly depend on distinguishing between fact and fiction, employing our "factual competence," as it were. When we are challenged by a narrative that presents itself as fact, but includes dialogue or events that we may doubt, our response is usually to challenge the text and determine its worth, not throw up our hands and surrender. We will continue to maintain the fact/fiction distinction at least as long as we find it worthwhile to conduct a collective search for the truths of our past.

One of the consequences of factual status is that it brings into play certain epistemological principles, variously codified for the different purposes of journalism, history, and law. When we pick up a work of nonfiction, we have in mind questions about access to information, first- and second-hand sources, and so on. If the text is clearly a piece of journalism, a history, or a courtroom transcript, we can narrow the appropriate responses even farther. However, in the case of an ambitious or experimental text, we will not be able to decide ahead of time which epistemological principles are to be in force—unless we privilege certain conventions. This is exactly what John Hersey does when he applies to the work of Norman Mailer, Tom Wolfe, and Truman Capote the strict standards of journalism. Not surprisingly, Hersey concludes that his fellow authors are poor reporters: "The writer of fiction must invent. The journalist must not invent." This neat aphorism is entirely correct, as long as it is intended only as part of a description of conventional journalistic practice. However, conventions are made to be challenged, in nonfiction as in fiction. As literary critics we have a special interest in innovation, and it makes more sense for us to begin reading with an open mind, discovering along the way which conventions will be adhered to and which ignored or tested by a particular text.

This does not mean that an author can get away with anything he pleases or can expect us to believe everything he says. I think that Capote damaged *In Cold Blood* by violating certain conventions of accurate presentation. But that belief is based on the conviction that Capote did not abide by his *own* rules, the principles which he indicates in his text to be in force. For instance, he employs an omniscient point of view, telling his story from the perspectives of a variety of characters but never entering the narrative as a character or making explicit value judgments as a narrator. He strongly implies that one or more of his characters provide first-hand evidence for every event and that words placed in quotation marks can be verified to virtually everyone's satisfaction. However, Tompkins found witnesses to dispute Capote's version of some of Smith's "exact words," including his final apology. . . . Either Capote completely made up key scenes, or he transferred his own experiences to another character. In either case he violated the principles he set up for himself in this book, reducing his accomplishments considerably. However, this does not mean that Capote made up all of *In Cold Blood* or that any nonfiction writer who makes up scenes would be cheating, or that Capote must have intended me to read his book without regard to whether he made things up. Factual status is crucial to the experience of reading *In Cold Blood,* which in turn means that we are invited to make a decision about its factual adequacy, not merely according to *a priori* principle but by the rules Capote indicates are in force in his book.

We might tentatively identify two different kinds of truth—accuracy and meaning—for which different principles are important. The former involves a kind of groundwork, a detailed and sufficiently neutral verbal representation of events, for which the goal is universal agreement or correspondence. The latter is much more nebulous, covering virtually everything one does with "the facts" once they have been given an accurate shape. In practice there is seldom any convenient way to distinguish a fact from its meaning, because facts are verbal models that always already participate in the infinite connotations of language. Moreover, facts can be variously broad, complex, and controversial, just as meanings can. Nevertheless, and without pretending to any sort of philosophical profundity, I think we can usefully talk about accuracy and meaning as different sorts of claims or strategies in nonfiction narrative.

We judge competition between true stories to be important because we believe that two people witnessing the same event could eventually come up with some shared version of that event, a linguistic model to which both would accede. . . . Fortunately, language is so flexible a tool that in daily life we manage to agree well enough on versions of just about everything, or at least on the kind of information that, if available, would produce such agreement. In the competition between Capote's and Tompkins' versions of events in Kansas, our concern thus far has been accuracy. Capote did not achieve the "immaculate" correspondence to events that he claimed. However, it is the influence of his inaccuracies upon the meaning of the book that is fatal. Complex truths may be well served by inventions, exaggerations, slanting, and other transformations of fact. But in the case of *In Cold Blood,* the inventions concern the character of Perry Smith, and his precise motivations are at the thematic and aesthetic heart of the book. Capote's meaning is flawed by his inaccuracies. If they had not been exposed by Tompkins, *In Cold Blood* would be a more important book, not merely for historical reasons, but aesthetically as well.

We have arrived at the issue of literary value, albeit by a very strange route. This whole discussion of accuracy and competition runs counter to the traditional notion of literary value as transcendent or a-contextual. As John M. Ellis puts it, "literary texts are defined as those that are used by the society in such a way that *the text is not taken as specifically relevant to the immediate context of its origin."* . . . I would argue that virtually everyone is interested in the origins of texts—in questions about authors, dates, influences, careers, and so forth—notwithstanding the fact that many critics, for various philosophical or rhetorical reasons, play down such matters in their writing and teaching. I think it would be more accurate to amend Ellis by saying that literary texts are not taken as *limited* in relevance or significance by the details of their origins.

What about *In Cold Blood?* To put it baldly, is it literature or not? This question, which I have frequently encountered in casual discussions about the book, is extremely frustrating because it indicates the degree to which an essentialist theory of literary value is alive and well. In order for me to participate in a discussion of the literariness of *In Cold Blood,* I first have to explain the view of Ellis, Searle, and others, that literature is a "family resemblance" notion and that members are certified over time. As Searle puts it, "the literary is continuous with the nonliterary. Not only is there no sharp boundary, but there is not much of a boundary at all." What good would it do to state flatly that *In Cold Blood* will or will not be taught in a few years? A more honest and more helpful version of that frustrating question is, what is valuable about Capote's book? Put another way, to make the connection between the two versions clearer, upon what grounds could one argue that *In Cold Blood* deserves literary status? Looking at the issue this way foregrounds the reader's role in the fluid (especially for contemporary works) question of literary status, without, I hope, taking the responsibility for that status out of the author's hands entirely. (pp. 484-87)

Eric Heyne, "Toward a Theory of Literary Nonfiction," in Modern Fiction Studies, *Vol. 33, No. 3, Autumn, 1987, pp. 479-90.*

Cyrus Colter

1910-

American novelist and short story writer.

Colter writes traditional stories featuring black characters from all social classes. Critics praise his work concerning the middle-class as an important complement to the canon of African-American literature. Colter's fiction is known for its gentle, bleak irony and deterministic position, which traps his characters in the repercussions of their past actions and denies them the power to change the course of their lives. Critics note that Colter's naturalistic settings and dialogue portray this powerlessness as a facet of the human condition rather than of racial discrimination. An attorney by profession, Colter began writing fiction at the age of fifty, inspired by his reading of such Russian masters as Fedor Dostoevski, Leo Tolstoy, and particularly Anton Chekhov, with whom he is often compared for his keen psychological observation and pessimistic viewpoint. Dudley Randall commented: "Colter illuminates familiar things and people . . . and makes you aware of the tragedy, the pathos, and the irony in the life around us."

Colter's first collection of short fiction, *The Beach Umbrella* (1970), was warmly reviewed for its rich variety of characterization. In such stories as "A Chance Meeting," "Black for Dinner," and "Overnight Trip," Colter employs a restrained and doleful irony that demonstrates the power of destiny over the lives of his characters. As in much of Colter's fiction, the protagonist of "The Beach Umbrella" becomes aware of the bleakness of his destiny and must accept the futility of seeking out relationships to diminish or alter that state. In other stories, awareness of sexual desire intensifies feelings of aloneness, and in such pieces as "A Man in the House" and "After the Ball," Colter portrays characters who experience desires society deems unnatural or immoral.

Colter's first novel, *The Rivers of Eros* (1972), focuses on the far-reaching implications of a sexual indiscretion. Clotilda Pilgrim, a morally respectable poor woman, is haunted by the affair she had with her brother-in-law thirty-five years earlier. Granted custody of her grandchildren after the violent death of their mother, Clotilda becomes obsessed by her granddaughter Addie's sexual awakening and subsequent affair with a married man, and is finally driven to murder Addie to prevent her from further transgressions. Colter substantiates Clotilda's conviction regarding the impact of the past on the present in a sub-plot that rejects both separatism and assimilation as viable solutions to racism in the United States. John O'Brien explained: "Colter is interested in the extent to which the history of the black man in America is a myth from which blacks cannot escape."

Colter's next novel, *The Hippodrome* (1973), is a surrealistic nightmare in which a religious man, attempting to escape the law, is forced into a slave-like existence in a Chicago brothel, performing sexual acts with other blacks for a white clientele. *The Hippodrome* received mixed reviews that questioned the originality and depth of its allegorical statement, although some commended the novel's suspenseful plot. *Night Studies* (1979), like Colter's earlier fiction, concerns the ways in

which the events of the past affect or determine the present. An ambitious novel in terms of length and complexity, *Night Studies* explores the range of African-American experience from the eighteenth century to the present through John Calvin Knight's meditations on his ancestry and present circumstances. Anthony K. Grosch remarked: "If I were to choose one word to describe the essence of Colter's edifying novel, that word would be *nobility*. Because he has so deeply touched 'the mystery of Blackness,' people of all races can know something of it through *Night Studies*."

Colter's second collection of short fiction, *The Amoralists and Other Tales* (1988), contains stories collected in *The Beach Umbrella* along with four new pieces. Critics applauded Colter's use of dialogue, action, and gesture to portray primarily non-introspective characters. Bert Atkinson added: "[Colter] shows an acute insight into human behavior and uses all of his senses to the fullest: he gives us memorable characters with authentic voices." Colter's most recent novel, *A Chocolate Soldier* (1988), takes perception of character as its theme. The narrator of this psychological drama is a childhood friend of the protagonist, whose zeal in pursuing his mission in life is variously perceived by others as inspired or insane.

(See also *Contemporary Authors,* Vols. 65-68; *Contemporary*

Authors New Revision Series, Vol. 10; and *Dictionary of Literary Biography,* Vol. 33.)

JOSEPHINE HENDIN

Cyrus Colter, who began to write ten years ago at the age of fifty, makes brilliant fiction out of uptightness, exploring the disease with the awareness and precision of a first-rate clinician. *The Beach Umbrella* is a remarkable collection of stories about the isolation and emptiness of the lower-middle-class black, and of those who rise to wealth and social prominence only to find the same despair at the very center of themselves. Whether his characters are rich or poor, lusting after expensive clothes or unattainable women, all are crushed by a sense that some vital force is missing from their lives. And this consciousness of loss most affects those industrious family men for whom life is an endless series of obligations.

Elijah in ["The Beach Umbrella"] is a white-collar worker who is ridiculed by his wife for not taking a more lucrative factory job. The more she complains, the more he yearns for his Saturdays on a beach at the edge of Lake Michigan, where he finds "life": those laughing, joking people whom he observes from afar seem to contain all the world's mirth under their beach umbrellas. Chased away from their parties, Elijah takes money from his hard-working twelve-year-old son to buy a beach umbrella of his own, and the day a group gathers around his umbrella he comes as close as he can to joy.

Colter powerfully conveys the fervor of Elijah's longing, and the force with which his emotional tightness strangles his single day of fulfillment. This is a fine and tragic tale of how deadening are the ways of decency, and how hard it is to ward off gloom.

> *Josephine Hendin, in a review of "The Beach Umbrella," in* Saturday Review, *Vol. 53, August 22, 1970, p.55.*

JERRY H. BRYANT

One school of black and white literary critics has for a long time urged black writers to write about blacks as people rather than as blacks. What they mean by that is illustrated by [*The Rivers of Eros* by] Cyrus Colter. His characters are black. It is important that they're black. But their blackness does not raise issues restricted to politics or sociology.

Colter has a passion for the interior lives of ordinary, unnoticed people. He doesn't psychoanalyze them, or have them engage in long and self-revealing interior monologues. His characters are too inarticulate for that, or else shy and unsophisticated. They find it hard to admit the truth to themselves, much less to anyone else. So we see their inner turmoil mainly in their outward behavior, and at this Colter seems to be a natural master. There is no straining after glib psychological explanations, no reducing the purity of the individual's agony to theoretical causes.

The world of this novel is a narrow one. The experiences of its characters are related to no national or international currents of fashion. Mrs. Clotilda Pilgrim runs a rooming house. She supports her two grandchildren, Addie and Lester. The

16-year-old Addie brings her grief by taking up with the 28-year-old Dunreith Smith, who is wild and married. Gradually, Clotilda goes insane. Addie's misdoings are only the occasion of her derangement. Her simple mind deteriorates under the pressure of a life that has thwarted and cramped its natural liveliness and spontaneity. In flashbacks we see Clotilda's ill-conceived marriage to the plodding, uninteresting Eugene; her affair with her sister's husband Chester by whom she conceives her only child, Ruby; and Ruby's painful marriage to the philandering Zack, which ends in her death.

There is violence here, and sex and guilt. But Colter doesn't subscribe to the literary commonplaces of either the market or the intellectual establishment. He consistently underplays his potentially sensational themes. In *The Rivers of Eros,* it is life itself, unexplained and unexplainable, that strikes the reader with such force. And this is all carried through with the economy of drama—a single flashback and a whole pattern of feeling is conveyed; a few lines of dialogue and a minor character is vividly illuminated. When we first meet Dunreith Smith, after only hearing about him for more than half the book, we get a nearly perfect paragraph capturing his contradictory character:

> Dunreith was a garish wreck. Bareheaded, his bushy mustache now somehow drooping, he wore a gaudy dashiki and really looked insane. The still-inflamed stitches over his left eye were a lurid red against his olive complexion as he squinted at Hammer and suddenly roared a laugh—"Prof!" He put out his damp, limp hand. "You don't know me, but I know *you.*" He wilted in another gravelly laugh. "You made that dogass speech the other night! Right?—*Hey!*" His eyes were wild one moment, glazed the next, as Hammer took the limber hand. "Hey! Yeah, the Professor!"
>
> (p. 727)

[Colter's] style is neither exceptionally graceful nor notably clumsy. A sentence of his may call our attention to itself. We think, the image isn't right. No, that isn't the problem. We think, there is strain here, a reaching for effect. No, not that either. We think, that sentence is O.K. We move on. We become more and more confident that we're in capable hands. It's just that they aren't hands we're *used* to. When we read a book like this, we realize that even though novels are written by people as different as, say, James Baldwin and Saul Bellow, James Joyce and John A. Williams, Henry James and Flannery O'Connor, there is a kind of novelistic language. We recognize it, and feel comfortable with its familiar cadences and rhythms.

Infrequently, a true innocent comes along, one who reads in that language but has not adopted it as his own. Cyrus Colter is like that, altogether the creator of his own language. He is to the contemporary world of educated readers what the teller of folk tales was to his communal auditors. That is, he has no *technique.* His contrivances are all innocently transparent, left uncovered with a childlike trust in the reader's honesty and interest in the life the words describe. This is an unusual book, a kind of folk tale told by a man sophisticated about life but not about the literary process. It is a novel of truly rare parts.

Those parts, when catalogued, seem commonplace and stereotyped. Old Ambrose Hammer, a widower, is successfully pursued by Miss Letitia Dorsey, rail-skinny spinster tenant of Mrs. Pilgrim's rooming house, who woos Ambrose with "brilliant" smiles and girlish ways. Middle-aged Titus Neeley, another roomer, still mourns his long-dead mother. Addie tries to commit suicide when Dunreith tells her they must break up. Clotilda worries about her grandchildren growing up respectable. But in Colter's hands this is not a commonplace world. Even such a sentimental stroke as having Ambrose quote, when pushed, Gray's line about "some mute, inglorious Milton" becomes enormously moving.

Colter's prize-winning short stories, collected in **The Beach Umbrella** (1970), have been compared with the work of some of his favorite continental writers. But such comparisons do little to convey the essence of this novel. It is completely its own. Don't expect glitter, or to be compelled and fascinated by every page. The novel is quiet, sometimes even monotonous. But we're carried along by Colter's own calm certainty that what he is writing about is important. And there are two scenes of violence that blast the reader with the unexpectedness and power of a hidden bomb. This I think makes for the peculiar quality of the book—its occasional unapologetic monotony and the relationship of that monotony to several scenes that stop the heart. This novel is one that I would recommend unreservedly. It deserves literary prizes, though it may be too good to win them. (pp. 727-28)

> *Jerry H. Bryant, "Without Benefit of Technique," in* The Nation, *New York, Vol. 214, No. 23, June 5, 1972, pp. 727-28.*

WALTERENE SWANSTON

In the autobiographical novel, white America has discovered some of its best pictures of how black America lives. Claude Brown, Maya Angelou, Ralph Ellison, and others have told of their black brothers and sisters in Harlem and elsewhere with the kind of insight that enriches everyone.

Cyrus Colter's **Rivers of Eros** is *not* an autobiographical novel, and that's too bad; if it were, Colter could have added a new dimension to this store of understanding of the black experience. . . . Instead he wrote about a stereotyped black woman—an aging big mama of the matriarchal black world. A well-to-do, establishment, black male, Colter wrote about a poor, black woman. The result is an inconsequential novel consisting of thinly drawn characters that provides little insight into the black American experience.

Not that every novel by a black person must provide insight, of course. Black novelists and film makers and playwrights do, and should, turn out pure fun, escapist fare. But **The Rivers of Eros** clearly didn't intend to be that: it intended to be a serious examination of the "inward struggle" of a black woman "at the complex and illusive place where culture and personal identity meet."

The book centers on Clotilda Pilgrim, apparently a strong, self-reliant woman who has taken her tragedies in stride and makes the best of supporting herself and two grandchildren in Chicago's black ghetto. In reality, Clotilda is haunted and eventually destroyed by a secret guilt that she has kept locked within herself for 35 years.

In the summer of 1935, Clotilda and her husband move from Kentucky to Chicago so they can be near her only sister. Once there, Clotilda has a one-time sexual encounter with her sister's husband and bears a child as a result. She never reveals that her husband is not the father of the child, and her

secret haunts and torments her. The child grows up and marries; when she is murdered by her husband, Clotilda takes in her two children. . . .

Colter writes of the destruction of these three generations in such cold, blunt language and with such dispassion that it is difficult to know the characters well or to care what happens to them. They remain little beyond stereotypes, and their dialog rings false. ("Oh, Tish! You got taste, girl. Wow. My, ain't you fancy.") The language of the ghetto is rich in expletives for an enormous range of emotions, yet Colter rarely deploys them.

If Colter were young, his book's weaknesses could be overlooked. But he is 62, with a perspective on being black that no young writer can bring to a novel. And thus his failure is doubly disappointing.

> *Walterene Swanston, "If Colter Were Younger . . . But He Isn't," in* The National Observer, *July 8, 1972, p. 21.*

PUBLISHERS WEEKLY

[In **The Hippodrome**] Yeager, a black writer of religious articles, has just murdered his wife and her white lover. On the run, exhausted, numbed by his bloody act, he stumbles towards refuge: Bea takes him to her place. . . . Bea's place is a pornographic theater (the hippodrome), where a handful of blacks perform sexually for a white clientele. Yeager is to replace an absent trooper. Prisoner of his own violence as well as of Bea's enforced degradation, the fugitive fears, despairs, comes to see the facts of his own dehumanization. What happens is totally involving, surprising, shocking. Colter, a distinguished criminal lawyer, shades the depths of his characters with such skill, creates a world of such immediacy, suspends the reader so unbearably that one lives the hippodrome with him. Out of the inferno comes humanity. A mature talent that bears watching, Colter published his first novel (**The Rivers of Eros**) at 62. This new one merits serious literary attention.

> *A review of "The Hippodrome," in* Publishers Weekly, *Vol. 203, March 5, 1973, p. 73.*

JOHN S. PHILLIPSON

Two centuries ago the Gothic novel stirred the hearts of readers with its suggested or depicted horrors, its sinister and sometimes supernatural (or seemingly supernatural) goings on. In [**The Hippodrome**], Cyrus Colter has given us a modern Gothic tale that we may or may not be willing to accept. I wasn't.

Briefly, we have here an account of one Jackson Yeager, a black, who murders both his wife and his wife's white employer in a hotel room, then takes off with his wife's severed head done up in paper. A chance meeting with two women in a restaurant takes him to a house where orgiastic rites are performed thrice weekly for the pleasure of a paying audience in a circular amphitheater.

As in Anne Radcliffe's *Mysteries of Udolpho*, the horrifying rites are never portrayed explicitly; we are left to imagine them. At the end, we are to suppose that Yeager (alias Willie Carter), who is basically a good guy, finds happiness and peace once more as he flees from the house with a female inmate, whose change of heart is never quite explained. Presumably she just felt pity for poor old Jackson-Willie and was tired of the whole setup. The jacket of this book quotes enthusiastic approval of Mr. Colter's first novel, *The Rivers of Eros,* and the *Saturday Review* is even cited as declaring, "This powerful writer should win the attention of every serious reader of fiction." I have not read the first novel, but I feel its encomiums inapplicable to this second one. Mr. Colter . . . apparently considers himself a writer of serious fiction. Unfortunately, *The Hippodrome,* an excursion into twentieth-century Gothic, just doesn't fit into this category.

John S. Phillipson, in a review of "The Hippodrome," in Best Sellers, *Vol. 33, No. 5, June 1, 1973, p. 102.*

JOHN O'BRIEN

If one had to speculate on the kind of black writer who would go unrecognized in the 1970's, Cyrus Colter would possess all the requirements. Unlike some of his young contemporaries, Colter has struck no new formal experimental paths in his fiction. His closest literary relatives are Nathaniel Hawthorne and Anton Chekhov. The writers he most admires are Melville, Dostoevsky, and Joyce. And despite the fact that the characters in his stories are black, Colter has a singular disinterest in polarizing the so-called "black experience" as the subject of his fiction. Almost ignoring social and political themes, he turned his fiction towards the perennial philosophical problems he finds in thinkers as disparate as Hobbes, Camus, and B. F. Skinner. And unlike his younger contemporaries who came to their writing after a few frustrating years in a university or the New York publishing world, Colter began writing in his fifties after a successful life in Chicago law and politics. . . . In spite of his unusual journey, Colter has arrived. With his prize winning collection of short stories, *The Beach Umbrella,* plus his recently published first novel, *The Rivers of Eros,* and two others nearing completion, Colter has announced himself as one of the most serious literary figures to emerge from the 1960's.

As one of Colter's characters stands on Chicago's 32nd Avenue Beach and looks out at the confusing maze of bathers, he asks, "Could you any longer call that a *race* of people?" The question suggests many of Colter's pervasive themes. Elijah stands before this fragmented crowd wondering what is necessary to unite them, to personalize their haphazard and accidental gathering, to break down the isolation he feels so intensely. But all Colter characters discover that attempts at such union end in futility. Alienation is a fact of human existence, and the modern world in its technological efficiency constantly reminds man of this. It is, however, not the modern world which has caused this condition. Environment and personality have always determined man to a life of unfulfilled expectation and frustrated ideals. Overshadowing the pessimism of such a fate is the sense of how absurd and pointless are all these human efforts at achieving some meaning; how painfully obvious it is to the reader that were these characters able to escape their mechanized and controlling pasts, they still would be faced with a universe that held no meanings and offered no home.

It is because of this sense of the underlying meaningless of their lives that his characters are pushed into creating the illusions with which they try to sustain themselves. And, for a time, they are able to live under those illusions. The illusions take the form of sexual fantasies, romantic idealizations, self-imposed martyrdoms, spiritual reform or social status. They are invented by characters of all ages and social standing. Inevitably each must awaken to the unreality of his aspirations and the hopelessness of his situation. Without relief Colter shows them discover that the premises they have built their lives on are false, and then implies the disillusionment with which they must live out the rest of their uneventful lives. A part of their tragedy is that they are "innocents," acted upon by forces inside and outside themselves that prevent them from achieving their rather meagre dreams. They carry within themselves certain unarticulated expectations of what life must yield them; yet, as becomes clear, even those expectations are less chosen than imposed by internal forces that they have had no part in creating. Oftentimes their conditions are the result of traumatic past events which, once having occurred, cannot be undone. In **"Moot"** Matthew was betrayed early in his marriage by an unfaithful wife. The discovery leaves him "an empty shell" so that years later when his only son is killed in war, Matthew was "callous and uncaring." Scarred by this one attempt at human love, he steals a dog and tries to develop with it the kind of relationship that is denied him with people. But the relationship, in accordance with the pattern that has already been determined for Matthew, is one of torment. His real reason for stealing the dog is to save himself from "boredom and loneliness." Deprived of the dog's company, he would be alone in facing a universe that is threatening and alien to him. When the dog finally dies, Matthew tries developing a relationship with the objects in his room, but even his television stops working. A short time later he dies of "a kind of ennui." In their professional indifference, the workmen who clean out his room and prepare it for the next tenant, judge all its contents "absolutely worthless."

But past event is only one form of determinism that is at work in Colter's fiction. In **"A Man in the House,"** Verna is an eighteen year old who has come to stay with her aunt and uncle in Chicago for the summer. Without preparation she is catapulted out of the innocence of her childhood and into a world of sexual passion and guilt. Unable to distinguish between natural desire and her sense of what is right, she ends the story by stripping naked and fantasizing that she is a whore. Although no outward affection has been expressed between her and her uncle, she is convinced that she is guilty for the sexual attraction that appears to be mutual. In Colter love only becomes the ground on which is built more barriers between human beings. At eighteen she "felt *her* dreams were in the past already." . . . In **"Girl Friend"** the sexual encounter between two quickly aging people, one a widower and the other a wife of an invalid, leads them to discover how emotionally sterile their lives have been and will be: " 'We're twins like that, we haven't felt, we haven't lived.' " She wearily submits to going home with him again as "an old terror gripped her heart." The sexual, which for a time seems to hold out hope for Colter's characters of overcoming their deep sense of alienation, becomes a kind of metaphor for the emptiness and lovelessness they cannot escape from. (pp. 24-5)

The most painful expression of Colter's determinism appears in **"The Beach Umbrella."** Elijah is in search of love and is relatively free to experience it if the world outside has it to offer. His quest leads him to purchase a beach umbrella because they seem to attract crowds on the beach. Though the day he plans his last desperate attempt at finding love is cold and overcast, he is unwilling to yield to what promises to be another uneventful day and he plants his umbrella on a nearly deserted beach. Eventually a middle-aged woman with her two children and a few young girls arrive. Elijah begins his noble efforts at establishing a community with them. And, of course, the sacramental union he seeks is met with suspicion by the mother and indifferent and mocking gestures by the girls. When one girl goes for a swim with him, Elijah is elated in his frantic desire to make the day equal to his imagination. But the group soon breaks up and Elijah realizes that he must face the world away from the beach. When he tries to sell the umbrella to repay his son who lent him the money for it, the lifeguard shouts at him to " 'get the hell outa here! An' I mean it! *You thievin' bastard, you!* " He returns to his car knowing that he must now, as his wife has nagged him to do, go to work in the steel mills of Gary.

In another age Elijah's simple faith in the possibility of love might have resulted in sainthood. In this age he's a dupe of commercialism. His best efforts at breaking down his anguished isolation only result in a banal day with swimmers on a Chicago beach, who neither desire or need the love that he wants to share. Instead of becoming a breakwater against the spiritual isolation of the outside world, the day turns into a nightmare where even his dreams cannot endure. In this dark and growing awareness, Elijah perfectly reflects the hopelessness that colors the Colter world, where hope is illusion and love is dream.

The Rivers of Eros afforded Colter the breadth in which to explore many of these same themes on a greater scale, by providing the opportunity to consider how history works together with personality and environment to determine man. Although he does not write within the myth, Colter is here interested in the extent to which the history of the black man in America is a myth from which blacks cannot escape. Overtly, the novel concentrates on the destruction of Clotilda Pilgrim as she is driven insane by guilt. Once again the guilt is directly related to sexual experience. As a young woman she had relations with her sister's husband and bore his child. This sinful act set into motion a chain of tragic events which, in her mind, is about to climax thirty-five years later. The first victim was the illegitimate daughter herself who, years later, was senselessly murdered by her husband. The second victim is Clotilda's sixteen year old granddaughter, Addie, who witnessed the murder. Clotilda accidentally finds a box of contraceptives in Addie's dresser and senses that the whole tragic past, begun by her own sexual transgression, is repeating itself. The rest of the novel, as it relates to Clotilda, is about her growing madness amid her attempts to prevent Addie's moral downfall. Her efforts culminate in suffocating Addie and nearly decapitating her. The novel ends just after she has been committed to a state mental asylum.

Colter parallels Clotilda's fated action with that of the history of the black man in America. As with the characters in his short stories, Clotilda cannot avoid what has been determined for her. Seemingly, all these events would have been prevented had she not committed that one act. But it is just Colter's point that, given Clotilda's unhappy marriage and her instinctive romantic conception of life, there was no way that she could not have committed that act. And for the rest of her life she must live in the fatal knowledge that she is responsible for all the evil that results: "Addie . . . Addie. A mere child—not yet seventeen. Gone to the devil in hell already. Could it be that one life, one sad, sinful life, hers, Clo-

tilda's own, had brought on all this misery. . . . Her mind was fogged now with murky riddles, disorder—guilt." Her private tragedy suggests the nature and development of America's racial tragedy. One of the roomers in Clotilda's house is a retired post office worker who is compiling a momentous volume entitled "History of the Negro Race." He tries to prove that the black man in this country has played a vital role in its military struggles and has made a glorious but unrecognized contribution to America's military history. Ambrose Hammer hopes that his book will persuade Americans that, contrary to the way American history has portrayed him, the Negro has served his country with honor and distinction. Hammer believes that by awakening Americans to this fact, they will no longer consider blacks a burden on the country and will accept the truth of their history.

Hammer's work, however, is doomed from the start. His tenacious and industrious devotion is unequal to his lack of education which prevents the book, as he later discovers, from having any scholarly value. One of the other roomers continually chides him for his blatant inaccuracies. Further, his work is made ludicrous because of its naive notions of racism. It assumes that racism arises from a simple misunderstanding about what the black man has contributed to his country. In other words, he tries to treat a problem which is essentially irrational by presenting what he hopes will be indisputable rational proof that white people have made an innocent mistake. What Hammer is trying to accomplish is unacceptable or misunderstood even by other blacks in the novel. When he reads a selection from his manuscript to the Sons of Ezra Lodge, most of what he reads appears to be over the heads of the few people who come to hear him speak. The two who do understand heckle and call him an "Uncle Tom." They argue with Hammer that there is no reason the black man should want to be recognized and accepted by white America. The only way of changing the racial climate in America is through violence and separatism. Colter succeeds in making both attitudes equally foolish because each believes that there is some possibility for change. And, of course, there is none. The past utterly determines the nature of the future. Once the myth of blackness was created there was no way, either peacefully or violently, lawfully or through revolution, that it could be altered. Just as Clotilda has had no choice in what was fated for her, the black man can not change his historically determined role as slave. Once decided, there was no way of reversing it. Ironically, Hammer, in effect, proves that once the myth is established, despite the fact that it is based on a lie, it must be fulfilled. His work only demonstrates that racism has persisted even though there has been nothing in the black man's history to warrant it.

In typical Colter fashion, the ending dispels any possibility of hope. Hammer, Clotilda's grandson, and Hammer's middle-aged bride are returning in the rain from visiting Clotilda at the asylum. His wife tries to dissuade him from working on his book that night, dotes upon him, and makes simple-minded remarks about the rain. He pulls his hand away from hers and "withdrew into himself again." Rather than reducing the sense of alienation, such intimacy with another human being only serves to remind Colter's characters of their unbridgeable separation and how short-lived their hopes for love are. In the closing lines of the book Hammer knows that "Now the riddle would never be solved." The riddle is both Clotilda's fate, which she has never revealed to anyone, and the black man's fate in America, which remains just as inscrutable to Hammer as it ever had.

The gloom that pervades all of Colter's fiction does not result solely from the fact that his people are so utterly manipulated by accident, time, and personality. Such determinism is made terrifying because the reader also perceives something which is hidden from, or only dimly suspected by the characters themselves. One sees that even were they more free, were they more able to understand and control things in the realm of their own lives, still some fatal misfortune overshadows all their efforts. Their lives are negated and made ridiculous, not simply because they are without freedom of any kind, but because life itself is without meaning. The characters are striving for meaning which must elude them as individuals just as it eludes man collectively. As his characters muddle through life with meagre expectations of what lies ahead, whether it be love or the hope of self-reform, the reader knows that they are being innocently lured to their doom. They are lost and determined in a world that is absurd. (pp. 26-8)

> *John O'Brien, "Forms of Determinism in the Fiction of Cyrus Colter," in* Studies in Black Literature, *Vol. 4, No. 2, Summer, 1973, pp. 24-8.*

EILEEN KENNEDY

[*Night Studies*] is an old-fashioned slice-of-life novel, like Zola's *L'Assommoir* on a contempory theme: the various shades of black identity in American life, from the black bourgeoisie to the downtrodden and dispossessed. In examining the roots of his cast of characters, the author has gone back into history to make their present condition comprehensible. For instance, there are long, detailed sections on the blacks in Africa, their kidnapping by slave traders, and the nightmare voyages endured, even before they emerged into the nightmare of American slavery. There are also large chunks on life as an ex-slave exposed to the brutality and hatred of Ku Klux Klansmen riding through rural Georgia in the dead of night.

This panoramic novel searches the past to shed light on the lives of its characters. They are John Calvin Knight, messianic leader in the struggle for black power who is loved by the partly black (though initially she is unaware of it) Griselda, moody temptress, disturbed and disturbing, who pursues Knight wildly and threatens the black organization he is effectively building. Knight becomes involved with Mary Dee, daughter of an affluent black surgeon, when she returns to Chicago from her art studies in Paris. In France she had had a passionate but ultimately unfulfilled love for the white son of a Philadelphia Main Liner. Despite her mother's disapproval, she is drawn to Knight by her idealism and her guilt about feeling more white than black. Around these three characters stretches a near-infinite array of minor characters whose stories are closely intertwined with the major ones but who are also used to portray various aspects of black life in the present and past (hence, the large segments of eighteenth and nineteenth century history).

The story is too epic in scope, too rich in sub-plots, and too wide-ranging in design to summarize succinctly. The author's intention is admirable, his achievement considerable though uneven. His ending—and, presumably, his conclusions about the black struggle—is equivocal. One sympathizes often with the characters, even the less admirable ones because they grow in strength; certain incidents are done with verve, skill, pace, and suspense; others seem contrived and wooden. This overlong novel is worth reading, but it is not equal, let's say, to *Invisible Man,* in its portrayal and assessment of the black experience.

> *Eileen Kennedy, in a review of "Night Studies," in* Best Sellers, *Vol. 40, No. 2, May, 1980, p. 46.*

ANTHONY R. GROSCH

[In *Night Studies*] Colter aspires to do nothing less than to penetrate the essence of existence for black Americans. But the essence of Blackness will forever remain a mystery beyond man's powers. For Blackness is an abstract word expressing a common element in the manifold lives of millions in the present and of millions upon millions who lived, worked, rejoiced, suffered, and died in the past. It is given to any of us to know but little of the immensity of all this. Yet just as man from his beginnings has sung in story and poem from the depths of his soul, Colter speaks profoundly of his vast and grave subject.

Embracing this enormous subject, Colter must portray both its breadth, suggesting the variety of current black experience and attitude, and its depth, suggesting the principal historical aspects of its development. *Night Studies* achieves this, but not flawlessly. A lesser flaw is Colter's occasional lapse from admirable diction into expressions such as "highlight," "maximize," "role model," "prodigious feats," and "veritable maelstrom." A greater flaw is a touch of melodrama in character and plot. A beautiful white woman falls in love with a handsome black man, a race leader. A beautiful black woman falls in love with a handsome white man, a wealthy blue blood. To preserve his leadership, the black man rejects the white woman, who leaps off the Golden Gate Bridge. To preserve his status, the white man rejects the black woman and marries one of his own kind. Knowing that he has betrayed himself, the white man drinks heavily and dies in a car accident. The black man falls in love with the black woman. She rejects him to study art, and he withdraws from leadership into study and contemplation. The intentions are obvious.

Yet Colter transcends melodrama because through his characters he truthfully renders life in its complexity. Set in the early 1970's, the novel traces the development of John Calvin Knight's Black Peoples Congress, a national organization advocating xenophobic passion toward the white world. The relationship of various characters—ghetto dwellers, workers, professionals, intellectuals—to this organization shows the range of black adjustment—from separation through assimilation—to life in America. The early parts of the story are set in San Francisco and Paris. The Parisian scenes, eloquently described, are lovely and symbolize an interracial Eden without Blackness. The remaining contemporary scenes, except for occasional short passages, shift to Chicago, where no one escapes Blackness. Colter's narrative of his own city shows the keenness of long observation. There is, for example, an intense scene in a ghetto restaurant during which a black policeman, because of strength, experience, and compassion for his people, averts violence. Embodying practical wisdom, the policeman represents Colter's implied belief that the progress of black people greatly depends upon those who do the humble work of the world. (pp. 398-99)

On three lengthy occasions the past interrupts the present to tell of Knight's progenitors during crucial stages of American history. The first, set in the late eighteenth century, depicts the capture and enslavement of Knight's African ancestor. A harrowing account of the middle passage includes a slave revolt that is probably without equal in American fiction since Melville's "Benito Cereno." The second shows the plight of the former slaves during Reconstruction, when the Klan chases Knight's forebears across Georgia. The third recalls the Red Summer of 1919, when Knight's cousin is lynched in Ohio. These episodes represent the terrible history of injustice that forms so indelible a part of Blackness. The linked past and present unquestionably constitute an epic about the meaning of Blackness.

In all of his writing, Colter has evinced great faith in the mind's capacity for truth and in the soul's capacity for virtue. By the end of the novel John Calvin Knight's experiences have led him to reject as simple and superficial his organization's rhetoric and ideology. He then begins a deep study of self and history in an attempt to understand the true significance of Blackness. Knight's final position suggests Colter's threefold theme: the meaning of Blackness is subtle and complex and requires much study and thought; every black person has the right to decide how to address the issue of Blackness; and, although it must be considered in relationships between the races, Blackness in some way unites rather than divides humanity.

If I were to choose one word to describe the essence of Colter's edifying novel, that word would be *nobility.* Because he has so deeply touched "the mystery of Blackness," people of all races can know something of it through **Night Studies.** (pp. 399-400)

> Anthony R. Grosch, in a review of "Night Studies," in The Old Northwest, Vol. 6, No. 4, Winter, 1980-81, pp. 398-400.

ROBERT M. BENDER

Justly celebrated for his short stories, fourteen of which were brought together in **The Beach Umbrella** (1970), winner of the first Iowa School of Letters Award for Short Fiction, Colter began his writing career with a clear sense of purpose. As is well known from a number of interviews, Colter did not start writing fiction until he was fifty. Struck by the range of characterization in the great 19th century Russian writers—Turgenev, Gogol, Dostoevsky and Chekhov—Colter determined to see what he could do to depict the range of black experience in America.

Collectively, the stories published in **The Beach Umbrella** provide us with a glimpse of every level of black life. They are very much in the manner of Chekhov. Ordinary people pursue their lives, go about earning their living, dream of happiness and success, while everything is about to tumble around them. At one end of the social spectrum, Dave Hill, a wealthy Chicago real estate broker, in **"Black for Dinner,"** participates in the empty social life of the "posh Hyde Park-Kenwood black community," so dear to his wife of thirty years upon whom he dotes. Despite Dave's request that she wear something "gay," Anita insists on putting on a new black dress for a dinner party she has assembled. The party is a great success but Dave is preoccupied and Anita thinks it's the dress. After the guests have gone, she tearfully cuts the dress to shreds and promises, "I'll never wear black again, honey," hardly guessing what we know, the opinion of a "hell

of a cardiologist," as one of the dinner guests thinks of his colleague Dr. Cartwright, "that a man with Dave's clogged aorta was a walking miracle."

At the other end of the social ladder, in **"An Untold Story,"** Lonnie pathetically tries to tell the story of *Hamlet* to the men assembled at a murky bar, and only ends in providing the provocation for one man to murder another. (pp. 93-4)

In between, there are all manner of people, men and women, of whom Colter tells a moving story. The stories are filled with humor, but there is always a sense of tragedy which hangs over these characters. Indeed, the viewpoint of this fiction is that of naturalism, akin to the Russian masters Colter so much admires. Colter has sometimes been criticized for being an old-fashioned writer. Fashions, of course, change. In his short fiction, Colter is a superb story teller, always in control of his material. Nor is he an overbearing moralist; the stories are permitted to tell themselves. What he tells us about one character or another, however, always says something about general human nature.

Having set himself the task of portraying the entire range of black culture, concentrating largely on the neglected middle class, and having succeeded so well in his short stories, it was inevitable that Colter turn to the novel to allow himself greater scope. By comparison with the short stories, however, the first two novels, **The Rivers of Eros** (1972) and **The Hippodrome** [1973] are somewhat limited. Both are quite short, both display the same tautness of the shorter fiction, both are carefully crafted. Good as these two novels are, they both are rather tentative, revealing a writer in search of something larger.

In **The Rivers of Eros,** Colter sets out to tell the story of Clotilda Pilgrim, a sixty year old woman, trying to raise her two grandchildren to a life of respectability. The children live with her on the first floor of a well tended house, in which Clotilda ekes out a living through her sewing. To supplement her earnings, she lets out the upstairs rooms, rationalizing that her tenants "were the kind of people, if she must have roomers, she was proud to have—'educated' people." The boy, Lester, at eleven, devoted to his "Grammaw," finds a fairly easy time of it; Adeline, at sixteen, coming to full sexual awareness, having to sleep in the same bed with her grandmother, finds the would-be genteel atmosphere of the home stifling. It is with Addie that the problems begin for Clotilda.

Her respectability is based on the suppression of what her past life has been. Addie's sexuality reminds her of her own contact with "eros." At twenty-five, childless, she had moved with her husband, seventeen years older than Clotilda, from Paducah, Kentucky to Chicago, where her younger sister Pearlie had gone years before as the maid for a white family. Clotilda eventually has a child by her sporting brother-in-law, Chester Jackson. Disappointingly, her daughter, Ruby, marries at nineteen, but Clotilda makes the best of it and dotes upon her two grandchildren. When Ruby is brutally murdered by her husband in a fit of sexual jealousy, in front of the young Addie, Clotilda relives her own sin. Ultimately, she finds herself unable to control Addie. Clotilda, feeling that "one life, one sad, sinful life, hers, Clotilda's own, had brought on all this misery," grows more and more deranged, and ends by brutally suffocating her granddaughter with a plastic bag. The fact that Addie has at last seen the error of her ways and has resolved to reform only adds to the irony of the story.

There is, in this domestic tale, the sense of tragedy one finds in the Greek dramatists, or in the plays of Ibsen and O'Neill, but Colter provides another context for his story. One of Clotilda's roomers is Ambrose Hammer, a Post Office clerk who has retired early to spend his days deep in study, at the public library, or in his room in Clotilda's house. He is obsessed with his "History of the Negro Race," a litany of the unsung black heroes of American history. He is asked to make a speech at the Sons of Ezra lodge and for his title chooses, "The Need for Greater Emphasis on the Contribution of the Black Man to the Early Struggle for American Independence." The speech, of course, is a fiasco. Dunreith Smith, a married man who is Addie's lover, and his friend, a young militant, James Potts, who has assumed the name Alexis, are in the audience, avoiding the police, and they sneer at Hammer, crying out, "Where'd they *get* this God-damn white folks' nigger, man?"

Clotilda's story, then, takes on a clearer meaning in the context of the conflict of the moderate views of Hammer and the militant position represented by Dunreith and Alexis. And Colter refuses to take sides. Hammer is a bumbler; Dunreith is involved with drugs and alcohol, and when he finally comes to understand why he must give up Addie, the decision comes too late and only compounds the girl's despair. Clotilda's story is seen as part of a larger conflict, one which will not easily be resolved. (pp. 94-6)

The stories and this first novel not only provide a view of the black middle class, they present a strong sense of place. Chicago is the setting. Colter not only chronicles a people, but details the place they live. One of the great strengths of his fiction is precisely this precision of place. Just as the stories are so well crafted, careful attention is paid to physical locale. This sense of place is missing in *The Hippodrome,* which is something of a departure for Colter. It is more experimental than his other writing, and, indeed, has the surreal cast of nightmare. The action seems to take place in a fairly small city which is perhaps somewhere between but clearly is *not* St. Louis or Chicago. Like *The Rivers of Eros* it is the story of characters who cannot run from their past.

Colter is less concerned here with his usual themes. Though his characters are primarily black, we are not so much concerned with their race as with the metaphorical sense of the blackness of all human experience, as in the writing of Melville or Hawthorne. The characters, moreover, all appear as grotesques. Jackson Yeager, dazed and bloody, the man in flight to nowhere, carries a strange package under his arm. Meeting with Bea and Darlene, apparently a madam and a whore, he is forced to reveal the package's contents. It holds the severed head of "a yellow, flat-nosed, youngish woman," Yeager's wife. We quickly learn that Yeager has worked on the staff of the "Black Christian Publishing Company" where he "did a column on New Testament interpretations—and wrote inspirational articles sometimes." He and his wife had moved to the area just two years ago, and now, having caught her in bed with a white man, committed his horrid crime, and as we can easily guess from his confession to Bea, mutilated the white man too, commenting, "he'll never climb in bed with anybody again—not even with his *own* wife."

Thus, Yeager comes under Bea's power and is skirted off to "The Hippodrome," a kind of house she runs. He is given a new name and trained to replace one of the former members of the household in the strange performances given for crowds of nightly visitors. "The Hippodrome" resembles a brothel as much as the house Genet presents us with in his

play *The Balcony;* it is a house of illusions, what the unspeakable rites are we are never told. (pp. 97-8)

The white owner of the house soon discovers that Yeager has killed a white man and is on his way to destroy the house. Bea struggles to put Yeager out and he ends by strangling her. Finally, outside the house, on another night, once more in flight, he is joined by Darlene, who has also escaped from "The Hippodrome," and together they attempt to get away.

Impressive as Colter's performance is in this experimental novel, he is not on his own ground. With *Night Studies,* he returns triumphantly to his own territory in an ambitious and panoramic study cutting across all levels of society. The novel focuses on John Calvin Knight who as a young man had worked in the civil rights movement with Martin Luther King, Jr., and now, at the age of thirty-five, perhaps five years after the assassination of the great leader, finds himself at the head of the Black Peoples Congress. The present action of the novel covers a period of little more than two years, but within the novel, as part of Knight's struggle to understand himself and his failures, there is the tale of his ancestors, how they were brought from Africa, how they fared during reconstruction, and in the aftermath of World War I.

The title of the novel derives from a speech King made to his followers some ten years earlier. In it, King refers to "blacks' history as 'our long night of suffering.' " Knight becomes obsessed with his own night studies, and, indeed, King's words serve for the central theme of the novel. (p. 98)

In the brief "Epilogue" to this massive novel, Knight, alone, examines and "collates" the texts of prominent writers and thinkers—Garvey, Malcolm X, DuBois, King. Their answers do not quite satisfy him and he turns to thoughts of his father, William Goforth Knight, whom he earlier had condemned as a failure. Tentatively, sadly, Knight accepts his father's explanation: "We are what we were made." It is too easy an explanation for what Colter has presented to us in his novel, for he is concerned with the suffering of a great many people, black and white. Colter, who obviously knows his Sartre, presents Knight's resignation with sympathy, but suggests that the really important question does not lie with "what we were made," but rather with what we do with what has been done to us.

Organized in four large sections together with a brief Epilogue, *Night Studies* examines the present in the light of the past. Book I, "Convergence," presents us with all the major characters, revealing the shape their lives have taken thus far, before they all come together, in Chicago, for the working out of their individual destinies.

The story opens at a Ray Charles concert in San Francisco, where Marvin Freuhlinghausen, a misshapen "runt," president and founder of Career Commercial College discovers a strange passion for Griselda Graves, a beautiful young widow, formerly married to a black who has died in Viet Nam. Refusing Marvin's precipitous offer of marriage, Griselda nevertheless agrees to live with him, an arrangement her mother, Nancy Hanks, once an opera singer, wholeheartedly agrees to in her desire to be rid of her daughter. Griselda moves in that very night and thus begins her bizarre relationship with Marvin. She soon becomes irresistibly drawn to the Black Peoples Congress, headquartered in San Francisco. To all appearances a white woman, Griselda finds difficulty in being accepted by the organization, but she forces herself upon the central staff, and eventually, deserting Marvin, follows the organization to Chicago for its relocation. Griselda does not know that her father was part black, yet still feels drawn to this nationalistic movement.

Having introduced Griselda, who will figure largely in John Calvin's struggle, Colter moves on to Mary Dee Adkins, the beautiful daughter of a wealthy black surgeon from Chicago. Just as Griselda is drawn to blacks, Mary Dee is drawn to whites. Our first glimpse of her is as an art student in Paris. At a cafe in Paris, she is observed by a fierce black man, while sitting with her French professor, Raoul, and her white boyfriend, Philip Wilcox, a member of a wealthy Philadelphia family. Mary Dee's affair with Philip has been problematic because of the racial problem, which has overtaken them even in Paris. Mary Dee's father dies suddenly, forcing her return to Chicago, breaking off any relationship with Philip and her plans for a career as an artist. Such is chance in this naturalistic novel, that she scarcely dreams the black man who has observed her so scornfully is none other than John Calvin Knight with whom she will become very nearly fatally bound. (pp. 99-100)

John Calvin Knight remains a shadowy figure throughout this first part of the novel. For all his acumen as a leader of a black nationalist organization, he too is uncertain of his future, even of his place in the world, much like Ellison's nameless hero in *Invisible Man.* By the end of Book I, he is the victim of an attempted assassination, and the lives of his followers, of Ferdinand Bailey, his chief assistant, Mamie Campbell, his secretary, as well as Ornette and Griselda, become suspended as we await the outcome of this attempt on his life.

Book II, "Chronicle," by far the longest section of the novel, presents the story of Knight's heritage. Colter places this story within the historical perspective of western "culture." As he is lying in the hospital, the story filters through Knight's consciousness. The tale begins with Bymba, a young boy, who in a journey reminiscent of the story Melville tells in "Benito Cereno," is the first of Knight's forebearers to come to America. The story of Bymba's capture in Africa and his nightmarish voyage to America is told with a compelling sense of detail. It starts out at the end of the 18th century, in a context we often forget: "Mozart was to die late that year in Vienna and be borne to an unmarked grave, while, in the New World, George Washington served his first term as president of the new slave-importing nation of freedom zealots." (p. 101)

To some readers, the historical account of slavery and the subsequent story of black life during the reconstruction may seem forced, but it is essential to the tale Colter has to tell. There can be no understanding of the present without an awareness of the past. What emerges here is not only Knight's bond with his racial past, but his even more problematic relationship with his father, Goforth, from whom John Calvin has learned of his past. Later in Book II, when John Calvin comes to see his dying father, a portion of the story that takes us back nearly a decade, we learn of the sons of Bymba, Acts and Aaron Knight, and their struggle to gain freedom after the official act of emancipation. The war torn south is not so very much different from the ravages of the present even if the problems are more visible. Again, the focus is on character and so many people seem dislocated. Harrison Donaldson, a southern gentleman who has fought with Lee at Gettysburg, clearly a racist, but also an honorable man, is attacked by fellow whites when he attempts to aid the fleeing blacks. Colter's point is clear: everyone suffers in an unbalanced, violent society.

Colter's technique is to use the past to inform the present. While dealing with the past, Colter moves his tale forward in the present toward a mighty climax which occurs at the end of Book III, "Canticle," at a national meeting of the Black Peoples Congress. Knight has become hopelessly tangled in his feelings for Griselda as well as for Mary Dee as the movement develops a more and more militant position. . . . At the meeting, with Mary Dee seated behind him and Griselda secretly present in the audience, John Calvin attempts to preach a moderate line amidst an audience driven to frenzied cries of "ZENAPHOBIA! ZENAPHOBIA!" as they mistake the term in their enthusiasm for a cause. Knight vainly uses the answer he has gotten from his father, "we blacks are what we were made," it has no impact, he faints and is taken from the hall in an ambulance, Griselda crying out over his prostrate form.

Book IV, aptly titled "Crucible," presents us with Knight's struggle as a leader and more simply as a man who must face and understand his own life. Eventually, he will come to see that the rejection of his father has been a rejection of a larger sense of his past, but this will not be enough. After an engagement she is not wholly committed to, Mary Dee deserts him and returns to Paris to marry her professor, Raoul. Knight once more suffers collapse, loses his position of leadership and retreats to his apostate isolation to pursue, at last, his night studies.

There is a good deal of melodrama in this novel, but it is all very much in the naturalistic tradition. We are never quite sure what to make of Mary Dee's escape from her responsibility as a black to fulfill herself personally. Philip Wilcox dies in an automobile accident; Griselda commits suicide by jumping from the Golden Gate Bridge. Colter is not a militant writer in the usual sense, but he is surely militant about the results of living in a society where freedom is denied to specific groups. His work, of course, is in many ways comparable to the great novels of Richard Wright and Ralph Ellison, but it is also, as theirs, part of the major traditions of western writing. (pp. 101-03)

Resisting the writing of fiction in the currently fashionable modes, Colter has insisted on grand themes. . . . Concerned with the sweep of history, **Night Studies** can be compared with the panoramic tales we are given in Naipaul's *A House for Mr. Biswas* or Nadine Gordimer's *Burger's Daughter.* We see a society in which individuals are swept up by causes, struggling to know themselves. Colter's writing here is intentionally grandiose and elevated, fitting with the issues with which he deals. **Night Studies,** finally, is a novel in which Colter has brought to bear the skills at characterization so evident in his short stories within the framework of a major exploration of life in our society. The range of characterization is altogether remarkable; women and children are portrayed with special skill. We are made to see the problems of being black, but we are also made to see that these are not isolated nor need they be isolating. The struggle of the individual against the overwhelming odds of the universe is what lends dignity to all our lives. It is the stuff of great fiction; it is at the heart of all Colter's writing. (p. 103)

*Robert M. Bender, "The Fiction of Cyrus Colter,"
in* New Letters, *Vol. 48, No. 1, Fall, 1981, pp. 93-
103.*

ROBB DIMMICK

Cyrus Colter prowls the recesses of our souls. He did it in 1973 in his dark novel, *The Hippodrome* and he does it again in his darker still *A Chocolate Soldier.* In it he makes us walk the tightrope of our conscience along with the narrator who divulges a story which haunted him for 35 years. This book is his final attempt to exorcize his demon. Unlike *The Hippodrome* which gripped the reader only by the sheer horror of its circumstances, *A Chocolate Soldier* holds the reader with horror and with well-defined characters, diagrammed with a psychoanalyst's detail. Where *Hippodrome* moved by the pressure of plot necessity, *A Chocolate Soldier* is propelled by the natural forces that occur in the collision of strong characters. Nothing is manufactured in Colter's text. The events have to happen because of who and what his characters are.

Cager is a man with a mission, a mission with no definition. Its meaning emerges in stages. . . . As a young man in college, Cager discovers he is sexually underdeveloped. Stunned, his academic excellence slides and he becomes preoccupied with forming a liberation army out of the local townsfolk. It is a farce, but it is his passion—especially the smart Germanic uniforms he scrapes to buy. It is here that the narrator comes to know Cager and here that the book takes on epic proportions. As a friend the narrator becomes inextricably bound to Cager's life, vision and goals. In dark, ruminating passages the narrator talks deep into the night seeking to clarify his friend as hero or madman, all the while fighting to maintain his own frail grasp of reality. This is where Colter is his most dazzling and disturbingly realistic.

Later, as a servant to a wealthy white woman, Cager surreptitiously reads volumes of war related documents. It is in this mansion, the bastion of white supremacy, that Cager fully discovers his blackness and unearths the purpose behind his mission. In his most feverish prose Colter delineates one of the most electrifying racial relationships in literature.

In cinematic fashion, Colter cuts from past to present, from external action to internal turmoil while beguiling us with shimmering episodes of childhood, college days and night-club activity that rival anything he has written before. With five books to his name, Cyrus Colter is still a relative unknown. *A Chocolate Soldier* should finally bring him into the arena of writers to be remembered.

> Robb Dimmick, in a review of "A Chocolate Soldier," in Small Press, Vol. 5, No. 6, August, 1988, p. 30.

LARRY KART

Analogies between the arts can be tricky, but one of the ways Cyrus Colter's fiction works is so much akin to one of the ways the music of Duke Ellington spreads its magic that a little analogy-drawing seems worthwhile.

In any number of Ellington pieces ("Harlem Airshaft" and "All Too Soon" immediately come to mind), a musical-dramatic statement made by one or more members of the orchestra is answered by another soloist or instrumental choir until several different "stories" are being told at once—the results of that emotional counterpoint being a further story that includes all the others but is more than their sum, because it also is about the act of storytelling.

Consider, in that light, two of Colter's most powerful tales [collected in *The Amoralists and Other Tales*]. In **"A Chance Meeting,"** Ford and Spivey, former servants of a wealthy denizen of Lake Forest named Mrs. Cates, meet on a South Side Chicago street and retire to Ford's apartment to compare notes about their deceased employer. Ford has never married ("that's for you fellows that know all about women"), and his reminiscences suggest that he saw Mrs. Cates through a romantic haze—believing her to be a "real artistocrat" who shared his love of classical music and never had "an immoral thought in her life." But Spivey, the ex-chauffeur, counters with unimpeachable facts about Mrs. Cates' affair with a concert pianist—to which Ford's feeble reply is, "of course, when he played for her . . . she was greatly moved. But by the *music,* Spivey!—by the music."

At the end of what is virtually a compressed novel, Ford sits crushed and silent. But his romantic dreams are not really debunked, nor is Spivey's cynical realism endorsed—the story's dramatic truth residing instead within the sweet-sad music of their encounter.

"An Untold Story" finds Colter rounding back on himself—as Lonnie, a barroom habitue, recites a soliloquy from *Hamlet* and fondly recalls his immersion in the play many years before, at "Wirebridge State Training an' Industrial School" in Mississippi. Again, a man's pretensions are torn at—this time by a chorus of fellow drinkers who demand that Lonnie tell them what happens in *Hamlet*. But when he refuses to do so ("Th' story's only for the unthinkin' . . . That's whut Prof said"), a fight breaks out between Lonnie's sole supporter and one of his antagonists—and a man dies.

"He wouldn't tell us the story!" is the final cry, as though Lonnie's refusal were the direct cause of the crime. But buried within this fiercely comic tale are Colter's profound doubts about the value of storytelling—which then, remarkably, become part of the story as well.

A prophet of humane regret, Colter has collected all his short fiction [in *The Amoralists and Other Tales*]. Included are the 14 stories previously published as *The Beach Umbrella* and 4 new tales—one of which, **"Macabre,"** strikes me as a masterpiece.

Its theme is the unexpected eruption of desire, the perpetual underground stream that only the foolish try to repress. (The title of one of Colter's novels is *The Rivers of Eros.*) In fact, from the vantage point of **"Macabre,"** it is worth looking back to note in how much detail Colter's near-omnipresent erotic vision is, so to speak, fleshed out.

Quite often, what he detects is perverse, in the literal sense of the term: a "turning away" from the norm. But the erotic stream cannot be denied—may be the only norm, as Colter sees it. So we find Verna, the teenager of **"A Man in the House"** who is, unknowingly, in love with her uncle, brushing her hair "with one of those harsh little passions she directed at certain special things in her life"; Abby of **"After the Ball,"** telling her father, a distinguished jurist, that "if I caught any other man looking at me like that, I wouldn't like it a bit". . . . and the hothouse world of **"Macabre,"** in which impatience, fear, bigotry and rage somehow lead to a mutual seduction.

It is tempting to say that Cyrus Colter, at age 78, is one of Chicago's most important writers. But a man who writes as he does would be important no matter where he lived or how long he had lived there.

Larry Kart, "*The Truth-Telling Music of Cyrus Colter's Short Fiction*," *in* Chicago Tribune— Books, *December 25, 1988, p. 4.*

BERT ATKINSON

Collecting all of a writer's short stories enables the reader to follow the development of his work and then arrive at some conclusion about how he has forged his esthetic vision. In addition, a careful reading of **The Amoralists & Other Tales** by Cyrus Colter, a 79-year-old black writer who lives in Chicago, also reveals his considerable skill as a storyteller. . . .

Mr. Colter's themes are universal and familiar, but he gives them refreshing twists. For example, in the opening story, **"A Man in the House,"** Verna, a young girl from Memphis, spends a summer in Chicago with her aunt and uncle. Living with her caring uncle gives her the poise to make an important decision that will take her from adolescence into womanhood. Another story, **"After the Ball,"** also explores family relationships, but uses them to probe even deeper, more complicated emotions. Here Abigail Rivers, the daughter of a retired judge and the apple of his eye, becomes aware that her bond with her father is perhaps too close, thus threatening her relationship to the rest of her family. In the process, Mr. Colter explores love and hate, and how closely the two are intertwined. Abigail becomes, in her father's eyes, almost a personification of evil; he, in turn, becomes to her a leering sensualist.

The title story, **"The Amoralists,"** is a subtle piece, disturbing in its psychological and social implications about differing concepts of what is right and wrong, and about alienation. . . . A brother and sister, in Chicago to attend their sister's funeral, are mugged while walking back to their hotel. The dead woman, Nell, dominates their lives in death even as she did in life. In fact, the bitterness the living sister wishes the undertaker could have removed from Nell's face is everywhere present in her own voice. This is just one glimpse of the thread of irony that runs through Mr. Colter's fiction.

In **"An Untold Story,"** Lonnie, a young man whose formal education was cut short, translates soliloquies from *Hamlet* into street language at a bar—with tragic results. A tender counterpoint to this violent piece is the story called **"Rapport."** In it, Alf Sewell, who is widowed and childless, spends his days watching the antics of children in a park. One evening he sits near an unkempt woman and her small daughter. When Alf speaks kindly to the child, who obviously is abused and cowed by an overbearing mother, she cries and wants to remain with him. But he returns to his room alone, overcome with emotion, with a sense of love that he hasn't felt in years.

In the story called **"Moot,"** an old man and his aging dog (Matthew and Mark) live in a cluttered and unkempt apartment. Both die within a short time of each other. The old man deposits the dead dog at the city dump; when he dies, the old man is taken to the cemetery, without a single mourner. Afterward, a member of the crew that clears out his belongings remarks that an old man and his dog once lived in the apartment, but now that all the evidence of his occupancy has been removed, his life is moot.

The final story, **"The Frog Hunters,"** is the only piece in the collection that is not primarily concerned with blacks. In fact, the only black character is a man named Luther, who is presented to the reader through the eyes of his wife, Rita, and her son, Raymond. Luther has gone to California; Rita is talking about divorcing him and planning to marry a third husband. Raymond, a perceptive boy of 15, is away at summer camp while all this is going on. He dreams that his mother and an unrecognizable escort meet disaster at Luther's hands, an upsetting nightmare that takes the form of a surreal water ballet—and in the aftermath Raymond becomes obsessed with frog hunting. "If his forebodings were right," the story concludes, "then there would be no future. If they were wrong, there would be none still." While Raymond's emotions are dueling to a draw, he needs to catch at least one bullfrog before he leaves the camp, to have one tangible accomplishment in a summer that has brought the dissolution of his family.

A strong aspect of Mr. Colter's fiction is his predilection for the third-person point of view. The author, like an objective reporter, seldom imposes himself on the scene. In Mr. Colter's stories, characters are developed through action and dialogue interlaced with deft narrative; the result is often dramatic. But although most of the pieces are very satisfying in themselves, it is the echoes they create that strengthen their appeal. Mr. Colter not only engages his readers, he invites us to participate in his story world beyond the point at which he leaves us. He shows an acute insight into human behavior and uses all of his senses to the fullest: he gives us memorable characters with authentic voices. In **The Amoralists & Other Tales,** the literary menu is varied and delightful.

Bert Atkinson, "*When Life is Moot,*" *in* The New York Times Book Review, *February 12, 1989, p. 16.*

Michael Cook

1933-

English-born Canadian dramatist and scriptwriter.

In his plays, Cook focuses upon volatile relationships among inhabitants of Newfoundland, Canada, and often stresses the need for a human affinity with nature. Through vivid metaphors, striking imagery, and his recreation of local dialect, Cook depicts the Newfoundland people as extensions of the rugged, natural environment surrounding them. Although occasionally faulted for weakly structured plots, Cook is regarded as one of Canada's leading contemporary dramatists. Martin Fishman observed: "Cook is a playwright of great compassion and humanity. . . . His vision, though bleak and stark, is touched with a feeling not only for the characters themselves but for the human condition in general. . . . [Cook] makes excellent use of the theatre of language and emotion. He touches us deeply and presents the world with a compassionate view of man."

Born and raised in London, England, Cook emigrated to Newfoundland in 1966 and has set all of his plays there. He refers to the region as "the source of my imagination and the seat of any joy I have ever found." Cook wrote numerous radio scripts for the Canadian Broadcasting Company prior to completing his first theatrical work, *Colour the Flesh the Colour of Dust* (1971), a study of war's consequences and humanity's strong instinct for survival. Set in 1762, when Britain and France struggled for control of Canada, the production revolves around the British military's misguided attempts to tame an already civilized town and the differing attitudes of each country concerning integrity and survival. Brian Parker asserted: "[*Colour the Flesh* conveys] Cook's intuition of a double-edged vitality in existence itself, destructive yet enduring, and his sense that this may be our last defence against spiritual collapse." Cook continues his exploration of humanity's desire for power in *The Head, Guts and Soundbone Dance* (1973). In this play, elderly Skipper Pete, who detests the idea of progress, spends his time reminiscing about his triumphant past as a fisherman. Obsessed with dominating his ineffectual son-in-law and retarded son, Skipper Pete creates his own reality and slowly goes insane. Throughout the play, a thickening fog symbolizes Skipper Pete's increasing derangement. In a tragic climax, drunken Skipper Pete ignores the cries of a drowning child because he is engrossed in telling a sailing story. Although some critics commented that Cook failed to adequately convey his characters' idiosyncrasies, *The Head, Guts and Soundbone Dance* was lauded for its blend of realism and symbolism.

Skipper Pete's character is manifested in many of Cook's later protagonists, including the dying Skipper Blackburn in *Jacob's Wake* (1974), which chronicles the Blackburn family's Good Friday observances. The three generations gathered at Skipper Blackburn's house have become progressively more removed from nature and, consequently, more cynical; the elderly man's grandsons are there for the sole reason of committing him to an asylum. As the Skipper dies, a powerful storm that has been heard outside the Blackburn dwelling throughout the play rises in intensity, and the Skipper's ghost steers the home through the ensuing squall. Cook's fascina-

tion with the relationship between people and the natural conditions that envelop them is evidenced by the complex personalities of the characters and the anthropomorphic qualities of the tempest, which creates an allegorical effect in *Jacob's Wake*. *Tiln*, originally a radio play in 1971 and staged in 1975, has been compared to Samuel Beckett's drama *Endgame*. Both works take place within a symbolic, isolated setting and feature the interaction of two debilitated men. In Cook's play, the demented title character is a lighthouse keeper whose mania increases to the point that he ignores ships in peril; instead, he uses the bright light's beam to blind sea gulls. Fern, a badly injured survivor of a bombed ship, has attempted for ten years to coax Tiln out of his monomaniacal world. Finally, as Tiln buries Fern alive in a barrel of salt brine, he becomes distraught over his solitude. Cook's unconventional style of drama is further reflected in his next two works. In *Quiller* (1975), an eccentric retired sea captain carries on a rambling monologue about his deceased wife and God, and in *Thérèse's Creed* (1977), which features Cook's first female protagonist, a fisherman's widow speaks directly to the audience about her difficulties in confronting the past and the present.

Cook's plays often include strong social criticism and convey a sense of Canadian history. *On the Rim of the Curve* (1977) concerns the extinction of Newfoundland's Beothuk Indians, and *The Gayden Chronicles* (1978) examines the life and death of William Gayden, a British sailor who was court-martialed for mutiny and hanged in 1812. Cook centered *The Gayden Chronicles* on the hypocrisy and deceptive charm he discovered in Gayden's diaries.

(See also *Contemporary Authors,* Vols. 93-96 and *Dictionary of Literary Biography,* Vol. 53.)

PATRICK TREACHER

[*The excerpt below was originally published in the April 5, 1973 edition of the* St. John's Evening Telegram.]

Michael Cook is a comparative newcomer to the Newfoundland scene, and, like many of us who are not native, feels that he has something to say about Newfoundland that Newfoundlanders have not said for themselves.

Some will say that this is impertinence. This, of course, is probably quite true.

However, his play [*The Head, Guts and Soundbone Dance*], the title of which is deceptively repellent, is one of the most perceptive things I have ever seen. It's rather like peeping through a window. A church window.

Skipper Pete is an old man—old, knowledgeable, Master of his community, obsessed by his own power. Skipper. What a powerful word that is in Newfoundland.

The entire play is set on a stage-head and it is all about power—a Newfoundland obsession. Who is master, who is not? Particularly, the remembrance of things past. Things like great catches of cod. King Cod they used to call it, like mastery over all the beasts of the earth, cold, protestant style, where pigs can be dropped from the mast and splatter all over the deck and everybody laughs, if they are not Master, that is. (p. 78)

Skipper Pete, an old man, remembers his past glory, which consists entirely of shoals of fish, and his ability to appear an iron master of lesser men. That they were men in their own right is not relevant—he was Master. How many, who have lived under these circumstances, can deny this? But the Skipper makes the supreme mistake—he believes his own fantasy, and goes mad.

Not observantly mad, of course. His adopted son loves him. He loves all the primitive strength Skipper Pete possesses, his quality of mastery over boats, fish and women. His blind, idiot courage and the ignorant assumption that such courage existed nowhere else. . . .

The stage-head becomes the Skipper's life, and his adopted son Uncle John . . . joins the fantasy. What else can he do? Saved from drowning by the old man, kicked in the backside whenever he stepped out of line, married to the old man's daughter, dedicated to the Skipper's concept of what is true—"the old way is the only way". He must do what is expected of him.

He hates it all—the word of God, as interpreted by the Skipper, the lies he must swallow in the name of tribal memory,

the whole sorry ritual so well described by T. S. Eliot in *Murder in the Cathedral.*

> This is the last temptation, the final Treason.
> To do the right thing for the wrong reason . . .
>
> (pp. 78-9)

The function of a playwright is to observe, to understand and finally present his conclusions, with sympathy and tolerance. Mr. Cook does almost all of these things, but perhaps because his dedication gets in the way, his tolerance tends to slip sometimes.

At times . . . he reminded me of J. M. Synge, with only this difference. Synge only recounted, he never consciously commented. Mr. Cook has not yet mastered this art, but he is near enough to the thing to becoming an important person in the theatre. (p. 79)

> *Patrick Treacher, in a review of "The Head, Guts and Soundbone Dance," in* Canadian Drama/ L'Art dramatique canadien, *Vol. 11, No. 1, Spring, 1985, pp. 78-9.*

MYRON GALLOWAY

[*The excerpt below was originally published in the April 29, 1974 edition of the* Montreal Star.]

[In *The Head, Guts and Soundbone Dance*] Cook has obviously absorbed a great deal of the atmosphere of Newfoundland (though still not nearly enough) and observed the external characteristics of some of the more rugged of its individualists. What he has failed to do however is get beneath the surface idiosyncrasies of these people and invest them with a degree of dimension. Unable to illuminate their personalities with a single saving grace his characters remain cold, hard, unyielding and ultimately unsympathetic.

The result is we watch them from a great distance as peculiar oddities we are unable to identify with, or feel for them. Newfoundlanders are hardly likely to feel flattered.

The central character is Skipper Pete, an elderly fisherman who is lost in the past dreaming of outmoded methods of bringing in a good catch which no longer work. Rendered to the sound bone, this is all the play is really about.

In the course of the hour we learn that he rules with an iron fist a middle-aged son-in-law and a mentally retarded son and succeeds in casting a mindless spell over both. At the same time he treats his daughter, who recognizes the futility of his reactionary attitude to progress, with bitter contempt. Long before the play opens he has come between daughter and husband until they now all but despise each other. On the other hand the daughter has little to offer her husband as an alternative to her father's empty dreams apart from a cosy chair in front of the television and an electric blanket on his bed at night.

Having established this much, Cook then concocts a feeble and totally unconvincing piece of business concerning the drowning of a neighbour's child which both men might have prevented had they been less preoccupied with the past. It is as a result of this thin device that the husband becomes aware he should pay more attention to what is going on around him, escapes the old man's spell of a lifetime and joins his wife in front of the telly, to watch the CBC, no doubt.

To sustain our interest, the playwright tosses in a number of visual gimmicks, such as the gutting of fish (the stench which permeates the theatre is sickening), the mending of a net, the sloshing of water about the stage and several scenes in which both men urinate, none of which can, in all honesty, be considered adequate compensation for the play's complete lack of any real drama. (p. 80)

Myron Galloway, in a review of "The Head, Guts and Soundbone Dance," in Canadian Drama/ L'Art dramatique canadien, *Vol. 11, No. 1, Spring, 1985, pp. 80-1.*

MARION OWEN-FEKETE

[*This excerpt was originally published in the October 22, 1974 edition of the* Fredericton Daily Gleaner.]

Michael Cook's **The Head, Guts and Soundbone Dance** is a queer play. It upsets one, knocks one off-keel. I don't like it because it's pessimistic and contains some unpleasant things, yet I like it because it doesn't prostitute itself to any tradition, and just because it does unbalance me and make me think.

What is a good tragedy supposed to be, we ask. Must we be Aristotelian and conclude that the good guy must be considerably noble, one way or another, that after seeing the hero's downfall we must feel purged, experience a quiet after a storm? Can't a good tragedy have a hero who's pretty lousy? And can't the play be good even if we do leave the theatre feeling as low as all Hades?

I've always held with Aristotle, myself, but **The Head, Guts and Soundbone Dance** causes me to reconsider the basis for my criticism. And anything jolting our ensconsed notions, even if only in their settling in with securer hold, is surely worth a lot in that regard alone.

Once I have accepted the pessimism in the play and the lack of moral uplift, I find the main fault to be a structural weakness. Near the end of Act I, the main character in the play, Skipper Pete (age 90), and his son-in-law and sidekick, Uncle John (age 60), are looking out the back door of a stage-head (structure built over the sea) talking about a little boy they once knew who fell overboard into a school of dogfish and was devoured. (The play is full of this sort of disagreeableness.) Just then a child appears, crying that little Jimmy Fogarty has fallen into the water. The men continue their reverie, paying no attention to the child. In the play as it was written, the child tugs the men's clothing. In . . . [the] production, the child hardly comes onstage. In the written version, with the child making himself quite obvious, the lack of response by the men is extremely difficult to accept as realistic action. In the produced version, at the expense of heightened drama, Skipper Pete and Uncle John are made more natural and likeable. The play is weak here. Rewriting doesn't help.

About three old Newfoundland fishermen who find themselves out of the water, with fish no longer abundant, as they once were, the play contains enough to set pens of letters-to-the-editor writers wriggling. There are swearing, urinating (but not quite on stage), and the throwing of fish guts to the four corners. (Those six huge fish caught by Skipper Pete's son Absalom smell to low Hell. One's nostrils are assailed, and there's the fear of getting splattered with an innard. In places the play turns into something nigh like an Aldous Huxley feelie.) (pp. 81-2)

Marion Owen-Fekete, in a review of "The Head, Guts and Soundbone Dance," in Canadian Drama/L'Art dramatique canadien, *Vol. 11, No. 1, Spring, 1985, pp. 81-2.*

MICHAEL COOK [INTERVIEW WITH ROTA LISTER]

[Lister]: *Michael, one of the things I noticed about your dramaturgy is that it seems to seek to bring out by whatever formal means the holiness, not only of the human spirit, but of the human flesh.*

[Cook]: I suppose you made me conscious of something that I didn't particularly want to be conscious of, but I happen to know it's there. It seems to me that the body confirms that immense dignity of the human experience in its relation to environment. A lot of the people I write about are people who might be considered by many to be inarticulate, to be poor, to be on the edge of a kind of poverty and yet their physical approach and involvement with their landscape is something which is fluid, which is total. They give, they take back, and they are extensions of the world in which they live and the things they make are extensions of those worlds, and they are extensions of themselves and there is that sense, really, of the body as church.

Would you say that you think of yourself as somewhat similar in that sense to Dylan Thomas, the Welsh poet-playwright?

I hadn't thought of that either, Dylan Thomas, of course. I suppose, because I'm very familiar with his work but I think, my response would be as in his own preface for the collected poems, where he asked why the shepherd in the 20th century still making ritual kinds of movements to the moon. And the shepherd's reply was, I'd be a damned fool if I didn't, I suppose that my observation comes with a very joyous kind of recognition of people who do things because they have to be done.

I notice that your titles tend to be very earthy in confirmation of what we've just been saying; **Colour the Flesh the Colour of Dust** *and* **Head, Guts and Sound Bone Dance** *and that sort of thing; was there anything in perhaps your childhood experience that predisposed you in this direction?*

No, I don't think so, I think that what really happened is that most of my life was spent in tearing about hither and yon in boarding schools and the army for twelve years, never any kind of settled identification with a landscape, or a place or a sense of time until I was about 28 or 29. So I discovered the earth at 28 or 29 and I suppose that's why it's so strong. I'm still discovering it. I didn't know anything about it until then. (pp. 176-77)

You remember Eliot's famous line about seeing eternity in a handful of dust and, no doubt, he was harking back to Blake's seeing the universe in a grain of sand. Well, then, you were more a city creature, and Canada taught you how to think about the land. Do you think that perhaps it is the rediscovery, the second birth that shapes the artist's vision, that the artist in a way is a New Adam, a Second Adam?

Well, I didn't have a vision. That's the point. I'd always been a writer; it sounded bloody pretentious and every now and again I'd write a book and write a novel which was lousy, and I'd write poetry which was lousy. And, you know, I just didn't have a fixed point. It was Newfoundland, in fact, very specifically, that gave me that focal identity and it was the sea and the sea's response to the land and people's response to the sea and the land and it was really like someone opening the shutters. I no longer looked inward as in Plato's parable of the cave—I'd been looking at the shadows all the time and I turned outwards and there it all was.

It seems almost as if, when poetry or drama or any literary form becomes fairly artificial, then writers seem to feel impelled to go back to the basics, to the earth, the sea, the great eternities. Browning goes back into primitive sounds; would you see yourself in the line of the great so-called rebarbarizers or civilized culture?

I don't really see myself in the line of a great anything. You know, some people work with wood, I happen to work with words, that's a craft. But I think there has been a tremendous pursuit of the initial kind of rediscovery of the soul, an age of magic which precedes one of religion. And I think we are now back to some kind of age of magic. Our gods have gone. We're in this rediscovery kind of process. Even the visual arts that have come up in Canada and North America in the last ten years have exploded in a rediscovery of things as they are, not as we would like them abstractly to be. I think that is symptomatic of what we are all doing. (pp. 177-78)

One of the problems a dramatist has, of course, is to take whatever vision he has and to find a form that renders that vision accurately. Sartre solved this problem in one way, he made his form work against his vision; he had a vision of the chaos of life pitched on the edge of a nothingness, yet he creates a very rational form in such plays as No Exit. *Other writers, such as Eliot, have tried to express the vision they had in their very form. How do you feel about the kind of formal compromises you have had to make to mediate your vision into the theatre?*

I don't make those kind of compromises because I don't think at that level. I simply listen and see what's around me, so I've never consciously thought about form. I have made everything as simple and realistic as possible.

In other words, you work essentially the way the Romantic poets worked when they said that they wanted an organic form that would grow out of the subject itself. Do you feel that each time your decision has been largely unconsciously made, after the subject was chosen?

It really is much simpler, it's that the form arises from the subject without any conscious imposition. The subject is the form. (pp. 178-79)

I notice that as I look over the progression of your plays, certainly those about Newfoundland, there has been a gradual narrowing down of focus. You began with a great panorama, then you had a slightly smaller panorama; you began with history, now you are dealing with the present. In your latest play you have only the central character, a monologue with a few incidental impingements, in **Quiller.**

I think that's because the particular type of character or point of view I was looking at has become focused really upon a final individual kind of expression. I think that's the end of that particular form of expression. I really want to write a massive play with about seventy people in it next, probably go back into history again. You go back into history to renew your sources all the time. I think that immediate contact with an absurd reality has probably come to some kind of pause, so I'm going to have to go back.

So you see your creative patterns as perhaps more of a systole-

diastole movement, not a one-directional line. Now you contract, now you expand and perhaps you need both to act as counterbalancing forces.

This is the age of Proteus, isn't it? We change and shift identities. So I guess I do the same thing. When you reach the end of one particular identity or one *persona* you discard it like a lizard and you take another; as a playwright I guess that's what I'm going to be doing.

Do you think that you are definitely lodged in the Newfoundland experience or do you have other plans for widening your focus?

I've been lodged in the Newfoundland experience, but I'll probably need to look at other things; I have a funny idea that the really critical thing is how much Newfoundland has become home to me, because I discovered it late. I'm going to have to leave it as we all have to leave home. I suspect I'll be writing out of that experience for the next twenty years but not necessarily living in it. (pp. 179-80)

Rota Lister, in an interview with Michael Cook, in Canadian Drama/L'Art dramatique canadien, *Vol. 2, No. 2, Fall, 1976, pp. 176-80.*

MARTIN FISHMAN

We have living in Newfoundland a playwright of immense stature and ability, a playwright who understands the conventions of the theatre and who uses the theatrical medium with expertise to convey to his audience his vision of man. Michael Cook is the name of this master playwright. As his plays gain the recognition they deserve, he will most certainly be compared to [Bertoldt] Brecht, [John] Arden and other great artists of the modern theatre. However, before these comparisons can be made, one must first examine Cook's work as it stands on its own, for Michael Cook is first and foremost a playwright in his own right. His first play, ***Colour the Flesh the Colour of Dust,*** is an excellent example of the unique philosophy and style of Michael Cook.

In ***Colour the Flesh the Colour of Dust*** Cook has, in a theatrical and well structured manner, juxtaposed the ideas and themes of honour and survival and recorded poetically the resulting human actions and reactions. The play is set in Gibbet Hill, St. John's, in 1762. Into this town made up of mainly Irish immigrants comes the British army, led by the Captain. The result is a clash between the townspeople, who understand the way of nature and the meaning of survival, and the soldiers who are attempting to bring ideals, order and concepts into what appears to them to be a savage and desolate land. This conflict is almost classical in its implications. Although Cook does maintain a sense of the inevitable, all the characters in the play are desperately attempting to protect their own way of life, that is to survive the best way they can in what is a hostile and harsh environment.

The concept of honour so important to the soldiers when they arrive is upheld by the young Lieutenant who, because he has been in Newfoundland for only seven years, still clings to his ideals. His struggle, however, is a losing one, since he realizes that he will eventually succumb. . . . [The] Lieutenant continually tries to maintain his dignity, which to him is a sense of duty to God and Country, as a means of survival: "We weren't born clean. It's something we have to work for." Because the Lieutenant has been stripped of his personal life, forced to leave his wife and home to take up his duty in New-foundland, his loyalties, obligations and contracts are all he has left. Without them he is as good as dead. And he believes that he alone stands as the last bulwark against the rage of the sea, the victory of land and nature over man. He is the only soldier who wants to fight the invading French rather than surrender, even though he knows that it is a foolish thing to do. Cook, however, does not make the Lieutenant a fool in any way. Treating him, as he does all the characters, with humanity Cook sensitively portrays the loneliness, heartache and desperation of a man who just does not and cannot reconcile his ideals with the harsh reality of the environment in which he lives.

The Lieutenant's struggle, though filled with universal implications, is a personal one. He begins a sexual relationship with a whore in an attempt to procure some security, some protection. He clings wildly to the whore but in the end realises that her love is not enough. He cannot find anything to relieve his emptiness and despair. . . . As he grows more desperate, he becomes more fanatical. It is important to him that one of the soldiers who was killed rather unheroically by a crowd leader be reported as having died in battle and be given a 'decent burial.' Honour even in death is an ideal which helps the Lieutenant rationalize his existence in this foreign land. The Lieutenant's choice becomes increasingly clear: either to succumb to the laws of the land—which to him would mean spiritual death—or to die a physical death. As the whore perceptively notes: "You'll die you know—that's the only way you can redeem yourself in the cold eyes of the men who will judge you." Cook, with a touch of irony, allows the Lieutenant to die in battle. But the honour that the soldier struggled so hard to preserve is denied him in his death. As the battle draws to a conclusion and with the British victorious over the French, the Lieutenant is shot in the back by one of his own soldiers. (pp. 181-82)

Captain Gross, on the other hand, is a soldier who has sacrificed his ideals and has, as a consequence, died a spiritual death. Coming to Newfoundland twenty-three years ago, leaving behind a wife and a baby from whom he hasn't heard in ten years, the Captain was at one time like the Lieutenant: "Spit and Polish. Serve King and Country. Encourage harmony and goodwill." But he has arrived at the painful realisation that all of that is useless, inapplicable to a country filled with "fish, guts and excrement and stinking hovels and lice and vermin and the pox. . . . " The only duty he now has is to himself, to his struggle for survival. He is more of a pathetic figure that the Lieutenant, since, although he has given up all his ideals and beliefs, although he has tried to maintain himself, he has found nothing to replace the justice, fairness and humanity he once held as firm beliefs. His awakening came with the discovery that no matter what he did, good or evil, no one would remember him. . . . The Captain's only sanctuary is the fog which washes off the sea, hiding life and all its trappings. Man cut off from the ties which once identified him as a man, as a human being, is adrift. The image of man adrift on an island is used by both the Captain and the Lieutenant to explain the hopeless desperation and solitude they face in this country. At the end of the play the Captain, a shell of a man taken to musings and melancholic ravings, disappears into the fog.

Cook does not condemn nor condone any character in the play. He creates an environment and reports the actions, refusing to take sides. Everyone has a clear reason to act and react the way they do. No one ideal is better than another, no one morality is correct. Certainly some characters are more able to survive, though by dubious means. Cook does not denounce them for it. The point is they survive.

Two such characters are the Merchant and the Magistrate, both of whom are driven by reasons of money and power. Their philosophy is a simpler one. They do whatever is necessary in order to survive and in their case, survival means comfort. . . . The Merchant and Magistrate also speak of honour and dignity; but these ideals are perverted and manipulated to fit the occasion. . . . While many other playwrights might be tempted to turn these characters into stereotypical Uriah Heeps, Cook invests them with a great deal of credibility. We clearly see the motives for their actions, and their understanding of the land and its people: The Magistrate advises the Merchant: "No matter how much they [the people] hate you—at the moment of violence, weaken—be generous—it destroys the flame of the spirit." And in the end they emerge victorious. As much as we may dislike the Magistrate and the Merchant, as much as we may disagree with what they do, we have to admire them because they have the know-how and the ability to survive. (pp. 182-84)

The third group of people examined by Cook are the townspeople, the ones who live in this environment and who have learned to cope with their existence. It is their world which the soldiers, merchants and magistrates invade. They are the ones who are exploited, pillaged and killed and yet they are also the ones who will be left to continue the struggle, not against man, but against nature. . . .

The townspeople have accepted their lot in life. They must go on with the knowledge that they can no longer survive in terms of honour. In order to exist they too must do whatever is necessary. They lack the shrewdness and the perceptions of the Magistrate and Merchant and, as a result, they suffer more. However, unlike the Lieutenant and the Captain, they have come to the conclusion that they must not allow themselves to think but rather live life from moment to moment, never pausing to look at themselves. They are almost nihilistic in their attitude; but it is this attitude which will pull them through. (p. 184)

To give us a greater insight into the townspeople, Cook is careful to reduce the universal to the personal by creating human relationships. The character of the Woman, in her relationship with the Lieutenant, brings us closer to a comprehension of the attitudes and feelings of the people. The Woman understands life in this country in a personal way. She is willing to turn away from her Irish people and join the Lieutenant because she sees in him the dignity which is so lacking in her own people. But although she desires this dignity, she also knows that it is impractical. She is trapped because she sees the good and evil of both sides, both ways of life. Her solution is to transcend these issues through a human deed—the birth of a child. However, she knows that this is really not enough. The Woman can accept anything in the environment except humanity because it is the knowledge of humanity which points out and isolates the faults of the people. It forces them to draw back and see how they really are; and as she says: "It's not possible to live very long once you accept that." She is, therefore, involved in a strange attraction-repulsion relationship with the Lieutenant, attracted by his ideals and repulsed by their impracticality. Importantly, she does not attempt to change the way of life because to her the struggle for survival is not one of rebellion against the ways of man and nature but rather a battle to accept life as it is and reconcile oneself to it. Speaking to the Lieutenant, she exclaims: "We exist. . . . And you think you'll win peace in some bloody parody of heroics; but I tell you—I will tell you—that the bravest people are the ones who endure." To her the important idea, the only ideal, is survival. Despite the odds, despite morality, the people exist because they have to. It is the Woman we see at the beginning of the play, crouching below the body of her hanging lover. It is also the Woman we see at the end of the play, clutching her pregnant body and swaying to and fro. The birth-death cycle implied by these images reinforces the idea that these people will endure and, whether we like it or not, they have no other choice. Survival means acceptance and reconciliation—acceptance of oneself and the ability to adapt oneself to the environment and to one's fellow man.

Cook has chosen the epic style to come to terms with the large and encompassing nature of *Colour the Flesh the Colour of Dust.* Almost filmic in its progression, the play employs an episodic structure, switching the action from the battlements to the Merchant's store, to the sea and back again. This quick succession of scenes not only provides an exciting rhythm and flow but also enables Cook to juxtapose two scenes together in order to achieve an effect greater than the whole. It is an interesting use of montage in the theatre. (pp. 184-85)

Not only does the montage demonstrate cause and effect, it also serves to heighten mood and develop the theme of survival. For example, on the upper level deals are being made with the French to ensure the commercial survival of the Merchant and Magistrate, while below a soldier does a song and dance around the body of Willie [a British soldier], whose death satisfied the blood-thirstiness of the mob and thereby guaranteed this soldier's survival. It is an example of the perfect match of form and content.

Cook also employs a narrator figure, usually in the form of the Spokesman, to fill in exposition and to bring the immediacy of the situation to the audience by direct address. This convention is used not to alienate but rather to punctuate. An example of this occurs in Act Two where the Spokesman turns directly to the audience—"good people"—and explains in an eloquent and poetic speech the exact feelings of the people. This not only involves the audience in the play but also provides a break in the action, a time to digest the rapid succession of events on stage. (pp. 185-86)

Song is used to increase the emotion and mood values. Importantly, a la Arden, the songs fit into the action and do not in any way stop or impede the flow of events. As was mentioned before, the play opens with a stark poetic image of a man hanging from the gallows while below his whore sings the "Song of the Woman." The words and music, which are beautifully poetic, not only serve to explain the Woman's thoughts but also create the desired mood of desolation and bleakness. It is perfectly natural for the Woman to sing this ballad because it is simply the best way she can express herself. To further the naturalness of song, Cook divides the stanzas of the song with prose. The transition, therefore, between music and prose is made easily and fluidly. The play is filled with examples of this kind.

Perhaps the best way Cook creates mood and atmosphere is through his use of language, a language which is at the same time poetic and earthy. Once again there is the feeling that the characters would express themselves in this way. An example of this is the First Soldier's speech in Act One:

> You and me now, we're still warm, breathing. Like bloody cattle in a pen. And it doesn't seem to matter—when you see somebody dead—whether it's a pig-sty, a mess of fish guts—or linen sheets that you sleep in. You sleep easier 'cos someone else's blood drips on the stones and it isn't yours.

This poetic use of language elevates feelings with images which are earthy and raw.

The problem of language fitting character is one which Cook does not completely solve in this play. Occasionally one is struck by the feeling that the poetry of expression is incorrect for a certain situation or character. This usually occurs in a personal situation. In these moments, the confrontation of the individuals in a one to one situation is powerful enough and the poetry tends to heighten the moment beyond credibility. This happens specifically in the scenes between the Lieutenant and the Woman.

Cook's use of the poetic device extends to what I term the poetry of the senses, that is, the use of colour and sound. This particular use of the theatrical medium not only helps create mood but also places the emphasis on the personal rather than the spectacle. In his stage directions Cook describes a large cyclorama used to show outlines of various locations of the scenes. We never see a complete picture but rather sparse, exact glimpses. This creates a stark mood and allows the audience to focus their attention on the stage. When battles occur, Cook wisely resists the temptation to portray them on stage. Instead he selectively shows flares flashing on the cyc accompanied by the sounds of gunfire and cannons. The emphasis therefore, is not on the war itself but on the characters' reactions to the events of war. Our total attention is on the people on stage who are the victims of the war. Their personal feelings, their dreams and ideals stand alone. And we as spectators and emotional participants watch with sympathy and understanding.

Michael Cook is a playwright of great compassion and humanity. He portrays the human dilemma in an exciting theatrical manner. His vision, though bleak and stark, is touched with a feeling not only for the characters themselves but for the human condition in general. Although the play is set in Canada and touches our Canadian sensibilities, the ideas and feelings displayed go far beyond one country or one people. Cook is a playwright who makes excellent use of the theatre of language and emotion. He touches us deeply and presents the world with a compassionate vision of man. (pp. 186-87)

> *Martin Fishman, "Michael Cook: A Playwright in His Own Right," in* Canadian Drama/L'Art dramatique canadien, *Vol. 2, No. 2, Fall, 1976, pp. 181-87.*

BRIAN PARKER

Michael Cook has weaknesses as a dramatist that have drawn down upon him the obloquy of critics, and it is perhaps as well to consider these first. He thinks of himself basically as a poet, and has explained that plays occur to him not in the form of Aristotelian "action" but poetically as "a series of images, dramatic scenes, and circumstances." The obvious difficulty he has in organizing his work, perhaps his most serious defect as a dramatist, reflects this centrifugal habit of imagination. None of his plays has much conventional plot and all tend to be wordy and overwritten. At one extreme, he uses overlong "realistic" monologues, as in *Quiller* and *Thérèse's Creed,* which reveal the effect of his apprenticeship to radio drama; at the other, he throws heterogeneous materials loosely together in quasi-historical Brechtian structures with huge casts, like *Colour the Flesh the Colour of Dust, The Gaydon Chronicles,* and *On the Rim of the Curve,* where social caricature, historical or regional realism, and poetical philosophizing all clash. He compensates for his plays' verbosity with rather obvious stage effects: either by the detailed recreations of everyday routines—cooking, washing, net making—or by vaudevillean songs, dances, and allegorical tableaux, according to whether the bias of a particular play is realistic or presentational. His work can be thematically confusing because it combines an almost reflex sympathy for any underdog with a more existentialist concern with the strain that isolation imposes on human relationships. And these imprecisions are reflected in unevennesses of rhetoric. Cook is capable of genuine poetic intensity, but too frequently he falls into philosophical overexplicitness or poetical overwriting, both of which can strain characterization.

Nevertheless, Michael Cook remains an important dramatist, because beneath the technical crudities, at the poetic heart of his work, lies an intensely imagined experience of Newfoundland life, presented with such integrity that at its best it rises to comment on the human condition.

Paradoxically, Cook is helped in this because he is not a Newfoundlander by birth, but a Briton of Anglo-Irish descent who arrived in Canada as recently as 1965. Thus he brings to Newfoundland an outsider's eye like that of the original settlers. What he sees is the "survival" experience which critics such as Northrop Frye and Margaret Atwood have argued is the central Canadian literary theme: confrontation with a relentlessly hostile environment which undermines all confidence in human institutions and even in identity itself. By its very nature drama finds it more difficult to represent this experience than poetry or the novel because it can only represent reactions to the experience, not the confrontation itself, and Cook is perhaps the most successful dramatist so far in conveying the experience in stage terms. (pp. 22-3)

[Pre-eminently] for Cook artistry is to be found in the Newfoundlanders' retention of "a language colourful, new, musical, scatological . . . full of the power of ancient metaphors."

Experience on this primitive, existential plane appeals, Cook thinks, to men who have come to realize that "somewhere in the transition between rural and industrial man they left behind a portion of their souls." His main purpose as a playwright is thus twofold: to reaffirm the validity of the traditional Newfoundland way of life, while also exploring the tragic cost of such "Satanic" assertions of order, and, at the same time, to record its demise beneath the pressures of a shallow, regimented, urbanized civilization with which Cook has little patience. He has explored these themes in some forty plays, but his strengths and weaknesses and the range of his technique can be discovered by looking in some detail at his so-called "Newfoundland Trilogy"—*Colour the Flesh the Colour of Dust* (1971), *The Head, Guts and Soundbone Dance* (1973), and *Jacob's Wake* (1974)—recognizing, however, that they are not strictly a trilogy at all, since there is no continuity of action or characters between them and they are written in wholly different modes. . . . What binds the plays together is their common concern with unmediated experience "on the edge of the world."

Colour the Flesh the Colour of Dust was Cook's first stage play and is something of a mess. Ostensibly it is a Brechtian "epic" about the surrender of St. John's to the French in 1762 and its subsequent recapture by the English. However, as the "Spokesman" character in the plays points out, "Historically, this has been a pretty inaccurate play." Its interest lies in Cook's reactions to Newfoundland, but the overall effect is incoherent because he has tried to cram too much into it without a clear sense of priorities.

Perhaps the simplest element—the one that the reviewers seized on with relief—is the broad satire directed against a hypocritical merchant called Tupper and his ally, magistrate Neal, who manipulate the political situation for their own advantage ("Wars may come and wars may go, Tupper . . . but trade . . . "). This concentrates in two main scenes. In Act I Tupper adulterates his flour with sawdust only to discover that he must now purify it again in order not to antagonize the French, and in Act II he tries to learn French in order to trade with the new garrison and insists on teaching his shopboy what he does not know himself. But the comedy of these situations is complicated by other elements. In the first act a more savage level of satire comes into play when Tupper cheats the pathetic Mrs. McDonald whose family is starving, and justifies himself with selfconsciously villainous irony:

> It wouldn't be right now, for me to give you something and you worrying about whether you'd ever pay it back. . . . it's a terrible thing in these times to have a working conscience, Mrs. McDonald; and I'm afraid yours will drive you to the grave.
>
> (pp. 23-4)

Basically, *Colour the Flesh* conveys a sympathetic awareness that history does not interest or affect ordinary people except for the worse. Their concern is always for survival: whichever side governs, the drudgery of work must go on; social inequalities will continue; at most, war provides a break in bleak monotony and perhaps the chance of a cathartic outburst of violence. (p. 25)

The play shows . . . spiritual demoralization in various ways. At its simplest it is seen in the British soldiers of the opening scene, who have lost all hope for the future and all pride in their profession, yet at the same time hate the pointless brutality they have fallen into. More thoroughly, this state of mind is explored in the characterization of Captain Gross, the garrison commander. Gross tells Lieutenant Mannon that he was just as keen for "law" and "honour" as the Lieutenant once, "But this rock now . . . something in it defeats the spirit." Squalor, insubordination, separation from his family, sexual infidelity, a growing sense of isolation, the harshness of the land, and the drink with which he has tried to dull his sensibility, have eaten away his self-respect.

At first the remnants of the man he was are reflected in a rather dandyish, epigrammatic turn of speech, . . . but when a whore breaks in to shame him with her scolding, this brittle elegance snaps and Gross drops abruptly into a more symbolic mode of speech: "I see icebergs in my sleep. All the time." The switch of rhetorical levels is shocking but quite deliberate: it reflects Gross's surrender to a different plane of experience; and this poetic style becomes his norm for the rest of the play. At times it seems a bit selfconscious, as when he answers Tupper, who has said he tries to avoid the sea:

> But we are at sea, Tupper. At this moment . . .
> Can't you hear it? We're adrift, man. Helpless. The
> whales and ice thrash about us. Without a rudder,
> what can a man do? Drifts, Tupper. Only his head
> above the wave. Limbs, loins . . . ice cold . . .

—where poetry and dandyism seem to mix. But this, too, may be deliberate, since there is always a certain posing quality in Gross, a need to have his situation appreciable by others.

Gross's speeches play a large part in establishing the special Newfoundland *angst* of *Colour the Flesh,* as in the lines already quoted where he describes his pain at human impermanence, evoking despair in terms of the environment that caused it; and in that particular scene, which is a key one, the setting strengthens the link, because Gross speaks the lines to the Lieutenant when the two meet in a fog. Like the tattered uniform that he insists on wearing even after St. John's has been recaptured, the fog becomes a conscious symbol for the Captain. It represents his sense of isolation and spiritual drift, but at the same time, as he recognizes, it provides comfort by insulating him from reality ("The fog, I find, always makes life more bearable"); moreover, it also leads to greater self-knowledge ("a man learns things walking alone in the fog"), since it is in the fog that he recognizes that the seed of his collapse was already in him before he came to Newfoundland: "[My spirit] was defeated before I got here." (pp. 26-7)

The Captain's breakdown is interestingly complex but not quite clearly worked out, and as he is not the play's protagonist, he is slightly offcentre in our interest anyway. Potentially more interesting than Gross, though even less developed, is the character of Lieutenant Mannon. He, too, feels the isolation of their position:

> We are stranded on some island at the edge of time.
> There's the sea. And the fog. . . . We can't gentle
> it in any way . . . impose order or a universal design upon it. . . . Ultimately we respond to the ferocity of the sea. And the impermanence of life.

His hobnobbing with the common soldiers in scene one suggests that this experience has already begun to corrupt the Lieutenant's concern for "spit and polish," but the challenge of the French invasion apparently revitalizes his sense of "duty" and "honour." During the action, however, he discovers that he does not believe in these values for their own sake but because, without them, he, too, would face a moral collapse: "It's all I've got, see. Certain loyalties. Certain obligations and contracts." The strained nature of such ideals forces him into unnecessary rashness and falsifies his relationship with the Woman. Significantly, at the end he is shot in the back by one of his own men. A major flaw in the dramaturgy is that the reason for this killing is never made explicit, but there are sufficient hints for us to assume that it must be because of the pressure that the Lieutenant's idealism puts on others, a certain selfserving quality in his "honour" that Cook would later develop more fully in the monomaniacal skippers of *The Head, Guts and Soundbone Dance* and *Jacob's Wake.* (p. 28)

As a work of art *Colour the Flesh* is exasperating yet memorable. There are striking scenes, passages of vividly evocative poetry, and some shrewd insights into behaviour; but the overall structure is incoherent. . . . The presentational elements—the Spokesman's address to the crowd and a voice-over reading of the official report of the surrender (which was cut in production)—are not adequate to establish a truly

"epic" mode; the songs can be tangential (as in the ballad of "Old Noll Cromwell") and sink sometimes to pretentious doggerel; the rhetoric is uncertain, with no attempt at the Newfoundland dialect used so effectively in the other two plays of the trilogy; and the symbols of the hanged man, the fog, and the *pietà* (made more explicit in the original draft by comparisons to Christ, the Romans, and Mary) are all rather too obvious.

Nevertheless, for all its faults, *Colour the Flesh* stays stubbornly in the mind because it does manage to convey Cook's intuition of a double-edged vitality in existence itself, destructive yet enduring, and his sense that this may be our last defence against spiritual collapse. These intuitions are developed further in *The Head, Guts and Soundbone Dance,* which is his most powerful stage play to date.

Whereas *Colour the Dust* is very loosely organized, *Dance* has a form that is almost perfectly suited to its theme. At its core is the same harsh Newfoundland experience, but confrontation with it is now more active and heroic. Moreover, the focus has been shifted to the tragic price exacted for such heroism, and the main threat is no longer nature itself but the modern world that renders heroism obsolete. Cook summarizes the plot as "Two old men trying to keep the past alive to the exclusion of the rest of the world."

The action centres on a Newfoundland fisherman, Skipper Pete, an "Ancient leader of a savage pack with the instincts still there but the ability in pitiful repair," who in his "splitting room" on a fishing stage jutting into the Atlantic tries to keep tradition alive by remembering past glories and ritualistically making preparations for "one more trip." Pete stands uncompromisingly for

> The old way. The only way. The proper way to do
> things. Greet the day at cockcrow. The sea, no matter what the weather. Stack the gear. Mend the
> nets. Make the killick [a stone anchor]. Keep the
> store in order. There's nothing without it.

His son-in-law, Uncle John, once the cook on the Skipper's fishing boat, aids him, and so does his simple-minded son, Absalom, a sixty-year-old who is the only one of the three still physically able to go fishing. For most of the play, John's wife tries unavailingly to free her husband from the Skipper's domination, until a fatal accident convinces him she is right.

Our attitude to the Skipper is contradictory. He is admirable in his intransigent insistence on natural truths that lie beneath the surface of contemporary society; but, at the same time, he is a monomaniac like Melville's Ahab, who refuses to recognize change or alternative styles of life and is prepared to sacrifice everyone to his own stark vision. Though in the past he was famous for never losing a man, Uncle John accuses him of tyrannizing over his crews for self-aggrandizement . . . and he reminds the Skipper that (like the Magistrate in *Colour the Flesh*) he never showed humanity except to disarm men on the brink of mutiny. This same brutal imposition of personality continues into the present with the Skipper's vendetta against seagulls; his sneer that, if John had gone to the war, "You'd never have survived. Unless I was with you"; and, more comically, with his insistence that his son-in-law must urinate decently, as though he were still on board his ship. Most strikingly, it is shown in the elaborate work rituals—preparing equipment, cleaning, salting, and cooking the fish, and careful cleaning up afterwards—that he enforces before he will allow his companions to celebrate, also ritualistically, his son Absalom's "end of voyage" and miserably small catch. (pp. 29-31)

The egotism of the Skipper's need to impose order is qualified, however, by a strain of mysticism in him. He holds that it is useless to demand meaning, as Uncle John does at one point; life can only be accepted: "It doesn't matter what it means. It's enough that it's there." Fishermen in the past knew their proper place in nature: "We understood each other—the sea, the cod, and the dogfish, and the sculpin and the shark and the whale. They knew us and we knew they. . . ."

And in spite of the fish's disappearance, Skipper Pete believes—or wishes to believe—that this state of things will return, ousting the modern world of relief, welfare, and education, for which he has total contempt: "We waits. . . . And one day, they'll come back in their t'ousands. . . . They's waiting for the old days like we is."

These two sides to his attitude—the "Satanic" compulsion to an order based on egotism and his mystique of man's relation to nature—are given religious overtones, which are handled much more skilfully than the hanged man and *pietà* devices of *Colour the Flesh.* On the surface, the Skipper is an intolerantly conservative Catholic who will not attend his sister-in-law's funeral because it is to be held in a Pentecostal church, nor welcome the visiting bishop because he has come by car instead of boat and the traditional floral arches have not been built to welcome him. The Skipper's orthodoxy is wholly superficial, however. He warns Uncle John that "God is not merciful. Don't ye ever forget that," and seems to substitute his own authority for the bishop's when he defends the sternness of his regime by claiming "I made an arch for ye." When the Skipper boasts of never changing a habit or opinion, Uncle John replies with irony: "You and the Pope 'as got something in common after all then, Skipper . . . ," and John's wife pushes the implications of this a stage further when she says her father is "Only one breath away from God or the Devil himself." On the other hand, the Skipper's reaction to the news of young Jimmy Fogarty's death is wholly pagan and fatalistic, deifying not himself but the sea: "The sea wanted him. Old Molly. She took him in her good time. . . ." (pp. 31-2)

For a while, with memories, work rituals, drink, and snatches of song, the Skipper and his two companions manage to create their own reality within the shack, culminating in the drunken dance of triumph that gives the play its title. A stage direction tells us that during this dance "For a moment they are all one. All free"; and one implication of the title is, of course, the celebration of a sense of life in the raw, a dance of fundamentals. But as the title also implies, it is a dance of discarded remnants as well, the pieces of the fish that are thrown away: the dance is ultimately a dance of death. All along, the emphasis on heroic individualism has been balanced by a recognition of the sterility of the Skipper's way of life. His is a world with no place for women or children. (p. 32)

Uncle John and his wife have only daughters themselves, their son having been stillborn; and John blames this on the Skipper, who, he claims, killed their sex-life by his expectations of a grandson. We hear that when the Skipper's own son, Absalom, was young, his father sent him back into a fifteen-below blizzard to gather five more sticks of firewood and, when the boy's horse returned alone, refused to go to

look for him because "Ye know ye had to bring 'em up hard or else they wouldn't survive."

Absalom is now retarded, a sixty-year-old with the face of a child, still unable to look his father in the face. When he asks the Skipper to sing, his uncle underlines the significance of his name by repeating the psalmist's cry for the son he has destroyed, "Oh Absalom, my son. Absalom. Absalom."

This destructiveness focuses in the action round the death of Jimmy Fogarty, which alters the relationships within the play. When at the end of Act I another child comes to the shed to beg aid for Jimmy, who has fallen off a wharf and cannot swim, the Skipper and Uncle John ignore him, continuing drunkenly to gaze through the church window, discussing a drowning that happened in the past. This callousness looms behind the subsequent celebration of Absalom's catch, as the noise of the search party is heard increasingly outside; and at the end it is Absalom who finds the body and brings it to his father: "Look what I caught by the side of the boat . . . I nivir caught a boy before. What shall I do with him, Father? . . . Can I have him?" (pp. 32-3)

Uncle John had genuinely not noticed the child's plea, in fact, because the Skipper's arm had kept him turned towards the church window, but now he realizes that Skipper Pete had heard and had deliberately ignored the cry for help. The doubts and rebellions that have worried John throughout the play come to a head, and he breaks at last from his father-in-law's dominion, taking Absalom with him ("he don't know nothing about boys. Only fish"). The play ends with Skipper Pete alone, stubbornly returning to the ritual of his evening chores by lamplight, as the sun dies out in the shack's church window.

Except for the rather forced situation where the child's plea is ignored, *Dance* is remarkably economical and successful in fusing realism and symbolism. Cook admits that the Skipper's disregard of the child's request is "unrealistic," but says "The scene was intended to drive home the Skipper's character." . . . (p. 33)

Apart from this particular incident the ingredients of the play are admirably coherent. The characterization of the four main personages—Skipper Pete, Uncle John, Absalom, and John's wife—is sharply individualized; the set, while realistic, has rich symbolic suggestiveness; sounds-off—the sea itself, the mocking cry of seagulls, the bells for Aunt Alice's funeral, and the encroaching noise of the searchers for Jimmy Fogarty's body—all acquire thematic significance; and the elaborate rituals of preparing equipment, feeding the stove, making tea, cleaning and cooking fish, and preparing a celebratory drink, do not substitute for action, mere visual filler, but reflect the old men's attempt to use routines to recreate the past. This culminates in the grotesque dance, which, like the shanties sung by Pete, absorbs "presentational" techniques into the play's realism yet also carries a level of symbolism. The use of a modified Newfoundland dialect which is sparse, proverbial, coarsely comic, and repetitive, gives a sense of authenticity which can rise effortlessly to poetry—as, to give one brief example, Uncle John's comment that Absalom dreams "Of the mackerel thicker'n on the water than moonlight, whispering together." And the result is a powerful, credible picture of the end of an heroic tradition.

The Head, Guts and Soundbone Dance is bracketed by two of Cook's shorter plays, each centring on a character like Skipper Pete, which were written originally for radio but subsequently staged: *Tiln* (1971) a very successful piece which takes the symbolism of *Dance* a step further, and *Quiller* (1975), a less interesting, mainly realistic monologue. A brief comment on these pieces is pertinent before turning to the final play in the trilogy, *Jacob's Wake.*

The setting of *Tiln* is a lighthouse—"a platform on the very edge of space and time"—inhabited by the keeper Tiln, "a crazy old man . . . living on the exposed edge of his soul," who has come to believe that he is God, and by Fern, the dying survivor of a bombed ship from the south (the direction of dangerous civilization where Tiln has refused to go), who with his bible, phonograph, and single record of "Eternal Father, strong to save," has tried for ten years to keep alive some human feeling in Tiln's monomaniacal world. The language of the play is wholly poetic, combining Beckett's stripped down repetitions with lusher passages that show a debt to Dylan Thomas:

> I, Tiln. God of Light. Of the tilting universe.
> Lord of the bladderwrack and the black sea moss.
> Keeper of the pearled and fishy parables of the sea.
> Master of sailing barns.
> Executioner. Jonah's hangman.

Tiln's rituals to impose order and their eventual undermining by a sense of lost humanity constitute what action there is. Like Skipper Pete, Tiln wages war against the mocking sea gulls; he ascends and descends his ladder ceremoniously, counting the rungs and pausing on every third step; he decides to light the lamp in a fixed position to blind the gulls, instead of letting it revolve to warn off shipping ("There are no travellers. There are none to save or destroy"); and climactically he refuses Fern's request to have the burial service read over him, repudiating his appeal "we have been good to each other" (as Pete repudiated his debt to Aunt Alice), tearing his bible and breaking his record of "Eternal Father," and finally "burying" him still dying in a barrel of salt brine: "You are no martyr but my sacrifice. Me. God Tiln. . . . Tiln giveth. Tiln taketh away. That's your service." Once alone again, Tiln finds his isolation unbearable, and the play ends with a tableau like the *pietà* with which *Colour the Flesh* began: Tiln cradling Fern's head in his arms and sobbing "You've cheated me."

Quiller goes to the opposite, realistic extreme. Apart from very brief incursions from some children and two passing women, it takes the form of an old sea captain's rambling monologue and hallucinations about the past, lusting after a neighbour woman, waging war against the mocking children (like Pete and Tiln against the gulls), and conducting folksy conversations with God ("Mornin', Lord. Dis is your servant, Quiller") and his long-dead wife, Sophie. Its mixture of reminiscence, gossip, simplistic philosophizing, and attempts at earthy humour show a good ear for Newfoundland speech and a compassionate understanding of character, but the piece is too long and too static for the stage, without any of the symbolic excitement of *Tiln.* It does show a new aspect of Cook's technique, however, which is important in *Jacob's Wake.*

Whereas *Colour the Flesh* is in presentational "epic" form and *Dance,* for all its realistic elements, operates symbolically, in *Jacob's Wake* Cook relies mainly on contemporary realism. . . . Yet this concern for realism is combined with a variant of the Newfoundland experience that is difficult to present realistically. Cook's object now is apocalyptic. He wishes to convey the destruction of a humanity that has tried

to turn its back on nature. . . . [Cook achieves this through] a sense of the steadily increasing storm outside the outport house which is the setting for the play: "It is essential . . . that the storm becomes a living thing, a character, whose presence is always felt, if not actually heard, on the stage."

For most of the play, however, this storm is strictly background for the human failings displayed within the house, where the celebration of Good Friday has brought together three generations of the Blackburn family, who represent successive stages of alienation from nature. The traditional heroic fatalism of Newfoundland is represented by Elijah Blackburn, an old sealing skipper very like Skipper Pete of *Dance,* who lies bedridden upstairs, confusedly mingling past and present as he has his log books read aloud and barks out orders as though he were afloat. (pp. 34-6)

Like Skipper Pete, he also has a mystic belief that the vanished seals will return and that somehow he will be able to hunt them again: "They'll come back. The swiles'll come back in their t'ousands and when they do, I'll go greet 'em just like in the old days." But his attitude to nature is "Satanic" ("Swiles is bred and killed in Hell, boy"). He defies the storm like Lear in his madness—and his attraction to sealing lies not in the value of the catch but in the excitement of the hunt itself, the risking of one's own life to have the primitive pleasure of killing.

Like Skipper Pete, he scorns his daughter, Mary, an old-maid schoolteacher whom he wishes he had never begotten, and considers her a "poor substitute" for his second son, Jacob, who was lost while hunting. But Elijah is more complex and sensitive than his predecessor. Offsetting his dislike of Mary is his comfortable rapport with his daughter-in-law Rosie; and he is still remorseful over his dead wife's grief for their son, and distressed by her refusal to believe that he did all he could to save him. Indeed, as the title indicates, Elijah's overriding sorrow is the abandonment of Jacob to the ice, a sacrifice that ended the family's capacity to face nature with traditional defiance.

The Skipper's other son, Winston, and Rosie, his wife, are utterly non-heroic but have a capacity for love which provides an alternative to Elijah's pride. This centres on Rosie, whom Cook presents as an almost too perfect Irish-Catholic mother, loving, undemanding, and self-sacrificing. Rosie lacks grandchildren, however, and like Elijah mourns the death of a child, a daughter Sarah, who might have carried on her kind of values.

Sarah was also Winston's favourite ("Everytime I gits afflicted with me family I thinks of the one that might have been different"), and her birth galvanized him for once to a courage in defying the elements that reminded Rosie of Elijah: "I never see ye like it. Ye were like a wild man. Like yer fader almost. . . . I believe ye'd 'ave faced the Divil dat night and gone on."

For Winston, life collapsed after his daughter's death ("It was never the same after she died. I doesn't know why . . ."), and he has since been left believing in nothing: "They's nothin', Rosie. Nothin'. They's madness and they's death and they's some who work at it and some who wait for it."

Winston, in fact, is the most complex character in the play, to whom our attitude changes radically. At first he seems merely idle, vulgar, and malicious, drinking heavily, hazing his returned sons, and teasing his spinster sister with indecencies. There is a sense of violence in the man, moreover, which culminates in his ineffectual firing of a shotgun after he hears that his son Alonzo has forged his name. His cry on hearing of this—"My name! 'Tis all I've got left"—reveals the damaged self-respect beneath this coarseness. (pp. 36-7)

Our sympathy for him grows as we realize . . . [his] sensitivity and note his tenderness not only for Rosie and the dead Sarah but also for the tragic Mildred Tobin, who froze to death with her illegitimate child when her father turned her out into a storm. Moreover, though he knew the culprit was really his own son Brad, Winston loyally kept this quiet even when gossip fathered the child on himself. . . . [He] resists the move to commit the old man to a mental home, and by the time his sister rejects his offer of reconciliation, throwing beer in his face, our sympathies for the two have switched completely.

In the Blackburns' degeneration Mary has a position between that of Rosie and Winston and that of their children, and our attitude towards her balances exactly our attitude to Winston. Initially, we are sympathetic to her pride in teaching standards, her contempt for her coarse brother and the nephew Alonzo, her opposition to her father's tyranny and to all the men's exploitation of Rosie's good nature, and the pride she shows in her favourite nephew, Wayne. But gradually the narrowness and lack of generosity in her nature emerge. Laudable independence shades into closefistedness, distaste for sexual coarseness becomes a chilling condemnation of the pathetic Mildred Tobin, and pride in Wayne shows itself possessive and even snobbish, as she exults in the impression they will make riding in his car to church. It is she who is ultimately behind the move to put the Skipper in an asylum—a move that denies the values of both Elijah and Winston—though it is Wayne who is her willing instrument in this treachery, just as he has been responsible for the final breakdown of his brother Brad by getting him dismissed from his parish.

The third generation of Blackburns has degenerated completely from the heroism of the Skipper, in fact: the "time of the seal" has given place to "the day of the dogfish." Winston describes their attitudes to Elijah without illusion: "One of 'em pretends ye don't exist and the other wants to save yer black soul. And the third waits fer yer will." (pp. 37-8)

The realism of these family relationships (which have more than a whiff of O'Neill about them) is deepened by religious symbolism. Placing the action on Maundy Thursday and Good Friday not only provides a realistic excuse for the family's reunion but is also meant to relate to Elijah's sacrifice of Jacob on an April 5th many years before. Thus the mourning for Christ is also Jacob's Wake, and their parallelism is driven home by the crucifixion image, borrowed from David Blackwood's striking series of Newfoundland etchings "The Lost Party," in which the Skipper recalls his last sight of his son: "The way dey was, so far away, dey seemed to form a t'in black cross on the ice. Den the ground drift swallowed dem up. . . ." This image is recapitulated later as a premonition of disaster: " 'Tis the shape of death, boy. I kin see'n jest like that first time, rising out of the drift, moving across the ice widout a sound, a man like a cross growing up into the sky." (p. 39)

As usual in Cook, there is . . . an attempt to use the set to

suggest several levels of response. Wayne's type of society is represented by the blandness of the radio's music and its stilted weather forecasts, which gradually give place to the real thing as the storm increases in violence, screaming round the house and finally overwhelming the radio and the lights. Within the house itself a distinction is established between the ground floor and the bedrooms. On the ground floor the ordinary aspects of outport life are conveyed by realistic conversation and methodical processes of quilting, cooking, drying firewood, playing cards, and even preparing drinks—"a traditional part of the family ritual." The bedroom level, by contrast, is appropriately the realm of vision—Brad's nightmares of the last judgment and the Skipper's reliving of his sons' death and premonitions that the house is a ship drifting to disaster.

At the end these levels are suddenly reversed. While the apparent corpse of the Skipper is visible on his bed above, his "ghost" enters below to take charge of the house like a ship, impressing his son and grandsons as part of the crew, and heading, he says, defiantly into the truth of the storm: "Comes a time. . . . When ye has to steer into the storm and face up to what ye are." There is also the sound of seals, and Elijah exults, "The swales is back. Newfoundland is alive and well and roaring down the ice-pack. . . ."

But then the play ends with nature triumphing in "a blackout and the sound of a cosmic disaster . . . the final release of the insensate fury of nature that has been building throughout the play." When the lights go up, the fragile house is empty save for the death mask of Elijah, and "All fades into the lone quiet crying of a bitter wind." (pp. 39-40)

[The significance of the conclusion] is clear in the context of Cook's other work; he has mingled realism and symbolism in all his plays; and *Jacob's Wake* itself has a persistent symbolic level, with the identification of house and ship repeated many times before the transformation. Nevertheless, the experiment fails: the reversal of levels is too extreme, and the significance of the end remains unclear. . . .

The failure is an instructive one, however, because of its very boldness. The dilemma Cook faces as a playwright is that the experience he wishes to convey arises from an only too actual reality—the awesome environment of Newfoundland—which he cannot present on stage. He is forced to convey its significance poetically, through heightened language and stage symbolism, but this has an allegorical effect, removing the experience from the actuality that is its very essence. Only in *The Head, Guts and Soundbone Dance* has he found a form to fuse these levels, and even there it is at some cost to the realism. *Jacob's Wake* switches between the levels too abruptly; while the "epic" looseness of *Colour the Flesh* allows realism and symbolism to coexist without a proper fusion. Perhaps the problem is insoluble in stage terms; but unless it is solved, Michael Cook's imagination itself remains "on the edge," its undeniable power denied an adequate dramatic form. (p. 40)

Brian Parker, "On the Edge: Michael Cook's New-foundland Trilogy," in Canadian Literature, *No. 85, Summer, 1980, pp. 22-41.*

Douglas Crase

1944-

American poet.

In his acclaimed first collection, *The Revisionist* (1981), Crase assesses the physical and moral condition of America. As he delineates a beloved landscape that is threatened by literal and metaphoric erosion, Crase argues for an imaginative "revisioning" of the country that emphasizes its wild, natural beauty and unique cultural heritage. Like Walt Whitman, Crase combines scenic description and philosophical meditation in free verse forms to create a nationalist aesthetic, and, like John Ashbery, Crase employs a discursive, effusive tone to convey his impressions. While some reviewers commented that Crase's formal, iambic verse induced obfuscation, most praised his intelligent, graceful style. Vernon Shetley concluded: "For a first book to show at once as much achievement and as much invention as this one marks it as an important event. This is a poetry that convinces us not merely by an assured and masterful style, but by its ability to acknowledge its own limits without bitterness or nostalgia, by its ingenuity in turning the losses of experience into imaginative gain."

PHOEBE PETTINGELL

Until the American renaissance of the mid-19th century, our writers looked primarily to English literature for their models. Ralph Waldo Emerson, while lamenting this parasitic tendency, nevertheless declared confidently that "America is a poem in our eyes; its ample geography dazzles the imagination, and it will not wait long for metres." His words were heard by the young Walt Whitman, and soon the hopeful prophesy was being fulfilled by a vital home-grown poetic tradition. (p. 14)

"If I could raise rivers, I'd raise them / Across the mantle of your past: old headwaters / Stolen, oxbows high and dry while new ones form, / A sediment of history rearranged." Thus the central voice in Douglas Crase's ***The Revisionist***. . . . Crase has a painter's eye and embodies his ideas in landscapes. Titles such as **"Six Places in New York State"** or **"Great Fennville Swamp"** might suggest Currier & Ives prints translated into verse, but Crase's real goal is to restore America to its original beauty—if only he can discover what that would look like. In one section of the long title poem **"The Revisionist,"** he catalogues his methods for righting sundry wrongs: Asphalt parking lots will be torn up to restore lost buildings, interstates scribbled across the plains will be erased, foreign trees (and their blights, like Dutch elm disease) will be deported, and European art treasures will be sold to buy back American paintings in museums abroad. "I can see that my intervention is required, / The more urgently as your prospects alter and disappear," this fanatic proclaims to scattered Americana. "As you are dispersed, / Return and inhabit me." . . .

Bemused to discover that the very ground of America, not merely its people, partakes of melting-pot pluralism, the poet despairs of ever recapturing the primal continent. Out of this disappointment, however, comes the realization that America is constantly renewing itself. "The heat of the fires / Which burned over your logged-out heart released / The seed of the jack pine and gave it a delayed / But native start." In the end, the poet transcends his own grudges to conclude that "Although the past / Seems to be level in its place there's room for more / And the ragged additions polish the previous days."

Crase creates dramatic tension by concentrating on the fluid interplay between history and our changing perspective on it. **"America Began in Houses,"** for example, traces the Colonial architectural style from its inception to its debased revival in modern subdivisions. Still, Crase's outlook remains hopeful, and even here he foresees the possibility of valid new forms; "Strangely, as the pilgrim / Aspirations increase they seem to diminish in promise / Yet who can say that out of these borrowed fashions / Won't come a suburban mutant enlarging nature / Once again. The Federal fanlight opens in the sun. / And on the gateleg table is a treaty to be signed."

The Revisionist is a remarkable first book of poems, an audacious attempt to put Emerson's poem that is America into "metres." That Crase's invocation of the Whitmanian poetic tradition can be so powerful after all these years of overuse and abuse is a small miracle of revisionism itself. **"The Continent as the Letter M"** shows Crase able to take on not only Walt's expansiveness but the musicality of Wallace Stevens as well. He uses both to capture the spirit of America's "ample geography":

> So many centuries thicken its animal sound,
> This mammoth that holds us between its knees,
> *Maumee, Menominee, Michilimackinac,*
> Deep, past Appalachian deep
> The inarticulate lives in its hold on me.

(p. 15)

> *Phoebe Pettingell, "America in 'Metres'," in* The New Leader, *Vol. LXIV, No. 11, June 1, 1981, pp. 14-15.*

LOUIS SIMPSON

The gulf is widening in American verse between poetry that speaks from experience and makes its appeal through sensuous images, narrative, and drama, and poetry that is highly mannered, aiming to derive pleasure from words alone. . . .

The subordination of feeling or drama to a formal arrangement is as marked in Douglas Crase's *The Revisionist.* I don't mind a poet's using a mannered style—Yeats, for instance, could be very grand—but I object to verbosity, and Crase is verbose. And he uses abstract language . . . so that his argument is obscure—and he is always arguing. But in fact, what this writing produces is not a line of argument but a sound. It is what philosophy sounds like. As with the later poems of Wallace Stevens, to understand what Crase is saying you would have to study the poem—you cannot grasp it as a whole, sound and meaning both, while his ponderous sentences are unrolling. That is to say, there is the disassociation of sensibility, split between sound and meaning, Eliot pointed to 50 years ago. Some poets and critics actually seem to prefer it—this is why Stevens has been having a vogue. They prefer ratiocination to the kind of involvement that lyrical and dramatic poetry demands. (p. 4)

Throughout his book Crase refers to topography, geology and the weather in order to raise questions about the nature of perception. But we don't arrive at any insights, for ideas in poems have no effect unless they are realized in images or embodied in an action we can see and feel. (p. 5)

> *Louis Simpson, "The Down-to-Earth and the Acrobatic," in* Book World—The Washington Post, *June 7, 1981, pp. 4-5.*

CHARLES MOLESWORTH

Douglas Crase's excellent book, **The Revisionist,** is even more impressive considered as a first effort. Mr. Crase has what it usually takes several books to achieve: an important subject; a consistent and supple attitude toward it; and a style rich enough to answer to it. His subject is America, more specifically the spirit of place, for he writes of geology, colonial history, Federal architecture and a variety of landscapes. His attitude is probing, tenacious, and he conveys it without too much cynicism or weariness and with an occasional sprightliness. Stylistically, his work uses a free loose verse that comes

close to musical prose. Like Merrill's and Ashbery's, his writing argues sinuously, often subordinating sentence elements and juggling contexts in an almost baroque way. His failures are what usually count as virtues, but virtues overdone: too much elegance; too much richness of reference, which leads to obscurity. But the large proportion of Mr. Crase's poems succeed, in whole or in part.

Imagine, paradoxically, Auden as the guiding spirit of style and Williams as the instructor of concerns, and you have a sense of Mr. Crase's richness. He can be accurate and nimble with metaphor and description. . . . He can also be discursive, boldly minimizing imagery when required. . . . Douglas Crase writes of the nation, materially and mythically. Some may say he writes more as a Horatian poet than in our native grain. But that draws the boundaries too narrowly. It's more important to note that he has written on a large scale, and with considerable authority. (p. 12)

> *Charles Molesworth, "Three American Poets," in* The New York Times Book Review, *August 23, 1981, pp. 12, 29.*

HELEN McNEIL

So many of John Ashbery's idiosyncrasies crop up in Douglas Crase's **The Revisionist** that Crase's topographical, hortatory and even nationalist address to the reader comes as a sharp surprise. The powerful and witty title-poem addresses an America which Crase wants to "revise." . . . The tone of **"The Revisionist"** varies eccentrically but convincingly between ecological indictment, descriptive natural history, high-cultural whimsy, and the eroticism of Hart Crane's *The Bridge:* "I've wondered to find you waiting there tethered / and dreaming". In another long poem, **"Six Places in New York State",** Crase meditates upon landscape and character, shifting skilfully from philosophy to sensation to memory. Crase's poems take their strong visual sense from nineteenth and twentieth-century American art, with Jackson Pollock's *Blue Poles* seen as "seismic totems" of the continent. Crase's parodic homage to William Cullen Bryant (and to Ashbery) in **"To a Watertower"** makes another link between the topographical, the nationalist, and the aesthetic. Yet Crase is least convincing when he most resembles Ashbery. His fondness for first lines referring to "it" and "things" indicates an Ashbery-like fastidiousness about naming the object too soon. But the technique is over-used to the point of mannerism. Crase is the unusual case of a contemporary poet whose most public, expansive voice is his most authentic.

> *Helen McNeil, "In the Line of the Image," in* The Times Literary Supplement, *No. 4113, January 29, 1982, p. 113.*

JAY PARINI

[**The Revisionist** is] an amazingly good book. . . . For sheer ambition, ingenuity, and wit, Crase stands alone [among new American poets]. He writes with dizzying confidence, gently alluding to his various precursors—Whitman, Stevens, and Ashbery—but in a style utterly his own. An intelligent poet above all else, he can sustain an argument throughout a relatively long poem, such as the title poem, where he addresses America itself in bold, fanciful terms. . . . This intimately discursive tone carries through the eight sections of Crase's opening poem [**"The Revisionist"**] which might be called a crazy love poem for a threatened landscape that originates somewhere in the poet's mind and demands imaginative reconstruction, or revision: "I can see that my intervention is required," he writes, "the more urgently as your prospects alter and disappear."

Crase's "conclusion" in **"The Revisionist"** is that "everything allows itself to be seen again / In the focus of its possibilities." And he proceeds to revise the world by seeing it again, closely, turning it over in the mind's eye until its metaphoric potential is realized. In **"The Winter House,"** a brilliant poem about the artist's necessary progress from literal to imaginative vision, Crase observes that

> in the seasons there is a kind of law
> Of conservation of fullness and vision
>   that takes over
> And as things disappear they leave
>   behind the clear
> Outline of the immensities they
>   occupied, their cool
> Horizons.

Crase allows these immensities to grow inside of him, to become him: "Beautiful, / Our actions depend upon finding their objects / And growing around them / Until one or the other is forced to bloom." That comes from **"The House at Sagg,"** in which Crase declares that "The simple things / . . . exist." In taking their measure, we "emulate their still extent." This emulation, of course, involves us in the delicate process of limitation, and limits—Crase explains elsewhere—"apprise you / Of where things are likely to end." But limitation does not mean restriction, and while celebrating limits Crase somehow manages to revise the world in such a way as to admit endless possibility. "A poet's subject," Wallace Stevens once said, "is his sense of the world." And Crase offers a sense of things so fresh and vigorous that he can afford to end his book with this sentence: "There is nothing to fear." (pp. 37-8)

Jay Parini, "A New Generation of Poets," in The New Republic, *Vol. 186, No. 15, April 14, 1982, pp. 37-9.*

VERNON SHETLEY

The poets who mean the most to us are those who tell us about what we cannot see by reason of its very proximity. What we look for in the voices of young poets is news of the freshest modifications of our consciousness. . . .

So we scan the emerging poets of this country for signs "of the metaphysical changes that occur / Merely in living as and where we live," to use Stevens's phrase. What we find mostly, of course, is evidence of changes in the models used for imitation. The best of our young poets, however, show us the various paths open to the contemporary mind.

The disconcerting quality of Douglas Crase's poems [in *The Revisionist*] seems to lie in their straightforwardness. Crase states even his most peculiar propositions in a tone so matter-of-fact that one is likely to be caught off guard, forced to retrace one's steps to grasp the import of some seemingly unarguable statement. The self in Crase's poems does not make its own performance the matter of the poem, does not indulge in gestures trying to expose or erase the self. Even Crase's "I," because it addresses a "you" at once personal and extended, seems to take on that extension, and present us not with opinions, but with statements of fact. Statements of imaginative fact, to be sure, but information, nevertheless, delivered in a broad summarizing way that tends to submerge peculiarities of voice and viewpoint.

The intense and steady concentration with which Crase grasps and works at his subject suggests attention to the Emersonian admonition to "Ask the fact for the form." Crase seems to give us the energy of thought brought directly to utterance:

> Nothing is ever over in a place like
>   this, which is one
> Of the reasons why people come to
>   look at it. As an
> Exhibit the waterfall is naturally
>   unsurpassed: part of
> Its fascination must be in the way it
>   demonstrates how
> An event can be still permanent
>   when it depends for its
> Definition on continually going
>   over the edge. . . .

The revisionism that Crase announces in his title lies in his attempt to read, in the "sediment of history," the crucial points of contact between the past and our own situation. Crase has an exact sense of the pressures of historical time and cultural place, neither diminishing those forces to elements of an autobiography nor reducing them to abstractions. Whether in his frequent poems about places, or in poems about love, Crase defines his subject to include its broadest imaginative possibilities, then proceeds to reveal and examine those possibilities. . . . Crase views things from an unusual angle but his vision nowhere obtrudes as merely a peculiarity. [In **"The Revisionist"**], the "you" addressed seems at once a former lover and America itself, a conception that in other hands surely would seem a tour de force; Crase treats it so naturally that one is convinced he really does conceive of love affairs and his relation to America in the same terms. . . .

Crase's trick is to accept the impoverishment of the imagination, to acknowledge its contingency on the history and culture that surround or engulf it. The poetic self surrenders its privileged position, opening itself to the pressures that limit the imagination. Yet having accepted this diminishment, Crase goes on to locate the imagination outside himself, outside imagination, in the very realm of facts that seemed to confine and suffocate it. If "Our imaginations have let us down" in the face of the world, we must renounce sublime aspirations, and the world itself must grow imaginative. . . . First books of poetry show promise more often than achievement. For a first book to show at once as much achievement and as much invention as this one marks it as an important event. This is a poetry that convinces us not merely by an assured and masterful style, but by its ability to acknowledge its own limits without bitterness or nostalgia, by its ingenuity in turning the losses of experience into imaginative gain.

Vernon Shetley, "Ask the Fact," in The New York Review of Books, *Vol. XXIX, No. 7, April 29, 1982, p. 43.*

ROBERT von HALLBERG

[In *The Revisionist*], Crase has found a way of talking that sounds plausibly contemporary, unpretentious, and humane, and that enables him to move easily and rapidly, as in conversation, from one topic to the next. His writing is lively, imaginative, and often thoughtful. . . . Perhaps *smart* is the right term: at his best Crase brings intelligence to bear on areas of experience that seem to have been undeservedly neglected. These lines from **"Sagg Beach,"** the most acute explanatory poem in the book, show how Crase can deploy intelligence casually, with a kind of effortless reach for homely figures:

> In them
> The present seems a firm result, in us the endless shame
> Of a model manufacture that went wrong. We dream
> On our potential as if nothing had happened since
> As if we each were the parents of our specifications
> And not their child. It's an anxious excursion,
> Red-pencilling your infancy.

Yet often the pressure to be intelligent leaves the writing merely smart, in the sense of stylish, clever, self-aware.

The Revisionist is a longish book of notably uneven quality. Crase allows himself time, even in individual poems, to turn up something good. In most of the poems, he is as unconcerned with concision as his masters Whitman and Ashbery are. One could delete several poems from the book without pain; the workshop exercises **"The Continent as the Letter M,"** with *m*-sounds in nearly every line, and **"Great Fennville Swamp,"** which includes more than a dozen clauses beginning "The thing about" or "The thing is" would be at the top of my list, because they are smart after the fashion of Ashbery's "Into the Dusk-Charged Air." Throughout the book phrases and lines could be excised, if force or point were what one were after. Sometimes redundancy is a problem, as when he says that "the ocean / Not only surrounds us *on both sides,* it meets in the middle, too, / Because half the ocean is the ocean air" (my italics). More often, the style just seems loose. . . . It takes Crase a good many words to make a point, yet he always has one. A young poet who can begin his career in this Whitmanesque mode of explaining everything in his country has a powerful claim on one's patience.

Economy is not Crase's thing, to use one of his preferred words. Like Ashbery, he seeks an air of irrelevance that, however diffuse it renders poetry, calls to mind how most of life is routinely passed. The book begins with a catalogue of natural quick-changes (hurricanes, frost, volcanoes), but erosion is Crase's main theme. . . . Finding a style fit for this theme involves some difficulties: one may be drawn toward a slow-moving, uneventful manner of writing; in which case, little jokes, flashes of wit ("people don't wish on erosion"), will seem a way of forestalling tedium. Then, too, only a geologist thinks that a landscape requires explanation; poets are customarily content to describe landscape. . . . Crase has a good landscape-poet's eye for changes of quality, those shifts that are entirely palpable but hard to fix.

Crase, however, is only partly a descriptive poet; his more constant ambition is to explain moral life. As he himself says, one does not watch the erosion of a landscape; one sees only the results and is told of the process. Insofar as moral life can be treated in similar terms, there is danger in a poem trying to explain much more than it shows. A few poems in *The Revisionist* (**"The House at Sagg"** and **"Toronto Means the Meeting Place"**) do not get beyond pontifications, old Creeleyisms about the adequacy of the visible, and so on. A still greater peril for Crase in this erosion figure arises from the fact that, even for geologists, explanations of erosion bottom out rather sooner than explanations of moral life: a geologist

takes more for granted than a moralist does; one does not ask exactly why a landscape should change, or when. (pp. 556-59)

Like Ammons, Crase looks to the landscape for a way of talking almost philosophically about the meaning of life. [**"Genessee Falls"**] makes the point that life is like a waterfall. At the end of this 41-line poem, it is plain that Crase has a way of talking and thinking in verse. (Most of the poems are written in loosely iambic six- or seven-beat line. The distinctive feature of the prosody is the way that the beginnings and ends of lines often chip off a few syllables . . . to undermine—or erode—the firmness of the line.) But as explanatory verse the poem is shallow and repetitive. That a waterfall cannot be frozen into segmented scenes, that events in life are inextricably connected to each other in series, are true but not searching statements. ". . . You won't find it, though." The pressure to explain life is insufficiently great to move Crase far beyond the obvious. A merely smart poet can be too easily satisfied to hear himself talk engagingly; this is a difficulty that Crase needs to resolve. But a poet as vigorous and generous-spirited as Crase will very likely find a compelling way around this and other problems in the future. (p. 559)

Robert von Hallberg, in a review of "The Revisionist," in Contemporary Literature, *Vol. 23, No. 4, Fall, 1982, pp. 556-59.*

WILLIAM H. PRITCHARD

[*The Revisionist*] was highly touted by that poet of whim-wham and filigree [John Ashbery], also by the official designator of "strong poets," Harold Bloom. So I was doubly on my guard, only to be charmed and awed—in a way I seldom am with Ashbery—by Crase's elegant procedures, his command of name and place, his inventive scope and generosity. He is excellent at sweeping you up and into the poem with a rush of breathless but patiently extended assertion:

> Nothing is ever over in a place like
>   this, which is one
> Of the reasons why people come to
>   look at it. As an
> Exhibit the waterfall is naturally
>   unsurpassed; part of
> Its fascination must be the way it
>   demonstrates how
> An event can be still permanent
>   when it depends for its
> Definition on continually going
>   over the edge.
>
> **("Genessee Falls")**

This sounds like Ashbery, but is less wilfully and flashily discontinuous; in reading Crase you don't constantly have to be saying, oh *wow,* what will he do next that we never could have expected? On occasion, one can even read through a poem and feel at the end of it some confidence about its development—that it *has* a development. . . . [**"Summer"**] is one of Crase's more modest efforts, though modesty is typically in his air and manner, for all the freedom effected so daringly by his language.

Things can become oppressive at times, since poem after poem conducts itself at the same leisurely pace, never a rhyme or the shape of a stanza to provide any formal limits within which the voice must discipline its unfoldings. And every so often the manner seems rather too-too preciously accepting of it all. . . . The volume's *tour de force,* which I've reread many times with pleasure, is called **"Great Fennville Swamp,"** and essays—again and again—to describe what is "The thing about the Great Fennville Swamp," developing into among other "things" the following: "The thing about sounds is the way / The swamp sounds at night, a blank tape hissing with too / Much gain, and nothing but background in the background you / Can hear."

Crase flirts with the possibility, indeed can nicely demonstrate, that poems are "sounds"; but, as with Whitman (a presence in this volume) poems are also about things, about America. One of the book's best poems is **"Abraham Lincoln in Cleveland,"** which beautifully renders the concrete in a larger abstract:

> Dead center: it's one of a thousand capitals
> In this abstract territory of ours, its dominant
> Structure departing, arriving, as if a terminal
> Was the best that anyone could do.

But this is a place that "things" have happened to, somehow:

> the department store was once an opera house,
> Fat trains moved for a hundred years, the river's
> been
> Altered by Republic Steel.

Evocations of Lincoln's funeral train passing through alternate with glimpses of the city today ("At night after work we see how / The white people are beginning to disappear") and the poem ends with a fine, felt response to the exhilaration and the peril of life in these United States:

> It's true, the terrible
> Body stopped here on its way to a living grave,
> Gathered mourning around it as it went and left
> For us this bared unbearable heart with the logic
> Gone out of it: one of thousands to be built
> All alike across the indecipherable land from which
> Every road leads home and none is getting there.

This seems to me the voice of a potentially major talent, but certainly, at the least, that of a rewarding and original new poet. (pp. 182-85)

William H. Pritchard, "Intelligence and Invention," in Salmagundi, *No. 60, Spring-Summer, 1983, pp. 176-85.*

RICHARD TILLINGHAST

[In ***The Revisionist,***] Mr. Crase's subject is nothing less than America—her landscape, her history, her buildings, her soul. This is a staggeringly ambitious book, and its author sets about his task manfully, with no bashfulness or false modesty, even addressing the country (though not, let me add, by name) in the second person—a form of address which is more familiar to us through the medium of the television commercial. The title poem, about two hundred lines long, admirably detailed and informative, with its stated purpose of revising the course of American thought, begins: "If I could raise rivers, I'd raise them / Across the mantle of your past: old headwaters / Stolen, oxbows high and dry while new ones form, / A sediment of history rearranged." Though he never quite makes clear the future he has in mind, his treatment of particulars is both impressive in its breadth and delightful in its vividness. (p. 474)

Crase's poems are often dense and difficult, and must be read several times. This poetry does not sing. Crase instead achieves a tone that is equally cerebral and conversational. He worries away at his subject—or comes at it obliquely, backs off, then tries again—until a deeper understanding or strikingly novel point of view is achieved. His style owes much to the poetry of John Ashbery and has some of the same faults, including a tendency toward obfuscation—as in his use of the word *mantle* in the first passage quoted above—sometimes seemingly pursued almost for its own sake. An arresting poem, **"In Memory of My Country,"** devoted to weather and the landscape, begins "As the land lifts / The weather begins at once to wear it down." The obscurity of the ending, however, leaves one with a vague feeling of dissatisfaction: "Hard as granite, the weather levels the record / Of the toughest past whose moments unfasten / In confusion with the active land."

The Revisionist nevertheless is a book to be reckoned with. I can hardly think of another poet who convinces us so well of the significance of what Richard Wilbur calls "the things of this world":

> The way physical things add up,
> The plain practical shapes of them. . . .
>   Our bodies, of course, but also
> The space they agitate in a just right bed,
> The doorways that make you stoop and the ones
>   that don't.

(pp. 474-75)

Richard Tillinghast, "Ten New Poets," in The Sewanee Review, *Vol. XCI, No. 3, Summer, 1983, pp. 473-83.*

FREDERICK GARBER

The cover of [***The Revisionist***] shows an old Kodak print of the face of an abandoned factory. The sky is visible through its back windows because the factory is empty, between businesses or, more likely, ready to be supplanted by a new structure. In front is a river pool which becomes a broad and busy falls, a place where (as Crase puts it in **"Genesee Falls"**) "nothing is ever over," where "an event can still be permanent when it depends for its / Definition on continually going over the edge." Hints of allegory are in the print as well as the poem; indeed, they are everywhere in Crase's book, where meaning is often singular but never single. We could, then, take the print as pairing artifact and natural fact, the water brightly busy at its permanent falling, the building busy only with its own undoing. Put that way the pairing makes a comfortable cliché, an easy way of engaging things, useful when we need comfort, fascinating because it makes for a special kind of seeing, the kind that platitudes prompt. In **"The Pinnacle Range"** and **"Chimney Bluff"** (the poems which straddle **"Genesee Falls"**) Crase takes up the way in which old bundles of words—"the spirit of place," "blood, sweat and tears"—can be determinants of seeing, just as waves always "troop" toward you. Yet there are other kinds of seeing both in the print and the poems, for example the kind where we look through the building's emptiness to the greater emptiness of the sky. The places we build are calendars, Crase says in **"To a Watchtower."** To keep them from destruction means to keep old calendars going, "even when plunder redeems piecemeal." And that, it seems, is the only kind of redeeming we can do: "You, you are under an acid rain, / A skyline more notable for the gaps in it, / A history, the too many places / Where much of the sky shows through." The old shoe factory is one of those places, not only something we see but an instrument of seeing, a mode of vision which we envision as, at once, both thing and process, object and means. *The Revisionist* is not only about revising history but revisioning it, seeing it again and anew, in buildings we see and see through, in thick swamps or in water that always "begins (or just begins) to fall," in places where we meet old lovers as well as the remnants of those old events that make new events comprehensible ("After a few hundred years / A shipwreck becomes a way of seeing things"). And since nothing is single in Crase, that revising which is revisioning is only one of the kinds of vision seen in his book.

Yet seeing, in the largest revisionary sense, is also a kind of hearing: what is seen is not only old places but old ways of speaking as well, ways which had as much to do with our beginning as did the places which were lived in and looked at. Voices were as good as edifices for getting things going. In **"America Began in Houses"** Crase goes over Colonial and later styles, wondering about taste and originality "when this meeting of artifice and artifact occurs": "could they really have planted lilacs / By the door, had Sheraton sideboards when they were the rage, / Stencilled the dining room till only the wainscot / Had been spared?" And should we really continue these styles, these old ways of saying what we were, ways lived with so long that they keep on having an effect? Styles are ways of speaking, artifactual voices. Maybe, if we work at it, there will come from "these borrowed fashions . . . a suburban mutant enlarging nature once again." Crase shows us how that can happen through his own handling of artifactual voice. The comment about lilacs by the door brings in Whitman as theme but Whitman had been a theme and a voice from the first page of the book. The first poem, the title poem, begins with an urge for remaking the face of America, a revision of its look through a hand-made apocalypse, generated by the speaker, that would make it a new home, "a place returning and a place to turn to whole." The remaking takes place in a kind of conditional boasting ("If I could . . . If I had") which would unlock lakes, move sunspots around, push tides. The tone, the sweep, the American area in which he would work, the ambiguity of the addressee (who may be America or a lover or both)—all this is Whitman but not so much Whitman echoed as Whitman used, Whitman drawn in as a voice which had spoken of such things. He is not a feared predecessor but a welcome one, a seer who is part of what is seen, part of the material with which one works. In much of Crase there are long Whitmanesque lines with a rich inner music. We are aware of the music because of its richness but it never becomes oppressive, never too much of what is not always a good thing. Crase knows that his music has to do with the rhythms of his world and the movements of the self in that world, just as music did for Whitman. It is thus that Whitman comes into Crase's experience. His ways were ways of rendering what Crase now sees. When they appear in Crase's poems, they are as much about annals as about seeing, as much about how things were done as about current doing. To use them as Crase does is not only to offer homage but to make Whitman a subject as well as a voice, that which one watches as well as that which one speaks. Whitman, like the factory on the cover, is both thing and process, object and means. His way of speaking is part of the history Crase ponders, much like the oak at Cuylerville to which the Indians tied a sadistic lieutenant's intestines. To touch the oak, to sound Whitman's speech, is to do what Crase hoped old styles would do: to offer "that suburban mutant enlarging nature once again."

And it is, in some ways, a curious mutant indeed. There is a great deal of Ashbery here, perhaps as much as there is of Whitman, not stressed in the way that Whitman is, present openly in a few poems like **"Création du Monde,"** more subdued but steadily perceptible through many of the other poems. It is not only that Crase can handle a classical contemporary obscurity, that mode which Ashbery defines, its import always at the edge of our reach. With all the Whitmanesque expansiveness there is a laid-back quality in Crase, a cool reminiscent of Ashbery in many of his modes and, for this reader, of the early Miles Davis. His effusiveness never turns to self-preening, as Whitman's sometimes does. His yawps are always civil. If there are times when we meet pure Ashbery there are none when we meet pure Whitman. That point says much about where Crase is at and what he is doing, his own making of suburban mutants.

Where one is at is always where others have been, some for as long as they could manage, others only for what they could just get away with. The lieutenant whose intestines unravelled around the oak had an unparalleled attachment to place. Crase takes the poem close to a mockery of his own insights and methods, his own obsessions with the relations of self, seeing and place: "you should expect the novelty to increase / As proof of your own similar involvement comes unwound." He plays with grossness and a kind of enforced empathy ("this clear interior, / So beautiful it turns you inside out to look at it"), his mastery of tone taking in puns which shock but never sicken, all at the service of seeing: "there's more than one way to look at a place and this / Is one of them." His way is one of the ways one could look at Cuylerville, at the particulars which he ponders with a profound existential awe because they were there at the lieutenant's time: "*that* feature, *this* one, these same / Horizons were really here." To touch such truths is to enlarge nature by linking what was and what is. Old and new ties to place are tied to each other by what could and can still be seen. In **"Blue Poles,"** a poem on a painting by Jackson Pollock, he talks of tracing erratic riverbeds down between canyon walls which still speak brightly of their own making. Though they seem outside of our possible experience "they are instead the particulars surrounding present / Consciousness," ways—the only ways—of making contact with what was, links to line up points for present seeing. Crase uses them as a surveyor uses particulars, and to much the same effect: **"Blue Poles"** grows out of a conceit on Pollock's painting as a road map. One knows places partly by knowing how things hold themselves within them. That is especially so for things and settings so fitting and fitted that they make an incomparable match, each one knowable only when we know the other. And it is as true of present fittings as of old ones. **"In Defense of Ellis Hollow Creek"** puts that point precisely: "in their surroundings one gets to know / The lively specificity of things." No knowing is quite as unique as that, "exclusive as things are where they grow / Exact." To get at history, then, one has to envision the iridescence of the lieutenant's guts but note, in addition, how the specificity of the oak, the being it has in that context, surrounds, commands and partly surrenders to present consciousness. We come to know a place not only through what went on (and out) there but what grew and still grows fitted, fittingly, there. Seeing is hearing and saying but it is also, and perhaps as a result, a mode of the sort of knowing that only places can give. In **"Ellis Hollow**

Creek" Crase recognizes "the claim of knowledge abandoned at its source." In **"Blue Poles"** the seismic totems "advance / On the waking extent of the world, what it knew."

To know such fittingness is clearly a marvellous instrument for the revisionist but, in a series of poems on present occasions, Crase delves lovingly into fittingness in itself, what it is like, what it entails. **"Locale," "The House at Sagg," "Gunpowder Morning in a Gray Room"** and **"Sagg Beach"** (these among others) show Crase probing the immediate relations of self and place, what it means and it is like to *be* in a place. In **"Locale"** the speaker seeks out the essence of a sound, the sound of the place being a place: "For something / Which is part of life it's attached / In a funny way and yet there's no danger / Of it ever flying off to someplace else." In **"The House at Sagg"** we hear how "the minutes / Reach for footing" in physicality, in our bodies but also in the spaces they occupy (beds, doorways); and those spaces, and the physicality other than ours which fills them, show how where we are and what touches us become what we are and do: "Beautiful, / Our actions depend on finding their objects / And growing around them / Until one or the other is forced to bloom." In **"Gunpowder Morning in a Gray Room"** Crase envisions what it would be like to be so at one with oneself that rearrangement is never needed: "Not to feel the weather, / How would that feel? To be tuned to a shape / Long since assumed, sure, single, *in from the wind.*" The relations of shape and being come up again in **"Sagg Beach"**: "The form you have / Is just what you are, real, and when you shine / It is with this delivered fact." That comes after a pained pondering of what we have become, "the endless shame / Of a model manufacture that went wrong," the anxious uselessness of "re-pencilling your infancy." To see Crase whole we have to see that such speculations are basic to his entire work, that they take form in revisionary actions but also in a vision of the meaning of presentness.

The point of those speculations involves both history and immediacy. All actions in the book, all of its visions and revisions, are acts of homemaking, of the self's making a place for itself to be in the world; and that is so not only for what Crase sees (both around him and in history) but for his own seeing of those subjects. The ultimate import of his seeing, the essential business it is about, is the same as that which he looks for in places. **"Life in a Small Neighborhood,"** like **"Blue Poles,"** gets quickly into a conceit, "the cat of behavior," and it tracks the cat through its neighborhood as it learns to persuade, "by persuasion making a place for itself, / Survived." The wish in **"Gunpowder Morning"** for a shape, wonderfully positioned, in from the wind, takes a different turn in **"The Winter House"** where "in the middle of this remoteness I am alone." Now we hear not Whitman but Thoreau, the poem echoing the winter chapters of *Walden* though without Henry David's contentedness at the drawing-in which winter entails: "The outside light contracts, the inside one expands / Out of necessity from this zero center." Of course to each season there is the seeing thereof, "a kind of law / Of conservation of fullness and vision," which means that in this case he will look out through the cold window at the plentitude of absence. That is the self's wintry at-homeness. His seeing is what makes that at-homeness and the seeing becomes, in itself, a part of what it makes. Home-making is thus not only the historical activity he looks at but the present activity he performs. He performs it in both gestures, the looking-back and the looking-out.

And yet all that making is never completely accomplished, never to be finished. In **"Genesee Falls"** he says that "nothing is ever over in a place like this." In **"Abraham Lincoln in Cleveland"** he wonders if "things only happen / When they stop"; and that in a city whose dominant edifice is a terminal, a place where there is only coming and going, one of thousands in an "indecipherable land from which / Every road leads home and none is getting there." Homes are only for the moment, terminals are absurdly named, America is never over and is always a cipher.

We are, it seems, always open, the movement of America coming to no closure. That way of regarding our openness can be taken with the kind of warmth that Whitman assumed when he embraced possibility. Crase takes it so at times though never without tinges, one tint of which comes out in the poem on Lincoln. Similar tinges emerge in his reading of the openness at the other end of history, the equal and opposite openness that led us to where we are now. This is not to say that the past is not fixed—it is pinned to its result as firmly as the lieutenant is to his tree—but that all that never happened inhabits Crase's poems with a subterranean vigor that makes much of their life. Aristotle saw how poetry could be made out of what might have happened but did not. Emily Dickinson made poetry out of the other kind of possibility, that which might well come and whose prospect alone makes living bearable ("I dwell in Possibility"). Traces of the later turn up in Crase though he is far more taken with exploring the past conditional. And what he sees in it most of all is the plenitude of potentiality, knowing as he does that what occurs is the smallest slice of what could have happened. The slightest shift in perspective, a move of a degree or two toward another segment of the horizon, would have made a very different set of conditions. In the sixth section of [**"The Revisionist"**] he speaks of "the grace of potential union" with a being who, again, may be America or a lover or both. The horizon, that "rim of temporal capacity," is always closing behind him, reminding him and his land/lover of "the world / We could have created a degree or two away." A constrained poignancy emerges from the meeting, in the speaker's mind, of the many might-have-beens and the irrevocable event: "even my memories of you *as is* / Take shape in the width of once possible days." That encounter of possibility and permanence, the mix of the missed and the made that leads to the shape of the present, comes out as much in the pebbles on Sagg Beach as it does in the labors of lovers: "A thousand surfaces / And each might have been exactly else, / As sure as any raw material, but comes to us / Shined as it is, to be." The end is in being, what lovers and pebbles become. The getting there is in possibility, what history could make. What we are is a tiny point on the horizon that is everywhere, the rim that hems us in while offering only a segment of itself.

Indeed, the world the horizon enfolds cannot offer us (or at least we cannot make sense out of) more than a segment of itself. Part of the problem is the seer's own presence. As Crase puts it in the fifth part of [**"The Revisionist"**], the seer too has a history and what he has been gets in the way of his seeing things in themselves: "in the most natural / Of flowers it's possible to read the account / Of my interferences instead." Which is not to say that the flowers themselves don't interfere: he is sometimes surprised that they do in fact have a history and that he cannot see them here separately from what and where they were, how they got here, what they grew into. Their past and present motions are so intertwined that he cannot unmake their mingling: "These have combined so I may never untangle / Their effects." With all his love of the land/lover there is a cloud of unknowing in their relationship, a difficulty of access which his interference and the presentness of history create and entangle. Crase quests everywhere for the meaning of place but its canny stubbornness keeps much of its content on the other side of his reach. "What's indigenous is also by nature recalcitrant"; so it went in **"Chimney Bluff."** In **"Great Fennville Swamp"** we are shown to be better at pondering what is doing in the swamp than at seeking to undo the meaning of its signifying. The swamp outdoes any meaning we can make of it, always eluding our attempts at possession; thus, perhaps, the fear with which he leaves the Fennville swamp and its overwhelming plenitude. Thus also the paradox of plenitude and unknowing which informs this and other poems. Still, if he cannot get at more than what is begrudged to him, acknowledging the unlikelihood of fuller access, he does know where meaning re-

sides. It is, of course, in the things and events and places in themselves but it is also, so very much of it, in the way these reach out to each other, the way each has a spot in a context, is defined by the context, enlarged by it. The meaning for which Crase seeks is so largely contextual that the business of the revisionist comes to be, in great part, the redefining of contexts and the relations that make them up, that make them contexts. Crase's book is a kind of geography not only of American places but of American contexts, fields of connection. Finally, though, it explores what contexts are in themselves, what they do and will give, and it does so remarkably well. *The Revisionist* would be impressive as the third or fourth book of a well-blooded poet. As a first book it is an extraordinary achievement, one of the best to appear in some time. (pp. 18-19)

Frederick Garber, "Territorial Voices," in The American Poetry Review, *Vol. 14, No. 1, January-February, 1985, pp. 18-22.*

William Golding

1911-

(Born William Gerald Golding) English novelist, short story writer, dramatist, poet, and nonfiction writer.

The following entry presents criticism on Golding's novel *Lord of the Flies* (1954). For discussions of Golding's complete career, see *CLC*, Vols. 1, 2, 3, 8, 10, 17, 27.

The winner of the 1983 Nobel Prize in literature, Golding is among the most popular and influential British authors to have emerged after World War II. Golding's reputation rests primarily upon his acclaimed first novel *Lord of the Flies*, which he described as "an attempt to trace the defects of society back to the defects of human nature." A moral allegory as well as an adventure tale in the tradition of Daniel Defoe's *Robinson Crusoe* and Richard Hughes's *A High Wind in Jamaica, Lord of the Flies* focuses upon a group of British schoolboys marooned on a tropical island. After having organized themselves upon democratic principles, their society degenerates into primeval barbarism. Although the novel initially generated little attention outside Great Britain, *Lord of the Flies* has subsequently achieved a notoriety among high school and college readers rivaling that of J. D. Salinger's *The Catcher in the Rye*. While often the subject of diverse psychological, sociological, and religious interpretations, *Lord of the Flies* is consistently regarded as an incisive and disturbing portrayal of the fragility of civilization.

Golding composed *Lord of the Flies* following his experiences as a naval officer in World War II, when he witnessed what he regarded as the fundamental immorality of apparently civilized nations. Similar in setting and characters' names to R. M. Ballantyne's nineteenth-century novel *The Coral Island, Lord of the Flies* subverts Ballantyne's assumption that such virtues as resourcefulness, piety, and compassion are inviolate. Set in the near future when nuclear war has devastated Europe, the novel opens after a plane evacuating schoolchildren from England crashes on a deserted island and kills the adults on board. Ralph, a charming if not shrewd twelve-year-old, is the first survivor to emerge, followed closely by Piggy, an overweight, bespectacled child whose serious demeanor contrasts markedly with Ralph's buoyant attitude. When, on Piggy's urging, Ralph blows on a conch shell found on the shore, other children appear. Among them are quiet, enigmatic Simon; Jack, who leads the black-robed choirboys onto the beach; and the preschool "littluns." During this first assembly and in keeping with their background, the children establish a democratic society and elect Ralph as their chief. Among his first acts, Ralph placates Jack by accepting his proposal that the choir function as hunters for the group. Initially, the children agree to build huts on the beach, gather fruit, and maintain a signal fire on the island's mountain, but the routine becomes tiresome and is soon abandoned by the majority. This disregard for rules ultimately reaches a crisis point when Jack, while pursuing a wild boar, allows the fire to die while a ship passes by the island.

That night, Ralph calls a meeting, intending to "put things straight" concerning the lack of discipline within the group. This chapter, titled "Beast from Water," is considered among

the most incisive episodes in the novel. A discussion regarding the day's events degenerates into speculation concerning the evil "beast," a figure originating in the dreams of a littlun that also functions as an externalization of the group's unacknowledged fears. While contemptuously dismissing the idea of the beast, Jack asserts that if such a creature exists, only he and his hunters can protect the group. In defiance of Ralph and Piggy, Jack breaks up the assembly, leaving with his steadily increasing band of followers. Critics have variously interpreted the symbolic importance of Ralph, Piggy, and Jack in *Lord of the Flies*. Several contend that their personalities and actions represent the fundamental political struggle between democracy and totalitarianism. Accordingly, the rational democracy of Piggy and Ralph and their promises of future rescue must compete with Jack's dictatorship, which offers the immediate satisfactions of food and security in exchange for the unquestioning loyalty of the recipients. Other critics, however, regard the trio as representing Freud's divisions of the psyche: Ralph exemplifies the ego that mediates between Piggy, the intellectual superego, and Jack, the animalistic id.

Left alone with Piggy after the assembly, Ralph longs for a signal from adults, who, he believes, would neither argue amongst themselves nor fear the beast. His wish is ironically fulfilled that night when a military plane is shot down over the island while the children sleep and the corpse of a dead pilot, a victim of adult evil, descends by parachute to the mountaintop. The following morning, two boys discover the decomposing body, which, through a combination of the wind and the parachute's tangled lines, appears to move independently. Terrified, they return to the beach and tell the others that they have seen the beast. Mounting an expedition, Ralph and Jack reach the mountaintop by nightfall, where they witness the figure moving in the moonlight. Retreating, Jack declares that they must surrender the mountain to the seemingly invincible beast and sacrifice pigs to ensure its benevolence. Ralph and Piggy again protest, asserting that only in concentrating on the signal fire will they be delivered from the island and thus from the beast. Jack, however, has finally undermined Ralph's authority, and he leads the majority of the children into the jungle to hunt for pigs.

Among those who remain with Ralph are Piggy and Simon. Unlike Jack, Ralph, and Piggy, Simon is not a parody of a character in Ballantyne's *The Coral Island,* and he is generally regarded as the single example of purity in *Lord of the Flies.* Although epileptic and frail, Simon possesses an artistic sensitivity, evidenced in his meditative retreats into the jungle, which allows him to initially visualize the beast as "a human at once heroic and sick." At the final assembly, he meekly proposes to the other boys that they climb the mountain again to discover the truth concerning the beast but is caustically dismissed. Returning to his private place in the jungle, Simon encounters "the Lord of the Flies"—the head of a pig swarming with insects, which the hunters have impaled on a stick as an offering to the beast. Then, in what is regarded as among the most overtly symbolic episodes in the novel, Simon suffers an epileptic attack, during which he hears the head speaking to him in the voice of a reproving schoolmaster. Its name a literal translation of Ba'alzevuv, a Hebrew term for the devil, the Lord of the Flies reveals to the boy that evil does not exist as an externalized "beast" but dwells within the soul of every person. Simon, ultimately hallucinating that the head is about to swallow him, loses consciousness.

When Simon regains his senses, he climbs the mountain and recognizes the figure not as a fearful beast but as a corpse at once "harmless and horrible." Although initially sickened, he untangles the parachute strings, freeing the body "from the wind's indignity," before returning at dusk to tell the others. However, the other children, including Ralph and Piggy, have begun to panic in Simon's absence, and, when he stumbles onto the beach, they mistake him for the beast and kill him in a frenzy. Simon's death as well as his actions have prompted several critics to regard him as a Christlike figure sacrificed to save a fallen humanity within their ruined Eden. Others, however, eschew any strictly religious interpretations and perceive the events in moralistic terms. Patrick Reilly observed: "Ralph and Piggy both fail to see that, in silencing Simon, they are in effect delivering themselves into Jack's hands. The book traces three routes for mankind: Piggy's commonsense, Jack's irrationalism, and Simon's mysticism. But commonsense is intimidated by irrationalism—Piggy is terrified in Jack's presence. The paradox is that the mystic way, which strikes Piggy as outrageous mumbo jumbo, is the only sensible, practical solution. . . . [We must] face and outface whatever we fear or be afraid forever."

Following Simon's death, the airman's corpse is blown from

the mountain and into the sea, and Jack and his painted "savages" seize control of the island, ultimately isolating Piggy and Ralph on the beach. Several nights later, the hunters steal Piggy's glasses, which had been the only device for starting fires on the island. Still believing Jack capable of redemption, Piggy searches him out and, with Ralph, demands the spectacles back while holding the conch, the symbol of authority. Jack and his band, however, break the conch and murder Piggy, hurling him from a cliff. While initial reviewers characterized Piggy's actions as heroic, subsequent critics regard his refusal to confront the evil within humanity as cowardly. Arnold Johnson observed: "Piggy's actions immediately before his murder are brave in conventional terms; but his rationalist's faith in order and human perfectibility, ironically undercut throughout the book, seems nowhere more misguided. . . . The mystic's intuitive recognition that good and evil coexist within man is the spark of his divinity; but the rationalist's denial of such intangible forces chains him forever to the material world of earth and organism."

Now alone, Ralph is attacked by the other boys, but he momentarily escapes into the jungle. Jack subsequently orders that a stick be sharpened so Ralph's severed head may be sacrificed to the beast, then sets fire to the island to force his prey from hiding. Trapped, Ralph flees to the beach where the adult world unexpectedly intrudes in the form of a British naval officer. In a complete shift in perspective, the savages, once made immense in their violence, are reduced to crying, bewildered youngsters in the presence of this adult. Ralph, upon being congratulated by the officer for acting like the boys of *The Coral Island,* begins to sob as he mourns Piggy and "the end of innocence, the darkness of man's heart." While several critics faulted the novel's ending as contrived, most agreed with Golding's assertion that when "adult life appears, dignified and capable, [it is] in reality enmeshed in the same evil as the symbolic life of the children on the island. The officer, having interrupted a man-hunt, prepares to take the children off the island in a cruiser which will presently be hunting its enemy in the same implacable way. And who will rescue the adult and his cruiser?"

When *Lord of the Flies* initially appeared, critical commentary focused less upon the novel's fictional merits than on its symbolic realization of a pessimistic psychological and sociological outlook. While some original reviewers dismissed *Lord of the Flies* solely for its bleak assessment of humanity, others lauded the novel as an ominous parable for the nuclear age. Recent commentators contend that *Lord of the Flies* best illustrates Golding's innovative synthesis of traditional allegory, intricate description, fast-paced plotting, and realistic characterization. Bernard S. Oldsey and Stanley Weintraub commented: "Although it is enough to say that the fabulist must be permitted pegs upon which to hang his fable, it is Golding's richly novelistic elements of the telling that call attention to the subtle dissonance. Paradoxically—yet artistically—this very tension between realistic novel and allegorical fable imparts to *Lord of the Flies . . .* its unique power."

(See also *Contemporary Authors,* Vols. 5-8, rev. ed.; *Contemporary Authors New Revision Series,* Vol. 13; and *Dictionary of Literary Biography,* Vol. 15.)

THE TIMES LITERARY SUPPLEMENT

During an atomic war an aircraft carrying a number of small boys crash-lands on a coral island. The crew have been killed, and the boys are left alone. There is fruit to eat for the picking, there is a clear pool for swimming, in the forest there are piglets to be caught and eaten. What will happen to these children, the youngest of them about six years old, the leaders perhaps twice that age? In a remarkable fantasy called *Lord of the Flies* Mr. William Golding answers that question. The story is fantastic in conception and setting: but with so much of strangeness granted, *Lord of the Flies,* like all successful fantasies, enlightens and horrifies by its nearness to, rather than its distance from, reality. Accept the idea of children being set down on an island in conditions that preclude the possibility of starvation, and this is really how they might behave. A leader is elected, Ralph; a boy honest, tenacious, not highly intelligent but aware that the first requirements are to build shelters and to keep a fire burning day and night. A routine of duties is arranged; there will be fire stokers, shelter builders, hunting parties to catch pigs. But the routine becomes tiresome and is not maintained; the smaller children believe that there is a beast in the forest, and it is only one step from belief in the beast to worship of it, one step more to the idea that the beast must be propitiated by a human sacrifice. A new chief is chosen who fulfils the children's desire for a reversion to primitivism, and the old chief becomes in the natural course of things a scapegoat.

Perhaps this makes *Lord of the Flies* sound too much like a variation on a Frazerian theme. It is that, incidentally; but taken purely as a story it is beautifully constructed and worked out, with the various children just sufficiently individuated and with tension built up steadily to the climax in which the scapegoat is hunted over the island.

"Tales of Imagination," in The Times Literary Supplement, *No. 2751, October 22, 1954, p. 669.*

LOUIS J. HALLE

[In *Lord of the Flies*], the oldest of the English schoolboys was twelve and the youngest six. Finding themselves plane-wrecked on an uninhabited tropical island, without grown-ups, they had to manage for themselves. English political experience since Runnymede, however, made its contribution. An assembly was called, a leader elected, rules established, assignments distributed. Civilization had come down out of the sky with the children.

But so had savagery, and fear of the unknown brought it out. Parliamentary procedure, after all, cannot propitiate the beast in the dark. For that you have to paint your face with colored clays, chant incantations, dance ritualistically, and offer blood sacrifices. So the struggle between civilization and barbarism began.

William Golding tells all this in his first novel, *Lord of the Flies.* One is impressed by the possibilities of his theme for an expression of the irony and tragedy of man's fate. Against his majority of little savages he places a remnant that convincingly represents the saving element of human heroism, thereby posing the eternal moral conflict. But he cannot quite find his meaning in this material. The heroes come to a bad end, having contributed nothing to such salvation as the society achieves. There is a great deal of commotion, and the last page is nothing more than a playwright's contrivance for bringing down the curtain. One is left asking: What was the point?

In 1929 Richard Hughes's *The Innocent Voyage* (also published as *A High Wind in Jamaica*) set a standard for accounts of savage-civilized children (who are simply grown-ups more plainly written). The Bas-Thornton children were such fiends that even the pirates who captured them were shocked; but the angel still lay hidden in each. Hughes had simply turned the Victorian view of childhood upside down. The brutality with which he did this, however, revealed his humanitarianism. His inverted world was still a world for God's pity.

The integrity of *The Innocent Voyage* was perfect. It represented the single vision of a literary artist who knew human nature from personal experience. In Mr. Golding's novel, however, the novelist's vision conflicts with that of the textbook anthropologist. The novelist sees good opposed to evil; he recognizes the existence and the utility of heroes. But the social scientist deals only with amoral phenomena. In his termite society the novelist's heroes are social misfits who must come to a bad end, one suspects, to confirm the tacit assumption that maladjustment is undesirable. The intimidated novelist, thus opposed by the misplaced authority of science, dares hardly suggest even that his heroes save the honor of mankind. The best he can do, at last, is to find a meaningless fulfilment in thrills and horror. His rocket explodes in the air, spectacular for the moment, but leaving only the memory of a light that went out and the dead stick of an academic conception.

Louis J. Halle, "Small Savages," in The Saturday Review, *New York, Vol. XXXVIII, No. 42, October 15, 1955, p. 16.*

JAMES STERN

The title of this highly original first novel [*Lord of the Flies*] is the name given, symbolically, to the head of a wild pig which has been slaughtered for food by a horde of English schoolboys stranded on an uninhabited island somewhere in the Pacific. The noun "horde" is used advisedly, for by the time the pig's skull has been impaled on a stick, where it is promptly infested by flies . . . the majority of these well-brought-up boys, none of whom has reached his teens, have retrogressed from the civilized state to the primitive. They have become, in a word, savages. Having slowly discarded the habits acquired at home and school, and discovered the "liberation" brought about by paint on the naked body, these children, faced by primeval conditions, are soon ready to torture, ready to kill. And not only animals.

As is probably clear by now, *Lord of the Flies* is an allegory on human society today, the novel's primary implication being that what we have come to call civilization is, at best, no more than skin-deep. . . . [This] brilliant work is a frightening parody on man's return (in a few weeks) to that state of darkness from which it took him thousands of years to emerge.

Fully to succeed, a fantasy must approach very close to reality. *Lord of the Flies* does. It must also be superbly written. It is. If criticism must be leveled at such a feat of the imagination, it is permissible perhaps to carp at the very premise on which the whole strange story is founded.

How did these children come to be on the island at all? And why, among them, were there no grown-ups? Although Mr. Golding's answer is simple, it may not convince everyone. The boys have been "dropped" in the "passenger tube" of a plane during an attack in an atomic war: the pilot has been seen to vanish in flames. This possibility once accepted, even the most skeptical reader will surely be carried away by the story's plausibility and power, by its skillfully worked-out progress, by the perfection of its characterization, dialogue and prose.

In an ovenlike and adultless jungle, clothes, of course, are the first things to be discarded. Slower to be shaken off are national characteristics: "After all we're English; and the English are best at everything. So we've got to do the right things." Faced, however, by brute Nature, by no power of authority and little hope of rescue, the "right things" seem, particularly to the older boys (the "biguns"), to lose what purpose they may once have had. So two chiefs—Ralph and Jack—are appointed; meetings are held; rules drawn up. . . . [But] authority is undermined, the common spirit split. Two camps are formed, and the fatal seed of rivalry, of hatred, is sown.

From the terror that follows one figure stands out, a character known to us all: the Fat Boy, commonly called "Piggy." This boy, however, has brains, and he is almost blind. And it is his blindness, by excruciating irony, that finally saves the lives of the surviving boys while failing to save his own. Piggy is the hero of a triumphant literary effort.

James Stern, "English Schoolboys in the Jungle," in The New York Times Book Review, October 23, 1955, p. 38.

C. B. COX

William Golding's *Lord of the Flies,* published in 1954, is a retelling in realistic terms of R. M. Ballantyne's *The Coral Island.* A group of boys, shot down during some kind of atomic war, are marooned on an island in the Pacific. In contrast to the boys in Ballantyne's story, who after a number of exciting adventures remember their time on the island as an idyllic interlude, the children in *Lord of the Flies* soon begin to quarrel, and their attempts to create an ordered, just society break down. On one level the story shows how intelligence (Piggy) and common sense (Ralph) will always be overthrown in society by sadism (Roger) and the lure of totalitarianism (Jack). On another, the growth of savagery in the boys demonstrates the power of original sin. Simon, the Christ figure, who tries to tell the children that their fears of a dead parachutist are illusory, is killed in a terrifying tribal dance. The Lord of the Flies is the head of a pig, which Jack puts up on a stick to placate an illusory Beast. As Simon understands, the only dangerous beast, the true Lord of the Flies, is inside the children themselves. Lord of the Flies is the Old Testament name for Beelzebub.

Lord of the Flies is probably the most important novel to be published in this country in the 1950s. A story so explicitly symbolic as this might easily become fanciful and contrived, but Golding has mastered the art of writing a twentieth century allegory. In contrast to the medieval audience, the general reading public today does not believe that correspondences exist between the material and spiritual world, and they do not automatically expect every incident or object to have symbolic importance. No conventions of allegory exist. . . . In these circumstances, many novelists have given objects an arbitrary symbolic meaning. . . . There are other methods of writing twentieth century allegory, of course, as in Kafka's use of fanciful situations to explore psychological and religious experiences; but if a story based on real life is used, then there must be no unlikely situations or fanciful embroidery. A modern audience will accept the underlying meanings only if they are conveyed in a completely convincing, true to life series of events.

To find an exciting, stimulating plot which is both dramatically credible and capable of allegorical interpretation is exceptionally difficult. The idea of placing boys alone on an island, and letting them work out archetypal patterns of human society, is a brilliant technical device, with a simple coherence which is easily understood by a modern audience. Its success is due in part to the quality of Golding's Christianity. He is neither puritan nor transcendentalist, and his religious faith is based upon his interpretation of experience, rather than upon an unquestioning acceptance of revelation. Although his four novels deal with the depravity of man, he cares deeply about the condition of human life, and shows great compassion for men who suffer and men who sin. His religious sense does not make him turn from life in disgust, but proves to him the dignity and importance of human action. In development of plot, descriptions of island and sea, and treatment of character, he explores actual life to prove dramatically the authenticity of his religious viewpoint.

Lord of the Flies is a gripping story which will appeal to generations of readers. It is easy to despise the power of a good story, and to think of moral implications as an alternative to the obvious devices of surprise, suspense and climax. But to succeed, a good story needs more than sudden deaths, a terrifying chase and an unexpected conclusion. *Lord of the Flies* includes all these ingredients, but their exceptional force derives from Golding's faith that every detail of human life has a religious significance. This is one reason why he is unique among new writers in the '50s, and why he excels in narrative ability. Typical of the writers of the '50s is an uncertainty about human values, a fundamental doubt about whether life has any importance whatsoever. In contrast, Golding can describe friendship, guilt, pain and horror with a full sense of how deeply meaningful these can be for the individual. The terrible fire which kills the young children, the fear of Ralph as he is pursued across the island, and Piggy's fall to his death on the rocks make us feel, in their vivid detail, Golding's intense conviction that every particular of human life has a profound importance. His children are not juvenile delinquents, but human beings realising for themselves the beauty and horror of life.

This faith in the importance of our experiences in this world is reflected in Golding's vivid, imaginative style. He has a fresh, delightful response to the mystery of Nature, with its weird beauty and fantastic variety. The conch, which Ralph and Piggy discover in the lagoon and use to call the children to assemblies, is not just a symbol of order. From the beginning Golding does justice to the strange attraction of the shell, with its delicate, embossed pattern, and deep harsh note which echoes back from the pink granite of the mountain. When towards the end of the story the conch is smashed, we feel that sadness which comes when any object of exquisite beauty is broken. The symbolic meaning, that this is the end of the beauty of justice and order, is not forced upon us, but is reflected through our emotional reaction to the object itself.

In this way Golding expresses his passionate interest in both physical and moral life. His narrative style has an unusual lucidity and vitality because he never forgets the concrete in his search for symbolic action:

> Now a great wind blew the rain sideways, cascading the water from the forest trees. On the mountain-top the parachute filled and moved; the figure slid, rose to its feet, spun, swayed down through a vastness of wet air and trod with ungainly feet the tops of the high trees; falling, still falling, it sank towards the beach and the boys rushed screaming into the darkness. The parachute took the figure forward, furrowing the lagoon, and bumped it over the reef and out to sea.

With admirable simplicity this passage conveys a multitude of effects. The incident is part of an exciting story, a surprising climax to the murder of Simon; at the same time the dead parachutist is the 'beast' to the children, a symbol of adult evil, which, by their own act of killing, they have shown to be part of themselves. But the passage achieves its strong emotional impact because it is so firmly grounded in physical awareness. Water cascades from the forest trees, the parachutist 'furrows' the lagoon. These precise words describe with physical immediacy a situation which is real and dramatically poignant. And the picture of the man treading the tops of the high trees recalls the mystery of human life, with its incredible inventions, and yet also makes us feel deep compassion for the ungainly feet, the horror of death.

The island itself is boat-shaped, and the children typify all mankind on their journey through life. In the opening scenes the island has the glamour of a new-found paradise. . . . But soon the terrifying fire transforms the island, and illusion gives way to reality. In nightmares the children begin to be afraid that this is not a good island; they become accustomed to the mirages, "and ignored them, just as they ignored the miraculous, throbbing stars". The beauty of the earthly paradise grows stale to their eyes. At the end they leave behind them "the burning wreckage of the island", whose loveliness has been degraded by their presence.

As his attempts to discipline the boys begin to appear hopeless, Ralph, on a search for the illusory beast, sees beyond the lagoon out to open sea:

> The lagoon had protected them from the Pacific: and for some reason only Jack had gone right down to the water on the other side. Now he saw the landsman's view of the swell and it seemed like the breathing of some stupendous creature. Slowly the waters sank among the rocks, revealing pink tables of granite, strange growths of coral, polyp, and weed. Down, down, the waters went, whispering like the wind among the heads of the forest. There was one flat rock there, spread like a table, and the waters sucking down on the four weedy sides made them seem like cliffs. Then the sleeping leviathan breathed out—the waters rose, the weed streamed, and the water boiled over the table rock with a roar. There was no sense of the passage of waves; only this minute-long fall and rise and fall.

This creature becomes a part of Ralph's consciousness, a symbol of a reality he tries to avoid. As he watches the ceaseless, bulging passage of the deep sea waves, the remoteness and infiniteness of the ocean force themselves upon his attention. By the quiet lagoon he can dream of rescue, but the brute obtuseness of the ocean tells him he is helpless. It is significant that the two boys who are killed, Simon and Piggy, are taken back to this infinite ocean.

As the waves creep towards the body of Simon beneath the moonlight, the brilliantly realistic description of the advancing tide typifies all the beauty of the world which promises eternal reward to those who suffer:

> Along the shoreward edge of the shallows the advancing clearness was full of strange, moonbeam-bodied creatures with fiery eyes. Here and there a larger pebble clung to its own air and was covered with a coat of pearls. The tide swelled in over the rain-pitted sand and smoothed everything with a layer of silver. Now it touched the first of the stains that seeped from the broken body and the creatures made a moving patch of light as they gathered at the edge. The water rose further and dressed Simon's coarse hair with brightness. The line of his cheek silvered and the turn of his shoulder became sculptured marble. The strange, attendant creatures, with their fiery eyes and trailing vapours, busied themselves round his head. The body lifted a fraction of an inch from the sand and a bubble of air escaped from the mouth with a wet plop. Then it turned gently in the water.

Here we become aware of the Christian meaning underlying the story. For Ralph the sea typifies the insensitivity of the universe, but this is to see it from only one point of view. The multitudinous beauties of the tide promise that creation was not an accident; after our suffering and confusions are over, a healing power of great beauty will solve all problems. The advancing waves are like moonbeam-bodied creatures, gently washing the body of Simon free from all stain, and dressing him in pearls, silver and marble in token of the richness of his love for the other children. Instead of seeking to introduce ancient myths into the modern world, Golding creates his own, basing his symbols on the actual wonder of life itself. The intricate beauty of the waves is not merely a pleasing arrangement of light and matter, but an incredible manifestation of the wonder of creation, with a valid life in our consciousness. As Simon's body moves out to open sea under the delicate yet firm lifting of the tide, it seems impossible that his sacrifice has had no ultimate meaning.

The island, the sea and the sacrifice of Simon all show Ralph the truth of the human situation. His mind finds the burden of responsibility too great, and he begins to lose his power to think coherently: "He found himself understanding the wearisomeness of this life, where every path was an improvisation and a considerable part of one's waking life was spent watching one's feet". Jack's return to savagery, taking all the children with him, is portrayed with frightening realism. The lust for killing grows too strong, and Ralph's inadequate democratic machinery cannot keep it in check. Behind their painted faces, the children can feel a security, a lack of personal responsibility for the evil they perpetrate, and this desire explains the growth of Jack's prestige. When he tells them they will not dream so much, "they agreed passionately out of the depths of their tormented private lives", and he is amazed by their response. Only the intelligence of Piggy is not tempted by the tribal dances, and his character is presented with great compassion. His fat, asthmatic body is a natural butt for children, and continual mockery has taught him to be humble and to enjoy being noticed even only as a joke. But he has a powerful belief in the importance of civilised order, and gradually Ralph learns to appreciate his value. His death is a poignant reminder of the unjust and cruel treatment given by society to so many good men.

Simon is perhaps the one weakness in the book. We see his friendship for Ralph, when he touches his hand as they explore the island, and his love of all people when he ministers to the dead body of the parachutist, but alone among the characters his actions at times appear to be motivated not by the dramatic action, but by the symbolic implications of the story. At the beginning, when he withdraws at night from the other children, his motives are left uncertain. But the scene where he confronts the lord of the flies is most convincing. In this pig's head covered with flies, he sees "the infinite cynicism of adult life". He has the courage to face the power of evil, and, knowing that the beast is in all of them, he climbs the hill to find out the truth about the dead parachutist.

The whole story moves towards Simon's view of reality. The growth of savagery forces Ralph to make strange speculations about the meaning of human identity. . . . He faces the possibility that there is no absolute perspective to human life, and that all experience may be meaningless. He longs to return to the world of adults, and the irony of this illusion is shown when, after a battle in the skies, the dead parachutist comes down "as a sign from the world of grown-ups". At certain stages of the story, Golding deliberately makes us forget that these are only young children. Their drama and conflict typify the inevitable overthrow of all attempts to impose a permanent civilisation on the instincts of man. The surprising twist of events at the end of the novel is a highly original device to force upon us a new viewpoint. The crazy, sadistic chase to kill Ralph is suddenly revealed to be the work of a semi-circle of little boys, their bodies streaked with coloured clay. But the irony is also directed at the naval officer, who comes to rescue them. His trim cruiser, the sub-machine gun, his white drill, epaulettes, revolver and row of gilt buttons, are only more sophisticated substitutes for the war-paint and sticks of Jack and his followers. He too is chasing men in order to kill, and the dirty children mock the absurd civilised attempt to hide the power of evil. And so when Ralph weeps for the end of innocence, the darkness of man's heart, and the death of his true, wise friend, Piggy, he weeps for all the human race. (pp. 112-17)

> *C. B. Cox, in a review of "Lord of the Flies," in* Critical Quarterly, *Vol. 2, No. 2, Summer, 1960, pp. 112-17.*

CLAIRE ROSENFIELD

In analyzing William Golding's *Lord of the Flies,* the critic must assume that Golding knows psychological literature and must then attempt to show how an author's knowledge of theory can vitalize his prose and characterization. The plot itself is uncomplicated, so simple, indeed, that one wonders how it so effortlessly absorbs the burden of meaning. During some unexplained man-made holocaust a plane, evacuating a group of children, crashes on the shore of a tropical island. All adults are conveniently killed. The narrative follows the children's gradual return to the amorality of childhood, and it is the very nature of that state of non-innocence which makes them small savages. Or we might make the analogy to the childhood of races and compare the child to the primitive.

Denied the sustaining and repressing authority of parents, church, and state, they form a new culture the development of which reflects that of the genuine primitive society, evolving its gods and demons (its myths), its rituals and taboos (its social norms). On the level of pure narrative, the action proceeds from the gradual struggle between Ralph and Jack, the two oldest boys, for precedence. Ralph is the natural leader by virtue of his superior height, his superior strength, his superior beauty. His mild expression proclaims him "no devil." He possesses the symbol of authority, the conch. . . . Jack, on the other hand, is described in completely antithetical terms; he is distinguished by his ugliness and his red hair, a traditional demonic attribute. He first appears as the leader of a church choir, which "creature-like" marches in two columns behind him. All members of the choir wear black; "their bodies, from throat to ankle, were hidden by black cloaks." Ralph initially blows the conch to discover how many children have escaped death in the plane crash. As Jack approaches with his choir from the "darkness of the forest," he cannot see Ralph, whose back is to the sun. The former is, symbolically, sun-blinded. These two are very obviously intended to recall God and the Devil, whose confrontation, in the history of Western religions, establishes the moral basis for all actions. But, as Freud reminds us . . . , gods and devils are "nothing other than psychological processes projected into the outer world." If Ralph is a projection of man's good impulses from which we derive the authority figures— whether god, king, or father—who establish the necessity for our valid ethical and social action, then Jack becomes an externalization of the evil instinctual forces of the unconscious. Originally, as in the more primitive religions, gods and devils were one; even Hebraic-Christian tradition makes Satan a fallen angel.

The temptation is to regard the island on which the children are marooned as a kind of Eden, uncorrupted and Eveless. But the actions of the children negate any assumption about childhood innocence. Even though Golding himself momentarily becomes a victim of his Western culture and states that Ralph wept for the "end of innocence," events have simply supported Freud's conclusions that no child is innocent. On a third level, Ralph is every man—or every child—and his body becomes the battleground where reason and instinct struggle, each to assert itself. For to regard Ralph and Jack as Good and Evil is to ignore the role of the child Piggy, who in the child's world of make-believe is the outsider. Piggy's composite description not only manifests his difference from the other boys; it also reminds the reader of the stereotype image of the old man who has more-than-human wisdom: he is fat, inactive because asthmatic, and generally reveals a disinclination for physical labor. Because he is extremely nearsighted, he wears thick glasses—a further mark of his difference. As time passes, the hair of the other boys grows with abandon. "He was the only boy on the island whose hair never seemed to grow. The rest were shock-headed, but Piggy's hair still lay in wisps over his head as though baldness were his natural state, and this imperfect covering would soon go, like the velvet on a young stag's antlers." In these images of age and authority we have a figure reminiscent of the children's past—the father. Moreover, like the father he counsels common sense; he alone leavens with a reasonable gravity the constant exuberance of the others for play or for play at hunting. When they scamper off at every vague whim, he scornfully comments, "Like a pack of kids." Ungrammatically but logically, he tries to allay the "littluns" fear of a "beast." . . . He has excessive regard for the forms of order:

the conch must be held by a child before that child can speak at councils. When the others neglect responsibility, fail to build shelters, swim in the pools or play in the sand or hunt, allow the signal fire on the mountain to go out or to get out of hand and burn up half the island, he seconds Ralph by admonishing the others vigorously and becomes more and more of a spoil-sport who robs play of its illusions, the adult interrupting the game. Ralph alone recognizes his superior intelligence but wavers between what he knows to be wise and the group acceptance his egocentricity demands. Finally, Piggy's role—as man's reasoning faculties and as a father—derives some of its complexity from the fact that the fire which the children foster and guard on the mountain in the hope of communicating with the adult world is lighted with his glasses. In mythology, after all, the theft of fire brought civilization—and, hence, repression—to man. As the new community becomes more and more irrational, its irrationality is marked by Piggy's progressive blindness. (pp. 93-4)

The history of the child Piggy on the island dramatizes in terms of the individual the history of the entire group. When they first assemble to investigate their plight, they treat their island isolation as a temporary phenomenon; they want to play games until they are rescued—until their parents reassert the repressive actions of authority. This microcosm of the great world seems to them to be a fairy land. . . . They compare this reality to their reading experiences: it is Treasure Island or Coral Island or like pictures from their travel books. This initial reaction conforms to the pattern of play which Johan Huizinga establishes in *Homo Ludens*. In its early stages their play has no cultural or moral function; it is simply a "stepping out of real life into a temporary sphere of activity." Ironically, the child of **Lord of the Flies** who thinks he is "only pretending" or that this is "only for fun" does not realize that his play is the beginning of the formation of a new society which has regressed to a primitive state, with all its emphasis upon taboo and communal action. What begins by being like other games in having a distinct "locality and duration" apart from ordinary life is—or becomes—reality. (pp. 94-5)

The games of the beginning have a double function: they, first of all, reflect the child's attitude toward play as a temporary cessation from the activities imposed by the adult world; but like the games played before the formation of civilization, they anticipate the ritual which reveals a developing society. So the children move from voluntary play to ritual, from "only pretending" to reality, from representation to identification. The older strictures imposed by parents are soon forgotten—but every now and then a momentary remembrance of past prohibitions causes restraint. (p. 95)

The younger children first, then gradually the older ones, like primitives in the childhood of races, begin to people the darkness of night and forest with spirits and demons which had previously appeared only in their dreams or fairy tales. Now there are no comforting mothers to dispel the terrors of the unknown. They externalize these fears into the figure of a "beast." Once the word "beast" is mentioned, the menace of the irrational becomes overt; name and thing become one. At one critical council when the first communal feeling begins to disintegrate, Ralph cries, " 'If only they could send us something grown-up . . . a sign or something.' " And a sign does come from the outside. That night, unknown to the children, a plane is shot down and its pilot parachutes dead to earth and is caught in the rocks on the mountain. It requires

no more than the darkness of night together with the shadows of the forest vibrating in the signal fire to distort the hanging corpse with its expanding silk 'chute into a demon that must be appeased. Ironically, the fire of communication does touch this object of the grown-up world only to foster superstition. Security in this new situation can be achieved only by establishing new rules.

During the first days the children, led by Jack, play at hunting. But eventually the circle of the playground extends to the circle of the hunted and squealing pig seeking refuge—and it is significant that the first animal slain for food is a nursing sow—which itself anticipates the circle of consecrated ground where the children perform the new rites of the kill.

The first hunt accomplishes its purpose: the blood of the animals is spilled; the meat, used for food. But because Jack and his choir undertake this hunt, they desert the signal fire, which is dictated by the common-sense desire for rescue, and it goes out and a ship passes the island. Later the children reenact the killing with one boy, Maurice, assuming the role of the pig running its frenzied circle. The others chant in unison: " 'Kill the pig. Cut her throat. Bash her in.' " At this dramatic representation each child is still aware that this is a display, a performance. He is never "so beside himself that he loses consciousness of ordinary reality." Each time they reenact the same event, however, their behavior becomes more frenzied, more cruel, less like representation than identification. The chant then becomes, " 'Kill the beast. Cut his throat. Spill his blood.' " It is as if the first event, the pig's death, is forgotten in the recesses of time; a new myth defines the primal act. Real pig becomes mythical beast.

Jack's ascendancy over the group begins when the children's fears distort the natural objects around them: twigs become creepers, shadows become demons. I have already discussed the visual imagery suggesting Jack's demonic function. He serves as a physical manifestation of irrational forces. After an indefinite passage of time, he appears almost dehumanized, his "nose only a few inches from the humid earth." He is "dog-like" and proceeds forward "on all fours" "into the semi-darkness of the undergrowth." . . . Already he has begun to obliterate the distinctions between animals and men, as do primitives; already he thinks in terms of the metaphor of a ritual drinking of blood, the efficacy of which depended on the drinker's assumption of his victim's strength and spirit. Ralph and Piggy confront him with his defection of duty.

> The two boys faced each other. There was the brilliant world of hunting, tactics, fierce exhilaration, skill; and there was the world of longing and baffled commonsense. Jack transferred the knife to his left hand and smudged blood over his forehead as he pushed down the plastered hair.

Jack's unconscious gesture is a parody of the ritual of initiation in which the hunter's face is smeared with the blood of his first kill. In the subsequent struggle one of the lenses of Piggy's spectacles is broken. The dominance of reason is over; the voice of the old world is stilled. The primary images are no longer those of fire and light but those of darkness and blood. The link between Ralph and Jack "had snapped and fastened elsewhere."

The rest of the group, however, shifts its allegiance to Jack because he has given them meat rather than something useless like fire. Gradually, they begin to be described as "shadows" or "masks" or "savages" or "demoniac figures" and, like Jack, "hunt naked save for paint and a belt." Ralph now uses Jack's name with the recognition that "a taboo was evolving around that word too." Name and thing again become one; to use the word is to incite the bearer. But more significant, the taboo, according to Freud, is "a very primitive prohibition imposed from without (by an authority) and directed against the strongest desires of man." In this new society it replaces the authority of the parents. Now every kill becomes a sexual act, is a metaphor for childhood sexuality. . . . Every subsequent "need for ritual" fulfills not only the desire for communication and a substitute security to replace that of civilization, but also the need to liberate both the repressions of the past and those imposed by Ralph. Indeed, the projection of those impulses that they cannot accept in themselves into a beast is the beginning of a new mythology. The earlier dreams and nightmares can now be shared as the former subjectivity could not be.

When the imaginary demons become defined by the rotting corpse and floating 'chute on the mountain which their terror distorts into a beast, Jack wants to track the creature down. After the next kill, the head of the pig is placed upon a stake to placate it. Finally one of the children, Simon, after an epileptic fit, creeps out of the forest at twilight while the others are engaged in enthusiastic dancing following a hunt. Seized by the rapture of reenactment or perhaps terrorized by fear and night into believing that this little creature is a beast, they circle Simon, pounce on him, bite and tear his body to death. He becomes not a substitute for beast but beast itself; representation becomes absolute identification, "the mystic repetition of the initial event." (pp. 95-7)

Simon's mythic and psychological role has earlier been suggested. Undersized, subject to epileptic fits, bright-eyed, and introverted, he constantly creeps away from the others to meditate among the intricate vines of the forest. To him, as to the mystic, superior knowledge is given intuitively which he cannot communicate. When the first report of the beast-pilot reaches camp, Simon, we are told, can picture only "a human at once heroic and sick." During the day preceding his death, he walks vaguely away and stumbles upon the pig's head left in the sand in order to appease the demonic forces they imagine. Shaman-like, he holds a silent colloquy with it, a severed head covered with innumerable flies. It is itself the titled Lord of the Flies, a name applied to the Biblical demon Beelzebub and later used in Goethe's *Faust, Part I,* to describe Mephistopheles. From it he learns that it is the Beast, and the Beast cannot be hunted because it is within. Simon feels the advent of one of his fits and imagines the head expanding, an anticipation or intuition of the discovery of the pilot's corpse. Suddenly Golding employs a startling image, "Simon was inside the mouth. He fell down and lost consciousness." Literally, this image presents the hallucination of a sensitive child about to lose control of his rational faculties. Metaphorically, it suggests the ritual quest in which the hero is swallowed by a serpent or dragon or beast whose belly is the underworld, undergoes a symbolic death in order to gain the elixir to revitalize his stricken society, and returns with his knowledge to the timed world as a redeemer. Psychologically, this narrative pattern is a figure of speech connoting the annihilation of the ego, an internal journey necessary for self-understanding, a return to the timelessness of the unconscious. When Simon wakes, he realizes that he must confront the beast on the mountain because "what else is there to do?" He is relieved of "that dreadful feeling of the pressure of personality" which had oppressed him earlier.

When he discovers the hanging corpse, he first frees it in compassion although it is rotting and surrounded by flies, and then staggers unevenly down to report to the others. Redeemer and scapegoat, he becomes the victim of the group he seeks to enlighten. In death—before he is pulled into the sea—his head is surrounded by flies in an ironic parody of the halo of saints and gods.

Piggy's death, soon to follow Simon's, is foreshadowed when the former proclaims at council that there is no beast. " 'What would a beast eat?' " " 'Pig.' " " 'We eat pig,' " he rationally answers. " 'Piggy!' " is the next word. At Piggy's death his body twitches "like a pig's after it has been killed." Not only has his head been smashed, but also the conch, symbol of order, is simultaneously broken. A complex group of metaphors unite to form a total metaphor involving Piggy and the pig, hunted and eaten by the children, and the pig's head which is at once left to appease the beast's hunger and is the beast itself. But the beast is within, and the children are defined by the very objects they seek to destroy.

In these associated images we have the whole idea of a communal and sacrificial feast and a symbolic cannibalism, all of which Freud discussed in *Totem and Taboo.* Here the psychology of the individual contributes the configurations for the development of religion. Indeed, the events of **Lord of the Flies** imaginatively parallel the patterns which Freud detects in primitive mental processes.

Having populated the outside world with demons and spirits which are projections of their instinctual nature, these children—and primitive men—must then unconsciously evolve new forms of worship and laws, which manifest themselves in taboos, the oldest form of social repression. With the exception of the first kill—in which the children still imagine they are playing at hunting—the subsequent deaths assume a ritual form; the pig is eaten communally by all and the head is left for the "beast," whose role consists in sharing the feast. This is much like the "public ceremony" described by Freud in which the sacrifice of an animal provided food for the god and his worshippers. . . . So we see that, as Freud points out, the "sacrificing community, its god [the 'beast'], and the sacrificial animal are of the same blood," members of a clan. The pig, then, may be regarded as a totem animal, an "ancestor, a tutelary spirit and protector"; it is, in any case, a part of every child. The taboo or prohibition against eating particular parts of the totem animal coincides with the children's failure to eat the head of the pig. It is that portion which is set aside for the "beast." Just as Freud describes the primitive feast, so the children's festive meal is accompanied by a frenzied ritual in which they temporarily release their forbidden impulses and represent the kill. To consume the pig and to reenact the event is not only to assert a "common identity" but also to share a "common responsibility" for the deed. None of the boys is excluded from the feast. The later ritual, in which Simon, as a human substitute identified with the totem, is killed, is in this novel less an unconscious attempt to share the responsibility for the killing of a primal father in prehistoric times, than it is a social act in which the participants celebrate their new society by commemorating their severance from the authority of the civilized state. Because of the juxtaposition of Piggy and pig, the eating of pig at the communal feast might be regarded as the symbolic cannibalism by which the children physically partake of the qualities of the slain and share responsibility for their crime. (It must be remembered that, although Piggy on a symbolic level represents the light of reason and the authority of the father, on the psychological and literal level of the story he shares that bestiality and irrationality which to Golding dominate all men, even the most rational or civilized.)

In the final action, Ralph is outlawed by the children and hunted like an animal. Jack sharpens a stick at both ends so that it will be ready to receive the severed head of the boy as if he were a pig. Jack keeps his society together because it, like the brother horde of Robertson Smith and Freud, "is based on complicity in the common crimes." In his flight Ralph, seeing the grinning skull of a pig, thinks of it as a toy and remembers the early days on the island when all were united in play. In the play world, the world of day, he has become a "spoil-sport" like Piggy; in the world based upon primitive rites and taboos, the night world where fears become demons and sleep is like death, he is the heretic or outcast. This final hunt, after the conch is broken, is the pursuit of the figure representing law and order, the king or the god. Finally, Jack, through misuse of the dead Piggy's glasses, accidentally sets the island on fire. A passing cruiser, seeing the fire, lands to find only a dirty group of sobbing little boys. (pp. 97-9)

But are all the meanings of the novel as clear as they seem? To restrict it to an imaginative re-creation of Freud's theory that children are little savages, that no child is innocent whatever Christian theology would have us believe, is to limit its significance for the adult world. To say that the "beasts" we fear are within, that man is essentially irrational—or, to place a moral judgment on the irrational, that man is evil—that, again, is too easy. In this forced isolation of a group of children, Golding is making a statement about the world they have left—a world, we are told, "in ruins." According to Huizinga's theory of play, war is a game, a contest for prestige which, like the games of primitives, or of classical athletes, may be fatal. It, too, has its rules, although the modern concept of total war tends to obscure both its ritualistic and its ennobling character. It, too, has its spatial and temporal limitations, as the new rash of "limited" wars makes very clear. More than once the children's acts are compared to those of the outside world. When Jack first blackens his face like a savage, he gives his explanation: " 'For hunting. Like in war. You know—dazzle paint. Like things trying to look like something else.' " . . . (p. 99)

[The dead pilot is] the analogue in the adult world to the ritual killing of the child Simon on the island; he, like Simon, is the victim and scapegoat of his society, which has unleashed its instincts in war. Both he and Simon are associated by a cluster of visual images. Both are identified with beasts by the children, who do see the truth—that all men are bestial—but do not understand it. Both he and Simon attract the flies from the Lord of the Flies, the pig's head symbolic of the demonic; both he and Simon are washed away by a cleansing but not reviving sea. His position on the mountain recalls the Hanged or Sacrificed god of Frazer; here, however, we have a parody of fertility. He is dead proof that Piggy's exaggerated respect for adults is itself irrational. When the officer at the rescue jokingly says, " 'What have you been doing? Having a war or something?' " this representative of the grown-up world does not understand that the games of the children, which result in two deaths, are a moral commentary upon the primitive nature of his own culture. The ultimate irrationality is war. Paradoxically, the children not only return to a primitive and infantile morality, but they also degenerate into

adults. They prove that, indeed, "children are but men of a smaller growth." (p. 100)

Claire Rosenfield, " 'Men of a Smaller Growth': A Psychological Analysis of William Golding's 'Lord of the Flies'," in Literature and Psychology, Vol. XI, No. 4, Autumn, 1961, pp. 93-101.

PAULETTE MICHEL-MICHOT

William Golding's *Lord of the Flies* (1954) calls to mind both Ballantyne's *The Coral Island* (1858) and Defoe's *Robinson Crusoe* (1719). In each they isolate people on an island: a group of children in *Lord of the Flies,* three adolescents in *The Coral Island,* and a young man in *Robinson Crusoe;* and the characters they present, what they are and what they undertake, so strikingly reflect the problems and ideas of the age in which each book was written.

Lord of the Flies is obviously intended as a counterpart to *The Coral Island.* Golding wanted to explode the myth of the innocence of the child living, as in Ballantyne's romance, in harmony with nature on a desert island, and leading brave civilized and even civilizing lives. In whatever situation they find themselves, Ballantyne's children never show any impatience with one another; the understanding is perfect, practical difficulties are easily overcome; there is no question of their ever failing in what they undertake for they are 'Britons', a term they use to congratulate each other. The only two things that prevent them from considering their island as Paradise are the existence of cannibals and of pirates. *The Coral Island* is of course a romance but, as we shall see later, it is also a sign of the age.

Golding chooses the same situation as Ballantyne's. His main characters are, like Ballantyne's, called Ralph and Jack. But though, at first, his children delight in their freedom and in the beauty and the pleasures of the island—plenty of food, fruit, drink, and plenty of 'fun'; one of them even observes "it is like Coral Island"—the situation soon deteriorates, and when at the end the naval officer taking in the horror of the situation, remarks "I should have thought that a pack of British boys—you're all British aren't you?—would have been able to put up a better show than that", Golding strikes the final blow at Ballantyne's conception of the child and by extrapolation of Man.

In *Lord of the Flies* a group of schoolboys aged between six and twelve, evacuated from England where an atomic war is raging, are accidentally stranded on a desert island in the South Pacific. They are left on their own, without adult guidance, to organize their own society. Their first aim is to abide as much as possible, in spite of their isolation and of the primitive way of life they have to adopt, by the standards of life that the civilized world of adults has infused into them, and to wait for rescue. The fire which they try to keep going on the top of the mountain is the symbol of their attachment to civilization for it embodies their hope for rescue. . . . At first it is fun, a boy-scout adventure. But gradually more sinister elements in their nature take control. They imagine that there is a beast on the island, that it comes from the water and moves at night, unseen. Some of the boys have seen it in the mountain. The beast quickly becomes the sign of the children's unrest, of their superstitious fear which becomes so overwhelming that it eventually takes control of the situation. The boys in charge of the hunting have become so intent on killing that they no longer understand that the aim of hunting was originally to provide the community with food. They mistake the means for the end. The community splits into two groups: the hunters deviate further and further from the standards of civilized life that the other group strains to preserve. The hunters become a savage group of outlaws giving themselves up to primitive rites: they paint their faces and perform horrible ritual dances round the Pig's head they have actually deified or round a boy playing the part of a chased pig, but finally they perform their killing dance on one of their former comrades, and kill him on the rhythm of their murderous song 'kill the beast! Cut his throat! Spill his blood!'. The hunters' deification of the Pig's Head, which becomes the Lord of the flies himself, and the horror of their rituals stress the fact that the children have fallen into a state of savagery in which evil is all-powerful. . . . The situation deteriorates more and more until the hunters, drunk with frenzy, kill Simon when he brings them the 'good news'. For Simon has discovered the truth about the beast. Simon is a visionary who wants to find out the nature of that 'beastie'; he is given a deeper insight into the situation than the others: "When discussing the identity of the beast Simon explained: 'what I mean is . . . maybe it's only us' "; or "however Simon thought of the beast there rose before his inward sight the picture of a human at once heroic and sick". Alone in the mountain, Simon saw a humped thing slightly moving in the wind and he understood then that this thing was the corpse of a pilot, rotting away with his parachute still fixed on his back. The wind blew and the "figure lifted, bowed and breathed foully at him". This is the beast, it is Man himself "at once heroic and sick", a fallen creature, dead, a symbol of war and decay, a reminiscence of the state of the adult world when the children left it, and a symbol of what is threatening the boys' community. Simon now holds the clue to their situation: there is no 'beastie', the evil is in the children themselves. This is made explicit when Simon, looking at the pig's head, is granted a moment of insight: the head is speaking to him: "Fancy thinking the Beast was something you could hunt and kill. You knew didn't you? I'm part of you? Close, close, close! . . . This is ridiculous, you know perfectly well you'll only meet me down there (on the beach, among the others) so don't try to escape!" Simon hurries down to the boys and wants to tell them the 'comforting' news but he is savagely murdered by the frightened boys who perform their beast-killing-dance on him. After this more or less deliberate sacrifice they lose all sense of control. The 'littluns' have long before joined the hunter group because they feel more secure among them. They declare war on the last few powerless representatives of civilized living. They torture and murder them. And when a naval detachment eventually comes to rescue the last survivors, the hunters are madly chasing Ralph, their former elected leader, across the island, burning everything on their way.

The appearance of the naval officer at the end and the sudden shift in point of view throws the story into focus. Though the characters are children they had to deal with problems that have their exact equivalent in the adult world. Now they are dwarfed to children again, they are crying little boys held in control by an adult presence. Yet we cannot forget the cruelty and the savagery of what they have done and of what they were up to, had the rescue been delayed a little longer. We cannot forget the potential evil that will come to the surface again whenever the circumstances permit it: "In the middle of them, with filthy body, matted hair, and unwiped nose, Ralph wept for *the end of innocence, the darkness of man's*

heart" (italics mine). The innocence of the child and of man is a fallacy; by nature man has a terrible potentiality for evil. The fact that Golding chooses children as protagonists, makes it all the more striking and terrifying. It explodes for ever the view that man is originally good or even neutral and that society is the source of all evil. Neither does Golding allow us to believe that the evil a child is born with can be annihilated in the child's process of growing up or that it can be eradicated by a pattern of rules imposed by civilization or by a social or political system. For, though the appearance of the naval officer seems to restore order, we cannot forget that the war carried out by the boys on their island is neither better nor worse than the atomic war that was raging over the world at the opening of the book; and in a way the children with their painted faces are no different from the naval officer in his uniform with his gilt buttons.

The children's community is in fact a microcosm of the adult world. Golding has isolated his children on an island and has deliberately magnified the problems and issues at stake. The situation is first presented as a 'game' enacted by children, but we are gradually led to forget that the characters are boys; it then assumes the seriousness and the gravity of our contemporary world. Golding works out his themes by means of symbols. The conch which regulates the assemblies is the symbol of democracy, of free speech; but the defect of the system is mercilessly pointed out: "we have lots of assemblies. Everybody enjoys speaking and being together. We decide things. But they don't get done". The conch is inadequate and powerless confronted with violence and tyranny: Piggy, the fat intelligent boy is savagely murdered while holding the conch.

The fire which must be kept burning is the symbol of their hope for rescue, of their attachment to civilization, for it will reveal their presence on the island to the outside world. But it can be otherwise interpreted, and this makes for the richness of Golding's work. It is a distant end that will be reached only at the price of an everyday effort; it is a duty that must be done for no immediate end: it can be culture and education. But the fire remains unattended for the first time when Jack prefers to go hunting wild pigs and forgets everything about the fire; as some boys and all the 'littluns' gradually come to join Jack's tribe, it becomes more and more difficult to keep the fire going because the interest of the majority lies elsewhere i.e., in the urge to satisfy a lower and cruel instinct which gives them the illusion of security. The hunters no longer hunt to provide the community with food but because they like the killing itself, first the killing of wild pigs and finally the killing of their former comrades.

The same symbolism is also to be found in the characters; Golding makes them work out archetypal patterns of human society or of different conflicting tendencies within the individual. Ralph, the elected leader, and Jack, the hunter and final chief and tyrant, are the two polarizing figures. Ralph is a 'decent' chap, a natural leader but is not very intelligent. He is assisted by Piggy, a fat asthmatic intelligent boy who is always a butt for the others; he represents thoughtfulness but is unable to communicate his ideas to a vast audience; hence he becomes Ralph's adviser. Jack on the other hand is arrogant, proud, boastful, unscrupulous and finally becomes a murderer. Simon has insight but is diametrically opposed to Piggy. The majority thinks he is 'batty' because he is an individualist who goes his own way; he is ready to face anything to find out the nature of the beast; he goes alone into the mountain and discovers the truth about it. The way he meets his death . . . makes him a martyr. The twins, Sam and Eric, who always act in concert, represent the average man of good will who will stick to his principles as long as possible, but who will eventually join the majority when it is too hard to stand alone on his own ground. The 'littluns' stand for the mob the leaders work on: neglectful and idle when they are on Ralph's side and are asked to contribute to the welfare of the community; frightened of the dark and a prey to superstitious fears, but disciplined and obedient when they become part of the hunter tribe and are under Jack's drastic military and tyrannical leadership. Jack is assisted by two or three evil-minded boys, one of them being the official torturer.

This brief analysis is intended to suggest the vast scale of human values and social or political problems both universal and contemporary that are dealt with in *Lord of the Flies.* It is also worth mentioning that if this is an allegorical story, it is nonetheless deeply rooted in the physical and psychological world of the child. The story can be read as a story and the allegorical meaning emerges from it.

Golding's wish to use the same situation as Ballantyne's is obvious; but the final result is just the opposite. Ballantyne's characters are children free of evil—as F. Kermode so rightly put it, they belong to the period when "boys were sent out of Arnoldian schools certified free of Original Sin". They fear nothing and behave like gentlemen towards each other, not like adolescents. They embody the blind optimism, the assurance and sometimes the pompousness of the 19th century. (pp. 510-14)

In *The Coral Island* the natives' faces "besides being tatooed, were besmeared with red paint and streaked with white"; in *Lord of the Flies* there are no native cannibals, it is Jack's hunters who paint their faces: "Jack began to dance and his laughter became a bloodthirsty snarling . . . the mask was a thing of its own, behind which Jack hid, liberated from shame and self-consciousness". Golding knows that the distinction is not merely a simple one between good Christians and bad cannibals.

When Golding writes in detail about the life on the island, it is often to stress the cruelty and the intolerance of the boys: Simon is 'batty' and, though Ralph and Piggy make a good pair, Ralph can't help teasing or laughing at clumsy Piggy: "there was always a little pleasure to be got out of pulling Piggy's leg, even if one did it by accident". It is not necessary to dwell on the savagery of Jack's tribe.

To destroy Ballantyne's pastoral picture of life on a tropical island where everything is so delightful, Golding speaks of the diarrhea of the 'littluns' who eat too much fruit, of the sweat, of the flies that cover the pig's head which in Simon's delirium becomes the Lord of the Flies himself. Golding creates sympathy in the reader for a group of children and gradually uses the reader's repulsion for dirt and brutality to increase his horror at discovering the true nature of man.

Instead of Ballantyne's blind faith in the superiority of the white race, Golding asks how superior we are to savages and he points to the superficiality of our civilization: indeed it seems to be powerless against the innate brutality of man, against his fear which is in fact the expression of the evil that pervades the world.

Ballantyne's characters do not develop, they go through a se-

ries of exciting and heroic adventures and are left unchanged at the end of the novel. On the contrary Golding shows the deterioration of the initial situation and of the characters; but the book is not altogether pessimistic: though Ralph is on the point of defeat, he has learned much in the process of growing to maturity, he has learned to recognize the quality of Piggy's mind—"Ralph wept for . . . the fall through the air of the true, wise friend called Piggy"—he has learned much about his enemies and about himself, that is, how short he fell of his own standards. The book can also be read as a metaphor for human experience. (pp. 515-16)

Robinson Crusoe and *Lord of the Flies* stand in contrast to *The Coral Island,* for Ballantyne's characters are presented as fundamentally good whereas Defoe's and Golding's are depraved. Crusoe is the depraved 18th century nonconformist; he has led "a dreadful life destitute of the knowledge and the fear of God" but he comes to accept his unfortunate condition as God's punishment for his misspent life and to see a sign of God's mercy in the fact that he alone has survived the wreck of the ship and is allowed to live fairly comfortably on his island. He meditates constantly and sees the hand of God in the smallest events of his daily life, for he is not free of evil and needs the help of God to resist temptation. Yet compared to Golding's view of man, the depraved 18th century nonconformist is far less depraved. Defoe's presentation of evil belongs to the puritan tradition: the main issues of life are often reduced to a mere choice between good and evil i.e., between God and the devil. Defoe is thus far from exploring the problem of evil as thoroughly as Golding whose theme in *Lord of the Flies* is before everything else, the exploration of evil from a metaphysical point of view.

After the creative energy of Robinson Crusoe, his constant struggle against his depraved nature, his ability through work and inventiveness to solve his problems, came the complacency of Ballantyne's characters, for whom no problem actually existed and who enjoyed a position which they had inherited; they were innocent Christian adolescents going through 'exciting' adventures and bringing the 19th century truth—Christianity—to the barbarians of some distant island of the Pacific. Then came *Lord of the Flies,* the savage destruction of the myth of innocence, presenting us with a society of children which is a microcosm of the adult world. Golding points to the deterioration of the values fought for by Robinson Crusoe and blindly taken for granted by the boys of *The Coral Island.* He explodes the myth of innocence and takes us back to the problem of Evil ignored by Ballantyne and oversimplified by Defoe. (pp. 519-20)

Paulette Michel-Michot, "The Myth of Innocence," in Revue des langues vivantes, *Vol. 28, No. 4, 1962, pp. 510-20.*

KENNETH WATSON

It is the close-knit texture and significant pattern, even more than its most obvious quality of immediate vividness and force, which makes William Golding's *Lord of the Flies* worth the detailed study not many novels stand up to. As it seems to me to have been too often and too easily assumed to be essentially a religious work, I should like to modify this assumption, for its outstanding place among post-war novels invites and justifies as close a reading as possible.

The clearest tribute I know to the power and realism of *Lord of the Flies* is the shock of its impact on even non-literary students, precisely because it is not 'literary' but unfalteringly tough-minded. Its first reading is for most people a frightening experience, arousing a sense of uncanny and even supernatural evil like that which almost—but never quite—engulfs Simon. This subjective but common experience is a relevant critical reaction in distinguishing the quality of the novel, if it is consolidated by objective analysis. The immediacy of the writing is at once apparent in the imagery, with metaphors often embedded in the verbs, in the observant eye firmly on the object, and in an at times poetic transforming imagination:

> The eye was first attracted to a black bat-like creature that danced on the sand, and only later perceived the body above it. The bat was the child's shadow, shrunk by the vertical sun to a patch between the hurrying feet.

> This sweaty march along the blazing beach had given them the complexion of newly washed plums.

The tropical detail combines with an occasional reminder of its effects on the boys to give an awareness of their physical plight. Even the sea plays surprisingly little part in their lives and the reef is completely inaccessible. The only escape from the confines of the island and the march of events is Ralph's remembrance of having once lived in a Devon cottage on the edge of the moors.

Even more important than this restriction to the island is the entire absence of adults. This, together with a refusal ever to release the reader by intruding with personal comment, produces an utterly claustrophobic effect, spiritual as much as physical. It is this spiritual claustrophobia which makes the hunting of Ralph so terrifying, so that one experiences such a sudden shock of contrast when the mob of merciless and howling savages suddenly shoots down to child size. . . . (pp. 2-3)

Both the sensory accuracy and the emotional concentration are essential foundations for the reader's fuller experience of the work. As in *The Ancient Mariner* they give firmness and clarity to the symbolism, which arises directly from character and event. Mr. Golding's novels are usually called fables; it is this exactness in both action and description (the description is never static or separate from event) which supports us in experiencing and therefore accepting the moral fable.

Obviously the progress of the plot can be compared to the Fall. But once any tendency, especially towards chaos or lawlessness, establishes itself, it progresses at ever-growing speed towards its climax. Any accomplished writer would give increasing pace to the narrative through the need for increasing tension. Nor is the plot in the form of a single unbroken movement: the episode which is both the most important and the most moving, though not the most purely terrifying, is the death of Simon. . . . To take it as symbolizing the Fall may be a valid personal interpretation, but I do not find it a necessary one—though this is not of course to exclude interpretation in terms of religious *ethic*. But 'the darkness of man's heart', deterioration into fear and cruelty, do not necessitate a reading based on 'original sin'. To say so is no more valid today than is the old free-will and determinism antithesis. And if the island is the paradise within which the 'Fall' occurs, it is so only in a very limited sense of unrestricted fruit, warmth, and enervation. It is far from an ideal environment even physically. The fruit is an inadequate diet which pro-

duces diarrhoea, the littluns exist in squalor and neglect, and it is problems of discomfort and trying to organize obvious needs, such as the fire, and shelter from both rain and fear, which soon cause the first splits and outbursts of ill feeling.

But the deeper levels of meaning can, I think, be identified more precisely. The novel works most vitally in moral, not religious or theological, terms. Ralph has even been described as a father figure who represents virtue and light. But he is too clearly flawed. The beginning of cruelty, unthinking as always, must be important in a work so tightly constructed as this. And it comes from Ralph. . . . As for light, it is Piggy and later Simon who hold up the torch. They alone resist the growth of superstition; Piggy through rational thought, Simon by the strength of his own conviction, which unlike the intellectual literal-mindedness of Piggy grows under the stress put upon it. He has faith: but in what? By holding fast to the power of his own mind he interprets the evidence of his senses in the light of what he knows.

There is evidently not only a moral and intellectual fable but a social and political one. Ralph is *l'homme moyen sensuel* but even more clearly the 'liberal' politician who has found he can talk fluently and enjoys the applause of the crowd.

> The assembly was silent.

> Ralph lifted the conch again and his good humour came back as he thought of what he had to say next.

> "Now we come to the most important thing. I've been thinking. I was thinking while we were climbing the mountain." He flashed a conspiratorial grin at the other two. "And on the beach just now. This is what I thought. We want to have fun. And we want to be rescued."

This is an epitome of the political oratory, based on emotion but nothing else, which carries the speaker along with it as much as the hearers.

> The passionate noise of agreement from the assembly hit him like a wave and he lost his thread. He thought again.

> "We want to be rescued; and of course we shall be rescued."

> Voices babbled. The simple statement, unbacked by any proof but the weight of Ralph's new authority, brought light and happiness.

This cannot be satisfactorily read on the narrative level alone: the parallels are too close and insistent. His words induce simple euphoria; 'important', 'thinking', and especially 'light' are ironic and the happiness is without foundation or possibility of endurance. This represents the quality of his mind in contrast to Piggy's while also implying its common quality with his audience's. Later, in another mood 'he found himself understanding the wearisomeness of this life where every path was an improvisation and a considerable part of one's waking life was spent watching one's feet'. (pp. 3-4)

It is enlightening to read the accounts of the four assemblies successively and notice how increasingly, as the shutter comes down and the curtain flaps in his well-intentioned mind, Ralph has to be prompted by Piggy to save him from completely losing his grip on the clue of the actual.

The most explicit symbol is the conch. Since it carries the right to be heard, the mandate to speak even for a littlun if he holds it, it implies that the rule of law still exists. Jack, who epitomizes the course of political change followed by most authoritarian demagogues, is the first to demand rules for his own advantage, but the first to shout them down later. When the conch is smashed—it and Piggy, the rational nonviolent person, are wiped out at the same moment and by the same blow, for Piggy's separateness leaves him no other protection—then all attempt to maintain social order is ended and barbarism is loose. Piggy has been established at once as a realist: while Ralph stands on his head at the thought of no grown-ups, Piggy says the plane will not be back—and why. Ralph's belated recognition of him—forging a link which till then had been with Jack—comes because Piggy shows he can think: see essentials, criticize, and make suggestions. . . . It is Piggy who first says they must have a meeting, and he is the organizer who tries to collect names—and at this stage is obeyed. Indeed only the myopic Piggy is clear-sighted enough to see what their problems and needs actually are and how they are failing more and more to meet them. 'Like a crowd of kids', he says repeatedly. His is the particular agony of the mature in mind.

> We could experiment. We could find out how to make a small hot fire and then put green branches on to make smoke. Some of them leaves must be better for that than others.

This is the scientific attitude, the intellectual emancipation that applies empirical thought and experiment to any new problem, making comparisons and establishing priorities and values, even in changed circumstances. 'Only Piggy could have the intellectual daring to suggest moving the fire from the mountain.' In ironic contrast to his physical timidity and social ineffectiveness is his intellectual courage in facing facts even when horrified by them, about people as well as things. . . . Finally, in a book where every close-packed detail has significance, there should be meaning in the fact that he is the only boy who does not come from a conventional middle-class background. It is not his grammar but his lack of the social conventions; he speaks of his 'auntie', which is very non-U. Helpless in the absence of protection, he seems to stand as the representative social democrat and intellectual, over against both the conventional member of the 'officer class' presumed to have automatic powers of 'leadership' and those who take ease and affluence for granted.

Social attitudes and types are plain behind the remarkable individualization of the boys. Characters emerge. They do not change, but traits grow as changing circumstances feed them. Irony plays most on Ralph and Jack. What they have in common is vanity, but where there is a 'mildness' about Ralph, Jack's eyes are frustrated and ready to turn to anger at our first sight of him. . . . His mortification when not in the full limelight and his lust to hunt and kill, rationalized as providing meat, feed each other till he is swallowed by his own mad unreal world in which everything is transformed with the ingenuity of the paranoiac to fit his fantasy, and Simon's body becomes the beast—disguised. In the completest possible contrast to Piggy he says, 'Forget the beast and sacrifice to it.'

The others do, sooner or later. Samneric, their identities lost not just because they are twins, become in the face of power the ordinary good-hearted nonentities most of us are, who protest at first and remain loyal, then defect under increasing, and finally physical, pressure, but retain their humane impulses and will take risks at times, as in warning Ralph. (pp. 4-5)

'A slight furtive boy whom no one knew', [Roger] finds the beginnings of ecstasy in the stone-throwing, and becomes the eager executioner of the cruelties decreed by the Leader who does not need to carry them out himself. . . . One knows from this why the concentration camps could always be staffed, as through Jack's 'numberless and inexpressible frustrations' one has an insight into the psychology of a Hitler.

And the littlun with the birthmark, who disappears in the fire, leaving no trace and remembered only by Piggy (he was never even noticed till he resisted notice): does he not represent the anonymous millions, the Unknown Citizen who has existed throughout history and before it, and still exists till obliterated by forces, part human, part natural, which he can neither control nor even understand? It is remarkable that at the end when the naval officer, 'who knew as a rule when people were telling the truth', asks if anyone has been killed, Ralph's answer is 'Only two'. The point is that this is truthful as far as he or anyone else is aware. The memory of the very existence of a littlun (the word is always written as a common noun) has been repressed, as presence at the murder of Simon becomes taboo even to Piggy. I have been more than once struck by the fact that in reading *Lord of the Flies,* many students, not usually careless readers, accept at first Ralph's statement and themselves forget the third death, simply because, I think, their minds work like most people's.

But all this is moral, psychological, social; not theological. While the spreading evil emanates from the boys themselves, they deteriorate not under any inner compulsion of original sin, but through a failure of imagination and therefore a neglect of thought, which leads them to ignore their own opportunities and the plight of others alike, so that they refuse to co-operate even for their own advantage. That is to say, they are a microcosm of the adult world; incomplete, but one which, since it excludes all manifestations of sex, which is essentially individual, emphasizes still more powerfully the elements of society. This is the world of which Piggy and Ralph say pathetically that grown-ups would not quarrel or talk about a beast, and their belief may represent the unwisdom of relying on the unaided intellect. The ironic comment on it is the uncomprehending naval officer's cliché: 'I should have thought that a pack of British boys—you're all British, aren't you?—would have been able to put up a better show than that', which is no better than Jack's rabid nationalism: 'After all, we're not savages. We're English; and the English are best at everything.' Above all, in their frenzy the boys are unable even to hear the truth, that is, the plain facts, that Simon brings them from the hill. Cruelty has crept in as always in intrinsically small ways, through imaginative laziness and failure of sympathy, till callousness hardens more and more. Even the killing of the pig, made worse by the emphasis at this point on the beauty of the surroundings, is shown as a brutal act and the animal as needing compassion.

The hunting of Ralph is the final example of the construction which builds up such emotional intensity by the resonance of incidents repeated with added, or different, significance. The pushing over of the rocks, Roger's repeated stone-throwing, the assemblies, the fires, the hunting scenes, and the dances are merely the more obvious of these 'repetitions with a difference'; there are many smaller ones. The most important is the sight of the 'Beast', first by Samneric, then by Jack and Ralph, and lastly, and with so different a response, by Simon.

Simon is tough-minded, emotionally reliable though physically handicapped; and it is he, not Ralph, who is nobility and light.

> "As if," said Simon, "the beastie, the beastie or the snake-thing, was real. Remember?"
>
> The two older boys flinched when they heard the shameful syllable. Snakes were not mentioned now, were not mentionable.

But 'However Simon thought of the beast there arose before his inward sight the picture of a human at once heroic and sick.' Only he stands apart, not simply intellectually like Piggy, but by his very nature; his innate qualities prevent his being smirched like the others. . . . Like each of those who die, he is set apart by physical defect, but more intensely so. The littlun has 'one side of his face blotted out by a mulberry-coloured birthmark'; Piggy is myopic and asthmatic; Simon is epileptic, and even Piggy says he's cracked. But his strength is that of the martyr he becomes: moral and emotional, a part of him, not an externally sought conviction or faith. (pp. 5-7)

'Pig's head on a stick'—the gift for the *darkness*. If faith today might be summed up as a belief in explicability together with a belief that everyone is ultimately emotionally educable, then Simon has faith in this sense. Here is the central example in the novel of art as what Joyce Cary called a proposition for truth. In his lonely, half-conscious nightmare he clings to the fact that there is—must be—an explanation, and fights off the inert acceptance of the supernatural. The title marks this as the key, the central scene, and this is not all. Recovering consciousness after his fit, 'Simon spoke aloud to the clearing'.

'What else is there to do?'—but keep on. (Piggy at almost this moment is repeating 'We just got to go on, that's all. That's what grown-ups would do.' But Simon relies on something more integral, less external, than does Piggy.) 'He saw a humped thing suddenly sit up on the top and look down on him.' But 'he hid his face and toiled on.' He not only finds, faces, and understands the 'Beast', 'the mechanics of this parody', which is 'harmless and horrible', but 'he took the lines in his hands, he freed them from the rocks and the figure from the wind's indignity.' There is no supernatural, only the unknown, the not yet understood, the potentially knowable. There is no Beast, either from air or water (for the broken bodies when released are carried out to sea), only ignorance which with fear begets evil in the human imagination and which needs help. So, though 'to speak in assembly was a terrible thing to him', 'the news must reach the others as soon as possible'. Once again 'he felt a perilous necessity to speak', and though once before 'his effort fell about him in ruins; the laughter beat him cruelly', in the moment of death 'Simon was crying out something about a dead man on a hill'. But this is not a clear religious symbol. The dead man on the hill is not Simon who has been tempted in the wilderness and who strives to the death to bring release and salvation from 'mankind's essential illness' to his fellows—through rational understanding.

On the book's first appearance, rather naturally what was first noticed was the parallel with primitive communities. . . . [However, Golding] is concerned with the continuing human predicament of living in *this world*, in which modern technology or primitive attempts at weapons or tools are only the attendant circumstances. The world of civiliza-tion is a world of savagery still. One of the clearest indications of the social meaning is the war paint and the incantations, reflecting not tribalism so much as the depersonalization, the shedding of identity and therefore of responsibility, which is particularly a modern problem and which is made easy by uniforms, songs, and slogans:

> The mask was a thing on its own, behind which Jack hid, liberated from shame and self-consciousness.

It is Mr. Golding's conviction that man's destiny is his own responsibility, and man must face this hard fact. . . .

[The boys in *Lord of the Flies*] are children, immature, undeveloped yet for good or ill. But even more important, there is the non-mystical individual integrity, at once intellectual and emotional, of Simon. (p. 7)

> *Kenneth Watson, "A Reading of 'Lord of the Flies'," in* English, *Vol. XV, No. 85, Spring, 1964, pp. 2-7.*

R. C. TOWNSEND

The rise of William Golding's *Lord of the Flies* to the top of best-seller and required reading lists should suggest to the teacher of literature and the social sciences important insights into his students', and perhaps his own, willingness to be taken in by false profundity and false art. When the book was first published in 1954 it had an interestingly mixed reception. Reviewers sensed that it was by no means flawless, but they retreated from literary grounds and ended up praising or condemning the book on the basis of their agreement or disagreement with Golding's thesis about what lies beneath the thin veneer of civilization. (p. 153)

The present enthusiasm for Golding's book in America dates back primarily to 1959 when it was reissued in a paperback edition. This edition contains a supplementary essay in which E. L. Epstein makes apologies for the superficial nature of previous criticisms of Golding's books and goes on to set the sober and laudatory tone of almost all subsequent English and American criticism of *Lord of the Flies.* The theme is defined by Golding himself ("an attempt to trace the defects of society back to the defects of human nature"); the symbolism is worked out (" 'The lord of the flies,' is, of course, a translation of the Hebrew *Ba'alzevuv,* [*Beelzebub* in Greek] which means literally 'lord of insects' "); the book is seen as a cultural monument. . . . (pp. 153-54)

In January 1962 the book review section of the *New York Times* began to carry accounts of the novel's race to the popularity it now enjoys: "In the Ivy League, at any rate, William Golding's *Lord of the Flies* is edging up on Salinger." Seven months later another reviewer looked out upon a less exclusive scene and found that it "has been pressing J. D. Salinger's work in popularity, particularly among students, running a close second to *Catcher in the Rye* in campus bookstores." . . . By the time the newspaper strike was over [in April 1963] the race was won; the *Times* announced that *Lord of the Flies* had become the best-selling paperback in America.

In that first post-strike issue the novel was described in terms that suggest *King Lear* or the Book of Revelations: "Apocalyptic, harrowing, shatteringly dramatic, it is a novel of the beginning and end of things." That the book could be placed in the category of Great Books was made even more apparent by a publisher's announcement of a forthcoming selection of *Literature from the Bible:* " . . . each introduction includes a list of suggested readings—ranging from Homer to William Golding—which are pertinent to that particular section of the Bible." On a lower plane, *The New Republic* invited "faculty members of four universities to account for this popularity" and only one told of (or shared) the dissatisfaction of some students with the novel's "pretentiousness, obviousness, and oversimplification." A film has been made of it and in a cozy advertisement in *The New Yorker* the producers and the director describe what is the usual response: "it has become required reading in schools, and is the unchallenged darling of the sensitive literati." Because this is so, another look at *Lord of the Flies* can help us not only to judge the book but also to suggest some things about the malleability of students, teachers, and other "literati." And to compare this book . . . to what may well be another source besides Ballantyne's *Coral Island,* Richard Hughes' *A High Wind in Jamaica,* is to see how the same theme can be treated with tact and integrity.

Presumably one starts with the hope—if not the belief—that Golding's thesis is wrong, that finally man is more than a beast, but to object to the book on these grounds is to make the mistake of the first reviewers. Yet it is understandable why they retreated to the "very premise" on which the story is based; at least that is just where Golding wants to engage his reader, and on first reading the book one is more concerned about Piggy's glasses or Ralph's rescue than about how Golding is luring his reader up a path which leads only to an acceptance of his thesis. But after a second reading it becomes clear how unsure Golding is of that thesis and of his ability to make his fable suggest it. He thinks he would be unable (or he knows we would be unwilling) to move from the terms of one to those of the other and so he continually makes the jump for us. Thus Ralph and Jack become, he tells us, "two continents of experience and feeling, unable to communicate" and are later opposed as "the brilliant world of hunting, tactics, fierce exhilaration, skill" and the "world of longing and baffled commonsense." Piggy, the most intelligent of the boys and the possessor of the only recognizable voice in the novel (though ironically because of his bad grammar) looks into the fire and, it is claimed, "glanced nervously into hell." At one point Simon tries "to express man's essential illness," and the eyes of the pig's head into which he gazes are "dim with the infinite cynicism of adult life"; at another point Sam and Eric protest, Golding says, "out of the heart of civilization." And on the final page, as is well known, the cause of Ralph's tears is supposed to be "the end of innocence, the darkness of man's heart." It is as if Aesop had told us that the fox really liked grapes but was calling them sour because he was unable to reach them.

But Aesop was clear about the separation of his fable and his moral, and consequently so are we. He does not expect the fox's hunger pains to upset us; we can go on to join him in his conclusions about man's rationalizations. But we do care about children's hunger pains and about bullying, and realizing this, Golding is quick to name our concern as one for "mankind's essential illness." He does not trust us to move from the terms of one to those of the other, so he forces children into moral positions and attitudes they could never take and that he could not come out and make explicit in the novel itself. (pp. 154-56)

In objecting to what Golding is doing in *Lord of the Flies* there is no need to invoke Jamesian principles about intrusive narrators or more modern edicts about impersonality. Golding is obviously violating these, but we are learning not to rely too heavily on them and he is doing much more. For not only is he exploiting Ralph and Piggy and Simon but he is also exploiting the thousands of students who are committed to the book. Carried along by the excitement of a first reading it is not clear where the voice is coming from (thus Walter Allen's nice phrase, "too easily affecting"). If Simon is trying to "express mankind's essential illness," it may seem plausible that we don't amount to much after all, that the effort isn't really worth it. It is an age in which the voice of despair is particularly seductive to the ears of a student, so Golding's easy cynicism usually goes unchallenged. And it is no more than "easy cynicism." That reference to "the infinite cynicism of adult life" need apply to no one else but to him. "When I was young, before the war," he said breezily in a recent *New Republic* interview, "I did have some airy-fairy views about man . . . But I went through the war and that changed me. The war taught me different and a lot of others like me." Students are also willing to be "taught different"; indeed, Golding once admitted that they have "a vague sense" (only "a vague sense" unfortunately) that "he too has it in for the whole world of organization."

One might account for the popularity of *Lord of the Flies* only in terms of Golding's exploitation of student bewilderment, but teachers of literature and political science, and, conceivably, "anthropologists, social psychologists and philosophical historians . . . " have contributed greatly. It is they, after all, who assign the book and it seems that the book was first read (and still is read) as "required reading." It would be too harsh to say that they also "have it in for the whole world of organization," but though they may not be looking for prophecies of doom they are all too eager to find some sort of significant statement or some symbolic use of language. And so a facile comment on the human condition is heard as an apocalyptic voice. Should the ear need convincing, there is the students' eager acceptance of the book; should the teaching of the book need some justification or some "tone," there is all that Symbolism—conch, glasses, parachutist, or the lord of the flies who "is, of course, a translation of of the Hebrew. . . . " The book is eminently teachable: it "speaks to students," the symbolism can be "worked out." But what does not get demonstrated, apparently, is that in order to force its dubious conclusions upon us the voice that speaks relies not on any authority it possesses but on our inattention, and that Golding's symbolism emanates from a desire to support the conclusions rather than from a total commitment to his subject, whether that subject be defined as the fate of a handful of boys after a nuclear attack or the defects of society and human nature.

There is no need to contrast Golding's book to truly harrowing works about "the beginning and end of things" or to deft handlings of the child's world like *What Maisie Knew.* A relatively minor work like Richard Hughes' *A High Wind in Jamaica* is sufficient, and it is of especial interest here because Hughes' book reversed the optimistic conclusions of Ballantyne's *Coral Island* thirty years before *Lord of the Flies.* Although Golding said in a Third Programme interview that he saw little point in writing a novel, "unless you do something either you suspected you couldn't do, or which you are pretty certain nobody else has tried before" (a principle that would have silenced Shakespeare), it seems clear to me that he knew about *A High Wind in Jamaica,* a novel in which another band of children is cut off from the world of organization in a fabulous way (this time on a pirate ship), but a novel in which children are handled with refreshing care and respect.

Whereas Golding continually intrudes into the child's world in order to extract his own moral, Hughes continually asserts that there is a gap between their world and ours, that it is all but impossible to translate their thoughts into adult terms. . . . The pirates do not understand them: "What on *Earth* were the children's heads made of, inside?" the captain asks. When they do speculate about the children's actions they go as far astray as Golding, though somber edicts like his are presented with wry irony. (pp. 156-58)

[At the end of *A High Wind in Jamaica*] whatever turmoil exists in the minds of the children is undiscernible. (p. 159)

At the end of *Lord of the Flies,* on the other hand, a caricature of a British naval officer (i.e., civilization) rescues the boys, and barbarous Jack does not protest fair-haired Ralph's assertion that he is their leader. One critic has read the ending as an indication that "civilization defeats the beast"; another asserts that "only an idiot will suppose that the book ends happily" and defends the ending as "a deliberate device by which to throw the story into focus," a device by which Golding "underscores the argument of the narrative: that Evil is inherent in the human mind itself, whatever innocence may cloak it." Yes, we may step back and wonder at the thinness of the cloak, but we are still relieved that the book ends, if not happily, at least far less unhappily than it might have had Golding either carried its fable out to the conclusion that would be most natural to it or followed the implications of his thesis to the end. And we are also left wondering: if it takes no more than that to reestablish the world of organization, is the darkness not so powerful after all? or is Golding unable to face the implications of the thesis he has flirted with throughout the novel? We do see that once again Golding has manipulated his fable arbitrarily. Whether it be to support his thesis indirectly or to avoid its implications is not of primary importance. What is of primary importance is that he has used a delicate subject in this way and that thousands of readers have been used in their turn. (pp. 159-60)

R. C. Townsend, " 'Lord of the Flies': Fool's Gold?"
in The Journal of General Education, *published by
The Pennsylvania State University Press, University
Park, PA, Vol. XVI, No. 2, July, 1964, pp. 153-60.*

BERNARD S. OLDSEY AND STANLEY WEINTRAUB

Lord of the Flies (1954), Golding's first novel and the one that established his reputation, is still most widely acclaimed as his major work. Not only has it captured a large segment of the popular and academic imagination . . . , but it has also attracted the greatest amount of critical attention directed toward Golding.

To date, that critical attention has proven various, specialized, and spotty. A remarkable "first novel" on any terms, *Lord of the Flies* has been praised on literary grounds much less often than as sociological, psychological, or religious tract, as "pure parable," fable, or myth. The terminology of Frazer and Freud are more often brought to bear upon the novel than the yardsticks of literary criticism. As literature, however, it has been—even while praised—called unoriginal and derivative, filled with "gimmickry," devoid of character-

ization, and lacking in logic. Only twice has it been blasted as insignificant art encased in bad writing.

Certainly *Lord of the Flies* is derivative, in the sense that it falls well within the main stream of several English literary traditions. It is a "boys' book," as are *Treasure Island, The Wind in the Willows, High Wind in Jamaica,* and other books primarily about juvenile characters which transcend juvenile appeal; it is in the tradition of the survival narrative, along with *Robinson Crusoe, The Swiss Family Robinson,* and even Barrie's *Admirable Crichton;* it is in the tradition—best exemplified by Conrad, Cary, and Greene in our century—that examines our culture by transplanting it harshly to an exotic locale where it prospers or withers depending upon its intrinsic value and strength; it is in the long tradition of antiscience writing in England, where authors for centuries have equated scientific progress with dehumanization; and it at least appears to be in the Nonconformist English religious tradition, which assumes mankind's fall from grace.

If all these traditions lead back to one key source of inspiration, it may be no accident. The traditions embodied in *Lord of the Flies* can be discovered in *Gulliver's Travels*—Swift's version of the primeval savagery and greed which civilization only masks in modern man. It seems no coincidence that we also find in Golding a Swiftian obsession with physical ugliness, meanness, and nastiness (sometimes bordering on the scatological), and with the sense of how tenuous is the hold of intelligence, reason, and humaneness as a brake upon man's regression into barbarism.

Eventually, of course, Golding must be judged according to his individual talent rather than tradition or polemical appeal. Other critical visits to his minor devil's island have been accomplished mainly at a distance, through special field glasses. Here we revisit the island armed only with the knowledge that Golding is essentially a literary man who uses scene, character, and symbol (not to mention an exceedingly fine style and some admittedly tricky plot methods) to achieve imaginative literary effects.

The scenic qualities of *Lord of the Flies* help make it an imaginative work for the reader as well as the author. Although Golding occasionally provides consolidating detail, he more commonly requires the reader to pull narrative and descriptive elements into focus. For example, he provides no endpaper map or block description of his fictional island. The reader must explore it along with the participants in the story and piece together a usable concept of time and place. What we learn in this way is just enough to keep the work within the realm of fiction, but not enough to remove it from the realm of allegory. *And the essence of Golding's art resides exactly within the area of overlap.*

Fable-like, time and place are vague. The Queen (Elizabeth?) still reigns, and "Reds" are apparently the vague enemy. It is the postcatastrophic near-future, in which nuclear war has laid waste much of the West. ("They're all dead," Piggy thinks. And "civilization," corroborates Golding, is "in ruins.") The fiery crash of the boys' plane upon a tropical island has been the final stage of their evacuation from England. The island seems to lie somewhere in the Indian or Pacific Ocean. . . . (pp. 15-18)

When the details are extracted and given order under an analytical light, Golding's island looks naturalistic in specification. But matters are not at all that clear in the book. The location of the island, for example, is kept deliberately vague:

it is sufficiently remote to draw only two ships in a month or so, yet close enough to "civilization" to be the floor above which deadly, and old-fashioned, air battles are fought miles high (the boys' plane itself has been shot down). The nearby air and naval war in progress, with conventional weapons, is somewhat out of keeping with earlier reports of utter catastrophe. Equally incongruous is the smartly attired naval officer and savior of the closing pages, whose jaunty mien is incompatible with catastrophe. Yet he is as important to the machinery of the allegory as the earlier crash, which is equally difficult to explain on rational grounds. During the crash the fuselage of the evacuation plane has apparently broken in two: the forward half (holding pilot and others, including more boys) has been cleanly washed out to sea by a conveniently concomitant storm; and the after-section (which makes a long fiery scar as it cuts through the jungle) tumbles unscathed children onto the island. As incompatible, obscure, askew, and unrealistic as these elements may be, they are no more so than Gulliver's adventures. And Golding's graphically novelistic character and topographic details, both poetic and naturalistic, tend to blur the fabulous qualities of the narrative's use of time and setting in its opening and close. Although it is enough to say that the fabulist must be permitted pegs upon which to hang his fable, it is Golding's richly novelistic elements of the telling that call attention to the subtle dissonance. Paradoxically—yet artistically—this very tension between realistic novel and allegorical fable imparts to *Lord of the Flies* some of its unique power.

Golding's characters, like his setting, represent neither fictional reality nor fabulistic unreality, but, rather, partake of the naturalistic and the allegorical at the same time. As a result, they emerge more full bodied than Kafka's ethereal forms, more subtly shaded than Orwell's animal-farm types, and more comprehensibly motivated than Bunyan's religious ciphers. Bit by bit we can piece together fairly solid pictures of the major figures in *Lord of the Flies.* And since a number of commentators have fallen into interpretative error by precipitously trying to state what these characters "mean," perhaps it would be best here to start by trying to state what they "are."

Ralph, the protagonist, is a boy twelve years and a "few months" old. He enters naïvely, turning handsprings of joy upon finding himself in an exciting place free of adult supervision. But his role turns responsible as leadership is thrust upon him—partly because of his size, partly because of his attractive appearance, and partly because of the conch with which, like some miniature Roland, he has blown the first assembly. . . . [There] has been some reader tendency to play down Ralph as a rather befuddled Everyman, a straw boy of democracy tossed about by forces he cannot cope with. Yet he should emerge from this rites-of-passage *bildungsroman* with the reader's respect. He is as much a hero as we are allowed: he has courage, he has good intelligence, he is diplomatic (in assuaging Piggy's feelings and dividing authority with Jack), and he elicits perhaps our greatest sympathy (when hounded across the island). Although he tries to live by the rules, Ralph is no monster of goodness. He himself becomes disillusioned with democratic procedure; he unthinkingly gives away Piggy's embarrassing nickname; and, much more importantly, he takes part in Simon's murder! But the true measure of Ralph's character is that he despairs of democracy because of its hollowness ("talk, talk, talk"), and that he apologizes to Piggy for the minor betrayal, and that—while Piggy tries to escape his share of the guilt for Simon's death—Ralph cannot be the hypocrite (this reversal, incidentally, spoils the picture often given of Piggy as superego or conscience). Ralph accepts his share of guilt in the mass action against Simon, just as he accepts leadership and dedication to the idea of seeking rescue. He too, as he confesses, would like to go hunting and swimming, but he builds shelters, tries to keep the island clean (thus combating the flies), and concentrates vainly on keeping a signal fire going. At the novel's end Ralph has emerged from his age of innocence; he sheds tears of experience, after having proven himself a "man" of humanistic faith and action. We can admire his insistence upon individual responsibility—a major Golding preoccupation—upon doing what must be done rather than what one would rather do.

Ralph's antagonist, Jack (the choir leader who becomes the text's Esau), is approximately the same age. He is a tall, thin, bony boy with light blue eyes and indicative red hair; he is quick to anger, prideful, aggressive, physically tough, and courageous. But although he shows traces of the demagogue from the beginning, he must undergo a metamorphosis from a timidity-shielding arrogance to conscienceless cruelty. At first he is even less able to wound a pig than is Ralph, but he is altered much in the manner of the transformation of the twentieth-century dictator from his first tentative stirrings of power lust to eventual bestiality. Although Golding is careful to show little of the devil in Ralph, he nicely depicts Jack as being directly in league with the lord of flies and dung. . . . Jack is a compelled being; he is swallowed by the beast—as it were—even before Simon: "He tried to convey the compulsion to track down and kill that was swallowing him up." Jack's Faustian reward is power through perception. He perceives almost intuitively the use of mask, dance, ritual, and propitiation to ward off—and yet encourage simultaneously—fear of the unknown. Propitiation is a recognition not only of the need to pacify but also of something to be pacified. In this instance it is the recognition of evil. "The devil must have his due," we say. Here the "beast" must be mollified, given its due. Jack recognizes this fact, even if he and his group of hunters do not understand it. Politically and anthropologically he is more instinctive than Ralph. Jack does not symbolize chaos, as sometimes claimed, but, rather, a stronger, more primitive order than Ralph provides.

Jack's chief henchman, Roger, is not so subtly or complexly characterized, and seems to belong more to Orwellian political fable. Slightly younger and physically weaker, he possesses from the beginning all the sadistic attributes of the demagogue's hangman underling. (pp. 19-24)

Simon is perhaps the most effectively—and certainly the most poignantly—characterized of all. A "skinny, vivid little boy, with a glance coming up from under a hut of straight hair that hung down, black and coarse," he is (at nine or ten) the lonely visionary, the clear-sighted realist, logical, sensitive, and mature beyond his years. We learn that he has a history of epileptic seizures—a dubious endowment sometimes credited to great men of the past, particularly those with a touch of the mystic. We see the unusual grace and sensitivity of his personality crop up here and there as the story unfolds until he becomes the central figure of the "Lord of the Flies" scene—one of Golding's most powerful and poetic. We see Simon's instinctive compassion and intelligence as he approaches the rotting corpse of the parachutist, which, imprisoned in the rocks on the hill in flying suit and parachute harness, is the only palpable "monster" on the island. Although

Simon's senses force him to vomit with revulsion, he nevertheless frees it "from the wind's indignity." When he returns to tell his frightened, blood-crazed companions that, in effect, they have nothing to fear but fear itself, his murder becomes the martyrdom of a saint and prophet, a point in human degeneration next to which the wanton killing of Piggy is but an anticlimax. In some of the novel's richest, most sensitive prose, the body of Simon (the boys' "beast" from the jungle) is taken out to sea by the tide, Golding here reaching close to tragic exaltation as Simon is literally transfigured in death. . . . (pp. 24-5)

With his mysterious touch of greatness Simon comes closest to foreshadowing the kind of hero Golding himself has seen as representing man's greatest need if he is to advance in his humanity—the Saint Augustines, Shakespeares, and Mozarts, "inexplicable, miraculous." Piggy, on the other hand, who, just before his own violent death, clutches at a rationalization for Simon's murder, has all the good and bad attributes of the weaker sort of intellectual. Despised by Jack and protected by Ralph, he is set off from the others by his spectacles, asthma, accent, and very fat, short body. Freudian analysts would have Piggy stand as superego, but he is extremely id-directed toward food: it is Ralph who must try to hold him back from accepting Jack's pig meat, and Ralph who acts as strong conscience in making Piggy accept partial responsibility for Simon's death. Although ranked as one of the "biguns," Piggy is physically incapable and emotionally immature. The logic of his mind is insufficient to cope with the human problems of their coral-island situation. But this insight into him is fictionally denied to the Ralphs of this world, who (as on the last page of the novel) weep not for Simon, but for "the true, wise friend called Piggy."

How many children originally landed on the island alive we never learn; however, we do know that there were more than the eighteen boys whose names are actually mentioned in the course of the novel. Census matters are not helped by the first signal fire, for it goes out of control and scatters the boys in fright. (pp. 26-7)

Of those who remain, at least a dozen of whom are littluns, a significant number come alive through Golding's ability to characterize memorably with a few deft lines. Only two have surnames as well as Christian names: Jack Merridew, already mentioned as Ralph's rival, and the littlun Percival Wemys Madison. Jack at first demands to be called, as at school, "Merridew," the surname his mark of superior age and authority. Percival Wemys Madison ("The Vicarage, Harcourt St. Anthony, Hants, telephone, telephone, tele—") clutches vainly at the civilized incantation, learned by rote—in case he should get lost. And he is. His distant past has so completely receded by the end of the novel that he can get no farther in self-identification than "I'm, I'm—" for he "sought in his head for an incantation that had faded clean away." We learn little more about him, and hardly need to. Here again, in characterization, Golding's straddling the boundary line between allegory and naturalism demonstrates either the paradoxical power of his weakness as novelist or his ability to make the most of his shortcomings.

Whatever the case, Percival Wemys Madison epitomizes the novel and underlines its theme, in his regression to the point of reduced existence. In fact, most of Golding's characters suggest more than themselves, contributing to critical controversy as well as the total significance of the novel. In the years of exegesis since publication of *Lord of the Flies,* critical analysis has been hardening into dogmatic opinion, much of it allegoristic, as evidenced by such titles as "Allegories of Innocence," "Secret Parables," and "The Fables of William Golding." . . . The temptation is strong, since the novel is evocative and the characters seem to beg for placement within handy categories of meaning—political, sociological, religious, and psychological categories. Yet Golding is a simply complicated writer; and, so much the better for the novel as novel, none of the boxes fits precisely. (pp. 27-8)

Jack may appear to be the demagogic dictator and Roger his sadistic henchman; Ralph may be a confused democrat, with Piggy his "brain trust"; but the neatness of the political allegory is complicated by the clear importance of the mystical, generalization-defying Simon. Although Simon, who alone among the boys has gone up to the mountaintop and discovered the truth, is sacrificed in a subhuman orgy, those who have seen a religious allegory in the novel find it more in the fall of man from paradise, as the island Eden turns into a fiery hell, and the Satanic Jack into the fallen archangel. But Ralph makes only a tenuous Adam; the sow is a sorry Eve; and Piggy, the sightless sage, has no comfortable place in Christian myth. Further, it is an ironic commentary upon religious interpretations of *Lord of the Flies* that of an island full of choirboys, not one ever resorts—even automatically— to prayer or to appeals to a deity, not even before they begin backsliding. And the Edenic quality of the island paradise is compromised from the beginning, for, although the essentials of life are abundant, so are the essentials of pain, terror, and death. . . . (p. 29)

As a social allegory of human regression the novel is more easily (perhaps too neatly) explainable as "the way in which, when the civilized restraints which we impose on ourselves are abandoned, the passions of anger, lust and fear wash across the mind, obliterating commonsense and care, and life once again becomes nasty, brutish and short." The island itself is shaped like a boat, and takes on symbolic proportions, not simply in the microcosmic-macrocosmic sense, but as subtle foreshadowing of the regression about to take place among the boys: "It was roughly boat-shaped. . . . The tide was running so that long streaks of foam tailed away from the reef and for a moment they felt that the boat was moving steadily astern." This sternward movement not only conjures up the regressive backsliding away from civilization that constitutes the theme of the novel, but is imagistically associated with Piggy's "ass-mar" and the general note of scatology—as with the littluns being "taken short" in the orchard—which prevails in this book on Beelzebub, lord of the flies *and* dung. Later, when Simon asks the assembly to think of the dirtiest thing imaginable, Jack answers with the monosyllable for excrement. This is not what Simon means at all: he is thinking of the evil in man. But the two concepts merge in Golding's imagination—covertly in *Lord of the Flies* and manifestly in *Free Fall,* which is a literary cloaca, full of that revulsion psychologists try to explain in terms of the proximity and ambiguity of the apertures utilized for birth and excreta.

Some critics who see the allegory of evil as just the surface meaning of the novel have been led into psychological labyrinths, where Jack appears as the Freudian id personified; Ralph the ego; and Piggy the superego, conscience of the grown-up world. . . . [But] the Freudian *ménage à trois* fails to accommodate the vital Simon. Indeed, the problem in all attempts to explain *Lord of the Flies* as some kind of parable is that the novel is not a parable: it is too long, and lacks the point-by-point parallelism necessary to meet the definition. Nor, in the precise sense, is it a fable, since it deals primarily with human beings, since it does not rely upon folkloristic or fantastic materials, and since it does not provide the convenience of an explicit moral. It *is* allegoristic, rich in variant suggestions, and best taken at the level of suggestive analysis.

This novel has been taken, too, as a straight tale of initiation, with Ralph as hero—an interpretation to which the book's ending is particularly susceptible. Yet there is more to it than Ralph's facing a brutal adult world with a lament for his lost childhood and for the innocence he thinks has been stripped from him. What Ralph dimly fathoms, the naval-officer "rescuer" cannot possibly understand—that the world, in the words of Shaw's Saint Joan, is not yet ready to receive its saints, neither its Simons nor even its Piggys and Ralphs. Whether he means it or not Golding provides a hopeful note, for even at mankind's present stage of development Piggy and Ralph, the latter with shame, relapse only slightly toward the barbarism of their contemporaries (and that of the officer, who is engaged in a no less barbaric war "outside"); while Simon withstands the powerful regressive pressures completely. That these three represent three-quarters of the novel's major characters defeats any explanation of the novel in totally pessimistic terms.

Almost endlessly, the four major characters are thematically suggestive, and are usually identified in the book with certain imagery and talismanic objects: Jack with blood and dung, with the mask of primitive tribalism (imagistically he is in league with the Lord of the Flies); Piggy with pigs' meat (his physical sloth and appetite and eventual sacrifice), with his glasses, which represent intellect and science (though they could hardly coax the sun into making fire); Ralph with the conch and signal fire, with comeliness and the call to duty, with communal hope (all shattered when the conch dwindles in power and is finally shattered, and the signal fire dies out). Again, however, it may be Simon—not so thematically suggestive as the others—who provides the best clues to the un-Swiftian side of Golding's intentions, for we recall not only his mysticism, his intelligence, his fragility, but also his association with the bees and butterflies that hover sweetly and innocently (by comparison with the flies) about the island, and the tragic beauty of his transfiguration. Perhaps it is Simon who best suggests Golding's optimism in the face of his apparent allegory of regression. "The human spirit," writes Golding, "is wider and more complex than the whole of the physical evolutionary system. . . . We shall have . . . to conform more and more closely to categories or go under. But the change in politics, in religion, in art, in literature will come, because it *will* come; because the human spirit is limitless and inexhaustible." Just around the corner, he promises, are the Saint Augustines, Shakespeares, and Mozarts: "Perhaps they are growing up now."

What can be said of *Lord of the Flies* eventually is that, in structure and narrative method, it is Golding's simplest novel. It lacks the ironic mystification of *The Inheritors*, which results from the necessity of working through primitive brains making simple and often erroneous "pictures" of situations. It escapes the often cryptic involvement, the sudden wrench of context, that come from the stream of consciousness and recall methods of *Pincher Martin* and *Free Fall.* But it is not an obvious novel, as sometimes claimed. It shares with his other books an ending technique that constitutes a reversal—a sudden shift of viewpoint. Here the timely

arrival of the naval officer acts as no concession to readers demanding a happy ending. What we get instead of "gimmick" or conventional *deus ex machina* is a necessary change of focus: the boys, who have grown almost titanic in their struggle, are suddenly seen again as boys, some merely tots, dirty-nosed and bedraggled. And then a retrospective irony results, since the boys deserve to be thought of as titanic: if they have been fighting our battle, we realize—with both hope and dismay—that mankind is still in something of a prepuberty stage. Thus *Lord of the Flies* ends as no act of hope or charity or even contrition. It is an act of recognition. The tone is peculiarly clam: Golding keeps his distance from his materials; he does not interfere or preach; and the material is made to speak for itself through a simplicity of prose style and a naturalistic-allegorical form. The vision of Golding is through both ends of the telescope. (pp. 29-33)

[Any] analysis or evaluation of Golding's fiction must revolve around the compound question of originality and derivation, for although Golding has been called the most original English novelist of the last twenty or thirty years, it is becoming increasingly clear that his originality in prose is much like that of T. S. Eliot's in verse. Golding, in fact, stands as a remarkable example of how the individual talent operates within a strong tradition. Tradition (the English novelistic tradition primarily, but with elements derived from American, French, and Classical sources) leaves its mark on his work, but his work leaves its individual mark, and sometimes excoriatingly, on tradition. What has become apparent is that Golding is a literary counterpuncher. Put another way, *he is a reactionary in the most basic sense of the word.* Reacting strongly to certain disagreeable aspects of life and literature as he sees them, he writes with a revolutionary heat that is contained rather than exploded within his compressed style. Restoration rather than preservation is his aim: he would restore concepts of Belief, Free Will, Individual Responsibility, Sin, Forgiveness (or Atonement, anyway), Vision, and Divine Grace. He would restore principles in an unprincipled world; he would restore belief to a world of willful unbelievers.

From the outset of his career, Golding received critical recognition on the basis of his providing something new, something original (most early commentators put it down to his renovation of parable and fable as literary modes of serious expression). One early reaction to his work was that here at last the Home Counties had succeeded in bringing forth a voice capable of contending with the universal wilderness and the everlasting whirlwind. It might not be the voice of a Dostoevsky or Melville or Conrad or Camus, but certainly it was not the voice of still another angry young man. (pp. 34-5)

Aside from his novels, which did their own attesting, Golding himself lent credence to the idea that he was indeed original, something of an experimenter in the making of modern myths. In a Third Programme radio discussion, for example, he expressed a wish to make each book say something different, and in a different way each time:

> It seems to me that there's really very little point in writing a novel unless you do something that either you suspected you couldn't do, or which you are pretty certain nobody else has tried before. I don't think there's any point in writing two books that are like each other. . . .
>
> I see, or I bring myself to see, a certain set of circumstances in a particular way. If it is the way ev-

erybody else sees them, then there is no point in writing a book.

This self-portrait of Golding as literary experimenter is fairly accurate, but it needs expansion. In this connection, we should remember that he spent his first years at Oxford as a student of science before he switched emphasis to English literature. And there remains in his literary efforts something of the scientific stance—that of a white-coated experimenter working in the isolation of a laboratory, isolating in turn his literary elements on islands, promontories, and rocks, in closets, asylums, and prison camps. But in doing his experiments Golding inevitably has a finger stuck in someone else's lab book, along with a marginal note indicating what is wrong or at least what remains to be done. If we were allowed to expand Golding's statement about himself, we would have to—on the basis of what proves to be his practice—add this presumptuous comment: "I often see what others have been getting at, and disagree strongly. So I conduct counter-experiments with results that state: 'Not that way, but this.' " (pp. 35-6)

What remains to be said is that this reactive method of composition has become the *modus operandi*. It provides a key as to what Golding has derived from others and what he has provided that is original. Yet Golding has insisted, "But one book never comes out of another, and *The Coral Island* is not *Lord of the Flies*." And, adamantly, that *"one work does not come from another unless it is stillborn."* Nevertheless, with Golding the process may be, if he has created counter-experiments which are original fiction, not stillbirth but birth.

The process begins with *Lord of the Flies,* and here the critical documentation has been fairly solid. In separate essays Frank Kermode and Carl Niemeyer make it quite apparent that a strong connection exists between Golding's novel and one published almost exactly a century earlier, R. M. Ballantyne's *The Coral Island* (1857). Golding reworks Ballantyne's basic situation, setting, and narrative episodes. Like Ballantyne in each respect, he isolates a group of English boys on a coral island that seems an earthly paradise, with a plentitude of fruit and coconuts. He introduces pig killings, cannibalistic tendencies, and the question of ghosts. He names three of his major characters Jack, Ralph, and Piggy in honor of Ballantyne's Jack, Ralph, and Peterkin Gay. . . . (pp. 36-7)

If Golding works closely to Ballantyne's outline, it is mainly to show by contrast to his own findings how inane the nineteenth-century experiment in youthful isolation was. Eventually the contrast shows through strongly. While Ballantyne's characters, for instance, are stout English lads who overcome evil introduced into their worldly paradise by natives and pirates, Golding's characters find evil within themselves and almost go under, until finally extricated by a *deus ex machina*. The officer who is the long arm of that godly machine underscores the difference between Golding's novel and Ballantyne's when he says with Old Boy naïveté: "Jolly good show. Like the Coral Island." Ralph looks at the officer dumbly, uncomprehendingly, and his look measures the distance between generations as well as the distance between the fictional visions of 1857 and 1954. (p. 37)

[These] related books of Ballantyne and Golding can be used as documents in the history of ideas, Ballantyne's contribution belonging "inseparably to the period when boys were sent out of Arnoldian schools certified free of Original Sin,"

ready to keep the Empire shipshape. Golding writes with a vivid sense of paradox, with the eyes of someone who has seen the Empire crumble and witnessed twentieth-century manifestations of Original Sin.

Although it has gone unnoticed or unmentioned in comparisons of Golding and Ballantyne, both authors use similar conclusions involving the technical assistance of the *deus ex machina*. Jack, Ralph, and Peterkin are in the clutches of savages near the conclusion of *Coral Island;* they believe they will never more see home, and await death, only to find their bonds severed, and themselves set free. A "teacher," who stands in the place of the naval officer in *Lord of the Flies,* acquaints them with the miraculous fact that their captor, chief Tararo, "has embraced the Christian religion." This is no less a miracle in its way than the appearance of the naval officer who arrives just in the nick of time to save Golding's Ralph. Religion also appears in *Lord of the Flies* in truncated form: as already mentioned, some of the boys are choir members, but no prayer is ever heard. Religion enters only by way of hindsight and moralistic impingement from the outside, as the reader considers a hidden theme. In *The Coral Island,* as we can see by the quite Christian ending, it plays a central, well-advertised part. Not only are Ballantyne's youths invincible Britons, as they often call themselves, but they have faith, in the usual sense of the word. The Ralph of that group could be speaking for them all when under difficult pressures he remembers his mother's parting homily: "Ralph, my dearest child, always remember in the hour of danger to look to your Lord and Saviour Jesus Christ. He alone is both able and willing to save your body and soul." This is exactly what Golding's children do not do. Golding made clear why in an interview in which he explained his approach to the efficacy of *Coral Island* morality:

> What I'm saying to myself is "don't be such a fool, you remember when you were a boy, a small boy, how you lived on that island with Ralph and Jack and Peterkin." . . . I said to myself finally, "Now you are grown up, you are adult; it's taken you a long time to become adult, but now you've got there you can see that people are not like that." Their savagery would not be found in natives on an island. As like as not they would find savages who were kindly and uncomplicated and that the devil would rise out of the intellectual complications of the three white men in the island itself.

Although Golding does not provide easy answers to all the questions he raises in *Lord of the Flies,* it is clear that his religious answer is not Ballantyne's. The real savior in *Lord of the Flies* is not the naval officer, but Simon—and his voice goes unheeded, as once again the crucifixion takes place, this time without redemption or resurrection. (pp. 38-40)

Bernard S. Oldsey and Stanley Weintraub, in their The Art of William Golding, *1965. Reprint by Indiana University Press, 1968, 178 p.*

HENRI TALON

Lord of the Flies is a web of ironies. The very nature of this fable is ironic since it reveals cruelty and perversity where one expects to find gentleness and innocence—in childhood. Moreover, the children's sole intention at the start is to play: 'Until the grown-ups come to fetch us, we'll have fun,' says Ralph and, to begin with, he stands on his head. Can one imagine anything more harmless than the freedom from care, the roguishness and the joy of these new Crusoes? And yet, playing will prove to be a source of evil for them. It will bring about their regress and disaster. Thus irony—an essential discord in the story—is the form assumed here by the author's creative urge. Morally wounded by the extreme barbarity and sadism that the Second World War disclosed in the heart of supposedly civilized Man, Golding chose to project his spiritual uneasiness into a picture of children's hatred and deadly combats. But the intensely disturbing force of his own fiction came to him as a surprise. He was the first horrified observer of the ruthless boys he gave birth to. Embodying his anguish in his characters awoke in him a keener sense of it. Only then was the full significance of his outlook upon life brought home to him.

Before we analyse the irony that lies in games that degenerate, let us point out that the coral atoll is an exceptional spot on which to play. Isolated as it is, it constitutes that closed space which . . . the player needs and never fails to create. It is true that a child can always draw an ideal boundary line, and decree, for instance, that the lawn is an island and the path around it the sea, but how much more exciting the play-world is when reality itself is like one's most ambitious dream come true! And how well one can understand Ralph's enthusiastic exclamations and capers! (p. 296)

But next to Ralph is Piggy for whom playing is absurd. He declines to enter an imaginary universe which appears as the negation of common sense, thought, responsibility and worry. (p. 297)

The meaning of play as an interruption of the normal course of existence, as disregard and oblivion of time, is so foreign to him that he once suggested to the other boys, astonished and mocking, that they should make a sundial.

The moment Ralph gets the conch out of the water, Piggy proposes to establish a society inspired by that of the grown-ups. 'We can use this to call the others. Have a meeting. They'll come, when they hear us'. And when this proposal is enriched by Roger's hint that they ought to have a vote, Ralph is provided with just those factors of seriousness which make a game truly funny. A good game demands discipline. The harder the trial the greater the fun. . . . [Thus] Ralph is delighted to make his escape from the adult world a sham image of that very world, in accordance with the invariable exigency of all play—to see what is going to happen, or, as philosophers put it, to experience *Freude am Schein.*

But, very soon, acted seriousness, seriousness for fun, if I may bring together words that seem to clash, becomes real earnestness. The game is a game no longer. The role of chief Ralph has assumed involves obligations that exclude pretence. The existence of time cannot be ignored or denied after all. Like Piggy, Ralph is torn between regret for the past and the hope of a doubtful return home, while Jack and his tribe are engrossed by the hunt and the dance and the swim which make their lives a continuous present.

Against all expectations, playing proves to be a school for Ralph, since it conduces to a keener sense of duty instead of blurring it; since it makes him realise his limitations instead of giving a glorious feeling of freedom and power. This is one of irony's many faces.

As for Jack, playing the part of chief of the hunters gratifies his love of physical effort and leadership, and his impatience

with all but his own rules. However, for him also the game soon ceases to be mere play, a temporary forgetting of the serious business of life. Certainly playing ever involves seriousness too, as I have already remarked, yet the player is always aware that the importance of the game is of his own making and therefore different from the seriousness that life enforces upon us. But the seriousness of the game becomes the only one that Jack wishes to, and eventually can, recognize. (pp. 297-98)

Golding has not read the philosophers and other authorities to whom we owe thrilling analyses of playing, yet he has found for himself a well-known psychological truth that serves his end in his fable—namely, that playing may give birth to obscure forces which overwhelm reason. And thus, when fear of the unknown and dread of the on-coming storm have brought the frenzy of the dance to its highest pitch, the children, half believing that Simon is the Beast in disguise, murder him.

Playing, Suzanne Lilar has said, offers a choice between self-possession and mental confusion, between consciousness and delirium. And Eugen Finck, in his important essay *Towards an Ontology of Playing,* has shown that playing may tear the player away from the real world and cause his alienation. Playing, he says, gives rise either to the Apollonian light of free *Ipseitas* or to the Dionysiac rapture of a mad surrender of human personality.

How grim irony is here! inherent in man's state. In the very process of his quest for the happy illusion (*inludere*) involved by games, he brings about his own degradation and misery.

But let us go further into the irony that lies in the degenerescence of the children's play. Normally, a child at play experiences a rare pleasure: he is two persons in one. Of course, he does not forget that he is Johnny Smith or Dick Martin, but he is also Robin Hood or Robinson Crusoe. He is himself and he acts like someone else. But in that coral island, which seemed to have been created to make innocence possible, the child's very games disclose in him an undreamed-of perversity. One can no longer distinguish being from doing, and the being that action reveals is monstrous.

This insane game, in a paradisial spot gradually being laid waste, is presented as a bitterly ironical metaphor for the normal course of the world, of which Heraclitus has said that it is like 'a playing child moving pawns—a child's kingdom'.

Perhaps Golding would say that the function of his art is to make his reader sensitive to the ironic discord that he finds at the heart of existence. His fable acts both as a condenser to store up the energy of his thought and feeling, and as a developer that brings out the latent images of his inner vision.

But let us carry further the analysis of a story in which human beings finally do harm although they first meant to do good, in which gestures falsify intentions and action appears as a caricature of design.

The children decide to build a society whose foundations will be freedom and justice. Whoever wishes to speak may do so, provided he respects the ritual and holds the conch, and everyone has a right to vote. Rules set down by unanimous consent should have been obeyed unreservedly. The discipline which Piggy and Ralph imagine is voluntary submission, the highest form of liberty, that which sets bounds to its own expression.

Such is the original purpose and option, but what happens? The right to speak leads to idle talk. . . . They agree to build shelters and then go bathing instead of working. They agree to keep up a fire on the mountain top and forget it. They agree to observe elementary hygiene and to use as a lavatory rocks which the tide cleans up; but they soon use anywhere, even—supreme derision!—near the platform where they hold their meetings. They planned order and allowed disorder to settle. The hopes that initiate action are baffled by it in the end. The human being appears as an invalid whose rebellious hand plays his spirit false when the spirit is not first unfaithful to itself.

All this makes clear the nature of the irony that runs through the whole work. It is made manifest by contrast and conflict and is characterized by ambiguity, for the children's failure is nonetheless funny, but the fun is no true joy. The association of merriment and sadness is naturally paradoxical, but irony flourishes in paradox—it calls up a smile and turns it into a grimace.

Why is this so? The reason is because we are divided against ourselves in the presence of irony. We readily perceive the comic in a social and political organisation which is but an apish simulacrum. Yet we also detect in those brats' negligence and confusion a scaled-down version of adult disorder. Undecisive meetings, barren debates, misapplied or unenforced resolutions, we have experienced all this, and we feel the sadness of it all.

It is sad because disorder is prejudicial to everybody, and because it should never have been. The principles are good, the conduct they inspire deplorable. The beginning is full of promise, the end is a catastrophe. Between what is and what ought to have been there is a great gulf, and the cause is to be found in the very nature of man who is fated to fail for he is 'sick', as Simon puts it; and the heroism which this intuitive little boy also perceives is of no avail. Therefore, the irony of man's destiny is potentially in his own being. (pp. 298-300)

Having shown the general orientation and scope of irony, we must further examine the structure of the narrative, since irony breaks out between contrasted scenes somewhat distant from one another, and even as far apart as the beginning and the end of the story.

For instance, when we first catch sight of Ralph, he is neat, handsome and laughing. He prepares to live an adventure that seems to have leapt into existence from one of his books. When we last see him he is dirty, in rags and sobbing. He had looked forward to a fine, clean game and he has lived a sordid, terrible drama. He had anticipated an episode as good as a dream and he has been through a nightmare. But in the interval the little boy has matured and he knows 'the darkness of man's heart'. . . .

The irony which breaks forth between the early picture of innocence and that of ultimate experience is therefore not altogether distressing. He who was but 'un bon petit diable', as the Comtesse de Ségur would have put it, has grown a soul. But here irony is not merely linked to the structure of the story; it has an existential significance which I shall analyse later.

Jack also provides an instance of the irony that is discharged when scenes loaded with opposite meanings and as it were with different electricities clash in our memory—'After all,' he says soon after he has joined Ralph and Piggy, 'we're not

savages. We're English; and the English are best at everything'. At each stage of his regress we remember his proud words. When, having bedaubed his face with paint, he looks at the image reflected in a coconut shell filled with water, it is not himself he sees but 'an awesome stranger'. Ths incident underscores the mistake he made in denying his kinship with savages, for, *in potentia*, he was a savage even at the beginning. (p. 301)

In parts, the irony comes of the self-ignorance of a boy who thought that he was a law-abiding, righteous human being whereas, beneath the black coat adorned with a long silver cross, there was an uncivilized brute. The image of the togged-up choirboy contrasts with that of the undressed hunter ever brandishing his knife. Naked man, 'unaccommodated man' is no poor forked animal but a blood-thirsty brute. (p. 302)

Jack did not try to deceive anyone. He believed in his own inborn virtue as an Englishman. Had his vocabulary been larger, he might have said, like one of G. B. Shaw's characters, a foolish young man in whom his father feigns finding genius: 'I pretend to nothing more than any honest English gentleman claims as his birthright'.

On the theme of chauvinistic pretentions Golding has developed various comic effects, and the naval officer's words at the end echo those which the boy utters at the beginning: 'I should have thought that a pack of British boys—you're all British aren't you?—would have been able to put up a better show than that.' Here irony spreads out like a fan.

It was impossible for the officer to guess what happened on the island. This is not a question of either self-deception or lack of imagination, as is often asserted by readers. This is the normal ignorance of one who never had any opportunity of observing the lawlessness to which small boys can yield when they are left to themselves for long. He sees dirty boys in rags, but precisely such slovenliness is what one expects from children. (pp. 302-03)

For the reader, the irony results from the contrast between the picture of puerile innocence which the officer thinks he is beholding, and our memory of their insane cruelty. It is untrue to say that the officer reminds us of what we had forgotten—that these devils were only children. No, the irony comes of the contradiction between the data of vision on the one hand, and those of memory on the other; it comes of the clash between what seems likely to the officer—namely that schoolboys have availed themselves of an extra vacation to indulge in pranks and games usually forbidden—a pleasant likelihood which is false—and the children's perversity which has been revealed to us—a terrible unlikelihood which is the truth.

The next ironic effect is due to the fact that the boys' rescue is no salvation, since they leave an island scorched up like dead wood to return to a world that is in the process of being burned down too. . . . The naval officer does not know either whether Ralph, whom he has snatched from the jaws of death today, will not be killed tomorrow. The boy leaves a demented society to join another, whose folly is not a whit less cruel. And can precociously corrupted children regain balance and normality among men equally perverted and abnormal?

There is to be found in this story a form of irony which is even more bitter, which no longer raises a smile, however wry, because of the discord of which we are made aware rends both our heart and intellect. It is related to Simon's fate, the child who stands for *Agapê,* whose courage springs from love, whose insight into man's heart is charismatic, and whose loneliness is great, precisely because he is exceptional.

When he is bold enough to say that they should seek the Beast in themselves—'What I mean is . . . maybe it's only us'—he causes indignation and laughter. They say he is 'cracked', he is 'batty'. They might have listened to a fluent, handsome, athletic boy, for they are as sensitive to physical strength and charm as indifferent to moral virtue and beauty. Simon cannot be understood, for he speaks the language of truth to the blind, that of humility to the proud. And when he endeavours to save his friends from their own passion by telling them that the Beast is harmless, he is assaulted not only by the wicked, but also by the righteous—the temporarily bewildered Ralph and Piggy—and he dies.

Here irony calls forth at once compassion for the victim and terror of the murderers, as it also does a two-fold moral judgment: respect for Simon, contempt of Jack and Roger. Indeed, the resonance of irony goes even deeper, for Ralph and Piggy are spared our scorn, although they are guilty. Our pity suspends condemnation.

Again, we can observe that irony is associated with both doing and being. The contingent cause of Simon's murder lies in his misconception of the boys' state of mind and of the temper in the tribe, but he was predestined to such mistakes by his very selflessness. He is a victim because he is what he is. Irony is also related to the moral solitude of the innocent person among sinners. Nobody understands Simon, Piggy least of all, for whereas Simon is prompted by moral vision, Piggy only believes what can be explained and demonstrated—'Life's scientific'.

But Piggy is very lonely too, although he soon wins Ralph's pity and later deserves his regard. He is despised for he is not fit to play games. Should he make no mistakes he would nonetheless be spurned by the other boys; for being different amounts to a kind of culpability in their sight. Moreover, his very loneliness occasions his blunders. As he desperately needs sympathy, he rashly confides in Ralph, whose amiable unconcern towards him he mistakes for fellow-feeling. When Ralph's face brightens up because he is dreaming a happy dream, he interprets the light in the dreamer's eyes as the dawn of friendship, and responds by a cheerful laugh to a smile that was not meant for him.

Piggy makes mistakes because he is too unlike the others and left too much on his own to understand them. He lacks the experience that intelligence needs to operate successfully. His reasoning is often vitiated because his premises are wrong. When he makes up his mind to challenge Jack about his spectacles, it is obvious that he does not have an inkling of the other boy's motivation. His words are at once touching because they reveal how exacting his sense of justice is, and ridiculous, because they are unrealistic. 'I'm going to him with this conch in my hands,' he says, 'I don't ask for my glasses back . . . as a favour . . . but because what's right's right'.

This is an instance of the conflict between the *Eiron* and the *Alazon* which, in various forms, is a recurrent theme in comedy as in tragedy: *Eiron* being used here not in its original denotation—'a dissembler', but in its derivative meaning—'a naïve' or even 'foolish' person. The honest, guileless one, backed up by Ralph, stands against the 'Impostor', whom we

see on one occasion, sitting on his throne like an idol. The 'Impostor' wins the day, irony arises, and once again we are divided against ourselves. We grieve because justice is flouted and trampled down, but we cannot help smiling because Piggy is as short-sighted intellectually as physically. We are moved because his faith in democracy is admirable, but we are amused because he proclaims it when democracy is no longer.

Piggy stands for intelligence made inoperative because he is unaware of its limitations and starved by his ignorance of usual human intercourse. To a large extent his life is one of misunderstanding, and not only his. In this fictional universe, misunderstanding is general. . . . (pp. 303-06)

Piggy's intelligence, valuable in spite of its shortcomings, is not recognized, neither is Simon's vision, which could have redeemed them, nor Ralph's good will and common sense, which should have enabled them to survive. The dead parachutist, a victim of man's folly, is not recognized for the poor, harmless thing he has become. Instead of uniting them in a common pity, he intensifies the irrational fear which brings about hatred and division.

Indeed the ironist is a stern Prosecutor. He condemns both Piggy who only believes in what is reasonable and Simon who fails to realise its necessity. He indicts Ralph who thinks that it is enough for a community to ensure the practical welfare of all. The rationalist, the visionary, the eudemonist are all guilty because they all are mistaken. Golding's fable calls to mind the destructive character of irony considered strictly in itself (even when it is used, as it was, by Socrates, to find out the truth). Within the framework of the story it is hard to see on what values the author would lay a faith in the future of the human city.

Irony scours surfaces tarnished by routine use, it opens a man's eyes, it raises questions, but it answers none. It is, or should be, a turning point in the development of critical thinking before one comes to a new affirmation. Because it makes one's vision keener and more delicate it is an important state in the life of the spirit, but it cannot gratify the very needs it contributes to awaken.

Against all expectation, one of the characters, young though he is, develops that ironic vision I have just begun to analyse—irony as a mode of thought, as a critical attitude towards life, which, Kierkegaard says, is like a frontier zone between two states of existence, the aesthetic and the ethic.

Indeed the time comes all too quickly when Ralph becomes ironically aware of the contrast between his early hopes and happiness and the wearisomeness that followed. . . . Thus irony operates first and foremost at the cost of the ironist. Ralph does not spare himself. Because he has matured, he finds the little chap he was not long ago at once touching and laughable. Now he knows what it means to age: he can look back and survey his short life; he has a history.

Later, when he and Jack have grown bitter enemies, he hesitates to summon an assembly for fear Jack and his tribe will not come. He feels that the breach will be irreparable the moment his authority is openly flouted. If he does not know whether or not to blow the conch, the reason is because, ironically, cowardice and courage look alike all of a sudden. Is it dastardly to refuse to acknowledge the secession that has taken place, or is it moral strength, the strength of a ruler who temporizes as long as there is a hope for the better? 'If

I blow the conch and they don't come back, then we've had it. We shan't keep the fire going. We'll be like animals. We'll never be rescued'.

Ralph also experiences the grim derision that lies in that last effort of his to bring the boys together, when only 'the littluns'—a useless audience—turn up. And when Piggy says to him: 'You're still Chief,' the loyalty of his one friend gives a sharper edge to his loneliness, for nothing remains of the former order except the now unavailing conch and that vain, inept title in which Piggy still believes.

He laughs sharply, and Piggy is frightened. This is the laughter of that brand of irony which is sometimes called romantic, that of lost illusions; an irony that may be light and gentle but that sometimes expresses despair. If Piggy asks Ralph to stop laughing, it is because he feels that his friend is on the brink of tears.

However, Ralph's spiritual development does not quite conform to the Kierkegaardian process. It is not irony that brings about his ethical outlook upon life. His critical irony does not occasion his choice, it follows it. It is the bitter fruit of his experience of responsibility.

I have deliberately neglected a number of ironic effects, even when they are associated with dramatic development. Such is, for instance, the final conflagration which was meant to allow the capture of Ralph, but which, in fact, is the means of his deliverance. A conflagration, we remember, which was lit by those who had no wish to be rescued and refused to look after the small signal fire on the mountain top. As the ultimate manifestation of evil, that conflagration is very important indeed, but its significance does not lie in the attendant irony. (pp. 306-08)

Golding's irony is that of a moralist who exposes aberrant conduct and multiform evil, but opens no vista into a world to which man could aspire. Of the ironic ending of the story, that rescue which is perhaps only a brief respite granted by death, and which, anyhow, does not lead to an *ordo salutis,* one cannot say, as has been said of tragedy, 'not a happy, but the *right* ending'. Indeed we might contend that what I. A. Richards feels about tragedy applies to Golding's fable. In tragedy, Richards says, we are so overwhelmed that we become temporary agnostics. Now, is not **Lord of the Flies** (whatever the author's private beliefs may be) the kind of nightmarish fiction which utter agnosticism could produce with murderous children leaving the earthly paradise they have ruined to return to a fundamentally sick, and therefore incurable world, in which intelligence is the handmaid of crime? (pp. 308-09)

> *Henri Talon, "Irony in 'Lord of the Flies'," in* Essays in Criticism, *Vol. XVIII, No. 3, July, 1968, pp. 296-309.*

DAVID SPITZ

In a statement to the American publishers of his book, Golding described the theme of **Lord of the Flies** as

> an attempt to trace the defects of society back to the defects of human nature. The moral is that the shape of a society must depend on the ethical nature of the individual and not on any political system however apparently logical or respectable.

In a lecture to American students some years later he restated the overall intention of the work as follows:

> Before the Second World War I believed in the perfectibility of social man; that a correct structure of society would produce goodwill; and that therefore you could remove all social ills by a reorganization of society. It is possible that today I believe something of the same again; but after the war I did not because I was unable to. I had discovered what one man could do to another. I am not talking of one man killing another with a gun, or dropping a bomb on him or blowing him up or torpedoing him. I am thinking of the vileness beyond all words that went on, year after year, in the totalitarian states. It is bad enough to say that so many Jews were exterminated in this way and that, so many people liquidated—lovely, elegant word—but there were things done during that period from which I still have to avert my mind lest I should be physically sick. They were not done by the head-hunters of New Guinea, or by some primitive tribe in the Amazon. They were done, skilfully, coldly, by educated men, doctors, lawyers, by men with a tradition of civilization behind them, to beings of their own kind. . . . I must say that anyone who moved through those years without understanding that man produces evil as a bee produces honey, must have been blind or wrong in the head. . . . I believed then, that man was sick—not exceptional man, but average man. I believed that the condition of man was to be a morally diseased creation and that the best job I could do at the time was to trace the connection between his diseased nature and the international mess he gets himself into. [**The Hot Gates**]

To realize his purpose Golding patterned his book after a nineteenth century work on a related theme, R. M. Ballantyne's *The Coral Island,* whose three characters carried the same names as some of the protagonists in **Lord of the Flies.** In this way, he thought, he could show that little had changed though much had changed in that century. He chose British schoolboys because, as he said, he knew them best—he had himself been a schoolmaster for many years—and because they were the stuff of which British gentlemen were made; hence it was to be expected that they would know how to conduct themselves. (pp. 22-3)

He removed them from civil society and isolated them on a remote island, an earthly paradise, beautiful and with an abundance of food, water, and the materials for shelter. He kept them below the age of overt sex, for he wished to exclude this issue as a causal factor. He excluded too private property and the struggle for survival—neither work nor robbery was essential for existence—and hence avoided the controversy that engaged Dühring and Engels over the Robinson Crusoe story: whether political power (force) or economic power (exploitation) should be given the higher priority. Along with Freud and Marx and Darwin, he banished Caesar; for there was no danger of external aggression and hence no need for an army. Finally, there were no classes, no divisions, no inequalities based on previous status; except for Jack, who initially appears as the head of a group of uniformed choirboys, a relationship and a dress that are quickly terminated, the only significant sign of difference is that of age.

Everything, then, was there for a calm and peaceful and contented life. It was a veritable utopia: "Here at last was the imagined but never fully realized place leaping into real life."

It was, if you will, a state of nature inhabited by free and equal individuals. If anything were to go wrong, as it tragically did, it could only come, then, from within; the only enemy of man was himself. (pp. 23-4)

One of the many questions that has plagued political thinkers throughout the ages is the question of the legitimacy of power. In every society known to man, some men exercise power over others. Some issue commands that others are expected to obey. But when we look at those who command, it is not immediately evident that they and not some others should occupy the seats of power. They are not all wiser or better, more intelligent or more informed, richer or stronger, than the rest of us. Why then should *they* stand at the top, rather than kneel at the base, of the ever-existing pyramids of power? What makes this right? What makes their retention and exercise of power legitimate?

The quest for this principle of legitimacy is the quest for authority. We obey the policeman, or the tax collector, or the sanitation inspector, not because he has persuaded us of his superior wealth or might or intelligence, but because we recognize his authority. His power is a function of his authority, not the reverse. Hence we need, and have long sought for, a principle other than power that will make power right.

It is a commonplace that this quest has yielded a plenitude of answers. Authority, it has been said, comes from God; so proclaimed the prophet Samuel when he anointed Saul king of the ancient Hebrews. Authority comes from reason; so said Socrates when he insisted that philosophers ought rightfully to be kings, or at the very least counselors to kings. Authority comes from consent; so said Hobbes and Locke and Rouseau and the fathers of the American Republic. Authority comes from might; so said, and still say, the victors in every war. Which of these, not to speak of other claims, shall we heed? Which is right? How shall we know?

This is the political problem squarely confronted in **Lord of the Flies.** Consequently it is as representatives or symbols of these diverse responses to the question of authority that I would respond to Golding's leading personages. And it is a considered answer to this question that I would interpret and apply the moral of his fable.

Simon, it is clear, is the Christ-figure, the voice of revelation. He is "queer" but "always about." He sees the bushes as candles, unlike Ralph who thinks "they just look like candles," or Jack the materialist who dismisses them because they can't be eaten. He was one of the original choirboys, like Peter a member of a group of believers (or apparent believers) and then a defector. He goes into the jungle to pray, to build a church; "he knelt down and the arrow of the sun fell on him." He alone speaks to the beast, the Lord of the flies, and learns that the beast is not something outside of man but is an actual part of man, always close to man, and hence not something to be killed or run away from. Indeed, he had been the first to anticipate this: "Maybe there is a beast. . . . Maybe it's only us." He alone does not fear the false god, the messenger from heaven, the slain airman—a metaphor for history—who is dead but won't lie down. Ralph and Jack see him but turn and run away before discovering his true identity. Simon sees him and understands; he knows that "the beast was harmless and horrible; and the news must reach the others as soon as possible." Like Moses, then, he comes down from the mountain bearing the truth—which in Simon's case is that the beast is Man himself, the boys' (and man's) own natures. But

when he comes out of the darkness, bringing the truth, he is not heard—for what ordinary man can live with so terrible an understanding? Like Jesus, he is killed. . . . (pp. 24-5)

Thus men, Christian men, even—as Dostoevsky's Grand Inquisitor would have understood—those who had once worn priest-like robes, reject the authority and the truth of revelation. They dance and chant and kill; they revel in their passionate joys; they exercise power; but they do not heed the voice of God.

Piggy I take to be Socrates, the voice of reason. Like Socrates, he is ugly, fat, and—to men unappreciative of reason—a bore, with a disinclination for manual labor. He is the "outsider." He alone shows marks of intelligence; he can think; he has brains. He not only thinks; he knows himself as well as other men. "I done some thinking. I know about people. I know about me. And him." When he wears his spectacles he can see; he is like Plato's philosopher who has emerged from the cave. Those same spectacles not only shed light; they make possible the lighting of the fire which is meant to be seen. And when he is deprived of those spectacles, he loses his rationality too. He has a sense of what is required for society. He calls for order and justice—"put first things first and act proper"—and appeals to what is right. Though Ralph discovers the conch, it is Piggy who understands its significance as a symbol of legitimacy, an instrument of reason and order. . . . Like Socrates in the *Phaedo* seeking to remove the child-like fears of Simmias and Cebes, it is Piggy who reminds the others not to act like children but to behave like grown-ups. Above all, it is he who recognizes that there is no beast and no fear—"unless we get frightened of people." All in all, he is indeed "the true, wise friend."

But Piggy too is killed, and with his death all sense, all reason is gone; the ultimate in madness sets in. Authority must be found elsewhere, for men accept reason no more than they do revelation.

Ralph is democratic man, the symbol of consent. "There was a mildness about his mouth and eyes that proclaimed no devil." He was "set apart" not by virtue or intelligence or other sign of personal superiority—though he may well have been the tallest and strongest of the boys—but by the fact that it was he who had blown and possessed the conch, who had exercised the symbol of legitimacy. Chosen chief by an election, he sought always to maintain parliamentary procedures, to respect freedom of speech, to rule through persuasion, with the consent of the governed. He was not an intellectual, but he "could recognize thought in another." He could gain understanding from Piggy and had "the directness of genuine leadership," as he demonstrated when he consoled and (temporarily) won over the opposition candidate by naming him second-in-command, by putting him in charge of the hunters.

But Ralph too is rejected. The boys secede from his rule; they destroy the conch; and ultimately, their passions inflamed, they seek even to put him to death. Thus consent, like reason and revelation, is abandoned as a principle of authority. The "three blind mice" having been shunted aside, what finally is left is force, naked power. (pp. 25-7)

Jack then, is authoritarian man. Like Hitler and Mussolini, he came out of an authoritarian tradition; himself a Satanic figure with his red hair and black cape, he was also the leader of a black-capped and black-cloaked gang that marched in step—"something dark [that] was fumbling along"—and followed orders. His "was the voice of one who knew his own mind," and when it was suggested that there ought to be a chief he immediately and arrogantly demanded that position for himself. Defeated in an election, he took command of the hunters, the forces of naked power. "We'll have rules!" he cried excitedly. "Lots of rules! Then when anyone breaks 'em—" But his desire for many controls did not of course extend to controls he disliked, to those over himself. Then he rejected the rules and claimed the right to decide for himself. . . . Madness came often into his eyes, and when as hunter and warrior he again cloaked himself, this time behind a mask of paint, he lost all inhibitions; "he was safe from shame or self-consciousness"; he gave full vent to his passions. The conch, as Piggy said, was "the one thing he hasn't got"; and when he sought to assert his leadership through its use he blew it "inexpertly" and then, finding that he could not have his way, set it aside "at his feet." Eventually it was shattered by his henchman into a thousand fragments.

Yet he prevailed. "Power lay in the brown swell of his forearms: authority sat on his shoulder and chattered in his ear like an ape."

Who and what, then, is the Lord of the flies?

He is Beelzebub—a Greek transliteration of the Hebrew Ba'al Zevuv, which means Lord of the flies; or, as it is rendered in some New Testament texts, Beelzebul, which means Lord of dung, or Lord of a fly-ridden dung heap. As such, he is the personification of evil. He is the beast that is part of man. Having rejected God, man can look only to himself. Having rejected reason and consent, what remains within himself is only savagery and force. The boys are the flies and the beast, the evil, the senseless passion that is in man; in each and every man—in Jack, in Roger, even (under special circumstances) in Ralph and Piggy, even in you and me—is the Lord.

This is possible because the boys live in the dark. In the light they would be ashamed; and he who has common sense, who—like Ralph—would live in the light, is an outcast. [The conflict between light and dark is a theme that seems to have absorbed Golding almost to the point of obsession. Recalling his youthful days, for example, he speaks of the moment when he realized that the dead in the neighboring graveyard lay with their heads under his wall, their bodies under his lawn. "The lawn, almost the only uncontaminated place in that ancient neighborhood, had been sunny and innocent until my deliberate exercise of logic had invited the enemy in. Who was that enemy? I cannot tell. He came with darkness and he reduced me to a shuddering terror that was incurable because it was indescribable." (*The Hot Gates*) But to Golding the child, as to Piggy, the solution lay in science. "Science was busy clearing up the universe. There was no place in this exquisitely logical universe for the terrors of darkness. There was darkness, of course, but it was just darkness, the absence of light. . . . God might have been a help but we had thrown Him out . . . (*ibid.*). To the mature Golding, of course, science too ceases to provide the answer (*ibid.*).]

With the triumph of the Lord of the flies, the darkness in man's heart, Ralph weeps for the end of innocence. But the final, most devastating, most ironic note has yet to be sounded. For at the very moment when Ralph thinks he is saved, when all the children are saved, by the appearance of adults on the island, *we* know that he and they are not really saved. For the man who heads the adults who have come to rescue them is a naval officer, also a leader of hunters; and the ship

to which he will take them is a battle cruiser, which cannot carry them back to the safe shore (England), since that shore is now in ruins, but will itself soon be engaged in a hunt for the enemy—man—in the same implacable way as Jack and his deranged followers hunted Ralph. The boys move not from one evil to another evil, but from one aspect or level to another of the same evil; they go from the Lord of the flies writ small to the Lord of the flies writ large. For power based on the authority of force has been supplanted not by a different principle of authority, but only by another, though greater, power based also on the authority of force. And who, or what, will control this greater power?

So the moral remains the same: when all else fails, clubs are trumps. And all else must fail.

So, at least, Golding would have it appear. But is this really so? Has Golding proved his case?

His case, let it be recalled, is that evil is innate in man; that even the most suitable environmental conditions, unmarred by all the customary factors that have distracted and corrupted men in the past, will not suffice to overcome man's capacity for greed, his innate cruelty and selfishness; and that those, therefore, who look to political and social systems detached from this real nature of man are the victims of a terrible, because self-destructive, illusion. His method is to create a civilization out of innocence, to detach a group of the best of our very young and to put them into a state of nature, there to found a civil society on such principles of decency as seem to them appropriate, and to follow with a close and careful eye their inevitable course of destruction. His evidences are the events that constituted that course.

Now a novelist is not a historian; much less so is the author of a myth or fable. We cannot submit his work, therefore, to the standards and tests of historical or anthropological research. (For this reason I omit from consideration here what would otherwise be, I think, a telling criticism of Golding's argument: namely, that evil inheres not simply in man but also in collectivities; institutions, and social forces.) But we can judge him by his own method and evidences. And here, while I do not doubt that Golding has called our attention to a profound but partial truth, to what he has strikingly and properly called "the terrible disease of being human," I would contend that—precisely because he has built on but a partial truth—he has fallen short, far short, of establishing his case.

For what Golding has forgotten is that a state of nature is not necessarily a state of political and moral innocence. The boys who inhabited the island did not spring up full-blown, as did Athena from Zeus's head. They were the carefully chosen products of an already established middle-class society. They were socialized in, and were a partial microcosm of, twentieth century English (or Western) civilization; and they had brought that civilization, or what fragments of it they could remember, with them. Hence the values they possessed, the attitudes they displayed, the arrangements they established, and the practices in which they engaged, were all in some degree or other a reflection of the world into which they had been born and within which they had been educated and fashioned.

Jack and the choirboys, for example, had brought with them a system of order based on authoritarianism, and had been habituated to the wearing of masks (their uniforms) which set them apart, and enabled them to act differently from other men. Piggy brought his spectacles, an artificial aid provided by the civil society in which he had lived; and so conditioned had he been by that society that with those spectacles he saw precisely those democratic and middle-class values that that society esteemed, he appealed repeatedly to science and to what grown-ups would think. Maurice, who in his other life "had received chastisement for filling a younger eye with sand," now, despite the absence of a parent who might let fall a heavy hand, felt the unease of wrong-doing when he committed the same act, and hurried away. Even Roger, around whom the hangman's horror was later to cling, was initially bound by the taboos of the old life. (pp. 27-30)

Hence we still don't know, any more than we know from the story of Robinson Crusoe, what man, innocent, naked, non-socialized man is really like. We still don't know what is innate and what is environmentally conditioned in man. Nor can we ever hope to attain this sort of knowledge; for the individual apart from society is an inconceivable thing—he is always, no matter how peculiar or unique a person, still a social animal. And if it be said, despite this, that all societies are evil, or that there is evil in all societies, which means that men however created or evolved are necessarily the source of that evil, it is still not shown what in man or in his circumstances produces that evil, or why, and whether this is irredeemable.

Golding's truth, if truth it be, is thus true only for his English schoolboys, and those of like circumstances. It is not necessarily true of the products of other cultures and civilizations, or of other times.

This point merits pursuit. If Golding is right, if "the shape of a society must depend on the ethical nature of the individual," and if that nature is innately evil, then every society must be rooted in naked or arbitrary force; every society must be evil; every society must be, in this sense, the same.

But every society is not the same. Horrors and indecencies abide, to be sure, in every society; but the horrors and indecencies that Golding encountered in the concentration camps of Nazi Germany were outrages of a different degree, perhaps of a different order, than those to be found in some other states. Does this not suggest that the problem of human bestiality is more complex, more factor-bound, than the single-factor explanation Golding makes it out to be? That the customs and traditions of a people, their ethical precepts and practices socialized through education and over time, even perhaps their social and political arrangements, make a difference?

Plato's Socrates was clearly wrong in looking only to the rule of good men, on the ground that such men, precisely because they were good, would act virtuously and need not therefore be restrained by laws. Good men will not always be at the helm, and in any case they are not likely to remain good very long; they too are subject to the temptations and corrosive effects of power. Hamilton and Madison, influenced by Hobbes and Hume, did not make that mistake; but by leaping to the other extreme they made a mistake of their own. With Golding, they seized on a partial truth and extended it to a universal falsehood. Thus Hamilton, following Hume, argued that it must be accounted a maxim

> that, in contriving any system of government, and fixing the several checks and controls of the constitution, *every man* ought to be supposed a *knave;* and to have no other end, in all his actions, but private interest. By this interest we must govern him;

and, by means of it, *make him co-operate to public good,* notwithstanding his insatiable avarice and ambition. Without this, we shall in vain boast of the advantages of *any constitution.*

(pp. 30-1)

Whether the auxiliary precautions devised by the framers of the American Constitution have in fact been the best, have in fact been adequate to curb the injustices that men have tolerated or indeed have visited upon other men, is not here at issue. Clearly, they have left all too much undone. What is crucial, however, is not Hume's statement that all men must be considered knaves, which they are not, but the perception by Hamilton and Madison that many are in fact so and others might well become so; hence it behooves us to build our political arrangements with a careful regard to this danger, with a view to preventing, so far as we can, some at least of the consequences that readily flow from "the terrible disease of being human"; and that they may well have succeeded in mitigating those dangers. It would be foolhardy for contemporary man not to go on from there, as have Tocqueville and John Stuart Mill and a host of other theorists.

Now Golding has himself admitted that intelligence and historical knowledge are of supreme importance and relevance in meeting this problem. It is, he has said, in "that attempt to see how things have become what they are, where they went wrong, and where right, that our only hope lies of having some control over our own future. [*The Hot Gates*] If this is so, if there is *some* hope of controlling our future, then the hypothesis of innate evil is but partly right, and therefore partly wrong. It cannot by itself explain the governance of mankind.

The matter cannot rest here. Every society does indeed, in some measure at least, rest on force. We may appeal to God, even claim (as we now officially do) that this is a nation "under God." . . . But we, along with every other so-called civilized nation, nonetheless maintain an army and police force. Without them, or so it is believed, the state cannot survive, or do the job it purports to do. Without them, or so it is believed, we cannot resist the will of greater powers or impress our will on those with lesser force.

Yet it remains true that while a people may do many things with bayonets, they cannot sit on them. Force alone is not enough: it neither unites the nation that employs it, nor sustains the nation that is formed after its use, nor controls a people that has been subjugated by it. (pp. 31-2)

We are caught, then, in a pathetic dilemma: we cannot seem to do without force, and in this respect every society runs the risk of being oppressive; but we cannot do without justice, and in this respect force becomes not an end but a means, an instrument in the service of right. But the use of violent means tends always to corrupt the user and may well distort, and render unattainable, the desired end. Suppression even in the service of right is still suppression, and that, if not wrong, is but painfully right.

So we seem to be back where we began. There is power, and there is authority; and how to bring them together in the name of justice—whether of reason, revelation, or consent— may well exceed, if not the imagination, at least the practical capacities of mortal man. This, too, may be a part of the terrible disease of being human.

However, what is perhaps more astonishing is not that there

is so much evil in the world but that there is a measure of good; not that there is so much violence but, occasionally, a period or a place that knows a degree of amity and peace; not that there is so much selfishness and greed but, from time to time, a touch of altruism—and it matters not here whether this is called enlightened self-interest or sacrifice—and decency. . . . It is also true that in our social and political arrangements and practices we are far from realizing our avowed democratic ideals; but to confuse this dreadful failure with the worst practices of totalitarian or repressive systems is hardly an expression of responsible judgment.

This is not to excuse evils, or fatuously explain them away. It is merely to say that while no human society is completely without evil, the fact that there are differences in the levels of evil among societies indicates that factors other than "man" or "evil in man" play an important role. They make a real difference in the quality of human existence. They warrant the hope, expressed by prophets and democratic thinkers, that in principle an ideally good society may be approximated if not attained.

Some societies, some political and social systems, are in fact less vile than others. The evil that is common to them all cannot causally account for that which distinguishes them from each other. (pp. 32-3)

David Spitz, "Power and Authority: An Interpretation of Golding's 'Lord of the Flies'," in The Antioch Review, *Vol. XXX, No. 1, Spring, 1970, pp. 21-33.*

VIRGINIA TIGER

[Over two decades, *Lord of the Flies* has] received superb, sustained attention; to judge from recent criticism, it continues to demand critical vigour and, best of all, aesthetic frankness. As is the case with Doris Lessing's fiction, serious readers seem compelled to account for their initial astonishment and appalled recognition that finally a novelist was confirming what had only been privately understood about human behaviour. For just as Lessing's *Golden Notebook* made public the private tone of female grievance, so Golding's *Lord of the Flies* tugged at one's private hunch that males—even small boys—enjoyed aggression, group hierarchies, and the savour of blood.

Powerful thematic conceptions like these govern the narrative action throughout. As many of us now realize, much of the book's persuasive resonance comes from its strong structural shape. While this form has eluded easy categorization—terms such as allegory, parable, fable, science fiction, romance, have been variously suggested—its element of arbitrary design obviously makes it akin to allegory. Judging from his comments in the essay **"Fable"** in **The Hot Gates,** Golding's own preference is the term fable, which he once defined for me as 'allegory that has achieved passion.' I take this gnomic clue to imply the peculiar conjunction of contrived pattern and fictional freedom which is a characteristic feature of Golding's work. As readers we sense strongly our own freedom from complete iconographic control, yet we judge as pertinent the author's intellectual effort to bring together generalized significance and a direct rendering of life. In protean fictional modes like this, the story's conceptual machinery antedates its imaginative expression; nevertheless, such a fable must be distinguished from parable (Orwell's *Animal Farm,* for example), the purpose of which is wholly didactic and the agents and adjuncts of which are more often than not supernatural or preternatural. Gregor and Kinkead-Weekes put the matter rather more cleanly in their introduction to the school edition when they described *Lord of the Flies* as 'fable and fiction simultaneously'.

Another persistent classification has attended to the book's intellectual schema—its affinity to neither romance nor realism, its definition as neither parable nor fable, but its relation to the Christian apologia. . . . The notion that *Lord of the Flies* in particular was somehow intellectually or philosophically contrived became, in fact, one of the major critical assumptions about the rest of his work. Ignoring the fictional landscape altogether, many commentators constructed explications of 'meaning' more relevant to social and literary history than the analysis of fiction. . . . Despite the numerous interpretations, religious, political, psychological, anthropological, the story itself seems rather simple. And it would seem that one of the main reasons for the many contradictory critical interpretations of this fable is that while the meaning of the fable is coherent at so many different levels critics have isolated for discussion only one or two of these levels. Against this we must put Golding's own statement to Kermode that 'it was worked out very carefully in every possible way, this novel.' (pp. 39-41)

Lord of the Flies tells a totally absorbing adventure story but like another sort of island story, *Robinson Crusoe,* it seems susceptible of various interpretations. It has been read as a moral fable examining personal disintegration, a social fable which explores social regression, and a religious fable which offers a variant account of the Fall of Man. As a moral fable, *Lord of the Flies* seems capable of endorsing a number of mechanico-psychological theories of behaviour, or at least commentators have argued so—and in discussion these have ranged from Aristotle's *Ethics* through Jung's *Psychological Types.*

It is possible to view the boys as representatives of various instincts or elements of the personality. 'The catastrophe occurs because the qualities of intelligence, address, bravery, decency, organization, and insight are divided among Piggy, Jack, Ralph, and Simon. Each of them lacks some vital gift; none of them is a complete person.' E. M. Forster declares that it is just this fragmentation that is responsible for their regression. One critic argues that the fragmentations correspond to Plato's division of the human soul. . . . Offering a variant *schema,* E. L. Epstein believes Freudian psychoanalytical theory is relevant: 'The Devil is not present in any traditional religious sense; Golding's Beelzebub is the modern equivalent, the anarchic amoral, driving force that Freudians call the Id.'

If seen as a moral fable, *Lord of the Flies* appears to emphasize the inadequacy not the depravity of the solely human. In this light, the power and potential of individual human responsibility becomes a workable index for moral actions, and a legitimate abstraction from this is that people are governable inasmuch as they can be the responsible authors of their own actions. Simon is a 'saint'—Golding's term for the boy—precisely because he tries to know comprehensively and inclusively; he possesses a quality of imagination which forces an 'ancient, inescapable recognition.' Before the obscene decapitated pig on the spike he comes to acknowledge the existence of his own evil. In contrast, Ralph because of a failure of moral imagination exhibits only a 'fatal unreasoning *knowledge*' (italics added) of his approaching death which is directed towards his own survival not that of the community's.

Such a moral account of the fable posits the duality of man: man is, in Swiftian terms, not *animale rationale* but only *rationis capax*. Individual recognition of unreason is symbolic of order; failure is symbolic of decay. A legitimate inference, one that Piggy and Ralph keep voicing, is that society—the *Noumos*—does not confine and deform but is man's only proper habitat: its influences, however faulty, are the bonds that free him from unreason and disorder.

Viewed from another perspective, which concerns itself generally with social correspondences, *Lord of the Flies* might be seen to shift from moral fable to social fable. Here it becomes what some commentators call an anti-Utopian satire. For the island society is microcosmically a human society, related all too ironically to the 'grown-up' society that occasioned the original fall from the skies. Anthropologically the society is a mirror of the first, primitive societies of prehistoric man; its progress illustrates a biological maxim now fairly well discredited: that the development of the individual recapitulates in capsule time the development of the species. . . .
 (pp. 42-3)

The critical danger in discussion of this sort is again to start treating the boys as men, since in their terms they appear less as autonomous characters than as images of social ideas. Thus one critic sees the tale in social psychological terms and decides it 'shows how intelligence (Piggy) and common sense (Ralph) will always be overthrown in society by sadism (Roger) and the lure of totalitarianism (Jack)' [see excerpt above by C. B. Cox]. Seen in political terms it is a dramatization of 'the modern political nightmare' in which responsible democracy is destroyed by charismatic authoritarianism: 'I hope', writes V. S. Pritchett, 'this book is being read in Germany.'

If seen as a social fable, *Lord of the Flies* appears to stress not the capabilities of the boys but their depravity and man's apparent inability to control aggression within a workable social order. Seen from the perspective of the moral fable, morally speaking Piggy and Ralph do exercise good will and judgment; from the angle of the social fable they are inadequate politically. Much more damaging is their participation in the murder of Simon, a murder effected by the tribal society which Jack leads.

Many of the accounts of *Lord of the Flies* place the fable in a mythic frame, rather than the social or moral one, for ultimately 'it derives from—displaces—a familiar myth, that of Earthly Paradise which it handles ironically.' Here the Christian tradition has been by far the most popular mythic framework cited by critics, though the fable itself makes no immediate or direct allusion to orthodox Christianity. Many critics write that *Lord of the Flies* dramatizes the Fall of man. As Adam unparadised, the boys cradle within themselves the beast of evil, 'Beelzebub' (the Hebraic original for its English translation, lord of the flies [II Kings i.2]; 'the chief of the devils' in Luke ii.15). They turn the Edenic island into a fiery hell. When he discussed his notion of the morally diseased creation in 'Fable', Golding himself admitted that in 'theological terms' man is a 'fallen being'. 'He is gripped by original sin. His nature is sinful and his state perilous.' Such a statement merely describes metaphorically a general condi-

tion, it does not place it within a constricting metaphysic, a constricting scheme of theology. (pp. 44-5)

Other mythic contexts seem equally relevant to the image of evil in *Lord of the Flies.* One such commentary sees the titular lord of the flies as a primary archetype for the destructive element, a Dionysian irrationalism that Jack celebrates and Piggy ignores. Baker regards Piggy in what he takes as a Promethean aspect and argues Piggy's empirical disavowal of the 'beastie'—'Life . . . is scientific, that's what it is. In a year or two when the war's over they'll be travelling to Mars and back. I know there isn't no beast . . .'—is evidence of intellectual *hubris* which must be punished. (p. 45)

Suggestive analogies have also been seen in variant anthropological myths: thus the dead man is not so much an ironic parody of the Crucifixion as a parody of the fertility god of Frazer, the Hanged or Sacrificial god. As Claire Rosenfield suggests [see excerpt above], Simon is the ritual hero who is metaphorically swallowed by a serpent or dragon 'whose belly is the underworld; he undergoes a symbolic death in order to gain the elixir to revitalize his stricken society, and returns with his knowledge to the timid world as a redeemer.' (pp. 45-6)

[Conceptual analyses] obscure—even destroy—the primary strength of Golding's fable. For *Lord of the Flies* is first and foremost a gripping adventure story. . . . It is related ironically to various literary conventions: science fiction, Utopian fantasy, boys' south-sea adventure, survival narrative, and desert island tale. Readers now are familiar with the most important source, R. M. Ballantyne's *Coral Island* (1858), a nineteenth-century Victorian boys' story which Golding has admitted has a 'pretty big connection'. . . . Golding defuses Ballantyne's conception of the civilized child and by extension civilized man. *Lord of the Flies* represents in its recasting of the situation not only an inversion of a popular literary model—a strategy of reversal which Golding adopts in the three subsequent fables—but a refutation of *Coral Island* morality which Golding obviously regards as unrealistic.

Ballantyne's island is a nineteenth-century island inhabited by English boys in the full flush of Victorian smugness, ignorance, and prosperity. (pp. 46-7)

Now obviously Golding's island is a twentieth-century island, inhabited by English boys just as smug about their decency, just as complacent and ignorant as the boys in Ballantyne's story. Talking about its genesis in *Coral Island,* Golding explained to Kermode:

> What I'm saying to myself is "don't be such a fool, you remember when you were a small boy, how you lived on that island with Ralph and Peterkin", who is Simon by the way, Simon called Peter, . . . I said to myself finally "Now you are grown up, now you are adult . . . you can see that people are not like that, they would not behave like that if they were God-fearing English gentlemen, and they went to an island like that, their savagery would not be found in natives on an island. As like as not would find savages who were kindly, and uncomplicated, that the devil would rise out of the intellectual complications of the three white men."

It is Golding's intention in *Lord of the Flies* to tell a true story—to cite the beast within and tell a realistic story—'a book' as he put it, 'about real boys on an island, showing what a mess they'd make.' Ballantyne's children are children free of Original Sin. They epitomize the optimism, the certitude, and perhaps even the pomposity of the Victorian Age; they not only play at being empire-builders: they are. (p. 49)

Instead of Ballantyne's unshaken faith in the superiority of the white race, Golding questions civilization itself; against man's innate savagery it seems contemptibly weak. While in *Coral Island* the natives' faces 'besides being tattooed, were besmeared with red paint and streaked with white', in **Lord of the Flies** it is the choir boys, Jack's hunters, who colour their faces so their primitive selves can be released from shame. . . . To qualify Ballantyne's pastoral evocation of life on a tropical island where everything is glamorous, Golding stresses such things as the diarrhoea of the 'littluns', who 'suffer untold terrors in the dark and huddle together for comfort'; the densely hot and damp scratching heat of a real jungle; the remote and 'brute obtuseness of the ocean' which condemns the boys to the island; of the filthy flies which drink at the pig's head; and the hair grown lank: 'with a convulsion of the mind, Ralph discovered dirt and decay; understood how much he disliked perpetually flicking the tangled hair out of his eyes.' Perhaps the most important recasting of *Coral Island* optimism is Golding's inversion of Ballantyne's cheerful notion of the psychology of the child. One evening, Ballantyne's boys hear a distant but horrible cry; at the suggestion that it might be a ghost, Jack answers:

> I neither believe in ghosts nor feel uneasy. I never saw a ghost myself and I never met anyone who had; and I have generally found that strange and unaccountable things have always been accounted for, and found to be quite simple, on close examination. I certainly can't imagine what *that* sound is; but I'm quite sure I shall find out before long. . . .

Golding's boys, of course, do grow frightened of the unknown. In fact, it is just the fear of a beast—and its ambiguous existence on the island—which forms the dramatic and symbolic core of **Lord of the Flies**. (pp. 50-1)

Had Golding simply recast *Coral Island* morality, **Lord of the Flies** might well be a derivative fable along the lines of Richard Hughes' *High Wind in Jamaica* demonstrating a twentieth-century belief that, without the discipline of adults, children will deteriorate into savages. No such rigorous allegory emerges, it seems to me. To the initial source reversal, Golding has sewn a structural reversal which makes the fable question even its own ground. A superb coda elevates **Lord of the Flies** above diagrammatic prescription to something like 'an allegory which has achieved passion.' There is no essential difference between the island world and the adult one and it is the burden of the fable's structure—what I call its ideographic structure—to make it clear that the children's experiment on the island has its constant counterpart in the world outside. Both the occasion of the boys' landing on the island and the parachutist remind us that 'the majesty of adult life' is another childish delusion. As the narrative progresses the reader is lulled into the unguarded belief that adults may save the situation; yet, one detects certain ironic clues which the coda will confirm. Take the reiteration of motifs—for example the phrase 'Let's have fun' that Ralph as liberal leader introduces and which later the Head obscenely throws back at Simon—these force one to reconsider what earlier seems innocuous. The heaving of logs by Sam'eric, the rolling of larger and larger stones, the several gifts to the sea, the several pig hunts, the two desperate races by Ralph—these sequences of repeated actions, placed at intervals during the story, intensify the ambiguous threat and give the illusion of a vastly speeded-up dénouement. The cumulative effect on the reader is to create a vague yet familiar threat, a sense of doom which cannot be adequately located in the narrative's thrust until its confirmation in the coda.

In **Lord of the Flies** the ideographic structure consists in two movements; in the first, the story is seen from the point of view of the childish protagonist, Ralph, as he gradually grows more and more aware of the island's disintegration. In the second movement, the coda which concludes the fable, we see events from a new point of view, that of the adult naval officer, who is completely unaware and largely indifferent to the suffering. The coda, in conjunction with such symbols as the parachutist, indicates that adulthood is also inadequate to prevent destruction. The dead parachutist shows man's inhumanity to man; he is a legacy of barbarism in both ancient and contemporary civilization who, Golding says, represents history; thus he haunts the boys, a haunting appropriately represented by his uncanny position and motion: 'the figure sat on the mountain-top and bowed and sank and bowed again.'

The children reveal the same nature as the grown-ups whom some invoke and try to emulate. In fact the child's world on the island is a painful microcosm of the adult world, for the ruin they bring upon themselves is universal—recall that it is atomic warfare in the air that brings about their initial descent to the island. The cruel irony of the matter is made all the stronger by the sudden switch in perspective. Here the officer's dismal failure to comprehend the 'semi circle of little boys, their bodies streaked with coloured clay, sharp sticks in their hands' is itself testimony to 'the infinite cynicism of adult life' and silent witness to the Lord of the Dung's general sway. It is as though he has sailed straight from the pages of *Coral Island,* moments after we have witnessed the consequences of that novel's banal optimism.

In fact, the story is more striking precisely because Golding chooses wonderfully real children as protagonists, children who yank up socks, stamp feet, and quarrel over sand castles. The arrival of the officer at the end with its sudden shift from Ralph's agonized eyes to the benign view of the adult throws the story back into grotesque miniature. The children are dwarfed to children again. . . . Throughout the narrative's first movement—and with appalling momentum—the children appear to have been adults dealing with adult problems. Now they are whining little boys held in control by the presence of an adult. Yet the reader cannot forget the cruelty of what has gone before. For the conch of order has been smashed; the spectacles of reason and rescue have been used to destroy the island. A tribal society has hunted down and killed two individuals. Nor can we forget that Ralph's piteous weeping at the end transcends the smug cynicism of the rescuer, for Ralph knows the real nature of the 'pack of British boys.'

Ralph is saved only because the adult world intervenes; yet his rescuer is on the point of returning to 'adult' war, a nuclear war which is in numerical terms infinitely more extravagant in its potential disaster. Given the barbaric chaos the boys have been reduced to, the officer appears to them (to us) as order. It is only on reflection that the reader remembers that the officer is involved in a nuclear war and yet is still 'order'. This brings up Golding's own explication of the thematic content of his fable:

The whole book is symbolic in nature except the rescue in the end where adult life appears, dignified and capable, but in reality enmeshed in the same evil as the symbolic life of the children on the island. The officer, having interrupted a man-hunt, prepares to take the children off the island in a cruiser which will presently be hunting its enemy in the same implacable way. And who will rescue the adult and his cruiser?

The meaning of *Lord of the Flies* is not, then, allegorically simple but instead ideographically suggestive. The moral operation on the reader of the fable's ideographic structure—when the two patterns clash—makes such a symbolic density possible. For *Lord of the Flies* suggests a large scale of human values, social, political, moral and mythic which are relevant in both universal and contemporary terms, but it isolates and roots these concerns in a boy's world, a world where real boys make a mess of things. Finally, that child's educated view of things is crossed by an adult's uneducated view and the reader must join the two perspectives and probe the question Golding poses above: 'who will rescue the adult and the cruiser?'

Perhaps a useful elaboration on the contrast between what I am implying about an ideographic response and an allegorical one would be to examine here one allegorical feature of the fable upon which no doubt is cast. In Golding's view, the innocence of the child is a crude fallacy, for *homo sapiens* has by nature a terrible potentiality for evil. This potentiality cannot be eradicated or controlled by a humane political system no matter how respectable. Thus, in 'Beast from the Water', one of the fable's most allegorical chapters, the fundamental inadequacy of parliamentary systems to deal with atavistic superstition is portrayed. In this episode, the scene's physical and psychological atmospheres are as schematically constructed as the major characters' different pronouncements on the 'Beast.'

A parliamentary assembly begins at eventide; consequently the chief, Ralph, is merely 'a darkish figure' to his tribe. Light is, at first, level and only Ralph stares into the island's darkness; his assembly before him faces the lagoon's bright promise. But light gradually vanishes, accompanied by increasing spiritual blindness and fear. The place of assembly on the beach is described as 'roughly a triangle; but irregular and sketchy, like everything they made.' Obviously it is like a receding boat, a kind of mirror image of the island-boat itself. . . . (pp. 51-5)

Since Ralph sits on 'a dead tree' that forms the base, no captain occupies the boat's rightful apex: where 'the grass was thick again because no one sat there.' Like the island that appears to move backward, the assembly-boat is pointed to the darkness of the jungles not the brightness of the navigable lagoon behind. Hunters sit like hawks on the right of Ralph; to the left Golding places the liberals, mostly children who giggle whenever their assembly seat, 'an ill-balanced twister', capsizes. And Piggy stands outside the triangle, ironically showing the moralizing ineffectuality of the liberal: 'This indicated that he wished to listen but would not speak; and Piggy intended it as a gesture of disapproval.' Darkness descends on the shattered assembly, and for the first of many times the 'beastie' is ritually appeased. Island boat, assembly boat, and the ship of civilization itself, rational government, all drift bleakly into blackness. (pp. 55-6)

[In **"The Ladder and the Tree"**], Golding dramatizes an atavastic quest through darkness which is central to all his fiction. Pondering over the church graveyard at the foot of his garden, the child, Billy, grows terrified of some enemy he imagines is lurking there to harm him. A similar mythopœia of a beast is central to *Lord of the Flies* though its implications are by no means fully worked out in this fable. They are dramatized in the crucial confrontation scene where two apparently irreconcilable views of one situation are brought slap up against each other.

Ultimately, the meaning of the fable depends on the meaning of the beast—the creature which haunts the children's imagination and which Jack hunts and tries to propitiate with a totemic beast. Simon's quest, then, is the fable's major pursuit, for he is used as a mouthpiece for what Golding, in conversation, has called 'one of the conditions of existence, this awful thing.' Simon, the strange visionary child, encounters and recognizes the beast. In this confrontation scene he recognizes his own capacity for evil as well as his ability to act without evil. He is thus able to release the parachutist and try to tell the boys below about 'mankind's essential illness'. . . . The confrontation scene brings about a single crystallization of the fable's total structure since it brings together the concepts of evil-and-innocence as does the ideographic structure.

At the heart of the fable's mythopœia is the visual hieroglyphic or symbol of the severed Head of the pig, to which Simon turns in distaste and awe, and from which he first tries to escape. Grinning cynically, its mouth gaping and its eyes half-closed, the Head is placed on a rock in a sea-like clearing, before Simon's cabin-island. The Head here is like an island surrounded by sea. It is, of course, a symbol which operates macrocosmically as well as microcosmically. A larger macrocosm, the Castle Rock, at the island's end is like a severed head too—it mirrors the pig's head. Described as a 'rock, almost detached,' this smaller landmass is separated—a point, it should be noted, which Golding makes repeatedly—from the island's main body, by a 'narrow neck.' 'Soon, in a matter of centuries', this Head will be severed too. At the story's conclusion giggling black and green savages swarm around and over it as the black and green flies swarm around the Lord's head.

Piggy's death occurs at this Head; it is the slaughter of a pig for he is decapitated by 'a glancing blow from *chin* to knee' (italics added). Travelling through the air, with a grunt he lands on the square red rock in the sea, a sacrificial table. And the monster-sea sucks his body, which 'like a pig's after it has been killed, twitched.' Presumably the emblematic name of the character is now pretty obvious. His head is smashed and Ralph, running along the rocky neck, jumps just in time to avoid 'the headless body of the [sacrificial] sow.' The preparation is clear; a Head is needed.

From a traditional point of view, this symbolism suggests that the Head—the centre of reason—is destroyed with the death of Piggy and, as the island society regresses, the 'bridge' between rationality and irrationality is cut. But rationality is, for Golding, a suspicious concept. The severed Head of the sow is not the Lord of the Dung either; it does not symbolize an evil external to the individual. Rather, it is a symbol of corrupt and corrupting consciousness. It is a symbol for the malaise of the human consciousness which objectifies evil rather than recognizes its subjectivity: the kind of moral distancing the officer commits. This intellectual complication is 'mankind's essential illness' which Simon discovers in the severed Head; it prospers on the island's Head, Castle Rock.

Three ambiguous confrontation scenes formulate the mythopœia: Simon before the Head; Ralph before the skull of the pig; Ralph before a savage. However, the scenes function by symbolic cluster on a symbolic level and they have little dramatic necessity. Golding himself, in **"Fable"**, suggests a reason for this fragmentation: 'I don't think the fable ever got right out of hand; but there are many places I am sure where the fable splits at the seams and I would like to think . . . they rise from a plentitude of imagination.' Clearly he cherishes these 'splits' for he adds warmly: 'May it not be that at the very moments when I felt the fable to come to its own life before me it may in fact have become something more valuable so that where I thought it was failing, it was really succeeding?' And significantly he quotes the passage of Simon before the Head to illustrate these comments.

Simon alone recognizes the real Beast and like Moses with the tablets of the law brings the truth down from the mountain. What is the truth? Simon broods before the totemic sow's Head, having witnessed the anal rape and decapitation. Suddenly the pig's head speaks in 'the voice of a schoolmaster' and delivers 'something very much like a sermon to the boy.' It insists that the island is corrupt and all is lost: ' "This is ridiculous. You know perfectly well you'll only meet me down there—so don't try to escape!" ' Shifting by the ironic motif of 'fun' into schoolboy language, the Head assures him: ' "*We* are going to have fun on this island" ', (italics added) even though 'everything' is 'a bad business.' Such counselling of acceptance of evil is 'the infinite cynicism of adult life', the cynicism of the conscious mind, the cynicism that can ignore even 'the indignity of being spiked on a stick', the cynicism that 'grins' at the obscenities that even the butterflies must desert; recall that the butterflies 'danced preoccupied in the centre of the clearing' during the sow's mistreatment—the Head then represents something a great deal more obscene than simple blood-lust. It is the cynicism and easy optimism of the naval officer at the end who *'grinned* cheerfully at the obscene savages while muttering "fun and games" ' (italics added).

But this Lord of the Dung *is* Simon: the Head that counsels acceptance is his own strategic consciousness. Evil exists but not as a Beast. To interpret incorrectly the Head as an objective symbol for evil, independent of consciousness, would be to make the same mistake as Jack of externalizing and objectifying one's own evil. The identity of the two is worked out very carefully indeed. Speaking in schoolboy language, the Lord's head has 'half-shut eyes' and Simon keeps 'his eyes shut, then sheltered them with his hand' so that his vision is partial. He sees things 'without definition and illusively' behind a 'luminous veil.' Simon feels his own savagery: he 'licks his dry lips' and feels the weight of his hair. Later, after his epileptic fit, the blood 'dries around his mouth and chin' in the manner of the 'blood-blackened' grinning mouth of the Head. The flies, now that the butterflies have dismissed them, detect the identity and—though they are sated—leave the guts and 'alight by Simon's runnels of sweat' and drink at his head. The Head grins at this indignity. By a profound effort of will, Simon forces himself to penetrate his own loathing and break through his own consciousness. . . . (pp. 56-60)

It is himself he is looking at. His face (i.e., the Head) grins at the flies of corruption and he acknowledges it as himself. Rather like Golding's Egyptian mummy, he prepares 'to penetrate mysteries' and 'go down and through in darkness'. He looks into the vast mouth of hell, and thereby submits to the terror of his own evil.

> Simon found he was looking into a vast mouth. There was blackness within, a blackness that spread. . . . He fell down and lost consciousness.

He penetrates here his own evil. Returning from non-being, he awakens next to 'the dark earth close by his cheek' and knows that he must 'do something.' He approaches the beast on the hill to discover that 'this parody', ringed as well by green flies, is nothing more 'harmless and horrible' than the Head. Both are man as he is. In releasing the figure 'from the rocks and . . . the wind's indignity' he frees himself.

Twice Ralph is confronted with just such a primal confrontation, face to face, eye to eye. We earlier see that he cannot connect with primal nature. For example, standing at the island's rocky shore 'on a level with the sea', he follows 'the ceaseless, bulging passage' of the waves and feels 'clamped down', 'helpless,' and 'condemned' by a 'leviathan' monster with 'arms of surf ' and 'fingers of spray.' Nor can he accept Simon's intuitive and correct faith, when the latter whispers 'you'll get back all right', that man can escape the 'brute obtuseness' of nature. Much later, after the deaths of Simon and Piggy, Ralph stands in the clearing confronted by the same offensive Head. He looks steadily at the skull that 'seemed to jeer at him cynically.' Once again the darkness is depicted as resting 'about on a level with his face' and the skull's 'empty sockets seemed to hold his gaze masterfully and without effort.' But unlike Simon, he turns away from acknowledging his own nature and makes a monster there:

> A sick *fear* and *rage* swept him. Fiercely he hit out at the filthy thing in front of him that bobbed like a toy and came back, still grinning also into his face, so that he lashed and cried out in loathing. (italics added)

And no more than Jack can recognize his own image behind the 'awesome stranger's' mask of warpaint when he looks into the water-filled coconut, can Ralph recognize his own face, though he keeps 'his face to the skull that lay grinning at the sky.'

For Ralph cannot penetrate this 'parody thing' which in its motion amalgamates the parachutist's bowing, the 'black ball['s]' bobbing, and the sea's 'breathing.' All three motions are those of an ancient primal rhythm that does not so much 'progress' as endure 'a momentous rise and fall.' It is the rhythm of man's darkness. . . . It is the rhythm that transfigures Simon in death, that engulfs the parachutist on its way to sea . . . and the rhythm that imparts to Piggy some beauty: the water becomes 'luminous round the rock forty feet below, where Piggy had fallen.' Yet for Ralph, the ordinary man, it is a terrifying rhythm, 'the age-long nightmares of falling and death' that occur in darkness, intimating the 'horrors of death.'

Golding seems to be indicating that once atavistically in contact with this dark rhythm, at the centre of the self, man will no longer be, in Ralph's words, 'cramped into this bit of island, always on the lookout.' If man is prepared to face his face, he may escape (in symbolic terms) the Island.

Ralph, in fact, is given just such an opportunity. In his last desperate race (depicted in the penultimate scene where many of the earlier symbols are recapitulated) Ralph hides himself in Simon's cell, 'the darkest hole' of the island. Like Simon he connects in terror with primal nature: 'He laid his cheek against the chocolate-coloured earth, licked his dry lips and closed his eyes' and feels the ancient rhythm: 'Under the thicket, the earth was vibrating very slightly.' Jerking his head from the earth, he peers into the 'dulled light' and sees a body slowly approaching: waist, knee, two knees, two hands, a spear sharpened at both ends.

A head. Ralph and someone called a 'savage' peer through the obscurity at each other repeating in their action Simon's scrutiny before the Head:

> You could tell that he saw light on this side and on that, but not in the middle—there. *In the middle was a blob of dark* and the savage wrinkled up his face, *trying to decipher the darkness.* (italics added)

Just at the moment his eyes connect with those of the savage, Ralph repeats Simon's early important admonition 'you'll get back' and with this partial acknowledgment of his own savagery he breaks through the cell. Expecting nothing he strikes out. . . . Rushing, screaming through the fire that undulates 'forward like a tide', screaming and rushing and *'trying to cry for mercy'* (italics added), he trips, and fallen on the ground, sees, before him, the officer. In a manner of speaking he is saved; in a manner of speaking he is given mercy. (pp. 60-2)

A germinal eschatology of the scapegoat/sacrificial victim seems to be emerging here. Simon's recognition of evil—and all mankind's complicity—occasions his ritual death. He meets the fate of those who remind society of its guilt; man prefers to destroy the objectification of his fears than recognize the dark terrors and evil of himself. In **"Fable"** Golding declares this a 'failure of human sympathy' which amounts to 'the objectivizing of our own inadequacies so as to make a *scapegoat*' (italics added). It is, by the way, the only time he has mentioned the term. Thus the ritual enacts the confinement and destruction of the boys' own terrors. They kill Simon as a beast, yet paradoxically his death exorcizes (for a short while at least) their fears. Piggy is killed on the other hand because he is an alien, a pseudo-species. And his death marks the essential inadequacy of the rational, logical world; the conch is smashed as the blind Piggy falls into the sea. But Ralph, the ordinary man, can only operate within the community's pattern; he cannot exorcize it. There is no way for him to release fully the fear even in himself. He can weep 'for the end of innocence, the darkness of man's heart.'

Now while this eschatology is implicit in the narrative texture, little of it is explicit in the narrative plot. True, Simon's encounter with the airman brings about his death, while unravelling the mystery of the bobbing figure. Ralph's foray with the savage does release the dénouement; the fire sweeps through the island thus signalling the naval ship—a not implausible arrival given the earlier ship—and the ultimate ironic rescue. Nevertheless, charges of 'gimmickry', some technical manipulation, obscurity, and inconsistency seem not ill-considered. Such lengthy and tonally weighted episodes as those before the Head do not contribute directly to the drama nor do they adequately suggest the rather simple dictum that mankind is evil.

Experienced at the level of sensation, however, these episodes seem to me to be extremely significant. By their density and ambiguity, and yet familiarity, these confrontation scenes all draw the reader into the imaginative act the characters themselves make. For the confrontation scenes here construct a parallel between the focusing of the individual character's vision and the focusing of the reader's vision. Point of view is so skillfully handled that what Simon recognizes, when he affirms his face, the reader is forced to recognize. The fable's

total structure brings about a similar fusion in the readers' focusing of events. By means of its ideographic structure, *Lord of the Flies* portrays its thematic meaning. (pp. 63-4)

Virginia Tiger, *in her* William Golding: The Dark Fields of Discovery, *Calder & Boyars, 1974, 244 p.*

JEANNE DELBAERE-GARANT

Water and rocks, ebb and flow, angles and circles, microcosm and macrocosm, reason and intuition, good and evil, flies and butterflies: rhythm beats in *Lord of the Flies,* sometimes loud, sometimes with "an undertone less perceptible than the susurration of the blood," but always with the regularity of waves against the reef. This continual back-and-forth motion, the rhythm of life, is complemented by a rhythmic use of gradation suggesting the constant progress of evil. The killing of pigs and the throwing of rocks, two important activities of the boys on the island, provide a metaphorical structure for the illustration of the author's theme.

In the description of the setting is a basic opposition between sea and island, liquidity and hardness, flux and fixity, roundness and angularity. The "circular horizon of water" contains the "square motif of the landscape." This pattern, however, is not closed upon itself. It expands upwards, outwards, inwards in a never-ceasing reproduction. Sea and sky, islands and stars answer each other: the sky mirrors itself in the water together with the "angular bright constellations." At a mile's distance from the island and parallel to it lies a coral reef, against which waves break so that the beach is duplicated in the sea. . . . Finally, there is a reminder of the water motif in the island, a reminder of the rock motif in the sea. As in the yin and yang of the Chinese, there is a black patch in the white surface and a white patch in the black, a piece of squareness in the liquid element and a pool in the island. . . . (pp. 72-3)

There is rhythm also in the abrupt succession of night and day and even in the configuration of the island itself. The boys, having come with their rhythmic changes set to the time of the clock and of their European tradition, must now adapt to the physical cycles of their new abode: "The first rhythm that they became used to was the slow swing from dawn to quick dusk." Time is no longer measured by the clock but by the regular movement of sunlight from the horizontal at dawn to the perpendicular at noon and back to the horizontal in the evening. On the island the sandy beach is interrupted by the "square motif" of the mountain. . . . As this rhythmical alternation of vertical and horizontal planes measures the tropical day and underlies the structure of the island, so contrastive and repetitive patterns govern the structure of the novel, which is built on a contrapuntal balance of opposites and on repetitions, echoes, parallels, which blend and culminate in the last chapter.

The action starts smoothly. The first chapter consists of an alternation of pictures and scenes according to whether Golding describes the place or presents the characters. From the beginning we are aware of correspondences: a bird's cry on the first page is answered by Piggy's voice, and the noise emitted by Ralph's blowing of the conch is echoed by the mountain. Even the fundamental patterns of the geophysical world will be unconsciously imitated by the boys in their activities: the contrast between the circular horizon of the sea and the angular shape of the island is reproduced in the circles and triangles into which they fall when they come together. When they hold meetings the boys form a triangle which eventually deteriorates into a sketchy and empty shape. When they hunt, Jack's choir-boys form a circle around the pig, and this pattern becomes neater as the boys revert to savagery. On the evening of Simon's death the circling movement has become so regular that it begins "to beat like a steady pulse." The conch, reconciling roundness and angularity, the irrational and the rational, in its "slight spiral twist" is a symbol of wholeness. The boys do not know this but take it as a talisman and feel that it is precious and rare.

The basic opposition between sea and reef corresponds to a contrast between the two groups of boys. Ralph's group—the democratic one—is characterized from the start by its heterogeneity, Jack's—the authoritarian one—by its organization. The boys of the first group come one by one, adding individual face to individual face. . . . The choir-boys, however, are first perceived as "something dark," a creature whose blackness interrupts the clear sand as the square motif of the mountain interrupts the beach. The geometrical elements suggest strict organization: "The creature was a party of boys, marching approximately in step *in two parallel lines* and dressed in strangely eccentric clothing. Shorts, shirts, and different garments they carried in their hands: but each boy wore *a square black cap* with a silver badge in it. Their bodies, from throat to ankle, were hidden by black cloaks which bore *a long silver cross*" (italics mine).

As a rock stands detached amid the water and a pool stretches on the island, a boy is singled out on each side: Simon and Piggy do not really belong to their groups. They are first noticed because of physical particularity which sets them apart and is commented on by the other boys: Simon because of his fainting fits, Piggy because of his obesity. They are outsiders: Piggy is laughed at and rejected; Simon goes off to meditate in the jungle. These two boys play a more important part in the novel than Ralph and Jack, who are most often set against each other. Indeed, in their opposition and complementariness Piggy and Simon epitomize all that exists in the universe: Simon is the passive element; like the candle-buds in his shelter opening their white flowers to meet the night air, he is always open, ready to let the world enter his soul and fill it. Piggy's protruding belly is the image of his affirmation, of his determination to change the world instead of accepting it. He is the rational mind opposed to intuition and insight. The two boys die significant deaths: Piggy's skull breaks into pieces against the rock which stands apart at the other end of the island, a symbol of himself keeping forever outside the triangle of the other boys' meetings or the circle of their ritual dances. Simon's body is lifted gently by the tide that fills the pool—an empty receptacle like himself—and takes him away to the open sea. The event manifests a larger rhythm into which it is integrated. . . . (pp. 73-5)

By introducing correspondences between setting and characters Golding intimates that the same law governs the geophysical world and the world of man. Human nature is an aspect of nature at large. Man is neither worse nor better than nature: the same evil principle permeates and harms both. Before the boys came to the island "some unknown force" had split the rocks and given the place its present aspect. When the boys scramble up these rocks they notice a scar across the landscape, probably made by the fuselage of their plane when it crashed. They smash a deep hole in the canopy of the forest by dislodging a boulder in order to reach the top of the mountain. The place is wounded successively by "some unknown force," by the civilized world of grown-ups, and by the boys themselves. At the end of the novel Ralph, with his bruised flesh and a "swollen and bloody scar where the spear had hit him" is identified with the island. The metaphorical scar of the first chapter was real after all.

In chapter 4 Golding concentrates on this rhythm of life in which each living creature is the victim of a force larger than itself. The littluns are on the beach, building castles in the sand. Two bigger boys, Roger and Maurice, look for a while at the castles and start kicking them over. The littluns do not protest any more than a grown-up would if his town had been suddenly destroyed by a typhoon. One of them, Henry, leaves the place and goes to the edge of the water. There his attention is caught by little organisms which come scavenging over the beach, and he starts poking about "with a bit of stick *that itself was wave-worn and whitened and a vagrant*" (italics mine). He is fascinated because he can exercise control over these tiny transparencies which, though embryonic, are endowed with life. Absorbed in his play he fails to notice Roger, who has remained near the scattered castles and observes him with the same attention as the littlun observes the scavengers. Suddenly a breeze shakes a palm tree sixty feet above Roger's head and nuts fall like stones about him. Roger is not touched but looks "from the nuts to Henry and back again": "The subsoil beneath the palm tree was a raised beach; and generations of palms had worked loose in this *the stones that had lain on the sands of another shore.* Roger stooped, picked up a stone, aimed, and threw it at Henry—threw it to miss. The stone, *that token of preposterous time,* bounced five yards to Henry's right and fell in the water" (italics mine). Man and nature are in turns victims and victimizers. It is this confused new knowledge that Jack brings back from the hunt: you "feel as if you're not hunting, but—being hunted; as if something's behind you all the time in the jungle." The same blind force moves Henry's hand when he destroys the work of the scavengers on the beach, Maurice's when he scatters the sandcastles, Roger's when he throws stones at Henry, the wind's when it looses nuts around Roger, and the afternoon sun's when it "emptied down invisible arrows" on Henry's head. The fact that the stick is wave-worn and that the stones have lain on the sands of another shore situates the whole process in a larger perspective not limited in time or space.

To remind us of this general rhythm, of which the action of *Lord of the Flies* is only a miniature manifestation, Golding selected his material with care and reduced the episodes of the book to two types of opposite activities developing inversely. On the positive, rational side are expeditions and assemblies; on the negative, irrational side, throwing rocks and killing pigs. Keeping the fire is not for the boys a regular activity since they soon neglect it. A symbol of man's reason and intelligence (there could be no fire without Piggy's glasses), the fire can be either positive or negative according to how it is used. Meant as a signal fire for passing ships or planes it becomes, through misuse, a wild beast with a life of its own which invades the whole place, kills the little boy with the mulberry-colored birthmark, and threatens to destroy them all. What happens by accident in the second chapter is done deliberately at the end by the boys turned savages.

Each of the three expeditions on the island is made by a three-boy party: successively, Ralph, Jack, Simon; Ralph, Jack, Roger; Jack, Maurice, Roger. Jack, the red-haired devil figure, is present in each. The first aims at exploring the place to make sure it is an island. The worlds of common sense (Ralph wants to draw a map of the island), of action (Jack wants to kill a pig), and of imagination (Simon sees candle-buds among the bushes) are united in the joy of common discovery and experience. About the middle of the book a second group of boys decides to climb the mountain to look for the beast. Ralph and Jack remember their first exploration, and "consciousness of the bad times in between came to them both." Ralph senses the rising antagonism between himself and Jack. Roger now replaces Simon; hatred replaces love. The third expedition takes place after Jack has formed his own group and has decided to steal Piggy's glasses to light their own fire. The forces of evil (Roger, Maurice) gradually replace love and common sense (Simon, Ralph). The constructive aim degenerates into robbery and destruction. At the end Ralph is alone against an expedition made by savages and conducted against himself. (pp. 76-8)

[The meetings held by Ralph] indicate the gradual deterioration of the civilized element, as Ralph's confident talk turns into a lamentable stuttering and the neat geometrical pattern of the first assembly wears off into a sketchy triangle before becoming a mere shape emptied of people. The meetings are in direct connection with the explorations, which are presented directly and then commented upon in the assemblies, so that the same event is seen from two different angles. Besides, each new meeting accretes new meaning by being charged, in Ralph's mind, with memories of the previous ones, which gradually awaken him to the consciousness of something he did not know before. He becomes more and more silent, conscious of the increasing evil but unable to stop it.

With the throwing of rocks and the killing of pigs the movement is first confused and only gradually asserts itself as the boys lose control of the rational in themselves. The memory of punishment received for throwing sand in a younger boy's eyes holds back Maurice's hand on the beach. The interdictions from his former life keep Roger from throwing stones at Henry. . . . When Jack raises his hand to kill his first pig, "There came a pause, a hiatus, the pig continued to scream and the creepers to jerk, and the blade continued to flash at the end of a bony arm. The pause was only long enough for them to understand what an enormity the downward stroke would be." At the end of the novel the same boys, Maurice, Roger, and Jack, have become real forces of evil, intoxicated with their own power and impatient to exercise it.

Indeed, the throwing of rocks begins with Roger's first stone in the sea, which is a perfect diagram of Golding's technique to depict the progress of evil. The same act recurs with an amplification similar to that of waves spreading in larger and larger circles around a stone thrown in the water. When he kills Piggy, Roger makes the same gesture as when he threw stones at Henry. Only the stone has become a "monstrous red thing" and Roger a murderer. Yet at the beginning the boys mean no harm. If they roll a rock through the forest, it is because it bars their progress; they join efforts to move it and are happy when they succeed:

"Heave!"

Sway back and forth, catch the rhythm.

"Heave!" . . .

The great rock loitered, poised on one toe, decided not to return, moved through the air, fell, struck,

turned over, leapt droning through the air and smashed a deep hole in the canopy of the forest. . . .

"Wacco!"

"Like a bomb!"

After that, the way to the top is easy. Although this is only a first step in deterioration, the boys' exclamations point to the future and a further expansion of evil which, like the rock, will gather pace as it tumbles down. From the start the boys are aware of their power. . . . The second throwing of rocks takes place in chapter 6 when the hunters decide to look for the beast. The antagonism between the chiefs makes them think of war and see the pink bastion as a fort. Jack suggests that a palm trunk might be shoved as a lever under the last broken rock so that it can be launched more easily at an imaginary invader. Meanwhile the hunters are heaving and pushing rocks for fun. Under them the grass is "dotted with heads."

Once they have imagined a weapon, the hunters are not satisfied until they use it against a real enemy. They do so as soon as the opportunity offers: Roger, leaning all his weight on the lever, lifts the big rock and propels it at Piggy. A change of perspective takes place at the end, when the throwing of rocks is seen from the point of view of one of the insectlike figures. Because he is now one of them, Ralph knows that nothing will stop the tumbling monster. (pp. 79-81)

There is the same tidelike amplification in the killing of pigs. After he has overcome his repulsion, Jack thrusts his knife into the living flesh of his victim. The reader does not witness the scene directly; it is related by the hunters when they come back from the forest. Ralph is waiting for them, furious and helpless on the ashes of the signal fire which they have let go out. They are so excited they fail to notice his anger and speak all at once:

"We got in a circle—"

"We crept up—"

"The pig squealed—"

Again, as after the throwing of the first rock, there is perfect harmony between the boys who have been caught in the same rhythm ("so then the circle could close in and beat and beat—"), who have shared the same experience and are now rich with the same knowledge and memories. But the world of Jack ("of hunting, tactics, fierce exhilaration, skill") and the world of Ralph ("of longing and baffled common sense") part here. (pp. 81-2)

The mock hunt is repeated in chapter 7. The hunters have just missed a boar and console themselves by organizing a game in which Robert enacts the pig while other boys dance and chant around him. As in the second throwing of rocks, the hunters are disappointed because it is just a game: the desire to spill blood possesses them, and they see this as only a surrogate for the real thing. Once more Jack is the instigator of evil when he suggests that a boy might be used as a substitute for the pig. . . . (p. 82)

Again what Jack conceives in imagination and presents as a joke will become reality. When they hunt the third time (the reader now witnesses the scene directly), the game turns into murder. It begins with the killing of a sow surrounded by her young piglets. The hunters pursue her to the open space where Simon, concealed by the leaves, has retired to meditate. The violence of the hunt contrasts with the fragile beauty of the butterflies which, as usual, occupy the center of Simon's clearing. Jack orders Roger to "Sharpen a stick at both ends" so that they can impale the sow's head and leave it as an offering to the beast. It is some time before the butterflies desert the open space and are replaced by flies that alight on the sow's dripping head and Simon's sweating face. Identification with the sacrificial victim foreshadows his fate. After the hunt the boys' excitement is increased by the stifling heat and the menace of an approaching storm, and they fall back on their ritual dances to protect themselves. . . . Even Ralph and Piggy, "under the threat of the sky, found themselves eager to take a place in this demented but partly secure society." The tension grows, the need to kill becomes urgent, and when Simon comes out of the forest to tell them that the beast is a dead parachutist he is assaulted and slain.

In the last chapter, everything is seen from Ralph's point of view. He hears the chant that accompanies the killing of a pig and is told by the twins that Roger has "sharpened a stick at both ends." It takes him some time to make sense of this enigmatic sentence, which the reader immediately understands; he then remembers that the hunters needed such a stick to impale the sow's head and that they now want another for his own.

The throwing of stones and the killing of pigs develop in similar ways: both pursuits are initiated out of necessity, repeated for fun, turned against a human being (significantly, Piggy and Simon, who represent the two poles of the human mind) and finally against Ralph, who has become the center of consciousness and learns to decipher, now that he is its victim, the darkness of the human heart. (pp. 83-4)

After making clear, through a rhythmical balance of opposites recalling the waves of the ocean, that all things, animate and inanimate, are governed by the same law, that evil does not spare man any more than it does nature, that each living creature is in turn hunter and hunted, Golding shows, through a series of repetitions expanding like the movement of the tides, that there is no stopping evil. When he shifts the focus of the novel in the last chapter, he anticipates a device used later in *The Inheritors* and *Pincher Martin*. In the last chapter of *The Inheritors* there is a switch in point of view; the action is no longer seen through the eyes of Lok but through those of a new man. In *Pincher Martin* the sudden intrusion of the naval officer—a duplicate of the one that rescues the boys—gives a twist to the novel and generalizes its effect. These gimmicks are combined in Golding's first novel: after focusing on Ralph to present the action through the boy's consciousness, the author focuses on infinity and universalizes his theme. Not only is this contraction-expansion in keeping with the movement of the novel, but the metaphorical structure itself is borrowed from the two main activities through which the progress of evil has been illustrated.

The killing of the pigs provides Golding with his first metaphor: all the concentric circles of the novel now close in on Ralph—identified with the pig and the place—in a climactic high tide of evil that threatens to engulf him and the island alike. He has become the prey of the evil force which he had so far observed from the outside: he is the boar tracked by the hunters and considers the possibility of bursting the line; he is Piggy menaced by the great block above his head; he is Simon used as a sacrificial victim by the savages; he is the littlun who perished in the fire at the beginning of the story. . . . Finally he is the island itself, "scorched up like dead wood." And then, when the scar is no longer a metaphor but is felt in his own bruised flesh, he weeps for the end of innocence.

This contraction is immediately followed by an expansion when the officer appears. His "fun and games" echoes Ralph's words at the beginning of the novel and suggests, like the white beach line reproducing the contour of the island in the sea, a further duplication of the whole story. This time it is the throwing of stones that provides Golding with his metaphor: the movement is no longer centripetal but expands from the center outwards, from the world of the children to the world of the grown-ups, from the island to the world at large. The island is a microcosmic stone thrown in the middle of the ocean with waves of evil radiating around it in larger and larger circles. The events witnessed in *Lord of the Flies* do not end when the book does. If Roger's first stone leads to his murderous gesture, there is no reason why the rock thrown at Piggy should not also lead to the bomb launched against an enemy's country and ultimately to the atomic bomb that will destroy mankind. At this stage not only Ralph but the reader himself is aware that once the process has started there is no stopping the enraged monster. (pp. 84-6)

Jeanne Delbaere-Garant, "Rhythm and Expansion in 'Lord of the Flies'," in William Golding: Some Critical Considerations, *edited by Jack I. Biles and Robert O. Evans, The University Press of Kentucky, 1978, pp. 72-86.*

ARNOLD JOHNSTON

Lord of the Flies falls into that hardy genre of accounts of shipwreck and survival on tropical islands: *Robinson Crusoe, The Swiss Family Robinson, The Coral Island,* and so forth. Golding particularly wishes the reader to associate his novel with Ballantyne's *The Coral Island.* The two main characters in both books are named Ralph and Jack, and the relationship between the names of Ballantyne's Peterkin and Golding's Simon needs little elaboration. Then, too, there are two direct references to *The Coral Island* in Golding's book, one near the beginning—

"It's like in a book."

At once there was a clamour.

"Treasure Island—"

"Swallows and Amazons—"

"Coral Island—"

and one near the end—

The officer nodded helpfully.

"I know. Jolly good show. Like the Coral Island."

(p. 9)

[In an interview with Frank Kermode, Golding] had this to say of his book's connection with *The Coral Island:*

What I'm saying to myself is, "Don't be such a fool, you remember when you were a boy, a small boy, how you lived on that island with Ralph and Jack and Peterkin. . . . Now you are grown up, . . . you can see people are not like that; they would not behave like that if they were God-fearing English gentlemen, and they went to an island like that." Their savagery would not be found in natives on an island. As like as not they would find savages who were kindly and uncomplicated and that the devil would rise out of the intellectual complications of the three white men on the island itself.

Golding's remark about kindly, uncomplicated savages stacks the anthropological cards a bit heavily against civilized man, and ignores a number of basic facts about primitive cultures. Of course, *Lord of the Flies* doesn't allow the reader any "real" savages with whom to compare the boys, as Golding's artistic sense evidently told him to avoid confusing the central human issue with such anthropological quibbles. However, the aforementioned remark does underline Golding's moralistic bias, and points toward a more serious charge that might be leveled against the novel: that his authorial presence is often overly obtrusive, either in didactic interpositions or, more seriously, in unconvincing manipulation of his characters.

In this connection Lionel Trilling says that Golding succeeds in persuading the reader that the boys' actions result from the fact that they "are not finally under the control of previous social habit or convention," but adds that he "should not have credited this quite so readily of American boys who would not . . . have been so quick to forget their social and moral pasts." For my part, I am unable to see why Mr. Trilling is unwilling to carry his pertinent critical comment to its logical conclusion, without involving himself in speculations about the relative acculturation processes in Britain and the United States. Had he pursued his doubts to an expression of dissatisfaction with the credibility of the boys, he would have been on firmer ground, since there are several points at which Golding's manipulations of narrative and dialogue do ring false.

Two interrelated but discernibly distinct threads are evident in *Lord of the Flies.* One is the actual narrative, detailing meticulously the boys' descent into savagery; the other is the gradually developed symbol of the "Beast" that is first suggested by the wholly natural night fears of the "littluns" and that eventually becomes the object of worship by the boys-turned-savages. The Beast is an externalization of the inner darkness in the children's (man's) nature, and its ascendancy is steady, inexorable, as is the path to savagery, increasing in intensity with each new regression on the part of the boys. But despite his often brilliant handling of this apposite motivating symbol of the book, it is especially during scenes involving the Beast that Golding becomes particularly intrusive.

At one point, for instance, when the assembled boys are discussing the problem of the Beast, Piggy (the pragmatic rationalist) explains: " ''Course there isn't a beast in the forest. How could there be? What would a beast eat?' " And the answer, supplied by the chorus of boys, is " 'Pig!' "—to which the unmistakable voice of Golding (by way of reminding the reader just what his symbol represents) can be heard to add, " 'We eat pig'." And a few pages later Simon, the convulsion-afflicted mystic, says of the Beast: " 'What I mean is . . . maybe it's only us'." This rather subtle interpretation of human nature from a small boy demonstrates further that Golding is so intent on his moral message that he will not hesitate to make the youngsters dance to his tune.

This assembly scene is central to the novel's development in that it marks the last point at which "civilized" rules and procedures can be said to dominate the boys' words and actions. Grounds for the breakdown of the rules are furnished by dissent among the representatives of order (Ralph, Piggy, and Simon), as Piggy, with his unimaginative rationalist's intelligence, answers Simon's observation with a resounding " 'Nuts!' " Even among the "civilized," communication is lacking, and when Jack—leader of the forces of disorder—shouts " 'Bollocks to the rules!' " chaos and darkness are ushered in.

However, Golding cannot let the matter of the Beast rest here, and after the assembly has dispersed, Ralph, shaken, turns to Piggy and asks, " 'Are there ghosts, Piggy? Or Beasts?' " And here the ventriloquist's lips can be seen to move, as Piggy answers: " ''Course there aren't. . . . 'Cos things wouldn't make sense. Houses an' streets, an'—TV—they wouldn't work'." Although beautifully camouflaged in boyish diction, the implication that a boy of about ten can reason that the existence of supernatural phenomena challenges the validity of natural law is simply too much to swallow.

A major objectification of man's inner Beast appears in the shape of a pig's head on a stick that Jack and his "hunters" leave as an offering for the Beast. Unknown to the hunters, Simon has been nearby during the killing of the pig, having hidden himself in some bushes at the onset of one of his fits. He is then left alone with the head, thus setting the scene for the most self-consciously symbolic incident in the book. At this point the significance of the book's title becomes evident, as the head, swarming with flies, enters into an imaginary conversation with Simon, a conversation in which Golding, speaking through this grotesque agent, removes any doubts that might still have lingered in the reader's mind with respect to the novel's theme or the source of the evil described therein:

> The Lord of the Flies spoke in the voice of a schoolmaster.
>
> "This has gone quite far enough. My poor, misguided child, do you think you know better than I do?"
>
> There was a pause.
>
> "I'm warning you. I'm going to get waxy. D'you see. You're not wanted. Understand? We are going to have fun on this island! So don't try it on, my poor misguided boy, or else—"
>
> Simon found he was looking into a vast mouth. There was blackness within, a blackness that spread.
>
> "—Or else," said the Lord of the Flies, "we shall do you. See? Jack and Roger and Maurice and Robert and Bill and Piggy and Ralph. Do you. See?"

The above scene, which places perhaps the greatest strain on the reader's credulity, may be defended as the book's clearest indication that human guilt is pervasive, including even the "good" characters, Ralph and Piggy. However, by comparing this strained encounter between Simon and the head with the scenes immediately preceding and following it, one may see that Golding makes his point there just as clearly and much more effectively.

The killing of the pig by Jack's hunters is a case in point. The pig-hunting of former days has been relatively innocent, but to fully dramatize the deep inner evil that takes possession of the boys after they accept the Beast as their god, Golding depicts more than a mere killing. Conjuring up the most shocking imagery he could use to show the degeneration of these preadolescents, he describes the slaughter of a mother sow in terms of a sexual assault. How better to portray the children's loss of innocence (since children are no strangers to killing) than by picturing them as perpetrators of an Oedipal violation . . . ? The vividness of [the] scene makes it both a powerfully realistic component of the essential story and a major contribution to the novel's symbolic scheme. The episode involving Simon and the head, however—especially the "conversation"—is difficult to view in other than symbolic terms, marking it as another nagging flaw in a book that—whatever its thematic concerns—seems committed from the outset to creating believable boys on a believable island. Actually, the mere physical presence of the pig's head, the Lord of the Flies, would have served well without the didactic pronouncements, since "lord of the flies" is a translation of the Hebrew *Ba'al zevuv* (Beelzebub in Greek), implying quite effectively that the head is representative of man's "inner devil."

In any event, the most successful symbolic portrayal of the Beast as man appears earlier in the novel in the form of a dead airman whose parachute carries him in the night to the top of the mountain, where, tangled in the complication of strings, he becomes lodged in a sitting position, the upper half of his body alternately rising and falling as the breeze tightens and slackens the lines. Sam and Eric, the twins, are horrified by this grisly figure when they come to tend the fire, and when a subsequent expedition (headed by Ralph and Jack, but notably excluding Simon and Piggy) climbs the mountain to confirm the twins' garbled report, the following powerful passage shows the Beast impressed forever on the minds and hearts of the boys:

> Behind them the sliver of moon had drawn clear of the horizon. Before them, something like a great ape was sitting asleep with its head between its knees. Then the wind roared in the forest, there was confusion in the darkness and the creature lifted its head, holding toward them the ruin of a face.

This is the experience that accelerates the deterioration of civilized procedures, bringing confusion to the final assembly and committing Jack fully—in a parody of his initial appearance as leader of the choir, or perhaps an oblique commentary on the ritualistic mind—to high priesthood in the dark new religion. And it is to determine the truth of this experience and the nature of the so-called Beast from Air that Simon, after his ghastly interview with the head, courageously ascends the mountain, where he frees the wasted body "from the wind's indignity."

Simon, whom Golding has called quite explicitly a "Christ-figure," comes down from the mountain to carry the truth to the others, but—still weak from his recent attack—he stumbles instead into a ritual reenactment of the pig-killing and is killed by the frenzied and fear-maddened boys, who ironically mistake him for the Beast. And here Golding's sweeping indictment of humanity becomes most nearly complete, for Ralph and Piggy, lured by the prospect of food, have temporarily joined with the hunters and take part, albeit unwittingly, in the murder of Simon. And here, too, at the moment of Simon's death, in the midst of a storm that thunders within

as well as around them, the boys are visited by the spectre of human history, embodied in the form of the dead airman. Dislodged from atop the mountain and carried again into the air by the winds, the grotesque figure of the decaying parachutist plummets to the sands, scattering the terror-stricken boys, and sweeps far out to sea. The beach is left desolate save for the small broken body of Simon, which follows the parachutist into the sea:

> Along the shoreward edge of the shallows the advancing clearness was full of strange, moonbeam-bodied creatures with fiery eyes. Here and there a larger pebble clung to its own air and was covered with a coat of pearls. The tide swelled in and over the rain-pitted sand and smoothed everything with a layer of silver. Now it touched the first of the stains that seeped from the broken body and the creatures made a moving patch of light as they gathered at the edge. The water rose farther and dressed Simon's coarse hair with brightness. The line of his cheek silvered and the turn of his shoulder became sculptured marble. The strange attendant creatures, with their fiery eyes and trailing vapors, busied themselves round his head. The body lifted a fraction of an inch from the sand and a bubble of air escaped from the mouth with a wet plop. Then it turned gently in the water.
>
> Somewhere over the darkened curve of the world the sun and moon were pulling, and the film of water on the earth planet was held, bulging slightly on one side while the solid core turned. The great wave of the tide moved farther along the island and the water lifted. Softly, surrounded by a fringe of inquisitive bright creatures, itself a silver shape beneath the steadfast constellations, Simon's dead body moved out toward the open sea.

The amount and kind of description devoted to Simon's death is ample indication of his saintly role even without Golding's identification of him as a Christ-figure.

All of the obvious parallels to Christ are there—from Gethsemane to Golgotha—and one may easily identify Simon's story with that of many a martyred mystic. But why are they there? Why is Simon there? Is Golding merely speaking with the voice of moral and religious orthodoxy? As his subsequent novels have shown, Golding is not to be labeled so easily. But in those novels one sees a consistent preoccupation with the artist or artist-figure, someone actively engaged in interpreting the human condition. . . . (pp. 9-15)

Viewed in this light, Simon's habitual isolation from the other boys, his obvious inability to communicate to them the "truths" that he grasps intuitively, and finally his death at their hands, reflect the all-too-frequent fate of the artist in society. Of course, all that can be said of the artist's role may be applied to that of the religious or mystic; but again and again in his later works, Golding demonstrates that the nature of his unorthodoxy is its basis in that highly eclectic form of mysticism called art. Like many artists before him, he sees the artist as priest, as interpreter of life's mysteries and possible savior of mankind. Unlike many of his predecessors, though, Golding faces squarely the historical fact that the artist—like other saviors—has met with little success. And in this first novel, Simon should be recognized as the first of Golding's "portraits of the artist," embodying both his pride in the high calling and his frustration at the artist's inability to defend himself against the weaknesses of others, or to transcend his own human frailties. Even more important to a reading of his works as a whole is the realization that, for Golding, the artist is representative of humanity at large, and that Golding finds in creativity the source of man's strength and weakness, his good and evil.

In any case, the aftermath of Simon's death is the last point at which *Lord of the Flies* can be said to picture the existence of a calm and ordering vision. Total disintegration of the civilized forces follows swiftly, beginning with the theft of Piggy's glasses—the source of fire and symbol of intellectual power—by Jack and his hunters, and proceeding through Piggy's murder by the brutal Roger to the final hunt for Ralph, who is to be decapitated and sacrificed like a pig to the Beast.

The description of Piggy's death provides an informing contrast to that of Simon's, showing quite clearly, though subtly, Golding's antirationalist bias:

> The rock struck Piggy a glancing blow from chin to knee; the conch exploded into a thousand white fragments and ceased to exist. Piggy, saying nothing, with no time for even a grunt, traveled through the air sideways from the rock, turning over as he went. The rock bounded twice and was lost in the forest. Piggy fell forty feet and landed on his back across that square red rock in the sea. His head opened and stuff came out and turned red. Piggy's arms and legs twitched a bit, like a pig's after it has been killed. Then the sea breathed again in a long, slow sigh, the water boiled white and pink over the rock; and when it went, sucking back again, the body of Piggy was gone.

One notes here the same studious reportage of physical fact as in the passage quoted earlier. But this time Golding concentrates on matter-of-fact particulars, eschewing the angle of vision that might place Piggy's death in universal perspective: whereas Simon is described in language befitting a dead saint, Piggy is pictured as a dead animal. Of course, Piggy's actions immediately before his murder are brave in conventional terms; but his rationalist's faith in order and human perfectibility, ironically undercut throughout the book, seems nowhere more misguided than in this scene. The mystic's intuitive recognition that good and evil coexist within man is the spark of his divinity; but the rationalist's denial of such intangible forces chains him forever to the material world of earth and organism.

After Piggy's death, Ralph finds himself being hunted by the other boys. But at the book's climactic moment, just as the "savages" are about to descend on Ralph, a "rescuer" appears in the person of a British naval officer. And at once, in a passage laden with irony, the shrieking painted savages become "a semicircle of little boys, their bodies streaked with colored clay, sharp sticks in their hands . . . standing on the beach making no noise at all." The officer, confronted with this scene of filth and disorder, rebukes the boys lamely (as Lionel Trilling might have noted): " 'I should have thought that a pack of British boys—you're all British, aren't you?— would have been able to put up a better show than that—'." And Ralph, the book's Everyman, representative of the world of "longing and baffled common-sense," is left to weep "for the end of innocence, the darkness of man's heart, and the fall through the air of the true, wise friend called Piggy."

Several early critics and reviewers of *Lord of the Flies* assailed the book's ending as too neat, if not actually as a question-begging compromise with lovers of happy endings. How-

ever, a reflective reading shows that the "rescue" is no rescue at all: throughout the novel Golding is at pains to point out that the major human predicament is internal; the officer solves Ralph's immediate problem, but "the darkness of man's heart" persists. Practically, of course, as Golding says, in a book "originally conceived . . . as the change from innocence—which is the ignorance of self—to a tragic knowledge . . . If I'd gone on to the death of Ralph, Ralph would never have had time to understand what had happened to him." And on a more sophisticated thematic level he observes, "The officer, having interrupted a manhunt, prepares to take the children off the island in a cruiser which will presently be hunting its enemy in the same implacable way. And who will rescue the adult and his cruiser?"

Returning to the Simon-Piggy contrast discussed earlier, one might also note that it is Piggy, the misguided rationalist, for whom Ralph sorrows, not Simon, the "saint." Besides subtly underscoring Golding's concern for the fate of the artist-mystic, this fact seems to indicate that Ralph's tragic experience has not finally brought him to the sort of self-knowledge that can save him as a man. The implications for humanity at large are clear and unencouraging. Thus, although the officer seems to suggest a deus ex machina, one will be hard pressed to find a happy ending here.

On a broader front, the plot of *Lord of the Flies* has been attacked as both eccentric and specious, either too far removed from the real world or too neatly microcosmic to be true. The first of these charges, that of eccentricity, may be put aside for the time being. After all, removing one's setting and characters from the larger sphere of civilization has long been an acceptable, if not honorable, practice in almost every literary genre and tradition. . . . However, the related charge—that Golding oversimplifies complex truth through manipulation of his microcosmic world—is on firmer ground. And in speaking to this point, one must necessarily return to John Peter's identification of Golding as a fabulist, as well as to Golding's own wish to be seen as a "myth-maker."

The main concern, then, of both opponents and supporters of *Lord of the Flies* is whether or not it functions adequately on its primary, or "fictional," level; or more simply, is the story told convincingly? Peter, in "The Fables of William Golding," assails the novel for its "incomplete translation of its thesis into its story so that much remains external and extrinsic, the teller's assertion rather than the tale's enactment before our eyes." And indeed, I have detailed several instances of such didactic obtrusions, including some aspects of character and action that seem more concerned with theme than credibility. However, I would qualify Peter's observation rather strongly, noting that such instances seem more vulnerable to the charge of being extraneous than of betraying Golding's "incomplete translation" of his thesis, which is more than adequately communicated by the rest of the novel. (pp. 15-18)

[Here], Golding's style becomes a major concern. As Kinkead-Weekes and Gregor demonstrate, Golding's descriptive prose carries the burden of his meaning and—coupled with the inexorable narrative of the boys' descent into chaos— provides the reader with a naturalistically concrete and complex surface world against which to view the symbolic drama. One need only note passages already quoted—the killing of the sow, the deaths of Simon and Piggy—to be convinced that the realities of *Lord of the Flies* live in the flesh, as well as in the abstract, comprising a universe not oversimplified, but paradoxically diverse, in which beauty and ugliness, good and evil, precariously coexist. The main features of Golding's best description are scientific accuracy and objectivity, combined with a felicitous use of simple adjectives and verbs that can transform his tersely pictured scenes into powerful evocations of transcendent beauty or obsessive ugliness. One thinks here of the extremes of such effects before the sow-killing, when "she staggered into an open space where bright flowers grew and butterflies danced round each other and the air was hot and still," and after, when "the pile of guts was a black blob of flies that buzzed like a saw." Without doubt, Golding's world exists compellingly on its primary level: its strained moments seem more like surface blemishes than structural defects, blemishes that catch the eye because of their dissimilarity to the skillfully woven fabric of the whole.

As for Golding's stature as a maker of myth, one must grant him a considerable measure of success. Certainly, if myth "comes out from the roots of things" and evokes age-old and recurrent human patterns, *Lord of the Flies* is much closer to myth than to simple fable. One may trace its literary roots alone back through the more immediate past (*The Coral Island*), to the ancient past (*The Bacchae*), and on a broader plane one may easily see in the story echoes and parallels from both the political and social dynamics of contemporary civilization (the rise of Fascism, anti-intellectualism) and the religious and philosophical foundations of Western culture (the Old Testament, the Fall, the New Testament, the Crucifixion, as well as nineteenth-century rationalism). Indeed, the very profusion of suggestive patterns in the novel should demonstrate that here is no simple allegorical reworking of the materials of *The Coral Island,* and that irrespective of Golding's initial plans, Frank Kermode properly observes: "In writing of this kind all depends upon the author's mythopoeic power to transcend the 'programme.' " And in this first novel, William Golding displays "mythopoeic power" of an impressively high order. The flaws, the didactic interjections and manipulations remain. But, all in all, one may compare Golding to a puppet master who has wrought his marionettes meticulously and beautifully and led them skillfully through a captivating and frightening drama, while only occasionally distracting the audience by the movement of his strings. (pp. 19-20)

Arnold Johnston, in his Of Earth and Darkness: The Novels of William Golding, *University of Missouri Press, 1980, 132 p.*

PATRICK REILLY

[*Lord of the Flies*] reveals Golding as the supreme revoker, the most obvious abrogator in modern literature, employing the dark discoveries of our century to disclaim the vapid innocence of its predecessor. The target is R. M. Ballantyne's *The Coral Island* and Golding points up the ironic contrast by lifting even the names of his boys from the earlier work. Ballantyne's book could be used as a document in the history of ideas, reflecting as it does a Victorian euphoria, a conviction that the world is a rational place where problems arise so that sensible, decent men can solve them. God has his place in this world but his adversary is pleasingly absent and, with him, the sin which is his hold on humanity. (pp. 139-40)

Lord of the Flies was conceived in a very different moral landscape and Golding himself tells us that the horrors of the Second World War were crucial in producing this

alteration. . . . *Lord of the Flies* springs from the cultural catastrophe of our times and not, as has been foolishly alleged, from the petty rancour of an arts graduate peeved because the scientists today have all the jobs and all the prestige. To attribute the book to a sullen distaste for the contemporary world, to see Golding as another Jack, who, when he can't have his own way, won't play any more and goes off in a huff, all because the scientist has displaced the literary intellectual as leader of society, is dignified by describing it as a *niaiserie*. But it does, at least, help us to focus our attention on Golding's attitude to science. He had started to read science at university on the twin assumptions that 'science was busy clearing up the universe' and that 'there was no place in this exquisitely logical universe for the terrors of darkness'. But the darkness stubbornly refused to scatter and Golding came to suspect . . . that science by itself could not be our saviour and might well, in the wrong hands, become our enslaver. The war confirmed that 'the darkness was all around, inexplicable, unexorcised, haunted, a gulf across which the ladder (science) lay without reaching to the light'. (pp. 140-41)

Golding's explanation of how his book came to be written seems infinitely more convincing: 'I set out to discover whether there is that in man which makes him do what he does, that's all . . . the Marxists are the only people left who think humanity is perfectible. But I went through the War and that changed me. The war taught me different and a lot of others like me.' Among the lessons learned was that Ballantyne was retailing illusions: namely, that man is basically noble and decent, that reason must extend its empire over darkness, that science is the prerogative of the civilised man. *Lord of the Flies,* by contrast, 'is an attempt to trace the defects of society back to the defects of human nature. Before the war, most Europeans believed that man could be perfected by perfecting his society. We saw a hell of a lot in the war that can't be accounted for except on the basis of original evil.' . . . [Golding] seeks to discover 'that in man which makes him do what he does'; to dismiss these men as a literary cave of Adullam, a gang of petulant and disaffected *littérateurs* miffed at a scientific takeover, is as foolish as it is impertinent.

Golding has perhaps encouraged his own devaluation by describing himself as a parodist and parody as depending on the mean advantage of being wise after someone else's event. There is a similarly ungenerous self-depreciation in his allusion to a pint-sized Jeremiah, almost as though he were colluding with those who dismiss him as a peddler of doom, content to describe the ruins around us. But *Lord of the Flies* is more than just an inversion of *The Coral Island,* a retelling in realistic terms of a nineteenth-century fantasy, and it is when Golding is most creative that he is also most interesting. . . . The real triumph of *Lord of the Flies* is not its parodic demolition of Ballantyne but the innovative skill that is most evident in the creation of Piggy, Simon and Roger; it is this that makes it an original work of art, the authentic expression of its age, and not simply a spoof deriving its second-hand force from the work of another era. How sin enters the garden; it is, after all, the oldest story in western culture and Golding's contemporary rendition is a worthy continuation of the tradition.

Piggy is a much more complex character than the simplistic interpretations so regularly adduced will allow; the very fact that his unhesitant commonsense would have chimed in so well with Ballantyne's ethos might make us pause before acclaiming him as the book's hero. This commonsense is evident from the start as when he organises the meeting and tries to make a list of everyone present. It is, significantly, the first question put by the rescuing officer; he wants to know how many boys there are and is disappointed and a little shocked to hear that English boys in particular have not made even this elementary calculation. Yet Piggy is a doubtful hero who, no sooner met, has to rush away from us in a bout of diarrhoea; in addition, he wears spectacles, suffers from asthma, is fat through eating too many sweets in his auntie's shop, can't swim, and, most important of all, his abysmal English reveals him as unmistakably working-class. What, one wonders, was he doing on the plane with boys so clearly his social superiors? (pp. 141-42)

Yet it is he who has a monopoly of commonsense and practical intelligence. Jack, instinctively recognising him as an inferior and a target of abuse, orders him to be quiet, yet no one else talks such consistent good sense. Ironically, in the increasingly hysterical atmosphere, that turns out to be as much a handicap as his bad eyesight. Yet nowhere is Orwell's description of England as a family with the wrong members in control more visibly demonstrated than in the way the leadership contest becomes a straight two-way fight between Ralph and Jack, with Piggy not even considered, far less chosen. Yet who better to elect, given that clear thinking, with a view to maximising the chances of rescue, is the main priority? Jack knows that he should be leader and tells the others why: he can sing high C. The utter irrelevance of this is not meant to expose Jack's folly but his menace: the *Führer's* lust for power needs no other justification than his own irrational conviction of merit. Yet the choice of Ralph, as Golding makes plain, is just as irrational. Ralph becomes leader because he looks like one—he gets the job on appearance and not ability. His very stillness is charismatic; he only has to sit and look the part.

Piggy lacks the looks but has the know-how. The trouble is that he knows but cannot do, and is relegated, in accordance with Shaw's dictum, to being at best a teacher. He cannot blow the conch himself—the asthma again—but he sees its possibilities and shows Ralph how to do it. He never advances his own claims to leadership nor even thinks of doing so, but is happy to be Ralph's adviser, the thinker and framer of policy. **Lord of the Flies** does not, like *The Admirable Crichton,* depict the rise of a meritocracy, when, following the social upheaval of shipwreck, the supremely efficient butler takes over as leader from the feckless aristocrats and only relapses into subordination when the party is rescued and taken back to the Home Counties from the jungle. Ralph and Jack are the leaders in the jungle as they would be in England. Barrie's aristocrats, recognising the demands of reality, resign themselves to accepting a social inferior as their natural leader; Golding's boys would laugh at the idea of taking orders from Piggy.

What is interesting is the skilful way in which Golding employs the prejudices of the English class system to support his allegorical intention. The allegory requires that the boys should undervalue, ignore and even despise commonsense. How shrewd, in that case, to embody commonsense in a fat, bespectacled, unathletic, working-class boy who is the natural target of upper-class contempt. The language barrier is the crucial thing. . . . Piggy can aspire, at most, to advise and he is to begin with the best adviser that Ralph could get. We must not, of course, push the allegory to the absurd extreme

of saying that the working-class have all the commonsense, but we are entitled, even obliged, to point out that the task set commonsense in the book becomes infinitely more difficult by making its representative a working-class boy among upper-class companions.

The allegorical insistence throughout the book that men prefer passion to practicality and glamour to commonsense (*plutôt la barbarie que l'ennui*) is reinforced by the realism of social antipathy. Piggy, trained to know his place, does not protest, far less rebel against this. From the moment Jack turns up, commonsense takes a back seat, and the reason is unarguably connected with the English class system. . . . Piggy knows he is inferior just as Ralph and Jack take their superiority for granted. It is this sense of inferiority that makes him deliver himself into the hands of his class enemies right from the start when he foolishly tells Ralph his derisory nickname and even more foolishly asks him to keep it a secret. It is perhaps unfair to say that Ralph betrays him, since betrayal implies a confidence solicited and a promise broken, and Ralph does neither, but at almost the first opportunity Ralph blurts out Piggy's secret to the whole world. Even Ralph, so straight and decent, is not above meanness, and his tears at the close for Piggy are an act of contrition for all the insults and injuries, climaxing in murder, which the boys have inflicted right from the start upon their inferior companion. In Ralph, at least, class contempt is gradually and thoroughly overcome; he weeps for the true, wise friend who came to him originally in such an unprepossessing guise.

That Piggy does to some extent bring his troubles upon himself leaves unchallenged his claim to be *the* sensible person on the island. He himself never makes this claim because he only partially realises it. One of his limitations is a tendency to credit others with his own good sense. . . . He shares Ballantyne's confidence that commonsense can master any problem and he believes that most people, given the chance, are as logical as himself. When, after Ralph's first speech—Piggy admires it as a model of succinct good sense—the other boys, led by Jack, run off in disorganised excitement to light the signal-fire, Ralph and Piggy are left alone with the conch; then Ralph, too, scrambles after 'the errant assembly', leaving disgusted commonsense on its own. All Piggy can do is toil breathlessly after them while venting his exasperation in the worst reproof he can imagine: 'Acting like a crowd of kids!' But that's what they are. The book shows that you only get an old head on young shoulders when the shoulders are those of a podgy, unhealthy boy. The adult the boys so desperately need is among them but disguised so impenetrably that there is no hope of his being recognised, let alone heeded. Piggy's continual annoyance and even less justified continual surprise at the foolish behaviour of his companions should surely have led him to suspect that his own commonsense was not so widely distributed as he had imagined, yet right up to his destruction he goes on believing in the power of reason to tame the beast. His most fervent exhortation to the others is that they should stop being kids and instead try to think and act as adults do, for he believes that therein lies salvation. One of the book's major ironies is that the boys finally take his advice: they act like adults and kill him.

Yet in this ambivalent book in which everything is double—fire is both good and bad, faces lit from above are very different from faces lit from below, nature is both beautiful and menacing, the human being is at once heroic and sick—it is fitting that Piggy's handicaps, most notably the asthma, all those things which qualify him as the target for ridicule, should be, in another sense, compensations. Sickness brings its own insights—Simon is, of course, an even more dramatic exemplification of this psychological truth. Long before anyone else Piggy senses the menace of Jack and the element of self-interest in this intuition makes it no less valid. Allegorically, it represents the fact that reason and commonsense are the prey of fanaticism. Piggy is stricken when Ralph talks despairingly of surrendering to Jack: ' "If you give up", said Piggy in an appalled whisper, "what'ud happen to me? . . . He hates me. I dunno why." ' On the naturalistic level this is perfectly credible; a little boy, with every cause to be frightened of a bully, expresses his own personal fears, but allegorically we note the impotence of commonsense to check the progress of demented totalitarianism. . . .(pp. 142-45)

Piggy perceptively associates his fear of Jack with the sickness from which he suffers: 'You kid yourself he's all right really, an' then when you see him again; it's like asthma an' you can't breathe.' When Ralph tries to pooh-pooh this as exaggeration, Piggy confides the source of his superior insight: 'I been in bed so much I done some thinking. I know about people. I know about me. And him.' If the grammar is faulty, the psychology is sound: Piggy does know about Jack, long before anyone else does, and his knowledge springs from the kind of boy he is. The same thing that has stopped him from being an athlete has encouraged him to be a thinker, though, as we shall see, a thinker of a limited kind.

There is certainly much to admire in Piggy. His liberal-democratic outlook and sense of fair play lead him to the honourable idea that everyone, however lowly, has a right to speak—even a littlun who wants the conch must be given it. Again Jack is the adversary: 'We don't need the conch any more. We know who ought to say things.' This leads straight to a kind of Asiatic court where only the tyrant's voice is heard because all dissenters have been put to death; Piggy supports a polyphonic society, Jack a society of mutes, since men require only ears to hear the master's command.

Piggy, too, is the first to recognise that life entails making certain choices and establishing certain priorities. Ralph, by contrast, tells the boys what mankind has always wished to hear: that there is no troublesome competition among our desires but that all can be simultaneously gratified, that the world will complaisantly minister to all our wishes. . . . 'We want to be rescued; and of course we shall be rescued.' Such brash optimism is presumptuous enough, for even though the assembly is 'lifted towards safety by his words', we know that words alone are futile and that the comfort they provide is delusive. But Ralph compounds his offence by presuming still more: 'We want to have fun. And we want to be rescued.' (Fun is a word worth watching in *Lord of the Flies* for on the three important occasions when it is used—here by Ralph, by Beelzebub in his warning to Simon, and finally by the unseeing officer—it sets alarm bells ringing.) The conjunction used by Ralph implies a confidence that we can have both things—fun *and* rescue—together. The boys have had a happy accident: they will have a delightful, unexpected, adult-free holiday, with rescue just around the corner the moment boredom begins.

It is the practical Piggy who jarringly introduces the reality principle into this dream of pleasure: 'How can you expect to be rescued if you don't put first things first and act proper?' The grammatical solecism should not conceal the psychological wisdom. . . . It is the Judaeo-Christian premise upon which western civilisation once rested. You can eat the apple or stay in Eden; not both. You will reach the Promised Land but only after the discipline of an arduous journey through the wilderness. Do you want fun *or* rescue? Piggy introduces the unpleasant idea of an incompatibility between desires; if rescue is our first priority, then fun must come a poor second. . . . Civilisation, says Freud, is based upon the renunciation of instinctual gratification and Piggy is the only Freudian on the island. *Lord of the Flies* depicts, initially, the disintegration of a society whose members play rather than work.

Self-denial is the infallible litmus-test. When Jack goes hunting, he is clearly doing something that is both demanding and dangerous—instinctual gratification is not necessarily immersion in sybaritic hedonism. The point is that Jack is doing what he wants, not what he ought; he relishes the danger of the chase and the excitement of the kill. Piggy does not criticise Jack for doing what is easy, but for putting his own pleasure above the priority of rescue. Stalking pigs is thrilling, tending a fire is dull, so Jack opts for Yahoo excitement in preference to Houyhnhnm tedium—that's what makes him the foe of civilisation and Piggy alike. The trouble is that Jack is more representative than Piggy and his outlook prevails. . . . It is hard to be civilised, deleteriously easy to be savage. Work is irksome, and, in terms of this Kantian definition, Jack is a layabout, even if he chased pigs from dawn to dusk.

We must, accordingly, be careful not to be too harsh on Piggy for being such a bore; even Ralph, despite their growing friendship, sees this failing: 'his fat, his ass-mar and his matter-of-fact ideas were dull'. Piggy *is* depressingly literalist, totally lacking in a sense of humour, taking everything so seriously. But the book exists to demonstrate the superiority of dull decency to the heady intoxication of evil—the Yahoos pay a swingeing price for all that life they are supposed to possess. The two worlds are strikingly contrasted when Jack, the bloodied knife in his hand, fresh from his first, elated kill, confronts Ralph, fuming because the chance of rescue has been lost: 'the brilliant world of hunting, tactics, fierce exhilaration, skill' versus the antithetical world of 'longing and baffled common-sense'. We *must* choose between pigs and huts, hunters and builders, fun and rescue. If Piggy is dull, he is also right.

Only to a certain degree, however, because Piggy's intelligence is seriously limited. The sole, damaging occasion when he agrees with Jack is to deny the beast's existence. Jack initially insists, with fine positivist arrogance, that there is no beast—he has hunted all over the island and 'if there were a beast I'd have seen it'. Piggy ominously joins his enemy in scouting the idea of a beast—'of course there isn't nothing to be afraid of in the forest'—though he approaches Simon's intuition in stating that 'there isn't no fear . . . unless we get frightened of people'. But Piggy is handicapped by an unfounded trust in a rational universe administered by rational man: 'Life is scientific, that's what it is. . . . We know what goes on and if there's something wrong, there's someone to put it right.' Everything comes right in the end: it is the root fallacy of the liberal mind that Orwell identified and pilloried in *Nineteen Eighty-Four*. Piggy has joined up with the complacent optimists he formerly rebuked.

It is Simon, a character not to be found, however faintly, in Ballantyne's story, whom Golding uses to highlight Piggy's shortcomings. The distance separating Piggy from Simon (who clearly embodies Golding's highest values) is indicated in Piggy's shocked incomprehension when Simon hesitantly suggests that perhaps there *is* a beast and that 'maybe it's only us'. Piggy indignantly rejects this as 'Nuts!' Simon's mystical speculations are beyond Piggy's limitedly sensible mind; he cannot and, more to the point, will not assist Simon in the latter's inarticulate effort to express man's essential illness. For Piggy, man is *not* ill—he just has a foolish but corrigible habit of following Jack when he should be taking Piggy's sensible advice. Piggy is still handing out this sensible advice when the stone crushes him to death. Simon's stumbling attempt to explain the beast provokes general derision in which Piggy participates, but, as the book shows, it is Simon who is right and the mockers who are wrong.

Ralph reveals a similar incapacity for Simon's insight and reproaches him for voicing such a distressing thought: 'Why couldn't you say there wasn't a beast?' Tell us what we want to hear or say nothing at all. But Piggy characteristically supplies the rationale for dismissing Simon as demented. There is no beast for the same reason that there are no ghosts. "Cos things wouldn't make sense. Houses an' streets, an'—TV— they wouldn't work'. Piggy will pay for this empty faith with his life, but, even as he speaks, the argument is sorrily unconvincing. Golding ironically emphasises this by having the other boys, led by Jack, chant and dance like savages while Piggy is making his pitiful profession of faith.

Ralph and Piggy both fail to see that, in silencing Simon, they are in effect delivering themselves into Jack's hands. The book traces three routes for mankind: Piggy's commonsense, Jack's irrationalism, and Simon's mysticism. But commonsense is intimidated by irrationalism—Piggy is terrified in Jack's presence. The paradox is that the mystic way, which strikes Piggy as outrageous mumbo-jumbo, is the only sensible, practical solution. That the mystic is, astonishingly, the practical man is made evident when the boys huddle in crazed despair after the appalling discovery of the beast on the mountain. Ralph has just gloomily announced that there is nothing to be done when Simon reaches for the conch. Ralph's irritation is plain: 'Simon? What is it this time?' Bad enough to be leader in such a predicament without having to listen to a crackpot, but what Simon says takes the all-time gold medal for sheer looniness: 'I think we ought to climb the mountain.' Piggy receives this with open-mouthed incomprehension and no one even bothers to answer the idiot when he asks, 'What else is there to do?' Piggy's solution, applauded by the boys as a stroke of intellectual audacity, is to concede the mountain to the beast and shift the signal-fire to a safer place. Yet Simon's is the truly intrepid invitation in every sense of the word, intellectually, morally and psychologically, for it *is* the only thing to do: we must outstare Medusa, face and outface whatever we fear or be afraid forever. Either the beast rules us or we rule it—surrendering the mountain to the beast is admitting that the contest is over. One might as well go the whole way and join Jack in devil-worship, in full propitiation of the demon.

Simon knows how to deal with the beast because he knows who the beast is: 'However Simon thought of the beast, there rose before his inward sight the picture of a human at once heroic and sick.' Piggy is incapable of such an intuition. In his secret place among the leaves Simon's recognition of the beast enables him to solve the problem that leaves the others in baffled anguish. It is while Simon is unlocking the secret that Ralph is asking why things have gone so terribly wrong and making one more vain appeal to commonsense. Surely if a doctor told the boys to take medicine or die, they would do the sensible thing? Why, then, can't they see the equal importance of the signal-fire? Why do you have to beg people to save themselves? The mystery tortures him without respite. . . . Ralph appeals piteously to Piggy: 'What's wrong? . . . what makes things break up like they do?', but Piggy's answer shows how sadly limited his own understanding is, for all he knows is to blame Jack. This is true only in the allegorical sense, but Piggy, of course, not knowing that he's a character in an allegory, blames Jack as an individual and this is totally inadequate. Jack is to blame only in the sense that he lives in all of us, that we are all guilty because mankind is sick.

Simon is the one exception to this general condemnation. The epileptic is the one spiritually sound person on the island, and, further paradox, it is his sickness that helps to make him a saint. Simon is not interested in leadership or any other form of competitive self-assertion—the nature of reality, not the promotion of the self, is his preoccupation. He is one of the meek, of the poor in spirit, who are promised the kingdom of heaven, not the congratulations and rewards of earthly assemblies. He is a surprising and anachronistic addition to the one-time commonplace tradition which affirmed the peculiar sanctity of the sick, the weak and the dying. His very debility is to be seen as a mark of the divine at work in him. While Ralph and Piggy wrestle in vain with the *mysterium iniquitatis,* Simon is shut up in audience with the Lord of the Flies. Piggy is only partially right: there is nothing to fear in the forest because the beast is within man; the only forest to fear is the heart of darkness. . . . Beelzebub warns the boy who has broken the secret not to interfere with the 'fun' about to take place or else 'we shall do you', and it is significant that the 'we' includes Piggy and Ralph as well as Jack and Roger; Simon is the sole immaculate conception in Golding's fable. When he ignores the threat and tries to bring the good news to the other boys, Beelzebub's promise is hideously fulfilled.

'What else is there to do?' Despite Beelzebub's warning and the indignation of his companions, Simon climbs the mountain to face the beast and finds instead the rotting parachutist, 'harmless and horrible'. He at once sets out to bring to the others as quickly as possible the news of salvation, and, stumbling into the predicted 'fun', is murdered by his frenzied friends, Piggy and Ralph included. The representatives of commonsense and decency are just as eager as anyone else to take a place in the ritual of 'this demented but partly secure society'. Simon is killed while 'crying out something about a dead man on a hill', and, however different from Christ the parachutist is, the words cannot fail to evoke an image of the corpse on Calvary, with Simon's own death just as clearly intended as a recapitulation of that ancient sacrifice. Nothing changes in the way men treat their redeemers.

Despite the fact that *Gulliver's Travels* was written by the Dean of St Patrick's, and despite [Camus's] *The Fall,* with its significant title and its pervasive Christian themes and images, it is, of all the texts we have considered, ***Lord of the Flies*** that is closest in spirit to Christianity. . . . ***Lord of the Flies*** is different and the difference is Simon, for either he is imbecile or he has a 'supernatural' insight into reality denied to the other boys. The novel forbids the first alternative. Simon clearly *has* some mystical, prophetic power, as when he tells Ralph that he *knows,* in some incommunicable way, that Ralph will get home again—Ralph, be it noted, not him-

self. Simon is awkward in that he confounds all simplistic interpretations of the novel, for example, that it is an Augustin-
ian or 'tory' book, arguing for law and order against anarchic
misrule and licentious freedom. All of the boys, so it is argued, removed from the pinfold of civilisation, inevitably regress to savagery. But Simon doesn't regress to savagery; it
is in the jungle that he becomes prophet and redeemer, and
it would be foolish in the extreme to argue that he inherits
these roles as a result of a sound education in the Home
Counties. Simon is not one up for civilisation in its quarrel
with nature—if anything, the beautiful resumption of his
body by the ocean might lend support, here, if nowhere else,
to nature's advocates.

But it is misleading to use him as a counter in the culture versus nature debate, for he transcends both to become, in the
religious sense, a new creation. Why did Golding create him
and why is the hideous death followed by so beautiful a *requi-
escat,* in almost brutal contrast to the curtly realistic disposal
of the dead Piggy? Only the determinedly deaf will miss the
religious reverberations echoing through the passage describing the transfiguration of the dead Simon . . . [It] is, to begin
with, beautiful in the way that the transformation described
in Ariel's song in *The Tempest* is beautiful. But more than
simply a sea-change is depicted in Simon; this beauty is clearly the servant of some greater purpose—it points to an alternative world opposed to the nightmare world of blood and
taboo, a world, in Hopkins's words, charged with the glory
of God. The passage provides a sacramental guarantee that
creation is not just some haphazard collision of atoms but the
product of an organising power, a power which promises not
simply rest but resurrection to those who sacrifice themselves
for its sake. The rhythm and imagery make it impossible to
believe that Simon's death is merely another bloody atrocity,
pointless and inane, clinching proof in this dark book that life
is a tale told by an idiot. The sense of peace informing the passage is not simply that which Macbeth envies in Duncan.
Simon *is* out of the madness, *is* at rest—after the fever of the
island he sleeps well—but not just in the negative sense of
Macbeth's longing; the peace that concludes Simon's sacrifice
is much more akin to the promise of the Sermon on the
Mount: blessed are the pure in heart for they shall see God.
Simon is now at one with whatever strong, beautiful power
it is that sustains creation, the power that will continue to
maintain 'the steadfast constellations' when all the hagridden
acolytes of Jack have followed Macbeth to vacuous death. It
is an arresting *peripeteia:* the dark epiphany is pierced by a
shaft of light from that other epiphany promising salvation. . . . (pp. 145-53)

But only momentarily. We are taken from the glory of resurrection back to fallen humanity, to the 'befouled bodies' of
Simon's friends, Ralph and Piggy. It is now that Piggy's
moral limitations are most fully exposed: the failure to climb
the mountain is a metaphor for the failure to face truth. He
will not even talk about Simon: 'We got to forget this. We
can't do no good thinking about it, see?' Truth must be placatory or it is unwelcome. He searches desperately for any defence against the accusation, for the essential thing is to maintain one's innocence. The darkness, the dancing, the storm
all combined to thrust the boys into an act they never intended. One recalls Swift's icy disdain for the shifts of alibi-
seeking men, incriminating Satan for their own misdeeds.
Ralph, more honest than Piggy, denies that he was afraid and
seeks in vain to name the emotion that drove him to attack
Simon—the reader has no difficulty in identifying it as

bloodlust. 'Didn't you see what we—what they did?' The
change of pronoun deceives no one, himself included, for
even as he speaks 'there was loathing, and at the same time
a kind of feverish excitement in his voice'. Piggy denies com-
plicitly: he wasn't in the circle and his poor eyesight prevented him from seeing what happened. By now he is hopelessly
entangled in evasions, contradictions and lies. . . . (p. 153)

Ralph is frightened 'of us', but Piggy still insists that he is victim and not culprit, and he finally persuades Ralph to tell the
lie that preserves innocence: 'I was on the outside too.' We
did and saw nothing; Jack and the others committed the
crime—it is always the others who are guilty. Yet the Lord
of the Flies included Ralph and Piggy among those who
would 'do' Simon, and this is one occasion when the father
of lies speaks true. And the boys know it: when Piggy touches
Ralph's bare shoulder, Ralph shudders at the human contact.
Simon in death is proved correct; there is no salvation for
those who will not climb the mountain. Jack is just as evasive;
they didn't kill Simon, for it was really the beast in disguise
and the beast is unkillable. But Piggy's self-deception is much
more hurtful, for, while Jack's irrationalism thrives on lies,
Piggy's practical intelligence must respect truth or it is good
for nothing.

Piggy starts off short-sighted, becomes one-eyed and, finally,
his glasses stolen, is completely blind; it is, in terms of the allegory, a depressing view of the value of commonsense. His
reverence for the conch is at once exemplary and absurd,
touching and ludicrous. As with his commonsense, he tends
to attribute his own values to everyone else. Thus, despite
Jack's unconcealed contempt for the conch from the start,
Piggy foolishly believes that the purpose of Jack's raid was
to seize the conch and not the glasses. To the end Piggy clings
to the delusion of legitimacy. . . . Piggy's passionate willingness to carry his talisman against all the odds is at once a tribute to his liberal commitment and the guarantee of his eventual destruction. No wonder the savages giggle derisively
when Ralph tells their chief that he isn't 'playing the game',
that in stealing Piggy's spectacles Jack has broken some
schoolboy code. . . . Piggy insists on treating the savages
like a crowd of scatter-brained kids, implying that if only they
behaved like adults all would be well. When Roger, looking
down on the bag of fat that is his view of Piggy, releases, 'with
a sense of delirious abandonment', the great rock that kills
the advocate of adult commonsense, he is not acting like a kid
but like the corrupt adults who have plunged the world into
atomic war in the first place. Commonsense and the conch
perish together and there is nothing healing or transfiguring
about this death.

Yet, even after all this, the frenzied slaughter of Simon and
the calculated killing of Piggy, Ralph still tries to persuade
himself that the savages will leave him alone. His first
thought, remembering his dead friends, is to assume that
'these painted savages would go further and further', but it
is a thought too hideous to entertain and he instinctively rejects it: 'No. They're not as bad as that. It was an accident.'
It is easy to believe what we want to believe. His wish to think
well of his fellows, despite all the contrary evidence, springs
from fear for himself, for if they *are* as bad as their actions,
he is as good as dead. . . . Both Golding and Orwell know
that the worst thing in the world can and will happen unless
man unearths some undisclosed resource, some as yet untapped or neglected potency, to deflect the disaster.

This deliverance is shown by the text to be far more difficult than some of its more simplistic interpreters will allow. It is facile to present the book as a straight opposition between civilisation and savagery, city and jungle, with Golding upholding the former and all its salutary disciplines against the chaotic free-for-all of the latter. Certainly, this opposition is present but the solution is not nearly so easy as the mere election of one over the other. The first page presents the two states, jungle and Home Counties, which are apparently so remote from each other. The boys are ecstatic at their miraculous relocation. (pp. 153-55)

Almost immediately reality breaches the idyll. The marvellous sun burns, the convenient fruit causes diarrhoea, irrational fears come with darkness. The bigger boys deride the littluns' terrors—'But I tell you there isn't a beast!'—but privately they share them. Soon taboos have infiltrated paradise: 'snakes were not mentioned now, were not mentionable'; 'the glamour of the first day' wears increasingly thin. The jungle is now threat rather than playground. . . . Life in a real jungle educates the boys to appreciate civilisation: the rescue once so casually postponed is now ardently desired, the missing adult supervision is no longer cause for celebration but grief.

'With a convulsion of the mind', Ralph discovers dirt and decay. Everything breaks down: the shelters collapse, the simplest repairs are too taxing, the basic rules of hygiene are ignored, the habit of disciplined work is lost as lazy, feckless man succumbs to nature. The boys understandably blame this collapse on the absence of adults, but the text denies the reader so simple an explanation. Ralph, Piggy and Simon, left alone as the others slide into savagery, can be forgiven for craving 'the majesty of adult life', for believing that with adults in control none of the insanities would have occurred. Adults, they assure themselves, would not quarrel or set fire to the island; what the boys fail to see is that children are but men of a smaller growth, that the child is father to the man, for they would not be on the island at all but for the fact that adults have quarrelled in an atomic war which may set the whole world ablaze. . . . When the boys pray for a sign from the adult world—'if only they could get a message to us'—their prayer turns into an ambush. 'A sign came down from the world of grown-ups'; the dead parachutist descends upon the island and is catalystic in toppling the already disintegrating society into gibbering demon-worship.

Everything has come full circle. Ralph pines now for the once unheeded benefits of civilisation like a bath or toothbrush, while Simon the prophet can bring Ralph no more joyous tidings than to assure him that 'you'll get back to where you came from'. The island is now a prison, Eden become Gehenna. . . . *Lord of the Flies* was clearly not written to encourage a flight to the jungle, and the nature it exhibits is certainly very different from that mediated by Wordsworth or Rousseau. Yet it would be unwise to conclude that it must be a plea for civilisation, at least in its existing form, for, just as clearly, it exposes the delusion that 'civilisation' is civilised and that Jack can only be found in the jungle.

Jack is not a proponent of savage disorder but of stern totalitarian discipline. Far from disliking rules, he loves them too much and for the wrong reasons. . . . From the outset his authoritarianism is glaringly evident. That is why it is such a disastrous concession when Ralph, to appease his defeated rival, tells him that 'the choir belongs to you, of course'. Jack, as leader of the hunters, becomes invincible as the lord of the food supply. The need to hunt and kill leads to the formation of an army and the democratic process is undermined by this alternative power-structure. Ralph's bitterness when he lashes the hunters for throwing away a chance of rescue should include himself as target, for he is not blameless. Nor does he emerge with credit from his showdown with Jack, for he finds the lure of meat as irresistible as anyone else. His resolve to refuse the costly meat crumbles and he is soon gnawing as voraciously as the others. It is a crucial victory for Jack, as his triumphant cry announces; 'I got you meat!'

This is not, as is sometimes mistakenly said, a slide from society into savagery, but the replacement of one kind of society by another. Jack's exultant claim is the announcement of a new totalitarian contract in which freedom is the price of meat. The Grand Inquisitor (who was certainly not advocating a return to nature) declared that men will fall down and worship anyone who guarantees to feed them and his chief complaint against Christ is that he will not use food to secure obedience. Jack would have won the Grand Inquisitor's approval. The provision of meat becomes a key element in the establishment of his new society. The democrats can stay and get diarrhoea with Ralph or defect to Jack and a full table, at the trifling cost of their freedom. The meat-giver wins hands down; a hungry democracy cannot compete with a well-fed tyranny. The meat which in Ballantyne is the means of redeeming cannibals becomes in Golding the infallible resource for transforming citizens into slaves—slaves rather than savages. Even Ralph and Piggy, all their fine principles notwithstanding, are driven by hunger towards Jack's camp where he sits among piles of meat 'like an idol'. (pp. 156-58)

Those who cite the book as proof of how people, removed from the ramparts and reinforcements of civilisation, so easily regress into savagery, have failed to see that, for Golding, our much vaunted civilisation is little more than a sham in the first place. 'We're English; and the English are best at everything.' Such hubris is asking to be chastised and the book duly obliges. Our alleged civilisation is, at best, a mere habit, a lethargy, a conditioned reflex. Jack, longing to kill the piglet yet unable to do so, is simply unlearning a tedious half-taught lesson; three chapters later he has overcome the rote indoctrination as he sniffs the ground while he tracks his prey, obsessed with a lust to kill, more avid for blood than for meat. The island, like a truth-serum, makes us tell the truth about ourselves, the truth that hitherto lay hidden within—it is, in the etymological sense, an education, and its prime lesson is to confirm Renan's belief that we are living on the perfume of an empty vase. Roger is simply the most frightening instance of the emptiness of civilisation; to say that he retreats from it misleadingly implies that he was ever there at all. But the island does not change people so much as liberate them to be their real selves. Jack would be just as arrogant in England, though his aspiration to command would necessarily take a different route. Roger would have the same sadistic drives at home but the island allows them to be indulged with impunity, as he finds himself in the serendipitous position of a psychopath promoted to chief of police. It is, however, not only in the jungle that psychopaths become chiefs of police. (pp. 158-59)

[Roger] is a much more frightening figure than Jack, for whereas the latter's cruelty springs from fear—the unfortunate Wilfred is going to be beaten because the chief is angry and afraid—Roger's sadism is the pure, unadulterated thing, with pleasure as its motive. When he hears the delectable news of Wilfred's beating, it breaks upon him like an illumination and he sits savouring the luscious possibilities of irresponsible authority; it is a sadist's elysium—absolute power and a stock of defenceless victims. The rescuing officer arrives just in time to prevent a supplantation, for, as the connoisseur in pain, Roger is already beginning to shoulder the chief aside to practise his hellish craft. Significantly, the sharpened stick meant to take Ralph's life is carried by Roger and not Jack. But we do the island an injustice if we blame it for producing Roger, for he exhibits, rather, the two ostensibly contradictory truths which the book advances: how far the boys have moved away from civilisation and what a tiny journey it is. By the book's close little Percy Wemys Madison has completely forgotten the talismanic address chanted throughout to console him in his ordeal; it is a sign at once of how perilously fragile the civilised life is and of how thoroughly abandoned it can become.

Whatever flimsy excuse can be offered for missing the implicit indictment of civilisation recurring throughout the text is irreprievably cancelled by the unmistakable irony of the climax. . . . [This] final startling change of perspective is integral to the book's meaning. Ralph, fleeing in terror, falls, rolls over and staggers to his feet, 'tensed for more terrors and looked up at a huge peaked cap'. The long desiderated adult has finally arrived and the bloodthirsty savages seeking Ralph's life dwindle to a semicircle of little boys indulging in fun and games; Jack, from being a manic dictator, is reduced to a dirty little urchin carrying some broken spectacles at his waist. This has been astonishingly misinterpreted as an unprincipled evasion of the problems posed by the fable: the horror of the boys' experience on the island is finally only a childish, if viciously nasty, game; adult sanity has returned and the little devils will have to behave themselves again. Human nature cannot be so irremediably bad if the arrival of one adult can immediately put everything to rights—the problem is, apparently, a mere matter of classroom control.

But such obtuseness in face of the text's irony is inexcusable. Ralph is saved but that does not exempt us from scrutinising his saviour or assessing the fate that awaits the rescued boy. The officer seems a doubtful redeemer; his cruiser and submachine gun are the sophisticated equivalent of the primitive ordnance used by Jack and his followers. Killers are killers, whatever their implements. . . . We must be gullible indeed to be taken in by evil simply because it comes to us well groomed and freshly laundered. The officer stands embarrassed as Ralph weeps—English boys should surely behave better than this—but this merely betrays his imperception, which is replicated in that of certain critics. Ralph, weeping for the end of innocence and the darkness of man's heart, is weeping for all men, the officer and his crew included. Because the officer cannot see this does not entitle the reader to be equally blind. The idea that when the cruiser arrives the beast slinks back abashed into the jungle to wait for the next set of castaways is so preposterous that it scarcely deserves refuting.

There is no happy ending nor anything optimistic about the final scene. Whatever we may wish, it is not legitimate to infer from the text that society, the *polis,* is man's salvation. The book is not an implicit tribute to the humanising power of social institutions nor does it offer us the city as a refuge from the jungle. Perhaps the city *is* essential, but it very much depends what kind of city it is—Cain's city will not help us. If man regresses in nature, that does not mean that social man is necessarily good. . . . Of course, man needs a structured community in which to develop his humanity; of course, the city should be the safe and decent haven. But 'should' is not 'is.' . . . [Golding] knows that all too tragically in our century the city itself has become, paradoxically, a jungle, the wild place in which man finds himself born. In any case, Golding's concern is with the defects of man and not those of society, because man is more important than society. Simon is again the decisive figure, for, while not anti-social, he cannot ultimately be defined in social terms—when he goes apart from his fellows to meditate alone, Golding is affirming the superiority of man to men. . . . [Salvation] exists, if anywhere, within man himself, the individual human being transcending social roles, however important those may be. From Swift to Camus we have contemplated the darkness of man's heart. *Lord of the Flies,* continuing this tradition, supplies yet another striking instance of the dark epiphany, but shows, too, the possibility of a brightness within. It would be presumptuous to demand more. (pp. 159-61)

Patrick Reilly, " 'Lord of the Flies': Beelzebub's Boys," in his The Literature of Guilt: From "Gulliver" to Golding, *University of Iowa Press, 1988, pp. 138-61.*

John Haines

1924-

(Born John Meade Haines) American poet, essayist, short story writer, and editor.

Best known for works in which he draws upon his experiences in the wilderness, Haines often presents impressionistic and metaphorical observations on solitude, pristine landscapes, human interaction with animal life, and various means for coping with harsh environments. The poems in *Winter News* (1966), his first and most celebrated publication, are based on his background as a homesteader in Alaska, where Haines resided from 1947 until the 1960s. Blending descriptions of the rugged terrain and wildlife with subdued meditations, and juxtaposing the quietness of isolation with the violence of such basic activities as fishing, trapping, and hunting, Haines explores sense of place as it relates to the physical world and individual inhabitants. Paul Zweig stated: "Haines has discovered in Alaska a world that corresponds to something at the center of his character: quiet, slow moving, contemplative, ready to display, under the calm surface, a kind of sober murderousness." In such poems as "A Moose Calling," Haines evokes a sense of sacredness in the relationship between hunter and prey, while other pieces, including "If the Owl Calls Again," focus more explicitly on the skills and traits necessary for survival. Several critics noted that Haines's interest in the visual arts is evinced in his careful attention to color and his blending of dreamlike imagery and concrete detail.

In his later verse, Haines continues to examine conditions in the wilderness while expanding his thematic interests to other areas of contemporary life. Prominent topics in *The Stone Harp* (1971) include social issues of the 1960s and Haines's return to the continental United States. *Twenty Poems* (1971) contains musings on art, memory, and experience, while human relationships are frequently examined in *Cicada* (1977). The poems in *In a Dusty Light* (1977), many of which offer extended meditations on areas in the western United States, are longer than Haines's typically short, free verse forms. "News from the Glacier," one of Haines's most respected later poems, combines impressions of a landscape with literal and metaphorical observations on its geologic history. Pieces from all phases of Haines's career are collected in *News from the Glacier: Selected Poems, 1960-1980* (1982).

Among Haines's prose works, *Other Days* (1982) features contemplations on nature, and *Living Off the Country* (1983) collects essays on poetry as well as the importance and influence of place on experience and the imagination. Critics praised Haines's commentary on the uses and effects of history, ideas, media, and personality in contemporary American poetry. *Stories We Listened To* (1987) is a collection of short fiction pieces examining human interaction with the natural world.

(See also *Contemporary Authors,* Vols. 17-20, rev. ed.; *Contemporary Authors New Revision Series,* Vol. 13; and *Dictionary of Literary Biography, Vol. 5.*)

RICHARD TILLINGHAST

John Haines writes poems about Alaska, where he is a homesteader. He is clearly a follower of Robert Bly, and his poems have the faults of the poems published in *The Sixties* and *Kayak*. Aiming for simplicity, he sometimes achieves only flatness and prosiness. Sometimes a poem of his will sound, with the lack of grace in its language, like an uninspired translation from a foreign language. His poems often lack any sense of the line as a unit, and could be printed as prose. This stanza, for example, from **"The End of the Summer,"**

> We will not storm what barricades
> they erect on the Cuban beaches,
> or set forth on the muddy
> imperial water—
> at least we shall go to hell
> with open faces.

seems to be to go just as well (though not much better) as prose: "We will not storm what barricades they erect on the Cuban beaches, or set forth on the muddy imperial water—at least we shall go to hell with open faces."

But Haines is much better than that. He has a real tone of

213

voice that builds up throughout *Winter News,* and a presence that gains in force the more one reads him. Above all, he has the gift of writing poems that are believable, with the utter simplicity of "The stories they told us were true, / we should have believed them." For me, the most interesting thing about Haines is the way he balances a concrete, knowable world with an approach that can only be called surrealistic. We may as well get used to that word, for surrealism is becoming a definite and undeniable force in our poetry. See how Haines combines levels of existence in this short poem, **"The Gardener:"**

> His hoe makes a hush
> as of a stone rolled away.
>
> We who are standing here
> in rows, green men,
> small handfuls of death,
> we hardly know this one
> who tends us—
> dark, inscrutable angel
> whose step passes by.

The grim Alaskan life seems to fit Haines's own bent of mind—grave, terrible, with an eye always on death. . . . Haines's faults and virtues are combined [in the title poem, **"Winter News"**]: the prosiness, particularly in the first stanza, barely getting off the ground; yet the combination of plainness and oddness, too—"They say the wells / are freezing . . ." The sound evoked by "Oil tins bang" is curiously accurate; and the uninsistent horror of "the stiffening dogs". Haines will inevitably be compared with Frost, the Frost of **"Desert Places"** and **"Directive,"** and there is some accuracy in the comparison. In both men there is a kind of trouble that does not call attention to itself, the real thing. (pp. 121-22)

> *Richard Tillinghast, "A Prizewinner, the Real Thing, and Two Others," in* Poetry, *Vol. CIX, No. 2, November, 1966, pp. 118-22.*

MILLEN BRAND

John Haines' turning away from the city must be called total. Born in Norfolk, Virginia, he went on a visit to Alaska in 1947, and in 1954 returned and found a place for himself some seventy miles from Fairbanks, on the border of the wilderness: "I framed a house of moss and timber, / called it home, / and sat in the warm evenings / singing to myself as a man sings / when he knows there is / no one to hear." He makes his living by berry picking, hunting, fishing and trapping, and he grows some vegetables in the short summer before "the resurrection of Silence."

He gives a report on his new home in his first book of poems, *Winter News,* a report at its best incantatory and ravishing, with such self-surrender to the primitive world around him that he seems to dissipate himself into it by some shaman act of identification.

Just as he issues out to the natural world in mists and identifications, becoming an owl or a mole, calling the moose by rubbing a piece of horn against a tree and feeling himself into that creature's raging challenge, he repudiates the world he has left, the city, wars, and the "muddy imperial water," all the smoldering threat beyond the mountains, beyond the shelter of snow that holds him in its arms. The repudiation

seems to derive not from the part of the soul that goes backward to archaic violence, but to a yearning for quiet.

When he turns to the transitory summer, to the wraiths of millennial Indian or Eskimo, to lynx, wolf, or caribou, to the wave of sustaining natural life around him, he is a magician. . . .

> *Millen Brand, "New Pastorals," in* Book Week— World Journal Tribune, *November 13, 1966, p. 16.*

PAUL ZWEIG

The news that John Haines brings us is of deep winter indeed. His poems describe a world that is limitless and vastly empty, where all the sounds have been stifled, and where those movements that still resemble life are accomplished with a slowness that is familiar to us, perhaps, only in dreams. It is the massive winter of Alaska, where Mr. Haines has lived for nineteen years, scraping together his living as a homesteader on the frontier, 70 miles from Fairbanks. His poems [in *Winter News*] are the shape he has given to his very real isolation; the words—and there are so few of them—which have survived our decision to renounce our complicated violence and our civilities. Unlike Thoreau, he went more than the symbolic mile from home. The quiet brutalities of winter, which Haines describes, occur at an incalculable distance from the anxieties and the familiar pleasures of our lives: not a mile but a world away. The poems are like messages in a bottle, launched half-distrustfully from the far side of this isolation; the reader is an accident, a piece of unexpected good or ill fortune, yet somehow not part of the plan.

> I came to this place,
> a young man green and lonely.
>
> Well quit of the world,
> I framed a house of moss and timber,
> called it a home,
> and sat in the warm evenings
> singing to myself as a man sings
> when he knows there is
> no one to hear.

This simple description points to what is best and worst in Haines's poetry. He speaks as a man "well quit of the world," who has swept aside the cluttered surface of his emotions in order to sing only to himself. Every object he describes to us, every rhythm of speech and landscape in the poems, embodies this retreat—or is it, on the contrary, an adventurous journey?—into what is utterly cold. . . . (pp. 281-82)

Haines reminds us that he made a voyage once; that his removal to this world of winter was in its time difficult and painful, but it has been accomplished. Now he is there, on the other side of life, where the events of winter are a constant illumination: "As if Death were a voice made visible." At their best, his poems *are* that voice. The violence and the dislocations of the voyage are behind him; what remains is the soft-spoken authority of a style which, when it is most effective, convinces that its quietness is a strength; as if the imposing vastness of this winter had made the loud voice impertinent—shouting is as quickly drowned as a whisper in such endless snow—and gesticulation a sign only of bad nerves.

In the dozen or so poems that are carried through successfully from beginning to end—but also in lines and stanzas of many other poems—Haines explores a world of quiet, brutal reversals: a lamp filled with shadows that burns on a table; another flickering in a "drafty cave . . . walled with visions." The lamp is an image for the poems themselves. It describes an uncertain perimeter of light in which men sit "gazing past the limit of fire into the towering darkness," or where they "awaken and listen in darkness, / guarding a smoky candle / against the silent / and relentless cold." The puddle of clarity—the life and the poem—are small moments in the hugeness of the frozen landscape.

Although the texture of the poems is simple, and their style subdued, they render the winteriness of Haines's vision with a kind of sparse detail which comes surely from the lived experience itself. . . .

Several of Haines's strongest poems describe an unexpected dialogue, which is at the same time a kind of metamorphosis. What he cannot say to men the poet says to animals, with the controlled but deadly energy of the hunter who is "haunted by the deaths of animals," for "they listen / as though I had something to tell them." . . . [In **"Horns,"** the] poet's message is one of violence, mingled with a strange, lonely sexuality; and he talks it to the proper inhabitants of his winter: the moose, the salmon, the owl, as if by killing them he too could become indigenous, not an exile or an intruder but a changed being, a member of the snowy "abyss." That is the change he imagines in one of the most beautiful poems of the book, where he listens to an owl at nightfall and, when he hears it, dreams that he will glide to meet it over the river. . . . (p. 282)

Haines has discovered in Alaska a world that corresponds to something at the center of his character: quiet, slow moving, contemplative, ready to display, under the calm surface, a kind of sober murderousness. "Well quit of the world," singing only to himself, he imagines this pure circumference of which he is the center: a vacillating, smoky candle, half in love with the frost that is its only interlocutor and that may, at any moment, put it out.

But isolation has another aspect: not only does it reveal—it also conceals. And this too is apparent in the poems. The question is: what kind of language does a man use when he is talking only to himself? What happens to such circular discourse? Words are sharpened by the situations they create; in order to convince a reader, a lover, a father, one must not only know the truth, one must use good arguments. The words, straining against real incomprehension, must be crisp and effective.

Yeats wrote that poetry is made out of the argument with oneself, rhetoric out of the argument with others. But this argument of poetry is made, nonetheless, in the presence of others. In some sense, the drama of self-discovery must then become another drama which takes shape in the reader's imagination. In Haines's poetry, one feels the lack of this other. His argument with himself is made too often, in the presence of no one. It is surely no accident that many of his strongest poems are those which describe an exchange of messages— **"If the Owl Calls Again," "The House of the Injured," "Poem of the Wintery Fisherman,"**—I mean those animal poems where owl, moose and salmon provide the drama and articulation which elsewhere may be lacking. There is a danger in being too well quit of the world: the messages that drift back lose their sharp human resonance; they may become undecipherable or just boring.

Haines escapes this danger often enough to have written a number of distinctive poems which are like little that has been written in recent American poetry. The cumulative effect of **Winter News** is, however, muffled by a number of poems whose vague imagery and blurred emotions cannot but disappoint; as if Haines had taken the shadow for the living object, the surface movement for the singular discovery it only half indicates. This indecisiveness is surely the danger of Haines's vision, and of the very real isolation in which it is rooted. Yet it is clear that **Winter News,** John Haines's first book, contains, at its best, an achieved style and a degree of insight which make it well worth reading. (pp. 282-83)

Paul Zweig, "Messages in a Bottle," in The Nation, *New York, Vol. 204, No. 9, February 27, 1967, pp. 281-83.*

LAWRENCE RAAB

For fifteen years John Haines lived as a homesteader in northern Alaska. The poems in his first collection, **Winter News,** drew themselves from this life. They were stark, dreamlike and mysterious, always solitary, often lonely, and possessed by whiteness, which has not only the whiteness of the snow, but the whiteness of speech itself, and, finally, of silence:

> Now, in the white shadow
> of those streets, ghostly newsboys
> make their rounds, delivering
> to the homes of those
> who have died of the frost
> word of the resurrection of Silence.

Haines continues this voice in his second book, **The Stone Harp.** He commands an effortless and almost transparent style. The best poems are like small streams into which the words fall, like stones, gathering color and revealing their markings as water passes over them.

But this book lacks a certain tension and precision. Many of the poems do not speak with the authority that distinguishes **Winter News.** They remain incomplete, as if they had not discovered the real necessity of their being. Particularly weak are the political poems of "America," the book's middle section, which sound as though they had wanted to break into a passion that they could not bear. The landscape here has changed, and moves from Banner Dome to New York to California, where the author now lives. Something is lost in the journey. Haines is at his best when he is in nature, really inside of it, inside the skins of animals and inside their dreams, giving his voice over to their silence. In this new work he is too often at the edge of nature, or looking back at it, as to an abandoned country.

Still, there are lovely poems here, some with an intensity equal to that of anything he has done. These possess an incantatory impersonality. Reading them, one feels that the poet, through the act of the poem, is reaching toward something as basic and as necessary as food or shelter. In one poem Haines speaks of "the mystery of a shared country,/ never completely whole." If many of these new poems are not "completely whole," the best create the likeness of that country, and grow out of its solitude, into the shapes of what we know—wind, water, smoke, stones—the things of the world seen with a clarity that touches their mystery and the possibility of their magic. . . . (p. 538)

Lawrence Raab, "On the Edge of Silence," in The

American Scholar, *Vol. 40, No. 3, Summer, 1971, pp. 538, 540, 542.*

CLIVE WILMER

[Haines's] long period of withdrawal [in Alaska] would seem to have been justified, for, in spite of some serious flaws, the poems in *The Stone Harp* reveal more basic poetic power than we have seen in a new writer for a good many years. . . .

As his superb little parable **"The Cauliflower"** suggests, Haines is by nature a visionary poet whose imaginative impulse is constantly held in check by the accuracy of his observation. This balance, his most distinctive virtue, is most in evidence in the first of the book's three sections. Here, in the flux of the natural world, he finds microscopic analogies for larger human conflicts and disasters. His metaphors and personifications are so extended that they issue in a kind of metamorphosis, the effect of which is to implicate humanity wholly in the processes of nature. At the same time, human society is revealed as temporary and precarious. For Haines, as for so many of his contemporaries, our civilization is now defunct, persisting as a mere charade, a grey succession of shadows that blind us to the Nature that underlies them. In the political poems that occupy the middle section of the book, he more or less welcomes the disintegration of American society. Neither ideologically nor sceptically reasoned, most of these poems are either assertive parables or streams of images unharnessed by ideas or understanding. "There will be many poems written / in the shape of a grenade— / one hard piece of metal flying off / might even topple a government." It is hard to believe that lines so crassly simplistic could flow from the same pen as the title-poem, with its superbly modulated imagery depicting the poet as a near-tragic figure, 'a drifter,' uprooted from a culture now frozen in anticipation of its own nemesis. . . .

The book picks up in the third section where **"The Middle Ages"** and **"The Wreck"** stand out for their greater objectivity and exactness of form. All apocalyptic in theme, the poems in this last group have a hallucinatory power, that occasionally degenerates into portentousness.

His imagery is Haines's clearest strength. What one remembers from his work are the landscapes, vast icy wastes, and "the figures of men and beasts" that float across them: the beasts especially, inhabitants both of the wilderness and of the imagination, alien yet familiar. But poetry cannot live by evocation alone. Rejecting both conceptual language and formal syntax, he is unable to develop or substantiate his vision. He merely *states.*

It would seem that for Haines the conventions of verse and language are infected by a moribund culture; he would start from scratch and construct a language for survivors in a cultural void. Too often this necessitates a thinness of language and an imprecision of form and rhythm that make the poems sound more like translations than the real thing. In theory this could be admirable, but one should remember that there are poets whose work, informed with a similar disquiet, remains composed and articulate.

Clive Wilmer, "Alaska and Orkney," in The Spectator, *Vol. 227, No. 7478, October 23, 1971, p. 591.*

JOHN R. CARPENTER

I greatly admired John Haines's *Winter News,* which appeared in 1966. *The Stone Harp* is a very different book; the setting has changed, and so has the mind of the author. Haines's imagery is often highly subjective, corresponding to impulses inside the mind rather than to outer reality, like the surrealists:

> around the straining tent
> of your life there prowls and sniffs
> a fallen black star who overturns
> stones and devours the dead.

There is a tendency—more so than in *Winter News*—for metaphors to originate in the *desire* to distort, rather than in the object itself, which, when looked at long enough, contains the seeds of its own distortion. There is much concentration in these poems but they are often highly reductive, obscuring object and subject alike. **"In Nature,"** for instance, is about human qualities in animals and insects, but they are exclusively warlike, hostile qualities. John Haines's manner of looking at animals is diametrically opposed to that of Gary Snyder.

When Haines writes poems about human society—and there are many in this book—his subjectivity often gets in his way, producing poems radically out of focus and not really about society at all. They are often misanthropic; society *as a whole* is indicted: "humanity / strolling like an overfed beast / set loose from its cage" (**"The Way We Live"**). Many people are selectively misanthropic, of course, especially toward those they blame for inflicting damage and suffering on others. But it is important to make distinctions, and not to confuse those who inflict suffering with the victims. Poetry may not be the keenest analytical tool for making these distinctions, but they can be made. (The Polish poet Zbigniew Herbert is instructive here.)

While reading many of these poems I had a feeling of waste; there are so many things wrong, so many legitimate targets, but Haines hits none of them. To use his own metaphor, the poem "like a grenade" goes off in the poet's own hand. The poem **"From the Rooftops"** recommends political assassination, without caring in the least about its consequences. When Haines writes "state", the reader is obliged to interpret it as "state of mind". The talk about revolution is rhetorical; it takes more than a knowledge of headlines and resentment to make a revolutionary.

The problem with this book, I think, is primarily one of *setting.* Haines's best poems have strongly realized settings; many of the poems about "society" lack a visualized setting, and "society" is curiously absent. Alaska provided Haines with a convincing background for his vision; now, in his new habitat, he has chosen an easily available "political" stance as a means of orientation, but the poems remain apolitical. Can fine poetry be made out of purely negative feelings? Personally, I doubt it. There was Robinson Jeffers; and the small group of readers who like their poetry misanthropic will also like Haines. On the other hand there are fine poems of protest, outrage, sadness, and disgust, but the good ones always have an ideal behind them, even if it is unstated, lurking in the background. Poems of *pure* disgust tend to be purely subjective, and very narrow.

Haines's technique is impressive; he can turn almost any poem into a highly compressed vehicle for strong emotion.

But in what service will this technique be used in the future? I ask the question with some anxiety, because Haines's success is assured and he can count on receiving praise. But what kind of success? What kind of praise? (pp. 167-68)

> *John R. Carpenter, in a review of "The Stone Harp,"*
> *in* Poetry, *Vol. CXX, No. 3, June, 1972, pp. 167-68.*

JAMES HEALEY

In a recent article titled **"Roots"** (*Quarry,* Winter 1971/72) John Haines writes that without roots good poetry cannot be composed. Roots are not necessarily related to a certain geographic region, but rather to a place of belief or conviction to the poet: "The poet believes in, or he is in the process of becoming a believer in, or he may be letting go of a belief in, a self, a way of being, a way of seeing and feeling." Haines's latest volume of poetry, **The Stone Harp,** shows the poet in the process of striving to define some new way of being. The universe which Haines attempts to construct is less clear than the world from which he is departing.

The Stone Harp is divided into three sections: "In Nature," "America," and "Signs." The poems in the first section grow out of Haines's Alaskan experiences and show the poet as he listens to nature for some clue to the direction he should take: "I waited on a corner of the earth / for the wind to move me" **("Beginnings").** But, like a stone harp, the natural world offers only disjointed sounds: the howling wolves, the drifting wind, the drops of rain on leaves, or the croaking frogs around a pasture pond. Without a firm conviction or belief, the poet will remain at the listening stage, never comprehending what he hears. Nature by itself cannot give the poet his roots.

The "America" poems are the most powerful in this volume because Haines has a clear notion of the beliefs which he is rejecting. An intense dissatisfaction with the American way of life and values pervades these poems. (pp. 270-71)

In "The Sign" poems Haines presents an apocalyptic vision of the transitional stage between the universe he is destroying and the universe he is creating. Once the poet has listened and comprehended, he is left to discover his new role in this changing world. . . .

At the end of the **"Roots"** article Haines writes of finding a cave where one can sit for a time and construct a universe: "We must find that place in ourselves. And we must begin now." **The Stone Harp** becomes Haines's declaration of his sense of roots; the poet has listened and understood. Now he must begin to construct that new world out of the ashes of his old beliefs. Hopefully, Haines's future poems will do this. **The Stone Harp** stands as a fine tribute to a poet in transition, a poet who deserves to be read and listened to. (p. 271)

> *James Healey, "Roots," in* Prairie Schooner, *Vol. XLVI, No. 3, Fall, 1973, pp. 270-71.*

RICHARD SCHRAMM

John Haines' third book, **Twenty Poems** . . . looks back again on his long stay in Alaska. The sparse features of Haines' landscapes, familiar to readers of **Winter News,** are here again in the guileless economy of poem after poem. They are added to by two studies of Klee and Ryder, and then there are a handful of lyrics difficult to group under any heading—

domestic might do, since they bring in closely tied people, childhood memories, and other warming presences foreign to much of his other poetry—which are . . . simply gotten at and . . . unpretentiously achieved. . . . For all its compactness this is a beautiful volume, winsome in the purest sense of the word. I can't imagine anyone not being taken into its quietly drawn illuminations, like the face in **"A Winter Light"** which ". . . by candle or firelight / . . . still holds / a mystery that once / filled caves with the color / of unforgettable beasts." (pp. 397-98)

> *Richard Schramm, in a review of "Twenty Poems,"*
> *in* Western Humanities Review, *Vol. XXVI, No. 4, Autumn, 1972, pp. 397-98.*

HAYDEN CARRUTH

Haines knows more than any poet alive about real wilderness, having homesteaded for years in the remote part of Alaska, living off and with the land. His love is fierce. Once he said: "I'd rather live in Alaska than anywhere, but I wouldn't work on the pipeline to do it. I couldn't." And in a poem:

> now on the high tundra,
> willows and water without end,
> come shade and a noise like death.

What shade? It doesn't matter; we know well enough— airplane, earthmover, oil rig, quonset, they all cast shadows and they make "a noise like death." The last wildernesses are going. No indignation can serve now, only the countering creative urgency of art, the lyric voice. And then what is that worth? Sorrow behind sorrow behind sorrow, the song goes on. *Cicada* contains poems of the past six years, while *In a Dusty Light* is a smaller sequence written last year . . . Both books give us the mature work of one of our best nature poets, or for that matter one of our best nature writers of any kind, best because he is so much more than a naturalist. Haines knows the ecological crisis as well as anyone, and he knows it is more than that. It is a crisis of consciousness, the human mind in ultimate confrontation with itself. (pp. 87-8)

> *Hayden Carruth, "The Passionate Few," in* Harper's, *Vol. 256, No. 1537, June, 1978, pp. 86-9.*

PETER STITT

John Haines has been widely praised for the lonely purity of his earlier work, a meditative verse which grew out of the life of isolation he lived as an Alaskan homesteader. . . . *Cicada,* is in many ways a book of changes. The poems are longer, more discursive, much more often about the poet's relationships with other people than about his deep relationship with the wilderness and with himself. Haines no longer lives exclusively in Alaska; he has divorced and remarried; his new poems directly reflect this spirit of transformation. As he says in **"Goodbye to the Flowerclock"**:

> It was time to push away
> the four walls of the years,
> to go to the end of the path
> and go beyond . . .

The book is divided into four sections and is clearly designed to move from a point of emptiness, failure, an emotional dead end, through a rebirth, and into the fullness of a new life. Among the many images which help to carry this pattern is that of the tree. **"Poem about Birch Trees"** presents a metaphorical look at an unfulfilled life, a "life held back in secret": "too long withheld, the heartwood / sours and slowly rots . . . // Until one day, . . . / . . . that hollow life breaks down." The first section of the book concludes with **"There Are No Such Trees in Alpine, California,"** a poem which describes an unsuccessful search for a full and satisfying family life. The pattern achieves a positive climax in a poem in section II, **"The Tree that Became a House"**:

> They came to live in me
> who never lived in the woods before.
>
> They kindled a fire
> in my roots and branches,
> held out their hands
> never cramped by the weight of an axe.

The result of this process is a long series of poems in section III celebrating domestic happiness. That many of these poems are also somewhat saccharine is perhaps inevitable. As Allen Tate pointed out long ago, poetry thrives on tension; once the basis for polarity has been removed, the tension—and often the poetry—is gone. This stanza from **"Jonna"** is typical:

> The depth of the evening
> sank blue in your eyes.
> I have never seen a mountain
> so small, never watched
> in so clear a window
> a forest, a sky, and a rock.

A pretty tribute to his lady's eyes, but heightened just that much too far. Haines seems to be presenting literal truths and events from his life in these poems; the rite of passage which he describes is his. The truth of the human heart often leads to sentimentality in poetry; it can also lead to didacticism. When in **"The Stone Bear"** Haines assesses his present position—"Before me the unclimbed summit / of my life"—one gasps at the didactic artlessness.

At heart John Haines would seem to be a romantic poet, and not just for the sentimentality of his love poems. In his nature poems, Haines bathes his scenes in a more than real glow, attempting to heighten and transform. . . . [In **"The Lake in the Sky,"** his] desire for an ethereal prettiness carries Haines much too far; the effect for the reader is akin to trying to eat a tablespoon of sugar.

This attitude of breathless reverence at times calls to mind the group with which Haines is most generally classed—the Northwest school. The Northwest poets love Indians even more than the rest of us do, of course, and write lots of poems about their mystique. In **"Fourth of July at Santa Ynez,"** Haines presents a sentimentalized portrait of a dignified old Indian caught in a fading world full of loud, insensitive, white yahoos. As the poem ends, this noble savage fades into the sunset:

> Slowly, too slowly, as if returned
> from a long and difficult journey,
> the old man lifted his bucket
> and walked away into the sunlit crowd.

It is hard not to see, when reading this poem, the Indian who appears in those anti-pollution messages on television. At the end of one segment, the announcer intones something like "let's make this land beautiful again," as the Indian, a tear running down his cheek, looks out over a junk-littered freeway.

Curiously, what is probably the best poem in the book is almost identical to this one in pattern, though with crucial differences in tone and strategy. In **"Victoria,"** Haines, through the use of a half-Indian girl, again contrasts the white culture—commercial, shallow, exploitative of the land—with the Indian culture—which, through its reverence of the land, attains a greater spiritual depth. In reality, the girl simply makes bead curios; but in the poet's imagination she is seen taking flight on a horse, returning to the wilderness and to the earlier way of life of her people. In answer to the question—"Will we ever again be at home / on earth?"—Haines asserts that the essential wilderness must be allowed to live on inside of us, even though we lost touch with it outwardly:

> Wilderness survives at the camp
> we have made within us,
> a forest filled up with night,
> its ancient sounds
> and floating, starlit images.

John Haines is a skilled lyricist writing in a minor, romantic mode. His earlier work appeals to me more than do these newer poems. But *Cicada* has all the marks of being a transitional volume, and it is only by breaking the constricting conventions of his earlier work that a poet may truly progress. Haines will bear continued watching in the future. (pp. 476-78)

> *Peter Stitt, in a review of "Cicada," in* The Georgia Review, *Vol. XXXII, No. 2, Summer, 1978, pp. 476-78.*

GREG SIMON

The poetic reputation of John Haines will continue to ride on the strength of his first and most unified book, *Winter News* (1966). The lucidity and stillness of the prosody in this book belie the fact that something enormous and strange to most of us has been contained there. "I could walk north from my homestead at Richardson," Haines wrote recently, "all the way to the Arctic Ocean and never cross a road nor encounter a village." His first book contains the devotional records and meditations of twelve years spent at the violent edge of a place unchanged for centuries, unlimited by the conventions of progress. In Alaska "the rising and setting of the sun, the coming and going of birds and animals, the sources of food and light, became for me not a passage in a book of histories, but a matter of daily occurrence."

Haines, "well quit of the world" in his own disarming terms, nevertheless entered eagerly and often into the struggle to maintain a foothold before the arctic abyss. And all the time he was coincidentally watching and recording furtive shapes slipping by him "past the limit / of fire into the towering / darkness."

The snow simply accepted these fellow travellers, as it always has. They fell through holes in the ice and returned haggard and changed. Or did not return. Or took root beside Haines, and learned how to survive as caribou, moose and wolves have survived in the cold, and as Haines himself was learning to survive. Their homesteads of memory and dream, brought with them from the cities, were soon invaded by the bright-eyed northern slayers—the fox, the lynx, the Indian trackers and their quarry.

John Haines did not flee from the giant moose, but in **"Horns,"** a poem from the farthest edge of courage and wonder, explored the possibility of luring one closer. Only Haines himself can know how many times he had to go where the moose lived, and repeat his hunter's tricks until he captured the noises perfectly and his images of the bull moose were filled with the reality of one. (pp. 130-31)

Haines's voice in the poems from his second book, **The Stone Harp,** which was written during the period of greatest turmoil over Viet Nam, speaks much more directly than the mythical snow-covered voice of **Winter News.** The words move strongly outward and outward only from the page, and in this way they echo the protests and rhetoric of thousands of other despairing and raging citizens.

Haines's own sense of outrage, however, was predicated on a deeper premise. "I can still remember the intensity of my feeling of actual pain and outrage," he wrote recently, "seeing the landscape of Southern California once more after twelve years in the wilderness." The solutions that Haines pointed to in his anger and frustration were as harsh and unrelenting as his previous experience in the north. The poems from this period glitter with rough uncut kernels of radical policy, so radical in fact that they made even the poet himself uneasy. I am convinced that in many ways Haines's uninsulated life in Alaska had much to do with the violence of his reaction to what he found harmful or lacking in the south. He became outraged when others around him did not because "the securities of our civilized life put to sleep in us a much needed sense of peril; it requires the nearness of disaster to awaken us again."

Even if the advice that Haines gave at this time ("With rifle or pen, / take aim at the state") seemed destined to fail against the military powers behind the war, we must always keep in mind while reading Haines that he has unsparing respect for any enterprise that can turn necessity and turmoil into a prelude to higher life. In giving such militant advice, Haines had merely turned his attention to the affairs of life in the south in the same passionate way he had attended to what needed to be done in the north. Instead of toppling trees for lumber and firewood, he studied ways to topple governments. He wrote soon afterward that he had considered "leaving such poems out of a book, or at least rewriting them. I haven't done so, not only because they appear to be honest expressions of the mood I was then in, but also because they seem to form important stages of an inner journey."

This inner journey, as Haines has written many times now, is the reconciliation of dream journeys with actual life. The result is an intense and more genuine form of human reality in which we realize that the full scope of each of our actions, due to the tremendous advance in our genetic and scientific powers, must be measured for its effect on whole continents, not towns or neighborhoods. It is Haines's contention, based on his reading of poems being written now, that "the world of the poet has shrunk many times since Williams and Stevens took for their concern the whole of life, or at least the whole life of a place." But it is also his belief that the potential world of the poet is as large as ever, both in an interior and exterior sense, and that it has never been in more need of steady hands to find it. The image throughout his work is of a writer who immerses himself in the spaces and powers of his interior dream places, and then steps into his place in the world and takes up a pen to describe it.

Haines's newest poems spill out of his recent books like talismans from the knapsack of a traveller bent on changing the nature of the ground beneath his feet. They are, in one of his own phrases, "heavy with iron and distance." The iron in this instance would be the hardened sorrow and disappointment accompanying contemporary life. The distance is the true loneliness of one who has exhausted his courage on what he perceived to be the correct path, only to see everyone else passing by him with fearful and discontented faces in the opposite way.

The poems in **Cicada** (1977) and **In A Dusty Light** (1977) represent a personal, almost magical fusion of the forces and powers fostered by a life clinging to the wilderness experience. In order to live any kind of harmonious and productive life in our society, it also seems necessary to nurture an open pioneering spirit of mind. Haines's discoveries in this vein have been prompted by his belief that someone should make a record of what has or will fade away. This is not sudden, but slow and stubborn fading. It is a world unresigned to defeat, like the magnificent bear from **"The Stone Bear"** in **Cicada** in whom Haines sees (as he sees in himself) "an aging strength," and who is looking ahead even in the moment of his greatest loss:

> Before me the unclimbed summit
> of my life, the rock where
> I may stand in the biting air
> of another, far-off October.
>
> There in a wind spilling down
> from wintry pastures,
> I'll pull my fur around me
> and freeze into living stone.

For Haines, the evidence of this kind of power all points behind us. He has been learning "an ancient track, / scar of the wilderness that sings / around lighted towns . . ."

This plunge back into the sacred, now mythical holding of darkness is the theme of the strongest poems in **Cicada,** and of Haines's first venture into the long poem—**"News From The Glacier,"** which is the centerpiece of [**In a Dusty Light**]. . . . (pp. 131-34)

In poems like this Haines joins a select few who have chosen to look behind them for inspiration and resources. The list includes Andre Malraux (ancient art); Gary Snyder (myths and gene pools); Charles Simic (proverbs and folklore); and Loren Eiseley (mammoths, mastodons, plants, outer and inner space). Haines follows them into the world of archaeological time, communing with the rocks and skulls stashed away in caves and trenches, the once-living safes of information. The resulting poems are stunning examples of their motions and secrets, revealed to his interested, practised scrutiny. The revelations from his travels in ancient and unchanged parts of Oregon, California and Montana compare favorably to those he found in Alaska. (p. 134)

Haines is not simply a voice standing against the march of progress, urging all of us to begin collecting cave art or fossils. The ghosts, according to Haines, are very much present in everyone's daily life. In a series of autobiographical sketches that are just now appearing in [journals] . . . , Haines has begun to delineate the exact details of the life he led for two decades in the Alaskan wilderness. The claims he makes for this life are sublime. He claims it fused the dream artist within him with a respondent challenging landscape and "something of the original life of the continent"; and that this closeness to the details of human reality caused him to lift his own concerns toward the life of the planet itself. In this demanding and startling prose, the poet changes and grows before our eyes, and learns to see in accordance with the powers he uncovers and comes into contact with. And he goes further to show us that nature can no longer progress along with us without our full co-operation and care. Man's indifference and unhappiness has become a kind of glacier, threatening to sweep the earth clean of all that fails to amuse him. (pp. 134-35)

Greg Simon, "The Endless Present: On John Haines," in Northwest Review, Vol. XVIII, No. 2, 1979, pp. 130-35.

WILLIAM STAFFORD

It was back in 1947 that John Haines moved to Alaska and homesteaded a place near Milepost 68 outside of Fairbanks. Educated as an artist, he turned to hunting, trapping, fishing and writing, a brief biography of him says. Being quiet up there in the north for a while, he began to register what he learned about basic human existence; and his poems—viewing civilization lengthwise and estimating its curve—began to show up like spear points in little magazines. By 1966 when his first collection, **Winter News,** appeared, his insistent vision of life in the city as a life oblivious to important things had distinguished him.

[**News from the Glacier: Selected Poems, 1960-1980**] brings together the best from five collections that span 20 years of that decidedly individualistic accomplishment.

The vision behind these poems illuminates a judgment upon civilization: Before it came, and hovering at its edges now, ready to come again, is primitive life—a life that, though brutal, satisfies the reader through its clear hard focus.

Definite as that embracing of primitivism is (and it shows up again and again, at the center of Mr. Haines's work), the poems are not merely assertions; in fact, emphasizing their content could distort what the experience of reading this book feels like.

For an extra ingredient derives from that doubleness hinted at when Haines moved north: "Educated as an artist . . . he turned to hunting." Wherever these poems turn for their topics, they turn artfully. Each time the attention shifts, it makes its way by phrases and cadences that lean toward conclusions; the trajectory of the message signals the presence of someone under a spell, falling toward knowledge while maintaining a balance, as in **"Poems of the Forgotten."** . . . (p. 12)

Typically the poems drift down the page in free-falling, three-beat lines that play accompaniment to one another with recurrent gritty words, as in the **"Cold Journey"**—"dry," "bitter," "close," "inward," "darkness," "cold."

Comforting in the actual, wintry scenes that dominate the pages is something to be cherished and carried along—a human endurance, a sturdiness in confronting what is out there. There are ideas, anticipations and remembrances that bolster the human spirit, voiced in phrases that imply an understanding between writer and reader. It is not surprising, in view of Mr. Haines's early training, that many of the allusions connect with art: "faces like broken bowls" in a poem titled **"Hunger"**; "a pale horse of torment flying" in a poem

titled **"Ryder"**; "The hot mice feeding in red" in a poem titled **"Paul Klee."**

Humanizing the whole collection are stray hints of autobiography—places and acquaintances in Alaska, fragments from the poet's naval background, traces of university towns. But because cold is where the years go, and because what surrounds us ultimately dominates us, the most compelling parts of this book regularly attach to the sensibility that is alert to the big scene in the background: There is a poem about an Eskimo walking one evening "on the frozen road from Asia"; one about the mole dreaming of spring when "the rising sun slowly dries / his strange, unruly wings"; one that says, "Little Rabbit, you are bleeding again"; one in which all the sounds of history pass and become only the wind sweeping leaves and dust, and one about hearing the dinosaur tread. (pp. 12, 34)

William Stafford, "The Self-Contained Traveler," in The New York Times Book Review, October 31, 1982, pp. 12, 38.

LEX RUNCIMAN

For some twenty years John Haines's Alaskan poems have formed a constant and valued portion of the landscape of contemporary American poetry. With [**Other Days**], Haines further explores a new form: the prose meditation. Haines's outward subject continues to be the Alaska he homesteaded, yet to a greater degree than ever before what astonishes one is the simple fact that this is no nineteenth-century account of wilderness experience. Our living contemporary, Haines has done things few of us have; he has lived our American primitive dream of self-sufficiency. . . . (p. 70)

If Haines's physical life in Alaska—the trapping, fishing, gardening, the making of nets, tools, moccasins—constitutes one side of these essays, the other side has to do with the psychic struggle inherent in Haines's essentially solitary life. The struggle is, in part, to retain a humanness—to preserve a distance between landscape and man, between the animal and the human. For instance, Haines looks at his hands, hands which "have gone deep into the hot body of the animal, and torn from it the still-quivering tissue of lungs, heart, liver and guts." Looking at those hands, Haines finds "a troubling thought . . . having done so much, would I kill a man?" It is a question with no easy answer at any time, a question made even more difficult by Haines's Alaskan life.

But Haines's most basic struggle is to retain a sure sense of "I" in a landscape which on the one hand demonstrates no regard for his personal existence, and yet nonetheless faithfully supports and records the evidence of his presence. It is a duality Haines is aware of, for he deals with its two halves in separate, back-to-back essays. In **"Lost,"** a series of anecdotes about people who died in the wilderness anonymously and often without trace, that sense of disregard is foremost, amounting to "a drowsy, half-wakeful menace [that] waits for us in the quietness of this world."

In **"With an Axe and an Auger"** only a page or so later, Haines writes of how the land once changed by human habitation then preserves the fact of such habitation: "the people live in these hills, in the shape of their ditches, their mounds and cellars." What survives, and what Haines celebrates here, is the physical landscape's testimony to the Alaskan settler's strength of spirit. . . . For John Haines, as these essays make clear, to live in Alaska, off the land, with the land, is "a way to touch the world once more"—in its largest sense, an act of love. That startling and useful concept lies at the heart of this book. (pp. 70-1)

Lex Runciman, in a review of "Other Days," in Western American Literature, Vol. XVIII, No. 1, May, 1983, pp. 70-1.

SAM HAMILL

These "essays on poetry and place" [collected in *Living Off the Country*] date back as far as 1969, when Haines wrote a controversial review of Paul Carroll's anthology, *The Young American Poets*. Haines had not been reluctant to view recent American (*North* American) poetry with a critical eye. "There is," he says, "no adequate substitute for ideas. Having ideas doesn't guarantee anything, either, but lack of them has contributed to the demise of a number of poets in our time." And he offers Roethke as an example of the prototype:

> full of energies directed all over the place, but relying in the end, perhaps, too much on personality, making of private life and the fantasies of childhood and adolescence a small world of his own to replace the greater one he could neither feel at home in nor find adequate terms to describe. These limitations have since come to typify a mode made prominent by much of Lowell, Plath, Sexton, and Berryman . . .

The cults of personality and neurosis are all-too-much with us. This is evident, as Haines points out in an interview, in the recent application of show-business techniques in the presentation of poetry to the reading public: it is not at all unusual to see the photograph of the poet in [*American Poetry Review*] take up more space than his or her poems. Consequently, we are, however subconsciously, invited to judge the poet by his or her appearance before we ever get to the poem. One cannot help but wonder, thinking back over the centuries, whether the reading public might not have been put off by the rather harsh, uninviting countenance of Dante, or, more recently, by the indelicate appearance of Amy Lowell.

And, coincidentally, Haines points out the intractable fact that fewer and fewer of our younger poets seem to have read the literature of the past. It is hardly surprising that one finds almost no sense of tradition in so much of the poetry of the last quarter century. There is only the monotonous sameness. The best seem to write descriptive prose. The most write flat reflexive prose of a rather low order. . . .

Another recurring complaint is the absence of a sense of history in our poetry. In the best commentary yet on the poetry of Tomas Transtromer, Haines justly praises the poet's strong historical sense that binds him to the modern European tradition, and says, "It is not a thing we find frequently in North American poetry, though something like it can be found now and then in the poems of Philip Levine, Robert Bly, Denise Levertov, and Hayden Carruth. . . ." And while one may leap to include Gary Snyder and Kenneth Rexroth to this brief list of exceptions (or the one or two others one may suddenly remember), the exception remains just that. . . .

For a poet, for any active intelligence whatever, the way to find meaning, and thus engagement, lies in establishing connections with the drift of human history. In **"Homage to the Chinese,"** Haines places himself on the Tanana River in the late fifties, and begins to reveal some very important, and unlikely, influences. He felt "disengaged" and isolated from current literature. And then came a copy of Kenneth Rexroth's *One Hundred Poems from the Chinese.* "I began reading the Chinese poems in the evenings," he says, "in time spared from fishing and cutting wood. The poems seemed to speak for something in my own life, as I sat reading late by lamp or candle in the small cabin I kept on Tenderfoot Creek, an old, reclaimed camp with a dirt floor and mossy roof-poles."

Rexroth's translations from the Chinese, along with those of Robert Payne and Ezra Pound, filled Haines with a sense of "renewal and rediscovery." He wrote poems again, "direct (and weak) imitations of Chinese poems" that he would come to see as "trials." Later, he would add the powerful influences of Machado and Trakl. Finally, we begin to glimpse the years and years of study and deliberation that preceded the calm, easy grace of the Haines style of *Winter News* and *The Stone Harp:* the T'ang poets, especially Tu Fu, the early 20th Century poems of Georg Trakl, the poems of Machado, Stevens, Williams, the poems of Transtromer and Milosz. Haines's essays on poetry are superb. His is a very serious sensibility that manages not to become weighty or burdensome, that refuses intractable formulae. His evaluations of the work of other poets are generous without becoming weakened by their generosity. And his essay on the poetry of Robert Bly may well be the best critical writing on Bly ever.

And when Haines talks about "place" and poetry, "place" and the development of sensibility, he reverses the cliche to say, "a place of sense." A sense of place is one of the rarest events in modern North American poetry. Most often, it is simply a shopping list of *things* inserted into a short lyric by a shallow imagination, it is the poet's version of the traveler's postcard from a literary cruise through the country. Haines makes connections between the imagination and the "real world" that lead toward an ever-expanding "place of sense." . . .

Living Off the Country is a compelling book. . . . [We] are left with the prose of one of our best poets, only to find that his prose, his critical faculties, and his perception of the *use* of poetry are all as finely tuned as his ear for the line in speech. As he says, "There is nothing so useful in art as a vital form." *Living Off the Country* is cold, crisp, and clear like the air following a week of winter snow.

Sam Hamill, in a review of "Living off the Country," in The American Book Review, Vol. 5, No. 5, July-August, 1983, p. 16.

ROBERT HEDIN

News From The Glacier brings together 127 poems selected from five of Haines's previously published collections: *Winter News* (1966), *Stone Harp* (1971), *Cicada* (1980), *Twenty Poems* (1971) and *In A Dusty Light* (1977).

Typically these poems are short, the language relatively simple. As a poet Haines is distrustful of conceptual language; consequently he never strays far from the many elemental sources—the stones, the cold, the snow—to which he has deep allegiance. His interest lies with the brief epiphanal moment when an experience reveals its shadow world where our lives link up with myth, ritual, and dream. And what we get are glimpses of our earlier selves when we were nothing but "grass people" standing "patient and obedient" to the natural cycles, when the only shelter was a "drafty cave . . . walled with visions," when the rituals of hunting and wandering meant more than escapes from the weekly grinds of the office.

Perhaps the most striking quality of these poems is their haunting silence. **"Fairbanks Under the Solstice"** is a typical example. . . . Despite its direct and matter-of-fact beginning, this poem drops us into a vision of austere beauty. It is as if Haines is purposely quieting the world around him in order to reveal what he calls, the "inspired glimpse into the other." It should be said too that throughout *News From The Glacier* Haines takes on the role of one of these "ghostly newsboys." And some of what he delivers hardly bolsters the spirit.

Speaking from a world stripped of its technological apparatus and void for the most part of any community other than the most elemental, Haines's vision is as stern and as uncompromising as the Alaskan landscape. The poems come as terse reminders of the gross injustice we have done to the land, our cultural dreams, and by extension to ourselves. Look at the conclusion to **"Rolling Back"**:

> Everything we have known for so long,
> a house at ease, a calm street
> to walk on, and a sunset
> in which the fire means us no harm . . .
>
> Rolling back from the blocked summit
> like an uncoupled train
> with no hand on the brake,
> gathering speed in the dark
> on the mountain grade.

In **"Driving Through Oregon,"** the poet carries on a dialogue with our cultural past and, in the course of the exchange, dismantles many of our country's myths and illusions—Whitman's declarations of the Open Road being one. (pp. 250-51)

In many ways this collection is a sustained longing for home and reconciliation—with ourselves and our native ground. This alone is sufficient to provide necessary warmth to an otherwise cold vision. If there is a general movement to this book, it is toward the inseparability of subject and object, land and speaker, until it can be said that Haines fulfills William Carlos Williams's dream to "reconcile the people and the stones."

Not every poem in this collection is first-rate. Some, such as **"The Rain Glass"** and **"The Mirror,"** are so steeped in particulars that they are unable to expand out of their original groundwork of imagery. In others such as **"In the Middle of America"** Haines bails out too quickly with summarizing images that fail to bring the poems to either their rightful conclusions or their rightful points of departure. At their best, however, the poems of *News From The Glacier*—so quiet and dignified, so distilled to their purest moment—reach the essential clarity that we ask of our best literature. Under their deep resonant voice, the poetic terrain changes, gradually and with assuredness, toward self-scrutiny and the honest governing of the self. (pp. 251 52)

Robert Hedin, in a review of "News from the Glacier," in Western American Literature, *Vol. XVIII, No. 3, November, 1983, pp. 250-52.*

ROBERT McDOWELL

Long ago the poet, critic, and literary journalist Donald Hall decided to do something about the fashionable assumption that his generation lacked opinions. He did not agree, though he realized that opinions were not frequently expressed in the traditional form of the essay. . . . [Such essays] were found in the pages of miscellaneous little magazines in the form of interviews, tossed-off reviews, and casual notes. As years and magazines passed away, these opinions settled into the dusty anonymity of bookshelves. Hall's idea was to retrieve these documents, bring them out of the archives and make them available to a larger audience.

What he did with this idea is a triumph of small press production and courageous editing, and this triumph vindicates, in some ways, the generation in question.

Hall went to work lining up poets who agreed to collect their essays, interviews, reviews, recollections—their critical documents—in individual volumes which together would constitute a series. After failing to sell the series proposal to a large New York publisher, he approached the press at The University of Michigan.

Today there are twenty-one volumes in the Poets on Poetry series with more planned. (p. 507)

Living Off the Country opens with six pieces focusing on John Haines's homesteading experiences in Alaska. As a group they convey the impression that we are in the presence of a complete citizen; poetry is one of many essential activities in a full and responsible life. This practical awareness forms the basis of all Haines's literary judgments. It distinguishes his opinions from those of the professional opinion-grinder and makes us yearn for a literary environment where more voices like his were possible. Instead, we exist in a world in which "poets seem too much centered on themselves. Not in a deeply inward way, for that takes the individual away from his everyday self. But as people who are inwardly bored, for whom the outside world of nature and humanity, the great landscape which includes everything, is of no more than slight interest . . . The larger thing is missing, the message, the tale to tell, the personal story of one touched by God or Fate."

In nine pieces ranging from notes on the poet's vocation to book reviews to letters to the editor, Haines celebrates the "separate and perceiving" vision of a poet like Jeffers, laments our lack of regard for the past and the sterile character of much of his generation: "One notices how few actual people there are in contemporary poems; only the poet and his personality seem capable of life."

Haines repeatedly stresses the importance of *place* and the "conviction of circumstance" in poetry, and he concludes this austere volume with twenty-five priceless pages of autobiography. Everything in this book will act as a balm relieving the itch of self-satisfaction. Because Haines is by no means a "mainstream" poet, his book might be overlooked by many. Nevertheless, it is *the* sleeper in the series. (p. 509)

Robert McDowell, "The Mum Generation Was Always Talking," in The Hudson Review, *Vol. XXXVIII, No. 3, Autumn, 1985, pp. 507-19.*

DAVID MURRAY

To the question "Why on earth would anyone want to live in the wilderness?" John Haines provides a lyrical answer in this short book of essays about life in Alaska [*Stories We Listened To*]. His is not the ooh-and-ah prose of travel writing, or the macho rhythm of outdoor magazines or even the Linnaean detail of nature books. Rather, Mr. Haines, a poet-homesteader who worked and wrote for 15 years in the bush, sets his scenes and tells his stories from the point of view of someone who loves his demanding environment deeply but still is somewhat in awe of what it can do. He has the eye of an Audubon and the style of a Thoreau. He describes an encounter with a grizzly bear in terms that graphically communicate his barely controlled fear. . . . But, as if fearful that we will think him sentimental, he goes on to describe the killing and dressing-out of a moose, and in so doing gives us a peep into the ecological cycles of death and rebirth. . . . In Mr. Haines's wilderness, the seeker will find "a freshness denied him in the place he came from." This wondrous land is lighted by a major talent telling his stories in a haunting minor key.

> *David Murray, in a review of "Stories We Listened To," in* The New York Times Book Review, *March 29, 1987, p. 23.*

ROBERT HEDIN

On one level, *Stories We Listened To* tells of living off the land, of the passing of seasons, of the rituals of hunting and fishing. Haines repeatedly strikes a dark and resonant chord about what it means to live in the heartland of one of North America's last great wildernesses. In the process, he displays a familiarity with the natural world that few writers since John Muir have achieved and one that could only come from having lived in an area for a long period of time.

On another level, however, it is a book of recovery and reconciliation. Though set almost exclusively in the interior of Alaska, in and around the Tanana River valley, it goes well beyond its local geography and history to rescue the mysterious and oftentimes terrifying intimacy that comes about when the old psychic links between man and the natural world are re-established. The result is a book both haunting and memorable, one that ultimately devotes itself to the retrieval of what William Carlos Williams called "the ground sense necessary."

The real character in *Stories We Listened To* is the land, the extensive and peculiar geography of the north. It can be felt in Haines's relentless and exacting imagery of the cold, the snow, and the wind—a land so stubborn that it is oftentimes broodingly indifferent to anything human. We are constantly reminded that we are part of a larger, more significant context than our daily routines suggest—one defined by seasonal turnings and the yearly migrations of animals. *Stories We Listened To* takes a strong moral stance against the often mindless excitation of our technological age. Like many writers before him, Haines reminds us again that with the death of the wilderness comes the death of something in us, a psychic link to our original home ground.

Beneath all the snow and the cold of these essays lies the vision of a world locked in natural unity, one so fully integrated that little or no distinction exists between subject and object, land and speaker. Through Haines's quiet and unpretentious prose, we are able to look into the original grandeur and mystery that has been lost to us since the frontier closed and our culture turned toward industrialism and urbanization. (pp. 74-5)

> *Robert Hedin, in a review of "Stories We Listened To," in* Western American Literature, *Vol. XXIII, No. 4, May, 1988, pp. 74-5.*

David Hare

1947-

English dramatist, scriptwriter, and filmmaker.

Hare is a leading figure among a group of English play-wrights who gained recognition during the 1970s for works that depict the social and political ills of contemporary Britain. Often focusing upon moral, ethical, and political issues and choices faced by characters as they pursue careers, romance, and personal goals, Hare has employed varied settings and scenarios that serve as microcosms of post-World War II English society. Frequently, his characters represent or struggle against ineffectual or corrupt authority figures, and they encounter deceit, self-interest, and greed in their relationships. Blending farce, witty dialogue, and cinematic techniques, including abrupt transitions of place and time, Hare has used such forms as epic theater, the musical, and character studies to satirize idealistic and progressive-minded individuals as well as members of the existing social order. Colin Ludlow stated: "[Hare's] plays are refreshingly understated for modern political and social drama. They cannot be reduced to a simple message, for his characters are not manipulated simply to provide a thesis. The power of his work is to provoke thought and disturb complacency."

During the late 1960s, Hare was a founding member of the Portable Theatre, a forum for experimental drama that staged original plays in such unusual sites as storefronts and gymnasiums. Several playwrights who established their reputations in the early 1970s, including Howard Brenton, Trevor Griffiths, Stephen Poliakoff, and Howard Barker, were associated with this group and are frequently categorized as Fringe Playwrights, since their early works were staged in small London theaters and generally expressed radical views. By the mid-1970s, these writers were connected with London's National Theatre, receiving government funding and contributing controversial and commercially successful works, several of which were directed by Hare. Hare has collaborated on plays with these writers, most notably with Howard Brenton. Hare and Brenton cowrote *Brassneck* (1973), which explores local government corruption as well as criminal behavior that derives from materialism, and *Pravda* (1985), a comic farce that reproaches contemporary journalism. In *Pravda*, a ruthless, wealthy man acquires major London newspapers and proceeds to compromise journalistic ethics. He promotes such practices as sensationalism, slanted editorializing in favor of particular groups, and trendy, style-oriented formats that emphasize superficial coverage rather than in-depth reporting, all of which prove popular and financially successful and are met with varying responses by the other characters. While some critics regarded *Pravda* as a humorous and poignant indictment of the journalism industry, others found the presentation exaggerated and ultimately ineffective.

Critical reception to Hare's work is often contingent upon whether or not commentators believe the settings and characters accurately reflect the larger social problems they suggestively illustrate. In *Slag* (1970), for example, the decline of a private school is generally interpreted as representing the decay of English society. Three female teachers challenge the

school's traditions and leadership, but their revolutionary struggles accomplish nothing. *The Great Exhibition* (1972) concentrates on an isolated and suspicious socialist Member of Parliament who entered politics for dubious reasons. One of several works in which Hare examines the relationship between theater and reality, this play exposes the shallowness of the politician while emphasizing his ability to perform roles and manipulate appearances. In *Knuckle* (1974), Hare parodies the thriller genre as practiced by Raymond Chandler by depicting a man who investigates the disappearance of his sister, falls in love, and encounters the seamier elements of society. The play suggests that greed, lack of ethics, violence, and materialistic lifestyles are corrupting influences of capitalism that gradually disillusion idealistic individuals. *Teeth 'n' Smiles* (1975) is set at a college around the final performance of a rock 'n' roll band that has been undermined by alcohol and drugs, a manipulative agent, and failed relationships. According to critics, the band represents the hopes of 1960s popular music as a force for social change, and the college audience serves as a model for privileged members of society. Both groups are overcome by their own excesses.

Hare wrote three plays during the mid-1970s that were collected in *The History Plays: 'Fanshen,' 'Plenty,' and 'Licking Hitler.' Fanshen* (1975), which is based on William Hinton's book, *Fanshen: A Documentary of Revolution in a Chinese Village,* centers upon the transformation of a feudal-like community to a collective based on socialist ideals. One of Hare's most optimistic works, *Fanshen* presents social and political groups working together for positive change. The title of *Plenty* (1978) comments ironically on post-World War II Britain, which, according to Hare, entertained illusions of prosperity and abundance. In this work, a woman who experienced great dangers during the war while working for the French resistance attempts to assimilate into an ordinary postwar lifestyle but experiences boredom, despair, and a mental breakdown. While *Plenty* is generally considered Hare's most important work, it received mixed reactions from critics, some of whom question whether the woman's breakdown results from personal or social problems. John Simon queried: "Was postwar England totally whacked out, or was it the heroine who was bonkers? Or were they both crazy?" *Licking Hitler* (1978) is a teleplay concerning a group that produced propagandistic radio broadcasts during World War II from an English estate with intentions of demoralizing German troops. Deceit in public and private relationships are among the themes examined in this work.

Among Hare's later plays, *A Map of the World* (1983) is set during a United Nations conference in Bombay, India that addresses poverty and injustice in the Third World. This play examines the pursuit of truth in art and journalism, primarily through conflicts between a sardonically cynical Indian novelist and an idealistic British journalist. A film concerning the conference is presented during this play, showing how actual occurrences can be recreated through various media to achieve specific political, commercial, and artistic purposes. Hare's abiding interest in individuals whose values are profoundly influenced by the social and political systems in which they live is evidenced in his two one-act plays, *Bay at Nice* and *Wrecked Eggs* (1986). The former drama, set in the Soviet Union in 1956, concerns an art aficionado who acts rigidly and unresponsive in her personal relationships. *Wrecked Eggs,* which takes place during a divorce party for two young urban professionals, comments upon materialism and the "success ethic" in America of the 1980s. Michael Billington noted: "Like most of Hare's plays, these two are about the attempts to salvage a personal morality from an immoral system."

The Secret Rapture (1988) depicts personal and professional conflicts between two sisters, one a junior Tory Minister, the other a small business owner. Love, good and evil in human behavior, the relationship between political and personal values, and Christian beliefs concerning death, martyrdom, and redemption are among the motifs explored in the play. Douglas Kennedy stated: "*The Secret Rapture* is a stunning example of complex political argument taking place on the intimate battleground of tangled, inter-familial relationships. . . . It leaves one cautiously optimistic about the future of a theatre which still challenges, argues, and provokes—in short, a theatre which is bracingly political." While *The Secret Rapture* was a popular and critical success in London, the New York production closed after a few performances. A controversy erupted when Hare took issue with a negative review of the play by *New York Times* drama critic Frank Rich; Hare opined that Rich's review was ascerbic and mean-spirited. Rich defended his style and intentions, and the dramatist and critic presented their views in several pieces printed in the *Times.* The fray also drew attention in such periodicals as *The Village Voice, Variety, 7 Days,* and *Newsweek.*

(See also, *CLC,* Vol. 29; *Contemporary Authors,* Vols. 97-100; and *Dictionary of Literary Biography,* Vol. 13.)

MICHAEL RATCLIFFE

'Editorial freedom,' murmurs the Press tycoon Lambert Le Roux to his sacked protégé Andrew May as if evoking some lost garden of Eden in Howard Brenton and David Hare's brilliant new comedy [*Pravda*]. 'You never used it when you had it. It is fast gone. Why should you deserve freedom any more?' What we deserve if we are not prepared to defend what we have is the major theme of the play.

For *Pravda* is not merely about a Fleet Street in which the clenched fists of independence have slackened into the limp shrug of the balanced view; it honours a rich tradition of monster-theatre in which Lucifer is superstitiously believed to have been reborn; the resistible rise of Lambert Le Roux is a parody of the Second Coming. Like *Richard III* and *The Jew of Malta,* *Pravda* demonstrates the skill with which ruthlessness, energy and brute wit contrive to make all opposition look pathetic, self-seeking and absurd.

Lambert is a South African businessman who believes only in making money and achieving success. He has diversified into newspapers from sportswear, acquiring first *The Tide,* a tabloid, then *The Victory,* a national institution losing one million pounds a week. (They exaggerate? Very well, they exaggerate.) His progress goes virtually unchecked. 'I come to this country,' he tells Andrew in the same climactic scene during a grouse shoot on a Yorkshire moor, 'to organise your lives. I do nothing. People fall before me as if they had been waiting. . . . Sell their property, emigrate, betray their friends even before I ask them. Give in.'

Only Andrew, as he is raised from decent provincial obscurity to prize-winning eminence at *The Victory,* followed immediately by the sack, guerrilla warfare from without and final humiliating submission, offers much resistance, but Andrew lacks the urge to kill. 'You should hit a man in the face to make his face disappear,' Lambert reminds him. 'In England you can never fight because you do not know what to believe.' Why should the Press be expected to tell the truth? Nobody else does.

One by one, the old believers fall or are bought off: a joke bishop, an absent ornithologist, a venial MP, a printer with implausibly fancy views on editorial quality, dozens of scared hacks. . . .

All this is good knockabout stuff and the play contains many wonderfully funny lines. Its great weakness is that those who are given a chance to counter the power and force of Lambert's arguments with more than allusive waffle or frustrated rage are so ineffective. Andrew is a sketch.

His wife Rebecca exemplifies the frequently preferred view of male English dramatists that a woman's instinct can be relied on to prescribe the correct moral course in any tricky situation but that a man's refusal to take it is the more interesting subject to pursue; this is disappointing from the authors of *Weapons of Happiness* (Brenton), ***Licking Hitler*** and ***Plenty*** (Hare). Men like Lambert must be fought not with foolish conspiracy, says Rebecca, but with ideas. What ideas? They will have to be pretty good ones to clobber a man out to destroy the power of the argued word as fast as Lambert Le Roux.

That Brenton and Hare are more interested in Lambert's destructive energy than in any sort of debate to match, certainly makes for a sulphurous and crackling entertainment. . . .

Michael Ratcliffe, "Life Under Lambert Le Roux," in The Observer, May 5, 1985, p. 23.

MICHAEL DAVIE

When it became known that two formidable marksmen-playwrights, Howard Brenton and David Hare, had Fleet Street in their sights, it looked as if at last Fleet Street was going to be brought down. Now art was going to hit a target barely touched by fusillades from politically motivated members of the National Union of Journalists, authoritarian politicians and discontented lecturers in media studies at provincial polytechnics.

Alas, **Pravda: A Fleet Street Comedy** is a show that any journalist—even the editors of the *Sun* and *The Times,* whose papers, lightly disguised as *Tide* and *Victory,* are prominent in the play—could recommend to his aunts without a second's misgiving.

The comedy is certainly there, as advertised, especially in the first half, which contains many good jokes and one-liners. It is a funny idea that a newspaper proprietor should first sell his paper and only then inform his assembled staff that he is beginning a "process of consultation" to ascertain their wishes. "Not everyone is fired", he says. "It's not as simple as that." The play is brilliantly staged, with newsrooms looking like newsrooms, and journalists, for once, looking and even sounding like journalists. [The dominant character is Le Roux,] a South African outsider-tycoon who buys first a tabloid and then the organ of the Establishment. . . . Politician, gangster boss, police chief, company chairman—Le Roux behaves like all of these, so that through him the authors do occasionally approach their stated purpose, which is to illuminate the workings of power in general and of Fleet Street in particular. . . .

The action, a succession of short scenes, resembles a series of clever revue sketches put on in a university. The authors perhaps did too much research; they are too up-to-the-minute. As at a university revue, the audience is distracted by allusion-spotting. . . .

The high-jinks on stage, and the fun that all concerned must have had in putting on the show, obstruct any substantial intellectual examination of the nature of the press, as at present owned and conducted. The play scores a few flesh-wounds about the way sub-editing can transform a story, about the reluctance of papers to correct mistakes, about the lobby system, and about the way journalists can avoid thinking about substance by becoming obsessed with lay-out. But the jabs and jokes are not armour-piercing.

The point being made about power is not so much that a powerful man forces others to do his will as that others prostrate themselves before him. . . . The climactic scene puts an editor on his knees before Le Roux. Earlier, he has been too weak to publish a leaked document that proves the Minister of Defence is a liar. He becomes editor of another paper and

exposes the misdeeds of Le Roux. But this information is false and has been planted by Le Roux himself, who issues a libel writ. The editor, outwitted and defeated is destroyed.

All this is highly implausible. Why did not the editor, instead of falling to his knees, return to his office and write the story of the way the misinformation had been planted by Le Roux's right-hand man? The editor had four witnesses. Even under British libel laws, no jury would have found for Le Roux.

The play's central charge against newspapers appears to be that they pretend, like *Pravda,* to be about truth, but in practice have no connection with truth. "Nothing can be said through these things", exclaims the editor's idealistic wife, as she scrumples up newspapers in fury and despair. It was she who got hold of the leaked document that her husband failed to publish. Like many attacks on Fleet Street, this speech is based on the proposition that somehow, despite appearances to the contrary, vital political information in Britain is consistently suppressed by a conspiracy that includes newspapers. Yet even in the play the bullet misses the target by a mile, since the editor's wife takes the document to another paper, which publishes it.

Michael Davie, "Urban Ire," in The Times Literary Supplement, No. 4285, May 17, 1985, p. 551.

WILLIAM A. HENRY, III

Reporters have delighted in seeing themselves depicted as figures of quixotic integrity in plays ranging from the Broadway musical *Woman of the Year* to Tom Stoppard's rueful tragicomedy *Night and Day.* But the current wave of antipress feeling in the U.S. may have spread to Britain as well. Audiences at London's National Theater, which in 1972 staged an acclaimed revival of *The Front Page,* are cheering now for **Pravda,** a coruscating, comic attack on Fleet Street that portrays reporters as timid, trivial and truckling and that describes a newspaper as "the foundry of lies." . . .

Unlike American attacks on the press, which tend to come from the right and assail reporters as too skeptical toward government, **Pravda** lambastes London's journalists from the left, as tame toadies of deceitful politicians. The handful of reporters in the play who show glimmers of decency are hounded out of the trade or nullified by their editors or derailed by their own greed and ambition. In the climax of the plot, the forces of virtue, somewhat tarnished themselves, are gulled into printing a libel that undoes their chances of stopping an evil publisher. Like too many journalists, these dubious heroes simply believe what people tell them and thus are easily misled.

The malign publisher, Lambert Le Roux, is the captivating antihero of the piece. By cunning, he takes over both a populist tabloid and a stately, ultra-upperbrow daily. The character has been assumed by many people in Britain to be a burlesque of Australian Press Lord Rupert Murdoch. . . .

Whatever real-world parallels the playwrights may have had in mind for this shrewd, calculatedly savage entrepreneur, Le Roux has a life of his own, and on the grand scale. . . . [He] is a comic creation as monstrously beguiling as Tartuffe. He shares with Molière's sham holy man the gift of ever renewed plausibility. Time and again, just as the audience is ready to withdraw its sympathy in disgust, Le Roux exposes the hypocrisies of opponents so tellingly that he becomes persuasive anew. When outraged employees confront him, his retort is blunt and seemingly unanswerable: If an unfettered press is crucial to a free society, then why have Fleet Street journalists squandered their energies on look-alike rags compounded of crime, cleavage, gossip about royalty and page upon page of sports?

In that moment, it becomes clear that *Pravda* is not merely lamenting the newspapers that are but pining for newspapers that might be. The play is not foremost a preachment, however, but a superb high-energy entertainment, with a cast of 33, lavishly detailed sets, throbbing music and an urgent, propulsive style set by Co-Author Hare, who directed. It recalls the morally assertive best of warmhearted Broadway satires like *The Solid Gold Cadillac* in every regard save one: *Pravda* does not and, given its bitter convictions, could not have a happy ending.

> *William A. Henry III, "Savaging the 'Foundry of Lies'," in* Time, *New York, Vol. 125, No. 23, June 10, 1985, p. 81.*

HERB GREER

When it comes to sending up journalism in the theatre, you had better know your stuff. The American classic *The Front Page,* based upon the shark-pool ambiance of 1920s popular newspapers, was a product of playwrights who did know their stuff—and not just theatrically. They had first-hand experience of the people and the business they were writing about. . . .

The sins of the press are still a public commonplace, which means that our playwrights in London have naturally got around to taking them up. John Osborne wrote the unfortunate *World of Paul Slickey,* and recent plays by Tom Stoppard (*Night and Day*) and Michael Frayn (*Clouds, Alphabetical Order*) have dealt more successfully with journalism. All these playwrights worked as journalists, so Osborne's special failure may have been due to a slight oversupply of caricature and bile.

This salutary warning was not taken in by David Hare and Howard Brenton. Their *Pravda* "play"—it is actually more of a three-hour undergraduate sketch—shows very little (if any) experience or direct knowledge of journalism. Instead the authors have evidently relied on hearsay from Fleet Street (very dangerous), on what they have selected from reading the newspapers (even more dangerous), and on a collection of coarse and shallow bromides which have become the staple fare of media chat about the press and so-called Press Barons or Fleet Street Lords. On top of these disadvantages, the authors suffer from a virulent strain of what Lenin, with no patience for puerility, called infantile leftism. (p. 36)

For some time before it opened, *Pravda* was given a deal of hype by the British press and other media. At one point this extended to an obsequious *Observer* colour-magazine interview with Hare, in which this much-praised playwright held forth on his motives for committing *Pravda* to paper and then to the stage. "I found", he said, "that the big social plays I want to see on the English stage don't exist. Writers seem to have become ghettoised, and make no claim on a large audience. . . ." On these extraordinary assumptions (has Hare never set foot inside the various houses of, say, the Royal Shakespeare Company?) he and Howard Brenton wrote what the enthusiastic interviewer called "a coruscating satire on Fleet Street." The title stems from Hare's conviction that "modern British newspapers are little more than government organs. In fact, it's really about the political climate, where competition reigns unchecked. And about how people *want* evil—a wonderful theme for a play. . . ."

The contempt for people and the suggestion that political competition should in some way be checked accord nicely with Hare's recipe for the press, which I will come to in a moment. But first the play: *Pravda* shows more signs of Brenton's comic-strip technique than of Hare's penchant for suburban *angst* and second-hand theorising. It is a clod-hopping attempt to satirise Rupert Murdoch (thinly disguised as a South African corporate psychopath) and his takeover of *The Times.* . . . As in most radical-chic agitprop, the villain is omnipotent and everyone else is totally helpless. This puts a severe strain on the rest of the cast, who try to compensate for their watery parts in any number of ways: they caper, huff and puff, sneer a lot, run about, mug and grimace, pose furiously, roll on the floor, frown severely, and climb on to furniture and wave their arms. Most of all—apparently with the director's encouragement—they shout. Time and again Hare ranges his actors in a row facing the audience and makes them bellow at the stalls. Alas, for all the gymnastics and noise, the good guys . . . remain a dull pack of posturing ninnies.

The plot-line, barren of conflict and therefore of drama, is devoid of interest. Theatrical moments, when they occur (not often), spring from incidental sketches like Lambert Leroux playing at martial arts in his Japanese garden and costume. Some humour comes out of remarks—mostly by Leroux—which score off the ninnies. There is a strong nudge-wink or *entre nous* element in the play which draws laughter from Hare-Brenton *aficionados* in the audience. A character had only to stand erect and say "I am a journalist" for a knowing guffaw to ripple through the house. Otherwise this effect operates through a display of the above-mentioned bromides, or samples of What Everybody Knows—i.e. Press Barons are awful crypto-fascists who exercise direct, absolute control over everything their papers print, but don't really care about the press, and are mad as hatters anyhow. Their editors are cynical tuft-hunters and don't care about the truth; the ranker-journalists are liars perforce, who may care about the truth but are too corrupt or weak to do anything about it. In short, from top to bottom Fleet Street is (in Beatrice Lillie's old phrase) all of it just rotten to the core. As a *soidisant* satire on Fleet Street and/or journalism, *Pravda* never gets above the level of trite, facile prejudices already flogged to death a generation ago and before, not only in the theatre (by much better men than Hare and Brenton) but in other media, and currently over pints of beer in local pubs.

I found much more of interest in the post-opening public discussion of the play—an event staged at the Olivier Theatre, in which Hare and Brenton talked about *Pravda* and about journalism. Their guest onstage was Donald Trelford, editor of *The Observer*—whose paper bestowed such generous advance praise upon the play. Trelford is an important figure in journalism who could have put the two playwrights and their work into some professional sort of perspective. Instead, he read out a prepared statement, rather flattering to the play, declaring that most reviewers had praised it. Indeed, some had. . . . Trelford's dissertation, later published in part on his paper's editorial page, hinted at the play's superficiality without openly condemning it, and in the spoken version made the astonishing assertion that *Pravda* "raised serious issues" about journalism. He was not very specific about these, but seemed to refer to those old chestnuts about bad barons, cynical editors, sullied truth, and so on.

Actually the play and the discussion did raise serious issues, though not, I think, the ones suggested by Trelford. Really at stake were the authors' qualifications for attempting such a piece, and their prescriptive views on journalism. During the discussion Hare recounted a solemn anecdote about the *Daily Telegraph:* a lady journalist's front-page report on China (which pleased Hare) clashed with an editorial inside the paper (which did not please Hare). He urged the lady to agitate for a Hare-approved change in the paper so that editorials would at least have to agree with the reportage. Her comment was, "That way madness lies. . . ." A more acute reply would have noted that a Stalinoid uniformity also lies that way, for that surely is the real implication of Hare's complaint. This anecdote reflected a bitter scene in the play, in which a cynical editor altered a left-slanted story to tilt it the other way, making it clear that Hare and Brenton do not object to bending news as such—only to news that is not warped the way they want to warp it . . . to wit, against the Police, the present Government, and other *bêtes noires* of the Left. After the anecdote an amusing question, unasked by Trelford or the discussants, hung in the air: the play's "evil" South African magnate is naturally Right-wing. But suppose, just suppose that this secular pantocrator should change his mind and decide to propagandise the Leftist cause of Messrs Hare and Brenton, and even to use his power and resources to back it politically? (Such things have happened.) Would they still disapprove of his dictatorial style? Or would they be out there with their clenched fists raised, cheering with the rest of the true believers?

There is a short scene in *Pravda* which brings a print-union official onstage to justify the notoriously exorbitant pay-rolls of print-workers in Fleet Street. If the paper is going to print "shit"—so his argument goes—then why shouldn't working men make a couple of thousand a week out of it? Now, Hare and Brenton blame the Fleet Street Barons for all these sins. Are they really unaware that union greed and workfloor malpractices make it impossible for anyone but multimillionaire "barons" to own a newspaper in Fleet Street? Had they ever stumbled across the point during their "research"? The title of *Pravda* fits their play just a little bit better than Hare and Brenton may have intended. (pp. 37-8)

However, the most fundamental issue raised by *Pravda* was not the Left twists and turns of the authors, nor even that a great deal of public money (something like £100,000) was spent to produce a chunk of knee-jerk revolutionary agitprop. (This sometimes happens at the Royal Shakespeare Company and does not seem to have affected the quality of its good work.) The basic question is whether a superficial, ill-informed and entirely sophomoric piece of theatrical *dreck* should be dressed up as major work, and then given the full great-playwright treatment by the National Theatre of Britain. (p. 38)

> *Herb Greer, "A Play about the Press," in* Encounter, *Vol. LXV, No. 3, September-October, 1985, pp. 36-8.*

BERNARD LEVIN

It is a matter of much more than theatrical interest that *Pravda,* the play by David Hare and Howard Brenton at the National Theatre, is a very considerable popular hit. The interest that it has aroused is, among other things, a reflection of our national obsession with newspapers, and in particular our attitude, ambivalent to the verge of schizophrenia, of simultaneous fascination and revulsion at the antics of the mass-circulation ones, with their gossip columns, their trivialities and their very remarkable ability to give the most detailed and colourful accounts of things that never happened.

We live in a time when both the popular hatred of journalists and the avidity with which the worst of them are read have never been more intense, and a play which set out to analyse and depict this astonishing state of affairs, a mass addiction to a drug which is simultaneously denounced by its users as poison, would have been, if well done, a valuable contribution to the continuing debate on the standards and effect of "the media". So would a play which looked into the ambitions, power and ethics of the new breed of newspaper proprietors—Murdoch, Maxwell, Rowland. So, for that matter, would an insider's newspaper-play as entertainingly cynical as *The Front Page.*

But *Pravda* is none of these things. Nor is it anything else that might, while we are wrestling with the paradox of our newspapers, move us, as we contemplate them, the width of half a column of type closer to understanding, scepticism, fear, tolerance, anger, resignation or contempt. It is an illiterate strip-cartoon, cruder by far than the worst excesses of any newspaper possessed of photographs depicting a trouserless vicar in the company of the chief bellringer's wife. . . .

Pravda is the story of how a wicked newspaper proprietor corrupts and destroys newspapers and journalists alike. The character is intended to make the audience think of Mr Rupert Murdoch, and the central story is likewise reminiscent of his purchase of *The Times;* I like to envisage the moment when, thinking that it might be best not to make "Lambert Le Roux" an Australian. Hare and Brenton made him a South African, and sat back hugging themselves with admiration of their own brilliance.

Come; let us speak with unforked tongue. Hare and Brenton are guilty of every one of the sins and crimes they attribute to journalists, newspapers and newspaper-proprietors.

Is there bad writing, full of clichés, in newspapers? There is, there is; much of it, indeed, is as bad as *Pravda.* . . .

Or is much of the writing in newspapers childish, an insult to the intelligence of their readers? Hand on heart, I cannot deny it. But hear the rebukers. The last editor but one of *The Times* was William Rees-Mogg; the deputy to Harold Evans, Rees-Mogg's successor, was Charles Douglas-Home, who is the present editor; in the play the outgoing editor of *The Victory* is called Elliot Fruit-Norton and his deputy Cliveden Whicker-Baskett. (And I swear that these names are genuinely representative of the level of the play's wit and sophistication.)

Much journalism is inaccurate, is it not? Verily. But not as inaccurate as this play depicting it.

Hare and Brenton talk about the "research" that went into the play; there is no evidence that they have done any research into journalism at all other than reading Arnold

Wesker's silly and self-serving book on the subject. They cannot construct a plausible parody of the mass-circulation papers' headlines, though they have no fewer than *thirty-five* shots at it.

But there is more to come. The climax of the story concerns evidence, passed to the one man who has really defied Le Roux, which shows the monster to have been guilty of shameful and criminal behaviour. His opponent publishes it, whereupon, in the most ridiculous and bathetic scene of the play, Le Roux reveals that it was all false, deliberately planted by Le Roux's henchman on the man he wants to destroy. The published revelations are now seen to be undefendable libels, and Le Roux's adversary is served with the fatal writ. But there were witnesses—*four* of them—to the original planting of the fraudulent charges; not only would Le Roux never have been able to get the case on its feet, he could have been prosecuted for attempting to pervert the course of justice if he had tried to.

It is inconceivable that Hare and Brenton failed to notice this. But they could not be bothered—because they did not need to be bothered—to tear up the scene and find a way of making their play work. . . . [Brenton and Hare] knew they could do what they liked with the National Theatre; much more significant, *they knew they could do what they liked with the audiences,* who are proving them right as they greet every packed performance with resounding applause.

For the audiences are not composed of those who read *The Sun, The Mirror* or *The Star.* They are the soft underbelly of the middle classes, and Hare and Brenton are mirrors to them all. Beneath the trash of *Pravda* there runs a darker stream, composed of hatred not for journalism's excesses, but for the very idea of the clash of opinions and hucksters in the marketplace, for a world in which millions want to look at pictures of pretty girls with no clothes on, and millions to read of the exploits of a randy Duke, and millions to play newspaper Bingo in the hope of riches.

If only the masses were ours to command! We would soon stop them eating things that are bad for them, and smoking and drinking things that are worse for them, and viewing things that are worse still for them, and reading things that are worst of all for them. . . .

I forget who said that the only result of spitting into the wind is an eyeful of spit. The audiences will continue to throng to the National Theatre to see *Pravda,* and the authors will wax rich on their royalties. And why shouldn't they? Certainly I can have no objection to their success; they have created a genuinely popular entertainment, and are entitled to ignore those, more ideologically pure, who will condemn them for selling their wares to the infidel, as the NT was criticized for staging, and—worse—succeeding with, *Guys and Dolls.*

Besides, they are serving their audiences as faithfully as the popular newspapers serve their readers. For where those give breasts, these offer reassurance; where the one provides titillation, the other makes a gift of flattery; where the ungodly spread Bingo, the righteous lay down a soft carpet of mutual admiration.

I cannot pretend that the choice is a particularly comfortable one, but at least it is not unclear. I have been a journalist for more than 30 years, and will probably die still exercising my inky trade. In the years of my servitude, I have seen newspapers do things that shamed not only my profession but my very country. But never yet did I read a newspaper story that was simultaneously as ignorant, erroneous, unchecked, ill-written and reckless as *Pravda.* And even if I had, it would not have lasted for three hours.

Bernard Levin, "The Truth about This Play," in
The Times, *London, October 29, 1985, p. 16.*

MOIRA HODGSON

[*Les Misérables,* a hit play in London,] is due in New York City in the fall. It is certain to be a hit.

I wish we could get . . . *Pravda,* a play by Howard Brenton and David Hare, instead. *Pravda* is a hilarious satire about Fleet Street and what happens when one newspaper after another is bought up by a right-wing South African entrepreneur who manipulates them all to his own end. This will no doubt sound familiar to anyone who has followed the fate of *The Sun,* the *News of the World, The Times* and *The Sunday Times.*

Pravda is a provocative play of clockwork cunning, directed at a brisk pace by David Hare. Sir Stamford Foley the owner of a provincial newspaper, the *Leicester Bystander,* has sold out to Lambert Le Roux, the South African businessman, so that he can buy shares in a racehorse. "Le Roux is of impeccable liberal credentials," Sir Stamford reassures his shocked staff. "So he's black," replies Andrew May, an idealistic young journalist, after a pause. "That's interesting."

Le Roux, who is in fact white, proceeds to take over the *Victory,* a national newspaper reminiscent of *The Times,* firing journalists whenever he appears in the newsroom. "Who wrote this article on Central America?" he asks, grinding a piece of paper to a pulp in his fist and holding the journalists at bay like a bulldog in front of a herd of antelopes. A nervous journalist raises his hand. "You're fired. No gringo should have to read this kind of stuff."

Andrew marries Rebecca, Sir Stamford's daughter, and is appointed editor by Le Roux. Rebecca, who is the only incorruptible character in the play, acts as his conscience. When she produces a compromising government document, he must decide whether to publish it. But Le Roux shows up in the nick of time, angry at having been interrupted over dinner "on the royal train," and fires Andrew. (pp. 26-7)

Andrew is approached by other disgruntled journalists who have fallen under Le Roux's ax, and becomes editor of the independent *Usurper.* "I don't know why they don't have the manhood to shoot me," Le Roux wonders, referring to his departed editors. "They could get me from the street. A point 44 in the back of the neck. But what do they do? They publish books which are all remaindered in Foyles."

Andrew does attempt to take revenge when Eaton Sylvester, Le Roux's smarmy Australian manager, pretends to betray his boss and feeds Andrew malicious lies about him. When Andrew, unaware that they are false, publishes these stories, against Rebecca's advice, he is destroyed. (p. 27)

Moira Hodgson, in a review of "Pravda," in The Nation, *New York, Vol. 243, No. 1, July 5-12, 1986, pp. 26-7.*

VICTORIA RADIN

In keeping with his fondness for foreign climes, David Hare has set these two conversation pieces [*The Bay at Nice* and *Wrecked Eggs*] in Russia and in the USA respectively. The Leningrad of *The Bay at Nice* is dated 1956, the year of the occupation of Hungary and, presumably, the dawn of an era of greater restrictions on personal liberty. *Wrecked Eggs*— the title refers to a character's assessment of her culinary skills but may have something to do with revolutions, hopes and marriages—takes place in New York State in the present, more a condition of mind than a setting, characterised by a denial of the past. In both plays Hare is concerned with countries, and people, who try to obliterate their histories: each links a marital break-up to the erosion of a wider moral order. (p. 30)

Like all of Hare's plays—or, indeed, any work which questions moral standards—[*The Bay at Nice*] is basically a piece about authenticity: what constitutes a true work of art? love? decent work? a valid life? and the author's characteristic urge to stop the action and offer us his well shaped thoughts (love, says Valentina, is 'a bet placed by two shivering tramps at the racetrack') seems more obtrusive than in his larger plays. His heroines, however, are infinitely more appealing and recognisably of humankind. Sophia, Valentina's homely and plodding daughter (conceived in one of those Parisian moments of 'lying around in beds with men in studios' and a thorn in the formerly unfettered maternal flesh ever since), arrives in the hope of enlisting her mother's help in her divorce from her 'model husband of the State'. She introduces Valentina to her new lover, a tall, gentle, aged and improbable suitor who toils on the outskirts of upward mobility for the sanitation department. After many savage utterances on Sophia's person, her amateur and merely 'photographic' painting, her lack of ambition and misapprehensions of love, Valentina most implausibly offers to sell her own flat to pay for her daughter's divorce. Then, alone, she removes the drapes from the painting and, from her expression and her series of happy feints round it (almost a matador's with a bull), we know the picture to be the real thing: a relic, we suppose, of an age of idealism, when personal definitions of freedom and discipline weren't state-controlled.

We also feel public beliefs to be controlling private lives in Reagan's America—or Hare's idea of Reagan's America—in *Wrecked Eggs*. . . . Grace is a disaffected public relations representative, a veteran of many affairs and only slightly fewer abortions. We may recognise her as a descendant of *Plenty*'s Susan Traherne: a rather romantic and non-aligned investigator of the why of things, who earns her living by dirtying her hands in Hare's detested journalism. I would have said that Loelia, one half of the couple whom Grace visits in a posh poolside house along the Hudson River, shares some of Grace's quest, if Hare, who directs these works himself in typically stylised and formal manner, hadn't made [Loelia] a tennis coach who pads about in running shorts and speaks in a soap-opera drawl. (pp. 30-1)

These are hardly blindingly new, or useful, ways to look at Americans, and Hare wastes a lot of time in familiar satire. Loelia is an ex-hippy who used to 'fuck anything in jeans'; she is also a Buddhist who goes to classes in croissant-making at the New School. Robbie has a way with cooking soft-shell crabs and finds death 'very negative'. This weekend they are holding a 'splitting-up party' to mark the 'rite of passage'.

Such is their unlikely life that Grace, an acquaintance of Loelia's for a couple of weeks through the tennis, is the only person to show up. However, in this self-proclaimed 'heretic'. . . Hare has created a person who does tell us a bit about life in New York: young lovers who turn nasty, property developers who want to tear down blocks of 'life' and a cult of personality which never asks, 'Is he right?', but, 'What's he like?' 'Everyone behaves as if everything's normal,' muses Grace.

She could be anyone in a large city anywhere; and I wonder, apart from its vein of satirical possibilities, why Hare chose New York rather than our own London Yuppieland. Yet, in Grace and in Valentina, Hare has been able to find a gentler, less hysterical female embodiment of his own moral quest than he was able to deliver in the heroines of *Plenty* and of *Map of the World,* respectively mad and inane. Though these two plays show him still to be more interested in ideas than in character, I find them much more attractive than those earlier works and, perhaps, evidence of a new direction. (p. 31)

Victoria Radin, "Put Asunder," in New Statesman, *Vol. 112, No. 2896, September 26, 1986, pp. 30-1.*

JULIAN GRAFFY

In a back room of a Leningrad museum in 1956, a mother and her daughter are waiting to see a painting recently bequeathed to the museum which may or may not be by Matisse. An assistant curator brings the painting but the mother, Valentina Nrovka, who had been Matisse's pupil in Paris almost forty years previously, is not yet ready to look at it, and commands that it be stored, draped in a cloth, in a corner, on the floor, against a fire-bucket. In *The Bay at Nice* this fake, this masterpiece, which we the audience will never be allowed to see, presides enigmatically over talk of painting: of painting and enjoyment, of painting and discipline, of painting and the state; but also over talk of personal life, of feelings, and fate. For the daughter, Sophia, wants to leave her successful headmaster husband for a new lover, Peter Linitsky. . . .

The history of Russia in the twentieth century is alluded to in *The Bay at Nice.* The characters speak of the emigration to Paris in the 1920s, of the Party and of socialist realism. These questions are not obtrusively dwelt upon, however; Hare's concerns transcend his context, and his eloquence and wit provide an absorbing variation. . . .

In a weekend cottage in Rhinebeck, New York State, Robbie and Loelia are having a "splitting-up party" after ten years of marriage. In *Wrecked Eggs* the talk is of sex, money, food, possessions, success—as good, as much and as often as possible. The talk is also more about America and the absurdity of foreigners, a reminder of Hare's earlier metaphorizings of the individual into the national.

Parallels and contrasts between the two plays soon become apparent. In the first a couple are attempting to come together, in the second about to part. In each a third character, a woman, questions the rightness not just of this action, but of all the couple's assumptions. There are quotations of the concerns of the first play in the second. The third character in *Wrecked Eggs,* Grace, the only guest, is a disenchanted press agent (here Hare re-treads old ground from *Pravda*) who does offer some eloquent rejoinders to Robbie: "Is there nothing? Is everything allowed?" (Hare quoting *The Brothers Karamazov*); "I hate this idea that we're all just sensation. 'I feel good, I don't feel good' ", but overall she lacks Nrovka's gravity and intelligence.

Hare writes about Europeans and Americans, about deprivation and excess, culture and consumption. For a European audience it is unsurprising, perhaps even initially flattering to find his Americans trite and vulgar, his Europeans intense and complex, but, to quote Hare, "Is it right?" One cannot help noticing that the dice are loaded. The main Russian protagonists are an artist and her teacher daughter; the American couple a lawyer and his tennis coach wife. The Russian sanitation engineer responds with radiant joy to talk of Matisse. Would Hare let his American equivalent do likewise? Does he believe that European sanitation engineers are more cultured? Is he right? The weaknesses of the second play are obvious. There is an inappropriate and undeveloped melodramatic subplot which reveals Robbie to be the son of a spy and some crass over-writing in Robbie's reaction to the mention of death. More importantly the doggedly clichéd view of Americans, unengagingly vulgarian in the pursuit of sensation, casts doubt upon Hare's whole enterprise. *The Bay at Nice* alone is a more satisfying offering than with *Wrecked Eggs* to follow.

> Julian Graffy, "Culture and Consumption," in The Times Literary Supplement, *No. 4356, September 26, 1986, p. 1064.*

CHRISTOPHER EDWARDS

[*The Bay at Nice* and *Wrecked Eggs*] make a complementary paid. The first is set in a museum in Leningrad in 1959, the second in present-day America in a well-appointed summer house overlooking the Hudson River. As we shall see, although divided by time and place, they share certain common moral assumptions.

In *The Bay at Nice* an old woman, Valentina, is brought to a room in a Soviet state museum by her daughter. The point of her visit is to identify a picture that has been bequeathed to the nation by an exiled White Russian Count. The old mother, who studied in Paris under Matisse, is *persona non grata* but recognised as an authority on Matisse. At the end she identifies the picture as, indeed, by her old master.

The audience never sees the picture. Nor does it need to, for the drama does not really turn upon the verification of a picture. Indeed, we could have done without some of the faintly absurd quivering which leads Valentina to her intuited conviction that the picture is original. The play is really a moral argument. Valentina, is a woman of high principle. When she conceived her daughter in Paris (by one of her several bohemian lovers) she returned home to Russia instead of having an abortion and continuing her life of instruction and pleasure. She wanted her child to be Russian, despite the cost to her own career. And the White Russian's bequest to his country represents a more obscure form of duty—this time to his country.

Matisse's duty to his genius is described by Valentina in a series of grandiloquent and occasionally sentimental speeches. Essentially she applauds his dedication to his craft and his disregard for the relatively unimportant demands of the ordinary self; in other words he had no time for love. This is a harsh doctrine to put before her untalented daughter, who

wants to 'fulfil' herself by leaving her husband and children for a kind, 60-year-old civil servant. A shrill, and familiar, self-righteousness confirms to us that she will take that step even at the expense of her family. She claims a 'right' to happiness.

The debate, although it resists schematic analysis, seems to favour the uncompromising mother; an unfashionable resolution. (p. 47)

Whereas in the first play Hare laboured, at times, to create an authentic idiom for his Russian characters, [in *Wrecked Eggs*] he shows a fine ear and eye for the modern American yuppy. Robbie . . . appears as the all-American, bluntly materialistic lawyer—although in fact he has a secret that this identity seeks to conceal. Loelia, his girlfriend, is a long-legged tennis coach whose promiscuous hippy past is no secret to anyone. Grace's role, in between passing amusing and baffled observations of the morality of public and private life, is to act as the catalyst that brings the couple back together. Again, an appeal to a sense of duty lies at the heart of the piece and if at times *Wrecked Eggs* has something of the situation comedy about it, it is, nevertheless, often funny and acute.

Taken together the plays represent interesting essays in a genre—the play of ideas that English playwrights do not usually handle well at all. Both examine the conflicting demands of personal fulfilment and responsibility; themes that confirm Hare to be a moralist. And the unmodish way in which these themes are resolved here suggests what sort of moralist he is becoming. (p. 48)

> Christopher Edwards, "Moral Imperatives," in The Spectator, *Vol. 257, No. 8255, September 27, 1986, pp. 47-8.*

JACK TINKER

However worthy the impulses and motives which impelled David Hare to write his bleak play for the Eighties [*The Secret Rapture*], the impulses and motives which drive his characters are ultimately about as deep and rewarding as in your average pulp novel.

In the parlance of the age, the marketing is A1 while the product is actually C4. I don't want to patronise a playwright of Mr Hare's proven stature, but really! Are we asked to believe that a Junior Government Minister, quite blatantly displaying every crass surge of self confidence that has turned Edwina Currie into a form of national toothache, will melt overnight into the arms of her wimpish husband—a caricature of Born Again piety moreover. . . .

Mr Hare has so specifically spelled out the nature of his shock Nemesis that one has practically prepared oneself for the big bang (in this case of the literal kind) a whole scene before it comes.

It is, of course, one of the sad facts of life that passivity of nature, especially one's nearest and dearest, is a sure incitement to extremes of behaviour in those with whom they deal. So the blind and callous anger with which [Marian French] is called upon to conduct not only her politics but her private life is in glib psychological terms mitigated by the self-contained calm of her sister [Isabel Glass]. . . . , (p. 1386)

The events of the play follow the death of their father and

roughly chart how each deals not only with their grief, but also the young alcoholic wife whom he apparently adored. (pp. 1386-87)

[Other] plays have informed us how both power and profit-motive corrupt without having clients stabbed for turning down a deal, lovers shot for saying No and sister asset-stripped by sister.

Sadly what Mr Hare is saying gets rather lost beneath how he chooses to say it. (p. 1387)

> *Jack Tinker, in a review of "The Secret Rapture," in* Daily Mail, *October 5, 1988. Reprinted in* London Theatre Record, *Vol. VIII, No. 20, 1988, pp. 1386-87.*

PETER KEMP

As the title of his television play **Licking Hitler** memorably indicated, David Hare is engrossed both by those who fight viciousness and by those who have a taste for it. **The Secret Rapture,** his exciting new work. . ., demonstrates this double interest particularly clearly. Seriously concerned with a struggle against destructiveness, it is simultaneously a caustic comedy about modern modes of corruption.

At first, in fact, it seems an elegant addition to the rapidly expanding genre of drama that explores and deplores the aggressive acquisitiveness holding sway in 1980s Britain. As in *Fashion* or *Serious Money,* you are taken into a world of new norms: one where compassion is equated with feebleness and it is considered natural to revel in a kind of predatory prosperity.

The main exemplar of this attitude here is Marion, a Tory Junior Minister first seen thriftily retrieving a ring from her father's corpse. Commandeering and domineering, she is at the opposite extreme to her sister Isobel, a graphic designer who is self-effacing, sympathetic, liberal.

It is a contrast that could easily seem crude: a caricature of materialism ranged against an icon of idealism. That it never becomes too schematic is due to the dialogue, crackling with contemporary authenticity, which Hare gives the two women and the wealth of detail he has worked into their characterisation. . . .

Twists of plot pull Isobel into the familiar-looking territory of yuppy perfidy. Machinations by Marion and her pious financier husband lead to first a takeover, then the asset-stripping, of the design agency Isobel has run with her lover Irwin. The transformation of this homely outfit into something soulless is signalled by those now standard indicators of mercenary depravity: black leather furniture, chrome fitments and computer terminals. Completing the picture of a morally downward slump into the upwardly mobile, Irwin briefly succumbs to the worldly wiles of Marion's assistant: a blasé siren. . . .

Interlinked with the suave satire on modern rapacity is a morality play. For much of **The Secret Rapture** is about the challenge of—and challenges to—decency. Isobel's unselfishness and honesty unsettle those around her. Feeling shamed or rebuked by her behaviour, shoddier characters attempt to label it neurotic, unnatural or old-fashioned. Sometimes, this generates scenes of comic unease. Eventually in Irwin . . . something more desperate is triggered off.

The Secret Rapture's closing moments boldly make play with notions of martyrdom and redemption. There is a slightly over-elevated air to this; but, everywhere else, Hare's wry dramatisation of unselfishness and its repercussions is always accompanied by the saving grace of tough, humane psychological acuteness.

> *Peter Kemp, in a review of 'The Secret Rapture,' in* The Independent, *October 6, 1988.*

DOUGLAS KENNEDY

Marion and Isobel are sisters. And yet, though they share a common familial and national identity, the fact is that they ultimately inhabit two very different countries within the same country. For Marion's Britain is the no-nonsense, technocratic world of Thatcherism triumphant. In fact, she's a junior minister in Madame's government and—besides possessing a husband who heads up an organisation called Christians in Business, and will happily tell you all about his personal relationship with Jesus Christ—she is also a testament to the coolly clinical ethos of self-interest which rules supreme today. . . .

Isobel, on the other hand, lives in a rapidly vanishing Britain: a Britain of humane and liberal tendencies. She is a partner in a modest three-person design studio—a business in which the participants accept that nominal financial reward is the price one willingly pays for job satisfaction. She is also in love with one of her associates, Irwin—a man who readily admits that his talents as a graphic artist are limited, but who sees his relationship with Isobel as a far more important *modus vivendi* than the need to be a careerist. And, more importantly, she is someone who understands that the landscape of people's lives is a convoluted one, and therefore one must always be prepared to come to the assistance of anyone who seeks help.

Two radically different sisters. Two radically different Britains. And in David Hare's remarkable new play, **The Secret Rapture,** these two spheres collide when their father—a Gloucestershire bookseller of high ideals and low business ability—dies, leaving behind a young second wife, Katherine; a woman whose life has been one continuous loose end. And when Katherine imposes herself on Isobel—begging her to manufacture for her the professional identity that she has always lacked—Isobel cannot bear to say no. It's a decision that inevitably wreaks havoc, for Katherine possesses a destructive personality which gradually poisons and undermines Isobel's life.

But **The Secret Rapture** is not simply a contemporary study of good undermined by evil. For this corrosive and brilliantly written examination of the fragility of human relationships in an age of Social Darwinism is also very much a play about people inhabiting a vast set of contradictions. And, as such, it constantly reminds one that this sort of robust, passionately political play is, in itself, potentially inhabiting a contradiction in the world of Thatcherite Britain today. (p. 36)

The Secret Rapture is a stunning example of complex political argument taking place on the intimate battleground of tangled inter-familial relationships. But it is also, very much, a play that shows the way in which an individual or a society which negates the idea of human fragility—and of the need to care for others—will end up mourning the loss of its own capacity to love.

And though Hare himself sees the clinical principles of Thatcherism turning this country into "a perfect imitation of life", there's a peculiar optimism to his play; a belief that the destruction of our capacity for goodness will eventually leave us desolate, and force us to rebuild it again.

Indeed, it's a play that also leaves one cautiously optimistic about the future of a theatre which still challenges, argues, and provokes—in short, a theatre which is bracingly political. (p. 37)

> *Douglas Kennedy, "Two Britains," in* New Statesman & Society, *Vol. 1, No. 19, October 14, 1988, pp. 36-7.*

JOHN SIMON

Have you ever come into a small gathering a bit late and found an animated conversation going that you couldn't quite cotton to? All are vitally involved, and what is said makes perfect sense to them, yet you are utterly at sea? That's how I felt at David Hare's *The Secret Rapture.* There is a rapture there, all right—perhaps even several—but what about remains a mystery. So the title, at any rate, makes sense.

There is a note appended to the text of the play—but not to the program—saying that the secret rapture is the moment when a nun goes to be united with Christ, i.e., death. I'm afraid that doesn't help me much, either. I understand that Isobel, who runs a tiny graphic-design studio with her lover, Irwin, is something of a saint; that when her kindly bookseller father dies, she feels she must take his very young and very crazy widow, Katherine, into her business and the small flat from which she runs it. I also understand that her sister, Marion, a Thatcherite junior minister, is a pain in the butt, jealous of her and riding her, and yet Isobel loves her. That Marion's husband, Tom, is a henpecked businessman who has found Christ and become some sort of Anabaptist. And that Tom and Marion bully Isobel into expanding her business under Tom's supervision. Maybe for a tax loss. Maybe not. . . .

A fine plot for Feydeau, you may think, but can Hare handle farce? You are barking up the wrong tree; this is tragedy. The question is, Can Hare handle tragedy? I think his earliest plays were his best, things such as *Knuckle* and *Slag.* Even about them there was something perverse, something hocuspocusy, but there was energetic fun, too. I could endure even Hare's Maoist-Brechtian phase, sort of; but with *Plenty,* things became irksome. Was postwar England totally wacked out, or was it the heroine who was bonkers? Or were both crazy? And did *A Map of the World* have to contain its own movie version right there on stage? And does the hero of the recent Hare film *Strapless,* following his romantic compulsion, marry all the women he makes love to? In which case, he must be a very advanced polygamist. But he seems to be only a bigamist and a shady financier, which doesn't seem to bother anyone much, not even the authorities.

Perhaps it's Hare who is bananas. He certainly gives most of his characters elaborately sculptured speeches—something out of an Oxford-Cambridge debate, with a touch of High Church sermon and a dash of absurdism thrown in. Then, as his own director, he has the cast orating at the audience, very slowly, very deliberately, as if doing a special matinee at a mental hospital. Aha! So it is we the audience who are crazy. Perhaps that is why we wonder about what the saintly Isobel

could have seen in scruffy Irwin in the first place. And if she saw so much, why she was so ready to fall out of love at one all too human misstep of his. What Hare has been writing lately is an intelligent man's follies. Individual scenes have bravura, or perception, or humor, but the whole doesn't add up, jell, communicate.

> *John Simon, "Rapture Under Wraps," in* New York Magazine, *Vol. 22, No. 44, November 6, 1989, p. 132.*

JACK KROLL

David Hare writes probably the strongest women's roles of any playwright anywhere. Such roles are rare for male playwrights, but Hare sees the world primarily through women—whether it's the three school teachers in *Slag* who decide to abstain from sex, Maggie, the self-destructive rock singer in *Teeth 'n' Smiles* or Susan Traherne in *Plenty,* who's driven near madness by the decline of Britain after World War II. So it was inevitable that Hare, with Tom Stoppard the outstanding British playwright of his generation (he's 42), would be fascinated by Margaret Thatcher and the climate of Thatcherism. His new play, *The Secret Rapture,* explores that climate through several women (and their men). It's the best play of the year and the most compelling British import in years.

"A great deal has been written about the politics and economics of Thatcher," says Hare, "but nothing about the psychology of Thatcherism. I started from wondering why she was angry all the time. She'd been in power for an eternity, she got all her measures passed. Why was she in such an appalling temper?" The question led Hare into deep waters. *The Secret Rapture* deals with politics, human goodness (and its opposite), spirituality, greed, sex and something close to saintliness. . . .

Hare, a superb craftsman, orchestrates this intricate action in a form that echoes upon the comic polish of Noel Coward, the slashing dialectics of Shaw and the mystical overtones of T. S. Eliot's plays. Each character has a prismatic humanity. Tom is a fatuous born-again who thinks that Jesus even supplies him with sparkplugs for his car, but he's also a decent man. Marion, the bellicose apostle of Thatcherite self-interest, clings to such simplicities because she has always feared the uncertainties of passion. Isobel, driven by a seemingly pure virtue, hurts her lover mortally by her unbending morality. Katherine is helpless, but there's also a taint of pure evil within her. Hare includes a fourth woman, Marion's aide Rhonda, a sexy technocrat who's given the play's most withering indictment of the emotional inadequacy of men.

> *Jack Kroll, "The Women of Thatcherland," in* Newsweek, *Vol. CXIV, No. 20, November 13, 1989, p. 89.*

MIMI KRAMER

Toward the middle of the first act of David Hare's *The Secret Rapture,* . . . two characters have an argument about how to deal with crazy, manipulative people. The heroine, Isobel, has given a job to her deceased father's second wife, Katherine, an unbalanced, destructive young woman with a history of substance abuse and unemployment. Now Katherine is wreaking havoc at the small London studio where Isobel and her lover/partner, Irwin, design book jackets and record-album covers. Trying to persuade Isobel to throw Katherine out, Irwin quite accurately characterizes a certain kind of neurotic: "chronically dependent . . . on other people's good will," who looks for suckers to take advantage of and then proceeds to behave badly, "always at somebody else's expense." Listening to this description, anyone who has ever had a troublesome relative, friend, or lover (and which of us hasn't?) might identify with the situation in the play and think that Hare is grappling with something real. But the moment passes. The heroine's position ("I can't just abandon her") proves to amount to little more than pious righteousness, and you find yourself thinking, No, my life is more complicated than that—this is baloney.

The central character of *The Secret Rapture,* the terminally good Isobel, seems a woman afflicted by a congenital inability to say anything interesting about anyone. She is surrounded by curious enough people: her sister, Marion, is a brawling martinet; her brother-in-law, Tom, is a religious fanatic; her father's widow is an alcoholic dropout who married a man twice her age. But Isobel can't seem to pass judgment on any of them. As a matter of fact, the heroine of *The Secret Rapture* is not all that different from the character that Blair Brown—for whom David Hare created the role of Isobel—portrays in the television sitcom "The Days and Nights of Molly Dodd." Like Molly Dodd, she is the still center of a universe in which crazy, objectionable people orbit about her, and her function, like that of the television character, seems to be to stand around looking hurt or bemused while others systematically let her down. (pp. 106, 111)

On the face of it, Hare's theme seems to be family relations; unfortunately, he approaches his subject so complacently as to make a mockery of character and human experience. The people who inhabit his play are more than just caricatures; they're political stereotypes. Marion isn't just a selfish and dictatorial person given to parading her narrow-mindedness and greed; she's a junior minister in Thatcher's Department of the Environment. The good-natured, conciliatory Tom isn't just ineffectual; he's a born-again Christian. What Hare is presenting—disingenuously or not—as a family thrown into disarray by the death of a beloved father is really a blueprint of contemporary society as he views it, with Marion as the blinkered, right-wing figurehead . . . and Tom as the hypocrite fundamentalist who flies from moral ambiguities, taking refuge in personal salvation. The bribable boyfriend, Irwin, who comes on the scene advertising his dislike of blood sports and jesting about right-wing politicians but winds up cheating on Isobel with Marion's administrative aide, clearly stands for liberals seduced by the go-for-it ethos of supply-side economics, and Katherine for that unstable element of society known as the underclass. We are probably meant to equate the dead father with that vanished breed of truly good person, the old-style intellectual. As for Isobel, she is the martyred do-gooder, left by the Marions, the Toms, and the Irwins to care for the disadvantaged and forsaken, and in the end destroyed by them all.

That Hare wants us to take his little family drama as an allegory of what has happened to political idealism in England and America (socialism in his country, liberalism in ours) is only too clear. In Marion's advice to Isobel on how to deal with Katherine—"You have to pretend . . . keep her calm. String her along . . . lie to her"—he wants his compatriots to hear the voice of Thatcher speaking about those neglected elements in British society "the blacks" and "the unemployed" just as surely as he wants Americans to take Irwin's definition of "growing up" (giving up one's "integrity") to heart. Where all this breaks down is on the level where allegory, no less than drama, is supposed to represent realistic human action and discourse. What happens to Isobel's design firm may or may not constitute an accurate representation of the way in which Thatcher's economic policies have destroyed small businesses, promising them subsidy in the name of job creation and abandoning them when they have proved unlucrative or have failed as a result of unsound management. But Hare hasn't bothered to establish any plausible motivation—personal or financial—for Tom and Marion's decision to buy into the firm. He gives them reasons—it's "to help Katherine through this very difficult time," or because "there's money to be made"—that echo policy statements but make no sense in the context of character and situation as they have been established. Allegory, in order to work, has to be revealing on two levels, and Hare's play, in order to state any more than the obvious (that it's selfish not to care about those we should care about), would have to explain something about why people think and feel and behave as they do. But, just as Hare's is not an interesting analysis of why masochistic people put up with the demanding, destructive, and confrontational dependents that life has dealt them, there is room in his microcosm of British and American politics for no subtlety of thought or motive. (pp. 111-12)

There are really only two effects I can see this play having: it could alienate those who entered the theatre agreeing with Hare (either by boring them or by insulting their intelligence), or it could make converts of a sort to an anti-Thatcherite position. If it weren't for Margaret Thatcher, after all, David Hare probably wouldn't have written this smug and obvious play. (p. 113)

Mimi Kramer, "Anti-Nuclear-Family Drama," in The New Yorker, *Vol. LXV, No. 39, November 13, 1989, pp. 106, 111-13.*

ROBERT BRUSTEIN

The only thing I found provocative about *The Secret Rapture,* David Hare's new play . . ., is its title. Since the characters are far from rhapsodic and leave little undisclosed, why identify this gray slab of English masonry with a title more appropriate to dime-store romance? One clue comes in the epigraph to the published version, also included in the program—a quote from Rebecca West about that uncontrollable strain of insanity buried in the most normal lives that "loves pain and its darker night despair, and wants to die in a catastrophe that will set life back to its beginnings."

So the "secret rapture" is what Joseph Conrad (in a better phrase) called the "destructive element," those dark, unconscious forces that pulse under the smiles and nods of daylight life. Hare's recognition of those forces in *Plenty* is what occasionally elevated that play from a plateau of earnest moralizing to heights of poetic surprise. But they're only an epigraph to *The Secret Rapture.* Hare may acknowledge the irrational side of life, but here he dismally fails to dramatize it.

Part of the problem is the playwright's political agenda. Whatever his feelings about the intrinsic nature of evil, Hare believes behavior to be deeply influenced by the social environment. This endows his personal relationships with a dimension beyond the domestic, but it also imprisons his characters in representative roles. The play's heroine (once again, Hare's central character is an idealistic woman) is Isobel Glass—liberal by persuasion, therefore warm and decent and independent by nature—while her sister, Marion French, is a Conservative politician and businesswoman, thus hard-nosed, frugal, unfeeling, Darwinian. Hare makes some effort to complicate these characters—Isobel is oddly unforgiving of her boyfriend's infidelity, Marion has an uncharacteristically soft and passionate moment with her husband. But essentially, like everyone else in the play, they exist primarily as symbolic reflections on life and character in Margaret Thatcher's England.

Opinions about the play may therefore very well divide along political lines, and I suspect its great success in Britain may have less to do with Hare's artistic gifts than with his sympathetic convictions, particularly his belief that the conservative climate of the past decade has helped to harden human feeling. *The Secret Rapture* is not a political primer, but it's hardly a triumph of negative capability either. As a play of ideas, it's always threatening to fade off into schematism. The neurotic heroine of *Plenty* managed to leave us in mystery and ambiguity; the remorselessly virtuous Isobel Glass does not.

What's missing from *The Secret Rapture* is a plausible plot. The play begins around the body of Isobel and Marion's father, an antiquarian bookseller who lived a life of thought. Isobel has been mourning him in the dark; Marion's primary interest is to retrieve the expensive ring she once gave him. Isobel is a partner in a small design studio and loves her designer-partner, Irwin; Marion is a junior minister in the Thatcher government, married to a Jesus-loving businessman. Isobel has compassion for her father's addictive wife, Katherine; Marion would just as soon consign her to an alcoholic ward.

Marion and her husband manage to persuade Isobel to expand her company, which they then plunder through a series of manipulations, investments, and mergers. Possibly corrupted by this atmosphere of opportunism and greed, Irwin goes to bed with Marion's assistant, Rhonda, and when Isobel refuses to absolve him, he shoots her. Too late, Marion acknowledges the decency of her sister—at the same time that the audience is acknowledging the collapse of decency in a time of corroded values.

Despite the echoes of *Heartbreak House* reverberating throughout the play (Isobel as the disillusioned, heartbroken Ellie Dunn; Marion as Lady Utterword, the flinty conservative from Horseback Hall), Hare does not leaven this matter with wit, and his language is surprisingly flavorless and plain, oddly crusty and dry. The style is so telegraphic it sometimes approaches parody (Marion: "I was wondering . . ." Isobel: "What?" Marion: "No, it's just . . . no, it's nothing."), which makes the speakers appear repressed, anemic—the lawn sculpture of a desiccated bourgeois landscape. The play is showy in only one respect: the way it so colorlessly proclaims its own integrity. (pp. 29-30)

David Hare is one of a growing number of male playwrights regarding manner and mores from a female point of view, on the assumption that what is happening to women is the best indicator of the current social climate. Susan Traherne in *Plenty,* with her ferocious disenchantment, lacerated character, and blistering tongue, vindicated this assumption because Hare conceived her as an interesting character in her own right; Isobel Glass is too full of the milk of human kindness to take on convincing dimension. Because she is never much more than an allegorical abstraction in a masque of contrivance, one ends up loving her virtues without being touched by her fate. (p. 30)

Robert Brustein, "No Secrets, No Rapture," in The New Republic, *Vol. 201, No. 21, November 20, 1989, pp. 29-31.*

Václav Havel

1936-

Czechoslovakian dramatist, essayist, and poet.

Havel, a major figure in Czechoslovakian culture and society, is considered his country's foremost contemporary dramatist. His plays are powerful condemnations of the bureaucratization and mechanization of modern Czech society and their effects on the individual. His trenchant satires depict the prevalence of cliché and official doublespeak under a totalitarian government and the chaos engendered by the resulting disintegration of meaning. Many of Havel's works are considered absurdist black comedies because they incorporate grotesque and ludicrous elements, giving expression to humanity's fundamental discomfort in a Godless universe. This focus on the absurd nature of existence in the modern world lends to his works a universality that augment his particular exploration of the Czechoslovakian experience.

Havel was born into a wealthy family in Prague. As a young man he was denied more than a basic education due to the Communist policy of discrimination against the bourgeoisie under Soviet leader Joseph Stalin. Havel worked in a chemical factory and attended classes at night in order to finish secondary school. He later took menial jobs at a theater, began writing, and eventually gained admittance to the Academy of Arts in Prague. During the 1960s, Havel became associated with the highly respected avant-garde Theatre on the Balustrade in Prague, which produced his *Zahradní slavnost* (1963; *The Garden Party*), *Vyrozuměni* (1965; *The Memorandum*), and *Ztížená možnost soustředěni* (1968; *The Increased Difficulty of Concentration*), plays which brought him international attention.

In the early 1960s, Czechoslovakia experienced a gradual relaxation of government controls on culture which abruptly ended following the Soviet invasion in 1968. Although his works were subsequently banned and Havel himself prohibited from working in the theater, he refused to defect to the West and continued to write plays and political tracts. His resistance to the Communist regime, which included cofounding the human-rights organization Charter 77, resulted in his arrest several times during the 1970s. In 1979, Havel was sentenced to four-and-a-half years in prison. *Letters to Olga: June 1979—September 1982* (1988) collects Havel's weekly letters to his wife from prison and contains meditations on theater, politics, literature and art. The social and economic reforms implemented by Soviet premier Mikhail Gorbachev in the mid-1980s were not adopted by Soviet Bloc countries until 1989, when large demonstrations forced Communist ruling parties, including Czechoslovakia's, to resign *en masse*. Havel's steadfast opposition to human rights violations in his country contributed to his election in December, 1989, to the presidency of the first non-Communist government to rule Czechoslovakia since the mid-1940s.

Although unable to have his plays produced in his homeland, Havel continued to write throughout the 1970s, performing what are known as "the Vanek plays" in private homes and acting in the title role himself. Produced in the West under the collective title *A Private View,* the Vanek plays are three one-act pieces, *Audience* (1975; produced in Great Britain as *Interview*), *Vernisáz* (1975; *Private View*), and *Protest* (1978), all of which feature Ferdinand Vanek, a dissident playwright. In *Audience,* Vanek's supervisor at the brewery offers him an easier job in exchange for composing the supervisor's weekly report on Vanek to authorities. In *Private View,* Vanek visits a well-to-do couple who flaunt the material possessions they have gained by renouncing their previous opposition to the government. They attempt to convince Vanek to recant his dissent as well. *Protest* features an extended monologue by Stanek, a successful scriptwriter, in which his refusal to sign a petition protesting the arrest of his daughter's boyfriend is presented as being in the best interest of all concerned. Throughout these plays, Vanek is a nearly silent figure who functions as an external conscience for his guilty interlocutors, prodding them to inadvertently confess their cowardice and hypocrisy. Although several critics observed an element of self-righteousness in Vanek's silence, most praised Havel's portrayal of some of the ways in which political oppression erodes human values. Mel Gussow remarked: "While the plays [in *A Private View*] lack the linguistic complexity of Havel's earlier full-length works such as *The Memorandum,* each is a finely wrought cameo, and the political subject matter does not lead the author into didacticism."

Václav Havel; or, Living in Truth: Twenty-two Essays Published on the Occasion of the Award of the Erasmus Prize to Václav Havel, edited by Jan Vladislav (1987), is a collection of essays in honor of Havel by such writers as Tom Stoppard and Samuel Beckett. The volume also includes several pieces by Havel in which he expounds upon the difficulty of "living in truth" under a totalitarian society that makes lying necessary for survival for its citizens. Havel's *Largo Desolato,* which made its American debut in 1986, is a semi-autobiographical play about a philosopher driven to alcohol and pills due to the pressure both from officials, who want him to recant his writings, and from friends who are unable to support his efforts but urge him to continue. The play was not well received by critics, many of whom found only weak echoes of powerful works by Franz Kafka and George Orwell. *Temptation* (1988) is a variation on the Faust legend, in which a man sells his soul to the devil in exchange for unlimited knowledge. Dr. Henry Foustka, Havel's updated Faust, is a social scientist who becomes fascinated by black magic and accidentally conjures up Fistula, Havel's version of Mephistopheles. In this allegory, the state is portrayed as the true devil because it corrupts science in the service of political ends. Linda Winer commented: "[*Temptation*] is a fairly simplistic update on the Faust legend—more polemical than most Havel, though not without some of his wry insights on the broader nature of dogma."

(See also *CLC,* Vol. 25 and *Contemporary Authors,* Vol. 104.)

MEL GUSSOW

The dehumanizing effects of totalitarianism are demonstrated with wounding honesty and irony in Vaclav Havel's *Private View.* This triptych of interrelated short plays . . . is an event of artistic and political urgency.

Convicted of subversion for his defense of human rights, the dissident playwright was twice imprisoned in Czechoslovakia. The plays, written in 1975 and 1978, are banned from public performance in his native country, along with other works by Havel. However, the author has played as his own protagonist in a private performance, and in a production on BBC radio in England the role was played by Harold Pinter. . . .

A Private View reminds us of the importance of the artist as provocateur. Despite his victimization, Havel has retained his comic equilibrium and his sense of injustice. Confronted by public and private absurdities, the artist clings to first principles: self-respect and an unquenchable morality.

In Samuel Beckett's *Catastrophe,* [see Havel's entry in *CLC,* Vol. 25] a play that is dedicated to Havel, we see a Havel-like hostage silently willing his audience into an awareness of his—and their—predicament. Something similar occurs in Havel's three plays, with the addition of the fact that these are first-hand experiences.

The author's alter ego is a playwright named Vanek, who is an alien in his own homeland. In each of the plays we see how others react to him and to his martyrdom, how each wears his guilt as a badge of identity: the price of prosperity is the loss of humanity. Vanek has become a public conscience and his very presence is a "living reproach" to those who are com-

promisers and cowards. People play up to him, trying to win his absolution with favors. . . . [He] is a man who has weathered the tempest and is determined to weather the aftermath.

In the first of the plays, [*Interview*], Vanek is working as a laborer in a Czechoslovak brewery—as Havel himself did—and is called in for an interview with the head maltster. Feigning conviviality, the boorish employer, a diehard bureaucrat, plies Vanek with the house brew while tempting him with the possibility of a less arduous office job. In return, he would like Vanek to furnish him with reports of his own political activity. Astonished, Vanek explains that he cannot inform on himself. Such a dilemma reminds us that Havel's national and artistic antecedent is Kafka. Strange are the labyrinthine intrigues of a society trying to repress its people.

The play is a comedy. . . . [The employer] is a self-styled "brewery mug," and that description can be taken as a pun. In common with his own product, he foams to overflowing as he tries to win the dissident as confidant.

The second play, which gives the evening its title, finds Vanek in the bourgeois household of a married couple who have survived in high style. Their lavishly decorated apartment and their lounge clothes would be leisurely at home in an affluent American suburb. Vanek, on the other hand, looks frayed.

With a farcical fury that rises to surrealism, the couple attempt to entertain their "best" friend. The guest is eager to be pleased and is resistant only when personal questions are raised. He allows himself one moment of introspection: "I sometimes have a feeling of futility." That futility is endemic to his existence. There is nothing he can do except endure and try to play the game of social engagement.

In the third and most moving play, *Protest,* Vanek visits a former friend, a novelist who has sacrificed his art as well as his honor. The novelist wants Vanek to publish a protest against the arrest of a young revolutionary. From the beginning, we know that Vanek will ask him to sign the petition and we know that he will refuse, which he does with a convoluted logic that turns every positive into a negative as he assures himself of the rectitude of moral abdication.

Havel's analysis of the novelist's self-induced quandary is richly detailed. . . .

While the plays lack the linguistic complexity of Havel's earlier full-length works such as *The Memorandum,* each is a finely wrought cameo, and the political subject matter does not lead the author into didacticism. The plays are highly theatrical, an aspect that is embellished in performance.

> *Mel Gussow, "Havel's 'Private View'," in* The New York Times, *November 21, 1983, p. C16.*

DON NELSEN

Three one-acts under the umbrella title *A Private View* offer a salutary example of political theater as fine entertainment. They were written by Czech dissident playwright Vaclav Havel, who has suffered imprisonment for his importunings on behalf of human rights. The plays are semi-autobiographical and many of the names mentioned belong to real people, Havel's fellow playwright, Pavel Kohout, for example.

This blending of the actual with the semi-fictional lends Havel's trio an extra dash of immediacy because we are reminded that we are dealing with real humans, not just a playwright's puppets artfully manipulated. Moreover, *View* is no mere polemic against the total state. Its humor, arising from the contradictions that beleaguer our behavior, rounds the figures.

Havel's concern is the frightened citizen—here a brewer, a businessman, a writer—whose only defense against the repressive state is to agree with it—at least publicly. If that means conformity, compromise and guilt, Havel does not flail them with it. To those who cannot stand against odds like himself and other dissidents, Havel's reaction is not enmity nor even anger. It is sorrow, which, unfortunately, only brings these people to a greater realization of their toadying. As one character laments, those who sacrifice integrity for security attack the dissidents because "they see them as their guilty consciences. . . ."

Interview shares a good deal of common ground with the two other plays, *Private View* and *Protest.* In each, Vanek says relatively little, allowing his hosts to talk on and, in the process, convict themselves of cowardice. In each, Vanek's self-justifying hosts try to tempt him to their cause by means of forcing drinks on him, then offering him easy jobs, political favors or creature comforts to win his approval of their behavior.

A businessman and his wife in *Private View* seek to persuade him that their prosperous existence—all the latest records and gimcracks plus a "perfect" sex life—is the only way to live. The seedily dressed Vanek is unimpressed, which drives them nuts.

The novelist and TV script writer in *Protest* questions at great length the wisdom of signing a petition condemning the imprisonment of his own daughter's boyfriend. He does not, of course, sign, preferring the safer alternative of contributing—secretly, of course—to the cause. He shouts, "It's sickening the way everybody looks after Number One." But he and they keep doing it.

Yes, these people are pitiable but they are also understandable. How many of us would, faced with danger to our security or family, stand up for the right? Not many; so these characters elicit our sympathy, if only because we suspect we might do as they in the same circumstances.

This is what makes *A Private View* so absorbing. . . . *View* is a cautionary tale that reminds us that the practice of people collaborating in their own destruction is not limited to Czechoslovakia.

Don Nelsen, " 'Private View' of Socialist Hell," in Daily News, *New York, November 24, 1983.*

LEO SAUVAGE

The first and last [plays in *A Private View*], *Interview* and *Protest,* are short tales of extraordinary dramatic power, exemplary in the sense Cervantes gave to the word. Rather unexpectedly, Havel concentrates with bitter, yet only slightly sarcastic understanding—not on people like himself but on those who have more or less reluctantly adapted to the totalitarian system. What the conformists are still able to feel, and how they cope with it, is revealed when they are faced with a dissident playwright named Ferdinand Vanek, who is obviously Vaclav Havel himself. . . .

Vanek is a quiet, steady, sturdy symbol of human resistance. Havel, a permanent victim of the Prague regime even if he is out of jail for the moment, intends to demonstrate that the authorities have not entirely succeeded in extinguishing the emotional and moral life of their servants. Deep, or not so deep, inside, some of the submissive majority cannot help admiring, indeed envying, the dissident, however they try to wriggle out of the discomposure this causes them.

Unfortunately, there is also the second play, the title piece. Placed between the two small masterpieces, *Private View* comes close to spoiling the whole evening. Certainly, it upsets Havel's demonstration. (p. 16)

Interview begins when the "head maltster"—as the program identifies him—summons Vanek to his office. Looking like a George Grosz drawing of a fat bureaucrat, the chief is a former blue-collar worker who has managed to climb to a position that allows him to drink beer, fall asleep at his desk, snore, and dream of spending a night in the arms of a beautiful actress whom, he learns with rapture, Vanek knows. Though vulgar and well aware that he has to be very careful to retain his cushy spot, he is neither brainwashed nor mean. Vanek's political status doesn't seem to disturb him, except for one problem: *They* want him to write a weekly report on his worker, and he doesn't know what to say.

Eventually, he thinks of a solution. After long, embarrassed, circuitous small talk punctuated by the opening of beer bottles and interrupted by frequent trips to the toilet, he suggests that perhaps Vanek would be willing to concoct the entries to his own dossier. After all, he is a writer by profession. An easy desk job, it seems, could be arranged in exchange for these innocent flights of imagination.

Interview is a farce—thick, coarse, uninhibited. . . . But it is not devoid of meaning. When Vanek tries to slip out of the office without having relieved his superior's headache, the "interviewer" arouses himself from a moment of drunken stupor and, forgetting the previous conversation entirely, invites the disgraced intellectual in to start all over again. And Vanek, who has until now carefully kept his distance, is ready to join the man in his revels. In the eyes of Vanek/Havel, then, the dull-witted bureaucrat is not an enemy, only a sad example of Czechoslovakia's "new society."

In *Protest,* Vanek's presence unravels a quite different member of the unhappy group who once thought they could reap the benefits of satisfying the regime without becoming dissatisfied with themselves. Stanek, a novelist and television scenarist, and a former good friend of Vanek, has given up all independent writing in favor of his well-rewarded hack work. He has suddenly called Vanek, whom official intellectuals of course prefer to avoid, because a young songwriter lately placed under arrest happens to be the boyfriend of Stanek's daughter. Maybe, Stanek tells Vanek, a protest signed by well-known dissidents would help the young man.

Vanek, although previously ignorant of his ex-friend's personal connection to the case, has come to Stanek's comfortable villa with a briefcase containing precisely such a petition. By asking Stanek whether he wants to sign it himself, he launches an exquisitely peculiar dialogue wherein the accommodationist, pen in hand, details all his good reasons for refusing. It's a great scene.

Like the head maltster who represents the industrial bureaucracy, the opportunist from the intellectual bureaucracy is not hopelessly corrupt—for he is as little at ease with himself as with Vanek. In *Private View,* by contrast, Michael and Vera, the husband and wife whose apartment Vanek is visiting for the evening, have no conscience. They are soulless, perhaps brainless, certainly tasteless profiteers. Thanks to Michael's position in the upper-class bureaucracy, they have recently traveled to the U.S., bringing back every American gadget, record and piece of furniture they could lay their hands on.

Although Michael would have access to luxuries unknown to his ordinary comrades, it is difficult to believe a high-ranking Communist would openly lead such an "Americanized" life. Surely Michael would understand that he was putting an end to his career.

More important, because it lacks the leitmotif of guilt and embarrassment that carries the other plays, *Private View* introduces an element of incoherence into what is supposed to be an interrelated trilogy. Michael and Vera conspire to seduce Vanek into relinquishing his principles out of friendship—or, as becomes increasingly evident, out of desires that reach beyond the bounds of normal friendship. There is an incredibly ludicrous scene where [Vera] exhibits her breasts to Vanek while Michael vaunts their beauty. No less grotesque is the concluding sequence. When Vanek is told that breaking with fellow dissident playwright Pavel Kohout (throughout, Havel refers to the various offstage characters by their real names) would make life easier for him, he takes his coat and prepares to leave. With Vera crying hysterically on the sofa, however, and Michael swearing at his guest for turning his back on their longstanding bond of affection, Vanek comes back, not to drink beer with a head maltster this time, but to join in what is obviously going to be a triangular sex party.

[*Private View*] is bad. . . . I recommend, therefore, walking out after *Interview,* without going too far away to be back in time for *Protest.* (pp. 16-17)

Leo Sauvage, "Dramas in Two Worlds," in The New Leader, *Vol. LXVI, No. 24, December 26, 1983, pp. 16-17.*

ROBERT BRUSTEIN

I am late in reviewing Vaclav Havel's *A Private View* . . . for reasons that suggest how political considerations can inhibit one's critical judgments. I have not greatly admired Havel's dramatic writings in the past (I found *The Memorandum,* for example, a post-Absurdist contrivance hamstrung by crude linear plotting), but in view of the courageous public actions of this Czechoslovakian dissident, it somehow seemed insensitive to be making aesthetic judgments on his techniques. How does one criticize the art of a man exemplary enough to draw tributes from Samuel Beckett and Tom Stoppard without seeming to mitigate one's admiration for his personal heroism? Still, Havel is not just a symbol of political persecution, he is also a serious writer who both seeks and deserves an honest assessment. The problem is that Havel's new play is compromised by the very virtues that make him a hero to the West.

A Private View consists of three short playlets unified by its central figure, Ferdinand Vanek. When we first see Vanek, he has arrived, cap in hand, for an interview with his bibulous boss, the head malter in a brewery. An intellectual and a playwright, Vanek has taken this job for reasons partly economic (he needs money), partly political (a troublemaker banned from editorial jobs, he needs to identify himself with working people). But his beer-soaked interrogator, alternately menacing and friendly in the manner of a Kafka bureaucrat, views him as a condescending creature from another class whose friendship with such dissidents as Pavel Kohout is compromising his credibility with the authorities. Guzzling bottles of brew and interrupting their conversation for frequent piss calls, the boss holds out promise of a better-paying job if Vanek will fix him up with an actress and admit his dissident sympathies. Always humble and agreeable, Vanek will arrange the assignation, but stoutly refuses to inform on himself. The boss grows more sloshed; Vanek makes another entrance to start the interview again, this time assuming the coarse macho manners appropriate to his environment.

"I am a swine and the swine go home," says Brecht's Kragler of *Drums In The Night,* another character who learns that the best defense against authority is pliancy. The second playlet, [*A Private View*], however, suggests that Vanek's self-denigration is more a modest authorial pose than a strategy for political adaptation. Here Vanek visits two friends from his past, a swinging middle-class couple in a trendy apartment festooned with vulgar objects purchased abroad. "We're having our own little private view here this evening," they tell him.

Soon they get down to the real subject of the visit, which is to rebuke him for his unorthodox politics and his dissident associates (Kohout is again mentioned as a dangerous influence), meanwhile suggesting that if Vanek would only conform he could be enjoying similar luxuries and privileges. Throughout this colloquy, Vanek remains silent, unprotesting, a figure whose very impassivity seems to make his critics furious. Finally, Vanek confesses he is sorry to have caused his friends so much trouble and anguish, and just as he adapted earlier to the proletarian camaraderie demanded by the head malter, he now sits contentedly listening to his bourgeois friends' rock records and drinking their bourbon. (p. 28)

[Although] Vanek is undoubtedly an autobiographical figure, there are significant differences between the dissident Havel and his unprotesting hero. These are even more evident in the third and final playlet of the evening, *Protest,* which takes place four years later, in 1979. Here Vanek—just released from a year in prison for his political activities—visits a successful writer, Stanek. . . . Stanek greatly admires Vanek's integrity in regard to art and human rights, even though, having read his play about the brewery, he disapproves of the "unrealistic" ending. Now a young friend of his daughter (she is pregnant by him) has been arrested for political reasons, and Stanek wants Vanek to submit a petition for his release.

Vanek has already written such a petition and collected some signatures, including that of Pavel Kohout. It never occurs to Stanek to sign it himself. Instead he makes suggestions about how to make the document milder, less provocative, and then offers Vanek some money for his persecuted comrades (naturally he doesn't want this known). Still preternaturally mild-mannered, Vanek finally asks Stanek to become a signatory to his own petition. The panicked Stanek responds with an outpouring of shame and remorse. He had always assumed that only dissidents made protests, that when you wanted something dangerous done you turned to agents—"Can everybody become a fighter for human rights?" Filled with self-loathing, he determines to regain his lost honor and self-respect, and sign, then rehearses all the reasons why he shouldn't: he will lose his job, his son will be unable to continue with his studies, he will no longer be able to do any "backstage maneuvering." Inevitably, Stanek decides to withhold his name, and when he asks Vanek, "Are you angry?" receives the reply, "I respect your reasoning."

This Christ-like response enrages Stanek. He accuses Vanek of "benevolent hypocrisy," of "moral superiority," of hiding his contempt behind a mask of reasonableness. Still impassive, Vanek refuses to defend himself against these charges, but the issue resolves itself at the end of the play when news comes that the young man has already been released and the petition is unnecessary. Vanek assures the relieved Stanek it was his "backstage maneuvering" that produced the happy results, and, considering for a moment whether to return Stanek's donation, decides to keep the money and leave.

Clearly, Havel has created for himself an insoluble problem: how to dramatize the cowardice of others and contrast it with your own heroism, without appearing impossibly self-righteous. The playwright's strategy is to make Vanek at times a "swine who goes home," scraping before authority and conforming to whatever is demanded, at other times a model of compliant sweetness. Still, the savagery of Havel's satire on the moral dilemmas of those who lack his courage raises doubts about whether he shares his hero's charitable nature, and the difficult sacrifices he has made on behalf of human rights suggest that whatever his faults, conformity is not among them. Vanek, the character, is exonerated from Stanek's accusation of "moral superiority" by the uncritical way he behaves toward others; but the man who invented him cannot entirely escape the same charges.

It is a problem compounded by a conflict between the public and private aspects of Havel's character, between the hero who acts and the playwright who creates. I can't begin to suggest how it could be avoided, except to avoid writing about yourself altogether. But since political protest is at the very center of Havel's obsessions, this alternative would rob him of his subject. Brecht escaped the problem because he had a much less exalted view of human character ("Unhappy is the land that needs a hero"), including his own (he was willing to adopt any strategem for survival). But without personal heroism, a once proud, progressive nation would be doomed eternally to slavish servility. (pp. 28-9)

Robert Brustein, "Private Views, Public Vistas," in The New Republic, Vol. 190, No. 10, March 12, 1984, pp. 27-9.

MICHAEL SCAMMELL

About one-third of the way through this collection of Vaclav Havel's prison letters to his wife, [**Letters to Olga**], there is a brief discussion of a Polish movie Con Amore that Mr. Havel has just seen:

It was essentially about how there are times when an artist must put his art aside in order to do something positive in life, something modest that may not earn him a place in history but which is the expression of a moral imperative or simply a love for

people. At the same time, this film put forward the rather optimistic notion that the artist who is capable of subordinating his art to life—temporarily at least—is ultimately more interesting than the artist who sacrifices everything to his art. The latter will end up sacrificing his art as well, because he strips it of meaning.

It is not surprising that such a movie should have attracted Vaclav Havel's attention, for it seemed to describe the very predicament he was then trying to cope with—a four-and-a-half-year jail sentence precisely for subordinating his art to life—that is, for joining the Committee for the Defense of the Unjustly Persecuted (known as VONS in its Czech acronym) and distributing documents regarded as "subversive" of the Czechoslovak republic. The letters cover a period of just over three years (June 1979 to September 1982) out of the three and a half years that Mr. Havel served of his sentence; half fearful and half optimistic, they represent a sustained effort to make sense of his decision and to assimilate its meaning into a larger theory about the nature of society, politics, morality, art and the artist's responsibility to himself and others.

Certainly there was a majestic logic to the series of events that had led Mr. Havel to jail. Having achieved an international reputation with his three absurdist plays of the 1960's, *The Garden Party* (1963), *The Memorandum* (1965) and *The Increased Difficulty of Concentration* (1968), Vaclav Havel had been one of the first Czechoslovak writers to speak out against President Gustav Husak's "normalization" campaign after the Soviet invasion in August 1968. As a consequence, he himself was "normalized" out of Czechoslovak theaters, magazines and publishing houses, and encouraged to vanish from his country's literary life. (pp. 10-11)

One of the key discoveries that Vaclav Havel seems to have made during the 1970's was that although his human rights activities carried obvious risks, they were not necessarily inimical to, or at odds with, his literary goals. On the contrary, in three beautifully written and painfully funny one-act plays, *Private View, Audience* and *Protest* (known collectively as "the Vanck plays" after the name of the central character), Mr. Havel gave the finest dramatic expression yet to what it means to be a dissident in Eastern or Central Europe. Far from being simple additions to the literature of political protest, or flights from the literature of protest, they elevate, broaden and deepen protest into a metaphysical category, relevant to all times and places.

It is clear from many self-conscious comments in *Letters to Olga* that these reflections were intended to continue this quest for meaning in the experience of dissidence while Mr. Havel was still in jail, and it is equally clear that his friends expected this of him too. . . . [In the introduction to *Letters to Olga,* Havel is quoted as saying]: "The letters gave me a chance to develop a new way of looking at myself and examining my attitudes to the fundamental things in life. I became more and more wrapped up in them . . . to the point where almost nothing else mattered."

The letters get off to a slow start: there are endless reproaches to Olga for not writing enough, lists of items to include in parcels, instructions on what color to paint their summer house, and repeated complaints about his chronic hemorrhoids. It is only when we get to the summer of his second year, about 100 pages into the book, that Mr. Havel arrives at his main themes. Even then they are often clothed in the language of phenomenology and existentialism, which is not always easy to follow, and are complicated by the need for indirect expression to evade prison censorship. But the closer Mr. Havel comes to his own work, the role of the theater and the nature of the literary profession, the better he is. On the death of an actor friend (Jan Werich), for instance, he writes:

> He had one exceptionally important influence on me: he helped me realize . . . that theater can be something incomparably more than just a play . . . it is a special focus of social and intellectual life . . . a living instrument of social self-awareness, one that is, in an unrepeatable way, lodged in its own time.

He is also interesting whenever he has a concrete film or a book to discuss, or is commenting on the work of other artists (he has some excellent things to say about the meaning of the death of John Lennon); and on those rare occasions when he is allowed to touch upon the details of his situation (for example, in a superb little essay about the role of tea in a prisoner's life), he is absolutely fascinating. As he writes elsewhere: "In some ways, there is far more truth in this world than in the world outside. Things and people manifest themselves as they really are. Lies and hypocrisy vanish." To this reader's taste, some of the philosophical and speculative passages strike a less authentic note.

In the increasingly large volume of prison literature spawned by our benighted century, the work that *Letters to Olga* irresistibly calls to mind is the Russian author Andrei Sinyavsky's *Voice From the Chorus,* which was also made up of letters written to the writer's wife while he was serving a sentence slightly longer than Mr. Havel's on similar charges. Once out of prison, Mr. Sinyavsky ruthlessly selected and pruned his letters and rearranged them using a collage technique, to produce a work of high literary distinction. Vaclav Havel, on the other hand, was dissuaded by his friend Jan Lopatka from committing such an act of "self-censorship" and was persuaded to publish his letters (in Czechoslovak *samizdat,* of course) more or less as written as a human and social document.

If this is so, one can only lament Vaclav Havel's good nature (amply illustrated in his letters), deplore Mr. Lopatka's erratic taste and wish that Mr. Havel had allowed his artistic instinct to prevail. We would then have had a book at least one-third shorter, more succinct, more shapely—and more like one of Vaclav Havel's plays. (p. 11)

> *Michael Scammell, " 'Normalized' in Prague," in* The New York Times Book Review, *May 8, 1988, pp. 10-11.*

CARY FAGAN

Vaclav Havel, the Czech playwright and political activist, was arrested in 1977 for membership in the human rights groups Charter 77 and the Committee to Defend the Unjustly Prosecuted. During almost four years in prison Havel worked at hard physical labour and suffered a plethora of physical complaints, most painfully a case of hemorrhoids that eventually required an operation. But as he told his wife, Olga [in a letter collected in *Letters to Olga*] (the only person he was allowed to write to), he entered prison with an almost euphoric desire for a "self-reconstitution" that would bring a new "inner freedom." He planned to study German and English, write a play, and overcome the humourless self-

obsession that had fallen on him in past years. Not surprisingly, these plans proved too ambitious. Pain and fatigue, and lack of time, solitude, and intellectual stimulation all conspired against him.

What became the centre of his existence was the weekly letter to Olga and, slowly, the working out of a remarkable personal philosophy. (pp. 30-1)

The letters do have a form and a sort of intellectual plot. They begin with Havel's obsessive requests for detailed information from Olga in an attempt to maintain a relationship with the outside. Some of the early letters have a patronizing tone, even when Havel writes that "this temporary emancipation from my domination is allowing you to develop your personality." But the strength of the relationship was never in doubt.

After Havel was transferred to Hermanice prison, his meditative letters began. Some were rejected by the censors, and Havel had to develop a style that was convoluted and peppered with abstract terminology. But despite some tiresome repetitions as Havel was working out his ideas, the letters reveal an astonishingly positive system of belief. Havel employs the jargon of existentialism and phenomenology, yet he holds not to a philosophy but to a faith. In essence he came to believe that the crisis of modern man's identity arises from his separation from immortal Being. Man can define himself and see beyond the material world to Being only through a sense of responsibility. Havel's imprisonment, then, became a realization of his self.

The letters on other subjects do come as a relief from the abstract letters. There is a lovely dissertation on the significance of tea in prison. John Lennon's murder is called "the death of the century." Olga's visits are prepared for in letters before and analysed after. And Havel, deprived of visual beauty, tells how a banal television film can move him to tears.

Given his renown as a playwright, Havel's comments on the theatre are mildly disappointing. (Of course the difficulties under which Havel wrote must be remembered.) This absurdist's ideas are not always radical: every good play must have structure; the audience cannot respond to something too removed from its range of experience. He notes (and theatregoers in the West can relate) that the social and communal quality of the theatre is too often merely a formal exercise. Nevertheless, he believes in the effect that even a small production can have on society, with the same faith that draws him to the notion of eternal Being. . . .

Letters to Olga gives us a welcome rewriting of the end of Orwell's *Nineteen-Eighty-Four.* It shows us that even one person, by remaining fully human, can rob his persecutors and achieve a very real victory. (p. 31)

> *Cary Fagan, "Prison Mail," in* Books in Canada, *Vol. 17, No. 6, August-September, 1988, pp. 30-1.*

ANDREI CODRESCU

Having been but a baby dissident myself, I never did get to experience the formative hells of a political prison in a workers' paradise. I have no doubt that given time (or *the times,* those wild mid-sixties) I would have been in an excellent position to do so. In Romania, where I was born, bred, and precociously thought myself a poet, I had been headed that way, along with other writers of my generation, ever since the first thaw of 1963, when Khrushchev's de-Stalinization speech let some savage ghosts out of the bag of authorized history, including the unspeakable Gulag. It was a heady time, filled with the beat of that *esprit du temps* that saw young people from Bucharest to Detroit shed futures planned by Central Committees in the East or social convention in the West to plunge headlong into the unknown. The hair curtain suddenly became more important than the iron one. (pp. 57, 59)

The termination of the Prague spring of 1968 was for Central Europe the distinct end of a great adventure.

From 1968 until 1979, the date of Vaclav Havel's last arrest, paranoia and repression entrenched themselves in the hungover survivors of the sixties. Many writers and intellectuals chose exile to the West or made their apologies and crawled back into the still-warm cells of the Party. But hardier souls had also been forged during the golden era of dissidence, people who refused to abandon the struggle for democracy and human values. They found themselves locked in a fight with the security apparatus, a body notoriously lacking in subtlety and humor.

Havel, author of this collection of prison letters to his wife [*Letters to Olga*] was a central figure of the gradually darkening years of the seventies. In 1978 he co-founded (with Jiri Hajek) Charter 77, an organization formed to further democracy in Czechoslovakia, including monitoring the cases of people indicted and imprisoned for their political views. The Charter's typewritten reports, documenting human rights violations, were widely circulated and carefully read. The philosophical basis of Charter 77 (so named for the number of people who signed it) was an amalgam of the best of sixties ideals: nonviolence, openness, tolerance, democratic participation.

In 1979, six signatories of Charter 77 were brought to trial in Prague. Havel received four-and-a-half years in prison for disseminating unacceptable writings. (At the time of his arrest, Havel was a well-known playwright who had received world-wide attention for *The Garden Party, The Increased Difficulty of Concentration,* and *The Memorandum,* plays that captured the imagination of the Czech public with their savage dissection of a hopelessly bureaucratic society where the absurd is part of everyday life . . .). (p. 59)

Letters to Olga contains the majority of his prison letters to his wife. Some were censored and never delivered. The letters are numbered and dated, to give notice to prison censors that record-keeping was going on. Taken as a whole, they help elevate the abstraction "dissident," or even "dissident writer," to the status of being human, with all its incumbent flaws.

Vaclav and Olga's relationship (her letters are not published here) is not likely to please feminists. It is in many ways a typical sixties relationship, in which a so-called progressive husband grudgingly makes room for the personality of his spouse. The endless instructions, both particular and general, are often embarrassing:

> Be cheerful, level-headed, healthy, and sociable, do your tasks conscientiously, keep track of what goes on, don't let trivial matters upset you, think about me and keep your fingers crossed for me, try to get along well with everyone.

Elsewhere, he instructs Olga on how to do her hair.

But as the letters go on, the relationship changes. The irritations of the first letters, which must have been the tenor of their pre-prison relationship, give way to respect and even affection. I was reminded that the feminist critique in the United States began with an analysis of what was wrong with precisely such committed couples as Vaclav and Olga. I couldn't make up my mind whether I liked the writer of these letters enough to go on, until I became slowly captivated by the story of Vaclav's mind as it rediscovers itself in prison.

Introspection is simple self-defense in prison, and Havel examines himself rigorously, chronicling and classifying his every mood. When the news of John Lennon's assassination reaches him, he experiences that chill of recognition familiar to all of us for whom the music and style of the sixties were an intrinsic part of our thinking. Havel compares Lennon's death to John Kennedy's and finds that he is moved more profoundly by it because Lennon is more intimately a part of himself.

Meditating on the meaning of Lennon's death, he has a generational epiphany. "I do not believe that certain values and ideals of the sixties have been discredited as empty illusions and mistakes . . . ," he writes, "though it is a history of repressions, murders, stupidities, wars, and violence, it is at the same time a history of magnificent dreams, longings, and ideals."

Having come to intellectual maturity during the decade that ended in the Prague Spring, Havel, like his contemporary Milan Kundera and many others, is a firm believer in certain givens of that generation: the world is ruled by fearful old men whose vested interests lie in protecting a corrupt power structure; youth and love are the chief enemies of this grotesque tribe of bureaucratic vampires. (pp. 59-60)

Born among the shards of post-war Europe under the totalitarian absence of thought imposed by rigid Marxist revision, the children of the sixties availed themselves of all culture. Havel's eclecticism is not solely philosophical. We hear him discoursing seemingly at random on every book that falls into his hands, whether it is a Soviet history book or an old French novel. Kafka's name comes up quite often, and not accidentally. To Central European writers, Czechs in particular, Kafka was not a writer of allegories or parables. His writings are "truth," pure and simple. Kafka described for all times our bureaucratic nightmare.

Vaclav Havel's letters deliver the reader to a pivotal moment in the history of Central Europe. In what seems like only a few moments before talk of glasnost became commonplace, a voice from the inside is speaking clearly and intelligently about personal and political freedom. What happens next in Gorbachev's experiment depends very much on how freely voices like Havel's will be permitted to speak. As we've seen from recent events in Poland, demands for change may still exceed the goodwill of the Party. At those times it is useful to remember—particularly in the beguiled and easily charmed West—that true change cannot come from the top. Democracy has to unsettle society to much deeper levels. It probably won't be necessary for the whole of Czech or Russian society to be unsettled to the depths to which Havel unsettles his mind. But the honest exploratory spirit that landed him in prison and that produced this book ought to be held exemplary. (p. 60)

Andrei Codrescu, in a review of "Letters to Olga,"

in The Washington Monthly, *Vol. 20, No. 9, October, 1988, pp. 57, 59-60.*

STEVEN LUKES

[Vaclav Havel's] voice speaks through his plays, but only to theatre audiences abroad (including Poland). In his own country since the end of the 1960s his plays have been privately circulated and read, and performed only in private apartments. One of Czechoslovakia's finest living dramatists is thus (like others of his generation, such as Ivan Klíma, Milan Uhde and František Pavlíček) cut off from the artistic discipline he sees as having "the greatest potential to be a social phenomenon in the true sense", from "common participation in a particular adventure of the mind, the imagination and the sense of humour, and a common experience of truth or a flash of insight into the 'life of truth' ", from producers, actors and audiences.

The plays are personal in a number of ways. Intense, concentrated, yet playful and blackly funny, they project a distinctive vision of a world Tom Stoppard has described well: "an absurd society raised only a notch or two above the normal world of state bureaucracy; the absurdities pushed to absurdity compounded by absurdity and yet saved from mere nonsense by their internal logic". Yet they are also about the pressures of the impersonal on personal character, about personal disintegration and the struggle for personal integrity: "all my plays", Havel writes to Olga [in a letter collected in *Letters to Olga*], "circle around the theme of the breakdown of identity and continuity".

The theme, moreover, is always explored from the inside: "in all my writings", he recently said, "my starting point has always been what I know, my own experience of this world I live in, my experience of myself ". This is most evident in the trilogy of "Vanek" plays (*Audience, Private View* and *Protest*), whose "hero", a polite, soft-spoken intellectual who says "No", is a thorn in the flesh both to the authorities and to the once-critical intellectuals who have made their peace with them, yet is speechless before the voiceless brewmaster who asks "Who's gonna help me? Who can give a shit? I'm just the manure that makes your fancy principles grow."

It is evident, too, in his recent plays *Largo Desolato* (completed in 1984) and *Temptation* (1985). In the first, a philosopher, disintegrating under official pressure to renounce his work and thus himself, while moralizing "friends" urge him to go on fighting, is condemned in the end not to be arrested or imprisoned. In the second, Havel's "Faust play" (whose progress he periodically reports on to Olga), the Faust figure is a scientist dabbling in black magic who is tempted by an old tramp with rotting feet into doing deals, losing his soul by trying to save his skin.

Havel's personal experience is, of course, no ordinary one. Ludvík Vaculík mischievously suggests that Havel has cornered for himself the two "extreme advantages" of being born rich (his grandfather was an architect—the Lucerna Palace in Wenceslas Square is by him—and one of the few self-made millionaires in the First Republic) and having the character-strengthening experience of prison. To Olga, Havel recalls the effects of his privileged background and his fatness as a child: "instinctual mistrust of a classmate from a rich family found in my chubbiness a marvellous opportunity for unwit-

ting 'social revenge' ". In consequence, he always felt "a little outside the given order, or on its margins", and that

> I'm always running along (like that well-fed piglet) a short distance behind my marching classmates, trying to catch up and take my place with the others as a fully fledged and equal member of that moving body, and that I am powerless to do otherwise.

"I have", he adds, "understandably, a heightened sense of order (wasn't that, too, characteristic of Kafka?)". . . .

The reference to Kafka is significant. In Kafka he recognizes "an intensely personal and existential understanding of experience that borders on spiritual kinship . . . ". For Havel, what mattered was "the quite trivial and 'pretheoretical' certainty" that Kafka "was 'right' and that what he writes is 'exactly how it is' ". "I have always been intensely aware", he tells Olga,

> of matters like the alienation of man from the world, the dehumanisation and incomprehensibility of "the order of things", the emptiness and unintentional cruelty of social mechanisms and their tendency to become ends in themselves, how things get out of control, fall apart, or, on the contrary, evolve to the point of absurdity, how human existence tends to get lost in the mechanised contexts of life, how easily absurdity becomes legitimate, the apparent nature of the "real" and the ludicrousness of the "important" etc. This experience of the world (at many points so akin to Kafka's) would obviously show up in my writing no matter what I wrote.

It is just this personal, existential evocation of experience that gives life, and indeed argumentative power, to Havel's political and cultural essays. In **"The Power of the Powerless"**, for instance, the image of a greengrocer who puts in his window, among the carrots and onions, a sign saying "Workers of the World, Unite!" is the focus of an extraordinarily rich and suggestive analysis of the interior life of state socialism in Eastern Europe—its seductions and entrapments, its subterfuges and alibis, its "as if " ideology of make-believe, its blurring of distinctions between superiors and subordinates, between "them" and "us", so that all are drawn into the same plot. The greengrocer, in short, declares his loyalty (and he can do no other if his declaration is to be accepted) in the only way the regime is capable of hearing; that is, by accepting the prescribed *ritual,* by accepting appearances as reality, by accepting the given rules of the game. In doing so, however, he has himself become a player in the game, thus making it possible for the game to go on, for it to exist in the first place.

As an account of the dynamics of impersonal power, of the workings of ideology and of the potential of the powerless, this essay is unrivaled in the academic "theoretical" literature. Not that it is un- or pre-theoretical. It is, rather, a reflective reconstruction of lived experience. (p. 327)

In *Letters to Olga,* the playwright and essayist is forced into a new form of expression by the censorship imposed by a fanatical prison commandant, a professed admirer of Hitler, who saw his rule over Havel and his co-prisoners as a welcome return to the good old Stalinist days. The constraints were tight: one letter a week to his wife, and only about "family" and "personal" matters (though nothing about prison conditions, which happened to be the most personal matter at the time), no humour, no corrections or crossings out, and (at various times) no reference to the "order of being" ("The only order you can write about is the prison order"), no philosophy ("You can only write about yourself"), no more numbering your moods (when Havel started to explore some sixteen of these), no foreign words, no exclamation marks, and so on. Letters failed to get through and those that arrived move back and forth between the immediacy of prison life, his anxieties about Olga and friends outside, his frustrations over the lack of news, and contemplative passages, interspersed with powerful introspection, and, as the letters proceed, a taking-on of ever larger themes. The last cycle of letters is a sustained series of speculative and sometimes lyrical meditations, largely inspired by the French philosopher, Emmanuel Levinas.

It is an extraordinary book, a coherent series of reflections on all the central themes of Havel's life and work. Here, as Heinrich Böll remarked in a review of the *Letters,* "the author of spiritually absurd and 'humorous' dramas . . . reveals the brooding seriousness on which his work is founded". A word of caution, though. As we have seen, humour was forbidden (there must be a play in that!) and Havel has himself acknowledged that some of the more abstruse philosophical vocabulary was a code to elude the rather non-philosophical censor: for example, instead of writing "the regime", he would refer to the "social collective manifestation of the not-I".

At one point Havel remarks,

> I'm no philosopher and it is not my ambition to construct a conceptually fixed system; anyone who tries to understand it that way will soon discover that I am perpetually contradicting myself, that I leave many things unexplained or explain them differently each time, etc.

It is an intriguing disclaimer, of which the Czech philosopher Ladislav Hejdánek has aptly said that if they do not expound philosophy, these letters certainly raise weighty philosophical issues. They do far more, for they are fresh and powerful reflections of an exceptionally active and acute mind on the nature of responsibility and its links with personal identity, on the necessity of a non-relative basis for moral judgments (which he calls the "absolute horizon"), on the rational truth in religion, on the origins of fanaticism, on the nature of the theatre, on the reasons why human beings do good deeds, even when they do not gain from doing so and feel guilt at failing to do so, on what answer one can give to the question "what is the meaning of life?" and on the desperate importance of caring about the question, and on many other such matters. Small wonder that these texts circulated among his friends, and more widely, as soon as they were received. As one of them recalls, "not even while incarcerated behind prison walls did Havel allow his friends and acquaintances to rest".

Havel has made his voice count. It speaks in a moral vocabulary, with great precision and vividness. It is secular in tone ("I am a child of the age of conceptual, rather than mystical thought"), though respectful and cautious in matters of religion ("I admit to an affinity for Christian sentiment and I am glad it's recognisable; nevertheless, one must be extremely cautious in such matters and weigh one's words well"; "God . . . behaves too much like a person for me").

What it says is not, however, always comfortable or even palatable. To his fellow citizens he offers an overtly moral challenge to lead a "life-in-truth", and to those that have left he offers the thought that the totalitarian systems of Eastern Europe are "a convex mirror of all modern civilisation and a harsh, perhaps final call for a global recasting of that civilisation's self-understanding" and the suggestion that "what is called 'dissent' in the Soviet bloc is a specific modern experience, the experience of life at the very ramparts of dehumanised power". To the left, and to the peace movement in the West (whose brother if not comrade he has always been), he offers in **"An Anatomy of Reticence"** an exceptionally subtle account of the deep reasons behind East Europeans' scepticism and reserve, and the difference between the anti-political politics of the dissidents and what he sees as the utopian politics of his interlocutors. To western intellectuals seduced by the current fashions of postmodernist scepticism and nihilism about "metanarratives" and "foundations", he offers an unfashionable belief that the question of what life actually means is capable of an answer—and that both question and answer are to be found in personal experience. . . . Havel's final message is not to propose answers, least of all a definitive one, but that we should find ways of "living with the question."

"The tragedy of modern man", he writes to Olga, "is not that he knows less and less about the meaning of his own life, but that it bothers him less and less". *That* is Havel's distinctive voice. It will not easily be silenced. (p. 328)

> Steven Lukes, "The Meaning of Life at the Ramparts," in The Times Literary Supplement, No. 4487, March 31-April 6, 1989, pp. 327-28.

CLIVE BARNES

There is no doubt that on one level at least, Vaclav Havel's *Temptation,* . . . is fascinating.

Joseph Papp's Public Theater has had an ongoing relationship with Havel since 1968, when it presented his absurdist picture of obscurantist language and social lethargy in *The Memorandum.*

In *Temptation,* the writing is sharp as ever, and you keep on wanting to know what is happening—or rather what is the meaning of what is happening. The text is clear enough, but it is the subtext that grabs the attention.

Then if, like myself, at the end you can discover little more about the meaning of the meaning than you had at the beginning, then, like myself, you will doubtless feel cheated.

Havel, one of Czechoslovakia's leading playwrights and banned in his own country, is a notable civil rights activist, at present shamefully imprisoned by the Czech government.

This is, in the final count, irrelevant to consideration of the play, yet it legitimately suggests the kind of political, or at least moral, coloring it might possess.

Equally important are the odd circumstances of a playwright being banned in his own country, which means that he can potentially reach every audience except the one for which he is essentially writing.

Perhaps the seeming ambivalence of this contemporary version of the Faust legend would speak more clearly to the Prague audience that cannot see it than to the outside audiences which can. Not that this helps anyone.

As the play says at one point; "You have to take a side." Yet to a large extent, taking a side is precisely what the play fails to do. It ends with a bacchanale of chaos, which resolves nothing, except to suggest nihilistically that nothing can be resolved.

Our Faust, Dr. Foustka, is a high-level scientist at some Scientific Institute, run by a Director, busy spinning webs of meaningless phrases, heading up a research laboratory where bureaucracy, as in *The Memorandum,* runs very wild and intensely civilized.

Foustka, for reasons which are never very clear, is tempted to dabble in the occult, and his dabbling is eventually interrupted by a mysterious stranger, calling himself Fistula, who tempts him with . . . well, it's not quite certain what he tempts him with, but certainly this foul-smelling, tramp-like visitor offers him a collaboration.

At the Institute's Garden Party, Foustka wins the apparently undying love of a secretary, called Marketa, firmly rejects the homosexual advances of the Director, and goes home with his mistress, another scientist, Vilma, to the savage excitements of their jealousy-fired, sado-masochistic relationship.

The next morning, Foustka is exposed and accused of black magic. He wriggles on the hook of the accusation, and tries to suggest that, acting independently and unwisely, he was attempting to infiltrate the occult ranks, and set himself up as a double agent.

The play's conclusion, such as it is, is best left to the playwright. That there is some kind of allegory going on here is clear enough—although our own simplistic temptation to identify the bureaucratic scientists with the Czech political regime, and the demonological charms of the occult with Western ideology should probably be resisted.

Presumably Havel is busy here showing us the moral tergiversations of a decent man correctly accused of something he cannot in his heart regard as wrong.

The Faustian paraphernalia, complete with a Faust, a Mephistopheles and even, in a half-hearted fashion, a Marguerite, merely adds symbolism without depth, pretentious puzzlement without solution.

> *Clive Barnes, "Puzzling Prague Politics," in* New York Post, *April 10, 1989.*

FRANK RICH

There is no glasnost for the dissident Czechoslovak playwright Vaclav Havel, who has once again been thrown in prison for championing human rights in Prague, and there is no glasnost in *Temptation,* the Havel play now having its American premiere at the Public Theater.

Set in the malevolent scientific institute of a totalitarian state, *Temptation* is a reworking of *Faust* in which the devil you don't know is always worse than the devil you do know, and the devil you do know is at best a party apparatchik, at worst a thug. In *Temptation,* as in such past Havel plays as *The Memorandum* and *A Private View,* even simple words (starting with "morality") are inverted in meaning by a state that demands intellectual conformity and that governs by fear. It's Mr. Havel's incredible gift—all the more incredible given his inability to see his own works in production—that he

spins out the nightmare of repression in intricate verbal comedy to match that of Tom Stoppard, his longtime friend and admirer.

Perhaps it's a small mercy that Mr. Havel cannot see [this] shabby version of *Temptation,* because it might break his heart. . . .

The listless production only accentuates the author's repetitions and the laborious setup of his less-than-startling final twist. But if *Temptation* seems lesser Havel, it would be absurd to make any conclusive judgment on the basis of this staging—just as it was impossible to evaluate the Havel play *Largo Desolato* on the basis of the distorted rendering it, too, received at the New York Shakespeare Festival in 1985.

Temptation is actually the second Havel presentation [in New York] this year. Shortly after the writer was arrested in Prague in January, leading American playwrights joined representatives of Helsinki Watch and the American Center of PEN in a celebrity-studded program of readings to demand his release. It might be worthwhile if these influential citizens returned to [this theatre] to bear witness, as Mr. Havel cannot, to this production of *Temptation.* While the plight of the playwright in Czechoslovakia may be beyond the reach of concerned Americans, the plight of his plays in New York, at least, is not.

> *Frank Rich, "A Cry of Anger from an Enemy of the State," in* The New York Times, *April 10, 1989, p. C13.*

JOHN BEAUFORT

Repeatedly jailed by one of communism's most repressive police states, Czech civil rights activist Vaclav Havel nevertheless continues writing plays and getting them produced—but only abroad. . . . In [*Temptation,* a] modern version of the Faust legend, Faust becomes Dr. Henry Foustka, member of an institute whose high-tech environs and assorted displays (from skeletons to two white rabbits) seem designed to camouflage its emptiness of purpose.

A secret occultist, Dr. Foustka is furtively immersed in bell, book, and candles when he receives a visit from a repulsive stranger named Fistula. Although Henry does not leap immediately at the Faustian bargain, he acknowledges that his supernatural dabblings have already enhanced his powers of eloquence. In fact, Henry's philosophical flights have captured the heart of innocent Marketa, the institute's resident slavey.

In the course of 10 intricately plotted scenes, Mr. Havel traces the progress of Foustka's dilemma as he becomes ever more deeply involved in satanic pursuits and is regarded with increasing suspicion by his gossipy institute colleagues. Henry himself begins to believe that Vilma, his brutally treated mistress, may be betraying his secret.

Henry's public undoing occurs at an office inquisition presided over by the institute's director, whose homosexual advances Foustka had earlier rejected. The accused scientist fails to convince his colleagues that he has been using the occult rather than being used by satanic forces. Meanwhile, poor little Marketa has lost her job, attempted suicide, and suffered an Ophelia-like derangement. To celebrate Foustka's unmasking, the director proposes a victory celebration in the form of a witch's sabbath masquerade. . . .

For all its symbolism and topical allusions, Havel's sardonic attack on the inane emptiness of the regimented bureaucracy proves more wearisome than entertaining.

John Beaufort, "An Updated, High-Tech 'Faust'," in The Christian Science Monitor, April 21, 1989, p. 10.

JACK KROLL

Vaclav Havel started working on *Temptation* in prison. In his moving collection of letters to his wife from various jails, *Letters to Olga,* the celebrated (everywhere but in his own country) Czech playwright and dissident refers several times to his "play on Faust." That play, *Temptation,* a literally diabolical comedy, just had its American premiere. . . . It seems inevitable that Havel would apply the Faust theme—the man who sells his soul to the Devil in order to obtain ultimate knowledge—to the brutally absurd authoritarian regime in Czechoslovakia. Havel's Faust figure is Henry Foustka, a scientist at a government "institute" engaged in mysteriously unspecified research. In the laboratory, pumps gurgle, computers clack, a heart beats inside a glass case, cute bunnies await their fate. Whatever this Frankensteinian farrago is all about, it has something to do with crushing political dissent, as the institute's director makes clear in Stalinoid speeches to his cowed staff.

Outside the lab, Henry is conducting secret occult experiments when he's not pursuing a kinky affair with one of his colleagues, the sumptuous Vilma. During one of Henry's black-magic sessions a tattered, evil-smelling stranger named Fistula barges in. Fistula, of course, is Mephistopheles, just as Marketa, the institute's virginal secretary, represents the innocent Margaret in the Faust legend. With fiendish logic and biting wit, Havel fuses the Faustian original with the reality of today's Czechoslovakia. Henry discovers that the true devil is the state, which has corrupted science into a tool of political and spiritual oppression. But Havel's real target is not the satanic state but Henry and all the modern mini-Fausts who have made their miserable pacts with power.

Havel is a master of irony, but the supreme irony is that *Temptation* cannot be produced in his own country. It will be circulated through *samizdat,* the underground network, through typescripts, tapes and possibly even performances in living rooms. One can imagine the raw impact of such an experience.

Jack Kroll, "The Devil in Eastern Europe," in Newsweek, Vol. CXIII, No. 17, April 24, 1989 p. 77.

VACLAV HAVEL [INTERVIEW WITH MARK FRANKLAND]

Vaclav Havel is not only Czechoslovakia's best-known playwright, 'dissident', and organiser of the unprecedented mass petition for democratic rights published in Prague last month. He is East Europe's most compelling philosopher of moral resistance to Communism, and already talked about by serious men as a possible president of his country. Although Havel's own government only let him out of prison in mid-May [1989], half way through an eight-month sentence, his callers these days come from East as well as West. . . .

Short of stature, in jeans and brown sweater, [Havel] bustles about getting drinks for his guests: he is famous for his sociability and good manners ('deep rooted, indestructible and profoundly unhealthy' is his own description of his politeness). Nevertheless an Englishman's gift of a large tin of Earl Grey, whose praises Havel sings in *Letters to Olga,* provokes the hint of a frown. Earl Grey, he says, was his favourite drink in prison. In freedom—he is grinning now—he prefers alcohol.

Conversation demonstrates his compulsion to commit himself to whatever he does. Answering questions he concentrates hard, talks slowly, repeats key words. The brainwork is almost audible. Answer finished, he takes a drink, lights a cigarette and makes a joke. He does not want to be kept apart from anything: from the company around him; from everyday pleasures; from the world of the mind—and ultimately, and the root of his steadfastness, the mind of the world.

• • • • •

[Frankland]: *Are you still Vaclav Havel the playwright or have events forced you to be almost entirely Vaclav Havel the public figure?*

[Havel]: If this question concerns what I feel myself, I have to say unequivocally that I still feel the same person I have felt myself to be for the last 30 years, namely a writer and a playwright. If it concerns the role I am playing, or what takes the most of my time, I have to say that an ever-increasing proportion is occupied by my civic and public activities, and that for many people in Czechoslovakia I am known more as a citizen than as a writer. Personally, I regret this, and it explains my feeling that the more I'm forced to be active in politics, the more I enjoy doing theatre.

Your father and grandfather were well-known architects, builders and entrepreneurs in pre-Communist Czechoslovakia. Is there a link between this and the man you are today, perhaps in the dislike you've expressed of the privileges of your well-to-do childhood?

It was only later in my life that I thought about the influence of my so-called bourgeois origins.

I would say it had a paradoxically favourable influence on me in terms of my productivity and work. When I was young and enjoyed the advantages that my background entailed, I felt humiliated by this elevation through privilege. I felt there was a barrier between myself and my environment and social surroundings, and I longed to be equal with others.

The situation changed suddenly after the Communist takeover when I was 12, and since that time I have been persecuted for my origin, or at least it has been publicly held against me. But I felt the same about it both when it was a source of privilege and when it became a cause of suffering and trouble for me.

It helped me as it helps all people who are in some way alienated from their surroundings, in that one can keep a distance, a certain perspective on things, which I also think is the source of the aesthetics of my plays. It is one of the basic, existential influences which was later projected into my work. . . .

What is the link between Havel, the man of the theatre, and Havel, the man of public affairs?

Under conditions like ours where society cannot organise itself naturally, and where politics in the original sense of the word have been abolished, everything becomes crypto-political or semi-political. Politics are thrown out of the door only to come back through the window. Having been abolished as a specific form of human activity, politics spread around and affect everything. In this country everything from a rock group to a concert to a religious Mass can become political.

If a writer attempts to speak the truth all his life he too becomes a political phenomenon, even more so than anybody else because he works with conceptual language, and from time to time names specific things directly. This is the way I understand my political position and my political role.

I have never done any practical politics. I have only written, be it plays, or essays, or manifestos, but I can understand why under these conditions I ended up being considered a political figure *par excellence*. For this reason I feel no split myself, no schizophrenia, no sense that I am jumping from politics to writing or culture and back. It only becomes a problem in everyday life where I'm addressed and sought out increasingly as a political phenomenon rather than as a writer. (p. 31)

You've written that during your first spell in prison you were 'frightened out of your wits.' Did it get any easier?

It is a strange thing. Sometimes I have a feeling—it's quite absurd and irrational—that my place is there, and that I'm on a kind of visit here, in freedom. I think this is perhaps one of the mysterious markings that prison has left on me. Olga was amazed by hearing me talk six months or so after I was released about 'our ward', meaning the prison ward that I had been in.

You've mentioned your wife. In **Letters to Olga** *she is like a character built up by a dramatist throughout his play, but who never makes an appearance. (Havel laughs: 'We'll call her and get her to come in.') Will we ever read her letters to you?*

Those letters, if they exist, are in the archives of the Ministry of Justice because the custom is that if you get a new letter you have to hand in the previous one to be destroyed. But Olga would never approve of their publication, because she does not feel herself to be a writer and she finds it very difficult to write.

You gave up writing poetry because you dislike 'disrobing in public', but can you sum up your marriage to Olga?

I have lived together with my wife for 30 years, and I take her as my lifelong partner. (Silence. Havel smiles.) Today I would say it is an even deeper relationship than an erotic one. . . .

You have in your workroom a card saying, 'Here will stand my computer named Harold.' Will you have time to use it for the writing you really want to do? And why Harold?

It's a present that several Western writers contributed to and by coincidence the first of the donors I spoke to was Harold Pinter. That's why I decided to call the machine Harold. The gift was an act of public protest against the police having confiscated my previous computer. Recently they gave it back to me, and naturally I don't need two so I shall give the old one to someone else. But I not only don't have time for creative writing, I don't even have time for reading, not even for reading all the letters I get. In spite of this I've not lost hope that I shall finish a play I started writing last year.

What are your main opposition activities?

I feel duty bound to participate not only in writing petitions like the latest one on 29 June, but also in other forms of pressuring the government. But I want to have this under my control, and to do it only to the extent that it does not make it impossible for me to exist as a writer. . . .

I have many times made it clear to the ruling powers—most recently during my last time in prison—that they should realise that the people around the Charter 77 are their last chance for peaceful dialogue, and that if they don't take this chance, they can expect an onslaught of fundamentalists.

Are there no signs of compromise?

When the police came here last month very sternly and seriously to warn me for 'the last time', the hard mask with which they started the interview gradually melted. Perhaps that was my doing. In the talk that followed they said they assumed I wanted to be performed as a playwright and that this could even happen quite soon; and that as a writer who wants to be performed I should remember this and be more careful in my public activities.

I had to laugh. This was an enormous concession on their part, because for 20 years they had been saying I wasn't a writer at all, that I had betrayed this country, that I had no right to be published here and that anyway I don't write much and what I do write is rubbish; and that if they perform my plays at all in the West it's only because the theatres there were instructed to do so by what they call the centres of imperialism.

But the situation is complicated by the fact that my plays are now being performed in some socialist countries. It is very hard to suspect one of the applauding spectators of my recent first night earlier this year in Warsaw, namely the then Polish Prime Minister Mieczyslaw Rakowski, of being an agent of imperialism. This retreat from the thesis that I do not exist as a writer to the plea that I should exist only as a playwright bears witness to a subconscious rearguard strategy. How come they appeal to a person who does not exist as a playwright to devote his energies only to the theatre?

Have you ever been tempted to give up?

I am often depressed, and I even have states of desperation, but it is never in the form of a temptation to give up the struggle. I have become involved with my own conscience.

What was the happiest part of your life?

The Sixties, when I could work in a small theatre and do things that reflected my aesthetics, things that I wanted to do. In the 53 years of my life there have been only seven when I could be published here officially. I am not fascinated by being published. It is something that goes deeper. That was a period when I could take time to do what I enjoyed. . . .

You wrote in the **Letters** *that people who do not lose hope and faith in life never come to a bad end. Isn't this too optimistic for a European writer at the end of this of all centuries?*

I always distinguish sharply between hope and optimism. An optimist is a person who thinks everything will turn out for the best. A pessimist thinks everything will turn out for the worst. I don't know how things are going to turn out. That is why I am neither an optimist nor a pessimist. I have a hope inside me, which is something different from optimism or pessimism because these two are a kind of estimate, or prognosis, of the future. Hope is a state of the spirit. It is a state without which life loses any meaning. If I want to live, I have to have hope. (p. 32)

Mark Frankland, *"Necessity of Hope," in* The Observer, *July 30, 1989, pp. 31-2.*

MERVYN ROTHSTEIN

"History has begun to develop very quickly in this country," Vaclav Havel said on Nov. 28, the day Czechoslovakia's Communist Government pledged to give up its 41-year monopoly on political power. "In a country that has had 20 years of timelessness, now we have fantastic speed."

Yesterday [December 29, 1989], with a speed that perhaps even Mr. Havel could not have dared hope for, the 53-year-old playwright and human rights campaigner was elected Czechoslovakia's first non-Communist President since 1948.

Mr. Havel has fought his country's dictatorial abuses for more than 20 years. . . . Until last month, he had been reviled by the Government as an enemy of socialism. Even some of his neighbors would not talk to him.

But throughout the harassment and imprisonment, he has been writing plays to international acclaim for 25 years, though not one of them has been performed in Czechoslovakia since the Soviet-led invasion of 1968. . . .

The British playwright Tom Stoppard, who was born in Czechoslovakia and has known Mr. Havel for years, described him yesterday as "rather like his plays, he's a man who's got a sort of humorous stoicism, without any bitterness in it."

Mr. Havel's plays have long been noted for their absurdist, ironic humor, reflecting the repression that has existed in his country and others in Eastern Europe. His plays often deal, directly or indirectly, with the suffocating life under Communism, and with characters who try to rationalize their collusion with an oppressive system. They live their real lives indoors, in private, but in public, they must go along with the evil that surrounds them.

Mr. Havel, asked about the irony and absurdity of his plays, once said that they were not absurd but "parables of human life itself," or rather life for East Europeans under Communism.

"It seems that in Central Europe, what is most earnest has a way of blending, in a particularly tense manner, with what is most comic," Mr. Havel told *The New York Review of Books* in 1985. "It seems that it is precisely the dimension of distance, of rising above ourselves, that lends our concerns just the right shattering seriousness." . . .

The Government often pressured Mr. Havel to emigrate, but he refused, even declining to go abroad to accept drama prizes in the Netherlands and Sweden out of fear he would not be allowed back into his native country. . . .

"I am Czech," Mr. Havel said in an interview in 1988. "This was not my choice, it was fate. I've lived my whole life in this country. This is my language, this is my home. I live here like everyone else, I don't feel myself to be patriotic, because I don't feel that to be Czech is to be something more than French, or English, or European, or anybody else."

"God—I don't know why—wanted me to be a Czech. It was not my choice. But I accept it, and I try to do something for my country because I live here."

Mervyn Rothstein. *"A Master of Irony and Humor: Vaclav Havel," in* The New York Times, *December 30, 1989, p. 10.*

Chester Himes

1909-1984

(Born Chester Bomar Himes) American novelist, short story writer, autobiographer, and essayist.

Primarily recognized for the serial detective novels he wrote toward the end of his career, Himes also won praise for his significant contributions to African-American postwar fiction. While his earliest literary endeavors are often identified as works of social protest, Himes's later writings, in which he frequently set characters in alien environments to comment on the consequences of social intolerance, are regarded as pleas for social reform. Although Himes's works are often violent, critics commended his satire and his impartial approach to volatile issues. James Sallis noted: "[Himes] is a marvelous observer and prodigious inventor, working by instinct and feeling towards his singular vision. . . . I do not know of any other American writer who has created vivid, memorable scenes in the quantity Himes has, scenes which are hard-edged and durable like a footprint in cement, and with an astonishing economy of dialogue and language."

Himes was born in Jefferson City, Missouri, but his family moved throughout the South before settling in Cleveland, Ohio, when he was fifteen. A dominant character in his novels, the belligerent white woman, was based on his mother, a light-skinned black who berated and humiliated her dark-skinned husband and children. While enrolled in Ohio State University, Himes was angered by discrimination and quickly established a raucous reputation which led to his dismissal. He became involved in gambling and drugs, exhibited a violent temper, and committed petty thefts and forgeries. Himes was arrested for armed robbery in 1928 and sentenced to twenty years in prison. While incarcerated, he began writing short stories based on his experiences there. "To What Red Hell," which appeared in a 1934 issue of *Esquire,* concerns the 1930 fire that killed over three hundred convicts in the Ohio State Penitentiary. Other stories, including "Crazy in the Stir" (1934) and "The Night's for Cryin' " (1937), examine loneliness and fear in the brutal, angry prison environment. Granted parole after serving seven years, Himes moved to California in search of greater employment opportunities. His ill fortune and encounters with blatant racism there formed the basis of his first novel, *If He Hollers Let Him Go* (1945), which critics have described as Himes's most embittered work.

Written in Southern black dialect and set in Los Angeles during World War II, *If He Hollers Let Him Go* centers on Bob Jones, a young black man who is demoted from his factory supervisory position for retaliating against Madge, a coarse white woman who abuses him verbally and taunts him sexually. Bob vows to punish Madge by raping her but rejects her after realizing that she has always desired him. When Bob attempts to apologize to Madge, the scorned woman screams that he is raping her. Madge eventually drops the fabricated charges, and the book ends ironically as Bob is forced to join the army to fight overseas for freedom. Himes continued his exploration of interracial relationships in *Lonely Crusade* (1947), the story of a black man, Lee Gordon, who becomes involved with a white woman, Jackie Falks. After an extend-

ed period of unemployment, Lee becomes a union representative for black workers and surprises a prejudiced society with his intelligence and integrity. When he defends Jackie against threats of expulsion from the union for being a Communist, Lee's wife forces him to leave their house, and Jackie also rejects him from fear of his wife's wrath. As with his first novel, Himes concludes *Lonely Crusade* ironically, as Lee, charged with a crime he did not commit, is shot by the police while leading a union parade.

In *Cast the First Stone* (1952), a highly autobiographical confessional work with a white protagonist, Himes began to balance his racial themes. Set entirely in an unidentified jail, the story is related from the perspective of Jim Monroe, a young man from Mississippi who is incarcerated for armed robbery. He discusses the inhumanity of both the prisoners and the guards, and, in a sequence reminiscent of "To What Red Hell," describes a fire that nearly destroys the jail. Jim breaks prison rules by becoming involved in a homosexual affair with another inmate. In order to be sent to the minimum security prison farm, he concedes that the relationship was a mistake, but his lover commits suicide. In *The Third Generation* (1954), Himes scrutinizes the racial strife he experienced during his childhood. The Taylors, a thinly disguised version of Himes's family, are constantly embroiled in familial and class struggles. Although Mr. Taylor is a respected college professor, his ancestors were slaves, and his wife considers her white lineage and light skin color to be more impressive than his career achievements. She urges her three sons, particularly the youngest, Charles, who narrates the story, to ignore black culture. The psychological turmoil that Mrs. Taylor precipitates ultimately destroys the entire family. Stephen Milliken observed: "The characters of *The Third Generation* have a largeness of size that is without parallel in the rest of Chester Himes's fiction. They are creatures of epic, of romance, of allegory—and of life itself, remembered with love and anguish." Himes's next work, *The Primitive* (1954), is considered a skillfully plotted exploration of the ease with which stereotypical judgments can destroy society. Jesse, a black man, and Kriss, a white woman, are old friends who reunite for a weekend of celebration when Jesse gets a cash advance for his novel. Quite drunk, Kriss demands sexual favors of Jesse, whom she has always envisioned as the stereotypical libidinous black man, and Jesse, who has pictured Kriss as the personification of white feminine beauty, complies. Neither can fulfill the other's expectations, however, and Jesse murders Kriss in an angry, drunken stupor. The novel ends as Jesse, complying with social sterotype, telephones the police to inform them that a black man has killed a white woman.

Frustrated by racism, Himes left the United States in 1954 and traveled through Europe, eventually settling in Spain, where he lived until his death. As an expatriate, Himes had the opportunity to write more freely of racial concerns. He achieved international success with *Pinktoes* (1961), his only nonviolent novel. Again, Himes confronts racism, but through a radically different thematic approach. A sex farce, this novel probes the doctrines of Mamie Mason, a white society matron who believes that she can end prejudice by hosting desegregated sexual orgies. In reality, the guests are merely interested in interracial sex and not social change. Widely popular in France, where readers were amused with the satire of American high society, *Pinktoes* is regarded as Himes's most daring work of fiction. During this time, Himes was encouraged by his agent to write the series of detective novels that would become his most famous works. Between 1957 and 1969, he published nine books, all of which, with the exception of *Dare-dare* (1959; *Run Man Run*), are set in Harlem, New York, and feature the same pair of black detectives, Coffin Ed Johnson and Grave Digger Jones. The two are fiercely loyal to each other and to the white and black Harlem residents they protect. Of the series, James Sallis asserted: "I admired their singular voice, the precise economy of Himes' imagery and description, the outlandish rightness of his characterizations and the velocity he generated in his narratives, their sheer force of imagination." Throughout the novels, Himes ironically depicts oppression within black society as the detectives' gravest problem. Each plot involves an enigmatic object or an amount of money that the detective duo inevitably locate. The formula is reminiscent of the novels of Raymond Chandler, whose works Himes admitted to reading and admiring while in prison. Extreme violence, vivid descriptions, and dry wit characterize the series, of which *Retour en Afrique* (1964; *Cotton Comes to Harlem*) is perhaps the best known volume. In this work, Coffin Ed and Grave Digger must recover the eighty seven thousand dollars that Harlem families lost as a result of a swindle by a religious group. The story's light, farcical style and Himes's ability to enrich the tale with symbolism and elements of African-American history contributed to its overwhelming success. A film version of *Cotton Comes to Harlem* was produced in 1970.

Himes also wrote *Black on Black* (1973), an acclaimed volume of short stories, which includes "Baby Sister," a brutal tale of an incestuous affair between a poverty-stricken brother and sister. He published an autobiography in two volumes, *The Quality of Hurt* (1972) and *My Life of Absurdity* (1976), which offer glimpses of friendships and relationships, discuss influences on his writings, and chart the bitterness and rage Himes felt toward the uncertain status of blacks in America. Of *The Quality of Hurt*, Richard H. Gaines commented: "[Not] only does one discern in these pages the spirit of vengeful evil that seems to assist Himes in achieving his goals . . . but the presence of innate good. He is at once menacing and admirable, darkly tragic and luminously human."

(See also *CLC*, Vols. 2, 4, 7, 18; *Contemporary Authors*, Vols. 25-28, rev. ed., Vol. 114 [obituary]; *Contemporary Authors New Revision Series*, Vol. 22; and *Dictionary of Literary Biography*, Vols. 2, 76.)

EDWARD MARGOLIES

Chester Himes is one of the most prolific of all Negro novelists. . . . [Yet] for the most part the American critics have dismissed him as being of the [Richard] Wright school of naturalism, whose "protest" is no longer fashionable. Such criticism is not altogether fair. Himes's interests are considerably different from Wright's, and his firsthand knowledge of certain areas of American life is more developed. His protagonists are generally middle-class, fairly well-educated, somewhat sophisticated in the ways of the world, and often intellectually oriented. They are concerned with ideas and the application of ideas to their experience; they are constantly searching out rational explanations for the irrationalities of their lives. They move with considerable aplomb among white liberals and radicals of both sexes, and engage them in dialectics on their own terms. Himes is also a more deliberate prose stylist than Wright. He seldom intrudes, moralizes, or explains. His characters are usually sufficiently articulate to say what they mean—and what they mean issues often enough from their character and intelligence. (pp. 87-8)

In an autobiographical novel, *The Third Generation* (1954), Himes relates the growth into young manhood of Charles Taylor, the son of genteel, decorous Southern parents. Charles grows up in Cleveland, attends public school with white children, and spends some time at Ohio State University. As the novel progresses, Charles and his family disintegrate under the pressures of modern urban life and of the insidious racism that underlies their social and familial relationships.

Although generally well-written, the novel is more interesting as a psychological study than as a finished work of fiction, since Himes never really focuses in on his theme. He does, however, very delicately and compassionately attempt to understand his characters. On the surface, rank bigotry seldom intrudes as the direct cause of their suffering; they appear to be defeated by their own incapacities, weaknesses, blindness, and obsessions. But Himes makes clear that in order to understand them, one must understand the generations that preceded them, black and white: they are doomed not simply by their own psychic drives but by the history that created them and forced them into self-destructive channels. (p. 88)

Himes feels the trunk and roots of American society are so corrupted as to make normal growth and development impossible. His concern is not primarily with social protest, as has so often been alleged, for protest implies some hope of appropriate reform, and Himes, one suspects, regards the American scene as beyond redemption. His principal subject is the human consequences of a distorted and diseased civilization. His characters, on the other hand, prefer to interpret their warped and maddened psyches in terms of the society that has conditioned them. Being Negroes, they are more attuned to social abuse, and being middle-class or intellectual, they are all the more aware of their frustrations since their aspirations, though similar to those of the white bourgeoisie, are blocked by their color. "Successful" professional Negroes are frequently more embittered than persons of lower socioeconomic strata, whose expectations are not nearly so great. And it is men like Himes who are often the bitterest enemies of their own social class for having compromised their values in submission to caste mores.

Somewhere James Baldwin has written that Chester Himes is the only Negro writer who has described male-female relationships in other than violent terms. This is not altogether accurate, since Jessie Fauset and Nella Larsen probed along these lines in the 1920's, as have some latter-day novelists, notably Kristin Hunter and Paule Marshall. Nor is Himes's treatment of love without its elements of sadism and self-laceration. But it is undoubtedly true that Himes, in each of his major works, has focused much of his attention on lovers, and has attempted to track down the vagaries and nuances of their emotions. He has, in addition, an unabashed eye for the physical and sensual. It is true as well that he appears to be devoting more and more of his work to material hitherto regarded as taboo—interracial love. Perhaps Himes feels, like so many other Negro authors and intellectuals, that underlying the structure of American society is an unresolved residue of erotic racial guilt that manifests itself, among other ways, as "the Negro problem."

Himes's first novel, *If He Hollers Let Him Go* (1945), is related in the first person, in hard-boiled, Hemingwayesque prose, by a young Negro who works in a Los Angeles shipyard during World War II. In the course of the novel, Bob Jones loses his girl, is demoted in his job, becomes involved in a brawl in which he is unjustly accused of attempted rape, and ultimately promises to enlist in order to avoid imprisonment. But his declining fortune is forecast in the first pages of the novel by a near paranoid state of mind—and in that sense there is no real progression in the novel. Everything that happens to Bob—and there are humiliations, rebuffs and insults from beginning to end—only serves to justify the extremity of his emotions. Had Himes shown Jones to be more trusting from the start, the effect might be cumulative rather than tedious.

What intrigues the reader, however, is not what his first novel might have been, but rather his discovery of the themes that he would employ to greater advantage later on. This is a race novel in the purest sense of the term. Bob's tensions are produced and aggravated by the bigotry he meets everywhere. He lives from one moment to the next on the edge of violence, terrified not only of what others may do to him, but of what he feels about himself. Specifically, systematic racism has

awakened in him deep castration fears—has indeed psychologically emasculated him, robbing him of his self-esteem since he is constantly being reminded of his "place" in the scheme of things. In compensation, Bob drives his car furiously, drinks hard, fights hard, and makes love to the wife of one of his friends. But his principal torment is that he is intellectually aware of what is happening to him, but cannot muster sufficient strength to save himself as he watches his fate overtake him.

His dreams of crippled men and tethered dogs describe to him metaphorically the realities of his waking condition.

> The alarm went off again. . . . I groped for it blindly, shut it off; I kept my eyes shut tight. But I began feeling scared in spite of hiding from the day. It came along with consciousness. It came into my head first, somewhere back of my closed eyes, moving slowly underneath my skull to the base of my brain, cold and hollow. It seeped down my spine, into my arms, spread through my groin with an almost sexual torture, settled in my stomach like butterfly wings. For a moment I felt torn all loose inside, shriveled, paralyzed, as if after a while I'd have to get up and die.

Bob himself never employs clinical language to explain the erotic implications of the psychosocial roles he knows he plays—but the meaning is never far from the surface. Not only does white society emasculate him, but it tends simultaneously to regard him as an envied symbol of sexual strength from which white women must be protected. Implicit here is Himes's view that the sexual insecurity of the white American male impels him to suppress the Negro in order to bolster his shaky masculine ego. (pp. 89-91)

In his next novel, *Lonely Crusade* (1947), Himes extends the fantasy one step further to the white woman. The white mistress of a Negro man often unknowingly experiences feelings of smug *noblesse oblige* in giving herself to an "inferior." At critical moments, however, she will retreat behind caste barriers rather than risk social disapproval. Lee Gordon, for example, learns that his white mistress will not condescend to fight over him with his wife—not out of tender considerations for his family life, but because it would offend her sense of racial superiority to squabble with a Negro woman. The white woman finds the Negro eminently desirable as the forbidden embodiment of her sexual yearnings; on the other hand, he also stands for her guilt and shame about these feelings. She punishes herself by taking the Negro at the same time that she gratifies herself physically. Or should she be rebelling against social conventions, she may use the Negro as a symbol of her defiance. Whatever the combination of motives, in no case is the Negro's essential humanity recognized. Rather do white and Negro lovers play games with one another, using one another as objects of wish fulfillment.

Lonely Crusade is a sprawling, uneven novel of ideas dealing with the life of an uncommitted West Coast Negro union organizer, Lee Gordon, who after a series of mishaps learns to overcome his deep-seated caste-conditioned fears and suspicions and achieve a sense of identity. There are lengthy passages relating to dialectical materialism, anti-Semitism among Negroes, and Negro attitudes toward labor unions—and some of these have a certain intrinsic value. Moreover, Himes has been able to create a few authentic characters who manage to stand out in vivid contrast to a somewhat strained, at times oversentimentalized plot.

But Himes is really at his best in portraying Lee Gordon's relationships to his wife and mistress. He shows the gradual deterioration of a marraige as Lee Gordon discovers his wife is better able to provide for herself than he. Conversely, he shows how Lee temporarily regains an illusion of manhood with a white woman whose demands are primarily sexual. The emasculating effects of racism are again the deepest source of Lee's misery, and Himes traces these in graphic emotional detail. But the story resolves itself in a strange upbeat ending (resembling the proletarian novel of the thirties), in which Lee decides he cannot blame race for everything and throws in his lot with the struggling working man for the betterment of white and Negro alike.

The novel is thus clearly derivative, but Himes's insights are good, particularly as regards the Negro's attraction to the white woman. On the most obvious level, she is an object of fear, since any suspicions of interracial sex may lead to death and castration. When Lee Gordon, as a young boy, is discovered hiding in a girls' locker room, he and his family scurry out of town in order to avoid possible ghastly consequences. Yet because of the mysterious taboo aura with which she is endowed, Himes's Negro men find the white woman all the more desirable. This desire is often mixed with hate, since she is viewed as the original cause of their pariah status; moreover, possessing a white woman may serve as an act of clandestine revenge on the white man who persecutes them. Finally, the white woman may provide the Negro with the sense of masculinity which he fails to achieve with women of his own race. In a society where the man is expected to support and protect his women, the Negro male who finds himself unable to do so for caste and economic reasons may turn for solace to the white woman. (pp. 91-3)

On the surface, **The Primitive** (1955), appears to be far less ambitious than Himes's previous undertakings. For one thing, he narrows his scope considerably, focusing on two rather atypical characters and their circle of estranged Bohemian acquaintances. The setting of the novel alternates between a shabby Harlem tenement and a Gramercy Park apartment, lending the story a kind of staged theatrical quality. Finally, the concentrated time span—six days—within which the narrative is encompassed, forcibly limits the range of action of its participants. The novel does, nonetheless, explore many of the same problems as his previous works and represents Himes's best artistic effort to date.

The two major characters are an unsuccessful Negro novelist, Jesse, and a white woman, Kriss, who holds a responsible administrative position at a Madison Avenue foundation called the India Institute. The first few chapters alternate between Kriss and Jesse—Kriss in her apartment, at her job, and among friends; Jesse in the dreary Harlem rooms that he shares with disreputable tenants, or out on the streets wandering aimlessly from one bar to the next. They meet, having not seen each other for several years, and each uses the other for his own neurotic needs. The latter portion of the novel describes a week-end drinking party at Kriss's house, where Kriss and Jesse are visited by a number of "liberal" intellectual friends, white and Negro. The presence of these exacerbates their feelings of defeat and failure, and each turns on the other with increased hate and venom. Jesse apparently kills Kriss in a state of drunken oblivion (the scene is not described but alluded to after the event), and the novel closes on Jesse calling the police to inform them of her death.

Himes endeavors to relate their own emotional chaos to corresponding absurdities in world affairs. From time to time Kriss tunes in a television interview with a chimpanzee who can predict the news. The monkey responds to specific questions by reciting news dispatches that will be broadcast at some future date. The effectiveness of this device is somewhat compromised by the fact that Jesse and Kriss provide no suitable reference point of sanity. Their imbalance appears too much the product of their own peculiar backgrounds, so it remains for the reader to, link up the madness within and the madness without.

It is not that Himes has not made the effort. He traces their history in terms of the environment that has fashioned them. Kriss was brought up in North Dakota, the only daughter of an alcoholic German nobleman and a mother of Scandinavian peasant stock. When she was sixteen, she was seduced, and the abortion that followed rendered her sterile. Later she works in Chicago as an assistant to a Negro sociologist researching race relations. The interracial, Bohemian group with whom she associated during this period pressured her into marrying a white Mississippian, who turned out to be a homosexual. Her numerous subsequent liaisons with men of both races were an attempt to compensate for the terrifying hurt and loneliness she had felt all her life. . . . On the surface Kriss appears to be a very elegant and successful career woman, but in truth she is despairing and hysterical, and uses drink and promiscuity to stave off her loneliness. Kriss is a well-realized character, but the extremities of her situation appear to have been induced by her environment only in the most general way. Rather does she seem to be the victim of chance circumstances and a certain central weakness of character. She is not a racist, but she does resort to racial fantasies to compensate for feelings of inadequacy, and she uses the racial fears of her white and Negro lovers to exact her revenge on men—on whom, usually, she places the blame for her psychological undoing. Nor is she a racial "radical" advocating miscegenation and free love as a social cure-all. Her dearest wish is to marry into the respectable white middle class and live a normal bourgeois life. To imagine Kriss as a reduced version of the absurdities she watches on television is somewhat far-fetched.

Jesse, on the other hand, is more understandable. His bitterness stems in part from the racial humiliation he has suffered all his life, in part from the fact that he cannot support his wife (and has, as a result, left her), and in part from the sordid conditions in which he lives. Jesse's third novel, on which he had been working for more than a year, has been turned down for publication. The reading public, he is told, is tired of protest; he should try writing novels with more "uplift." When Jesse observes that he can write only about the life he knows, he is advised to write about successful Negroes like himself. (pp. 93-6)

When [Jesse and Kriss] meet again, their story becomes a dance of death wherein the black man and the white woman tease and taunt and thrust at one another until both are destroyed. Within this macabre framework, Himes projects varying degrees of alcoholic murk through which his two principals attempt to grope their way. On occasion, however, he will introduce flat documentary prose in order to keep his characters in some kind of touch with reality. (p. 96)

The title of the novel, **The Primitive,** of course refers to the role Jesse plays in his affair with Kriss. From the world's viewpoint Jesse lives up to this image by murdering Kriss. But the irony lies in the fact that, far from being primitive,

Jesse kills because he is overcivilized. His sensibilities have been stretched to the breaking point, and it is precisely because he feels his individual humanity is never recognized that he finds his existence unbearable. In killing Kriss, Jesse strikes back at the primitivism of "civilized" whites who deny him his dignity. His "primitive" act of violence thus makes him civilized in their eyes. When he realizes he has murdered Kriss, he muses sardonically to himself that he can now join the human race.

Himes's point is basically that anything that dehumanizes is primitive, and the racial attitudes of American society are symptoms of a dehumanized culture. . . . The dehumanized lives of all Americans, from the exploited poor to the characterless sophisticates of Kriss's circle, torment Jesse in drunken dreams. Perhaps most symbolic of all is the prophetic monkey forecasting the news. It is as if this nonhuman, precivilized creature really expresses the nature of American life.

It is in the area of sexual relationships that the theme of the novel makes its greatest impact. Kriss and Jesse perceive one another in primitive images—not as individuals but as projections of their own inchoate impulses, desires, and terrors. For Kriss, Jesse is at once a symbol of sexual power, a whipping boy for all her self-loathing and frustration, and an instrument to taunt the sensibilities of white men who have rejected her in the past. But Kriss, by a strange twist of logic, tends subconsciously to blame Negroes for the failure of her marriage. In taking a Negro lover, she can also direct her anger toward Negro men generally. For her, an act of love is as much an act of hostility as anything else. Jesse, in turn, is motivated by certain primitive and dangerous elements in his nature. . . . Without acknowledging it to himself, Jesse is seeking out his physical destruction, but just as significantly he is seeking out the cause of his destruction. For him Kriss represents the white world that has crushed him, and, unconsciously, Jesse decides to kill her. (pp. 97-8)

It is difficult to do justice to this novel. Parts are extremely well-written and Himes's cast of characters is authentically conceived. Jesse is especially interesting. His self-pity—of which he has plenty—is seldom irritating, and this is a remarkable feat for any author. Himes laces Jesse's gloom with a kind of dry wit, a sad intellectual humor that saves him from sentimentality.

> No more worrying about what's right and what's wrong. Just what's expedient. You're human now. Went in the back door of the Alchemy Company of America a primitive, filled with things called principles, integrity, honor, conscience, faith, love, hope, charity and such, and came out the front door a human being, completely purged. End of a primitive; beginning of a human. Good title for a book but won't sell in America with the word *human* in it. Americans sensitive about that word. Don't want to know they're human. Don't blame them, though. Poses the only problem they've never been able to solve with all their gadgets—the human problem. But they'll know damn well you're human. Be in all the newspapers: *Black man kills white woman.* Not only natural, plausible, logical, inevitable, psychiatrically compulsive and sociologically conclusive behavior of a human being, but mathematically accurate and politically correct as well. Black man has got to have some means of joining the human race. Old Shakespeare knew. Suppose he'd had Othello kiss the bitch and make up. Would have dehumanized him.

This is Himes's most pessimistic work. He has lost faith in the human capacity to reason its way out of its dilemmas. Jesse and Kriss, two intelligent human beings, are as muddled and distressed about their own identities as the worst racists. But here lies the trouble. Himes has, in a curious way, written two books—one about Jesse and Kriss, and one about racist America—and the two do not quite mesh, because Jesse and Kriss are too atypical and too idiosyncratic. Himes's ideas require a novel with a wider scope than one shabby Harlem tenement, one Gramercy Park apartment, and a few decadent intellectuals. Whether or not he will succeed in writing such a novel remains to be seen.

Himes's latest work on similar subject matter is a broad comic farce, *Pinktoes* (1965). Ironically, *Pinktoes,* the least of Himes's novels, has gained him his widest popularity in America. It deals with a Machiavellian Harlem hostess, Mamie Mason, whose most towering ambition is to win a place in society. She entices a variety of figures from the white and Negro establishments to parties intended ostensibly to improve race relations. But Mamie believes that race relations are best improved in bed, and so the guests at her soirees generally manage to seduce one another away from husbands, wives, lovers and so on without any special regard to race.

The satire is presumably aimed at the pretensions of certain elements of the Negro bourgeoisie and the race-relations "moderates" who dominated the New York scene a decade or so ago. The danger in writing novels of this sort is that caricature implies a certain singleness of purpose that makes the plot predictable. Himes must therefore place his characters in more and more outrageous situations in order not to bore his readers. This nearly succeeds, but the trouble is that too many of his characters, black and white, male and female, are cut from the same mold. They are all lesser Mamie Masons, ambitious and unscrupulous and with only one thing, more or less, on their minds. (pp. 98-100)

Pinktoes is not without its moments. Himes has a slap-stick imagination and can write wildly funny scenes. . . . But there are too many . . . definitionlike statements, too many explanations: how Negroes are defined in America, and why; how persons happen to be in such and such a place when some unseemly event occurs; where certain streets and houses are located in various parts of New York; and so ad infinitum. Himes is constantly interposing his own voice, sometimes condescending, up and down the narrative line, like some roué schoolteacher instructing his prurient students. (The novel was originally published in France, where such an account of the absurd and funny ways Americans conduct their sex lives would match a good many chauvinistic preconceptions.) (p. 100)

[Himes's] long absence from America . . . is beginning to tell on his novels. Some of the details of his American setting are no longer quite accurate (in *Pinktoes* he places railroad tracks on West 10th Street in the Village.) And some of the attitudes he attributes to his white and Negro sophisticates are no longer fashionable (not publicly, at least), and in any event would no longer be generally articulated. Yet Himes has considerable narrative power and startlingly clear psychological insights. Perhaps what his novels now require is a European setting. It would be a shame if he were to allow his latest success to impair his progress as an artist. (p. 101)

Edward Margolies, "Race and Sex: The Novels of

Chester Himes," in his Native Sons: A Critical Study of Twentieth-Century Negro American Authors, *J. B. Lippincott Company, 1968, pp. 87-101.*

A. ROBERT LEE

Despite his persisting and highly particular talents, Chester Himes continues to be footnoted a Wrightian exponent of Black American literary protest given to reworking an inherited vein of angry naturalism. This blunt evasion of his forty years of craft and resource speaks worlds of criticism's stubborn unseeing before Black imaginative achievement and of its insistence of notions of hierarchy and diagnosis largely inappropriate, dull and racist. Although his imagination is hardly without flaw or unsteadiness, Himes has written fiction of considerable claim which explores a vital nerve in American life and which records with extraordinary eloquence racism's waste and damage. Acerbic in tone, firmly angled for the most part, subvertingly funny and threat-laden of late, his novels are addressed to the unflagging play of violence in America, its encasing pressures for those obliged to live out an aggregate identity determined by the crude basis of skin rather than by individual presence and need. The reaches of Himes' abilities, diverse and frequently compelling, deserve far better attention than that long remarked by a small enthusiastic readership. . . .

Himes has recently awakened in America enthusiasm of a kind more usually granted to Richard Wright, Ralph Ellison, and James Baldwin of the immediate post-war American circuit and to John A. Williams, Imamu Baraka, and Nikki Giovanni of younger Black moderns. In some degree this belated recognition for a talent reputed to be of minor key has been the by-product of Black cultural recovery during the 1960s, but more directly it has been caused by Himes' enormously popular, almost cultist, Coffin Ed/Gravedigger Jones novels. . . . (p. 13)

The Harlem Himes puts on the page in the Coffin Ed/Gravedigger fables goes well beyond merely appropriate backcloth to a run of lively potboilers. It approaches inspired surrealism. Harlem comes through as an urban hothouse mean with exotic hustle and violence, a tangible asphalt jungle with its own abrasive laws of motion and boundaries and at the same time a mythical kingdom with properties of magic and violent farce. Though forever unlikely to earn comparison with, say Dickens' London or Joyce's Dublin (Chandler's Los Angeles, Claude McKay's Harlem, or Imamu Baraka's Newark might offer more precise frames of comparison), Himes' Black Upper Manhattan is charted with rich, if somewhat bizarre, authenticity.

With the exception of his *jeu d'esprit*, **Pinktoes**, . . . violence identifies all of Himes' fiction, violence both quietly corrosive and loudly expansive. The nine "Harlem domestic stories," as Himes terms the detective novels (only **Run Man Run** excludes Coffin Ed and Gravedigger), take up and magnify the violence of the earlier books. Himes has rendered the Harlem world they chart as one approaching an unprecedented total racial explosion. His Harlem explores an enclave of Black urban life constrained into exquisite heat and masquerade with the two Black detectives fighting a holding action against what, in the two most recent works, threatens as terminal violence, the holocaust of outright racial war. (pp. 13-14)

Read collectively, Himes' first five novels, not always without laboriousness, trace through an unfolding graph of injury and loss and of vital energies sapped and corroded. They chronicle fear, exhaustion, pursuit, individual need, and rebellion as decisive qualities in the lives of his major Black figures. With an unequivocal eye to the stab of controlling whiteness upon Black skins and psyches, Himes' fiction maps out interior landscapes of entropy, the process whereby unnourished selfhood runs down before its own impotence.

Himes' men and women in the early books, nearly all of articulate middle-class stock, find their very sharpness of consciousness punitive. By counterpointing the inner and outer textures of the violence that Willie E. Abrahams aptly calls "the language of white manliness" [in the introduction to William Melvin Kelley's novel *dem*], Himes avoids formulaic angry novels (though there is anger in all he writes) and achieves a notable density and impetus to his writing. His detective novels are really logical points of arrival for an author to whom violence is both the essential condition, and the essential abuse, of the life before him. Himes should rank as a writer of serious, if uneven, accomplishment, a longstanding connoisseur of violence whose fiction achieves its own vital and challenging voice.

If He Hollers Let Him Go (1945) on first view might rank unambiguously as a race narrative, a fable of persecution written in brittle Hemingwayese. Its story is that of Bob Jones, an intelligent young UCLA graduate given token authority over an all-Black work crew in the World War II shipyards of Atlas, one of California's super-industries. Fighting to keep the affections of Alice, the daughter of Black professional parents, and hounded on all fronts by white authority, Bob gets trapped into a spurious rape charge by Madge, an abused but succulent Texan redneck. Beaten half to a pulp by Madge's avenging white menfolk (imported cheap Southern labor like herself), then pursued by police and put to trial, Bob is given the choice of Army or prison.

Reviewing *If He Hollers* . . . the year of its publication, Richard Wright perceptively noted the book's ordering paradoxes, the careful means by which Himes takes his first novel beyond casebook realism. Having described Bob as a man "reacting . . . with nerves, blood and motor responses," Wright pointed to "the transformations by which sex is expressed in equations of race pride, murder in the language of personal redemption and love in terms of hate." These transformations in fact contribute to the novel's thick tissue of existential metaphor, the dreams, images and fantasies which express the introverting consequences of racism. Bob, for instance, suffers the paradoxical ability of Atlas's white workers and the society of which they are a part, to transform him from a castrated Black fugitive into a sexually daemonic superman. And when he reflects grimly, "I had to get ready to die before I could leave the house," his comment is that of a worker whose working vitality is exhausted, a Black whose daytime life is the quarry for his night-time dreams of emasculation. Instead of self-freeing relationships with women and the application of craft skills at Atlas, he feels only a cycle of control. Forced to hold two views of himself—on the one hand a conscious human being and on the other a mechanical functionary, a lover and yet a fiend of imposed sexual myth, a "man" who dreams endlessly of his own unmanning—Bob indeed personifies a living paradox, both in flight from and in combat against, his own finely tuned consciousness and the emasculating realities it reports. (p. 14)

Like all of Himes' novels, *If He Hollers* opens up the sexual fibers of race, those flashes of taboo and myth which invest racial violence (and in this novel, most racial contact) with a sexual iconography. At a prime level, Bob's confrontation with Madge, Himes plays off against his encounters with Alice, his slightly androgynous, genteel girl. And as a man among men, Bob seeks endlessly standards of useable manhood. His search takes various forms—his bid for dignity before Atlas's white overseers, his adolescent machismo in driving to the shipyards with his Black workmates in a souped-up car. But fevered manlessness dogs his every turn. Not only does he endure dreams of being without work-tools, but his mind roams back to a Black audience he once saw applauding blind white acrobats performing at, of all places, the Lincoln Theatre. His desperation takes the form of hunting down a white "nigger-baiter," violence Himes depicts as possibly manning, up-grading. Finally, the pursuer turns pursued as the Los Angeles police narrow in on his lonely flight. These different tensions of flight and pursuit, role and rolelessness, amount to a sexual catalogue of violence. . . .

The sharply unmanning directions of his life, with Alice as much as Madge, away from and inside Atlas, lead almost inexorably into the Court's reductive formula of the "rape and run" charge. Bob's emotions have been primitivized. His anger and despair turn self-destructively inwards. Throughout the novel Himes makes violence the reaction of both inner turbulence and the multiple external ways by which white society expresses its will over Blacks. Bob's relentless inner dream life and his own final act of external flight are made to match perfectly. For a first novel, *If He Hollers* offers a formidable log of violence's damage.

Heavy industry also forms the donnée of Himes' second and longest novel, *Lonely Crusade* (1947), a work which grants more comprehensive range to his diagrams of violence but which sags as an organic and formally arranged whole. The matrix out of which the novel grew is clearly discernible—Himes' direct involvement with the then newly minted C.I.O., his acid distrust of the Communist Party, and his close sense of Wright's *Native Son*. As an imaginative essay on unionism. West Coast politics, race and violence, it achieves far more than *If He Hollers.* The parts, however, lack the unified drive, the tautness, of the first novel.

Lonely Crusade recounts the troubled passage of Lee Gordon, a Black labor man hired to unionize the Black workers of Comstock Aircraft, like Atlas, a California war industry. Against the conspiring odds of historical communism, mainly personified by Luther McGergor, an opportunist Black brother and the Capitalist Right (Louis Foster, Comstock's boss), Gordon fights an uphill fight towards democratic unionism in company with a tough and by no means unracist assortment of union officials. Gordon's passage takes him through political chicanery on a number of fronts, through Hollywood parties and private sexual humiliations, a route of fear and emasculation which leads into a false murder charge. Finally, in a closing dramatic strike march outside Comstock, Lee seizes the union's banner from a fallen comrade and, with a policeman's gun leveled on his body, opts for the violent recovery of his right to a revolutionary destiny by rallying the strikers behind him.

Himes again links up the larger movements of violence at the surface of white-controlled society—murder, police brutality, bossism—to the inner trials of his main figure. Gordon's private struggle is to redeem his sexually injured manhood in the eyes of himself and his wife, Ruth, a woman who has long earned more money than he has and whose body he has come to regard as a source of pain rather than love. He abandons Ruth temporarily for Jackie, a young and attractive white Party agent eventually denounced by the Party to protect Luther's selling out the union to Comstock, an act which jeopardizes the loyalty of the Black workers. Himes thus keeps the narrative of Gordon's life alive at two primary levels, the first that of his struggle for attention and function in the world of Comstock, the second that of his inner life, the life of his battered psyche.

Despite the energy and intelligence of Himes' excursions into Marxism and race, especially his views of the Party's expedient uses of the American Black, and his scrutiny of labor and capital (scrutiny which extends to Jew and Black, color and sex), he doesn't altogether seat such concerns comfortably within the novel's imaginative structure. They tend to enter the narrative too stagily—in letters, newspaper clippings, heavy confessional scenes, party conversations in the Hollywood belt and in the long polemics of Rosie, a Jewish Party man closely derived from Max in Richard Wright's *Son*. The effect on the narrative is to retard the book's imaginative flow, veering it woodenly towards overt thesis fiction. But the novel does have filaments of great strength, amplifying Himes' enquiry into the racist technologies of white power, specifically in the violations of Lee Gordon's psyche and manhood. (p. 15)

Himes never explicitly acknowledges the hero of *Cast the First Stone* (1952), Jim Monroe, as Black, but his account of time-suspended claustrophobia in a Federal prison is loaded with analogies to the isolative and imprisoning sentences imposed by white society on Black. At the beginning of the novel the prison deprives Jim of name and history: "After ten days all information relative to my past and future, my body and soul, had been carefully recorded and filed. It had been done grimly and without sympathy." An ingénu, Jim gradually learns the ecology of prison routine, the high-temperature emotions of men placed under monitored physical constraint. He works first as a laborer in the prison's power-house (as a workhorse at the bottom of the machine, he is a part of a number of parallels to Black American history active throughout the novel). By a series of sexual and hustling moves he gains a position of handsome sufficiency, even triumph, among his fellow-prisoners. . . . The fixed limits of Jimmy's universe Himes terms "stone and steel and concrete." A sensation of total control guides his sense of time: "Almost all the days belonged to the prison. They were steel-laced and unvarying, shaped and moulded for eternity. Another day. And then another . . . " Only the solace of Jimmy's lovers reaches certain wellsprings of emotion—Mal Steater especially, who becomes his "cousin," and Duke Dido, the artistic queen who finally hangs himself. Trying to write, wrestling down sexual self-contempt, and playing the card-school boss, Jimmy staggers through his sentence, a man without privateness or the fostered confidence of identity. Like the Biblical injunction from which the book takes its title, the prison envisions life as a storehouse of private miseries running down into spasms of hate and violence. The massive fire which kills a large number of prisoners acts as a powerful emetic to the congested cycle of abusive power in the prison, a further Himesian violent image of how repressive systems turn volcanic and eventually erupt. The analogies with racial repression, though implicit, are clear.

The outside world Himes only marginally keeps in view. Jimmy gets letters from his mother. Clothes, cigarettes and food are smuggled in on the prison underground. In the main, however, the prison is its own total world, inverting all normal canons of behavior. . . . Like other fables of self-enclosure and escape, the novel is beautifully authenticated by Jimmy's reportorial "I." The recording consciousness as witness has a particular strength in Black American writing—stretching from oral slave narratives through the autobiographies of Booker T. Washington, Frederick Douglass, and James Weldon Johnson to the work of Malcolm X, Baldwin, Cleaver, Claude Brown, and yet more recently to the letters of George Jackson. So pervasive has this autobiographical mode been that it may well represent the most forceful province of Black letters. Survival in *Cast the First Stone* is elemental and deeply existential. In treading the paths of prison violence, Jimmy Monroe belongs patently enough with Bob Jones and Lee Gordon in Himes' special gathering of violated men. (pp. 16-17)

[*The Third Generation* (1954)] lies near to Truman Capote's category of the non-fictional novel, personal history only lightly fictionalized. Crowded, at several points slack in laying out its heavy texture of detail—Himes was possibly too close to parts of the story—it maps out the dereliction of the Black bourgeois Taylor family, "Professor" Willie, his wife, and three sons. The Taylors take a downward journey from South to North involving dislocation which is a direct consequence of the mother's blighting pride in the lightness of her skin (she can pass) and the conviction that her white heritage confers a mark of racial specialness (it does, a victimizing mark), a reprimand to her husband's Black and artisan lowliness. The mother's implosions of anger and pain and their impact on her darker-skinned husband, a personable teacher of ironcraft, bequeaths to Charles, the youngest son, on whom the novel comes to focus—he is 18 in the late 1920s—a new set of embitterments. The family's sober picaresque travels from town to Southern town—Himes offers several excellent lyric vignettes of childhood—and their eventual migration into urban Cleveland give spatial definition to Charles' private awakenings and the parents' domestic storms. (p. 17)

Of the Taylors as individuals, the father, deprived of his professor's status on the Black campuses of the South, dies in a knifing. Tom, the eldest boy, drifts into obscurity. Charles, self-accusing, lonely, an artist manqué, drops out from college into the petty crime which puts him in prison and into the charge of the courts. The mother, for whom the legacies of color have reserved their most ingenious devising, slows down finally, a female Sutpen alone in the city who broods over her dynastic embers and fades sadly into senescence. Only William Lee, Jr., the son blinded in a gunpowder accident, finds an accommodation with his life. Like Himes' own blind brother he moves into academia. The cruel freak of blindness removes from his sight, at least, the disabling spectacles of segregation, the thrash of Lilian Taylor to de-negrify her family.

The Third Generation, in fact, amounts to an anthology of experiences which pain and violate, though the book has sweeter rural moments—the slow drive into Delta Mississippi, for instance, or the hilarious hallelujah sermon "Dry Bones in the Valley." The mother's wedding night ("She was never able to separate the blackness of his skin from the brutality of his act") and the unrelieved fury she feels at the Black part of her racial heritage ("she wasn't white like other white people, because she lived with Negroes") make up the central spine of this anthology of pain, though Himes draws supporting detail from the slangings of husband and wife (he "a shanty nigger," she "white men's leavings"), from William's question to his mother, "Are we bad because we're colored?" and her answer, "You have white blood—fine white blood—in your veins," and from the array of incidents which educate the children into the different grammars of racism. . . . Himes gives his firmest attentions to Charles' adolescence (*The Third Generation* is something of a portrait of the artist as a Black disaffiliate) and to the Jim Crow equations which stiffen the boy's evolving consciousness. The sight in childhood of a cart puncturing the body of a woman haunts him like a spectre. Within him lurks a feeling for art and possible imagined worlds. The frustration of these creative drives blisters out into petty crime and his ventures on Cedar Avenue, the city's numbers and red-light district. The despair brought on first by the divorce, then by the death of his parents and his resorting to the bright-eyed rapacities of the block, a recess of hustlers, pimps and whores, brings on a final enervation. His obvious energies and creativity lie in abeyance, tired and unrealized. In any event Charles/Himes, we now know, loosened the blockage with a cascade of short stories in the Thirties. The novel ends on a temporary and foreboding note of quietness.

The Primitive (1955) is Himes' best novel. It an interior life which outstrips anything in the previous work. The circuits of failure and exhaustion which connect Jesse Robinson and Kriss Cummings, veteran isolates, even by Himes' standards, are laid out through careful shifts of viewpoint and interior flashback. Robinson, who might well be a grown Charles Taylor, and his equally ravaged, self-avenging white woman, fight literally to the death a sexual battle whose weaponry is racial taunt and the broken relationships which scar them and their frenzied inter-racial circle. The booze-laden weekend they spend together at Kriss's New York apartment, intensified by visits from other friends and lovers and by fresh deliveries of drink, Himes works as a memory-theatre for their two lives. His knit of recollection, dream, and live battle is set to a fluent and accelerating rhythm. The net of mutual revelation spreads painfully wide, into a hate which was once love for each other and into an accusing past of bad marriages, Kriss's conquests at parties and in bed, and Jesse's struggles to get published. Himes pulls together the whole with considerable narrative astringency.

From the parallel first two chapters which diagnose the linked insecurities of Kriss and Jesse, Himes matches the line of their sexual and racial experience to an interior psychology of ravage. (pp. 17-19)

These two troubled isolates move together inexorably. Their intricate afflictions of race and sex finally break out into a savage, sometimes comic, sexual dance, ritualistic violence which anticipates the acerbities of Edward Albee's *Who's Afraid of Virginia Woolf?* Taunted, provoked, and denied by Kriss's white body, Jesse drinks more and more, seeing in her the bitter manipulation of his manhood. His inner drives to revenge drunkenly take over. He stabs Kriss in a miasmic trance. His act registers Himes' most complex instance of risen violence, identity seized confusedly at an almost inevitable price of murder. (p. 19)

Killing her certifies [Jesse's] membership in the human race; he believes himself to have joined the mainstream American norms of violence. Jesse muses, "You finally did it. . . . End product of Americanism on one Jesse Robinson—black man. Your answer, son. You've been searching for it. *Black man kills white woman.* . . . Human beings only species of animal life where males are known to kill their females. Proof beyond all doubt. Jesse Robinson joins the human race." A considerable distance from Bob Jones' dream of impotence, Himes thus completes the graph of violence in his first novels with an appropriate diagram of what has brought murder into Jesse's soul. Himes' skills with tone and with declarative prose that traps the stinging edge of sensation gives concentration, and just the right engraving, to *The Primitive's* envisionings of violence. When Jesse phones the local police precinct with news of what he has done, the cryptic idiom he drops into could well come from a voice out of Gravedigger's Harlem: " 'I'm a nigger and I've just killed a white woman,' Jesse said, giving the address and hung up. 'That'll get the lead out of his seat,' he thought half-amused." The detective work lies close ahead.

Some of the groundwork for the Coffin Ed/Gravedigger fiction was prepared in *Pinktoes,* Himes' light-hearted mixture of Harlem anecdotery and erotica. An odyssey of double-entendres, sexual puns and scandal, it makes of inter-racial liberalism, the parties and good-mixing especially, a bed-hopping comedy to be ranked, perhaps, with Terry Southern's *Candy* or with the lighter sexual badinage of Henry Miller or William Melvin Kelley. Mamie Mason, "the hostess with the mostess," the presiding, and overweight, genius of "la Société des Mondaines du Monde de Harlème," gathers about her a motley of publishers, artists, college, and foundation presidents, actors and clerics in hues from the pinkest of pinks to the jettest of blacks. Together with their various paramours and wives she conducts, with appropriate Rabelaisian bravura, a sexual barn dance whose antics beautifully undercut the usual solemn masquerades of concern with "the problem." *Pinktoes* performs an attractive exercise in scatology, a bawdy tilt at middle-class American urban liberalism. It romps through the sexual and emotional manners of racial good-feeling, an extravaganza with the usually unmentionable premise that sexual fascination is the prime mover for most bourgeois racial contact.

Read in sequence, Himes' detective novels unveil a far meaner underside of Harlem. Coffin Ed Johnson and Gravedigger Jones, his two rough-hewn law-marshals with their own approximate standards of justice, patrol an overcrowded kingdom of Black life, a gallery of the living violent and bizarre. With the Harlem he has called "the Mecca of the black," Himes has taken enormous care. He displays a geographer's scruple for accuracy and detail even to the point of having made regular trips from Europe to New York in a bid to keep his knowledge of the changes in Harlem's landscape up to date.

A laconic archivist, he successfully puts on view the feeling of Harlem's pulse and argot, its music, dishes and flavors, the sweltering summer landscapes of brownstone and tenement, the motley of bars, whorehouses, churches and pawnshops. Himes abundantly knows his Jazz and Blues, his soul-food and pig-knuckles. Book after book offers a milling population of preachers and politicians, sober matriarchs and mock religious prophets, pimps, and their chippies, drug-pushers and wheel-thieves, transvestites and con-men, shysters of every kind and sex. . . . From this carefully observed domain Himes authenticates the complex—sometimes hilarious, at other times scarcely credible—spirals of violence and crime unraveled by his two Black cops.

Each of Himes' (to date) eight Coffin Ed/Gravedigger Jones novels is, he has rightly insisted, a barely fictive essay in violence, a witty, complicated, often anarchically grotesque and funny tale of detection bulging with mayhem, predatory hustle, and murder. Each individual narrative he writes to an involuted but rigorous logic. "Those two Harlem Sheriffs," as he calls his detectives in *The Crazy Kill* (does Loop Garoo in Ishmael Reed's mock frontier novel *Yellow Back Radio Broke-Down* owe anything to Himes' uniquely conceived pair?), have the unenviable task of bringing to some level of tolerable order the eruptive undergrowth of crime and communal self-violence which result from straight-jacketing half a million people into a suffocating urban enclave. Of his novels and their violence Himes has remarked, "They're based on one thing; black people want money through crime. They don't have any choice." Himes' eight novels (and *Run Man Run* is no different in this respect) propose ingenious map-readings in violence, decipherings of a mask-ridden world whose sober baselines he nevertheless insists upon, as in this description of a Harlem street in *The Crazy Kill:*

> Unwed young mothers, suckling their infants, living on a prayer; fat black racketeers coasting past in big bright-colored convertibles with their solid gold babes carrying huge sums of money on their person; hard-working men, holding up buildings with their shoulders, talking in loud voices up there in Harlem where the white bosses couldn't hear them; teenage gangsters grouping for a gang-fight, smoking marijuana weed to get up their courage; everybody escaping the hot-box rooms they lived in, seeking respite in a street made hotter by the automobile exhaust and heat released by the concrete walls and walks.

He almost invariably makes the foreground of the novels an act of macabre violence, an event outrageous to at least one of the five senses. (pp. 19-20)

Between them Coffin Ed and Gravedigger Jones run a curious show. Although they live outside Harlem they have it cross-webbed with stool-pigeons and informants and know its every crevice. Their inwardness with Harlem represents an endless bafflement to their white precinct officer, Lieutenant Anderson, who suffers the kind of inadequate racial vision which underpins Ralph Ellison's *Invisible Man* and which William Melvin Kelley develops into surreal comic nightmare in *dem* (1967). They keep to certain guidelines, laying off brothels, numbers, houses and bars intrinsic to Harlem life, but pistol-whipping their way over anybody bringing violence upon an already violated community. Their code Himes explains in *A Rage in Harlem:*

> Gravedigger and Coffin Ed weren't crooked detectives, but they were tough. They had to be tough to work in Harlem. Colored folks didn't respect colored cops. But they respected big shiny pistols and sudden death. It was said in Harlem that Coffin Ed's pistol would kill a rock and that Gravedigger's would bury it. They took their tribute, like all real cops, from the established underworld catering for the essential needs of the people—gamekeepers, madams, street walkers, numbers writers, numbers bankers. But they were rough on purse snatchers, muggers, burglars, con-men, and all strangers working any racket. And they didn't like rough

stuff from anybody but themselves. "Keep it cool," they warned, "Don't make graves."

Himes' two latest contributions to the sequence, *Cotton Comes to Harlem* (1963) and *Blind Man with a Pistol* (1969), strike me as noticeably widening both the range and violence as a theme in his work and the straight, however distinctive, thriller-detective format which identifies the run from *A Rage in Harlem* (1957) to *The Heat's On* (1961).

[*Cotton Comes to Harlem*] spans out from a death-strewn Back-to-Africa caper into more inclusive considerations of race-war in Harlem and America at large. Underpinning Himes' customary recipes of death and violent mayhem lies a pressing regard in this novel for Black American history which he brings to focus by making his central and reverberative point of reference a bale of white Alabama cotton. Himes frames his gun-battles and violent inflections of the comic-grotesque (the "Holy Dream" pitch deserves a special mention—a thief cuts the skirt from a Church-sister's backside in a bid to get her hidden purse while his accomplice enthralls the good woman with details of a conversation he has held with Jesus in a dream), within a subtle historical parallel. . . . Harlem is made a point of intersection, deeply explosive, between a chattel slave past, a future bound up with the politics of negritude, and a highly dangerous urban present. The task of Gravedigger and Coffin Ed, apart from sorting out the gory complexities of the Reverend Deke O'Malley and Colonel Robert L. Calhoun and their respective gangs, is to keep a harder-than-usual rein on a situation which brings into visible clash white retrenchment and the political arms of Black Power (the Black Muslims, significantly, appear for the first time in his work). In other words, *Cotton Comes to Harlem* takes the subject of violence beyond the immediate demands of the detective yarns into the wider reach of the political, or perhaps racial-political, parable.

This widening of theme and narrative kind applies even more to *Blind Man with a Pistol,* a title Himes deliberately chose to emblematize the unseeing thrust of "all unorganized violence." Retitled *Hot Day Hot Night* in the American re-issue, this latest novel, probably the richest imaginatively in the detective series, binds together a number of seemingly disparate themes: an inter-racial sex scandal which brings into play Himes' unflagging genius for the grotesque and comic; a rejuvenation caper with a Black Mormon and his wives with leads into Syndicate crime; and a spate of Black protest marches, political and religious, which put Harlem on a nervous, insurrectionary edge. For the first time in the series, Gravedigger and Coffin Ed are barely able to contain the flare-ups; and their ambiguous status as Black cops is challenged by new-wave militants. Tired, obviously aging, the pair learn more clearly than ever that Black ghetto crime derives, in large part, from the wider national equations of racism and power. The "Afro" explosion, the Sixties moves to alter and revolutionize Black Consciousness, lie pressingly to hand. *Blind Man with a Pistol* makes copious reference to Black Power, to the heirs of Malcolm X, and to the rising energies of confrontation and shoot-outs. Gravedigger and Coffin Ed inject a more explicit political character to their musings when they talk of Malcolm:

> "You know one thing, Digger. He was safe as long as he kept hating white folks—they wouldn't have hurt him, probably made him rich; it wasn't until he began including them in the human race they killed him. That ought to tell you something." "It

does. It tells me that white people don't want to be included in a human race with black people."

The violent train of events which Himes weaves and counterpoints throughout the novel comes to a turbulent close with a berserk pistol-firing of a blind man. As he flails about at the end of a bizarre chain of events, his contortions articulate the absurd, apocalyptic threat Himes reads in his times. His gun blasts off indiscriminately, and "Everyone thought the world was coming to an end; others that the Venusians were coming. A number of white passengers thought the niggers were taking over; the majority of the soul people thought their time was up." The blind man suggests confusion and sightless riot. Himes uses him as a living token of what can ensue from white supremacist dreams. The detective novels have almost ceded their place to a prophecy of anarchic racial apocalypse in which not even Coffin Ed and Gravedigger can exert a restraining hand.

Two recent observations by Himes offer useful angles on his writing. On the origins of violence as a root and branch theme in his books he comments: "If I had wanted to express my revulsion for violence then I would have made the violence even more repellent, really repellent. I am simply creating stories that have a setting I know very well. . . . " In drawing from "a setting I know very well" Himes, obviously enough, is transcribing violence personally witnessed which he takes to characterize the pervasive racist grain of Black American experience. The life which gives shape to his writing undoubtedly is violent enough—at an inner level in terms of racist damage to personality and at an outer level in the matching landscapes of ghetto, color-line, and sheer human blight. We might be grateful for being spared "really repellent" violence. Among other things, Himes undoubtedly has in mind, as always, the terminal violence of unconstrained racial warfare.

Himes' other comment links violence to the narrative disposition of his detective works:

> My French editor says, the Americans have a style of writing detective stories that no one has been able to imitate. . . . There's no reason why the black American, like all other Americans, and brought up in this sphere of violence which is the main sphere of American detective stories, there's no reason why he shouldn't write them. It's just plain and simple violence in narrative form. . . . American violence is public life, it's a public way of life; it became a form, a detective story form.

"Violence became a form" might stand more widely for nearly all of Himes' novels. In opening up his vistas on violence with so careful a controlling lens, Himes has mounted a record, both in terms of a major theme and in the resources of his narrative form, not to be put aside with complacency. His novels, lexicons of the workings of racist violence, can lay persuasive claim to our attention. (pp. 21-2)

> *A. Robert Lee, "Violence Real and Imagined: The World of Chester Himes' Novels," in* Negro American Literature Forum, *Vol. 10, No. 1, Spring, 1976, pp. 13-22.*

RICHARD YARBOROUGH

The experience of Afro-Americans in this country has been marked by two major ironies which would seem to preclude any widespread, long-term endorsement of that body of cultural ideals called the American Dream. The first is the disappointing fact that the society which claims to be founded upon the principles of freedom and equality nonetheless supported a brutal chattel slave system for over two hundred years. Abolitionists like Frederick Douglass and Martin R. Delany frequently alluded to this tragic inconsistency. With emancipation and the victory of the North in the Civil War, however, it seemed to blacks that America was finally beginning to fulfill the promise of its bright conception. Afro-Americans felt that they would only have to follow the rules which white society prescribed in order to attain the American Dream. It was at this point that blacks on a large scale began to confront the second, galling irony regarding their status in the United States. They discovered that essentially the same racist distortions which had been used to justify slavery now served to thwart the Afro-American's participation in the great national drive toward prosperity and apparent fulfillment. (p. 33)

Afro-American fiction in the twentieth century reveals the increasing difficulty black writers have had in maintaining both an unflinching willingness to confront white America's treatment of blacks and faith in the American Dream. After four decades of innumerable promises upon which America has almost inevitably reneged, the dialectical tension in Afro-American thought between hope and despair begins to produce a new synthesis: the agonizing recognition that white racism may forever keep the American Dream out of the black's grasp.

The first modern Afro-American novel to embody this despair, pain, and rage is Richard Wright's *Native Son* (1940). It is no coincidence that three black writers deeply influenced by Wright—Chester Himes, Ann Petry, and Ralph Ellison—share an acute sensitivity to the frustrations of the black individual striving for the American ideal of success. . . . [The resolution of Chester Himes's *If He Hollers Let Him Go* (1945) defines] the predominant reactions evoked by the failure of the Dream: the cynical acceptance of defeat; explosive rage and then despair; and, finally, the desperate hope that something of the American Dream can be salvaged. (pp. 34-5)

If He Hollers Let Him Go is the powerful examination of one black man's painful growth from naivete to cynicism as he searches for the American Dream in Southern California. Bob Jones, the protagonist, moves to Los Angeles from Cleveland in the early 1940s, not just for better employment opportunities but for something far more elusive and difficult to define—a secure sense of his own manhood. Bob has become quite familiar with white American racism. Early in the novel, he describes his previous encounters with prejudice: "Cleveland wasn't the land of the free or the home of the brave either. That was one reason why I left there to come to Los Angeles; I knew if I kept on getting refused while white boys were hired from the line behind me I'd hang somebody as sure as hell." Los Angeles, however, promises to be an open society which will allow him to start over. Arriving in California, he optimistically believes that he has left his troubles behind: "I felt fine about everything. Taller than the average man, six feet two, broad-shouldered, and conceited, I hadn't a worry. I knew I'd get along."

What makes Bob's experiences in Los Angeles particularly troubling is that his expectations are merely those shared by most of his fellow countrymen. While he acknowledges the restrictions imposed upon him because of his race, Bob cannot help but partake of the same values and goals as other Americans:

> I'd learned the same jive that the white folks had learned. All that stuff about liberty and justice and equality. . . . All men are created equal. . . . Any person born in the United States is a citizen. . . . Learned it out the same books, in the same schools. . . . I was a Charles Lindbergh fan when I was a little boy, and thought George Washington was the father of my country—as long as I thought I had a country.

His inability to abandon the notions that "being born in America gave everybody a certain importance," that he does indeed have "a country," and that he is fully an American predetermines his fate.

His first major disillusionment in California involves his search for work. He comments: "It was the look on the people's faces when you asked them about a job. . . . They just looked so goddamned startled that I'd even asked. As if some friendly dog had come in through the door and said, 'I can talk.' " If, in Cleveland, he found it difficult to be recognized as an American citizen, he finds his very humanity denied in Los Angeles.

His anger and frustration turn to fear and anxiety with the internment of the Japanese-Americans during the war. The sight of "little Riki Oyana singing 'God Bless America' and going to Santa Anita with his parents next day" epitomizes for Bob the awesome power white society holds over his own head and the frightening ease with which that power can be exercised. After Pearl Harbor, Bob becomes especially sensitive to the "tight, crazy feeling of race as thick in the street as gas fumes." He admits: "Every time I stepped outside I saw a challenge I had to accept or ignore. Every day I had to make one decision a thousand times: *Is it now? Is now the time?* " The sheer nervous tension of maintaining a state of constant mobilization frays Bob physically and emotionally.

After his initial disappointment, Bob strikes an uneasy truce with the hostile white society in which he finds himself. He still believes that some accommodation can be reached, that he can attain some degree of success, American style. This qualified optimism is grounded in Bob's sense of his own manhood, and his tough, desperate pride is tied directly to three possessions which have typically buttressed the confidence of American males throughout the twentieth century: his car, his job, and his relationship with a woman. Himes describes how, in each case, white America flaunts its power over Bob.

In wartime Los Angeles, Bob's '42 Buick Roadmaster is a sign of his superior status; he comments, "rich white folks out in Beverly couldn't even buy a new car now." Further, in his daily confrontation with the whites who can flourish their ascendancy with a condescending glance, Bob's car is a tool of aggression and an outlet for his frustrations. The limitations of his Buick as a symbol of prestige and as a source of power are brought home, however, the night he and his girlfriend, Alice, are pulled over by two white motorcycle policemen. The officers' insults and the fact that it is Alice who, using the political clout of her father, finally gets the police off their backs, both remind Bob of his impotence. After he and Alice have been taken to the police station and fined, Alice exclaims angrily: "I wish I was a man." Bob's cynical retort—"If you were a man what would you do?"—is directed as much at himself as at Alice.

The second important evidence of his own worth is his job as a "leaderman" at the Atlas Shipyard. His feelings as he dresses for work in the morning suggest the degree to which his position as a "key man" in the war effort defines him as a valuable and potent man and assuages somewhat his sense of helplessness: "Something about my working clothes made me feel rugged, bigger than the average citizen, stronger than a white-collar worker—stronger even than an executive. Important too. It put me on my muscle." Despite his title, however, Bob is confronted daily with the nominal nature of his authority. Not only must he put up with members of his own black crew who blame him for their mistakes, but he finds that he is the subordinate of every white worker. His union representative is ineffective; his superior insults him by telling a "darky" joke in his presence; and he must acknowledge that a less qualified white leaderman can get the black crew better jobs than he can. He learns his true status in the yard when he calls Madge, a white, Texas-bred tacker who insultingly refuses to work for him, a "cracker bitch." As a result of this exchange, he is downgraded and threatened with the loss of his military deferment.

His most precious source of masculine pride and the situation that most convinces him that he has a foot up on the ladder to American middle-class prosperity is his relationship with Alice. While Bob is an inveterate flirt with most of the black women he encounters, he believes that Alice Harrison is something special: "It gave me a personal pride to have her for my girl. And then I was proud of her too. Proud of the way she looked, the appearance she made among white people; proud of what she demanded from white people, and the credit they gave her; and her position and prestige among her own people." Yet Bob abhors the pompous superficiality of Alice's parents and her fatuous friends, and he is equally exasperated by the stiff social worker manner Alice cannot seem to leave at her office. Their relationship is further strained by a series of events, each of which seems designed to mortify him. The first involves the harassment they receive when they go to an elegant hotel for dinner. Then comes the confrontation with the police. The ultimate insult stems from the more direct intervention of white society in their relationship several days later. Incensed by the racist behavior of whites, Bob seeks refuge at Alice's house, where he must endure the glib comments of her white co-worker, Tom Leighton. Bob is particularly aggravated by the white man's condescension, which makes him "look like a goddamned fool" in front of Alice. When he later encounters Tom and Alice on their way to a date, he feels that he is in danger of losing everything which defines his masculinity.

In his desperate need to retaliate for his humiliation, Bob first decides to get revenge on a young white who struck him during a crap game. Determined to make the man "feel as scared and powerless and unprotected as I felt every goddamned morning I woke up," Bob finds that having "a peckerwood's life in the palm of my hand . . . made all the difference." Soon, however, merely threatening the white man no longer seems either satisfying or practical; confronting white America's ultimate racial taboo, Bob turns his attention to Madge.

While there is something of the appeal of the sexually forbidden underlying Bob's obsession with Madge, revenge is the strongest motive: "I was going to have to have her. I was going to have to make her as low as a white whore in a Negro slum—a scummy two-dollar whore. . . . I was going to have to so I could keep looking the white folks in the face." Despite his resolution to get back at white society through Madge, Bob is denied even this satisfaction, however, when her aroused cry of surrender—"All right, rape me then, nigger!"—literally unmans him: "I let her loose and bounded to my feet. *Rape*—just the sound of the word scared me, took everything out of me, my desire, my determination, my whole build-up." Having been thwarted in his every attempt to assert his manhood, Bob surrenders: "I was through and I knew it; the white folks had won again and I wanted out."

At the height of his pride, Bob has contended: "If I couldn't live in America as an equal in the minds, hearts, and souls of all the white people, if I couldn't know that I had a chance to do anything any other American could, to go as high as an American citizenship would carry anybody, there'd never be anything in this country for me anyway." Now, however, his goals are much simpler: "All I want is peace." Admitting defeat, Bob seems willing, at long last, to resign himself to his second-class status. Alice and her circle of bourgeois blacks exemplify how such an adjustment might be made: "They hadn't stopped trying, I gave them that much; . . . but they had recognized their limit—a nigger limit." As agonizing as it is for him to accept this "nigger limit," Bob also acknowledges: "(A)s long as I was black I'd never be anything but half a man at best." Determined to make the best of his unavoidable plight, Bob promises Alice that he will swallow his pride, and he accepts the patronizing advice of his white department supervisor, who tells him: "Take your punishment like a man, then make a comeback. That's the *American way,* my boy. Prove yourself " (emphasis added).

In Himes's pessimistic view, however, Bob's decision to resign himself to the crumbs white society offers does not prevent the ultimate destruction of his remaining ambitions. Accidentally trapped with Madge in a locked cabin aboard a ship, Bob is victimized by her second cry of "Rape," an accusation used for years to justify the emasculation of black men. While, for a short time, he naively expects to be somehow vindicated, Bob finally admits that he has no chance: "The whole structure of American thought was against me; American tradition had convicted me a hundred years before." The idealism which has carried Bob to California is dead. He ends up "pressed, cornered, black, as small and weak and helpless as any Negro sharecropper facing a white mob in Georgia."

Mauled physically and spiritually, Bob is finally bereft of all idealism, hope, anger, and even hatred. In the closing scenes, when he is offered the choice of going to prison or taking part in a war about which he cares little, he must fight down hysterical laughter at the bitter irony of his fate. After traveling West in the attempt to attain his portion of the American Dream—"just to be a man," he must enlist in the Jim Crow Army which has long advertised its ability to "make" men. His final words—"I'm still here"—mark the nadir of his aspirations; he has survived: that is all he can claim. (pp. 36-41)

Richard Yarborough, "The Quest for the American Dream in Three Afro-American Novels: 'If He Hollers Let Him Go,' 'The Street,' and 'Invisible Man,' " in Melus, Vol. 8, No. 4, Winter, 1981, pp. 33-59.

ANGUS CALDER

The publisher's blurb inside the front cover of Himes's *The*

Crazy Kill . . . cites a gentleman otherwise unknown to me called Anthony Boucher on Himes's 'Perverse blend of sordid realism and macabre fantasy humour'. What interests me here is the suggestion that 'macabre fantasy' is necessarily different from 'realism'. Alas, I fear it isn't. I would refer, if there were space, to first-hand accounts of tortures enacted upon slaves before 'emancipation', of the conduct of staff in German concentration camps, and of the bombing of Dresden, Nagasaki and Hiroshima.

I suspect many readers will react to Himes as critics for so long reacted to Dickens; they will enjoy him, but will find him an author who departs too far from 'realism' to be taken 'seriously'. (p. 5)

[Himes] is an author of best-selling detective stories, but this does not mean he need be taken lightly. He is an 'abnormalist', [a passionate moralist whose work shows the dubiousness of human nature], but this does not prevent him from being, in the best sense, a realist. His presentation of Harlem is densely detailed, to the point of apparent redundancy, but this richness of 'background' is associated, as in Dickens, with a view of character in which character and environment are morally indistinguishable. He is a 'societal' novelist, employing the useful convention of the crime thriller in order to ransack Harlem (conceived by him as a distinctive community) from east to west and from top to bottom. And he is a 'committed' novelist whose thrillers embody a splendidly intransigent refusal to come to terms with contemporary American values, to accept even one lie or subscribe to even one illusion. His crime stories are powerful fables presenting the dehumanisation extant in any capitalist-racist situation. He is a major novelist, as good as Wright, I think, and very much better than Baldwin or Ellison, to name the most fashionable Black American writers in White American circles. But even this comparison does him the obvious injustice which is bound to occur when a Black writer is compared only with other Blacks. (pp. 11-12)

It is time Himes is set in his proper place. One critic who made a start towards putting him there was Leroi Jones, a few years ago, when he wrote, 'One can find more moving writing in any of Chester Himes's bizarre detective novels than in most more "serious" efforts by Negroes, just because Himes's main interest must be in saying the thing like it is.' For those who think thrillers 'unrealistic' by definition, this verdict will seem self-contradictory. But it gathers weight from Himes's own remarks on the thriller form in a recent interview:

> . . . No one, *no one*, writes about violence the way that Americans do. As a matter of fact, for the simple reason that no one understands violence or experiences violence like the American civilians do. . . . American violence is public life, it's a public way of life, it became a form, a detective story form. So I would think that any number of black writers should go into the detective story form.

So in his own view, the thriller offers Himes not merely a suitable vehicle, but perhaps *the* most suitable vehicle for exposing and discussing the violence which he holds, with evident plausibility, to be the dominating and distinctive feature of American society. (p. 12)

It was for money that he began to write his Harlem detective stories, for a French publisher; all but the last of the series appeared initially in French. So did *Pinktoes* (1961), a 'por-

nographic' burlesque, on the theme of miscegenation (with variations), which finally established Himes as a best-seller in the USA. *Pinktoes,* like all Himes's writing, radiates magnificent intelligence, and from the sexual romping 'serious' satirical points emerge. But it must be regarded as thoroughly good fun rather than major fiction.

However, there is no necessary contradiction between writing for money and writing as an artist. As Himes himself reminds us, Dostoevsky produced major novels under extreme financial pressure: 'There was a man who wrote very rapidly and very brilliantly all the time, and the reason that he did so was that he needed money all the time.' (p. 13)

Which brings us to Himes's critical status, as reflected in current works of reference by (white) academics. Robert A. Bone (in *The Negro Novel in America*) and David Littlejohn (in *Black on White*) concentrate on *If He Hollers Let Him Go* and establish something like a consensus with [Edward] Margolies over that novel. It is seen as belonging to the 'school of Wright' [see Margolies's excerpt above], as a 'protest' novel and as a 'race-war' novel. It is critically identified by Bone as 'an impressive failure with accent on the adjective' and dismissed more lightly by the ineffable Littlejohn, who describes the hero as 'race-mad almost to the point of hysteria' [see Himes's entry in *CLC,* Vol. 7].

Several kinds of unhelpful preconception are involved in these verdicts. One involves the white predilection for casting black novelists as 'race' writers and then turning round to complain that they're nothing more. . . . There is a refusal to accept that the fact of race prejudice in the USA is no more intrinsically a 'narrow' theme than the factual relationship between marriage, money and class in early nineteenth century England which provided Jane Austen with virtually her whole subject matter. The typecasting of Himes as 'school of Wright' suggests, quite falsely, that he is imitative. In fact he is a very different novelist. He has what Wright lacks most of all, a gift for humour and satire, and the density of social detail which he offers contrasts sharply with the spareness of *Native Son.*

There are also the false assumptions which make many critics separate 'form' from 'content' before judging a novel in terms of its 'form'. Margolies makes the point that *If He Hollers* begins with such intensity that the build-up of tension desired in a novel cannot take place; so much, one might say, for *Crime and Punishment.* If the situation is diagnosed by Himes as one which produces constant tension, how can he honestly present it otherwise? Bone's conclusion is worth quoting:

> At bottom the problem is ideological: neither revenge nor accommodation is acceptable to Himes, and as a result, the novel flounders to an inconclusive finish. . . . The novel suffers ultimately from a one-to-one correlation between form and content: in portraying a divided personality, Himes has written a divided novel. But formless and chaotic is precisely what art cannot afford to be.

But what if life is 'formless and chaotic'? And what about those notoriously 'formless and chaotic' writers, Dickens and Dostoevsky? Why *can't* form correspond to content? If Himes can see no immediate resolution of the problem he presents in the novel, must he lie, in effect, in order to satisfy the demands of academic aesthetics? Bone should be clear (but isn't) that when he objects to Himes's anti-climactic ending his objection is to the *content* of Himes's book. In my own opinion this ending is much more convincing than Ralph Ellison's consolatory word-play at the end of *Invisible Man,* which Bone considers 'quite possibly the best American novel since World War II.' (pp. 13-14)

It is worth looking at **If He Hollers** now, in order to defend Himes against such irrelevant criticism, and to present the positive virtues of his style, which are virtues still present in the Harlem thrillers.

The novel deals with Robert Jones, a well-educated black who is the first of his race to be employed as a 'leaderman' in a certain West Coast shipyard during the Second World War. Though in theory he has the same authority as a White leaderman, in practice he does not, and he is bitterly aware of the fact, which is proven when he is demoted for swearing back ('cracker bitch') at a white woman employee who calls him a nigger. He has a near-white, bourgeois girl friend, Alice, who urges him to accept the limitations imposed on coloured people by white racism and to become a successful black lawyer. 'You need some definite aim', she tells him, in her social-worker's idiom, 'a goal that you can attain within the segregated pattern in which we live. . . . There is no reason a Negro cannot control his destiny / within this pattern.' Bob, in a calm moment, replies, ' . . . I've already made up my mind to conform . . . But please don't tell me I can control my destiny, because I know I can't. In any incident that might come up a white person can use his colour on me and turn it into a catastrophe and I won't have any protection . . . ' What follows proves his point, and makes it simply impossible for him to conform. The white girl employee, Madge, frames him, putting him in a position where he seems to be raping her. The white workers beat him up. He runs from the police. Alice refuses to help him escape. The authorities, realising that the false charges against him won't stick, but not prepared to let him off, 'release' him on condition that he joins the army. The book ends with him marching off to join the army, Though the rape motif of *Native Son* is repeated in this book, Bob is nothing like Bigger Thomas. He is a tough and intelligent man who should clearly be accepted as free and equal in any society, not, like Bigger, a pitiful creature depraved by the slums. He is torn between conforming, accepting inferior status, and the futile revolt which his rage and frustration urge him to. At one moment he resolves to kill a white who has hit him and go, like Bigger, a proud man to the electric chair. He plots to seduce the white woman who insulted him, but in the end humiliates her by *not* taking her.

Meanwhile, Himes's subtle and moving presentation of Alice makes his point that compromise desn't really solve anything very clear. Her brittle socialite poses mask a strain as constant as Bob's, and her Lesbian proclivities reflect the distortion wrought by this strain upon her personality. Himes views racism and its effects clinically, but with surprising compassion. He diagnoses its many varieties, from the Southern white 'cracker bitch', through the Fascist leaderman who takes Bob's job, to the pseudo-liberal employer and the well-meaning but uneasy Communist. It is a deforming disease, and the diagnosis seems to be that only the knife, only violence, can cure it.

This sober and powerful book already displays the essentials of Himes's style and vision. There is the 'brutal' realism beloved of . . . blurb-writers, though I would prefer to call it 'clinical'. There are also vast resources of psychological sub-

tlety, and of humour, which Himes deploys so easily that one takes them for granted. His very fine ear for dialogue is shown in the inconsequential exchanges between Bob's fellow black shipyard workers. They yield a strong flavour of the particularity of black culture, which is something Himes emphasises strongly; but they are also there to assist the making of another stern Himes point. Early in the novel, Bob thinks, 'We're a wonderful, goddamned race . . . Simple-minded, generous, sympathetic sons of bitches. We're sorry for everybody but ourselves; the worse the white folks treat us the more we love 'em.' Sure enough, Bob's black co-workers do nothing to support him when he is demoted, and work gratefully for the racist white replacement who is able, because he is white, to get them a cosier job in the yard. Himes diagnoses another disease; the black disease of feckless, happy-go-lucky indifference to the true interests of black people. The Harlem thrillers are concerned throughout with this disease.

My contention is that when the thrillers are set beside **If He Hollers** it is plain that Himes, in adjusting his methods to the pace obligatory in the thriller genre, does not violate the essentials of his serious style. The realism is as clinical, the dialogue is as vivid, and the view of character is essentially the same.

Himes has the gift of bringing a character to life in a few strokes. Here are two examples from **If He Hollers:**

> She was a small, compact, black-haired woman with sharp brown eyes and skin that was constantly greasy. She looked thirty and she was hard as nails. (The Boss's secretary)

> Dr Harrison answered my ring. He was dressed in a brown flannel smoking jacket with a black velvet collar. He waved a soggy cigar butt in his left hand, stuck out his right. (Alice's father)

The knack, as with any good novelist, is to give just enough detail to make the character vivid and distinctive, without slowing the story to a halt, and to make this detail significant. (pp. 14-16)

Both descriptions direct us towards a definition of man as animal, and as creature of his environment, rather than man as a spiritual entity capable of free motion.

In the Harlem thrillers, Himes presses on in this direction to the point where the possibility of free spiritual life is almost completely ruled out in our first meetings with his characters:

> Imabelle was Jackson's woman. She was a cushioned-lipped, hot-bodied, banana-skin chick with the speckled-brown eyes of a teaser and the high-arched, ball-bearing hips of a natural-born *amante.* (**A Rage in Harlem**)

> He was a small, elderly man with skin like parchment, faded brown eyes, and long gray bushy hair. His standard dress was a tail coat, double-breasted dove-grey vest, striped trousers, wing collar, black ascot tie adorned with a gray pearl stickpin, and rimless nose-glasses attached to a long black ribbon pinned to his vest. (**A Rage in Harlem**)

In the first description, of the fickle sex-pot who is probably the chief character in the novel, exact definition of the body, and appraisal of it in purely sexual terms, leaves no room for moral comment. H. Exodus Clay, the undertaker, *is,* essentially, his clothes, which define his function and his place in society. To repeat my earlier point; character and environment are morally indistinguishable.

The quick-fire style of the Harlem novels, where Himes is handling a vast number of characters in a small number of pages, certainly depends on something close to 'caricature'. But the underlying viewpoint is the same as in the remarkable second chapter of *If He Hollers,* perhaps the most original in the novel.

It is just Bob driving to work, picking up his workmates on the way, listening while they chaff each other. He is tense; his exposed position in the shipyard is giving him bad dreams. The manner of his driving illustrate his tenseness, but also his power, his capacity:

> . . . I was coming up fast in the middle lane and some white guy in a Nash coupe cut out in front of me without signalling. I had to burn rubber to keep from taking off his fender; and the car behind me tapped my bumper. I didn't know whether he had looked in the rear-view mirror before he pulled out or not, but I knew if he had he could have seen we were a carful of coloured—and that's the way I took it. I kept on his tail until I could pull up beside him, then I leaned out of the window and shouted, "This ain't Alabama, you peckerwood son of a bitch. When you want to pull out of line, stick out your hand."

It takes an abnormalist to recognise how car driving exposes the sharp edges of character; simply as a 'realistic' description of traffic behaviour, the passage is very good. But it also establishes the character of Bob, who unlike Clay or Imabelle is subjected to depth study, in relation to his environment, which is seen to surround him and also to trigger him. An image of California is established; a place where everyone wants to get ahead fast, like Bob, and where friction and collision are inevitable. The physical ambience and the moral ambience are identical; they dominate Bob and determine his behaviour. California is a trap. Only if he escapes and redefines himself in a different environment can he begin to exercise the control over his destiny which he craves. Hence our relief (I think) when Bob marches off to join the army. Perhaps we have here the motive underlying Himes's own self-exile. In America he was doomed to be another 'Black Protest' novelist; in France, Jean Cocteau and Jean Giono might (and did) acclaim him as a remarkable novelist in his own right. The insider desperately looking out, in *If He Hollers,* with its many pages of agonised 'visceral' description of Bob's emotions, becomes the much more mature Himes of *Run Man Run,* an outsider calmly looking in, 'saying the thing like it is,' more clinically than ever examining the fears and confusions of an educated young black, much like Bob in some respects, trapped in a similar claustrophobic ambience of race prejudice, and rescued by his own resourcefulness and by a slow, almost grudging application of elementary justice on the part of a hard, but decent, white cop. (pp. 16-18)

> Angus Calder, "Chester Himes and the Art of Fiction," in Journal of Eastern African Research and Development, *Vol. 1, No. 1, 1981, pp. 3-18.*

EDWARD MARGOLIES

When the black expatriate author, Chester Himes, submitted his first police novels to his French publisher in 1957, he was not immediately aware that his two hot-tempered, fortyish,

Harlem plainclothesmen were in any essential way different from the ordinary hardboiled breed. To be sure Coffin Ed Johnson and Grave Digger Jones were nominally cops, good family men with homes in Queens. But this fits the demands of the setting, for who in Harlem would have been able to afford private eyes, and besides, readers would never get to see them at home with their families. In most other respects they looked like old-fashioned independent operatives of the Hammett-Chandler variety. After the postwar decline of the pulps, tough, quirky, individualistic dicks were becoming less fashionable; still Grave Digger and Coffin Ed carried on in the old tradition doing what *they* thought was right. They often acted outside the law, manhandling suspects and criminals, and they usually found themselves free to pursue their prey without too much interference from their police bosses.

But Coffin Ed and Grave Digger made their literary debuts at a critical period when civil rights and black nationalist movements were underway. They were torn, almost from the start, between their desire to protect Harlem's exploited citizenry and their feelings that the white power structure for whom they worked was the real enemy. Like most other popular heroes, they entertained a healthy distrust of organized society, but their aroused black consciousness added new elements to their uneasiness. The rift in their loyalties would become more and more pronounced in each succeeding book until finally they were unable to perform.

Himes seems to have viewed the pulps as reflecting certain basic truths about his mother country and rather than attempt to avoid the outmoded conventions of the hardboiled formula, he employed the tough-guy genre to record his own political, social, and racial perceptions. And by the time he wrote his last novel, he had transformed the genre into an expression of the absurdities of American society. Indeed, he came to believe that absurdity was the central principle of black life. (pp. 53-4)

Himes's admittedly autobiographical novels may provide more reliable accounts of the life and attitudes that shape his thrillers than either his interviews or his two volumes of memoirs, *The Quality of Hurt* (1972) and *My Life of Absurdity* (1976). The latter pass too quickly over important events (like his seven years in prison, and his personal and literary relationships to writers like Louis Bromfield and Ralph Ellison) and dwell often inordinately on such less significant matters as his pets, his cars, and his casual sexual encounters. His fiction is more revealing. *The Third Generation* tells of his childhood and youth, and some of his later prison years are described in more disguised fashion in *Cast The First Stone,* while *The Primitive* depicts him as a "failed" black novelist in his early forties just prior to his departure for Europe.

Himes was born in Jefferson City, Missouri in 1909, the youngest of three sons. His father, Joseph Sr.—whom he describes in *The Quality of Hurt* as short and very black, with bowed legs and an ellipsoidal skull—taught metal trades, blacksmithing and wheelwrighting at southern Negro technical colleges. Himes does not, as a rule, portray him in a flattering light. His memoirs describe him as having inherited a slave mentality "which accepts the premise that white people knew best." Joseph's marriage to Himes's mother, née Estelle Bomar, a light-complexioned woman, was unhappy, but being a teacher he was regarded as rather a success in small Southern Negro communities. It was only after the family moved North during Himes's adolescence that Joseph Sr. experienced a shattering of his self-respect.

According to Himes, his mother had long felt she had married beneath her station—in part because her husband was so much darker than she and in part, presumably, because of his docility when white people were about. (pp. 54-5)

[Estelle Himes] attempted to instill in her children a love of music, literature, and culture. Her efforts bore fruit, for if Himes and his brothers rebelled as adolescents, each in his own way made his mark in the world: Himes's brother, Joseph Jr., became a well-known sociologist at the University of North Carolina and his oldest brother, Edward, became an official in the waiters' union in New York City. But her concern also became a problem. In *The Third Generation,* Himes tells how his fictional mother, Lillian Taylor, lavished so much love on him that he would from time to time erupt in hysterics. He clearly wanted to free himself of her smothering possessive ways, while at the same time he would be furious at himself for desiring her. Himes carried some of these attitudes into his adult years. In his memoirs, as well as in his novels, he tells of alternately tender and turbulent relationships with women (mainly white), and in his detective books he portrays a number of very strong-willed, seductive women who are threatening if not murderous to their male companions. As a popular novelist, Himes was, of course, working within the Hammett-Chandler tradition of treating beautiful women as troublemakers, but here tradition seems to have suited Himes's psychology and outlook. (pp. 55-6)

Himes's adolescent years in Cleveland were fraught with . . . self-torment. He adopted coarse and superficial friends in the Negro bourgeois community and afterwards befriended peripheral elements of the Negro underworld in the black slums. Later on, as a first-year student at Ohio State University he was suspended for taking other students to the Negro ghetto to visit prostitutes, an activity he had been indulging in himself for some time. Meanwhile he had begun a career of crime, at first associating with professional gamblers (the name of one of whom, Bunch Boy, reappears as that of a numbers racketeer in his 1960 novel, *All Shot Up*), and then pimping, bootlegging, stealing cars and weapons, and forging checks. Finally he tried armed robbery, was apprehended, and though only nineteen, sentenced to twenty years in the Ohio State Penitentiary. (p. 56)

Long before his incarceration Himes had begun thinking about divine responsibility for life's injustices. After the [chemical] explosion that took his brother's vision, Charles, in *The Third Generation,* thinks bitterly, "God didn't even know the difference" between right and wrong, for it was Charles who should have been punished. Indeed the title, *The Third Generation,* contains an ironic Biblical allusion to the sins of the fathers—in Himes's case, slaves!—being visited on their children and their children's children. Himes's ironic attitude toward religion is also reflected in his detective stories where religious messages are constantly being used to delude black humanity. But, curiously, many of Himes's characters possess something akin to religious fervor themselves, however antisocial their behavior. There is a driven quality about them, as if their lives are beyond their control and they must behave as they do regardless of consequences. Crooks relentlessly seek elusive fortunes that they know will destroy them, innocents persistently pursue women who have betrayed them and will do so again, and even Coffin Ed and Grave Digger risk their lives far beyond the call of duty. The wounds they incur for causes they no longer believe in defy rational explanation.

One can see then why the hardboiled genre with its emphasis on action rather than plausible motive would appeal to Himes. There was something compulsive about his own behavior as well as about the behavior of others he knew. Nothing can be more illustrative of this than Himes's several accounts of his own capture and arrest after the crime that would send him to the penitentiary. He writes that he attempted to sell his loot to a well-known pawnbroker. But the broker went into a back room on some pretext and Himes knew instinctively that he was calling the police. Himes says that he could easily have fled but did not. He was unable to move. In two of his short stories of the 1930s and in his prison novel, *Cast The First Stone,* he comes back again and again to these frozen moments. What caused his paralysis? Was it courage or fear—or an overactive conscience asking for punishment?

Himes spent seven and a half years in prison and was paroled in 1936. These years provided him with a gold mine of material for his later detective books. Many of the stories told him by convicts and guards return in one way or another in his fiction. It was in prison too that he decided to become a writer. Possibly he thought of it as a way of acquiring an identity that would win him respect. In *The Quality of Hurt* he says that convicts looked with awe at anyone who could use a typewriter, and in one of his first short stories he tells of a convict who wrote because he wanted "others to see his name." To a certain extent he succeeded. His first pieces appeared in 1929 in the *Pittsburgh Courier* and later he turned to other Negro publications. By 1934 *Esquire* had begun printing his short prison fiction, putting him in the company of such august white authors as Hemingway, Fitzgerald, Dos Passos, and Ring Lardner. What may be more important is that Himes found he need not totally despair of his criminal past and incarceration. At least there was material here for literature—something he would remember in the late 1950s when his situation once again seemed precarious. His prison years may even have been liberating since, despite humiliations and cruelties, he arrived at a sense of himself apart from his parents.

Emotional survival was not the only challenge of prison life. Himes lived through one of the worst fires in prison history when on Easter Monday, 1930, much of the Ohio State Penitentiary went up in flames, and more than three hundred convicts died. Himes describes the holocaust in grisly detail in his first *Esquire* story, **"To A Red Hell"** (1934), and again years later in his 1952 novel, *Cast The First Stone.* The latter work, significantly, deals with a young convict's growth to maturity as a consequence of adversity. . . . He learned whatever he had to learn well, for survival—physical, mental, and emotional—continues as a central theme in all of Himes's work.

None of Himes's first *Esquire* stories contains identifiable black characters. Presumably Himes and his *Esquire* editors implicitly agreed that white readers would not be interested in stories written by a Negro author. Such pandering to prejudice probably seemed senseless to Himes but by now very little could have surprised him. Prison life—especially the violence of prison life—had reconfirmed his sense of the absurd. In the first volume of his memoirs he tells how convicts stabbed, cut, slashed, brained, maimed, and killed each other for the most nonsensical reasons. "Two black convicts cut each other to death over a dispute as to whether Paris was in France or France in Paris." (Grave Digger tells the same story about two blacks to an Irish police lieutenant in *The Crazy Kill,* but the lieutenant tops it with a more nonsensical story about two Irishmen.) Blacks directing their violence against one another, when their real oppressors lie elsewhere, strikes Himes as the ultimate irony. But beyond that, such violence describes in physical terms the absurdity of the black situation in America. There is even something funny about it—as if by definition violence somehow defies the laws of nature. "What's funny when a man falls on the ice and seriously hurts himself is to see the limbs flying all ways," he told an English interviewer in 1969. The plethora of violence Himes witnessed as a prisoner would become the informing metaphors, both humorous and grisly, of the absurdist vision of his detective stories many years later.

Although most of Himes's early stories had prison settings, he was apparently influenced at least in part by tough-guy pulp fiction. Among the magazines that reached him in prison, he says, was *Black Mask,* and some of his first pieces probably owe something to *Black Mask'*s prose economy and penchant for flagrant simile.

> He moved down to the other end of the latrine, took three rapid drags from his cigaret. He could feel the smoke way down in the bottom of his lungs. His skin was tight on his face.
>
> But it was quiet down here. He tried to relax. And then sound creeped into his mind. A broken commode leaked with a monotonous gurgle. The skin crawled on his face like the skin of a snake's belly. **("Crazy in the Stir," 1934)**

He was also capable of writing as violent a woman-beating scene as any of his hardboiled contemporaries. In this regard one notes the pulp influence even after his release from prison.

> He never said a word, he just reached around from behind and smacked her in the face with the open palm of his right hand. She drew up short against the blow. Then he hit her under the right breast with a short left jab and chopped three rights into her face when she turned around with the edge of his fist like he was driving nails. **("The Night's for Cryin'," 1937)**

Himes says that one of the writers he read as a convict was Chandler, but Chandler's portrayals of Watts Negroes embarrassed him. The pulp writer he obviously admired most was Hammett whose relentless, obsessed criminals foreshadow, in their way, Himes's relentless and obsessed thieves and murderers. The treasures that Himes's and Hammett's crooks seek are lame excuses for the existential pleasure they derive from committing and plotting crimes. Himes may also have borrowed from Hammett the device of having his criminals kill one another off in order to resolve the complications of the plot. Where they differ principally is in their conception of detective heroes.

Precursors of Coffin Ed and Grave Digger appear in **"He Knew,"** a story Himes published in 1933 in *Abbott's Monthly Magazine.* It tells about two middle-aged, tough police detectives, one of whom is called John Jones. (Jones, it will be recalled, is Grave Digger's last name. It is also the last name of the tormented protagonist of Himes's first novel, *If He Hollers Let Him Go.*) In the short story, the cops kill two burglars who turn out to be their sons. Aside from its O. Henry-like ending and its reverse Oedipal implications—

fathers killing sons—the story embodies the implicitly autobiographical situation of the criminal son writing about the upright fathers of criminal sons. Insofar as one may say an author identifies with his main characters, Himes here becomes his own father. Some twenty-six years later Himes would return to the subject of fathers and their children in his novel, *The Real Cool Killers* (1959). Here Coffin Ed discovers that his daughter is associating with a gang of Harlem delinquents. Although practically all the other kids in the gang are killed, the life of Coffin Ed's daughter is spared at the last moment. Perhaps Himes had become somewhat more forgiving. (pp. 57-60)

Another characteristic of Himes's early short stories that anticipates his subsequent thrillers is his creation of grotesques. In *The Quality of Hurt,* Himes alludes to Lenny, the gentle but simple-minded murderer in John Steinbeck's *Of Mice and Men,* who reminds him of some of the convicts he knew in prison. People not unlike Lenny are found in Himes's fiction of the 1930s but then all but vanish until the first of his detective stories. Each of the latter contains at least one such creature. They are like nightmare figures—libidinal, unafraid, and unrestrained. Himes seldom tries to explain them. He simply describes something of their pasts and then permits them to run loose. An early version of this type is Pork Chop Smith of **"Pork Chop Paradise"** (1938), an ex-con evangelist. Like many of Himes's later criminals, Pork Chop uses religion to exploit the poor and vulnerable. He is obviously modeled on Harlem's Father Divine, but his ogreish appearance could just as easily come out of a child's fairy tale. He appears "half frog" and "half ape" with "huge muscle roped arms and weird long-fingered hands of enormous size" that "could scratch the calf of either leg. His immense flat splayed fantastic feet . . . grew from abnormally small legs as straight as sticks." Oddly, he bears a caricatured resemblance to Lillian Taylor's vision of her husband, Fess, in *The Third Generation.* Mrs. Taylor sees Fess as a "short, black man with a wiry, simian body [with] bowed legs and pigeon-toed stance. . . ." Also like Fess, Smith is a marvellously aggressive performer when black people are about but grins obsequiously in the presence of whites. It would seem therefore that if Himes transformed his father into a kind of fictional policeman, he also transformed him into a kind of criminal monster.

On his release from prison in 1936, Himes was paroled in the custody of his mother in Cleveland, but he shortly slipped back into his old ways, associating with gamblers and prostitutes and taking drugs. He later moved in with his father who now lived in Canton and the change improved his prospects. The following year he married Jean Johnson whom he had known before going to prison. He says in his autobiography that he had wanted to marry her earlier but feared his mother's disapproval of her dark skin. . . . In 1939 he moved to Los Angeles seeking steadier income and stayed there through most of the war years. (pp. 60-1)

Himes has related something of his own racial experiences during the 1940s in his memoirs and in interviews. When he arrived in Los Angeles, he sought work as a screen writer, but despite a recommendation by the popular novelist, Louis Bromfield, he had little luck in any of the studios. He tells of overhearing Jack Warner snarl he "didn't want no nigger" on his lot. Himes's other efforts to find steady work were not much happier. In *The Quality of Hurt,* he mentions twenty-three defense jobs he held during the first three years of the war, nearly all of them low-paying despite his skills and intellectual capacities. He was held back, he is convinced, because of his color. The strain affected his marriage, and it is not surprising that the angriest of his novels, *If He Hollers Let Him Go* (1945), was written during these years. Many of the same feral passions that characterize *If He Hollers* reemerge in the last of his fictional works, the crime thriller *Blind Man With a Pistol* (1969), which was also written at a time when racial confrontations were becoming widespread on American city streets.

If He Hollers Let Him Go is a first-person, tension-fraught account by a wartime shipyard worker, Bob Jones, who tells of the racial humiliations he faces day after day. It fuses the genre of protest novel with the violence and style of tough-guy detective stories.

> She was a peroxide blonde with a large-featured, overly made-up face, and she had a large, bright-painted, fleshy mouth, kidney-shaped, thinner in the middle than at the ends. Her big blue babyish eyes were mascaraed like a burlesque queen's and there were tiny wrinkles in their corners and about the flare of her nostrils, calipering down about the edges of her mouth. She looked thirty and well sexed, ripe but not quite rotten. She looked as if she might have worked half those years in a cat house, and if she hadn't she must have given a lot of it away.
>
> We stood there for an instant, our eyes locked, before either of us moved; then she deliberately put on a frightened, wild-eyed look and backed away from me as if she was scared stiff, as if she was a naked virgin and I was King Kong.

Few of Himes's other pre-detective novels adhere so consistently to hard-boiled prose, but they resemble the first in that the lives of his main characters are constantly being threatened. (pp. 61-2)

[After he moved to France in 1953, it] was Marcel Duhamel who in late 1956 first advised an impecunious Himes to try writing detective books. Duhamel, long an admirer of Himes, had translated *If He Hollers Let Him Go* into French and was now editor of Gallimard publisher's enormously successful *Série Noire* police novel series. Himes at first demurred. He said he did not know how to write detective books, but Duhamel insisted, suggesting Himes's own life experiences could provide him with sufficient characters and background. Duhamel advised Himes to begin with some dramatic or criminal event in Harlem and then simply allow his imagination free rein. (pp. 63-4)

Himes knew too that he was addressing primarily a French audience for whom Harlem was an exotic landscape filled with jungle blacks who were passionate, violent, and joyous. He could say things to them that he dare not say at home. He could appear to indulge their fantasies, confirm their preconceptions, and still perhaps instruct them. For if Himes believed he was writing "straightforward violence," he was also writing in the Afro-American tradition that aims to tell readers, black and white, the hard truths about black life. And these truths may sometimes demand something more than a literal rendering:

> in the murky waters of fetid tenements, a city of black people . . . are convulsed in desperate living, like the voracious churning of millions of hungry cannibal fish. Blind mouths eating their own guts. Stick in a hand and draw back a nub.
>
> That is Harlem. (*For Love of Imabelle*)

These books, Himes states, represent a breakthrough because French readers had hitherto regarded all Negroes as "victims" and thought of detective stories as the exclusive province of white writers like Simenon, Peter Cheney, Raymond Chandler and Dashiell Hammett.

At first glance Himes's thrillers appear artless. They are related in the third person by an omniscient author who shuttles back and forth in time and locale at will. Plots are bewilderingly interwoven; like Chandler, Himes places more emphasis on individual scenes than on construction. Often Coffin Ed and Grave Digger do not appear until the narrative is well underway and several grotesque crimes have been committed. When they are called to duty it is sometimes because white police authorities fear bad publicity for Headquarters. A number of very violent confrontations take place before they succeed in ferreting out their criminals, but the layers and layers of graft, greed, and betrayal they uncover reveal an incorrigibly corrupt society.

Like their white predecessors, Coffin Ed and Grave Digger are skeptical that things can remain clean very long. But whereas white detectives often blame society's failures on the moral lapses of individuals, Himes's cops vent their social outrage. Exploitation and racism lie at the very heart of the system, they say, and the violent and absurd crimes blacks inflict upon one another are simply a microcosm of what goes on in the larger white world. Their fury mounts with each succeeding book as their author observed from afar the civil-rights struggles on American city streets. Without doubt Himes identified with that anger, but was he also partly furious because now he felt too physically removed? Oddly, one of the characteristics of Himes's later fiction is that the longer he is away from home, the angrier he gets—this at a time, paradoxically, when American racism appeared to be on the wane. Was he now reacting as well to European racism, which he says in his autobiography was not really so very different from what he knew in America?

Himes's Harlem is allegorical, a Hogarthian colony of exploited black people. Many are victims of violence, who themselves shoot, throttle, maul, slice, whip, and stab others. Among their number are hired killers, pimps, addicts, pushers, quacks, prostitutes, crooked cops, numbers racketeers, madams, pederasts, transvestites, and hustlers of all descriptions. They rejoice in such names as Sugartit, Ready Belcher, Uncle Saint, Sister Heavenly, Sweet Prophet, Dummy, Sassafrass, and H. Exodus Clay (an undertaker). Often their physical appearance betrays their monstrous or freakish nature. Consider, for example, Himes's semisardonic, semihumorous description of Sweet Prophet, an enormously successful religious cult figure.

> Sweet Prophet sat on a throne of red roses on a flower-draped float. . . . Over his head was a sunshade of gold tinsel made in the shape of a halo. . . . His tremendous bulk was impressive in a bright purple robe lined with yellow silk and trimmed with mink. Beneath it he wore a black taffeta suit with white piping and silver buttons. His fingernails, untrimmed since he first claimed to have spoken with God, were more than three inches in length. They curled like strange talons, and were painted different colors. On each finger he

wore a diamond ring. His smooth black face with its big buck teeth and popping eyes was ageless; but his long grizzly hair, on which he wore a black silk cap, was snow-white. (*The Big Gold Dream*)

Or Fats, the proprietor of Fats Down Home Restaurant:

He resembled the balloon that had discovered stratosphere, but hundreds of degrees hotter. He wore an old-fashioned white silk shirt without the collar, fastened about the neck with a diamond-studded collar button, and black alpaca pants; but his legs were so large they seemed joined together, and his pants resembled a funnel-shaped skirt. His round brown head, which could have passed for a safety balloon in case his stomach burst, was clean-shaven. Not a hair showed above his chest—either on his face, nostrils, ears, eyebrows or eyelashes—giving the impression that his whole head had been scalded and scraped like the carcass of a pork. (*The Crazy Kill*)

But Himes's humor is not confined to description. The crimes his characters commit will at times become a kind of grim joke they play on themselves; there is a macabre quality to their violence that one associates with the Keystone Cops or the more sadistic animated cartoons. . . . [To illustrate]: A sneak thief who has just managed to scissor carefully through the back of a church lady's skirt in order to snip off the money bag that hangs from her waist (while his partner engages her in "holy" conversation) is shortly thereafter hit from the rear by a truck and sent flying through the air like a bird (*Cotton Comes To Harlem,* 1965). A long wicker basket filled with loaves of bread stands in front of a supermarket. A young man lies down on the mattress of bread and is promptly stabbed to death (*The Crazy Kill,* 1959). A crook who is simultaneously trying to kill a goat and crack open a safe accidentally shoots off a half-pint bottle of nitro-glycerine that blows himself up with the goat, the safe, and the entire house (*The Heat's On,* 1965). A bartender leans over the counter and axes off the arm of an unruly knife-wielding customer (*The Real Cool Killers,* 1960). A gunman, Big Six, shuffles through the streets of Harlem with a hunting knife stuck through his head. A woman with two children on their way to see a horror movie shouts at him. "You ought to be ashamed of yourself frightening little children" (*All Shot Up*). (pp. 65-7)

Himes's humor is verbal as well as physical. He burlesques some of the old-fashioned moral platitudes of the pulp writers. In *For Love of Imabelle,* for instance, a con man who has been passing himself off as a federal agent "apprehends" Jackson, the simple-minded victim of a gang of thieves that has promised to convert his real money into counterfeit money ten times its value. In order to avoid jail, Jackson bribes his captor with money he steals from his boss. Upon receiving the payoff, the marshall admonishes: "Let this be a lesson to you, Jackson. . . . Crime doesn't pay." Himes's humor reflects the hard cynical wit of the urban poor who know how to cheat and lie to the white world to survive physically, and cheat and lie to themselves to survive psychologically. It is this kind of humor that passes in acerbic exchanges between Grave Digger and Coffin Ed as they await criminal payoffs or pay off crooks themselves for information leading to larger prey. Here are Coffin Ed and Grave Digger as they approach one of their information centers, an East Harlem brothel in a filthy tenement.

"What American slums need is toilets," Coffin Ed said.

Smelling the odors of cooking, loving, hair frying, dogs farting, cats pissing, boys masturbating, and the stale fumes of stale wine and black tobacco, Grave Digger said, "That wouldn't help much." (*Cotton Comes To Harlem*)

Himes's portrayal of Harlemites shows them lying somewhere between open-mouthed gullibility and tough-minded sophistication. Often they exhibit bawdy, earthy qualities mixed with a kind of urban hipness. The following exchange takes place in a diner between a black counterman and a white homosexual who has come looking for a "sissie."

I know what you want.
How you know that?
Just lookin at you.
Cause I'm white?
Tain't that. I got the eye.
You think I'm looking for a girl.
Chops is your dish.
Not pork.
Naw.
Not overdone.
Naw. Just right. (*Blind Man With a Pistol*)

The adventures in Himes's Harlem are wild, slapstick, violent, and improbable, but Himes says the improbability of his tales corresponds to a realistic vision of black life in America: "Realism and absurdity are so similar in the lives of American blacks, one cannot tell the difference." Himes does realistically convey the sights, sounds, and smells of Harlem: the extremes of weather, the grey streets and buildings, the loving delights of soul food, the names of taverns, nightclubs, restaurants, the look of alleys, junk shops, butcher shops, bars, gangster pads, brothels, gambling dens, subway stations, furnished rooms, tenement flats, department stores, warehouses, bridges, police stations, and "shooting galleries" where addicts service themselves. But in his 1976 autobiography, Himes says he now thinks of himself not primarily as a realist or as a protest writer, but as an "absurdist"; by revealing blacks absurdly oppressing one another, he was much more of a modernist than he had at first imagined. Although they had begun as nothing more than potboilers, his books have become parables.

Yet if he is an absurdist, he is not without compassion for some of the victims of oppression—whether they have been used by people of their own race or by outsiders. One thinks of the female domestic in *The Big Gold Dream* who stabs her minister, Sweet Prophet, after she learns he wanted her killed. She says she had known all along that he had been trying to steal her money but she remained devoted to him because in her otherwise dreary world she had to believe in someone. Or even more absurdly, there is the giant albino Negro, Pinky, in *The Heat's On,* who kills his father when he learns the latter is planning to emigrate to Africa without him. The father, it seems, feared that African blacks would reject Pinky because he is too light-skinned.

Himes's Harlem remains largely an inner vision, a crazy maze of frustration and evil through which Coffin Ed and Grave Digger must thread their way. To do this, they obviously make their compromises. For them, violence, cupidity, treachery, and brutality are norms of human behavior, and they rarely delude themselves about the true nature of their jobs.

They took their tribute, like all real cops, from the established underworld catering to the essential needs of the people—gamekeepers, madams, street-walkers, numbers writers, numbers bankers. But they were rough on purse snatchers, muggers, burglars, con men, and all strangers working any racket. And they didn't like rough stuff from anybody else but themselves. "Keep it cool," they warned. "Don't make graves." (*For Love of Imabelle*)

Still, they have their own peculiar code of honor: they are fiercely loyal to one another (indeed their personalities are scarcely distinguishable), and they possess a high-minded zeal to protect the downtrodden poor from their worst exploiters, black and white. But if beneath their rough exteriors they are Lochinvars, they are nonetheless ambivalent about the roles they play. They recognize that the police department that employs them is an extension of the larger society that has brutalized and degraded their community, which may in part explain the excesses of violence they employ on persons (almost always black) whom they suspect of wrongdoing. Are they directing their rage away from themselves for serving an oppressive society? Are they expressing subconscious hostility toward their own people? Must black cops be tougher on blacks than white cops? Or is their brutality really justified? Perhaps because he has been unable to truly answer these questions, and can only rarely even ask them, Himes has been unable to go on with his detective series.

To a degree the reason may lie in the contradictions of the hardboiled detective genre itself. Rather than transcend the formula as Hammett and Chandler would occasionally do, Himes carries the dime detective world view to its logical conclusion in absurdity—tough-guy fiction thereby becoming its own moral, metaphysical, and social comment. For Himes the genre *is* the message with its formula that depends upon unconscious assumptions about existence (violent), human behavior (irrational), sex (dangerous), power (malevolent), and society (corrupt). But, for all that, the genre also implies a modicum of faith in external justice. Despite the isolation of the hero, there must be some recognition somewhere that he has discovered truth and has brought his criminals to their just deserts. If society cannot validate truth and justice, there can no longer be any reason for the detective. What, after all, is the point of the hero pursuing crooks if no one is to confirm what is delusion and who is evil? For all his sense of being above the law and society, the detective needs law and society not simply to flaunt, but to give support to his values and substance to his identity.

All these contradictions come to a head in Himes's last novel, ***Blind Man With A Pistol*** (1969), for here he creates a society so corrupt and so venal that it becomes impossible for Coffin Ed and Grave Digger to track down their prey. ***Blind Man*** begins as his other books do, with Himes introducing us chapter by chapter to his usual gallery of Harlem low life, most of whom become involved with racist white cops as well as their black counterparts, the sour and cynical Coffin Ed and Grave Digger. The latter are required to investigate three major crimes, each of which may be related to the others, but before they are able to solve any of them, they are inexplicably taken off their assignments. The only thing clear about their situation is that their police superiors are obviously bowing to white and black political pressures in order to protect lucrative Harlem rackets.

The complete breakdown of social morality can only lead to chaos, and Himes is especially good at producing chaotic im-

ages in his absurd, upside-down Harlem mirror. Somewhere near the middle of the novel Himes describes the convergence from different directions of three parades at 135th Street and Seventh Avenue on Nat Turner Day. Each of the groups represents an opposing ideology: Brotherly Love, Black Power, and Black Jesus. The first, a mob of white and black marchers mindlessly gripping hands, is led by a simple-minded black youth and his dumpy, middle-aged Swedish mistress, while the latter two parades are headed by unprincipled black phoneys. At a critical juncture, all the marchers fling themselves madly on one another whereupon the confusion is compounded by an invasion of police. Himes paints the scene in broad comic strokes but below the surface one senses utter revulsion at the simplistic slogans and cure-alls that aggravate the sicknesses of the black community. Blacks who exploit other blacks do what whites have done to blacks from time immemorial. Only at the very end of the novel does a white/black confrontation take place, but characteristically, it is a confrontation that makes no sense at all. Cops and Negroes shoot it out with one another near a subway station without either knowing why. Meanwhile Coffin Ed and Grave Digger stand idly by shooting at rats fleeing a condemned tenement house.

Did Himes intend the rotting tenement as a metaphor for his country? Do the fleeing rats also bespeak an attitude toward some of Himes's fellow citizens? Whatever the answer, the detective thriller has come to a full stop. Clearly one cannot single out a rat in a house full of rats. (pp. 67-70)

> Edward Margolies, "Chester Himes's Black Comedy: The Genre Is the Message," in his Which Way Did He Go?: The Private Eye in Dashiell Hammett, Raymond Chandler, Chester Himes, and Ross Macdonald, *Holmes & Meier Publishers, 1982, pp. 53-70.*

JAMES SALLIS

In one early short story Chester Himes writes of a black man who, because he will not step off the sidewalk to let a white couple pass, has his feet doused with gasoline and set on fire, consequently losing them. At the end of the story another white man becomes enraged when at a movie theater [the black man] fails to stand for the playing of the national anthem, even though it is pointed out he has no feet.

A more recent story, **"Prediction,"** opens with the black janitor of the city's Catholic cathedral sitting astride the public poor box with a heavy-caliber automatic rifle, waiting at the end of "four hundred years" while six thousand white policemen parade in the streets below. The ensuing massacre is described with characteristic intensity and shocking detail: rank after rank of policemen are mowed down; shards of bone, lariats of gut and pieces of brain spin through the air. A riot tank is dispatched and, unable to find a target, turns its guns on black plaster-of-Paris mannequins in a nearby store window, then on the policemen themselves, killing 29 and wounding another 117. Finally the black janitor's location is discovered. The tank turns to the stone face and stares a moment "as if in deep thought," then levels the cathedral. But his symbolic action strikes a resounding blow: "In the wake of the bloody massacre the stock market crashed. The dollar fell on the world market. The very structure of capitalism began to crumble."

These two visions, the naturalist-didactic and the apocalyptic, largely define Chester Himes' career and work. The first of the stories, in its limning of the way in which white society makes demands on the black which that same society has assured he cannot fulfill, shares with the second a parabolic intensity common to Himes; each suggests, as do his later Harlem detective novels, that the forces of law and order only serve to amplify the disorder and chaos of American urban life. For Himes, the roots of our society are so thoroughly corrupt as to forbid anything approaching normal growth. Though he often has been labeled such, he is not a protest writer, for that term carries an implicit sense of meliorism, of redemptive change, a sense rarely manifest in Himes' work. The sense one *does* receive is that of a vast pall of futility, a huge sea of inaction and impotence relieved by sudden islands of violent, random motion: the crushing weight of centuries. And his interest from the first has been the individual human consequences of so distorted a society. Of his early naturalism he retains always determinism: if his people are monsters, misshapen, grotesque things, it is because the egg they formed in forced them to that shape.

In other respects Himes' naturalism has undergone a progression unique to American letters. Reminiscent of Richard Wright and proletarian work of the Forties, the early naturalist novels yielded, with their author's expatriation, to the serial exploits of a team of black Harlem detectives, Grave Digger Jones and Coffin Ed Johnson. (pp. 191-92)

Always together, Grave Digger and Coffin Ed prowl the streets in their beat-up, souped-up Plymouth, looking like "two hog farmers on a weekend in the Big Town," connecting with a broad network of junkies, stool pigeons, whores and pimps and maintaining law and order primarily by bashing heads and making deals, in the interim shooting off their mouths and identical long-barreled, nickel-plated .38 revolvers on .44 frames (they have a particular affinity for tracer bullets). Grave Digger, the more articulate of the two, has smoldering reddish brown eyes, a "lumpy" face and oversize frame, and always wears a black alpaca suit with an old felt hat perched on the back of his head. Coffin Ed's face, disfigured by thrown acid in the first of the novels, has earned him a second nickname, Frankenstein, and he often must be restrained from impulsive violence by Grave Digger. The two live near one another, with their families, on Long Island. They share a considerable courage, a sure knowledge of street ways, studied flamboyance—and an abiding pragmatism. They know that nothing they can do is likely to have much real effect, and maintain what order there is chiefly by improvisation, threat and brutality, generally adding appreciably to the toll of bodies and confusion. Here is their first appearance, from *For Love of Imabelle* (also issued as *A Rage in Harlem*):

> They were having a big ball in the Savoy and people were lined up for a block down Lenox Avenue, waiting to buy tickets. The famous Harlem detective-team of Coffin Ed Johnson and Grave Digger Jones had been assigned to keep order.
>
> Both were tall, loose-jointed, sloppily dressed, ordinary-looking dark-brown colored men. But there was nothing ordinary about their pistols. They carried specially made long-barreled nickel-plated .38-calibre revolvers, and at the moment they had them in their hands.
>
> Grave Digger stood on the right side of the front end of the line, at the entrance to the Savoy. Coffin

Ed stood on the left side of the line, at the rear end. Grave Digger had his pistol aimed south, in a straight line down the sidewalk. On the other side, Coffin Ed had his pistol aimed north, in a straight line. There was space enough between the two imaginary lines for two persons to stand side by side. Whenever anyone moved out of line, Grave Digger would shout, "Straighten up!" and Coffin Ed would echo, "Count off !" If the offender didn't straighten up the line immediately, one of the detectives would shoot into the air. The couples in the queue would close together as though pressed between two concrete walls. Folks in Harlem believed that Grave Digger Jones and Coffin Ed Johnson would shoot a man stone dead for not standing straight in a line.

In a later novel, urged by their Lieutenant to "play it safe" and avoid unnecessary violence, Grave Digger responds: "We've got the highest crime rate on earth among the colored people in Harlem. And there ain't but three things to do about it: Make the criminals pay for it—you don't want to do that; pay the people enough to live decently—you ain't going to do that; so all that's left is let 'em eat one another up."

As H. Bruce Franklin points out in an excellent piece on Himes in *The Victim as Criminal and Artist,* the varieties of violence inflicted on blacks by blacks, finally represented by the two detectives as much as by the criminals they chase, become the persistent theme of the Harlem novels. But, he adds, these two black cops know who the real enemy is. In **The Real Cool Killers,** after a rare exercise of traditional detective methods to discover the killer, Grave Digger conceals her identity, chiefly because she is one of the rare Harlem inhabitants who has struck out—in this case against a wealthy white sadist who comes uptown to beat young girls.

Though the Harlem novels develop in a fairly clear line from the modern detective novel as established by Hammett (particularly *Red Harvest*) and Chandler, they were never true genre pieces, fulfilling few traditional expectations, and as they continued, they in fact withdrew further from preconceived notions of the detective story. Specific crimes are solved in the early books (albeit rather incidentally), but there is a progressive movement towards concentration on the scene itself, on Harlem as symbol, using the detective story framework as vehicle for character and social portraiture. And as this shift occurs, absurdities, incomprehensible events and grotesqueries proliferate. The books close on greater disorder and confusion than they began with, as James Lundquist observes in his book-length study of Himes: "Order and reason are left farther and farther behind as the crimes Grave Digger and Coffin Ed must solve and the means of solution become ever more outrageous." This is of course nihilism— and a near perfect reversal of Gide's description of the detective story as a form in which "every character is trying to deceive all the others and in which the truth slowly becomes visible through the haze of deception."

Himes did not plan this evolution; it grew quite spontaneously out of the material he was working with in the Harlem novels, and what he himself was. In *My Life of Absurdity* he describes writing these novels:

> I would sit in my room and become hysterical thinking about the wild, incredible story I was writing. But it was only for the French, I thought, and they would believe anything about Americans,

black or white, if it was bad enough. And I thought I was writing realism. It never occurred to me that I was writing absurdity. Realism and absurdity are so similar in the lives of American blacks one can not tell the difference.

These trends culminate—there was a five-year delay between the final two, and it seems unlikely there will be more—in *Blind Man With a Pistol,* surely the apotheosis of Himes' detective novels. Assigned to find the killer of a cruising white homosexual, Grave Digger and Coffin Ed roar through a landscape of crazy preachers, children eating from troughs, the cant of black revolutionaries, and a gigantic black plaster-of-Paris Jesus hanging from the ceiling with a sign reading *They lynched me.* (Lundquist has called the first chapter of this book "one of the strangest in American literature.") Neither the original nor subsequent murders are solved; the sole connecting link is an enigmatic man (*or men*) wearing a red fez. The two detectives are confounded and frustrated at every turn: politically protected suspects, payoffs and neatly contrived "solutions," diversionary cleanup campaigns and bureaucracy. Halfway through the novel they are taken off the case, in fact, and assigned to investigate Harlem's swelling black riots. "You mean you want us to lay off before we discover something you don't want discovered?" Grave Digger asks point blank. But he already knows; they all do, and the rest is little more than ritual dance. This is where Himes' work breaks off most surely from its forebears. With Hammett, Chandler or Ross Macdonald, the corruption, however profound, would at last be penetrated; with Himes, it is so pervasive, its signature so universal, that it cannot be.

Towards the novel's end, in a scene paralleling that of their debut in *For Love of Imabelle,* Grave Digger and Coffin Ed are standing on the corner of Lenox and 125th shooting rats as they run from buildings being demolished. Their function, and efficacy, have been so abridged.

Meanwhile a belligerent black man who wants no one to know he is blind, walking streets and riding subways by memory, has become involved in an argument with a gardener (for whites, of course) who thinks the blind man is staring at him. Soon involved as well are a white truck driver and a black clergyman who intervenes to preach against violence. Attacked by the truck driver, the blind man draws a pistol and fires, killing the preacher. He continues to fire as the subway pulls into the 125th Street station, then staggers up onto the street close behind the gardener and truck driver, where he is shot to death by white police watching Grave Digger's and Coffin Ed's display of marksmanship. Immediately the cry goes out that "Whitey has murdered a soul brother!"

An hour later Lieutenant Anderson had Grave

Digger on the radio-phone. "Can't you men stop that riot?" he demanded.

"It's out of hand, boss," Grave Digger said.

"All right, I'll call for reinforcements. What started it?"

"A blind man with a pistol."

"What's that?"

"You heard me, boss."

"That don't make any sense."

"Sure don't."

Thus the book ends on a familiar theme: having abrogated their authority, the Lieutenant absurdly expects his detectives still to function. And just as Himes had discovered in his mythical Harlem a correlative for the absurdity of the urban black's life, so he found a final metaphor for the mindless ubiquity of violence against and within those same people. (pp. 193-97)

Himes is not a thinker, and his thought rarely penetrates to any significant level beneath the commonplace. When he does attempt discursive thought, outside his personae at any rate, it is often puerile, and even in the fiction what he *shows* sometimes subverts what he *says.* For he is a marvelous observer and prodigious inventor, working by instinct and feeling towards his singular vision; and that vision cannot be reduced to mere ideas. I do not know of any other American writer who has created vivid, memorable scenes in the quantity Himes has, scenes which are hard-edged and durable like a footprint in cement, and with an astounding economy of dialogue and language.

A passage from the second volume of autobiography, *My Life of Absurdity,* now seems to me emblematic of Himes' work, his description "of a painting I had seen in my youth of black soldiers clad in Union Army uniforms down on their hands and knees viciously biting the dogs the Southern rebels had turned on them, their big white dangerous teeth sinking into the dogs' throats while the dogs yelped futilely." The terrible ambivalence of the black's place in society, Himes' own bitterness and paradoxical rage, elements of graphic violence and *opera bouffe,* the contradictory, enigmatic and finally irreducible "message," the clarity of scene: the painting is a virtual mirror image of Himes' work. (p. 198)

James Sallis, "In America's Black Heartland: The Achievement of Chester Himes," in Western Humanities Review, *Vol. XXXXII, No. 3, Autumn, 1983, pp. 191-206.*

Paulette Jiles
1943-

American-born Canadian poet, novelist, short story writer, and scriptwriter.

Jiles blends humor, fantasy, and autobiographical elements into works that scrutinize and often satirize social conventions. Her first poetry collection, *Waterloo Express* (1973), focuses on the need for self-definition through actual and metaphorical travel; by horse, car, train, and boat, the speaker explores outer realities while probing inner feelings and thoughts. Reviewers commented that Jiles's long and complex works offer strikingly original observations. Themes relating to travel, self-identity, and human relationships are also explored in *Celestial Navigation* (1984), which won the 1985 Governor General's Literary Award for poetry. Critics lauded the intimate revelations and well-honed imagery in several poems and praised Jiles's skill with language. Dennis Cooley remarked: "Paulette Jiles's writing impresses immediately with the freshness of a peeled banana. Even in these days of acquired suspicion toward the referent, it strikes with the power of recognition. How fitting, how apt, how like it is. In image and metaphor we are grateful for the world brought new to us."

Jiles's first novel, *The Late Great Human Road Show* (1986), ventures into a fanciful but frightening post-apocalyptic future where orphans, professionals, vagrants, survivalists, and a pregnant cow roam deserted Toronto streets. While some reviewers faulted the novel as plotless and sentimental, most praised it for sharply depicted urban scenes, perceptive social commentary, and incisive humor. In *Sitting in the Club Car Drinking Rum and Karma-Cola: A Manual of Etiquette for Ladies Crossing Canada by Train* (1986), Jiles parodies detective novels and mystery films. In this series of short prose passages with individual titles and forms, Jiles unfolds the story of Our Heroine, a fugitive from credit-card debts and unsatisfying relationships who dresses like a 1940s movie star. On an eastbound train across Canada, she constructs a web of deceptions to fool an enigmatic investigator who becomes her lover. Some critics found the parody occasionally strained, but most deemed Jiles's work elegant, witty, and imaginative.

(See also *CLC,* Vol. 13 and *Contemporary Authors,* Vol. 101.)

JUDITH FITZGERALD

Paulette Jiles's third full-length publication [*Celestial Navigation*] contains much of her first book, *Waterloo Express* and a substantial selection of new poems. The effect of the juxtaposition is startling, demonstrating as it does that a consistent voice and vision have informed the poet's sensibility over the past decade. If elements of her writing have changed, the direction can only be described as fast-forward.

There are six sections in *Celestial Navigation.* The first, **"Waterloo Express,"** contains 21 poems from the earlier collection. Of these, **"Get Up in the Morning"** and **"Mass"** stand

out as exceptional examples of Jiles's incisive abilities. [**"Get Up in the Morning"**] fraught with a delightful system of *double entendre,* turns on its axis and then turns again:

> I get up in the morning and check out my feelings. . . .
> Even in this hour full of hushes,
> the shadows extending like tape measures,
> the stars, like amnesia, cancel themselves.
> I don't think I have ever seen you before in my life. . . .

The second section, **"Paper Matches,"** is the finest one in *Celestial Navigation.* Its 26 poems, including the title one, crackle with immediacy and an energy-charged surface. **"Late Night Telephone"** is electric; it drips with a taut edge of irony that goes on and on. **"Horror Stories"** surfaces as an intense and almost humorous examination of women's vicarious impulses. . . .

Celestial Navigation is a collection that derives its dynamic energy from Jiles's skill with language. Whether she focuses on interpersonal relationships or interplanetary movements, all things flourish where she turns her eyes. At her best, there is none better.

It is for precisely this reason that the remaining four sections of *Celestial Navigation* jar slightly. The first two succeed because they contain deftly constructed poems that derive much of their force from an inventive use of imaginative language. Yet, by the third and fourth sections, **"Griffon Poems"** and **"Northern Radio,"** there is a sense that many of these poems (and prose sections) have come into existence because of Jiles's abilities as a phrase-maker and dislocator. **"As The Night Goes"** and **"Turning Forty,"** unfortunately, offer much too much of the same. (p. 27)

Taken collectively, many of these poems might have made the passage from merely competent to truly great if they had been edited more closely. Jiles's dependence on similes becomes, after the first dozen or so poems, downright distracting. Further, her repeated use of the traditionally slow verbs (to be, to have) points to a laziness in the poems that a poet of Jiles's stature should have abandoned long ago. . . .

However, these are minor irritations that can be overlooked; on the whole, Jiles effectively marries form and content with unique style. *Celestial Navigation* is an impressive collection of tiny stars that burst into poems. (pp. 27-8)

> *Judith Fitzgerald, "A Star Reborn," in* Books in Canada, *Vol. 13, No. 8, October, 1984, pp. 27-8.*

DONALEE MOULTON-BARRETT

If you were to navigate the heavens, you would encounter some fascinating sights. But you would also, especially after several sightings, find part of the heavens mundane and ordinary. So it is with Paulette Jiles's collection of poetry *Celestial Navigation.*

The strongest section in *Celestial Navigation* is **"Waterloo Express,"** a selection of poems reprinted from Jiles's book of the same name. In these poems, Jiles is intimate with her subject matter and speaks from this very powerful position.

The least satisfying poems in the book are those where Jiles takes an issue (as opposed to an event, or even a character) and discusses it. These poems, and there are several, are bone dry and predictable. Also lacklustre are the **"Griffon Poems,"** about the 1679 loss of the ship, *The Griffon.* In **"Where They Disembarked,"** the opening poem of the section, Jiles writes: I drown and drown (you are here too, in / this flotsam, it's like being / killed by washing machine).

Here Jiles is trying to be clever, and it shows. There is none of the natural description or pounding rhythm of the Waterloo poems, for example. But perhaps these disappointing poems are so obvious, and so grating, because when Jiles writes well, as she often does, she writes very, very well indeed.

> *donalee Moulton-Barrett, in a review of "Celestial Navigation: Poems," in* CM: Canadian Materials for Schools and Libraries, *Vol. XII, No. 6, November, 1984, p. 252.*

DAVID O'ROURKE

[Paulette Jiles deserves] attention because she is unquestionably the real thing. [In *Celestial Navigation*], several of her similes are superb ("I feel like a land above some treeline"); her use of metaphor is very imaginative ("The aurora is a piano, playing blues / in green neon"); and many of these lines will not easily escape memory ("Texas is not my fault," "good-byes falling / away in flakes of dead skin," or "I took

a job on a / cigarette package"). She has the intelligence, the anger, the irony—all the right weapons. The first section includes a generous selection from *Waterloo Express,* her first work, and here her imagination runs in every direction, sometimes to the detriment of individual poems, but always there is something happening. Sections Three, Four, and Five are more seriously flawed. In the first she does the Canadiana thing, finding a sunken ship no one else has written on; in the latter two, she too often leaves the personal concrete for a dull abstraction. Sections One, Two, and the last three parts of Six, which is written in prose, display her at her very best. She has the right idea in **"Heatwave / St. Louis"**: "So this is life, we say, this is / not bad, give us more of this thunder." (pp. 138-39)

> *David O'Rourke, "Intelligent Anger," in* Canadian Literature, *No. 106, Fall, 1985, pp. 138-39.*

ANN MANDEL

[The poems of Paulette Jiles's *Celestial Navigation* share] an allegiance to seeing clearly and to resisting all prescribed identities and limitations other than those she imposes on or discovers in herself and in language. The universe observed ranges from the remote interior of the Canadian north to the remote interior of the mind, but the poet travelling its distances knows that borders are arbitrary, destination only a matter of time, and length of stay contingent on not being spotted "by any of the numerous accidents" that wait along the way. What real purchases we have on our lives reside in the imperatives of "speech and dreams" and the "lunatic assertions" of hope; everything else is unpaid-for and not ours. . . .

A photograph of an eighteenth-century quadrant prefacing the book, and a cover illustration taken from an eighteenth-century cosmological treatise . . . together emphasize the motifs of exploration, travel, and discovery in the book. Jiles has an acute sense of new worlds as both new possibilities and new responsibilities. In travel, one can measure one's ability to be at home in the world, to navigate seas and relationships, jettison unnecessary baggage and conclusions, leave one train of thought for another. . . .

While there is freedom and independence in moving to one's own rhythm, a responsibility exists to see truly and *be* wherever one is. As "Girl Friday" on an island, with "all this stone at close range," the poet knows that despite distant purposes and hopes, "this is the world, then," and "I am a caretaker." Sending a letter to someone she once knew, the poet in another poem writes "importantly," "I am far away." Then, becoming aware of the village where she is, the lights and people around her, she adds, "Actually, I am not so far away . . . I am extremely close." In the vastness of history, we can miss or forget details that both distinguish people from each other and bind them in common. (p. 19)

Jiles is much concerned with the uses people make of others, race of race, men of women, parents of children, especially by the imposition of unwanted roles. In families, for instance, everyone has a role in the **"Family Novel,"** in the **"Situation Comedy."** In the latter poem, "We got to where we were television . . . our parents watched us, relentlessly . . . and we began / entertaining them, relentlessly." Parents feed on children "as if [they] were Easter wafers," but there is no communion. Men, too, fix women in roles: wives who "carried and did things around the / house"; aunts who wash dishes inside while men play outside—women inscribed with the message " 'At Your Service,' like a book of / paper matches." . . . In one of the concluding prose poems, the poet remembers the starched, encumbering, constricting Sunday clothes "young ladies" wore to church in her youth, clothes that represent "innumerable systems" of social and sexual roles. But, like Huck Finn condemning himself to hell by choosing his intuitive sense of what is right over his society's teaching, the girl in Jiles' poem rejects the lessons she is being taught. (pp. 20-1)

Like Huck, too, Jiles trusts in her own sense of the perceptible world more than in some transcendent power. God is a symbol, for life, fate, or potatoes, and as "the Potato God" is "more desperate and more commonplace / than once thought." We can fly in planes like angels' arms, but we are earth-people and must return "to everything that is / unjust, unpaid-for and unwarranted, / claimed by our bodies like baggage"; must return to a world where people "guard themselves behind walls," separate themselves through wars, and, like stubborn horses, can be driven together only by stories of panic and burning barns.

The observable world to which Jiles gives her fealty is not only the visible landscape but the country of the mind as well, where communication and travel assume new forms. "The mind is an eye, it knows something / it tells only in dreams." "The remote interior" of the mind is another world, with its own moons, comets, stars, fireflies and deer, its jets and herons taking off and landing. It is a lake with "life below the surface"; it is "Hill 49, an arena for bad dreams," a war zone. It can rise above the earth and watch the "years fold up," old tribes disappear, a new time begin.

Like the mind, the body too can be a landscape. In one poem, Jiles writes, "I have become a wet brown root, my foot dripping out / and growing huge, clasping my barking tongue on the language / of pigeons." And in the book's final poem, **"Turning Forty,"** she writes,

> My imagination becomes an arctic,
> laced with jade rivers. I feel like a land above some
>   treeline,
> infinitely detailed, stripped by gale-force winds of
>   anything that
> gets in the way. I have everything I need except the
>   sun and it
> comes without warning. I seem to be growing
>   through latitudes,
> and in gales my single carbide light remains and
>   holds.

Jiles' poems are structured primarily on series of images, sometimes radically connected, sometimes developed into conceits. In **"Blacksnake"** the snake is "a tangle of black calligraphy," "a telephone cord," "a question mark," "a high-power line," "a black umbilicus," and a "voiceless and thin" glitter. In **"Rock Climbing"** an image of dangling on a rope over the Niagara Escarpment is extended to become an argument against mute resignation, for hope and communication. In **"Paul Revere"** the image of an accidental highway collision becomes a metaphor for a smashed relationship, much as sailing and navigation function in the book's title poem. The poems from **Waterloo Express,** in particular, work with startling images and witty reversals: church bells "have been hung alive / by their voices in the belfry"; a woman "swells with emotion like a revivalist's tent"; "a waiter, newly

washed and wrung out, is hanging on the roof to dry," and "time gets easier as I go by." The imagery of the more recent poems is both subtler and more complex, but all Jiles' poems are charged with high energy: the power station she imagines in her mind (in **"Turning Forty"**) sends out a constant high-voltage electricity.

Her tone can be by turns sombre, tough and ironic, colloquial and funny. The three prose poems, especially **"The Mad Kitchen and Dong, the Cave Adolescent,"** are wonderfully humourous interior monologues which use the interplay between an adolescent mind and the "real" world around it to suggest the many selves jostling and acting up within any one person.

All these selves are possibilities, left behind or still ahead. "When I was married," a woman comments in one poem, "I was / someone else, but all / the divorces were me." During the crisis in **"Night Flight to Attiwapiskat"** the poet thinks, "I used / to find myself a series of hostile strangers, startled / in doorways."

> Now they
> gather themselves up, the wives, daughters, friends,
> victims, perpetrators, the one with the pen and
> the other carrying a blank mask, another at pres-
> ent at the cleaners.
>
> They catch up and slam together like a deck of
> cards, packed into the present moment.
>   (pp. 21-2)

In whatever self or landscape one might be travelling, whatever power words and dreams are now generating, the present moment can promise nothing beyond itself. In **"Turning Forty,"** Jiles writes, "Whatever / I now possess is true and whatever I do not have is too bad." Therefore, what exists matters. "Everything the loon sings about is / monumental and jewelled. Everything matters and / floats." We are anchored between life and death and might without warning sink "towards whatever / the bottom holds." Like the 'turpentine pines' bent over the water, we must accept this with a "bitter grace." (p. 22)

Ann Mandel, "Night Flights," in Brick: A Journal of Reviews, *No. 27, Spring, 1986, pp. 19-22.*

NANCY ROBB

Sitting in the Club Car Drinking Rum and Karma-Kola and *The Late Great Human Road Show* are worlds apart in plot but similar in tone. *Karma-Kola,* a spoof of the macho detective fiction of the Raymond Chandler-Dashiell Hammett variety, follows a woman's flight from $50,000 in bad debts, while *Road Show* is pure satire, providing a fly's-eye view of how several oddball characters—including a cow—survive in Toronto's Cabbagetown after the nuclear holocaust.

The Late Great Human Road Show opens two months after the bomb has been dropped, and it's not long before the reader is introduced to the entire cast. There are the uptight high-rise dwellers (John and Heather, Marta and Larry, and Barry); there are the kids, from the innocent Benjamin to the delinquent Carl; there's the zany matriarch, Roxana Raintree; and there's the vigilante survivalist, Matt, holed up in a building at the zoo with his girlfriend Vicki, crazy Sarah, and impressionable Arco. Then there are the neighbourhood weirdos, Man-With-No-Nose and Cussing Man; the eccentric scientist Merlin; and two Indians, Mary Jo Akewence and her brother George. All of them slept through the evacuation, and they are forever trying to figure out what happened (except for Merlin, who's worked it out). The only hints of nuclear devastation are the dark clouds that invade the city and the too-frequent sounds of crashing glass. . . .

[*The Late Great Human Road Show*'s] biggest weakness is its lack of plot. The pages are brimming with astute social commentary—although some of it is heavy-handed—as Jiles enters the worlds of all the characters, analysing their foibles and penetrating their thoughts. Many of the scenes, especially those involving the children, are also funny: "Benjamin came into the lobby of the Parkview Apartments carrying a foot. . . . He felt that he ought to take it to an adult. . . . It meant something. He would take it up and give it to them, they would all throw up their hands, if not their lunch." But the humour isn't enough to carry the book all by itself. Jiles brings the characters into contact with each other too slowly and too methodically to keep the reader's interest.

The inspiration for *Sitting in the Club Car Drinking Rum and Karma-Kola* hit Jiles at the same time she was reworking *Road Show.* "I was fascinated with the zippy, courageous, working-class heroines of the 40s that you saw in the movies," she says, "just gutsy as hell." The Katharine Hepburns and Lauren Bacalls appeal to the protagonist in *Karma-Kola,* too, and they are her alter egos for the train ride across Canada. The woman, known as Our Heroine, is skipping out on massive credit-card debts, a relationship, and an unrewarding job in Seattle. The anonymity of train travel gives her the perfect cover until The Man From China Bar—the skip-tracer—embarks just when she's starting to feel safe.

At first the book is frustrating because, like its writer, it doesn't allow the reader inside the heroine, to discover her passions and motivations. Instead, Jiles only reveals the person Our Heroine is pretending to be, although her true history slowly unfolds as the trip progresses. When The Man From China Bar enters her imaginary world, she's thrown off guard and has to concoct more characters, more lies. But so does he, as he tries to deflect her suspicions and deal with the emotional tug-of-war that engages them. "What *Karma-Kola* is about," Jiles offers, "is the male figure moving in and taking over the visual fields, but he's also trying to get away from it. In the end, she gets out of the book. She says, 'You can have it. Take it.' "

Karma-Kola is a little rough around the edges. Some of the humour—the references to the game of Clue, for example—is too self-conscious and over-explained. Jiles also lapses into cliché and jargon ("astronomical debts", "extracted the max") and sometimes creates images that are just plain hard to take ("foaming liquid theologies of Hell's Gate").

But there are some great lines too, lines that are true and funny and original: "She is too tall to be of any comfort to short men," or "We've all had our moments of terror. They are usually when (a) we think we may be killed, and (b) we think we may be taken for who we really are." And most of the imagery is vintage Jiles, making the reader want to close her eyes, dream, and rock with the gentle motion of the train: "The catalpa tree throws up its hands, and the train whistles, and begins to move, and pigeons take off like applause."

Nancy Robb, "Paulette Jiles: From the Ozarks to Crossing Canada by Train," in Quill and Quire, Vol. 52, No. 12, December, 1986, p. 38.

DAVID HELWIG

The Late Great Human Road Show is perhaps best regarded as a fable, "ordinary people in the last days," to borrow the title of a poem by Jay Macpherson.

Toronto is full of wrecked and abandoned cars, streetcars, trash. There are constant storms of glass as the huge windows of the high towers come loose and fall to earth. There is a ceiling of low cloud, occasional moments of "piss-yellow" sun. Through the ruins move perhaps a dozen men, women, and children and a cow—a substantial and determined Holstein who is a wonderfully vital (one almost wants to say human) presence in the book.

The best thing about *The Late Great Human Road Show* is the precision and skill of its prose. ("The cow was black and white with an aluminum ear tab, and the grace of a circus tent, which is not without grace.") The empty city is imagined with a consistently sharp sense of detail. Those ominous cascades of glass become a central image of dangerous, half-beautiful deterioration. One feels vividly the empty streets, the animals from the little tame Cabbagetown farm wandering at large, searching for food.

In this bizarre and yet familiar landscape, we see human beings behaving in remarkably human ways. The first half of the book is largely about the way the few living souls adapt, or fail to adapt, to the new set of circumstances. Two middle-class young couples simply go on with their domestic lives, pretending that it hasn't happened, waiting for someone in authority to arrive and put things in order. Even the end of the world is not enough to break down their habits and assumptions, and their persistence is both fatuous and oddly sympathetic. There are worse things than superficiality.

One of the worse things is paranoia. Hidden away at the Cow House at the old Riverdale Zoo are two political fanatics and a couple of hangers-on. The suspicion and hatred of Matt, the journalist, we are led to believe, reflect the fanaticism that has led to nuclear disaster. One of the book's themes is that the anticipation of violence is, in part, a love of violence, a longing for it. Matt assumes that the children will turn feral, will hunt in gangs, that men and women will become maddened, cannibalistic. In fact most of those wandering the streets are sensible and straightforward, and it is Matt's projections that lead to insanity.

In the second half of the book, the violence that Matt prophesies and desires is gradually brought to occur, but by then we understand that all the characters are going to die anyway, of radiation poisoning. No happy endings here.

The book is thoughtful and cleanly constructed, but there is some sense of philosophical disjunction or incompleteness. An acceptance of the ordinariness of ordinary things, an attempt to reject melodrama—these make the first part of a moral statement, but none of the characters has the strength to go beyond this. The band of children watched over by the drunken Roxana is slightly sentimentalized. There are lovely moments when the children's reaction to Cow, their dumb love for her animal warmth, makes a statement, against the forces of death, about the goodness of merely living, but these moments are undermined by sentimentality and the presence of too many characters who seem to be constructed to allow the author to grind knives.

In *Sitting in the Club Car Drinking Rum and Karma Kola,*

Jiles creates something a good deal less serious, but more completely successful. Her story is articulated as a sequence of short prose passages, each with its own title, each having its own shape. They are inventively and elegantly written, and they are assembled to tell a story that is in part a fantasy, in part a game with certain story-telling conventions, in part a fragmented character study. Our heroine (named only Our Heroine) gets on a train in Vancouver, setting out for the East, dressed in the style of a 1940s movie star. Behind her, in Seattle, she has left a huge credit card fraud and a life that she needed to abandon.

Just into the mountains, at China Bar, a mystery man gets on the train, probably the detective who has been sent to find and capture her. In an ironic imitation of an old-fashioned detective story, they meet and become lovers. The train moves on. Half the width of Canada passes by outside the windows. Observation, wit, reflection—the story glitters with all these, and ends, in a new beginning, with a young woman in a Northern Ontario airport, waiting to depart and reading *Sitting in the Club Car Drinking Rum and Karma Kola.* "A bit of fluff," she calls it and in a way she's right, but if the book is slight, it's also beautifully realized at its own fanciful level.

There are worse things than mere high-spirited fun.

David Helwig, *"Starting Over,"* in Books in Canada, *Vol. 16, No. 1, January-February, 1987, p. 15.*

SUSAN J. SCHENK

[In *Celestial Navigation*], Paulette Jiles finds in storytelling a distinctively female, profoundly personal response to experience. In **"Horror Stories,"** Jiles' narrative voice states that "All women believe they are Scheherazade. They believe / they too will or are about to die / in burning buildings." In order to forestall fatal events, to displace them, women tell horror stories. Jiles' persona admits, "I have a collection of tales myself. There / are a couple I do not tell." The tales that are told, while perhaps less personal, more distanced, nonetheless reveal the fears that women share, including the fear of being left alone in silence. . . . The voice talking, beginning again, retelling its tale, is for Jiles a means of both displacing personal experience, locating it in the experiences of others, and revealing intensely personal thoughts and emotions. Indeed, the female voice that speaks in much of Jiles' poetry shares this doubleness, inviting us, on the one hand, to identify the "I" with Paulette Jiles herself as it relates apparently autobiographical experiences, while at the same time maintaining a tone of narrative distance.

This combination of personal focus and the narrative distance of storytelling is found in **"The Brass Atlas,"** where Jiles' persona relates her physical and psychological journey of self-discovery. In contrast to Jiles' later experiments with multiple voices in her narrative poetry, the story here is told predominantly by a single voice. This single voice, however, exhibits the doubleness discussed above; the persona, indeed, recognizes her own distance from herself: "I write this / with a peculiar hand that seems to belong neither to me nor anyone." This tension between personal focus and distance is also evident as Jiles' traveller herself becomes a continent, a map, the site of her own journey: "I am / a tracery of ribs, a map of veins, / the red coagulation of a heart." The persona is "bent on getting to unknown terrain," on "clarifying / the

limits of [her] territory"; to do so she must simultaneously explore her own experience from within and from without.

Among the newer poems in Paulette Jiles' *Celestial Navigation* which explore the tension between personal experience and narrative distance are those in the section entitled **"Turning Forty."** The section is comprised of four prose poems, all employing the first-person narrative voice, and three using Jiles' Missouri background as a source of personal legend. In **"The Mad Kitchen and Dong, the Cave-Adolescent,"** the narrative voice is not only self-conscious, but it is also double, both the voice of the girl in the story and of the woman remembering:

> I sit at the table (it is dinnertime) and read about cave-people and how they started making copper things. Dinner is partially large pieces of Velveeta cheese and I say "copper" to myself because it sounds weird with cheese in my mouth. Forever after I associate copper and cheese.

This movement from the young girl reading to the woman distanced by "forever after" signals the shifting narrative relationship between the "I" in its dual role as character and narrator. At once a part of, and apart from the events in the mad kitchen, the voice continues: "For once I see myself in repose. Around me people are yelling in defensive and accusative tones; in declarative sentences, imperatives, shrieks." Later, the voice asserts the fragmentation of her experience. . . . [In] the poem, it becomes difficult to separate the voice of the young girl from that of the adult narrator; they are inextricably interwoven parts of one complex voice. The persona's experiences with the "mad kitchen and its random occurrences" also become increasingly interwoven with the events in the book she is reading about Dong, the cave adolescent, adding another layer of narrative complexity:

> Dong has now discovered metallurgy and cries aiee! as he drops molten copper on his foot. The police arrive. Did your son shoot somebody in the leg? You bet. The police!! Everyone hides. The authorities! Dong has, then, discovered both metallurgy and cheese-product. Lightning strikes the tribal camp and blows the fur diapers all to flinders and thus they discover fused things.

The narrative itself is, in a sense, a "fused thing" composed of the "flinders" of the young child's experience, which are ordered, albeit rather randomly, by the controlling adult consciousness. This consciousness is also that of the storyteller who attempts to order experience, to understand and control it, like the women who tell "horror stories" to conquer their own fears by naming them.

In **"Going to Church,"** Jiles employs both personal history and the doubled narrative voice as she explores the experience of growing up female in the American South. As she sets the location for her story, the controlling voice moves from physical to personal geography, inviting the reader to accompany her on this journey through memory:

> This is Sunday morning, July 16, 1958, Cole Camp, Butler County, Missouri, population 100 and just look at all these people getting ready for church. We are only 150 miles from the Arkansas border down here, which seems to loom dangerously close. Whatever bad happens, happens to the south of us. There are too many layers of irrelevant dresses but it seems I and every other teenage girl down here

have been hired to play extras in *Gone With the Wind*.

Although the movement from Butler County to "layers of irrelevant dresses" might seem abrupt, the narrative voice repeatedly makes the connection between geography and the politics of fashion: "I look at my ironed and lacy dress laid out on the bed and I really want to be neolithic and hulk around the village in primitive weaves with beads made out of rocks and zircons. No dice, not in this town." The movement of the narrative itself fluctuates between the experiences of the teenage girl and the developing consciousness of the adult narrator who has returned in memory to the scene of these experiences. Although the two voices are sometimes indistinguishable, it is nonetheless clear that the adult persona has actually escaped the geographical and psychological limitations of "July 16, 1958, Cole Camp, Butler County, Missouri," while the teenage girl is suspended there in time, wondering, "Is there no other way to be? Out of this green and steaming town I suspect there are other modes of existence." Though this younger voice suspects, only the older narrative voice, in the very act of telling her personal legend, proves that she has located these "other modes of existence."

Like **"The Brass Atlas,"** then, **"Going to Church"** is another type of personal journey. Because it is more removed in time, more story than confession, it lacks the intensity and sense of struggle of the earlier poem; instead, there is a tone of irony which mounts to defiance as the tale reaches its conclusion. From the beginning, the young girl notices the unfairness of her restrictive clothing in comparison to that of her brother Elroy and the other men who "dress in simple, decent clothes" and whose "pants are held up by brown and honest belts which require no more than the brains of a two-year-old to fasten." Throughout she wonders, "Does God really want us to wear this crap?" and "Why do I take this so seriously? All this hot Sunday I take seriously the dreadful, precarious system of female clothes and shoes." At the end of the poem, she is defiant in her rejection of the passive female role:

> What will it avail a woman if she gain her own
> mind but lose her soul? All right, I will lose my
> soul. Not once but a hundred times. As many times
> as it takes. Turn now to page 145 and sing you are
> washed in the blood. No.

In this progression from ironic awareness to rejection, the voice of the teenage girl merges with the voice of the woman remembering, just as memory and story merge to create personal legend. (pp. 67-70)

More recently, Paulette Jiles returns to her Missouri heritage in a poem cycle entitled **"Desperados: Missouri 1861-1882 (or The James Gang and their Relations)."** As the title indicates, these poems are both historical and personal in nature; not only do they focus on the legendary figures of "The James Gang," but they also imaginatively explore the lives of "their Relations"—Zerelda, mother of Frank and Jesse, and Zee and Annie, their wives. In a sense, Jiles' retelling of the traditional tales surrounding the notorious James Gang is a feminist revision of history in its conscious creation of highly personal stories, not only about the men, but also about the women who are usually omitted from this Missouri mythology

This feminist, revisionist approach to legend is seen most clearly in **"Zerelda"** and **"Bandit's Wives."** In both poems, the controlling narrative voice, the voice of the storyteller, is acutely conscious of the way in which women are either transformed by or omitted from history and legend. . . . The restrictive social and legal forces that stifled Zerelda during her life, in the process of transforming her into legend have made her a monster—one of the few available roles for women in folklore.

The same restrictive forces cause Zee, as a bandit's wife, to be omitted from the legends that surround her husband's life. . . . Because Zee does not want to be either a whore or a monster, she is of no interest to the male historians who create legends:

> Zee never wanted to end up like Belle Starr or Cattle Kate or Poker Alice, those violent whores are attractive to male historians who can afford illusions but they are usually diseased or dead after a while, the whores I mean, and besides its no fun having people spit on your skirt.

Because Zee cannot "afford illusions," because she would have to live them, and illusions are difficult to sustain on a day-to-day basis, the narrative voice tells us that "her life and that of Frank's wife Annie is the kind of life you have to imagine or invent." Jiles' storyteller in this series of poems does precisely this; she imagines and relates the untold stories that form the personal, and female counterpart to the existing, predominantly male, historical legends about the James gang.

In **"Zerelda,"** then, we are told of the restrictions that stifle and enrage her, of her life as mother to Frank and Jesse, and of the hardships and pain she suffers. The voice that relates Zerelda's experiences is the voice of the oral storyteller, who occasionally interrupts her breathless tale with questions, and invites the reader to become involved in her story. . . .

The storytelling voice, conscious of the restrictions placed on women in the nineteenth century, goes on to say of Zerelda:

> She can neither vote nor sit on a jury
> nor go around without the ironclad corsets
> nor speak aloud of anything she knows to be true;
> she is alive and yet without
> a legal existence.

Zerelda, however, despite her restrictions, is spirited; we are told that "the law does not allow her husband to beat her / with a cane any thicker than his thumb. / She will get another husband / who is smaller; whose thumbs / are not so big." (pp. 71-2)

Despite the general tone of seriousness, these tales are not without their moments of humour. In **"Zerelda"** we are told of the reaction of Frank and Jesse to their mother's increasing outlandishness: "As the years go by Zerelda gets more dramatic / *Oh Mother* say the huge famous bandits." In **"Bandit's Wives"** we are presented with the picture of Zee as nineteenth-century housewife:

> she has to balance everything carefully, how to
> make Jesse the center of her life but yet not become
> too dependent, after all her husband's work takes
> him away from home all the time, she has to make
> some decisions by herself
>
> but then on the other hand she can't get too independent, Jesse likes to be the head of the household, you know how it is, the money she spends is not her own, it's not Jesse's either but let that go for now

The humour here is also touched with the irony that Zee's

tenuous position between dependence and independence is still a common, and problematic position for women in the twentieth century.

The oral tone of this passage in **"Bandit's Wives,"** with its run-on sentences and its casual, "you know how it is," is sustained in the stories within the poem that constitute the personal folklore of Zee and Annie. These tales are linked by variations on the phrase "such as the time" and function as personal, domestic counterpoints to the historical legends about Jesse and Frank. . . . Jiles, then, or perhaps more accurately her narrative persona, is working with storytelling and legend on two levels in this poem; she is imaginatively constructing both the personal equivalents to the historical legends surrounding the James Gang, and the family stories that are a sub-layer of these personal histories.

In **"Folk Tale,"** the narrative persona herself becomes involved in the tale; indeed, she is involved on two levels, for she is both storyteller and listener. Her voice is that of the young child listening as she says, "(They didn't have any restaurants in those days my mother explains)." As she relates the story of "Frank and Jesse and Bob and Cole" and their conflict with a woman over a chicken, she is once again the standard storyteller who begins her tale with "One day" and ends it with a moral: "The farmer's wife was trying to teach them that you have to eat what you kill." Throughout the poem, the narrative voice sustains the oral tone of a folk tale through the use of a vernacular dialect, the repetition of conjunctions, and narrative mixed with dialogue. . . . (pp. 73-4)

In **"The Last Poem in the Series,"** Jiles outlines a kind of ethics of storytelling, focusing on the sensitivity required of those who reconstruct people out of the past. The voice of the storyteller asserts that "the scholar who studies the life of Jesse and Frank needs solitude. This person approaches a cabin through fields and some woods, slowly, seriously, as if they were going to take vows." Using the bank robber as a metaphor for the storyteller, the narrative persona goes on to say, "Before you can step in the door, surrender and disarm. It is a kind of bank and can only be robbed by the antibandit." The storyteller must surrender any preconceptions about Frank and Jesse James, must enter the bank of history with empty hands, must give the stories back to the people in them, allowing them to speak their own lives. Jiles, in **"Desperados,"** gives these men and women their own voices, relates and allows them to relate their untold personal stories; in doing so she gives them back a dignity and humanity that history, with its reductive approach, had taken away.

More recently, Paulette Jiles' use of storytelling technique can be seen in her experimentation with performance poetry. Her most sustained effort in this medium, entitled **"Oracles,"** [which was performed in the Canadian Broadcasting Corporation radio network on October 27, 1985,] brings together many of the aspects of storytelling that she has been utilizing from the beginning in her written work. Jiles' interest in the unique relationship of women to storytelling, her concern with personal legend, and her attempt to create an oral quality in her work through the use of repetition, rhythm, and sentence variety, are united in this extended performance poem.

The relationship of women to storytelling is evident in the very premise of Jiles' "oracles," who are women in caves, women who speak prophetically. Like the women in **"Horror Stories"** who "believe they are Scheherazade," who believe in the diverting, life-saving power of stories for women, the oracles, who deem themselves "a sister act," introduce stories that are of particular interest to women.

The four stories connected by their prophetic, and often zany commentary, all have women as their central characters/voices. "One Sister" and "Susan Dangerfield" are both third-person narratives which share the first-person, autobiographical tone of the Missouri stories in the "Turning Forty" section of *Celestial Navigation.* "I used to live in the city" and "Following the muse" are first-person narratives which tell the same story of a woman living alone in the city from two slightly different perspectives. As the poem progresses, fragments from these stories become blended in the narrative babble/babel of the oracles, and the poem as a whole becomes one extended, self-reflexive story about women and storytelling.

Also linked to the earlier poem, **"Horror Stories,"** is the sense of circularity and continuation associated with the narrator's plea of "let me begin again." In **"Oracles,"** this cyclical pattern is achieved through the use of a frame narrative surrounding both the prophecies of the oracles and the four stories they introduce. The voice in this split section entitled "leading to . . ." begins her story, "There is road leading to the horizon; / and at the edge of the horizon is a house" and re-echoes this line at the poem's closing:

> There was a long escalator leading to
> the airport bus, which took the
> highway leading out of the city,
>
> which led to a road, and this
> road was leading to.

This rejection of closure suggests the ongoing nature of the oral tradition, the continued possibility of beginning one's story again. The repetition associated with continually beginning again is, of course, also a major component of oral storytelling technique. In performance poetry, without the visual aid of a text, this technical component becomes critical. Jiles' use of repetition, rhythm and sentence variety in her earlier narrative poems was central to her achievement of an oral tone in written work; in **"Oracles"** these same techniques function as replacements for the visual experience of connection available with the written word.

This oral connection is evident throughout the "leading to . . ." section with its repetition of such physical images as "path," "horizon," "house," "stream," and "cave." These images also mark the beginning of a progression from the visual to the aural:

> The path is leading to a cave entrance,
> and the cave entrance is leading
> downward into the heart of the
> mountain, into the earth, and the
> bones buried in the earth, and the songs
> buried in the bones;
>   songs of love
>   songs of desire
>   songs of mistaken identities.

Both the repetition and rhythm of this passage function to lead the listener on a visual and aural journey from cave to earth to bone; and finally to the songs/stories of "love," "desire," and "mistaken identities" sung/told in the poem by the oracles. (pp. 74-6)

This repetition and variation, then, is central to establishing both cadence and unity. In **"One Sister,"** the resulting phrasing is sometimes intensely repetitive:

> It is a matter of liquids
> it is a matter of being held up
> it is a matter of not falling
> it is a matter of keeping on with the swimming motions.

At other times, as in the last section of this story/poem, a more relaxed, sustained rhythm is achieved through a series of variations on the phrase "One sister died in the bombardments / and the other sister refugeed with her children to the countryside," which is transformed first into "Three sisters died in the bombardments / and the last sister made it to the countryside with / two mattresses, three blankets, four children and a frying pan," and then into "A hundred sisters died under the bombardments and a few made it / to the countryside and married tall dark men and they all / went underground." The story/poem ends with an almost infinite expansion of this phrase:

> A thousand, thousand, thousand, thousand sisters died
> in the fire and the falling buildings
> along with their fathers and their brothers
> and their sisters and their mothers
> and their children and their cousins
> and their neighbors
>
> and the unborn
>
> and the unborn
>
> and the unborn

The conscious variation of sentence types is another oral technique used to create texture in the poem. In **"One Sister,"** for example, Jiles combines interrogative, imperative and declarative sentences in one brief section. . . . (pp. 76-7)

Jiles also achieves a sense of the visual through her use of photography as a metaphor throughout the poem. Indeed, the photograph becomes a metaphor for the poem itself as we are first introduced to the oracles. . . . Through this metaphor, we are visually led from the margin of the photograph, the outer narrative frame, to the edge, where we "see" the oracles, and from there to the centre, where we meet the "she" of **"One Sister."**

The photography metaphor, in addition to introducing this visual aspect into an oral poem, also foreshadows the central theme of the "Susan Dangerfield" section. In this story, we are told that, "Susan Dangerfield, newsphotographer, is getting out of a taxi-cab with her camera-bag . . . A photographer is in love with images, and she's no exception." The narrative voice, in the repetitive, rhythmic phrasing heard earlier in "One Sister," explores the connection between women and seeing, a connection which is also implicit in the concept of the oracles as women who "see" and prophesy. . . . This voice also repeats, within and at the end of this story, in a kind of choric refrain, Susan's invitation to the listener to enter this visual world. . . . The listener who follows Susan through the image, like the listener who follows the series of voices through the poem, is returned first to the edge of the picture, where the oracles can be "seen," and finally to the margin, the outer frame narrative, and the road "leading to."

This ceaseless circularity, this need to continually "begin again," is more than mere technique in Jiles' poetry; it is associated, as in **"Horror Stories,"** with the fears and desires of women, as well as with the techniques of oral storytelling.

The female response to experience, for Jiles, is to transform that experience into story, and in doing so to reject silence and passivity. Thus she takes Scheherazade as her literary predecessor, and as the metaphoric mentor of all women who tell stories (sometimes about themselves) in order to survive. Her poems in the **"Turning Forty"** section of *Celestial Navigation* most clearly reveal Jiles in her Scheherazade-like role; her experience of growing up in Missouri is turned into stories, and thus put into the past, distanced as history, in order that she can go on living in the present. In the James poems, Jiles does the reverse—she brings history into the present in order to make it personal; her feminist revision of the legends associated with the James gang reclaims a place for, and restores the voice of, the women who were silenced by their omission from these stories. Finally, in **"Oracles,"** storytelling technique and story, the telling and the tale, are fused; here Jiles reclaims the oral, storytelling form and provides a poetic space for women telling stories of survival: a forum for the female voice, beginning again, repeatedly refusing, like Scheherazade, to lapse into silence. (pp. 77-9)

Susan J. Schenk, " 'Let Me Begin Again': Women and Storytelling in the Poetry of Paulette Jiles," in Canadian Poetry: Studies, Documents, Reviews, *No. 20, Spring-Summer, 1987, pp. 67-79.*

JUDITH CARSON

Post-nuclear Toronto, as portrayed in Paulette Jiles' first novel [*The Late Great Human Road Show*], has a *Twilight Zone* quality to it. Throughout the work, the cause of the recent wave of radiation and the disappearance of most of the population of Toronto is a mystery; the reason for the disappearance of the population of North America is never resolved. (p. 48)

The dialogue and description are vivid and evoke colourful pictures of a bizarre array of human flotsam and jetsam. Jiles creates tangible tension between her characters in several scenes. However, in spite of the use of children and animals and handicapped people, she fails to gain any sympathy for her characters; they remain two-dimensional caricatures. They are a hopeless lot, incapable of coping in society, and it seems very unlikely that they have any hope of surviving without it. This is a story about hopelessness and about dreamers.

Everything about the work is fragmented and the energy found in Jiles' poetry seems forced here. The snapshots that are effective in her poetic work don't work here. The scenes can't stand alone and they don't hold together significantly. The most effective character in the book is a pregnant cow, but Jiles doesn't make use of it, except as a prop.

The title of the book is misleading, to say the least. There is nothing great about her soon-to-be-dead humans and they never seem to set off on the road to anywhere. (pp. 48-9)

Judith Carson, in a review of "The Late Great Human Road Show," in The Canadian Forum, *Vol. LXVII, No. 771, August-September, 1987, pp. 48-9.*

PAUL JACOB

The grim irony of a nuclear age in which life everywhere has become equally conditional seems to favour post-apocalyptic fantasy displacing the coming-of-age novel as the dominant fictional genre for the late twentieth century. Paulette Jiles's contribution to the growing catalogue of speculative nightmare is more prophetic than most, having been written some ten years ago, well before the current spate of such fiction. Although similarly derived from a particular *genius loci, The Late Great Human Road Show* is contrary to [W. D. Barcus's *Squatter's Island*] in tone and scope as well as in kind—an urbane conspectus of folly in our time as witnessed by a range of inner voices refracted through a deadpan third-person overview. Like most worthwhile fantasy, Jiles's jeremiad is concerned less with the possible future that it projects than with the impossible present that it mocks, laments, and celebrates.

In such works, premise generally precedes plot and character is often dictated by concept. A mélange of some seventeen Torontonians has slept through a general evacuation of the city following an indefinite, presumably nuclear, catastrophe. Overnight one of the world's safest, most comfortable places is deserted and shorn of all civil amenities, its sky ominously streaked with greasy smoke, its unearthly silence punctuated by the alarming noise of windows as they pop out of downtown office towers and smash to powder in the street. Toronto's Cabbagetown makes an apt latter-day boneyard in which to reflect on the demons of gross selfishness, frenzied consumerism, and paranoid aggressiveness that in Jiles's view of history are driving us toward self-extinction. Her detailed rendering of the desolate neighbourhood provides an additionally eerie shock of recognition for readers familiar with the territory, a ready-made microcosm of urban North America in socioeconomic flux, its long-resident underclass either abandoned or shunted into warrenlike housing projects by the juggernaut of gentrification.

Jiles's gamut of characters is calculated to sound the basic intervals of the social scale. Most of them remain cartoonlike abstractions representing typical problems endemic to their respective situations, problems that emerge with dramatic definition as small groups of socially compatible survivors band together for mutual protection and consolation. Like Barcus, Jiles is most sympathetic toward, and most convincing in, her handling of the marginal and powerless, such as the aging street busker and the squad of singing orphaned street kids who adopt her as den-grandmother and artistic director. Conversely, characters who seem to have had their destinies well in hand before the disaster—right-wing survivalists who garrison a stronghold in the Riverdale zoo and the yuppie high-rise dwellers whom they seek out with predictable results—are observed with a mixture of amused detachment and manifest disgust.

Within and among these various groups (and a few individuals who fall between the cracks) the noble and sordid history of the race is re-enacted, even as the shadow of a common death, heralded by the proliferation of mysterious, unhealing bruises, promises to overtake the lot. For some readers, the cynicism of this sardonic farce will be counteracted by recurring evidence of an undefeated will to survive, to connect, to preserve our collective wits, however perverse or doomed the attempt. A pregnant cow who ambles through the novel attracting different characters toward their mutually conflicting ends, is a whimsical symbol of this tenacious life force. But unless we regard the story of universal destruction as a kind of existential allegory—after all humankind has always lived under the threat of imminent death—the novel's teasing

leaven of hope simply blackens the jest with a more brutal irony. Either way, Jiles's satire is usually too broad to be very instructive; but her imaginative empathy with her underdogs—especially the children—and her memorable evocation of an urban paradise after the nuclear fall animate what might otherwise have remained an amusing but inert anatomy of 1980's angst x-rayed in the flash of a generic apocalypse. (pp. 210-11)

Paul Jacob, "Island & Road," in Canadian Literature, *No. 116, Spring, 1988, pp. 209-11.*

DENNIS COOLEY

Paulette Jiles's writing impresses immediately with the freshness of a peeled banana. Even in these days of acquired suspicion toward the referent, it strikes with the power of recognition. How fitting, how apt, how like it is. In image and metaphor we are grateful for the world brought new to us, or anew. [In *Celestial Navigation* we] find shadows that extend like tape measures, a world where a train comes "ripping up the dawn like an old ticket," children sit "fixed in amber like / ancient hornets," ravens make sounds like bending metal, and someone "moves on the edges like a roll of dimes." In these snags on the imagination, years fold up, "they collapse like promises, like balloons."

Several of the best poems latch onto a strong central metaphor, often in honour of the romantic tradition with its convention of the possessed or stricken poet who taps special powers. **"Heat Lightning"** begins with a brief description of a commercial sign that pulses into a room like heat lightning, goes on then to extend our attention to the rest of the street: "And the streetcars creep by catlike on unbending rails / cracking electrical walnuts, blue-white and dangerous." The world crackles with power, cracks open, strange ghostly brains hover over it. And then the final two lines which, simple in diction, are heavily invested in principles of uncanny power and transgression: "a headful of voltage / a long trip to the end of town." All the references gesture toward the electrical, and to codes of crossed limits, as they figure, too, in the feminist poem **"Paper Matches,"** where women wait on table, "heads on fire." A strong poem, **"Ravens,"** works an inversion on this economy, one that would open a dark and subterranean force in service to the imagination. So does **"Dream III,"** where some unspecified presence "will walk out of the / nightmare with a tearing sound." Probably the most overt articulation of romantic poet as dangerous hero comes in a clever poem, **"Poetry Review."** Even as it celebrates its extravagant claims, this poem laughs at them. (pp. 127-28)

Several other poems work whimsically—whimsy is the word with Jiles—to elaborate a central metaphor or idea. This is especially true of a very witty set of generation poems, including **"Family Novel."** In it parents turn into perfect children who hoard their allowances and chocolate bars, and who dawdle home from school desultorily kicking leaves. Then there is **"Situation Comedy"** with its ingenious reversal in which humans—the children who "got to where we were television programs," and the parents who "watched us, relentlessly"—slide into becoming their own spectacle, as the world takes them over. Jiles develops this crazy notion with verve, bringing the parents' regression to a point of primal screams in the night. So, too, in **"Mass"** (an overt instance of many such religious references in Jile's work) she informs us that bells "have been hung alive / by their voices in the belfry," dexterously assigning powers of begetting to what ordinarily we think of as the consequence of some action, results turned cause.

One of the things that catches my joy is the casualness of the voice in this poem, a voice that is always nervy, nervous—about to spring something on us, catch us with a grin. Just where this voice breaks into the poems we get something more, and perhaps something other, than the poet as startling promoter of sharply focused imagination. The story I am telling will rapidly become familiar: poet finds or seeks no authority by which to measure things, poet enters into an anti-authoritarian rhetoric. Call it postmodern. It takes in Jiles its most characteristic features in mad humour and irreverence. Certainly it emerges in that breezy voice (one which D. G. Jones once oddly identified as an act of self-defence). No matter, there are many examples of it in Jiles. "But what if you drown, what if the / killer whales eat you, maybe you never / thought of that" Jiles writes, or somebody says, in ["**Celestial Navigation**"]. Elsewhere someone interrupts in sudden shift of register what has been another and a more sober rhetoric to ask, flirting with petulance, "where do we come in?" Who knows, don't come here, of course you could never do it—voices say, time and again. Expressive, pragmatic—they suddenly interfere with poems that are satisfied in making their way along in description and meditation. The noise pops up, emphatically declares the presence of someone who, though anonymous, makes it clear she is less committed to inwardness than perhaps we would expect her to be, certainly less consistent and 'serious' than any speaker we ordinarily would look for in modernist writing, however adversarial it might be.

The style upsets solemnity and bypasses the very sort of poet who presides over courts of metaphor. The speakers' subversions, in Jiles, often break out in mocking throwaway idiom, offhand expressions that deflate any gathering toward greatness. The tin woodsman from *The Wizard of Oz,* who contemplates killing himself and others with a shotgun, ends with a taunt to Dorothy: "Tough luck for you, you pink thing, / all full of corpuscles and organs. / The shotgun hollers in a big balloon of sound." These words—all full of, hollers, you you, tough luck—these inflections of casual speech belong to a speaker who will not long settle in high seriousness, who will in fact incorporate the lowly comic book. Jiles will not stick with the high because, it seems, she finds it neither credible nor interesting. And so they are cheeky, these talkers: "You'll have to line up for tickets and they'll cost you," "Do I ever." "So this is life, we say, this is / not bad, give us more of this thunder, / the floods, the buoyant paddlewheelers. / Give us not only this day / but the next." Everywhere there are raids on solemnities, poems that thumb their noses at Truth. They wash away Matthew Arnold's dream, schoolmaster's chalk on the cliffs of Dover.

They are parodic too, as here they play with the Lord's Prayer, undermining ready-made structures of knowing. Jiles lines up almost every piece of rhetoric she can lay her hands on, tosses it out on the counter like a kid emptying her pockets from the beach: have a look at this one. Who'd buy this stuff? Yet Jiles's world is dangerous, precisely because it continues to enlist our loyalties and to inscribe our perceptions. Comic book conventions; the language of direction and command; the cliches of love (especially as they drive true confessions) and departure; the grand heroic and the tragic; titles;

pop psychology and anthropology; American myths of history; the letter, the soaps, gossip; the gothic. They all take their lumps. So do the structures of logic. **"Inside from the Outside"** entirely foregoes the attractions of lyric and tilts us through a dizzying series of deictics, markers which normally would locate us in time and place, but which here have come unhooked and spin us therefore into disorientation. The same poem adopts a rhetoric that makes what would seem to be big claims, but it does so smirkingly, in banal terms: "Only a former shoe salesman knows what it is / to be free of shoes." The strategy, vaguely Kroetschean in its run of bizarre and barely related claims, is to prefer the structures of gnomic definition. Once Jiles has swirled us through a batch of these deliberately disjointed assertions, we must face the effect of quirky authority they engender. We seem to be presented with a fistful of truths, hard as turtle shells in their intact brevity, but then they are all undermined by the speed of their abandonment. Huh? What was that again? And before we can recover, snap, there's another. Banal as the first, but gosh it sounds good. Where'd it come from? The overall effect, I think, is to parody the language of definition and explanation (though Jiles herself, like so many other writers in this country, particularly female writers, practices its forms herself). (pp. 128-30)

[In] her off-tossing idioms, her casual burlesques of meaning, Jiles makes the most of slouchy imprecision. A macho sailor, who, in one of those exquisite reversals Jiles so rejoices in, appears in a job he has taken on a Players' cigarette package, tells us about what wives do: "They carried and did things around the / house." Did things? We can at once see the precision of the phrase, once it is read in an expressive circuit, where a willful not knowing comes home full force. Other vagueness directs us to the impossibility of naming the unknowable. And so some unidentified figure whose world looms menacingly, threatens in muffled words to call forces to her side, "whoever it is that / sees to these things." Again, it would be hard to imagine any expression that could more exactly work to convey the speaker's sense of helplessness in being able even to specify any source for her fear. The same for the stumbling mention of "something" on two other occasions when someone speaks not in parody but mystery. There is something, if I knew more exactly what I would tell you, but this, this is something: "We flew into darkness at the rim of the world, / where distant lights broke through and something / failed us." That's what it is: something. And it was "Something [that] arrived in the air / like a revelation, and then disintegrated." Out in the dark world things cannot easily be discerned, and so in it are "mountains and hashish, big things with fur," the words falling, much as do Margaret Atwood's, somewhere between exactitude and generality, and projecting us therefore into a realm that is felt vividly as sweat on the arm and unshakeable as echoes in the head are belled with symbols. The instability of pronouns on a few occasions, as in the unanchored "they" in **"Heatwave / St. Louis,"** where we cannot tell who these people called "they" are, further establishes the uncertainty of knowledge. . . . (pp. 131-32)

Easily one of the most delightful pieces in *Celestial Navigation* is one called **"Body."** In it Jiles mimics with lemon fresh ness a voice of childish petulance, including its stinging taunts (variants on the ready-made), the speaker's hope for some kind of pain waiting in the conditional verbs she reserves for her tormentor:

If only you could be punished
and left on a highway somewhere;
you would be so ashamed of yourself
with nowhere to go.
No one would speak to you,
no one would take you in.

And again there is that tag-along phrase, clinging like an appendix—"somewhere"—in imitation of speech where it comes as seeming afterthought, oh yeah, informationally unnecessary but tellingly expressive. A related point: as a consequence of wobbling through a syntax of self-correction and amendment—"his voice like / the white light of hydrogen, only long"—the language moves into rhythms of unfolding. It seems almost naive, childlike, as if the narrative or the sentence were coming into being as we follow it, mind finding its paths. In those trajectories it simulates a world in which things are not easily found or named. And in which, far from being grim or vacant, Jiles's world in chuckles hops.

Much of the mad undermining can be identified in Jiles's mix of the solemn and the casual. In her poems shipwreck sits alongside election ads, "satellites ring like cowbells," passengers fly "footloose in . . . the aurora," minds associate with toasters, passengers shuttle into corners "like cockroaches or lost change" and eggs bulge "full of troubles and protein." The mundane and the important clutch together in a crazy square dance of objects and extractions:

At the door to the great river we
watch our lives rush downstream in
the April floods, chicken coops, old
arguments, accusations, outhouses, the
gates of vanished fences.

You can see how the poems speed with incongruities and run from one domain to another, breathless as a kid opening presents. Take a look at **"Ravens."** It shows how Jiles rejoices in a capacity to amplify, to let go of brevity and reticence. As a result of that opening Jiles is able to generate a comedy of rapid incongruity. It too undermines forms of final authority that might oversee her world, as in the delightfully satiric **"A Letter to My Grandad on The Occasion of a Letter from Cousin Wanda Lee Saying Grandad Is Too Infirm to Feed the Cows and Is Not Long for This World."** Right from the start, with a wonderful sense of the ridiculous in the parodic title, the poem moves to parody cliché, conventions of the funeral and of mourning, and the gossipy rambling report. Herded up within a shaggy-dog parody of structure, a series of sardonic observations jab quickly at us in what we might think of as a humour of the radically elided. The sheer speed of the narration as it lurches from one irreverent idiom to another, jerky bodies in old movies, guarantees that what in our culture we expect to be sombre (a relative's death) will fall from its elevation into something approaching the macabre. . . . The combination of suppressed story and flippant gloss marks the poem as Jiles's. And those smartass idioms tip the poem into a peculiar projection, one where the poet-speaker no longer acts as sensitive soul or as visionary, refractory sage.

However, the rapid fire of language and its shifts from one discourse or level of discourse to another does not always produce comedy. In **"Blacksnake"** we trace a tumble of unexpected metaphors with quite different effect. The snake is compared to a whole range of startling phenomena, at least ten (one of the most powerful being snake as a "high-power line [that] dips in the pool"). All this within fourteen lines!

Here we don't laugh, but marvel at the bravado. This poem seeks not so much a singular gathering and focussing nor even a deliberate and sustained elaboration such as a modernist rhetoric might require, as a shooting off in all directions in virtuoso display of variety and plenitude. Look ma, no hands! We can discern here, too, a ludic impulse that de-centres and subverts forms of authority and control, at least ones that would override those very forays.

And yet, as I said a little earlier, we notice in Jiles a propensity for definition, a project that directs us elsewhere. In a sense we could argue that the very play which bounces through **"Blacksnake"** toys with the idea. So many of these poems build in additive ways upon runs of definitions. The poems often proceed, like Atwood's, by asserting something or other to be the case, and pivot therefore on copulas and generic verbs, i.e., those verbals which indicate characteristic and repeated gestures. Here in illustration is the opening of **"Far and Scattered Are the Tribes that Industrialization Has Left Behind"**:

Things never go out the way they came in yester-
    day.
        Years fold up;
they collapse like promises, like balloons, infinitely
repeatable.
Our bodies change under us, they do not want to
    lift up and go away
anymore, but sit on the ground. Our bodies are part
of
    something else.
Their allegiance is elsewhere. The air they once
    contained is a gaseous
concoction, we are full of it.

Look at the verbs: things never go, years fold up, they collapse, bodies change, they do not want, they sit, they are, allegiance is, air is, we are. And so on. The 'actions' do not represent transformations but states, they are habitual and therefore defining. That is what they do, these things, that is what they are. The book is full of similar constructions. Take one other example: "Depressed people are predictable, it's / always money or love, likely both. / People have always been terrible to depressives, / the truly mad take it all on themselves." These structures tend to become discursive and to migrate toward simple statement in their desire to establish, even whimsically, that this is the case, these are the situations.

It's not surprising that many writers in Canada, and above all women, should find this mode so congenial. When you are in colonized positions your rhetoric might well cycle on themes of identity, reality, knowing, identifying ([as in] *The Jesse James Poems* Jiles fastens on to the magical power of names). But still there is in these features a consistency with others we've noted. At every turn Jiles writes as one who finds her way and who dodges fixed forms of knowing and saying. It is important, therefore, who does the writing and whose stories get told. As we read in **"Horror Stories,"** "All women believe they are Scheherazade," saved if at all by their capacity to tell stories. Or as we read in **"Paper Matches,"** where like a *book* of matches a woman finds "Written on me . . . a message," she receives someone else's message, men's fictions in which she is to be enrolled as compliant character.

Little wonder then that Jiles should be so metalingual. Her frequent mentions of language and other texts do not serve, as some might suppose they serve, to keep up with the times. They are meant to register in yet another way the making and remaking of our lives that are so ridden by inherited structures, ensnared in the *déjà lu,* including certainly, **"The Family Novel,"** in which each plays or is asked to play a part. There is no point in itemizing all the mentions, they are easily found. But it might be useful to draw attention to a major instance. In one of a group of poems set in the north, Jiles very pointedly explores the consequences of losing stories, altering stories, the possibility even of knowing what it is you might want to say. And though one of the poems opens with resolve to get it right ("Nothing can jar me from this attentive position, this / pen hesitating over the paper is a cardiogram / needle, the page will be full of spikes and / indications," it ends in the speaker's mistaken reassurance that she will not betray her subjects. We see that language is destabilized, that promises will falter, the word cannot be kept.

Everywhere, then, we find a subverting of authority. It's there in the multiple voicing, the snappy shifts in register, their radical mix, the ridicule of sentiment and cliché, the wobbly trajectories, rambling structures, the outrageous speakers with their jibes and drolleries, sometimes at their own expense, their comic delineations. There is too their traffic in wit and surprise, as we witness in their lineations: "I am tired of this / heaven," "I don't think I will ever / see you again / in the same way," "Sometimes people come on in one / big unmuffled roar of engines." These are narrators who do not permit their characters the comforts of their stories, who will not allow themselves the assurance of belief. Always there are the jokes, the ironies, the parodies, spilling over into *The Jesse James Poems,* with its uncertain documents wedged in a nightmarish Ondaatjean world. All the instabilities in Jiles speak of rejoicing where there is no authority. Once high-mindedness collapses, and with it any possibility that meaning can be ensured and value fixed, we can go the way of Jiles. A child at play in the fields of poesey, quirky, smarty. Wicked. (pp. 133-37)

Dennis Cooley, " 'We Will Try to Act Like Human Beings': 'Celestial Navagation' as Anti-Authoritarian," in The Malahat Review, *No. 83, Summer, 1988, pp. 127-37.*

Joyce Johnson

1935-

(Born Joyce Glassman) American novelist, memoirist, editor, and short story writer.

Johnson's fiction often focuses on the external and intrinsic causes of the social repression of women during the late 1950s and the difficulties experienced by female protagonists attempting to abandon subservient roles. Through a blend of wit, pathos, and emotional insight, Johnson's novels illustrate American society's slow progress toward sexual equality. Although sometimes faulted for her limited thematic focus, Johnson is praised for controlled prose and deft character portraits. Anne Tyler asserted: "She has a way of characterizing people with a single stroke, allowing us to color in the rest—and therefore to invest ourselves more deeply."

While Johnson's first novel, *Come and Join the Dance* (1962), received little critical acknowledgment, her next work, *Bad Connections* (1978), amassed significant attention. The story revolves around Molly, a magazine editor in her thirties who defines her identity through her commitments with men. After summoning the courage to leave her boorish husband, Molly engages in two more destructive relationships before choosing an independent lifestyle. Reviewers applauded the narrative, which shifts between first and third person, noting that it further illuminates Molly's self-deprecating tendencies.

Johnson's reputation as a poignant commentator on youthful rebellion was established with the publication of *Minor Characters* (1983), a candid memoir of her involvement with the Beat movement of the 1950s and her romance with Jack Kerouac. Offering a rare female viewpoint of this disaffected culture, *Minor Characters* garnered extensive critical acclaim and won a National Book Critics Circle Award. Johnson's memoir begins with a discussion of her middle-class childhood in New York City's Upper West Side. A sheltered adolescent, Johnson became intrigued with the carefree lifestyles of Greenwich Village inhabitants and began frequenting popular bohemian haunts. On a blind date arranged by Allen Ginsberg, she met Jack Kerouac and began a turbulent two-year affair. Johnson examines the self-destructiveness of the male-oriented Beat society while also exploring the detrimental roles of the circle's women who, as its financial mainstays, voluntarily paid rent, lived on the periphery of the visionary clique, and became, as Robbin Schiff observed, "[minor] characters in their own as well as their man's life." Although Johnson confronts the suicides and untimely deaths that were consequences of this lifestyle, her tone is rarely bitter. Todd Gitlin commented: "*Minor Characters* glows with affection, as well as regret and pain for the waste of strong energies and high spirits in the Beat circles."

In the Night Café (1989) is similar to *Minor Characters* in its evocation of the Bohemian artistic and literary scene of New York City. Centering upon the theme of abandonment, this novel reflects on the doomed love affair of Joanna Gold, a former child actress, and Tom Murphy, an alcoholic painter. The crux of the work entails Joanna's attempts to rebuild her life after Tom's death and her relationships with his neglected

child and her own son, Nicky. "In the Children's Wing," a chapter which concerns Nicky's lengthy hospital stay, was originally published as an individual short fiction piece and won the O. Henry Award for Best Short Story of 1987. Critics were particularly impressed with Johnson's vivid characterizations of Nicky and Joanna. Phillip Lopate remarked: "[*In the Night Café*] sails on its first-person narration: a fiercely believable, testifying voice that is pungent, close to the bone, stinging with candor. . . . [The] poetry of this novel is in its quick psychological insights and the ability to make us shudder and feel along with it."

(See also *Contemporary Authors,* Vol. 125.)

BRUCE WOODS

Perhaps the newest, and certainly at this moment one of the most conspicuous, personas in contemporary literature might be called the "Jong-frau," the housewife loosed upon the fields of sexual freedom.

[In *Bad Connections*] Joyce Johnson's heroine, Molly, falls smack dab in the middle of this tradition. Leaving her unfaithful and insensitive husband, Fred, she stumbles, son

Matthew none too obviously in tow, into a romantic triangle. The term is, in this case, used very loosely.

Conrad, her "primary lover" (defined as being of the affair in ascendancy) is an overweight "radical" lawyer who is, himself, juggling Molly and another lover. He is the soul of unreliability, petty deceit, and indecision.

Malcolm, originally cultivated to promote Conrad's jealousy, later becomes a fixture in his own right. He is a dropout from marriage and academia, involved in teaching poetry to convicts, and usually impotent.

The narration shuffles between the first and third person. This is initially confusing, but does, perhaps, offer a greater perspective upon the happenings depicted.

It is possible that many people work their ways through relationships this sad, and perhaps there is even an emotional balm available in novels such as this that celebrate such sadness. ***Bad Connections,*** however, fails to produce a character that is any more appealing than a chronically complaining relative. There is little opportunity here for recognition, less for entertainment.

> Bruce Woods, in a review of "Bad Connections," in *West Coast Review of Books, Vol. 4, No. 4, July, 1978, p. 36.*

ELLEN WILLIS

Good or bad, serious or trivial, most novels inspired by feminism have focused on the sense of discovery that pervaded the movement's early years. These days women are more preoccupied with learning how to live with their discoveries in a world that has proved less receptive to them than anticipated. Caught in the middle of a historic transition, feminists must negotiate all sorts of painful and confusing gaps between their ideas and their feelings, their consciousness and their actions, their vision and the stubborn limits of their culture. The immediate literary result is likely to be novels whose values are feminist, but whose stance is more complicated and ambivalent than *eureka!*

Joyce Johnson's ***Bad Connections*** is clearly meant to be such a novel. Its heroine, Molly, is in the world's terms an independent woman. She is in her mid-thirties, works as a magazine editor, chooses to get divorced, lives and brings up her son alone. She is also a woman who defines herself and her life almost solely in relation to men. Worse, the relationships are terrible: in the course of the book, Molly leaves an appalling husband and is made miserable by two lovers. The novel centers on her obsessive passion for Conrad, who is brilliant, charming, terrific in bed, and a pig. He subjects Molly to continual petty humiliations, feeds her hopes for a commitment he will never make, lies about his involvement with another woman. Molly is no fool; she knows that putting up with this man is both self-destructive and, ah, politically incorrect. But she can't help it.

Molly's intelligence and self-deprecating irony make her both interesting and likable. Her tenacity in pursuit of what she wants has, even at its most misguided, a certain saving violence; she is not pathetic; she doesn't whine. As for Conrad, he is outrageous, but never such a villain that you don't understand his appeal. ***Bad Connections*** is often funny, sometimes cathartically angry, always skillful in rendering the small, excruciating moments that add up to the misery of love gone bad. Yet finally the book doesn't work, for besides being an exploration of post-feminist confusions, ***Bad Connections*** is an example of them. Both the author and her protagonist seem ambivalent on a level they never quite acknowledge; their overtly feminist assumptions—that women have a right to independent lives and equal relationships with men— coexist with a covert defense of traditional female values.

In a way, the feminist assumptions are a red herring. Molly's brand of grief is hardly peculiar to feminists, or to modern women: She is a loser in love; she can't get her man. Nor does she lose him by making onerous feminist demands. Molly demands nothing but the most traditional sort of commitment, in return for which she is prepared, if necessary, to sacrifice her job and her bias against trees and live with Conrad in the country; it is Roberta, the woman who gets him, who insists that he do his fair share of the housework.

If anything, it is Molly's devotion that puts Conrad off—a sexual dynamic no doubt as old as sex. Anyway, Conrad's particular weaknesses are beside the point. For reasons that remain mysterious, Molly consistently chooses men who don't come through for her. Where, the reader begins to wonder, is the kick-me sign? Is Molly perhaps more wary of commitment, more jealous of her independence, than she lets on? This is a plausible and politically satisfying explanation for which, however, there is no shred of evidence in the text.

What does become clear is that Molly's continual self-mocking references to her "unliberated" attitudes are disingenuous. Secretly, Molly believes that those attitudes are not only ingrained but superior. She equates being passionate with being antediluvian; in her mind to be a feminist is to be unfeeling. . . . For Molly, the issue is whether to pursue love on traditional terms, however oppressive, or to accept its absence with an indifference she imagines to be the approved feminist posture. It never occurs to her that there is a third possibility—to struggle for love on equal terms, a risky struggle but scarcely a cold one.

Ultimately, Molly sees her willingness to suffer on behalf of men as proof of her humanity—a traditional female value if there ever was one. That attitude has, as its complement, an equally traditional contempt for men: Molly is always going on about how men are little boys who don't know what they want, how she can't help feeling sorry for them and wanting to take care of them. It is with weapons like these—a moral investment in suffering, a self-deluded condescension of the powerless toward the powerful—that generations of women have fended off the scary recognition that they are not superior but oppressed.

If Joyce Johnson's view of reality diverges from Molly's, she gives no hint of it. And here is where the book gets trapped in its contradictions. Johnson obviously intends more than to add to the store of conventional novels that bewail woman's fate while assuming its immutability; her complaint promises to be more novel, and more ambitious, than "Men! Why can't they grow up? You can't live with them and you can't live without them!" By giving Molly an awareness of feminism— thus revealing her own—the author declares, in effect, that Molly's predicament has social and political weight, that it is to be taken seriously. But Johnson's failure to confront the self-deception at the heart of Molly's conservatism leads in the opposite direction: in the end Molly's fate does not disturb enough. The spectacle of a man who succumbs to an irrational one-sided love . . . evokes not ironic head-shaking but horror. Our culture assumes that for a man such a loss of self is tragic, while for a woman it is normal. To challenge this idea is by definition feminist. The alternative is resignation.

Bad Connections is, unhappily, a resigned book. Its underlying message is that feminist ideals are pie in the sky, that in the real world they just make life more difficult by providing new excuses for female self-hatred (we shouldn't crave men's love so much), handing men new weapons (if you're liberated, why are you so clingy?), and robbing women of their traditional strengths. There is a modicum of truth in this argument: a vision of freedom as yet unrealized does create new difficulties and, for that matter, sharpen old pains. But it also offers a good deal more sustenance than this book suggests.

> Ellen Willis, "The Trouble Is Not Just with Molly's Men," in The Village Voice, Vol. XXIII, No. 27, July 3, 1978, p. 86.

HELEN YGLESIAS

Bad Connections sets itself limitations; it is controlled, smooth, deftly written; it evokes scene and character with an admirably sure swiftness. But the bright, sexy, urbane young editor who takes a lover, sheds a husband, rears her child, takes another lover and sheds both, to end at a point of lonely liberation—this is no longer news. And it's dispiriting. "Don't tell me more," was my response; no matter how well told, it's too sad to bear.

Joyce Johnson's touches are all true: the husband complains in bed that the heroine's legs are too short; the radical lover is umbilically tied to a telephone cradled at his ear, his arrangements for political meetings punctuating and interrupting his lovemaking; he's solemn and selfish and a liar about his other woman lover. The heroine, Molly, has an enchanting little son—done perfectly, as is the older lover who inevitably commits himself to a nubile flower-child after announcing to Molly that he's a man who prefers not getting "involved." Molly is raped, on the West Coast, by a black man who performs so weakly he disgusts himself. "I can't do nothing," he says before he wipes himself on the sheet, zips up, and leaves her lying on the bed, slowly becoming aware that her belly is cold and that "her life will go on and on. On and on."

Too sad, too dreary, too sad for words—no matter how carefully Joyce Johnson has chosen them, one by one. (pp. 87-8)

> Helen Yglesias, "News from the Sisterhood," in Harper's, Vol. 257, No. 1539, August, 1978, pp. 86-8.

HERMIONE LEE

Bad Connections, though lively and poignant enough, is something of a disappointment. The plot is nothing new. Molly leaves egotistical unfaithful husband and goes off with cute precocious son only to become the victim of a prolonged, disastrous relationship with sexy, over-available radical lawyer who can't make up his mind to leave his other neurotic girl friend and commit himself to our heroine.

Molly's fits of jealousy and rage, mixed with rueful points of awareness—that what she really wants is a nuclear family, that 'there are some women who are my sisters and others who are definitely not'—are sympathetic, and her self-punishing dependence on the impossible Conrad will warm the heart of any reader who has ever left a good party to go home to a silent telephone.

But warming the heart is as far as it goes. This is not, even when Molly is statutorily raped or manages to leave Conrad, in the tough league of American feminist fiction. Quite the contrary: 'His small face trembled with hurt and indignation.' 'His blue eyes burned into mine.' It's hard to give credit to the book's acute, engaging qualities when the writing can be as fluffy as that.

> Hermione Lee, "Backwoods Messiah," in The Observer, August 19, 1979, p. 36.

HELEN CHASIN

Girl met boy early in 1957 on a blind date arranged by Allen Ginsberg. The rendezvous, which took place in a Greenwich Village Howard Johnson's, ended with fair-haired, 21-year-old Joyce Johnson picking up the tab and with Jack Kerouac, after wishing aloud that he were alone on a mountaintop, suggesting that he move in with her. When they arrived at her apartment he murmured into her ear his dislike of blondes. So much for the courtship stage.

Nine months later the publication of On the Road established Kerouac as the guiding spirit and spokesman of the beats. Johnson was, more and less, on and off for two years, the girlfriend. Since Kerouac did fame ("as foreign a country as Mexico," Johnson says) the way he did everywhere else—looked forward to it, enjoyed it briefly, found it intriguing, a drag, punishing, had to get out of there—Johnson was also the caretaker, the one who says, "It is time to go home," partly from a protective sense of responsibility and partly from feeling ignored. She was a buddy, fan, supporter, adviser. She was not a traveling companion (his mother was the only woman Kerouac made trips with), nor was she a grand passion, a role he reserved for dark, exotic women, "fellaheens."

And although Joyce Johnson (née Glassman) was working on a novel when they met and hanging out with artists and those subterraneans whose fugitive existences Kerouac chronicled, she couldn't be one of them. Like Robin Hood's and Peter Pan's, Jack's was a boy gang; among that crowd the opportunities for women in both fiction and life were limited.

The restricted membership appealed as it excluded, rendering her an appreciative audience for stories "of a hundred small occasions when in the ripening atmosphere of some midnight or endless beery afternoon came the moment when the absolutely right and perfect, irreducibly masculine thing was said or demonstrated unforgettably—an illumination worth waiting hours for." Her view was congruent with prevailing assumptions about where the action was and whose it was. There's an attitude, she writes, "that I'm responsive to in men. Some pursuit of the heightened moment, intensity for its own sake, something they apparently find only when they're with each other."

In fact, her acquiescent quiet was their loss as well as her own. Joyce Johnson too had stories, and hers are not only interesting and vivid but in several respects have more dimension than the adventure tales and clubhouse philosophizing that captured America's imagination in the late 50's.

The quest for significant experience is not related to gender or decade, and one person's minor character is another's sentient, perceptive self. Joyce Johnson's [**Minor Characters**] is a memoir of her childhood as well as of her coming of age in the counterculture during the period of cold war and other-directed gray flannel suits. It begins long before her love affair with Kerouac, whose interest here derives largely from his status as celebrity. Her portrayal of growing up bright and sensitive in Manhattan is the true heart of the book. What Johnson calls "the psychic hunger of my generation" characterizes the energy of youth, its emotional and intellectual excitement, and these, along with its concomitant isolations and conflicts, she evokes with feeling and wit.

Johnson refers to her middle-class, well-behaved eighth year as "the golden era of my career as a daughter," and to her 13th (during which she first encountered weekend folk singers in Washington Square Park) ascribes a quintessential adolescent leap: "It's as though a longing I've carried inside myself has suddenly crystallized. To be lonely within a camaraderie of loneliness." The Village was to be the main locus of this pursuit, a downtown of the mind which eventually included that part of the Upper West Side housing Columbia University's "outcast population." (pp. 9, 30)

As a high school student dismayed by the disparity between her interior life and her proper appearance, she acquired a pair of dangling copper earrings so she could turn herself instantly into a bohemian. The earrings are a means of making herself up. "I carry them with me at all times in case I need them. They constitute my downtown disguise." They are also the signs of her real, reprehensible identity, which must be hidden from parents and later from employers. Gentility is a "necessary mask," convention something to escape. "As a writer, I would live life to the hilt as my unacceptable self."

This intention survived her Barnard College writing instructor's pronouncement that if his students were going to be writers, they wouldn't be Barnard students; they'd be riding freight trains across the continent. In other words, if they were going to be writers, they wouldn't be girls. . . .

Aspiring to be neither warriors nor executives, rejecting power and competition, propriety and conventional success, the beats represented the other side of the mainstream values of their times but not a different currency. (Accounts of the group from other sources indicate that there was some crossing over: Kerouac liked Ike and subscribed to *The National Review,* Ginsberg was a talented promoter, and both were anti-Semitic.) Not only did they not challenge the pervasive masculinity of the decade's culture, they were exemplars of it. The issue of homosexual preference aside, their advocacy of the romance of transport (both geographical and psychic) and of the attractions of criminality and breakdown was incompatible with stable relationships and families, as was the lone voyaging of the visionary outsider. Sal Paradise, the narrator of *On the Road,* admires the protagonist's "hangjawed bony face with its male self-containment and absentmindedness." There's a warning here to women and children; nurturance is a virtue only if one is on the receiving end, and then only between trips. "Our battered suitcases were piled on the sidewalk again; we had longer ways to go. But no matter, the road is life." Which is not the same as saying that life is a road.

The road is freedom, in which a fellow can be spontaneous, impulsive, simultaneous, excessive, in progress. Its literary analogue emphasizes the colloquial and vernacular, immediacy, intuition. In each case the enemies of pure expression impose restraints; cleaning up, revision and what Sal Paradise calls "tedious intellectualness" are to be avoided. Editors are spoilers. Women can be useful, but they interfere with solitude and important work. In Johnson's case, Kerouac simply drifted off after a couple of years.

What Joyce Johnson relinquished by not becoming an aspiring artist's helpmeet was the opportunity

> to straighten him out a little, clean up the studio, contribute to the rent, have a baby or two, become one of those weary, quiet, self-sacrificing, widely respected women brought by their men to the Cedar [Bar] on occasional Saturday nights in their limp thrift-shop dresses made interesting with beads. Even a very young woman can achieve old-lady—hood, become the mainstay of someone else's self-destructive genius.

Johnson graphically conveys the squalor and disorder of the beat scene's marginal pads and gatherings, the underlying restlessness and movement that come to seem compelled rather than willed, a servitude instead of liberation. Her friends and acquaintances are given their due without sentimentality or claims for sanctity.

Her youthful sojourn through the 50's left Joyce Johnson with a "permanent sense of impermanence." It is her way of remaining unsettled. The 60's meant nothing to her except a diminishment of cultural vigor, the counterculture's disappointing falling away. She does not want, she says, to relinquish her youthful "sense of expectancy"—but in this she must also be disappointed, because that expectancy isn't synonymous with optimism or hope; youthful expectancy comes from having the greater part of your life ahead of you. It is impossible for adults to have such a sense, but they can have an appreciation of the now and of possibilities.

Joyce Johnson's enthusiastic loyalty to her days of heightened intensity has not prevented her from getting past them to realize her aim of giving up silence. The result makes for compelling reading. (p. 30)

Helen Chasin, "The Girl in the Boy Gang," in The New York Times Book Review, *January 16, 1983, pp. 9, 30.*

ROBBIN SCHIFF

When I first read *On the Road* as a teenager in the mid-sixties, I was sure my great loss was to have been born too late. High school, for all its rock 'n' roll and drugs, was just another conformist world compared to the intellectual and artistic passion of the Beat Generation. But my fantasies never took complete hold of me the way they did my male peers; it seemed that to truly understand the Beats one needed to be a male among males. Joyce Johnson's memoir [**Minor Characters**] tells what it was like to be there—for the first time from a woman's perspective. . . .

At 21, Joyce Johnson met and fell in love with the burnt-out, 34 year-old Kerouac and settled for the role of port in the storm rather than soul mate—to be the girl at the end of the road, but never on it. "I believe[d]," writes Johnson, "in the curative powers of love as the English believe in tea." Hers was a minor casualty of innocence. Others were less fortunate. Elise Cowen, for example, Johnson's astute and sensitive best friend, whose suicide ended her years of living on the edge, in hopeless love for the openly homosexual Ginsberg, and in real, if fashionable, despair at life's emptiness.

These women, though rarely mentioned in the histories that "[memorialized] a hundred small occasions when . . . the absolutely right and perfect, irreducibly masculine thing was said or demonstrated," had played integral roles in forming the new ethic before each faded away after a breakup. Johnson shows how the general atmosphere of misogyny as well as the very nature of the new vision served to exclude women from the legendary status of their men. In the 1954 "dream letter" (these guys communed even in their sleep) the critic John Clellon Holmes said to Ginsberg: "The social organization which is most true of itself to the artist is the boy gang," to which Ginsberg added, and "not society's perfum'd marriage."

Johnson sets the record straight about this new culture that rejected the dullness of conventional jobs and marriage and the women in it (many, like Hettie Jones, poets in their own right) who were willing to serve as mainstays for those visionary geniuses by holding straight, dull jobs, paying the rent on their pads, and raising their children alone. Minor characters in their own as well as their man's life.

Never again can I comfortably reconcile the lure of that time with what I now know of its boy-clubbiness and the silences of its women.

Robbin Schiff, in a review of "Minor Characters," in Ms., Vol. XI, No. 9, March, 1983, p. 36.

LAURIE STONE

In the span of [Joyce Johnson's] life, Jack Kerouac is a minor character, as she was in his life, and Johnson is perfectly aware of this. But Kerouac was a *significant* minor character, a Rosencrantz to her Hamlet, and her reminiscence in no way resembles the conventional fare on celebrated writers.

Minor Characters is a vigorous, stimulating meditation on why Joyce Glassman wanted Jack Kerouac, wanted him, in her early twenties, more than anything else in the world. The anecdotes recalled from childhood, the cast of characters selected for inclusion, all work to unravel this question. It gives the book its shape and sustained power, and Johnson's aim is consistently apparent, as tales of woolly Jack artfully counterpoint those of yearning Joyce. Johnson places Joyce Glassman in her times by unearthing conversations, remembering how she felt.

Some of this is familiar; stories similar to Johnson's are the meat and potatoes of grievance literature—that garrulous form whose message reduces to: "pity me; get angry for me." Johnson revitalizes the '50s confessional because her writing says as much about the past as about Joyce Johnson. She doesn't apologize for her actions—and thus doesn't betray her younger self, at the same time that she exposes her rawest feelings, the line to Kerouac about dyeing her hair to please him, for example. And by continually reaching for the larger meaning of her romance with Kerouac, Johnson reproduces a piece of consciousness.

In 1945, when Joyce Glassman was 10, she and her parents moved to 116th Street between Broadway and Riverside Drive—a steep hill that whips tears from the eyes in winter. Outside was Columbia University. Joyce roamed its red brick walks with the delicious hope that someone would think her a genius. Summoning her courage, she sneaked into the deeps of Riverside Park—her mother called it "down below," the same phrase used to describe "an otherwise unnamed region" of her daughter's body—and the child stared defiantly at forbidden traffic and brownish water. Inside was an immaculate, drape-fortified home, and governing that home was a marriage of heroic predictability and unsexiness. . . .

Joyce's mother prided herself on spending $20 a week to run the household. She also considered herself an arbiter of fine music, clothes, schools, and people. Joyce saw "permanent disappointment" in all her mother's gestures. It was sewn into the dresses she fashioned for Joyce. It drove the vacuum each day across the clean, worn carpet. This woman had no sense of where her own being ended and her fine daughter's started, and as she watched the little girl's hands on the piano, she conceived the marvelous plan to raise a composer.

The project warmed Joyce at first, made her feel special, but it had nothing to do with her desires and soon became a burden. What, Joyce wondered, was a girl supposed to want besides not pleasing her mother?

She was 13 and dying for something strong and sharp to happen when she began haunting Greenwich Village and hit on sex as a way into life. It was 1949, and squadrons of Lady Chatterleys and D. H. Lawrences were all at once converging and transforming sex from a sin, or a biological function, into a test of character. The Waldorf Cafeteria, smelling of greasy potatoes, was a kind of mead hall, Johnson recalls, where a girl could nurse a cheese sandwich for hours and overhear conversations with the names Kierkegaard and Sartre. It was a world of scruffy leather sandals, skinniness, guitars, and dangling earrings, of bad food, thin clothes, and rootless wildness—which added up definitively to sex.

A grizzled coal miner approached Joyce at a party one night, squeezed her hip, and announced: "Someday you will be a woman." She was transported. "To be seen as a woman, at least a future one," Johnson writes, "I couldn't get over it for weeks." Something was finally happening that qualified as experience. It was all so exciting, she did not pause to consider whether women who fucked around felt better than their mothers.

As she got older, Joyce fell into the habit of wanting remote, tantalizing men. Men who might have loved her approached, but she wasn't responsive. She didn't want the pain. She wanted the impossible: a nice anti-dad, a brutish, mercurial man who would *stay with her.* Frustration kept her hungry; yearning made her feel alive—it could fill up days, years. Active desire gave her a sense of power. And by being disappointed in a fever, she escaped her mother's dreaded fate of being frozen in disappointment.

Joyce felt her "life as a woman" beginning when her philosophy professor, a man with marriage and dissertation troubles, invited her to his bed. She could see from his angst and the purposeful clutter of his apartment that he was just too cool for her. She knew he'd break her heart, and he did, brushing her off with the line: "Promise me you'll get therapy."

Later, she was attracted to the Cedar Bar scene. It was a boy's party, clearly, but it seemed to Joyce the only party in town. The male artists and intellectuals ranted on rapturously about maleness, the sexiest subject in their lives, Johnson recalls. . . .

Through most of their relationship, [Kerouac] was in Europe or California. He was always expecting something wonderful to happen, but it never did, so off he went again. He liked yearning too. When he came to New York, he camped at Joyce's place, and they had unmemorable sex. "Someday you'll see Mexico," he wrote, moving on and breaking a promise, made at long last, that she could join him. He told Joyce he loved her only once. . . .

Kerouac's fame didn't strengthen his connection to Joyce. "Take care of this man," his editor told her, knowing how ill-equipped he was to handle TV and newspaper interviews. She watched, pained for his terror and awkwardness, as he numbly explained, for the 50th time, that "beat generation" came from the word beatific, signifying loveliness, not failure. "He could somehow cancel you out and make you feel sad for him at the same time," Johnson writes. When he was around, his lethargy said: "I'll stay if you'll have me." Eventually, he selected another undemanding lass who was duly passed the honor of slicing through parties and leaving whispers—"that's Kerouac's girlfriend"—in her wake. (p. 8)

Part of Johnson's purpose in **Minor Characters** is to show where she's moved since her affair with Kerouac, and she is just as admirably candid about her present state as her past. After 25 years, the small feminist battling away inside Joyce Glassman has evidently grown up and grown wise.

Feminism has given Johnson a subject in Joyce Glassman's life and times. It has focused her memory, sharpened her wit. The beat rebellion against authority and sexual repression laid some ground for the counterculture movements of the '60s, but, Johnson shows, women were sold out all the way down the line. Bohemians talked about overthrowing domesticity, yet somehow the women still wound up washing the dishes and taking the kids to school. It was a given, too, that beats loved freedom, but since all mothers were cops and all women were slotted to be mothers, women were more or less obliged to hate freedom—or their sex.

In the bohemian sexual idyll Johnson depicts, everyone was supposed to fuck for pleasure's sake alone; concomitantly, men had sex but women were sex. For women, then, there was no such thing as pleasure's-sake-alone, because sex was *their function.* When a woman didn't have an orgasm, she failed as a human being—not to mention how her body felt. (The man didn't much mention how her body felt.) Risk and destruction were glamorous, but while men were praised for conquering danger and for living, women often became famous for ending up dead.

Johnson's outrage about the waste of women's lives is by far the strongest emotion in her book. She evokes her predecessors, the '40s tough-girls who tended to crash-land. Edie Parker once shared her mattress and chili with Jack Kerouac and wound up threatening to expose Allen Ginsberg as a homosexual if he didn't help get her man back. Natalie Jackson, another Kerouac consort, jumped from a window one night shortly after he failed to convince her that life was "just an illusion." And witty Joan Vollmer fell for William Burroughs, the most serious outlaw in the Columbia pack (while still an undergraduate, he bought a submachine gun and became a dealer in morphine syrettes). Joan married Burroughs in 1945, grew marijuana with him in Texas, and in 1951, on crazy impulse, put a glass on her head in a Mexico City bar

and challenged her husband to blast it to smithereens with his .38. His aim, as Johnson puts it, "was off that night."

Elise Cowen was Joyce Glassman's dearest friend for 10 years, the secret sharer, ceaselessly interesting and sympathetic. They met at Barnard. Joyce identified a comrade in the anticollegiate clamor of Elise's drab sweaters and bad complexion. Elise was smarter about her sorrow than anyone Joyce had met; her middle name was Nada; "literally it means nothingness," she told Joyce, explaining the sort of people her parents were.

Elise was the first woman Joyce knew to drop out of school, the first one to hook up with the beats; on an odd date, she slept with Allen Ginsberg and was smitten, zapped. Ginsberg became her Kerouac, but there wasn't any more sex, only striving to be near, inside his adventure. She cut off her hair and became a lesbian; Ginsberg, Peter Orlovsky, and Peter's brother, Lafcadio, lived for periods with Elise and her lover, amid a collage of dirty plates and grayish sheets. Elise was the first one Joyce knew to get fired from her job for being a lesbian and to have the cops brought down on her when, incensed, she refused to leave the office. And Elise was the first one close to Joyce to exist on the California edge, eating one meal a day, sounding stoned beyond recognition on the phone, not eating at all sometimes, and sometimes turning tricks. She jumped out of a window and killed herself at 28.

Elise Cowen, not Kerouac, is Johnson's reference point, she says, and Elise's restless, inspiring ghost rides through the prose. Elise points to the future, one with nets and safe ports that might have rescued her, because her despair speaks with particular eloquence of the dead-endedness for women in this time. Johnson is unquestionably grateful to feminism—but she nonetheless feels troubling ambivalence.

Early in **Minor Characters,** she says that Joyce Glassman "still lives on in the most dangerous depths of myself," meaning treacherous longings are alive in her. It would be remarkable if they weren't. Kerouac looms up with a bad-boy smirk on his face, her pulse starts racing, and quite understandably, she heads for the heat. But it's not just erotic time-out Johnson craves; she wants the world that goes with it—despite everything she knows. She understands feminism, but feminism does not stir her. She has her own life, but it does not make her jubilant to have it. It feels like a consolation prize. So she remains caught, pitching between the perilous past that feels good and the pale good things of the present. That is who she is: a hybrid with a '50s heart and an '80s head.

Johnson describes her divided state, sometimes ruefully, at other times with a bit of defiance, as if addressing a militant task force intent on erecting road blocks across memory lane. Occasionally, perhaps unwittingly, she also illustrates how the mind turns away from its own knowledge when nostalgia takes over. She spends most of the 262 pages of her book discarding the past, but then she's moved, and in a flash she's rummaging through the trash heap, retrieving stuff she tells herself doesn't look so bad after all. She softens, forgets, fabricates.

"I hate Jack's woman-hatred," she writes, discussing *Desolation Angels,* and her usually detached, ironic voice starts quivering: "hate it, mourn it, understand, and finally forgive." Why forgiveness? Can't the man be worthy in parts and reprehensible in others? Forgiving woman-hate is a little like preparing to love it again.

In the book's final image, Johnson returns to the Cedar Bar in a grand, wishful flight. In her earlier description, she captures the posturing with acid and affection, and it comes out looking like a Feiffer cartoon. This time around, everything is bathed in a Rembrandt glaze. . . . (pp. 8-9)

The Cedar Bar is "the dead culture that needs wakening." When women speak, it shifts on its axis, and so does the earth. Maddeningly, poignantly, Johnson retreats from the remade world, even as she keeps summoning it. There is no grafting Joyce Johnson back onto this scene, whether or not she wishes to go, because as soon as she opens her mouth, her knowledge wipes it out.

To Joyce Johnson, feminism is a sobering protein drink, and she doesn't talk about alternate responses. She's not obliged, of course, to discuss feelings she doesn't have, but by depicting a progress toward feminism, *Minor Characters* inevitably evokes the women who loved it unreservedly, who got high as a kite on feminism. Their absence is a presence in this book. (p. 9)

> Laurie Stone, "Memoirs Are Made of This," in *VLS, No. 16, April 19, 1983, pp. 8-11.*

TODD GITLIN

It isn't Joyce Johnson's major purpose, but *Minor Characters,* her lovely, poignant memoir of her years in the Beat scene, makes plain just how fragile was the independence that so many male runaways thought they were living out. Her lover Jack Kerouac, the master iconographer of male revolt in the 1950s, was devoted to his mother and to male company in a way he could never be to a sexual partner. The touching cover picture—the photographic equivalent of Johnson's luminous prose—reveals a great deal: Kerouac in the foreground, illuminated by a neon BAR sign, head cocked back, heavy-lidded eyes gazing out with studied, studly arrogance; the "minor character," Johnson, in the background shadows, clutching her purse, eyes closed, facing off to the side, waiting for her man. Jack was always looking to new adventures with his buddies, though after some epiphanies and much booze and more despair, at the end of his open road the only home he could be counted on to return to was his mother's.

One moment of truth in Johnson's account comes when Kerouac agrees to drive a friend's car into town. Kerouac and Johnson get in the car; he crawls down the road until the friend's house is out of sight, and then he abandons it. "I was astonished," Johnson writes, "when he told me he'd always been a passenger rather than a driver." The apostle of the road couldn't run the archetypal American machine. What more pathetic symbol could there be of the dependency concealed within the freedom to keep moving?

The beauty of Johnson's book is that all the characters are for real. No one is either sentimentalized or brutalized by caricature. The female Rosencrantzes and Guildensterns—Elise Cowen, Hettie Cohen, Edie Parker—long mythologized (often self-mythologized too) as attendants and spoilsports in their famous boyfriends' courts, come into their own as women who stayed in the shadows of their men's freedom partly because they wanted their own but had no language for the desire. Fitfully coming to self-consciousness, they prefigured feminism. And Kerouac, however boozy or womanhating, isn't trivialized either. *Minor Characters* glows with

affection, as well as regret and pain for the waste of strong energies and high spirits in the Beat circles.

In the long, long haul toward mutual respect between the sexes, . . . [*Minor Characters* is] memorable for evoking the losses that grown boys have inflicted on women in the name of manhood—and for reviving, yes, the promise that someday we'll get it right. (pp. 664-65)

> Todd Gitlin, "Where the Boys Aren't," in *The Nation, New York, Vol. 236, No. 21, May 28, 1983, pp. 663-65.*

JAMES CAMPBELL

Joyce Johnson climbed into bed one night in 1957 with a likeable, immature, heavy-drinking hobo, and woke up with a celebrity. What happened in between was the publication in the *New York Times* of a review of *On the Road,* the first novel by Jack Kerouac (as opposed to "John", who had published one six years earlier). Agents and reporters started knocking on his door at breakfast, and by lunchtime it was, in a sense, all over: Jack was smashed and answering questions, with the drunken incoherence which was to become a trade mark, about the meaning of "beat" and the significance of "the road":

> "What was it really like, Jack? When did you first become aware of this generation? And how many people are involved in it? Is America going to go Beat? Are you telling us now to turn our backs on our families and look for kicks?"
> "Hey," Jack said. "Have some champagne."

While the first glasses were being filled, "Joycey", Kerouac's occasional girlfriend, the one who always understood and always forgave, was in the kitchen making coffee and having doubts about her own role in the coming drama of the Beat Generation. She was right, of course, as past experience told her. It was a boys' game: Kerouac and Cassady, Ginsberg and Orlovsky, Burroughs and his Tangier boys. . . . The myth of the freedom-seeking hero and his outcast sidekick is one of the most persistent in American fiction, from Fenimore Cooper's Leatherstocking and Chingagook, to Huck Finn and Jim, right up to the Lone Ranger and Tonto. By living it as well as writing it, Kerouac and friends became a legend.

Minor Characters is an attempt to tell the story from the side of the girl who makes the coffee and stays at home when the boys ride the range. Joyce Johnson cites, with a laconic bitterness, recent efforts by the novelist John Clellon Holmes to match the male characters in his novel, *Go,* with their originals, while admitting that the "centreless young women" were mere amalgams. Ms Johnson's purpose is to reveal the centre of at least one of them.

The Kerouac-Ginsberg-Burroughs legend has been the making of many books. Under her own name of Glassman, Joyce Johnson was one of the contributors to a compilation of interviews with friends of Kerouac, which was published four years ago. She was one of the few who retained a sense of reality in an otherwise indulgent exercise. "His mother made this big meal that everybody ate", she told the idolatrous interviewers, "except Jack. He ended up with his head in his plate." *Minor Characters* is better written than Carolyn Cassady's *Heartbeat,* although in places it is self-consciously lyrical, and also apt to rely on jargon: "hipster-angel Herbert Huncke"; "*naked,* that angelic word".

The book is composed, in effect, of two parts: there is the story of Joyce Glassman growing up in a polite New York suburb, struggling against her parents, coming to terms with nature's surprises (periods, sex), selling her first novel at the age of twenty-one; and, in counterpoint, the tale of Jack and Allen; eventually, Allen arranges a blind date—and Joyce meets Jack.

Whatever else it is, then, this is not a memoir in the mode of "Jack Kerouac as I knew him . . .". In the end, however, one's suspicions that "the boys" are its *raison d'être* are unallayed. Perhaps this is only because the stories of her own upbringing, though charming at first, are at length tiresome and contrived. Joyce Johnson has not the literary power to transform the mundane details of fussy mothers, severe fathers, discouraging teachers and fat friends into anecdotes with universal appeal. Naturally, then, one's ears prick up—as her publishers' must have done—when Kerouac enters. What was he really like? Did he always need to be free? How was he in bed?

In the act of filling in the centre, Joyce Johnson has also given the legend a bit of extra mileage. "As a lover he wasn't fierce but oddly brotherly and somewhat reticent." He told her about sex orgies, however, omitting to mention that he was the only one who had kept his clothes on. At bedtime, he sometimes went with his sleeping bag to another room. A good deal of the time, he is moving pointlessly from place to place; Joyce thinks of joining him sometimes, but he has already left. Had he had the courage to turn his back on America's desperate appetite for media stars . . . Kerouac might have written other books as good as *On the Road.* Instead, there was champagne, and all the holy-rolling phantoms he set in motion gradually coming home to roost. We could do with a book about that: a closer look at the delusions of these hipster-angels.

> *James Campbell, "Camp Follower," in* The Times Literary Supplement, *No. 4183, June 3, 1983, p. 576.*

PETER PRINCE

Minor Characters is much more than a worm's-eye-view of a famous man. Johnson's real subject is her own youth, the teenage Joyce Glassman who in the early Fifties began to make hesitant forays from the sterile, claustrophobic Jewish home on the Upper West Side down to the mysterious, burgeoning bohemia of Greenwich Village. It was a journey, an imaginative and physical adventure, that she shared with many of her contemporaries. But like the clearly marked BOYS and GIRLS entrances to old schools, the stream diverged sharply as it entered the new-found land below 14th Street. The boys for the most part went on to a world of experiment and ambition and, for a few, achievement and recognition. And the girls for the most part . . . ?

Well, look at the numbers. *Neurotica* was a small avant-garde magazine which began life in St Louis in 1948 and perished in New York at the end of 1951. It carried the early work of such future luminaries as Marshall McLuhan, Anatole Broyard, Allen Ginsberg, Kenneth Patchen, Chandler Brossard. But out of over eighty 'authentic' voices, exactly nine were female, and none of these was destined for future fame. As Joyce Johnson remembers it, these were voices that came essentially from the periphery:

> I see the girl Joyce Glassman, twenty-two, with her hair hanging down below her shoulders, all in black like Masha in *The Seagull*—black stockings, black skirt, black sweater—but, unlike Masha, she's not in mourning for her life. How could she have been, with her seat at the table in the exact centre of the universe, that midnight place where so much is converging, the only place in America that's alive? As a female she's not quite part of this convergence. A fact she ignores, sitting by in her excitement as the voices of the men, always the men, passionately rise and fall and their beer glasses collect and the smoke of their cigarettes rises towards the ceiling and the dead culture is surely being wakened. Merely being here, she tells herself, is enough.

The beat world was not exactly an exclusive male club. Indeed, as imaginative projections, women occupied high and varied positions as lovers, servers, whores, gypsies, virgins, jezebels, monsters of vengeance, angels of mercy. But the one truly important position was largely denied to them. They could not be seen as equals, fellow explorers, fellow artists. They might be ten miles high or ten miles deep, but they were not on the same level. . . .

Cut off from participating freely in the great creative excitement of their generation, the women waited and watched the men with varying degrees of resignation and desperation. The question Johnson probes at like a nagging sore throughout this fascinating book is why she and they were so passive. An obvious answer was that it was apparently much safer to sit on the side-lines. Kerouac's post-*On the Road* career was sufficient witness to the dangers of being noticed. But there did not seem to be much safety in passivity and obscurity either. The women suffered like the men, took to drugs and drink, and did desperate suicidal things like the men. Indeed, the most celebrated achievements of the beat women seem to have been their deaths. Dying was something they did rather well. William Burroughs's wife Joan placed a glass on her head one night and challenged her husband to shoot it off with his pistol. Unfortunately, as Johnson laconically puts it, Burroughs's 'aim was off that night'. Then there was Elise Cowen, Johnson's special friend and Ginsberg's one-time lover. She jumped to her death from her parents' apartment, a little while after being released from a mental hospital. Her passing won a poetic tribute from the hands of Ginsberg and Lucien Carr:

> How old was dear old Elipse when she went her
> merry
> way! I wish people I didn't like did that instead
> of her. I feel more loyalty than love for Elipse.

Thus by her leap to death, dear old Elipse, a poet herself but distinctly uncelebrated, finally won a secure place in the pantheon.

In some ways, the position of the women was far more vulnerable than that of the men. The beat world rejected and despised the old conformist 'bourgeois' models of male and female behaviour. But while the men had an alternative and rather splendid American role to fall back on—the outlaw, the lone pioneer conquering the wilderness—there was nothing similar available to the women, except perhaps for 'outlaw's moll' or 'pioneer's squaw-woman'. And they were still some years away from developing a feminist alternative. It irritates Joyce Johnson very much to look back on the abject silence in which she feels she passed too much of her young womanhood. But she is not inclined to pretend that things could have been much different, to dismiss the weight of opinion that lay on her generation. Nor, as she looks back at her personal submission to that culture, is she led to deny her youthful choices. She thought then that she was fortunate to be in touch with so many brilliant, exploring minds, to have at least a place in the vicinity of the boy gang. She thinks so now. It is not the presence of the girl Joyce Glassman at the edge of the charmed circle, while the voices of the men—'always the men'—rise and fall, that she wishes to forget: 'It is only her silence that I wish finally to give up.'

While it lasted, the affair with Kerouac clearly caused Johnson much pain. She was almost always in the difficult position of being the one who loved rather than the beloved. But this sad, dignified book is in no sense an attempt to get her own back. She writes of Kerouac with shrewd generosity, and leaves a convincing impression that behind the usually boorish public façade of the King of the Beats was a man of great sensitivity and sweetness.

> *Peter Prince, "Boy Gang," in* London Review of Books, *Vol. 6, No. 1, January 19-February 1, 1984, p. 23.*

PUBLISHERS WEEKLY

No one writes about the Bohemian New York art and literary scene of the late 1950s and early '60s with more affectionate and rueful insight than Johnson, and this novel [*In the Night Café*], about a doomed love affair with a painter, marks her strongest work so far. A whole era is flawlessly re-created as Joanna, onetime child actress turned Kelly Girl, remembers how she met the boozing, brawling Tom Murphy at a party; they began to live together while he struggled with his painting and his demons. Such characters in novels often become tedious, but here Murphy and Joanna, and their life together, seem to grow so inevitably from their milieu that the book achieves a genuine catharsis. Johnson's narrative tone, in the voice of Joanna, is meticulously maintained: unsentimentally self-aware, wryly observant, accepting without servility. There are wonderful portraits of Greenwich Village characters, with their lofts and odd obsessions. And the scenes with children—Tom's own, by an earlier marriage, and Joanna's son from a later affair—have a transcendent tenderness that is very moving.

> *A review of "In the Night Café," in* Publishers Weekly, *Vol. 235, No. 4, January 27, 1989, p. 454.*

ANNE TYLER

Anyone who's read *Minor Characters,* Joyce Johnson's award-winning memoir of her friendship with Jack Kerouac, will recall her special gift for evoking other times. That book was so hauntingly, delicately written that you could swear you were reading a novel. Rather than a painstaking chronology, it offered a series of catlike pounces upon exactly the right detail, the single sight or smell or sound that could bring a whole era flooding back into memory.

It should be no surprise, therefore, that when Johnson actually does write a novel, it's almost heartbreakingly evocative. *In the Night Café* summons up the New York of the early '60s. The Beat Generation has faded away, but her hero, Tom Murphy, would have felt at home among Kerouac and company. He's a tough, hard-drinking ex-Navy man who's ditched his wife and children to come to New York and paint abstract expressionist paintings; and when our young narrator, Joanna, meets him it is love at very nearly first sight.

Joanna's a bit more sedate than Tom—she works as an office temporary while rather desultorily pursuing an acting career—but she's cool enough, non-judgmental enough, so that they get along well together. In no time, they marry. But Tom is troubled by thoughts of the young son he abandoned, and he becomes increasingly self-destructive. Little more than a year after the wedding, he's killed. . . . Joanna eventually remarries and has a son, but she never gets over her attachment to Tom Murphy.

What gives this story its framework is the theme of the abandoned child. The book opens with a description of Tom Murphy's lifelong search for the father who left him in his infancy. Then we're shown Tom's small son—the child he himself left—meeting Joanna in New York a year after Tom's death and listening with pathetic concentration for any clue to his father. Only at this point does Joanna start telling us her own story in chronological order: her first encounter with Tom, their courtship and marriage, and Tom's death.

But his death is not the end. Joanna follows with a chapter called **"In the Children's Wing"**—a memory of her son's extended stay in a hospital years later. One of the other patients is an unaccompanied, overgrown boy from some kind of institution, and he's just threatening enough so that the mothers eventually assemble forces and protest his presence there. So Joseph is summarily hauled away while the other children watch. And Joanna's son? "Nicky got well," she concludes, "but he got old." This chapter was a co-winner of the O. Henry Award for best short story of 1987, and it's no wonder.

So *In the Night Café* is bracketed, you might say, by stories of lonely children. At the beginning you see Tom as a boy making his one and only trip with his mother to the candy store, walking in a "daze of joy, wondering if she'd be taking him to the candy store from now on." At the end you see the solitary young patient huddled alone on his hospital bed while visiting relatives deluge the other children with take-out food. And in between, the grown Tom Murphy agonizes over the child he's left behind.

"I'm hurting him," he tells Joanna. "Every day I'm hurting him." That he's right we already know, having been given that earlier glimpse of the sad little boy in New York after Tom's death—his "eerie dignity," his careful attentiveness to any word Joanna says about his father, his thin shoulder brushing Joanna's arm as he moves closer to her on the couch. (pp. 6-7)

A byproduct of this theme is that we're more tolerant of Tom's headlong rush toward ruin. Notice I don't go so far as to say we're sympathetic. That would be expecting too much, when the man willfully drinks his days away and makes constant veiled allusions to dying soon and fails to show up for supper. (And when the woman, one might add, keeps unaccountably preparing those suppers and reheating them.)

Such behavior seems less romantic to the reader than it does to his wife—or, one suspects, to the author—but it's at least explained, and so we do mourn Tom's passing. In fact, it's remarkable how moving the very last scene is, when Joanna revisits their old neighborhood many years after his death.

But the real reason for the book's effectiveness is the uncommon deftness and restraint of Johnson's writing. She has a way of characterizing people with a single stroke, allowing us to color in the rest—and therefore to invest ourselves more deeply. Of Tom's father we're told little more than that he "was addicted to cars and appropriated them when he could." Of his mother, that "a dangerous pitiless glint flashed off her like a knife." And of Tom himself, that he had "a face that had been used a lot, fierce eyes set deep in smashed bone, the right one angled down sharply."

Can't you just see him? And can't you see the "celluloid marcelled hair" of the aged mannequins in a cut-rate bridal store and hear the "dry, apologetic sputter" of Tom's motorcycle?

At one point, years after Tom's death, Joanna is confronted by a roomful of his paintings. The moment evokes a real ache in the reader; pictures we hardly noticed during their creation have become reminders of all that vitality, gone forever. But when I re-read that scene in order to quote it—imagining that some vivid, poetic description must have suddenly brought the paintings to life for me—it emerged that they weren't described at all.

Joanna decides to look for a certain picture that she particularly remembers. "I had the awful feeling I might no longer be sure which one it was," she tells us. "I walked across the room and started pulling the smallest paintings out. I found the one I was looking for right away."

That's all she says. What we knew beforehand—that the painting was red, that it was painted on an old canvas mailbag—we summon up for ourselves. And having summoned it, we find it as real and immediate as the room we're sitting in.

Here, I believe, is Johnson's secret: She trusts her readers. She holds up a slice of time, points out a single salient quality and then says, "Well, you know the rest." And to our surprise, we find we do know. It turns out we knew all along. (p. 7)

Anne Tyler, "Painting with Words," in Chicago Tribune—Books, *April 16, 1989, pp. 6-7.*

PHILLIP LOPATE

Joyce Johnson's third novel, **In the Night Café,** is a vivid romance set in that yeasty period of bohemian lower Manhattan, the early 1960's. Ms. Johnson has zeroed in on 1962 to 1963, portraying it as a time when painters and poets were wresting illegal living spaces from lofts, when Abstract Expressionism had already peaked but the new face of art had not yet presented itself, when everyone partied in an end-of-the-world insouciance. . . . The novel displays a gift for social history, for getting the period details right and not resorting to distortions of nostalgia. Joyce Johnson came of age in the 50's, as we learned from her engaging memoir, **Minor Characters,** about her time with Jack Kerouac, and she remains a champion of the era that shaped her moral and esthetic sensibilities. Indeed, one can read this novel as the ethos of the beat, starving-artist 50's reproaching the swinging, opportunistic 60's (and, by extension, the 80's).

"The sixties were never quite my time," says Ms. Johnson in **Minor Characters.** In this novel the narrator, Joanna Gold, declares: "I wasn't one of those who flourished at those famous downtown parties of the sixties. I knew what they were about, aside from abandon and ambition. You put yourself out there to be seen, to be taken up, to be judged in the flickering of an eye. I'd slip into watching and become, I thought, invisible." In both books, Ms. Johnson has staked out a territory all her own: the shy, observant young woman of that era, standing in a corner at the party, sensitive to humiliation, drawn to the handsome, tragically self-destructive male artist. This time, instead of Kerouac, Joanna's heart is stopped by a brooding older painter, Tom Murphy. . . .

> He was a very good-looking man, so I decided he would be dangerous, spoiled rotten by women no doubt. . . . He took me in, I don't know how else to say it. My tremendous uncertainty, my habit of watching, my ridiculously bright dress. It was as if he could read my bones, it wasn't that he wanted anything. 'Why do you hang back?' he said and walked away.

Considering how many of us hang back at parties, I am not sure why this mundane question should seem so revelatory to the narrator as to represent "the entire painful puzzle of my life," but it seems to do the trick. In this particular fairy tale, the passive, undervalued young woman must be found out, deciphered by the bruised older man's keen eye. Readers of **Minor Characters** may recall a painter named Jim Johnson, who also asked, "Why do you hang back?" and who married the author and died shortly afterward on a red Harley motorcycle, like Tom Murphy. So one is entitled to regard this as autobiographical fiction—within limits. Many details have obviously been altered in the novel, and the scenes have an intensity and shape not usually found in memoirs. Yet its overall manner still strikes me as a hybrid—a successful one, I might add—of novel and memoir.

The book sails on its first-person narration: a fiercely believable, testifying voice that is pungent, close to the bone, stinging with candor. Lyrical atmospheric effects aside, the poetry of this novel is in its quick psychological insights and the ability to make us shudder and feel along with it. Ms. Johnson is particularly good at conveying the tentativeness of adoration and the mute dependency of a young woman in love with an older, experience-scarred man. On the one hand, Joanna relies on Tom to teach her worldliness; on the other, she regards him with a precocious maternal protectiveness that is still too hesitant to demand that he take care of himself. Wildly happy with him, she admits it is a "happiness that had terror in it," and she cannot get over the presentiment that their days together are numbered. . . . The narrative style alternates between describing Tom in the third person and addressing him directly, with invariable tenderness: "I was still trying to keep you alive—that was really what we fought about. . . . I didn't have any other plan."

Joanna Gold is a complex and wonderfully realized character. The novel's major problem, as I see it, is Tom. He never really comes alive on the page; he remains a sort of simple Bogartian ideal of masculinity who calls her "kiddo" and tells her on their first date that he intends to marry her, carves her mother's turkey and reassures her that "wherever we go, we'll always be together.' . . . I never met another man who said 'always.'" Unfortunately, the men who put her down spring to life with resentful clarity, while the one who loves her remains sentimentally misty.

The solemnity of Tom's dialogue is especially hard to swallow, given as he is to irritating tough-guy pronouncements about art, truth and motorcycles. "I paint what I paint," he says, or "The el wasn't beautiful, but it was beautiful," or "The instinct's *there*, don't you see?" In a way he seems too perfect, with his willingness to love her unconditionally and forever: a wish-fulfillment hero in a romance novel. Even so, it's hard to share Joanna's enthusiasm for this inexpressive bore who drinks too much, forgets to come home, punches out people in barrooms and has already walked out on a wife and two kids. Yet Joanna seems to subscribe uncritically to the tired macho myth of the Abstract Expressionist painter who must heroically fight the canvas, get blind drunk and suffer martyrdom. . . .

Perhaps the reason why Tom remains so wooden is that the author is too reverently protecting the memory of her deceased husband—taking his side always, as a widow but not a novelist should. Or perhaps it is simply very hard to dramatize true love. "Found!" thinks Joanna when she wakes up the first morning in Tom's arms, and found she remains; but the description of their conjugal life has a suppressed, static quality, never quite achieving a daily sense of intimacy.

Whenever Joanna breaks away from moonily orbiting around the doomed Tom, she views the world with sympathy and wry amusement, and the prose soars. Fortunately, there are a multitude of digressions and sketches, including brilliant descriptions of her parents, her career as a child actress, her boyfriends, her city walks, her jobs ("It was the kind of office where people would create excitement by passing around homemade brownies"). In general, I loved the book whenever Tom was not around. I hasten to add that other readers who are more attracted to romances than I am will probably find him no stumbling block.

The novel's penultimate section, **"The Children's Wing"** (with Tom safely offstage, having already had his fatal accident), is Joyce Johnson's finest achievement as a writer, and one would have to search hard to find as powerful a 30-page stretch in recent American fiction. Here we follow the widowed Joanna to Paris, where she meets a displaced émigré film maker, Mikel. They console each other, marry and have a child, Nicky, then separate. It is the continuing responsibility for Nicky that forces Joanna to grow up, to trade in her footloose Office Temps definition of freedom for something more durable. What a pleasure to watch the interactions of mother and son (Nicky is a beautifully drawn character), and to see Joanna assert herself so comfortably. When Nicky is hospitalized, his mother is forced to summon all her strength while surrendering him temporarily to the medical staff. In grappling with the sadness of the children's wing, Joanna also faces her old tendency to shut out the suffering of other human beings. All her ambivalence is brought out by an emotionally disturbed child, Joseph, who moves her but who disrupts the ward and bothers Nicky. After Joseph threatens a child with matches, the mothers confront the supervisor:

"I spoke up, too. Irresponsibility, negligence, lack of consideration—the words came so fluently, as if I'd turned into the kind of person I'd always distrusted, someone with very sure opinions about rightness and wrongness and what was best for society." While Joanna is correct to distrust self-righteousness, the fact is that she *has* turned into a responsible, strong adult who is much better able to take care of her child than she had her first husband. She has come a long way from the silent, frightened wallflower whom Tom reproached for hanging back; and that progression, perhaps more than the story of their Big Love, is finally what ***In the Night Café*** triumphantly conveys.

Phillip Lopate, "Bohemia Died, but Life Went On," in The New York Times Book Review, *April 30, 1989, p. 11.*

James Kelman

1946-

Scottish novelist and short story writer.

Kelman's realistic fiction examines the psychological temperaments and obsessions of the working-class residents of Glasgow, Scotland and its surrounding areas. Writing in colloquial dialect, Kelman uses a laconic, stream-of-consciousness style to evoke a bleak atmosphere and vivid characters that reflect the biased social structure and urban decay he believes to exist in Scotland, and he recurrently uses obscenities as illustrations of this social collapse. Although his protagonists are often unemployed or trapped in menial jobs, Kelman avoids condescension by blending humor, pathos, and insight while rejecting contrived conclusions. Although critics sometimes fault Kelman's limited subject matter, they praise his adept use of interior monologue as a narrative technique. Mike Marqusee commented: "Experimental as they are, Kelman's stories are also highly accessible. The language gives life to bizarre anecdote, unexpected detail, and a deadpan sense of humor. . . . His work is fresh, honest, funny, and shouldn't be missed."

Kelman is primarily regarded as a short story writer, and critics contend that the widely varying length of these pieces allow him more imaginative freedom than the novel form. In his first collection, *Not Not While the Giro and Other Stories* (1983), Kelman examines day-to-day survival among luckless Glaswegians. Set in such places as pool-halls and race tracks, the stories reveal a characteristic casual desperation. "Not Not While the Giro," for example, features a protagonist perfunctorily contemplating suicide until his social security check arrives in the mail. Donald Campbell noted: "Kelman's ability to re-create this world so convincingly is a major achievement. [*Not Not While the Giro* is] full of satisfying insight, an economic eye for detail and a telling accuracy in the evocation of atmosphere." With his next volume of short stories, *Greyhound for Breakfast* (1987), Kelman attained international acclaim. While again exploring the prosaic interests of the working-class, Kelman injects more black humor and casual social protest, and has admitted that the volume is heavily influenced by the writings of Franz Kafka. As in Kafka's works, many of these stories examine the struggles of ordinary people in horrendous circumstances. In "Old Francis," for example, an elderly man on a park bench is menaced by drunkards. Kelman abruptly ends the story as the increasingly violent group surrounds the protagonist. "Greyhound for Breakfast" focuses on a jobless man who buys a dog with his unemployment check. Originally planning to race the greyhound, he is ridiculed by his friends and gradually realizes that he will not even be able to feed the dog. Despondent, he contemplates throwing the dog in the river or jumping in himself. "In with the Doctor" revamps Kafka's short story, "The Country Doctor," in which a physician becomes alarmed at a family's bizarre home medical practices. In Kelman's version, the patient is unnerved by the doctor's incapacity to fulfill his authoritative role.

Kelman's longer fiction shares the settings, thematic concerns, and unresolved crises of his short stories. His first novel, *The Busconductor Hines* (1984), revolves around the

dilemmas of the young title character and his family. With his life on the brink of several changes, Rab Hines feels a growing sense of disaster. Through a prolonged use of monologues, Kelman allows his protagonist to comment on myriad aspects of his existence and the world in general. Although several reviewers found these musings tedious, most considered *The Busconductor Hines* a realistic depiction of an individual in jeopardy. In *A Chancer* (1985), Kelman conveys the malaise of modern society through an account of Tammas, a young, philosophical gambler. Taking the guise of a series of short, related sketches, the novel follows Tammas through his everyday activities of betting, striking up casual friendships, and arguing with his girlfriend. Neville Shack stated: "Kelman's broad sympathy results in a vital depiction of everything stagnant as well as the possibility of a new beginning . . . much of it achieved through understated eloquence." *A Disaffection* (1989), featuring the author's first white-collar protagonist, was described by Brian Morton as "Kelman's most ambitious and sophisticated fiction to date." Patrick Doyle, a twenty-nine-year-old, unorthodox grammar school teacher, is bitter about the Scottish government and guilt-ridden about the social status he holds over his working-class family. Patrick attempts to maintain his ties with the proletariat by living in a tenement, eating poorly, and teaching his students about government suppression. The novel covers merely a week in his endless search for humanity and beauty in a dreary, unjust environment. Although wealthier than Kelman's other protagonists, Patrick experiences far more discontent.

DONALD CAMPBELL

The landscape of James Kelman's [*Not Not While the Giro and Other Stories*] is exceedingly bleak, a world of social inadequacy and squalor in which there is neither purpose, ambition nor even the least degree of hope. Kelman's characters wander through their lives rather haphazardly, living in temporary accommodation, working (when they can) in menial, often casual, occupations, their pleasures restricted to the odd scraps of good fortune which they occasionally encounter. At first sight, they seem feckless, superficial, depressing by dull people whose sense of proportion is almost non-existently narrow. The central character in ["**Not Not While the Giro**"], for instance, despairs of living but cannot bring himself to commit suicide because of the imminent arrival of his social security cheque!

Kelman's ability to re-create this world so convincingly is a major achievement. These twenty-six stories are full of satisfying insight, an economic eye for detail and a telling accuracy in the evocation of atmosphere. Set mainly in London and Glasgow, they reveal an entire sub-culture which has its own, quite distinctive, standards, ethics and priorities. For these people, money is unimportant, useful only for paying the rent, buying cheap food and drink, and betting on horses or dogs. Personal relationships, on the other hand, are extremely important, if somewhat transitory, while possessions and any kind of material security are totally disregarded. It would be all too easy to romanticize such a life-style, but Kelman avoids this by the simple device of assigning a character-role to the narration, effectively cutting out any need for judgement or even commentary.

Many of the stories are very short, some no longer than the anecdote one might tell over a couple of drinks. While Kelman is most adept at this kind of concentrated writing—his excellent "**Acid**" is restricted to a single paragraph—the best stories in the collection are longer and more fully developed. In "**The House of an Old Woman**" he makes a ghost story out of the tensions which exist between three single men sharing an abode, while in "**Remember Young Cecil**" he uses a curiously formalized dialect to evoke the legend of a snooker player. Some of the stories are what one might expect from a Glasgow writer: "**Nice to Be Nice**" is pure patois, while "**Away in Airdrie**" is the classic Glasgow tale of the boy being taken to a football match by his drunken uncle. All in all, however, Kelman achieves an astonishingly wide diversity of style and content within his chosen area of operation. As this is his first full collection, it will inevitably be seen as a staging-post in the development of a highly individual and intensely interesting practitioner of the art of the short story. (pp. 517-18)

> *Donald Campbell, in a review of "Not Not While the Giro and Other Stories," in* British Book News, *August, 1983, pp. 517-18.*

GERALD MANGAN

The narrators of *Not Not While the Giro* are often . . . solitary and insecure, but James Kelman's Glasgow accent places them squarely in . . . tangible surroundings. In one story he transcribes the vernacular at its most dense ("A hid fuck aw bar some smash . . ."), but elsewhere, by adopting only its rhythms and idioms, he keeps the prose readable as well as authentic. Speaking the same voice as his characters, yet avoiding all the pitfalls of condescension and nostalgia, he mines a rich ore from many unexplored seams of working-class life: tenements, dole-queues, dog-tracks, snooker-halls, football-grounds and so on.

In Kelman's closely-observed characters, this perspective is never altered or threatened: although work or hope often lure them south and north, very few of his workers, idlers, boozers and born losers display any ambition beyond the next winning-post. Kelman's stories can be as funny as Damon Runyon's, but his underworld is not a caricature. If it tends to be a male preserve, where women are mainly offstage wives or taciturn objects of conquest, this is perhaps just a less happy aspect of its realism.

The partiality of the vision is often its strength, in fact, and the briefest of the illuminations often the most intense. In three disciplined pages "**Wee Horrors**" turns up the underside of a half-demolished city like the insect-life under a stone. When a milkman is unhinged by a falling corpse in "**The Block**", Kelman makes a black comedy of his subjective vision; and by its very understatement, the single paragraph of "**Acid**", which Alasdair Gray cheerfully plagiarized for his novel *Lanark*, makes a horrible industrial accident unforgettable.

The humdrum readily breeds the fantastic . . . and confinement makes the fantasy poisonous. As a daydreamer and self-confessed "hopeless case", the unemployed narrator of the long title-story ["**Not Not While the Giro**"] typifies the failings and misfortunes of several others. Finally paralysed between his last smoke and his next Giro cheque, he nurses his hungers and grudges with grandiose pipedreams, but finds his initiatives cancelled out by the double negatives of poverty. This combines the keenest of Kelman's humour and pathos, but his perceptions in all these stories are acute.

> *Gerald Mangan, "The Short Fantastic," in* The Times Literary Supplement, *No. 4213, December 30, 1983, p. 1462.*

EDWIN MORGAN

James Kelman, who brought out an excellent volume of short stories, *Not Not While The Giro,* in 1983, has now followed this with his first novel [*The Busconductor Hines*], and a remarkable book it is. The bus conductor hero lives with his wife Sandra and small son Paul in a century-old, crumbling tenement in Glasgow. It is Rab Hines's third attempt at holding down a bus conductor's job, and he is already in the authorities' black book for turning up late, putting his feet on seats, not wearing his hat, and other misdemeanours; added to which, bus conductors are on their way out in any case. His wife works part-time in an office, while Paul is in a day nursery. The tenement will soon be due for demolition: will they be offered a house in Drumchapel (bad, but good in parts) or should they emigrate to Australia? The marriage, though a loving and surviving one ("the unit, the trio"), is going through a huge stress-field of uncertainties. There is an unresolved climax, when Hines refuses to attend a disciplinary tribunal under the conditions laid down, and a union meeting takes up his case and proposes a strike; the outcome is left beyond the scope of the book's last pages.

The circumstances are ordinary, and the central character's alienation is also ordinary, in the sense that it can be related to obvious causes in society—over-authoritarian employers, "a no-bedroomed flat", fear of his wife leaving him—but the novel has ambitions beyond the naturalistic. The naturalism is itself thoroughly convincing. . . .

But the book is deepened by the fact that Hines, while not ceasing to be "the Busconductor Hines" who has even had ambitions hypostatized as becoming "the Busdriver Hines", is also "predisposed towards speculative musings". These emerge in long monologues, some obsessively practical (the occasional househusband on how to cook mince and potatoes), some warmly associational in a Leopold Bloom manner (thoughts on backcourt middens and encroaching tenement demolition lead to a meditation on animals, the rats and mice "trying to stay one jump ahead of the demolition men", the dead rodents feeding smaller creatures, evolution going on), some political (warning his son to read history and know the robbers of the people "in their entrempenurial mejisteh") and some darkly symbolic.

Kelman takes risks with certain kinds of monotony and repetition: one soon begins to scream quietly whenever Hines "prised the lid off the tin" to roll himself yet another cigarette, and the ubiquitous taboo expletives, though perfectly realistic, will certainly irritate some readers. All the more interest, therefore, attaches to Hines's fondness for phrases like "a very perplexing kettle of coconuts", or to syntactic ironies like "what will be that which is not to be being accomplished". As hardly any authorial guidance is given concerning the characters' physical appearance, they have to be understood through their language, and on the whole this is brilliantly managed, if at times a jocular-columnist tone appears inappropriate ("prior to accepting the band of rolled gold", "during one's penultimate conducting moments"). This is, though, an intelligent, exploratory, and sometimes very touching novel.

> Edwin Morgan, "Musing on the Buses," in The Times Literary Supplement, No. 4228, April 13, 1984, p. 397.

JIM MILLER

[In James Kelman's *The Busconductor Hines*], Robert Hines lives with his wife Sandra and their son Paul in a mouldering, bathroom-less tenement in the Drumchapel district of Glasgow. He is a conductor on the city's buses, a job he doesn't like and to which he has returned for the third time; is it better than being on the broo, he frequently asks himself. Sandra has a part-time office job but is thinking of going full time. The four-year-old Paul attends a nursery when his parents are both at work, otherwise his father or mother takes care of him and the housework. We follow Hines on the buses, in the pub or the garage with mates, at home, visiting friends or in-laws, wandering the streets. His bad time-keeping leads to a show-down with the bus inspectors and a strike is narrowly averted. He pretends to be ill so he can take the day off. The plot is tenuous; what we have instead is a detailed

portrait of one man's life, one with a growing sense of crisis. This is a story of 'getting by', of overcoming the conspiracies of chance and the countless irritations fate throws in one's way, of dealing with the petty bureaucracies of desk clerk and inspector, of dreams—a holiday, a better home, emigration to Australia—foundering on the rock called 'more of the same'.

Through it all, Hines remains at heart a sentimental, almost romantic, soul. One senses in him a tension between the world of 'macho' convention and his realizations of lost opportunity; in this, he could stand as an archetype of the urban, working-class Scot. He worries that his wife will leave him because he can't achieve some of their goals; he has a sporadic ambition to become a bus driver so that he won't lose his job when one-man buses are introduced. Through Hines, James Kelman provides a brilliantly executed, uncompromising slice of Glasgow life: the banter and repartee of the 'punters' (an urban Scots term now almost synonymous with 'person'), religion, football, booze, the tenements and shopping centres, the smoke-filled union meeting—all in tough, authentic Glasgow speech. There is a vitality here and a boisterousness that sweeps the reader along—and humour, such as the splendid recipe for mince and tatties. With Kelman, and other writers such as Alasdair Gray, the great city of Glasgow and urban Scotland in general are finding the literary voices they deserve.

> Jim Miller, in a review of "The Busconductor Hines," in British Book News, June, 1984, p. 365.

KATE FULLBROOK

James Kelman is best known for his short stories, and in [*A Chancer*], his second novel, he brings the short-story writer's talents for compression and significant dialogue to a full-length story of working-class Glasgow. The novel is a highly original production in which Kelman conveys a brilliant impression of the malaise of contemporary life largely through the hundred-word basic vocabulary he allows his characters to speak. The 'chancer' of the title is Tammas, a shrewd twenty-year-old who takes the world philosophically, deciding that gambling gives him as good a chance as anything to fill up his days and to make his way in the world. The novel proceeds laconically from the betting shop to the track, from games of cards in the factory to the casino, as Tammas quietly learns his trade, and listens politely to advice that mates, family and acquaintances give him to stop his slide away from 'legitimate' work. But Tammas, living from cigarette to cigarette in a landscape of rubbish, chip shops, social security offices, football and factories, sees gambling as being as sound as other ways for getting 'cash in exchange for a slip of paper'. And this, he reckons, is, after all, 'what it is about'. The emotional climate of the novel rings absolutely true, with Tammas taking his losses and winnings and his human relationships with the same restrained response. While Kelman's ability as a notable stylist with an exact ear for contemporary speech has not been ignored, this understated novel about ordinary desperation should gain him an even larger readership. (pp. 684-85)

> Kate Fullbrook, in a review of "A Chancer," in British Book News, November, 1985, pp. 684-85.

NEVILLE SHACK

Gambling has its own etiquette: it matters a lot whether you win or lose, rather than how you play the game. . . .

Tammas, the central character of *A Chancer,* has already begun to lose sight of that elusive old magic, beginner's luck. He is a likeable youth who slouches around Glasgow's bare streets, meeting up with his mates, all of them fairly hopeless figures. Emigration, or just going south, are prospects borne half in mind, dim, distant aims; the outside world seems as far away as a chance of comfort and ease, always discussed in terms of rumour. This is the bleak landscape of dirty realism, where people are more redundant than the adjectives used to describe them. The no-frills prose itself creates a spartan picture: monosyllabic dialogue, minimal interiors and incidents which are apparently not brimming over with significance, allowing gloom to pervade instead.

Betty, Tammas's nondescript girl-friend, speaks of work opportunities in England. By means of a simple frown she also seems to suggest a dead-end relationship with a lifetime of boredom and domestic sanctimony to follow. One night at a casino Tammas meets Vi, an older woman who cashes in her winning chips. They strike up together casually. These are the warmest and most gently amusing moments: Vi, the resourceful, independent woman bringing up her young daughter alone; Tammas, diffident, slightly ridiculous, but stirred for the first time out of his usual apathy. Otherwise, not much happens. Bets are laid, good chances collapse and life is a spinning wheel with the odds generally stacked against.

Out of this dreary routine, a rough-and-tumble camaraderie develops, small glimmers of fellow-feeling—for instance, when Tammas acts as best man to a nerve-wracked friend—which are striking in their humour, antidotes to the grim environment. Tammas's air of vague discontent hints at intelligence and sensitivity adrift, while the rites of gambling are conveyed with finesse. The novel flows enjoyably as a series of episodes, some of them truncated bits of dialogue, often with a jerky syntax reflecting the way in which experiences are actually felt by the characters. James Kelman's broad sympathy results in a vital depiction of everything stagnant as well as the possibility of a new beginning at the very end, much of it achieved through understated eloquence.

> *Neville Shack, "Reckonings among the Rough-and-Tumble," in* The Times Literary Supplement, *No. 4314, December 6, 1985, p. 1407.*

FRANCIS SPUFFORD

There is a thing—call it the bastard high style—which has preoccupied some writers ever since [François] Villon found a fruitful union in the marriage of gutter argot and the language of the Schools. In English, in this century, it has mostly been used by Irish writers: by Joyce, with Vico and scatology, by Beckett, with velleity and bananas, and by Flann O'Brien, one paragraph of whose *At-Swim-Two-Birds* includes both an *argumentum* on Rousseau and the sudden eructation of 'buff-coloured puke'. Now there is a new practitioner, working with a different vernacular and a different elevated diction. The first of the 47 fictions in James Kelman's *Greyhound for Breakfast* finds old Francis on a park bench in Glasgow, menaced by vaguely circling winos trying to cadge a cigarette.

It was downright fucking nonsensical. And yet it was the sort of incident you could credit. You were sitting down in an attempt to recover a certain equilibrium when suddenly there appear certain forces, seemingly arbitrary forces, as if they had been called up by a positive evil. Perhaps Augustine was right after all? Before he left the Manicheans.

Kelman likes blending in a Latinate construction as much as his predecessors; he finds the correlative for it, as the Irish did, in the remembered shards of an imposed education. But it needs saying that in the case of **"Old Francis"** no confrontation of classes is intended, unless a confrontation between those like the winos who have fallen to pieces and those like old Francis who are still struggling to keep their souls and capacities in one bit: an important exclusion, because previous proponents of the style have always been jealous—often ironically jealous—for the leaven of high culture they strew in their gutter. Kelman's stories have no Dedaluses carrying secret aesthetic torches; nor do they have the Guinness-misted contempt for the poor that Flann O'Brien's narcoleptic narrators show. The style is potentially deeply patronising, using the language and world of derelict human fodder to feed the comedy or tragedy of the high culture. Kelman's use of it takes it in the other direction.

For the most part, these stories are about the Glasgow working class, with occasional excursions to Glaswegian colonies in London or Manchester or America, or into the Strathclyde hinterland of the city. Bets, paper-rounds, child-care, dole-money, industrial accidents, love, school-leaving, drinking and surviving are among their concerns. Sometimes, in monologues or narratives rooted entirely in the perceptions of a single character, he puts the style at his subject's disposal, as an articulating instrument; at other times, in more fantastic or more fragmentary pieces, it is imposed upon action to produce—through the inhumanity of its elaborations—a black, humane comedy. One of the latter, **"This Man for Fuck Sake"**, nine sentences long, has a guilty narrator describing someone's progress down a pavement in terms more appropriate to NASA: 'Then that rolling manoeuvre he performed while nearing the points of reference. It all looked to be going so fucking straightforward.' With a foreground alive with voices of fastidious clarity, and a distant commentary purged of sneers, Kelman frees himself completely from any possibly condescending editorial middle ground. His characters' voices are naturalistic; the compounded 'voice' of the style firmly realist in intent. Part of the reason for this lies in the high-cultural icon Kelman has chosen to hang on his wall and in his prose—not the Schoolmen, not the Symbolists, but Kafka.

Reviewing the South African writer Alex La Guma in the *Edinburgh Review* last May, Kelman called Kafka

> the greatest realist in literary art of the 20th century. His work is a continual struggle with the daily facts of existence for ordinary people. Kafka's stories concern the deprivation suffered by ordinary people . . . whose daily existence is so horrific other ordinary people simply will not admit it as fact.

As an interpretation one could disagree with that; as a declaration of Kafka's usefulness to Kelman, one cannot. One can only admire the use. The debt to Kafka in this book is multiple. A few stories—the least successful, I think—drink so deeply and directly from the spring that they are almost pastiche. In **"The Small Family"**, the small family (whose individual members 'were not especially small') arouse 'an ever-increasing burden of guilt. There is no one cause.' Benson's visitor in hospital, in **"Benson's Visitor"**, defines himself only as the person who visits Benson. When Benson asks who, apart from that, he is, he collapses, and as the story ends there is an alarming suggestion that he may now acquire a new role as a patient. Another group of stories takes up the Kafkaesque idea of a comedy based on the indescribable (**"The Red Cockatoos"**, **"The Failure"**): details accumulate not to clarify but to obscure, placing the protagonists in untenably false positions. Much more exciting—and more successful— are the pieces in which Kafka's influence has been digested, diffused and put to use in the Kelman style. The marvellous **"In with the Doctor"** pays explicit homage to "The Country Doctor" (Kelman's worrying doctor has been reading it— 'Gives me the fucking willies'). The Kelman story, though, is a realist rather than surrealist composition, because he has switched around Kafka's premise about authority: now it is the *doctor* who alarms the *patient* by failing to fill his authoritative role. The surgery is a half-dismantled hierarchy. The doctor uses his place of power to impose chatty chaos on the patient, while the patient, who is the narrator, has expectations of protocol at the same time as he fiercely resents the 'wee class games' in the doctor's authoritative failure to be authoritative.

> After a moment I say: So what've you dismissed me or what? It's hard to tell.
>
> He looked at me in an odd way, and I knew it was what to do next was the problem.

Obsession interests Kelman greatly. He excels at narratives slanted by unstated difficulties, à la Kafka, but is more concerned with when and how an obsessive eye can become the natural way to see. **"A Sunday Evening"** (about making sandwiches) and **"Getting Outside"** (about going for a walk alone) are narrated with the real deliberateness with which you do a difficult, small bare thing that really matters. The original innovation of realistic fiction was the presentation of domestic time: now Kelman is simply giving us un- or disregarded time—personal, tawdry and momentary—seen so closely and unremittingly that the attention itself almost begins to work as a distorting mirror. After all, one of the hallmarks of obsession is attention to a paucity of things, and to make use of obsession is a naturalistic procedure when describing the 'natural' world of dole and giro.

Who is this written for? Sadly, the reason 'why there are few good fictions about folk with low incomes' put forward by Alasdair Gray recently in his Postscript to Agnes Owens's *Gentlemen of the West* is also the reason why folk with low incomes are less likely to read what fictions there are about 'ordinary' lives: 'It is a horribly ordinary truth that our imaginations reject most of the living we do, so from the earliest days of recorded wealth we have lifted up our eyes to the wealthy.' Kelman's own statement of principles in the La Guma review is grittily optimistic: 'As long as art exists there are no areas of experience that have to remain inaccessible.' I hope James Kelman continues to believe what he said, and continues to write accordingly.

Francis Spufford, *"Dialects,"* in London Review of Books, *Vol. 9, No. 7, April 2, 1987, p. 23.*

ALISON FELL

[In the short story collection *Greyhound for Breakfast*], James Kelman homes in mercilessly on the tenements, hostels and [Department of Health and Social Service] offices of a Glasgow for the most part unemployed and used to it. From single killer paragraphs to longer, rambling tales of everyday inertia, Kelman catches the resilience of a class in the wit and spirit of the language.

Faced with the Scottish writer's perennial dilemma of standard English versus dialect, Kelman refuses to split himself off from his characters' language even as third-person narrator, and this is both his strength and his limitation. What he excels at is the baleful interior monologue: in the wretchedly funny **"Where but What"** a working-class patriarch stokes a vast and inarticulate grudge against the ex-wife who failed to treat him with all due slavishness and, worse, nagged him for looking at lassies in mini-skirts. He's also nursing a vast need to go to the toilet but he's too angry and idle to satisfy it. Beat that for masochism.

For the citizens of Kelman's Scotland, days dawdle past punctuated by small pleasures—the booze, the cards, the dogs—and irritations—the po-faced clerks at the Broo, the 'fucking wind that smokes your fucking fags'. These characters are virtuosos of abuse, hiding their tender parts behind great, irresistible explosions of swearwords. (You roll them around in your mouth for days. Imagine calling somebody an 'elitist wee shite'. Scottish aggro dies hard.) When there is love or tenderness—as in **"The Wean and That"** and **"Forgetting to Mention Allende"**, it's generally offstage. . . .

Even in the longer stories very little happens, and most of that is random. In **"Home for a Couple of Days"** expatriate Eddie intends to visit his mother bearing gifts, but instead fritters his money away on vodkas for his unemployed mates and never gets there; in **"Half an Hour Before he Died"** an old man becomes finally incensed by the noise of the main road he's lived beside all his life without complaint.

There are other stories which make more than one nod in Beckett's direction—**"The One with the Dog"**, for instance, whose truculent narrator is determined to uphold codes of etiquette among his fellow dossers, or **"An Old Story"**, wherein the teller of the tale is too depressed by what happened to the depressed girl to tell it. But Kelman is both angrier and funnier than Beckett, and his intentions are more specific.

If plot is minimal, so is character development, but then this is hardly Jane Austen country and Kelman is less concerned with individual heroes and their epiphanies than with a mass of people just about getting by. Like his refusal of the narrator's privilege of standard English, this may be a democratic project, but to me it's also a slightly claustrophobic and self-denying one, for I can't help feeling that to do justice to working-class Scotland writers need all the privileges and freedoms they can get. After all, Kelman's contemporary Alasdair Gray, another technician of dialect, has used all manner of fantastic, surrealistic and English narrations to explore inner life in the Scottish inner city, and he's no class traitor, either.

But if I shy away from the nose-grinding reality of it all, maybe it's just the rural Scot in me whimpering for a bit of sky and distance, for the closest Kelman lets us get to nature is a sooty park with alkies, and a sudden spring bird singing:

'D d d dooie. D d d dooie. Wee fucking bird. Its wee fucking heart and soul.' Really though, you've got to hand it to him.

Alison Fell, "Sound of the City," in New Statesman, Vol. 113, No. 2925, April 17, 1987, p. 30.

MIKE MARQUSEE

James Kelman is thinking of adding a glossary to the forth-coming American edition of his new collection of short stories, *Greyhound for Breakfast.* Some Home Counties readers may also require assistance with Kelman's intimate explorations of Glasgow's giro culture, but the writer denies any interest in 'Scottish problems' as such. His concern, he says, is for all those 'whose first language is English but whose speech falls outside what the self-styled arbiters consider proper literary usage.' . . .

'Most people's daily lives are full of drama,' he says, explaining why he takes such care to avoid the contrived twists which are meat and drink to most short story writers. 'There doesn't need to be something abnormal or special. Going to the DHSS to claim a benefit is dramatic, even if nothing is resolved. Working in an industrial job where you have to be careful to avoid death every day is dramatic.'

Kelman's stories, like his novels *The Bus Conducter Hines* and *A Chancer,* are far more than kitchen sink slices of life. They take place in the language in which the characters speak and think, the language which makes up their universe. This is not simply a question of including the odd bit of exotic Glaswegian slang, or faithfully recording dialogue overheard in the pub. Kelman revises his stories constantly and admits it's often hard work finding 'ways to attack the material.' At its best, his carefully-controlled style, using only the ready-to-hand materials of Glaswegian speech, blends pity and wit to achieve an adroit poetry. No line is drawn between dialogue and third person narrative—because both are cut from the same cloth.

Experimental as they are, Kelman's stories are also highly accessible. The language gives life to bizarre anecdote, unexpected detail, and a deadpan sense of humour. Despite the absence of climaxes or sudden revelations, the stories are full of action. His people are almost but not quite at the end of their tethers. He cannily charts their restless agitation through a babble of aimless conversation, personal abuse, and idle fantasy.

Kelman keeps close tabs on the makeshift rituals of the new poverty. The wives in part-time work while the unemployed husbands pick up the kids from school, the punters lamenting the closure of yet another greyhound track, the young migrants living in six-to-a-room London hostels. . . . Kelman doesn't waste time telling us about their personal history or social environment. He is not a scene-painter. He is concerned with the mechanics of psychic survival. . . .

'I don't earn much money,' Kelman explains, 'so I'm involved in the culture I write about. Glasgow's less broken up than London. There's more mixing in pubs. It's harder to become divorced from people.'

Some of Kelman's stories are no more than page-long narrative spasms. In **"An Old Story"**, the speaker begins talking about a young woman 'going about in this depressed state for ages' but breaks off after a paragraph, apparently either dis-gusted or bored with the whole business. Those who say Kelman's stories are 'not really a story at all' and deride his 'perversely non-literary' approach are victims of their own prejudice. His work is fresh, honest, funny, and shouldn't be missed.

Mike Marqusee, "Giro Culture," in Books, London, No. 2, May, 1987, p. 6.

TIM DOOLEY

[In the story **"In with the Doctor,"** from James Kelman's collection *Greyhound for Breakfast,* an] unemployed man with a back complaint finds himself unexpectedly at the head of a queue in his doctor's surgery. Equally unexpectedly the doctor offers the patient a coffee and begins to confide in him.

> Aye, he says, this job, it's worse than you think. He grinned suddenly, he reached to plug in the kettle, then returned to the chair. I was reading that yin of Kafka's last night, "The Country Doctor"—you read it?
>
> Eh aye, I says.
>
> Gives me the fucking willies. . . .

The comic incongruity (which intensifies as the story . . . develops) draws attention to two potentially conflicting tendencies—proletarian realism and experimental modernism—which James Kelman's fiction more typically attempts to resolve. The world of Kelman's stories is particular and limited. . . . His Glasgow men on the "broo" or in dead-end jobs drink, smoke, gamble and neglect or sentimentalize their womenfolk and "weans".

Ronnie in the title story [**"Greyhound for Breakfast"**] is a typical Kelman character. He has spent "eighty notes" on a greyhound which he realizes he is incapable of feeding, let alone racing. Now he wanders by the side of the Clyde [River] ashamed to go home and admit his mistake, worried that his wife and daughters will be worrying about him and worried about his son who has just left for London:

> London for fuck sake, what could happen down there, things were bad down there, weans on the street, having to sell themselves to get by, the things that were happening down there, down in London, to young lassies and boys, it wasn't fucking fair, it was just fucking terrible, it was so fucking terrible you couldn't fucking man you fucking Jesus Christ trying to think about that was Christ it was so fucking terrible, it was bad.

The breakdown of language, the repeated obscenities are symptomatic of a communicative collapse which besets many figures in *Greyhound for Breakfast,* and implies a wider crisis about meaning, a deeper obscenity in society at large. Kelman resists the temptation to make emotional or political capital out of exploited and impoverished lives. His stories are often deliberately inconclusive—as if rejecting the notion that an existence has been captured and understood. Some are fragmentary, others extraordinarily short—a paragraph or so in length. . . . Kelman's commitment to local patterns of speech, however violent or vulgar, is shared with other Glasgow writers—notably Tom Leonard. Where he is most his own writer, however, Kelman convinces his readers that something does need to be told, that there is something new to learn about what a story might "really" be.

Tim Dooley, "Living in the Filth," in The Times
Literary Supplement, *No. 4388, May 8, 1987, p.
488.*

MICHIKO KAKUTANI

In [**"Greyhound for Breakfast"**], the title story of this erratic
collection by James Kelman, the Scottish writer, the hero
buys an expensive racing dog and gets to thinking about his
new greyhound's profession. "Imagine being as easy conned
as that!" he thinks. "Letting yourself get lulled into it, racing
round and round" just to catch a "bundle of rags." "It made
you feel sorry for it. Dogs and all the rest of the animals. And
people of course, they were no different—they seemed different but they weren't." "They just thought they were, it made
you smile. Because there they were, running round and
round," trying to catch "a crock of gold" that would always
elude them.

Liberally spiced with four-letter words (one of which is used,
in various forms, as an all-purpose verb, noun, adjective and
adverb throughout this volume), this story of Ronnie's day
with his new dog is really a stream-of-consciousness chronicle of his downward-spiraling spirits told—for some reason—
in the third person. Although Ronnie starts off feeling somewhat optimistic about his dog's chances of winning some
"holiday money," his cronies at the local pub make fun of his
plans, and as he prepares to go home to his wife and children,
he begins thinking about his teen-age son, who's run away to
London. The dog suddenly starts to seem like a pathetic distraction from his own more intractable problems, and Ronnie
actually contemplates throwing the animal in the river or
even doing himself in.

Most of the pieces in [*Greyhound for Breakfast*] share this
depressive outlook, this sense of being trapped by circumstance. Whether they're set in London or Manchester or, like
the majority, in Glasgow, whether they're told from the point
of view of an adult, an adolescent or a child, they delineate
lives circumscribed by poverty, class and lowered expectations. It's a world of pubs and betting shops, rented rooms
and small furnished flats, a world where people pass the time
playing poker, making bets and lingering over beers. Many
of the characters appear to be out of work, and nearly all are
perpetually "skint" and forced to cadge cigarettes and free
drinks from their pals. Meals, for the most part, consist of
eggs and chips; cold tinned meat and instant coffee or tea.

Like one fellow who's lost his way and is just "bashing on,
hoping for the best," Mr. Kelman's characters tend to be passive creatures, dully getting by day to day, allowing others to
shape their lives. The panhandler in **"The One With the Dog"**
likes to "wander about the place, just going here and there,"
waiting for someone to come along who will give him "a couple bob." The woman in **"A Sunday Evening"** sits in a room
not listening to the wireless, "her mind gone, abstracted miles
away—a voyage to unknown parts, only brought back to reality by the occasional sips from her mug of tea." . . .

In many instances, this passivity seems to lead to a fear of victimization—or paranoia in one story after another, a threatening stranger follows someone down a street or alley or sim
ply arrives unannounced in a room. Violence occasionally
erupts . . . but more often than not a vaguely Pinteresque
menace just hangs over the characters, nurturing anxiety and
suspicion.

Occasionally Mr. Kelman provides his people with a tiny
glimmer of hope, the possibility of expanding their attenuated
lives. In **"Renee"** the narrator lands "a position of some authority offering scope for advancement," and, his hopes
buoyed, he attempts to woo a girl he fancies. In **"The Wee
Boy That Got Killed,"** a 15-year-old boy who's desperate to
drop out of school pinches 38 pence from his father, successfully eludes an annoying friend and imagines for a moment
that freedom is within his grasp.

Such escape, however, is usually elusive, at least for the characters who remain in Scotland. Taken together, in fact, Mr.
Kelman's stories give us a picture of Glasgow as a city that
suffocates dreams, snuffs out ambition. To live there is to resign oneself to "the stench of poverty, violence, decay,
death," to accept the deadening consequences of premature
middle age. In certain respects, this portrait of a moribund
land recalls the one Joyce drew of Ireland in *Dubliners,* and
Mr. Kelman's idiomatic use of local argot similarly reminds
the reader of Joyce's (and Beckett's) experiments with language. To draw comparisons with Joyce and Beckett, as some
British critics have done, however, seems highly inappropriate.

While a couple of the longer stories in this collection—most
notably **"Old Francis" "The Wee Boy That Got Killed"** and
[**"Greyhound for Breakfast"**]—give the reader a firm sense
of a time and place and demonstrate a certain ear for dialect
and vernacular, they never really become more than closely
observed sketches of fairly generic characters. As for the volume's shorter pieces (some of which are only a paragraph
long), they read like the sort of shapeless fragments a writer
might jot down on a napkin or in a journal. These flimsy bits
have no place in this collection save as obvious filler; and
worse, they point up Mr. Kelman's decidedly limited image
bank—his inability to come up with more than half a dozen
situations. By the time most readers have finished this volume
they will never want to hear about another person bumming
a cigarette, placing a bet or drinking a beer. They will feel
nearly as suffocated as Mr. Kelman's characters do.

Michiko Kakutani, "Down and Out," in The New
York Times, *January 16, 1988, p. 16.*

WILLIAM GRIMES

The 47 stories in *Greyhound for Breakfast* vary in length
from the eight lines of **"Leader From a Quality Newspaper"**
to the 24 pages of [**"Greyhound for Breakfast"**]. Almost all
of them, though, reflect James Kelman's devotion to both the
working-class speech of Glasgow and that peculiar area of the
brain where language roams free, where odd little turns of
phrase and the mere sound of words trigger intense mental
activity. . . .

Kelman's solipsistic art reveals a Glasgow of pinched circumstances and no hope. Its residents spend most of their time
talking to themselves, ruminating over nothing in particular,
strategically avoiding the deeper thought that would lead to
despair. Occasionally the women hold down pathetic part-
time jobs. The men work out little systems for stretching the
cigarette supply—thank God for the 10-pack, since no one
can afford the luxury of 20—and making ends meet until the
next government check. Mostly this is a matter of killing
time. There is much pre-noon drinking. Gallons of tea are
consumed. Better not even to mention diet on the dole.

The cigarette, basic unit of social exchange, seems far more satisfying, somehow, than food; if a "cunt" (i.e., bloke) can't give solace, he can at least offer a smoke. Hence the outrage of the penniless narrator in **"Samaritans"** when he helps an undeserving stranger.

> And out comes this gold lighter man and he flicks it and that and the flame, straight away, no bother. Puffs out the smoke. I'm waiting for the bank to open at half one, he says, I've got a checque to cash.

> Good, I says, but I'm thinking well fuck you as well, that's my last fag man I mean jesus christ almighty.

Kelman writes "bastard high style," in the phrase of one London reviewer. [See Francis Spufford's excerpt above]. He takes the humble material of common speech, half-conscious thought, and dull routine, fashions it into a brown-bag paper airplane, and, with a flick of the wrist, sends it flying. His prose, insistently aural, begs to be read aloud (take in a Bill Forsyth film to get the accent). In **"Samaritans,"** a half-pager, the payoff is the perfectly placed "jesus christ almighty." The Kelman eye is no less acute. In **"A Rolling Machine,"** the clincher is a worker's look of "astonished embarrassment" when he notices that the tip of his thumb has just been snipped off, "while the machine continued the rolling operation and out of the fleshy mess spiralled a hair-thin substance like thread being unrolled from a bobbin somewhere inside the palm."

The short short stories come in like a stray radio signal, clear and eerie for an instant, then gone. For the most part, we get a scrap of conversation, a bit of obsessive musing, a strange sight or dreamlike image. The longer stories, too, rely on the surrealism of the commonplace, the weird resonance of objects and gestures rendered with pinpoint precision. Antidramatic, they tend to pick up in the middle with little or no explanation and trail off inconclusively.

In **"Old Francis,"** a down-and-outer on a park bench finds himself surrounded by three drunkards, who alternately menace and banter with him. It's a tense, unsettling story, seen through the panic-sharpened eyes of Old Francis, whose thoughts circle around Augustine, good and evil, and a nearby bird, while he tries to jolly along his persecutors. Kelman pulls the plug on the narrative just as it seems to be approaching a violent resolution, so the old fellow is left sitting there, hands on knees, his knuckles white with terror. . . .

The stories in *Greyhound for Breakfast* were written over the last 16 years. During that time, Kelman has published three short story collections, contributed to two more, and written two novels. Only now is he being published in this country. Memo to [Kelman's publisher]: Please, sir, can we have some more?

> *William Grimes, in a review of "Greyhound for Breakfast," in VLS, No. 62, February, 1988, p. 3.*

ARNOLD WEINSTEIN

The Irish of the past 50 years have honed the short story into a national literary pastime. Now here's James Kelman, street virtuoso, out of Glasgow, where he was born in 1946. His books and his play about outsiders and inner cities are sheer art and wild wit. He's rightly been dubbed the crown prince of the Scottish avant-garde by its leader, the novelist, playwright and painter Alasdair Gray.

In *Greyhound for Breakfast,* a collection of 47 stories and prose poems, Mr. Kelman's tenements and boarding houses are prison camps, their derelict inmates are losers of the battle for existence. **"The Guy With the Crutch"** is a bag person who misplaces his artificial limb and hobbles in a "quite quick swinging motion" on a broken crutch, his last sliver of dignity.

He mixes and matches abstract slapsticks (**"Renee"**) and murderous farces (**"End of a Beginning"**), man versus mouse (**"A Hunter"**) and machine eats hand (**"A Rolling Machine"**). . . .

The mini-novel of the title, [**"Greyhound for Breakfast"**] is a fearsome piece of loneliness; **"Even in Communal Pitches"** is a wrenching one-reel comic masterpiece set in a seamy intelligentsia; **"Cute Chick!"** is what the "old lady with a polite English accent who roamed the betting shops of Glasgow being avoided by everybody" calls herself.

Mr. Kelman's eloquent thuggery can be dangerous. But obscenities are defanged by obsessive frequency; the poverty of vocabulary is an economic analogy. His street people drag his prose through the Glaswegian slums and he, and we, love it. His imagery may seem equally impoverished, featuring so many cigarettes, ashes, ashtrays, inhaling and exhaling that handling these pages could result in a severe case of yellow finger; but cigarettes here stand for smoldering.

His half-page prose poems echo like lost tragifarcical chords. They also echo Kafka, Beckett and somehow John Ashbery ("In the ensuing scramble the body will melt into undeciphered tremors"). But Mr. Kelman's originality assimilates all into his own hilarious genius for detail, his casual social subtext, his unique refreshing burr that echos the shivering slums, his and ours.

> *Arnold Weinstein, "Wee Prisons." in The New York Times Book Review, March 20, 1988, p. 19.*

PETER LEWIS

[The] Glaswegian writer James Kelman is more comfortable in short rather than long fiction, and in his case 'short' can mean 'miniscule'. Kelman has emerged in the 1980s as the Scottish chronicler *par excellence* of the other side of Thatcherite Britain, the waste land of inner-city dereliction, soul-numbing boredom and violence, and lives lived without hope. To convey his particular vision he has developed a hard-edged, laconic style rooted in the speech of his frequently unemployed lower-class Glaswegians. In a novel as long as his most recent one, *A Chancer,* the limitations of Kelman's ultra-realistic idiom become obvious after a time, despite the vividness with which he evokes the life style of his central character, Tammas, an inveterate gambler at the age of twenty, and the changes he rings by using an episodic structure with abrupt transitions. What makes his new collection of stories, *Greyhound for Breakfast,* a more exciting book is the sheer variety of its technical resources, even though the preoccupation with gambling, drinking and petty crime is much the same. One story is laid out like a concrete poem, another is virtually without punctuation, another is printed entirely in upper-case type. . . . [The] very short stories either hit or miss, and the longer ones, too, are distinctly uneven, but in a collection of forty-seven stories there are a significant number of successes: from the tiny **"Cute Chick!"** to somewhat fuller ones, such as **"The Red Cockatoos"**, to long ironic pieces including **"The Band of Hope"** and the title story itself [**"Greyhound for Breakfast"**]. No one could accuse Kelman of being an aesthete, but he is much more interested in the formal possibilities of short fiction than the widespread view of him as a social realist with a strong polemical streak gives him credit for.

Kelman's fictional world is predominantly, even obsessively, masculine: women exist mainly on its fringes and rarely feature in the consciousnesses of his characters, even as sex objects. (pp. 41-2)

Peter Lewis, "Recovering the Past, Uncovering the Present," in Stand Magazine, *Vol. 29, No. 2, Spring, 1988, pp. 34-42.*

NICHOLAS JENKINS

James Kelman is an exceptionally raw and, in his own way, ambitious writer. His stories move carefully and obsessively through demoralized Scottish lives, yet for all his narrow focus and use of jagged regional idioms, he is a prose stylist with international literary affiliations. Naturally, then, English reviewers have already gone down on their knees in front of *Greyhound for Breakfast.* And well they might.

The Scots in this collection are tired, aggravated and, for the most part, without cash. They circle, self-absorbed and powerless, in the crumbling inner city labyrinths of a derelict economy. In Kelman's vision, a daily round of frustrating, dulling trivia structures existence, as though in the wake of great national reversals, there can be facts but no events of any consequence. This helpless suffering is extended to an extreme in [**"Greyhound for Breakfast"**] where Ronnie, after contemplating suicide, decides instead to go home to his wife: "he would just tell Babs something or other . . . what did it matter, it didn't . . . matter."

Greyhound for Breakfast is most impressive taken as a whole, rather than line-by-line or even item-by-item. Many of the "stories" here are actually just sketches or jottings, but in a world where life itself is seen as so chronically inconclusive, some narratives are allowed to remain stunted or unresolved. "When she stopped outside the post office he paused. In she went. But just as you were thinking, Aw aye, there he goes. . . . Naw; he didn't, he just walked on." Out of such randomness, though, the sequence builds to a powerfully sustained description of modern urban life.

The representation of the dispossessed in fiction has always raised issues of class, language and artistic control. These problems, especially for a realist writer like Kelman, center on the difficulty of creating a voice for the inarticulate which is neither loosely comic on the one hand nor implausible or inexpressive on the other. His solution is a spare, harsh, colloquial style that never allows much distance to open between the speech and thoughts of a character and a story's narrative tone. It is a technique derived, however muzzily, from Flaubert and Kafka. The character is freed from an ironic authorial shadow, and the author is restricted by the limits of his character's mind.

How far, though, can such unflinching "realism" take Kelman? The occasional wild slashes of humor and grotesquerie

suggest a less restrained writer is lurking inside him. A few extended stories in this collection—like **"The Band of Hope"** and **"The Wee Boy That Got Killed"**—demonstrate a gift for delineation of the subtly altering balance in a situation. Kelman needs to develop people with more autonomy and "character" if his work is to deepen, and that process will probably involve some distancing from the world he has so faithfully presented here.

Nicholas Jenkins, "Scotland's Burning, Look Yonder," in Los Angeles Times Book Review, *April 10, 1988, p. 11.*

BRIAN MORTON

Describing Patrick Doyle as disaffected [in James Kelman's novel *A Disaffection*] is rather like saying that Young Werther was a bit morose latterly. Given a clear Saturday afternoon choice between Clyde v Raith Rovers and suicide, Pat takes a suspiciously long time to make up his mind. (And still gets it wrong; this is Kelman's one serious lapse of verisimilitude.)

There is a prevailing myth in Scottish literature that, just as the Highlands are peopled by immensely tall men in immaculate dress kilts, so the pubs of Glasgow are full of bauchly wee men with no teeth who read Kierkegaard and get into razor fights over the logical derelictions of the Ontological Proof. Only novelists ever meet these people.

Kelman has largely solved the problem by making Doyle a schoolteacher. The kids of 4B are largely unimpressed by references to Goethe, but they do like the fact that he says "fuck" a lot. (By my reckoning, Doyle—or Kelman—is on for some sort of all-comers swearie record.) It serves him, as it serves other stultified lives and minds, both as mental punctuation and as a way of insulating thoughts too painful or too tender to be exposed. *A Disaffection* borders on dysfunction, an inability to make decisions or connections between decisions and acts; between the two there always falls the shadow of rusty blades and high places, or the shorter oblivion of drink.

This is Kelman's most ambitious and sophisticated fiction to date. . . . [It's] important to recognise that it is also ironic and deeply humane. Reviewers of *The Busconductor Hines,* Kelman's first novel, instantly dived for the very useful *Oxford Book of Glasgow Stereotypes:* "grim", "bleak", "harsh", "hopeless", and thereby missed totally its comic edge and a warmth that bordered on sentimentality.

Doyle's expectations are simply greater than Hines's and therefore his disaffection is deeper and more representative. . . . Where Hines dreams of a driver's ticket, Pat dreams of turning his quotidian frustration into something like the inspired madness of [Friedrich] Hölderlin or even Werther; worse than a hopeless romantic, he's very nearly a hopeful one, shuffling his way toward some sort of declaration to Alison, a married fellow-teacher; he imagines coaxing music from discarded pipes he finds round the back of a local arts centre (alternative staff-room), takes home and paints exotically. (This is as close as Kelman comes to overt symbolism and it's uneasily done.) Just as the fractured interior monologue falls some way short of Hamlet and Mrs Dalloway, so the pipes produce gaseous parps that won't cause Charlie Parker any restless nights in heaven.

There is an apologetic critical shorthand for this kind of fiction—Céline, Beckett, Burroughs, Selby—that points to a measure of harshness, or at least diminished hope, a hint of scatology, but also a surface tension that resists the usual lit. crit. penetrations. If any one comparison holds water, it is with Hubert Selby Jr, most particularly *The Room,* which has the same blindly imploded rhetoric, the same sense of expectation thrown back by the boundaries of the text, the same painful reminders that we're all, somehow, characters in someone else's plot, reading poor scripts in borrowed dialects. (pp. 38-9)

Brian Morton, *"Greater Expectations,"* in New Statesman & Society, *Vol. 2, No. 37, February 17, 1989, pp. 38-9.*

GERALD MANGAN

"Patrick Doyle was a teacher. Gradually he had become sickened by it." The hero of James Kelman's third novel [*A Disaffection*], which opens with characteristic directness, is an unmarried twenty-nine-year-old Glaswegian who recalls so many features of the young unemployed misfit in his early collection of stories, *Not not while the giro* (1983), that we may regard Patrick Doyle as an essential Kelman character. The poverty that bedevilled the earlier hero has been dispelled by a salary, and Patrick's status as a professional with an MA has hoisted him one rung upward from a working-class background, but he is still recognizably the same restless and sardonic day-dreamer. A car and a credit card have done little to alleviate the frustration and existential discomfort of the earlier story; and *A Disaffection* can be read as a fuller orchestration of its solipsistic lament.

It recounts a week in Patrick's life, with the weekend in the middle. Few of its events would seem extraordinary to the colleagues, pupils and family who populate his humdrum world; but the internal monologue that dominates the book, in the Glasgow speech-rhythms which Kelman has long since perfected, describes the trajectory of a nervous crisis that hovers on the brink of breakdown. Deracination, self-repression, chronic boredom and paranoia are among the many sources and symptoms of his "disaffection"; and it is not mitigated by his job in an institution which he regards as the instrument of a repressive state. His candour on this subject makes him popular with his pupils, and occasions some of Kelman's most acerbic social satire; but Patrick is aware of an unhealthy dependence on his classroom audience. The chilly silence of his tenement flat, where inanimate objects conspire against him and the fish-supper remains his staple diet, is all too expressive of the emotional void he inhabits.

His astute self-analyses, which scrutinize the intimate relations between physical and moral unease, diagnose an acute case of sexual starvation. He is painfully aware of his lack of significant experience in this respect, and his craving has become so abject that he hankers for protective embraces more than for penetration. A major source of optimism and suspense is his tentative pursuit of Alison, an attractive fellow-teacher who is clearly not very happy in her marriage; but her responses are often as ambiguous as his own advances. His egocentricity appears to blind him to the aura of desperation he exudes, to the detriment of his erotic chances. Much of the novel's funniest pathos derives from the immaturity and fecklessness he displays in an elaborate affair of snakes-and-ladders, more mental than actual, which leads him gradually to a poignant hand-contact with Alison in a lounge-bar.

The unlovely urban background, which Kelman renders with the sharpness of broken glass, demands to be escaped from. Patrick finds solace on the football terraces, and dreams of Spanish exile in the course of frequent baths; but he disdains regret for juvenile ambitions, and an impulsive night-drive towards England proves abortive. His deepest comfort throughout the novel is an eccentric recreation that involves blowing a range of notes from a pair of discarded electrical pipes, picked up in a back-alley on the first page and adopted. . . .

His reliance on this creative release occasions much inner debate, and its value only narrowly survives a private performance for the non-committal Alison; but it reflects the extent of his hunger for harmony in a life of jangling discords. As "a good protestant atheist" he is reluctant to admit any mystical dimension in this, but it is the one act which begins to transcend his sterile "conceptualising". In a moving scene towards the end, where Patrick relates his discovery as a magical fairy-tale for his brother's young children, we recognize it as part of a larger longing for an innocence beyond experience.

Patrick's strong sympathy with Hölderlin adumbrates this theme, which gives a further resonance to Kelman's portrait of this latter-day Werther. The full effect of these early-Romantic echoes depends on the uncanny realism of his modern purgatory, and the self-effacing authenticity of his narrative voice; and the fusion of these elements makes *A Disaffection* the most complex of his novels so far. But the hero's ultimate failure to overcome his limitations by consummating a personal relationship in any sense does entail a drastic restriction of the novel's emotional scope. It is hard not to observe that Patrick is equally confined by an overlong fictional tradition, in which victims of Scottish society remain arrested in a pre-marital condition. It may be time for Kelman to direct his formidable capacities beyond this subject, and break new ground.

Gerald Mangan, *"Coming Down with an Acute Case,"* in The Times Literary Supplement, *No. 4482, February 24-March 2, 1989, p. 191.*

KARL MILLER

Studying the West Coast of Scotland from the yacht *Britannia,* the Queen is said to have remarked, not long ago, that the people there didn't seem to have much of a life. James Kelman's stories make clear what life is like in Glasgow, and what James Kelman's life is like. They are not going to change the royal mind. This is the queen who was greeted, on a visit to a Scottish university, by the sight of a student emptying down his throat, at top speed, the contents of a bottle of alcohol.

One of Kelman's stories, **"Greyhound for Breakfast"**, the last in the collection of that name which appeared in 1987, is, to my mind, a masterpiece. It's about a fellow called Ronnie who dumps down the notes for a greyhound, and, to the derision of his friends in the pub, gives his heart to it. He takes it for walks—a ritual activity, time out of mind, of the country's more optimistic male poor, the dog more expensively jacketed than the chap. 'It stopped for a piss. Ronnie could have done with one himself but he would have got arrested.'

The discovery is made that its withers will never win the prizes Ronnie is hoping for, and the story ends with a long defeated, dark-thoughted walk, from which he is reluctant to return to his wife and children. The story is wonderfully funny and depressing; the stroller's speech and soliloquy are perfectly gauged. Ronnie, I think, could be held to be a precursor of P for Patrick Doyle in the new novel, *A Disaffection.* Both works end on a possible return, on what might look like a bleak diminuendo but is really an anxiety state.

There are important differences, though. Kelman stands much closer to the new hero, and much more of the story happens in that hero's head. The new book is funny and depressing at considerable length, and there are moments when a wee terror comes of its expanded universe. *A Disaffection* is a problematical book—partly because of this closeness, the avoidance of developed perspectives on Doyle from those who surround him, those with whom he has his tender and abrasive dealings, with whom he airs his invectives and bitter ironies, with whom he conducts his antagonisms and ingratiations. But for all that, I feel that the book is pretty terrific, both truly challenging and nearly always very diverting.

Doyle—'Patrick' to his author—is of the bittersweet, fantastic-depressive Scots-Irish clan. He is a schoolteacher, 29 years old—the age of Christ at Calvary, whose name is often in his mouth, averse though he is to 'deities', and of Hamlet, whose words enter the novel. Doyle's greyhound is a pair of electricians' cardboard pipes, which he lights upon, paints and plays, producing a doleful sound that soothes him—it is like mumbling your mantra or telling your beads. He badly needs soothing. He has passed into crisis. He is lonely. His aged parents bore him ('Are all parents boring?'). His brother Gavin frets him, and he has a longing for Gavin's wife, together with a more urgent one for a teacher at the school, Alison Houston, who could be felt to lead him on a bit but doesn't want to have a 'relationship' with him. . . .

In such a setting his work as a teacher, to which he can often seem devoted, can only be betrayed. His work as a teacher doesn't involve much in the way of teaching. Homework is a thing of the past. His classes are soliloquies and Socratic teases in which his interest in Classical Antiquity, in Pythagoras and Heraclitus, and in Hölderlin, Hegel and Marx, and in James Hogg, is imparted to the young ones. He is the sort of Sixties dominie who keeps saying 'fuck' in class and inveighing against the system. His relationship with the kids is one between equals, but they also seem to expect him to be a wise man, and this is what he sometimes expects of himself. The kids are presented as decent and thoughtful, and there's an Arcadian absence of the stress and violence which some might look for in a class where the teacher free-associates and says 'fuck', and throws up and bunks off into the bargain. If the Queen's telescope were ever to reach into Patrick's classroom, there would be a surprise in store for her—but not for Patrick, who at least affects to believe the story that Orwellian minders are peering at the punters from the screens of the punters' television sets.

Kelman makes Doyle charming, and it is impossible to read the book without gaining the sense of a fully-developed authorial fellow-feeling. Not that Doyle isn't taxing and maddening too. His consciousness delivers paranoid images of aggression and hostility. He is against racism and sexism, but is capable of reflecting: 'He was in love with Alison Houston. And he wanted to grab a hold of her.' His crisis is precipitated by word of his transfer to another school; he staggers towards resigning from the school he's at, and maybe from the profession, and then bunks off for a long afternoon's superlager, home-brew and whisky with his brother, who is on the dole, and two of his brother's mates. Eventually, stone-cold-sober-seeming but perhaps too drunk to drive, he treks off through the dubs of a drizzle . . . back to his bachelor's tenement flat. . . . On the way, he is chased, or fancies he is chased, by Police who hate him. Kelman projects Doyle's state of mind virtually without framing or critique. The Queen will certainly need a glossary, but even then she may well be uncertain as to just how much Kelman likes his unlikely lad.

This kind of thing has been said about Hamlet, to whom, as I say, Kelman alludes. At one point, 'all he sought was death,' and the next paragraph has him aching to be 'out the road of trouble and strife and all things rotten and putrefied and shitey'. Later he reproves himself for an impulse to be rude to a 'good auld guy' encountered during his terminal search for a bus, and we think of the prating 'good old man' Polonius. And on the facing page, debating whether or not to go back to his brother's place, he utters some more of Shakespeare's words: 'To return to Gavin's or not. Whether it is nobler.' Whether or not he is sober enough to go back and fetch his fucking car. Hamlet kills his good old guy, makes mistakes and causes havoc, in pursuit of the right course. So does Doyle.

A high point in the novel is an altercation and huff with Gavin and his mates about the long holidays teachers get, or don't get, about the homework they withhold, and about the rights of weans—children—and the rights of parents.

> Patrick said: Do you know what I tell parents Arthur? I tell them to go and fuck themselves. Patrick held both hands up in a gesture of peace, he smiled for a moment; I'm no trying to get at you personally but I just fucking feel that you cant expect the teacher to be the everything, the heavyweight boxing champion of the world.
>
> Arthur stared at him.
>
> Know what I mean, I'm just being honest with ye. I dont think ye should expect the teacher to do everything. If you want your weans to get homework then give it to them your fucking self.
>
> Gavin said: That actually sounds quite right-wing ye know.
>
> Well it's meant to be the fucking opposite and it is the fucking opposite.
>
> Gavin nodded.

Then:

> Gavin gazed at him, then laughed briefly. He looked at Pat but Pat looked away. Nor was Pat going to say anything further because he was fucking off home as soon as he swallowed what he had lying. There was no point sitting here yapping to a bunch of fucking prejudiced right-wing bastards. And Gavin turned on him once more: What d'you mean ye deny ye get long holidays?
>
> I deny I get long holidays, that's what I mean.
>
> Back it up.
>
> What d'you mean back it up?
>
> Show me what you're talking about?

Naw. You show me what you're talking about.

I think I know what Paddy means, said Davie.

Good, tell me, replied Gavin.

I think I know what you mean Paddy.

Pat nodded.

Ye dont think ye get long holidays because when you're off from the school you're still doing other things connected with it, making up timetables and all that.

Patrick nodded.

By the end of it you're no all that sure whether teachers get long holidays or no (they do, though most of them have to work hard for it), and whether parents should go and fuck themselves. Soon after this we learn that Doyle believes he has sold his rights by serving the system as a teacher for 'a large wheen of pennies': 'He was an article that was corrupt . . . corruptio optimi pessima . . . ' This, as he recognises, is a form of self-praise. Throughout, Patrick is both the 'King of the World' that he wants to be—Glasgow belongs to *him*—and an abject sinner.

The rage of the novel's males would be enough to put the wind up Margaret Thatcher if it weren't so often the rage of those who believe themselves permanently beaten and cheated. The women are the vessels of a better spirit; the injury to them is greater, and it is from their own men that some of that injury has been sustained. Patrick rages and scorns in proportion to his frustration: Hamlet's 'weakness' has its counterpart here. 'Patrick couldni find a pen. It is most odd indeed how objects disappear in rooms wherein the only moveable entity is oneself.' (He slides into English here for a laugh.) Objects disappear, and for a man of 29 he seems to have grabbed hold of very little of anything except a glass and a book. Drink figures in the novel, in precisely rendered scenes, as a bastion of the culture which is also a slow death. And yet this man is very far from useless. What we are reading is the Book of Patrick Doyle. Whether or not it can be seen as Kelman's self-portrait, it is the portrait of an artist.

Karl Miller, "Shite," in London Review of Books, *Vol. 11, No. 5, March 3, 1989, p. 13.*

DOUGLAS DUNN

Disaffected characters pose the same problems as bored heroes. Dwelling on them at length can damage the reader's goodwill. James Kelman disregards the customary, old-fashioned restraints in his approach to this crude literary problem. A sense of humour saves [*A Disaffection*], but otherwise he certainly does risk the overexposure of Patrick Doyle, his disaffected Glasgow secondary schoolteacher. It is, I think, intentional. He wants us to know about Doyle and what he represents. To make this unavoidable Kelman writes in an alloy of external narrative and interior monologue, with the consequence that Doyle is insistently present on every page of a long-ish book.

Doyle is nearing 30. He thinks of his imposed pedagogic role as that of an educational constable whose function in the classroom is to suppress and misinform children on behalf of 'the Greatbritish Rulers'. As his sister-in-law says towards the end of the book, he is 'bitter, awful bitter'. Rancour has

boxed him into a corner where he can no longer tell what to do. Manic perseverance, rancid irresolution and an agitated loneliness dog his days, intellectually, professionally and in his highly unsatisfactory private life. . . .

Readers of Kelman's previous novels and stories will be familiar with his 'bad language'. It could be a disaffection of his own. All these expletives and epithets of f— seem part of what the book evokes as a 'male nightmare'. To a West of Scotland ear, however it can still sound as much like playing at wee toilets as a tactic for serving authenticity. But some sort of double ventriloquism is at work. Kelman's narrative style imitates the same idiom as his dialogue, which dispenses with any need for 'sympathy' in his point of view. It also identifies a literary self as a participant in the same life as his place and characters. He has founded a style of writing prose fiction on what, when seen against 'standard' English, looks worryingly close to perverse illiteracy. Anxiety caused by that closeness is exactly the destabilising effect on which his writing thrives. Doyle's ability to refer to ancient philosophy, or to Goya and Hölderlin, therefore looks laughably out of place—but that is only because you expect Hölderlin to be mentioned in a different idiom. Malapropisms, misspellings and wordy inventions are mixed into Kelman's up-tempo, syntactically confused or 'natural' speech and its wayward punctuation. He creates a verbal photography that looks for the status of a deviant language with which to identify a neglected citizenry and prove that they exist.

Particularly in a long, subtle evocation of an afternoon drinking session, or Doyle's long walk in the rain through the busless, taxi-less streets of outer Glasgow, Kelman succeeds brilliantly in showing at least part of a society crushed by its own inhibitions. It is connivance in that continuing unhappiness that Doyle rebels against, without knowing how to break free of 'a life of revolutionary compromise'.

Douglas Dunn, "Awful Bitter," in The Listener, *Vol. 121, No. 3104, March 9, 1989, p. 31.*

MARTIN KIRBY

We are in familiar psycholiterary country in [*A Disaffection*]. . . . [Patrick Doyle], a 29-year-old, risen-working-class Scot, has literary antecedents going back at least to Benjamin Constant's *Adolphe,* and ranging through Dostoyevsky's *Notes From the Underground,* on to the works of Kafka, Sartre and Camus, and into the mad proliferation of blossoms on the same branch that we see sprouting all around us today.

But James Kelman's apparently realistic portrayal of contemporary Glasgow gives the book an extra weight of novelty for the non-Scottish reader. The novel's other virtues include a skilled adaptation of Celtic torrent-of-words vernacular speech to narrative ends, somewhat in the manner of Sean O'Casey, and a carefully controlled seriocomic tone that holds interest without descending into mush, though, it must be said, without rising to very much dramatic excitement, either.

Mr. Kelman traces several days in Patrick's life mostly by means of a third-person interior monologue, the effect of which is to saturate the reader with knowledge of Patrick's character. We find that he is searching for beauty, meaning, truth and love while living in a dismal, poverty-stricken neighborhood and struggling with the handicaps of a highly self-critical personality and a not small load of class guilt.

The class-guilt motif is crucial. Patrick, a bachelor, is securely employed in a white-collar job, whereas his father is "a machinesetter in a factory" and his older brother, Gavin, married with two children, is a perpetually unemployed construction worker. Because he has gone to "uni," presumably Glasgow University, Patrick makes more than twice as much as his brother, even when Gavin is able to work. He feels guilty. He accuses himself of being "the tool of a dictatorship government. A fellow who receives a greater than average wage for the business of fencing in the children of the suppressed poor."

At the same time, he loves teaching. In the classroom he plays the fierce radical: "Now then, I want you all to repeat after me: The present government, in suppressing the poor, is suppressing our parents."

Patrick Doyle is a blocked intellectual, unable to make creative use of his knowledge. Much of his interior nattering consists of juggling bits of semi-digested information about thinkers and artists of the past that float around in his mind like alien substances injected into a laboratory animal. . . .

He drifts around Glasgow, worrying. He drinks in working-class taverns. He conducts a Prufrockian internal debate about whether to give up fried foods. He dares to miss an appointment with his headmaster, who he wrongly thinks is going to reprimand him. He snaps at his brother when the latter innocently makes a racist remark.

There are intimations that Patrick's life may be turning some ill-defined corner, symbolized by a pair of cardboard tubes that he finds by chance and calls "pipes." By carefully blowing on them, he discovers he can make musical sounds, and they come to dominate his inner life almost as much as his class guilt does. Somehow they are going to purify his soul, like a Hemingway hero's trout-fishing, a connection Mr. Kelman emphasizes with a bit of Hemingway parody: "He blew a sound, deep, long; a good sound. . . . He did another one and extended it. These sounds were good sounds. He was pleased with them."

Will Patrick chuck teaching in a desperate grab for class solidarity? Will he flee to Spain? Will he become a virtuoso cardboard-pipe player? Or will he kill himself? He broods on all these possibilities. Probably he will just go on drinking, worrying and teaching. At any rate, I am glad to have read this gently satiric novel.

Martin Kirby, "A Prufrock in Glasgow," in The New York Times Book Review, *June 18, 1989, p. 14.*

Maxine Hong Kingston

1940-

(Born Maxine Ting Ting Hong) American autobiographer, novelist, journalist, and short story writer.

A highly acclaimed memoirist, Kingston integrates autobiographical elements with Asian legend and fictionalized history to delineate cultural conflicts confronting Americans of Chinese descent. Frequently studied in a variety of academic disciplines, her works bridge two civilizations in their examination of social and familial bonds from ancient China to contemporary California. As an American-born daughter of stern immigrant parents, Kingston relates the anxiety that often results from clashes between radically different cultural sensibilities. Her exotic, myth-laden narratives are informed by several sources: the ordeals of emigrant forebears who endured brutal exploitation as they labored on American railroads and cane plantations; the "talk-stories," or cautionary tales of ancient heroes and family secrets told by her mother; and her own experiences as a first-generation American with confused cultural allegiances. From these foundations, Kingston forms epic chronicles of the Chinese immigrant experience that are esteemed for their accurate and disturbing illumination of such social patterns as Asian cultural misogyny and American institutional racism.

Winner of the National Book Critics Circle Award for general nonfiction, Kingston's first autobiographical volume, *The Woman Warrior: Memoirs of a Girlhood among Ghosts* (1976), is a personal, unconventional work that seeks to reconcile Eastern and Western conceptions of female identity. Kingston eschews chronological plot and standard nonfiction techniques in her memoir, synthesizing ancient myth and imaginative biography to present a kaleidoscopic vision of female character. The narrative begins with Kingston's mother's brief caveat concerning No Name Woman, young Maxine's paternal aunt, whose disrepute has rendered her unmentionable. Left in their village by her emigré husband, No Name Woman became pregnant—perhaps by rape—and was forced by the villagers to drown herself and her baby. Affirming traditional attitudes, Maxine's mother, Brave Orchid, describes such practices as foot-binding and the sale of girls as slaves, and she threatens Maxine with servitude and an arranged marriage to a retarded neighborhood boy. Subsequent chapters, however, provide sharp contrast to these bleak visions, for Brave Orchid also recites the colorful legend of Fa Mu Lan, the woman who wielded a sword to defend her hamlet. Kingston then describes Brave Orchid's own incongruent character; independent enough to become one of rural China's few female doctors, she returned to her customary submissive role upon joining her husband in America. Critics lauded Kingston's fanciful description and poetic diction, through which she imparts her fear and wonder of Chinese legacies. Jane Kramer remarked: "[*The Woman Warrior*] shocks us out of our facile rhetoric, past the clichés of our obtuseness, back to the mystery of a stubbornly, utterly foreign sensibility . . . Its sources are dream and memory, myth and desire. Its crises are crises of a heart in exile from roots that terrorize and bind it."

Kingston applies similar techniques to the plight of the immigrant male in *China Men* (1980), which won a National Book Critics Circle Award and an American Book Award. While her first autobiographical volume represents a daughter's endeavor to comprehend her mother's alien character, *China Men* constitutes her attempt to delineate her relationship with her silent, angry father. In China, her father was a handsome, gifted school teacher who longed for the "Gold Mountain," a fanciful appellation for gold-rush California. After settling in Stockton's Chinatown, however, he was reduced to unemployment, poverty, and depression. Kingston complements this narrative with imaginative, epic biographies of earlier male forebears—laborers in Hawaii and California who, despite strictly enforced anti-Chinese immigration laws and legalized abuse by their overseers, endured to establish family citizenship before returning to China. Concluding her history with an account of her younger brother's experience in the United States Navy in Vietnam, Kingston presents a multi-generational struggle to integrate cultural inheritance. Critics commented that Kingston's detailed technique elegantly blends the factual and the fantastic to create a magical, incisive depiction of Chinese-American identity. Mary Gordon observed: "*China Men* is a triumph of the highest order, of imagination, of language, of moral perception."

Kingston analyzes contemporary social and artistic values in her first novel, *Tripmaster Monkey: His Fake Book* (1989), a portrait of a fifth generation Chinese-American Berkeley graduate whose picaresque adventures as a dramatist in California's 1960s counterculture reflect Kingston's own experience. Wittman Ah Sing, one year out of college and puzzled about his future, imagines himself an incarnation of the legendary Monkey King, a trickster hero who brought Buddha's teachings to China. Roaming San Francisco, Ah Sing creates turmoil with his boundless energy; he reads poetry aloud on buses, marries on a whim, and convinces everyone he knows to perform in his improvisational play, which critics praise. Named for American poet Walt Whitman, Kingston's protagonist investigates his nebulous Chinese heritage, which has faded over the generations, while he rages against white Americans who regularly ask him if he speaks English. While some reviewers commented that Wittman's invectives were occasionally verbose and lacked the fevered eloquence of Kingston's earlier works, most lauded the book's dynamic pace and psychological depth. Herbert Gold concluded: "[Kingston] invigorates her novel with an avid personal perspective, doing what the novel is supposed to do—she brings us the news of the world and makes magic of it."

(See also *CLC*, Vols. 12, 19; *Contemporary Authors*, Vols. 69-72; *Contemporary Authors New Revision Series*, Vol. 13; *Something about the Author*, Vol. 53; and *Dictionary of Literary Biography Yearbook: 1980*.)

LINDA CHING SLEDGE

Maxine Hong Kingston has been widely praised by American critics for her two visionary biographical accounts of Asian-American life, **Woman Warrior** and **China Men.** Nevertheless, her reputation among some Chinese-American writers is still debated. The most serious allegation made by Kingston's detractors is that she does not paint an accurate portrait of ethnic culture and society. However, due to the currently undeveloped state of Asian-American literary criticism, this sweeping charge has yet to be fully supported by conventional historical methods of inquiry, by systematic literary theory, or by substantive analyses of Kingston's own writings. It already seems apparent that for sheer literary talent, originality of style, and comprehensiveness of vision, Kingston is a major American writer and the most formidable Asian-American writer in this nation's history. What is at issue is in part the question of genre. Are her works histories or novels? If they are histories, how realistic and verifiable is her evidence? If they are novels, why do they substitute separate, generally unconnected personal and family experiences for the contrivances of an "internal fiction" or "plot"? In some respects, **China Men** is so close to the "facts" of history that it can serve as a casebook for the evolution of Chinese-American family life over the last century; in other respects, it is wildly inventive and poetic.

Yet if it is an ethnic family history, **China Men** can only in the most limited sense be identified with the classic and definitive study in that discipline, Herbert Gutman's analytical and documentary *The Black Family in Slavery and Freedom*. Rather than accumulating and examining documentary evidence in a systematic fashion, Kingston in **China Men** attempts an imaginative reconstruction of one particular Cantonese family's emigration to America as the prototypical history of all immigrant American Chinese. That authentic, if idealized, family history is reified in the distinctive dialect of immigrant forebears; it is an extremely rich, consciously verbal style springing from a Cantonese village society that "talks" or "sings" its history, or what the distinguished linguistic scholar, Walter Ong, would call an "oral culture."

I would argue that **China Men** is neither novel nor history but represents the transmutation of "oral history" into cultural literary epic. It records a dramatization of real-life family stories in the form Asian-Americans recognize as "talk-story." As a chronicle of archetypal racial heroes, it is thus an "oral history" in the generic sense as well. Kingston is a sophisticated and contemporary artist, and her work is laden with eastern sources, but to my mind, **China Men** looks back to the traditional western epic, particularly the *Aeniad* in its cultural exegesis, its conscious formation of racial myths from earlier folk legends and its central theme of heroic wandering from "Troy" (China) to "New Troy" (America). It appears to imitate the epic's principal formal characteristics and functions. It is episodic in structure and told in a generally ceremonial, first-person voice. It continually intermingles supernatural beings with flesh and blood personalities, myth with history in a continuous present. It rehearses the exploits of wandering sojourner-heroes on whose actions depend the fate of a new nation or "race" and embodies in written discourse the oral poetic structures, customs, values, and psychology of a bardic community.

As a family history in epic form, **China Men** recounts the odyssey of a family of male sojourners across America and away from womenfolk and children in China. This dispersed arrangement of family members was the predominant form the traditional Chinese extended patrilineal family system took during the peak years of emigration, and although familiar to students of ethnic history and to Chinese themselves, it has not been the subject of any major scholarly study or literary work before **China Men.** Comparisons with pertinent findings of recent historians and sociologists of the family will show that Kingston remains faithful to the broad outlines of sojourner family history. Nevertheless, I hope to prove that her aim is not necessarily documentation but the celebration of the mystical continuity of the family, a triumphant vision that runs counter to the historical fact of family dispersion and dislocation. Thus without ignoring general historical trends and specific events, Kingston transmutes these into epic form with mythic content by idealizing selected values, problems, and personalities in her family's evolution. **China Men** also recalls the epic form in its stylistic recreation of "orality" or public verbal performance before a listening audience. The forefathers are poets, singers, tellers of tales. Song and story pervade the first-person voice of history, quicken the land and the sea, join past to present and homesick sojourners with loved ones far away.

The paradigmatic family in **China Men** functions as the principal arena in which universal human experiences such as birth, death, work, love, failure, and fear are tested, judged, and ultimately understood. So potent among ethnic women writers as a whole is this image of the family as touchstone of values and behavior that the ethnic literary critic, Edith Blicksilver, has designated it a chief literary theme of "female social protest" cutting across the boundaries of culture, race, and time. Kingston herself makes clear her lofty mission as "female social protester" (surely this, too, is the controlling notion of *Woman Warrior* as embodied in the narrator, Brave Orchid and Mu Lan): she intends to revise history from her race's point of view, to "claim America" for her male ancestors, a forgotten and misrepresented family of "American pioneers" and "Gold Mountain heroes." Their story unfolds as the retelling of exemplary tales composed by her forebears, preserved as accumulated family lore and handed down to the children. All concern family heroes driven by fate to seek an unknown destiny in barbarian lands. The ideal of family continuity gives these men strength to win at arduous "epic" tests of manhood. The traditional authority ascribed to male family members gives them a core of selfhood allowing them to withstand danger and defeat.

The preservation of these family values inevitably means the survival of heroes, their families, kin and clan, and the eventual proliferation of the larger community of sojourner families that constitutes their nation or "race." Just as the eccentric, feuding Dead family in Toni Morrison's brilliant novel, *Song of Solomon,* share a primal family bond that divides them from the black community yet grants them a generous vision of human possibility, Kingston's ancestors have a fierce family loyalty that isolates them culturally from mainstream America yet sustains them with a mystical belief in the oneness of all life. The fabled "Middle Kingdom" of T'ang heroes to which the family bears continued allegiance throughout its journey casts a long, protective shadow over lives lived in *Mei Kwok,* the "beautiful" but brutal new overseas home. Both places constitute the legendary frontiers which the author herself, in retracing the steps of her voyaging forefathers, hopes to explore.

> I want to talk to Cantonese, who have always been revolutionaries, nonconformists, people with fabulous imaginations, people who invented the Gold Mountain. I want to discern what it is that makes people go West and turn into Americans. I want to compare China, a country I made up, with what country is really out there.

In order to dramatize her ancestors' memories of a perfected homeland, a wandering race of family heroes and a legendary country of barbarian "demons" and spirits, Kingston recreates abstract versions of real-life family members and situations as I hope subsequently to show. Yet it is clear to me that the issue of authenticity that arose after the publication of *Woman Warrior* troubles the author. Kingston has thus included a lengthy central digression in *China Men* containing purely factual testimony of Chinese-American legal history ("The Laws") perhaps because some detractors have persisted in faulting her works for not being radical revisionist histories. Risking narrative discontinuity, the inclusion of this section balances the remaining chapters on "invented" or idealized history with substantial documentary material. But as a formal digression, it functions to provide the general American reading public, mostly ignorant of the history of Chinese in the U.S., with a brief chronicle of oppression against which the heroic deeds of the idealized fathers can be judged. . . . This brief chronology is a pertinent, persuasive reminder of America's long history of Sinophobia. It points to the harsh facts of peonage and discrimination under which Chinese were forced to labor for nearly a century. (pp. 3-6)

Despite the carefully drawn central digression on Chinese-American legal history, however, the overall design of *China Men* demonstrates that the author's intention is not to write a factual account of Chinese servitude but a celebration of her ancestors as protagonists in a triumphant saga of survival and family continuity. Except for the factual summary, the work is shaped more by the lives of individual heroes than by the passage of key events in Chinese-American history. Main characters are treated in separate narrative chapters identified by legendary patronyms ("The Great Grandfather of the Sandalwood Mountains"). These forefather portraits provide *China Men's* scaffolding: they offer vivid exemplary exploits that westerners can identify as "epic-like." They also embody the Confucian practice of ancestor worship and as such offer an eastern equivalent of what Greek rhetoricians called *epidexis,* ritual literary praise of renowned individuals. The legendary characteristics of these sojourner ancestors are enhanced by the proliferation of honorific titles and by the narrator's conscious obscuring of dates and locales of significant events. The circumstances surrounding the mental deterioration of "The Grandfather of the Sierra Nevada Mountains," for example, are purposely clouded so that his decline is not so much pitiful as noble and tragic. (pp. 6-7)

In between these narrative episodes are small literary myths based on Chinese folk legends that provide fictional parallels to the historical chapters. These are not definitive, "pure" myths in the textual sense but are consciously contrived literary imitations that may be ironic analogues of western tales ("The Adventures of Lo Bun Sun") or variations of actual folk tales ("On Mortality Again"). Some are the author's own private ethnic "myths" in the Yeatsian sense ("The Hundred-Year-Old Man"). Authenticity of sources and materials are not of paramount concern here. What is important is the function these myths serve as epic conventions widening the dramatic scope of the narrative in order to encompass a coexistent supernatural plane of existence and in thus aggrandizing the themes and characters of the historical chapters.

The ancestors who people this saga of journey and return are also characters of epic proportions. The two founding fathers in *China Men,* Bak Goong of the Hawaiian Islands and Ah Goong of California, are prototypes of the family hero, fashioned in the image of the valiant, long-suffering Prometheus. Both are Cantonese "explorers and Americans" who pit themselves courageously against monumental natural obstacles to win at epic tests of manhood based not on lofty achievement so much as the endurance of great physical danger and psychological stress. Great Grandfather (Bak Goong) "hacks a farm out of the wilderness" in the impenetrable Hawaiian backland. Grandfather (Ah Goong) literally moves mountains and hews through time with his bare hands along the rugged Pacific coast. Yet each tale has a different shape. Great Grandfather is the paradigmatic Chinese-American epic hero whose journey finally ends at home. . . . Like the wily Odysseus or the Nordic trickster Loki, he makes fools of his enemies, the "police demons" or the "pesky missionary Jesus demons." Finally, he returns to China to die, having endured and thus affirmed his manhood, his life harmoniously complete and "of a piece." By contrast, Grandfather's story plays a variation on Great Grandfather's theme of epic wandering and homecoming. He is both tragic and heroic: although he sacrifices mind and health in order to defy immovable rock, "dust devils," earthquake, and fire, his homecoming is tinged with gall for his family treats the ill and exhausted sojourner as an idiot. (pp. 7-8)

[Heroism] in *China Men* is not defined by the conventional Chinese standards of masculine authority nor by western standards of physical prowess. Kingston inverts the notion of masculinity and femininity in order to define "heroism" according to the standard of sheer survival of humiliating social and economic setbacks. The description of footbinding in the introductory myth of the captive "Tang Ao," a Chinese "Everyman," shows the hobbling of a male. Footbinding thus becomes a symbol for the immigrant male's "emasculation," his loss of power and position after his emigration to America.

> The women who sat on him turned to direct their attention to his feet. They bent his toes so far backward that his arched foot cracked. The old ladies squeezed each foot and broke many tiny bones along the sides. They gathered his toes, toes over and under one another like a knot of ginger root. Tang Ao wept with pain. As they wound the bandages tight and tighter around his feet, the women sang footbinding songs to distract him: "Use aloe for binding feet and not for scholars."

The womanization of Tang Ao is not to be interpreted as a diminution of stature or character. Like the crafty Odysseus biding his time in the land of the nymph Calypso, the Chinese hero's strength consists of an ability to find new methods by which to endure, in this case to acquiesce and hence to outlast his captivity. The myth also speaks of the growing equality of the sexes as a result of the male's adventuring into unknown territories.

If we compare the above myth with the chapters on "The Father from China" (BaBa), we see the father similarly "emasculated" or metamorphosed in a succession of unsuccessful male roles: talented scholar, village teacher, carefree American bachelor, ambitious entrepreneur. . . . He becomes the most fully realized "hero" in the work, for he is shown from many sides, as husband, son, "legal" and "illegal" father. He is heroic, too, in his ambitions for himself and for his family. It is he who defies the ancient edict that "a woman too well educated is apt to create trouble" by encouraging his wife to become a doctor, and by his heroic dream of achievement, he learns the realism of failure in American society. Even when he fails at his duty as father-provider, and retreats from his family in bitterness, he remains the family's *titular* authority by virtue of his wife's and children's love for him (**Woman Warrior** depicts the mother as the central figure and myth maker in the children's lives). They respect him even though they do not understand him. His belongings have for them a sacred aura despite their air of poverty and failure. His children regard his wingtip shoes, his expensive but threadbare suits, his private "father places" as touched with a special grace.

If Kingston's "Gold Mountain heroes" are heroic because they are survivors, despite having sometimes relinquished their responsibilities as male family authorities, her heroines too are special, for they redefine conventional notions of femininity within the sojourner family. There is strong historical testimony for this role-reversal. As historians have remarked, Cantonese women were forced to assume total family governance after the emigration of male villagers to foreign lands. Thus, there arose a strong tradition of womanly self-sufficiency and aggressiveness among Cantonese. Kingston shows the persistence of that tradition among those few Chinese women, like the mother, who were allowed to enter the U. S. during the lengthy period of exclusion.

In **China Men,** the Cantonese mother's independence and self-reliance is not simply a product of historical necessity

and village tradition but a way of preserving sacred family bonds even when the conventional function of the male collapsed. The mother from China is forced by the father's increasing passivity to take on "masculine" traits of aggressiveness and authority. . . . She preserves family solidarity by her never ending stream of advice, philosophy, stories, and reproaches, her energy, and her iron will. When her husband is psychologically immobilized by failure, it is she, a former physician, who supports the family by joining the hordes of migrant fruit and vegetable pickers in the fields of Stockton.

The inversion of sexual roles not only creates another notion of "heroism" based on the necessity of adapting to the conditions of poverty and unemployment in the sojourner family, it also illuminates the internal tensions accumulating in such families as a result of the erosion of sex differentiation in the household. The strain on husband, wife, and children as a result of the father's "emasculation" or failure as provider is clear. His silence and impotent rage deepen as the wife takes on more active power in the family. He screams "wordless male screams in his sleep." He erupts in furious misogynistic curses that frighten his daughter. Yet it seems to me that despite these tensions, the behavioral accomodations within the family enable it to remain integral and strong. Moreover, the ancient family values are still viable, for the mother's aggression is apparently born out of love and necessity, not frustration and shame, and through it, the father eventually finds a way of regaining his former authority. . . . Like the father, the heroism of the prototypical Chinese-American mother consists of an ability to alter traditional roles in order to prevent the dissolution of the family as an economic and cultural unit. (pp. 8-10)

Kingston's depiction of sojourner family life also takes into account the broad trends in western family which have undeniably influenced the course of ethnic family systems as well. *China Men,* to my mind, generally concurs with well known familists such as Philippe Ariès, Peter Laslett, Edward Shorter, and Christopher Lasch who have presented persuasive if varied historical arguments on the "crisis" of western family life in the twentieth century. Like these professional historians of western family structures, Kingston defines the family as a flexible domestic arrangement varying in intensity and configuration over time and buffeted by external forces beyond its control. One particular issue addressed by *China Men* is what the historian John Demos has called the "overloading" of the modern family "with the most urgent of human needs and responsibilities" due to the breakup of the reciprocal social relationships between individual and community. Pertinent details in *China Men* reveal that the sojourner family is like the western family described by recent historians of family life: it, too, is a nexus of shifting human relationships and deteriorating cultural values. (pp. 11-12)

Kingston also recounts occasional American accommodations of Chinese family traditions, such as the keeping of lunar holidays with special foods. These meals dramatize the family's shifting fortunes in the new world and the subsequent deliquescence of tradition. (p. 12)

However, the details and situations which attest to the historical fact of cultural erosion and family dislocation remain part of the background. Kingston, in the final analysis, gives an overwhelmingly heroic account of sojourner family life . . . Throughout **China Men,** the continuing hold of certain fundamental aspects of the primordial Confucian ideal of family unity, economic interdependence, and mutual help is maintained. (p. 13)

A closer look at the details which purportedly show the deterioration of traditional family and cultural values also affirms this impression. The leaf-wrapped legumes passed around by laborers in California are not merely substitutes for ritual feasts. They conceal secret political codes: the message to strike against the railroads which were cruelly exploiting their labor. The laborers have pressed holiday tradition into the service of another Chinese tradition—grass-roots rebellion against a hated oppressor. Ah Goong ties the strike plan into the bundles of food and happily recalls a precedent for their actions: "The time and place for the revolution against Kublai Khan had been hidden inside autumn mooncakes." These men are not slaves helplessly adrift in a hostile environment: they are heroes carrying their traditions into a new frontier.

Kingston's depiction of sojourner attitudes toward traditional Chinese family life may prompt some critics to accuse her of romantic nostalgia for an outmoded and unjustly authoritarian system that was "intended to extend the relations of domination and subordination." Yet this criticism would misrepresent her obvious intention to recreate mythic, not documentary, history. Nor does she espouse what Raymond Dawson has called the erroneous "fiction of 'eternal stand-still'" that led westerners for many centuries to extol the Chinese mind for its stability, "uniformity and unvariability" and the homogenous, family oriented Confucian state as "an example and model even for Christians." China men all too often drink deeply of loneliness, misunderstanding, and bitter despair as a result of their fidelity to ethnic and family unity. Such a loyalty has made assimilation into American society a long and painful struggle, as the father's saga of thwarted ambition and schizoid bicultural identities reveals. For China men, "home" is the absent and *real* family whose claims are continually reasserted in dreams, holiday feasts, mothers' and wives' scolding letters. Memories of home preserve their ethnic values and identities and teach them how to adjust to unexpected, even forbidden, social situations that may arise in the Gold Mountain. (pp. 14-15)

It is important to note the effect of Kingston's heroic method upon the thorny issue of miscegenation. It is well known that intermarriage was strictly forbidden to Chinese by Confucian teachings, for it went against the classical notion established in the *Li Chi* that marriage was a religious duty between consenting families "to secure the services in the ancestral temple for the predecessors and to secure the continuance of the family line for posterity." (p. 15)

Why does Kingston choose to exalt a controversial issue in Chinese-American history which Chinese commentators have generally avoided? To my mind, this pastoral treatment allows Kingston to explore typical and long ignored problems of sojourner history—loneliness, homesickness, sexual frustration—without cultural bias. We also come to understand and accept the emotional needs motivating these men to enter relationships which violated so profoundly cherished family and religious attitudes because we view such relationships from a sojourner's (Bak Sook Goong) own point of view. Literary myth is a way of dramatizing objectively the immigrants' general belief that their American experiences were illusory when compared with the more binding claims of the "real" family far away. (p. 16)

If Kingston's aim, then, in *China Men* is the celebration and not the analysis of racial and family history, how can the troubling question of her credibility even as "epic" historian be addressed? It occurs to me that through the forms and conventions of the epic, she comes closer than other commentators on the family to the actual truth about sojourner family history. Kingston proposes in *China Men* that the sojourner family is an indigenous American system whose evolution parallels but does not necessarily duplicate the major trends in family history in the west. The sojourner family is neither a "haven in a heartless world" nor an "encounter group" nor a simple domestic "construct designed for social purposes." Kingston, by contrast, shows that the special historical conditions and cultural traditions of sojourners have created unusually strong family ties that have intensified over the generations despite the reality of long-term separation of its members, the blurring of family and sex roles necessitated by economic hardship, even the gradual fragmentation of the ethnic American communities themselves. This development parallels in many ways that of the black family which survived despite slavery.

Nor does Kingston put forth the popular "mimetic" view that Chinese-American families are transplanted models of the traditional Confucian system. Rather, Kingston affirms that family traditions have always altered with the unique pressures of American society. The surprising result is that the sojourner family system has proven far more resilient than its counterpart in modern China where traditional family values have decayed markedly or have been wholly rejected. The unusual persistence of sojourner family unity was noted over thirty years ago by Olga Lang in her groundbreaking study of Chinese families: Lang notes that Chinese in foreign countries, particularly in the U.S. and Hawaii, show no weakening but a strengthening of family ties, and attributes this to their need for mutual protection. (pp. 16-17)

Finally, I would contend that Kingston's greatest achievement in *China Men* is her transmogrification of her forebears' language into a heroic tongue. To this end, she skillfully uses the myriad devices of the bard: mnemonic formulae; myths that parallel and enlarge the historical narration and are obviously stitched from the author's memories rather than taken from textual sources; a preoccupation with titles, recitations of names, name-calling; sensuous pictorial descriptions and descriptive catalogues; frequent authorial intrusions with translations of Sze-Yup terms (these are evocative conceptual translations, not literal translations); long summaries; and commentaries on previous action. These techniques are proof to me that Kingston's is above all a consciously verbal or oral literary performance of the sort described by Walter Ong in his seminal essay on ethnic language, "Oral Culture and the Literate Mind." Out of the indigenous Chinese-American tongue, Kingston recreates the spirit and beauty of the original myth-laden "oral culture" of her predecessors and fuses this with the rational "literate" craft of the western writer. It is not enough for her to embody in prose an authentic Asian-American diction by merely transcribing immigrant speech, slang, curses, clichés into English. She recognizes, perhaps, that the act of literal transcription is a mechanical exercise and results in lifeless, precious dialect. Her own characters do not speak in dialect or pidgin. Theirs is a simple, formal, generally grammatically correct diction that ranges from colloquial speech ("We need to go-out-on-the-road again," Kau Goong roared.), to flowery histrionics ("Old Uncles and Young Uncles, I have an appropriate story to tell. It cannot be left unsaid."), to monosyllabic chant ("I want my home," the men yelled together. "I want my home. Home. Home. Home. Home.") She depends not on dialect but on certain literary formulae, recognizable since Homer, to recreate the actual conceptual processes from which her ancestors' speech sprung, not reason and logic so much as memory and the psyche. (pp. 17-18)

The verbal character of Kingston's language is also reflected in the protagonists' preoccupation with poetry or song, an important thematic motif in the work. Song pervades the men's primary activity, work. Its presence or absence is a measure of their happiness and success as workers. Yet even when the men's voices fail, they find song everywhere around them. It is present in memory, in the voices of wives and children talking-story, and especially in nature. The singing of the ground, the cane, the rocks, the sea, even the railroad affirms that the new world, though often hostile, is governed by the same benevolent natural process as the old.

> He sucked in deep breaths of the Sandalwood Mountain air, and let it fly out in a song, which reached up to the rims of volcanoes and down to the edge of the water. His song lifted and fell with the air, which seemed to breathe warmly through his body and through the rocks. The clouds and frigate birds made the currents visible, and the leaves were loud. . . . He sang like the heroes in stories about wanderers and exiles, poets and monks and monkeys, and princes and kings out for walks. His arias unfurled and rose in wide, wide arcs.

The critic John Leonard somewhat misleadingly describes Kingston's prose as "sensual." Perhaps a better term is "sentient," for her "singing" language is identified inevitably with a monistic and animistic view of humanity and nature and with an idealized image of the family as an organism encompassing disparate traditions into itself. It is this evolutionary understanding of family and ethnic history as derived from "song" or oral culture that gives *China Men* its encyclopedic scope and architectonic vision. Song transforms what could well be interpreted as a cruel, randomly violent America into an elemental force, an opponent worthy of "Gold Mountain heroes," the author's preferred title. Song touches the harsh world of work with grace and transforms the most formidable obstacles—towering cliffs of granite, impenetrable stands of cane—into part of the cosmic order.

Like that other American singer, Walt Whitman, Maxine Kingston raises private experience to the level of American myth. The structure of her song is epic—that most heroic and elastic of literary forms—by which she is able to encapsulate the data of history, the deep dreams of myth, and the archetypal drama of one American family. (pp. 18-19)

> *Linda Ching Sledge, "Maxine Kingston's 'China Men': The Family Historian as Epic Poet," in MELUS, Vol. 7, No. 4, Winter, 1980, pp. 3-22.*

SUZANNE JUHASZ

Maxine Hong Kingston's two-volume autobiography, *The Woman Warrior* and *China Men,* embodies the search for identity in the narrative act. The first text places the daughter in relation to her mother, the second places her in relation to her father; they demonstrate how finding each parent is a part of finding oneself. For Kingston, finding her mother and fa-

ther is to name them, to tell their stories. Language is the means with which she arrives at identity, first at home, and then in the world. But because a daughter's relation to her mother is psychologically and linguistically different from her relation to her father, so is the telling of these stories different.

Although the two texts are superficially similar, they are generated from different narrative patterns. In *The Woman Warrior* alternating movements toward and away from the mother take place within a textual field in which a linear progression, defining first the mother, then the daughter, takes place. In *China Men* narrative movement goes in one direction only, toward the father. But because this impulse in the latter book is continually diffused into generalization and idealization, it begins over, again and again. Such narrative structures suggest the evolution of female identity, which is formed in relation to the mother through the achievement of individuation in the context of connection, in relation to the father through the understanding of separation, the creation of substitutes for connection. Taken together, *The Woman Warrior* and *China Men* compose a woman's autobiography, describing a self formed at the source by gender experience. (pp. 173-74)

The Chinese phrase for story telling is "talking-story," and it defines the narration of both books. It is as well the subject of both books, because finding words, telling stories, is in Kingston's writing the other major metaphor, along with home, for the process of achieving identity. Chinese into English, silence into speech: when they appear in her books, these themes are subject and technique. The narrator of *The Woman Warrior,* who literally could not speak in public as a child, later cries to another silent Chinese-American girl, "If you don't talk, you can't have a personality. You'll have no personality and no hair." The narrator's fantasy of the powerful woman, the woman warrior of the title, involves a female avenger with words actually carved on her back: "The ideographs for *revenge* are 'report a crime' and 'report to five families.' The reporting is the vengeance—not the beheading, not the gutting, but the words. And I have so many words—'chink' words and 'gook' words too—that they do not fit on my skin." That power, equated with the ability to talk-story, is specifically associated with her mother: "I saw that I too had been in the presence of great power, my mother talking-story."

Talking-story, discourse itself, is central to the difference between the two books, representative in turn of the difference in the relationships between daughters and mothers, daughters and fathers. . . . *The Woman Warrior* begins and ends with the narrator's mother talking-story. By the end of the book, the daughter's independent identity can be understood through her connection to her mother; talking-story is indicative of both parts of the mother-daughter relationship: "Here is a story my mother told me, not when I was young but recently, when I told her I also talk-story. The beginning is hers, the ending mine." Her father, in contrast, does not talk. Screams and curses define his speech, but more important yet is his silence: "You kept up a silence for weeks and months."

At the core of the relationship between daughter and mother is identification. The mother-child bond has always been the primary one, and girls never have to break it in the way boys do, by understanding that they are of different sexes. Through her stories, the narrator's mother passes on her version of reality to her daughter: "She tested our strength to establish realities," explains the narrator as *The Woman War-*

rior begins. The matter is complicated, however, by the fact that the mother often tells lies. In *China Men* the narrator specifically contrasts men's stories with "the fairy tales and ghost stories told by women." "No, no," says the narrator's mother to her in *The Woman Warrior,* "there aren't any flags like that. They're just talking-story. You're always believing talk-story." To find her own identity the daughter needs to ascertain the difference between herself and her mother. Discovering a separate identity for her mother is one way to help her find her own self. Discerning the relation between her mother's "truths" and "lies" is representative of this process.

With her father the narrator needs not to loosen a connection but to make one. His discourse, and especially the lack of it, is indicative of the fundamental separateness between daughter and father, a separateness that arises because the father is neither a daughter's primary love nor is he of the same sex. The narrator's father screams or curses at her, "Wordless male screams that jolted the house upright and staring in the middle of the night." His curses defile women: "Your mother's cunt. Your mother's smelly cunt." Worse are his long silences, whereby he "punished us by not talking . . . rendered us invisible, gone." To believe that her father does not mean *her* with his curses, to find out who he really is, the daughter has to invent him: "I'll tell you what I suppose from your silences and few words, and you can tell me that I'm mistaken. You'll just have to speak up with the real stories if I've got you wrong." In the face of silence, invention is her only possible recourse. Yet it cannot be trusted in the same way that the narrator of *The Woman Warrior* trusts her imaginings about the lives of women relatives. Furthermore, it would be better, in the end, if he would tell her himself.

Therefore, although the two texts are conceived of by their author as [one big book written more or less simultaneously], and although their surface stylistic features are similar, there is a profound difference between them. Whereas she "thought there would be a big difference between the men and the women," Kingston does not in fact "find them that different." On the surface, the texts do look and sound alike. Both tell stories of relatives, stories interspersed with memories of the narrator's own childhood, in a matter-of-fact tone and declarative sentences that permit the speaker a fluid interchange between fact and fantasy, reportage and poetry. Yet the results are different, indicating more profound differences in narrative structure. [In an interview published in *The New York Times Book Review* (June 15, 1980),] Kingston herself points to their different sources. "In a way," she says, "*The Woman Warrior* was a selfish book. I was always imposing my viewpoint on the stories. In *China Men* the person who 'talks-story' is not so intrusive. I bring myself in and out of the stories, but in effect, I'm more distant. The more I was able to understand my characters, the more I was able to write from their point of view and the less interested I was in relating how I felt about them." "More distant": This distance is, I think, a necessary result of the difference in finding a father rather than a mother, and it produces a text that creates not a universal or an androgynous but a female understanding of masculine experience. The essential separation between daughter and father is bridged by fantasy that, while it may do its work with intelligence and love, is never empathetic and is always idealized. For all its attention to detail, the text it produces is curiously—or not so curiously—abstract. *The Woman Warrior* is a messier book, but for me it is more satisfying than *China Men.* Yet, taken together as they are meant to be, they offer valuable insights into the na-

ture of female identity, as it is created in relation not simply to women, not simply to men, but to both sexes, both parents.

The Woman Warrior is "messy" insofar as its narrative patterns are several and intertwined. *Complex* is really a better word for the various kinds of narrative movements that taken together reflect the dynamics of the mother-daughter relationship. The move to individuate and the move to connect both arise from the essential attachment between daughter and mother; the need for separation thus exists in the context of connection. In consequence, the identity that the text establishes for its narrator is achieved through a process involving both individuation and attachment.

The largest narrative pattern has a linear direction. The first three stories move toward defining the mother, thereby distinguishing her from the daughter; the two final stories go on to define the daughter, distinguishing her from the mother. But within each of the stories other movements occur in alternating patterns, maintaining the necessary tension between separation and connection. The text as a whole, for example, can be seen as an alternation between the stories the mother tells and the stories the daughter tells. Each teller's stories, in turn, alternate between true stories and stories that are not true.

The mother creates her relationship with her daughter through the kinds of story she tells her, stories whose purpose is sometimes to keep the two women alike and sometimes to make them different, as when, for example, the mother tries to offer her daughter a life other than her own. Seeking to know her mother, the daughter begins by thinking that what she has to understand is the difference between her mother's "truths" and "lies." Ultimately, however, she comes to discover not so much which ones are lies but why they are lies, and it is this kind of awareness that helps her to see her mother as another person.

At the same time, the daughter's own narrative style also alternates between "truths" and "lies." Her truths are her actual memories of her own past; but to write her history beyond herself, she invents or imagines stories—of her dead aunt in China, of her mother's young womanhood, of the woman warrior. This process of imaginative empathy should be understood not as prevarication but as fiction. It is, however, not the literal truth, and it establishes both connection with her subject, by means of empathy, and separation as well—the story is, after all, her own creation.

In each of the stories, these alternating rhythms create the double movement of individuation in the context of connection that enables the narrator to establish identity. In the first story, "No Name Woman," for example, the mother's telling of the aunt's story gives rise to her daughter's version of it, yet the daughter's version is revisionary. The daughter's story, in turn, both deepens her connection to her female heritage and creates some separation from it and thereby control over it. (pp. 175-78)

But the daughter is not satisfied with her mother's account. "My mother has told me once and for all the useful parts. . . . And she senses in the very abbreviation of her mother's version a duplicity: "The emigrants confuse the gods by diverting their curses, misleading them with crooked streets and false names. They must try to confuse their offspring as well, who, I suppose, threaten them in similar ways—always trying to get things straight, always trying to name the unspeakable. The Chinese I know hide their names;

sojourners take new names when their lives change, and they guard their real names with silence." (p. 179)

[Once again, in "White Tigers,"] impetus for the narrator's imaginative reconstruction of the story of the woman warrior is given by her mother's version. Now the daughter begins to have some intimation that her mother's duplicity has a function other than to confuse or conceal. Chinese culture, as the narrator has described it in "No Name Woman," is strongly repressive of women. Yet, as she says in the opening lines of "White Tigers," "when we Chinese girls listened to adults talk-story, we learned that we failed if we grew up to be but wives or slaves. We could be heroines, swordswomen. Even if she had to rage across all China, a swordswoman got even with anybody who hurt her family. Perhaps women were once so dangerous they had to have their feet bound." In telling her daughter stories of female heroism that directly contradict many of her other messages about the position of women, the mother shows her daughter another possibility for women that is not revealed in her equally strong desire for her daughter's conformity and thus safety in a patriarchal system. (pp. 179-80)

In "Shaman" the narrator looks directly at Brave Orchid, the mother whose presence has infused and helped to create the stories that precede it. She tells not one but two stories, however—or tells the story twice: the "truth"—her actual memories of her mother, a laundress in America—and the "fiction"—the story of her mother who in China became a doctor. The fiction includes her own postulation of thoughts and feelings, added to the facts she has been given to create the character of Brave Orchid. But of course both kinds of story, the mother as ordinary woman and the mother as hero, are necessary, both kinds of knowledge, truth and fiction—each a corrective for the other, each a part of the reality of character.

Brave Orchid's heroism, as her daughter tells it, identifies her with the woman warrior, because her success, like the woman warrior's, is based on powers of the imagination. (pp. 180-81)

"At the Western Palace" offers the story of female relatives, once again, as the prelude or first step. The association of women with madness is shown as the alternative to their achievement of self-identity. Moon Orchid, Brave Orchid's sister who cannot change Chinese reality into American reality, goes mad. . . .

The narrator's own childhood silence—"a dumbness, a shame"—comes from the conflict between her Chinese upbringing and the ways of an American school, but in the story she represents it as symbolically caused by her mother (China), who seems to have cut her tongue, slicing the frenum, when she was a child. (p. 182)

Moving beyond [her] terrible shyness and silence demands the thing that happens at last, when the daughter starts to talk back. . . . In a fierce tirade against her mother she asserts her own American sense of independence and attacks, specifically, her mother's talk-stories. . . .

Establishing herself as a talker in opposition to her mother—as American instead of Chinese, a truth teller instead of a liar—makes it possible for her to define herself as separate from her mother. Leaving home at this stage means leaving China, and her mother's Chinese way of talking ("We like to say the opposite"), in order to understand difference. (p. 183)

Yet this way of seeing and talking, this complete sense of separation from her mother, from China, is not the whole truth either, the truth of her identity, and this fact the text itself has revealed. For the text is more complex and fuller of insight than any particular moment of understanding within it. Poised against the linearity of the narrator's progress is the recurrent alternation of movement toward and tugs against connection that takes place within the narrative field, as it were, in which the forward progress occurs. Thus, when the narrator discovers her independence from her mother, that fact is indeed a part of her process toward identity but is not its fulfillment. Independence must be understood in order that connection can occur again, but a connection, finally, between two different people rather than between two people who together make one identity.

The Woman Warrior ends with its narrator's perception of this achievement, with the story of the Chinese woman poet Ts'ai Yen, with a celebration of the woman who is powerful because she can speak, can write. The story is begun by her mother, finished by the daughter. "It translates well." In this way we see how the connection between mother and daughter, both storytellers, both women warriors, has been reestablished, but on terms that now both allow for separation and admit attachment.

China Men is less complicated textually than *The Woman Warrior*. As Kingston says, "the person who 'talks-story' is not so intrusive." Although here, too, the fact of memory is juxtaposed against the fiction of imaginative recreation, the memories are much fewer, and the imagining—the stories of male relatives, of grandfathers, father, uncles, and brother—is no longer urgent, no longer empathetic. These stories, lines thrown out across the chasm of separation, are more idealistic than realistic, more conceptual than kinetic, more parallel than developmental. The richness and tension created by the search for difference in the context of sameness—the mother-daughter relationship—is replaced by the clarity that distance offers, a lucidity that is at the same time monotonal. Only one person, after all, is talking here; narrative movement is in only one direction, not the tug toward and away from the mother but the yearning toward the father that goes so far but no farther, proceeding from anger and ignorance toward knowledge and admiration. (pp. 183-84)

The purpose of the text as a whole is to gain that knowledge by imaginatively entering the father's interiority—something denied to the daughter by actual experience—by replacing opacity and abstractness with concrete particularities, a technique that served the narrator well in *The Woman Warrior* to establish the identity of her mother. (p. 185)

To tell the story of fathers is to tell the story of China's coming to America. Both the mother and the father represent China to the American-born narrator, but there is a difference in their experience and therefore in the aspect of the homeland they embody. While the women were left behind in China, coming afterward to join their husbands, the men were the sojourners who came to America to discover the "Gold Mountain" there. In seeking to know her father the narrator looks as well for the experience of active appropriation, however painful, even humiliating some of its aspects may be, that has been denied to women, who find their power in the imagination, as *The Woman Warrior* shows, not in the public world. *China Men* confronts that public world, as grandfathers and fathers wrestle with nature and society from Hawaii to Alaska, from New York to California.

Yet there is in **China Men** a generality, an abstractness to all this experience that seems to bespeak the impossibility of the narrator's ever claiming male experience as an integral part of her heritage. Each character in the book has his own name, his own adventures, but all are referred to more frequently as "the father," "the grandfather," "the brother," a mode of appellation that is itself indicative of the generic character of the men, their normative function. In reading, it is difficult to keep them separate. They merge into the common maleness, a concept that the prose creates. (pp. 185-86)

What is most significant here is the combination of specific detail with a generalization of consciousness; the combination not only depersonalizes the individual man—in this instance it is Bak Gook, "The Grandfather of the Sandalwood Mountains"—so that he becomes akin to all the other male consciousnesses in the book, but also allows him, regardless of his immigrant status—he is a frequently brutalized sugarcane worker—to become heroic. All the Chinamen are capable of this kind of poetry, the result, I think, of an idealization of masculine experience representative of the daughter's approach to her father. Although the author seeks the humanizing middle ground between the father's generalized curses about the women and the daughter's idealized flights of poetic heroism, she creates such moments infrequently, despite many physical details, and these moments occur more often in actual memories than in imaginings. (p. 186)

After her father has lost his job at the gambling hall and becomes despondent, his children respond to his silence with a confusion—"I invented a plan to test my theories that males feel no pain; males don't feel"—that finally turns to anger:

> We children became so wild that we broke Baba loose from his chair. We goaded him, irked him—*gikked* him—and the gravity suddenly let him go. He chased my sister, who locked herself in a bedroom. "Come out," he shouted. But of course, she wouldn't, he having a coat hanger in hand and angry. I watched him kick the door; the round mirror fell off the wall and crashed. The door broke open, and he beat her. Only my sister remembers that it was she who watched my father's shoe against the door and the mirror outside fall, and I who was beaten.

Such experiences, informed as they are by powerful unmediated responses to the father's separateness, can be contrasted to the imagined experiences of the men themselves, sympathetic but lacking this intensity, experiences narrated through the creation of a masculine consciousness. Sympathy is not empathy, and the very distance between them seems to influence the nature of the knowledge that is available to the narrator.

China Men demonstrates that finding the father, for the daughter, means finding what one has always known: that distance. Fear and anger may be transformed into love, but it is a love based on knowledge laced with idealization. Over and over in **China Men,** in each of its stories, the daughter begins in ignorance, with silence, and fills the gap or void with the fruits of her own imagination to gain—just that—her own creation. Never having been able to encounter the true interiority of the father, she has, finally, only the stories she has told about him. She finds her identity as a storyteller, a writer, here as in **The Woman Warrior,** but here there is a suggestion that the imagination is less the embodiment of life itself than an alternative to it.

Consequently, the two processes—finding the mother, finding the father—seem less than parallel for the daughter. Regardless of its author's intentions, **China Men** is more of a postscript to **The Woman Warrior** than a complement to it. Because the mother is not only of the same sex but, by virtue of the familial arrangements of society, the infant's first and primary love, she remains at the center of the daughter's search for identity. The familial arrangements of society ask as well that the female be understood in relation to the male—as the word *female* itself suggests—so that Kingston is correct in seeing **The Woman Warrior** as a partial text, an incomplete autobiography. Finding the father may be understood as synonymous with ascertaining the woman's relation to the external world, or the other. Difference and distance, which produce ignorance, fear, and idealization, create boundaries that can be bridged imaginatively but cannot really be destroyed. The yearning to destroy them, perhaps the most important feature of the search, in both its intensity and its frustrations or displacement, propels the text of **China Men** but is also diffused by it. Kingston sees that text as an achievement for herself as a writer—not so "selfish," not so "intrusive." Perhaps she is right. Perhaps this is the success daughters can have with fathers—to displace the yearning for him with the creation of something in his place, to understand that her love must be informed by the knowledge of separateness.

Taken together, the search for the mother and the search for the father allow a person to find home, a place both inside and outside the self, in the way that, for a woman, the mother is always inside, the father always outside. Finding home gives a sense of such boundaries, of understanding not only what is eternally beyond the self but what is eternally within the self. The woman, as in **The Woman Warrior** and **China Men,** establishes her individual identity in this context. Recognizing this context, this meaning for *home,* she can leave it, go on into her life, while she recognizes that home can never be left but only understood.

Telling is the way to understand, so finally both volumes of Kingston's autobiography are about becoming a writer. Taken together, the two texts demonstrate the special power of telling and, especially, of the imagination for women. Traditionally denied access to the outer world by literal appropriation, women can nevertheless follow a different route. Language is symbolic action, and it becomes, in this autobiography, the route and embodiment of female psychological development. (pp. 187-88)

Suzanne Juhasz, "Maxine Hong Kingston: Narrative Technique & Female Identity," in Contemporary American Women Writers: Narrative Strategies, *edited by Catherine Rainwater and William J. Scheick, The University Press of Kentucky, 1985, pp. 173-90.*

MAXINE HONG KINGSTON [INTERVIEW WITH PAULA RABINOWITZ]

[Rabinowitz]: [*You have*] *said that you had not wanted to go to China before you had finished working on your two books* [**The Woman Warrior** *and* **China Men**]. *In an earlier interview you said you had not wanted to ask people to repeat their stories to you while you were working on the books, either. I saw some connection between the use of memory and the func-*

tion of imagination—the image of China, in particular for you as a writer, and in general for Chinese Americans.

[Kingston]: The artist's memory winnows out; it edits for what is important and significant. Memory, my own memory, shows me what is unforgettable, and helps me get to an essence that will not die, and that haunts me until I can put it into a form, which is the writing. I don't want to get confused by making new memories on top of the old ones which were already such a large vision—the mythic China. Going to China would have meant the creation of, and the beginning of, another memory.

So, when you subtitle **The Woman Warrior,** *"A Memoir of a Girlhood among Ghosts," "memoir" and "ghost" represent the same thing. And they both needed to be exorcised.*

Yes, but not *exorcised.* I have learned that writing does not make ghosts go away. I wanted to record, to find the words for, the "ghosts," which are only visions. They are not concrete; they are beautiful, and powerful. But they don't have a solidity that we can pass around from one to another. I wanted to give them a substance that goes beyond me.

Then memory is essentially a visual quality?

Visual, and emotional. Sometimes, there are words, too, like when someone says something that's violent and it echoes through time.

Like the father's insults in **China Men?**

Yes.

Well, in that context, memories have meaning for you in a sense very different from the Freudian notion that what we remember is what is insignificant, since what's significant is repressed and we never entirely get it back.

Yes, that makes sense, in a way, in that memory is really nothing. It's not substantial, and it's not present. It has to do with past times, and in that sense, it's insignificant, except when it haunts you and when it is a foundation for the rest of the personality. Somehow, though, words are a medium to get to the seemingly subconscious.

I think that these visions don't just come full-blown and with details such as chairs and clothes, and where everything is placed—the relationships between bodies in a room. All that becomes more and more accessible as I approach them with words. Words clarify the vision and memory.

When you think about it, words are also insignificant, insubstantial, not things. So we can use them to arrive at insignificant, insubstantial memories. As I paint part of a vision, the next part of it becomes clear. It's as if I am building the underpinnings of a bridge, and then I can cross it, and see more and more clearly.

So, memory is the starting point for your work, but once the writing begins, it's actually language that takes over the next level of memory, and words become traces themselves.

Because then you find the next memory, all of the time keeping an eye on what's happening in real life, right now. I think that my stories have a constant breaking in and out of the present and past. So the reader might be walking along very well in the present, but the past breaks through and changes and enlightens the present, and vice-versa. The reason that

we remember a past moment at all is that our present-day life is still a working-out of a similar situation.

Because the present reenacts the past. Memory becomes a structuring device to mediate past and present.

Understanding the past changes the present. And the ever-evolving present changes the significance of the past.

I was wondering about your decision to divide off your narratives in terms of a male and a female ancestry—dividing them off by gender. Did you feel that one narrative could not fully contain both kinds of memories?

At one time, **The Woman Warrior** and **China Men** were supposed to be one book. I had conceived of one huge book. However, part of the reason for two books is history. The women had their own time and place and their lives were coherent; there was a woman's way of thinking. My men's stories seemed to interfere. They were weakening the feminist point of view. So I took all the men's stories out, and then I had **The Woman Warrior.**

Historically, of course, the men went to a different country without their families, and so they had their adventures by themselves. It was as if they went to a men's country and they had men's stories. This is hindsight now; but it does seem as if the women's stories have a convolution and the men's stories have more of a linear passage through time. The men's myths and memories are not as integrated into their present-day lives, and that influences the structure of both those books. In **The Woman Warrior,** when the girls and women draw on mythology for their strengths, the myth becomes part of the women's lives and the structure of the stories. In the men's stories, I tell a myth and then I tell a present-day story, a myth, and then another present-day adventure story; they are separate narratives. The reason I think that happened was that those men went to a place where they didn't know whether their mythology was giving them any strength or not. They were getting very broken off from their background. They might not have even been drawing any strength, or they may have gone against the teachings of the myth. They were so caught up in the adventure of the new land that they thought, "What good are memories and the past?" Memory just hurts them, because they can't go home. So, the myth story and the present story become separated.

What you are saying, in a way, is that there is geographic difference in terms of genders. One might roughly say that China is a landscape inhabited, at least in the narratives, by the women and their myths, and the Gold Mountain, America, is really where the men are and that's where history is.

Yes, those men were making history. They were making a new myth, too. They were not so caught up in the old myths as the women were.

Yet, even in the narratives of the men, the sense is that these are narratives that have been retold through women. Perhaps, then, the women's voices and women's memories become a cultural connection between those China myths and that American history?

Yes. In fact, I wrote the characters so that the women have memories and the men don't have memories. They don't remember anything. The character of my father, for example, has no memory. He has no stories of the past. He is an American and even his memories are provided by the mother. She says that he went dancing, or whatever; he is so busy making up the present, which he has to build, that he has no time for continuity from the past. It did seem as if the men were people of action. (pp. 177-80)

Since I just reread them, I was struck by the way you played with intertextuality in the two books, where an insignificant reference in one of the books will be elaborated to a great extent in the other one. Some little statement that Brave Orchid makes in **China Men** *had been a whole section in* **The Woman Warrior** *or vice versa.*

It struck me that the way the two books work is the way that memory works, where some large memory often just comes out of the most ephemeral beginnings and then gets blown up from there. So that you don't ever really remember the whole picture. What you remember is a smell or a "sharp white triangle."

Yes. Yes, and then, that triangle turned out to be the trouser leg glimpsed on a ship while my father was stowing away. I think life works like that. There are various themes and people, and obsessions, that come and go and sometimes they take a major role in life. And then, on another day, you have to devote your whole day to going to the grocery store. . . . (pp. 180-81)

Your books also seem very American, even though they are about "China Men" or "Warrior Women" in China. I was wondering if you were also imagining America?

Oh yes. Actually, I think that my books are much more American than they are Chinese. I felt that I was building, creating, myself and these people as American people, to make everyone realize that these are American people. Even though they have strange Chinese memories, they are American people. Also, I am creating part of American literature, and I was very aware of doing that, of adding to American literature. The critics haven't recognized my work enough as another tradition of American literature.

What tradition?

I directly continue William Carlos Williams' *In the American Grain.* He stopped in 1860 and I pick it up in 1860 and carry it forward. When I was writing "No Name Woman," I was thinking about Nathaniel Hawthorne and *The Scarlet Letter* as a discussion of the Puritan part of America, and of China, and a woman's place. I use the title, "The Making of More Americans," from Gertrude Stein, because when I read *The Making of Americans,* I thought, "Yes, she is creating a language that is the American language; and she is doing it sentence by sentence. I am trying to write an American language that has Chinese accents; I will write the American language as I speak it." So, in a way, I was creating something new, but at the same time, it's still the American language, pushed further.

In that sense, then, there is a kind of political agenda to your writing.

Yes, there is. There has been exclusion socially and politically, and also we have been left out of literature.

I was thinking about the way, in your two books, the characters become Americans by appropriating bits of American popular culture.

Fred Astaire—yeah.

Or the comic books that the little girl reads, and I was wondering whether that appropriation is an example of a kind of subversion of the erasure of Third World cultures. In other words, instead of seeing it as, "Everyone comes to America and—

And we disappear"—

—rather it's a way of turning America into yet another aspect of one's own culture?

Yes, and I think that the highest form of that appropriation is art. In a sense, when I wrote these books, I was claiming the English language and the literature to tell our story as Americans. That is why the forms of the two books are not exactly like other books, and the language and the rhythms are not like other writers, and yet, it's American English. I guess my thought is, "If I can use this language and literature in a really beautiful, strong way, then I have claimed all of it for us." (pp. 182-83)

[The] idea that you are speaking out of a cultural community is crucial?

I don't see how I would live without a community, family, friends. But I am always very interested in how one can be an individual and be part of a collective people and a collective memory. Of course, that's very American too, because Americans strive to stand alone. I am always figuring out how the lone person forms a community.

Well, it seems that memory does that for you in a way. It becomes the translation between an individual narrator and the family, whose stories have been narrated, and the history in which that family has lived its stories.

Yes, and then that brings us to the tribal memory, the family memory, the cultural memory. Well, I guess I contain them all in my own individual memory, but some of the stories that I write began with memories that we all have. Those collective memories are the myths. For example, immigration stories about how you got through Angel Island—having four or five versions of your immigration—that's not just the way my head works, that's the way narration and memory and stories work in our culture. So, that's a gift given to me by our culture, and not something that I imagined on my own. I invented new literary structures to contain multi-versions and to tell the true lives of non-fiction people who are storytellers.

Your books are categorized as autobiography or cultural history and as fiction and I am wondering what you see as the relationship between fact and fiction?

It doesn't bother me very much; it bothers other people more than me. It has caused problems. When the British reviewed my work, they could not get past the question, "Is this fiction or non-fiction?" There have been articles that just addressed that, and never got to what I am talking about.

The question of fiction or non-fiction has become a very political debate. Some minority critics have really elevated the novel as the highest form. They say that autobiography is a lesser form because you are not using imagination, and you present yourself as an oddity, an anthropological specimen, not as a literary creator. Since both *The Woman Warrior* and **China Men** were called non-fiction, I have had attacks from that point of view. When people pointed that out to me, I said, "Sure, I could have classified them as fiction." Our usual idea of biography is of time-lines, of dates and chronological events; I am certainly more imaginative than that; I play with words and form.

After going back and forth on my classification for a couple of years, I've decided that I am writing biography and autobiography of imaginative people. I am writing about real people, all of whom have minds that love to invent fictions. I am writing the biography of their imaginations.

What are you working on now?

I am working on a novel [*Tripmaster Monkey*] that I should finish soon. It is definitely fiction. I mean, I made up everything; I invented the characters and the situations. I can tell the difference between fiction and non-fiction. In a sense, fiction is so much easier, because if the narration needs an exciting moment, I can invent the exciting moment. Whereas, in the other two books, structurally it may be time for an exciting moment, but if the characters decide to go do their laundry or something, then somehow I have to make that a compelling part of the whole narrative.

So you are saying that you felt constrained by the real people who were inhabiting those memories.

Yes, but they were an inspiration and a guide, too. They were always helping me shape the books; whereas in this fiction that I am writing, there is another kind of shaping, where I, as the writer, have a lot more power. In writing the other two books—finding the form, finding the language—I didn't always feel that it was me who was the most powerful. Some of the characters helped shape it, the way they spoke—

Certainly Brave Orchid looms—

Yes, she dictated it, dictated it.

So for the writer, fiction gives more power than writing autobiography. That's interesting, because one would think that if you are constructing the story of your life, you have a power; but you are suggesting the opposite.

Different kinds of power. Now that I have written fiction and two non-fictions, I just don't see why everybody doesn't do both. Each kind of writing draws on other kinds of strengths needed to find new ways to create a literary reality, to get at life. Just playing with another form, I feel that I am in another world.

Do you think that fiction comes out of the same locus of memory and imagination that generated the other two books?

There seems to be a fantasy at work that's different from memory and imagination. For fiction, we fantasize about what we would like to happen: I am making what I would like to happen happen. And so, this writing always feels new and going forward. If there is such a thing as reverse memory, maybe that's what I am getting into; because it seems to me, I'm writing the memory of the future rather than a memory of the past. (pp. 185-87)

Maxine Hong Kingston and Paula Rabinowitz, in an interview in Michigan Quarterly Review, *Vol. XXVI, No. 1, Winter, 1987, pp. 177-87.*

SIDONIE SMITH

A postmodern work, [*The Woman Warrior: Memoirs of a Girlhood among Ghosts*] exemplifies the potential for works from the marginalized to challenge the ideology of individu-

alism and with it the ideology of gender. Recognizing the inextricable relationship between an individual's sense of "self" and the community's stories of selfhood, Kingston self-consciously reads herself into existence through the stories her culture tells about women. Using autobiography to create identity, she breaks down the hegemony of formal "autobiography" and breaks out of the silence that has bound her culturally to discover a resonant voice of her own. Furthermore, as a work coming from an ethnic subculture, *The Woman Warrior* offers the occasion to consider the complex imbroglios of cultural fictions that surround the autobiographer who is engaging two sets of stories: those of the dominant culture and those of an ethnic subculture with its own traditions, its own unique stories. As a Chinese American from the working class, Kingston brings to her autobiographical project complicating perspectives on the relationship of woman to language and to narrative.

Considered by some a "novel" and by others an "autobiography," the five narratives conjoined under the title *The Woman Warrior* are decidedly five confrontations with the fictions of self-representation and with the autobiographical possibilities embedded in cultural fictions, specifically as they interpenetrate one another in the autobiography a woman would write. For Kingston, then, as for the woman autobiographer generally, the hermeneutics of self-representation can never be divorced from cultural representations of woman that delimit the nature of her access to the word and the articulation of her own desire. Nor can interpretation be divorced from her orientation toward the mother, who, as her point of origin, commands the tenuous negotiation of identity and difference in a drama of filiality that reaches through the daughter's subjectivity to her textual self-authoring.

Preserving the traditions that authorize the old way of life and enable her to reconstitute the circle of the immigrant community amidst an alien environment, Kingston's mother dominates the life, the landscape, and the language of the text as she dominates the subjectivity of the daughter who writes that text. It is Brave Orchid's voice, commanding, as Kingston notes, "great power" that continually reiterates the discourses of the community in maxims, talk-story, legends, family histories. As the instrument naming filial identities and commanding filial obligations, that voice enforces the authority and legitimacy of the old culture to name and thus control the place of woman within the patrilineage and thereby to establish the erasure of female desire and the denial of female self-representation as the basis on which the perpetuation of patrilineal descent rests. Yet that same voice gives shape to other possibilities, tales of female power and authority that seem to create a space of cultural significance for the daughter; and the very strength and authority of the material voice fascinates the daughter because it "speaks" of the power of woman to enunciate her own representations. Hence storytelling becomes the means through which Brave Orchid passes on to her daughter all the complexities of and the ambivalences about both mother's and daughter's identity as woman in patriarchal culture.

Storytelling also becomes the means through which Kingston confronts those complexities and ambivalences. In dialogic engagement with her mother's word, she struggles to constitute the voice of her own subjectivity, to emerge from a past dominated by stories told to her, ones that inscribe the fictional possibilities of female selfhood, into a present articulated by her own storytelling. Her text reveals the intensity of that struggle throughout childhood and adolescence and the persistance of those conflicts inherent in self-authoring well into adulthood; for, not only is that effort the subject in the text; it is also dramatized by the text. In the first two narratives she re-creates the stories about women and their autobiographical possibilities passed on to her by her mother: first the biographical story of no-name aunt, an apparent victim and thus a negative model of female life scripts, and then the legendary chant of the warrior woman Fa Mu Lan, an apparent heroine and positive model. But as she explores their fates, Kingston questions the very basis on which such distinctions are predicated. Uncovering layer by layer the dynamics and the consequences of her mother's interpretations as they resonate with the memories of her past, the daughter, as she too passes them on to posterity, circles around them, critiquing them, making them her own. Next she reconstructs out of the autobiographical fragments of Brave Orchid's own Chinese experience a biography of her mother, discovering by the way the efficacies of powerful storytelling for the woman who has fallen in status with her translation to another culture. In the fourth piece, an elaborate fabrication played on actual events, she becomes even more keenly attentive to all autobiographical and biographical representations, including her own. Looking back to the beginnings of her own struggle to take a voice, she traces in the final narrative the origins of her own hermeneutics. The apparent line of progress, which as it ends returns us to the beginning, becomes effectively a circle of sorts, a textual alternative to the constricting patriarchal circle Kingston has had to transgress.

" 'You must not tell anyone,' my mother said, 'what I am about to tell you. In China your father had a sister who killed herself. She jumped into the family well. We say that your father has all brothers because it is as if she had never been born.' " With that interdiction of female speech, uttered in the name of the father, Kingston's mother succinctly elaborates the circumstances of the sister's suicide. The concise maternal narrative concludes with forceful injunctions and powerful maxims inscribing the filial obligations of daughters in the patriarchal order: " 'Don't let your father know that I told you. He denies her. Now that you have started to menstruate, what happened to her could happen to you. Don't humiliate us. You wouldn't like to be forgotten as if you had never been born. The villagers are watchful.' " Kingston thus situates the origins of her autobiography in her recollection of the story her mother used to contextualize the moment of transition ineradicably marking female identity and desire. That event, as it proclaims woman's sexual potency, proclaims also woman's problematic placement within the body social, economic, politic, and symbolic. While her body, the locus of patrilineal preservation, will be contracted out to male authority to serve as the carrier of legitimate sons and of the order those sons perpetuate, it will always remain a potential source of disruption and disintegration in the community: It may provide no sons for the line of descent; or it may entertain strangers and thus introduce illegitimate children and an alternative genealogy into the order. Should a daughter opt for the latter (unfilial) alternative, warns the mother, the patriarchal order will work efficiently to punish her transgression of the contract, eliminating her body and name from the world of things and of discourse. Kingston's aunt has suffered this fate: Her family, like the villagers, has enacted its own cleansing ritual; and Kingston's mother has perpetuated the ritual in the very way she tells the story. The aunt's name remains unuttered; and her interpretation of events is sacrificed, within the mother's text, to concern for the villagers'

actions. Only her body assumes significance as it reveals the sign of its transgression, as it plugs up the family well.

The mother's cautionary tale at once affirms and seeks to cut off the daughter's kinship with a transgressive female relative and her unrepressed sexuality. Kingston acknowledges the effectiveness of that strategy by revealing later in the narrative that for a long time she accepted her mother's interpretation and kept her counsel, thereby colluding in the perpetuation of both her own silencing and the erasure of her aunt's name:

> I have believed that sex was unspeakable and words so strong and fathers so frail that "aunt" would do my father mysterious harm. I have thought that my family, having settled among immigrants who had also been their neighbors in the ancestral land, needed to clean their name, and a wrong word would incite the kinspeople even here. But there is more to this silence: they want me to participate in her punishment. And I have.

Now, however, at the moment of autobiographical writing, Kingston resists identification with mother and father by breaking the silence, returning to the story that marked her entrance into sexual difference and constituting her own interpretation of events. She comes to tell another story, seeking to name the formerly unnamed—the subjectivity of her aunt. As she does so, she imagines her aunt in a series of postures. . . . She imagines her aunt the victim of rape, fearful, silent, and vulnerable before her victimizer. But she suspends that narrative line, apparently dissatisfied with its unmitigated emphasis on female powerlessness and willlessness. Beginning again, Kingston enters her aunt's subjectivity from another perspective, preferring to see her as a willful woman after "subtle enjoyment." Contemplating this posture, she finds herself increasingly aware of the gaps in her mother's tale, which motivate her to ask further questions of the story and to piece together an alternative textual genealogy.

Instead of imagining her aunt as one of "the heavy, deeprooted women" who "were to maintain the past against the flood, safe for returning," and thus as victim, she imagines her as a woman attuned to "a secret voice, a separate attentiveness," truly transgressive and subversive. The fruit of her womb becomes the mark exposing the priority of her desire for sexuality and autobiographical inscription. Indeed, the expansion of her very body and of her sense of her own authority to define herself ultimately challenges the ontological roots of her culture—"the real"; for publicized female subjectivity points to the fundamental vulnerability of the patrilineage by exposing it as a sustained fiction. The alternative genealogy thus engendered breaks the descent line, subverting the legitimacy of male succession that determines all lines in patriarchy—descent lines, property lines, and lines of texts. "The frightened villagers, who depended on one another to maintain the real," writes Kingston, "went to my aunt to show her a personal, physical representation of the break she had made in the 'roundness.' Misallying couples snapped off the future, which was to be embodied in true offspring. The villagers punished her for acting as if she could have a private life, secret and apart from them."

While her journey across the boundaries that circumscribe the patriarchal order takes the aunt into the unbounded spaces of self-representation, Kingston acknowledges also that this "rare urge west" leads her into the vast spaces of alienation, fearfulness, and death. Expelled from the family circle, her aunt becomes "one of the stars, a bright dot in blackness, without home, without a companion, in eternal cold and silence." While the endless night proposes limitless identities beyond the confining borders of repetitious patriarchal representations, it promotes the "agoraphobia" attending any move beyond the carefully prescribed boundaries of ancestral, familial, and community paradigms of female self-representation. Overwhelmed by the vast spaces of possibility, the aunt returns to the genealogical source, reestablishing her cultural "responsibility" by giving birth in the pigsty— "to fool the jealous, pain-dealing gods, who do not switch piglets"—and then by killing herself and her child—"a child with no descent line would not soften her life but only trail after her, ghostlike, begging her to give it purpose." From one point of view, then, the aunt enacts on her own body and her own alternative genealogical text the punishment of the tribe, fulfilling her filial responsibilities to her circle by eliminating the source of contamination from its center and thereby restoring it to its unbroken configuration. She thus returns to the silence that defines her condition and her identity. From another point of view, however, the aunt's suicide continues her rebellion in a congeries of ways. First, she brings back with her to the center of her natal circle the two loci of greatest pollution in Chinese culture—the moments of birth and death. Second, by jumping back into the circle—the family well—she contaminates, in a recapitulated gesture of disruption, the water that literally and symbolically promises the continuance of patrilineal descent and the symbolic order it nourishes. Third, she takes with her the secret of paternal origins, never revealing the name of the father. Saving the father's face, she paradoxically erases the paternal trace, betraying in yet another way the fundamental fragility of undisputed paternal authority. Finally, by withholding from her natal family the name of the offender whose actions have caused such disgrace, she denies them the means to recover face by enacting their own revenge on the violator. Thus, while she seems to capitulate before the monolithic power of the order against which she has transgressed, Kingston envisions her as a "spite suicide," an antiheroine whose actions subvert the stability of an order that rests on the moral imperatives of filial obligations, including sexual repression. Her very silence becomes a powerful presence, a female weapon of vengeance. Toward the end of this imaginative portrait, Kingston returns once again to her mother's tale by repeating the earlier refrain: " 'Don't tell anyone you had an aunt. Your father does not want to hear her name. She has never been born.' " Yet while Kingston repeats her mother's words, she does so with a critical difference. Unlike her mother, she engenders a story for her aunt, fleshing out the narrative and incorporating the subjectivity previously denied that woman. Individualizing her mother's cautionary and impersonal tale, she transforms in the process both her aunt's text and her aunt's body from a maxim (a mere vessel to hold patriarchal signifiers) into a "life." Moreover, she ensures that she herself becomes more than a mere vessel preserving her mother's maxims, however deeply they may be embedded in her consciousness. For the story of this "forerunner," her "urge west" and her agoraphobia, becomes a piece in the puzzle of her own erased and erasable identity. . . . (pp. 150-55)

Kingston retrieves her aunt from the oblivion of sexuality repressed and textuality erased by placing her in an alternative narrative: the line of matrilineal descent to which she traces her origins and through which she gives voice to her subjectivity. Like her aunt's before her, this transgression of the injunction to filial silence challenges the priority of patrilineal descent. Allowing her imagination to give voice to the body of her aunt's text, Kingston expresses in her own way the excess of narrative (textuality) that links her intimately to that earlier excess of sexuality she identifies in her aunt. Indeed, her aunt becomes her textual "child," product of the fictions through which Kingston gives "birth" to her, and, by the way, to herself. Her story thus functions as a sign, like her aunt's enlarging belly, publicizing the potentially disruptive force of female textuality and the matrilineal descent of texts.

On the level of her mother's tale, then, the originating story of Kingston's autobiography testifies to the power of the patriarchy to command through mothers the silence of daughters, to name and to unname them, and thereby to control their meaning in discourse itself. On another level the opening piece displaces the mother's myth with the daughter's, thereby subverting the interpretations on which patrilineal descent and filial responsibilities are predicated and establishing a space in which female desire and self-representation can emerge. . . . Kingston does not yet know her aunt's name; and the subjectivity she has created for her remains only another interpretation, a fiction. Nor, by implication, can she be sure that she will ever know the truth about her own past. Her name is never uttered in the text; and her memories and stories may only be fictions too. This maternal trace, disruptive of the patriarchal order, may be potentially as threatening to Kingston as it was to her aunt. Indeed, she may be the child—"it was probably a girl; there is some hope of forgiveness for boys"—that her aunt takes with her to the grave. Ultimately, the full, the "real" story of woman may lead to madness and to self-destruction rather than to legitimate self-representation.

Kingston in the second piece engages another of her mother's representations of female autobiography, a story from which she learned that Chinese girls "failed if we grew up to be but wives and slaves." Here she does not distinguish in quotation marks the words of her mother; rather, she moves directly to her own elaboration of Fa Mu Lan's chant. But she goes further, appropriating not only the chant but also the very body of that legendary woman warrior: The identities of woman warrior and of woman narrator interpenetrate until biography becomes autobiography, until Kingston and Fa Mu Lan are one. Through this fantasy of mythic identification, the adult daughter inscribes an autobiography of "perfect filiality" through which she fulfills her mother's expectations and garners her mother's unqualified love. Simultaneously, this "life" enables her to escape confinement in conventional female scripts and to enter the realm of heroic masculine pursuits—of education, adventure, public accomplishment, and fame. Ironically, however, Kingston's mythical autobiography betrays the ontological bases on which that love, power, and compliance with perfect filiality rest.

The woman warrior gains her education beyond the engendered circle of community and family in a magical, other-worldly place where male and female difference remains undelineated. Her educators are a hermaphroditic couple beyond childbearing age whose relationship appears to be one of relative equality; and the education they offer encourages her to forge an identity, not through conventional formulations of woman's selfhood, but through a close identification with the creatures of nature and the secrets of natural space. In such a space female sexuality, signaled by the onslaught of puberty, remains a "natural" event rather than a cultural phenomenon situating the girl in a constellation of attitudes toward female pollution and contamination. Nonetheless, that education, while it appears to be liberating, presupposes Fa Mu Lan's total identification with the desires of her family, ubiquitously present even in its absence. For instance, she passively watches in the gourd as her own wedding ceremony takes place despite her absence, the choice of husband entirely her parents' prerogative. Ultimately, woman can be trained as warrior only in a space separate from family; but she can enter that space only because her sacrifice to the circle is the basis on which her education takes place at all. Consequently, her empowerment does not threaten to disrupt the representations of the patriarchal circle; on the contrary, it serves both the family and the discourse of gender. (pp. 156-58)

Fa Mu Lan's name, unlike the name of no-name aunt, is passed on from generation to generation, precisely because the lines of her story as woman warrior and the lines of her text as woman autobiographer reproduce an androcentric paradigm of identity and selfhood and thereby serve the symbolic order in "perfect filiality." Since both life and text mask her sexual difference and thereby secure her recuperation in the phallic order by inscribing her subjectivity and her selfhood in the law of the same representation, they legitimate the very structures man creates to define himself, including those structures that silence women.

The heroic figure of Fa Mu Lan thus represents a certain kind of woman warrior, a culturally privileged "female avenger." Embedded in Kingston's fantasy autobiography, however, lies a truly subversive "story" of female empowerment. Imaged as tiny, foot-bound, squeaky-voiced women dependent on male authority for their continued existence, the wives of warriors, barons, and emperors who haunt the interstices of the textual landscape are, in one sense, conventional ghosts. Yet those apparently erased ciphers become, in another sense, the real female avengers:

> Later, it would be said, they turned into the band of swordswomen who were a mercenary army. They did not wear men's clothes like me, but rode as women in black and red dresses. They bought up girl babies so that many poor families welcomed their visitations. When slave girls and daughters-in-law ran away, people would say they joined these witch amazons. They killed men and boys. I myself never encountered such women and could not vouch for their reality.

Such "witch amazons" are figures of all that is unrepressed and violent in ways both sexual and textual, in the narrator herself as well as in the social order. Wielding unauthorized power, they do not avenge the wrongs of fathers and brothers; they lead daughters against fathers and sons, slaying the source of the phallic order itself. Moreover, they do so, not by masking, but by aggressively revealing their sexual difference. Paradoxically, Fa Mu Lan has liberated the women who subvert the order she serves, just as Kingston the narrator has released the rumor that subverts the story she tells.

Kingston's memories of the real, rather than mythical, childhood also subvert the fiction she has created out of her mother's expectations. Juxtaposing to this autobiography of androcentric selfhood another self-representation that undermines the priority of the fantasy of "perfect filiality," Kingston betrays Fa Mu Lan's story as a fragile fiction only coterminous with the words that inscribe it as myth. And the jarring texture of her recollected experience—its nervous, disjointed, unpoetic, frustrated prose—calls into question the basis for the seamless elegance and almost mystical lyricism of Fa Mu Lan's poetic autobiography. (pp. 158-59)

In the end, there remains only one residual locus of identity between Kingston and Fa Mu Lan. . . . [Kingston's] appropriation of the pen, that surrogate sword, and her public inscription of the story of her own childhood among ghosts become the reporting of a crime—the crime of a culture that would make nothing of her by colonizing her and, in so doing, steal her authority and her autobiography from her as her mother's legend would do. In the tale the forces of exploitation remain external to her family; but in her own experience they remain internal, endemic to the patriarchal family whose existence is founded on the colonization and erasure of women in service to the selfhood of men and boys and whose perpetuation is secured through the mother's word. By simultaneously enacting and critiquing that legendary story of female power, Kingston manages to shatter the complacencies of cultural myths, problematic heroines, and the illusory autobiographical possibilities they sanction. By "slaying" the stories of men and boys and phallic women warriors, she allies herself with the true female avengers of her tale. Fa Mu Lan may have denied her identity with such women; Kingston does not.

Whereas the first two narratives explore the consequences of Kingston's appropriation of her mother's stories, the third goes through the stories to the storyteller herself. Three scrolls from China serve as the originating locus of this biography of her mother pieced together with "autobiographical" fragments. Texts that legitimate her mother's professional identity as doctor, the scrolls stimulate biography because they announce public achievements, a life text readable by culture. They also announce to the daughter another mother, a mythic figure resident in China who resisted the erasure of her own desire and who pursued her own signifying selfhood. In her daughter's text, Brave Orchid becomes a kind of "woman warrior," whose story resonates with the Fa Mu Lan legend: both women leave the circle of the family to be educated for their mission and both return to serve their community, freeing it through many adventures from those forces that would destroy it. Both are fearless, successful, admired.

Kingston's biography accretes all varieties of evidence testifying to her mother's bravery and extraordinariness. Portrayed as one of the "new women, scientists who changed the rituals," Brave Orchid bears the "horizontal name of one generation" that truly names her rather than the patronym signifying woman's identity as cipher silently bonding the patrilineage. Thus Kingston's awe-filled narration of her mother's confrontation with the Sitting Ghost takes on . . . synecdochic proportions in the text. . . . (pp. 160-61)

Embedded in the daughter's representation of her mother's extraordinariness, however, lies another, a palimpsest that tells of her mother's preoccupation with autobiographical interpretation. Even more important than the story of Brave Orchid's confrontation with the Sitting Ghost is the recreation of her narrative of the encounter. Skillful in creating compelling stories of her experience, Brave Orchid makes of the ghost a vividly ominous antagonist, thereby authoring herself as powerful protagonist. Such imaging ensures the emboldening of her presence in the eyes and imaginations of the other women (and of her daughter). . . . (pp. 161-62)

The mother's mode of self-authoring complicates the daughter's effort to reconstruct her mother's biography. Brave Orchid's stories about China become the only archival material out of which Kingston can create that "life"; and yet the stories are already "representations" or "fictions" of her experiences before she reaches an America where she is no doctor, where she works daily washing other people's laundry or picking fruit and vegetables in the fields, where she is no longer woman alone but a wife and mother, where she is no woman warrior dressed elegantly in silk. (p. 162)

Kingston's narrative, as it interpenetrates her autobiography with her mother's biography, reveals how problematic such stories can become for the next generation. From one point of view, they can be exhilarating, creating in children the admiration that is so apparent in Kingston's text. But from another, they generate confusions and ambiguities, since as a child Kingston inflected the narratives with her own subjectivity, attending to another story within the text of female heroism. For Brave Orchid's tales of bravery and exoticism are underwritten by an alternative text of female vulnerability and victimization. The story elaborating the purchase of the slave girl reaffirms the servile status of women and actually gives legitimacy to Kingston's fears her parents will sell her when they return to China. The stories of babies identify femaleness with deformity and suggest to the daughter the haunting possibility that her mother might actually have practiced female infanticide. The story of the crazy lady, scurrying directionless on bound feet, encased in the mirror-studded headdress, caught in her own self-destructive capitulations, dramatizes communal fear of the anomalous woman who embodies the threat of uncontrolled female sexuality and subversive alliances between women—always strangers within the community—and the enemy outside.

All these tales from her mother's past, by reinforcing the representation of women as expendable, resonate with Kingston's sense of displacement in her family and in the immigrant community in America, her confusion about her sexuality, and her fears of her own "deformities" and "madnesses." They leave her with food that suffocates her, a voice that squeaks on her, and nightmares that haunt the long nights of childhood. They also complicate Kingston's sense of identification with her mother by betraying the basis on which her tales of extraordinariness are founded, that is, the powerlessness of ordinary women and children and their cruel and insensitive victimization, even at the hands of Brave Orchid herself. In fact, in her self-representation Kingston identifies herself with the "lonely and afraid," a victim of her mother's stories, and thus no true heroine after her mother's model. Paradoxically, her mother, the shaman with the power of word and food, has, instead of inspiring her daughter to health and heroism, made the daughter sick, hungry, vulnerable, fearful.

In the closing passage of this third narrative, Kingston recreates her most recent encounter with her mother and, through it, her continuing resistance to her mother's victimizing presence. Ironically, the scene recapitulates the earlier scene of her mother's biography. The dark bedroom, the late hour recall the haunted room at the medical school. (pp. 162-63)

In the fourth narrative Kingston does not take the word of her mother as her point of narrative origin. She will reveal at the inception of the next piece that the only information she received about the events narrated in the fourth piece came from her brother through her sister in the form of an abrupt, spare bone of a story. . . . (p. 164)

In Kingston's designs Moon Orchid, like Brave Orchid in "Shaman," embodies her name: She is a flower of the moon, a decorative satellite that revolves around and takes its definition from another body, the absent husband. Mute to her own desire, attendant always on the word of her husband, she represents the traditional Chinese wife, a woman without autobiographical possibilities. . . . Unlike Brave Orchid, she is neither clever nor shrewd, skilled nor quick, sturdy nor lasting. Demure, self-effacing, decorative, tidy, refined—she is as gracefully useless and as elegantly civilized as bound feet, as decoratively insubstantial as the paper cutouts she brings her nieces and nephews from the old country. Having little subjectivity of her own, she can only appropriate as her own the subjectivity of others, spending her days following nieces and nephews through the house, describing what they do, repeating what they say, asking what their words mean. While there is something delightfully childlike, curious, and naive about that narration of other people's lives, there is a more profound sadness that a woman in her sixties, unformed and infantile, has no autobiography of her own.

When her husband rejects her, giving his allegiance to his Chinese-American wife, who can speak English and aid him in his work, he denies the very ontological basis on which Moon Orchid's selfhood is predicated and effectually erases her from the lines of descent. He also undermines with his negation of her role what autobiographical representations she has managed to create for herself. (pp. 164-65)

Through the "designs" in "At the Western Palace," Kingston confronts explicitly the problematics of autobiographical "fictions." Both Moon Orchid and Brave Orchid serve as powerful negative models for the perils of autobiography. Moon Orchid, bereft of the husband who defines her place and who sets the limits of her subjectivity within the structures of the patrilineage, succumbs to an imagination anchored in no-place, an imaginative rootlessness threatening Kingston herself. Overwhelmed by repetitive fantasies, her aunt vanishes into a world where alien males continually plot to erase her from existence, a preoccupation that resonates with Kingston's childhood fears of leaving no culturally significant autobiographical trace. A woman of no autobiography, Moon Orchid cannot find a voice of her own, or, rather, the only subjectivity that she finally voices is the subjectivity of madness. Brave Orchid, too, serves as a powerful negative model. She would write a certain biography of her sister, patterned after traditional interpretations of the identity of a first wife. In preserving her interpretations, however, she victimizes other women by failing to make a space in her story for female subjectivity in unfamiliar landscapes, by remaining insensitive to her sister's fears and desires, as she remains insensitive to her daughter's desires. Giving her unquestioning allegiance to language, she fails to recognize the danger in words, the perils inherent in the fictions that bind.

In the end Kingston, too, has created only a fiction, an elaborate story out of the one sentence passed by her brother through her sister; and she, too, must beware the danger in words as she constructs her stories of those other women, more particularly her mother. To a certain extent she seems to do so in this fourth narrative. For all the negative, even horrifying, aspects of Brave Orchid's fierce preservation and Moon Orchid's repetitious fantasies, both women come across in this section as fully human. Her mother, especially, does so; and that is because, releasing her mother to be her own character, under her own name "Brave Orchid," rather than as "my mother," the daughter penetrates her mother's subjectivity with tender ironies and gentle mercies. In doing so, she effaces her own presence in the text as character, her presence implied only in the reference to Brave Orchid's "children." Unlike her mother, then, who does not imagine the contours of her sister's subjectivity, Kingston here tries to think like her mother and her aunt. Yet even as she creates the fullness of her mother out of her word, she recognizes the very fictionality of her tale—its "designs" that serve her own hermeneutical purposes. She, too, like her mother within her story, negotiates the world by means of the fictions that sustain interpretations and preserve identities. In the persistent reciprocities that characterize Kingston's storytelling, her mother becomes the product of her fictions, as she has been the product of her mother's.

Kingston represents in the final piece, "A Song for a Barbarian Reed Pipe," her adolescent struggle to discover her own speaking voice and autobiographical authority. This drama originates in the memory of her mother's literally cutting the voice out of her. . . . Notably, Kingston remembers, not the actual event, but the reconstruction of the event in language, a phenomenon testifying to the power of the mother's word to constitute the daughter's history, in this case her continuing sense of confusion, horror, deprivation, and violation. Her mother passes on a tale of female castration, a rite of passage analogous to a clitoridectomy, that wounding of the female body in service to the community, performed and thereby perpetuated by the mother. It is a ritual that results in the denial to woman of the pleasure of giving voice to her body and body to her voice, the pleasure of autobiographical legitimacy and authority.

In her re-creation of the confrontation with the Chinese-American girl in the bathroom of the Chinese school, Kingston evokes her childhood confusion about speechlessness: "Most of us," she comments, "eventually found some voice, however faltering. We invented an American-feminine speaking personality, except for that one girl who could not speak up even in Chinese school." A kind of surrogate home, the Chinese school functions as the repository of old traditions and conventional identities within the immigrant community; and the bathroom is that most private of female spaces— only for girls, only for certain activities, which, as it locates the elimination of matter from the body, ultimately becomes associated with female pollution and shame. In that space, Kingston responds cruelly, even violently, to the female image before her, abhorring the girl's useless fragility: her neat, pastel clothes; her China-doll haircut; her tiny, white teeth; her baby-soft, fleshy skin—"like squid out of which the glassy blades of bones had been pulled," "like tracing paper, onion paper." Most of all, she abhors her "dumbness," for this girl, who cannot even speak her name aloud, is ultimately without body or text. (pp. 167-68)

Yet, while the girl stands mute before the screaming Kingston, they both weep profusely, wiping their snot on their sleeves as the seemingly frozen scene wraps them both in its embrace. Kingston remembers feeling some comfort in establishing her difference from the girl, taking pride in her dirty fingernails, calloused hands, yellow teeth, her desire to wear black. But the fierceness with which she articulates her desire for difference only accentuates her actual identity with the nameless girl: Both are the last ones chosen by teams; both

are silent and "dumb" in the American school. An exaggerated representation of the perfect Chinese girl, this girl becomes a mirror image of Kingston herself, reflecting her own fears of insubstantiality and dumbness (symbolized for her in the zero intelligence quotient that marks her first-grade record). In the pulling of the hair, the poking of the flesh, Kingston captures the violence of her childhood insecurity and self-hatred. Striking the Chinese-American girl, she strikes violently at her own failure to take a voice and at all her mother's prior narratives of female voicelessness. (p. 169)

[As] her narrative recollection reveals, taking a voice becomes complicated by her sense of guilt. She is ashamed to speak in public with a voice like those of the immigrant women—loud, inelegant, unsubtle. She is ashamed to speak the words her mother demands she say to the druggist ghost because she considers her mother's words, as they exact compliance with traditional beliefs, to be outdated. She is ashamed to keep the same kind of silences and secrets her mother would keep because such secrets command her duplicity before the teachers she respects. For all these reasons she would not speak like her mother (and Chinese women) in her American environment; but her own efforts to take the appropriate American-feminine voice fail, and that failure too gives her cause for shame. (pp. 169-70)

The landscape of her childhood, as she reconstructs it, reveals the underlying logic in Kingston's failure to overcome her symbolic disability. Seeing around her the humiliating representations of woman, hearing words such as "maggots" become synonyms for "girls," suspecting that her mother seeks to contract her out as the wife and slave of some young man, perhaps even the retarded boy who follows her around with his box full of pornographic pictures, she negotiates a nightmare of female victimization by adopting the postures of an unattractive girl, the better to foil her mother's efforts and to forestall her weary capitulation. Cultivating that autobiographical signature, she represents herself publicly as the obverse of her mother's image of the charming, attractive, practical young girl by becoming clumsy, vulgar, bad-tempered, lazy, impractical, irreverent, and stupid "from reading too much." She becomes, that is, a kind of fiction; and the psychic price she pays for orchestrating such a public posture is high. Publicly appearing as the "dumb" and awkward girl, she does not earn the affection and respect of her family and community. Moreover, she must convince herself of the reality of her mind by constantly attending to the grades she earns in the American school, those signs, unrecognized in her Chinese culture, that signal her access to other discourses. (p. 170)

The culmination of this struggle with voice comes when Kingston finally attempts to "explain" her silenced guilts, the text of which lengthens daily, and to represent her repressed desires to her mother, believing that by doing so she will establish some grounds for identification and overcome her profound isolation and dumbness. . . . Recapitulating the earlier castration, her mother cuts her tongue by refusing to acknowledge the daughter's stories as legitimate: " 'I can't stand this whispering,' she said looking right at me, stopping her squeezing. 'Senseless gabbings every night. I wish you would stop. Go away and work. Whispering, whispering, making no sense. Madness. I don't feel like hearing your craziness.' " In response, Kingston swallows her words, but only temporarily. The tautness of her vocal cords increasing to a breaking point, she later bursts the silence, uttering in a cathartic moment the text of her inner life before her mother. Finally, this girl takes of voice, albeit in great confusion, and thereby authors a vision, textualizes her subjectivity, and legitimizes her own desires. She embarks, that is, on the autobiographical enterprise, articulating her interpretations against her mother's.

In this battle of words, mother and daughter, products of different cultural experiences, systems of signs, and modes of interpretation, speak two different "languages" and inscribe two different stories—graphically imaged in the sets of quotation marks that delimit their separate visions and betray the gap in the matrilineage as the circle of identity, of place and desire, is disrupted. Unable to understand the mother, unwilling to identify with her, the daughter would, in ironic reciprocity, cut off her mother's word: " 'I don't want to listen to any more of your stories; they have no logic. They scramble me up. You lie with stories. You won't tell me a story and then say, 'This is a true story,' or 'This is just a story.' " But her mother's reluctant admission—" 'We like to say the opposite' "—forces Kingston to question, at the moment of their origin, her own interpretations and thus the "truth" or "fictiveness" of the autobiography she would inscribe through her memories of the past. As a result, the young Kingston comes to recognize the relativity of truth, the very elusiveness of self-representation that drives the autobiographical enterprise. "Ho Chi Kuai" her mother calls her; and, even to the moment in her adult life when she writes her autobiography, she cannot specify, can only guess, the meaning of the name her mother gave her from that culture she would leave behind. In the end she can only try to decipher the meaning of her past, her subjectivity, her desire, her own name: "I continue to sort out what's just my childhood, just my imagination, just my family, just the village, just movies, just living."

Kingston closes **The Woman Warrior** with a coda, returning it to silence after telling two brief stories, one her mother's, one hers. Notably, her mother's story is now a gift. Passed from one storyteller to another, it signals the mother's genuine identification with the daughter. Yet the two-part story also functions as a testament to difference, the simple juxtaposition of two words rather than the privileging of one before the other. Here, at last, Kingston lets her mother's word stand without resisting it. (pp. 170-72)

In that final juxtaposition of two stories, Kingston asserts the grounds of identification with her mother, affirming continuities rather than disjunctions in the line. She is her mother's daughter, however much she may distance herself geographically and psychologically, learning from her the power and authority that enable her to originate her own storytelling. Carrying on the matrilineal trace, she becomes like her mother a mistress of the word in a culture that would privilege only the lines, textual and genealogical, of patrilineal descent. With her text she gives historical "birth" to Brave Orchid, creating for her a textual space in the genealogical record, and she gives "birth" to herself as the daughter who has passed through the body and the word of the mother. (p. 173)

Sidonie Smith, "Maxine Hong Kingston's 'Woman Warrior': Filiality and Woman's Autobiographical Storytelling," in her A Poetics of Women's Autobiography: Marginality and the Fictions of Self-Representation, *Indiana University Press, 1987, pp. 150-73.*

HERBERT GOLD

[*Tripmaster Monkey*] blends the kind of magic realism familiar to readers of Latin American fiction with the hard-edged black humor of flower-epoch comic writers and performers—a little bit of Lenny Bruce and a whole lot of Gabriel Garcia Marquez. Kingston's energy, talent and unique perspective make an odd dish work, like some sort of hefty Chinese *nouvelle maxi-cuisine* stew.

The rhapsody of Wittman Ah Sing begins with a dolorous contemplation of suicide and ends in a good time, the poet and playwright happily sort of married to Tana, the blond free-spirit who promised she didn't really love him. Rilke-reading and tripping, Wittman lusts after the idea of America, sneers at the F.O.B.'s—fresh-off-the-boats—and follows a path familiar to other immigrants. He's in a hurry. In the Chinese tradition, the tripmaster monkey is a playful, all-knowing spirit. But here he is also a scammer, operator, hustler, a resentful friend, an ambitious artist, a street desperado. He is horny. He is, as he says, the King of the Monkeys.

Kingston writes accurately out of the persona of this young man, capturing his raving and his snobbishness, as when he describes another Chinese "bouncing about on his toes out of exuberance and shortness." She has some bitter fun with the notion that, because they aren't really looked at, all Chinese seem to look alike. Wittman's sense of apartness is soaked into the story, his resentment both of his old-country family in Sacramento and of his Bay Area friends with their unconscious racism.

But the familiar upward-striving immigrant's predicament is not what makes this story go. It's not a memoir or an argument. There is a marvelous magpie gathering of the evidence of the '60s, and a number of joyful improvisations upon memory and character.

Wittman drops in on a movie, *West Side Story,* and contemplates the Hollywood musical's falsifications while humming along with the song that goes, "I like to be in America. Everything fine in America." Then he comes blinking back into "the natural world that moves at a medium rate with no jump cuts to the interesting parts."

He lopes through life in his "metaphor glasses," which deliberately blur and fuzz the world into something imaginary. He wonders if he's "the only Chinese-American of his generation not in grad school." He is another Huck Finn, Henry Miller or Augie March in that western metropolitan village that is touched by the Far East in familiar, sometimes rude, places. He suffers adventures—movies, plays, romances, stories within stories—in a zany compost of tale, rap, invective, street poetry. (pp. 1, 10)

It used to seem that the Chinese of San Francisco lived apart from the flower-child madness of the '60s. Evidently Wittman (and perhaps Kingston) also was busy having fun. The dense anecdotes that rush through **Tripmaster Monkey** offer a crowded portrait of a man, a time, a city and of a misunderstood presence.

Waiting until middle life to publish her first novel, Kingston has combined a keen sense of recent history, a generous experience with fantasy fiction masters, a satirical meditation on the black humor picaresques of the '60s and early '70s, and something special, individual and captivating of her own. She invigorates her novel with an avid personal perspective, doing what the novel is supposed to do—she brings us the news of the world and makes magic of it. Her world is that of Chinese immigrants to America, and we don't yet have enough word of it. This report, funny, fast and touching, is more than testimony. (p. 10)

Herbert Gold, "Far-Out West," in Chicago-Tribune—Books, *April 16, 1989, pp. 1, 10.*

ANNE TYLER

[*Tripmaster Monkey* is] a great, huge sprawling beast of a novel, over 400 pages densely packed with the rantings and ravings and pranks and high jinks of one Wittman Ah Sing, a young Chinese-American (but how he would hate that term! Correction: American) rattling around San Francisco at some indeterminate point in the early 1960s. Just a year out of Berkeley, Wittman divides his time between writing poetry and clerking in a toy department, and when we first meet him he's considering suicide, but in such animated and slapdash terms that he doesn't have us worried for a moment.

A few of Wittman's mottoes are: "Better to be dead than boring," "Always do the more flamboyant thing," and "Do something, even if it's wrong." You see where all this could lead—and it does. Wittman's life is anything but dull. During the course of this novel, which encompasses just two months or so, Wittman gets fired for staging a pornographic scene between a Barbie doll and a battery-operated monkey, marries a virtual stranger in an impromptu ceremony performed by a mail-order minister, and produces a marathon play whose cast consists of nearly everyone he's ever met. And that's just the plot's stripped skeleton. There's much, much more, all of it related in his own highly exclamatory interior voice. . . .

Many of Wittman's most impassioned monologues, private or public, have to do with his resentment of the way white Americans perceive him. Why, he wonders, do readers always assume a character is white unless they're told otherwise? . . . And why, he asks his theater audience, do white Americans always focus immediately upon his Chineseness? . . .

Tripmaster Monkey is a novel of excesses—both the hero's and the author's. Wittman careens through the story with that oversupply of manic energy often found in bright, idealistic, not-yet-mellowed young men; and Kingston describes his adventures in a style equally manic, equally energetic. If we didn't know better, we could imagine this book had been written by, say, a 23-year-old newly graduated college student.

Sometimes this is dazzling. How does she do it? we marvel. Where, for instance, does she find the vitality to embark upon a minutely detailed five-page description of what a roomful of high and contact-high party guests sees while staring at a blank TV screen? How has she managed to summon the youthful quirkiness, the youthful sense of limitless time and entirely idle curiosity, that allows Wittman to delight in the reflection of his own naked crotch as distorted by the handguard of a fencing sword? Or, for that matter, the youthful cruelty with which he surveys his fellow human beings? (p. 45)

But at other times the effect is exhausting—much as if that 23-year-old had taken up residence in our living room, staying way too long, as 23-year-olds are wont to do, and wearing us out with his exuberance. The myths and sagas are particularly tiring. Wittman loves to tell lengthy stories that possess the grandiosity and the meandering formlessness common to folk legends. It's hard to believe that his friends, who tend to be as frenetic as Wittman himself, would sit still for what amounts to hours of this. Certainly the reader has trouble doing so. After a while, the merest mention of Liu Pei or Sun Wu Kong, the Monkey King, is enough to make our eyes glaze over.

No, what keeps us with *Tripmaster Monkey* (and we do stay with it, wholeheartedly) is not the larger-than-life sagas that Wittman finds so compelling but the tiny, meticulously catalogued details that fill his quieter moments. Just listen to the jumbled conversation of his mother and aunts as they play mah-jongg, or watch the hilarious lengths to which his father will go to save money, or observe Wittman's extended, gently humorous encounter with an elderly applicant in the Unemployment Office. When he lists the outward signs of a disintegrating marriage (the shrimp shells rotting on the dinner table, the off-the-hook telephone lost among the dirty clothes), or when he announces his resolutions for self-improvement ("decant the catsup . . . wash coffee cup between usings. . . . Peel an orange into the garbage bag, okay, but then walk a ways off, don't slurp over the bag"), the miracle is that we are riveted to his words no matter how long they go on. These passages refuel us; they remind us how infinitely entertaining everyday life can be when it's observed with a fresh eye.

Chinese, American, Chinese-American—Wittman is all three, whether he likes it or not, and the reader benefits. That Wittman is Chinese gives his story depth and particularity. That he's American lends his narrative style a certain slangy insouciance. That he's Chinese-American, with the self-perceived outsider's edgy angle of vision, makes for a novel of satisfying complexity and bite and verve. (p. 46)

Anne Tyler, "Manic Monologue," in The New Republic, *Vol. 200, No. 16, April 17, 1989, pp. 44-6.*

GERALD VIZENOR

"Got no money. Got no home. Got story," says Wittman Ah Sing, in this fantastic novel [*Tripmaster Monkey*] by Maxine Hong Kingston.

Ah Sing is an unemployed writer who encounters the '60s on a cultural rebound, a Chinese American determined to complete an ancestral Gold Mountain trunk, with his wild stories. "I can't die until I fill it with poems and play-acts." He lives in San Francisco as a splendid incarnation of the Monkey King from the popular 16th-Century fiction, *The Journey to the West.* . . .

The Monkey King is the paramount metaphor in these stories; the simian moves are comic transformations, rather than mere imposture. Ah Sing creates the scenes, directs the action and conversations; the author and narrator are obscure mediators in this urban trickster crusade. For instance, the unnamed narrator says to a woman in a restaurant, "Are you the one I can tell my whole life to?" Such narrative intercessions are comic duels; the narrator is the second and the mind monkey the duelist in a dramatic remembrance.

C. T. Hsia in *The Classic Chinese Novel* wrote that Monkey King is "always the spirit of mischief when he is in command of a situation." His sense of humor "implies his ultimate transcendance of all human desires . . . comedy mediates between myth and allegory."

The author mediates cultural myths and identities, the political allegories of the '60s, and comic themes from classical literature. This new monkey would overturn the world with his coarse beard and bizarre clothes; at least he could enchant women with his imagination. "This is The Journey *In* the West," said Ah Sing. "We have the eyes that won the West." Those "little squinny eyes" that scan the plains at high noon. (p. 1)

Anthony C. Yu, in his translation of *The Journey to the West,* noted that the classical monkey teaches enlightenment, "not simply the illusory nature of experience." Wittman is a postmodern monkey, a philosopher of coincidence: "Do the right thing by whoever crosses your path."

This monkey measured his mythic origins on stage, when "one big light blasted me." Zeppelin Ah Sing, his father, was a theater electrician, and later, a gold miner; his aunties were showgirls. "I was a mad baby from the start . . . a descendant of free spirits." . . .

Ah Sing is no moral master, but he is a resplendent commentator on scenes from cinema; in fact, there is more filmic hearsay than allusion to popular memories or political histories of the time. The cinema in this novel could be scanned as a revelation, the new dharma, a revision of classical scriptures. . . .

When the author encroaches on the narrative she can be hilarious: "Gary Snyder had gone to Japan to meditate for years, and could now spend five minutes in the same room with his mother." However, some intrusions are unsuitable, the diction awkward: "Anybody American who really imagines Asia feels the loneliness of the U.S.A. and suffers from the distances human beings are apart."

There is a wild humor and moral distance in the stories; coincidence seems to hinder the characters at times. The narrator bares the ironies in language, but seldom the intimacies; for instance, "Wittman's English better than his Chinese, and PoPo's Chinese better than her English, you would think that they weren't understanding each other. But the best way to talk to someone of another language is at the top of your intelligence, not to slow down or to shout or to talk babytalk. You say more than enough, o.d. your listener, give her plenty to choose from. She will get more of it than you can say." PoPo is his grandmother. . . .

[The] mind monkey is a contradiction; he is a comic trope, communal in imagination, but separated from histories, the '60s, and familial sentimentalism. "O King of Monkeys, help me in this Land of Women," said the narrator. "He wasn't crazy, he was a monkey."

Ah Hong Kingston, she got great stories. Enchanted stories that could fill a trunk. (p. 13)

> Gerald Vizenor, "The Triumph of Monkey Business," in Los Angeles Times Book Review, April 23, 1989, pp. 1, 13.

LeANNE SCHREIBER

[In *Tripmaster Monkey,*] Maxine Hong Kingston is writing with a monkey on her back, a chattering, squealing monkey-hero named Wittman Ah Sing. Wittman Ah Sing, whom the author clearly loves. Wittman is American, as American as Jack Kerouac or James Baldwin or Allen Ginsberg, as American as Walt Whitman, "the poet that his father tried to name him after," as American as five generations in California and a Berkeley education in the 1960's can make him. The problem is, if he's so American, how come everybody thinks he's Chinese? How can someone raised on Mickey Mouse and Life magazine still seem so exotic, so "inscrutable" to his countrymen?

Wittman, one year out of college, is in a tough spot, culturally speaking. His assimilation goes unrecognized, masked by appearances, and he can't be Chinese even if he wants to be. If first-generation Americans, like his author, have to make up China out of silences and ghost stories, imagine what little is left for Wittman to work with—"backscratcher swizzle sticks, pointed chopsticks for the hair, Jade East aftershave in a Buddha-shaped bottle."

Wittman is Maxine Hong Kingston's Stephen Dedalus, who wants to "forge in the smithy of my soul the uncreated conscience of my race." But unlike Stephen Dedalus, he needs an actual cast of thousands to fulfill his dreams, and much of this novel is the story of how Wittman meets people and fits them to his purposes. Mostly it is a book of talk, Wittman's talk. Nobody else gets a word in edgewise, not if Wittman can help it. He falls in and out of love, turns friends into enemies and enemies into friends, all under the steam of his own hot air. He tells movie plots, blow by blow, for pages at a time, and reads passages from Rilke out loud to a captive audience on a San Francisco bus. Sometimes he is spellbinding; too often he is just a windbag.

Luckily for him, everyone in the book—the girl he thinks he is in love with, the girl he doesn't love but marries on a whim, the parents he seldom visits and rarely mentions, the grandmother who might have stolen the show if he'd given her a chance, the old college friends he insults, everyone who has a walk-on in his life during the few months duration of it we are privy to—everyone agrees to serve his ambition. To love him, to listen to him, to put on his play.

Wittman's elaborately staged play is the climax of the book. The cast loves it. The audience grows bigger every night. The critics rave. But Wittman is unsatisfied, and so is given an encore, a final chapter called "One-Man Show," in which "we're going to reward and bless Wittman with our listening while he talks to his heart's content. Let him get it all out, and we hear what he has to say direct." Oh no, I thought, and then read on. What follows is a brilliant, maddening diatribe, a rant born of anger and pain at the racism that insists upon his exoticism, his inscrutability, the racism that denies him his Americanness. It only takes one generation to lose China. How many does it take to gain America?

Wittman is at times compelling, touching, wildly imaginative, and yet he made me long for another voice. He is indeed an American creation. For all his talk of community building, Wittman, like his namesake, sings a Song of Himself. No one else achieves any reality in his telling "I.I.I.I.I.I.I.I.I.," the aria of Monkey in *The Journey to the West,* his favorite Cantonese opera, is the refrain Wittman wants to make his. No more head-bowing me-talk, the "me no likee" talk of Hollywood movie Chinese. For Wittman there is only a resounding I.

Wittman's maniac monkey talk made me long for the less fevered but more exciting voice of Maxine Hong Kingston speaking for herself, as she did in *The Woman Warrior* and *China Men*. In *Tripmaster Monkey*, the ventriloquism is too complete. Except in occasional descriptive passages, I cannot hear the precise, sinewy, and, yes, let's admit it, beautiful voice of the author above the racket of her creation, the creation who speaks but never listens. It is as if James Joyce had let Stephen Dedalus run the whole show.

LeAnne Schreiber, "The Big, Big Show of Wittman Ah Sing," in The New York Times Book Review, April 23, 1989, p. 9.

JOHN LEONARD

We won't get much of anywhere with *Tripmaster Monkey* unless we understand that Maxine Hong Kingston is playing around like a Nabokov with the two cultures in her head. In *Ada*, by deciding that certain wars, which were lost, should have been won, Nabokov rearranged history to suit himself. There were Russians all over North America, making trilingual puns. This odd world was a parody of Russian novels.

In *Tripmaster Monkey*, America in the 1960s is looked at through the lens of a half-dozen Chinese novels, most of them sixteenth century. I will fall on this sword in a minute.

First, a disabusing. What everybody seems to have wanted from Kingston, after a decade of silence, is another dreambook, like *The Woman Warrior*. Or another history lesson, like *China Men*. Anyway: more magic, ghosts, dragonboats, flute music from the savage lands. Never mind that she's earned the right to write about whatever she chooses, and if she chooses to write about looking for Buddha in the wild, wild West, we'd better pay attention because she's smarter than we are. Nevertheless, the reviewers are demanding more memoir. Where's the female avenger?

Instead of the female avenger, we get Wittman Ah Sing, a 23-year-old fifth-generation Chinese-American male, Cal English major, playwright and draft dodger. . . . He wants to be an authentic American, but America won't let him. Racist jokes enrage him, but he also worries that a rapprochement of black and white might still exclude his very own yellow, which color determines his wardrobe, his slick performance. . . . He's done time at a dog pound, and among DNA biologists, and they all look alike: "A liberal-arts education is good for knowing how to look at anything from an inquisitive viewpoint, to shovel shit and have thoughts." He's into drugs, movies, comic books and modern masters. He wants to be, if not Lenny Bruce or Allen Ginsberg, at the very least "the first bad-jazz China Man bluesman of America." And what he'll do, like Judy Garland, is put on a show in his garage, a kind of Cantonese *Götterdämmerung*.

In other words: Huck Finn, Holden Caulfield, Augie March, maybe even Stephen Dedalus and probably Abbie Hoffman. Wittman is a "tripmaster," a friendly guide to the stoned in their travels through acid-time. But he's also, and this is where it gets tricky, an incarnation of the Monkey King in Wu Ch'eng-en's sixteenth-century *Journey to the West*, a kind of Chinese *Pilgrim's Progress*. He's the rebel/mischief-maker who helped bring back Buddha's Sutras from India; the shape-changer (falcon, koi fish, cormorant) who annoyed Laotse by eating the peaches of the Immortals, even though he hadn't been invited to their party. The weeklong play this

Monkey stages to finish off Wittman's "fake book" is nothing less than a reenactment of *Romance of the Three Kingdoms*, a kind of Chinese *Terry and the Pirates*. And the actors he press-gangs into service for that play—everybody he knows in California, including his Flora Dora showgirl mother, his "aunties" and a kung fu gang—are nothing less than symbolic stand-ins for the 108 bandit-heroes of *Water Margin*, a kind of Chinese Robin Hood—enemies of a corrupt social order, hiding out in a wetlands Sherwood Forest, like Chairman Mao in misty Chingkangshan or the caves of Yenan.

This Wittman is stoned on books. Imagine one culture, ours, reimagined in the classic literature of another's—late imperial Ming—so much older, no less bloody. Sixties grandiosity!

A word here about language. What so excited readers of *The Woman Warrior* and *China Men* was that shiver of the exotic, the Other's static cling. It was as if we'd eavesdropped on a red dwarf and picked up these alien signals, this legend stuff, from an ancestor culture that despised its female children, that bound their feet and threw them down wishing wells and killed their names. Kingston achieved such a shiver by a sneaky art—disappearing into people who couldn't think in English, and translating for them. She had to invent an American language commensurate with their Chinese meanings. In the way that Toni Morrison arrived at all the transcendence of *Beloved* by stringing together little words *just so*, rubbing up their warmth into a combustion, Kingston dazzled us by pictographs, by engrams.

She made it look easy, but imagine the price. She denied and abolished herself. There wasn't room for a grown-up Maxine in her portraits of a mother who devoured her children and a father who buried wine bottles upside-down in the garden so that "their bottoms made a path of sea-color circles." This grown-up Maxine, after all, was a Cal English major just like Wittman; a reader of Rilke and Proust, Pound, Joyce and Eliot, the original Whitman and his grandchild Ginsberg, Charles Olson and Gary Snyder and Brother Antoninus. From these books dissolved in brain, from a slang of be-ins and love-ins and trippings-out in the psychedelic 1960s, from radical chitchat and the calisthenics of Left Coast Zen, an adult Kingston had fashioned a language of her own. But she'd no place to put it in her first two books. Like Bak Goong in *China Men*, forbidden to talk on the Hawaii sugarcane plantation, she shouted into a hole in the ground. To sing herself, she needed someone like the unbuttoned Wittman.

The result in *Tripmaster* is less charming but more exuberant. Instead of falling into pattern or turning on wheel—there's something inevitable about everything in *The Woman Warrior* and *China Men*, something fated—this language bounces, caroms and collides; abrades and inflames. Instead of Mozart, Wittman's rock and roll. (pp. 768-69)

Wittman's too easily wowed. He's a one-man *I Ching*—"a book and also a person dressed in yellow," jumping from "reality to reality like quantum physics." He needs watching. And a female narrator—usually affectionate, always ironic, occasionally annoyed—looks down on him. Don't ask me how I know the narrator's female. I just do. She's as old as China, and remembers what happened in five dynasties and three religions. She's also foreseen the future: America will lose the war in Vietnam, which Wittman's dodging; the 1960s will be sadder than he hopes; feminism's in the works. She explains things Wittman has no way of knowing: . . . "Ho

Chi Minh's favorite reading was *Romance of the Three Kingdoms* and it's a text at West Point too. Uncle Ho and Uncle Sam were both getting their strategy and philosophy from Grandfather Gwan, god of war." Though seldom a bully, she does at one point tell Wittman to shut up.

It's a nice tension. Wittman is the ultimate innocent himself, the last romantic, all virtue and passion and energy and funk. He will go up like a balloon in every weather: "They hung over the balcony and watched the skaters going around. If we run downstairs and rent skates, could we be Orlando and the Russian princess zipping on the frozen Thames above the apple woman in the deep ice? Wittman, the fool for books, ought to swear off reading for a while, and find his own life." (p. 770)

Now about that play. *Romance of the Three Kingdoms* is required reading for every literate Chinese child. (If you don't already know this stuff, you probably wonder if you need to. Only if you want to get a tenth as much out of Kingston's novel as she's put into it.) It glorifies a third-century revolt of Liu Pei and his mentor, Chu-ko Liang, against the military dictatorship of Ts'ao Ts'ao. (pp. 770-71)

This, of course, isn't good enough for Wittman. As well as the god of warriors, Gwan was the god of actors, writers, gamblers and travelers. Wittman will rewrite *Three Kingdoms.* His play is a "fake war." He'll substitute his theater for all the wars in the history of the world. From Monkey King and Havoc Monster, Pure Green Snake and White Bone Demoness, Dwarf Tiger and Dry Land Water Beast, American movies and Peking opera, vaudeville and puppets and brothel music, fireworks and kung fu, he will ordain a Peaceable Kingdom: "Night mirages filled the windows reflecting and magnifying—a city at war and carnival. All aflare and so bright that we understand: why we go to war is to make explosions and lights, which are more beautiful than anything." (p. 771)

Well, the hippies wanted to be Indians. Why not Chinese, instead? And what, after all, was the trial of the Chicago Seven but Wittman's sort of theater? And wouldn't it have been something if the Quakers, Women's Strike for Peace, Martin Luther King Jr. and the vegetarians had prevailed? Instead, the garrison state, which had most of the violence, stopped this show, and the left regressed into little-league Leninism—a tantrum of cadres, Weatherpeople, Baader-Meinhof. And the rest is Heavy Metal. "It must be," says poor Wittman, "that people who read go on more macrocosmic and microcosmic trips—Biblical god trips. *The Tibetan Book of the Dead, Ulysses, Finnegans Wake* trips. Non-readers, what do they get? (They get the munchies.)"

You can stop looking for the Novel of the Sixties. It took 3,000 years on its journey to the West. But here are the peaches and the Sutras. (pp. 771-72)

John Leonard, "Of Thee Ah Sing," in The Nation, *New York, Vol. 248, No. 22, June 5, 1989, pp. 768-72.*

Ray Lawler

1922-

(Born Raymond Evenor Lawler) Australian dramatist and scriptwriter.

Among the first of Australia's playwrights to achieve international recognition, Lawler is best known for *Summer of the Seventeenth Doll* (1955), a play generally regarded as integral to the development of the country's drama. While traditional Australian theater had been faulted for its romantic social outlook and stilted dialogue, the naturalistic *Summer of the Seventeenth Doll* attacks the validity of nationally revered myths and stereotypes, and it inspired the satirical plays of such later acclaimed dramatists as David Williamson and Alexander Buzo. Throughout his work, Lawler also eschews clichéd dialogue as he authentically conveys distinct idioms through heroic yet ordinary characters. Although his subsequent plays have not achieved the success of *Summer of the Seventeenth Doll,* Lawler is nevertheless considered a seminal figure in contemporary Australian theater.

Summer of the Seventeenth Doll features Roo and Barney, two aging sugarcane cutters who for the last sixteen years have spent their annual five month lay off period with Nancy and Olive, two Melbourne barmaids. This seemingly idyllic arrangement, symbolized by the yearly purchase of a carnival kewpie doll, is destroyed in the seventeenth season when the realities of middle age expose the superficiality of their relationships. As the play begins, Barney, once a cavalier youth, loses Nancy to another man and later fails to win the attentions of Nancy's replacement at the bar. Roo, whose leadership in the fields has been successfully challenged by a younger rival, takes a despised factory job before proposing marriage to Olive. Unwilling to sacrifice her romantic vision of the layoff for the expected banality of married life, Olive vehemently refuses. Critics praised Lawler's indictment of such stereotypical Australian sentiments as the sanctity of male friendship, the superiority of the outback to the city, and the submissiveness of women to men, which he portrayed as vestiges of Australia's frontier past irrelevant to its urban present. Lawler later featured the characters of *Summer of the Seventeenth Doll* in the plays *Kid Stakes* (1976), a chronicle of their first season together, and *Other Times* (1976), set in 1945 when Roo returns to the bar after serving in World War II. While considered less effective than their predecessor, these dramas gained praise for their illuminating portrayal of events precipitating the final summer encounter.

In other plays, Lawler continues to explore Australian national myths. *The Piccadilly Bushman* (1959), for example, examines the colonial perception of British superiority. In this work, an Australian actor develops a neurotic contempt for his country after spending several years in England. *The Unshaven Cheek* (1963), unlike the more realistic *Summer of the Seventeenth Doll* and *The Piccadilly Bushman,* features the subjective recollections of a retired cooper, or barrelmaker who is forsaken by his family and society. In *The Man Who Shot the Albatross* (1972), Lawler portrays the complex inner life of William Bligh, the former captain of the HMS *Bounty* and governor of the Australian province New South Wales.

(See also *Contemporary Authors,* Vol. 103.)

WOLCOTT GIBBS

The play called **Summer of the 17th Doll,** by Ray Lawler, is principally concerned with the business of sugar-cane cutting in Australia—an industry that keeps its employees busily at work in the north of the continent for seven months of the year and then permits them a five-month lay-off, which most of them naturally devote to spending their wages in a cooler climate and among more festive surroundings. For sixteen years, the two workers . . . have been devoting their leaves of absence to a visit to Melbourne, where they have established a sufficiently cozy arrangement with a couple of barmaids who are game for practically anything, day or night. The action we see takes place in December and January of the seventeenth year, when things have begun to warm up down there at the bottom of the world. It is summer again, but somehow or other something has gone wrong with the old magic. One of the girls, with perhaps a rather chilly eye on the future, has gone away and got married, and her replacement, a widow, shows almost none of the proper spirit, being not only fairly supercilious about the entertainment projected for her but also disinclined to take much stock in her admirer's reputation as a Casanova. The other pair struggle heroically to recapture the past and all its remembered gaiety, but it is soon evident that the dream is slipping away, and the evening ends with the lady bitterly inconsolable and the gentleman resigned. It is clearly Mr. Lawler's intention to say something about age and diminishing powers (there is a younger, stronger cane cutter mixed up in it somewhere, as well as a fresher, prettier girl) and the sad, irremediable loss of the illusion of happiness. Probably only the incurable frivolity of a New York reviewer would suggest that the local conditions of seasonal employment are against the characters, too. Five months is a long time for any man or woman to devote exclusively to alcohol, sex, popular music, and easy card games, and it astonished me slightly that they had been able to stick it out as long as they did.

In spite of its rueful moralistic air, and the fact that the people in it are less moving than simply pitiful, *Summer of the 17th Doll* has its effective dramatic moments. Once, the mother of one of the girls, a fine old harridan, gathers the four of them around a tinny piano and starts to lead them in the songs they once sang so happily, and the ludicrous failure of this venture speaks more eloquently of what has been lost than all the explicit conversation that goes on about it. There is some pathos in the scene in which a man can find no other way to express the anguish in his heart than by destroying one of the collection of kewpie dolls . . . that he suddenly sees accurately as a sort of grotesque history of his life, and there is humor (I guess) in the odd dilemma of his companion, who claims to have had three illegitimate children up north but whose sense of fairness somehow deters him from proposing marriage to any of their mothers. On other occasions, too, Mr. Lawler writes movingly or divertingly, but altogether the principal quality of the piece is a kind of flat melancholy, which I'm afraid won't stir you very much. The trouble may be that the author's desolate purpose is plain very early in the evening and it is not much comfort to realize that things can hardly get anything but worse. (p. 53)

Wolcott Gibbs, "Off with the Old Love," in The New Yorker, *Vol. XXXIII, No. 50, February 1, 1958, pp. 53-6.*

TIME, NEW YORK

As Broadway's first newsworthy Australian play in history, [*Summer of the 17th Doll*] has its piquant side—plenty of local color, a working-class lingo, accents faithfully rendered by an all-Australian cast. As altogether honest work, it treats understandingly of believable people and of an odd patterning of human lives. But neither a fresh background nor a sound theme can give the play sufficient dramatic pressure or verbal leverage; if there are no false notes to the writing, there are no resonances or overtones either.

The play tells of two sugar-cane field workers, the one a Samson at his job, the other a Don Juan with the women. For 16 summers, during the long layoff period, they have come to Melbourne for a home-style spree with two barmaids. Each year one of them has given his girl a Kewpie doll, by now a symbol of gaily recurrent romance and absentee devotion. This 17th summer, with the other girl married and a new one in her place, with relations between the two men rather strained, and with various flare-ups and intrusions, all the fun fizzles out; the show goes bust. In truth, the revelers are has-beens, the one in brawn, the other in lure; their revels now are ended.

The last act sharply drives home with what deceiving colors and in what a dollhouse world they have staged their summer frisks. It drives home, too, their refusal, even with the dollhouse in collapse, to part with their illusions. The demonstration rings true, but Playwright Lawler has really had to take the audience by the hand and lead it up to the truth; somehow it has not the weight of the play behind it. Too many earlier scenes were flattish, too much writing was prosy; nowhere did 17 years leap out in a sudden glance, or a lifetime emerge in a comment. The play makes soberly clear the sad human arithmetic that twice two is four, and that mankind would make it five. What is beyond it is the magical creative arithmetic that can raise things to a higher power. (pp. 76, 78)

"New Play in Manhattan," in Time, *New York, Vol. LXXI, No. 5, February 3, 1958, pp. 76, 78.*

RICHARD HAYES

[*Summer of the 17th Doll*], Mr. Lawler's rueful investigation of the disguises of love, is the first Australian drama of consequence, and with a kind of fierce national pride, it has been sent about the English-speaking world all intact. This enforces some purity of actuality, it is true, but allows an obscure confusion as well, for the supreme irony of *Summer of the 17th Doll* is that in no unique nor, shall one say, biological way, does it draw on a specific Australian substance. Idiosyncrasies aside . . . the play is a restatement, with its own dominating potency, of themes and experience which have blooded the American imagination for decades. The British, who mark often—and often with a light fleck—the congruence of American and Australian temperaments, may have read the pattern more shrewdly than they know.

None of which need imply any lesion of originality, but is only to place *Summer of the 17th Doll* within a due scale and proportion of knowledge—to relieve it of the singular burden of the exotic, as if a kangaroo were loping about Times Square. Mr. Lawler, in truth, brings a great security of gift to his material: wholeness of sensibility and a deep masculine insistence. His quality is seen to advantage in the light of his American peers, all of whom work a comparable vein. He has some of Mr. Arthur Miller's dogged thrust, but a more acute ear and less doctrinaire social egotism; he shares with [Mr. Clifford] Odets the picturesque homeliness of the actual, and some wry delight in that, and there is a not inconsiderable affinity with Mr. Paddy Chayefsky: similar milieux, similar closeness and wit of perception, that same hovering tenderness—though here at a more austere removal—and altogether less smartness, less panicky clutching at tidy moralisms and therapies.

It is perhaps, and oddly, Mr. Tennessee Williams who is suggested by *Summer of the 17th Doll*, though a Williams blunt-fingered and indifferent to any aspiration of wider statement. Mr. Lawler's symbolism is pervasive yet not indulged, and he has a genuine instinct—rare in our theatre of the moment—for the image of resonance. If his variation of the Williams theme—indeed the theme of all literature, that of illusion and reality—marks no significant advance, it shows nonetheless a most impressive confidence in its own truth. This refusal of

Mr. Lawler's to evade the cost of things with a vague poetic deliquescence is a mark of his staying power as an artist; where *Death of a Salesman* and *A Streetcar Named Desire*, for all their sagacities, attack, bold demands upon art and life, wobble ultimately into vacillation, **Summer of the 17th Doll** drives through to its short, harsh lucidities with a brutal exactitude. It is this at the last . . . that one honors most in the Australian achievement: a certain unalterable finality of vision, however painful; ideas and images of value always committed, never small. (p. 540)

Richard Hayes, "The Disguises of Love," in The Commonweal, *Vol. LXVII, No. 21, February 21, 1958, pp. 540-41.*

RAY MATHEW

An Australian writer, in **The Piccadilly Bushman,** explains writing as 'the only way he feels he can get his hands on the sense of his own little hunk of the world' and the play is— surely—Mr Lawler's attempt to find the sense of *his.*

In an earlier play, **The Summer of the Seventeenth Doll,** the play that gave him an international success, Mr Lawler grasped at 'the sense of' the Australian's indulgent myth of himself as strong, bronzed, tough and free. He caught two cane-cutters, members of one of the few remaining seasonal occupations of the kind that gave birth to this nineteenth-century legend, and put them close against the claims of age, sex, suburbia. He showed them breaking against those claims and left them with nothing except a future of mutual pretence, rejecting and rejected by the world around them. This, he said, is what he-manliness and mateship mean. His play was the first serious questioning of those concepts—which still animate Australian politics, life and literature. (pp. 90-1)

[In Lawler's new play, **The Piccadilly Bushman,** an] Australian novel has been turned into 'a good international script' for an English film company. 'In other words, the film's being made for the overseas market, and it doesn't much matter that it should be true to us as we really are?' It is the novelist objecting, because he does care about 'the intangible difference of this one section of the world's population as compared with any other'. He is concerned with 'all the things' that 'anchor' people and although he may be, as the English suggest, 'a romantic with a national chip on your shoulder' he does have 'a way of looking at things' that is so much part of his background that he can be sure of himself. He has the kind of strength, apparently, that the play's principals need.

The hero, an actor, more English than the English, has starred at Stratford, etc. He has returned to Australia to make the film and a last effort at reconciliation with his wife. He is successful, famous, without friends. Before the play began, he betrayed his mate ('you know how close we were'), and that one friend is now dead. 'He and the few other good things out here that I could no longer fit into my life, I shoved them down and down until I lost all contact with them.' Now, 'I can't stand being on my own any more', and he wants his son back—son rather than wife, because she hurts.

The wife is difficult. In England, despite Stratford, etc., she drank, took lovers—not for love, as she explains, but for the comfort that there is in a 'huddling together of the rejected'. She tried then to force her husband into the intimacy of a confession. In Australia, 'with strong sunlight and sharp rocks', she succeeds: yes, he did 'obliterate' his mate, did marry her

for the ticket to England, did resent everything that anchored him to Australia;

> I loathe and detest this country with everything that's in me. . . . I never belonged here. This is the prison in which I spent my first twenty-four years. . . . I'm no special—freak. There are plenty of my sort out here, the throwbacks. But most of them manage to make an adjustment. Most of them. The rest of us fight tooth and nail for the happy chance of becoming an expatriate.

It is possible, indeed common, to grow up in Australia breathing 'this sweet smell of exile', as the wife calls it. She herself has felt it so intensely that she has had to cling to an extravagant and defensive Australianism.

> You know why I went down the gutter in London? Because in my heart I was certain that all the changes Alec was making in himself were right. Even though I hated them, I had enough of the poison in me to believe in what he was doing. But I couldn't match him in it, so I tossed myself in with what I thought were the other failures.

But her actor-husband she now realizes is the biggest failure 'of the lot'. 'Expatriate,' he says, 'the man who can never accept his own country, and finds that the country he hankers after never accepts him! If you ever want revenge for the fact that I married you as I did, you don't have to go past that one word.'

The *Australia* (and the English alternative) the wife tries to define is more than a name on the map; more than accent, position, idiom—things the play shows sometimes lightly and sometimes with clumsy vaudeville distaste. It is understood manners, attitudes, experiences. The English speak 'roughly the same language, but that doesn't mean they know what a bush-fire smells like on a hot day in February'. There is no one in the Sydney where the play is set who does not know that smell and something of what it means.

It is, of course, only the thinkers in the play—the creative or the uneasy—who are forced to consider their relationship with Australia; the English because they have to work there, the Australians because they are repudiating their class or looking for overseas markets. The two 'normal' characters are simply Australian; a press-agent with a surface toughness and cynicism about her own emotion and a 'servant' with a 'Give us a yell if you want us'.

As dialectic, however, the play is nothing (when does an expatriate become a migrant?). As a display of character in conflict, forced by that conflict to feel and to try to articulate, it is fascinating and it would be hard to exaggerate the skill with which Mr Lawler has packed his conventional three-act framework with plot, tension, humour, pathos and theatrical shock—shock that is always the result of character in action. The play ends tentatively, there is no 'easy comfort', but the actor and his wife have reversed their rôles of weak and strong, each of the characters has acknowledged the need to come to terms with the country where he finds himself and— *the* colonial problem—wonder whether playing for mother-England's approval is ever anything other than betrayal.

This last of course is Mr Lawler's problem. There are not enough theatres in Australia to support him. How is he to retain his hold on the overseas market and still be true to us, the Australians who are the facts he knows and is concerned with?

With Australian inhibition, he will not let us see him looking at his own emotion; he attempts to remove it from himself by giving it to his actor. This is the play's failing; the reason for its moral unease. For a creative artist, to be born in Australia (or some other colony) may well be the most important thing that happens in his life and to be removed from that country may be either life-crippling or life-making; it is certainly never easy. For a mere actor, like his hero, loss of accent and background is a simple technical problem unless he is a first-class neurotic. For Mr Lawler's hero to worry about and at it as he does must be a masking of some deeper self-unrest and Mr Lawler does not probe very far in any effort 'to get his hands on the sense' of *that*. (pp. 91, 93)

[*The Piccadilly Bushman*] seemed too rich in excitement, pleasure and pain for any serious questioning of its validity. It is, however, this failure in validity, this placing of writer's problems on to actor, that may prevent it reaching a wider audience. Again, although the characters are real anywhere and their feelings true of any society that shares a language with another, the detail of *The Piccadilly Bushman*—even the rhythmic certainty of its dialogue—is so precisely Australian that Mr Lawler may have to wait till native writers 'realize' his script before it can convey its excitements and relevances to audiences in other countries. (pp. 93, 95)

> *Ray Mathew, in a review of "The Piccadilly Bushman," in* London Magazine, *n.s. Vol. 1, No. 6, September, 1961, pp. 90-1, 93, 95.*

CLIFFORD HANLEY

The Unshaven Cheek is a study in decay of industry and ideals in a crumbling old cooperage. Its final message, if I'm right, is one of hope; that while the old dreams die in coming true, a new generation of dreams is waiting to be born. . . .

[In the play, a craftsman cooper is] brought all the way from Biddersley in England to make Australia's best barrels. In the by-going, he has also won the eight-hour day for his brother coopers. But wooden barrels are now out, steel and plastics are in, and the proud craftsman is reduced to caretaker of a factory slum. . . .

Then he has this trouble with his loyal spinster daughter, and different trouble with his cynical layabout son, and with his illiterate outback wife who did bird-imitations and kept going bush until she vanished; and his political young brother, and his burned-out mates; and so on. All this is splendid, Mr. Lawler's sheer creative exuberance will not allow him to offer us a thin little piece, and the stage is absolutely seething with human individuals and the dense atmosphere of place and time. . . . It is certainly his night, and what the play has to say is worth saying. But, cor, it goes on and on saying it, considering that hardly anything is actually *happening* for so much of the time. I should like it even more if it threw off some of the pure weight of its words and got into a higher gear. (p. 231)

> *Clifford Hanley, "Big Deals," in* The Spectator, *Vol. 211, No. 7052, August 23, 1963, pp. 231-32.*

J. C. TREWIN

[*The Unshaven Cheek* is] something that promised a lot to those who recalled *The Summer of the Seventeenth Doll.*

That was fresh, wistful, ultimately affecting: the best play Australia had sent to the English stage. Though we might use a few of the same terms for *The Unshaven Cheek,* which is also fresh, also wistful, also affecting now and then, it is far behind the *Doll:* maybe we should not have looked for so much. Still, it is by no mean negligible: the trouble, I think, is that Lawler's technique has failed him. . . .

In this new piece he has over-worked the flashback; past and present become intricately involved. The device is perilous: as Lawler employs it we seem to be moving along a snakes-and-ladders board, always likely to be switched back a dozen squares. It is a pity because we can believe in the old cooper . . . without having his past thrust at us so vehemently. His occupation—or his former occupation—is unusual. In the *Doll* we heard about the working conditions of cane-cutters in Queensland. Now in *The Unshaven Cheek* we hear a great deal about the working conditions of the Australian cooper (maker of casks, barrels, and so on) and the warning of a trade that apparently flourished in Roman Illyria.

The play is set in a derelict cooperage outside an Australian city: a superb lofty setting . . . of decaying timber work, rusty metal, range upon range of broken window-panes. Here the old foreman, who had emigrated in youth from the North of England—a fine craftsman and a natural leader—has dwindled to the caretaker of a building almost forgotten. His daughter looks after him; his son insults him; his brother badgers him; his former workmates call on him. But it is only half a life. His work is over, and he is plagued always by the anger of his son. The son is a dire oaf, arrogant and cruel. Here the dramatist has overburdened himself with some thoroughly implausible plotting.

We are asked, roughly, to believe that many years before, when travelling in the back-lands, the cooper had called at a remote sawmill. There he had seen a beautiful, illiterate girl worker carrying a plank. The sight, remarkably, confirmed him in his desire to improve labour conditions and to get an eight-hour day for coopers. He also married the girl and tried, without success, to get her to read and write. When her children were growing up, she ran away time after time, jealous of abilities she could not share. What she did achieve, before she vanished finally, was to teach her son a set of bird-calls (her own pathetic way of communication) which he turned later into an act for a touring vaudeville company. I need not elaborate all this. It is enough that the son, cherishing his mother's memory, apparently loathes his father for having tried to dominate her. The dramatist has not made this in the least persuasive. Indeed, though I can believe in the cooper's zeal for his craft and his fellow-workers, I cannot believe in the roots of the play, the father-son relationship (son attempting to destroy everything the father does), or the cumbrous mechanism used to explain the flashbacks, and at last to send the old man back to England.

The cooper himself . . . is someone I can credit, and the play throughout has speeches and insights that can reinforce faith in Ray Lawler as a dramatist. But he has both burdened himself with an awkward plot and found no satisfactory way of shedding the load. The more I think of *The Unshaven Cheek,* the more certain I am that there is a play here struggling to escape.

> *J. C. Trewin, "Moving About," in* The Illustrated London News, *Vol. 243, September 7, 1963, p. 358.*

PETER FITZPATRICK

[*The Summer of the Seventeenth Doll*'s] return to Melbourne in the summer of 1976-77 more than matched the euphoria of its first appearance; this time it was hailed as 'the masterpiece against which all other theatrical attempts to interpret universal truths in terms of specifically Australian situations must be judged and so far, found wanting'. And this time it was the third play of a trilogy, presented with *Kid Stakes,* the summer of the first doll, and *Other Times,* set shortly before the summer of the ninth.

When the Melbourne Theatre Company announced the return of Ray Lawler from Ireland with two new plays about the people of *The Doll,* it looked on the surface like an acknowledgment on Lawler's part of the loss of impetus that the comparatively disappointing seasons of *The Piccadilly Bushman* (1959) and *The Man Who Shot the Albatross* (1971) had suggested. But the completion of the trilogy seems to have been prompted by much more than a settling for the revisiting of proven themes and materials, and the excitement generated at its appearance seems to reflect something new in Australian audiences, and perhaps in Australian society. *The Doll* trilogy coincided with an apparent general concern for retrospection. (p. 19)

The makers of the new retrospection sought their myths not in the grim pioneering struggles of the colonial outback, but in the poignancies of small-town or suburban private lives from the generations of their parents or grandparents. Whether the toughness or the gentility of the subjects was the dominant impression, they depicted an Australia that appeared the more charming and the more innocent in the consciousness of its loss. (pp. 19-20)

Kid Stakes and *Other Times* were a part of this retrospection. Where *The Doll* is set in the year of its writing, the two new plays look back to a lost urban Australia; our impressions of the lives and values of Roo and Barney 'up north' are not advanced at all by our acquaintance with these early summers, but the values, and idioms and bric-a-brac of suburban Australia just before and during 'the war' are given a most affectionate re-evocation.

The values of this sort of retrospection tend to be self-substantiating, and in so far as they rub off on the major play of the trilogy they compound some of the problems of considering it critically. It is not simply the length of the play's title, but a kind of affection, that allows the use of the diminutive *The Doll,* and the play's reappearance confirmed how far it had become part of a popular cultural self-consciousness. The sense of occasion when the trilogy was staged in a single day had a number of aspects. As a theatrical tour-de-force by the company, and a landmark which suggested, momentarily, that a tradition of Australian drama had grown to sufficient strength and maturity to start honouring its heroes, it offered grounds for celebration. But there was also a sense of shaking hands with old friends. It was rather coyly reflected in a programme note which gave Lawler's barmaids and canecutters some of the special 'reality' of characters in long-running soap operas: 'By 1976, Olive would be 61 years of age, Barney and Nancy would be 63, and Roo, if he were alive, would be 64' (the ages, incidentally, are at odds with those given in *The Doll*). In looking again at *The Doll* it is difficult but necessary to disentangle these more spurious virtues; or, less hardheartedly, to recognize that Lawler's play has come to have a number of kinds of importance.

It may seem odd that characters so firmly grounded in stereotype should have achieved the kind of fictive life that would make anyone want to calculate their present ages (or write plays about them at earlier periods of their lives). The explanation is probably partly a matter of affectionate respect for the play, its historical significance, its familiarity, and its 'period' qualities. But it is also a consequence of the play's generosity of tone, and of the sense that each character plays a role which does not fully answer the needs of his personality; that each is known compassionately and intimately, if never fully, in a way that makes them more than acquaintances or simple representative types.

The most clearly realized gap of this kind is that between Roo's proud conformity to the values of the bushman-hero and the awareness of his new vulnerability which enables him to contemplate life as a suburban factory-worker and husband, and finally to confront the impossibility of even that readjustment. Roo's taciturnity is part of his sense of himself as a man, and it is a quality in which he takes some pride. In the self-sufficiency of his strength he has no need for 'blabbergutsing', and he appears reserved, even secretive, in all relationships. It is part of the determined independence which prompts his refusal to 'bludge' on Olive, his extension of the principle in rejecting the idea of 'taking oscar from wimmen' when Emma offers it, and his fierce resistance to Barney's offer of a loan. The values which support that independence are every bit as conventionally decent as Pearl's, though less calculating and flexible; the lay-off arrangement may be a bizarre one, but for Roo it runs by conventional moral rules—he angrily asserts to Barney the responsibilities it creates ('That's your rotten form, isn't it? Once the fun goes. . . .'), and on introduction to Pearl raises the conventional eyebrow:

> Roo.   Missus Cunningham, is it?
> Olive.   (*quickly*) Yes, she's a widow.
> Roo.   (*understandingly*) Ah.

Adultery and taking oscar from women are not a problem for Barney. But he too meets the requirements of male reticence at moments of emotional intensity, and Roo respects the feelings which drove him into privacy on the day of Nancy's marriage:

> Roo. . . . He went away on his own a whole afternoon—something I've never seen him do before. Whenever he's been in trouble he's always wanted someone standing by holding his hand. This time he didn't want even me near him.

Less sentimental, and more convincing in its ambiguity and deliberate off-handedness, is Barney's reaction minutes later to the photographs of Nancy:

> Roo.   Bubba brought them in for yer, some snaps of Nancy's wedding. You're not to show Olive.
> (*Barney opens envelope, takes out first photographs, looks at them a long moment, then says unemotionally—*)
> Barney. She must have been ravin' mad. (*He shoves photos into pocket.*) What's there in the paper?

More characteristically, Barney's gift of the gab, his readiness for melancholy self-analysis especially as a technique of seduction, throws the laconic responses of Roo into sharp relief.

Roo jokes complacently with Bubba about the incongruity of his having anything to do with a perfume counter. But the pressure of maintaining the role of strong, silent male is evident in an exchange with Olive, when his mixture of tenderness and defensive embarrassment is juxtaposed with the 'female' province of emotional and sentimental statement, as Olive cradles her new doll:

> Olive. . . . But the dolls—they're something you
>   thought of by yourself. So they're special!
>   (*He grunts, embarrassed. She fluffs out doll's
>   skirts.*)
>   And don't make noises at me, they are.
>   Where'll I put her?
> Roo. (*Glancing around*) Gettin' a bit crowded,
>   maybe you should start upstairs.
> Olive. (*crossing to vase*) No, I won't, she's staying
>   right here with the others. (*Places doll in vase*)
>   Look at her now, she just dazzles yer.
> Roo. (*touched but gruffly*) She's all right.
> Olive. Beautiful.

The reflex of understatement offers Lawler the same dramatic possibilities as those exploited by Esson in the terse emotional exchanges of *The Drovers,* and Lawler achieves a similar power through what cannot be said in Roo's meeting with Johnnie Dowd:

> Dowd. 'Lo Roo.
> Roo. 'Lo.
> Dowd. Y'look like you been paintin' the town.
> Roo. Yeh.

The tokenness of the dialogue throws weight on to the subtext, the evident crisis in Roo before he can bring himself to shake Dowd's hand.

But this play places the bushman's taciturnity in the context of a number of representative kinds of articulateness, and gives him the task of saying important things to a woman he loves. Consistent understatement is a limitation in the central crises of a long play, and there is the risk that to present the major griefs as unspeakable might simply become a complacent evasion of the task of presenting them. One of the real achievements of *The Doll* is Lawler's scrupulousness in bringing those griefs into relationship with a range of language that may be flippant or clichéd or flat, and his refusal merely to exploit an unresolved incongruity. Roo's speaking reflects a difficult learning process, which is part of his painful acknowledgment of the loss of self-sufficiency. By the third act his manner with Olive is no longer inscrutable or avuncular, but represents an effort to communicate with her at a new level of equality. The climax of this growth is the high rhetoric of his last lines to Olive:

> Roo. . . . Kill me, then. But there's no more flyin'
>   down out of the sun—no more eagles. . . . (*Going
>   down on one knee beside her and striking the floor
>   with his hand.*) This is the dust we're in and we're
>   gunna walk through it like everyone else for the rest
>   of our lives!

When that new kind of verbal intensity fails, Roo's response is the same as on other occasions when he has been overwhelmed by the frustrating inadequacy of words to do the things he wants them to do. His smashing of the seventeenth doll in a 'baffled, insensate rage' at the close parallels the quick resort to physical threat ('Cut it out or I'll bash your face in') of an earlier response to Barney's merely verbal effrontery. As in David Williamson's *The Removalists,* violence is presented as integrally related to the commitment to stereotypes of masculinity by the characters; it is legitimized by the

role, and fostered in the tension between powerful feelings and the insufficiency of words.

Barney, we are told, looks smaller for his 'constant association' with Roo, and similarly in their obvious differences we may underrate the extent to which the values of the two men are shared. Barney and Roo complement each other in a relationship which is in part that of straight man and clown; Barney looks the embodiment of what George Orwell describes as 'the Sancho Panza view of life', the 'little fat man' who is in all of us.

> He is your unofficial self, the voice of the body protesting against the soul. His tastes lie towards safety, soft beds, no work, pots of beer and women with 'voluptuous' figures. He it is who punctures your fine attitudes and urges you to look after Number One, to be unfaithful to your wife, to bilk your debts, and so on and so forth.

A great deal of Barney's activities during the play conform to Orwell's model. He has all the outrageousness and irresponsibility of the perpetual prankster, careless it seems of all kinds of obligation, and he is therefore the life of the party; he is heroic only in his amiability, in his persistent efforts to revive the spirit of the layoff in the face of the weariness and disenchantment of the others. Like Falstaff, Barney is all loveable clown as long as his is a holiday world, and he is vastly entertaining for the ingenuity of his efforts to resist responsibility and turn its claims to his own comic advantage. (pp. 20-3)

But Barney's conformity to that set of attributes is limited. Like Falstaff again, his comic function is complicated when others refuse to allow him the illusion of being young, and enough vulnerability shows behind the comic mask to make him a suitable subject for pathos. But it is also a product of his assent to Roo's heroic model and its pride in the values of masculinity and mateship. His 'de facto wives' provide material for comedy, but his lack of commitment looks sour when it appears in the more relevant infidelity of his sycophantic sales-pitch for Johnnie Dowd. Yet Barney appears resolutely to believe in the values that he can hardly begin to live up to. Barney describes his failure to stand by Roo 'up north' in the terms of the disillusioned hero-worshipper:

> Barney. (*disturbed*) I dunno. It was all messed up.
>   You know what Roo's always been to me, a sort of
>   little tin god. I've never seen him in the wrong before.

The story of Roo's bad luck is Barney's invention to cover Roo's shame and his own share in it; and the revelation of the truth behind that lie, for all the provocation, comes only when Roo tortures him into making it. Barney has a notion of what makes a man which not only makes him as reserved about his real emotions as Roo, but also constrains him to be loyal, up to a point, to his mate.

Olive's ecstatic vision of the canecutters includes Barney quite as fully as Roo: they are 'two eagles flyin' down out of the sun', even if the incongruity is greater in relation to the smaller man; Barney is presented as sharing equally an easy, wordless authority over the 'soft city blokes' when he and Roo walk into the bar, like 'a coupla kings'. This contrast is clear too in the way Olive speaks to Pearl of their virility, in her evident contempt for 'that book bloke' Nancy married, and the pointed 'These are a coupla sugarcane-cutters fresh from the tropics—not two professors from the university'.

Barney has a good deal to live up to in his reputation as 'the Cassa of the North', but he has it seems made a fair job of it till recently. The values of the bushman-hero, however, have clearly never fitted him well, and through him Lawler dramatizes another aspect of the tensions within that stereotype, alongside the more general truth of the limited durability of any way of life founded on physical prowess; its terms are always impossible for some, as well as being, in time, impossible for all.

At the final curtain, Roo and Barney make their exit in an apparent reaffirmation of the ties of mateship, despite all the points of conflict and failures of understanding that have been exposed in their relationship. Barney's response to Roo's outburst of speechless fury is a gesture and a form of address with which one might approach any dangerous animal—patting Roo's shoulder just once, in a suitably constrained touch of affection, he says coaxingly 'Come on, Roo. Come on, boy'. What we have seen in the play undercuts the optimism of Barney's reassurances in these final moments. His vision of Australia as a land of opportunity in which every man can come up a winner is at odds with the knowledge of human limitations which the people of the play have been forced to accept. It is true that 'there's a whole bloody country out there—wide open before us', but in this context there is nothing liberating in that concept. However, while the optimism and the heroism and the mateship are all much qualified by that context, **The Doll** does not close on a reversal of the frontier values; instead they survive in the cut-down, compromised forms of vague hopefulness and dogged resilience and the need for company.

The ambiguity of the ending is really founded in that respect for others' illusions which Lawler's compassionate view of his characters seems to demand. The plot unfolds an implacable truth, working through objective laws of consequence like the processes of ageing and the processes of disintegration in inflexible relationships, which make an irrelevance of individual human wishes. But to the audience the disillusioning here, as in [Ibsen's] *The Wild Duck,* is not a triumphant irony. And for that reason the irrational survival of apparently discredited hopes and values may seem more brave than foolish as a way of adapting to too much reality.

In the same way the sceptical chorus which Pearl and Emma provide throughout the play can hardly be seen as offering an encompassing wisdom; except perhaps in Emma's gnomic underlining of the moral lesson in her scene with Roo, neither of the women rises above a very accessible sort of commonsense which is neither dramatically very interesting in itself or founded on a complete understanding of the experience. Pearl's conventionality is for the most part a subject for comedy. . . . Her function as a butt of patronizing laughter is so well-established that she is kept safely upstairs through the emerging conflicts of 1:2 until Lawler brings her on for a scene with Barney in which her comic conventionality brings out all his comic outrageousness, and permits the scene to close on a precarious restoration of the 'lay-off' spirit. That comic function is maintained through the complacency of her knitting for Barney in Act Two, when it is the incongruity as much as the tactlessness of her part in proceedings that produces so much of the tension of New Year's Eve 'at home'.

While Pearl is allowed a little more perception than the early comic function assumes, her development is really a watering down of the elements of caricature rather than an observable growth in understanding, and the 'grown-up look at the lay-off' which she presents to Olive in Act III is not to be confused with maturity. Emma is a more reputable *raisonneur,* and more discriminating in her judgments; Lawler's directions refer to her 'satirical eye', and she is self-consciously a wryly detached observer of the things that go on in her house . . . . Her comic eccentricities are bound up with her craftiness, and do not preclude the gnomic role which Lawler gives her at the end:

> Emma. . . . How long did you think these lay-off
>   seasons were gonna last—for ever? They're not
>   for keeps, you know; These are just—seasons.
> Roo. I know, but whose fault was it we came a
>   cropper?
> Emma. Nobody's fault, yer melon!
> Roo. Don't be silly, it must be somebody's . . .
> Emma. (*exasperated*) Why must it be? All that's
>   happened is you've gone as far as you can go.
>   You 'n' Barney 'n' Olive, you're too old for it any
>   more.

This is to the point, and brings the obvious to Roo's attention. Emma's role becomes more questionable however when she labours the point in biblical terms; Roo and the audience surely needn't be as slow to grasp it as her lines assume:

> Emma. . . . You and Barney are two of a pair.
>   Only the time he spent chasin' wimmen, you put in
>   being top dog! Well, that's all very fine and a lot of
>   fun while it lasts, but last is one thing it just won't
>   do. There's a time for sowing and a time for reap-
>   ing—and reapin' is what you're doing now.

The authority given Emma here, which even demands that she pick up her final g's, is dramatically something of an embarrassment, if one takes it as the central moral statement of the play, and as Lawler speaking only just in character.

The situation depicted in the play is complicated enough to limit even this truth as a way of accounting for it, however, and so to lessen the embarrassment of the audience's apparently being offered a 'key' to the play. Emma is presented in Lawler's stage direction as having '*no illusions about humanity, expecting the worst from it, and generally crowing with cynical delight when her expectations are fulfilled*'. Her lack of illusions enables her to be clear-sighted in her judgments, but it is inclined to make them reductive as well. Her grasp of the individual conflicts within the general truth is a limited one, and this is nowhere more apparent than in her view of Olive, her daughter.

The meaning, and the cost, of Olive's commitment to Roo is not quite accessible to Emma. The cost she dismisses in her impatience over Olive's lament over the seventeenth doll—'Middle of the night Olive sat here on the floor, huggin' this and howling. A grown-up woman, howling over a silly old kewpie-doll. That's Olive for yer!' The dolls seem to mean a great deal to Olive, more even than a huggable emblem of the tinsel gaiety of the lay-off. At several points in the play Lawler has her cuddle the doll in a way that is quite baldly suggestive of its 'meaning' as child-surrogate. . . . Olive's tears over her doll intimate a terrible sense of physical loss. And that knowledge adds a dimension of horror to Roo's destruction of the doll at the end.

Emma is more discriminating in her judgments than Pearl, and testifies that the lay-offs were for sixteen summers all that Olive claims them to be. In her grudgingly affectionate remark to Roo in 1:2, 'It could have been worse. Seventeen years is seventeen years, even though they ain't nothin' but the lay-off season', she seems to foreshadow one of the questions one might ask at the end; whether, if life has the low ceiling which Pearl and Emma assign it, all those summers are not 'worth' the painful present and a barren future. Nancy, who was able to 'have her cake and eat it' by combining the joys of sixteen holidays with the future comforts of the serious business of domesticity, is the refutation of Pearl's position, and the ideal of Emma's. But a lesson in the importance of adaptation is useless in dealing with Olive, who cannot and will not adapt, and Emma has too firm a purchase on the homiletic potential of the situation to anticipate its real pathos.

The character of Olive differs from the others in being largely unrelated to social stereotype, and this at once makes her an intriguing study and accounts for some of the loose ends of the play's psychologizing. She is held in the same focus, within the same conversational limitations, as the other characters, but where our knowledge of them is supplemented by the familiarity of the stereotypes to which they accord, the terms in which Olive is presented are self-substantiating and in the end not fully knowable—that 'something curiously unfinished' which suggests her immaturity is true too of the dramatic conception. This is not to deny her vitality, and we learn enough about Olive to relate her actions to aspects of her nature that have previously been demonstrated; it is the relationship between these elements that Lawler's method leaves undeveloped. We learn immediately that this woman of 37 is a romantic schoolgirl, younger than Bubba in many ways, and much younger at the end; Roo, just before he asks her to marry him, speaks of that quality with great affection—'Y'know, a man's a fool to treat you as a woman. You're nothin' but a little girl about twelve years old'. Her first line in the play, 'Hang on to your hats and mittens, kids, here I come again', seems to take us very engagingly into a world of schoolgirl jollity, of party dresses and giggling over boyfriends' photos. The incongruity of Pearl's matronly complicity in all this, and the presence of a grown-up Bubba who used to be given 'lolly walkin'-sticks' by Roo and Barney until she got too old for them, and now is given gloves or perfume when Olive is given her doll, makes Olive's prolonged adolescence a source of uneasiness as well as delight.

Alongside that, though, Lawler invests Olive with a depth of passion which shocks at its abrupt first appearance . . . but prepares for the intensely physical response to Roo's harsh presentation of a future walking through dust. . . . It is not easy to reconcile this ferocity of feeling with the bobby-soxer hero-worship, or to relate those two qualities to the insight into Roo and herself which clearly makes her see the importance of her sustaining a role which will assent to his heroic self-conception. The connections are not inconceivable, just unsubstantiated. Olive's refusal of Roo's proposal is entirely consistent with her commitment to a romantic ideal and with the directness of her passion, and it works convincingly on stage—but in her lack of self-awareness (and considerateness) here Olive seems a little disconnected from the very wifely woman of Act II.

It is one of the qualities that distinguishes Lawler's play that so much of the complexity of the situation is so intimately and compassionately known, and that the ambiguity of its conclusion is not the ambiguity of evasion or vague confusion, but a challenging ambiguity accounted for in the convincing presentation of a range of contending perspectives. It is a quality that may seem at odds with the exploration of self-consciously Australian sets of values through recognizable stereotypes. And it raises some problems in critical judgment, which become acute in assessing the drama of the last ten years, but which it is relevant to consider now.

It is the notion of representativeness that gives most trouble—the value of familiarity in characterization and of mimicry in language, and the relation of satiric or sociological point to dramatic substance. Some comments on *The Doll* by P. S. Davison (in *Southerly,* 23, 1963) are symptomatic, in the way the strengths and weaknesses of the play are defined in terms of the clarity of its sociological analyses and prophecies. It may be true that, as Davison says, 'It is not difficult to see symbolized in the decline of Roo's physical powers the passing of the nation's youth', but it is also dangerous when the play is made to represent historical rather than personal change. The outsider Pearl is proposed as representing 'the carping migrant', and Olive is to be seen as one of the old guard who cannot believe that 'the Australian dream has ended'. Such a reading is inevitably concerned with the demonstrable, perhaps 'objective', truth of the representative stereotypes within the society at large, rather than with the meaning those stereotypes have for the people in the play itself; and it is inevitably hostile to the final ambiguity of tone:

> Whether such a dream can be lived now, whether the old myth is still relevant is considered by Lawler, but there is a lack of clarity in the examination . . . (their departure together) makes one wonder whether a suggestion of the reaffirmation of the values is being given, or whether the sentimentality of this moment makes its own pointed comment on the worth of such values in contemporary society.

Most of the wondering seems legitimate enough, but that the play's end allows space for it seems to be an aspect of its dramatic strength; for Davison it is a considerable limitation. Australian playwrights have often been expected to perform as public relations men for their country, or as its opinion-samplers, instant historians, and pundits. For some the latter functions are chosen ones, and for them the sort of demands Davison makes of *The Doll* are appropriate and not too confining. Lawler's is however a bigger play than that.

It is bigger too than the two plays with which it has come to share a trilogy; *Kid Stakes* and *Other Times* are quite as shrewd in social observation, but present much less urgent moral and personal conflicts than *The Doll,* and their mood of affectionate retrospection is more indulgent than challenging to their audiences. *The Doll* from the start makes us aware of the complexity of the business of judging what we see; Pearl is an outsider, asking questions for us through the exposition, and finding like the audience how difficult it is to share the in-jokes of an intimate group. . . . But Pearl's rigid and narrow conventionality is calculated by Lawler to prise us away from stock responses. When Olive rejects Pearl's anticipation of 'a nasty mess' by arguing that decency 'depends on the people', her moral relativism expresses the position to which Pearl's strait-laced pragmatism has surely manoeuvred the audience. And that, in its turn, is qualified by some disquieting impressions, even before the arrival of 'the boys' establishes that this lay-off is going to be very different from the rest. That complexity is sustained through *The Doll,* and there is nothing like it in the later plays. And while all three plays show the same mastery in controlling the movements of the small cast in its fixed set, through the rapid alternation of two-person exchanges and periodic moves into group focus, this is in the later plays not so clearly in the service of a sense of contrasts and shifts in mood.

Though *Kid Stakes* and *Other Times* seem founded partly in the kind of fascination which sometimes leads novel readers to grant the characters life beyond the scope of the action, there is little new to learn about the central people of *The Doll.* Barney at 23 in *Kid Stakes* is every bit the raconteur and old lag that he is at 40; Roo at 21 is already the strong and stable leader of men that he tries to be at 38; Olive at 20 seems no less mature, and not much softer, than Olive at 37. Roo's experience of war in *Other Times* foreshadows, in the pain of his inarticulateness, some elements of the conflicts of *The Doll,* but the difficulties for such a man of making himself known prevent any very substantial development.

Nancy, whose absence is so obtrusive in *The Doll,* is just as others remember her in that play—in *Kid Stakes* her resilient gaiety is already qualified by the pragmatism and love of reading which will lead her to marry Harry Allaway from the bookshop after the sixteenth summer. *Other Times* places her absolutely at the centre. Her uncertain commitment to Olive's lovely hedonist holidays is further developed, as dramatic subject rather than simply premise; we are constantly reminded, in the action and running jokes of the play, of Nancy's dependence on the whisky bottle, and Nancy's friendship with the Austrian Josef Hultz compounds that insecurity in her. Hultz, with his bookishness, and his elaborate propriety and social tentativeness, offers an alternative view of the lay-offs which is more telling, given Nancy's nature, than the conventional disapproval and incomprehension of Lawler's other outsiders, Dickie Pouncett in *Kid Stakes* and Pearl in *The Doll.* Hultz's objections are as much aesthetic as moral, and this strikes home with Nancy, whose understanding of beauty and ugliness is rather more subtle, and troublesome, than Olive's.

Other Times has distinctly the feel of an in-between play, borrowing its data and postponing its denouements, and for all the charm of its period flavour it is the least impressive of the trilogy. *Kid Stakes,* which takes as its plot the initial arrangements for the off-season, has even less in the way of moral and psychological conflicts to sustain it, but seems to stand more firmly as a play in its own right. Lawler makes of it a beautifully workable piece of affectionate recollection in three acts; the comedy and the nostalgia are an end in themselves, and it is accordingly more Emma's play than anyone else's. Most of the recognition laughs, at 'period' attitudes and vernacular, are hers. The tensions aroused by the conflict of her personality, her morality and the bitter experience which shaped it, as it opposes and then acquiesces in the spirit of holiday, are never met front-on; but they are handled obliquely, in incidents like the gift of the refrigerator, and are always speculatively interesting. It is her quaintness, though, which sets the prevailing tone of this play. (pp. 23-30)

Lawler's people speak credible and flexible idiomatic Australian in the trilogy, and it is perhaps in this area that *The Doll* offered the most fruitful kind of influence to its successors. This remains true despite the fact that most of the colour comes from Emma's archaisms, and despite the propriety of the dialogue. For all the furore caused by the notorious bloodies of *Rusty Bugles* in 1948, *The Doll* in 1955 offers only half a dozen of them; and *Kid Stakes* and *Other Times,* although the product of a more permissive theatrical genera-

tion, are quite as scrupulous. This contributes to that air of only slightly tarnished innocence which clings to the presentation of both the period and the lay-off itself in all three plays. (p. 30)

The Australian-ness of Lawler's speakers is more a matter of syntax than vocabulary. There are plenty of local tags in *The Doll*—Nellie Melba and Young and Jackson's and 'Phenyle decay, talk of smooging and being chockablock and knockin' around together—but it is the colloquial rhythms that make their language convincing and speakable. Lawler's script is a kind of score, giving the actor's voice a shape by eliding or omitting words ('go down the beach', 'We got home half-past seven') as well as offering a guide to pronunciation with some early 'Strine' spellings. It provides a model for the writing of 'Broad Australian'.

Lawler presented a different kind of speaker in *The Piccadilly Bushman,* the rather disappointing follow-up to *The Doll.* Disappointment might be appropriate in relation to the plot—the film-team politicking and the private sense of alienation which it exposes in the expatriate actor Alec Ritchie, seem lacking in real substance. But this play, which appeared early in Lawler's own long absence from Australia, contains some very perceptive sociology which redeems a little its dramatic thinness; in its probing of the repercussions for language of an awareness of difference from the received culture. Lawler's is among the first of the plays of the 'generation gap'.

Alec's disowning of his Australian-ness is explored through two central actions—his relationship with his estranged wife Meg, the country girl from Yanngoola who drinks and picks up lonely men as consolation for her husband's embarrassment about her background; and his treatment of the Australian writer O'Shea, whose novel has been doctored for 'home' consumption in the film Alec has come back to make. The latter test is the immediate focus for the plot, and it is one that Alec fails from the start. In response to O'Shea's view that the adaptation is 'as much on the ball as a eunuch's tunic' Alec takes the party line:

> Alec. . . . In my opinion, what you have there is a good international script.
> O'Shea. In other words the film's being made for the overseas market, and it doesn't much matter that it should be true to us as we really are?
> Alec. You're being extreme.
> O'Shea. Much more important to show us as the old country likes to think we are, eh? Coarse lovable larrikins roaming around in the great outdoors with not a complexity within ten thousand miles.

Complexities are thin on the ground in this situation, however, and O'Shea repeatedly brings out Alec's over-sensitivities. The last straw is a folktale which O'Shea tells after he has expressed his disgust at Alec's bland record of cute native legends; O'Shea tells of a mother country, who, upon finding that the children of whom she was so patronizingly fond were struggling free of her diamond-studded apron strings, turns on them with an 'icy bitchiness', in a language they can no longer understand. O'Shea's story seems the mildest of provocations, as well as a tedious excursion at the centre of the play. The Englishmen of the party are unoffended; for the scriptwriter Stuart it is positively appealing, while Vincent the director finds its gaucheness reassuring. But, predictably, for Alec it is intolerable, 'a rotten outburst'. His isolation at this point makes it clear to him that he is a man who belongs nowhere. . . . The play peters out in vague suggestions that Alec's sense of the dimensions of his real failure may somehow lead to the rehabilitation of his marriage, as perhaps the most helpless of all Meg's strays.

Language in itself becomes a more rewarding subject. Grace Clive points to Alec's verbal estrangement from his country in the play's first conversation:

> Alec. How did it go?
> Grace. In the words of a vernacular you've probably forgotten—bloody bottling.

But Alec hasn't forgotten. He soon shifts into a vein of parodic Strine which demonstrates the strength of the roots he despises:

> Alec. Surely Meg must have given you some idea?
> Grace. I haven't seen her. Ever since she came back she's been shut away in Yanngoola.
> Alec. Well, that's how it is. Yanngoola! What a name. It really needs the accent to get the full ugly flavour, doesn't it? (*he reproduces it with bitter accuracy*) Meet the missus. Comes from Yanngoola. Her dad owns a bit of property up there. Nice place, Yanngoola. Town's a bit on the small side, of course, just the one street and there ain't much around but lots of sky and the flamin' great red plains, but we do all right . . .

Alec's sense of himself disappears somehow, amongst all his clever affectation of national stereotype.

The problem of sliding registers is apparent too in the comic scenes involving the social-climbing Leggatts, who own the 'cult temple to the worship of ultra violet rays' in which the action takes place. Isabel takes pride in the fact that those three elocution lessons a week when she was a little girl in Broken Hill have saved her from all the horrible signs of an Australian accent, and enabled her to be 'mistaken as English all over the world'. O'Shea points out that her pronunciation of 'salt' and 'bream' is very un-English; Stuart Allingham reluctantly agrees that Isabel has 'a light accent', at which she snaps 'It's a bloody lie!' In the face of her pretensions, O'Shea reacts by drawing attention to himself as an early 'ocker'—'I not only say salt and bream but big slangy stuff like "Don't come the raw prawn" and "Fair crack of the whip" '. It is the sort of response which [David] Williamson and [Alexander] Buzo explore in the plays of the early 1970s, but the problem for Lawler is that his sociological acuteness comes in such a low-pressure dramatic container. In the little exchange about accents, for example, there is nothing much to be done apart from the juxtaposition. The social tension mounts, of course; Lew Leggatt leaves in a huff, and Stuart tosses the dregs of his drink in Vincent's face. But Lawler is forced to fall back on an old trick to complete the sequence, short-circuiting the tension with a joke by bringing on Scone Corcoran—with a plate of bream. That trick in *The Doll* was of a piece with the habits of its characters and the tone of the presentation, but here it has more to do with the problems of set-piece analysis and a lack of dramatic impetus.

One can see why Lawler did not return to this subject area, but it is rather a pity, too, that his plays give the members of the educated middle-class no more occasions on which to scrutinize themselves. *The Doll* gave to an older Australia a splendid valediction in bringing traditional forms to the exploration of traditional values. The major subject for his successors was the problem of overlapping or conflicting cultures which *The Piccadilly Bushman* defines, in which the new values and the old obligations were still to be sorted out. Lawler set an impressive and not altogether helpful precedent in *The Doll,* but if he left an inheritance which had partly to be lived down, he also established some standards, and some notions of the dramatic resources of Australian speech, by which that might be done. (pp. 31-3)

> Peter Fitzpatrick, "Ray Lawler," in his After "The Doll": Australian Drama Since 1955, Edward Arnold (Australia) Pty Ltd, 1979, pp. 19-33.

DENNIS BARTHOLOMEUSZ

When [*Summer of the Seventeenth Doll*] opens in a terraced house in Carlton in the summer of 1953, the garden has been allowed to become a wilderness, and overgrown ferns and shrubs on the front and back verandahs enshroud the house in a tangle of plant life. The overall effect . . . [is] not one of gloom, but of a glowing interior luminosity, of light filtered through subterranean greenery, as if one were in Queensland and not in Melbourne. . . . The main decorative items in the room [are] the sixteen kewpie dolls on walking sticks, glowing in the luminous interior with a curious radiance, stuck behind pictures on the walls, flowering from vases in twos and threes, and clustered in a pattern over the mantelpiece.

The cane-cutters Roo and Barnie have brought them down every summer holiday from Queensland for the barmaids Olive and Nancy, their summer mistresses for sixteen years. But in the December of 1953, when the seventeenth doll will arrive, Nancy has left, opting for marriage and sober domesticity with Harry Allaway. Allaway, who works in a bookshop, has seduced Nancy with books smuggled into the pub . . . ; his conquest of Nancy bears no resemblance to Barney's. Barney, all the evidence suggests, has never read a book in his life.

The pronounced anti-intellectual strain in Australian life, the admiration for pure physical athleticism, is given an undeniable glamour. As Peter Fitzpatrick points out [see excerpt above], 'Olive's ecstatic vision of the cane-cutters includes Barney quite as fully as Roo: they are "two eagles flyin' down out of the sun", even if the incongruity is greater in relation to the smaller man; Barney is presented as sharing equally an easy wordless authority over the "soft city blokes" when he and Roo walk into the bar, like "a coupla kings." ' Olive tells Pearl, the barmaid, who is being tried out as a replacement for Nancy:

> Listen, lovey, you better make up your mind. These are a coupla sugarcane-cutters fresh from the tropics, not two professors from the university.

In their cultural context—Australian society is not classless but has more social mobility than one finds in most other cultures—the words are plausible: cane-cutters and university professors may not be as remote from each other as they are elsewhere; there is no good reason why Olive should not speak of them in the same breath, or why she should not see the cane-cutters as infinitely more glamorous.

The tragedy in the play is that eagles age like anyone else, and Roo for sixteen years the fastest of the cane-cutters has lost his place in the cane-fields during this seventeenth summer. A new king of the cane-cutters has succeeded him. The play is contemporary and Australian but contains as well a ritualistic pattern which goes back to the earliest drama. The King is dead. Long live the King. Roo seems prepared to accept his fate, to settle for a stable domesticity, marriage to Olive and a drab factory job in Melbourne.

It is here that Lawler presents us with his greatest surprise. The alternative of living in harmony with the drab necessities of urban employment after the visionary glories of the high summers of the past is an alternative that Olive finds unthinkable for Roo:

> Seven months they spend up there killin' themselves in the cane season, and then they come down here to live a little. That's what the lay-off is. Not just playing around and spending a lot of money, but a time for livin'. You think I haven't sized that up against what other women have . . . Even waiting for Roo to come back is more exciting than anything they've got.

She rejects the whole notion of suburban marriage, but not without the most terrible anguish.

Olive at thirty-nine, Lawler tells us in a stage direction, has an eagerness that properly belongs to extreme youth despite her surface cynicism. It is in relation to Olive that the doll symbol becomes most telling, most awesomely powerful. At several points in the play she cuddles the kewpie doll with an affection that suggests it is a child surrogate. The seventeenth doll is particularly beautiful in her eyes as the conversation with Roo shows:

> (She moves away to pick up the seventeenth doll from the rocking chair, and stands stroking it tenderly.)
>
> Prettier than ever. You know, I think they take more trouble with them than they used to. There's more tinsel and—they're dressed better.

It is essential to the reality of Lawler's art that Olive cannot be aware of any irony that the word 'tinsel' inevitably must carry. . . . The symbol of the doll attains by a process of accretion, and suggestion, an imaginative presence, not merely for Olive and Roo, but for the audience, growing slowly, becoming more distinct and clear, until it sits perched on that ridge in the mind which rises between conscious and unconscious awareness.

The first rending shock comes at the end of the quarrel between Roo and Barney when, angry beyond measure, Barney seizes the object closest to him, the vase containing the seventeenth doll, and swings it at Roo's head. Roo rips it from his hands and throws it away into the centre of the room. Olive sinks to her knees with a strangled cry and holds the doll close. This piece of stage business [has] more than an emotional force; when I saw the production in 1976 it was felt not in the heart only, it had the impact of a physical blow. There was no difficulty in understanding why Olive came down in the middle of the night, as her mother tells Roo, and sat on the floor, hugging the doll and howling.

The destruction of the doll summons in a single moment the awesome power of devouring time. Olive has to confront the fact that the glories of the high summers are over and will not return. When she clears the room of the dolls, the brilliantly plumaged, stuffed North Queensland birds, the tinted coral pieces, and shells from the Great Barrier Reef, we experience the sense of finality with her.

Indeed the doll is a richly ambiguous symbol. A kewpie doll in particular is bodiless and legless, the seventeenth doll had 'more tinsel' and was 'dressed better'. It is associated with the glamour of seventeen summers, which Olive has looked forward to with an excitement that is in some ways like that of a child looking forward to the feast of Christmas, when tinsel and frills announce that Christ is born among the barbarous hills. When Roo at the end of the play beats the doll 'down and down again on the piano, smashing and tearing it until it is nothing but a litter of broken cane, tinsel and celluloid', the dream itself is torn to shreds and appears to have no reality any longer. But as Emma, the moralist in the play, confesses, it was, when it existed, more than tinsel. It was a richer, intenser life, not, as Pearl suspects, a mere indulgence in self-deception and delusion. The doll clearly has immense reality for Olive.

In the world to which she is confined she will not accept the dreary materialism of a suburban marriage with Roo, the depressing alternative to the romantic radiances of the high summer, or permit her eagle from the north to be imprisoned in a factory. The cage she refused to accept for herself is not even golden, and perhaps she does well to refuse it. The action she finally takes in refusing a dull marriage, freeing Roo to return to the cane-fields, keeping her own dream intact, is . . . dramatically convincing . . . : for behind the illiterate surface of the barmaid lives an exceptional spirit, a spirit both more childlike and more mature than we suspect. Her refusal to accept anything less than a special kind of 'livin' ', both sensational and visionary . . . despite the immense anguish that the rejection of marriage brings, is in its own way a kind of affirmation. In the end she reveals an unsuspected strength. Because the choice she makes goes against the grain of many of our comfortable preconceptions it has been imperfectly understood. She refuses certainly to be a doll herself. Like some of the great and stubborn heroines of drama she will have her eagle or nothing; though it must be said that Ray Lawler, through his imaginative deployment of the symbol of the kewpie doll, surrounds the whole proposition with the profoundest ironies.

Lawler's own comments on his play give no idea of its organic complexity; they are helpful in a very general way.

> I deliberately avoided laying stress on a manufactured plot line, determined that the play should stand on the merits of its characterization. There is a central theme to hold the pieces together, that of the unbearable nostalgia and bewilderment felt by a group of people when an enchanted private world, built almost entirely on a physical basis, crumbles away under the stress of years and changing circumstances. It is meant to be the tragedy of the inarticulate who feel more than they rationalize or express.

The play is inarticulate in a masterly kind of way. Peter Fitzpatrick [see excerpt above] draws our attention to the dramatic power Lawler achieves through what cannot be said when Roo, his overalls stained with red paint after a day in a factory, meets Johnnie Dowd, the new king of the cane-cutters:

> Dowd. 'Lo Roo.
> Roo. 'Lo.
> Dowd. Y' look like you been paintin' the town.
> Roo. Yeah.

Roo's "Lo' and 'Yeah' are the brief, brusque signs of the turbulence within, before he can bring himself to shake Dowd's hand. The words succeed in being both convincingly laconic and thoroughly dramatic, with emotion intensely understated.

Lawler has succeeded in conveying the tragedy of those who are made inarticulate by words. Tragedy, however, requires a more powerful expression than this laconic language can give, and the characters express themselves ultimately through silent symbols which are immensely expressive. Communication in **Summer of the Seventeenth Doll** is accomplished through the currents and whirlpools of feeling that move beneath language and find expression in complex, visual symbols. Lawler's play is firmly established within a naturalistic tradition, but its deeper tragic life has its roots in a central symbol, which is organic, and convincing on a naturalistic plane. . . . [The doll has] a believable, literal existence. (pp. 188-93)

A poem, Paul Valéry once said, is 'une sorte de machine'. The machine Valéry had in mind was the reverse of mechanical. And it seems to me that **Summer of the Seventeenth Doll** is still the most perfect machine devised for the Australian stage. (p. 193)

> *Dennis Bartholomeusz, "Theme and Symbol in Contemporary Australian Drama: Ray Lawler to Louis Nowra," in* Drama and Symbolism, *edited by James Redmond, Cambridge University Press, 1982, pp. 181-95.*

JOY HOOTON

The two retrospective plays which Lawler wrote in 1974/75 and 1976 to accompany **Summer of the Seventeenth Doll, Kid Stakes** and **Other Times,** were not received with enormous enthusiasm by audiences and reviewers when they were first staged independently in 1975 and 1976. It was a different matter, however, when the trilogy as a whole was presented . . . in February 1977. With an elation similar to the national mood at the winning of the America's Cup, audience, actors and reviewers apparently responded to the staging as a timely ritual, reaffirming patriotic pride and rediscovering the communal past.

Judging by the reviewers' use of such terms as 'landmark' and 'classic', the recent production of the trilogy . . . has evoked the same sense of occasion. In this instance, however, the mood of affectionate retrospection was reinforced by the excision of several critical speeches and scenes and even some interpolated material. (p. 335)

Like *Phar Lap* and *The Man from Snowy River,* the **Doll** has become part of a family of well-known features in the national consciousness. Familiar as the play is, however, certain aspects have always provoked a range of interpretations. Commentators have been by no means agreed on its actual stance towards such romantic ideas as mateship and the freedom of the bush, or on the quality of its intellectual engagement with these ideas. The implications of the closing scene, in particular, have been frequently debated. Perhaps the most contentious scene has been the last one between Olive and Roo. If the feelings of the past have been so deep, if the ritual of the past sixteen summers has been a warm and enriching one—as is implied within the four well-crafted corners of the original **Doll**—why, in this case, does Olive reject the idea of marriage? Is this a profound rejection of suburbia and all its con-

ventions? A magnificently quixotic commitment to her unconventional dream? A final pathetic demonstration of the extent to which she has been seduced by an illusion? A powerful representation of the backlash of male chauvinism? A scornful rejection of an offer which she recognizes as Roo's face-saving option to returning to the cane-fields? An initial refusal which will, or should properly, be succeeded by a more sensible acceptance of the gold band and the one suburban roof? Responses to the *denouement* have been nothing if not varied. Praised as powerful, logical, tough or tragic, the scene has also been criticized as tear-jerking, manipulative, sentimental, pathetic and melodramatic.

A minor ambiguity connected with the play's *denouement* is the question of the likely future of Bubba and Dowd. Does this relationship represent the play's only positive vision for the future, or is it destined to re-enact the same, ultimately destructive dream?

I would like to suggest that virtually all these ambiguous wrinkles have been ironed out by the two anterior plays. But strangely, so powerful has been the nostalgic period magnetism of everything connected with the **Doll,** that few reviewers have noticed that something has happened to the play, that it has emerged from the retrospective redesigning in neater, but drabber and darker clothes. As I hope to show, this 'reformed' text of the **Doll** is much more thematically consistent, although far less richly suggestive than previous texts; it is only indirectly concerned with Outback values, although these play an important structuring role in terms of character and action; it is less a universally relevant study of the effects of time than a specific study of a certain kind of infantile, but magnetic psychology; it has at least traces of a bald morality theme in which the wages of sin are very heavy indeed; and it is one in which all the characters appear far more clearly defined, although Olive undergoes the most extensive resculpturing.

Perhaps the most striking aspect of **Kid Stakes** and **Other Times** is the actual lack-lustre quality of the lay-off's past, a past which seemed to have such a magical resonance in the original **Doll.** In **Kid Stakes** there is a certain amount of youthful, semi-drunken skylarking, some mildly funny practical jokes, usually with Emma as Barney's easy victim, and a few tender love scenes, restricted solely to Olive and Roo and expressed almost entirely in physical terms. The contrasting relationship between Barney and Nancy is defined from the first as strictly casual, tailor-made by a partly-reluctant Nancy and a thoroughly-satisfied Barney to fit his shallow requirements. Meanwhile, what wit the play contains flows almost entirely from Nancy, and is frequently less a spontaneous outburst than an attempt to raise Olive's flagging spirits, to divert Barney's bursts of sour temper, or to rally her own commitment to the fast-congealing patterns of loyal ritual that the lay-off imposes. Even at this early stage of the game, the fun appears to be mainly the manufactured variety characteristic of the fun fair, accompanied by the inevitable chink of beer bottles and defined by such naive antonyms of gaiety as middle-age, work, intellectual interests, marriage and social convention. The fun fair, in fact, with its progeny, the Kewpie doll, is soon recognizable as a fully-fledged symbolic device, freighted with moral connotations and ominous forebodings. As far as the structure of the two plays is concerned, the **Doll's** 'well-made' pattern of anticipation, sharp reversal and precarious re-affirmation is reproduced in a minor key. Given Lawler's unavoidable commitment to the old-fashioned, realistic form, of course, some emotional movement is undoubtedly essential if this retrospective journey is to avoid tedium; even so, the alternation between hysterical highs and depressed lows is so marked that it is impossible to avoid an impression of the Carlton lay-off as, from the first, a remarkably tenuous arrangement. There are several threats to the continuance of the lay-off, but perhaps the most real is Nancy's equivocal response to the cut-down future Barney represents, following the disclosure of his Makarandi past. This reaches its most bitterly precarious and curious expression at the close of Act II, when she pours whisky over his unbuttoned fly while he is in a stupor. . . . At this point the emotional movement almost tips over into total rejection, but is saved by Olive's hysterical reaction, verging on laughter, which unites the girls in a feeling of relief.

At the same time, the theme of failed aspirations and betrayed possibilities which unites the three plays sounds an ominous note in the background. Not only are there occasional reminders of Emma's past hardships during the depression, but the theme of her disappointed hopes for Olive is also given prominence; for Emma, Olive's avoidance of marriage and choice of a bar-maiding future are betrayals of a spirited struggle for survival that has lasted twenty years. Other doomed aspirations range from the serio-comic, such as the failure of Barney's Makarandi 'wives' to net him, to the more bitter-sweet such as Nancy's failure to win a wedding ring other than one in a Christmas cracker and Olive's explicit acceptance of Kewpie dolls instead of children.

The atmosphere of *Other Times,* set in 1945 in the ninth year of the ritualized arrangement, is several shades darker than that of *Kid Stakes.* After the first Act's rather torpid movement, dominated by Nancy's persistent recourse to the whisky bottle and Barney's unglamorous preoccupation with his tropical ailments, the action quickens as external changes force the characters to confront some of the realities of their situation. The severe costs to Roo's self-esteem of preserving the ritual (a natural soldier, he had deliberately avoided promotion in the Army) emerge in the violent, mostly off-stage 'celebration' of his discharge; the full extent of Barney's emotional disabilities is measured in Nancy's bitter account of her backyard abortion. Meanwhile, although Olive and Bubba are still passionately devoted to the idea of the lay-off, they appear to be alone in their commitment. For Barney and Nancy, and even for Roo, the rituals of the arrangement have clearly ceased to be interesting. . . . At best, in the Roo/Olive liaison, the relationship carries a heavy burden of emotional repression; at worst, in the Barney/Nancy union feelings are a matter of habit, resigned acceptance and displaced maternalism. Adult infantilism and child destruction, sordid undertones in the 'lower' relationship, act as a serio-grotesque parody of the 'heroic' attitudes of the 'upper' pair; and the same curious effects are occasionally produced by the contrasting embraces of the two couples. Meanwhile, the theme of failed aspirations reaches a crescendo. By the end of the play the corpses of dead possibilities are almost palpable entities; they include the abandonment of Bubba's education; Nancy's abortion and accelerating decline into alcoholism; the frustration of Josef's hopes for a relationship with Nancy; the obliteration of Emma's opportunity to run a respectable boarding house and her consequent decline into a figure of elderly pathos; and the frustration of Roo's opportunities of a more satisfying career in the Army. . . . The final scene of the play, in which a weary, disheartened Emma lis-

tens to Bubba's rendering of the banal song that becomes one of the ghosts haunting the party in the *Doll*—'There's a Goldmine in the Sky'—is heavy with symbolic ironies.

Common to most commentaries on the *Doll* is a perception of Olive as the central figure of the lay-off, just as her point of view concerning the past is the one that has prevailed. Responding to her passionately defensive accounts of the past romance, audiences and reviewers have tended to align with what is seen as her heroism or idealism. Refusing to submit to the tame categories of social convention, and intrepidly carving out a bolder, alternative life-style, Olive has apparently fitted snugly into the seductive vitalist tradition. But, strangely, in *Kid Stakes* and *Other Times,* Olive never ascends the peaks of imaginative eloquence she achieves in the *Doll.*

The only child of a fiercely protective mother, Olive is shown from the first as having all the mixed instincts of an adolescent who both rejects and clings to home. The first scene of *Kid Stakes* presents Emma as fulfilling the familiar role of semi-disgruntled skivvy and possessive, indulgent parent while Olive smokes upstairs, complacently risking her mother's ineffective disapproval. And the relationship barely alters; even when Olive's preoccupation with the lay-off has imposed itself on the house, Emma remains as its and Olive's uneasy custodian while the iron fact of Olive's arrested teenage is hammered home again and again. . . . Strangely obedient to Olive's ego, the other members of the group carefully dispose the lay-off ceremonies to show her off as its centrepiece; Roo's early wartime purchase of an emergency supply of dolls which are secretly stored by Nancy, and the careful preservation of traditional outings, under the watchful eye of Bubba, the lay-off's pedantic historian, emphasize that these rituals belong to the birthday-party world of an indulged child. In *Other Times* Olive's enthusiastic anticipation of the men's discharge, an event which will fully reinstate the old cycle even though it will also mean the immediate departure of Roo for the North, is a minor irony. The lay-off is Olive's most cherished possession, providing a delightful range of self-regarding activities and a stable audience of five. In this dream world, Roo is no more than an essential ingredient, one of a group, and hence her stunned fury at Nancy's departure in the *Doll* and her petulant unease when Bubba is temporarily removed from the scene in *Other Times.*

In Act II of *Other Times* when Nancy tentatively attempts to enlighten her on Roo's sufferings in the Army, Olive complacently appropriates his refusal to take promotion as perfectly natural, given the importance of the lay-off: 'it would have *knocked the bottom out of everything.* The lay offs and our times down here and all the *things* that matter to him . . .' (my italics). Blind to Roo's inner life, it takes his violent outburst . . . to jolt her into the realization that the war for her, although not for Roo, has been just another lay-off. The same inability to appreciate Roo's inner life is a feature of the *Doll,* where Olive often appears more irritated by the *debacle* up North and its impact on the holiday mood, than interested in its actual content.

An interesting side-light on Olive's infantilism, implicit in the above interchanges, is her obsession with things. Proudly independent on the subject of money, Olive's world-view is nevertheless tainted by an incorrigible materialism that values sex, loyalties, people, parties, parent, moods and feelings as analogous, sensually-enjoyable or sensually-distasteful *things.* To such a consistently reifying mind a Kewpie doll can very well do service as a child. In some ways she is still enclosed in the world that Piaget has described as typical of the infant in that she does not seek to benefit at the expense of others, she has simply not fully grasped that there are other selves. At the same time, of course, there is a wide gulf between Olive's biological and emotional ages, so that there is something chillingly appropriate about the post-war Olive, wearing her 'badge of service', the silver fox jacket, and clutching her family of Kewpie dolls.

Thus, given the detail of Olive's infantile materialism, her rhetoric in *The Doll* on the subject of marriage, on the hurt inflicted by the breakdown, and, above all, on the reasons for her rejection of Roo: 'I want *what* I had before . . . You give *it* back to me—give me back *what* you've taken', is all dismayingly consistent. If we accept the *Doll* as part of the trilogy, there can be no further doubt about the *denouement.*

One of the indirect ways in which Lawler establishes Olive's immaturity is through her relationship with Bubba. Intrinsically casual and self-regarding in her treatment of the child in *Kid Stakes* and, with more serious effects, in *Other Times,* Olive is interested in Bubba only in so far as she relates to the lay-off. Not only does she represent another captive audience, but the history of her childish responses has become integral to the ritual. The symbiotic relationship between the two infantile viewpoints is seen at its purest, of course, in the stripped-down environment of the *Doll,* although the action of *Other Times* implies that Bubba's removal from her neighbouring lotos-eaters is essential for her emotional and economic future.

Kid Stakes and *Other Times* also provide less flattering insights into Olive's connection with the outback legend. Much of Roo's fascination for her, of course, stems from his manly occupation; as top ganger of a cane-cutting gang, he offers both the romance of the outback and the gaiety of the cyclical city spree. Hence her sulky dejection in the *Doll* when he takes a city job and her total dismay when he reveals his intention to abandon cane cutting permanently. Not only does Roo's eagle-like image provide a flattering mirror for her own ego, but she also attempts to appropriate some of his masculine freedom. Clearly, marriage is offensive, partly because it relegates her too firmly to a female stereotype; the lay-off alternative, however, provides all the 'female' security of marriage with an impression of 'male' sexual freedom. . . . The world that Olive seeks to enter on the equal terms of a pseudo-mateship is really a paler, 1940s version of the male, adolescent world of Williamson's *Stork.* Hence her choice of barmaiding, where she can most readily be one of the mob; if Nancy and Olive's father have succumbed to alcohol, Olive succumbs to the surface fellowship that alcohol offers. Similarly she fiercely rejects suggestions that she is a kept woman; it is not marriage, or even free love, that Olive seeks but mateship. Similarly, just as the tropical butterflies on the walls of her room are surrogates for the bush she will never visit, the room and the house itself provide a dual security and freedom, as a result of her implicit decision to remain a teenager in the parental home. Olive has a tenacious grasp of the practicalities of a range of deceiving dualities.

Much of this eccentric mixture of androgynous motives in Olive's attachment to Roo is curiously anticipated in the seduction scene in *Kid Stakes;* significantly it is Olive who does the seducing, but the introduction to the event takes the form of Roo's surrendering of the 'makings', which she attempts to roll. As always, the deeper currents of their relationship

can only be expressed in a physical way, but it is the pseudo-male implications of this key scene that are interesting.

If Olive's heroic status has been deflated by the later plays, Roo's has also been modified; qualities that were previously only sketched in the *Doll* are now fully shaded, deepening the picture of his virtues and self-destructive limitations. Lawler has perfectly caught the familiar mixture of naivety, gentleness and inarticulate chivalry, characteristic of the pre-war, backblock Australian, as well as Roo's individual rigidities which fatally fit the bronzed Anzac mask; his confused unease when its calcified contours bruise his deepest emotions emerges most frequently in *Other Times* and the *Doll,* although it is discernible in *Kid Stakes.* Even his names imply the disabling contradiction, (Kanga)Roo expressing the prosaically narrow outback type he emulates and Reuben, his inner individuality, which responds to the Bible's poetry as a parched plant to water.

His actual accommodation to the Roo-persona, however, is packed with ironies and contradictions, almost all its uncomfortable public postures concealing more congenial but opposed private alternatives. Presumably radical and egalitarian, he emerges as naturally authoritarian, conservative and even competitive. Again, he is apparently sexually nonconformist, but persistently betrays attitudes that are conventional and even Victorian. . . . Paradoxically, the lay-off arrangement both imposes the stereotype and allows him some room for individual movement, to have wife, family and home and the illusion of bachelor freedom. In the same way, he is publicly unburdened by the routines and materialistic pursuits of a market economy, but has a positive passion for routine and is fully alive to the demands of economic expediency, as his sacking of Tony Moreno demonstrates.

His taciturnity is contradicted by his love of verbal self-expression; his role as natural leader by his subservience to Olive's emotional demands; his severe masculinity by his strong 'female' or nurturing qualities, qualities that Olive incidentally lacks. Determinedly rural, anti-suburban and a fish out of water in Melbourne, Roo is as proprietary towards the Carlton house as Emma, and as adaptive to urban ways as the 'soft city blokes' Olive despises; it is not the bush that is his natural home but the city.

Thus the seventeen-year arrangement allows Roo, more homing pigeon than eagle, to reconcile the opposing needs of his Reuben and outback identities to some extent, although his chance of growing apart from the mask, made dramatically acute by the war, is frustrated. His commitment to the stereotype, however, is clearly insidiously wasteful, blinding him to the destructive effects of the lay-off, to Barney's viciousness and Olive's immaturity. The full brunt of the false image's power is only postponed, of course, to the moment when he realises that Olive is not equipped to see beyond it. Forced finally to remove his Roo-mask, he is appalled to find that Olive can relate only to the mask, not to the man; it is a delusion which the cult of taciturnity and the exclusive physicality of their love have fostered, of course. Roo's discovery, which is not unlike Nora's in [Ibsen's] *A Doll's House,* impels him appropriately to destroy the Kewpie doll, garish, tell-tale symbol of the false dream which has been Olive's real passion.

One of the most important of Roo's received ideas, but one that he never critically examines, is mateship. Indeed his attitude suggests that the very idea of criticism is opposed to the spirit of the relationship. Apparently equating mateship with unquestioning loyalty, physical aid in times of hangover and financial in times of debt, Roo often deliberately refrains from interfering in the sordid scenes Barney generates. On two particularly excruciating occasions, he actually leaves the room, apparently unable to resolve the moral dilemma: during the revelation of Barney's past in *Kid Stakes* and after Barney's reiteration to Nancy of his offensive advice to Hultz in *Other Times*. Meanwhile as far as the mates' inward lives are concerned, there seems to be little or no communication. . . . Barney's dependence on Roo is easy to understand, but more difficult is Roo's tolerance of his squalid mate, even granted the latter's parasitic powers and Roo's uncritical concept of mateship. Undoubtedly, the key uniting fact is the lay-off itself and its implicit stipulation of group activity.

Given the drab actualities of their relationship, then, the final scene is hardly an apotheosis of mateship. Indeed, Barney's last words—'there's a whole bloody country out there—wide open before us' and 'Come on, Roo, come on Boy'—are heavily ironic, grotesquely underlining their actual isolation in an empty country and their distance from the resilient camaraderie of boyhood.

But if mateship's ironic duality needs any other support, the figure of Barney is there to supply it handsomely. Often praised on his showing in the *Doll* as Falstaffian in his amiability and ingenious avoidance of responsibility, or even as having 'the humble, unpolished goodness of a simple philosopher', the Barney of the trilogy fully endorses Lawler's own description of him as living 'below the belt . . . and not much above it'. Philistine, racist, bigoted, complacently ignorant, incorrigibly chauvinist and gratuitously crude, he betrays all the aggressive weaknesses of his successors, Norm and Kenny. Although he shows flashes of wit in the *Doll's* less wittily competitive setting, he is quite overshadowed by Nancy's spontaneous originality in the anterior plays— obvious where she is subtle, crude where she is *risque,* and swaggering where she is self-deprecating. A show of humour, nevertheless, is often Barney's substitute for feeling and most of his relationships with Nancy, Emma, Bubba and even Olive are kept going at the level of raillery, though one that often becomes viciously abusive. Affectionately if uncritically accepted by Olive as complementary eagle and an indispensable part of the ritual, he is implicitly dismissed by both Emma and Bubba. (pp. 335-43)

Unpleasant as he is in *Kid Stakes,* Barney reaches new heights of ockerism in *Other Times.* A whining self-pity has joined his store of vices and he is now aggressively resentful of the least sign of superiority in others; of Nancy's education, Roo's pride in soldiering, Hultz's culture, Bubba's youth and even Emma's chance of making money. The most devastating explosion of his claim to amiability, however, is surely the scene which discloses the 'third' attribute of the ideal womanly spirit which is dangled before Pearl in the *Doll.* Nancy, who had received this crass repertoire at the very moment when she was on the point of confiding her pregnancy, repeats his words with a wry, hysterical laughter that is close to despair.

But Barney's Falstaffian features are perhaps most severely impaired by Lawler's full-bodied creation of Nancy. Quick-witted and acute, Nancy has a cool style that laconically attempts to adjust almost any situation to light comedy, expressing no doubt her sense that the situation's combination of emotion and casualness, care and negligence, demands a stylized nonchalance, an understated stoicism. In *Other Times* her humour has become wryly defensive, an often bitter acceptance of the lay-off's destructive ambivalences. (p. 344)

Shrewdness and wit notwithstanding, Nancy is no match for the literally simple minded Olive. Strangely submissive to her friend's moods, she is drawn into the arrangement's ritualizing half-reluctantly in *Kid Stakes,* partly in response to Olive's enthusiasm and partly in a characteristically placatory reaction to a minor breach in their relationship. The situation rehearses her sacrifice of Bubba's education to the lay-off in *Other Times,* after Olive has indulged in prolonged freezing tactics. And numerous other moments in the two plays emphasize her emotional commitment to her friend. Cast as happy party-goers in the play of the lay-off, Barney and Nancy have the role of extras to the feature romance starring Roo and Olive. At one point, they explicitly recognize that such is the case. Meanwhile, in this infantile fantasy there is plenty of room for mother-figures, and Nancy readily fills the role both with Olive and Barney. Vivid as Nancy is, she also has her shadowy side; the emotional actuality of her involvement is real enough, but its emotional history is left uncharted, the individual reasons for her spiritual, cultural and intellectual self-negation remaining unexplained, so that we are left with the bald fact of Olive's magnetism.

There is no doubt, however, that the two plays would have been greatly impoverished without Nancy's lively individuality. The flow of her earthy good humour waters the aridities of the specific and cultural situation; her involvement with Olive and indirectly with the lay-off has a convincing urgency that contributes to the fetid emotional atmosphere; her occasional frank comments on their relationships articulate the arrangement's costs; while the bitter fruit of her liaison with Barney, the sacrifice of her energy, is made dramatically manifest by the passive drift into alcoholism and the defensive wit. Nancy also adds credibility to the prolongation of this deformed set of relationships. For Nancy, as for Roo, Emma, and Bubba, Olive is the magnetic north; for Olive it is only the lay-off itself that matters; and for the lazy, self-centered Barney, the arrangement offers a range of accessible comforts. The noble Roo, deluded by his passion for the morally autistic Olive, fails to recognize Nancy, his moral and emotional equal, while she is condemned to the sterility of her liaison with Barney. And both Roo and Nancy are trapped as much by their capacity for tenderness, stoicism and selflessness as by their blindnesses and their cultural circumstance. As instinctive parasites, eternal teenagers and purveyors of a breezy charm, on the other hand, Olive and Barney are surprisingly alike. They both offer sex as their chief commodity, even though their individual appeals are remarkably different and evoke different responses, sex being interpreted as love in Olive's case. Nevertheless, Olive is not surnamed Leech for nothing. The situation's pattern of unrequited passion has a Racinean symmetry, if not a Racinean poetry.

Consistent as Lawler's psychological sequence is, it is necessary to add that it accords neither with his own *post facto* explanations of Olive, nor with interpretations in the theatre. Lawler has commented on what he sees as Olive's 'romance' and the 'heightened level' of her speeches in the *Doll,* where there is 'a spirituality, a purity in her way of looking at things'; to his surprise younger actresses apparently have found this spirituality difficult to see. In the theatre, meanwhile, actresses have so far chosen to draw out Olive's childlike frailty, which combined with her centrality in the play's emotional pattern, has masked her destructive infantilism. The depth of Roo's concern and Nancy's protectiveness, in particular, have seemed to invest her with a special emotional worth, while the physically-expressive love scenes have been accepted at face value. . . . I would like to suggest, however, that the text of the published plays supports the alternative interpretation which I have described. . . . Given the range of critical responses to the play . . . , an Ibsenite production of the **Doll** with Olive cast as unwitting villain should not be impossible. Whether audiences would be prepared to accept such a version is, of course, another matter. (pp. 344-46)

Joy Hooton, "Lawler's Demythologizing of the 'Doll': 'Kid Stakes' and 'Other Times'," in Australian Literary Studies, *Vol. 12, No. 3, May, 1986, pp. 335-46.*

Michael Moorcock

1939-

(Born Michael John Moorcock; has also written under pseudonyms of Bill Barclay, Edward P. Bradbury, and James Colvin; joint pseudonyms of Michael Barrington, James Cawthorne, and Philip James; and house pseudonym of Desmond Reid.) English novelist, editor, short story writer, scriptwriter, and songwriter.

A highly prolific author and a former editor for *New Worlds* magazine, Moorcock played an influential role in the New Wave movement in science fiction and fantasy that began in England during the 1960s. A frequent contributor to numerous periodicals and the author of over a hundred diverse books that combine elements of romance, science fiction, heroic fantasy, espionage fiction, and avant-garde literature, Moorcock is best known for his unorthodox variations on traditional fantasy themes and characters. In reaction to the "pulp" image associated with the "Golden Age" of science fiction that took place in the first half of the twentieth century, Moorcock and other writers of the New Wave advocated a wider range of subject matter and literary techniques to replace the adolescent and escapist emphases common to the genre. Moorcock commented: "We were trying to find a viable literature for our time. A literature which took account of science, of modern social trends, and which was written not according to genre conventions but according to the personal requirements of the individuals who produced it."

Moorcock attended ten different schools during his youth, several of which expelled him for rebellious behavior. His mother, exasperated with his poor scholastic record and noticing her son's habit of producing amateur magazines in his spare time, enrolled him at Pitman's College, where he studied for a career in journalism. At age seventeen, Moorcock became the editor of *Tarzan Adventures,* a fanzine for devotees of Edgar Rice Burroughs. By expanding the periodical's comic-book format to include his own fiction, modeled on the fantasy works of Burroughs, Moorcock increased circulation. He resigned this position in 1958, however, to become a full-time editor for Sexton Blake Library and Amalgamated Press, an association that published paperback thrillers. At the request of E. J. "Ted" Carnell, literary agent and editor of several fantasy and science fiction magazines, Moorcock began to produce long fantasy stories. In 1963, Moorcock succeeded Carnell as editor of *New Worlds* and expanded the magazine's format to accommodate a wide variety of contributors. Along with stories and criticism by leading science fiction writers, including Brian Aldiss, J. G. Ballard, and Samuel R. Delany, Moorcock also featured such experimental authors as Jorge Luis Borges and William S. Burroughs. Attacked by conservative proponents of science fiction for its explicit concern with such contemporary themes as sex and violence, *New Worlds* was eventually ignored by publishing distributors in Great Britain and suffered financial setbacks. Although Moorcock emerged as proprietor of *New Worlds* following the abrupt takeover and disappearance of an independent publisher who accepted the magazine's debts in 1968, *New Worlds* ceased publication in 1970 due to continued monetary problems.

Moorcock's early novels were initially published under various pseudonyms as serials in New Wave publications. During the 1960s, his output was considered uneven in quality, often divided between careful serious works and commercial novels written at an accelerated pace to support himself and *New Worlds.* Among Moorcock's most praised creations is Elric of Melniboné, a young fantasy hero whose adolescent problems appealed to romantic British youths of the 1960s. In contrast to the muscled heroes of conventional fantasy, such as Robert E. Howard's Conan the Barbarian, Elric is a frail albino who is dependent on his broadsword, Stormbringer, for his vitality. In later novels Elric's survival depends upon maintaining an uneasy balance between the Lords of Order and the Lords of Chaos, both of whom struggle to control his soul. Among the many books in Moorcock's "Elric" series are *The Stealer of Souls and Other Stories* (1963), *Stormbringer* (1965), *The Singing Citadel* (1970), *The Jade Man's Eyes* (1973), *The Bane of the Black Sword* (1977), and *Elric at the End of Time* (1985). Moorcock's later tetralogy, "The History of Runestaff," which includes *The Jewel in the Skull* (1967), *Sorcerer's Amulet* (1968; published in Great Britain as *The Mad God's Amulet*), *The Sword of the Dawn* (1968), and *The Secret of Runestaff* (1969; published in Great Britain as *The Runestaff*), is a commercial "sword and sorcery" novel that comments on the insufficiency of heroic action and the need for individual responsibility in human affairs. Although many critics have faulted his fantasy novels as implausible or juvenile, Moorcock commented: "All the characters in a Fantasy have to be childish or adolescent in order to function. Because they're larger than life their emotions are huge, their ambitions and their destinies are vast."

While Moorcock published many science fiction novels during the 1960s, he generally considered the genre limited and preferred to write fantasy novels that combine elements of different genres. In these works, Moorcock develops the idea of a "multiverse," a metaphysical concept common to works of science fiction, which posits that parallel universes coexist interdependently and offer a wide variety of alternative realities. As a result, characters may simultaneously occupy or travel between different universes, and characters from different series recur throughout Moorcock's oeuvre. In his "Corum" series, which features such novels as *The Knight of the Swords* (1971), *The Queen of the Swords* (1971), *The Bull and the Spear* (1973), *The Oak and the Ram* (1973), *The Sword and the Stallion* (1974), and *The Chronicles of Corum* (1978), Moorcock combines Arthurian romance and Celtic legend to relate the adventures of Prince Corum Jhaelen Irsei. Like many of Moorcock's protagonists, Corum journeys through space and time to help various cultures defeat mythical monsters and other figures of catastrophe.

Perhaps the most popular of Moorcock's series is that which revolves around Jerry Cornelius, a malleable character who, like many of Moorcock's protagonists, is reincarnated at various times and places and possesses the ability to change physical characteristics, personality traits, and gender. Combining elements of fantasy, science fiction, the espionage thriller, and satire, Moorcock offers Cornelius as an emblem of 1960s values while lampooning his inherent excesses. Jerry Cornelius appears under similar names in many of Moorcock's works, including *An Alien Heat* (1972), *The Hollow Lands* (1974), and *The End of All Songs* (1976), a trilogy collected as *The Dancers at the End of Time* (1980). The character of Cornelius was also taken up by several other New Wave writers, whose pieces appear with five stories by Moorcock in his fiction collection *The Nature of Catastrophe* (1971). Moorcock considers four major books that were revised and republished several times and finally collected as *The Cornelius Chronicles* (1977) to be a single work. In *The Final Programme* (1968), a surrealistic and satiric spy thriller in which a series of killings is traced to a microfilm that turns out to contain only incomprehensible laughter, Cornelius is merged with a woman by a computer and is reborn as a superior hermaphroditic being. *A Cure for Cancer* (1971) depicts Cornelius's travels through various historical periods of crisis and catastrophe, both recognizable and fictional. In one potential reality, Great Britain is napalmed by the United States. *The English Assassin: A Romance of Entropy* (1972), a novel interspersed with news items, offers eight alternative futures for England, while the *The Condition of Muzak* (1977) concludes the tetralogy. Of *The Cornelius Chronicles,* Angus Wilson commented: "The four books together form one of the most ambitious, illuminating and enjoyable works of fiction published in English since the last war."

Many of Moorcock's works of the late 1960s and 1970s offer satiric or ironic commentary on contemporary society in the manner of his "Jerry Cornelius" books. *Behold the Man* (1969), a novel expanded from a novella of the same title for which Moorcock received a Nebula Award in 1967, centers on Karl Glogauer, a Jewish man whose belief in the historical figure of Jesus Christ leads him to travel back in time to Jerusalem. Discovering that Jesus could never have been the Son of God, Glogauer allows himself to be crucified in the Savior's place. In *Breakfast in the Ruins: A Novel of Inhumanity* (1972), Moorcock juxtaposes a homosexual romance between Glogauer and a Nigerian tourist, each of whom seems to mystically merge identities with the other, with accounts of Glogauer's various historical incarnations during times of catastrophe in such cities as Capetown, Shanghai, Kiev, and Saigon. Praising Moorcock as "both bizarrely inventive and highly disciplined," Helen Rogan described *Breakfast in the Ruins* as "by turns puzzling, funny, and shocking."

During the 1980s, Moorcock garnered widespread critical attention for several works that seemed to depart from the concerns of his fantasy novels to address themes more characteristic of mainstream fiction. Set in Russia following the turn of the twentieth century, *Byzantium Endures* (1981) is a picaresque novel about Maxim Arturovitch Pyatnitsky, or Pyat for short, a megalomaniac who survives the Bolshevik Revolution by exploiting both revolutionaries and nationalists. An amalgam of contradictions, Pyat is both bigot and underdog, a devout Greek Orthodox Christian and anti-Semitist of Jewish ancestry who claims to have significantly influenced the twentieth century while others took credit for his achievements. In the novel's sequel, *The Laughter of Carthage* (1984), Pyat escapes from Russia following the ascension of the Soviet regime. After traveling through Western Europe, which he views as declining due to its abundance of impure nationalities, Pyat is finally arrested in the United States for delivering a supportive speech to the Ku Klux Klan. Many critics objected to Moorcock's compassionate treatment of such a negative protagonist, concurring with the opinion of Angus Wilson that "there is a serious danger for an author who creates such a hero: that in bringing alive with sympathy the divine idiocy of his character, the devil's advocacy inherent in so many of his views may be insufficiently stressed." John Clute, however, asserted: "As a tour de force and as a portrait of the century, *Carthage,* along with its intimate predecessor *Byzantium Endures,* sums up [Moorcock's] career and may mark a boundary beyond which the novel as a form cannot safely—or sanely—go."

In his recent novel, *Mother London* (1988), Moorcock experiments with the idea of constructing new myths for England's ancient capitol by centering on three psychiatric outpatients in London, two of whom are mentally capable of sensing the thoughts and feelings of the city's crowds. Although faulted by some critics as overlong, Iain Sinclair called *Mother London* "the achievement of a master craftsman at the height of his powers," and British reviewer Nigel Andrew asserted: "If this wonderful book does not finally convince the world that [Moorcock] is in fact one of our very best novelists and a national treasure, then there is no justice." Moorcock was also a songwriter and guitarist for Hawkwind, an English rock band associated with psychedelia during the 1960s, and has written songs for the group Blue Oyster Cult.

(See also *CLC,* Vols. 5, 27; *Contemporary Authors,* Vols. 45-48; *Contemporary Authors New Revision Series,* Vols. 2, 17; *Contemporary Authors Autobiography Series,* Vol. 5; and *Dictionary of Literary Biography,* Vol. 14.)

RALPH WILLETT

Michael Moorcock has emerged in the late sixties and early seventies as that rare phenomenon, the popular novelist whose work has also become a cult among the young and the avant-garde. . . . [Now] over 30, he is compared not only to Edgar Rice Burroughs but also to William Burroughs, especially with respect to the Jerry Cornelius books: *The Final Programme*, 1968, *The Chinese Agent*, 1970, *The Nature of the Catastrophe*, 1971, *A Cure for Cancer*, 1971, *The English Assassin*, 1972, *An Alien Heat*, 1972, and *The Hollow Lands*, 1974. Moorcock lacks William Burroughs' accurate and devastating satire, and his verbal experiments have been less radical, but in both artists can be observed a basic dissatisfaction with linear methods of representing space and time, a surreal sense of co-existing multiple worlds, and an emphasis on apocalyptic disaster.

Moorcock's eclecticism is a facet of his work that the reader cannot escape; echoes of other writers abound, even if the final result and total effect are Moorcock's own. And the very conception of Jerry Cornelius as a fluid, metaphoric being erodes the old convention of the "retrospective" novel (as J. G. Ballard calls it), in which characters were the property of their creator. Tales about Jerry Cornelius by writers other than Moorcock appeared in *New Worlds*, the magazine edited by Moorcock and Ballard, and were collected, along with some by Moorcock, in *The Nature of the Catastrophe*, edited by Moorcock and Langdon Jones. This collection is dedicated to Borges, and in the introductory discussion of the "real identity" of Jerry Cornelius, several references are made to the Argentine writer, and specifically to "The Immortal." The Cornelius chronology at the end of the book (1900-1968, but with mention of a reference in Vergil!) could well derive from a similar chronology (1066-1921) in "The Immortal." And the universe of the Borges story, in terms of history ("in an infinite period of time, all things happen to all men") and ethics ("all our acts are just, but they are also indifferent"), resembles that of the Jerry Cornelius novels.

The introduction, written from "New Mexico" by a "James Colvin" is itself a hoax, reminding us not only of Borges, but also of Poe. Incest (between Jerry Cornelius and his sister Catherine) with hints of necrophilia also evokes Poe, while in *The Final Programme*, Jerry's father's house, a fake Le Corbusier chateau on the coast of Normandy, seems sentient, like the House of Usher: "As he looked up at it, Jerry thought how strongly the house resembled his father's tricky skull."

Other writers come to mind, such as Donald Barthelme, who is also fascinated with the impedimenta of modern civilization and creates a tone resembling Moorcock's, both sad and nonchalant, and Ronald Firbank, especially in *An Alien Heat*, set in a "decadent" future in which people give themselves up to "paradox, aesthetics and baroque wit." But it is Borges' juxtapositions of the real and the imaginary, and above all, the dream-like fictions in which he plays games with space and time, that are most frequently called to mind. The following lines from "The Garden of Forking Paths" provide an apposite transition: "In all fictional works, each time a man is confronted with several alternatives, he chooses one and eliminates the others; in the fiction of Ts'ui Pên, he chooses—simultaneously—all of them."

Since time is relative, not absolute, any temporal reality is only a possible order of events. Moorcock clearly appreciates and responds to this perception, mixing "real" news items with fictive speculations, and in *The English Assassin*, offering a series of eight different futures, each in the form of "The Alternative Apocalypse." The reader is deliberately refused the comfort of sequential logic by different type faces or by short paragraphs with unrelated randomised headings. The arbitrary nature of literary beginnings and endings is indicated in *The Nature of the Catastrophe* where the opening of **"The Tank Trapeze"** repeats the end of **"Sea Wolves."** (Both stories are by Moorcock.) Moreover, **"The Delhi Division,"** also by Moorcock, begins with the identical sentences opening the chapter "The Hills" in *The English Assassin*, although the protagonist is different: "A smoky Indian rain fell through the hills and woods outside Simla and the high roads were slippery. Major Nye (Jerry Cornelius in **The English Assassin**) drove his Phantom V down twisting lanes flanked by white fences." Once again, the limits of the individual novel or story are challenged. The action is enfranchised and, in its mirror-image, made more ambiguous. Are we witnessing merely different points in time or events in identical universes? The knowledge of the two passages is unsettling like a recurrent dream. (pp. 75-6)

The element of the fantastic is compounded today by radio, TV, magazines and movies, so that our consciousness may be aware of a variety of time-zones at the same instant. Moorcock will place his characters in an airship with Art Deco furnishings, but equip them with modern gadgets such as needleguns and nerve-gas grenades. *The English Assassin* begins in 1975, but moves rapidly to the period of the Austro-Hungarian Empire, and later takes in Una Persson's appearance as a music-hall entertainer at the turn of the century, and Mrs. Cornelius' bank holiday excusion to Brighton in the 1930s.

Certainly, Moorcock shares in the nostalgia of the sixties; "camp" in the second half of that decade made all of the recent past available for evocation. But a sense of irony was retained, and Moorcock too knows where to draw the line, especially in *An Alien Heat*, where an omnivorous nostalgia assists the pursuance of hedonism. In that futuristic novel, the characters vie with each other to set "fashions" which will catch on universally and, while capable of visiting the past, prefer to re-create it. But the past will take its revenge, as the avatar of Jerry Cornelius, Jherek Cornelian, is plunged into the squalor and brutality of Victorian London's slums.

Yet despite the movements in time that characterize *The English Assassin* and *The Nature of the Catastrophe*, the world of Jerry Cornelius is basically that of the 1960s, "a gift-wrapped throwaway age," as Miss Brunner calls it in *The Final Programme*, a mixture of dream and nightmare, buoyant, élitist, androgynous, narcissistic, over-populated, and either violent itself (the Kray twins), or permeated by images of violence (Vietnam, the Kennedy assassinations). Although London in the 1960s was often said to be the most exciting city in the world, the decade still produced books with such titles as *Suicide of a Nation*. Something of that despair finds its way into *The English Assassin* (subtitled "A Romance of Entropy") with its newspaper reports of heroin addiction, car crashes, Vietnam killings, murder and rape, and *A Cure for Cancer*, the most anti-American of the novels with its materials of ubiquitous U.S. military advisers, American internment camps, and paranoid right-wing rhetoric.

Moorcock's time travellers act out his plots in a variety of exotic locations, ranging from Lapland to Cornwall, from Phnom Penh to Simla. At the centre of this world lies Cornelius's Time Centre, set up in a convent in Ladbroke Grove, west of Central London. All the leading characters in the novels and tales find their way to this part of Notting Hill (one centre for the Alternate Society in the Sixties), drawn, for one reason or another, to the Time Centre or to a huge social gathering: Jerry's party in *The Final Programme* at his Holland Park house or the Gala Ball at Hearst's San Simeon, rebuilt on the site of the old convent in *The English Assassin.* These events are ended by the breakdown of government and by personal violence, respectively, but it is national violence, along with anarchy and entropy, that Moorcock usually portrays. The squandering of resources and energy precipitates the death of the universe. . . . Wasteland images predominate: in **"The Sunset Perspective"** (*The Nature of the Catastrophe*), New York is described in terms of distant gunfire, collapsing neon signs and corpses on steel gibbets, and, as cities are destroyed or filled with refugees, a post-atomic vision like Bob Dylan's in "A Hard Rain's Gonna Fall" (1963) is produced ("guns and sharp swords in the hands of young children"; "I saw a black branch with blood that kept drippin' "). This fictional universe is inhabited, indeed "created," by agents and double agents, alternately manipulators and victims, not always in full control of their powers and technology. It is this random factor which renders Jerry and the Time Centre vulnerable.

Glamorous, bi-sexual, capable of colour change, resurrection, and, from book to book, metamorphosis (the seedy Jeremiah Cornell in *The Chinese Agent,* the child-like Jherek Cornelian in *An Alien Heat*), Jerry Cornelius would seem, as his initials suggest, to have many of the pre-requisites for a messiah. But only in *The Final Programme,* where he merges physically with Miss Brunner, does he take up this role—in *The English Assassin* such a suggestion is ridiculed by Colonel Pyat: "A bloody Teddy boy, more like." Even as a modern hero, Jerry departs radically from the Superman image of assertive masculinity. His function—the maintenance of equilibrium between law and chaos—precludes purposeful action; Jerry likes everything "how it comes." Enervated when he loses energy, he is ordinary enough to weep in self-hatred, to vomit and suffer from migraine, and to be captured by the enemy, at which point he is inclined to scream and whimper. (pp. 76-8)

To read the later Cornelius novels is a distinctly masochistic experience, and beneath the "guitars, guns and glitter," there is an underlying despair and nihilism. In *A Cure for Cancer,* that despair engenders a cynicism which is, in social terms, deplorable. Captured twice by Bishop Beesley and once by a U.S. government agent, Jerry abandons humanity to its fate in a private, romantic gesture, maximizing entropy and diffusion so that his sister Catherine will have sufficient energy to live a few days longer.

New art forms are called into being when new material or "content" needs to be articulated. Unfortunately, Moorcock's inventive structures (in such works as *A Cure for Cancer* and *The English Assassin*) seem only to celebrate and mock the Sixties "scene" (an ambivalence characteristic of the period) and to deplore the violence of the modern world, while recognizing its inevitability. *An Alien Heat,* a comparatively conventional narrative novel, is a more considerable affair, using the future and the past to make a dialectical examination of freedom and discipline. Even the emissary from the past, Mrs. Amelia Underwood, an intelligent, hymn-singing gentlewoman from nineteenth-century Bromley in Southern

England, has to admit the attractions of the leisured civilization of the future in which she finds herself: "It was hard, indeed, to cling to all one's proper moral ideals when there was so little evidence of Satan here—no war, no disease, no sadness (unless it was desired), no death, even." But despite this concession, Moorcock's scepticism towards this projected society, which lives off the achievements of the past and fails to invent anything genuinely new, is clear enough, and finds expression through another visitor, Li Pao: "What ghosts you are. What pathetic fantasies you pursue. You play mindless games without purpose or meaning, while the universe dies around you."

Jherek Cornelian, whose nostalgia for the nineteenth century takes the form of pictorial reproductions and an air car that resembles a small steam locomotive, falls in love with Amelia, follows her back in time and, Orpheus-like, arrives in the underworld. His experiences among London's down-and-outs teach him misery, cold, hunger and fear, so that, on his return, he is better equipped to to answer his mother's question (the book's first spoken words): "How do you mean, my love, 'virtuous'?" He has learnt that virtue has to do with corruption, which in turn has to do with "not being in control of your own decisions," a widespread circumstance in nineteenth-century London. With freedom comes the possibility of choosing responsibility and moral action.

Like John Fowles' *The French Lieutenant's Woman,* and the detective novels of Peter Lovesey, *An Alien Heat* (and its sequel, *The Hollow Lands*) demonstrates a recent and continuing interest by contemporary writers in the Victorian period, an interest at times devoted to the accumulation of documentary detail, but one which also permits the comparative study of British cultures. The Jerry Cornelius of **"Sea Wolves,"** dressed in a Diane Logan hat, a yellow Saks shirt, a brown Dannimac coat, and dark orange trousers from Italy, already seems dated. But the modernist techniques of the Cornelius books, and the seriousness and control shown in *An Alien Heat,* make Moorcock one of Britain's most promising novelists. (pp. 78-9)

Ralph Willett, "Moorcock's Achievement and Promise in the Jerry Cornelius Books," in Science-Fiction Studies, *Vol. 3, No. 8, March, 1976, pp. 75-9.*

ANGUS WILSON

[*The Condition of Muzak*] brings to a close the adventures of Jerry Cornelius. The four books together form one of the most ambitious, illuminating and enjoyable works of fiction published in English since the last war.

It is very hard to do justice to Mr Moorcock's tetralogy in a short review, for he is, above all, a generous, even prodigal writer (sour-puss critics, I have no doubt, will write: 'Self-indulgent; you must learn discipline' at the end of their reports). Let me begin by saying that *The Condition of Muzak* surpasses the other three. I have long been his admirer but I had not expected an ending as good as this. Indeed, I would urge new readers (and I hope they will be legion) to start with the last volume, then read the middle two, and, if they have liked it all, they will inevitably go back to the first. . . .

There is very little here . . . that recalls conventional science fiction and its usual themes, save for 'some amused play with modern technology and some serious play with time (only, however, between about 1890 and the near future) in order to explore men's hopes and dreams and the sad fate that too often awaits them.

Mr Moorcock is a master of narrative and he never does less than tell a good story: for this reason he has been compared to Joyce Carey and to Chandler. But he is also a master of fictional play with the reader; hence he has been compared to Bernard Shaw and to Ronald Firbank. But as striking as either of these gifts is his exact ear for nuances of speech and particularly for the language of popular fiction, newspapers, high class magazine ads and so on. He is, in fact, a splendid and subtle parodist. In all this I see him as the heir of Dos Passos and his neglected epic of the USA. And, like Dos Passos, he is that rare thing for England: an urban romanticist, a poet of London street life, of Notting Hill's slums and carnivals and markets.

Not surprisingly, then, his hero Jerry Cornelius begins (in the last volume) as a Notting Hill boy with rock group ambitions. And in the four volumes Mr Moorcock takes him through all the possible failures and successes of his dreams. We see him in a world broken down into chaos, bombed cities, guerrilla warfare, armament racketeers, where nerve bombs and needle guns speak more often than words. Violence in these books is real, absurd and shameful. . . .

Best of all are Mr Moorcock's characters, beautifully observed and exaggerated both in appearance and speech—the baddies: Miss Burner with her world dreams of order and discipline disguising her power-urges, Jerry's brother Frank, the envious, brutal grafter; and the good guardians and friends of Jerry. . . . Jerry's mother, the raddled old cockney Marie Lloyd, whose Dickensian death is as comic and moving a scene as I know.

It is typical of Mr Moorcock that he can send up his own scene ('Because it was conventional, Jerry held her hand. She pulled it away with a throaty chuckle. "Oo'd ya think I am— Little bloody Nell?"') and get away with it. He's a very tricksy, good writer.

Angus Wilson, "Notting Hill Dreamer," in The Observer, *April 3, 1977, p. 26.*

PHILIP OAKES

Anyone trying to measure the talent of Michael Moorcock has to reckon not only with *Gloriana*—his latest, most ambitious novel which Fontana published in paperback last week—but also with the merits of 52 earlier novels, innumerable short stories, several record albums on which Moorcock features with the rock group Hawkwind as singer. . . . It is like trying to evaluate an industry.

I have read about half his prodigious output . . . and on the strength of that sample Moorcock strikes me as the most prolific, probably the most inventive and without doubt the most egalitarian writer practising today. . . .

His early novels, typified by *The Jewel in the Skull* . . . belong to what Moorcock dubs his 'sword and sorcery' period. They are fantasies set in a mediaeval timelock, teeming with warriors, monsters and magicians; pulp fiction which rubs shoulders with Tolkien and frequently withstands the comparison. Moorcock prefers his adventure stories, especially *The Warlord of the Air* in which an Edwardian army officer

is projected into the future (our present day) and meets a half-Chinese buccaneer determined to bring down the British Empire. The vigour of the story-telling is tonic. It is a Ripping Yarn which, like the author, never condescends. I can think of no other contemporary writer so unself-conscious (Moorcock argues that his journalistic training is responsible), or one who so clearly enjoys the job of engaging and enthralling his audience. If Penny Readings were restored—those high-principled Victorian entertainments in which the printed word was made flesh—Moorcock would be king of the circuit. He is a magnificent ham.

At least, one side of him is. In 1967 he won the Nebula Award for his novel *Behold the Man* in which a modern time traveller is transported back to Roman-occupied Palestine to find Joseph a failure, Mary a slut and himself taken for and crucified as Christ. He hates the book now because it lacks humour, but it marked the point in his career at which critics began to take him seriously.

What also sparked their attention was Moorcock's quartet of novels starring Jerry Cornelius, an elf-locked hermaphrodite, who changes sex and colour according to his metabolic rate and survives death and transfiguration on several occasions. . . . Moorcock gave him an incestuous sister; a fake Le Corbusier château as his ancestral home; a 1936 Duesenberg with bullet-proof glass and a cast of lovers and/or adversaries (occasionally the roles are interchangeable) ranging from the sexually-avid Miss Brunner to the blubbery Bishop Beasley forever easing his *angst* with a Mars bar. The Cornelius saga continued with *A Cure for Cancer* and *The English Assassin* and came to a grand *finale* with *The Condition of Muzak.* . . .

A summary of the all-over plot is impossible. The references which stud the text form an extraordinary collage of pop, science and history (a passage from a military manual may follow a paragraph from a paper by Albert Einstein). The technique borrows heavily from comic books and the cut-up experiments of William Burroughs. The tone is sardonic and detached. "Brechtian" says Moorcock half-apologetically, and it is Brecht and Kurt Weill he acknowledges to be the influences behind an LP he's just made called *The Entropy Tango* which is based on *The Condition of Muzak.* It's almost too much, but what makes it both acceptable and enjoyable is the gusto with which Moorcock retails his mammoth fable. Where the stuff of most novelists is barely the equivalent of an austerity snack, Moorcock lays on a banquet and provides the cabaret, too.

He is a joker, but a serious one. He started *Gloriana* with the intention of writing an epic romance which would create a watershed in his work, dividing the past from future projects. It is nothing less than an audacious retelling of *The Faerie Queen* in which Chivalry ends up with pie in the face and a knife in the back and Vice not only triumphs over Virtue, but is seen to be the ideal and eternal tool for pragmatists. "I became so fed up with Spenser's moralising that I turned the tale upside down," says Moorcock. He does so in a style as rich as a syllabub, but sinewy, allusive and ironic at the same time. It is a long book—150,000 words—but it should, thinks Moorcock, be longer still.

He writes fast: *Gloriana* took him only three months to draft and re-write. But, he says, he has tried to slow down for his next novel, *Between the Wars* [retitled *Byzantium Endures*], a steadily blackening comedy about an anti-Semitic old-clothes merchant whose best-kept secret is that he's a Jew. Already, he fears, it is over-long. But he sees length as one kind of strength. Recently, he says, he was approached by a New York publisher who begged him to produce the best book possible for a huge advance. Certainly, said Moorcock, "What can you do me for a million dollars?" asked the publisher. *"War and Peace"* said Moorcock. It was a joke, of course. An even better joke is that he might prove as good as his word.

Philip Oakes, "Michael Moorcock," in The Sunday Times Magazine, *London, November 5, 1978, p. 100.*

MICHAEL MOORCOCK [INTERVIEW WITH IAN COVELL]

[Covell]: *Could you start by giving an autobiography?*

[Moorcock]: I was born in Mitcham, Surrey (on the outskirts of London) December 18th, 1939. . . . My father left my mother (he hadn't served in the war) around, I think, 1945. After VE Day, I think, but I'm not sure. My mother moved soon after, but not very far. . . . I was sent to Michael Hall school in Kent. It was a Rudolf Steiner school, for boarders. I don't think I lasted more than about a year (ages 7-8, probably) before, having run away a few times and got into other kinds of trouble, they asked my mother to take me away. . . .

I went next to a local (Norbury, London SW16) private school where all that I'd learned at Michael Hall (algebra, languages and so on) was dismissed. I wasn't very happy there and played truant a lot. Failed my 11-plus.

In desperation, my mother decided to give me a "business" education and equip me for a journalist's career (since I'd by now started to produce hand-done magazines like *Outlaw's Own,* using carbons for copies) by sending me to Pitman's College. I learned typing but all the other subjects were a mystery to me. I left at 15 and became an office boy in a shipping company. By this time I had produced a fair number of fanzines and so on. One was an Edgar Rice Burroughs fanzine, but most of them were fairly general, like Book Collector's News—a kind of polemical magazine for collectors of Old Boys Books and such things. . . . I was writing stuff from an early age (I could read adult books before I went to school and this also made school very boring for me) and after I was fired from the shipping company after a few months (for "insulting" the lady who turned out to be the manager's mistress, . . . I joined Harold Whitehead and Partners as an office junior.

This was a management consultants and everyone from the boss down was incredibly nice to me, encouraging me to do even more fanzines on the firm's duplicator and to write. My main job was going to the Times Library twice a week to get two books for the boss and one I thought he (and I) might like. The people there provided me with a more sophisticated education, more encouragement, more friendship than I'd ever had before. They encouraged me to take the job on *Tarzan Adventures* when it was offered. At 16 I'd started selling articles and stories to the magazine.

By 17 I was full time editor largely because nobody else would work for the low wages they were paying. I was unable to leave the magazine well alone and began to add text, stories—increasing the fantasy and SF emphasis and decreasing the amount of comic strip. The circulation climbed, I'm glad to say, but eventually (believe it or not) the magazine was clobbered by distributors who had rival comics (Marvelman and so on) which were doing badly. The publishers wished to reduce the budget by returning to more comic strips. I refused to do this and shortly afterwards left. (p. 18)

I got a job on Sexton Blake Library and began to work for Fleetway (then Amalgamated Press). . . . I worked on Sexton Blake Library (two 45,000 word thrillers a month were published), . . . as well as writing for comic books in the same department—Thriller Picture Library and Cowboy Picture Library, mainly. I worked on the last Robin Hood annual, the last Billy the Kid annual and various other annuals of that sort. So far I'd been in the folk-hero business since I began in professional journalism—Kit Carson, Buck Jones, Robin Hood, Buffalo Bill, Three Musketeers, Tarzan, etc. . . .

I'd been writing non-generic fiction of one sort and another and by 1958 had completed an allegorical novel called *The Golden Barge.* . . . I'd written a few SF and fantasy stories because I had various contacts in that world—the world of "fandom", which consisted of about fifty people, I suppose, in those days. But I had no particular ambitions in that direction, as I recall. I began writing long fantasy stories largely because Ted Carnell asked me for some and by that time I was a professional journalist willing to earn money in any way I could. Between 1960 and 1965 I earned most of my money from writing features and comic strips—an innumerable number of stories for such markets as *Bible Story Weekly* and *Dogfight Dixon RFC.* I began to specialize in "educational" features for such periodicals as *Look and Learn,* mainly because they were more interesting to research. I learned, if nothing else, an economy of technique and the ability to plan my stories in terms of scenes—running landscape, narrative and dialogue together so that each contributes to the other. I wrote a comic strip, *Life of Charlemagne.* A comic strip *Life of Alexander the Great* and another of Constantine. I wrote a lot of the *Karl, the Viking* strips which Don Laurence illustrated and I also wrote *Olac the Gladiator.* History and mythology was my speciality, as well as a certain amount of science. . . .

My first long SF story was the two-parter in *SF Adventures—The Sundered Worlds/The Blood Red Game*—and I discovered there that it was impossible to do much individual work in a hardened genre form. From then on, I became a proselytiser for what came to be called "new wave" SF and at that time hardly existed. In fanzines, at conventions, in guest editorials and book reviews, I attacked low standards and demanded more passion and care and integrity in the writing of SF. (p. 19)

By early 1964 it seemed that *New Worlds and Science Fantasy* were to fold forever. They had become amongst my only markets (although by this time I had my first book, *Stealer of Souls,* 1963, out)—at two guineas a thousand words! I was desolate. Then Ted Carnell told me the titles had been sold and he'd recommended me as his succesor. Roberts and Vintner contacted me and said that they'd already promised Bonfiglioli one magazine—which would I like. I chose *New Worlds* because there was more scope in the title for expansion. It was the only period in which I was actually paid (very badly!) to edit *New Worlds.* That period lasted for a couple of years, while it remained in paperback format. When *Roberts and Vintner's* distributors went bust, they had to dump

New Worlds. One of the *Roberts and Vintner* directors, impressed by Brain Aldiss's getting of an Arts Council Grant to "save" the magazine, decided to carry on as an independent publisher with me. We did, I think, four issues under his imprint. While I was away in America in 1967, he disappeared to Scotland and I haven't seen him since. I was left holding the baby. A firm called Stonehart, and well named, offered to take the magazine over. They did, but they were con-men and they also tried to "commercialise" *New Worlds* in silly ways. I refused to compromise and we parted company. By 1968 I was sole publisher. I never incorporated (i.e. formed a limited company) so was responsible for all the magazine's considerable debts. I had begun writing sword and sorcery in 1966 or even earlier . . . and was forced to take on more s&s books in order to keep *New Worlds* and myself funded, for there was no time for other kinds of work. This was how I came to plan and do the Hawkmoon books. Each one of these was written in three days. I had to do them in three days because the magazine was taking up so much of my time! My journalistic training enabled me to meet self-imposed deadlines, but at considerable personal cost—to my family relationships and to my health. While *New Worlds* stumbled along—being banned, having printing difficulties, staff difficulties and so on—I wrote very rapidly.

Stories written during this period included *The Final Programme* (written 1965), *Behold the Man* and *The Ice Schooner.* These two latter were written because the first book had met with general incomprehension on the part of most readers and all publishers and I felt I ought to "go back" to more conventional writing, because my enthusiastic and rather joyful attempt at slightly "experimental" writing had failed to entertain anyone. I was despondent for a while. I like to write for readers and I felt if I wasn't getting through to them, then there must be something wrong with me. (p. 20)

You mentioned a novel, **The Golden Barge,** *was this connected to the short story of the same title, and, if so, was the novel something like Edmund Cooper's* Firebird—*an allegorical tale of a man's life from birth to death as he pursues the mythical Phoenix?*

Yes, the bit printed is a fragment—a chapter—from the original novel. The Cooper story is probably quite similar, yes. It's a pretty conventional theme, I think.

You also mentioned the genesis of **The Chinese Agent.** *What were those two "Nick Allard" books—and was that the protagonist or the pseudonym?*

The LSD Dossier, by someone who's name I forget, was a heavy rewrite by me. It was the first "Nick Allard" book and not really humorous. **Somewhere in the Night** was the second—I threw away the book I had to rewrite and wrote a completely new one. **Printer's Devil** was the other. I never republished it. The two later books were done under my "Bill Barclay" pseudonym. (pp. 20-1)

New Worlds *seemed to publish works and authors spearheading the change toward the "New Wave"—what did you feel were the failings of "traditional" SF?*

We published for the first time a good many stories and novels no other publisher would touch. Also I worked hard to convince publishers to take on other books regarded as "doubtful"—which I admired. I've been instrumental in getting a good few novels published which never appeared in *New Worlds* and weren't always "imaginative". . . . We

were the first people to push the newer American writers like Zelazny, Delany and (though he wasn't exactly new) Ellison here. We helped get Philip K. Dick decently published here. We also supported various non-SF writers such as William Burroughs, Alan Burns, Boris Vian, Borges and a good many other foreign writers who were not at that time either well-known or understood in this country. What, a little later, Judy Merril and Harlan Ellison began to do in the States was not quite the same thing. We ignored the hard-core SF world altogether (unless it was to subject it to various polemical attacks!) and didn't think it was worth worrying about. . . . We never suffered from the constraints of commercialism found in even the best of the American markets. We didn't give a shit about money, circulation or public opinion. We were fundamentally idealistic and willing . . . to go all the way. We were, perhaps, more consciously literary than the U.S. movement—largely because SF was never quite the ghetto-taste it was for a long while in the U.S. There is much more snobbery in the U.S. (particularly in New York) than exists either in England or France. Raymond Chandler's talents (as Bester's, for that matter) were celebrated for their own sake in England long before they were treated seriously in the U.S. A number of our writers had hardly read any conventional SF and when they did read it were astonished by its badness. We didn't so much develop out of the SF world as alongside it. We were a generation of writers who had no nostalgic love of the pulp magazines, who had come to SF as a possible alternative to mainstream fiction and had taken SF seriously. The reason for our anger, our attacks, our idealism was because we genuinely did feel that a superior popular fiction could come out of SF. What united us, if anything, was our alienation from the SF world as well as from the mainstream world—our enthusiasm for many kinds of literature, from Jacobean drama to Nabokov—and we agreed about nothing. We argued and fought and despaired of one another. I, for instance, never could read Nabokov.

We were trying to find a viable literature for our time. A literature which took account of science, of modern social trends and which was written not according to genre conventions but according to the personal requirements of the individuals who produced it. *New Worlds* never had a policy, as such. When we tried to editorialise about one, we became confused. What we tried to avoid, in the large-size issues and later, was to take notice of the commercial SF world. We occasionally knocked the writers with reputations—Blish, Heinlein, Sturgeon and others—but only because the critics discovered to their astonishment that these people could scarcely write on any level worth reading. We came to these writers late (I had a crash-course in SF in 1963 when I read a run of *Astounding*s of the "Golden Age" and was horrified at how bad all these writers like Asimov, Del Rey and others were), usually because we had only a passing familiarity with SF. The potentiality of SF had sparked our imaginations. . . .

Did you ever try to lose the "New Worlds—used to be SF—must still be SF" label which was then attracting the SF reader?

I wanted a general audience, including SF readers. The sort of audience who could take imaginative fiction and other ideas for granted. I felt that SF had left the ghetto—that the kind of fiction we were printing was, in fact, mainstream to the generation who bought *New Worlds.* In the main the big size *New Worlds* stopped addressing the traditional SF audience, making our references general rather than relating to

SF (by and large). It depended, of course, on who was writing what. We had, as I say, no hard and fast "policy". (p. 21)

Perhaps the essential difference between "new wave" and "old wave" is that the former is consciously present-culture oriented and the latter attempts to explore a totally alien reality?

Some of the best aliens have appeared in so-called "new wave" SF—Barry Bayley's in *All the King's Men,* M. John Harrison's in *Settling the World,* Benford's in *If the Stars Are Gods,* all of which try to deal with the modern world in some form or other. For "alien" in old SF read "phobia" and you get a lot of the stuff identified. For "alien" in some SF read "alienation" and you get some of what the authors are about identified. I'm actually shocked and horrified by what's tacit in so much old SF—particularly an almost psychotic misogyny. You're inclined to weep for the terrors which must trouble Heinlein and Niven, for instance. Poor sods. Howard Hughes syndrome. . . .

You did much work in the fantasy field, an escapist literature; in what manner did you bend the rules of the genre to alter the result?

Most fantasy fiction is escapist and therefore misanthropic in a fundamental sense. What I tried to do in my fantasy fiction was turn the thing round and produce simple, humanitarian fables. They celebrate human strengths and weaknesses. That's all I've tried to do. Anything else would destroy the framework and fuck up the reader's expectations. If I'm using a popular form I won't fuck up those expectations. That would be a con-trick I'm not prepared (he said pompously) to employ. (p. 22)

Your major "hero" (in output) is "The Eternal Champion" (aka Erekose, aka Corum, aka Dorian, etc.). Where did the idea of the character originate? Are he and his milieu, symbols, Erekose being symbolic of "Everyman"?

The Eternal Champion idea was one of the first I had. The idea of a reincarnated hero isn't new, of course, and derives from folk-lore. Literary influences were Haggard, Merritt, Howard (in *Almuric,* I think) and Poul Anderson (*Three Hearts and Three Lions*). The "Everyman" aspect of the idea is, to some degree, my own. I used the symbolism implicit to the idea (and that of the "multiverse") to put some simple, sentimental, and, to my mind, worthwhile points across. To interpret any of my stuff like a cross-word puzzle or in "linear" terms is to miss the irony and the paradox. Interpretation is up to the reader. If the reader does not like doing that and doesn't like the work, that's fine. The "Cosmic Balance" is a crude form of symbol.

I'm attempting all the time to find equilibrium between unchecked Romanticism ("Chaos") and stifling Classicism ("Law"). Pinnochio and Jiminy Cricket. Pierrot and Columbine. Ego and Superego. Make your own choice. And in form I'm always looking for a combination (that will work) of the epic and the novel—or the romance and the novel. You will notice that I call very few of my books "novels" because they are not, classically speaking, novels. They are romances. Scene and idea (allegorical concerns) in general take precedence over characters. In the Cornelius books this is not the case, I feel. I've tried to combine "romantic" and "classical" methods there. Humour and irony can achieve the same result in some ways. That's why I'm attracted to comedy as a vehicle. The same moral arguments are debated again and

again from my earliest (***The Golden Barge***) to my latest (***Gloriana***).

The trick is to look at them from as many different viewpoints as possible. That was why I invented Jerry Cornelius and why other writers used him in order to join in the "debate" at one time.

I was just going to ask about Cornelius. Is he a satirical character, and if so, what on?

The Cornelius books are not satire. They are ironies. I don't like satire, by and large. There are, of course, satirical elements in a good many of my books—from the "Kane" stuff onwards—but satire isn't my main concern. Certainly, one hopes, as a writer, to hold a mirror to one's world, but I wouldn't call myself a satirist in any real sense of the term. . . .

Since Jerry Cornelius is a definite aspect of "The Eternal Champion", which war is Jerry fighting?

Jerry (a quote from the Hawkwind number I used to do) is "the veteran of a thousand psychic wars". That's what ties him in with the EC.

Erekose is a victim of his multiverse and Cornelius a victim of his own failings. These are two examples that prove much of your output is concerned—from Jesus Christ (another J.C.) in **Behold the Man** *to your finally publishing* **Moorcock's Book of Martyrs,** *which firmly established The Eternal Champion as a martyr. Why . . . Do you believe we are all martyrs?*

I don't think we are all martyrs. I am against the idea of martyrs as I say in the introduction to ***Book of Martyrs.*** I believe that people become martyrs at the will of other people because other people need martyrs as well as heroes. I don't believe in either. I believe in models—in examples. I have personal models of people who I think live well. That's the best you can provide in the place of "heroes". Christianity and its emphasis on martyrdom has produced in my view a somewhat weird kind of society. Self-denial, altruism and other positive virtues are not, in my view, the same as martyrdom as it's commonly understood. Martyrs do exist. I think they should not. I give Glogauer short shrift in some respects. He is turned into a martyr because he is too weak to find his own destiny. He had to follow a pre-existing one. (p. 23)

Michael Moorcock and Ian Covell, in an interview in Science Fiction Review, *Vol. 8, No. 1, January, 1979, pp. 18-25.*

THE NEW YORKER

[***Byzantium Endures*** is a] picaresque novel about how one Maxim Arturovitch Pyatnitski (to give him the first and the last of the several names he finds it expedient to use), born in Kiev in 1900, survived the Bolshevik Revolution. The author, a well-known English science-fiction writer, pretends that the story came to him from Pyatnitski—in conversations and autobiographical papers—in London just before the aged exile's death, in 1977. It is thus a tour de force, and an extraordinary one. Mr. Moorcock has somehow acquired an impressive understanding of Kiev and Odessa in the early nineteen-hundreds, of St. Petersburg (where Pyatnitski was an engineering student at the Polytechnic Institute) at the outbreak of the revolution. . . . He has also created in Pyatnitski a wholly sympathetic and highly complicated rogue—a gifted engineer, a linguist fluent in French, English, Polish, and German, a womanizer and cocaine user from the age of fourteen, an effortless role player, a devout Greek Orthodox Christian (hence the title), and a violent anti-Semite (though he is possibly half Jewish), anti-Roman Catholic, and anti-Muslim. There is much vigorous action here, along with a depth and an intellectuality, and humor and color and wit as well: "The Revolution had been a work of modern art: convulsive, undisciplined, emotional, and formless." (pp. 127-28)

> *A review of "Byzantium Endures," in* The New Yorker, *Vol. LVII, No. 51, February 8, 1982, pp. 127-28.*

FREDERIC MORTON

Usually writers try to cope with the Russian Revolution on a panoramic canvas as Mikhail Sholokhov did in *The Silent Don.* In ***Byzantium Endures*** one man's subjective paroxysms tell the story. Michael Moorcock has filtered a great upheaval through a supremely chaotic character named Maxim Arturovitch Pyatnitski—"Pyat" for short. Pyat really lived Mr. Moorcock claims. (p. 12)

The dust jacket, however, bills Pyat's chronicle as a novel. Furthermore, it informs us that Mr. Moorcock is an Englishman well known in his country for his futuristic stories. This suggests that his credentials for writing historical fiction set in Russia are as interestingly illogical as his hero's life. But it also suggests that Mr. Moorcock, again like his hero, is a whiz at running wild risks. His tale resonates even where it does not quite succeed.

Pyat was born on January 1, 1900, an emblematic date. From the start he burns with the ambitions and sicknesses of our century. First he must overcome a threadbare childhood. His mother is a laundress, his father a "radical" who deserted the family. Pyat feels himself afflicted not only by circumcision but by a Semitic visage. This curse leads him to profess— frequently, obsessively—pride in his "pure Slavic descent" and in the noble lineage he cannot divulge for fear of endangering cousins under Bolshevist rule.

To counter his disadvantages, young Pyat develops an exalted sense of mission. Russia has been infected by low Jewish corruptions oozing in from the West; but he, Pyat, bolstered by his talent as a budding engineer, will restore Russia's strength and, with it, her purity. He sees himself as a genius ordained to a high task. That vision is pursued with a quirky arrogance and a picaresque energy that take him through the crises of the Revolution. At the outbreak of the war he travels to Odessa, where he studies physics and bordellos and cocaine praxis. . . .He savors the dregs of Western-decadence while refining still further his conception of Holy Russia redeemed.

Then he returns to the Ukraine. There he is caught in the riptides of the Revolution. But he saves his hide (and keeps drinking good vodka) by playing mechanic-in-chief to whatever faction is occupying the premises. We find him repairing the rifles of anarchist guerrillas, fixing the treads of White Army tanks, doctoring the engine of one of Trotsky's armed trains, perfecting a violet ray gun for a Ukrainian hetman. Along the way he invents devices as earthshaking as Edison's. Yet again and again some villain or some mischance cheats him of his reward. Again and again Pyat gloats over the technical virtuosity of his opportunism without ever seeing him-

self as an opportunist. Again and again he views his expediencies as minor detours from his mission. And along the way men starve, bleed, perish, as he gets by. Not once—to give him his due—does he fail to give us an arresting view of the landscape of his survival.

But that very landscape painting becomes a problem. The book has two important virtues, and they conflict. Russia's great cities, before and during the Revolution, come alive in judicious renderings of sights and sounds, gestures and moods. Pyat, for example, ends his impression of the desolate majesty of St. Petersburg by saying, "It seemed one could not even raise one's voice here, unless it was to berate a servant."

The image works, and there are many others of like effectiveness. But these images are the product of a balanced literary sensibility attuned to moral ironies and to ethical counterpoint. As such they work against rather than with the book's major element: Pyat's other, more dominant voice, which mesmerizes just because it is so authentically unbalanced in its egotism, so dynamic in its lopsidedness, so amoral in its élan, so gorgeously maniacal.

If Mr. Moorcock had been able to resolve the dissonance, he would have come close to a masterpiece. As it is, ***Byzantium Endures*** is often *masterly*—and never more so, strangely enough, than when Pyat fantasticates away on the nature of divinity. The machines he invents may be altogether chimerical, but his private theology intriguingly underpins his ravings. In an original inversion of the Arian heresy, he posits that the Son is superior to the Father. Christ is the pure Grecian Godhead, revealed in Hellenized Palestine. Jehovah is an unruly Semitic demon. From the Byzantine Empire and the Greek Orthodox Church, Russia has inherited the truer faith in the Son. Byzantium endures as a mirage in his mind. His knight-errantry on its behalf makes his obsessions logical. . . . In his nostalgia for Russia, pre-Western and unstained, he harks back to Jesus's Virgin Birth.

Is this self-contradictory Christology? Or is it the sort of schizoid piety that, suitably tempered, applies elsewhere as well? Don't many of us in America still feel that tomorrow's supergadget will save us yet? And don't we at the same time long for that old hometown sunshine that has not shone since those television antennas went up? I think the power of this book rests on a disturbing fact. It is not only in Pyat's crazed mind that Byzantium endures. (pp. 12, 20)

> *Frederic Morton, "One Man's Revolution," in* The New York Times Book Review, *February 21, 1982, pp. 12, 20.*

PAUL WEST

When you open ***Byzantium Endures,*** a bulge forms down the middle of the two-page frontispiece map, all the way from St. Petersburg in the north to Constantinople in the south. A handy fluke, because it's along the time-line of this vertical bulge that Michael Moorcock's anti-hero whizzes up and down, from Kiev in the dead center of the map to Odessa, due south, then up to St. Petersburg, after which he goes to Constantinople, which is old Byzantium. Like mercury in a fine tube, he measures the revolutionary climate in the first decades of our century; a twisted H. M. Stanley looking for the source of Russia's pain.

But he's more than that: self-engrossed and self-serving, he is an accomplished liar and an anti-Semitic Jew whose emotional life is a series of agonized twists. Determined not to be what life has made him, Maxim Arturovitch Pyatnitski only becomes more so: for supposedly hygienic reasons his father had him circumcised, and this obsesses "Pyat." In fact, he is nothing but obsession, although some of the things that haunt him are more interesting than remembrance of a prepuce past: his love of aeronautics, for instance, comes bewitchingly through. As a mere boy, he devised a manned flying machine and, partly to impress Esmé his childhood sweetheart, jumped into the Babi Yar ravine, thus attaining premature fame as the Icarus of Kiev.

If you believe him, that is. A first-person narrative, **Byzantium Endures** has all the usual traps: no corroboration by witnesses, no interventions by an all-knowing authority whose mind is the novel's locus. Moorcock supplies an introduction which explains how Pyat's papers came into his hands, eventually to obsess *him* and drive him "half-mad." There is even a "a facsimile page from Pyat's manuscript" to thicken up the illusion, and Moorcock makes a tempting job of the preview, offering the image of old Pyat in London, his final retreat, tippling in favorite pubs with his mysterious mistress, a Mrs. Cornelius, who wafts through the book proper like some Cockney angel of mercy. . . . (p. 10)

A game of mirrors is going on here, a game whose rules extend beyond the immediate concerns of **Byzantium Endures.** As Moorcock says, Pyat "knew that I had already . . . 'exploited' [Mrs. Cornelius] in some books," and there are the several Jerry Cornelius novels to prove it, as well as **The Adventures of Una Persson and Catherine Cornelius in the Twentieth Century.** And, if you jump ahead to the last page of Moorcock's recent fantasy novel, **The War Hound and the World's Pain** you find a note saying that he "is working on an ambitious four-volume novel *Some Reminiscences of Mrs. Cornelius Between the Wars,* the first volume of which, **Byzantium Endures,** has already appeared."

Hence some of the huffing and puffing in the introduction, which is essentially a portrait of the artist as an inheritor of materials. He resists the opportunistic Pyat's demand that he write the life of Mrs. Cornelius but, eventually succumbing to Pyat's spell, ploughs through 11 shoeboxes of papers and ends up with the present text (1900 to 1920) whereas the papers go all the way to 1940, with Pyat in a concentration camp. The reader has to work out whether or not, granted the constraint of editing, the entire novel should have been cast in the mode of the preface, with Pyat given not raw and unmediated, but planted in the living tissue of authorial speculation. I wonder, because Moorcock as himself, or impersonating himself, is a subtler teller than Moorcock impersonating Pyat, who limps and drones and fumbles, enlarging what an expert novelist would have trimmed, and vice versa. If the gain is a greater realism, the loss is in technique; a loss which perhaps the other three volumes will justify.

As it is, some of the book foams along. The disastrous parabola of Pyat's cocaine-heightened private life is undeniably vivid, and it survives the log-jams of data allowed in by the putative editor. An odd mix of picaro, Cartesian diver, and thwarted pilot who flies all the time in his mind's eye, Pyat is someone to remember: a warthog of the Ukraine, a flunked Prometheus convinced he never had the life he deserved, a fake, a snob, a lover of machinery ("the sight of a simple English bicycle" ravishes him), and a misfit who says to Winston Churchill "How are you, you old bugger?" (pp. 10, 12)

Rasputin stalks through these pages while Pyat lurches from high to high in white suit, boater, walking with his silver-headed cane into and out of aliases, leaving only the "liquid steel" of his sperm behind him. He struts along the rim of history and topples off, a man who might have ruled the world (or so he thinks), an H. G. Wells figment who ends up in real Wells-land, living over a second-hand clothes shop in Notting Hill, surrounded by bits of old bicycle "petrol engines, old spark plugs, electrical bric-a-brac." . . . Something gritty and nasty about him keeps him at a slight distance, at exactly the distance where personification thrives; so he easily becomes what he thinks himself—the spirit of the age, an Ancient Mariner who's read Nietzsche.

A memorable though greasy creation, he puzzles me only if I try to figure out when he wrote things down. The blurb says "told . . . during the Russian Revolution," but it all feels as if set down much later, in the later '30s, perhaps. It will be uncanny to have him presented by yet another first-person narrator: Mrs. Cornelius, to be sure. (p. 12)

Paul West, "The Adventures of Colonel Pyat and Mrs. Cornelius," in Book World—The Washington Post, *March 21, 1982, pp. 10, 12.*

J. E. RUDD

The characterization of Pyat [in **Byzantium Endures**] is perhaps Moorcock's best to date as I found myself so absorbed by my reading that I forgot that this was a Moorcock book, and began to believe that these *were* the memoirs of Pyat, that it was Pyat who invented the laser and other mechanisms, Pyat that formulated Relativity. Only when Mrs. Cornelius made her entrance with her characteristic "Wotcher, Ivan, you ole bugger!", that I remembered that this was the fictitious story of Colonel Pyat.

Often throughout the novel I was reminded of Gunter Grass' *The Tin Drum.* Pyat is Oskar, deformed not in body but in mind, for despite his intelligence, the narrator's hatred of the Jew comes above all else. And it is an unhealthy hatred, for Pyat cannot admit to it. His relationship with his mother and the doubt about his father are similar in both stories, although the differences are obvious.

At the start of **Byzantium Endures,** Pyat comes across as very much an innocent. At one point he asks his childhood friend and "sister" if she has a sweetheart. Esme tells him that she is waiting for someone. Technically, this sequence is excellently written. The reader knows that she means Pyat, but Pyat does not, or if he does, only in retrospect, now that over fifty years have passed. The narrator's character develops from a boy to a man, physically and mentally, finally to the rambling, insane old man who writes the story. Towards the end of the book he deviates from the current story to his diverse religious beliefs and pieces together for us the major details of his later life.

I finished **Byzantium Endures** feeling that I had watched Pyat develop from a boy to a man, but at the same time sad at his misguided romanticism; feeling that Pyat's "memoirs" were merely wild exaggerations from pieces of the truth and an over-active insane mind.

I hope that Moorcock will continue to write as well as he has recently. For all the excitement that the Elric and Cornelius books gave us, his writing of **Gloriana, The War Hound and** *the World's Pain* and *Byzantium Endures* shows how he is beginning to write now with more skill and he seems to be enjoying it as much, I hope, as his audiences are. (pp. 16-17)

J. E. Rudd, in a review of "Byzantium Endures," in Science Fiction Review, *Vol. 12, No. 2, May, 1983, pp. 16-17.*

JOHN CLUTE

Michael Moorcock is 44. *The Laughter of Carthage* is his 55th novel, give or take a few. It has been a long career for a young man and, by the evidence of this book, it is a career, after a quarter of a century, that is only now attaining its full momentum. As a tour de force and as a portrait of the century, *Carthage,* along with its intimate predecessor *Byzantium Endures* (1981), sums up that career and may mark a boundary beyond which the novel as a form cannot safely—or sanely—go.

In science fiction circles, there has been a storyline about the life and works of Michael Moorcock. It has the virtue of simplicity. Fresh from the pits of *Tarzan Adventures* and the Sexton Blake Library, so the story goes, young Moorcock sprang around 1962 into the larger world of science fantasy as a kind of idiot savant. His relentlessly pliant ability to churn out dozens of myth-soaked novels—most notably the Elric tales—had little or nothing to do with the conscious premeditations of slower, more visibly crafty writers. In 1965, by some labile magic, he managed to create an icon for the Sixties in Jerry Cornelius, shape-changer, fetish-monger, murderous city-dweller, Bond and Pierrot irretrievably mixed.

By the end of the Sixties, so the story goes on, Moorcock began to retreat from the delirium of the good days and to produce, out of some dark abyss in his convivial innocent self, those problematical moral fictions about the nature of the catastrophe—the catastrophe being in short the history of the modern world—through which dance, like the masked players in a harlequinade, like dervishes, all the characters of the earlier books. . . . (p. 31)

Much of the early work is junk; the later work feeds off the earlier in ways difficult to analyse, though sometimes embarrassing to have to note. But this version of Moorcock's quite extraordinary career does fail to emphasise the fact that, from the very first, with conscious cunning and craft, he has put together a body of work the interconnections of which are primarily matters not of circumstance but metaphysics. At the maelstrom heart of his work lies a beguilingly slippery Pop Platonism, a constant shimmy of levels of reality, so that what is real in one book will seem only a parodic shadow of the real world as uncovered in the next book; and the book after that will introduce a yet higher and more real haven, in which, for a little while, there may be some peace between the wars.

But not for long. We come to *Byzantium Endures* and *The Laughter of Carthage,* in which all the Platonic cardsharping of Moorcock's entire career comes home to roost in this our own world, and there is no escape. In the Cornelius books, Colonel Pyat may have danced with the best of them; here, he is Maxim Arturovitch Pyatnitski, and the dance among realities of the earlier books becomes something far more punishing than one could have guessed, because Pyatnitski, who tells his own story, is perhaps the most appallingly unreliable narrator ever presented in a work of fiction of any stature.

But no matter what he says, the world does not shift. He remains caught red-handed in the holocaust of this century. The effect is terrifying.

It is all the more terrifying when we begin to realise, through the 600 pages of *The Laughter of Carthage,* that Moorcock has created in the hysterical foetor of Pyatnitski's self-serving personality a model of moral and cultural bankruptcy that can serve as a paradigm of the failure of Western civilization itself. The previous volume tells of his birth in 1900 of Jewish blood; of the education whose tenets he despoils; of the family and friends whom he betrays again and again; of his enormous greed for money, prestige, sex, drugs, food; and of his entering a panicked adolescence in the midst of the Russian Revolution. The new volume carries him to Constantinople, Rome, Paris and, finally, America. He has not changed. He remains an anti-Semite, a liar, a thief, a monster of greed, a ruthless manipulator of those weaker than he; and all the while denies any complicity in the 'nightmare' he constantly attempts to escape but which is nothing more, or less, than his own loathsome slippery self.

Strangely, he is also an innocent. Totally humourless, he is incapable of detecting the scams or impostures of anyone else. There are moments of high comedy in Paris and, later, in Memphis Tennessee, when he becomes unwittingly involved in the confidence games of others. At points he bears an uncanny resemblance to the Pooter of the Grossmiths' *Diary of a Nobody* or, more precisely, to the husband in Barry Pain's *Eliza* books, for Moorcock's impersonation of Pyatnitski has something of the manic, imageless, hysterical drive of Barry Pain at his best.

Because we never escape Pyatnitski's voice, *The Laughter of Carthage* is at points almost unendurable. But the sustained brilliance of the telling pulls us back. Though there are moments when the story merely repeats itself, the underlying moral grasp never seriously falters. In Pyatnitski's manic elatedness at moments of triumph or travel, we can see something of the insensate momentum of the technologies we inherit; and in his frantic hatred for everything that makes him what he is, we may see something of our own losses. (p. 32)

John Clute, "No Escape," in New Statesman, *Vol. 108, No. 2790, September 7, 1984, pp. 31-2.*

VALENTINE CUNNINGHAM

In every way, with Dmitri Pyatnitski *alias* Pyat *alias* Peterson there's a question of endurance. The egregiously pompous, bragging, illiberal, ranting remembrancer of Michael Moorcock's *Byzantium Endures* now puts himself and his readers through an even more bloated self-resurrection in *The Laughter of Carthage.* Nor is Pyat the only one of the earlier novel's huge cast to get out of recently Sovietized Russia. With the boy hero and engineer comes Mrs Cornelius, Falstaffian cockney bad-mouther and mistress of all the top revolutionary brass. Once in western Europe Pyat soon comes across his old chum the aesthetic princeling Petroff, conspicuous among the hordes of White Russians thronging the Parisian bohemian scene. . . . [In Paris], he thinks he glimpses his old adversary Brodmann tracking his every turn. The sinister Jewish Chekist/Bolshevik is bound, Pyat fears, to denounce him as a spy on one side or another. Pyat needs at least one of his former beloveds as well. His fiancée Esmé disappeared into the erotic squalor of the revolutionary mayhem, but in this novel Pyat recreates her in the person of a Rumanian tart he picks up in the cafés of Istanbul. Much of this narrative is about Pyat getting this second Esmé out of Turkey, through Italy, to Paris, and then scheming to transfer her to the United States.

Of course, for all the other old opponents who didn't make it through the Bolshevik terrors of *Byzantium Endures, The Laughter of Carthage* has hordes of ready replacements. For this is epic writing, explicitly devoted to the memory of the crowd-mastering cinematic arts of D. W. Griffith. As Griffith stuffed his movies with vast throngs and Promethean matter so Pyat's narration feeds hugely on the numerous people he claims to have met, the history he makes believe he has helped to shape, the many places his traveller's tales take him to. Pyat's story snorts up continents-full of things with much the same eager relish as Pyat evinces for his daily doses of cocaine. Together, Pyat and his story will be big, bigger, biggest. . . . His briefcase is always chock-full of plans for the vastest of flying machines. The stupendous airship hanger Pyat gets to build in France—like a medieval cathedral, he says—is intended at once to make his readers feel small and to aggrandize him.

The gargantuan sweep and hubristic excess of Pyat's story could not fail to be at least occasionally enticing—not least because Pyat's private variants on the post-First-World-War history we know better in other people's versions are so sexually engaging. If only schoolbooks expatiated as freely on the contribution to world events of the brothels of Istanbul or the posh and puritanical bordellos of Memphis! But for all this uplifting attention to cosmopolitan low life, it remains the case that after two chubby volumes even Pyat's Rabelaisian charms are getting rather worn, and the more irksome features of his recollections more intrusive. Increasingly, the epic appetite is making do with a fairly mundane fondness for mere lists of names, catalogues of things, Baedeker-like jottings and joggings about Constantinople, Rome, Paris, New York, San Francisco, wherever. The self-praised poet of the modern concrete-and-steel urbs keeps turning, in the event, into a much more ordinary traveloguist, tricked out in the occasional purple patch—on Paris the queen of whores, it might be, or the dream-factory of Hollywood. The would-be master of every contingency, the rider-out of a century's political storms is actually set on a peculiarly formulaic bout of journeyings, perturbed in the main by pretty predictable set-pieces, in an all-too *voulu* run from Constantinople (for the Russian-Greek-Orthodox reflections that Byzantine churches will incite), to Italy (for its Futurists in politics and art and the motor-industry), to America (the land God gave to Griffith). Worse, Pyat stretches the reader's confidence in the truthfulness of what he lays claim to. Worse still, in the end he challenges one's tolerance, the readiness to put up with, to endure, the views he presses on one's attention.

The shocking contrast between this old emigré's boasts about his glorious past and the grotty shop, in the shadow of London's grim Westway, in which he is now writing is, of course, nicely managed to cast doubt on his textual and sexual endeavours. The question of how much of his story is fantasy, spliced together at the behest of mere wish, is intended continually to intrigue. If he was so great an inventive genius, how is it that none of his grand designs got off the ground? If he's so pure an Orthodox Christian, how did he get circumcised, and why does he speak Yiddish so constantly, and why do people keep taking him for a Jew? Moorcock contrives a number of these inconsistencies to help undercut Pyat's claim on political and social wisdoms. But Pyat is given stretch after stretch of rope and still doesn't get hung; instead he obsessively and endlessly picks at the scabs of some of the nastiest ideological sores English fiction has ever been subjected to.

For Pyat goes on and on about what's wrong with most of the human race—Jews, Bolsheviks, Catholics, Blacks, Turks, Marx, Freud, Einstein, almost everyone except himself, a few other faithful Russians, and a handful of white Protestant Americans. Pyat has soft spots for Hitler and Mosley (only Mosley's breath smelt). He rhapsodizes over Mussolini and Senator McCarthy. He won't ever let us forget his private division of the world into Holy Russia, its Greek ideals, its brand of Christianity, its few supporters, on the one hand, and on the other the hunnish, semitic and "philosemitic", asiatic, negroid, nigger-loving, blues-caterwauling hordes of what he calls Carthage. White men let the Bolshevik-Hebrew-Moslem-Papist conspiracy overwhelm Byzantium, and now the West collapses into suitably terrible decline. Pyat has written to politicians, but in vain. He spends much of the period this novel covers stumping about America preaching to audiences of Klu Klux Klansmen the virtues of hating niggers, yids, papists, and the good sense promulgated by Griffith's *Birth of a Nation,* only to get into trouble with the FBI. So now he's turning on us, in page after page of extended, dismayingly unironic hate-laden rant.

To what end? This novel, like its predecessor, assumes that its protracted abandonment of stage-centre to this wicked crank will be of interest. Excuses or explanations are not thought necessary. "A genius of innocent vituperation", the blurb calls Pyat. But innocent is precisely what his vituperation is not. At best it might be just excusable as Swiftian—the granting of a hearing to immodest proposals that should be rejected by all sane readers. But the dearth of placing signals is as perturbing in Moorcock as it is in Swift. Pyat's "finest achievement (and that of his author)", the blurb-writer goes on, "is that his own warped and deluded vision is powerful enough to redefine reality". But which reality might this be? The reality of Hitler, or the Klan? It's an awesome thought that Moorcock might go along even a bit of the way with Pyat's denunciations; that even one reader can take seriously this sinister monstrosity Moorcock has so vigorously spawned, even for a moment.

Valentine Cunningham, "Incontinent Continents-Full," in The Times Literary Supplement, No. 4249, September 7, 1984, p. 1005.

ANGUS WILSON

Michael Moorcock is, I have little doubt, one of the most exciting discoveries that I have been able to make in the contemporary English novel during the 40 or so years that I have been publishing my own novels and reviewing those of my contemporaries. Exciting for myself and, as is becoming increasingly clear with the appearance of each Moorcock book, for a legion of other readers.

The fusion of fantasy and realism is surely the main advance now being made in the English language novel. The paths of this convergence are many: human individuals molded by the esthetic demands of strict formal shape as in Henry Green; the interlocking paths and journeys of magic and everyday life as in John Cowper Powys; the excitements and revelations of metaphysical adventure and legend as in J. R. R. Tolkien. . . . (p. 1)

For me [Moorcock's] Jerry Cornelius quartet (beginning with *The Final Programme*) assured the durability of his reputation. But if, as now seems likely, his career will take in many more multi-volumed novels we have a long, packed and exciting journey to make with him—and with such magic figures as Moorcock's beloved Mrs. Cornelius—for how can a novel go wrong with Mrs. Cornelius to meet again?—that strange haunting mixture of Sairey Gamp (for laughter) and the Talmadge sisters (for beauty and sex). And *The Laughter of Carthage* has other characters that promise as much for the future as Mrs. Cornelius has done from the start.

Moorcock covers such a wide field in *The Laughter of Carthage* (and its predecessor, *Byzantium Endures*). In this volume chronicling the life and adventures of the mythomaniac engineer Pyat or of Colonel Peterson or of Matt Pallenbury, the changes of name not only signal the hero's failure of scientific or mechanical invention (which makes his life one long pseudonym to avoid prosecution for fraud), but also establish Pyat's almost magical power to invent those new names and new personalities needed to sustain his absurd, childish life of imagined success. (pp. 1, 13)

Of course, all his hopes are dreams, and blighted dreams at that. He has to leave his wonderful little girl mistress from Constantinople in Paris to avoid prosecution, although by tricks and cheats he is able to end the book in New York awaiting her arrival to make an idyllic life in L.A. The pictures of life in all these places are no doubt measured somewhat by the reader's familiarity with the locales. Yet I must confess that though I do not know Memphis, life there with the Ku Klux Klan comes over most successfully. Indeed, all this world of shady deals and high hopes, likeable ladies of all classes and of high sexuality, insecure hotel living, dope and meetings with movie stars makes for a series of wonderful fast-moving scenes.

It is lucky that it is so, for with the best will in the world, one may sympathize with the hero's eroticism and even his absurd high hopes, but it is quite impossible for me to swallow any of his loyalties and faiths. Admittedly I am an old-time liberal, but I fear that like many other readers I cannot accept Pyat's philosophy which not only demands the absolute acceptance of a white, Western world of values but utterly condemns Jews, people of color, Moslems, Socialists, indeed all liberals, I think.

Luckily one is able to trust the irony of Moorcock's story, for he openly declares his own dislike for his hero's beliefs. But there is a serious danger for an author who creates such a hero: that in bringing alive with sympathy the divine idiocy of his character, the devil's advocacy inherent in so many of his views may be insufficiently stressed. Moorcock's disclaimer is outside the text. In the novel itself I believe that he just avoids the danger. (p. 13)

> *Angus Wilson, "The Picaresque Imagination of Michael Moorcock," in* Book World—The Washington Post, *December 23, 1984, pp. 1, 13.*

BRIAN APPLEYARD

Michael Moorcock sits comfortably amidst the happy chaos of his study. . . .

Like his head, the place is full of wild ideas, a hippyish profusion in celebration of . . . well, everything. It is also full of ghosts—of Colonel Pyat, the warped engineer, and of freedom-fighting Una Persson. But, most potent of all, there is the shade of Jerry Cornelius, the time-travelling dreamer of the 20th century.

With the four Cornelius novels, published in the Seventies, Moorcock established himself as a major writer. They were ambitious, fantastic and downright weird. They were the products of an imagination that could never be satisfied with the tight little conventions of mainstream British fiction. . . .

> To people of my generation, rock 'n' roll and SF were the two things that were yours—there was no body of criticism, they weren't occupied by academics or authority. There was something you could work with and nobody to tell you you shouldn't. . . .

The Fifties gave Moorcock two things: a vast range of material and a remarkable degree of literary fluency. For magazines he wrote series of stories and 15 20,000-word novellas. "I used to think if a book took more than a month, it wasn't worth writing."

The effect of all this was that, as his writing veered away from these "genre" novels and started receiving respectful "serious" reviews, he appeared to be a writer with a split personality. On the one hand he turned out fantasy potboilers, on the other he wrote *Behold the Man* or the Cornelius tetralogy.

Says Moorcock:

> I never did feel the split myself. The first novel I ever wrote was realistic—it was terrible—then I wrote an allegory. Only then did I start writing genre books. They turned out to be the kind of thing I had a talent for.
>
> When *Behold the Man* came out, that was regarded as a bit posher. But for a long time I was regarded as a barbarian interloper. I was treated as unsophisticated and naive—someone who had just wandered into the world of literature. All I know is I've read more than they have . . .

He chortles gleefully.

The Sixties were a Golden Age for Moorcock. He was writing as furiously as ever and he was playing and writing songs for the "progressive" rock band Hawkwind.

> That was the easiest thing I've ever done, and the most successful. But I was never very much good as a player, and I don't write music. I'm not Anthony Burgess.

With the Cornelius books, he began to slow down. *The Condition of Muzak* took all of six weeks. Angus Wilson, one of the few modern novelists Moorcock admires, thought they represented some of "the most ambitious, illuminating and enjoyable" fiction in English since the war [see excerpt above].

Moorcock was unquestionably at least a decade ahead of his time. Along with his friend J. G. Ballard, he had used the novel form generously and ambitiously to distil the preoccupations of the age. It was not until the Eighties that a new generation of similarly ambitious novelists was to emerge.

His own literary influences are almost entirely 18th and 19th century: he mentions Dickens, George Eliot, Conrad and Fielding. "My reading was largely 19th century. I did read modern novels, but only Jimmy Ballard and Angus Wilson were writing about experience I actually recognized."

He believes in the traditional role of the novelist of entering into the lives of others. The lives of himself, his friends and his relatives are absorbed and transformed into fiction with disturbing speed. He has often discovered to his horror that, with some secondary characters, he has even forgotten to change the names.

There are a few such cases in his latest novel, **Mother London.** But the main characters in the book are aspects of Moorcock himself. David Mummery shares his autobiography and Joseph Kiss some of his personality.

The book is a complex, layered history of London since the war, seen through the stories of a group of psychiatric patients. Moorcock describes its construction as "symphonic"—its interest derives not from any single plot but from the way each narrative resonates and echoes with the others. We are being shown a city of voices and of words—a landscape as invented as the real thing.

It took him four years. His relative slowness, he explains, was due to increasing age and to the need to allow the book to grow entirely out of characters.

After a bout of pneumonia he decided to turn to a book he had planned for some time about the mythology of modern London.

> We all have these myths—about the Royal family or the war. We deify certain people. The book is about the fictionalizing process, but not in a narrow sense. Everything is fictionalized. I actually do believe that if enough people believe something it will actually come true, even if only for a while—like the Third Reich."

> *Brian Appleyard, "Fiction of the Future," in* The Times, *London, June 18, 1988, p. 20.*

NIGEL ANDREW

London is a city of words. Her pull on the imagination is not visual but verbal in origin, the product of an immense literature and an equally rich oral tradition. . . . These are the strata on which the London of the imagination—as real as the city of bricks and mortar and historical fact—is built and rebuilt.

Michael Moorcock's new novel [*Mother London*] digs deep into those buried riches in a prodigious work of imaginative archaeology. One of his principal characters, David Mummery, is an expert in the arcane lore of the city and obsessed in particular by the mysteries of subterranean London, a forgotten world where, at one point, he even discovers a lost race of troglodytes. Josef Kiss, similarly, delivers impromptu lectures on London's history and myths to his Indian 'Boswell', Dandy Banaji, and breaks into song with snatches of old ballads and glees. Their London is thick with history, resonant with long echoes of the past.

Another character, Old Nonny, even claims to know Brutus the Trojan, the mythical founder of London: he is at present busy 'antiquing' furniture in the East End. But it is the more recent past that is the central concern of this book, and in particular the Blitz. Through David Mummery, the very first paragraph states the premise:

> By means of certain myths which cannot easily be damaged or debased the majority of us survive. All old cities possess their special myths. Amongst London's in recent years is the story of the Blitz, of our endurance.

Improbably, four decades on, the Blitz here bursts into abundant fictional life: but this is no conventional 'wartime London' novel.

Moorcock's central characters are all, variously, cracked; all survivors, all linked by strands of consequence and coincidence extending far into the past. . . . The novel begins and ends in the present, but builds its story by dipping into the lives of its characters at various dates, from the Blitz to the recent past. The cast list grows by accretion, the light of what has been spread over what is to come, and around these strange, damaged lives Moorcock gradually creates what amounts to a new myth of London and of the times we have lived through since the War.

This author has the sort of imaginative energy and ambition that largely died out with the great Victorians, and in **Mother London** he displays the generosity of spirit, the sweep and sheer gusto of Dickens. He mixes tragedy and farce in the most daring manner, even in the midst of his Blitz scenes, which are perhaps the most remarkable in the book, written with an unforgettable, hallucinatory vividness. He throws everything in, rather in the encyclopaedic manner of Joyce, but somehow the details only add to the grandeur of the informing vision. Reminiscent of Joyce, too, are the frequent bursts of unpunctuated 'noise' which are the inner voices either of the characters or of random Londoners, wafting momentarily across the narrative—the urgent voices, cumulatively, of the city itself.

Moorcock even dares to steer his novel to a full-dress, all-inclusive happy ending, complete with wedding scene. One feels that he loves his characters—. . . too much to do otherwise, and that love is infectious, as is Moorcock's humane and visionary optimism. He has created a city in which miracles happen, in obscure corners, amidst ruin and destruction. It is a various, rich, eloquent, sustaining city—truly **Mother London.**

Despite the formidable achievements of his last two large-scale novels, **The Laughter of Carthage** and **Byzantium Endures,** there is still a tendency to see Moorcock as a sci-fi maverick afflicted with the *cacoethes scribendi.* If this wonderful book does not finally convince the world that he is in fact one of our very best novelists and a national treasure, then there is no justice.

> *Nigel Andrew, "London Calling," in* The Listener, *Vol. 119, No. 3068, June 23, 1988, p. 31.*

IAIN SINCLAIR

Michael Moorcock, with transcendent modesty, brings to life the ravished and abused confederation of villages that make up his *Mother London* from the unregarded stock of some prelapsarian Portobello junk-pit.

He decorates its groves and dales with glittering toys and tricks, *Magnets* and *Gems, Strands* of detonated old boys' fiction, fire-damaged ephemera. He honours the underground rivers, forgotten music halls, parks, pubs and mythic fathers. This is a book that has been assembling itself for years, while Moorcock readied himself to discover it. It is the achievement of a master craftsman at the height of his powers: made possible by the length and diversity of his career, the training in compression, serial-composition, jump-cuts—and sheer elbows-on-the-table, hook-'em-hard narrative drive.

Mother London is an unhurried epic that calmly, and at conversational pitch, manipulates the stream of time between the twinned traumas of Blitz and Blight; from the stern alchemy of fire-storms to the corrupt transformation of the city as a fatally tainted heritage riverscape. The conscience of ruin invades our galloping entropy with mantic and urgent voices-in-the-head: "must stop this going back to I was happy why can't I accept the present." What was once heroic and human is now savage and self-serving. The threat is ourselves, our loss of nerve. These pilgrims are disenfranchised and, superbly, crazy like foxes.

It is, of course, a millennial version of where-did-we-go-wrong, but also, and primarily, it celebrates the journey, relishing the pricks of the flesh, the pains and joys of those who are condemned to live up to their own obsessions. They will not blaspheme against the self-mutilating impulses that are their only guide. So this tale of many voices is built up from the overlapping biographies of a group of perpetual outpatients who wander the limits of the city like exiles from Blake's *Jerusalem*. . . . (p. 39)

They are the lesser gods of Moorcock's *Mahabharata*, coupling, betraying, discovering and, endlessly, talking. They are richly and sensuously named, Joseph Kiss, Mary Gasalee, David Mummery—who seems, in part, an avatar of the author, "calling himself an urban anthropologist . . . lives by writing memorials to legendary London". They feed on epiphanous seizures that occurred during the fire-raids. They have alternately raged and sleepwalked through the dying fall of the years that followed.

Mary Gasalee walked, unharmed, from the inferno of her bombed home, with her infant daughter in her arms, only to pass through the welfare state in cyclic dreams of Gamages and a visionary Holborn Viaduct, guided and comforted by the presence of familiar afternoon stars, Katharine Hepburn, Janet Gaynor and Merle Oberon, whose name is as rich and strange as her own. Now the city of the apocalypse is invaded by angelic and demonic entities that touch and smile. Mary does not age, becoming a sister to her daughter, and when she wakes—the lover of both Kiss and the virgin Mummery.

The sympathetic strength of the women, and the delirious wanderings of the men, give the book a warmth that cannot disguise the knowledge that the city, Mother London herself, is doomed. The characters are somehow posthumous, glad ghosts. . . .

Beyond them, at the fringe, are the travellers, the immigrants, the criminals whose collective pasts are now denied and invalidated. Beneath them is a network of abandoned railway tunnels and dead rivers in which survive an underclass of mute tribesmen; a metaphor perhaps for the genre fiction that

Moorcock once practised with such distinction, before making his assault on mainstream literature.

He has the energy of a Golden Age author, whose belief in the validity of fiction as an agent of transformation is breathtaking in its optimism. If any of the debased literary prizes want to make a claim on credibility they had better put *Mother London* at the head of the list for 1988. (p. 40)

> Iain Sinclair, *"Fabulous Flotsam,"* in New Statesman & Society, *Vol. 1, No. 3, June 24, 1988, pp. 39-40.*

GREGORY FEELEY

Michael Moorcock has long been Britain's quintessential novelist of urban life, although it is only with his more recent works, such as the celebrated *Byzantium Endures* and *The Laughter of Carthage,* that this distinction has emerged clearly from the enormous body of his work.

Prolific author from the age of 16 of innumerable fantasies, thrillers, historical romances and science fiction, Moorcock has unsurprisingly been slow to receive critical attention in this country. Much of this output went to subsidize Moorcock's embattled magazine *New Worlds,* which in the late '60s espoused "speculative fiction" as the literature of modern times, a good decade before "magic realism" became respectable. *New Worlds* early published writers such as J. G. Ballard and D. M. Thomas, while Moorcock wrote his way indefatigably through a number of "periods;" the most recent an ambitious sequence of novels chronicling the moral course of Europe in this century, beginning with the above-mentioned two and continuing with the forthcoming *Jerusalem Commands.*

The magisterially titled *Mother London* has obvious affinities with the trilogy it interrupts, not least of all the witty slavicism of its title. . . .

Ranging from the beginning of the Blitz to the present day, *Mother London* chronicles the history of its great city through the eyes of three characters, all of them sometime mental patients and apparent psychics. . . .

The structure of the novel is unusual. After an opening chapter showing all three characters followed by a chapter devoted to each, the novel proceeds with a series of disconnected episodes running from the late '50s to the present day, then reverses direction and marches back to 1940. The second half of the book then produces a mirror image of this, running up and down the chronological scale once more before reprising each character and ending with a sentimental envoi. Only at the novel's center do two chapters run consecutively.

Moorcock's fiction has always been notably ramshackle in form, with variants of the same characters appearing in different books, or adventure series converging into each other or petering out. *Mother London* is unusual in being neither part of an ongoing sequence nor cobbled together from shorter works. The novel's interesting architecture in fact goes some distance toward reassuring the reader of the author's firmness of control, for *Mother London* is often sprawling and prolix, and would have benefited greatly from a firmer editorial hand.

In a recent essay Moorcock has written how early memories of the Blitz have shaped his emotional life, and the characters of *Mother London,* indeed the city itself, locate their defining trauma in that period of bombardment. For Moorcock, the Blitz presaged another and equally sinister devastation: of real-estate developers and yuppie interlopers from the surrounding Home Counties, now dispossessing working-class Londoners of their suddenly desirable neighborhoods.

This last point is of such evident urgency to Moorcock that he fairly swamps the chronologically late chapters with his rage. Josef Kiss, aging and splenetic by the 1980s, derides these developments at length, and although Moorcock seeks to escape charges of editorializing by presenting his harangues as comic, he also arranges corroborating evidence to appear on scene as needed.

If *Mother London* often indulges its author's crotchets and biases, it also proves warm and humane, often surprisingly funny, and moving in a way Moorcock has never before succeeded in being. Not every reader will retain patience through the various longeurs, but those familiar with Moorcock's earlier fiction will be heartened by its shapeliness and heart.

> *Gregory Feeley, "In the Heart of the Heart of the City," in* Book World—The Washington Post, *May 14, 1989, p. 8.*

Christopher Nolan

1965–

Irish autobiographer, poet, short story writer, and dramatist.

Internationally recognized for their literary merit and emotional impact, Nolan's autobiographical works depict a paralytic's quest for expression and acceptance. In an alliterative, inventive style critics often compare to that of such authors as James Joyce, Dylan Thomas, and Gerard Manley Hopkins, Nolan chronicles his singular experiences as a profoundly handicapped youth. Complications at birth, which did not harm Nolan's intellect, rendered him mute and unable to govern the sometimes spastic motions of his limbs. Able only to direct his eyes, he spent his first ten years with extremely limited means of communication. A new drug, however, allowed eleven-year-old Nolan enough muscle control to learn to type; with his mother supporting his chin, he would point a "unicorn" stick strapped to his forehead to select letters on a keyboard. This arduous method, wherein a single word can take the author up to fifteen minutes to type, freed him to record the poetry he had composed and memorized since age three. According to Nolan, the title of his first book, *Dam-Burst of Dreams,* expresses his elation at the release of his imprisoned intellect. His supportive family and strong Roman Catholic faith are often cited in his writings, which recount frustrations related to his impairments. Nolan has described himself as "castrated by crippling disease, molested by scathing mockery, silenced by paralysed vocal muscles yet ironically blessed with a sense of physical well-being."

Nolan began receiving recognition for his verse in the late 1970s, and *Dam-Burst of Dreams* (1981), a collection of poems, stories and plays, was published in England when he was fifteen. Critics deemed Nolan a literary prodigy, lauding his ornate phrasings and invented words. Pat Raine commented: "Christopher Nolan's work is characterized by flamboyance, alliteration, and a wild originality of approach. His descriptive phrases are striking and sometimes felicitous." Nolan's accomplishments generated interest in the British press, television, and radio media, and benefactors donated the use of a computer with a custom-designed attachment that allows him to type with a small movement of his chin.

Nolan's autobiographical novel, *Under the Eye of the Clock* (1987), relates the life story of Joseph Meehan, a severely disabled boy who surmounts extraordinary obstacles to earn an education and become a professional writer. Praised as exuberant and adventurous, Nolan's narrative is an unsentimental account both of the disappointments of a paralyzed boy and the determination of his parents, who engage him with stories, carry him on hikes in the Irish hills, and hold him up on horseback. Critics noted that, possibly because of his difficulty in typing, Nolan has developed a distinctive style; he often forgoes articles and employs intricate participle constructions to replace relative clauses. Many reviewers remarked that, while his prose was occasionally clotted, Nolan's elaborate syntax and creative wordplay demonstrates a remarkable literary facility. Other commentators asserted that such comparisons were excessive. Judges for the prestigious Whitbread Award, however, selected *Under the*

Eye of the Clock for best biography and later named it book of the year.

PUBLISHERS WEEKLY

Nolan was paralyzed and virtually speechless for 11 years. Then a new drug, Lioresal, gave him partial control of muscles and made it possible for him to use a mechanical attachment to type the extraordinary poetry and other works represented [in *Dam-Burst of Dreams*]. Many of the visions in the author's Celtic alliterations and Joycean invented words are somber but an equal number express hope, love and gratitude. Nolan pays tribute to his devoted family and the staff of the Central Remedial Clinic, Dublin, who helped release his "trapped intelligence." Collected here are his writings produced up to the age of 14, material which shows promise of even more impressive work yet to come from this gifted teenager.

A review of "Dam-Burst of Dreams," in Publishers Weekly, *Vol. 220, No. 7, August 14, 1981, p. 46.*

PAT RAINE

When Christopher Nolan writes in [*Dam-Burst of Dreams*] of "brilliant, bright, boiling words poured into his mind" he is describing the sense of elation which accompanied his discovery of a means of expression. Years of pent-up feelings had suddenly found an outlet—a very productive one. For it became clear, with the first lines he typed laboriously on his typewriter, that Christopher Nolan had been nurturing a rare literary talent. . . .

Christopher Nolan's work is characterized by flamboyance, alliteration, and a wild originality of approach. His descriptive phrases are striking and sometimes felicitous: "zany, bonny December", "the dolorous days of death". He can rise to irony, as when he describes himself in these terms: "a frightening handicap, a foolish facial expression and a doubtful public". He displays a sure feeling for the vivid and the dramatic: "In storms his sad looking Mam and his damned-angry Dad"—this stage direction refers to an interesting moment in one of his plays, when a couple of outraged parents are about to confront their delinquent son ("Look smart cur and feverishly give an honest account of your activities at school yesterday", it goes on). The poems at present have something of a hit-or-miss quality about them, but there are indications that this will be rectified when greater discipline succeeds the heady access of creativity.

Pat Raine, in a review of "Dam-Burst of Dreams," in The Times Literary Supplement, *No. 4133, June 18, 1982, p. 671.*

JOHN NAUGHTON

[In 1981], literary London was briefly stirred by *Dam-burst of Dreams,* a book of poems by a 15-year-old Irish spastic called Christopher Nolan. Extravagant claims were made for the lad at the time. It was said, for example, that he had a touch of Dylan Thomas about him, and perhaps even a smidgen of Joyce. In the normal course of events, these comparisons would have been enough to sink even the ablest young author, so it is one measure of Mr Nolan's quality that he has survived the great futures predicted for him to produce a premature but moving and engrossing autobiography.

Mr Nolan's condition derives from being almost asphyxiated at birth; and in a sense his writing is also a metaphor for his life, because it signifies an escape from the mind-numbing imprisonment imposed by near-total muscular incontinence. Being able to make a meaningful mark on a piece of paper was, for many years, an unattainable dream for him—which is why, when the barrier was finally broken by typewriter and computer, he approached words much as a child might approach an overturned lorry spilling its load of Smarties. The result is a wacky exuberance of style which [in *Under the Eye of the Clock*] is occasionally tedious but more often strikingly evocative. . . .

It is, as you might expect, a story of courage and resolution on the part of Mr Nolan. But it is also a heartwarming story of parental and sibling love, of schoolchildren who were surprisingly supportive and protective, of generous teachers, headmasters and professors. . . .

Those of us who touch-type without even thinking about it have a tendency to become maudlin and uncritical when confronted by the likes of Mr Nolan. We do not examine whether the thing is done well, so much as marvel that it is done at all. This is not Mr Nolan's fault, for his own attitude to his condition is exceedingly unsentimental and bleakly dismissive of 'casting renown on himself by dangling disability before the reader'. So the highest compliment one can pay him is to forget about his physical condition and ask whether his autobiographical writing measures up to the high hopes of his literary sponsors.

My personal judgment is that it is a bit early to say. It is always difficult to follow a hit like *Dam-burst of Dreams,* and *Under the Eye of the Clock* reads like a transitional work, bridging the gap between the precociously naive wordsmith of the early poems and the mature writer struggling to get out from underneath. Mr Nolan has been encouraged (in Trinity College, Dublin) to read a good deal of Lit Crit since he embarked on this literary business, and the iron has entered his style. The juxtaposition of long patches of conventional narrative, for example, with his patented stream-of-consciousness stuff, sometimes jars. On the other hand, there are clear signs of a new confidence. One sees it, for example, in the literary device of referring to himself as another person (Joseph Meehan) or in the craftsmanlike way the book is structured: the author's story is told in a sophisticated way which maintains dramatic interest (a perennial problem with precocious autobiographies, this) throughout. Mr Nolan has lost his innocence and not yet quite settled upon a style; but he is on his way.

John Naughton, "Post-Precocity," in The Listener, *Vol. 117, No. 3009, April 30, 1987, p. 31.*

DEBORAH SINGMASTER

"Nested" and "nutshelled" are words that recur frequently in Christopher Nolan's life story *Under the Eye of the Clock,* and they aptly describe the nurturing of his hidden literary talent before its liberation. . . .

Christopher Nolan is not an "easy" writer. The physical difficulty of committing words to paper is reflected in his syntax, his choice of words and his imagery: "He budded mental, hickory-hard gladness in his numb heart" is a typical example of his verbal complexity. He piles up participles and dispenses with articles. Sometimes his sentences are as clotted as a clumsy translation of a particularly difficult Latin text; at other times he can produce passages of spare, vivid narrative that could not be improved on, such as the description of the selection and slaying of the Christmas turkey. He has been compared to Joyce, but the resemblance is superficial; Hopkins, a fellow Catholic, is a far more obvious influence:

> Had he but known man's memory never seems to
> cap its can but rather hovers kestrel-like, wings out-
> spread, beady-eyed for any scent of despair, when
> swiftly it nosedives doleful buccaneers of venom to
> break the lonely flayed osprey, man's pent-up
> hurts.

The echoes of "The Windhover" are unmistakable.

Nolan's narrative, in contrast to his prose style, is straightforward; chronological transitions are smoothly handled and his theme, as the media were quick to realize in 1981, cannot fail to arouse sympathy and interest. He has written about himself with striking objectivity and this book, which could so easily have been an exercise in self-pity, is a vigorous and impressive literary performance.

Deborah Singmaster, "Nutshelled Gladness," in The Times Literary Supplement, No. 4400, July 31, 1987, p. 828.

JOHN GROSS

Under the Eye of the Clock, is an autobiography cast in the third person. Family names have been changed—Christopher Nolan himself becomes "Joseph Meehan"—and even though there is no suggestion of fiction beyond that, the decision to distance himself a little from his experience seems a wise one. It probably enabled him to write more freely, and it reflects the detachment of a writer who, far more than most, has had to learn to stand outside himself.

Many of the incidents in the book would be unremarkable in another context. A pony ride, a country outing, classroom jokes and rivalries, churchgoing, a visit to the theater, the small change of family life. Here, however, the slightest episode is liable to take on an epic quality, to become part of the unceasing struggle to draw forth words from "the depths of numbness."

All that one of the teachers can see, on Joseph's first day in high school, is "dull looks, dribbles and senseless sounds." But locked up inside, a keen intelligence is striving to express itself. *Under the Eye of the Clock* is the story of how it succeeded—and a reminder, since Joseph himself never forgets them for long, of all the imprisoned predecessors who failed to find a way out, or who never had a chance. "Think of the others gone before you," he muses. "Did they have fiery intellects?"

In telling his tale, Mr. Nolan has forged a bold, highly distinctive style. Or perhaps it has forged itself, since for all its oddities it almost always sounds appropriate and natural. He coins gleaming new metaphors, inverts conventional word order, compresses a wealth of suggestion into an image. Hell doesn't just mock him, it guffaws, and the sheets of typing paper that await him become "white sheets of life" (the very opposite of shrouds).

In case any of this sounds daunting, one should add that there is nothing very difficult about his wordplay. Reviewers in England have compared him with Joyce, but an apter comparison might be someone like E. E. Cummings.

At the heart of the story is Joseph's will to live—not simply to survive, but to be himself. The child begins by throwing out a mute challenge to his family: "Accept me for what I am and I'll accept you for what you're accepted as." (Mr. Nolan's irony, it will be seen, can be very cutting: he is emphatically not a writer to be patronized.) And his family responds.

His mother, first. She "tumbled to his intelligence, tumbled to his eye-signaled talk, tumbled to the hollyberries, green yet, but holding promise of burning in red given time, given home." Then, one weepy, never to be forgotten day, when he was 3 years old, she reassured him that the family loved him just as he was, and left him determined to fan "the only spark he saw."

After that his father and his sister, who is two years older, played almost as big a part. If there were sibling rivalries, they were quickly neutralized and overshadowed by sibling love: his sister caught his imagination with the little song-and-dance shows that she put on for him, just as his father was to do with his repertory of stirring, old-fashioned poems—"Barbara Fritchie," "The stag at eve had drunk his fill"—and the "ould" songs he sang at the top of his voice. Out of such precedents, Mr. Nolan shaped an artistic vocation.

Beyond the family, the child was to find a whole network of nurture—teachers, friends, doctors, a favorite priest, all lovingly and for the most part humorously evoked. Strangers, too, although eventually one of them came into his life with a reminder that the devil still walks—a journalist (an American, alas) who interviewed him and then published an article insinuating that he was a fraud, that his poems were written for him by somebody else.

It took him a long time to recover from the blow: not so much because he was afraid it would damage his reputation (it didn't) but because it was such a naked display of cruelty. His first—though temporary—reaction was to find that his firm Roman Catholic faith had been shaken: asking his father to wheel him into church, he took his anger out on God.

Even at this point, however, his sense of comedy didn't desert him. If there are many moments in *Under the Eye of the Clock* that had me close to tears, there are many amusing ones as well. And if there are occasional patches of overwriting, they scarcely seem to matter. All in all, a most touching and heartening piece of work.

John Gross, in a review of "Under the Eye of the Clock," in The New York Times, February 26, 1988, p. C33.

JACKSON COPE

[*Under the Eye of the Clock*] is not exactly an autobiography. Rather, it is the third-person history of one Joseph Meehan, a mute and paralyzed protagonist whose adventures may be poetically embroidered beyond the limits of Nolan's life history by excerpts from some understandable dreams of the future. This is what raises rancor with the publishers' exploitation of natural curiosity in yet another nonce-book about the unnatural circumstances in which a few of us live more desperately than the rest.

Nolan's proper instinct wanted to fictionalize experience, but [his publisher] saw fit to subtitle his fiction as "the life story of Christopher Nolan." Nolan's motive was to test himself and his literary powers in the time-honored genre of the *Bildungsroman,* those histories of budding maturation which have focused young fictionalists from Goethe to Joyce and well beyond these landmarks. The publishers' motive was to emphasize the sentimentality of Nolan's spectacular partial transcendence of immense difficulties. They succeeded beyond any measure of reasonableness or decency: Nolan's book was put into literary competition with the late Richard Ellmann's biography of another Irishman, Oscar Wilde, a work as permanent as any scholarly accomplishment is likely to become and Ellmann's last gracious contribution in a lifetime of meticulous preservation which made him the major historian of Irish literature. . . . The competition was for the British Whitbread biography prize, which Nolan has now won, but which has been permanently debased by the ballyhoo accompanying his book's candidacy. (He has also won a second and more lucrative prize, Whitbread's book-of-the-year award.)

It is too late and too futile to preach to the converted, but perhaps this sad yet sanguine young Irishman foresaw it all, even as he hoped for better things. There is an ironic cry early in his book of self which might serve as epigraph: "Don't let the media make a monster of me." They have succeeded where nature failed.

Not every college senior could have written this book, but many could have done, and done better (attune the ear to a thesaurus, real or imagined, of cliches and neologisms: "Plodding bravery abandoned him," intones the self-sentimentalizing victim, "Joseph Meehan now joined hushed criminals before the firing squad." He is, in fact, about to be interviewed for admission to prep school. I can offer no similar context for the outburst which begins "Beast and boy were emanating a wondrous Ness-like vraiment. Thirsty notoriety homme-like hiccuped individual hollyberries on all robbed moments of holly-leafed life."

A book full of such self-indulgence, parental-indulgence, youthful hope and the rare concomitant promise of growth deserves better than the author has been asked to give. Exploiting Nolan's handicaps to sell bad books indicts [his publisher]. A semi-literate youth cannot learn to transcend misfortune, even to become its articulate symbol, if he is told by St. Martin's authors of jacket blurbs that his "writing has been compared to Joyce, Yeats and Dylan Thomas." Held to such standards, Christopher Nolan will, as will we all, be found wanting.

Nolan's slight beginnings have suffered the indignity of phony kudos from an industry that swallows authors much abler to protect themselves than this one. But let us hope he emulates in a stronger, more self-subsistent manner the honored Irish predecessors of isolation, Joyce and Yeats. One need hold no one strictly to their standards. Nolan never approaches meeting them. But a little patience, thoughtfulness, self-extrication from the trashing of mind which has become common to those corporations exploiting print; maybe another young Irishman could become a writer. Not yet. (pp. 2, 10)

> *Jackson Cope, "No Joyce, No Yeats and No Dylan Thomas," in* Los Angeles Times Book Review, *March 6, 1988, pp. 2, 10.*

PATRICIA HAMPL

[Christopher Nolan's] stylistic hallmark has been a linguistic virtuosity that, at its best, is heady and acrobatic. It may be a style better suited to the compression of lyric poetry than to the discursive tendencies of narrative prose. But his prose has moxie, though it rushes and stumbles from a pent-up surge:

> Crying hurrah for lilysweet knowledge he frowned at the greatness of Joyce; wanting to emulate him for boyhood's fame, he nadir-aspired to mould his only gift into briny, bastardized braille so that fellows following never had to nod yes to mankind's gastric view that man speechless and crippled must forever be strolling as underlings to the yapping establishment.

A further eccentricity (one Henry Adams also chose for [his autobiography, *The Education of Henry Adams,*]) is that Mr. Nolan has written his life story [*Under the Eye of the Clock*] in the third person; he appears always as Joseph Meehan.

Like so much about Mr. Nolan's style, it is a risk. The third person works most effectively when it gives his autobiography the fresh, jaunty tone of a picaresque novel: "Baffled by beauty, slow to worry, able only to think, Joseph continued on his lively path through life."

One of the abiding pleasures of the book, in fact, is that while the reader is never allowed to forget Joseph's extreme disability and physical dependence, the story reads like an adventure, not a meditation. It is busy, active—and young even when it is wise.

A second, simpler style seems also to be emerging in Mr. Nolan's prose, more precise and immediate, less contorted than his "Joycean" manner. There is a tour-de-force rhapsody about his mother killing and cleaning a turkey on the family farm in which Nora, "wielding a sharp knife . . . cut off the lonesome, guilty-looking head, then she cut off the scaled-skin legs." Describing the layout of his new school, he says, "Great long corridors blossomed between the various school sections."

The act of writing itself is, for him, not simply laborious; it is heroic, and requires someone (usually his mother) to cup his chin in her hands while he attempts, amid spastic lurches he cannot control, to aim a headmounted pointer at the keyboard. "As he typed he blundered like a young foal strayed from his mother," he says. "Sometimes his head shot back on his shoulders crashing like a mallet into his mother's face."

He is aware of the vast ambition before him: "to find a voice for the voiceless." After all, "century upon century saw crass crippled man dashed, branded and treated as dross in a world offended by their appearance." Mr. Nolan has a sense of his historical importance; he maintains his sly, appealing good humor as he makes his contract with the able-bodied: "Accept me for what I am and I'll accept you for what you're accepted as."

But the sign that Mr. Nolan is a true writer comes not from his ability to describe his own locked world, compelling as that report is. Rather, it is the lasting portraits of his family and, to a lesser degree, of rural Ireland that makes his firmest claim.

And what a family! Nora and Matthew, his mother and father, and his older sister, Yvonne, display a relentless faith in Joseph. Their faith is clearly the buoyant wave he "crests"—to use a favorite Nolan verb. Yvonne, "nimble of wit, could never understand how folk failed to capture the mind hinting from her brother's eyes." And when Joseph's spastic arm lurches out to a passing stranger and the "hand flew in between the man's legs while his fingers tickled all before them," Yvonne is there. Her comment at such moments: "Let go, you sex mechanic!"

And the greatest compliment from son to devoted mother: "Nora never gobbled up her son." As for Matthew: "Placing his wobbling son on his knee he recited poetry, told nursery rhymes and later on bawdy vulgar stories. Joseph's mind was wallowing in his father's mire of memories." His father gave him "musical notation, intricate thought patterns and a merry love of writing. Literature was never mentioned."

The driving plot of Mr. Nolan's autobiography is Joseph's assault on the world of the able-bodied. The citadel Joseph rushes is the educational system. He makes one effort after another, moving from a school for handicapped children to a regular high school and then to Dublin's Trinity College itself.

The book's ironic triumph comes when Joseph decides to leave Trinity after all, although he's won the day and has been invited to work for a degree. "The grim rigours of his family" to see him through strike him, finally, as too high a price. He graciously liberates them, as their constant assistance has, earlier, liberated him.

It is the right, the honest, finish. Mr. Nolan does not pretend to conquer the province of the able-bodied. He knows he is outside. But this knowledge isn't a defeat. It is a choice, that most adult thing.

What is left is the truth of his testimony. His voice speaks, as a writer must, from the margin, the solitude where detachment encounters all the jangled emotions it must serve.

> Patricia Hampl, "Defying the Yapping Establishment," in The New York Times Book Review, March 13, 1988, p. 9.

JULIA O'FAOLAIN

Christopher Nolan's *Under the Eye of the Clock* draws the reader closer in emotionally than is usual with a purely literary enterprise—and indeed it is not purely literary. Instead it is that rare thing: a text which performs the action it describes. Writing is how the author's trapped consciousness finds release. . . .

This autobiography describes the quest for a better method as supportive relatives "brengunblasted his silence" and he was fired by a "volcanic wish to become more adept at communicating." Words were there, pent; it was a matter of finding an outlet, and this happened when a muscle-relaxing drug and a typing stick fixed to his forehead enabled him, albeit laboriously, to write. He was 10 years old. . . .

[Nolan] writes in the third person, giving himself the name Joseph Meehan (Me?), presumably so as to put distance between the free writer and his subject self, letting fancy evade "zoo-caged" confinement only to butt back, sooner or later, against the snib of reality. A feisty Quixote, he keeps battling this, and the most inspiriting moments come when Joseph, tackling matter head–on, succeeds in tasting some of the joys of the able-bodied.

After remedial school, he attends an ordinary one, then goes to university, making friends despite the odds. Notwithstanding his muteness, they come to see that "youthful adventures interested him just as much as able-bodied them" and the claim is not idle for, as a boy, Joseph insists on being set on a horse, floats in the ocean when on holiday with his family, has himself buried in sand so as to experience the sensation of being vertical and, at a school dance, gets girls to twirl him in his wheelchair "like the chairoplanes in a carnival."

Inevitably, these bittersweet venturings bring him up against his limits. Girls will never come closer.

> Youthful though he was, he had long ago snapped shut his challenging fees-fashioned future and humanhinded his woldway as a celibate pilgrim through life. Tickling his fancy always was the image of the breadbreaker's calling. Priestnamed, his fatherhood could be measured just as though he clasped healing power in his kernelled loneliness.

The breadbreaker is Christ, and Nolan—Meehan being temporarily forgotten—is "priest-named" because Christopher means "Christbearer." The passage is revelatory as it shows (1) how religion helps him keep a sound mind in an erratic body, (2) the sort of wordplay which has led critics to talk of Joyce and (3) the occasional obscurities which he lets spill into the prose like samplings of his darker moods.

Under the Eye of the Clock is many things: heroic record, manifesto on behalf of Nolan's fellow-disabled, protest—against society's readiness "to abort babies like him"—and a literary exercise which incorporates its own blurb since accounts of past successes include the critics' praise.

While saluting his prowess on all fronts, one should perhaps, after the Whitbread, raise some questions. What, for instance, about the comparison with Joyce? Is Nolan not usually "re-Joycing," i.e. borrowing a trick? Also: his word–forging often seems designed to achieve a compression dictated primarily by his typing stick. In particular, a quirky use of participles to replace relative clauses gives a clotted, spurty effect. Knotty syntax, fine in verse, can make the going laborious for a prose-reader.

Then too, while the book has some splendid and exhilarating passages, it also has cute, mock-heroic ones where words like "verily," "merrily" and "wondrous" are used either without irony or with the minimal sort which aims to disarm the reader's.

The book is uneven—yet why should it not be? Nolan is just 22. The Whitbread judges, in preferring it to Seamus Heaney's *The Haw Lantern* and the late Richard Ellmann's *Oscar Wilde*, were no doubt partly swayed by extra-literary considerations. But Nolan is far too good a writer to need anyone's indulgence.

> Julia O'Faolain, "The Freedom of the Word," in Book World—The Washington Post, April 10, 1988, p. 9.

KATHERINE DIECKMANN

It would have been enough if Christopher Nolan were simply a great story, but as it turns out, he's a great storyteller, too. A weep and a revelation per page, his autobiographical *Under the Eye of the Clock* is a lustrous, unsentimental account of how a spastic-mute-paralytic came to be a critically praised youthful scribe, all told with a prudent third-person distancing (Nolan recasts himself as "Joseph Meehan"). . . .

Under the Eye of the Clock begins with Joseph Meehan's triumphant return to Dublin after being embraced by literary London, then backtracks through his childhood up to his first year at Trinity College, Stephen Dedalus's former stomping grounds. It is impossible to understate how influential Joyce is on Nolan (comparisons have also been made to Yeats and Dylan Thomas, but they seem far less apparent), and the disciple is a bit too fond of Joyce-derived abrupt verbings like "bested" and heavy alliterative phrasings (Joseph "greeted gaping students' gombeen glances"), though the prose lightens as *Clock* progresses. Nolan's life also naturally traverses what we've come to think of as Joycean terrain— the schoolyard, the church, the coming to consciousness of the writer.

But Nolan surmounts this burdensome inheritance with a

strength of mind and insight that parallels and in some respects surpasses Joyce's own. What makes that variety of thick, incantatory prose so resonant (and makes mere imitators so immediately transparent) is that it's there to service complex ideas and feelings. Nolan's writing is directly emotional where his predecessor's was cerebrally preoccupied. An ideal cross between Joyce and former Smiths singer-songwriter Morrissey (his *Viva Hate* solo album is the ideal accompaniment for reading *Clock*), Nolan possesses a gift for verbal gymnastics, but isn't above tossing out a phrase like "bad vibes" when the occasion warrants it.

Joseph Meehan was reared by his parents, Matthew ("a psychiatric nurse by profession but a farmer at heart") and Nora (who "got on with her work" whenever a self-pitying Joseph "got on with his crying"), and his tough and much-admired older sister, Yvonne, who could exhibit such refreshingly bratty behavior as riding a pony around in front of her brother while he remained confined to his "little purple chair with the red leather pommel nestling between his legs." Joseph recounts the rich rural splendors of his parents' farm at Corcloon and, later, the pleasure of visits with extended relations at his grandparents' home at Clonbonny. Grounded by his family's humor and determination to treat him as normally as possible, Joseph is able to joke about the countless difficulties of his circumstances and enjoy the jokes of others: when his uncooperative mouth refuses to open and receive the host at church, a local pastor named Father Flynn accuses him of "riflin' the poor box" and thus is able to pop the wafer in the stunned boy's jaw-dropped mouth. The pragmatic Father Flynn becomes a key figure in Joseph's childhood, and it is a tribute to Nolan's sense of dramatic construction that he sets us up skillfully for the priest's unexpected demise. (Nolan plans to try a novel next, and from the evidence here, he's more than up to the job.)

The most remarkable aspect of *Under the Eye of the Clock* is how Nolan makes his life seem at once marvelous and reassuringly ordinary. Despite the usual cruelties confronting an aberrant "outsider" upon entering school, Joseph assimilates fairly painlessly. Tempting though it must be, he refrains from striking back at those who taunt him. Throughout his education, Joseph is included in outings and games and, in one great schoolyard sequence, he sneaks outside with his buddies to smoke his first cigarette, with hilarious results. . . . Thus another memory in Meehan's spectacular and unspectacular life is forged, and another striking passage rises from Christopher Nolan's *Under the Eye of the Clock.* This is a brave accomplishment from a young writer who bypasses the handicapped-testimonial genre to turn out a remarkable piece of prose.

Katherine Dieckmann, "The Artist as Young Man," in The Village Voice, *Vol. XXXIII, No. 16, April 19, 1988, p. 60.*

SUE M. HALPERN

Until now, with the publication of Christopher Nolan's novel, *Under the Eye of the Clock,* the entreaties made by the disabled to draw us into their world, to help us see what it is like to be blind or to feel the numbness of their limbs, have largely shut us out. Confessional and testimonial, these first-person narratives reinforce the distinction between them and us. They leave us mindful of our good fortune, knocking wood, thinking "there but for the grace of God. . . ."

Grace and God figure prominently in Christopher Nolan's writing. Nolan is twenty-two, Irish, devoutly Catholic, profoundly disabled. . . . [He] waited eleven years before he was able to communicate to those around him with more than an upward roll of his eyes. . . .

While he waited those eleven years he prayed, not for normalcy, but for recognition; he wanted others to know he was, as he called it, "sane." And as he listened for the answer he heard words and their nuances; their sonority became tangible.

Nolan memorized the sounds and meanings of the words he heard. He began to string them together, writing poems that he would recite to himself again and again, with the outrageous desire that some day they would be released from memory into the audible world. When the drug and the typing stick finally rescued Nolan from silence, he began to record his poems. He said it was as if a dam had burst. Poems that he had fixed in his memory since the age of three began to cascade over the barrier of his body. It often took fifteen minutes to launch each word.

"I Peer Through Ugliness" was the second poem he wrote:

> Years dead tears, peter down my face,
> Lucifer quietly plays me down,
> Out of a light there came Christ Divine,
> Peace always comes, reigns awhile.
> Day after dawn, raw quiet rested there,
> As I peered through rough pastures,
> Dew drops glistened in golden buttercups.

He wrote it, he said, "because every day I realized how more and more handicapped I was." Yet it is, like much of Nolan's subsequent writing, infused with a hopefulness that leads not to Lourdes but to the mystery of the Resurrection.

It was immediately apparent to all who read Nolan's first offerings that they were witnessing a kind of Athenian catapult—a poet sprung directly from his own mind. Despite his age, despite the limits of his education, there was no doubt that Nolan was a poet. He reveled in metaphor and poetic diction, he seemed to instinctively understand prosody, and he had a passionate, sensual grasp of language.

His poems and early writings were then collected and published in a volume called *Dam-Burst of Dreams.* His literary career had begun. He was feted in London and celebrated in Ireland. Critics, awed by Nolan's story if not his mellifluous voice, compared his work with that of other Irish writers like Joyce and Beckett, writers with whom he was largely unfamiliar. The comparison, while premature and self-congratulatory, was not wholly inappropriate. Nolan's use of language was inventive. It was sometimes inverted and arcane. His vocabulary could be obscure and private, his sentence construction baroque.

Alliteration took precedence over accessibility, particularly in Nolan's early prose writings. "All people must question the quelling quest quietly, quoting Milton's Paradise Lost, attempting all quarrelling quests quisling quintain qualms queenly quiz," he wrote at the age of thirteen in a story called **"A Mammy Encomium."** His poems from the same period, in comparison, are stark and unadorned. . . . The poems were of an earlier time when economy was necessary if Nolan was to remember them. His stories came later, when typing had given him greater license; they often read like verbal bacchanals. (p. 3)

Under the Eye of the Clock records Nolan's school days . . . , his gradual acceptance into the "denim corded world" of adolescence. It is pretty standard stuff—overnight class trips, illicit smoking (he couldn't grip the cigarettes with his numb lips), academic triumphs, the sexual pairings of his friends—which is why it seems extraordinary.

But what renders Nolan's story more remarkable than the sum of its facts, and more moving, is his telling of it. Nolan is a stunning writer. (Not a stunning disabled writer, a stunning writer who is inescapably disabled.) He combines a poet's devotion to language with a novelist's sense of time and place. If before he reeled as if drunk on words, in this book he is more sober. He makes constant raids on the province of the inarticulate where he dwelled alone for so long, recognizing that he will only succeed if he brings the reader with him:

> Can any sane, able-bodied person sense how it feels to have evil-intentioned limbs constantly making a mockery of you. . . . How can even the greatest expert rescue truth from your meagre writings, after all it's when you seem asleep that you're really thinking; game but really unable, harassed but not cheated, joyful but fractured, notorious but cowardly, man but still boy, boy-writer by birth but garnered in difficulty, yessed by daffodil moments but fated in dull colours, typhooned in dolorous landscape but not abandoned, hurt but desperate to survive; and stranger still, how can they hear your cry for life, your wish to be given a chance to look out on a world where heretofore your crippled brothers ebbed away on muttonfat crosses, where sun burnt passions and melted human hearts.

That we do hear his cry for life, that we listen without lashing ourselves to the mast of "normalcy" and plugging our ears, is owing to Nolan's ingenuity as a writer. He does not recount his history directly. Rather, he writes the autobiography of Christopher Nolan as a novel, unsentimentally, in the third person, through the persona of a boy called Joseph Meehan. (pp. 3-4)

There is no deception here. Joseph Meehan is Christopher Nolan—even the book jacket announces it—with more verisimilitude, perhaps, but in the same way, say, that Stephen Dedalus is James Joyce. Yet, while *A Portrait of the Artist as a Young Man* draws the reader into Joyce's mind, **Under the Eye of the Clock** projects Nolan's mute thoughts outward. Joseph is not only Nolan's invention, he is his medium. Speaking through Joseph, Nolan self-consciously becomes the author of his own life, not its subject.

> He saw life recoil before him, and using the third person he rescued poor sad boyhood and casting himself inside the frame of crippled Joseph Meehan he pranked himself a storyteller, thereby casting renown on himself by dangling disability before the reader. Look, he begged, look deep down; feel, he begged, sense life's limitations; cry, he begged, cry the tears of cruel frustration; but above all he begged laughter, laugh he pleaded, for lovely laughter vanquishes raw wounded pride.

And so, with this narrative device, he hooks us. The reader does laugh and cry and feel those limitations, but for Joseph, not Nolan. It is Joseph whose "chair [is] his throne, his feet his companions," while Nolan, the author, walks nimbly among us, guiding readers through Joseph's "zoo-caged" universe. It is Joseph Meehan who wins our empathy. Christopher Nolan wins our recognition. (p. 4)

Sue M. Halpern, "Portrait of the Artist," in The New York Review of Books, *Vol. XXXV, No. 11, June 30, 1988, pp. 3-4.*

Harold Pinter

1930-

English dramatist, scriptwriter, short story writer, novelist, and poet.

A major figure in contemporary drama, Pinter is best known for his enigmatic plays which blend absurdism and realism to illustrate the isolation and violence in modern society. Such topics as the ambiguity and subjectiveness of reality, the failure of interpersonal communication, and the primacy of power in human relationships figure prominently in Pinter's ominous yet humorous works. Central to Pinter's exploration of these concerns is a dramatic tension often attributed to the conflict between the meticulously preserved social pretenses of his characters and the subconscious desires they repress. While some commentators have derided Pinter's style as confusing and unintelligible, most laud his synthesis of fabrication, interrogation, confession, and silence as among the most original and perceptive expressions of communication in the contemporary theater.

Pinter's early plays are often described as "comedies of menace" in which mysterious strangers threaten the inhabitants of an insulated, seemingly secure environment. In Pinter's first production, the one-act play *The Room* (1957), a blind man invades the comfortable flat of sixty-year-old Rose, entreating her to come home even though she vehemently denies knowing him. Her husband later discovers the visitor and savagely beats him in front of Rose, who is then struck blind. Pinter's subsequent work, the full-length drama *The Birthday Party* (1958), focuses upon Stanley, a pianist living in a shabby seaside hotel, whose birthday celebration is transformed into a torturous interrogation by two strangers. Initially demoralizing Stanley with a litany of serious and absurd charges, the pair take him away to an undisclosed location for a "rest cure." Reviewers, daunted by the cryptic plots of *The Room* and *The Birthday Party,* generally dismissed these dramas as nonsensical, an epithet subsequently applied to *The Dumb Waiter* (1960). In this play, assassins Gus and Ben, waiting for instructions in the basement kitchen of an abandoned restaurant, willingly fill meal orders transported via a dumb waiter. When Gus leaves momentarily, the machine brings a new message, directing Ben to murder the next person who enters the room. The play ends as he confronts his returning partner, gun in hand.

During the time Pinter produced these plays, the British theater was dominated in part by the "Angry Young Men," a group of writers whose portrayal of disillusioned, working-class characters in bleak, mundane surroundings reflected the heightened social consciousness of the post-World War II era. This period also gave rise to the Theater of the Absurd, an experimental dramatic style typified by the works of Samuel Beckett and Eugène Ionesco, which replaced the traditional formulas of plot, action, and denouement with such elements as contradiction, indecipherable dialogue, and bizarre images and situations. While Pinter's early plays have much in common with these theatrical trends, critics emphasize that a combination of elements from these two movements distinguishes his work. *The Hothouse* (1980), written in 1958 but not produced until 1980, exemplifies such a synthesis. A

satiric, surrealistic portrayal of a government-run mental hospital and its sadistic, incompetent staff, this drama is often regarded as an implicit condemnation of modern bureaucratic institutions.

Following his radio plays *A Slight Ache* (1959) and *A Night Out* (1960), Pinter produced *The Caretaker* (1960), his first critical and popular success, which delineates a more recognizably realistic situation. Aston, a former mental patient, brings Davies, an opportunistic vagrant, to the house owned by his domineering younger brother, Mick. While Aston enthusiastically recommends the hiring of Davies as caretaker, Mick immediately detects the derelict's selfish motivations and abusively cross-examines him. Ultimately driven to distraction, Davies leaves, speaking incoherently about retrieving "his papers" in a London suburb. Critics discerned that *The Caretaker* differs from Pinter's earlier plays in that the atmosphere of menace arises not from a mysterious source but from the struggle for dominance between Mick and Davies. Later commentators also noted that *The Caretaker* introduces several themes developed by Pinter in his more recent work, including the subjects of reality and verbal communication. Daniel Salem stated that the reality of Pinter's characters "is double and always experienced on two levels. On the one hand there is a surface reality that everyone is led to believe in when trying to be guided by appearances. On the other hand, there is the hidden reality of secret emotions which contradicts surface reality, alters it, and gives each character his psychological depth."

In Pinter's teleplays *The Collection* (1961), *The Lover* (1963), and *Tea Party* (1963), those vying for power are spouses and family members rather than strangers. Similarly, Pinter's third full-length stage drama, *The Homecoming* (1965), concentrates on the exploitative relationships within a working-class London family. Regarded as one of Pinter's most effective works, this play centers upon the return from the United States of the eldest son and his attempt to dominate his depraved father and brothers. The son is rejected, however, in favor of his coolly detached wife, who gains control of the household, as the mother had, by agreeing to become a prostitute. Katherine H. Burkman asserted: "The men, on the whole, in Pinter's family plays are trapped in their ambivalent family relationships. Several of the women, though, who as whores seem to betray all that is sacred in the family, tend to find their way to freedom and to an authentic voice that is still a family one. . . . [They] find their way to a self-possession in which they accept their multiple roles as wife, mother, and whore, belonging to themselves and thereby offering new life to the family."

Pinter's subsequent dramas focus increasingly upon the subjectivity of memory. *Landscape* and *Silence*, two one-act plays produced together in 1969, feature exchanges of monologues in which intimately related yet isolated characters recall disparate versions of common events. Memory also plays a pivotal role in *Old Times* (1970), Pinter's next full-length drama. In this play, Anna welcomes Kate, her one-time roommate and, it is implied, her former lover, to the house she shares with her husband, Deeley. Apparently hoping to resume their affair, Kate competes with Deeley for possession of Anna by selectively recalling past events concerning his wife that will substantiate or negate their present claims upon her. Although Anna ultimately asserts her preference for Deeley by envisioning Kate as long dead, the trio prove to be inextricably bound by the past. In a review of this work, Harold Clurman observed that for Pinter "memory merges much of what has happened to us into things which we only imagined or dreamed as having happened. The reality of the past fades and memory transforms real events into shadowy remnants of experience which are no more substantial than reveries."

Pinter's recent plays, while still dramatically complex, are often considered more accessible than his earlier works. Critics generally contend that *Betrayal* (1978), for example, differs from other dramatic treatments of marital infidelity only in its reversal of chronological order. *Family Voices* (1981), which stylistically resembles *Landscape* and *Silence* in its use of alternating monologues, examines the repressive relationship between a mother and her son, who lives in a dissolute boarding house. *Family Voices* and the one-act dramas *Victoria Station*, which concerns the bizarre alliance between a taxi dispatcher and an uncooperative driver, and *A Kind of Alaska*, based on actual case histories of sleeping sickness victims who were revived after spending decades in comas, were combined to form a trilogy entitled *Other Voices* (1983). *One for the Road* (1984), which replaced *Family Voices* in later productions of *Other Voices*, reflects Pinter's growing concern for political and human rights in its realistic portrayal of the interrogation and torture of a family by a decorous government representative. *Mountain Language* (1988) also examines political repression. Based upon the alleged attempts of the Turkish government to eradicate the language and culture of its Kurdish minority, this work focuses upon a group of women waiting to visit loved ones in prison who are forbidden by guards to speak their own "mountain language."

In addition to his highly regarded original dramas, Pinter has won acclaim for his screen adaptations of such works as Marcel Proust's *A la recherche du temps perdu*, entitled *The Proust Screenplay* (1977), John Fowles's *The French Lieutenant's Woman* (1981), and Russell Hoban's *Turtle Diary* (1988).

(See also *CLC*, Vols. 1, 3, 6, 9, 11, 15, 27; *Contemporary Authors*, Vols. 5-8, rev. ed.; and *Dictionary of Literary Biography*, Vol. 13.)

BENEDICT NIGHTINGALE

If Harold Pinter's standing in the stockmarket of international taste remains higher than that of any other living British dramatist, it isn't because of his own unrelenting efforts to keep it there. In the whole of the 1970's, he produced only three works for the stage, and *Family Voices*, the first time he has broken his silence since, lasts a mere 35 minutes. . . .

[In the play, an unnamed woman] dictates what appear to be letters to her son. Where is he? What is he doing? Why hasn't he written her? Why no word from him even when his father died? The tone becomes increasingly hurt, recriminatory. "I miss you. I gave you birth" becomes "If you are alive, you are a monster." "I pray your life is a torment to you" becomes "You will be found, my boy, and no mercy will be shown to you" and, finally, "I've given you up as a very bad job."

Not five yards away . . . [a young man addresses the woman] as "Mother," yet giving no more sign of hearing what she says than she of hearing him. His letters, monologues, whatever they are, consist of breathless, bubbling descriptions of life in the kind of apartment house that could only have been created and peopled by Mr. Pinter. In one room is his landlady, Mrs. Withers, who drinks gin, reminisces skittishly about the war and calls him her "pet." In another is Lady Withers, who plays the piano, eats cake, and sips vin rosé "with an elegance of gesture and grace I thought long dead." Upstairs there festers Mr. Withers, whose specialty is giving unnerving and mainly incomprehensible advice. . . .

The speaker puzzles over these peoples' relationships to one another, but is persistently frustrated whenever he tries to find out what they actually are. Whose daughter is Jane Withers, a 15-year-old schoolgirl who interrupts her homework to put her feet on his lap and erotically wiggle her toes? And who is the big, black-haired man who calls himself Riley, enters the bathroom uninvited and ominously expatiates on his homosexual inclinations? . . .

The play's style is similar to Mr. Pinter's 1969 playlet *Silence*, in which three characters sat on chairs, remembering the history of their fraught encounters in fragmented monologues. But the content of *Family Voices* takes us still further back in his career, to *The Homecoming* in 1965. There, you may recall, a drab university professor came from America to his London birthplace in order to introduce his wife to his father and brothers, who proceeded not merely to steal her from him but to turn her, with her enthusiastic consent, into a professional prostitute. For her, it was a more profound "homecoming" than for him. In the dirt and stench of North London, in the sweat and turmoil of the family, she found her emotional home, the place she belonged.

So it is with the unnamed character [of the young man]. . . . Even when [his mother] is angry or distressed, her voice sounds curiously calm, even serene; the home life she remembers and foresees seems equally bloodless. Her son's past apparently consisted of going on "damn good walks" with his father; his future, she hopes, will be part of a cosy ménage à trois, consisting of him, herself and his "nice" young wife. No wonder the boy escaped, and no wonder he is attracted by these sinister, unsettling Witherses. Their household is sexy, inscrutable, frightening and fascinating, where his old one was sexless, predictable and dull. "Oh, Mother," he cries, "I have found my home, my family. Little did I ever dream I could know such happiness."

In other words, the play is largely about self-discovery, which in Mr. Pinter's strange yet subliminally plausible world usually involves the recognition and acceptance of very dark instincts and impulses. Maybe the boy will end up as what his mother suddenly, distractedly accuses him of being, "a male prostitute," rather like Ruth in *The Homecoming.*

Yet, this interpretation isn't sufficient to explain the play's peculiar form. After all, we don't meet a single member of the Withers clan, we simply hear the boy talk about them. We watch the widowed mother, and, toward the end, we hear the dead father, a sepulchral voice from the blackness, affectionate and accusing.

What is the purpose of these two characters, apart from giving us information about their son's past? It is surely to suggest that they are still very much part of his present, too. At one point the mother apparently turned up at the apartment house and was sent packing by Riley with all the hostility Mr. Pinter's characters reserve for unwanted intruders invading their territory. But her presence is usually less literal and more effective than that. She and her dead husband are internal voices, nagging projections, memories come to haunt their son and guilts to trouble him. . . .

They are the mental luggage their son has carried with him into his new home, and, try to ditch them though he may, they will no doubt continue to weigh him down. At the end, he talks as if he might give in to his mother, return to her, but that would, of course, present him with the problem of leaving the Witherses, who have clearly become equally inescapable. He sits there in a state of suspended tension, promising to "make the journey back to you" but doing nothing whatever, while his mother stares agonizedly ahead, his father reverberates balefully from the grave, and his new friends and neighbors beckon from somewhere offstage, like Venus flytraps. It is a teasingly ambiguous close to a subtle and skillfully succinct play.

Benedict Nightingale, "Pinter's New Play Evokes 'The Homecoming'," in The New York Times, March 1, 1981, p. 8.

ALAN JENKINS

Somewhere "in this enormous city" a young man thinks of his mother, who languishes somewhere on the south coast and thinks of her son. [In *Family Voices,* these] thoughts, formulated but not transmitted (their content tells us as much), mother and son address to each other in an unspecified mode, its ambiguities exploited to the full between unspoken monologue and unwritten letter. There is no suggestion of contact made, response secured, but only an overwhelming sense of solitary, echoless speaking. Harold Pinter's latest work is a play for two voices—and, at the end, a third voice, that of the young man's father—and for those voices' tones of voice. The young man tells himself entertaining, even exciting stories of his new "family", while the abandoned, widowed mother lives in her memories of the old. . . .

[*Family Voices*] is an exquisitely funny and plangent piece of theatre. . . . Much of it recalls "classic" Pinter—the writer of *The Homecoming* or *No Man's Land*—but refined almost to disappearing (we do not actually see, or hear, the grotesques in this play). . . .

Initially the boy is self-justifyingly, jauntily defensive about his move away from the nest; the mother anguished, plaintive, fondling memories as lovingly as she once dried the boy's hair, "so gently with my soft towel". Gradually, almost imperceptibly, a shift in emphasis occurs, the tone and burden of the utterances change direction. The mother grows accusing, embittered; the boy, regretful and increasingly doubtful about his substitute family/landlords, the Witherses, contemplates with joy the prospect of a return and a reunion. No home, for this writer, can fail to be charged with uncertainty or terror; no family can be without its private dreads, its history of pain and miserable struggles for domination or independence. In *Family Voices* these are complicated by a departure from home and the discovery of a new, very different "home"; all the horrors are present, ready to come home to roost, though conveyed indirectly, both through the shifts and contradictions of the touching/terrible picture that emerges of the boy's "real family", and through the more startling and comic dislocatedness of his reports or fantasies as regards Mrs Withers ("I was a right titbit, she said. I was like a piece of plum duff"), Lady Withers ("She asked me to call her Lally"), the alarming Jane and unspeakable menfolk.

The elements of puzzle and inconsistency, the circumambient sexual ambiguousness, the pervasive overtones of menace and perversion—there are no prizes for noticing these in any play by Pinter. But they are distilled in this short piece into some fine flashes of sinister and fantastic double-talk.

Pinter's verbal touch, at its surest on the boundary between politeness and derangement, the genteel and the thuggish, and his marvellous ear for the self-revealing phrase, for the detail or cadence that renders acute embarrassment or conjures a world of social posturing, is put to deft effect. "I had never seen so many buns. One quick glance told me they were perched on cakestands all over the room . . ."

The father's last words from the grave, "I have so much to say to you. What I have to say to you will never be said", do not contain within themselves the possibility of the hoped-for communion. They entertain the possibility only of final, irrevocable separation, a kind of unending poignancy, and unbreakable silence. Inevitably, given all that we have heard these family voices say; yet Pinter's inventiveness is so grimly and constantly surprising, his language so rich for all its economy and simplicity, and his best moments are so memorable, that it almost seems like the price we have to pay—not for lip-service to "realism" or a "view of human nature" but for fidelity to a governing shape and feeling, and for what a critic once attributed to Samuel Beckett, "the dramatist's equivalent of perfect pitch".

Alan Jenkins, "No Man's Homecoming," in The Times Literary Supplement, *No. 4069, March 27, 1981, p. 336.*

BENEDICT NIGHTINGALE

Harold Pinter writes so seldom for the stage nowadays that he'd only have to trace a line of dialogue in the dirt with his big toe for the world's theatrical scholars to jet in with cameras, spades and preservative; and [the short plays *Victoria Station, One for the Road,* and *A Kind of Alaska*] offer more to dig into than that. *Victoria Station,* about a taxi dispatcher first puzzled, then infuriated and finally converted to a sort of crazed camaraderie by an amiably uncooperative driver, may seem little more than an anecdote, a nostalgic throwback to the revue sketches its author wrote 20, 25 years ago. Yet it injects a strangeness, an unease, a distinctive Pinterishness into the kind of disembodied banalities every passenger must have heard bleated from office to taxi and back again. It leaves you wondering if you aren't hearing the two survivors of some unmentionable disaster playing out their last rituals in an empty, airless city. And the other two components of the triple-bill Pinter has called *Other Places* are certainly much more than anecdotal.

One for the Road, which has only just opened in London, also risks being categorized as a throwback. It has something in common with the early *Birthday Party,* in which the vengeful representatives of an unnamed "organization" reduced a seemingly harmless young man to a walking vegetable, and something with the only slightly later *Hothouse,* which recorded a similar piece of mental destruction, this time in a Kafkaesque asylum run by incompetents and sadists. Both plays clearly had political implications and reverberations. Indeed, there's much in Pinter's work as a whole to call into question the commonly held view that he's the most apolitical of contemporary British dramatists. Don't several of his plays involve more or less malign intruders invading more or less private spaces? Wasn't it Pinter himself who pointed out that the appearance of sinister strangers at the front door, with or without raincoats, search warrants and oversized dogs, hasn't exactly been an unusual experience in Europe over the past 50 years?

But *One for the Road* is altogether less guarded about its intentions. One might conceivable choose to interpret it as an allegory about a cruel and tyrannical Old Testament deity, a grim little gloss on Beckett's *Waiting for Godot,* but it's much easier to see it as what it appears to be, a study of political brutality and oppression, Pinter's version of Beckett's *Catastrophe.* A burly English apparatchik . . . quizzes a captive family: tortured father, bloodied mother, and their 7-year-old son, who has committed the only offense anyone mentions, kicking and spitting at some God-fearing dictatorship's legionnaires. Some of the menace is smiling and oblique, as so often in Pinter: "I'm terribly pleased to meet you," "Everybody here has fallen in love with your wife." Some is unwontedly direct: "How many times have you been raped?" By the end, when it becomes apparent that the little boy won't be ac-

companying his ruined parents back into the world outside, you've felt something unique in Pinter: indignation about the abuse of human rights guilelessly steaming off the stage.

This impassioned piece of propaganda . . . may not, of course, be to the taste of those who like their Pinter more artful or their drama less ugly. . . . [Yet] the last play, *A Kind of Alaska,* is quieter, gentler and unique in quite another way. Throughout his career Pinter has concentrated on the dark intestinal drives, giving the impression that the human animal was governed exclusively by a triple hunger for territory, power and sex. In *Alaska* and *Alaska* alone, he admits to the existence of something that could be dignified as selfless devotion.

The play was inspired by Oliver Sacks's *Awakenings,* a series of studies of patients struck down by Encephalitis Lethargica in earlier decades and reactivated in the late 1960's by the drug L-Dope. Rose R, for instance, dreamed at age 21 she was a statue imprisoned in a castle, became precisely that for the next 40 years, and, restored to reality one morning, could never entirely believe it wasn't 1926. Similarly, Pinter's Deborah has been mentally incarcerated in a vast series of glass halls, where she's alternately listened to faucets dripping and danced "in the most crushing spaces," for no less than 29 years. Now she must accept that her sister is an ample matron, her father blind, her mother dead, the clamor and bustle of adolescence long since over. . . . [This] gray-haired Sleeping Beauty squints and blinks from her bed, a 16-year-old consciousness incredulously, angrily, pluckily getting its bearings in a world way beyond anyone's emotional compass. She recites the few terrible facts she can grasp, and declares, with poignant dignity: "I think I have the matter in proportion. Thank you." . . .

[*A Kind of Alaska* is] a moving play, and maybe more than that. It might have been no more than a bizarre case-history from some spidery archive, appealing mainly to those morbidly fascinated by sensational medicine. It could conceivably have become a lurid horror-story from the locked ward. As it is, many will find something of themselves in Deborah, as she peers from the remote present into the vivid past, benignly watched by her sister and her sister's husband, the doctor who has given his life to tending her. There's loss and regret, the feeling that life has evaporated before it's been used. There's also courage and resilience and generosity, the generosity of others, those who care for us. Pinter sees the murk all right: witness *One for the Road.* The evidence of *A Kind of Alaska* is that he isn't altogether unaware of the light. (p. H3)

Benedict Nightingale, "Three Plays Illuminate the Range of Pinter," in The New York Times, *April 22, 1984, pp. H3, H6.*

STEVEN H. GALE

Pinter's plays exhibit the same ambiguity regarding the concept of family that the dramatist has displayed in his personal life. Although most of the scholarly consideration given to the subject as it appears in his dramaturgy has focused on *The Homecoming* (1965), the theme of family has been a central one in Pinter's work since his first play, *The Room* (1957), when Rose solicitously 'mothered' her husband, Bert. . . . However, it is not easy in examining all of . . . [Pinter's] works to determine exactly either what Pinter's definition of family or his attitude toward the family might be, for each work displays unique elements, some of which, as might be expected in the dramatist's canon, produce contradictory statements.

This is true of **Family Voices,** one of Pinter's most recent plays, and one which may indicate that he is finally drawing some conclusions about the nature of 'family'. . . . Along the lines of **Silence,** the play consists of a series of monologues spoken by three characters, two men and a woman. As in the earlier play, the three are separated, but in this case they are speaking about the present rather than the past, and while none hears the words of the others, the statements are directed to one another. The speakers are identified simply as Voice 1, Voice 2 and Voice 3. The only sound heard is their talk.

Voice 1 is a young man who seems to be reading aloud a letter that he has written to his mother. He describes the lodgings where he lives and the others who live there:

> . . . my room is extremely pleasant. So is the bathroom. Extremely pleasant. I have some very pleasant baths indeed in the bathroom. So does everybody else in the house. They all lie quite naked in the bath and have very pleasant baths indeed. . . . the landlady . . . is a Mrs. Withers, a person who turns out to be an utterly charming person. . . .

He concludes his letter affectionately, 'And so I shall end this letter to you, my dear mother, with my love.'

The mother, Voice 2, also seems to be reading a letter aloud, one to her son asking why he never writes to her, inquiring about his life away from home, and informing him that his father has died. Interestingly, she seems to be writing at the same time as her son is, for she remarks that she does not have information that he has just mentioned in his letter:

> Darling. Where are you? The flowers are wonderful here. The blooms. You so loved them. Why do you never write? . . . Do you ever think of me? Your mother? Ever? At all? . . . Have you made friends with anyone?

It is apparent that the two care for one another, and that they are trying to communicate; many of their comments are related, or at least parallel, yet there is never any connection. Occasionally, for instance, one says something that seems to be an answer to what the other has just said, but as the monologue continues it is clear that there has been no linkage, so the answer is not actually a response. It is, instead, merely that the two are talking about the same things. When the son observes, 'But I haven't forgotten that I have a mother and that you are my mother', for example, the second voice notes, 'Sometimes I wonder if you remember that you have a mother.' This is not a reply, though, for the son goes on to describe having tea with Lady Withers and Jane, while the mother continues to wonder where her son has gone and why he never writes—even though ostensibly we are hearing him compose a letter to her all along. What develops is a picture of a parent and a child who care for one another and who think about one another, but who lead separate lives and never communicate their mutual thoughts and concerns, a fairly commonplace occurrence.

As noted above, the concept of family appears to some degree in almost everything that Pinter has written from **The Room** on, and throughout **Family Voices** phrases, lines, and passages echo from previous works to the extent that the play almost takes on the character of a self-parody. When Pinter has dealt with the idea of family before, his focus has been on one or the other of two sets of configurations, that of locus or that of relationship, though often the two are interconnected. The locus set has to do with relationships between family members (family being defined either by blood or marital union) that are somehow tied to a particular location. For example, although **The Room** is not really about the concept of family and the legal relationship between Mr. and Mrs. Hudd serves merely as part of the setting and is not directly related to the play's meaning, still, Rose mothers her husband, Bert, in their room, and their relationship is clearly affected by her perception of the room as a sanctuary, a place where she and her younger husband will be safe and protected from outsiders. (pp. 146-49)

Rose's real concern is with their room, their sanctuary. Her husband's presence may be comforting, but her personal fear of whatever menace lies outside of their room is overriding, and it is this fear that is the focus of her attention, not the family itself. Rose constantly reminds both her husband and herself that 'The room keeps warm', and that 'you know where you are' in such a place. In contrast, the outside world is dark, damp and cold. Only when Bert returns home, she insists, does he 'stand a chance'.

Before Bert does return home, though, the doubly-dark blind, black man from the basement, Riley, intrudes upon Rose's sanctuary and proves her world vulnerable. Alluding to the family, Riley asks Rose to return home to her father. As a result of her confrontation with this intruder, Rose goes blind. Bert returns home to the wife who took care of him, but whom he was unable to protect from the consequences of the outsider's intrusion.

Although in **The Birthday Party** Meg and Stanley are not related, she and her husband, Petey, treat their lodger as one of the family, at least in part because he has sought refuge in their boarding-house after having lost track of his father. Actually, Meg treats the middle-aged Stanley not just as one of the family, but as though he is a child. . . . [Stanley] was superficially made a member of the family merely because he was on the premises; when he goes only Petey seems to feel even the slightest bit of sadness. Ironically, some of the accusations levelled at Stanley by Goldberg have convinced critics to refer to Goldberg as a representative of the familial element in society—Stanley is derided for murdering his wife, for never having married, for deserting his pregnant fiancee, and for defiling his mother, among other things.

In both **Night School** and **A Night Out** the protagonist is in a sense involved in a territorial battle with a relative.

In **Night School** when Walter returns home from prison he finds that his aunts have installed the school teacher Sally in his room and he has been relegated to a day-bed. . . . Walter contends that he has a right to the room because it is his home, that he has lived in it for years, even having bought the bed that they are arguing about. Nevertheless, it is only after he has scared the girl away by threatening to expose her questionable background that he can regain his room. Family is less important to the aunts than is the rent money, and Walter never seems as upset about being displaced by his blood relations as he is with the physical loss of his place in the house. In this drama the definition of family includes no sense of responsibility, let alone belonging.

In *A Night Out* Albert's family situation is just the opposite of Walter's. Where Pinter explores the questions of a noncaring family with Walter, in the person of Albert he demonstrates what can happen when the family becomes too confining because it cannot let go of one of its members, when there is too much concern and affection. Albert tries to break his mother's apron-strings, in *A Night Out,* to escape from her house, but blood proves stronger than his sexual desires and he remains a member of a very non-extended family. (pp. 150-51)

Finally, *The Homecoming* serves as the culmination of the locus set, for Ruth's husband's family home functions both as a sanctuary and simultaneously a location where blood relatives constantly battle, where the place 'home' is ultimately defined by the relationships of those who live there rather than by kinship or the physical structure itself. Thus, Teddy is rejected and Ruth embraced because the concept of family likewise becomes defined by inter-relationships and not by blood or marriage. Home is where the family lives and the family group is established by individuals who fulfil each other's psychological needs.

There has been a definite evolution in Pinter's drama from *The Room* to *The Homecoming* in terms of the concept of 'home', as implied by the difference in the titles of the two plays. The word 'room' refers to a physical structure; the word 'homecoming' implies an emotional connotation. . . . [The] movement reflected in the playwright's thinking is the difference between describing a symptom and discussing a disease. When, at the end of the play, Ruth says to the departing Teddy, 'Don't become a stranger', she is stating the major theme of the drama. She does not dismiss Teddy as a person; rather, she rejects him as a member of a family that does not need her, and she needs to be needed. Therefore, while she opts to remain with her new family, as her Biblical forebear did in the Old Testament, because she fills a need and her needs are filled regardless of the lack of legal or blood connections, she and Teddy still can remain friends.

In plays in the relationship grouping, as in *The Homecoming,* it often seems as though the concept of family is almost coincidental. Frequently a family unit provides the characters and circumstances through which the playwright's themes can be developed and his subjects expressed naturally. At the same time, it is clear that the concept of family impinges on the themes, for the action grows out of the characters' familial relationships. In *A Slight Ache,* for instance, a husband is unable to satisfy his wife's needs, and, much as in *The Homecoming,* Flora rejects Edward and seeks out a substitute for him. . . . As Pinter said in speaking of *The Homecoming,* 'If this had been a happy marriage it wouldn't have happened. . . . Certain facts like marriage and the family for this woman have clearly ceased to have any meaning.' These words could be applied to Flora as easily as they were applied to Ruth.

How does Pinter define family, then, so that we know what it is that has ceased to have any meaning for these women? Well, in *The Caretaker* two brothers provide a partial answer. Their relationship is emphasized by the fact that they always refer to one another as 'brother', never by name, and Mick is his brother's keeper, even though Aston is the older of the two. When Davies intrudes and tries to come between them, the two men redefine their relationship. Mick's love and sense of responsibility coalesce with Aston's trust and appreciation for having been allowed to move toward self-

sufficiency and self-confidence. This family unit survives intact and even is strengthened because the relationship has been reinterpreted in a way that recognizes potential disintegration, change and progress, and expells the disquieting agent. (pp. 152-54)

The same kind of reaffirmation also takes place in *The Collection* and *The Lover.* In the first of these two dramas the family unit is disturbed because the husband, James, has begun to take his wife, Stella, for granted. The introduction of an outside force in the form of an alleged affair between Stella and Bill threatens the marriage in an even more dramatic way and forces James and Stella to re-establish their relationship with new bonds and with new understandings. With James's reassessment of the situation at play's end, Stella has clearly reversed the circumstances to the point that she emerges as the dominant partner, the one who will control the relationship from now on. James's hapless pleading and Stella's enigmatic response underscores their new positions. . . . [Both] James and Stella, in their own ways, are willing to fight to maintain their relationship.

In *The Lover* an imaginary lover leads another couple to reassess the basis on which their marital relationship exists, and to conclude that it is sound. This reaffirmation re-enforces their union because Richard no longer questions its fundamental appropriateness. Having found himself enmeshed in a game that was devised to strengthen the marriage but that has taken control of the couple's life, Richard informs his wife, Sarah, that the game must end: 'Perhaps you would give (Max, the imaginary lover, Richard's alter-ego) my compliments, by letter if you like, and ask him to cease his visits from (*He consults calendar.*)—the twelfth inst.' The concept of family and marriage has been so important to this pair that they have been unable to reconcile their unrestrained, non-logical, passionate, sexual needs with their idealized definition of marriage. . . . [Richard's] attempt fails, though, and at the end of the play, while the marriage remains intact, it does so only because the couple is able to incorporate a new version of the game . . . into their lives. (pp. 154-55)

[In *Tea Party*], Disson's jealousy centres on his bride and eventually leads to his nervous breakdown. He is suspicious of everyone; he cannot trust Diana, her brother, his sons, his parents, or his best man. The apparent betrayals here foreshadow those in the play *Betrayal,* written fifteen years later. In the later play every type of betrayal takes place: husband betrays wife, wife betrays husband, friend betrays friend, and business associate betrays business associate. Ironically, all of these betrayals are possible because of the interconnections that develop out of the context of Emma and Robert's marriage. Whereas the family has been a source of strength until now, in these plays it provides the cause for destruction, something implied but not realized heretofore.

Relationships between individuals, family members or otherwise, concerned Pinter up to this point. From here on his emphasis shifts. Relationships are still his subject, but they are examined through a gauze of time and memory—and the nature of reality, how relationships affect and are affected by time and memory, becomes the centre of his interest. (p. 156)

Night features a married couple reminiscing about their first meeting, but their recollections do not mesh. This is somewhat like the differences in the descriptions of America given by Teddy and Ruth that serve to define the disparities in their needs in *The Homecoming.* . . . As in *The Collection,* the truth, the actual facts, of the original meeting are less important than the relationship established because of it, a relationship that led to a family and children and that has lasted.

Silence is the remembrance of how a marriage was prevented because of the nature of the individuals involved, individuals whose past relationships preclude the establishment of any new relationships. Rumsey, a man of 40, rejected Ellen, a woman in her twenties, because he felt that he was too old for her. Ellen in turn rejected Bates, a man in his thirties, because she could not marry Rumsey. Now the three remain isolated, alone in their rooms, remembering what they used to do together, imagining that they are still living those happier times. When their needs for a familial relationship were thwarted, the three characters became emotionally paralysed.

Pinter's best play, *Old Times,* recalls *The Caretaker* as an intruder attempts to come between a man and his wife, and Anna, like Davies before her, is expelled, the family remaining intact, albeit disturbed. *Old Times* illustrates the desperation of characters who attempt to restructure the past in order to provide themselves with a present in which they can establish a relationship that is vital to them. The husband and his wife's former room-mate [Anna] discuss each other's marriages, infidelity, previous relationships, and promiscuity, all in order to devalue their opponent so that they can control Kate and either maintain or replace the other in a relationship with her. Anna's attempt to destroy the marriage fails, even though Deeley is not strong enough to repel her, because Kate wants the marriage to continue. During the last two or three minutes of the play no words are spoken, yet the emotional power generated by the characters' exposed needs is so great that the audience is left overwhelmed. Deeley's sobbing reflects his sadness at having lost the sexual, passionate pleasures in life, his realization of his vulnerability, his recognition of Kate's power in contrast to his weakness, and his relief that he has been chosen to remain and that Kate has seen Anna 'dead' and, thus, the former room-mate can never threaten his marriage again. (pp. 157-59)

In this second set of plays the family is pivotal because it is the source of vulnerability. If the relationships survive whatever menaces them, they are revitalized and fortified. If the relationships cannot withstand the strain, not only does the family disintegrate but the individuals are cast into a no-man's-land of defeat, isolation and paralysis. When the family holds together, it is a source of strength; when it falls apart, individuals are left with nothing to support them. Kate remembers Anna dead, effectively excluding her from the family, and the voluble Anna for all intents and purposes is dead and never speaks again.

It is interesting, therefore, to note how *Family Voices* speaks out of the dramas that precede it, especially given the play's title. When the members of the family talk, they repeat sentiments from earlier plays. In this case location is unimportant, as suggested by the title, and the characters are concerned with their relationships with one another. In his first speech Voice 1 asks if his mother misses him, makes a joke, and describes those 'pleasant baths' taken by everyone in the house. The first two items are perfectly normal topics, but the depiction of the baths is reminiscent of Deeley's description of Kate luxuriating in her bath in *Old Times* that is part of his attempt to establish that his relationship with Kate is more intimate and familial than Anna's. Voice 1 later exults that he feels close to those who share a bathroom when he claims,

'I have found my home, my family. Little did I ever dream I could know such happiness.' Since this statement follows his description of sharing tea with Lady Withers and Jane and a recounting of his conversation with Riley, a fellow lodger, while taking a bath, in which Riley explains how he has turned away the inquiries of two women claiming to be Voice 1's mother and sister by denying knowledge of him, it can be assumed that the definition of family being dependent upon blood relationship is supplanted here by a definition in which emotional relationships are superior.

There are contradictory signals, however. First, Voice 1 claims that he is not lonely because, as in *Silence,* 'all that has ever happened to me is with me, keeps me company; my childhood, for example, through which you, my mother, and he, my father, guided me.' Then he talks of making new friends, after which his mother, besides asking why he never writes, wonders if he has made any nice friends, though like Albert's mother in *A Night Out,* she is worried that he might 'get mixed up with the other sort', a good, motherly worry. Furthermore, in spite of Voice 1's admiration for those living in the boarding-house, they seem a questionable lot. An old man named Benjamin Withers, in spite of echoing Goldberg's Polonius-like advice . . . , is summed up as someone 'to whom no one talks, to whom no one refers, with evidently good reason'. In *The Room* Riley was the blind Negro who emerged from the basement calling Rose Sal (Voice 1 is nick-named Bobo by the other lodgers) and tells her that her father wants her to come home, then switches to the first person, saying '*I* want you to come home' (italics mine), a switch that Rose apparently does not notice, implying that Riley might be her father. In *Family Voices* Riley is the name of the bathroom conversationalist who sent the two women packing (with a Davies-like 'Piss off out of it before I call a copper') and who admires the bather's 'wellknit yet slender frame' and admits that he fancies the younger man. His descriptive phrases recall Flora's gushing over the match-seller in *A Slight Ache.* A self-avowed policeman who seldom leaves the house, he must be a 'secret policeman', Voice 1 concludes. Mrs. Withers, who talks constantly about her experiences in the Women's Air Force during the Second World War, will not answer Voice 1's questions, but like Meg she entertains him and calls him her 'little pet'. His comment on Jane, who wears black stockings and juggles buns with her toes, is that she 'continues to do a great deal of homework while not apparently attending any school'. (There is also an echo of Spooner's remembrance of his mother's hot cross buns in *No Man's Land.*) Lady Withers wears a red dress (or maybe dark pink?), lives in an opulent apartment with 'sofas and curtains and veils and shrouds and rugs and soft material all over the walls, dark blue', where she drinks rosé wine and plays the piano during the day. At night she receives guests who whisper on the stairs and in other rooms. Unlike T. S. Eliot's whisperers, who represent romantic love, these night whisperers are probably visiting a brothel. It is also important to realize that in the end, in the last words that he speaks, Voice 1 informs his mother that 'I am on my way back to you. I am about to make the journey back to you. What will you say to me?'

Actually, it is easy to imagine what she will say. Throughout the play Voice 2 has repeated her questions—'Where are you? . . . Why do you never write? . . . Do you ever think of me?' She calls him 'Darling', reminds him that she is his mother, worries about his acquaintances, dreams of living 'happily ever after' with him and his young wife, remembers happy times together, recalls that she gave birth to him, curses him for abandoning her, assures him that she is waiting for him, reports his disappearance to the police, and wants to know if he thinks that 'the word love means anything'. The sometimes mutually exclusive statements are representative of the ambiguities in all of Pinter's work and, functioning as they do in the other plays, the contradictions are also a measure of how desperately Voice 2 needs to retain a familial relationship with her son and how destroyed she is without it. As if to emphasize this point, she also repeats a phrase that ties her reaction to the perceived loss of her son to the emotional sterility embraced by Hirst in **No Man's Land:** 'I sometimes think I have always been sitting like this, alone by an indifferent fire, curtains closed, night, winter.' Moments later she is reminded of shampooing his hair and knowing simultaneously that he was 'entirely happy' in her arms while she was 'sitting by an indifferent fire, alone in winter, in eternal night without you'. Past and present coexist and intrude upon one another, producing irony and a sense of prescience. All that is missing is Hirst's ice.

The third voice, which speaks only twice in the play, the first time after over 80% of the drama has transpired, is Voice 1's father. The intriguing thing about this, of course, is that it is on record that he is dead. He puts our minds at ease momentarily, saying that he is dead, as his wife claimed three months ago, and Voice 2 did admit that she sometimes heard his cough and step upon the stair, though this could be dismissed as simply memories or imaginings kindled by the loss of a family member whose presence is missed, and how can a dead man talk anyway? But, then he admits,

> Well, that is not entirely true, not entirely the case. I'm lying. I'm leading you up the garden path, I'm playing about, I'm having my bit of fun, that's what. Because I am dead. As dead as a doornail. I'm writing to you from my grave. A quick word for old time's sake. Just to keep in touch. An old hullo out of the dark. A last kiss from Dad.

Of course, although we only have his word for it, obviously Voice 3 would not lie to his son, although he just did, and a dead man would not lie, so he must actually be dead. This is reinforced by his statement that the only thing that he hears that breaks the absolute silence is the occasional barking of a dog—and this frightens him. Perhaps it is Cerberus? So what is he doing writing letters if he is dead? His second speech, the final words spoken in the play, may hold the answer. His wife has reported that his deathbed reactions to his son were ambivalent—on one occasion she recounted that his last words were of tenderness; elsewhere she describes his passing as in 'lamination and oath', dying with a curse. He states that his son has prayed for his death 'from time immemorial', but he sends 'Lots of love', and encourages his son to 'keep up the good work', too. The result of these contradictory statements is the lack of an unequivocal statement, something that has long been one of Pinter's trademarks, and it may be that he intends to connect ambivalence with the concept of family. The final words are 'I have so much to say to you. But I am quite dead. What I have to say to you will never be said.' . . . Voice 3 holds out the promise of special knowledge, too, but he never reveals his secret.

One interpretation of **Family Voices** would be that the concept of family itself is dead. In a sense, though, this is probably moot. The play presents a series of disembodied voices who, because they are disembodied, cannot connect. The image that we are left with is one of separateness. Essentially, family has become a hollow concept. Everyone, even family members (whether related by blood, marriage, or emotional dependence), is isolated and lives speaking to others who cannot hear them, and hearing no one's voice but their own. (pp. 159-63)

Steven H. Gale, "Harold Pinter's "Family Voices' and the Concept of Family," in Harold Pinter: You Never Heard Such Silence, *edited by Alan Bold, Vision Press, 1985, pp. 146-65.*

BERNARD F. DUKORE

Among the apparent atypicalities of **A Kind of Alaska** in the Pinter canon, as reviewers of the first production have been quick to observe, its programme note by the author . . . points to a literary source or inspiration: *Awakenings* by Oliver Sacks. Obviously, the chief—perhaps only—reason is to give credit where credit is due. Yet Pinter is so adept at concealing his tracks . . . that one wonders whether he points in a certain direction partly in order to draw attention from another. I doubt that it takes much imagination to speculate whether Pinter, recently married at age 50, recalling the Pinter who had been newly married in his mid-twenties, used his own emotions as a creative springboard to draw the central figure of **A Kind of Alaska,** a middle-aged woman whose memory and part of her present is her younger self. From this supposition one may easily move to others. Consider Teddy's statement to his father, uncle, and brothers (**The Homecoming**): 'You wouldn't understand my works. You wouldn't have the faintest idea of what they were about.' Might this be an inversion of what adult Pinter heard from his boyhood friends when, after his success as a dramatist, he met them again? He certainly read such statements about his own 'works' from reviewers. For a writer as meticulous as Pinter, it can hardly be accidental that the people to whom Teddy speaks 'wouldn't appreciate the points of reference'. Perhaps like critics of Pinter's early plays (and—why not?—later as well) those whom Teddy addresses are 'way behind'. One may also wonder the extent to which Stanley's account of responses to his piano recital (**The Birthday Party**) draws upon experiences of Pinter when he was a young actor.

The foregoing is certainly not to say that these characters are simply autobiographical. To cite one difference per play, unlike the character in the first Pinter is a man; unlike the figure in the second he has no brothers; unlike that in the third he is not a pianist. These personages are fictitious. Yet (axiomatically) the characters, situations and emotions a writer creates derive from his own experiences, emotions, observations and readings (which may be no less important to him than other, supposedly more personal experiences). One's interest in an artistic product leads to interest in its producer. Speculations or inferences like those in the previous paragraph are therefore inevitable. (pp. 166-67)

There is a point to these conjectures or ruminations—pronounced roominations, thus coincidentally linking Pinter's recent play, **A Kind of Alaska,** with his first, **The Room,** a play whose nonliterary genesis he also noted (two men he observed, one silent while the other chattered on). An apparently atypical work can suggest perspectives with which to regard other, more obviously typical works.

As quick as reviewers have been to recognize that it is unusual for Pinter to reveal a play's source, they have been equally quick to notice an uncharacteristic feature of the play itself, a psychological study of a woman in her mid-forties, Deborah, who through injection of the recently discovered drug L-DOPA awakens from sleeping sickness, which she contracted when a teenager. For Pinter, the situation is surprisingly clearcut and the ambiguities of a teenage consciousness in a mature woman's body receive an unambiguous explanation. We watch the tensions between two-people-in-one, a girl's response to her woman's body and to a fresh world, her unpractised efforts to conceal and to cope. After the play opened, . . . standard reactions included: 'the reality of the situation' marks 'a departure for Mr. Pinter' (Robert Cushman, *Observer*); 'He was never less obscure than here' (John Barber, *Daily Telegraph*); 'a new surge of realism', the play is 'more nakedly dramatic and certainly more accessible than anything he has written before' (Jack Tinker, *Daily Mail*); and 'Pinter, uncharacteristically, has chosen to write what is almost a documentary study of a patient recovering from sleeping sickness' (John Elsom, *Sunday Mail*).

Does *A Kind of Alaska* really represent a radical departure for Pinter? Despite the play's semblance of atypicality, its vista is that Pinterland to which a quarter of a century has accustomed us. The newly awakened girl-woman's complaint, on the second page of the printed text, 'No one is listening to me', echoes those works of Pinter in which characters, not listening to each other, talk at cross-purposes. The doctor's question that prompts her complaint, 'Who am I?', reiterated immediately after Deborah's lament by the more precise query, 'Do you know who I am?', repeats similar questions asked by other characters in Pinter's plays, for example: 'Tell me, Mrs. Boles, when you address yourself to me, do you ever ask yourself who exactly you are talking to?' (*The Birthday Party*); 'Do you know me?' (*The Collection*); 'I know him.' 'Do you really?' (*No Man's Land*).

In *A Kind of Alaska,* metaphysical resonances on the subject of identity seem to diminish. Does not the programme and prefatory note explain the situation, thereby accounting for the dialogue and permitting one to accept such questions at their face value? Take what would otherwise be Pinter's almost trademarked ambiguities, wherein a flat statement calls into question equally unambiguous assertions. Says Deborah:

> I am twelve. No. I am sixteen. I am seven.
>
> *Pause.*
>
> I don't know. Yes. I know. I am fourteen. I am fifteen. I'm lovely fifteen.

Our knowledge of what her situation is makes the statements of the awakened Deborah comprehensible. As the unfortunate girl-woman says, she does not know—though she immediately contradicts herself on this point. Despite her assertiveness, she guesses. We can see for ourselves that the 16-, 7-, 14-, or as she reiteratively concludes 15-year-old girl—who her sister later says was 16 when sleeping sickness struck—is in her mid-forties. The accuracy of her guesses does not matter. What matters is what happens; she herself in the present tries to ascertain the truth. This is part of the action of *A Kind of Alaska*, as it is of other plays by Pinter, in which what happens is dramatically more important than what happened. By placing his customary techniques and themes in what for him is a generally different context, the known or understandable, one might infer that one should observe earlier plays with them in ways similar to one's observation of *A Kind of Alas-*

ka. I say 'generally different' because he uses a related stratagem in another play, the relatively recent *Betrayal,* wherein the backward moving dramatic action gives us, though not the characters, a known or understandable context.

A Kind of Alaska provides the imprecise, unexplainable, unknown, or unremembered in a context that does not prompt spectators or readers to ask what really happened but rather to understand that certain matters are imprecise, inexplicable, unknown, or unremembered. See, for instance, this partly comic dialogue between doctor and patient:

> HORNBY. You fell asleep and no one could wake you. But although I use the word sleep, it was not strictly sleep.
> DEBORAH. Oh, make up your mind.
>
> *Pause.*
>
> You mean you thought I was asleep but I was actually awake?
> HORNBY. Neither asleep nor awake.
> DEBORAH. Was I dreaming?
> HORNBY. Were you?
> DEBORAH. Well was I? I don't know.

Deborah's last two speeches unquestionably demonstrate the unreliability of memory—a familiar Pinter theme. Note, however, the difference between our response to them and our responses to such passages as Stanley's recollection of his concert (*The Birthday Party*), Aston's account of his medical experience (*The Caretaker*), and both versions of seeing *Odd Man Out* (*Old Times*). While one might wonder the extent to which the victim of sleeping sickness was aware of what occurred about her while she slept or seemingly slept and while one might wonder about her dreams, which she claims not to remember, one does not question the accuracy of her claim—partly because of context, partly because few of us without sleeping sickness remember our dreams, and partly because those of us who remember them do not always do so.

In short, the unfamiliar yet familiar qualities of *A Kind of Alaska* suggest perspectives with which to regard Pinter's earlier plays. Just as we accept the doctor's inability to pinpoint the states of sleep, awake, and 'not strictly sleep', and just as the awakened Deborah does not know whether she dreamt, we may assume that the past is as imprecise and as unremembered for people who have not had sleeping sickness.

After all, as a voice-over says at the start of Pinter's movie adaptation of *The Go-Between,* a line that also begins L. P. Hartley's original novel, 'The past is a foreign country. They do things differently there.' Deborah's past is a foreign country which she no longer inhabits. In Dr. Hornby's words, her mind 'took up a temporary habitation . . . in a kind of Alaska'. She dwelt in frozen isolation in what Pinter calls in another play, whose title is the first phrase, 'no man's land. Which never moves, which never changes, which never grows older, but which remains forever, icy and silent.' *It* may never change, but its sojourner, however long he or she may remain there, changes. If nothing else, the resident ages. While the change is gradual, short periods of time lengthen: moment by moment, day by day, year by year, decade by decade. The Alaska-like deep freeze, a no-man's-land, is therefore both unchanging and temporary. One's view of it now differs from one's earlier view. Even Deborah's does, for she is no longer there and she has a different body. Now, that icy, silent past or Alaska or no-man's-land is a foreign country.

What does one remember of it? Has one's memory altered the actuality? Notice how a statement by the woman in *Silence* partly resembles Deborah's position: 'I'm never sure that what I remember is of to-day or of yesterday or of a long time ago.' What we accept at face value in *A Kind of Alaska* suggests that we might similarly accept statements in other plays by Pinter.

A Kind of Alaska is not a touchstone that enables us to regard Pinter's earlier plays in a simplistic way, as this proposal might appear. The new play's complexities raise questions about it and prompt further questions about Pinter's other plays. For example, more than halfway through the action Deborah becomes aware of a third person in the room, Pauline, who introduces herself as Deborah's sister. Only at this time does Pinter alert the reader to her presence. Does the spectator first see her then or is she visible from the start? Pinter does not say. . . . All that Pinter's printed text reveals is that Hornby is not cognizant of Pauline's presence until Deborah is. 'I didn't call you', he tells Pauline; but he permits her to speak to Deborah. Soon comes this crucial exchange:

> PAULINE. Shall I tell her lies or the truth?
> HORNBY. Both.

The sympathy with which one views the situation or the empathy one has with Deborah should not obscure the fact that what Pauline tells her, and implicitly what Hornby has told and will tell her, may be untrue.

Again we are on familiar Pinter terrain, the *terra incognita* that custom has made *terra cognita*—but with a difference that also exists, too often overlooked, in Pinter's other drama, as it does in the world his drama reflects. While people unconsciously distort the truth, for as much Pinter criticism reminds us their views are limited and their memories fallible, they also consciously lie. The performance implications of these factors are vital. Since a great deal has been written on ambiguities, unconscious distortions, and the like, I wish to focus on the issue of conscious lies. 'I am a widow', Pauline tells Deborah, a seemingly clearcut statement of fact. But is it? For us, there may be as much ambiguity in that statement as there is between sleep and wakefulness; but Pauline herself knows the truth. Two pages later, Hornby tells Deborah, referring to Pauline, 'When she was twenty I married her. She is a widow. I have lived with you.' Is she a widow because her husband has spent so much time away from her, caring for Deborah, that he has made her a *de facto* widow? Or was she a widow when they married? If so, her first husband would have died when she was extremely young and both her and Hornby's use of the present tense would, to say the least, be odd, considering that their marriage would have lasted some twenty years (Pauline is four years younger than Deborah). If the former is the case, Pauline's statement about her widowhood, literally untrue, may be intended more for Hornby than for Deborah and Hornby's support of that statement may be an attempt to clarify their relationship for Deborah's benefit and perhaps also to confess to his wife his understanding of what he has done to her. But might Hornby lie about the marriage? If Pauline is a widow in the conventional sense of the term, the lie and the statement 'I have lived with you' could be efforts to reassure Deborah by conveying a sense of familial stability. . . . Different interpretations result in different line readings, and at least in this section of the play the characters' relationships and motivations have widely diverse possibilities.

We have become so accustomed to ambiguities in both performance and criticism of Pinter's plays that now might be an appropriate time to consider production possibilities of the clearcut. From Pinter's very recent play, let us turn to his first. In *The Room,* Kidd mentions his sister. After he leaves, Rose's first words are, 'I don't believe he had a sister, ever.' Is she lying in order to create conversation with Bert? Should the actress make us aware that she lies? If Rose tells the truth, is she correct? Did she hold this belief before Kidd entered or did she acquire it during the scene in which he comments on his sister? Does Kidd consciously lie? If he does, does the actor who plays the rôle make us aware he is doing so? Whether or not he lies, does Rose make us aware of her disbelief? Does Kidd become aware of it? His first reference to his sister is in a context of his younger days, when he was more fit than he is now:

> That was when my sister was alive. But I lost track
> a bit, after she died. She's been dead some time
> now, my sister. It was a good house then. She was
> a capable woman. Yes. Fine size of a woman too.
> I think she took after my mum. Yes, I think she
> took after my old mum, from what I can recollect.
> I think my mum was a Jewess. Yes, I wouldn't be
> surprised to learn that she was a Jewess. She didn't
> have many babies.

If Rose expresses disbelief and makes Kidd aware of it, and if such expression and awareness occur after, let us suppose, the first and then second sentences, these affect the interpretation of the third sentence, which could be an effort to persuade Rose that the sister is dead. Or it could mean that while he really had a sister he cannot prove it to Rose because she is dead. Or he could invent lie upon lie to make Rose believe he had a sister. There are other possibilities: he could be oblivious to Rose's disbelief and either ramblingly reminisce about his real sister or continue to invent lies without being aware that Rose does not believe him; or Rose might not express her disbelief but instead egg him on. . . . One could continue at greater length, of course, but the point is that the reading of these passages and the reaction to them derive from answers to Pauline's question, 'Shall I tell her lies or the truth?'—an implication that the speaker can differentiate between them—and from the other characters' belief or disbelief—which may have a similar implication (it does for Rose, does not for Deborah). In *The Room,* Rose's four speeches that follow the quotation about Kidd's sister are all questions and all refer to her: 'What about your sister, Mr. Kidd?' 'Did she have any babies?' 'When did she die then, your sister?' 'What did she die of?' Kidd answers none of them. During the interplay between him and Rose, the issues of whether he lies about having had a sister, whether Rose does not believe him at that time, and whether she expresses her disbelief then are not merely academic. They affect the performance and through it our perception of the play. To tell the truth, I cannot definitively answer my own questions. Yet different answers will result in different performances, thus different interpretations of the play. (pp. 167-74)

I do not argue for simplistic interpretation. Rather, I propose that Pauline's question be asked of all Pinter's characters, together with the questions of whether the characters reveal deceit to the audience and whether other characters recognize they hear lies. To tell the truth once more, I do not know what the results would be. However, I can guess that they would differ from what one may call traditionalist ambiguity in productions of Pinter's plays. They might provide additional insights to his work, from *The Room* to *A Kind of Alaska.* (p. 177)

Bernard F. Dukore, "Alaskan Perspectives," in Harold Pinter: You Never Heard Such Silence, *edited by Alan Bold, Vision Press, 1985, pp. 166-77.*

DANIEL SALEM

To make the audience more aware of subconscious reverberations, Pinter blurs the signs of conventional theatrical grammar. He breaks the rules to which the passive spectator is accustomed and transforms classical rational speech. Like the musicians of the serial school, he suppresses the privileged functions of certain fundamental chords. He establishes no distinction between dissonance and consonance. He creates a kind of tension which is no longer based, as in traditional musical writing, on successive starts, suspensions and pauses, but on the absence of consonant chords (the non sequiturs) and on the continual subconscious fluctuations of characters who, constantly and secretly, modify the dramatic situation. Like Anton Webern, in particular, Pinter uses silence as an element of tension. . . . Like cricket players, his characters (in *No Man's Land,* they are even named after four champions) watch each other and react in abrupt, unexplained, sometimes threatening ways.

A Pinter character never analyzes himself lucidly. He never interprets psychologically what he feels. He lies and evades reality. . . . Like Beckett and Ionesco, Pinter renounces completely the heritage of rhetoric and perpetually underlines the ambiguity of words. Beckett encouraged him to express the human condition in its existential reality and to mock language. He showed him that a playwright shouldn't be afraid of disconcerting his audience. One finds in Pinter numerous elements which characterize Beckett's work: the absence of any real plot, the musical quality of the dialogue, memory games, the ability to charge words and silences with maximum meaning. Yet, unlike Beckett, Pinter doesn't deal with the theme of despair hidden behind the mask. His subject *is* the mask. Beckett expresses a truth. Pinter presents characters who experience it. Beckett doesn't encourage a willing suspension of disbelief. Pinter, on the contrary, plays upon fascination and suspense.

Pinter's characters are also different from Ionesco's. Pinter's art isn't based, like Ionesco's, mainly on exaggeration and caricature. It is founded above all on concentration and distillation. Martin Esslin was right in underlining that the dramatists of the "Theatre of the Absurd" have invented a new language—of rupture and distillation—to which Pinter is indebted. But the truth is that Pinter doesn't belong to such a theatre. The reality of his characters is quite different. It is double and is always experienced on two levels. On the one hand, there is a surface reality that everyone is led to believe in when trying to be guided by appearances. On the other hand, there is the hidden reality of secret emotions which contradicts surface reality, alters it, and gives each character his psychological depth.

Pinter is close to those dramatists who, like Strindberg, express the inner dialogue and watch for the moment when the obstacles of the subconscious are overcome and suddenly the truth of the matter is revealed. He is convinced that every perception is subjective: one doesn't perceive reality, reality is what one perceives. And there is total contradiction between what is said and what is felt. So in order to show reality, one has to show the mask and the distorted vision. Like the French writer Nathalie Sarraute, Pinter is interested in the exploration of imperceptible palpitations. He respects the complexity and variety of human emotions. He tries to catch the slightest intonation expressing the secret impulses, all the subjacent and complicated movements which propel language.

What makes Pinter's style different, "Pinteresque," is the fact that he says nothing explicitly. He finds people and things enigmatic. His presentation of an enigma therefore remains an enigma. Any meaning in his work must be guessed, grasped intuitively, read between the lines. His hermetic writing resembles the cabalistic style that seeks to generate an "obscure flame." Rather than explain truth directly, Pinter exposes the lies that the spectator believes to be the truth. He shows that these lies are contradictory and reveals indirectly that they *are* lies, so that the spectator can finally discover *by himself* that the characters are lying. To those who refuse the truth, Pinter shows just how contradictory the lies are that are accepted. Such an approach is a call for more lucidity. As Arthur Koestler explains: "The intention is not to obscure the message, but to make it more luminous by compelling the recipient to work it out by himself—to recreate it. Hence the message must be handed to him in implied form—and implied means 'folded in'. To make it unfold, he must fill in the gaps, complete the hint, see through the symbolic disguise."

The emotional repercussions of a Pinter play are all the greater as the audience witnesses the development of an ambiguous situation and must rely on clues in order to understand it. Each play puts the spectator in the position of a voyeur and asks him to relive subconscious conflicts. The meaning of the dialogue can be grasped only if the public is able to add to the words, the pauses and the silences a series of echoes, connotations, and undertones.

Pinter's work mirrors anguished confusion and belongs to a specific period—the era of suspicion. It calls upon a forewarned audience capable of distinguishing a play's oneiric elements. It brings a new awareness to spectators who are in connivance with the dramatist, who don't take words literally and who mistrust characters. Such work can't please an audience that requires entertaining "well-made" plays, that seeks only an amusing, conventional, and reassuring social game. On the contrary, Pinter's work is shocking and provocative. It has the power to disturb. This is why the spectator's reaction is often resistance, embarrassment, and fear. He refuses a secret reality which refers to something that he has experienced but also repressed.

By dealing with the subconscious, Pinter touches directly upon something essential and generates deep-seated emotions. His dialogue seems to be based on conventional phrases and innocuous non sequiturs. But as soon as the cues are exchanged in a given situation, the spectator guesses what happens behind the masks. A latent content contradicts appearances and preconceived ideas about what should and what shouldn't be revealed. In the name of morality, prudence, and modesty, members of the audience may condemn the illumination of the innermost recesses of the psyche. Sensing that the behaviour of Pinter's characters secretly alludes to their own repression, they fear the flashes of lucidity in which they might see themselves naked. Incapable of accepting the truth objectively, they resort to defence mechanisms which allow them to avoid the uneasiness generated by the dialogue and particularly by the silences.

An audience which, unexpectedly and abruptly, discovers the repression process immediately divides itself. Spontaneously, it chooses between humour (which consists in including oneself among the accused) and incriminating irony, mockery, or indignation. Humour allows acceptance, while irony is a form of impotence. It is guilt transformed into intellectual vanity in order to allow oneself to laugh at others and thus be excluded from the situation.

We can distinguish three types of psychological reactions. First there is *adapted behaviour.* It is based on a lucid perception of the global reality expressed in the play, including what is revealed without being explicit: the spectator controls his emotions while grasping the meaning of the work. Then there is *blind behaviour,* based on repression: the spectator's perception is distorted by lack of empathy, by prejudice. Truth is denied, suppressed, because it is too unpleasant to be acknowledged. Finally, there is *uncontrolled behaviour,* based on panic: the spectator's perception is distorted by excessive emotional involvement. He reacts excitedly, angrily.

To meet with incomprehension and indignation is inevitable when certain conventional beliefs are threatened. ***The Homecoming*** is particularly disturbing because the family is preeminently the experience from which all feelings of love and hatred originate. As he shows all the ugliness of an embittered family, Pinter incites strong opposition. The spectator is embarrassed, nay frightened. . . . Without taking into consideration the spectator's feelings, the dramatist confronts him with a painful truth. Therefore a self-protection mechanism is at work. Touched subconsciously, attacked, the spectator feels repulsion and protests against someone who shows him images that shake his innermost defences.

Blind behaviour is also linked to the deep-seated belief that it is always possible to perceive one's motives clearly. It is in the name of such conviction that Pinter is often taken to task for his obscurity. The spectator who admires only order, harmony, and beauty will reject anything diseased or adulterated because he will feel that it debases his taste. He will insist on being entertained and charmed and will refuse any sudden awareness of reality.

He will also be put off by Pinter's comedy as it is a comedy of deception that raises a grim laughter. Pinter is interested in tragicomic situations, in situations which are both funny and painful because they are experienced in a state of anxiety. His characters are tragic but their suffering is caused by their own vanity. They encounter laughable obstacles (a disconnected gas-cooker, a wasp) and, making mountains out of molehills, they become ridiculous. Pinter shows how tragic it is always to be forced to put on an act in order to save appearances. His comedy is not a comedy of situation but *the comedy of exposed repression.* Such comedy is aggressive and embarrassing because it reveals the characters' subconscious distress.

Pinter's comedy corresponds to Jewish humour, a desperate humour that often helps make bearable the unbearable. When Spooner, in ***No Man's Land,*** embarks on a long monologue to blow his own trumpet in the hope that Hirst will hire him as private secretary, the situation is tragicomic because it is hopeless. Lost in his frozen world, Hirst doesn't listen. . . . (pp. 71-5)

Pinter's plays generate two kinds of laughter: *a liberating laughter,* i.e., a lucid laughter conscious of the pain which is constantly mixed with the foolishness, and *a sneering laughter,* i.e., a blind laughter which considers the characters not as persons but rather as caricatures. It is a defensive laughter that Pinter defines thus:

> . . . where the comic and the tragic (for want of a better word) are closely interwoven, certain members of an audience will always give emphasis to the comic as opposed to the other, for by so doing they rationalise the other out of existence. . . . This indiscriminate mirth . . . represents a cheerful patronage of the characters on the part of the merrymakers, and thus participation is avoided. This laughter is in fact a mode of precaution, a smokescreen, a refusal to accept what is happening as recognisable (which I think it is). . . .

In so far as the spectator guesses, recognizes, and accepts the masks that the characters wear, he laughs because the absurdity of their self-justifications is suddenly exposed. He laughs at self-delusion. Tragicomedy derives from the distance between the character as he really is and the false image he tries to make other people believe. The greater that distance, the more it reveals the character's vanity, the more he looks ridiculous. On the contrary, the shorter the distance between his real self and what he believes he is, the more he shows his guilt and pain, the more he looks pitiful. Then laughter stops short. The spectator intuitively senses the character's suffering and the scene becomes tragic. Laughter stops whenever anguish appears. It stops in front of any tormented character seeking help and showing his subconscious open wound.

One rarely finds in Pinter the dramatic irony which allows the spectator to know more than the characters. Sometimes he even knows less than they do. He is confronted with characters who never display any true sense of humour, who never accept smilingly other people's limitations as well as their own. So when a character is unmasked, the spectator inevitably becomes conscious of the repression process. He can't avoid the subconscious depths. A Pinter play will never be a pleasant game as it invites the spectator to laugh at repression and denounces both the ridiculous and tragic aspects of vanity. Comedy is always closely linked to the intuitive knowledge that repression is mixed with pain.

Such is Pinter's relation with his audience. He refers the spectator to his innermost repressed feelings. If the spectator is too weak to tolerate that confrontation, he is petrified. If, on the contrary, he is able to acknowledge his own weaknesses, he will laugh at the revelation of what is behind the mask. He will be pleased with the breaking of the tacit pact of repression. He won't find it indiscrete or inopportune. The revelation of the subconscious will generate a liberating laughter.

Pinter's audience is finally divided in three groups: those who laugh lucidly, those who laugh blindly and those who are embarrassed, who do not laugh, who even sometimes can't stand other people's laughter. The performance of a Pinter play involves an exchange between two subconscious minds. At such a hidden level, depending on our own individual degree of maturity, on our ability to understand and recognize our own obscure thoughts and feelings, Pinter's work can be interpreted as either a series of painful and ironical grimaces or a series of intelligible images of reality. Each understanding is personal and unique. Some spectators immediately reject a Pinter play. It is a matter of self-protection. In order to preserve a precarious balance, they refuse to hear what transpires throughout the play. They shut themselves off from any experience liable to awaken their own guilt. Often, they counter-attack by blaming Pinter. A dramatist, they say, shouldn't be wily, intent on showing "sick" people and, at the same time, refuse to pass judgement on them. Indeed, Pinter explores his characters' subconscious (without realizing that he is projecting his own guilt) but never clearly commits himself morally. He expresses what he sees and feels without any profession of faith.

Pinter's work is often rejected or misunderstood not only by the public but also by the actors and directors themselves. Any spectator feels the fundamental need to be able to penetrate the secret of the characters. As this need is never fully satisfied in Pinter's plays, the temptation for the director and actors to fill that "void" is strong. Unfortunately, whenever they yield to it, it is always at the expense of the central truth of the play.

The actor is often wrongly convinced that he has *to speak* the text, that he must help "clarify" it. Yet Pinter's writing is never accidental. As a dramatist, he carefully orchestrates words and silences so that his plays may shape an image as complex as his own experience of reality. (pp. 75-8)

Pinter's dialogues cover up a "subconversation." . . . Words carry the weight of a whole underground world. They must be considered as nets through which the meanings may slip and get lost each time a useless gesture or intonation blurs the form that the dramatist has carefully chiselled. The underground world over which Pinter's words are fixed like boards is the characters' secret motivation. It can be detected only by studying the mood of the scene. If one refuses to make the effort of discovering and respecting it, one distorts the underlying meaning of the lines, the confrontation behind the words. What is important is not so much what is being said as the way it has to be said. Above all, it is *the right rhythm* which has to be found, a rhythm which fits the characters' secret emotions. . . .

The intentionality hidden under the characters' words is revealed by the subtle way in which those words are spoken, *without removing the mask.* (p. 78)

The opaque clue offered by silence is particularly significant. Pinter asks the spectators to supplement his dialogue with an immediate meaning, grasped intuitively. He asks them to decipher what is implicit in the words and to do it according to their individual reactions to those words. A recognizable current of intentionality circulates through and between the words. Each spectator vaguely identifies it since he also carries it within himself. Pinter's work is intelligible only because of the fugitive introspection we all constantly undertake, more or less unconsciously. (p. 79)

Pinter isn't committed to any particular political struggle. The image of society that he gives is favourable neither to the established ideology nor to one class as opposed to another. The complexity of life, in Pinter's opinion, can't fit into a political theory. His commitment is expressed through his work on language, the different levels of which he recreates to the point of parody. The slyness of characters such as Goldberg, Edward, Harry, Willy, Spooner, Hirst, and Robert is, in his eyes, a form of violence, a masquerade, which effectively denounces the mystifications of abstract language and the use of labels and stereotypes in order to devalue people and exclude them.

In Pinter's plays, language is more often than not a means to an end which is domination. Instead of communicating, language subjugates. Evasion and deceit lie hidden under the disguise of logical discourse. Conscious of the incantatory, "Hitlerite" power of words, Pinter shows how they can become instruments of cruelty or be replaced significantly by drum beats, nervous giggles, or inarticulate sounds. (pp. 79-80)

Pinter doesn't show political or social conflicts. But he does allude to the secret motives which engender inhibition and aggressiveness. He doesn't divide society into guilty oppressors and innocent victims. But he does divide it into individuals, couples, families, whose behaviour constitutes society. In his work, only individuals and their reactions, their friction, provocation, resentment and fury, exist. Pinter believes that social violence is due to resentment. So when showing the mask, the game of conventional repression, he is showing a diseased society where angry accusations unleash social conflict, revolution, and war in the same way as they devastate individual lives. And society grants him leave to speak just as princes and kings allowed their jesters to amuse them in the past.

Not always, though. It isn't surprising that in the U.S.S.R., where psychoanalysis is rejected, Pinter's plays are banned. They are officially considered as *too pessimistic.* In October 1976, an amateur performance of *The Caretaker* in Moscow was called off by the authorities at the last minute. True, Pinter *is* pessimistic. He is a gifted, talented dramatist who only expresses the darker side of life. His work is the testimony of a truncated vision. He shows the frightening results of subconscious deformation but ignores the joy which rewards conscious elucidation. His work lacks an essential dimension: the contrast between the pain of perversion and the joy of mastered suffering. (pp. 80-81)

Pinter can only point at vanity without being able to fight it. Quite understandably, the reality that he recreates seems unrelenting, disappointing, and difficult to endure.

Pinter's vision of life is, indeed, pessimistic. Yet it isn't desperate. When Pinter shows that the inner life of his characters is unhealthy, he shows at the same time that it might be made healthier. A clear vision of mental illness helps to cure or at least check that illness. A writer like Pinter has no theory about his work. He follows his intuition about people and the pain they inflict on themselves and one another. He must be judged according to the degree of responsibility he displays in his understanding and expression of that pain. Pinter is pitiless because he is convinced that discretion can only prolong the pain. To him, sentimentality is only a cover-up for brutality. Everything happens as a result of reactions that are camouflaged by language. Words prove to be highly dangerous when used to dominate, to assert one's superiority, to produce theories cut off from reality, windmills working on a lot of hot air. Pinter is an intellectual answering Marguerite Yourcenar's definition: "Every intellectual is limited by his temperament and the resources of his own intellect. The image of reality he offers may be partly inaccurate or false but it is the sincerity of his effort, rather than the result, that counts."

Pinter's work expresses a reality he has experienced and it meets with a powerful response. By focusing attention on subconscious mechanisms, it is both moving and thought-provoking. In a subtle way, it helps clarify human relations and encourages the progress from intuition to analysis. By giving an embarrassing image of men, it acquires a subversive power. It contributes to the shaking of stereotypes. It generates suspicion about an alienating language. It favours a different consciousness. The images in Pinter's work are indeed oppressive but they may free from anguish those who accept and recognize them. Similar to the images in dreams, they open "inner eyes" and verify the existence of a subconscious reality. It isn't the verification of such a reality which is traumatic but the ignorance of it.

The effort of understanding required by Pinter's work also leads to a beneficial awareness of the importance of symbolic language. The misunderstanding of Pinter's plays is often based on the confusion of oneiric images and realism, on the mistake which consists in reading the text literally without translating its symbolic data, without interpreting the characters' psychopathic symptoms. A misunderstanding is inevitable if the spectator forgets that the characters' behaviour, like any human behaviour, isn't a direct reaction to a stimulus but a symbolic reaction, a transformed reaction, worked out unconsciously.

The deciphering of Pinter's work reveals the essential human problem—the fight between lucidity and blinding affectivity. Pinter's whole work deals with repressed anguish. To analyze his characters is to become conscious of the harm they do to themselves. It is to understand the psychological meaning of their symptoms. Such a diagnosis allows a better knowledge of the vicious circle of repression and helps to avoid it.

Pinter is no guide. He mirrors our subconscious. Yet his work is fuelled by a moral effort, inspired by an appeal to patience. If it has the power to move us, the merit of alerting us, it is because it expresses not only a dramatist's inner life but also the life of each one of us, recognizable by all. By obstinately revealing the truth about our secret pains, by helping us feel the immanent justice of life, Pinter's work awakens our ethical responsibility. It makes us reflect on our own errors and urges us on to fresh efforts of self-control. It represents a salutary landmark in our slow evolutionary ascent to higher levels of consciousness and lucidity. (pp. 81-2)

> *Daniel Salem, "The Impact of Pinter's Work," in* Ariel: A Review of International English Literature, *Vol. 17, No. 1, January, 1986, pp. 71-83.*

RICHARD A. BLAKE

[*Turtle Diary* is] successful in using a thin and improbable narrative line to explore two people's search for meaning in their lives. Neaera Duncan writes and illustrates children's fiction, but she has run into a wall of writer's block. . . . William Snow works in a bookstore after the failure of both his marriage and his business. Both are lonely, both visit the London Aquarium and sympathize with the 30-year captivity of the giant sea turtles. Both independently resolve to kidnap them and set them free.

With the cooperation of the zoo keeper, they join forces in their plan and in the process unwittingly fashion their own liberation from loneliness. In an unlikely movie scenario, they do not fall in love with each other. In fact, although they collaborate in an adventure most uncharacteristic for each and even snatch a few hours sleep together in the back of a rented van after the work is completed, they remain oddly distant and formal in their relationship. For his part, William

awakens to the presence of Harriet, who also works in the bookstore, and Neaera turns toward a working man. . . .

Both the novel by Russell Hoban and the screenplay by Harold Pinter use the turtles as images for William and Neaera. They are confined for so long that they have begun to lose their natural color. Their shells offer only the appearance of invulnerability, for in fact they are relatively weak. . . . (p. 385)

[Hoban's novel] contains several comic sequences that could provide perfect material for visual slapstick. At one point, for example, William searches for relief from his anxiety by consulting a California cultist who wires his head with an alpha-wave detector and later by submitting to a woman wrestler-turned-therapist who nearly squeezes the breath out of her clients with a scissor lock. Hoban's satire flies in many directions at once.

Pinter's screenplay, by contrast, is much more tightly focused. He pares away all extraneous incidents to concentrate exclusively on his two main characters. He is a master of the elliptical sentence and the half-completed idea. . . . (pp. 385, 392)

[In *Turtle Diary*], the narrative is merely a vantage point for exploration. [It provides] wonderful characterizations and [asks] thoughtful questions about the human condition. . . . By choosing to say little, Harold Pinter was eloquent in the extreme.

Cocktail-party bores, take a note. (p. 392)

> *Richard A. Blake, "Two Fables," in* America, *Vol. 154, No. 18, May 10, 1986, pp. 385, 392.*

KATHERINE H. BURKMAN

Although Harold Pinter has claimed as the territory for his plays a place in which his characters exist "at the extreme edge of their living, where they are living pretty much alone," he also writes and has always written plays about living in families. Since his first play, *The Room* (1957), in which Rose is summoned home by her father's emissary, until this more recent play, *Family Voices* (1981), in which a young man writes his mother about a newfound family, Pinter has dwelt on the family; even the sole character in Pinter's television play *Monologue* (1973) has fantasies about family life. He would die, the man in *Monologue* insists, for his friend/rival's unborn children, whose uncle he imagines himself to be. In *Family Voices* . . . , Pinter has made explicit what has been implicit in all of his previous drama—the agonized isolation of the individual "living pretty much alone" at the same time that he lives in the midst of family, in this case a newfound family and his original one.

Pinter interweaves the voice of the young man, Voice 1, telling his mother about his new family, with the voices of the young man's mother, Voice 2, and of his father, Voice 3, dwelling on their relationship with him in such a way as to make the connection between the two families clear. Benedict Nightingale, in his review of the play for the *New York Times* [see excerpt above], considers the young man's original home life to be "bloodless." "No wonder the boy escaped," he writes, "and no wonder he is attracted by these sinister, unsettling Witherses [his new family]. . . . But as Nightingale himself perceives, the boy has not really escaped—the original family voices are ever present, even if he does not appear to hear them. While he seems, at play's end, to be caught between old and new family, as motionless, despite his announcement to his mother that he is returning to her, as the tramps who decide to leave are at the end of Samuel Beckett's *Waiting for Godot,* he is really imprisoned in what is fundamentally one family situation. The Withers family is not so different, it turns out, from his own. There is, in fact, as with the *Godot* tramps, no escape—no place to go.

The counterpoint of past and present in **Family Voices** reveals the love-hate relationships in the family that are typical of Pinter's other dramas. The young man, who writes with ostensible love to his mother, is, according to her voice, which he does not appear to hear, completely out of touch with her and has not even responded to news of his father's death. All three of the characters demonstrate their ambivalent feelings by juxtaposing clichéd statements of affection with outbursts of hostility.

The young man, for example, says that he is planning to meet a nice girl to bring home to his mother, but then he goes on to tell her of the far-from-"nice" girl he has met, Jane. Jane, whom he supposes to be Mrs. Withers's fifteen-year-old granddaughter, despite her dedication to homework—"She keeps her nose to the grindstone,"—tends to keep her toes in the young man's lap. . . . The young man's desire to offer himself as Jane's tutor is fraught with sexual innuendo. "She possesses a true love of learning," it seems. "That is the sense of her one takes from her every breath, her every sigh and exhalation. When she turns her eyes upon you you see within her eyes, raw, untutored, unexercised but willing, a deep love of learning."

The young man not only juxtaposes his ostensible desire to meet a respectable girl with his descriptions of Jane and her acrobatic toes, he also describes himself alternately as drunk and as a teetotaler. He first disclaims his drunken habits by pretending he was joking about them:

> When I said I was drunk I was of course making
> a joke. I bet you laughed. Mother? Did you get the
> joke? You know I never touch alcohol.

Several lines later, however, he indicates that his relationship with his landlady, Mrs. Withers, is one of drunken comradery:

> I get on very well with my landlady, Mrs. Withers.
> She tells me I am her solace. I have a drink with
> her at lunchtime and another one at teatime and
> then take her for a couple in the evening at the
> Fishmongers Arms.

Similar contradictory attitudes emerge from Voice 2, as the mother alternates effusive expressions of love with ferocious attacks of hate. She tells of her fantasy of living with her son and his "young wife," the nice girl she expects him to marry, and speaks of her longing and love for him and of his father's affection as well: "Darling. I miss you. I gave birth to you. Where are you?" Shortly thereafter, however, she speaks of him as a monster whom his father cursed on his deathbed. In one speech she makes, her alternation of attitudes comes together as she apparently recognizes her isolation, not just in her present deserted state but in her past state when her son was home and the family seemed to be intact:

> Sometimes I think I have always been sitting like
> this. I sometimes think I have always been sitting

like this, alone by an indifferent fire, curtains closed, night, winter. . . . What I mean is that when, for example, I was washing your hair, with the most delicate shampoo, and rinsing, and then drying your hair so gently with my soft-towel, so that no murmur came from you, of discomfort or unease, and then looked into your eyes, and saw you look into mine, knowing that you wanted no-one else, no-one at all, knowing that you were entirely happy in my arms, I knew also, for example, that I was at the same time sitting by an indifferent fire, alone in winter, in eternal night without you.

What the mother intuits, of course, is that she will have no place in her son's life with a nice wife. He is, she later asserts, depraved and has doubtless become a male prostitute. "I have declared in my affidavit," she informs him, "that you have never possessed any strength of character whatsoever." Women, she asserts, were his downfall; witness their French maid or his governess. Jealousy of her son is the paramount emotion that emerges. Far from sexless or bloodless, the mother seethes with sexual jealousy and prophetically fantasizes the worst, ensuring the realization of those fears with her domineering and repressive character.

Equally ambivalent is the allegedly dead father, who protests when his voice emerges quite late in the play, that he lives and then admits that he is dead. Alternately cursing his son for wishing him dead and expressing his love for him—"Lots of love, son. Keep up the good work"

> —the father has the play's last word. "I have so
> much to say to you. But I am quite dead. What I
> have to say to you will never be said."

In the context of the play, the suggestion is that the father has never been able to speak to his son; he has always, in the sense of communication, been the living dead. Now that he is dead, it makes little difference. Like Beckett's improperly born characters, the prototype being a child Mrs. Rooney refers to in *All That Fall,* because he has not been fully born, he cannot fully die.

The father, however, makes himself well understood through the young man's alternate fathers, Mr. Withers and Mr. Riley. When the young man asks Mrs. Withers to clarify her relationship to the bald, retiring man who, someone has told him, is called Benjamin Withers, she evades the question by calling the young man her pet and apparently offering him an embrace—"Sometimes she gives me a cuddle, as if she were my mother." But if the mother would ignore the father and possess the son, the father will not permit this to happen. Mr. Riley disposes of the original mother and Mr. Withers warns the young man away from the three Withers women with their provocatively sexual ways.

It is while bathing that the young man learns from the intruding Mr. Riley that his mother and sister have been sent on their way. From the outset, the bathroom has taken on symbolically surreal importance to the young man as the room the inhabitants of the house all brag of to everyone they meet because of the pleasant baths they may take in it "quite naked." Significantly, what the people brag about is the baths in the bathroom "we share." One gets the feeling that what is shared in his new family is a form of nakedness or exposure, one that worries the young man so much that he must assure his mother of the pleasantness of the room and bath four times in one brief description.

Mr. Riley is able to come through the bathroom door, which the young man thought he had locked, to inform him both of his dismissal of his mother and sister and of his own homosexual leanings. Denying any knowledge of the young man, Mr. Riley has sent his relations, in hilarious fashion, on their way. "I can smell your sort a mile off," he has apparently informed them, "and I am quite prepared to put you both on a charge of malicious mischief, insulting behaviour and vagabondage, in other words wandering around on doorsteps knowingly, without any visible means of support. So piss off out of it before I call a copper." The young man reacts to this outrageous treatment of his family and to the homosexual pass that Riley proceeds to make at him by commenting on his father's absence. "It interests me," he notes, "that my father wasn't bothered to make the trip." The father is both absent and ominously present in Mr. Riley, who later, having invited the young man to his room, dwells again on his homosexual inclinations, which he says he restrains only to keep on "the right side of God." He could, he asserts, crush the young man with his love.

> I'm a big man, as you can see, I could crush a slip
> of a lad such as you to death, I mean the death that
> is love, the death I understand love to be.

Sexual love, historically so often associated with death, is explicitly related to it here, but we have seen the dangers of love tinged with death throughout the play.

The other father figure appears with threatening warnings just as the young man prepares to settle into his new family. "I took a seat," he says, describing an elegant evening with the three Withers women. "I took it and sat in it. I am in it. I will never leave it." Almost immediately after so settling, the young man appeals to his mother for advice, worried by Mr. Withers's summons to his room and his seemingly senseless and mystifying speech. "Don't mess about," is one of his clear messages, and he informs the boy that he is in a "diseaseridden land." "I'm the only saviour of the grace you find yourself wanting in," he assures the young man, who, when asked to look at him and does, finds the experience "like looking into a pit of molten lava."

The young man collapses before the claims of the two father figures, the one threatening him away from women if he is to receive salvation, the other threatening the damnation of a crushing, homosexual love. To whom does he turn, then, when so threatened by the men but to his mother, to whom he decides to return. Back in his original home, at least in fantasy, he accuses his mother of doing away with his father. A final wish? A half-feared, half-anticipated fantasy?

The final irony of the young man's plan to return home, which is expressed in counterpoint with his mother's decision to give up on him and with his father's admission that he cannot reach him, is heightened by the audience's realization that the young man has clearly never left home. In essence, his two families, the new and the old, are one. The women are sexually available and possessive while the men are threatening, uncommunicative, and also sexually available. And so the young man's paralysis—he does not move—is given full psychological explanation. The family is a wasteland in which any move is fatal, and not to move, though safe, is stultifying.

Family Voices bears some resemblance, as Nightingale points out, to *The Homecoming;* the Withers family attract the young man because they act out the dark sexuality that is repressed in its own home, even as Ruth is attracted by her intellectual and repressed husband's unrepressed family. Ruth, however, elects to stay with her new family, who provide much more of an alternative for her than the young man finds in his new family. At the end of *The Homecoming* Ruth is not only at home but well in command of her situation. The young man, in contrast, seems quite lost at the end of *Family Voices* and is certainly not self-possessed.

Family Voices harks back more clearly to an early Pinter play, *A Night Out* (1960), in which another young man attempts unsuccessfully to break away from his mother. "Your father would turn in his grave if he heard you raise your voice to me," Albert's mother tells him when he wishes to spend one night "out." "You're all I've got, Albert. I want you to remember that I haven't got anyone else. I want you . . . I want you to bear that in mind." When Albert does go out, he identifies a girl he picks up with his mother. The girl poses as a mother but is actually a prostitute. "You're all the same, you see, you're all the same, you're just a dead weight round my neck," he complains to her.

While the images are richer and fresher in *Family Voices* than they are in this earlier play, the drama suffers from the same tendency, rare in Pinter's canon, to make something of a case history of its protagonist. Although the same oedipal tensions emerge in many of Pinter's plays, the characters and situations, however bizarre, do not give the impression of aberration or mental illness; they tend, instead, to suggest universal struggles for dominance, love, and identity, with the voice of the family operating as the ground on which the characters work out their salvation or suffer their damnation.

In most of his plays, as much as Pinter cares for some of his individual characters, he is as concerned with the family or the "tribe" as he is with those who make it up. Rarely involved with the kind of caricature that he played with in *A Night Out* and possibly *Night School* (1960), and that he has partially returned to in *Family Voices,* Pinter does not always give us three-dimensional characters, but he does, more often than not, create characters with archetypal resonance. The ritual rhythms and structures of his plays suggest Pinter's concern with the survival not just of the individual, but of the family within which the battle for survival and salvation takes place.

We have a touch of this universalizing tendency in *Family Voices* when Mr. Withers reportedly suggests himself to the young man as the source of salvation . . . ; focus remains, however, on the young man's psychology. Mythical overtones are clearer, however, in *No Man's Land* (1975), a play about a lost old man, in which Hirst, like the lost young man of *Family Voices,* cannot deal with his sexuality—Alan Jenkens has aptly titled his review of *Family Voices* "No Man's Homecoming" [see excerpt above]. Focus here is less on individual psychology than it is on a ritual struggle for renewal with Spooner, as Hirst's double or inner potentiality, playing out his spurious savior role until his, and consequently Hirst's, final defeat at the play's conclusion. (pp. 164-69)

While the young man in *Family Voices* is bound by his psychology in a family prison, the old man of *No Man's Land* elects his doom and ultimately defeats not Spooner but himself. Unable to accept his mortality (he refuses to accept his recurrent dream in which someone, either himself or Spooner, is drowning), he is beyond the possibilities of renewal. Indeed, Pinter's male characters, like Hirst, are rarely able to accept the opportunities that they are given for renewal; witness the Matchseller, who rises as Edward falls in *A Slight Ache* (1959), driven more by Flora's needs and the fatalities in his situation than by any visible choices he may elect to make. Richard in *The Lover* (1963) is a rare exception as he attempts to integrate the several roles he plays with his wife but is defeated by her need to continue to relate as a series of fragmented selves.

While women in Pinter's early plays are often caught as completely as the men are in the destructive nature of family relationships (Rose in *The Room* [1957]; Meg in *The Birthday Party* [1958]), Flora makes her tragicomic choice for renewal in *A Slight Ache;* and Ruth in *The Homecoming* (1965), Kate in *Old Times* (1971), and Emma in *Betrayal* (1978) are all women who take charge of their lives. Taking charge of her life, for Ruth, in what may remain Pinter's most significant family drama, involves the exchange of one family for another and the wresting of the rule of her new family from a weekend patriarch, Max. (pp. 170-71)

The self-possession of Kate in *Old Times* is achieved, like the self-possession of Flora and of Ruth, by discarding a husband, an effete, middle-aged artist, though in this case there is no new king-god to take his place. Kate must come to terms in this play, not only with the failure of her marriage but with a past self who comes back to haunt her in the form of an old room-mate, Anna. Victorious but alone at the end of the play, Kate moves away from the kind of possessiveness that characterizes family relationships at their worst in Pinter's dramatic world. "And someday I'll know that moment divine, / When all the things you are, are mine," Deeley sings in vain to his wife. Unlike the young man of *Family Voices,* Kate is able to deal with the voices of the past; "But I remember you. I remember you dead," she says in an annihilating speech to Anna. Startlingly and somewhat agonizingly alone at the end amid the ruins of her past, Anna and Deeley, Kate is, in contrast to *Family Voices's* young man, quite free.

Emma, too, in *Betrayal* is able to deal with the voice of the family, and though she does not take on the matriarchal tasks of *The Homecoming*'s Ruth, like Ruth, she plays out the roles of mother, wife, and whore within the family circle. Like *The Homecoming, Betrayal* is a play that would seem to shatter the family structure irreparably; yet it, too, has its homecoming—its celebration and affirmation of the family.

In the backward movement of the play, which begins with Emma's meeting with her ex-lover, Jerry, to tell him of the end of her marriage to his best friend, Robert, and ends some years earlier with Jerry making his first pass at Emma, we discover betrayal within betrayal within betrayal. Emma has betrayed Robert with Jerry, Robert claims to have betrayed Emma, and he has betrayed Jerry by concealing his knowledge of the Emma-Jerry affair from him. Since Emma and Robert have a child during the course of her affair with Jerry, Robert points out to her that she has betrayed Jerry as well.

Why, then, is a play suffused with sexual betrayal a family-affirming drama? Partly because the characters care very much about each other as family. Their very betrayals, wounding as they are, are desperate attempts at cummunication; they betray one another, paradoxically, to find that which is authentic within the family. (pp. 171-72)

The men, on the whole, in Pinter's family plays are trapped in their ambivalent family relationships. Several of the women, though, who as whores seem to betray all that is sa-cred in the family, tend to find their way to freedom and to an authentic voice that is still a family one. Because the oedipal rivalry that claims the young man as its victim in *Family Voices* is an inevitable part of the family dynamic that Pinter depicts, his family dramas always do have their victims. But in those plays in which the women, who are at the center of the rivalry, refuse to become either the possessive mother of *Family Voices* or the helpless victim of male wrath of *The Room,* they do sometimes find their way to a self-possession in which they accept their multiple roles as wife, mother, and whore, belonging to themselves and thereby offering new life to the family. (pp. 173-74)

Katherine H. Burkman, " 'Family Voices' and the Voice of the Family in Pinter's Plays," in Harold Pinter: Critical Approaches, *edited by Steven H. Gale, Fairleigh Dickinson University Press, 1986, pp. 164-74.*

DOUGLAS KENNEDY

It could be argued that one of the great intellectual trivial pursuits of the 1960s was playing the Harold Pinter Guessing Game. This was an after-dinner game which became fashionable in the wake of Pinter's early success as a dramatist, in which the well-educated participants attempted to excavate some sort of "meaning" or "subtext" from his plays—even though his plays "refused to broadcast a message" in the first place.

And indeed, Mr. Pinter himself helped fuel his own mystique by taking a sort of Greta-Garboesque—"I want to be alone with my enigma"—stance towards his work. Consider his explanation (given in a 1962 lecture) about why his first full-length play, *The Birthday Party,* only ran a week in London, while *The Caretaker* (his second major play) lasted a year in the West End:

> In *The Birthday Party* I employed a certain amount of dashes in the text, between phrases. In *The Caretaker* I cut out the dashes and used dots instead . . . So it is possible to deduce from this that dots are more popular than dashes and that's why *The Caretaker* had a longer run than *The Birthday Party.* The fact that in neither case could you hear the dots and dashes in performance is beside the point. You can't fool the critics for long. They can tell a dot from a dash a mile off, even if they can hear neither.

A clever statement, no doubt, yet one which perhaps underlines a basic reason why Pinter has been elevated to the major league division of 20th-century dramatists. For it could be argued—albeit sarcastically—that if you write inexplicable plays which nonetheless work dramatically, then you might just achieve literary guru status during your own lifetime. Especially if you also win favour with the academic fraternity as well. And become a subject of innumerable critical studies. And have your work dissected in that overblown language of "doctoral-candidate-speak". . . . (p. 38)

[Pinter's] work has almost always found an audience. Which, of course, is a reminder that, whatever the supposedly puzzling nature of his plays, the fact is that they *do* succeed as theatre. A one-time actor, Pinter not only has an instinctual understanding of what works dramatically onstage, but also how to make even the most ambiguous of situations hold an audience.

But, perhaps, the ultimate reason why Pinter's first plays captured one's imagination was due to the fact that he was the first contemporary dramatist to confront the "stale dead terminology" of language today, and discover a profound dramatic power behind the ambiguous nature of words and how we manipulate them. And therefore, though you can attach labels like "theatre of menace" or "theatre of noncommunication" to describe the atmosphere which underscores a play like, say, *The Birthday Party,* Pinter himself believes that what he is ultimately writing about in his early work is silence:

> There are two silences. One when no word is spoken. The other when perhaps a torrent of language is employed . . . We have heard many times that tired, grimy phrase: 'Failure of communication' . . . and this phrase has been fixed to my work quite consistently. I believe the contrary. I think that we communicate only too well in our silence, in what is unsaid, and that what takes place is a continual evasion, desperate rearguard attempts to keep ourselves to ourselves. Communication is too alarming. To enter into someone else's life is too frightening. To disclose to others the poverty within us is too fearsome a possibility.

Silence has largely characterised Pinter's work as a playwright during the past ten years. For though he has directed frequently during this period, and has written several screenplays, he has not tackled a full-length stage play since *Betrayal* in 1978. And yet, during this period, Pinter-the-Obscure has become Pinter-the-Political—a transformation which began in 1984 when his last piece for the theatre, *One for the Road,* was produced. It was a short, sharp shock of a play, in which an interrogator in a nameless totalitarian country systematically berates a tortured prisoner, his wife and their seven year old son. And Pinter—in an interview which accompanied the public text of the piece—not only acknowledged that the work grew out of his concern with the "official torture subscribed to by so many governments"; he also stated that he was doing something in the theatre that he had never done before: namely, jabbing an accusatory finger at the audience, and engaging in a theatrical genre he had previously despised—better known as agit-prop.

Of course, in that same interview, Pinter rightfully argued that a political undercurrent always existed in his work. *The Birthday Party,* for example, had a "central figure who is squeezed by totalitarian forces", while *The Hothouse* (another late fifties play) was "essentially about the abuse of authority". And it is images of authoritarianism which pervade his new play [*Mountain Language*]. (pp. 38-9)

Mountain Language is a highly condensed guided tour through state tyranny. Set in an unspecified country, the play drags us into that nether-world of malevolent officialdom and casual terror. It's a place where a group of women are kept waiting eight hours in the snow outside a prison before being allowed in to see their men (whom one prison officer refers to as "shithouses . . . enemies of the state"). A place where those same women are informed that the state has classified them as "mountain people" who speak a language that has been prescribed. A place where an elderly woman—whose hand has been savaged by a prison guard dog—is not allowed to communicate with her political prisoner son because she speaks only the "mountain language". And a place where that same prisoner is beaten for casually mentioning to a guard that—like him—he too has a wife and three kids.

In short, *Mountain Language* presents us with a series of stark, rather atypical images of political repression. But—of course—like his earlier work, this is also very much a play about the language of silence and its relationship to the language of tyranny. And therefore, in this tightly constructed, yet uncomfortably hollow play, Pinter seems to be reminding us that silence and tyranny form a limited partnership in any totalitarian state.

Obviously it's a subject which Pinter cares for passionately enough about to break his extended period of theatrical silence. For here, the playwright—who was once called (by an over-enthusiastic pair of academics), "a communicator in the paradoxical position of having nothing to say"—makes his political concerns terribly clear, and the result is worthy, yet terribly predictable in its vision of state terror. . . .

Mountain Language could be ultimately seen as more of a pronouncement of Pinter's new-found political activism than as a polemical statement about the brutal grammar of totalitarianism. It's as if the master of the unspoken has met up with an eager convert to an artful sort of agit-prop, and the result leaves one wondering whether Pinter wasn't a far more effective political writer when he left you baffled, but unnerved. (p. 39)

> Douglas Kennedy, "Breaking the Silence," in New Statesman & Society, Vol. 1, No. 21, October 28, 1988, pp. 38-9.

DAVID PRYCE-JONES

Harold Pinter's *Mountain Language* consists of four short scenes, in effect tableaux, lasting altogether about twenty or twenty-five minutes, set around the visit of some women to their men-folk in prison. Not an ordinary prison either, but one wholly outside the rule of law. Nobody will dissent from Pinter's central purpose, which is to show what an unspeakable horror it is when one human being has unrestrained power over another.

In each tableau gaolers callously abuse and insult prisoners and their visitors. In particular they forbid them to use their own language and brutalize them for doing so, only to relent when it is too late. This is actually the state of the Kurds, a people who cling to their language and culture in more than one Middle Eastern country where such expressions of independence are not tolerated. Although Pinter has denied that the play is specifically about "the fate of the Kurdish people", it is clear that in their plight is a metaphor of oppression which he has sought to realize. How to project a pro-Kurdish manifesto beyond its context is a very real difficulty. Members of minorities imprisoned elsewhere are not forbidden the use of their language. Some sort of generalization valid for humanity had to be devised, or else the tableaux would prove a sport of politics, in themselves curiosities. . . .

[In the play], Pinter has chosen English references. Clothes, looks, manners, swearing, are all homegrown. . . . Names to emerge among either visitors or gaolers are also English, Sara Johnson, her husband Charley, Joe Dokes. . . . Distressing as prisons in the land may well be, they are not in fact outside the rule of law like this one. These English references do not make for a generalized condition in which compassion for the Kurds and all oppressed people is natural, but only for implausibility and exaggeration.

What little there is by way of speech is contrived, maybe with the deliberate intention to dramatize the metaphor implicit in forbidding the use of a language. "Lady Duck Muck" is what one gaoler calls a visiting woman. Another of the women has been bitten by a Dobermann pinscher and the gaoler asks about the guard-dog in this strained style: "They are given a name by their parents, and that is their name, that is their *name!* Before they bite, they *state* their name. It's a formal procedure. They state their name and then they bite. What was his name? If you tell me one of our dogs bit this woman without giving his name I will have that dog shot!" Caught between what might equally well have been the irony of an oriental despot or the rigmarole of an English joker, the audience can only titter nervously, unable to decide what the level of fright is supposed to be.

The tableaux begin and end with imposing silences, one or two of them perhaps as long as a minute. There is tension and threat in such freezing, of course, but it seems self-indulgent to have a silence speaking louder than words.

> *David Pryce-Jones, "Expressions of Independence,"*
> *in* The Times Literary Supplement, *No. 4466, No-*
> *vember 4-10, 1988, p. 1228.*

Dennis Potter

1935-

(Born Dennis Christopher George Potter) English dramatist, scriptwriter, novelist, and nonfiction writer.

Potter's controversial novels, films, and television plays often focus on such themes as the consequences of sin, insincerity in love and sexual relations, political disenchantment, and the decay of English culture. Black humor and a strong belief in the power of imagination are prominent in Potter's writing, which he refers to as "non-naturalism," a fusion of fantasy and reality that explores intrinsic worlds and challenges traditional narrative techniques. Praised for his verbose commentaries on social ills, Potter is generally regarded as one of England's most innovative television dramatists. Vincent Canby asserted: "Potter seems to have liberated the conventional narrative to such an extent that one might think he has discovered a new form. He hasn't, but he has . . . set a new standard for all films. . . . He's made writing for television respectable and, possibly, an art."

Potter was born and raised in the Forest of Dean in West England, a coal-mining community where many of his works are set. As a student at Oxford, he became interested in politics, and during his last year there wrote *The Glittering Coffin* (1960), a biting critique of England's social system. After graduation, Potter joined the Labour Party and ran unsuccessfully for a seat in the British House of Commons. This experience forms the basis of his first play, *Vote, Vote, Vote for Nigel Barton* (1965), a political satire that launched Potter's controversial reputation. The British Broadcasting Company (BBC) deemed the play offensive to the Labour Party and changed the ending. Potter's career switch from politician to dramatist was inspired by the onset of psoriatic arthropathy, an excruciating hereditary disease that combines the symptoms of arthritis with psoriasis. Bedridden, Potter began writing as a means of supporting his family. He continues to suffer from the illness several months a year and describes it as the "strange, shadowy ally" that shaped his life.

Many of Potter's television productions have provoked outrage. One of his early works, *The Confidence Course* (1965), brought threats of a lawsuit from the self-improvement programs of the Dale Carnegie school. Potter was nearly prosecuted for blasphemy for *Son of Man* (1969), which depicts Jesus Christ as a hippie carpenter, and *Brimstone and Treacle* (1976) was banned from the BBC for eleven years for its portrayal of the devil bringing a paralyzed, brain-damaged girl out of her catatonic state through rape. *Only Make Believe* (1973) was attacked by critics for indecency but was generally better received than Potter's previous works. In this play, a young angel has been sent to earth to establish credibility with the human race but achieves this only through a perfect sexual performance with a bored housewife. Critics praised Potter's technique of enacting events that are being imagined by an angst-ridden writer and dictated to his secretary. In *Schmoedipus* (1974), Potter maligns humanity's fear of emotion through the account of a middle-aged woman's first confrontation with her illegitimate son. He probes the Oedipal

complex again in his film *Track 29* (1988), a black comedy about an illegitimate boy who becomes his mother's lover.

Potter has achieved popular and critical success with three television mini-series. *Pennies from Heaven* (1981), which is set during the 1940s, revolves around a sheet-music salesman's quest for happiness. Arthur Parker, a libidinous Cockney who roams the country searching for a life as rosy as those in the sentimental songs he sells, ends up going to the gallows for a murder he did not commit but returns from the grave for the happy ending he desired. Critics found the blend of music, humor, and pathos complex and arresting, and *Pennies from Heaven* established a cult following in the United States, inspiring a film version. Potter's custom of having his somber characters lip-synch upbeat songs of the Depression era was repeated in *The Singing Detective* (1988). Philip Marlow, a failing pulp-detective novelist, is stricken with psoriatic arthropathy and occasionally retreats into fantasy to cope with his pain and the hospital's tedium. In his imagination, Philip becomes the hero in his own novels, gives his unfaithful wife her comeuppance, and turns the doleful doctors into a swing band. Acclaimed for its lucid complexity, *The Singing Detective* was described by John J. O'Connor as "an astonishing tour de force." Potter's recent production, *Christabel* (1989), departs from his usual themes. Based on Christabel Bielenberg's memoir, *The Past is Myself*, this play concerns life's uncertainties and the strength of love during World War II. Christabel, a wealthy young British girl, marries a radical German who is captured by the Nazis after his failed assassination attempt on Adolf Hitler. During her efforts to rescue her husband, Christabel becomes more politically conscious of the country's suppressed awareness of Hitler's brutality. Critics observed that Potter's factual plot made *Christabel* more accessible than his other works.

Potter has also written several novels, each characterized by subtle detail and intertwined narratives that reflect the chaotic mood of his plays. *Hide and Seek* (1973), his first novel, examines the essence of creativity. While writing a book, Daniel Miller discovers that he is a character in another writer's novel, with no control over his own life. The writer destroys Miller's marriage and ruins his career before his own fictitious status is also unveiled. A third author, Potter, declares responsibility for the turmoil and hints that he himself is controlled by yet another individual. Reviewers considered *Ticket to Ride* (1986) a more restrained approach to a similar theme. In this work, an amnesiac who arrives in London with no identification but plenty of money sets out to regain his identity. He believes he may have committed a murder, and Potter explores the dark side of human nature as the search for the present uncovers ominous details from the past. *Blackeyes* (1987) is a interweaving of stories that Lorna Sage described as "a whoundunnit." Septuagenarian author Maurice James Kingsley has published his first successful work in nearly twenty years, a novel called *Sugar Bush*, which is based on the life of his niece, Jessica, and her work as a model. Kingsley concludes his novel by having Jessica's fictional counterpart, Blackeyes, drown herself in a shallow fountain with a waterproof list of men who abused her rolled into her vagina. Angry about her uncle's triumph and Blackeye's demise, Jessica determines to redeem herself. Peter S. Prescott commented: "In the way of much contemporary English comedy, *Blackeyes* is clever, intricate and cold as a coroner's chisel."

(See also *Contemporary Authors*, Vol. 107.)

PETER PRINCE

Television dramatist Dennis Potter has chosen to start his career as a novelist by writing a book about writing a book. *Hide and Seek* also presents the spectacle of the author—or rather 'the Author'—and his main character directing remarks at each other and at the reader. By now the general drift of the book will be cosily familiar to most readers of contemporary fiction, though curiously Mr Potter seems to believe he is breaking totally new ground. There are one or two good scenes—I liked especially a little comedy of mistaken identity set in a Shepherd's Bush café—and the dialogue is often sprightly. But on the whole this is a rather modest debut, and Mr Potter's publishers should have thought twice before dubbing it 'the most exciting and impressive novel to be published in this country for years.' Such clumsy putting really does an author no service.

Peter Prince, "Darkest SW3," in New Statesman,
Vol. 86, No. 2224, November 2, 1973, p. 658.

THE TIMES LITERARY SUPPLEMENT

Dennis Potter's first novel [*Hide and Seek*] is a Pirandelloesque re-examination of the themes of his most successful television plays, a dense elaboration on the nature of creativity and the reality of invented things. Yet it is not Pirandello of whom the reader is first reminded during the novel's initial section, but Muriel Spark. As in [her work] *The Comforters*, the central character is aware that he is in a novel. The tone of *Hide and Seek*, however, is not comic but desperate and embattled: Daniel Miller's life, which has led him to a psychiatrist and to separation from his wife Lucy, has been piloted by his author into an obsessive series of contacts with prostitutes; to escape his author he abandons his flat in Shepherd's Bush, his book on Coleridge, and Lucy to flee to a cottage in the place of his birth, the Forest of Dean. So much is the matter of the novel's first section, and it is represented in a language characterized by a ponderous, deliberate awkwardness: Miller's universe, tainted by the author's mind, has a perverse, troubling suggestiveness he can elude only by escaping into that space between word and writer.

The rest of the novel deals with the author's self-justifications, as he first describes events in his life and then attributes them to Miller. The author also lives in Shepherd's Bush, is in the midst of a blocked book on Coleridge, has separated from a wife named Lucy, suffers like Miller from psychotherapy and psoriatic arthropathy, and was born in the Forest of Dean. Although he is at pains to separate himself from his character, the author is driven by the images of degradation and sexuality which bedevil Miller. Indeed, the figure of the writer is wholly successful; scribbling hotly in a room without light, warmth or telephone, he is rancorous, suspicious, jealous, and has a large portion of writer's paranoia.

Coleridge chimes in and out of his life and his novel. As the narration switches from first to third person and back, the writer seeks images of imaginative and semi-religious Glory, echoes of Kubla Khan's Pleasure Dome. Writing—the burrowing into imagination—is the most immediate of these images; others are the Forest, a girl the writer sees in a coffee bar (not recognizing that she is a prostitute), and a Guyanese prostitute. . . . Physical purity, unattainable, is itself linked to Coleridgean caves of ice and spaces of crystal. But even the purity of childhood and nature is soiled: the narrator and the girl in the coffee bar were as children sexually abused by adults in the Forest of Dean, the Guyanese plies her trade in the room where her son sleeps: and only the invention and formal intricacy of fiction offer escape. Towards the end, the writer acknowledges that he too is fictive and will be released into the freedom of the page when the book finishes.

All of this is carefully and complexly done; and if *Hide and Seek* escapes being stifled by its own self-consciousness it is chiefly due to its insistent truth to its own condition as a work of fiction. Yet the final effect is of airlessness, even of aridity; as if the intricacy were in the end really only trickiness.

"Fictitious Freedom," in The Times Literary Supplement, *No. 3740, November 9, 1973, p. 1361.*

ROGER GARFITT

Dennis Potter's first novel [*Hide and Seek*] is an ingenious structure built on a triteness of insight. Daniel Miller is driving desperately across the pages of a novel to escape the manipulations of The Author, who has wrecked his marriage and lost him his job. The Author, for his part, is desperate to deny any connection with that terrible character Miller. What identifies them, however, is the total inability to do anything but read Coleridge to their wives in bed, coupled with visits to a rising number—or should I say, a mounting toll—of prostitutes. But Dennis Potter fails to establish a credible dynamic of identity, which in this case requires a dynamic of style, between Miller, whose taut anguish *is* convincing, and The Author's platitudinous flatulence. (p. 675)

> Roger Garfitt, "Safe Audacity," in The Listener, Vol. 90, No. 2329, November 15, 1973, pp. 674-75.

CLIVE JORDAN

The playwright and polemicist Dennis Potter's first novel **Hide and Seek** is unfortunately . . . a confusing paranoid game played between the Author and his main character, complete with alternative endings and gobbets of literary quotations. Somewhere in it all are fragments of true narrative, glimpses of a rural childhood in the Forest of Dean swamped by the urban experience of lonely coffee-bars and isolated rooms. Marital problems gradually emerge into importance, and the Author who finally takes over is full of a puritan self-disgust partly provoked by that weary old standby of introspective fiction, the sinful encounter with a prostitute. Through the self-questioning stridency comes the feeling of a novel behind the novel, aching to be written if only Dennis Potter would let it—of an innocent childhood which is indescribable for a novelist corrupted by cities. In this form, though, this is the Novel as therapy, for the writer rather than the reader. (p. 65)

> Clive Jordan, "World Enough, and Time," in Encounter, Vol. XLII, No. 2, February, 1974, pp. 61-5.

GARRY O'CONNOR

Dennis Potter's **Only Make Believe** has the basic comic situation of a middle-aged man—in this case a writer—whose wife has left him and who is engaging a secretary in order to begin his latest work, a television script. The script itself . . . has the recondite theme of the existence of angels, and the main character in the script, which the author dictates to his temporary secretary, is a young angel boy, called, appropriately enough, Michael. Michael has great difficulty in establishing his credibility as an angel. It is only a highly dissatisfied housewife who finally experiences his perfection in bed in revenge for her own husband's highly priggish attitude towards permissive sex on television.

This central scene—and a very good one it is—resolves the preoccupation both at the centre of the play within the play, and of Mr Potter's own author, namely whether angels have sex. Sex they have, but whether they really enjoy it is another matter. The funniest section is when the angel Michael is outraged by his rape by the militant woman and flees her bed refusing even to wear the socks she has given him to cover his naked feet.

Mr Potter calls his writer Christopher George. Christopher has mutilated his right hand before the play begins. This affords a further scene exploring the writer's process (apart from seeing it in action when he dictates: excellent mental work all too rarely depicted on the stage) when a doctor comes to dress the burn and tells him he ought to see a psychiatrist. Christopher refuses, as he wishes to guard all his precious interior torment for the play he is writing.

The message Mr Potter seems to be putting across is that, quite opposite to the generally held view of permissiveness in our society today, modern man is imprisoned by his sex, by his energy which is constantly thwarting him and dulling his faculties. It may be that the message is only too lightly portrayed in action—of the angel holding back, crucified on his own sex—yet it would seem to be crucial. But unfortunately in expressing it, Mr Potter has, in my opinion, relied too much on an abrasive form of dialogue which often on the stage comes over as a kind of posture which the nobleness—and interest—of the theme, does not need or warrant. It is this self-conscious abrasiveness, deliberately virile and cynical, which leads one to suspect at its centre a deep sentimentality and a thinness of material, though in the case of **Only Make Believe** the material is far from thin.

Only Make Believe awakens many a wry smile with its intelligence over current attitudes, but it hardly manages very often to awaken a unified response in its audience: it is armchair theatre, enjoyed in solitude.

> Garry O'Connor, in a review of "Only Make Believe," in Plays and Players, Vol. 22, No. 5, February, 1975, p. 39.

RUSSELL DAVIES

The sight of another "novelization" of a television series does not uplift the heart, and those forbidding words "Now a major film from M.G.M." simply pile dread on melancholia. The odds, clearly, were always against Dennis Potter, and this book duly transforms one of his successes into a defeat. It is a great shame. In its original form, **Pennies From Heaven** was called "a personal triumph" for Potter, and that was truer than the cliché allows. Many of us have watched Potter's work—in the last decade at least—with an eye for the drama beneath the drama: the sight of a sensitive man doing battle with a terrible disillusionment which will never quite submit to the process of being spread among the dramatis personae. One feels always for Potter as an individual, for between hope and raging despair there does not seem to exist, for him, the intervening net of cynicism which breaks the fall for most of us. When political faith collapsed and religion rushed in with a damagingly clumsy first-aid, the dramatist was left to fight off nihilism more or less from memory. With memories, indeed. His "nostalgia" puts the word to shame; it is the most strenuous form of spiritual yearning, by which Potter urges us back to an Edenic state which, his intellect recognizes, was never really there. He has acknowledged, for example, that childhood innocence, the Eden of the poets, was always surrounded by the same world of exploitation and betrayal and *selling* (Potter is a fundamentalist in his disgust with commerce) that we see around us now.

But **Pennies From Heaven** found a device—trivial, slight, but vital—to get round all this. The cheap little tunes on its soundtrack, punctuating the action (by stopping it) and filling the head of the music-salesman "hero" Arthur, were perceived to be in some fragmentary way immune from moral decay. It was hard to argue that they really *were* immune: what could be more damning, after all, than the fact that you could sell them across a counter? But there was something, some primeval chirp in these silly old refrains, that kept hope alive. Some unreachable optimism, and even goodness, was kept going in the grooves of the old shellac. You saw it in people's faces within Potter's play, and his present-day audience responded commensurately. Every song embodied a declaration of faith by the beleaguered playwright, and if it was nothing more than "I sing, therefore I am"—a barely verbalized equivalent of whistling in the dark—then so be it.

A novel perforce must cast this device aside. The page is not alive to the sound of music. The primitive sense of release—sob into song—which the television drama offered cannot be provided by third-person narrative. Besides, the very sound of the music filled out the character of Arthur in his role as a song-sheet vendor. It explained things about him, it accounted for the soul we were supposed to sense within his shell of bluff. In the novelized version, for all that tunes may still run through Arthur's head, he might as well be selling soap. The scene, moreover, has been transported away from the leafy lanes of England to the chill of Illinois (presumably for the benefit and comfort of the major film-makers at M.G.M.). Potter is ill at ease here, his dialogue uncharacteristically turbid with unintended colours. " 'You're a—what they call it—? A *fatalist,* right?' he said, touched by awe. 'That's the only word that's left, lover, she smiled . . . ' ". Exchanges like this merely remind one that Potter faced the task of concocting American speech. Under the Hollywood tags, there's an earnest English heart-to-heart in progress, and you can hear its distracting echoes all the time. " 'That's all right, honcy', he responded, with evident relief. 'I've got enough moxie for both us!' " Sadly, he doesn't have it at all.

Potter is not a natural prose narrator, not in a faked America anyway. Partly it's because an element of stage-direction survives in the wooden wording ("Arthur began to shift about again, both in actual physical movements and in his mind . . . "), especially when description is called for. "An early juke was quivering its own brand of music" is a line written from the television scene-setter's point of view: it makes a hole in the atmosphere and involvement drains away. More serious again—though I think this might not have happened if Potter hadn't felt obliged to lay on the verbal vigour for the American audience—is his habit of trying to jazz up exhausted forms of words. "It was already too late. His goose was cooked, and basted with sizzling hot fat" is not better but worse than the original bare cliché.

At least two false endings prolong what is by now an agony. Nothing in the book has helped persuade us that "Arthur, after his fashion, and deeply flawed as he was by his own compromises and evasions, nevertheless retained . . . 'some memory of the Garden of Eden'." . . . It's getting to the stage where we're dealing in memories of memories of memories; but something of the kind will have to suffice if we are to rescue a fragment of uncompromised hope from this recycled matter.

> *Russell Davies, "Memories of the Primeval Chirp,"*
> *in* The Times Literary Supplement, *No. 4108, December 25, 1981, p. 1488.*

MARTIN HOYLE

Dennis Potter is so admirably against all the correct things—the modish, the meretricious, the manufactured, [the critic] Bernard Levin—that one only laments his inability to be *for*

anything except the haziest concept of unspoilt nature and uncorrupted values. The old-fashioned puritanism he professes is one thing; the arid jeering of myopically pharisaic smugness quite another.

The motive force of [*Sufficient Carbohydrate*], his 'first original stage play', is the rage of one Jack Barker, given to tirades against, *inter alia,* adultery, Americanisation and synthetic food—the last despite his employers' mass manufacture of edible junk. A Greek island holiday, engineered by an American colleague to dissuade him tactfully from his bolshie attitude or his job, provides the setting for Anglo-American wife-swapping, a number of clichés and much queasy symbolism.

Jack enunciates sentiments accepted as respectable by parties as divergent as the *Telegraph,* the Greens and worried middle-class liberals, against the dehumanising vulgarity of an increasingly synthetic way of life. His verbal rockets recall a Jimmy Porter sold out, guilt-ridden and on the hard stuff, over twenty years on.

The suspicion that near-hysterical over-statement is the last resort of a playwright uncertain how to develop character or plot is borne out by Mr Potter's creakingly cumbersome stage mechanics. Evidently missing TV's flexibility, he has characters eavesdropping, spying and making unseen but all-observing entrances to chime in with the onstage chat, with an artifice that would have made [Sir Arthur Wing] Pinero blush.

An unexceptionable if familiar message is underlined by stock characters—wistfully quoting Keats, Jack represents declining European culture, ironic, self-lacerating; his colleague's teenage son, all coltish vulnerability and inarticulate sensitivity, even comes out with 'You used me!' to his unwisely tender step-mother—and whopping poetic metaphor (a sporadically passing ship, initially visible only to the yearning Jack).

Not quite witty ('Moderation can be an intolerable vice'), not quite incisive ('He's going to seed faster than dear old England'), not quite symbolic ('People like to eat other people'), laced with fourth-form subtlety (of cigars: 'Putting one of those in my mouth always makes me feel vaguely homosexual'), this not quite necessary play has enough of 'What are you trying to say?' and 'What are we going to do?' and plain 'What?' (I lost count) to make one wonder how familiar the writer is with advances in theatrical convention over the past thirty years.

Finally the bewildered author drifts rudderless through sex-comedy and domestic drama before running aground on valedictory symbolism in the most embarrassing conclusion to any play I have seen. As the cast, gazing into the centre stalls, revealed that they too could see that distant freighter—except for the nasty American, by implication beyond redemption—I realized that the craft contained neither God nor salvation nor hope but a nice TV crew from a drama department with a cargo of that cake that writers of technically adroit shallowness have long since learned both to have and to eat.

> *Martin Hoyle, in a review of "Sufficient Carbohydrate," in* Plays and Players, *No. 365, February, 1984, p. 25.*

BRYAN APPLEYARD

It is impossible to ignore the clinical details. Dennis Potter suffers from psoriatic arthropathy, a disease which combines the symptoms of arthritis and psoriasis. . . .

Potter discusses his disease with detailed enthusiasm. He regards it with wry detachment—after so many years he has sublimated it into a kind of hobby. His family tell him he talks about it a lot, but then that is probably what keeps it out of his work.

Instead there are the familiar Potter qualities: an insistent, melancholic yearning, a ferocious seriousness and a formal awareness which separate him from the English literary pack. It is a willed separation. Potter is rare among the practitioners who depend on the tightly-knit film and television world in that he is perfectly happy to dislike a good deal more than he likes.

"The characteristic mode of modern literature of all kinds is irony", he explains.

> Irony presupposes a form and a convention which is of our time, certainly, but it means you can very seldom do anything other than step back from it. Your facial response is that of the wry smile. Anything truthful, anything painful, anything emotionally threatening gets the same treatment. Only political commitment has escaped and only at the terrible price of having to preach to the converted.

With **Sufficient Carbohydrate** Potter took a risky stand against the ironic mode. He adopted the form of a soap opera with a conventionally pleasurable setting—a Greek island—and with heightened characters and exaggerated plot. It is the kind of package which is daily thrust at us in dozens of different ways; any freshness of response should in theory have been buried long ago.

> But I don't think as a form it is totally redundant [observed Potter]. It allows the release of emotional truths that you couldn't get at in any other way. I wanted the play to live inside the shell of a soap opera. I am sure there's something people like Ibsen and Chekhov would recognize in the form.

The idea is that, instead of ironic distance, the form will offer an unusually direct contact with the energies behind the play. Potter compares the effect he has aimed for to that of religious prose—behind Jack Barker's vision of transcendence lurks the Pauline conception of a conversion in the twinkling of an eye. . . .

[With **Dreamchild**, a film examining the relationship between Lewis Carroll and his inspiration for *Alice in Wonderland*, Alice Hargreaves, Potter] is in high spirits. . . . "I think it's the best thing I've ever done—it's the most complex and yet the most accessible."

The battle between complexity and accessibility is one which, of course, every serious writer in film and television faces. Potter's rarity arises from his uncompromising adherence to the formal challenges of modernist art and yet his insistence on working in these high-cost, and therefore necessarily high-audience, arts. He tried one novel but is now unable to believe in the medium: "I feel the form hasn't got the mileage, the guts, the bravado to be of its time. Nabokov's *Pale Fire* is magnificent of course but each time something like that happens it seems like one more cul-de-sac, one more door closed." Yet he maintains a burgeoning belief in the importance of story-telling and imagery.

It is finally a belief in the imagination and its power to suggest a higher, alternative reality combined with the appalling poignancy of the fact that it can never deliver. The love-songs which magically transformed the milieu of **Pennies from Heaven** and Jack Barker's obsessive pursuit of the vision of a ship crossing the farthest reaches of the horizon gain energy from their artificiality. They are true neither in fact nor in fiction but they evidently possess a more elusive truth.

For them to leap beyond the confines of the art and become true in any wider sense requires a religious commitment which Potter seems perpetually on the verge of making—"I felt sort of vaguely Christian without taking the title". Yet the imagery is now clearly striking closer to home: "Cardinal Hume said, let us find God in the cancer. It caused a lot of offence among so-called Christians. But that is the sort of voice I am willing to attend to."

> *Bryan Appleyard, "A Risky Stand against the Ironic Mode," in* The Times, *London, February 14, 1984, p. 17.*

W STEPHEN GILBERT

It's 13 years since Dennis Potter gave us a novel, though the publishers of his second, **Ticket to Ride,** do not acknowledge even the existence of the first, **Hide and Seek.** Both books reveal a natural novelist, a novelist with the focus and control of a screenwriter, a screenwriter with the subtlety and detail of a novelist.

[The publishers] do Potter a disservice by blurbing the new tale as 'a brilliant psychological thriller'. The expectations thereby set up draw attention to the less engaging aspects of the writing. After parody, disclosure is the least satisfying literary gambit unless done by such stealth that you perceive it only in hindsight. Opening the novel with a protagonist in the grip of amnesia, Potter here fights a long and debilitating battle holding back the full measure of obsession's grip on events. In a simile that rings with defiance he even has his protagonist peer 'like a detective' in the search for history and identity.

John is in obscure flight from home and past. Flight turns to quest. Dream and hallucination fuse memory and encounter. Images turn experience to symbol, symbol to experience. We are full-pitch into obsession and breakdown, paranoia and schizophrenia, priapism and death.

You can't simulate the terror of these things and hope to get there. Potter is the most compelled of writers. His prose—even more than his dialogue at its most anguished and driven (**Double Dare, Angels Are So Few, Only Make Believe** and, for me his finest play, **Follow the Yellow Brick Road**)—is a fury and a fever. It is not overwritten but in every sense it is overwrought and superbly so. Potter is a genius at articulating the intricate, febrile constructs of the inner voice, the possession of the instant. And there is no let-up. 'There could be' he writes 'no escape into silence'.

Even so, **Ticket to Ride** is much more orderly than the broken-backed and over-literary **Hide and Seek.** This time you can feel Potter's movie experience, sense him 'seeing the shots' and panning for you, tracking, pulling focus, dropping in filters and cutaways and, especially, editing with a highly developed rhythmic grasp. He *must* direct a movie.

In the midst of the delirium, Potter places a burst of exquisitely timed and turned dinner-table comedy, followed by black family ritual. Here the central imagery comes into focus. John's sexual disgust stems from the obsessional, smothering knowledge of wild flowers that so exercised his cleric father. The flower/genital axis—Potter writes for instance of 'the recollection of a breathless descent into the tendrils of a plant, and the seep of mauve which came from its bloom' and he has John's father chide the boy with the highly resonant interdiction: 'Please don't say um. Never say um. You are not a bumble bee'—this pollination/penetration correspondence directs us to the book's epigraph and its author, D. H. Lawrence.

The quotation is from Lawrence's poem "Shadows" wherein that equally perfervid novelist/playwright weaves a wee shiver of flower-dream-God-renewal magic. I am irresistibly reminded too of that vivid scene in the "Classroom" chapter of *Women in Love* where the predatory Hermione intrudes on Birkin's lesson about catkins and asks 'When we have knowledge, don't we lose everything but knowledge? . . . If I know about the flower, don't I lose the flower and have only the knowledge?'

In *Ticket to Ride,* Potter writes most deeply and surely about the urge to know and the loss that knowledge brings. His conclusion, corresponding to the end of "Shadows"—'[God] is breaking me down to his own oblivion / to send me forth on a new morning, a new man'—comes out of a, for me, *too* orderly wish to resolve the patterns of hurt. The arrival is less than the journey.

One part of his writing in heat is unusually difficult to come to terms with—again it touches hands with Lawrence—and that is his preoccupation with woman as whore. Perhaps emboldened by the conspicuous success of his depiction of Mrs Hargreaves in the movie *Dreamchild,* Potter here makes a rare attempt to write from a woman's perspective (though, I think, formally filtered through the imaginings of a man) in the interweaved torments of John's seemingly abandoned wife Helen. That Helen used to be a prostitute in a literal sense may be only an obsession of John's, though 'only' hardly does justice to the obsession. But it puts a limit to the role of women in John's breakdown, making all of them actual whores or women who, to a wracked heterosexual puritan man, *behave* like whores (a quibble perhaps on 'abandoned').

The only woman not so characterised is John's fleetingly recalled mother, a woman reduced by a cleft palate to a private sound-language like that of the paralysed Pattie in *Brimstone and Treacle.* Nothing, you feel, is desultory in Pottering—the absent gardener, 'a jobbing Scot', is called Milne and that's neither private nor a joke—and even this disability of the mother's resonates with notions of secret silence, violence and perversion.

The torment of Potter's protagonists is so frequently that of sexual possession that I long to read a comprehensive feminist assessment of his work.

> *W Stephen Gilbert, "Potter's Field," in* The Listener, *Vol. 116, No. 2980, October 2, 1986, p. 23.*

PHILIP SMELT

Dennis Potter is famous for his television plays such as *Pennies from Heaven* and *Blue Remembered Hills,* but he is less well known as a novelist. His latest work of fiction, *Ticket to Ride,* is a confusing psychological thriller about John, an art director who has been sacked from a London advertising agency. The novel opens with John losing his memory while he is on a train journey to London. Having no ticket and no means of identification, just a pocketful of money and a suspicion that he has committed some crime, John books into a Paddington hotel.

From there on, the novel lurches into a sequence of flashbacks: John's former life in the country and his unhappy childhood, punctuated by powerful descriptive passages set in London, and the strange goings-on of his wife, who is portrayed as a fallen woman. When he was sacked from the agency, John began drawing wild flowers in painstaking detail. This obsession is traced back to his tyrannical and meticulously oppressive father, who forced John to study and memorize all the native plants of the woodlands around their vicarage home. But John's attempt at a new career also fails when his publisher rejects the drawings. John's amnesia may be the result of problems with his work; although there is a suggestion that his memory loss is a reaction to some unspeakable (and effectively unspoken) act of violence. The only certain thing is that Potter avoids any kind of clarity.

What results is an impressionistic collection of disjointed episodes, all beautifully described but studiously and disappointingly vague. The author obviously dislikes what he sees as the dissipation of London life—the litter of fast-food hamburgers, the "sardonic . . . working-class males" and the jaded prostitutes—all part of "A scum left by the receding bilge". But the countryside retreat of the amnesiac anti-hero is also the scene of desperate unhappiness. John's wife, Helen, whom he first met in a London hotel in some fold of his tortured memory, wanders from crisis to crisis, identified, enigmatically, with the London whores, with their "heavy eyelids and a crimson gash of a mouth", who form the multitude of "soiled creatures passing up and down the street". Bemused by the emotional waywardness of her husband, and frightened by his sudden changes of mood, Helen takes comfort in the dark possibilities presented by a kitchen knife.

There is no resolution of any of these anxieties. By the end of the novel, John's memory may or may not have returned; and Helen may be the victim, or the perpetrator, of a chilling crime. This is a depressing novel, but the psychological thrill is watered down by its mannered style and complex structure, which promise an exciting journey but never seem to get us very far.

> *Philip Smelt, "Among the Soiled Creatures," in* The Times Literary Supplement, *No. 4359, October 17, 1986, p. 1169.*

JOHN SUTHERLAND

The situation of Dennis Potter's *Ticket to Ride* (like the title) has a slightly used feel to it. A man comes to consciousness on an Inter-City train. He has no memory, and no clues to his identity on his person. 'I? Who is I?' he asks himself. On arrival at Paddington the station announcer gives details of a train departing for Cornwall 'and Estrangement'. To his alienated (or new-born) eye, 'the station forecourt was a gaseous swamp in which noisy and ungainly bipeds moved with difficulty, baying and grunting, stickied and unclean. How do such shambling creatures reproduce themselves? Sticks of bone and sinew poking into hairy holes.'

One grits one's teeth expecting pages of Gabriel Josipovici or Martin Amis-style prose of defamiliarisation. But, gratefully, the narrative promptly exfoliates into a series of hard and sequential plot lines. Intercut scenes to his deserted wife and house reveal that the traveller is John, an advertising man. John has just been let go from his agency. But there is another murderous John within him: bred by childhood rebellion against his puritanical father. This newly released self has come to London to kill a whore, Penny. Penny is, it emerges, the previous (and murderous) self of John's respectable wife, Helen. The bloody purging of their pasts moves the novel from experimental fantasia to conventional thriller.

Ticket to Ride introduces a number of familiar Potter themes, devices and situations: guilty paid-for sex in hotels, doubles, the indelible residues of childhood guilt, love, murder, and the insubstantiality of middle-class decencies. But the amnesia gimmick suggests a direct inspiration in the *film noir* of the Forties and Fifties. It was used, for instance, by Hitchcock in *Spellbound,* where the hero loses his memory so as to repress the childhood killing of a brother. Less celebrated is Victor Savile's blacker than black *The Long Wait* (1954), where the amnesiac hero comes to by a car wreck, with even his finger prints burned off. And (not to give it away) the ending of *Ticket to Ride* seems to owe something to the tricksy last scene of Fritz Lang's *The Woman in the Window* (1945). Potter's addiction to Hollywood musicals is well-known. I suspect his art may be as steeped in the sinister screen melodramas he watched in his boyhood. (pp. 14-15)

> John Sutherland, "Fiction and the Poverty of Theory," in London Review of Books, *Vol. 8, No. 20, November, 1986, pp. 14-15.*

JULIAN SYMONS

Blackeyes, like Potter's recent TV success *The Singing Detective,* offers an elaborately layered structure of interlaced stories. Blackeyes is a character in a commercially successful novel written by the 77-year-old Maurice James Kingsley. She is a model much in demand for commercial advertising, and also in sexual demand among the producers, photographers and other showbiz figures who have dealings with her. She drowns herself in the Round Pond in Kensington Gardens, her naked body containing a rolled-up bit of paper in her vagina listing the names of all the men who have used her.

That is Kingsley's novel. But we are concerned also with his niece Jessica, whose experiences as a model have provided Kingsley's material, unwisely given to him by her in a series of letters and lunches. Kingsley induced his niece to masturbate him when she was a child, and she fed him material in the expectation that the novel would be regarded as 'a ludicrous fantasy of his testosterone imperialism'. Infuriated by the success the book has brought him, she sets out to write the work that will expose him. The work in hand goes further, however, than Jessica's imagination. There are scenes providing a postscript to Kingsley's book, in which the sexual villains have roles as murder suspects, for Jessica emulates Blackeyes by putting the deadly roll of paper into her vagina and drowning herself in the Round Pond. And that is still not quite all, for near the end of the book D. Potter appears (well, an author writing in the first person), saying things like 'it ill becomes the present writer to make snide remarks about his elderly colleague', and when Jessica as well as Blackeyes has drowned, this voice tells us that he is 'waiting outside her door, ready to claim her' as a character in his own novel *Blackeyes. . . .*

[The Singing Detective's] travails in hospital were much more interesting than the subordinate theme of his imagined incoherent thriller, and here the personality of Kingsley and the occasions surrounding his novel have a vividness lacking in the rest of the story. The scene in which Blackeyes gets her first job as a model by making love to a bottle of body lotion is marvellously done. Kingsley dragging his ancient body out of bed, caressing the teddy bear he takes under the covers with him, being interviewed by a crass New Journalist, are all truly imagined and seen, where Jessica's divergence from 'Kingsley's version' seems no more than an ingenious device.

The basic theme is the humiliation of women by men. Blackeyes/Jessica is drooled over by almost every male who looks at her, sexually abused in childhood, rebuked when she resists rape, in general treated simply as an object to be penetrated. When Kingsley hears from Jessica at lunch the story of that first model session he 'practically dribbles over the Roquefort', and other men are similarly affected. This would-be moral tale, however, surely finds its resonance and interest in the very material it deplores, lingering over Blackeyes/Jessica's caressing gestures with the body lotion, the attempted rape, the sticky snake that Kingsley makes Jessica stroke. The literary cartwheels and handstands with which Potter dresses up a hot-eyed sexual puritanism about what might be called the Monroe syndrome may succeed in a television version, but to use the theme as basis for an effective novel calls for subtleties of a different kind from those Dennis Potter can command.

> Julian Symons, "Literary Cartwheels," in The Listener, *Vol. 118, No. 3031, October 1, 1987, p. 22.*

NICK KIMBERLEY

Jessica is a model whose life has been turned into fiction by her uncle, Maurice James Kingsley. The book's success revives his ailing literary career, but Jessica's not pleased with what he's done with her experiences. Blackeyes (her fictionalised name) ends up drowning herself in the Round Pond at Kensington Gardens. No wonder Jessica plots revenge, rewriting the narrative in real life, producing a new ending.

That's the skeleton of *Blackeyes;* the three narratives (Jessica's life, Kingsley's novelisation of it, the real-life rewrite) produce a fourth, the novel we're reading. Towards the end, Potter reminds us that 'the present writer' is using Kingsley's story just as Kingsley used Jessica's. Wheels within wheels; Potter doesn't want us to forget that fiction is artifice. But artifice at a price: at one point, Jessica wonders, 'How many times . . . would allegedly sympathetic accounts of the manifold ways in which women were so regularly humiliated be nothing more than yet further exercises of the same impulse, the identical power?'

Good question; but there's a bit of self-congratulation here, as if Potter were saying, 'I know how these terrible men work, girls, but you can count on me to do it differently.' Yet in order to achieve that purity of intent, he has to play lascivious games with Blackeyes' modelling career. To chastise the awful male novelist, he presents us with Maurice James Kingsley (who has three names, while Jessica has only one, and Blackeyes almost none), an old windbag who peppers his speech and prose with orotund quotations. But, of course,

Potter's the only one who can identify all the quotes, and has to alert his less erudite readers by doing a Kingsley himself.

I should say that this is all done with skill. Potter layers his narrative so that we're never sure which of the four (or more) stories we're reading. His years of TV experience show up in the way he uses televisual devices: voice-overs, dissolves, flashbacks. (p. 29)

Perhaps the story would best have been told on television. The jocular irony that runs throughout would have had to find a more subtle form; the presumably deliberate recourse to cliché . . . might seem less glaring; and poeticised infelicities (a sentence with the words 'silver . . . sliver . . . slither . . . shimmer' in quick succession) could disappear altogether.

But we haven't got a TV play, we've got a novel—one which, while bemoaning the fate of women in men's fiction, still achieves narrative symmetry by sacrificing Jessica. And one which, in order to explain away Kingsley's grubbiness of spirit and Jessica's vengefulness, takes refuge in Jessica's childhood experience of sexual abuse, replayed in hazy flashback. The mistreatment of women has to take the form of physical trauma, whose Freudian resonance does nothing to explain the spectrum of abuse Jessica suffers. *Blackeyes* teases us with its knowingness, dazzles us with its virtuosity, but in the end is only a hollow act of auto-deconstruction. (p. 30)

Nick Kimberley, "Oh My Darling," in New Statesman, *Vol. 114, No. 2949, October 2, 1987, pp. 29-30.*

LORNA SAGE

A 'thriller' in the literal (not the publishing trade) sense, *Blackeyes* is a richly devious tale. It has plenty of those woozy, vertiginous dissolves which fans of *The Singing Detective* will recognise with groans of joy, plus the cutting—in the end self-lacerating—edge that distinguishes Dennis Potter from most of our other dealers in nostalgia.

The villain of the piece is 'veteran' novelist Maurice James Kingsley, a beautifully characterised, pompous old devil who, not having written anything (except in the *Spectator*) for 20 years, suddenly comes up with a topical, sentimental-sadistic study of the wasted life of a model girl, Blackeyes. Kingsley's novel *Sugar Bush* (of which we're given nasty-but-nice slices) enables readers to eat their cake and have it, and is hotly tipped for the Booker [Prize]; it is also stolen from the experiences of his niece Jessica, who realises that she violently resents his pandering display of her as a passive, 'enigmatic' victim, and who sets about unravelling his story and liberating Blackeyes from the old man's wet dreams.

It's the usual detective formula turned inside out, a 'whoundunnit.' Jessica has to fight her way out of the script already written, a set of images of herself that aren't just Kingsley's, but most men's, common property:

> Kingsley's narrative had ended with the water smoothing itself out over the black hair of the girl . . . The . . . additions to *Sugar Bush* . . . were like a ramshackle annexe built on to the side of a small Georgian house . . . hammer and nails and hardboard brought to the now muddied-up site by Jessica.

Jessica is armed only with her fugitive memories and fanta-

sies, or (of course) those Potter chooses to lend her, delving back into childhood, into those old songs that constitute for him the music of time, into Nabokov, into Mills and Boon . . . The new ending is ingenious, impossible, and very persuasive—though evidently not Georgian enough for the Booker.

Lorna Sage, "Old Man's Dream," in The Observer, *October 4, 1987, p. 27.*

FRANCIS KING

[In Dennis Potter's *Blackeyes*], Maurice James Kingsley, a 77-year-old author, has stolen his niece, a model called Jessica, for the central character, Blackeyes, of the novel, *Sugar Bush,* which has amazed everyone, not least Kingsley himself, by its success. (As Potter puts it: 'He had not sunk so low as to have one of his now very occasional Occasional Pieces rejected by the *Spectator* or accepted by the *Daily Telegraph,* but there had been little hint that his dried-up old frame was going to produce such a late bloom').

But if Kingsley has stolen his niece, she, in the manner of one of those people who deliberately leave out money on a table in the hope of incriminating a maid or a cleaner, has all but forced him to do so. She has done this in the expectation that he will suffer the humiliation of having the resulting novel, so far outside the range of 'a rather unsavoury eccentric with odd opinions, bizarre habits, and dated, almost *fin-de-siècle* mannerisms', either rejected or dismissed with scorn by reviewers. When, on the contrary, his tale of a model from her first audition to her suicide, ten years later, by drowning in the Round Pond (surely a difficult feat in waters so shallow?), has become a strong contender for the Booker Prize, Jessica sets about 'deconstructing' it (the buzz word is Potter's) in order to put the truth—or, at least, *her* truth—back into his subversions.

The book therefore constantly shifts—often so abruptly that it takes some time for the reader to grasp that a shift has taken place—between Kingsley's story and Jessica's. Jessica's story is the truer of the two, since it derives directly from memory, whereas Kingsley's derives from memory through the mediation both of another person (Jessica) and of his own creativity. But in no absolute sense can Jessica's story be true, since memory itself can never be absolutely true. In addition to this pair of stories, there are two others. One is the story, occupying only one chapter, of an infatuated young man, Jeff, who recounts in the first person how he pays a visit to Blackeyes in her flat. The other is the story of Potter himself, who tells the story of how Kingsley, Jessica and Jeff tell their stories.

It will be clear that Potter is here up to what has now become a fashionable novelistic exercise or game. The blurb characterises this shuffling of conflicting realities as 'a manipulation of genres and . . . teasing interplay of fictional narratives'—which will do well enough. At the close of Kingsley's narrative, he kills off Jessica, in her fictional persona of Blackeyes, by that improbable act of self-drowning in the Round Pond. But in her narrative, Jessica kills Kingsley first, stamping him to death beneath a high-heeled shoe; then makes out a list of all the men who have ever exploited her, which she stuffs, in a small water-proof pouch, into her vagina, to be found by the police; and then sets off to drown herself. But in what sense is this murder of Kingsley any more 'true' than anything else in the book? Does Jessica dream it? Or does it really happen? No definite answer is possible.

Kingsley, the half-forgotten, septuagenarian writer who briefly becomes as much of a cult as the yo-yo or pogo-stick, is an entertainingly repulsive creation. Jessica's hatred of him derives from her childhood when, having bought her an expensive doll, he then sexually abused her. Now, in impotent old age, he in effect sexually abuses a pet, one-eyed teddy-bear, which he addresses, in the manner of W. C. Fields, as 'my little chickadee'. But if one tries to find any real-life prototype for this exemplar of Potter's dictum, 'Old men do not forget, they fumble. And grope,' it can only be in the past.

This ingenious and often entertaining novel suffers from another, graver flaw. If a book is to consist of the interweaving of narratives by wholly different people, then those narratives should surely be wholly different from each other in style. Potter lacks the ventriloquial ability to achieve this. Whereas the subject-matter of the narratives varies brilliantly, their styles hardly do so. The rhythms have the same kind of choppiness, the images spring the same kind of brutal surprises. This sense of sameness is fatal.

Blackeyes is at once nobody and all body. In creating her out of the stuff of Jessica and his perverted dreams, Kingsley has produced what is, in effect, a beautiful doll, as incapable of an orgasm (as she repeatedly tells people) as of any true emotion. Jessica herself hardly seems more real, except in that final act of revenge against all the men, Kingsley above all, who have exploited her.

Except when the works cough up an occasional spanner—for example 'like' used instead of 'as' as a conjunction—this is a meticulously engineered book, full of acrid satire at the expense of the literary world and advertising. It also has a lot of interest to say on the fashionable subject of male exploitation of women and, in particular, of beautiful women. (At one point, a woman says to Blackeyes, 'Don't you think you'd be better off in bed, my dear?' This is what, in effect, men are constantly saying to her). But it remains a book more to puzzle over than to enjoy, more to admire for the dexterity of its dissection of the dead than to love for the eloquence of its celebration of the living. (pp. 38-40)

> *Francis King, "Drowning in Shallow Water," in* The Spectator, *Vol. 259, No. 8308, October 10, 1987, pp. 38-40.*

JOHN J. O'CONNOR

These are not the best of times for those of us who are convinced that television has the potential to be something more than a receptacle for slick formula entertainments. But then, every so often, a production comes along to demonstrate conclusively that the medium can indeed be every bit as challenging and compelling as the very best of film and theater to be found on the contemporary scene. The latest conspicuous example is **The Singing Detective**. . . .

The plot cannot be summarized in one of those tidy one-line concept "bites" treasured by television executives. At the heart of the story is Philip E. Marlow, a British writer of cheap detective fiction. With that last name, the first name of Philip may have seemed inevitable, but he would have been happier with Christopher. In any event, he has been hospital-

ized with an excruciatingly acute case of psoriasis that has left him looking as if his entire body was scalded.

Plagued with high fevers, he drifts between the present and the past, between reality and fiction, specifically the fiction of his first novel, *The Singing Detective,* which he now sets about rewriting in his mind. So we get Marlow as hospital patient, trapped in his diseased skin and railing like some modern-day Job; Marlow as a 10-year-old, reliving key events that will haunt the rest of his life, and Marlow as the hero of his own novel, pursuing 1940's villains who may or may not be Nazis and occasionally pausing to sing a song as leader of a small dance-club band. Layer is placed upon layer, interweaving and overlapping, until Marlow is finally realized whole and inevitable. It is an astonishing tour de force.

The Singing Detective is written by Dennis Potter, who long ago decided he would work in television as opposed to film or theater because, at least for a time, the newer medium offered a mass audience and "the possibility of a common culture." As his television credits have accumulated over the years, Mr. Potter has made clear that he is not afraid to break the rules. Indeed, he is quite insistent about it. . . .

As in *Pennies From Heaven,* the characters in *The Singing Detective* are, at the most unlikely moments, apt to break into song, or at least to begin miming the words to popular recordings from the 1940's, everything from "Sunny Side of the Street" to "Don't Fence Me In," as interpreted by Bing Crosby and the Andrews Sisters. In one scene . . ., for instance, the smug, ignorant doctors who examine the embittered Marlow suddenly break into a full-scale production number of "Dem Bones, Dem Dry Bones" featuring all the patients and the entire staff of the hospital ward. Marlow has a wicked imagination.

Here is a television mini-series that is definitely not for the kiddies or perpetual adolescents of any stripe. Mr. Potter is very serious, even about his humor, which tends to have a Swiftian kick. Getting a therapeutic body greasing from an attractive young nurse and trying desperately to forestall any erotic urges, Marlow strains to think of something boring. Among his candidates: A speech by Edward Heath; a sentence, a very long sentence by Bernard Levin; everything in *Punch;* the bloody Irish; the Bible. The language occasionally is, to put it mildly, quite vivid, and some of the sex scenes are as explicit as family television is likely to get, even in these permissive days. . . .

The Singing Detective is strong stuff. It can be argued, I suppose, that the drama is intentionally ugly in its use of a protagonist covered with sores. Perhaps it is as ugly and as devastating as the Iran-contra scandal, say, or the AIDS epidemic or the phenomenon of the homeless. This is not just another serving of television escapism.

> *John J. O'Connor, " 'Singing Detective,' BBC Series," in* The New York Times, *January 6, 1988, p. C26.*

VINCENT CANBY

Philip E. Marlow, 10, sits high in a tree in the Forest of Dean, which, with its abundant, heavy foliage, looks as if it might once have sheltered Robin Hood, Will Scarlet, Friar Tuck and the others. The Forest of Dean is, instead, a kind of seed covering for West Gloucestershire's sooty, barren coal-mining villages, where lives are as bleak as the forest is rich.

The boy turns toward the camera. He stares at it without self-consciousness. "When I grow up," he says, "I'm going to live forever and ever, since, in my opinion, you don't have to die unless you want to." When he grows up, he's also going to have books and shelves just for books and a whole tin of evaporated milk and a whole tin of peaches—"I bloody be mind, I bloody damned buggerin' well be. And I shall curse." When he grows up, everything will be all right. When he grows up, he shall be a detective. "I'll find out things. I'll find out."

Nearly 40 years later, Philip Marlow is not a detective. He's a wreck of a man, but he's still trying to find out things.

What is one of the wittiest, wordiest, singingest-dancingest, most ambitious, freshest, most serious, least solemn movies of the year isn't, strictly speaking, a movie at all.

It's *The Singing Detective,* Dennis Potter's BBC-Television mini-series. . . . John J. O'Connor, of *The New York Times* [see excerpt above] and other television critics have, with good reason, already raved about the show. Now it's the turn of the rest of us. (p. H1)

It is not a film for the *Forsyte Saga* crowd. A lot of it is as nasty as the imagination of a furtive, guilt-ridden 10-year-old boy. When men and women come together in *The Singing Detective,* they don't make love. They grunt and sweat and are in such hurries they never have time to remove any clothing except the immediate impedimenta.

"Do you think sex is dirty?" someone once asked Woody Allen. The answer: "Only when it's fun." It's not fun in *The Singing Detective.* It's often mean, at best joyless. Betrayals, real and imagined, are cruel. The language sometimes sounds like elevated graffiti.

This is not to say that *The Singing Detective* is perfect.

Toward the end of the sixth hour, wrong decisions are made. The timing goes awry. The psychiatrist achieves his therapeutic effects, it seems, almost instantaneously. Deliverance is won with more ease than one has a right to expect from all that has gone before. The story concludes before the cameras stop.

These are minor reservations about a work that is truly innovative, partially for its heedless length on behalf of a script that was never a literary classic or an overweight, pre-sold best-seller, and partially for the invigorating way that it fuses the past with the present, the fantastic with the real. The result is a film of a density more often associated with the literary form than with the cinematic.

The Singing Detective is a writer's movie. . . . [It] seems almost drunk on the technical possibilities available only to film makers.

Sequential events are seen out of all order and sometimes so quickly that the effects are subliminal. Unrelated shots are intercut without, initially, apparent purpose. The wrong sounds are connected to the wrong images. (pp. H1, H8)

The Singing Detective is more of a movie than anything one is likely to see in most theaters these days. It enters the intellect not as a series of received ideas. It works on the senses first, through an accumulation of visual and aural impressions. They evoke everything from the helpless laughter of

burlesque and the satisfying confusion of an utterly incomprehensible mystery story to the elation of hearing words turned upside down and inside out, as if understood for the first time.

The film proceeds simultaneously on three and sometimes four levels. Philip Marlow, now in exhausted middle age, lies in a London hospital ward, his crippled hands bandaged, his arms, legs, torso and face a mass of scaly skin and sores that, when greased by cold cream, burn like wounds doused with iodine.

Philip has retreated into his body and become its raging prisoner. He suffers from arthritic psoriasis, which is, it seems, psychosomatic in large part. In the outside world he was a writer of paperback mysteries (now out of print) featuring a beefy, dime store-suave private eye who, being the leader of a 1940's dance band, is known as the Singing Detective.

Philip is at the end of his tether, but he can't let go. He lies on his bed, furious, humiliated, swearing at the imbecilities of the doctors and nurses who address him with the collective "we." His mind won't rest. It goes careering off into a rewrite of his first *Singing Detective* tale, into fantasies about his unfaithful, scheming wife, Nicola, and into memories of his childhood in the Forest of Dean as the son of a stoic coal miner and a desperately unhappy mother.

Sometimes the memories, fantasies, suspicions and present circumstances become hopelessly muddled in his brain. Fictional characters become real and real characters become fictional. He takes great pleasure in imagining the dialogue for his wife's trysts with her lover, who plans to steal an old screenplay Philip once wrote based on *The Singing Detective.*

When, finally, the lover turns on Nicola, who had wanted to play the lead in the screen adaptation, Philip laughs out loud as he has the lover say to the double-crossed, double-crossing wife, "Don't you think you're just a tiny bit old?"

In his restless imagination, Philip himself is the Singing Detective, wearing what seems to be an unconvincing, dark auburn toupee with a pencil-thin, dark auburn mustache to match. . . .

[He] is caught up in a caper involving the body of a nude woman fished out of the Thames and his latest client, who seems to be a Russian agent with mysterious ties to the Nazis. The body sometimes looks like his wife, sometimes his mother, sometimes like a beautiful hooker.

When the hospitalized Philip is really up against the wall, when he might will himself dead if that were possible, he retreats still further from the ward. With his eyes wide open, smiling at his own deviousness, he watches the patronizing doctors who, for his delight, suddenly break into a syncopated, furiously funny, lip-synched version of "Dem Bones, Dem Bones, Dem Dry Bones."

In the middle of the night, a palsied, senile old man, who usually can't walk without help, manages to crawl over to Philip's bed and, in a ludicrous confirmation of everything Philip thinks about sex, attempts to rape him in the fond belief that Philip is his wife.

How did Philip come to this hysterical, doomed corner?

The question is: Who dunit?

From Sophocles and Shakespeare, through Ibsen, O'Neill,

Beckett and *As the World Turns,* a large portion of our dramatic literature depends on events, usually terrible, that have taken place before the lights come up on the imperfect world of the present. What happened? Why? Who is responsible?

The past holds the answers. In most plays and films, the answers remain immutable, frozen in time like fossils in deposits of asphalt. All one has to do is dig in the right place to find them.

In Dennis Potter's view, this is a rather too comforting concept of the past. It is why he calls nostalgia "a very second-rate emotion." It preserves the illusion of chronological sequence and progress, with the past kept safely to the rear. Time is tamed. For all of its unpleasant secrets, which can rise up to transform the present, the past remains fixed. It is an orderly, knowable ghost.

Not so in *The Singing Detective* in which the past, as Mr. Potter once said in a television interview, rides alongside the present and flails at it. In return, the present twists and reshapes the past for its own ends. . . .

Mr. Potter and Jon Amiel, the director whose huge contribution should not be underestimated, evoke what might be described as the non-present-tense portions of *The Singing Detective* in an exhilarating, freewheeling way. They out-dare other film makers. *The Singing Detective* has an exuberance more often found in the contemporary musical theater, where the leapfrogging over reality is taken as a matter of course. Along with everything else, the film is an entertainment.

The time covered reaches from the final days of World War II ("War Rushing to Its End!" says one headline in Philip's memory, to which he responds, "I've always liked a good exclamation mark") to Margaret Thatcher's England, which Philip loathes. As real, imagined and remembered images succeed one another, sometimes to be repeated somewhat differently, there comes into view a world of extraordinary texture.

There is, first off, Philip Marlow's hospital ward with a cast of characters that includes a cheerful, dying Pakistani who understands Philip's "Hey, nig-nog" as the term of endearment it is under such circumstances; a pretty, exceptionally wise nurse, whom no ward should be without; a prissy cardiac patient, who fusses about the temperature of his tea and attempts to teach manners to a slob of a younger man, who has the next bed and moves his lips as he reads (by coincidence) an ancient copy of *The Singing Detective.*

None of the people is more understanding than the hospital psychiatrist, a Scotsman who finally takes on Philip Marlow's case, matching each of Marlow's hilariously scathing put-downs with one in kind. . . .

Most works of fiction about writers remain as remote to the rest of us as novels set in academe, written by people who, during sabbaticals from their sanctuaries, attempt to reinvent the world on a university campus the size of the head of a pin. They are parochial, self-referential. *The Singing Detective,* however, has less to do with the lot of the blocked writer than with a particular man in the grips of a gigantic depression, and who just happens to have the gift of gab of a dark, roaring angel. . . .

Mr. Potter's screenplay is remarkable not only for its achieved seriousness and lucid complexity but also for having (in American eyes, at least) achieved production. It couldn't

happen here. This is an original work, not an adaptation, but something conceived as a television play by a writer who has spent most of his career working in television. . . .

In the course of an interview with Mr. Potter, which was broadcast . . . to introduce *The Singing Detective* last January, clips from earlier Potter works were shown, including his *Follow the Yellow Brick Road* (1972). In it, Denholm Elliot, playing a maniacal actor who has become popular as a television product spokesman has a memorable speech in which he defends the kind of commercial television that Americans know best.

"Commercials are clean," he says with fury at those who look down their noses at commercial television.

> There are happy families in commercials. Husbands and wives who love each other. They have sunshine and laughter, and kids playing in the meadows. Nobody mocks the finest human aspirations. There's no deliberate wallowing in vice and evil.

In *The Singing Detective* Mr. Potter demonstrates that television needn't be a wasteland inhabited solely by commercials, sitcoms and crime shows. There are other possibilities, both for television and, by extension, the theatrical film. . . .

Mr. Potter seems to have liberated the conventional narrative to such an extent that one might think he has discovered a new form. He hasn't, but he has used his freedom to set a new standard for all films. He has also, single-handedly, restored the reputation of the screenwriter, at least in television. He's made writing for television respectable and, possibly, an art. (p. H8)

> *Vincent Canby, "Is the Year's Best Film on TV?"*
> *in* The New York Times, *July 10, 1988, pp. H1, H8.*

GRAHAM FULLER

Like *The Singing Detective,* Dennis Potter's *Blackeyes* unfurls an elliptical mystery about a beautiful young woman discovered naked and drowned. In each, she is the fuck-fantasy scapegoat of a writer "hero" embittered by sexual disgust and professional mediocrity—except here her creator is not a psoriatic author of pulp thrillers, but a foul relic of the London literati who, at 77, has hit the best-seller lists with *Sugar Bush,* his first offering in 27 years.

For his storyline, Maurice James Kingsley has purloined the former career of his niece, Jessica, a fashion plate—known as Blackeyes—licked clean of emotion by every advertising executive and photographer (and, of course, by Kingsley and Potter) who feasted on her pliant flesh. Jessica volunteered her confessions to Kingsley hoping for catharsis but, enraged by the fictional Blackeyes's watery fate (she's found with her hate-list of lovers tucked into her vagina), she decides to reinvent the novel's ending in life and force Kingsley into his own novel.

Never one to neglect the miasmic sway of the past, Potter informs us that—surprise, surprise—Uncle Maurice molested the child Jessica at the very moment he realized he was a failure. It's the sweeping of this primal dirt under the carpet which has resulted in Jessica's self-destructive promiscuity, just as Marlow's mother's adultery inspired his sex-loathing in *The Singing Detective.*

As in much of Potter's work, the miseen-scène loops around the now and the before (both real and imagined). The overinflated *Sugar Bush* meshes with Jessica's current musings, her sordid recollections, and the happy ending, culled from the Barbara Cartland school, which she appends to Kingsley's original—and which, if you want, you can choose as *your* ending.

Potter is a misogynist who gives men even shorter shrift than women. Jessica is abused by her lovers, by the sententious driveler Kingsley, and even by the one decent male character, the adman Jeff. Her main persecutor, however, is Potter. Sardonically intruding into the last quarter with a God-like "I," he implicates us by his prurient narration of Jessica. In the very last line of *Blackeyes,* it's Potter who is the stranger "waiting outside her door, ready to claim her." . . .

In the words of the caricatured New Journalist who interviews Kingsley, Potter is satirically "mediating sexism and style"—although that's beyond Kingsley's ken. Potter has denied that *The Singing Detective* is autobiographical, but as a writer who writes about writers he is a front-runner in the reflexivity stakes. Kingsley (with his teddy bear and touching personal habits) is a self-detonating portrait of the artist as an old man. Of course, neither he nor Marlow is in Potter's league.

Blackeyes delights in its own ingenious artifice. Trouble is, the spin and gloss Potter puts on every phrase undercuts any real sympathy we may feel for Jessica. She may yet be screwed more palpably when an actress plays her in the miniseries Potter is adapting from the book. That his characters are fleshier on the screen than they are on the page is of little comfort to Jessica.

> Graham Fuller, "Panty Raid," in The Village Voice, *Vol. XXXIII, No. 44, November 1, 1988, p. 62.*

RICHARD CORLISS

A sheet-music salesman reels through the Depression with murder on his mind, adultery on his conscience and a song in his heart. A young man walks into an English home to burgle a loveless couple and rape their brain-damaged daughter. An American woman, troubled by fantasies of her lost child, walks out on her philandering oaf of a husband, whom she may have stabbed to death. An aging British novelist pilfers the life of his beautiful niece for the plot of his new book. Another novelist, strapped to a hospital bed with a grotesquely disfiguring skin disease, plots deadly revenge on all those who have loved him not quite enough.

Welcome to the world of English writer Dennis Potter: a nightmare realm of domestic violence, scored to the haunting lilt of pop standards. His output embraces dozens of television plays, half a dozen screenplays and two novels. But the range of Potter's work is less impressive than its searing ferocity and compassion. His haunted characters dwell in the surreal land we all inhabit, as we float vagrantly from suffocating reality to liberating fantasy, from pessimism to possibility, from fear to hope—and then back, always back again, when we realize that the conditional tense holds even more horror than the present. Ultimately a Potter protagonist is likely to realize, like Dorothy back from Oz, that life is best endured at home. Just plant a bitter smile on your face and whistle something sweet in the dark. (pp. 90, E6)

Novelist Julian Barnes has described Potter as a "Christian socialist with a running edge of apocalyptic disgust." And Potter's works have provoked disgust in the more easily shockable segments of the British public. The tabloid press denounced the [*Singing Detective*] series as pornography, and as Potter recalls, "one Member of Parliament got up on his hind legs and said that he'd counted the number of swear words and bare bums. But that's partly because television is taken more seriously in England, which means more seriously by the fools as well." One scene—a flashback of a desperate encounter between the writer's mother and her husband's best friend—was sexually explicit, even by the liberal standards of British TV. "There was a debate about it at BBC," Potter says, "but they decided to let it go uncut. And in fact the consequences of that particular adultery were illness and death and great misery. So it could hardly be held up as an invitation to promiscuity." (pp. E6, E8)

On the suppurating surface . . . , Philip Marlow is every bit as tortured and brilliant as the man who created him. Marlow, who relishes the cheap irony that his name echoes that of Raymond Chandler's famed sleuth, is a failed novelist hitting 50 with a terrifying thud. His career has been sidetracked by illness and bile. His marriage to an actress is just an awful memory. Now he lies in a London hospital, racked with psoriatic arthritis, a crippling condition of the skin and bones. The pain and the pain-killers force Marlow's mind down strange old country lanes and treacherous culs-de-sac. Figures from the past make cameo appearances in his nightmares, and traumas from his Gloucestershire childhood mingle with the plot of his first novel, *The Singing Detective.* This time, he is the hero—and, maybe, the murderer. Doesn't each man kill the thing he loves most? Himself?

In one sense, Potter is no Marlow. His works—novels as well as plays—are lionized, though the author is unawed:

> I think novels are rather easier to write than plays. You can dance around without any thought for the proprieties of physical space: of actors making noises and opening doors, and of being corralled with an audience on either side of me. Years ago I loved the theater—until television came along, until I really saw it, saw what you could do with it. I love what television could be if they left it alone.

Exemplarily, British television has left Potter alone to create his emotionally atonal rhapsodies, whereas Marlow suffers the gnawing impotence of creative failure. And yet, Potter knows Marlow well; the author's biography crosses his character's life at crucial points.

Potter was born, the same year as Marlow, into a poor family in the Forest of Dean, those sprawling West Country woods where young Philip spots his mother copulating. Potter moved to London, as his character does, was graduated with honors from Oxford, ran unsuccessfully for Parliament in 1964, then began writing teleplays. For half his life he has suffered from the same disease as Marlow, and must stay occasionally in the sort of hospital he lances so vigorously in the series. Potter insists that *Detective* is not autobiographical, "except for the illness, with which I'm overly, sickeningly familiar. And yet there's something about it that comes closer to the bone than I ever wanted or intended. I realized this when I first watched the rushes. I started to get clammy-handed!"

The sympathetic viewer feels that way too, tracing Marlow's life and fantasies like a truth-seeking gumshoe. "I wanted to make an odyssey," Potter says,

> in which a man in extreme pain and anguish tries to assemble the bits of his life. That's the way you have to deal with physical pain, you know. You have to stand outside it and say, "O.K., destroy me if you must, but I'm going somewhere else." Those acute, extreme forms of illness almost force you to divide yourself between the suffering animal and the human being who has to moderate the suffering with intelligence and stoicism. And, if not kill it off, at least control it, put the dog on the leash.

The fantasy Marlow is, remember, a *singing* detective. As he did in **Pennies from Heaven,** Potter scatters period songs to make ironic points. A quartet of doctors turns Fred Waring's "Dry Bones" into a sardonic production number; "The Teddy Bears' Picnic" plays over memories of a forest seduction. "No matter how sugary and banal they might be," Potter says,

> old popular songs are in a direct line of descent from the "Psalms." They're saying that the world is other than the thing around you—other than age, other than sickness, other than death. These songs are chariots; they take you somewhere. The little bounce of the music can deliver you back, or forward, into some of your finest emotions.

So the music is a psalm and, for Philip, a therapeutic balm. In the final shot of **The Singing Detective,** Marlow the writer is able to walk out of the hospital in the guise of Marlow the slick detective. "He's stopped lying there moaning and suffering," Potter observes, "ready to deal with the world as a detective would—tough-minded and able to manipulate it." In the pain-streaked world of Dennis Potter, that counts as a happy ending: hero cured, beautiful woman on his arm, and Vera Lynn warbling "We'll Meet Again" in the tuppenny jukebox of his soul. (pp. E8, 91)

> Richard Corliss, "Notes from the Singing Detective," in Time, New York, Vol. 132, No. 25, December 19, 1988, pp. 90, E6, E8, 91.

JOHN J. O'CONNOR

Whether exploring or exploiting the horrors of World War II, television drama is at a disadvantage. Certainly the Holocaust cannot be conveyed by obviously healthy actors whose brightly capped teeth keep twinkling through their makeup. The mere effort is generally embarrassing. The story of the death camps is perhaps told most effectively when approached indirectly, through individual, contained incidents—*The Diary of Anne Frank* for example, or John Hersey's *The Wall.* . . .

Christabel looks at the war from a similarly constricted but rarely dramatized point of view—that of those who remained in Germany during the war and attempted to offer resistance. Adding an intriguing dimension to the project, the writer and executive producer is Dennis Potter, whose somewhat autobiographical **The Singing Detective** almost single-handedly made last season a memorable one for television.

The subject of Adolf Hitler and the Nazis remains a conundrum for Germany and the rest of the world. Scholars and historians are still trying to explain how a highly civilized so-ciety could revert so quickly and thoroughly to barbarity. And, as was illustrated so vividly by the ferocious reactions to a speech given in November by Philip Jenninger, the Speaker of the West German Bundestag who has since resigned, emotions still run high on all sides. . . .

Commenting on the attitudes of the broad public toward the atrocities of Kristallnacht . . . , he pointed out that "only a few collaborated in these excesses, but there was also no rejection of them, no resistance worth the name." He added: "Everybody saw what was going on, but the great majority looked away and kept their silence. Even the churches were silent."

This is the hard nugget of truth at the heart of **Christabel**, based on the true story of Christabel Bielenberg, which she told in her book *The Past Is Myself.* Christabel Burton, the Anglo-Irish daughter of wealthy and influential parents, married Peter Bielenberg in 1934. She had met the law student in Hamburg while studying to be an opera singer. She became a German citizen and, despite already ominous Nazi rumblings, they settled in Hamburg. The television drama jumps quickly to 1938, when Hitler was clearly in control of the country and aggressively on the march.

The attitude of Peter and his friends toward a complete takeover by the Nazis is that there will be a nightmare "if people like us allow it to happen." Christabel insists that she is concerned only with maintaining a home and raising her young sons. "If you're talking politics," she will say, "count me out." Yet, she is the one whose behavior is later fiercely political, even going so far as to lend encouragement publicly to a group of British POWs. And in the end, as the war is winding down in 1945, it is Christabel who brazenly confronts the Gestapo authorities, willing to say anything they might want to hear in her bid to get her husband out of prison. Peter has been arrested in a failed plot to assassinate Hitler. . . .

Christabel is, admittedly, slow going. Its four hours might have been reasonably squeezed into three. . . . And even enthusiastic admirers of Mr. Potter may be disappointed. His special signatures, familiar from both **Pennies From Heaven** and **The Singing Detective,** are not in obvious evidence here. The action does not suddenly stop to allow a character to mime the words to an old Bing Crosby recording. **Christabel** unfolds, more or less, in a straightforward, traditional manner.

More or less. There are, in fact, ingredients that are distinctively Potter. A period song called "I'm Following You" is used as a motif throughout the film. Mr. Potter's fascination with popular music and its special reverberations is apparently irrepressible. One scene features elegantly turned out Germans listening and dancing to Cole Porter's "Nacht und Tag." And certain themes surely attracted Mr. Potter to Christabel's story: the pervasive sense of dislocation; her boys experiencing a childhood of love and menace, and the strong sense that life will at any moment turn into a nightmare.

Perhaps for this reason, many of the scenes in **Christabel** have a dreamlike quality—spare, suspended, uneasily threatening. At times, the action slips briefly into outright fantasy. Christabel's horror at what the Nazis are teaching her children in school is as genuine as her love for her husband. But occasionally even he becomes the brunt of her anger. "Why? Why? I can't even begin to understand," she cries. "What sort of people are you?" She must cope with the little old gardener who suddenly puts on his Nazi uniform, and then she must learn to trust the generous Black Forest villagers who protect her and her sons until war's end. . . .

In some ways, Christabel's story is puzzling. Why did she insist on staying in Germany? But as she tells her parents, "I'm afraid being sensible has nothing to do with it." Her husband is adamant: "All Germans must accept the blame, but not all Germans must not accept the guilt—not if they resist."

Christabel and Peter turned out to be among the very few who did. Mr. Potter treats them with deserved respect.

John J. O'Connor, "Dreamlike Tale Recalls the Nazi Nightmare," in The New York Times, February 19, 1989, p. H33.

GRAHAM FULLER

Dennis Potter writes as if he is purging his soul: "to empty myself until I can't carry on emptying myself." The author of 28 TV dramas, three original miniseries, four adapted miniseries and now, at the age of 53, a first-time director, he is not only dauntingly prolific but the most resourceful innovator in British screen drama.

"I think any writer has a small field to keep plowing," Potter says, "and eventually you turn up the coins you want. I know I always return to the same motifs." Since his first play, *The Confidence Course,* was broadcast in February 1965, Potter has unearthed his fair share of "coins"—a treasure trove, in fact, of pennies from heaven and hell. His early work broached the themes that he has continued to explore and define: political disillusionment, England's decay, the role of popular culture, sexual disgust, the illusion of romance, faith and betrayal in all their forms, the interplay between past and present, life and fiction, reality and imagination. Religious but ungodly, Potter is obsessed with the consequences of sin. He has also turned his plowshare inward, writing scathingly about the omnipotence, or impotence, of writers. His vision is puritanical, morally ambiguous, ultimately optimistic. (p. 31)

By consistently challenging his audiences' assumptions about what they are watching, Potter has pioneered nonnaturalism in British TV—more out of necessity, he says, than design. In questioning their attitudes, and perhaps some of his own, he has dangerously utilized the bilious imagery of misanthropy and sexism. However, Potter's concern for the common good usually shines through. It is in *The Singing Detective* that the troubled schoolboy, Philip Marlow, makes his heartfelt appeal astride the branches of an oak tree: "When I grow up . . . everything ool be *all right.* Won't it? Won't it, God?" This is exactly the utopian sentiment that, as Potter acknowledged in a 1987 BBC interview, inspired his brief political career and drew him toward television, where "all sorts and conditions of human being could share the same experience . . . because anyone or everyone could see it." (p. 32)

Potter is logical about his jettisoning of narrative conventions. "All writers are aiming at a sort of realism," he contends,

but naturalism assumes we sense the world *out there* to be exactly as it is—and I know that not to be the case. If they really examine themselves, most people know that their own aspirations, moods, memories, regrets and hopes are so tangled up with

the alleged reality of the *out there* that it is actually interpenetrated by those feelings. Naturalism leads you to believe that you are just a creation of all the imperatives of the world—whereas the nonnaturalistic dramatization of the inside of your head is more likely to remind you of the shreds of your own sovereignty.

Where other writers have been constrained by the limits of the exterior "here and now," Potter has trademarked a number of bountiful and profoundly unsettling techniques for navigating the crosscurrents, streams and sewers that flow through his protagonists' minds. Typical is the "stranger outside the house who's really inside your head." In both the BBC's *Schmoedipus* and [director] Nicolas Roeg's *Track 29,* the infantile son/seducer is conjured up by a sexually frustrated housewife embarking on an Oedipal revenge fantasy. Similarly, when the devil rapes a catatonic girl out of her stupor in the BBC teleplay (banned for 11 years) and movie, *Brimstone & Treacle,* it is a classic Potteresque act of liberating violence. (pp. 32-3)

Potter's most celebrated nonnaturalistic device is his use of "cheap songs." In both 1978's six-part *Pennies From Heaven* . . . and *The Singing Detective,* "real" time is interrupted when actors spontaneously lip-sync the lyrics of '30s and '40s pop songs. Potter says he used them in *Pennies* as a kind of "psalmistry," as when . . . the self-deluding songsheet salesman, Arthur Parker, serenades his frigid wife with "The Clouds Will Soon Roll By" in their suddenly floodlit suburban bedroom.

Potter employed such songs, sparingly and more ironically, in *The Singing Detective,* less as escapist epiphanies—where the world is a better place—than as unbidden hallucinations in Marlow's brain, harbingers of poison or poignant musings or memories. "Chariots of ideas," he calls them, but denies they are intended to elicit bittersweet nostalgia. . . .

Never one to settle into predictability, Potter surprised his admirers, and critics, with *Christabel* . . . , a fact-based adaptation of Christabel Bielenberg's memoir, *The Past Is Myself* (1968), about her experience as a spirited, upper-class young English woman married to a liberal German lawyer during the Third Reich. "It felt like World War II in a matchbox, with the great events surging around the domestic and the personal," says Potter, who also saw in it "a deeper need for me to do a piece of naturalistic, chronological narrative as an act of writerly hygiene, just as you might wash your brain under the tap." (p. 33)

[*Christabel* is] big and romantic, without being glossy, and probably more accessible to American audiences than his maze-like *The Singing Detective.*

Potter's concern was to examine the war in microcosm—focusing on the emotional journey of an apolitical housewife, who must enter the heart of darkness to rescue her husband from the Ravensbrück concentration camp—and to show how far decent people will be pushed before they fight back. Rare for Potter, it's also a celebration of married love and a woman's self-determination. . . . (p. 54)

[Potter's novel] *Blackeyes* spies on a retired fashion model as she seeks to reclaim her identity from the pages of a bestseller, written by her decrepit novelist uncle, about her history as an emotionally empty sexual plaything for men. As she drags her uncle into his own scenario, her real and fictional lives appear to interchange. In a screenplay that adds fresh layers to the voyeuristic dimensions of the book, Potter's theme is the objectification of "young and attractive women as consumer goods in a way that brutalizes both sexes." Like much of his work, it's ripe for controversy.

"There's a relationship between the two versions I've written that fascinated me, and I decided I couldn't bear to hand it over to anybody. But I'm turning director in a spirit of melancholy resolve, because I won't be able to write while I'm doing it," Potter concludes. "That means killing off my old self. I've got to crack the shell of my reclusiveness, my working habits, my medication habits. But I just feel that there's no place else for me to go. I feel compelled, and all I can say is that I think I'll do it properly." (p. 55)

Graham Fuller, "Dennis Potter," in American
Film, *Vol. XIV, No. 5, March, 1989, pp. 31-3, 54-5.*

PATRICK McGRATH

Discussing his television serial ***The Singing Detective,*** the author and screenwriter Dennis Potter spoke in a BBC television documentary of using illness as a dramatic device to strip his main character down, leaving him nothing but "pain and a cry and a hate." From these rudimentary materials the character then begins to *rebuild* himself; by means of memories and fantasies that are transformed into facts and realities, he slowly forges a workable identity. In John Buck, the protagonist of ***Ticket to Ride,*** the crisis that sets in motion a similar process of reconstruction is sudden and total amnesia. John Buck's task is to find out who he is; our task is to separate, in a wealth of narrative matter, the spurious from the genuine, to isolate the clues that will enable us to understand not only what "John Buck" has done (and there are early hints that he has suffered a homicidal and sex-related psychotic breakdown), but also *why* he has done it. In this sense the book is more about pathology, about madness, than it is about character.

The story begins in the dining car of a train traveling to London, where John suddenly loses "all connection with his previous self." Arriving in London, he checks into a good hotel (despite having no clue to his identity, he does have three or four thousand pounds in his wallet), then sets about trying to discover who he is. . . . [As John] maneuvers among the various modes and strata of his imaginative world, the reader begins to question the reliability of the information being given. Dennis Potter has argued that events in mental life occur simultaneously and nonsequentially, and this is part of the difficulty; the novel is functioning as a sort of analogue of mental experience, which in most of us is a happy muddle of past and present, fantasy and reality. But what makes for a particularly dark complexity in this book is that the mental experience may well be that of a madman.

It is important to recognize what Dennis Potter is doing here, for in terms of narrative technique it is both unorthodox and frighteningly effective. While, for example, John Buck will seem to be remembering an incident concerning his wife, Helen (whom he may have rescued from a life of prostitu-

tion), midway into the memory we find we are seeing from *Helen's* point of view; at this point John, the remembering subject, becomes the *object* of his wife's thoughts, a shift into the sort of radical depersonalization that's found in acutely schizoid conditions. Dennis Potter does not explicitly signal what he's up to, and this too helps create in the reader an almost vertiginous loss of balance and certainty, in effect giving him an echo, a dim, faint comprehension, of the panic and terror involved in going insane.

So, advancing tentatively, we learn that John Buck, a man in his 30's, has lost his job in a London advertising agency and decided to devote his life to painting wildflowers. He goes at this new work with an obsessively rigid discipline, becomes cold and hostile to his wife and loses his sense of humor—he seems, in fact, to be undergoing the sort of rapid personality change that can prefigure psychotic illness. But there is a blank between this period and his reawakening, in another self, on the train to London; the question is, what happened during this black period? The answer, it seems, has to do with John's extreme ambivalence about sex, more specifically his intense fascination with and disgust for prostitutes.

The theme is not a new one for Dennis Potter. In much of his work, sex is an exclusively commercial transaction; John Buck, like others of Mr. Potters's male characters, is deeply conflicted in this area, his appetite for bought pleasure uneasily cohabiting with the guilt and revulsion he feels at his enjoyment of it. This disturbance is the true root and cause of John's breakdown, though at this point it must be said that a breakdown may not have occurred; other readings of the novel are possible, and close to the end John does wonder whether he has "herded such thoughts into [Helen's] head? Were both of them infected by his sick fantasies?" But whatever "really" happens, it pivots on John's memories—true or false—of the prostitute he employed in London and later married. And it is here that Mr. Potter uses to greatest effect his technique of taking what we feel confident is a *projection* of John's mind, then allowing Helen, within the projection, to turn the tables and project her own fantasies upon him.

The process thus developed is a good model of what the narrative imagination routinely does in creating fiction. It's a mark of Dennis Potter's tremendous technical assurance, his expertly tight weave of the book's many rich symbolic and thematic strands, that he can suggest that these complex operations of projection and denial, doubling and imposture, are analogous to normal mental life—that all of us, in other words, are constantly and energetically constructing fictions from our experience. But the real accomplishment of ***Ticket to Ride*** is not merely to depict these complicated psychic processes, but to demonstrate, with chilling plausibility, what they might look like in the mind of a mad murderer.

*Patrick McGrath, "How Violent Is He? Memory
Fails," in* The New York Times Book Review, *October 15, 1989, p. 37.*

Alice Walker

1944-

(Born Alice Malsenior Walker) American novelist, short story writer, essayist, poet, critic, editor, and author of children's books.

An acclaimed writer whose controversial novel *The Color Purple* (1982) won both the American Book Award and the Pulitzer Prize, Walker writes powerful, expressive fiction in which she delineates the black woman's struggle for spiritual wholeness and political autonomy. Viewing the African-American woman as a symbol representing hope and resurrection for humanity, Walker stresses the importance of bonds between women as a means to contend with racism and sexism. Although most critics categorize her writings as feminist, Walker dismisses the label, describing her works and social convictions as "womanist." She defines this term as "a woman who loves other women. . . . Appreciates and prefers woman's culture, woman's emotional flexibility . . . and woman's strength. . . . *Loves* the spirit. . . . Loves herself. *Regardless.*" While some commentators fault Walker's fiction for its polemical tone and excess of negative portrayals of black males, most applaud her lyrical prose and skill at rendering beauty, grace, and dignity in the lives of ordinary individuals.

Much of Walker's fiction is informed by her Southern background. She was born in Eatonton, Georgia, a rural town where most blacks worked as tenant farmers. At age eight Walker was blinded in her right eye when an older brother accidentally shot her with a BB gun. Because her parents had no immediate access to an automobile, Walker did not receive medical attention until several days after the accident, and the resulting scar tissue that completely covered her eye was not surgically removed until she was fourteen. Walker spent most of her childhood withdrawn from others because of her disfigurement and began writing poetry to combat her loneliness. Walker commented later that due to this incident, she "began to really see people and things, to really notice relationships and to learn to be patient enough to care about how they turned out." Upon graduating from high school with honors in 1961, Walker won a scholarship to Spelman College in Atlanta, where she became involved in the civil rights movement and participated in several sit-ins at local business establishments. In 1963, she transferred to Sarah Lawrence College in New York City and graduated in 1965. She spent the following summer in Mississippi as an activist and teacher and met her future husband Melvyn Leventhal, a Jewish civil rights attorney. Walker and Leventhal married in 1967 in New York City and resumed their activist work in Mississippi, becoming the first legally married interracial couple to reside in Jackson, the state capital.

Walker's first novel, *The Third Life of Grange Copeland* (1970), introduces many of her prevalent themes, particularly the domination of powerless women by equally powerless men. In this work, which spans the years between the Depression and the beginnings of the civil right movement in the early 1960s, Walker chronicles three generations of a black sharecropping family and explores the effects of poverty and racism on their lives. Because of his sense of failure, Grange

Copeland, the family patriarch, drives his wife to suicide and abandons his children to seek a better life in the North. His legacy of hate and violence is passed on to his son, Brownfield, who eventually murders his wife. At the novel's conclusion, Grange returns to his family a broken yet compassionate man and attempts to atone for his past transgressions with the help of his granddaughter, Ruth. For Grange, Ruth symbolizes hope because she has survived the Copeland's history of brutality and despair. While some reviewers accused Walker of reviving stereotypes about the dysfunctional black family, others praised her use of intensive, descriptive language.

Walker's next novel, *Meridian* (1976), a tale of perseverance and personal sacrifice set during the civil rights movement, is generally regarded as one of the best novels depicting that era. Walker explores conflicts between traditional African-American values handed down through slavery and the revolutionary polemic espoused by the black-power movement. The title character is a college-educated woman who commits her life to aiding southern blacks in gaining political and social equality. She joins an organization of black militants but is forced to leave the group when she refuses to condone its violent actions. Meridian continues her activist work, however, and later becomes a legendary figure throughout the South, resembling such historical figures as Harriet Tubman and Sojourner Truth. In a subplot involving Meridian, her lover and compatriot Truman, and Lynne, a Jewish activist whom Truman eventually marries, Walker also addresses sexual politics within the movement and hypocrisy among some black nationalists. While several critics admonished Walker for portraying Meridian as a mythic figure, Marge Piercy responded: "Is it possible to write a novel about the progress of a saint? Apparently, yes. With great skill and care to make Meridian believable at every stage of her development, Walker also shows us the cost."

The Color Purple placed Walker among the most important contemporary American writers and made her a literary celebrity. Presented in an epistolary style, the novel traces thirty years in the life of Celie, a poor southern black woman who is victimized physically and emotionally by both her stepfather and her husband. While in her teens, Celie was repeatedly raped by her stepfather, who sold the two children she bore him. Celie is eventually placed into a loveless marriage with Albert, a widower whom she addresses as "Mister," and who for the next three decades subjects her to beatings and psychological torment. Celie writes letters describing her ordeal to God and to her sister Nettie, who escapes a similar fate by serving as a missionary in Africa. Celie eventually finds solace through her friendship and love for Albert's mistress, Shug Avery, a charismatic blues singer who helps her gain self-esteem and the courage to leave her marriage. At the novel's end, Celie is reunited with her children and with Nettie.

Walker earned nearly unanimous praise for *The Color Purple,* especially for her accurate rendering of southern black folk idioms and animated characterization of Celie. Peter S. Prescott echoed the opinion of most reviewers when he called Walker's work "an American novel of permanent importance, that rare sort of book which (in Norman Mailer's felicitous phrase) amounts to a diversion in the fields of dread." *The Color Purple* subsequently became the source of controversy among the black intelligentsia, however, particularly for its negative portraits of black men. Darryl Pinckney unflatteringly equated Walker's novel with Harriet Beecher Stowe's *Uncle Tom's Cabin,* stating: "[Like] Stowe's, Walker's work shows a world divided between the chosen (black women) and the unsaved, the 'poor miserable critter' (black men), between the 'furnace of affliction' and a 'far-off, mystic land of . . . miraculous fertility.' " Richard Wesley, however, disputed charges of bias against black males in Walker's novel. He contended that Walker "is reminding many of us men of our own failures. She is reminding women of *their* failures as well. She is saying that Black is Beautiful, but not necessarily always *right.*"

Walker's recent work, *The Temple of My Familiar* (1989), is an ambitious novel recording 500,000 years of human history. Eschewing a conventional linear plot structure and three-dimensional characterizations in favor of multiple settings and narrative voices and abrupt shifts between past and present, Walker offers a profusion of observations on such diverse issues as the ecology, spirituality, and animal rights. The novel's central character, Miss Lissie, is a goddess from primeval Africa who has been incarnated hundreds of times throughout history. She befriends Suwelo, a narcissistic university professor whose marriage is threaten by his need to dominate and sexually exploit his wife. Through a series of conversations with Miss Lissie and her friend Hal, Suwelo

learns of Miss Lissie's innumerable lives and experiences—from the prehistoric world in which humans and animals lived in harmony under a matriarchal society, to slavery in the United States—and regains his capability to love, nurture, and respect himself and others. Unlike the acclaim conferred upon *The Color Purple,* critics generally dismissed *The Temple of My Familiar.* Most reviewers took issue with Walker's speculative interpretation of the origins of patriarchal societies and found her discourses on racial and sexual relations pretentious and offensive. However, J. M. Coetzee commented: "We should read [the novel] as a fable of recovered origins, as an exploration of the inner lives of contemporary black Americans as these are penetrated by fabulous stories. . . . Nevertheless, history is not just storytelling. . . . Africa has a past that neither the white male nor Ms. Walker can simply invent." Coetzee concluded that *The Temple of My Familiar* "is a novel only in a loose sense. Rather, it is a mixture of mythic fantasy, revisionary history, exemplary biography and sermon."

Walker is also considered an accomplished poet. Darwin Turner described her verse as "moderately open forms which permit her to reveal homespun truths of human behavior and emotion." Walker's first collection, *Once* (1968), includes poems written during the early 1960s while she attended Sarah Lawrence College. Some of these pieces relate to the confusion, isolation, and suicidal thoughts Walker experienced when she learned in her senior year that she was pregnant. In her second volume, *Revolutionary Petunias* (1973), Walker addresses such topics as love, individualism, and revolution while recounting her years in Mississippi as a civil rights activist and teacher. *Goodnight Willie Lee, I'll See You in the Morning* (1979) contains verse that celebrates familial bonds and friendships. Michael Dirda commented that Walker's poems "sometimes . . . address the reader directly; often they carry morals and are written as allegories, somewhat reminiscent of Stephen Crane's little symbolic story poems." *Horses Make a Landscape Look More Beautiful* (1985) focuses upon contemporary issues.

In addition to her novels and poetry, Walker has also published two volumes of short stories, *In Love and Trouble: Stories of Black Women* (1973) and *You Can't Keep a Good Woman Down* (1981), both of which evidence her womanist philosophy. *In Search of Our Mothers' Gardens: Womanist Prose* (1984) and *Living by the Word: Selected Writings, 1973-1987* (1987) are collections of essays written throughout Walker's career and relate to issues and problems concerning the environment, animal rights, nuclear war, and include several autobiographical pieces. Walker is also the author of two books for children, *Langston Hughes: American Poet* (1974) and *To Hell with Dying* (1988).

(See also *CLC,* Vols. 5, 6, 9, 19, 27, 46; *Short Story Criticism,* Vol. 5; *Contemporary Authors,* Vols. 37-40, rev. ed.; *Contemporary Authors New Revision Series,* Vol. 9, 27; *Something about the Author,* Vol. 31; and *Dictionary of Literary Biography,* Vols. 6, 33; and *Concise Dictionary of American Literary Biography: Broadening Views, 1968-1988.*)

THADIOUS M. DAVIS 1983

[The essay excerpted below was originally published in The Southern Quarterly, *Summer 1983.]*

Walker's heritage and history provide a vehicle for understanding the modern world in which her characters live. "Because I'm black and I'm a woman and because I was brought up poor and because I'm a Southerner, . . . the way I see the world is quite different from the way many people see it," she has observed to Krista Brewer: "I could not help but have a radical vision of society . . . the way I see things can help people see what needs to be changed." Her vision, however, is a disturbing one to share. Walker relies upon sexual violence and physical abuse to portray breaches in black generations. Typically, she brings to her work a terrible observance of black self-hatred and destruction. While Walker does not negate the impact of a deleterious past, she rarely incorporates white characters as perpetrators of crimes against blacks. Her works simply presume, as she states, that "all history is current; all injustice continues on some level." Her images of people destroyed or destroying others originate in a vision of cultural reality expressed matter-of-factly, such as in the poem from *Revolutionary Petunias*, **"You Had to Go to Funerals"**: "At six and seven / The face in the gray box / Is nearly always your daddy's / Old schoolmate / Mowed down before his / Time." Walker's racial memory of a tangible, harsh reality succeeds in focusing experience, holding it fixed, and illuminating some aspects of brutality that might well be overlooked or obscured. (p. 40)

One scene in *Meridian* delineates the everyday quality of familial rage in Walker's fiction. A woman who believes that her family and community, as well as the racial barriers and social order of the South, have all combined to rob her of a full life irons into her children's and husband's clothes her frustrations and her creativity. Instead of loving her family openly or accusing anyone explicitly, she uses her ordinary domestic chore to enclose her children in "the starch of her anger," as Walker labels it. This character, Mrs. Hill, includes her children in her victimization, and in the process she excludes them from any meaningful, close relationship with her. The result is a tension- and guilt-ridden existence, both for Mrs. Hill and for her family. The scene suggests how personal outrage and anger stemming from social and historical forces (particularly ignorance, discrimination, racism, exploitation, and sexism) become warped and distorted in Walker's world.

In fact, Walker has discussed her writing, and need to write, in terms that articulate her deflection of rage and her reconciliation with it. After the birth of her daughter, she put her frustrations and her energy into her work: "Write I did, night and day, *something,* and it was not even a choice, . . . but a necessity. When I didn't write I thought of making bombs and throwing them. . . . Writing saved me from the sin and *inconvenience* of violence—as it saves most writers who live in 'interesting' oppressive times and are not afflicted by personal immunity." She does not have to add that her writing absorbed the violence, especially emotional violence, in the lives of her characters. Walker's recollection and the scene from *Meridian* add a situational context to the prevalent violence and excessive pain found in all of her fiction, but they do not fully address the motivational context for the choice of family as the expressive vehicle.

Walker creates a multiplicity of permanently maimed and damaged souls within the family structure who feel no pressure for responsible living or assume exemption from the demands of responsibility. There may be occasions of optimism or hope; for example, when Sarah, a Southern black art student in **"A Sudden Trip Home in the Spring,"** returns from New York for her father's funeral, she comes, with the help of her brother, to understand her father's life after years of resenting his flaws, and she resolves to learn how to make her grandfather's face in stone. But more pervasive in Walker's fiction is despair: women who commit suicide, such as the wife in **"Her Sweet Jerome,"** who sets fire to herself and her marriage bed; men who maim or kill, such as the father in **"The Child Who Favored Daughter,"** who cuts off his daughter's breasts; people who allow themselves to become animals, such as Brownfield in *The Third Life of Grange Copeland,* who, accepting a "nothingness" in himself, shoots his wife in the face while his children watch; and people who simply give up on life, such as Myrna in **"Really, Doesn't Crime Pay?"** who spends her days softening her hands and thwarting her husband's desire for a child.

Walker assumes that by revealing negative actions and violent encounters, she may be able to repair the damage done by unreflective people who are unable to recognize that their actions have more than personal consequences, that they may rend bonds between generations and thus affect all members of a family, community, race, or society. In her depictions of abuse and violence, Walker takes the risk of misrepresenting the very people whom she seeks to change. Yet her unrelenting portraits of human weaknesses convey her message that art should "make us better." . . . Her message, postulated in her novels, is that the breaches and violations must be mended for health and continuity, for "survival *whole,"* as her character Grange Copeland declares.

Reparation or redemption may be undertaken by a single individual in whom Walker vests the responsibility for survival, because it is the action of a single individual that has caused the breakdown of experience or identity in private lives, and ultimately in the public or social life of the group. Individual characters acting alone become repositories of decent behavior, as well as harbingers that the messages embedded in the lives of generations of blacks will not be lost. One example is Elethia, a young woman who masterminds the retrieval of "Uncle Albert," a mummified black man who is all teeth, smiles, and servitude as a decoration in the window of a "whites only" restaurant, despite the reality of his having been a rebellious slave whose teeth were knocked out for his efforts to remain human. Elethia knows that Uncle Albert's denigration to a subservient happy waiter cannot be allowed. She and her cohorts break the plate glass, reclaim the mummy, burn it, and save the ashes. She aims to rid the world of all false, stereotypical images of blacks, especially men, and to recover the past, rectify its misrepresentations, and preserve the truth for future generations. Elethia realizes that the work will not end with rescuing Uncle Albert, but that it will extend over her lifetime. Walker's individual Elethias understand that breaches may have occurred between succeeding generations, but that progress in the present and towards the future depends upon reconstruction of the bridges that, as Carolyn Rodgers says in her poem "It Is Deep," one generation has "crossed over on." Although **"Elethia"** is not one of Walker's most successful stories, it adheres to her belief that the world, her reality, is filled with connections, oftentimes unsuspected connections, which she as an artist can illuminate.

Walker believes that as a writer she must work towards a larger perspective, which she describes as "connections made, or at least attempted, where none existed before, the straining to encompass in one's glance at the varied world the common thread, the unifying theme through immense diversity, a fearlessness of growth, of search, of look, that enlarges the private and the public world." For her, one way of structuring "the common thread" is by means of generations; she values the strength and purpose black generations have given to her writing, but she refuses to reduce their meanings to platitudes or to ignore the complexities of their lives. (pp. 41-3)

Walker treasures and preserves in her works not merely her parents' faces and her own, but those of her grandparents and great-grandparents and all her blood and social relatives as well. For instance, in the poem from *Goodnight Willie Lee* entitled **"talking to my grandmother who died poor (while hearing Richard Nixon declare 'I am not a crook'),"** she concludes: "i must train myself to want / not one bit more / than i need to keep me alive / working / and recognizing beauty / in your so nearly undefeated face." It is in her grandmother's "so nearly undefeated face" that Walker reads at what cost her people have survived. (p. 44)

Because of her conception of art and the artist, as well as her recognition of the value of her mother's stories and her family's faces, Walker displays an enormous sympathy for the older generation of Southern women ("Headragged Generals") and men ("billy club scar[ed]"), whose lives were sacrifice. . . . The poem ["The Women"] celebrates the generation that preceded Walker's own, those men and women who opened doors through which they themselves would never pass and who were unafraid to attempt personal and social change in order to restructure subsequent generations. Walker acknowledges their achievement, but also their adversities.

Her older men, in particular, have experienced troubled, difficult lives, such as those of Grange Copeland and Albert in *The Color Purple.* These men have been abusive in their youths, but they come to an essential understanding of their own lives and their families' as they learn to be reflective, responsible, and expressive individuals. Although they may seem to reflect her anti-male bias, they are more significant as portrayals of Walker's truth-telling from a particular perspective that is conscious of their weaknesses—weaknesses that they distort into violence against other blacks, especially women and children—and conscious, too, of their potential for regeneration. Walker's men to whom sexuality is no longer an issue are redeemed by learning to love and assume responsibility for their actions. In presenting these men, Walker first depicts what has come to be the stereotypes of blacks, essentially those set destructive patterns of emotional and psychological responses of black men to black life, their women, children, friends, whites, and themselves. Then she loosens the confines of the stereotype and attempts to penetrate the nexus of feelings that make these lives valuable in themselves and for others.

Much of the redemption, nevertheless, is only potential as Walker portrays it. The nameless husband in *The Color Purple* becomes "Albert" in his later years, because, like Grange Copeland in Walker's first novel, he discovers reflection which makes him a defined person who can accept the responsibility for his mistakes and the suffering he has caused, especially his abusive treatment of his wife whom he had

denigrated. . . . Despite his contemplative demeanor at the end of the novel, Albert remains in the realm of potential. His apparent psychological return to roots, though inadequately motivated, is primarily a portent of a healing process.

Walker names this healing a "wholeness" in her essay, **"Beyond the Peacock: The Reconstruction of Flannery O'Connor,"** in which she, like her characters, returns to her roots in order to regenerate herself and to comprehend the pervasive impact of social environment. Her attitude is clear in the poem from *Once,* **"South: The Name of Home,"** which opens: "when I am here again / the years of ease between / fall away / The smell of one / magnolia / sends my heart running / through the swamps. / the earth is red / here— / the trees bent, weeping / what secrets will not / the ravished land / reveal / of its abuse." It is an environment that is not without a history of pain, but it nonetheless connects generations of blacks to one another, to a "wholeness" of self, and to "the old unalterable roots," as in **"Burial"**: "Today I bring my own child here; / to this place where my father's / grandmother rests undisturbed beneath the Georgia sun / . . . Forgetful of geographical resolutions as birds / the farflung young fly South to bury / the old dead." One key to "wholeness," even if it is rarely achieved, is the development of self-perception by means of generational ties to the land.

The achievements and dreams that emerge from the connected experience of generations are expressions of freedom and beauty, of power and community. The primary dream, usually voiced in terms of the creation of art, is that of freedom to be one's own self, specifically to be one's own black self and to claim, as do Walker's blues singers Shug Avery in *The Color Purple* and Gracie Mae Still in **"Nineteen Fifty-Five,"** one's own life for one's self and for future generations.

Walker transforms the individual, so much a part of the special characteristics used to define the white South, into a person who is black and most often female. In the one-page story **"Petunias"** from *You Can't Keep a Good Woman Down,* she individualizes an unnamed woman with a history and a sense of herself. The woman writes in her diary just before her death in an explosion of a bomb her son intends for the revolution: "my daddy's grandmama was a slave on the Tearslee Plantation. They dug up her grave when I started agitating in the Movement. One morning I found her dust dumped over my verbena bed, a splinery leg bone had fell among my petunias." This woman and others in Walker's canon are the stereotyped, the maimed, the distorted blacks who still rise, as Maya Angelou entitles one of her works, "Still I Rise." These characters become redeemed as individuals with an indelible sense of self. But that act of rising out of the depths of degradation or depression is accomplished by means of the person's coming to terms with the truth of his or her community, with his or her social and historical place among others who have suffered, grieved, laughed, and lusted, but who miraculously have held on to dignity and selfhood. Characters, such as Sammy Lou, a woman on her way to the electric chair for killing her husband's murderer, pass on a powerful legacy of individual identity; Sammy Lou leaves her children the instructions: "Always respect the word of God," and "Don't yall forget to *water* my purple petunias."

Walker operates within this legacy. She keeps before her the vision of her own mother, who cultivated magnificent flower gardens, despite her work from sun up to dark either in the fields or as a domestic for less than twenty dollars a week. Walker refers to her mother's gardens as her "art," "her ability to hold on, even in simple ways." That garden is her recurrent metaphor for both art and beauty, endurance and survival; it is essentially, too, Walker's articulation of the process by which individuals find selfhood through examining the experiences of others who have preceded them. (pp. 45-7)

In her first novel, **The Third Life of Grange Copeland,** three generations of Copelands converge to create Ruth's identity, and three generations form the stages or lives of the patriarch and title character, Grange Copeland. When any one member of the Copeland family or of a particular social generation of blacks (from 1920 to 1960) ignores the dynamics of family structures or forgets the historical perspective that the structures are maintained through necessity and love, he or she loses the capacity for primary identifications with race, family, and community, and loses as well the major basis for defining one's self and one's humanity. The most detailed illustration presented in the novel is Brownfield, the son of Grange and a member of the middle generation in the work.

Brownfield Copeland becomes one of "the living dead, one of the many who had lost their souls in the American wilderness." He reduces his murder of his wife to a simple theorem: *"He liked plump women. . . . Ergo,* he had murdered his wife because she had become skinny." Because of his twisted logic, Brownfield "could forget (his wife's) basic reality, convert it into comparisons. She had been like good pie, or good whiskey, but there had never been a self to her." Not only by means of the murder itself, but also by the process of his reasoning about it, he strips himself of his humanity when he negates his culpability with the negation of his wife's existence as a human being.

Brownfield's physical death sadly, though appropriately in Walker's construction, comes at the hands of his father Grange and over the future of his daughter Ruth. But his spiritual death occurs much earlier "as he lay thrashing about, knowing the rigidity of his belief in misery, knowing he could never renew or change himself, for this changelessness was now all he had, he could not clarify what was the duty of love." He compounds one of the greatest sins in Walker's works, the refusal or inability to change, with his dismissal of meaning in family bonds. Ironically, his death makes possible the completion of change in his daughter's life that had been fostered by his father, who late in his life understood the necessity of moving beyond the perverted emotions constricting the lives of the Copelands.

In *Meridian,* Walker's second novel, the heroine divests herself of immediate blood relations—her child and her parents—in order to align herself completely with the larger racial and social generations of blacks. Meridian Hill insists that although seemingly alone in the world, she has created a fusion with her generation of activist blacks and older generations of oppressed blacks. The form of the work, developed in flashbacks, follows a pattern of Meridian's casting off the demands made by authority and responsibility within the conventional family and traditional institutions. Unlike Brownfield's rejection of responsibility, the rupture in this novel is ultimately positive, despite its being the most radical and mysterious instance of change and acceptance in Walker's fiction. It is positive because the novel creates a new basis for defining Meridian's self and for accepting responsibility for one's actions. In fact, the controlling metaphor is resurrection and rebirth, an acting out of the renewal impossible for Brownfield. By the end of the novel, Meridian's personal identity has become a collective identity. . . . In spite of her

painful private experiences, Meridian is born anew into a pluralistic cultural self, a "we" that is and must be self-less and without ordinary prerequisites for personal identity. And significantly, because she exemplifies Walker's recurrent statement of women as leaders and models, Meridian leaves her male disciple Truman Held to follow her and to await the arrival of others from their social group.

Truman's search, structurally a duplication of Meridian's, is part of personal change that is more necessary for men than for women in Walker's fiction and that becomes social change through the consequences of actions taken by individuals who must face constraints, as well as opportunities, in their lives, but must also know why they act and what the consequences will be. Truman resolves to live the life of an ascetic so that he might one day be worthy to join Meridian and others "at the river." (pp. 48-50)

Perhaps Walker's third novel most effectively conveys her messages and evidences her heritage as a black Southern writer. In *The Color Purple,* which won the Pulitzer Prize for fiction in 1983, she takes a perspectivistic or "emic" approach to character delineation and cultural reality. She sees and portrays a world from the inside outward; she uses the eyes of Celie, a surnameless, male-dominated and abused woman, who records her experiences in letters. Celie is not a "new" character in Walker's fiction; she is similar to one of the sisters in **"Everyday Use,"** the bride in **"Roselily,"** and the daughter in **"The Child Who Favored Daughter,"** but unlike these other silent, suffering women characters, Celie writes her story in her own voice. She tells her life as only she has known it: a girl, merely a child, raped by her stepfather whom she believes is her natural father; that same girl bearing his two children only to have them stolen by him and to be told that they are dead; the denial and suppression of that girl's actual background and history, as well as her letters from her sister.

In Celie's epistles, Walker makes her strongest effort so far to confront the patterns in a specified world and to order and articulate the codes creating those patterns. In effect, she uses the uncovered patterns to connect, assimilate, and structure the content of one human being's world and relationship to that world. Celie writes letters—her story, history—to God and to her sister Nettie. She writes out of desperation and in order to preserve some core of her existence. In love and hope, she writes to save herself. . . . Celie writes from the heart, and grows stronger, more defined, more fluent, while simultaneously her intensely private, almost cryptic style develops into a still personal, subjective style, but one which encompasses much more of the lives surrounding her.

While social interactions and institutions typically define human reality, these do not ultimately define Celie's. She is isolated and alone, despite the numbers of family members and others impinging upon her world. Slowly and cautiously, she builds a reality that is different, one based upon her singular position and the abstractions she herself conceives in the course of her everyday life. Her inner life is unperverted by the abuse and violence she suffers. Only when she has formulated the outlines of her private identity in writing does her interaction with others become a significant factor in making sense of social codes in the public world. When she reaches her conclusions, she has rejected most of the available social models for personal identity; she is neither Shug Avery, the hardliving blues singer who gives and takes what she wants in being herself, nor is she Nettie, her sister who can experience the wider world outside the social environment of her childhood. Yet, Celie passionately loves both of these women, and has tried at different stages to emulate them. Celie's own subjective probings lead her to confirm her individual interpretation of herself and of her situational contexts. Nonetheless, she does arrive, as invariably a Walker bearer of responsibility must, at her place in the spectrum of life, her relationship to others, and her own continuity.

Celie affirms herself: "I'm pore, I'm black, I may be ugly and can't cook, a voice say to everything listening. But I'm here." Her words echo those of Langston Hughes's folk philosopher, Jesse B. Semple (Simple): "I'm still here. . . . I've been uɪːderfed, underpaid. . . . I've been abused, confused, misused. . . . I done had everything from flat feet to a flat head. . . . but I am still here. . . . I'm still here." Celie's verbal connection to Hughes's black everyman and the black oral tradition extends her affirmation of self, so that it becomes racial, as well as personal, and is an actualization, rather than the potentiality that most often appears in Walker's work. Celie *is,* or in her own black folk English, she *be's* her own black, nappy-haired, ordinary self in all the power and pain that combine in her writing to reveal the girl, the female becoming totally a woman-person who survives and belies the weak, passive exterior her family and community presume to be her whole self. Her act of writing and affirming is magnificent. It is an achievement deserving of celebration, and perhaps not coincidentally, it is Walker's first "happy ending," not only for her character Celie, but for most of her fictional family as well. (pp. 50-2)

Despite her concentration on the brutal treatment of black women and the unmitigated abuse of children, Walker believes in the beauty and the power of the individual, and ultimately of the group. And because she does, she is willing to gamble on ways of articulating her unique vision. She is not always successful; the experimental stories of **You Can't Keep a Good Woman Down** are an example, as are the unconvincing letters from Celie's sister Nettie in Africa. However, even in the less effective works, Walker validates the necessity of struggling out of external constrictions to find meaning in one's own life. It seems quite appropriate that both her dedication and statement at the end of **The Color Purple** reaffirm and invoke the spirits of people who fill her head and her work with their voices and their presence, with the selves that come to *be* within the pages of her writing.

Certainly, in the composition of much of her work so far, Alice Walker must have felt as she did while writing **"The Revenge of Hannah Kemhuff,"** a work inspired by one of her mother's own stories: "I gathered up the historical and psychological threads of the life my ancestors lived, and in the writing . . . I felt joy and strength and my own continuity. I had that wonderful feeling that writers get sometimes . . . of being with a great many people, ancient spirits, all very happy to see me consulting and acknowledging them, and eager to let me know through the joy of their presence, that indeed, I am not alone." Perhaps this consoling vision of interconnections is one reason why Alice Walker can capture the deep layers of affirmative and destructive feelings in human beings who must live and make their lives known, and why she can compel readers to heed their messages. (pp. 52-3)

Thadious M. Davis, "Alice Walker's Celebration of Self in Southern Generations," in Women Writers of the Contemporary South, *edited by Peggy Whit-*

man Prenshaw, University Press of Mississippi, 1984, pp. 39-53.

THE VIRGINIA QUARTERLY REVIEW

[**Horses Make a Landscape Look More Beautiful**] is Alice Walker's fourth volume of verse and her first since she won the Pulitzer Prize for **The Color Purple.** Using short, nonmetrical lines, these simple lyrics meditate on love and lovers, Afro-American experience and heritage, Walker's own family past, women, Indians, hunger, the Third World, and poetry itself. "I understand how poems are made," she tells us, and perhaps she does, but the poems assembled here seem more posed and self-conscious than those of her powerful first volume **Once** (1968) in which she successfully combined detached observation, emotional urgency, and understatement. Here many of the poems read more like exercises than necessary utterances.

A review of "Horses Make a Landscape Look More Beautiful," in The Virginia Quarterly Review, *Vol. 61, No. 2, Spring, 1985, p. 57.*

L. M. ROSENBERG

[**Horses Make a Landscape Look More Beautiful**] has many of the virtues and flaws of her fiction—a breezy dogmatism, the tendency to oversimplify the world, a remarkable sweetness. Whatever else the book may be—often touching, sometimes irritating; a little stiff, a touch preacherly, with gems of wisdom inserted parenthetically—it is almost never poetry. Miss Walker's best effects are koan-like, stripped-down:

> I am the woman
> offering two flowers
> whose roots
> are twin
> Justice and Hope.

Set against this quality, often mixed in it, is pop poetry in truncated lines:

> When I no longer have your heart
> I will not request your body
> your presence
> or even your polite conversation.

These abbreviations have their meaner side in good guy versus bad guy poems where the world is set up to divide neatly, us against them, black against white; poems full of self-righteous rage against the other—the voice of the "murderous and lazy," the "small, white man," she writes, is "Coming from nearly inside me"—but rarely do her cries of anger rise into something that truly sees into the world, beyond irony, pity or mere regret. But **Horses Make a Landscape Look More Beautiful** has two fine strengths—a music that comes along sometimes, as sad and cheery as a lonely woman's whistling (in poems like **"Love Is Not Concerned"** with its echoes of Langston Hughes) and Miss Walker's own tragicomic gifts.

In my opinion Alice Walker's work has been generally overpraised, but you can't stop people from loving what they love, and no sane reviewer would try. Those readers who praised her novel **The Color Purple** will find qualities to admire in this book of poems.

L. M. Rosenberg, "Largesse, Erudition, Wit and

Sweetness," in The New York Times Book Review, *April 7, 1985, p. 12.*

DERRICK BELL

For a year or so, back in the early 1970s, before she gained deserved fame as one of our finest writers, Alice Walker lived next door. She had published her first book of poetry, ***Once,*** and her first novel, ***The Third Life of Grange Copeland.*** Her talents though were hardly certain signs of the tremendous success she would achieve with her award-winning novel, ***The Color Purple.***

Even then, Alice was her own person, ready to withdraw an article rather than subject it to editing she felt violated her integrity. Warned by one magazine that she would have to accept their changes, Walker told the editor, "All I have to do is save my soul."

Living by the Word, a slim volume of 27 short essays, is not only vintage Alice Walker: passionate, political, personal, and poetic, it also provides a panoramic view of a fine human being saving her soul through good deeds and extraordinary writing.

The style of this book is mainly conversational and relaxed, but there is plenty of Alice Walker, the militant activist. She is present at the 1984 trial of Indian Movement leader Dennis Banks. She is arrested for participating in the 1987 anti-war protest at the Concord Naval Weapons Station. And, in a deeply moving essay, **"Try to See My Sister,"** we learn of her persistent but unsuccessful efforts to visit Dessie Woods, serving a long term in a Georgia prison for defending herself and another black woman from rape and possible death.

Unlike ***In Search of Our Mothers' Gardens***—"womanist" prose dealing with gender, class, and race—the essays in ***Living by the Word*** cover a broader range of the problems facing the planet. They express many spiritual themes that she credits to learning more about Native American philosophies. . . .

Walker responds at some length to the severe and sometimes personal criticism leveled at ***The Color Purple.*** For those who attacked her use of black dialect as degrading to black people, she reports that her character "Celie's" unique speech was patterned on the dialect spoken by her step-grandmother. She adds: "Language is an intrinsic part of who we are and what has, for good or evil, happened to us. And, amazingly, it has sustained us more securely than the arms of angels."

About her black, male critics, she says, "It is nearly crushing to realize there was an assumption on anyone's part that black women would not fight injustice except when the foe was white." That response carries real weight, though Walker may underestimate both the power of her pen and the willingness of that white foe to enlist even her undeniable truths in ways quite the opposite of the love and respect in which she wrote them.

Walker's truths about the worth of black men are contained in a very personal memoir titled simply, **"Father."** This essay, unself-conscious and filled with spiritual insight, reveals her struggle to find a father she can love, . . . a struggle that continued after her father's death.

Living by the Word serves notice of Alice Walker's determination to protect her integrity against black critics for the same reasons she gave magazine editors. The harsh criticism of black critics saddened and disappointed her, but she writes:

> The infinite faith I have in people's ability to understand anything that makes sense has always been justified, finally, by their behavior. In my work and in myself I reflect black people, women and men, as I reflect others. One day even the most self-protective ones will look into the mirror I provide and not be afraid.

> *Derrick Bell, "The Word from Alice Walker," in* Los Angeles Times Book Review, *May 29, 1988, p. 11.*

NOEL PERRIN

If you're one of the men, black or white, who felt offended by the description of your sex in ***The Color Purple,*** you are going to be even more offended by some of the essays here [in ***Living By the Word: Selected Writings, 1973-1987***]. You'll be reading shallowly, of course, but you were then, too.

If you're a radical feminist, you're going to be disappointed by Ms. Walker's refusal to see men (with the possible exception of President Reagan) as the enemy. If you're an environmentalist, you will instantly recognize an ally. If you're a Georgia prison official, your first thought will probably be to challenge some of her statistics. If you're an editor, you'll itch to cut two or three of the 27 pieces the book contains. And to ask her to expand some of the others.

Living by the Word is an extraordinarily diverse collection. It's not a ragbag, but it's no finished quilt, either. It includes about a dozen true essays, five journal entries (two of them are prime candidates for cutting), several speeches and several page-long pieces of the sort that in medieval Japanese literature were called *zuihitsu,* or scattered thoughts.

Ms. Walker herself, she tells us, sees the book as the record of a journey. The journey is partly physical—she goes to China, to Jamaica, to Milledgeville, Ga.—but mainly spiritual. She has two goals. One is to reconnect herself with all living creatures in the immediate way that children do, and the other is to report with full adult intelligence on the health of the planet. Her original interests centered on black women, and especially on the ways they were abused or underrated. Now those interests encompass all creation.

About half the book records various aspects of a physical journey, and generally it is the better half. The trip to China, for example, gets recorded as the captions to 15 imaginary snapshots. (p. 42)

More interesting than the geographical travel, though, is the spiritual journey. It leads Ms. Walker, through a path distinctively her own, smack into ecology. In the essay **"Am I Blue?"** her attention is devoted mainly to a white horse named Blue who lives alone—much against his will—in a pasture next to a house she is renting.

In another essay she attempts with considerable success to imagine how she would feel about human beings if she were a tree, in particular a Western conifer suffering from air and ground pollution. In the best of the journal entries, an extended account of an antiwar demonstration she helped to lead at the Concord Naval Weapons Station at Port Chicago, Calif., in June 1987, she can look sympathetically at the long line of police with riot sticks. She can think that from their point of view *they* are oppressed. "Many of them are angry, because they feel they are poor and have to work while the demonstrators appear to be playing." A fine and a rare insight for a demonstrator to have.

In none of this has Ms. Walker abandoned her concern with downtrodden black women. She has merely expanded her view to see the planet itself as downtrodden: "It cannot tolerate much longer the old ways of humans that batter it so unmercifully," she says. And, of course, unlike the fictional protagonist Celie at the end of *The Color Purple,* it cannot rise and free itself unaided. We have made the earth our slave, and it cannot survive unless we free it. Rachel Carson, meet Alice Walker.

The rest of *Living by the Word* is miscellaneous. Ms. Walker being the gifted writer she is, there's nothing here that doesn't offer some pleasure in the reading. Certain pieces offer quite a lot. A speech she gave in April 1987 at Spelman College in Atlanta (**"Oppressed Hair Puts a Ceiling on the Brain"**), entirely devoted to how to wear one's hair, is both funny and charming. (pp. 42-3)

But what is the talk she gave in 1981 to the Atlanta Historical Society doing here? It's a denunciation of Joel Chandler Harris and the Uncle Remus stories, which she feels Harris stole from blacks. It's specifically not an essay, just notes. Ms. Walker explains at the beginning of the talk that she started out years ago to write a full essay, and because of the white man's theft found the subject too painful.

Her talk appears as the fifth entry in the book. By the eighth entry, written in 1987, the subject has become considerably less painful. She has now studied Native American folklore, and remarks casually that the Uncle Remus stories, "which I had assumed were from Africa, could as easily be from the Cherokee, since the very same tales abound in their folk 'literature.' " Those two quilt pieces don't fit together at all. One could even say they clash.

Living by the Word is subtitled *Selected Writings 1973-1987.* It's a short book for a collection that gathers material from a 15-year period—less than half as long as her first book of nonfiction, *In Search of Our Mothers' Gardens.* One possible reason is that most of the early material has already been picked over. In her preface to the earlier book Ms. Walker says that the pieces in it were written between 1966 and 1982. That's a huge overlap. It may be that this new child was born a year or two prematurely. (p. 43)

Noel Perrin, "Another Sojourner," in The New York Times Book Review, *June 5, 1988, pp. 42-3.*

BARBARA CHRISTIAN

By now, *Living by the Word* has been reviewed in many mainstream journals and newspapers. But many readers may have been misled, as I was, by most reviewers' characterizations of this book. Almost invariably they have read it as a collection of traditional essays and compared it, usually unfavorably, to Walker's 1983 collection of nonfiction, *In Search of Our Mothers' Gardens: Womanist Prose;* but in fact, I think that Walker's careful selection of the writing for *Living by the Word* is a clear signal that she is experimenting with a form she has not used before. . . .

Although many of the pieces in *Living by the Word* have been previously published, when arranged as they are in this volume each of them does not seem so much a finished product as writing in process. What Walker gives us is an opportunity to enter into the way she lives with words, how words live and breathe for her, and how, for her, writing is a living process rather than primarily the production of artifacts for publication. Walker's writings are a continuing whole; for her, writing is a healing process as well as a communing with various audiences, human and nonhuman, in the past as well as the present. She often explores apparently similar ideas, feelings, images, in various genres; her use of one form, say the essay, is sometimes complementary, in dialogue, with a poem or short story she'd previously written. It is as if she is an orchestral composer who uses different instruments and arrangements to get inside the nuances of an apparently simple sound.

Living by the Word, Walker's fourteenth book, cannot be appreciated, *heard,* unless it is set in the context of all of her works. Her meditation on her father in the essay **"Father"** recalls, sometimes revises, poems about him published in *Once* (1968), her first collection of poetry, as well as in *Horses Make a Landscape Look More Beautiful* (1984), her most recent. A reminiscence, **"The Old Artist: Notes on Mr. Sweet,"** evokes the personal context for her first published story, **"To Hell With Dying"** (1967) which has just been released as a beautifully illustrated children's book. **"Coming In From the Cold,"** named after one of Bob Marley's songs, is a sensual analysis (the best I've read by anyone) of Celie's language in *The Color Purple,* while Walker's recounting of her visit to Bob Marley's grave in **"Journey to Nine Miles,"** reminds us of her previously published 1975 essay, **"Looking for Zora."**

Even the form of *Living by the Word* resonates with other Walker works—the arrangement of short stories, many at different stages of development, in *You Can't Keep a Good Woman Down* (1981), the use of short units to create different kinds of quilts, a unique characteristic of her three novels. And in many ways Walker's most recent publication complements *The Color Purple,* for in *Living by the Word* she writes *her* letter to God—to her ancestors, to the trees, rocks, animals, to her sisters and brothers, to all that is the universe she'd so succinctly symbolized by the image of the color purple.

Seeing connections among Walker's many works is not merely formal counting, it is integral to what she calls "living by the word." To live by the word is to be on a continuing journey, exploring oneself as part of the universe, the universe as part of oneself where one knows "everything is only a human being." Perhaps because so many of us tend to look at writing primarily as an intellectual product rather than as a spiritual journey, it is not surprising that some reviewers devalued Walker's exposing of work not yet finished, still evolving.

The *New York Times* reviewer was particularly annoyed by her inclusion of the apparently unfinished memoir, **"The Dummy in the Window,"** [see Perrin's excerpt above], whose title refers to the dummy of an "elderly kindly cottony-haired darkie" that was featured for many years in the window of her hometown's Uncle Remus restaurant. Walker begins **"The Dummy in the Window"** with the explanation that she was asked to write an essay on folklore and what it meant to her writing; but because her hometown, Eatonton, was also the home of Joel Chandler Harris, author of the Uncle Remus stories, it was too painful for her to write. Instead she shares with us her notes, her research—not the completed essay. And yet it is the piece's unfinished quality that is so meaningful to me. From such sharing have come the narratives of ex-slaves—of Linda Brent, for example, who could write only that which she could bear to remember, to expose, to craft. It is from this apparent contradiction of not being able to *bear* one's "subject matter" that we reach for understanding and renew the word, even history—for example, most recently, Sethe's path to rememory in Toni Morrison's *Beloved.*

While there are unfinished pieces in *Living,* the work is coherent in its tone and meaning. Walker first speaks to us with a journal entry: "The universe sends me fabulous dreams." By beginning with that most private of experiences, the dream, she sets the tone of the intimate, which is the particular sound of this book. And by sharing with us a dream in which she asks a two-headed woman whether the world will survive and what "I/we could/should do," Walker announces the theme that unites the various pieces of *Living:* that the universe responds to what we do and how we do it. (p. 9)

Walker writes about a variety of subjects that are often labeled topical: animal rights, Our War in Central America, Apartheid, Dessie Woods, homosexuality, vegetarianism. For those who associate African-American women's writing with specifically gender or race issues, or for those who define the political as antithetical to the spiritual, some of these essays may be startling. Has Walker abandoned the political stance she is known for? In writing about animal rights or vegetarianism, has she succumbed to the California New Age diversions of the eighties? What I think is remarkable about these essays is the way she shows that "political" struggle is firmly rooted in the honoring and appreciation of life—a theme some readers may recall as being the focal one in her second novel, *Meridian.* (pp. 9-10)

"The Universe Responds," the last piece in *Living by the Word,* circles back to the beginning of her journey even as Walker has moved beyond that point. There she gives her answer to the question she'd asked the two-headed woman in the dream at the beginning of the book: Will the world survive? "What you ask of the universe it gives"; "Peace will come wherever it is sincerely invited." In sharing with us her journey, Walker invites us to pay attention to our own. (p. 10)

> Barbara Christian, "Conversations with the Universe," in The Women's Review of Books, *Vol. VI, No. 5, February, 1989, pp. 9-10.*

J. M. COETZEE

Readers of *The Color Purple* will remember that part of the book—the less convincing part—consists of letters from Miss Celie's missionary sister about her life in Africa.

The Temple of My Familiar again bears a message from Africa, but this time in a far more determined manner. The message reaches us via Miss Lissie, an ancient goddess who has been incarnated hundreds of times, usually as a woman, sometimes as a man, once even as a lion. Less a character than a narrative device, Lissie enables Alice Walker to range back in time to the beginnings of (wo)man.

Here are just three of the ages in human evolution that Lissie lives through:

First, an age soon after the invention of fire, when humanfolk live in separate male and female tribes, at peace with their animal "familiars." Here Lissie is incarnated as the first white-skinned creature, a man with insufficient melanin, who flees the heat of Africa for Europe. Hating the sun, he invents an alternative god in his own image, cold and filled with rage.

Next, an age of pygmies, when the man tribe and the woman tribe visit back and forth with each other and with the apes. This peaceful, happy age ends when men invent warfare, attack the apes and impose themselves on women as their sole familiars. Thus, says Ms. Walker (rewriting Rousseau and others), do patriarchy and the notion of private property come into being.

Third, the time of the war waged by Europe and monotheistic Islam against the Great Goddess of Africa. The instrument of this warfare is the slave trade (Lissie lives several slave lives). Its emblem is the Gorgon's head, the head of the Goddess, still crowned with the serpents of wisdom, cut off by the white hero-warrior Perseus.

These episodes from the past of (wo)mankind give some idea of the sweep of the myth Alice Walker recounts, a myth that inverts the places assigned to man and woman, Europe and Africa, in the male-invented myth called history. In Ms. Walker's counter-myth, Africa is the cradle of true religion and civilization, and man a funny, misbegotten creature with no breasts and an elongated clitoris.

The impact of Lissie's revelations upon modern black consciousness is traced in the lives of Fanny (Celie's granddaughter) and her ex-husband, Suwelo, a middle-class academic. Suwelo finds his authentic self by absorbing Lissie's message; Fanny finds hers by opening herself to her dreams—her archetypal memories—and by journeying back to meet her African kinfolk.

Suwelo learns that there are better things than philandering and watching football on television. By the end of the book he has rejoined Fanny and lives with her in a house shaped like a bird, in which they have separate wings. As for Fanny: "The women in her consciousness-raising group had taught her how to masturbate. Suddenly she'd found herself free. Sexually free, for the first time in her life. At the same time, she was learning to meditate, and was throwing off the last clinging vestiges of organized religion. She was soon meditating and masturbating and finding herself dissolved into the cosmic All. Delicious."

Such cliché-ridden prose is not representative of the best of *The Temple of My Familiar,* but there is enough of it to give one pause. How deep can Fanny's liberation run when its very language is secondhand? At another level, how seriously can we take Lissie's Europe, whose aboriginal "dark peoples" have been exterminated by white invaders, or her Africa, which reads like an overlay of South Africa over a vaguely realized Nigeria?

The immediate answer is that we betray the book by demanding this kind of realism. We should read it, rather, as a fable of recovered origins, as an exploration of the inner lives of contemporary black Americans as these are penetrated by fabulous stories.

But this answer strikes me as too easy. History is certainly written by people in positions of power, and therefore principally by men. The history of the world—including Africa—is by and large a story made up by white males. Nevertheless, history is not just storytelling. There are certain brute realities that cannot be willfully ignored. Africa has a past that neither the white male historian nor Ms. Walker can simply invent. No doubt the world would be a better place if, like Fanny and Suwelo, we could live in bird-shaped houses and devote ourselves to bread making and massage, and generally adopt Fanny's mother's gospel: "We are all of us *in heaven* already!" Furthermore, I readily concede that inventing a better world between the covers of a book is as much as even the most gifted of us can hope to do to bring about a better real world. But whatever new worlds and new histories we invent must carry conviction: they must be possible worlds, possible histories, not untethered fantasies; and they must be born of creative energy, not of dreamy fads.

There is an element of the book I have neglected thus far, in many ways its most serious element. Fanny's crisis is the crisis of an oppressed woman, but also the crisis of a black person living in the gunsights of white racism who does not want to turn into a hatefilled racist herself. "What do you think of white people?" asks her therapist. In reply, she recounts a terrible recurring dream. A feast is going on at which white people are endlessly eating. Sometimes she is present at their feast as an emaciated, chained slave. Sometimes she is the one being devoured. And sometimes she sees herself participate in the joyless eating. . . .

Revulsion against the death feast of the West and equal revulsion against a countervailing black violence—this is the agony at the root of *The Temple of My Familiar.* Its fierceness erupts at many places in the text. It is an agony experienced by all too many black people across the world. But the brand of salvation discovered by Fanny and Suwelo will help few of them. The words of Fanny's father, in whom there are elements of Wole Soyinka and Nelson Mandela, carry a greater if more chilling conviction: "I have been responsible for the deaths of whites. It did not 'liberate' me psychologically, as Fanon suggested it might. It did not oppress me further, either. I was simply freeing myself from the jail that they had become for me, and making a space in the world, also, for my children."

The Temple of My Familiar is a novel only in a loose sense. Rather, it is a mixture of mythic fantasy, revisionary history, exemplary biography and sermon. It is short on narrative tension, long on inspirational message.

> J. M. Coetzee, "The Beginnings of (Wo)man in Africa," in The New York Times Book Review, *April 30, 1989, p. 7.*

PAUL GRAY

Alice Walker ascended from the realm of mere literature after Steven Spielberg's film adaptation of her novel *The Color Purple.* The movie's huge commercial success—and the controversy that arose over its portrait of black males—ensured Walker's public renown as a woman with a cause, an author who, when she has a message, would rather write a book than call Western Union. Indeed, her poetry and fiction have always been, to some extent, polemical. Now that her potential audience has increased many times over, Walker . . . has become more forthright about the burden

of her prose: the horrors that whites have historically imposed on blacks and that men have inflicted on women. Perhaps these lamentable subjects cannot be exaggerated. But in her latest novel, Walker tries.

The Temple of My Familiar is almost all talk—monologues and dialogues, chiefly by and among black women. The skeletal plot is an excuse to get the conversations going. Suwelo, a black professor of American history, travels from his California home to attend an uncle's funeral in Baltimore and to dispose of the house that comes as his inheritance. . . .

His spirits lift when he meets Mr. Hal and Miss Lissie, two old and aged friends of his uncle's. These two drop by regularly to talk and reminisce; they prove themselves remarkable founts of memory, particularly Miss Lissie, who confides that she has lived in countless incarnations dating back to the dawn of time. Relating her experiences as a slave girl being transported to America, she interrupts herself to warn Suwelo, "You do not believe I was there? I pity you."

Suwelo believes. Short of hustling Miss Lissie out the door, that is probably his only option. For her voluminous story, to which a growing chorus of other voices gradually contributes, is an extended myth that must be taken on faith or not at all. Parts of it are enchantingly beautiful. She remembers primeval Africa as the Edenic cradle of life, when women and men lived separately and thus at peace and when lions killed only to put ailing fellow creatures out of their misery. But then the men decided to force their way into residence at the women's encampments, which Miss Lissie sees as the first of many tragedies: "In consorting with man, as he had become, woman was bound to lose her dignity, her integrity."

More evil followed. Ancient Africa was home to white people as well, but they were driven out because their pitifully pale skins could not protect them from the blazing heat and light ("The white man," Miss Lissie notes, "worships gold because it is the sun he has lost"). Thus was conceived whites' envy of blacks and a determination to crush them, a process that began, at least symbolically, in Greek mythology when Perseus beheaded Medusa, who was really the Great Mother, the Black African Goddess.

None of this admits argument, of course; legends, old or new, are not susceptible to logic. But when Walker's characters venture into more recent history, their opinions, to put it discreetly, seem open to debate. Is it, for instance, true that the white colonial powers driven out of Africa have tried to undermine the liberated countries by flooding them with pornography? . . . [Suwelo's father-in-law], the Minister of Culture of a newly emerged nation, claims that "the reason millions of Africans are exterminating themselves in wars is that the superpowers have enormous stores of outdated weapons to be got rid of." Is this really the whole, or even a valid, explanation of the current slaughters across the continent? . . . [Another character] discusses the viciousness that people, especially white ones, display as the consequence of cruelties done to them when they were young. "I shudder to think," she says, "what Hitler's childhood was like. But anyone can see that the Palestinians and their children are reliving it under the Israelis today."

The most hateful aspect of this last comment is not its content but its smug, self-righteous assurance ("anyone can see"). Ultimately, all of Walker's principal narrators reveal themselves as dictators manqué, people who believe that the truth is whatever they happen to say and who will tolerate no dissenting opinions. Fortunately for them, their author provides none. She rewards her actors with the good life, California style. . . .

Walker's relentless adherence to her own sociopolitical agenda makes for frequently striking propaganda. But affecting fiction demands something more: characters and events in conflict, thoughts striking sparks through the friction of opposing beliefs. The cumbersome ideological weight of *The Temple of My Familiar* will lead some, probably many, to praise it as a novel of ideas. But it is something else entirely, and disturbingly: a novel of allegations.

Paul Gray, "A Myth to Be Taken on Faith," in Time, New York, Vol. 133, No. 18, May 1, 1989, p. 69.

DAVID NICHOLSON

With *The Temple of My Familiar,* Alice Walker seems to have been striving to write a *big* book, the kind writers used to feel they had to write at a certain point in their careers—a significant book jampacked with compelling characters and dealing with the great social and political issues of an age. It would be nice to report that Walker has succeeded, but reading this new novel is much like watching a little girl on parade, all dressed up in her mother's clothes and high heels. One may applaud her cuteness, but it is awfully hard to take her seriously.

The central problem is that this is not a novel so much as it is an ill-fitting collection of speeches, a *faux*-hip tract for the New Puritanism, a manifesto for the Fascism of the New Age. *The Temple of My Familiar* has no plot in the conventional sense of the word, only a series of strung-together stories in which things happen without rhyme or reason. There are no characters, only types representative of the world Walker lives in or wishes could be. And there is no dialogue between these characters. Instead, there are politically correct speeches grounded in knee-jerk feminism (which Walker calls "womanism") and the same catalogue of goofy California enthusiasms—vegetarianism, crystals, massage, psychology, talking to plants, trees and animals, past life regression—that characterized to wretched excess her recent collection of essays, *Living by the Word.*

As it has no conventional structure, it is difficult to summarize *The Temple of My Familiar.* There are several couples: Carlotta (daughter of a widowed Latin American refugee) and Arveyda (a musician reminiscent of the rock star Prince); Hal and Lissie, two older people originally (though this is never quite made clear) from the South Carolina Sea Islands and now living in Baltimore; and Suwelo (a professor of American history who has adopted an African name) and Fanny, his former wife, a woman in search of herself.

Walker's theme appears to be the difficulty of love, the pain men and women must pass through to find themselves and each other, for each of these couples must confront and overcome some internal crisis. It's worth noting here that, as this is womanist fiction, women suffer, but do no wrong. Men, though, are dangerous children infatuated with power and violence, except for those few willing to allow their mates the "space" to search for some mysterious personal fulfillment, and those (even fewer) who have given up their anger and aggression for the satisfaction of bread-baking, vegetarianism, shawl-wearing and soft, plant-fiber sandals.

All of this—the individual passages from fragmentation to wholeness, even the New Age inanities—might be more meaningful had Walker made the characters' dilemmas more powerful. But nothing is dramatized sufficiently, only told flatly with a marked absence of passion. We are told, for example, that there is something missing in Arveyda's life because he does not know who his father is, but not shown how this loss affects him. We are told, not shown, that Carlotta is bereft when she learns that her mother and Arveyda have slept together. And we are told of, and not shown, the disintegration of Suwelo and Fanny's marriage because of Fanny's quest for freedom.

Then, too, Carlotta and Arveyda and Hal and Lissie and Suwelo and Fanny spend page after tiresome page talking to each other. . . . Yet somehow, despite all the talk, despite the ranging among the centuries and from country to country, none of the conflict, none of the dilemmas these people find themselves caught between ever becomes very real. One reads, but does not believe.

It is hard, of course, to be moved by the despair of characters blessed with such material goods as saunas, whirlpool baths, sailboats, country homes in Marin County and recording studios in town homes with views of the Golden Gate Bridge. In the end, however, it is of more consequence that the characters fail to move us because Walker has denied them their integrity—their contrariness, their freedom to be wrong. Instead, she has imposed her consciousness upon them. Many of the stories are told in the first person but, oddly enough, none of the characters sounds like himself; all—from Guatuzocan-born Carlotta to Hal to Fanny—sound alike. After a while the reader realizes that this is the voice of a West Coast intellectual, perhaps even the voice of Walker herself.

The Color Purple, Walker's best-selling novel, was also told in the first person and contained, in germ, some of the same themes. The difference there was that Celie's and Nettie's voices were so real, so right, the reader was willing to overlook the shift in point of view midway through the novel and its dishonest, anachronistic happy ending. Here there are only glimmers of the tough forthrightness that characterized *The Color Purple,* glimmers of what might have been, had Walker not fallen victim to her own publicity or had her editor been courageous enough to save her from her own excess. What Walker has given us [in *The Temple of My Familiar*] is a fragmented hodge-podge, and that is all the more sad because so much of her earlier work was so good, breaking ground that allowed black women (and men) to look at themselves and their lives in new ways. (pp. 3, 5)

David Nicholson, "Alice Walker Trips," in Book World—The Washington Post, May 7, 1989, pp. 3, 5.

RHODA KOENIG

If the statement "Let me tell you about this dream I had" brings from you the response "Why, of course, how lovely," and you *mean* it, then I heartily commend to you *The Temple of My Familiar.* Numerous dreams and remembrances of past lives are related in it, mostly by Miss Lissie, a sort of black Shirley MacLaine who tells of her experiences in the jungle as a boy, her experiences in the jungle as a girl, and the time she visited a temple with her familiar, a creature part bird, part fish, part reptile, which she caged and which, resentfully, broke out and flew away.

The moral of this last story seems to be the one so often seen on inspirational posters—that if you love something, you should set it free, etc. It's a mushy moral, but, then, so much else in *The Temple of My Familiar* is runny tapioca. Readers who were moved by the tough, biting, thrilling voice Walker used in *The Color Purple* will be greatly disappointed by all this yammering about sex, oppression, and the cosmos, all the sanctimony and, literally, sermonizing. . . . (p. 76)

Walker's novel appears at a time when the sixties are being reexamined, with nostalgia and contempt. One's feelings about the period are complicated by its characteristically vexing tendency to express worthy ideals in repulsive language—vulgar, oversimplified, full of strident slogans, goofy slang, or bureaucratic jargon. With the passage of time, one would have thought, the ideals would shine through these tatty disguises and burn them away. But Walker's book is only one of several recent releases that take us back to the preoccupations of that time in the same tiresome language, as if the years had produced no reflection or detachment. Carlotta visits Fanny's massage parlor and thinks, when handed a crystal and promised she will feel its vibration, "This kind of talk seemed the very babble of witches to me." But her next thought—"I couldn't understand why she'd taken such a service-oriented, low-prestige job when she had such solid academic credentials"—is itself a kind of babble. It is a moronic compilation of over-consonanted clichés and belongs in a novel not as a neutral statement but as an object of ridicule, both of the banality itself and of the sort of person it evokes. Walker even reproduces a T-shirt comment of the time, "A woman without a man is like a fish without a bicycle," as an example of feminine wisdom; it may still be, for lesbians, but otherwise it's a pretty threadbare bit of bravado.

In *The Color Purple,* Alice Walker was bitter and defiant about the injustices visited on her race and her sex; that tone made her book effective, and made it possible for readers who had suffered injustice to identify with it, whatever their sex and race. But her new novel is sullen and murky, as her characters drone on about their problems and their feelings and their feelings and their problems. (pp. 76-7)

> *Rhoda Koenig, "Dream On," in* New York *Magazine, Vol. 22, No. 19, May 8, 1989, pp. 76-7.*

LUCI TAPAHONSO

The origin stories of tribal people long ago were accounts of hardship, optimism, love and finally, of endurance. These stories are still told today in various contexts and to listen to the storyteller is to participate in the re-creation of an entire people. It is to participate in the rhythm of ancient voices, complete with nuances and laughs of delight. Or cries of grief. It is to participate in songs, to listen to stories animals have to tell and to believe worlds other than this one exist. Through the storyteller, we experience the dreams, the hopes, pain and the love of a people. We understand it is this love that will outlast us all.

The storyteller in this account is Alice Walker, the acclaimed poet and writer. She asks us to suspend learned literary expectations and become part of the evolution of a people. *The Temple of My Familiar* is technically a work of fiction—it is also the moving account of the outside forces imposed upon

a tribal people, the fears and grief thereof and it speaks directly to the strength of love and the resilience of all living parts of this world—humans, animals, birds, and the Earth itself. This mode of storytelling has nothing to do with linear time, detailed maps or chronological order. It is as simple as telling stories in one's kitchen (which does happen) or over iced tea on the back porch. In this setting, gestures, nuances in narration and facial expressions make it clear as to who is speaking.

The novel begins with Zede, who weaves beautiful peacock feather capes for celebrities in America. This once-revered art was taught to Zede by her mother, who also learned from her own mother. The capes were once part of the ritual ceremonial regalia worn by her ancestors in South America. In San Francisco, Zede sells the exquisite capes to support herself and her daughter, Carlotta. The capes have become a fashion showpiece and available only to the rich and extravagant. Zede is one of the last remaining survivors of her aboriginal community and the stories following are heartwrenching accounts of the colonization of a people. Through Zede's and other characters' voices, we experience the effects of Christianization on native people and the effects of "civilization." The stories are first-hand accounts and draw us in immediately and the events are not obscure historical facts, after all. It is real and painful. The power of the oral tradition is overwhelming. We understand the loss and pain when American Indians speak today of the Cherokee Trail of Tears or the Long Walk of the Navajos, their eyes glistening with tears. Walker intends it to be this way as history creates us, and centuries or decades have no meaning in this context.

The six major characters in this book tell their stories to each other. We are eavesdroppers. We are fortunate as their voices are distinct, poetic at times, and always filled with the love of language and of humor. This is particularly true with the elderly characters—Lissie, Hal, Shug and Celie. (pp. 1, 13)

Fanny and Lissie are two of the strongest characters in *Temple.* They are very intuitive and their stories are bursting with innate strength, incredible psychic abilities and a belief in more than this world. Through them, we learn of other life forces and other planes of existence. Through them, we examine the evolution of gender roles and the possibility of an existence of a true egalitarian society before the institutions of family, marriage and patriarchy were established.

This book is a celebration of ordinary life and of everyday emotions. Whether it is Lissie and Hal cooking gumbo and telling stories, the aroma of fresh homemade bread or the sounds of children in the next room—our senses are alert. . . .

Racism is a daily issue for many people of color and this is addressed deftly and with compassion. For instance, when Mr. Hal tells Suwelo about the purchase of a home: "No doubt the neighbors thought the house too fine for 'niggers' . . . I don't think black people were allowed in that part of town then. But we were so discreet they hardly ever saw us. . . .

Walker explains that anger and violence will not change the world, but an appreciation of each other will improve our lot here.

Finally, *The Temple of My Familiar* is a novel about love—in all its forms; love for spirits and spirituality, love for the land and plants, love for all people—regardless of color, sexual preference or age—and love for all living things. It is about compassion for the oppressed, the grief of the oppressors, acceptance of the unchangeable and hope for everyone and everything.

Alice Walker has written beautifully about dreams, the power of stories—and about the remarkable strength of our own histories. (p. 13)

Luci Tapahonso, "Learning to Love through Storytelling," in Los Angeles Times Book Review, *May 21, 1989, pp. 1, 13.*

JAMES WOLCOTT

Cover to cover, Alice Walker's **The Temple of My Familiar** is the nuttiest novel I've ever read. (And I read [Norman Mailer's] *Ancient Evenings.*) Helpful, talky, **The Temple of My Familiar** subordinates fictional interest—character, plot, atmosphere; stuff like that—in order to function as a workshop. It's many workshops in one.

A civics workshop. "I realize . . . that there is not a single government in the world I like or trust. They are all, as far as I'm concerned, unnatural bodies, male-supremacist private clubs."

A Middle East workshop. " 'I shudder to think what Hitler's childhood was like,' she said. 'But anyone can see that the Palestinians and their children are reliving it under the Israelis today.' "

An our-friends-the-animals workshop. "The animals can remember; for, like sight, memory is renewed at every birth. But our language they will never speak; not from lack of intelligence, but from the different construction of their speaking apparatus." (p. 28)

And—could everyone please be seated? people, *please*—a wardrobe workshop.

> I watched my mother magically create garments in that particular shade of blue, which she eventually dubbed "Power Blue."

> I was fascinated by her. . . . By the way she invariably wore pants, even to church. But pants so subtle only other women noticed they were pants.

Baby, when you wear those subtle Power Blue pantsuits, my bad James Brown self breaks out in a (song cue!) "Cold Sweat."

The Temple of My Familiar could use a little James Brown backbeat, a soulful bit of butt-funk to stir the dead air droning from the workshops. But Walker's book is New Age in its non-stop om toward oneness. In her earlier novels (the most famous being, of course, *The Color Purple*), Walker was a storyteller with a message; **The Temple of My Familiar** finds her an oracle with a mission. Her characters are merely mouths at the workshop mikes. She uses the squelch knob on her sound board to maintain a level tone. Take Arveyda, for example. A Jimi Hendrix voodoo chile festooned in headband, cape, and feathers, Arveyda makes women weep and moan with his guitar and flute. But his music is a tamer call to communion than the mortar barrage and air raid siren unleashed by Hendrix's amps. No cock-rock pagan, Arveyda is "a deeply spiritual person" who plays "softly and prayerful-

ly." The angels dote on every suspended note. Blessed are the meek, for they shall inherit the Power Blue pantsuits.

It's the women who wear most of the power pants in **The Temple of My Familiar.** The Force is with them. Unlike men, women are centered. Precivilization prospered when women straddled their curve of the planet. Via a long monologue by Arveyda's mother-in-law, Zede, Walker transports us back to our matriarchal beginnings, to that matriarchal Eden so dear to mystical feminists. Back then man was not the measure. Man mirrored woman. A man's penis was simply an "elongated clitoris," dangling without significance. Man's prowess on the hunt was also a paltry show. "The men . . . were better hunters than the women, but only because the women had found they could live quite well on foods other than meat. . . ." Like all green idylls, this one was doomed to spoil. The meat went to the men's heads. They began to mutter. To seethe. To scheme. Zede suggests that the real reason men rebelled was that women laughed at them for lacking dress sense. "The finery the women wore seemed to prove their supernaturalness. The men, lacking the centuries of clothing and adornment experience of the women, were able to make only the clumsiest imitations."

How mortifying it must have been, to strut into the village square in your sharpest-looking pelt, acting, *feeling* good, only to hear snickers from every corner of the bazaar. What a bringdown! Small wonder the menfolk got testy. "The men grew sick of the women they worshiped. And by now they had made an important discovery about women's ability to produce life. That discovery was—and it had been kept well hidden by woman for a very long time—that the life that woman produced came out of a hole at her bottom!" To copy this capacity for childbearing, some men begin chopping off their penises, "trying to fashion a hole through which life could come." These guys really didn't have a *clue.*

Not that modern men are any more attuned. White men in Alice Walker's writing are mostly offstage, waging war, ruining economies, bleeding nature. It's the black man who carries the oppression indoors. . . . Walker has been accused of being opportunistic in her slam-dunk of black men. In his hilarious, rampaging satire *Reckless Eyeballing,* Ishmael Reed (without naming names) suggests that black feminists such as Walker, Nzotake Shange, and Michelle Wallace are sellout stooges for their white sisters, cashing in on society's fear of the black man. By melodramatizing the dark side of Mister moon, Walker is able to titillate and wow a crossover audience of white readers wanting to think the worst of black men. Reed claims that the black feminist (who is often a middle-class softie trying to act African-militant) makes a phony show of her scarred hide to say what a white feminist would find too impolitic to say—namely, that the black man is part of the problem rather than the solution, more oppressor than oppressed. In other words, Alice Walker is taking in Gloria Steinem's dirty laundry.

The thesis isn't all paranoia. Alice Walker and Gloria Steinem *are* friends, and white women *do* make up the bulk of the book-buying public. Walker sells loads more books trashing black men than John Edgar Wideman does dramatizing their plight. . . . Yet black male authors can't come on all so miffed and innocent at this turn of events. There *is* a savage streak of misogyny in large stretches of their writing, from the rape exploits of Eldridge Cleaver in *Soul on Ice* to the barely suppressed cry of "bitch" in even Ishmael Reed's best work, not to mention the pimp chronicles of Iceberg Slim. Black women can back up their right to glare.

Without trying to be accommodating, Walker lowers the glare in *The Temple of My Familiar,* engaging the black man/black woman problem non-confrontationally, through talk therapy. ("Talking," says one character, "is the very *afro*-disiac of love.") Gone is the fear-mongering of *The Color Purple.* The black men may be simple meatloaf compared with the women, but they aren't menacing; they're left behind and ineffectual, even sheepish about their shortcomings. "His generation of men had failed women—and themselves, he mused, taking off his tortoiseshell glasses and stroking the ridge of his generous and somewhat shiny nose."

The sheepish owner of that shiny nose is Suwelo, a black historian who Toms in his profession, teaching history as the record of "What a few white men wanted, thought, and did." Suwelo isn't a total Tom. He takes a pathetic sneaky pride in pencilling in a few black men's names on the scorecard of this Caucasian all-star team. Men's names, because women don't rank on his roster. He doesn't even read women writers, white or black. In his complacent myopia, Suwelo is a stand-in for those black male writers Walker chastised in her essay collection *In Search of Our Mothers' Gardens* for dissing their black sisters. In your face, Ishmael Reed: "Though black women have religiously read every black male writer that came down the pike (usually presenting black females as witches and warlocks), few black men have thought it of any interest at all to read black women. As far as they're concerned, they have the whole picture."

One of this novel's workshop tasks is to re-educate Suwelo and by extension all black men who think they have the whole picture. First, Suwelo's sense of history is humbled . . . , then his sexual pride is shot down. . . . He learns to bend. He learns to extend. "Here's my hand in strugglehood," he says to a black woman named Fanny. "Let's shake on it." Suwelo grows as a person, but his growth is entirely on Walker's terms—he comes around to her way of thinking. The book tutors him and in tutoring him becomes tedious.

No such tutoring is needed for Arveyda, the New Age avatar who knows that woman is of herself entire. One night after a concert he sees a woman sporting a T-shirt that reads "A Woman without a Man Is like a Fish without a Bicycle." That tired old line!—if I had a dime for every time the black feminist Flo Kennedy has croaked it over the years, I could buy that pair of Power Blue pants I've been eyeing. But because Arveyda is secure with himself, man enough to be a woman, he's rewarded with the novel's showcase prize of penetration. He and Fanny fuse, she on top. (He's no colonizer.) Predictably, their happiness is a cosmic happening. . . . (pp. 28-9)

All this starshine doesn't obscure Walker's long-term political agenda. Her conception of multiethnic society is an Indian corncob with white, black, red, and yellow arrayed side by side like kernels. (Ideally, the cob is then used to cornhole capitalism.) But sometimes the kernels have their own ideas, and being a hard-line radical means having to sweat out the deviations. Revolution is a permanent workshop. (pp. 29-30)

The Temple of My Familiar is an attempt to mindbend the stubborn vanities of human nature . . . by intoning an earth-mother mantra. Like that masturbation workshop, Walker's book seeks to dissolve personal/political tensions in the cos-

mic All. Etherealizing to the nth degree in her novel, Walker constructs a cosmology that unthrones the male order. Zede's monologue about matriarchal Eden is more than a matter of auld lang syne. It serves to build the basis of Walker's mythos, to truly locate our mothers' gardens. The geographical center of this mythos is Mother Africa, its moral and spiritual center the black African woman.

Mother Africa's kharmic ambassadress in *The Temple of My Familiar* is Lissie, a woman whose past lives are as thick as a pack of cards. . . . In her restless odyssey the quintessence of black womanhood rejoices to the glory not of—well, certainly not that old fraud, God. God Himself has been unthroned in this grand scenario. The mother of Mother Africa is "the Great Mother, Creator of All, Protector of All, the Keeper of the Earth. *The* Goddess." The Goddess is nothing less than the immortal face of feminism. In the late 20th century, lesbians are Her light brigade. . . .

If *The Temple of My Familiar* undulated, it would be a hootchie-cootchie dance to castration. It's too high-minded for that. Pantheistic plea, lesbian propaganda, past-lives chronicle, black-pride panorama, *The Temple of My Familiar* doesn't really gel at any junction. Its counterculturalism is too dreamy-floaty to connect with the crackhead immediacies of the times. Not that Alice Walker doesn't have as much right as Swedenborg or Blake to construct a cosmology. If she wishes to indulge in pantheism (she has confessed to being a tree-hugger), that's her prerogative too. The catch is that *her* cosmology doesn't transcend the self but reeks of ineffable egotism. Walker carries on in *The Temple of My Familiar* as if she were Mother Africa's flower-power favorite. Her hippie prose is a form of handicrafts, tie-dyed and dated.

Walker is herself a hippie artifact. In a credit note at the end of *The Temple of My Familiar,* she writes, "I thank the Universe for my participation in Existence. It is a pleasure to have always been present." Like Lissie, Walker is her own astral projection. The drumbeat of her Word reaches beyond barriers of race, sex, time, space, and species. Asked by *USA Weekend* about the reactions to her books, Walker replied, "The ancestors were really happy with *The Color Purple.* The animals are pleased with *The Temple of My Familiar,*" and at the end of the invitation to the New York publication party for *The Temple of My Familiar* is the request: "Please come in the spirit of the animal who is your twin." A party of animals! But animals don't buy a lot of books, and the first printing of *Temple* is 175,000 copies. (Which means a lot fewer trees to hug.) Oh, well, back to the Ouija board. (p. 30)

James Wolcott, "Party of Animals," in The New Republic, *Vol. 200, No. 22, May 29, 1989, pp. 28-30.*

URSULA K. LE GUIN

The richness of Alice Walker's [*The Temple of My Familiar*] is amazing, overwhelming. A hundred themes and subjects spin through it, dozens of characters, a whirl of times and places. None is touched superficially: all the people are passionate actors and sufferers, and everything they talk about is urgent, a matter truly of life and death. They're like Dostoyevsky's characters, relentlessly raising the great moral questions and pushing one another towards self-knowledge, honesty, engagement. . . .

As I read *The Temple of My Familiar,* the kalei-doscope of

people and relationships occasionally daunted and confused me. I wanted just to slow down and get to know somebody better. There were times I felt like saying, "Dear Genius, please—you don't have to get it *all* into one book!" But it's her book, and she gets it all in. It isn't a novel of observation or of meditation, it's a story of transformation, and the essence of transformation is that it goes on. It's not a matter of "conflict" and "resolution" as in the laboratory-novel, but of urging, asserting, and recording *change*. Every character in the book bears witness that if we don't change, we perish.

The characters all tell one another fiercely, tenderly, how the world is and why and who they are and who they ought to be. Often they lecture. The book would go stiff, go dead, at these points, except that even the lectures are borne and buoyed by the current of passion and sympathy. The anger is great but not rigid, not self-righteous. It explodes. It unbuilds. Some of the characters are more mouthpiece than person, but even if they're all talk, their talk is powerful, vivid, funny, and also what one says another may contradict just as vehemently. They are all trying (as Shug puts it) "to keep their feet on the goddam Path." (p. 12)

Lissie's memories carry us back several times to prehistoric lives, Africa of the human dawn, lovingly and fearfully imagined. So many women are writing such imaginations now that it is surely a communal undertaking responding to a communal need. Those whose minds are locked in the conservatism of "growth," and even "higher" technology based on unlimited exploitation, see these tribal societies (real and imagined) only as escapist regressions; they cannot understand that women are studying such societies in a radical and subversive effort to think back to before things went wrong. What went wrong, they say, was Civilization—Western Civ—The White Man's World. (By the way, Asia is notably lacking from this book; it's Africa, Europe, and the Americas, and I don't think one of all the many characters is East or West Asian. But now here I am asking her to get it all in!) To get away from or back before all that takes a long mental journey, and a hard one, since the evidence of what went before white patriarchy has been systematically defiled and destroyed. But the women writing these books are going back so we can go forward, so we can realistically try to get our feet on the goddam Path. No more temples, they say, built on the bones of our children: we are trying to get down to the sacred earth, and build right. Not easy, and anything but a simplification. The complexity of Alice Walker's book—a rainforest tangle, the front and back of the tapestry seen all at once—perfectly embodies its vision of life, not alienated, rigid, hierarchized, bleached, "the color of cheap false teeth," but life interlocked, multiple, multiplying, endless, desirous, vociferous, and gorgeously peacock-colored.

Virginia Woolf said that "the words ride on the back of the rhythm." The rhythms of Alice Walker's prose are beautiful and characteristic, flexible, vigorous, easy, the gait of a hunting lion. Even when the pace of the story crowds and races and the words are choked with meaning and intent, the rthythms never falter. The lion goes her way. (p. 13)

Ursula K. Le Guin, "All Those at the Banquet," in San Francisco Review of Books, *Summer, 1989, pp. 12-13.*

CHRISTOPHER ZINN

The Temple of My Familiar, centers on three pairs of characters: Suwelo, a professor of history, and Fanny, an academic administrator, have divorced but continue to live alongside each other in San Francisco while sorting out the tangled threads of their lives. Carlotta, a professor of women's studies, and her husband, Arveyda, a famous and successful musician, live in the Oakland hills. A third, older couple, Hal and Lissie, enter the story when their friend Rafe dies and his nephew Suwelo comes to Baltimore to meet them. The young people's marriages have temporarily broken down while each of them follows perilous and surprising paths of self-discovery. Fanny becomes a masseuse and eventually travels to Africa to find her father, a mysterious figure who turns out to be a controversial playwright in the independent nation of the Olinka. Arveyda abandons Carlotta and accompanies her mother Zede to her South American homeland. Left alone, Suwelo and Carlotta pursue a turbulent affair.

But these incidents are hardly presented in a straightforward and incidental way; rather, they emerge from the many stories each of the characters is involved in some way telling. Fanny writes beautiful letters to Suwelo, full of the marvelous discoveries she makes in Africa concerning her own lineage. Arveyda tells Carlotta about his own painful childhood. Carlotta resorts to a therapist until Fanny becomes her friend and confidante. When Suwelo meets Hal and Lissie in Baltimore, he learns about the unconventional bonds of love and affection that these two friends shared with Suwelo's Uncle Rafe. Suwelo, in turn, starts to tell these remarkable old people about his own problems, and in so doing begins to understand the full significance of his actions.

In dazzling fashion, the novel moves along these various streams of conversation, storytelling and memory, recovering the various combinations of ancestry and incident that, pasted together, form the long foreground of these contemporary African-American lives. . . . The novel draws to a close as the two younger couples, having struggled separately through discord and perplexity, become friends and intimates, and seem destined to share their lives in trust and affection, as Lissie and Rafe and Hal had done before them.

At the center of this collective recovery is Lissie, "the one who remembers everything." This great "rememberer" teaches Suwelo the story of the African race while counseling him on the conduct of life's enigmas. Her own memories extend through several reincarnations and include what she calls "dream memories" of earliest human time, when, she says, humans and animals lived together as "familiars" in an Eden-like African paradise. Like Zede, Lissie remembers the ways in which women once conducted their lives and taught their traditions to their daughters.

She recalls as well how successful men attempt to mimic and eventually usurp the prerogatives of women, and their subsequent invention of various misogynous regimes with which to keep women in their hurtful place. Hence, her "memories" are also a critique of the power relations that govern the interaction of blacks and whites and of women with men. Such profound probing of the racial memory, of the species' collective experience, seems the special prerogative of women in this book. (p. 90)

Lissie's memories at times seem more typical than personal. When she recalls that "I was sold to one planter, my sisters and brothers to others. We never heard from each other again," she also recapitulates the archetypal if seldom commemorated experience of black African women during their enslavement and transportation to America. Nor can she be far from the catastrophic norm when she remembers that "my weakened body gave up the ghost—in other words, I died." It seems difficult, at times, to separate vivid memory from prophetic invention in Lissie's narratives. Her story, for instance, of a painful expulsion from a kind of Eden ("We lived at the edge of an immense woods. . . . We had fire by then . . . a recent invention. . . . I wish the world today could see our world as it was then.") is also an impressive attempt to rewrite the Book of Genesis from the perspective of a feminist anthropology. Yet Lissie's insistence on the mysterious operations of deep memory ("Some people don't understand that it is the nature of the eye to have seen forever, and the nature of the mind to recall anything that was ever known.") tends to mask Alice Walker's own artful transactions with such authoritative texts as the Bible and Milton's *Paradise Lost.*

Lissie's visions emerge as much from the modern writer's explorations in the archive as much as they emanate from the superhuman recesses of Lissie's memory. Hence it is appropriate that, although she begins speaking to Suwelo in person, Lissie later writes letters to him in disappearing ink and, in her final remove, addresses him through a cassette recording after she has died. There are times in this book, indeed, when the outlines of the characters dissolve and we have a clear view of Alice Walker the essayist. Even so, this voice—however much simply Walker's "own"—is never uninteresting, often mesmerizing and occasionally awe-inspiring. When Fanny explains to Suwelo that "men must have mercy on women," her wisdom reverberates with Lissie's as much as Walker's own. In a similar way, what Lissie "sees" in the ancient garden turns out to be what Fanny and Arveyda glimpse when they make love. . . .

Thus the lives of those distant ancestors in the great forests of Africa are in a sense remembered whenever their descendants draw close to each other in happiness and love. For this artist as for her characters there exists an almost mystical affinity between memory and imagination, just as there obtain hidden connections between the lives of these individuals and the spiritual and physical continuity of the African people. And although it would be ill-advised to underestimate the importance of her identity as a woman and an African-American to Walker's artistic vision, that vision applies to human culture in the broadest sense. (p. 91)

In this remarkable novel, Walker summons her considerable store of fable and tragedy, of historical insight and passionate argument, to convey similar strengths and joys to her reader. (p. 92)

Christopher Zinn, in a review of "The Temple of My Familiar," in America, *Vol. 161, No. 4, August 12-19, 1989, pp. 90-2.*

Christa Wolf

1929-

(Born Christa Ihlenfeld) East German novelist, essayist, short story writer, and editor.

Among the most respected and popular German postwar novelists, Wolf probes issues of individual identity, artistic expression, and personal accountability under authoritarian regimes. Her internationally acclaimed works reflect her own experiences as a former Hitler youth, a socialist critical of Communism, and a woman disillusioned with male-dominated Western culture. Suppressed artistically and politically, Wolf's protagonists often defy social and governmental dictates as they strive for identity, truth, love, and integrity. In her presentation of everyday human dramas set against a background of war, repression, or environmental threats, Wolf stresses an intrinsic relation between personal concerns and political action. For example, she urges her peers to examine their own complicity in Nazism and to employ an analytical, balanced approach toward both capitalism and Communism. From the beginning of Wolf's career through the 1980s, her dissenting political views and her refusal to write in the objective Socialist-Realist mode generated controversy within the German Democratic Republic (GDR). Denouncing Wolf's political convictions, East German authorities limited public access to her work. West German officials, however, honored Wolf with their country's most prestigious literary award, the Georg Büchner Preis.

In Wolf's first work of fiction, *Moskauer Novelle* (1961; *Moscow Novella*), a love affair between an East Berlin doctor on tour in Moscow and her Russian translator serves as an allegory for political relations between Germany and the Soviet Union. Wolf's second work, *Der geteilte Himmel* (1963; *The Divided Heaven*), earned substantial critical notice, government support, and a wide readership in both East and West Germany. While recovering from a suspicious accident, protagonist Rita Seidel reevaluates her decision not to join her lover Manfred, who fled to the West just before the erection of the Berlin Wall in August, 1961. Manfred's cynicism toward socialism has driven him to the West, but Rita's deep loyalty to her homeland precludes her emigration, and the building of the Berlin Wall seals her decision. Western reviewers, who interpreted Rita's accident as an unconscious suicide attempt, lauded the novel as a timely discussion of East German anxieties. Conversely, GDR government reviewers, who awarded the novel the Heinrich Mann Prize, commended Wolf's portrayal of an earnest heroine who affirms socialist tenets.

Official disapproval accompanied the limited East German publication of Wolf's *Nachdenken über Christa T.* (1968; *The Quest for Christa T.*), a fictional memorial of the title character—a frustrated writer and housewife who died of leukemia. The novel is narrated by Christa T.'s college companion, who searches for meaning in her deceased friend's life by examining Christa's education, her marriage, and the prevailing literary conventions that thwarted her sensitive, subjective mode of expression. Because Wolf presents Christa as an ordinary woman representative of her generation, government reviewers reproached the novel's lack of an exemplary

socialist heroine, but West German scholarly and popular audiences celebrated the book as a probing study of individual development and disillusionment.

In the autobiographical novel *Kindheitsmuster* (1976; *A Model Childhood,* later published as *Patterns of Childhood*), Wolf again addresses a topic often avoided in East Germany, the acceptance of national guilt. This work, considered Wolf's most ambitious in its integration of past events and present realities, involves the narrator's trip back to the village where she lived as a youth during the Nazi era. The narrator grows in self-knowledge as she attempts to confront and explain her acceptance of Nazism to her daughter, who is similarly involved in ideological confusion—in her case, the differences between capitalism and communism. Margaret McHaffie remarked: "This is a disquieting novel, not least in its revelation of how easy it was to hoodwink many ordinary people about the nature of the Nazi regime. The narrator depicts the insidious advance of Nazism among the innocents of the 1930s, the naïveté with which often decent people succumbed to the appeal of romanticized brutality, the lure of banners, songs and emotional rallies." Reviewers in both German states esteemed the novel as a frank and persuasive argument that equates individual apathy with personal complicity in murderous policies from fascism to such contemporary hostilities as the war in Vietnam and Middle-Eastern conflicts.

In *Kein Ort. Nirgends* (1979; *No Place on Earth*), Wolf creates a fictional encounter between two nineteenth-century German literary figures, Heinrich von Kleist and Karoline von Günderrode. These Romantic writers, both of whom later committed suicide, meet in Wolf's novel to discuss the artist's place in modern society. Joyce Crick remarked: "[*No Place on Earth*] takes the form of a dual stream-of-consciousness, and an imaginary conversation between Kleist and Günderrode composed of a complex collage drawn from their writings, letters, journals, metaphors: a duet on the importance and vulnerability of creation in dark times, on male and female sensibilities, on death, friendship and hope." While some critics found this historical, erudite novel objectionably obscure, others commented that Wolf's obfuscation allows her to discuss issues her government considers inflammatory, such as social alienation, limitations on writing, and suicide.

As she recasts the Greek myth of the prophetess Cassandra in *Voraussetzungen einer Erzahlung: Kassandra* (1983; *Cassandra: A Novel and Four Essays*), Wolf again manipulates a historical setting to allegorically address modern anxieties. The essays and novel, all initially presented in West Germany as a lecture series, relate Wolf's reaction to her reading of Aeschylus's *Oresteia,* her trip to Greece, the process of writing her reinterpretation, and Wolf's tale itself. Considered by many critics to be an effort at establishing a feminine poetics, the novel disavows the violent heroic epics of Homer and the male-centered literary traditions he founded. Less a gifted prophetess than a clear-sighted daughter of a corrupted monarch, Wolf's Cassandra evolves from loyal princess to disillusioned outcast because she refuses to espouse her father's immoral policies. Cassandra escapes from a Trojan prison into the comfort of a colony of ostracized, goddess-worshipping women, then forsakes her lover Aeneas because he will become an epic hero and thus a subscriber to the belligerent, fraudulent precepts that have destroyed Troy. While some commentators considered Wolf's feminist themes doctrinaire, many lauded her depiction of an individual's struggle against conformity and her reassessment of cultural foundations. Ernst Pawel concluded: "Christa Wolf has brilliantly rewritten history, and in viewing the past through the eyes of the doomed seer, she traces its link to our own imminent future. The question she leaves eloquently unasked is whether mankind—men, women and children alike—will this time listen to Cassandra before the Trojan horses already in their silos deliver a final answer." The accompanying essays, which directly discuss current threats to the individual from restrictive governments and nuclear weapons, were not originally intended for publication within the GDR, but were later printed with substantial deletions.

In *Störfall* (1987; *Accident: A Day's News*), Wolf openly recounts her reaction to the nuclear accident at Chernobyl. Published just one year after the Soviet reactor meltdown, this novel chronicles the terror-filled day in which the narrator first learns of the radiation damage to her environment. Such routines as visiting grandchildren, picking garden produce, and walking in the countryside are now potentially dangerous, and her anxiety is compounded by concern for her brother, who is undergoing delicate brain surgery that same day. As she awaits news of her brother's condition and reports on radioactive clouds, the narrator meditates on the power and peril of technology; her brother may survive his ordeal only to discover a contaminated world. Mary Gordon observed: "*Accident: A Day's News* has the grandeur of a noble labor. The woman, the writer, the sister, the mother, the cook, the gardener, the citizen of the world must use her whole life to keep back the lie of separateness: the poison of the lie that fission is to be desired, the disease of schizophrenia with which each modern man and woman lives, forgetting that terrible forces shape our lives."

(See also *CLC,* Vols. 14, 29; *Contemporary Authors,* Vols. 85-88; and *Dictionary of Literary Biography,* Vol. 75.)

MICHAEL NAUMANN

Cassandra—daughter of the Trojan King Priam, prophetess, madwoman, murdered as a slave in the house of the victorious Atridae—is the title, and the heroine, of a slim novella by the East German writer Christa Wolf. In the stillness that has prevailed within German literature for some years, this work about the Trojan catastrophe has the sound of a distant but nonetheless unmistakable sigh. (p. 40)

Cassandra is, on the face of it, a feminist revision of Aeschylus's *Oresteia.* Christa Wolf believes neither in fate nor in the gods, and most decidedly not in their childish imitators, the heroes in shining armor. But it is the book's other truths, its private laments about love and about men, its pain and its thousand precisely catalogued sentiments, that weigh more heavily. They reflect German, not Hellenic, anxieties; and also the traditional German difficulty of transmuting those anxieties into practical political actions. The preference is for a new world. *Cassandra* foretells a downfall of existing political institutions. This land and its artists love downfalls.

Wolf has brought back to life the *Bildungsroman,* that typically German genre that seemed to have been buried with Thomas Mann. Her novella's heroine has the same elevated style as its author. The book resounds loudly with the thumpings of bronze swords on leather shields; it is written with the pathos of a funeral oration. The gods and heroes of Greece are once again fixed in the firmament of German spiritual life—this time, though, as failures. There is an admirable device at work here, as old as the dramatic competitions of Athens themselves: Christa Wolf, who grew up on Karl Marx, himself a lover of the classics, transposes her German themes—fear of war, loneliness, spiritual flight in a world administered with icy exactitude—to the distant cosmos of Greek myths. Thus she gives modern anxieties a classical aura, and literary authority as well. Whatever seems timeless by virtue of its costuming in an age-old tradition must also be true.

Because her modern Cassandra believes neither in the gods nor in any authorities above and beyond her own prophetic frenzy, Wolf is able to imbue her work with the charm of startling anachronism. Glaring neon light shines upon this book as if to proclaim over the entrance to the Temple of Apollo: "The prophet is in." On the compact stage of Greek mythology this Cassandra disports herself with the skeptical, ironic, scornful, and vulnerable awareness of a disappointed peace activist toward the close of the twentieth century.

Wolf's Cassandra arraigns the military—that is, masculine—decisions of Troy, and wants to convince the royal parents that war for the sake of the beautiful Helen is senseless. The contemporary reader should realize, however, that Homer (and his listeners) did not employ such terms as "sense," "decision," or even "psyche"—and that in the god-ruled world of the Atridae there were no concepts (and no commensurate experiences, either) that would correspond to what the sociological jargon of Marxism might term "the autonomy of Cassandra as a subject." Thus it happens that Wolf's heroine now and then suggests one of those eccentric Anouilh productions of the 1950s—Antigone in a Dior dress, or Odysseus in a double-breasted suit. This proclivity to modernize may well be rooted in the author's own disappointed experience of the classics: "To whom shall I confess," she asks in an essay appended to the book, "that the *Iliad* bores me?" The Cassandra of Aeschylus foretells fate, the ineluctable. Wolf's Cassandra pours out her scorn upon people blind to their own fate and unable to confront it. She is not the daughter of Hecuba, but of Rosa Luxemburg.

The narrative begins with an interior monologue of the enslaved Cassandra in front of the Lion's Gate at Mycenae, a few hours before the sacrificial death that fate has determined for her. Anamnesis—recollections of the decisive experiences at Troy—is the technique, and at the same time the path of the book through the thicket of associations, fragmentary experiences, and rediscovered emotions. Cassandra recollects her childhood at the court of Troy. She remembers her young lover Aeneas, who did not dare to touch her—a mythological lover indeed. She recounts the magic religious world of her slaves, the gods that failed before all others. And she chronicles the events that led to the downfall of her city: how her brother Paris kidnapped Helen from the Greeks, how on his way home he lost her again to the enthralled king of Egypt (no, this is not the official version of Homer). It was a cruel joke, perpetrated by Troy's royal politburo—a whole city fighting for an idea, for Paris's honor and Helen's beauty, when in reality the lady was not there at all. Is this what Wolf is trying to tell her readers: that ideas are not worth fighting for?

At the close Cassandra stands before the reader as a whole person, calmly awaiting death, without hope, but replete with pleasure at the fulfillment of the downfall she had foretold: "For I drew pleasure from all things I saw—pleasure, not hope! And lived on to behold." This is the pleasure of being proved right, a German propensity that also permeates the day-to-day doings of the nation's peace movement. Cassandra, who has foretold the downfall of Troy, who saw through what was happening—the sclerotic politics of Priam, the Gestapo mentality of the besieged Trojans, the psychopathology of "Achilles, the brute"—she, the prophetess, believes she has uncovered the secret of her city, even of the Greeks themselves: "O, that they don't know how to live. That this is the real misfortune, the truly fatal danger—I came to understand this only gradually." For a prophetess that last remark is a rather curious admission.

This Cassandra, and not the one chosen by the gods, totters between epileptically induced frenzies and feminist meditations. In her many roles—eye-witness and member of a conquered people, daughter, culprit, citizen of Troy, mother, intellectual, outsider—she fulfills all the analytic burdens the author has loaded upon her. In her accompanying essay Wolf writes, for instance, that Cassandra "is one of the first feminine figures whose destiny has had a predetermining effect on

what was to happen to women across three thousand years: that she is transformed into an object." (Supposedly she was raped by the Achaean Ajax the Lesser at the sanctuary of Athena.) As a good Marxist intellectual, Wolf treats the half-mythical, half-historical princess "as a vibrant, socially and politically committed person," who wants to find out about things for herself. The only possible profession for her caste—that of priestess—is seen as part of the "emancipation process" from her aristocratic family background. Happily such nonsensical interpretations didn't find their way out of the essay and into the fiction itself. In her literary guise Cassandra remains less categorizable, and what Wolf threatens—"To lead her back out of the myth and into the (apparent) social and historical coordinates" of the ancient world—does not happen, owing to her own poetic power.

What remains is a *roman à clef* setting forth German anxieties in a manner that could not be more intense:

> The future speaks to me in only this one sentence: I will be murdered no later than today. . . . The thought occurs to me that I am secretly following the course of my fear. Or more accurately, the course of its unbridling, or still more accurately, its liberation. Yes, fear, too, can be liberated, and thus is shown to belong together with everything and everyone that is oppressed.

Argos and Troy, Agamemnon and Priam: in Wolf's **Cassandra** these are terms for war preparations, self-deception, the madness of male heroism—not what is discovered in the dim past but striking symbols of the German present, in East and West.

While Cassandra could still give shrill voice to her anxieties, however, Wolf virtually gives up on language in her essay: "What these anonymous planning staffs have in mind for us is unspeakable; the language that could encompass it appears not to exist." (pp. 40-2)

"Anxiety," Europe's sense of life in the war years up to 1945, seemed until recently to be no longer a characteristic of the Germans—at most an obsession of Woody Allen (whose modest art has been enormously celebrated in Germany). But today German teachers, artisans, students, and apprentices take out half-page advertisements to proclaim that "We are afraid." A nation of Cassandras searching for the experience of Troy? Wolf may be on to something. (p. 41)

Into [the] empty chamber of the German spirit, into the self-imposed uneventfulness of the past two decades, economic and political malaise has forcibly penetrated. . . . [There] has been nothing in recent years to raise the spirits of the nation. It's as if the enemy were already at the gates.

The realm which German poets and philosophers—Goethe, Schiller, Hölderlin, Kleist, Novalis, the Schlegels—discovered two centuries ago, and which German archeologists dug up and German classical philologists interpreted, blooms anew in Christa Wolf's book. They called it simply "Greece"—a land in which freedom was always conceivable, as rebellion against the Gods. Antigone as the Jane Fonda of German idealism. A nation sought aesthetic sanctuary in the Greece of its illusions, at a time when the anachronistic absolutism of its petty principalities afforded insufficient civil freedom. Wolf's **Cassandra** represents Germany's renewed reverence for a Greece that has been reconstructed for one main purpose: to serve as sanctuary for those oppressed by the present. Yet behind the archaizing tone of voice, behind all the olive trees and city ramparts of its Greek background, there lies concealed a tormenting experience of the German present: "No way out, all emergency exits are closed." Or, to maintain the classical context, the thread of Ariadne has been lost. (pp. 42-3)

> *Michael Naumann, "A Prophetess and the Pershings," in* The New Republic, *Vol. 191, No. 5, July 30, 1984, pp. 40-3.*

CHRISTOPHER LEHMANN-HAUPT

I found *Cassandra: A Novel and Four Essays* a compelling narration of the Trojan War. Instead of celebrating "the wrath of Achilles," as Homer did in *The Iliad,* it despairs over Troy's betrayal by its leaders, particularly King Priam. Instead of being told by the side that won, the history of the war is recalled by the cursed prophet Cassandra as she rides in a Mycenaean chariot to meet her death at the hands of Queen Clytemnestra.

In Miss Wolf's handling, Cassandra is a psychologically plausible figure whose visions of Troy's doom come in seizures that resemble madness. . . .

Just as realistically portrayed are Apollo's gift of prophecy to Cassandra and subsequent curse: he comes to her in a dream and, after conferring his gift, "with a casual gesture which I did not dare to feel was disappointing," transforms himself into "a wolf surrounded by mice" and spits furiously into her mouth when he is unable to overpower her.

But why "a wolf surrounded by mice"? Why does Menelaus's Helen, the putative casus beill, turn out not even to be present in Troy during the war? Why does Queen Hecuba insist that the real bone of contention is the toll the Greeks must pay to bring their goods through the Hellespont?

In short, I found it hard not to anticipate what was coming in the following two-part **"Travel Report,"** the **"Work Diary"** and **"A Letter about Unequivocal and Ambiguous Meaning, Definiteness and Indefiniteness, about Ancient Conditions and New View Scopes, about Objectivity."** And sure enough, in these four lectures Miss Wolf explains her growing obsession with the figure of Cassandra and develops her thesis that the prophetess represents the residue of a feminist *Poetics* that was suppressed and abandoned.

It is, of course, impossible in this space even to hint at the intricacy of this thesis. One can only guarantee that as a work of scholarship it far transcends in subtlety its somewhat familiar conclusion that if what Cassandra represents to the author had been allowed to survive, we might not now be stuck in the reign of nuclear terror that Miss Wolf seems to regard as the triumph of masculine thinking.

But a reader is left with several dissatisfactions. One of them is summed up in the inevitable question provoked by all such revisionist histories of the development of human consciousness. If the present fix we are in can be blamed on the triumph of rationalism, where then do we go from here?

Another complaint is the degree to which Miss Wolf has reduced the figure of Cassandra. For if she is really "the first professional working woman in literature," as Miss Wolf at one point somewhat playfully proposes, then it becomes difficult to see her in her grander mythic role—as symbolic of that pact of our unconscious minds that perceives certain tragic truths but is denied by our will to believe in immortality.

Finally, there's the structural problem that this volume presents. Originally, Miss Wolf offered an early draft of *Cassandra* as the fifth and final talk in her series; she then revised and expanded it, and published it in a volume separate from the one containing the four introductory lectures. That procedure makes sense. But its primacy in this edition is too great a burden for the novel. One reads it nervously, wondering what Miss Wolf is going to tell us it means.

> *Christopher Lehmann-Haupt, in a review of "Cassandra: A Novel and Four Essays," in* The New York Times, *July 31, 1984, p. C17.*

MARY LEFKOWITZ

To the East German novelist Christa Wolf, Cassandra is the symbolic representative of women in the Western world, whose talents and intelligence have been suppressed in order to serve the interests of men, power and destruction. [In *Cassandra*], Mrs. Wolf arrives at this ambitious equation by a series of imaginative leaps. She sets the familiar and unfamiliar characters of Trojan legend in a world she reconstructs not from ancient myth but from the speculations of archeologists and historians—and even more, from her own perceptions of the modern world, especially the capitalist West.

Formed of such diverse components, Mrs. Wolf's Troy becomes, especially in the eyes of the sensitive Cassandra, a society whose original innocence is repeatedly violated by corruption, deception and violence. . . .

Mrs. Wolf gives a vivid impression of life in the preindustrial age when days are marked by sunrise and sunset and one butchers and disembowels the animals one sacrifices and then eats. But in no other respect does *Cassandra* resemble a historical novel, since Mrs. Wolf has selected only those facts about the ancient world that suit her political purposes. She believes in the myth of an egalitarian matriarchy usurped by a male hierarchy—a utopian fantasy without historical basis. Her research methods, as she frankly tells us in the accompanying essays and diaries, are eclectic, unsystematic and intuitive; modern Greece suggests to her the character of the ancient Greeks, especially in its superstition, bureaucracy, corruption and repression of women. She seems able to recapture her own innocence only at home, behind the Iron Curtain, where she can see the West as a kind of Greece writ large.

If Mrs. Wolf had looked more closely at Aeschylus instead of relying on a 19th-century handbook's recasting of the myth, she would have seen that in the original story Cassandra chose her own fate. Apollo offered her, the most beautiful of Priam's daughters, whatever she wanted if she would have intercourse with him. She asked for the gift of prophecy but then refused to keep her part of the bargain, so the god punished her by keeping her from being believed. If she had slept with him, she would have been able to prophesy and to bear a son who would have become a famous hero—not a bad deal considering what the gods were capable of doing to men and women if they felt like it. The ancient Greeks, whatever their limitations, believed in freedom of choice; their women were no more victimized by the world around them than their men; they recorded not only the oppression of individuals and groups but of humanity.

The fate of Aeschylus' Cassandra strikes us as unjust and cruel because she speaks succinctly and directly of the forces that will bring about her death. Mrs. Wolf's Cassandra, brooding about her past in a disjunctive stream of consciousness, stirs up not so much reflection as revulsion; we are asked to react, not think, and to imagine that Mrs. Wolf's random thoughts about life and literature constitute informative discourse, while in reality they represent only the mental anguish of a woman trying to understand the world around her but lacking the knowledge and mental discipline to offer persuasive and practical solutions.

> *Mary Lefkowitz, "Can't Fool Her," in* The New York Times Book Review, *September 9, 1984, p. 20.*

ERNST PAWEL

Despite a penchant for privacy and an admirable disdain for self-promotion, Christa Wolf has established herself in the course of the past two decades as one of the foremost figures in contemporary German literature. . . . [Though] she is indeed a woman writer, not just by gender but by conscious and articulate affirmation, her feminism defies easy definition. Instead of merely challenging established institutions, she examines their underlying assumptions and presumptions in a deceptively low key and in a rational voice far more subversive than that of her more strident counterparts. For in the final analysis, what she calls into question is nothing less than our collective memory of the past. (p. 246)

[In] a totally politicized society, writers can never be apolitical; what they fail to write about will be held against them as much as what they choose to express. Christa Wolf, a woman thoroughly at home with the minutiae of daily life in both city and country, seems more than capable of measuring the gap that separates demagogic promises from actual fulfillment, and banal slogans from day-to-day reality. Her concerns, however, center not on politics and politicians but on the much broader issue of the individual at odds with society. In Eastern Europe, the pressure to conform is brutal, open and ubiquitous; Western society exerts its pressures far more indirectly, but whether this makes resistance and the cultivation of true autonomy significantly easier is at least arguable.

In *A Model Childhood* she made a highly personal effort to come to terms with the collective past by explaining to the generation of her own children what growing up in Hitler's Germany had meant to her. At 15, she witnessed the collapse of Nazism and the installation of the Ulbricht regime. Although different in their goals and methods—to minimize the differences between those two strains of totalitarianism distorts the meaning and memory of a time and place—both regimes proved equal in their zeal to reward conformity and extirpate individuality as an antisocial vice.

This conflict between collective and individual selves was explored with great subtlety in *The Quest for Christa T.,* written in 1970. Despite its thoroughly nonpolitical and nonpolemical tone, the book triggered instant reactions from the censors as well as from the public at large, most notably from young people on either side of the wall. The fact that it had so clearly touched upon a subject of passionate concern in both East and West Germany made its suppression impracticable in the long run.

But the struggle for a balance, or at least a livable compromise, between alienation and rootedness, between social integration and individual freedom, inevitably led Wolf to discoveries that opened up much larger and far more disquieting perspectives: the individual, in this instance, was a woman seeking personal autonomy as well as artistic independence within a power structure not only all-male but shaped almost exclusively by male myths, laws, traditions, customs and prejudices. The consciousness of Western civilization, quite irrespective of political systems, grew out of the highly selective historical memories of what happened in history as seen and recorded by the self-styled lords of creation.

In *Cassandra,* . . . Christa Wolf tackles nothing less than the skein of myth, tradition and belief inherent in the gods and heroes of the Homeric universe. The four essays that form the second half of the book provide fascinating glimpses of a first-rate mind searching for truths beyond the platitudes of tradition, a mind at once restless and serene. There are some marvelous descriptions of people and places in Greece, particularly in Crete. In luminous prose, Christa Wolf writes about Easter in a Greek village, about Athenian cops, Minoan palaces and the wrath—or temper tantrums—of Achilles. But hers is travel with a purpose. Painstakingly, with a determination rivaling that of the archeologists she learns to envy and admire, she digs up shards and fragments of Homeric myths and tries to fit them into her emerging vision of that ancient world.

Cassandra, the novel itself, which precedes the essays in this combined edition, closes in on the last few moments in the life of the legendary prophetess. (pp. 246-47)

One hesitates to call it a feminist version simply because Wolf's whole outlook is militantly prohuman and wise enough to discern the virus of reverse male chauvinism in much of what passes for feminist militancy. But in this magnificent prose poem of a counter-*Iliad,* it is Cassandra, cursed with the gift of prophecy and fated to earn nothing but contempt and ridicule for her predictions, who becomes the tragic heroine. Her prophetic gifts are ultimately no more—and no less—than the ability to see the obvious. By exposing the vapid rhetoric of greed and murderous ideals, and by denouncing the primitive fears and stunted emotions that make men exalt senseless butchery as a sacred duty—"the honor of our house is at stake"—Cassandra earns her death as a true heroine, while Homer's gutless heroes go on to spawn an endless line of equally craven conformists who "fear murder less than they fear disapproval."

Brief as it is, this terse and moving work defies summary. With knowledge, insight and foreboding, Christa Wolf has brilliantly rewritten history, and in viewing the past through the eyes of the doomed seer, she traces its link to our own imminent future. The question she leaves eloquently unasked is whether mankind—men, women and children alike—will this time listen to Cassandra before the Trojan horses already in their silos deliver a final answer. (p. 247)

> *Ernst Pawel, "Prophecies and Heresies," in* The Nation, *New York, Vol. 239, No. 8, September 22, 1984, pp. 246-47.*

SHEILA MacLEOD

Try rewriting the *Iliad* from a woman's point of view. It is not a task to be lightly undertaken and yet Christa Wolf, the distinguished East German writer (now based in West Germany), has managed to create in a mere 138 pages something approaching a feminine epic. *Cassandra,* seer and prophetess, stands not only for the woman writer who perceives intuitively and unheard in the male world, but also for all women struggling towards that elusive synthesis of autonomy and responsibility: women who cannot make things happen, but to whom everything happens; women who invoke the power of the mothers, only to be silenced or stigmatised as mad by the fathers; women who bear children, only to see them raped or slaughtered in man-made wars.

Christa Wolf sees the Trojan War—and, by extension, all war—as the systematic murder of the female principle, the very principle which seeks to prevent war in the first place. Her Trojan women have much in common with their latter-day sisters at Greenham and Cassandra herself with the Doris Lessing of *The Golden Notebook* or *The Summer Before the Dark,* daring to claim a position of central importance for female experience. Of course she suffers for it. But then she would have suffered anyway—unless she had been born and bred in the 'alternative' female culture which flourishes in secret, isolated groups outside the walls of the citadel of Troy.

In a sense this is all familiar territory and the stuff of many a feminist text. But there is more here. To judge only by the translation Christa Wolf handles language with all the precision and sensitivity of a poet: a lyric-intellectual poet intent on soaring with no middle flight. The background essays (and for those whose recollection of the Trojan Wars is a trifle hazy, it would be as well to read these first) are fittingly less concentrated, more speculative, while never departing from the mode of high seriousness. They will also have an unfamiliarly urgent edge for British readers, emanating as they do from a divided Germany which sees itself as the prime target of nuclear annihilation.

Sheila MacLeod, "War Cry," in New Statesman, *Vol. 108, Nos. 2805 & 2806, December 21-28, 1984, p. 52.*

JOYCE CRICK

Christa Wolf's [*Cassandra*] is a black parable of the painful disengagement of a loyalty, and of the recovery of humane values among the peaceable women beyond the pale. Once—though it now seems a long time ago—the favourite daughter of the East German literary establishment, and still a committed and humane Socialist, Wolf has moved very close to the peace movement and its feminine supporters. With *Cassandra* she has moved on from her experiments in contemporary fictional biography and autobiography, to an allegory of corruption and war from the beginnings of Western culture. . . .

The four lectures leading up to [*Cassandra*] are an account of the premises, public and private, of its writing. They take the form of travelogue, diary, letter. Their apparent casualness is an illusion created by careful art: everything is thematic, from the little boys playing soldiers in the airport lounge to the radiant cherry-tree in the Mecklenburg garden. "Prose" is the non-committal term by which Wolf describes the continuum of essay and fiction in her writing—though it is often very poetic. She uses the personal genres of letter and journal to convey that "fourth dimension" which, she claims, is nowadays as important in a text as the traditional triad of

narrator-story-reader: that is, the latent or overt presence of the author as subject. If her Cassandra has a higher profile and seems far more independent than most of Wolf's earlier figures, it is because the matrix of reflections out of which she emerged has been presented separately and distinctly in the first four lectures. It seems inappropriate, therefore, that the English publishers should have printed the story first and the preliminaries second.

In *Cassandra* there is none of the blurring of self and character that is produced when Christa W. writes about "Christa T." in her earlier novel, *The Quest for Christa T.* The transition from author to narrator here is accomplished in a single line, indeed in a single pronoun: "As I tell this tale, I approach death." And the story is no longer set in the modern GDR, but in a Troy whose self-induced beleaguerment functions as a model for the tensions of modern world. The threat to the individual from the states, and the threat to the species from war, hang over all. The private pleasures of hospitality and talk with friends are vulnerable. Like her near-despair at the arms race and at preparations for war, Wolf's obsession with Cassandra, which takes her to Greece and leads to her quarrel with Aeschylus and Homer, also engages with man-made images of women and man-made modes of writing. The lectures are an approach towards a feminine poetics: she rejects the forward march of the heroic epic in favour of the web of memory, and a style which anticipates, darts backwards, catches up on itself. "Alongside the river of heroic songs this tiny stream may reach those . . . faraway people in times to come."

Into this short work Wolf has woven most of the mythological and historical sources of the tale of Troy, bending them to her new purposes, shifting the emphasis away from the heroic to the horror and the harm done to women. . . .

Cassandra herself is not a visionary, but an intelligent, clear-sighted daughter who moves from loyalty to disillusion because the reigning house will not listen to her truth and want her to tell their lies. When she refuses, she is cast out into the darkness of prison and despair, recovering only as she shelters with the other outcast women, the worshippers of the Magna Mater, outside the walls. The gloom is lit by such figures as old Anchises, whose shrewd humanity resists the universal corruption, and by Aeneas, Cassandra's lover (and the token good partner), who leads the survivors away. But Cassandra will not go with him, for she knows he will have to become a hero like the rest, enter a new epic—the founding of Rome—and commit himself willy-nilly to the corrupting values that destroyed Troy. She would rather die than collude with that.

The anti-heroic mode is not new, but this work is remarkable in both its density and its darkness. It confronts the extremities of experience, violent, erotic, despairing, in ways that are new to Wolf, and perhaps only possible within the distancing frame of ancient tales, however contemporary the values which inform her reading of them.

Joyce Crick, "The Darkness of Troy," in The Times Literary Supplement, *No. 4311, November 15, 1985, p. 1298.*

LINDA SCHELBITZKI PICKLE

The Cassandra whom tradition has handed down to us is a good vehicle for the exploration of the history of alienation in our culture. Between the creation of Homer's *Iliad* and the writing of Aeschylus's *Agamemnon,* the originally unremarkable daughter of Priam acquired the gift of prophecy and the curse of never having her prophecies believed. It is as the tragic prophetess that we know Cassandra. Misunderstood and reviled by those about her, she would have had to struggle to maintain a sense of her personal integrity. As an early victim of historical and political forces beyond her control, Cassandra experienced the alienation and abuse of the individual that in Wolf's view have led to the present state of things. In addition, her fate highlights the beginnings of the materialistic, rationalistic tendency that, Wolf believes, has caused the subjective side of human nature and those events and individuals thought to be connected to it to be perceived as "outside" the mainstream of the Western historical tradition. The realm of the subjective and everything connected with it, women above all, have been rendered powerless and voiceless. In *Voraussetzungen einer Erzählung: Kassandra,* Wolf attempts to give a voice to one of the earliest representatives of this hidden historical tradition. Wolf also uses the figure of a female seer in a preliterary age to represent the female writer. Cassandra's road to self-knowledge, as Wolf presents this to us, leads her toward that subjective openness which is a precondition for the committed writing Wolf advocates. Finally, the novel that Wolf creates around this figure is an example of the kind of literature that, written "from below," that is, from the vantage point of those who have had no literary voice, can assist in a new understanding of Western myth, culture, and history that might change the suicidal course humankind seems bent on.

I want to focus particularly on the way in which Wolf attempts to "scratch away the entire male tradition" that has been attached to the first recorded female voice, that of Cassandra. She does this by letting Cassandra speak for herself and by placing her as fully as possible in an historical and personal setting that seems realistic to the reader. The setting is not primarily that of the Trojan battlefield celebrated or eulogized in classical literature, but that of the everyday world into which the war intrudes ever more destructively and changes forever. In Wolf's novel, Cassandra is not the ranting half-mad woman of the literary tradition. Instead, she is a fully rounded figure: daughter, sister, lover, mother, priestess who gradually loses her belief in the gods, resident of an Asia Minor kingdom caught in the throes of cultural and political transition. She is an individual who changes and grows and finds new alternatives for living as the world around her disintegrates.

Significantly, Wolf prefaces her novel with a quotation from Sappho, the first identifiable woman writer in the West. These lines on the bittersweet experience of that "untameable dark animal," "limb-loosening Eros," may seem a puzzling beginning to what is essentially the interior monologue of a woman about to die. But they introduce themes and set a tone that will be important in the novel. There are certain surface similarities: the erotic shudder celebrated by Sappho is reminiscent of the epileptic sort of attack that accompanies Cassandra's direst prophecies. More importantly, these lines, like the monologue to follow, are the words of a woman, and of a woman in the grip of the hidden, darker, subjective forces of life. The "little death" of orgasm is related to the real death Cassandra faces, and to the waves of fear she must combat as she waits outside Agamemnon's palace and reviews her life. The overpowering experience of sexuality is also parallel to the way a flood of reminiscent sympathy for Cassandra

sweeps through the narrator/author as she stands in front of the now ruined lion-gate of Mycenae. All three female voices of the novel's first page give controlled, thoughtful, literary expression to subjective experiences: Sappho to that of sexuality, Cassandra to the confrontation with the self and with death, and Wolf to an overwhelming sense of intimacy with her protagonist. (pp. 34-5)

The voice Wolf gives Cassandra is one marked by intimacy and immediacy, and yet also by the attempt at cool detachment. There is no hint of madness in her intelligent, thoughtful, yet often passionate monologue. Her first words declare her recognition that she was fated to end as she has, but there is no despair in this recognition, only acceptance. She goes on to wonder at the inexplicable tenacity with which mortal beings cling to life, even when they know, as she has long known, that their feeble attempts to counterpose the "ice cold indifference" of the supernatural with their "little bit of warmth" are in vain. She explains this at first by her desire to continue to see all that is still possible, and this leads her, in the elliptical fashion that is so typical of Wolf's narrative style, to ask herself the most fundamental question in the novel: "Why did I want the gift of prophecy unconditionally?" This is a woman who still has questions to ask herself on the threshold of death, and indeed, this is the fundamental reason she has chosen to live until the end: to think, to comprehend, to satisfy as completely as possible her curiosity about herself. Indeed, she feels that "never was [she] more alive than now, in the hour of [her] death". Cassandra goes on to define what she calls being alive: "Not avoiding the most difficult thing, changing the image of one's self." This is why most people are not truly alive: they lack self-knowledge or even the will to know themselves and thus others more fully. The significance of self-knowledge is the most important thematic element in the novel. Wolf shows us what self-deception and alienation lead to in Troy. In contrast, Cassandra wants to retain her consciousness to the very end, and in so doing, to be a witness to what has happened, even if there is no one to hear her testimony.

Cassandra's attempt to gain fuller self-knowledge and resist the alienation from the self typical of her times is the constant structural element in the novel. Her progress in this vein provides the forward motion of the plot, while her remembering the various stages in the development of such knowledge is the framework to which the sometimes confusing chronology of the novel refers. As is the case with human memories, Cassandra's are complex webs of interconnected persons and events, and it is some time before the reader begins to understand the significance that such figures as Aeneas, Penthesilea, Polyxena, Achilles, Arisbe, Priam, and Hecuba have for her, or can identify characters and circumstances that Wolf invents or transforms, like Marpessa, Panthous, Eumelos, and the women who live on the slopes of Mt. Ida. This is only proper, for Cassandra herself is still in the process of learning the meaning of her past and of comprehending her past actions. It is only now, as she is about to die, that she understands why she did not go with her beloved Aeneas and his followers when Troy fell, although she does not answer this question for us until near the end of her monologue: that she cannot love the hero, the lifeless statue of an idol, that he will be forced to become. Cassandra's self-examination allows us to follow the process of enlightenment she experiences, and at the same time reveals the complexity of the reality in which Wolf embeds her protagonist.

As part of her attempt to establish the reality of Cassandra below the layers of myth and antagonism that the male-dominated literary tradition has laid upon her, Wolf demystifies Cassandra's role as priestess and her special gift of prophecy. We learn that Cassandra had always been different from her brothers and sisters. Her mother Hecuba, "the ideal queen," recognized Cassandra's self-possession from the beginning and stated: "This child doesn't need me," for which her daughter admired and hated her. There grew in Cassandra a desire to be something other than a wife and mother, partly because of her favored place with her father—and therefore concurrence with her mother—and partly because of the death of a beloved half-brother. This brother, Aesacus, committed suicide when his young wife died in childbed, and Cassandra, in her first attack of mad-seeming grief, formed the unspoken wish never to have a child. Such psychological motivations in Cassandra's becoming a priestess of Apollo are primary in Wolf's novel. Cassandra wished to maintain the physical distance from men and all others her personality requires, and she wanted "to be on an intimate footing with the deity." But there are other reasons as well. She also sought the dignity and the power the office could give her, for "how was a woman to rule otherwise?" Of her desire for the gift of prophecy, Cassandra asserts at the beginning of her monologue that she only wanted "to speak the uttermost," but she realizes immediately that she is attempting to justify herself. Less noble reasons gradually emerge. She sees now, "at the outermost point" of her life, that she tried to use her position as priestess and prophetess to gain power within her family and to punish them for what she saw as insufficient respect. Ironically, as Cassandra realizes, it is the Greeks who spread her frame as prophetess; the Trojans had long considered her a madwoman, and she herself finally rejected prophecy and the attempt to influence people that went with it. (pp. 35-7)

[Instances of deception for political purposes] are part of the chain that results in the disastrous Trojan war. They also cause the inner conflict in Cassandra, that between the member of the royal family and the individual who seeks to be of wider social value through her vocation. . . . Loath to turn her back on her family and especially on her beloved father, she is unable and unwilling at first to see through the cloud of deception that becomes increasingly thick at the court and in the city. Cassandra's early prophecies erupt from her in epileptic-like fits which the others find easy to interpret as madness. But we discover a plausible psychological explanation for the manner in which Cassandra utters her prophecies when we consider the inner conflict that spawns them. Cassandra herself finds "Insanity as the end of the torment of dissimulation." From her descent into madness that follows the sailing of the ship taking Paris to Sparta, Cassandra emerges as a person on the road to self-knowledge. This "rebirth," as Cassandra terms it, contains many back-slidings, however, for she is still torn between her "inclination to agree with those in power" and her "longing for knowledge." (p. 39)

In *Voraussetzungen einer Erzählung,* Wolf asks why the odium of doom-saying should have attached itself to Cassandra and not to Laocoön, the Trojan priest of Apollo who prophesied the same dire consequences as she. Part of the answer is that her seeing through the reality of the situation is perceived as an act of treachery performed by a member of the king's family, especially by Priam's favorite daughter. The rest of the answer is that in Wolf's novel the Trojans come to consider it improper for a woman to arouse fear, and to prevent this, they allow women no voice. This has the perverse effect, however, of causing more anxiety to the men who claim all power and authority for themselves, for "what one excludes and bans, one must fear." Wolf shows how men try to render women powerless by refusing them their full humanity, by making them objects. This layer of distortion, too, by which a woman becomes the scapegoat for men's fears, Wolf seeks to remove from Cassandra.

In a plausible manner, Wolf's novel examines one small part of the history of how women may have come to be treated as objects, as the feared and reviled "other" in Western culture. Changes in Trojan religious beliefs show this first. Within human memory, the patriarchal gods of the feared, yet envied, Greeks have replaced the female gods of Asia Minor. It is dangerous to speak of these old gods now, for this is tantamount to treason. (pp. 40-1)

In contrast to the traditional image of the men of Troy as valiant defenders of the city, Wolf's novel portrays them also as oppressors of the female half of society. *Kassandra* shows how changes in attitudes and practices gradually force women into a defensive position outside the social mainstream. Individual women experience this in different ways. The Amazon queen Penthesilea is an extreme example of the antagonism to men and the destructive attitudes that this development can arouse. From "the abyss of hopelessness in which she lived," Penthesilea is willing to have everything about her destroyed, including herself, to purge men from the earth. Although she is "a bit too shrill" for Cassandra, the latter senses that Penthesilea "had behind her what we still had ahead of us": the diminishment of women's rights, their gradual enslavement. . . . Some of this development Wolf ascribes to the influence of the Greeks, who rape and pillage on the outskirts of the city regularly, and who are used to dealing with women as commodities. The fate of Briseis—in Wolf's novel the daughter of Calchas and beloved of Cassandra's brother Troilus—is one of the most glaring examples of a woman destroyed by men's desires, envy, and aggression, but Priam's own daughters are not exempt. The Trojans use Polyxena to obtain the plans of the Greek camp from Achilles and then to lure him to his death, taking advantage of Polyxena's own sense of worthlessness and degradation, and of her wish to punish her family by destroying herself. . . . The fleshing out of Polyxena's otherwise shadowy figure in all its psychological complexity and tragic fatefulness is one of the most interesting aspects of Wolf's novel. It contributes a great deal to bringing Cassandra and her world to life, and also provides another specific example of the degradation of women into objects.

Cassandra herself suffers all the violations of her independence and personal integrity possible to a daughter who does not obey Priam: he declares her insane, imprisons her, and forces her into an unwanted marriage. The last was unheard of in Troy before this, and Cassandra asserts that this break with tradition, the blatant use of a woman as an object, is a sign that Troy is lost. More than this, now in all the Trojan women "there was laid the contradiction that they had to hate Troy, whose victory they wished." As the war goes on, and their men grow to resemble the Greeks more and more, the Trojan women feel that "the men of both sides seemed to be allied against" them.

In her recreation of the world of the Trojan war, Wolf goes beyond the portrayal of women's growing powerlessness in this male-dominated world. She also posits the formation of an alternate female subculture as part of the hidden but absolutely spontaneous and natural reaction to it. This subculture predates the war itself, and stems from the exiling of the old female gods from Troy. . . . The life in this community is the third alternative that the Greeks, and increasingly the Trojans also, do not recognize: "Between killing and dying is a third thing: living." The Greeks, says Cassandra,

> think differently. Whatever cannot be seen, smelled, heard, touched, does not exist. It is the other, that they crush between their sharp distinctions, the third thing, that does not exist according to them, the smiling, living thing that is capable of creating itself ever anew out of itself, the undivided, spirit in life, life in spirit.

Cassandra spends the last two years of the war among the women outside the wall. The women sing and talk together, tell each other their dreams, lead a life of outer poverty but inner richness, learning from each other and always "moving toward the main thing, [themselves]." There are men here as well: men like Aeneas and his father Anchises, who respect women's autonomy and have self-knowledge, and young men "wounded in body or soul by the war" who are made whole again by the women's "plump life." But it is a community dominated by women who live in utopian harmony among themselves, free of distrust and strife.

In her essay **"Berührung,"** Wolf spoke of "the spirit of the real, existing utopia, without which every reality is unlivable for human beings," and found in Maxi Wander's collection of oral interviews of East German women, *Guten Morgen, Du Schöne,* the "forefeeling of a community" characterized by "sympathy, self-respect, trust and friendliness." In **Kassandra,** Wolf imagines that such a community existed in the past and implies that this gives reason for hope for the future. It is significant that Wolf accords the Trojan women awareness of the potential lesson they have to give later generations:

> actually, most of all we talked about those who would come after us. What they would be like. Whether they would still know us. Whether they would make good what we had neglected to do, would correct what we had done wrong. We wracked our brains about how to leave them a message, but we didn't know how to write. . . .

The primitive pictures and hand prints the women press into the walls of the caves they close off when the Greeks come, the trickling female oral tradition Cassandra posits as an alternative to the mighty stream of heroic songs—these inarticulate or nonexistent messages have a utopian import that Wolf seeks to reveal to us through her novel and its recreation of Cassandra and her world.

In the context of the German Democratic Republic, this utopian import has potentially subversive implications. Wolf's continued interest in utopian themes has made her work suspect to the East German establishment. The concept of a "real, existing utopia" ironically inverts the government's oft repeated appeal to the people to be content with "real, existing socialism," i.e., the status quo. Wolf's criticism of bellicosity in both East and West has not been greeted favorably by party-liners. Nor have they approved of her locating the Western cultural tendency to devalue and deny the attitudes and modes of expression of the powerless, especially of women, in her own land as well as in capitalist societies. At best, her attitudes have been seen as weak-minded, unhistorical romanticism, and at worst as subversive criticism of the Marxist-Leninist socialist state. By asserting a need for a female aesthetics (see especially the final essay in **Voraussetzungen**), Wolf is not only criticizing the Western "bourgeois" literary tradition. She is also challenging the much-vaunted claims of sexual equality in the GDR, specifically in its male-dominated literary establishment, but also in the society as a whole. Her novel and its accompanying essays thus have a particularly admonitory significance in the land in which she has chosen to live and work.

In regard to the broader literary heritage Wolf is dealing with, we may ask if she is successful in scratching off the male tradition that adheres to Cassandra. She certainly places her in a setting stripped of its mysterious and vainglorious trappings. The motivation for the war is unmasked as economic: control of the Dardanelles. Helen is merely another woman used as an excuse, an object, to give both sides an "honorable" motive for war. Wolf also gives us an alternative, negative view of the men of the heroic tradition, both Greek and Trojan. (pp. 41-5)

In the diary she kept while working on **Kassandra,** Wolf wondered what would happen if one tried putting women in the place of men in "the great patterns of world literature." In her novel we see the result. Here are women who are realistic alternatives to the traditional heroes: women who act (Hecuba, Arisbe), women who commit violent deeds (Penthesilea, Clytemnestra), women who attain knowledge (Cassandra). What is more pertinent to Wolf's stated intentions, however, is that she achieves her objective of "leading [the figure of Cassandra] back out of myth into the (imagined) social and historical coordinates." Since she could not base her recreation of Cassandra and her times on a female literary tradition, nor on a long-lost "trickle" of female oral literature, Wolf had to rely on scholarly works on classical myth and culture, on her subjective interlinear reading of texts from the male literary tradition, and on her own artistic creativity. In this way, she fills in the picture of the everyday events, the domestic and familial background so little evident in the classical literature that deals with the Trojan saga.

By stripping Cassandra of the layers of misunderstanding and antagonism that the male literary tradition has laid upon her, Wolf does more than offer an alternate view of the historical origins of an important Western cultural heritage. She also clarifies the connection between the overvaluation of objectivity and rationality to the exclusion of the subjective in a patriarchal culture and the tendency of such a culture to develop a propensity toward self-destruction. . . . In Wolf's novel, a believable everyday reality speaks through a woman whose search for herself leads her to see the truth of the world around her. In spite of Cassandra's conviction that she is bearing witness only to herself, Wolf evokes a powerful sense of the wider, contemporary significance of this legendary figure's final thoughts. The imagined reality of a long-distant past has personal and political meaning for contemporary readers. (pp. 46-7)

> *Linda Schelbitzki Pickle, "'Scratching Away the Male Tradition': Christa Wolf's 'Kassandra'," in* Contemporary Literature, *Vol. 27, No. 1, Spring, 1986, pp. 32-47.*

EDITH WALDSTEIN

[In the story **Kassandra**] the picture of Cassandra that Wolf paints for herself and offers the reader is not so much the result of the unearthing of new "facts," something in which Wolf has never placed much value, but rather of viewing this legendary figure from a different perspective. She attempts to understand Cassandra by first allowing her to represent herself, rather than be portrayed by others who have traditionally been more interested in people and events surrounding her. For this reason, Christa Wolf feels compelled to rewrite this tale in the first person, after having written sixty pages in the third. . . . With a first-person monologue, Wolf begins to undo the silence that Cassandra has suffered under for centuries.

To make the point stronger, the narration is formally handed over to Cassandra at the beginning of the story. . . . Wolf begins with a third-person narration, but even the last lines of the first paragraph indicate a transition away from this. Because the three sentence fragments at the end of the paragraph lack a grammatical subject, they lend a sense of immediacy that neutralizes the third-person narrator. They mark the final deviation from the third-person narration and the transition to the "I" introduced in the following paragraph. This "I" remains somewhat ambiguous for just one sentence, that is, one paragraph. Who is "keeping step with the story, the author, the third-person narrator, the main character? While this intentional ambiguity remains throughout the story, Cassandra dominates the first-person monologue from this point onward until the end, where the third-person narrator appears once again in the three closing sentences. From a narrative point of view, Cassandra has told her story. She has spoken with her own voice.

Cassandra's circular monologue recounts and reflects on personal concerns and political events. The process of "Subjektwerdung" [subject-formation] begins with memory and continues with the painful struggle to find a language that both describes the horror of the present, namely war, and that gives expression to the dreams of a better future. Wolf believes in language as a revolutionary force, an avenue of invention. At times silence itself becomes the language of protest for Cassandra, but more often than not she steadfastly pursues her quest for subjectively authentic speech. This sometimes entails uses deemed inappropriate by others. For example, Cassandra clearly speaks out to the council against her father's military plans and adamantly resists the pledge of silence to which her father wants her to swear. Moreover, she refuses to use politically "correct" terminology.

Fantasy, sensitivity, and subjectivity characterize Cassandra's attempt at a new discourse. These are the elements Christa Wolf believes are necessary to keep our society from annihilating itself. "We have to start being very creative and think of the most impossible things first, because we're trying all the possible things right now." How creative and revolutionary Cassandra's language is, compared with that of the other characters and with what we understand language to be today, is metaphorically expressed through the trances and seizures that accompany her prophetic visions. In these moments, when images are clearer and more accurate than words, Cassandra loses the ability to speak in a language we and the other characters can understand. She thereby forces us to grope for a new expression of the impalpable elements that comprise individual lives and political history. Though we know the "facts," we do not know how it really happened; we do not know about the "inconspicuous" dynamics and motivations that determined Troy's history. To Christa

Wolf's mind, this story must relay the "sinnlich(e) Erfahrung des Alltagslebens" [the sensual experience of everyday life], if it, as literature, is to fulfill the subversive function of changing our vision of "reality."

The innovative nature of this voice is, of course, characterized by much more than the narrative stance. Cassandra's account incorporates silence by giving expression to concepts generally associated with it and by giving a voice to silenced groups. Her monologue, for example, is motivated by fear, more specifically, by fear of death. It is fear that forces her to recollect, to think, to feel. And simultaneously, it is this fear that she wants to "set free" by sharing it with others who are oppressed. She does this by giving expression to it as a positive force. Instead of associating fear with weakness and something one tries to conceal, Cassandra reinterprets fear as "a means to counter experiential closure." Her people have been annihilated; she stands on the brink of her own destruction. She must become an acting subject, rather than a passive object in her people's history, if complete hopelessness is not to be the author's message. Cassandra begins this process by scrutinizing herself. She does not eliminate herself from an analysis of Troy's fate but allows her subjectivity to inform this reflective process. Her memory "does not allow for the objectification of its own subject." (pp. 194-95)

Through the process of reconstructing her life, which is about to be taken from her, [Cassandra] is able not only to see clearly for the first time the true nature of her society, but she is also able to express these perceptions. Cassandra's introspection enables her to recognize her own creative powers. With these, she hopes to alter a course of destruction. This, of course, is not possible for herself because Troy's fate has been sealed, but Cassandra's visions are relevant to the future. . . . (p. 195)

Here Christa Wolf returns to a theme that predominates in all of her works. How can the individual who is capable of viewing society from a utopian perspective integrate these perceptions within a society whose history has proven harmful, if not devastating, to humanity? In *Kassandra,* more than in any other work, Wolf moves her main character in the direction of looking for an alternative collective, a new society in which or through which such utopian goals could be put into practice. The search for this alternative begins with Cassandra's distancing herself from her familial/societal background, specifically her father/king. (pp. 195-96)

"No" becomes the key word with which to describe Cassandra's relationship to the palace. She ultimately rejects everything it stands for—hierarchy, insensitivity and violence—without denying that she has been a part of it. This recognition of complicity is what makes Cassandra's use of the pronouns "I," "we" and "they" difficult. Her quest for her-self is very much dependent upon how she defines "we" and "they." Through her contact with the cave dwellers, Cassandra is able to use a "we" with which she feels comfortable. After "Achilles the Brute" (as he is called almost exclusively by her) kills and then rapes Penthesilea, the Amazon warrior, Aeneas carries Cassandra, who has been run over and is unconscious, to the women of the caves. When she awakens, she can finally utter the word "we" and know that it means humanity. Here among the cave dwellers Cassandra is able to reconcile the "I" and "we" with which she had been struggling. Her entire life takes on new meaning because she is now also able to posit a utopian future. (p. 196)

With this prophetic voice, Cassandra has reached Christa Wolf. Not only has the author given Cassandra a voice, but this has, in turn, generated a certain creative power within Christa Wolf. The synthesis of the past and present is then what makes possible a vision of the future. Thus, ". . . the cave is not just the place from which the past is retrieved but the place where the future is conceived. . . . "

The emphasis on process, on coming to authorship is underscored in the four accompanying lectures, which bear witness to the genesis of the story. These also reflect Wolf's concern with silence, for they share with the reader a part of the creative process that normally remains hidden. . . . Through these lectures, it becomes clear that the impetus for the writing of **Kassandra,** the book, is fear, a fear so great that it threatens to silence Wolf totally. . . . The only way to counter this is to speak, to find a voice that will authentically express both the threat and the fear. For Wolf, this happens through the rediscovery of Cassandra. This figure's contemporaneity lies in the way she learns to deal with pain. Although Wolf poses this as a question in her own reflective process, an affirmative answer is given throughout the book. (p. 197)

She reminds us that Cassandra prefigures the fate of women for 3,000 years and that it is necessary to reject traditional literary genres because of their complicity in the silencing of women and their concomitant inability to express that which has been silenced. Wolf mixes genres in order to allow for a maximum of expression. The story itself is primarily a reflective monologue that incorporates dialogue from the past. Wolf's untraditional use of punctuation, which often excludes quotation marks in relayed conversation, for example, adds a sense of immediacy, despite the dialogue's setting in the past. The lectures, on the other hand, have a literary quality that makes possible the integration of fantastic elements into forms, such as the travelogue, that are typically used to convey more practical information. Personal and more emotional expression is also made possible through the letter and diary, as genres that have traditionally been used for the expression of subjective thought and feelings. Not only does Wolf mix these genres, she also incorporates untraditional content into them. . . . Wolf's mixing and untraditional use of genres subverts traditional aesthetics in an attempt to develop "[d]ie Ästhetik des Widerstandes" [an aesthetics of opposition], an ongoing process that will allow for changes in the perception of one's world and only thereby make social change possible.

According to Christa Wolf, it is the writer's duty to "bear witness," (to "see" in Cassandra's case). In **Kassandra,** this means to reevaluate and give expression to various forms of silence. Cassandra, who is silenced by force, first by Apollo, then by her father and society, finds strength in silence through introspection and learns not only to refuse to be silenced but to begin to create something new from this experience. She creates a language that incorporates the silence she has experienced, but it also gives a voice to those who have not been heard. Most importantly, however, it allows for new silences as an expression of that which has yet to be created (both aesthetically and socially)—a utopia that Christa Wolf purposely only shades in, leaving the outline to be drawn by us and future readers.

The process of changing optics is perhaps what Wolf perceives to be the "aesthetic of resistance." But one is left anxious and somewhat isolated after reading the book. Cassandra and Wolf do find a voice appropriate to their *Seh-Raster* [frame of reference] but it sometimes borders on resignation and leaves little room for resonance. . . . There is no real dialogue, and one therefore begins to question the purpose of the voice that has been found. It most certainly is authentic, but does it posit hope, as the author states is the intention of this book?

The reader is not successfully drawn into a dialogue with the text, although some recent analyses have maintained the contrary. The narration is for the most part quite linear and closed, especially if one compares this book with earlier works by Wolf, such as **Kein Ort. Nirgends** and **Kindheitsmuster,** in which dialogue both within the text and with the reader is the driving force behind the novels' narration. The question is, then, not whether Christa Wolf "has given up on language," but whether she has given up on the reader. This leaves one with a sense of despair. Wolf herself admits to despair but attempts to redefine it as hope through a quotation from Thomas Mann's correspondence. . . . The hope Wolf posits through the life of the cave dwellers is fragile. As Leslie Adelson has argued, Wolf allows Cassandra to perceive the utopian alternative this collective offers but not to appropriate it entirely as her own. The reader is confronted with the same dilemma and must question whether there is an alternative to the arms race and nuclear war which s/he would be able to appropriate. As a result, s/he suffers from unproductive anxiety because the text has left neither a character nor the narrative space required to "discuss" the issues raised. Christa Wolf has handed silence back to us, and we must look for the voices of our future—a difficult task, if we must do it alone. (pp. 197-98)

> *Edith Waldstein, "Prophecy in Search of a Voice: Silence in Christa Wolf's 'Kassandra'," in* The Germanic Review, *Vol. LXII, No. 4, Fall, 1987, pp. 194-98.*

JÜRGEN LIESKOUNIG

In **Kassandra,** three major elements may be identified as the essential components of Wolf's revaluation of the [Cassandra] myth: her portrayals respectively of Cassandra, of Troy and the Trojans before the war, and of the Greek enemy camp.

Christa Wolf radically reinterprets her central character, revealing Cassandra's development from childhood as the daughter of a king (queen?), through the priestess and seer, to the woman in love and a kind of 'Green', or alternative drop-out. Her life and biography may be summed up and simplified as one of radical emancipation, taking her from the initial *emancipatio* from the *paterfamilias,* through her self-liberation as a woman and priestess (who is still a privileged part of the 'system' of the royal palace), to the ultimate liberation from Aeneas, the man she loves but whom she is not prepared to follow after the fall of Troy because he 'will soon have to be a hero.' As Cassandra asserts, 'a hero I cannot love' since for her this heroism resembles the heroism of the victorious Greeks and must necessarily lead to death and destruction. Christa Wolf tries to give Cassandra's death a meaning, making it appear a conscious and self-determined decision. This amounts to a rather heavy-handed attempt to 'salvage' Cassandra from her negativity and death-wish, and it turns her into a 'positive' feminist-conscious tragic figure.

We follow Wolf's Cassandra as she reflects on her life that has led her from the corridors of power in the paternal palace (a power eventually corrupted, affecting everyone, including herself) to what seems to be the only viable alternative to a male-dominated world of killing and dying: life with the uncomplex women of the ordinary people, a life-style that exists outside the palace, outside the beleaguered city. This alternative and essentially 'humane' and unassailed life is characterised by female solidarity; by living, singing and working together in the caves of Mount Ida, worshipping the old goddess of the earth, Cybele.

Cassandra's liberation process leads her to provocative insights into the male world: '. . . men are self-centred children', she says, 'they are all afraid of pain.' As the almost inevitable consequence of Cassandra's 're-mythologisation', she who throughout her self-recorded life is determined to conquer her feelings through *thinking* (as distinct from the male *reasoning*), arrives finally at the point where she *wants* Troy to fall. For Cassandra realises that the Trojans have become indistinguishable from their enemies—in the course and through the dynamics of the war they have taken over the same heroic-tragic, destructive and murderous principles in order to beat the enemy. In short, in the attempt to be victorious, the Trojans become like their Greek enemies. This however does not present a 'livable alternative' to Wolf's Cassandra.

There are other, more questionable, traits in Cassandra: there is an underlying 'lust' for self-destruction that seems to contradict her search for a 'humane', peaceful and sane life. Wolf's Cassandra seems secretly to triumph at the thought of total and final destruction. At the same time the prophetess is quite explicit in her belief that she sees through everything, unmasks everyone (including herself), and is aware of all the contradictions that others as well as herself have to live with. 'Now there was embedded within me, and even in all the women of Troy, the contradiction that we had to hate Troy whose victory we desired.

War to Wolf-Cassandra represents *the* male occupation; it is utterly non-female. Whether this kind of absolutist simplification in any way furthers the radical change in thinking that Christa Wolf so much desires, remains in doubt. Consequently Cassandra in her increasingly militant, feminist rebellion arrives retrospectively at the conclusion that the men on *both* sides, Greeks and Trojans alike, have been united against the women of Troy. Not surprisingly, then, in the final years of the war, Cassandra attempts to renounce all connections with the world of men, including her family. Instead, she and the other like-minded women worship Cybele; they weave, they make pottery, they harvest fruits, and in general live a simple and impoverished life, experiencing one another's physicality: in a word, they 'sensitivise' themselves.

All this indeed leads to the social and historical coordinates into which Christa Wolf intended to repatriate Cassandra and her myth, with the small but significant modification that the reader is in fact presented with Christa Wolf's *own* socio-historical coordinates and *her* reality. This kind of alternative life corresponds more or less exactly with the prevailing *Zeitgeist* of the late seventies and early eighties. In those years we find all the ingredients of the New Sensitivity, the New Physicality, the feminist emancipation movement, the alternative 'muesli-and-seed' generation with chunky, hand-knitted sweaters, and the 'Green' movement—with all the attendant myths of dropping out and alternative living that were rife in West Germany at that time.

Christa Wolf's Cassandra is a contemporary woman, even if she seems to represent the proto-'Green' movement that, according to the book, was started by women in the ancient city of Troy. Wolf's Cassandra-figure corresponds almost fatally to the 'headwoman' of an intellectually inclined and poetically sensitive, alternative *Frauenhaus* such as existed in West Berlin by the hundred, in about 1980.

The second major component in Christa Wolf's revaluation of the myth is Troy and the Trojans as they were before the war. They represent, for Cassandra, the 'humane' counter-world to the heroics of the Greeks (that is in itself a myth, of course). In the course of the war a metamorphosis takes place. Troy becomes identical with the enemy for the war, according to Cassandra, deformed the men in a dehumanising process. The war grows to become a (mythical) monster that effectively makes the Trojans 'dead' before the actual fall of the city, to the extent that they even hope for the end—an ancient death-wish syndrome?

Helen, whose abduction conventionally caused the whole war and Troy's destruction, according to the de-mythologising intentions of Wolf-Cassandra has never set foot in Troy, and in fact becomes a kind of substitutional myth for the Trojans. 'In Helen, whom we invented, we defended everything that we did not possess any more.' By extension, Paris is painted as an infantile macho-type who craves prestige to an excessive degree. The only acceptable (in the sense of positively portrayed) Trojans are Aeneas and Anchises. The latter incidentally appears quite unintentionally comical as the *Übervater* of all the alternative and 'Green' rebels, who argues with amazingly Brechtian logic. In her version of Aeneas, Cassandra's beloved who is almost too good to be true, Christa Wolf steers dangerously close to a type of bitter-sweet love story.

The final component which is the depiction of the enemy camp of the Greeks, Wolf-Cassandra unmasks and de-mythologises perhaps most radically of all. Here her target is, of course, *the* (male) heroic epic of all times, the *Iliad*. The Greek heroes appear without exception weak, infantile, cruel and cowardly. Cassandra singles out Achilles and Agamemnon in her denunciation. The latter is portrayed with some fine feminist psychology as a pathetic weakling who has serious problems of impotence, for which he compensates by being particularly cruel in battle. To Cassandra, Agamemnon appears as the idiot compared with Clytemnestra whom she views as the true sovereign, an independent and emancipated woman (and a professional one at that!). Cassandra sympathises with her—and applauds her slaughtering of Agamemnon, as a fair revenge for his butchering of her daughter Iphigenia in the name of sacrifice. Achilles is also dealt with mercilessly by Cassandra, being introduced in the book as 'Achilles the animal'; and hated by her more than anyone else because he embodies the male combination of lust and murder, of destructive barbarism and inhumanity. To Wolf's Cassandra, Achilles is a homosexual who has relations with women only as an alibi; he is a butcher with no finer feelings.

At the same time Cassandra realises that all of the Trojans, including herself, harbour 'an Achilles within'. It appears that Wolf-Cassandra is determined to destroy the Achilles-myth above all others as the most influential and far-reaching male heroic myth. Her anti-heroic, anti-tragic perspective is very consciously perceived and clearly defined. On the whole, the Greeks represent the 'moderns', the 'enlightened' and efficient ones to whom the (male-dominated) future belongs. They are the determined and thorough ones, the brutal, successful and inhuman victors—and they are all men.

Returning to the point of departure of Christa Wolf's claim to anti-mythological writing, one comes to perhaps the most fundamental conclusion that she effectively replaces ancient myths with other myths. If one takes, for example, her notion of a feminist counter-world in the sense of a non-heroic 'earth-culture' (as practised in her book by the women who worship Cybele), does the Utopian concept of a redeeming, more 'humane' and unheroic alternative world not belong to the stock of well-known myths? And what of the belief in the healing powers of female thinking that would counter the present, seemingly desperate situation? However true and however necessary, surely this must inevitably imply a kind of unhistorical regression that approaches dangerously close to a substitute religion.

For Cassandra, the livable alternative to the world of the palace and the world of men and war, exists in the world of mountains, caves and forests. It is the simple, natural life that is characterised by the transition from the world of tragedy to the world of what Wolf calls the 'burlesque'. By this she means a peaceful, 'humane', complete and ordinary kind of world where people do not take themselves tragically seriously, as happens in the male-dominated world of heroes and war and its unavoidable self-alienation. All this, too, is a well-used myth in our century that proclaimed the impossibility of tragedy and the tragic hero in the face of a mass-society with increasingly Orwellian characteristics.

Christa Wolf's belief that the *naming* of dangers in itself might be able to work some kind of magic, reveals a romantic belief in the powers of poetic language which is in turn another myth. Further myths emerge in the book, one of the most common in our times being the one about the end of all myths—the myth of the end of the world, the myth of catastrophe that has its roots in the negative myth of the failure of the Enlightenment, the failing of belief in the power of rational thinking and all its consequences. This belief in the end-of-the-world-through-man's-own-doing—that is, the believing religiously in the infallibility of rationality—is perhaps a particular German favourite. The apocalypse is the only remaining 'story' that can still be told and this, of course, constitutes another myth, the 'final' one perhaps. A myth can be counteracted only by another myth—it can, however, be replaced by another, more successful, myth.

Thus one might say that Christa Wolf, far from demythologising Cassandra and her context, is rather engaged in rewriting old myths and re-directing their complex history of reception. Whether her version will eventually replace the ancient version seems doubtful in a world where the voice of Cassandra has been reduced to computer-printouts whose matter-of-fact horror-prophecies we consume with the daily newspaper. (pp. 70-4)

Jürgen Lieskounig, "Christa Wolf's 'Kassandra': Myth or Anti-Myth?" in Theoria, *Pietermaritzburg, Vol. LXX, October, 1987, pp. 67-75.*

MARY FULBROOK

Christa Wolf has attained international stature as a writer. This recognition acknowledges not least her directness of approach, her "subjective authenticity", the "dimension of the author" referred to in the title of this book [*Die Dimension des Autors: Essays und Aufsätze, Reden und Gespräche 1959-1986*]. In grappling with the specific problems of her generation, her society and her gender—the psychological effects of fascism, the development of socialism, the social roles of women—Wolf's writing reaches a much wider audience. This comprehensive collection of essays, speeches and conversations gathers together material—including some which has until now been relatively inaccessible and a few new pieces—permitting a sustained engagement with Wolf's reflections on a range of themes.

Wolf believes that the process of writing is in some ways more important than the product, allowing the author to work through and come to terms with the distortions and repressions of the past and the problems of the present; that good literature can heighten sensibilities in the reader; and that it can actively contribute to the humanization of social relationships and the building of a better society. More specifically, "subjective authenticity" does not mean any return to "subjectivism" or "bourgeois idealism"; Wolf argues that the achievements of socialist realism and Marxist socio-economic theories now permit the exploration of the inner workings of personality in an honest way, avoiding clichés.

For Wolf and her generation, a key question is that of the formation and channelling of personality under fascism. This exploration has relevance for the present, in that a whole generation has not yet adequately confronted, and emancipated itself from, a suppressed past. Wolf's reflections on the social conditioning of personality, the layers and levels of consciousness, the meaning of memory, as expressed in many of the pieces in this collection and as explored at length in her masterly novel, *Kindheitsmuster,* put into question the very notion of an unchanging "I", while yet endorsing the existence of an inner self which—even when treated in the third person—can still stand back and insist "das nicht!". In her writings on these questions, Wolf develops a subtle and persuasive case on the complex inter-relations between a developing self and social environment.

However compelling Wolf's views on these central themes which inform her work, certain inconsistencies appear. On the subject of gender, for example, she appears to be developing a less subtle form of biologism. From her insistence in the early 1970s that both women and men needed emancipation from the dehumanizing division of labour in industrial society—an insight only gained once women had achieved equal rights and opportunities and could then ask what it was that men actually did—Wolf now perceives intrinsic, persistent differences between male and female, and suggests that men have played the villains, supressing women throughout most of western history (see the new piece on **"Krankheit und Liebesentzug"**). Similarly, there are inconsistencies in Wolf's reflections on her own society. Wolf—a committed socialist—insists that the deference to authority and the tendency to conform evident in the GDR is to some extent a legacy of fascism which must be worked through. Wolf appears to assume that heightened awareness can in itself help to overcome constraints. She does not directly confront the central question of whether the sociopolitical organization of the GDR itself serves to foster certain tendencies, and whether indeed—or under what conditions—socialism can combat the effects of bureaucratization and centralization on social relationships. . . .

[*Die Dimension des Autors*] is an invaluable source; and, most importantly, the "subjective authenticity" of Wolf's voice, here as elsewhere, stimulates in the reader processes of increased awareness, questioning and change, as Wolf herself intends.

Mary Fulbrook, "Authentically Active," in The Times Literary Supplement, No. 4409, October 2-8, 1987, p. 1075.

ANTHONY STEPHENS AND JUDITH WILSON

[One may see Christa Wolf's] whole artistic development as a continual experiment, in the sense that it is determined by the need to create fresh possibilities of existence, but always through what Ingeborg Bachman called the 'Widerspiel des Unmöglichen mit dem Möglichen' ('the interaction of impossibility with the possible'). (p. 277)

What determines the possibility or impossibility of an existence, the spuriousness or authenticity of a piece of writing is for Christa Wolf the specific form the play of opposites takes. It may be the political opposition of East and West, the discrepancy between vision and reality in socialist society, the dilemmas posed by censorship and self-censorship, the tension between an authentic inner self and a public personality; increasingly in her later works it is the tension between a patriarchal order of society and its possible alternatives or . . . the dissonance produced by deliberately confronting writing that is the immediate expression of the self with the posed attitudes of artistic self-consciousness.

In *Nachdenken über Christa T.* [1968] the dualism appears in the constant emphasis on dimensions of the main character's life which remain unrealised; in this novel and in *Kindheitsmuster* [1976] the possibility of narration itself is repeatedly called into question because of its tendency to fix and thus deform the characters it creates; in the case of the longer narrative works, no longer designated as novels, which follow *Kindheitsmuster,* namely *Kein Ort. Nirgends* (1979) and *Kassandra* (1983), the tension between her determination to push back the limits of what can be said, to recover lost areas of experience or explore new ones, and her scepticism about the adequacy of simple narration, leads to a splitting off of the fictional text from discursive explanations: the essays on Karoline von Günderrode and Bettina von Arnim and the *Voraussetzungen einer Erzählung: Kassandra.* In *Kindheitsmuster* the sheer amount of questioning of the probity of narrative is clearly related to the stresses set up by the enormity of the events it tries to encompass, a childhood and adolescence spent in the Third Reich, but the fabric of the novel ultimately manages to withstand these pressures. With the later works, Christa Wolf has apparently moved away from the novel form, separating off the exposition of ideas in order to articulate a greater range of possible forms of existence and to allow a greater freedom of formal experimentation.

Her practice of cultivating both a range of possibilities and their opposites within a given context produces in her work a certain lack of fixity. . . . This may well account for the continued, although uneasy, co-existence of her work with the demands of the regime in East Germany and for the sharp divisions in the critical response to it in both Germanies. On the one hand, the cat-and-mouse game she plays with official disapproval has a proven strategic value in opening up new territory for East German fiction. On the other hand, she generalises specific human difficulties to the point where they become intractable problems of existence and this has resulted in her going over much the same ground several times. It is fair to say that since *Nachdenken über Christa T.* she has shifted much the same set of problems into increasingly distant dimensions of the past: firstly into the recent past of *Kindheitsmuster;* secondly into the early nineteenth-century historical setting of *Kein Ort. Nirgends;* thirdly into the mythic past of *Kassandra.* (pp. 278-79)

[This] process goes hand in hand with a growing detachment from the doctrinaire views of social and historical progress to which the regime in East Germany expects writers to adhere. In *Der Schatten eines Traumes* (1978), the fate of Kleist, Günderrode and their generation is blamed on the perversity of historical processes, the disjunction between exceptional individuals and the confusion of society: . . . 'The new middle-class society, still inchoate and already debilitated, uses them as drafts, preliminary versions that are all too rapidly rejected'. Despite the claims of the present socialist state to be the summation of everything good in history, Kleist and Günderrode have fared no better at the hands of contemporary East German literary orthodoxy. By *Voraussetzungen einer Erzählung: Kassandra,* history in both Germanies seems to have reached a stalemate in the conviction that: . . . 'The young intellectuals on both sides of this border are exhausting themselves in the pursuit of the impossible . . . And that the older members of my generation, those who no longer have any illusions, have been aware for some time: there is no room for change. There is no revolutionary situation.' Further on in the same text, all the doubts about the morality of fiction, which are familiar from *Nachdenken über Christa T.* and *Kindheitsmuster,* culminate in the formulation of a nexus between linear narrative and male dominance in history and society:

> Not until private property, the rule of priests and the patriarchy arise, is that one blood-red thread torn out of the fabric of human existence, is it reinforced at the expense of the wholeness of the fabric: the story of the heroes' combat and victory or of their defeat and death. Fiction is born. The epic, a product of the struggle to establish the patriarchy, becomes *by virtue of its very structure* as well an instrument to use in its development and consolidation.

A programmatic statement such as this seems to confront the reader with various inconsistencies. Not only has Christa Wolf in the same work defined narrative as 'making meaningful' what is narrated, but the story she finally tells of Kassandra is itself linear in the extreme. Moreover, its purpose is clearly to make Kassandra's life and convictions significant despite the inevitability of her violent death. It is in fact the narrative process itself which produces this meaning, whereas the bare facts of the myth, to which Christa Wolf adheres, would ultimately deny it. The possibility of existence which *Kassandra* makes tangible can only emerge—because of the way in which Christa Wolf has chosen to tell the story—both in opposition to the myth itself and to the author's own programmatic condemnation of linear narrative.

In all of Christa Wolf's work there is a problematic mixing of such contradictions as are clearly strategic with others that have every appearance of being unintentional. It is in a sense the conceptual intransigence of the 'either/or', which she develops as a response to a given historical, political or personal situation, that rebounds on both her theoretical statements and her fictional characters. (pp. 279-80)

Her first published fiction, *Moskauer Novelle* (1961), was written in 1959. Described by the East German critic Peter Gugisch as 'an exemplary gesture towards maintaining German-Soviet friendship', the story endeavours to come to terms with German guilt for the past by working through the complications of an abortive love affair between Vera, an East German pediatrician visiting Moscow, and Pawel, a former officer in the Soviet occupation forces and now an interpreter. In addition to the guilt she bears as a German, Vera also bears some responsibility for the accident which has prevented Pawel from realising himself as a doctor. Its modest scope and marked sentimentality makes the *Moskauer Novelle* fall far short of Christa Wolf 's own vision of East German literature at the time and it resembles instead some of the works of others she criticised harshly in print. (p. 282)

When her first novel, *Der geteilte Himmel,* appeared in 1963, the initial East German reviews were in the main hostile. . . . But these negative voices soon gave way to official approval, as such prominent establishment critics as Alfred Kurella, Dieter Schlenstedt and Hans Koch, First Secretary of the Writers' Union, found it quite ideologically acceptable. (pp. 282-83)

The success of *Der geteilte Himmel* with official circles can be attributed in large part to its seeming to fulfil the requirements of the programme enunciated at the Bitterfeld conference of 1959: that writers and artists should participate in the building of the socialist state by, in particular, experiencing the life of the workforce and reflecting workers' concerns directly in their artistic production. . . . In the 1950s, the primary task of literature was seen as promoting the construction of the new social order; in the 1960s, there was a call to reflect a socialist society which had come of age. The ghosts of the past could be taken as exorcised, and instead the focus was to be on the everyday reality of the worker, in which conflicts were no longer taboo. While the solutions themselves remained unquestioned, it was open to portray more difficulties in achieving them than in the previous phase. (p. 283)

There is little disagreement in academic criticism on [*Der geteilte Himmel*] that its positive socialist character is more apparent than real. While Rita does her best to affirm the sacrifice she has made, her own interactions with figures representative of socialism are on the whole less convincing than Manfred's disaffection with the system. John Milfull has suggested that Manfred is basically no more than a projection of Rita's difficulties in coming to grips with reality and other critics have argued that her process of reflection still leaves her strangely passive and dependent on external influences. In terms of the model of possibility/impossibility we have proposed, it is certainly made clear what values are meant to represent which of the polarities, but what is lacking is any convincing mediation of them. In a way that anticipates all Christa Wolf 's later works, self-realisation is shown to be a problem that resists all the pragmatic solutions available, whether these be joining Manfred in the West or reintegration into socialist society. Prophetic also is the mythicising of nature in the novel which tends to create epiphanies of feeling that short-circuit the reflective process. Furthermore, by standing in opposition to the drabness of contemporary urban existence, nature in *Der geteilte Himmel* becomes the prototype of those later idyllic settings which are at once es-

capist and oppositional, such as the utopian community of women on the banks of the Scamander in *Kassandra.*

In the twentieth-century German novel, there appears to be a strong correlation between complication of the narrative perspective and emotional rejection of the narrative present. . . . If one may see in *Der geteilte Himmel* some correlation between the complication, in East German terms, of narrative technique and the ambivalences which undermine the dogmatic socialist perspective, then her next work, *Nachdenken über Christa T.,* makes the connection quite explicit. For the novel is full of agonising over the dangers of fiction's manipulating and falsifying human reality, and it singularly fails to reconcile either the main character or the reader with the present dimension of the plot.

The novel sets out to explore a life that is not so much impossible as unfulfilled, but does so in a way which raises wider questions as to the possibility or impossibility of existence—largely because of the extremely problematical relationship of the unnamed narrator to the main character Christa T. Critics continue to disagree as to the extent to which the narrator can be identified with Christa Wolf and the author has deliberately blurred the issue. The issue is, in fact, of minor importance for an understanding of the novel itself; it only becomes significant once one tries to analyse the concept of personal authenticity, which from *Nachdenken über Christa T.* onwards becomes dominant in all her theoretical statements, replacing the orthodox concept of 'Parteilichkeit' ('partisanship'). What is important for understanding the novel, as the author herself has said, is to grasp the relationship between the narrator and Christa T. as two characters within a fiction. (pp. 284-85)

The real impossibility in the novel, and one which is not easy to understand, is ultimately that of the narrator's becoming the full character which she is by implication. There seems to be a strange taboo on her talking about herself except in relation to Christa T., and the effect of this is that she projects a good deal onto the figure of her dead friend which sits rather uncomfortably. In fact the narrator seems to want to become the 'other' of herself, as the text strongly implies in the following two passages. The first instance occurs when the impending separation of the narrator from Christa T. is seen as a division of the self: . . . 'And that we were shortly to lose contact with each other and ourselves . . . , until a moment comes when this alien self will return and become part of me again'. The second passage, in which this theme emerges significantly, links the possibility of otherness with the tensions between East and West: . . . 'To make the distinction between "us" and "the others", with complete intransigence, irrevocably: that way lay salvation. And yet to know inside: not much more needed to happen and not one step would have separated us from "otherness", because we would ourselves have changed. But how do you divide off from yourself? We never spoke of this. But she knew it'.

This passage could stand as a motto for her next novel, *Kindheitsmuster* (1976), the main subject of which is a childhood and adolescence in the Third Reich. The novel also includes two dimensions of the narrative present: the one recounts a visit to Poland by the narrator and her family in 1972 and the other mirrors the composition of the novel itself, with many reflections on the problematics of fiction and the relation of present to past. The last segment of the novel is dated 2 May 1975, three days after the end of the war in Vietnam. As in *Nachdenken über Christa T.,* the relation between the narrator and her material is complicated by the question of otherness. In political terms, this is inevitable, since there can be no simple identification with a childhood spent under Nazism. If one of the criticisms made by Max Walter Schulz of her previous novel was that it failed to recognise the past of the Third Reich had been effectively dealt with by the socialist present, *Kindheitsmuster* shows Christa Wolf's determination to contradict this attitude, as summarised by her quoting with approval Freud's maxim:'He who does not remember his past is condemned to repeat it.'

In exploring the childhood of Nelly Jordan, Christa Wolf explicitly rejects the practice of projecting all negativity onto 'the others'. Reconstructing the development of Nelly's identity, she confronts directly the issue of the childhood self's adaptation to a system which the adult personality must reject. She is far from succumbing to the temptation to present this as one brutalisation after another, and maintains the credibility of the character by allowing the childhood talent for dissimulation to go for long stretches uncensored by the ideological strictures of the present. While she frankly declares her projected narration to be a 'Such- und Rettungsaktion' ('a search and rescue operation'), she is nevertheless so nervous of evoking the past in too glowing or sombre colours that she hardly succeeds in resurrecting anything of the essential anarchic feelings of childhood. An incident from the autumn of 1943, in which Nelly, to the narrator's own discomfiture, maintains a steady indifference towards the Ukrainian women she is working with in the fields, is typical of her emphasis on the neutrality of which the adolescent self is capable:

> What she felt towards the foreigners was not pity, but fear, a strong feeling of alienation . . . Would it ever have occurred to her to get up, to walk the thirty paces across the abyss separating her from the workers from the East . . ., and to give one of them her own bowl of soup in which there were pieces of meat? The dreadful secret: not that she didn't dare do it, but that she hadn't even thought of it.

(pp. 287-89)

To us the main deficiency in the novel seems to stem from one of the implications of its title. Christa Wolf has emphasised the experimental connotations of the word 'Muster'—'pattern' in the sense of a model to be tried out—, but the more basic sense of a patterning of the individual through childhood experiences poses problems for a work bent on realising an ideal of authenticity. For there is a real need for the novel to scrutinise the detailed consequences of this patterning for the adult personality, and this is not answered by the endless questionings of the probity of narration itself. When it comes to the further questions of how such patterns may have persisted in German society and been confronted in the post-war decades, the reader is left with little to go on but the narrator's intense anxiety. Given that this does nothing to offset the aura of inevitability which surrounds Nelly's apparently normal development, we are left wondering just what alternatives, socialist or otherwise there might be, and this is not helped by the narrator's reticence in pursuing her own relationship with Lenka, her daughter.

Wolfgang Emmerich, in his account of East German fiction of the 1970s, sees a general loss of the belief in a non-antagonistic relationship between the individual and society and a tendency towards constructing self-conscious narratives that must remain incomplete, as *Kindheitsmuster* indeed does. Even before the exclusion of the poet Wolf Biermann in 1976 and the subsequent hardening of attitudes on both sides, the problem of self-realisation tends to be posed in more insistent terms than previously and even the negative resolution of it that an incomplete story represents is cleary preferable to a formula which is too general to impress one as authentic.

While criticism cannot ignore the contradictions in Christa Wolf's works which appear unintentional, they do not constitute grounds for undervaluing her achievement. Both *Nachdenken über Christa T.* and *Kindheitsmuster* are important novels because they give voice to the experience of a particular segment of the post-war generation in both Germanies, and this experience itself cannot help but be contradictory. If the reception of both novels in East and West comes to different conclusions about what message is being conveyed and what aspects are most or least successful, this does not alter the fact that the novels are landmarks, in the sense that they crystallise particular possibilities and impossibilities of coming to terms with present and past which have found a resonance among a wide readership in both Germanies. (pp. 289-90)

Kein Ort. Nirgends, which tells of a fictional encounter in the year 1804 between Karoline von Günderrode and Heinrich von Kleist, builds its plot around a single significant occurrence in the style of the classical German *Novelle*. Its structure has close affinities with Kleist's two *Novellen, Das Erdbeben in Chili* and *Die Verlobung in St. Domingo*. The key to understanding the author's intentions in the story really has to be found in the essay on Günderrode, *Der Schatten eines Traumes* (1978), rather than in the story itself, as critics were not slow to point out. While *Kein Ort. Nirgends* is very tightly written and coherently structured, it makes even fewer concessions to the expectations of the average reader than *Kindheitsmuster.* Read together with the essay, it makes a satisfactory whole, but the question remains whether Christa Wolf has ceased to find the form of the novel adequate to contain the range of perspectives she now finds essential. (p. 291)

Determining what genre *Kassandra* belongs to presents similar problems. . . . It is designated as an *Erzählung* [tale] rather than a novel. In the *Voraussetzungen* [essays], discursive statements are mixed in with various narrative forms, such as an account of the author's stay in Greece, extracts from a working diary and a long letter to a friend. Here the foundations of a wide range of possible new versions of the myth are laid. Clearly, only some of these can be realised in the final narrative, whose closed nature contrasts markedly with the openness achieved in the *Voraussetzungen*. While much that Christa Wolf says in them would lead the reader to expect something like the later novels of Virginia Woolf, the story that is told adheres to the tragic ending of the myth and is both linear and convergent in its narrative technique. One explanation for this is that Christa Wolf has, in the *Voraussetzungen,* committed herself to taking the tragic pattern of the myth as a paradigm of the fate of women in history. Whereas much in her own narration, such as the feminist interlude on the banks of the Scamander, seems to demand a different kind of ending, to depart from the tragic conclusion may have seemed tantamount to a falsification of history. Such meaningfulness as there is in the life of Kassandra must therefore be extracted, by a process of reflection, from the impossibility of her final situation. As Sigrid Weigel points out, this makes her very like the type of heroine popular in German Classicism, which hardly coincides with the author's stated intentions. In our view, the fundamental conflict is between the different demands of the psychological portrait and the myth. Psychological elaboration is unavoidable, if the story is unfolded as a reflection on the past, and is essential for bringing the figure of Kassandra close to the reader. However these improvisations cannot affect the ending of the myth, since this has already been reinforced by assigning it the status of historical inevitability. Trying to meet both sets of demands produces an unevenness in the narrative which has been widely castigated.

It is necessary to conclude our discussion of Christa Wolf's work with some analysis of the concept of authenticity which she introduces in 1966 and which from 1968 onwards, with the publication of *Nachdenken über Christa T.* and the *Selbstinterview* in which she defends her position, becomes central to all her literary theory and evaluations. As we have shown elsewhere, the main difficulty of using authenticity as a criterion is that it is for Christa Wolf, on the one hand, a distant goal towards which her writing aspires, while on the other it is a kind of essence whose presence or absence can be instantly detected in virtually any piece of writing. As other critics have pointed out, this can lead to the effect that when her fictional characters embark on voyages of self-discovery they seem in very little doubt as to their destination, and this in turn undermines the credibility of the reflective process. Already in *Nachdenken über Christa T.* the narrator seems to know in advance what she will claim for the figure she is reconstructing, and in *Kassandra* the fact that the heroine narrates the story from a point just before her inevitable murder means that all possible developments are stigmatised as leading ultimately to this end.

Part of the difficulty stems from the fact that Christa Wolf has developed the concept in opposition to a number of different things: the increasing alienation of the individual from society; the structures of power, be they political, technocratic or partriarchal, which restrict self-realisation as she has come to define it; and the complicity of literature over the centuries in this process. Contrary to what critics such as Bernhard Greiner have said, authenticity is not simply an aesthetic principle but is rather a set of moral imperatives which extend beyond the sphere of art. In point of fact, it means the importing into the realm of fiction of an ethical norm, requiring a renunciation of the narrator's traditional position of power *vis-à-vis* both the fictional characters and the reader. This leads to the setting up of various models of communication which, as Gerhard Neumann has shown, have in common the abdication of dominance.

Communication of this kind necessarily involves a high degree of empathy, such as Christa Wolf praises in the dialogue between Bettine von Arnim and Karoline von Günderrode, or between Kassandra and Arisbe in her story, but when this is applied to the relation of reader to work, there is a tendency for the reader to have no vision beyond that of the main character, as also happens in *Kassandra. Kein Ort. Nirgends* is a more successful work in this respect because it presents a genuine dialogue between Kleist and Günderrode, and includes a third position as well, that of the narrator, thus offering the reader perspectives that are somewhat less convergent than in *Kassandra.* So one is left, in the case of Christa Wolf's last work to date, with the uneasy tension between the wide range of strongly critical perspectives offered in the *Voraussetzungen* and the narrowing of perspective in the story itself.

While the principle of authenticity has met with a reasonably sympathetic reception in East Germany, Ursula Püschel, writing in *Neue Deutsche Literatur,* has complained about what she sees as a restriction of freedom on the part of the reader by precisely this close-focusing. While her criticism is explicitly aimed at the underdevelopment of the minor characters in *Kein Ort. Nirgends,* it certainly can also be applied to the story of Kassandra. Despite its undoubted good intentions and the successful fiction it has produced, there is some risk that the cult of authenticity, since it ultimately produces its own ideology, ends up by manipulating the reader. The problem of imposing a non-fictional criterion on fiction is in some ways similar to that of writing to ideological recipes, a difficulty that has beset East German literature from the outset. While Christa Wolf's position has become more and more oppositional over the last two decades and while she takes infinite pains to preserve an openness of experience, the danger of ideology is present as soon as any concept is built up, by sheer repetition, to mythical proportions.

If the concept of authenticity has been worked through to the point where it no longer seems susceptible of further development, it none the less remains essential as a guarantee of the value of her literary project in its present form, since it is its integrity which differentiates her own myth-making from that much more questionable sort which the Trojans in her *Kassandra* practise on the figure of Helen of Troy. The attitudes expressed in the *Voraussetzungen* have taken her even further out of the mainstream of East German literature than the abnegation of historical progress in *Der Schatten eines Traumes.* What is clear is that the path she has taken has been determined by her sincere resolve to keep certain possibilities of self-realisation alive in her fiction, to guard against their being lost sight of in either of two German societies. The pessimism of *Kassandra* and the *Voraussetzungen* is very obviously a product of the deterioration of the political climate in Europe in the first year of Reagan's presidency, with the corresponding Soviet inflexibility offering no amelioration. It is not clear how the feminist position which she adopted at this time will develop. It may well come to dominate her responses to political and social realities. We began by presenting a model of possibility/impossibility, and it has become evident that it is the devaluation both of the present and of the notion of historical progress as well that makes the impossibilities of existence come through more strongly in her fiction and those possibilities dearest to her be projected increasingly into a utopian or mythical dimension. Even so, what Ingeborg Bachmann called the 'Widerspiel des Unmöglichen mit dem Möglichen' ('the interaction of the impossible with the possible') is likely to remain one of the mainsprings of Christa Wolf's writing, for essentially it gives her room to move. (pp. 291-95)

Anthony Stephens and Judith Wilson, "Christa Wolf," in The Modern German Novel, *edited by Keith Bullivant, Berg Publishers, 1987, pp. 276-95.*

SUZANNE RUTA

Both in method and content, Wolf's novels pay history its due. They are a blend of invention, autobiography, documentary, narrative, and essay. Wolf has praised the diary as a literary form and she incorporates it into her novels. Lowly, traditionally feminine, fluid, and open-ended, the diary allows paradoxes to stand unresolved, decisions to hang in the balance. It's suitable for honest confusion as opposed to the deadly complacency of ideologues.

Wolf found her form in **The Quest for Christa T.,** a beautifully allusive and lucid portrait of the generation that came of age after the war. The tone is elegiac, mourning a real friend, the novel's main figure, who died of leukemia in her thirties. It's also an elegy for the hopes the liberation raised and then dashed or, worse, betrayed into cynicism and lip service. Christa T. is no heroine of socialist productivity. At the university in Leipzig she cuts classes to read Dostoevsky or flirt with strangers in bars. (p. 9)

From her professors' point of view, Christa was a particularly weak specimen of the so-called weaker sex, complete with moods, caprices, depressions, neuroses, and suicidal tendencies. By a transvaluation that will become more explicit in her later work, Wolf takes Christa T.'s female complaints as a sign of her moral worth. She's incorruptible. Others go along with what the times require, become not only teachers but principals and department heads. Christa T. can't compromise with the truth. Her death is both a biographical fact and the inevitable outcome of a contest between the real and the ideal.

"She believed that you must work at your past as you work at your future," the narrator says. By "future," her German public would understand the radiant future of socialist slogans; "past" would mean, among other things, Nazism. Wolf began to work on this past in the '70s. In 1971, she visited her hometown for the first time since the war. On her return to Berlin, she began to write her own private history of the Nazi years, **Patterns of Childhood,** perhaps her greatest work.

German denial of the years between '33 and '45 tends to take two forms. It's either what Wolf calls the "everybody is always blaming the Germans" mentality—a compound of self-pity, resentment, and blindness that sees the Hitler years as a logical response to the Bolshevik threat—or, especially in East Germany, an exclusive focus in public life and school history books on the heroes of the anti-Nazi resistance.

Wolf abjures both strategies with a detailed and immensely moving portrait of her large, close-knit, hard-working, Nazi family. These very qualities made it easier for them to shut their eyes to what was going on around them after '33. As a witness to this period, she's the equal of Milosz. The portrait of her long-suffering father, an infantryman in World War I and later in Hitler's army, buttresses Milosz's poignant observation on the amount of silent human fortitude it took to produce a catastrophe such as Verdun.

In 1945, with Soviet troops advancing on her hometown, Wolf and family fled westward. In a field by a campfire, her mother offered a bowl of soup to a concentration camp survivor also in flight. She asked gently what they'd put him away for. For being a Communist, he replied. "But just because you were a Communist they didn't put you in a concentration camp!" she insisted. "Where on earth have you been living?" the man asked. **Patterns** is Wolf's answer to that question, an attempt to explain "how one could be there and not be there at the same time, the ghastly secret of human beings in this century."

A memoir, even a fictionalized memoir, is a hybrid form, grafting the adult writer to the clumsy child. When that child thrilled to radio broadcasts from Vienna during the *An-*

schluss, aspired to leadership in the girls' branch of the Hitler Youth, kept a diary of her favorite Nazi songs even after the German defeat, how is the adult, cosmopolitan, politically aware citizen of a socialist state to bridge the gulf? She worries about condescending to the child no longer able to defend herself. The writer's solution is to admit defeat and give up the use of the integrated first-person singular. The child "Nelly Jordan" is described in the third person, the grown-up narrator, like someone who needs encouragement to complete a distasteful chore, is addressed throughout as "you."

Although **Patterns** further develops the shifting and mobile form of delivery Wolf first tried in **Christa T.,** she can't avoid talking about her family in set pieces: the day Father got his draft notice, the day the synagogue burned down, the day Nelly got scared she might have Jewish blood. The anecdotes follow in roughly chronological sequence, but they've been deliberately frayed at the edges, allowed to bleed into one another, cut through with reflections on brain physiology and current events in Chile and Vietnam. Wolf's overt didactic aim in veering between '33 and '73 is to suggest a recurring pattern that might, if one recognized it in time, be resisted by future generations. But her detours and parenthetical comments also serve a deeper purpose. "Memory," she says (the book is seeded with aphorisms), "is . . . a repeated moral act." Talking about the brain or Chile or President Nixon is an evasion, a needed respite before another of those moral acts. Critics complained of the book's complex structure. It's less a structure than a rhythm, that of memory and release, guilt and forgiveness.

Wolf can't bring herself to tell her 14-year-old daughter that the Nazi flag hung from the roof of her grandparents' house on the required holidays. (There was no flagpole; they had to rig up a bunch of ropes.) Can't tell her about going to look, the day after *Kristallnacht* in November '38, at the remains of the burned-out synagogue in Landsberg. The sight of the destroyed synagogue made her sad, she remembers, but she resisted compassion. German girls, she'd been taught, were hard, and bathed their breasts in ice water. (The girl berates her mother because their bathwater doesn't run ice cold, as the teacher recommended.) (pp. 9-10)

The year **Patterns of Childhood** appeared, '76, was the year of Biermann's expulsion. Instead of following him abroad, Wolf took up residence in another century, among the early German Romantics. Her next novel, **No Place on Earth,** is set in the Rhineland village of Winkel in 1804. It is a brief tour de force of scholarship and poetry. . . . Abandoning the discursive mode, Wolf subjects these Romantics with their boundless longings to the strict classical laws of dramaturgy: one place, one day, one theme. In the space of an afternoon Kleist and Günderrode meet, overcome their shyness, bare their hearts to one another, and separate forever. The text is woven from direct quotes, biographical allusions, and Wolf's own insight into the affinity between these two artists who are apparently so unlike. . . .

The salon chitchat flirts with big issues: poets versus statesmen, idealism versus realism, the impossibility in Germany for a man of vision to find a field of useful activity. . . . Asked to make three wishes, Kleist says at once, "Freedom. A poem. A home." "Irreconcilable things which you want to reconcile," the clairvoyant Günderrode remarks. The parallel is clear between 1804 and 1976. The country still has no use for its artists, deporting them or driving them to despair. The tight form Wolf has chosen for this book suggests that the despair is her own. The tone is darker and more inward than in *Christa T.* Landscapes are not invitations to build, but correlatives of tormented inner states, as in the frozen-sea paintings of Kaspar David Friedrich. All the writer at 50 can do is to record the self-hatred and paralysis that afflict free spirits in a country that prizes other qualities, embodied in the character of Savigny. Günderrode sums him up: "He knows only one kind of curiosity, curiosity concerning that which is incontrovertible, logically consistent, and soluble." In other words, he is a technocrat. Wolf will have more to say about his type in later works.

What would it take to break the deadly pattern in German history? Looking for an answer, Wolf broadens her focus in *Cassandra: A Novel and Four Essays,* her major work of the 1980s and her first novel set wholly outside Germany. But why take ancient Greece as her allegorical cover? Perhaps the more far-reaching her critique of GDR policies, the more remote the setting becomes. *Cassandra* is her thoughtful response to the panicky climate of the early '80s in central Europe. . . . This she does with a vengeance, looking in Greek and prehistoric times for the origins of our dangerous ideas about war and peace, men and women.

The *Cassandra* essays, first delivered as lectures on poetics at the University of Frankfurt am Main in 1982, make explicit the radical feminism implied in Wolf's earlier novels. Her thinking is ironic, profound, and eclectic, drawing together Robert Graves, Engels, Goethe, Aeschylus, Thomas Mann, and Ingeborg Bachmann. Her feminism is not reformist but revolutionary or Utopian; equal rights are a side issue in a world on the verge of nuclear destruction. Was there, she speculates, a period in human history when matriarchy prevailed? She quotes Engels. Men learned to enslave other men by first subjugating women within the confines of monogamous marriage. She rereads Aeschylus, wondering if the Greek fear of female monster-divinities isn't the projection of a guilty conscience for some prehistoric crime—namely, the subjugation of women by men. What would matriarchy have been like? Communitarian, living in nature rather than seeking mastery of it. The mode of thought magical rather than abstract. In this manner, perhaps, humankind survived on the same level of technological progress for thousands of years. But whether or not the longest part of human history was organized under women's rules, it's clear that the last few millennia have been male-dominated. And that this regime won't work anymore. The survival of the race depends on righting the balance between male and female qualities, on women finding the confidence to stand up for what they know.

The last lecture in the series became the novel *Cassandra.* While the essays are a provocative mixture of travel diary and philosophy, recipes and textual criticism, the novel is not completely successful. Legend has it that Cassandra got her gift of prophecy from Apollo along with a curse that no one would believe her predictions. Wolf sets out to do for her what she's done for the other women she has written about. She disengages the historical figure from the encrustations of legend. It's an inspired insight to make this legend a piece of Greek war propaganda. She explains Cassandra's clairvoyance not in supernatural terms but as something akin to her mother's deep pessimism during World War II (In 1944, the Gestapo visited Wolf's mother to investigate reports that Frau Jordan had been heard to say in front of her customers, "We've lost this war, even a blind man can see that.") Ex-

cluded from the National Security Councils and battlefields of the world, women maintain an independence of judgment that men compromised ages ago.

Can women save the world? Troy burned, as every schoolchild knows. Wolf invents a group of slave and servant women living outside the city walls, worshipping the mother goddess Cybele, and learned in the healing arts rather than the destructive. It's thanks to this band, which Cassandra eventually joins, that her lover Aeneas survives to found Rome. But the evocation of an alternative culture, matriarchal instead of male-dominated, has the weakness of the later chapters of *The Color Purple.* Just because women are nicer than men, do they have to brew herbal teas and throw pots? Is Wolf nostalgic for the neolithic? Maybe a little bit. But the Nazi years taught her the danger of nostalgia for an imaginary simpler, purer era. The problem is primarily one of form. In the essays, she is free to weigh all sides of a question and leave it in suspension. The novel, Cassandra's dramatic monologue, is a closed construction that sometimes reduces Wolf's thinking to self-parody.

Yet allegory has its own force; it conveys a sense of looming destiny. We're meant to be as certain of our own impending destruction as we are of the holocaust in ancient Troy. Wolf is Cassandra and we are the people she identified in her Nazi memoir, those who "could be there and not be there at the same time." "When, if not now?" she pleads in *Christa T.* To live in the present with our eyes wide open is the most difficult thing of all. (p. 10)

Suzanne Ruta, "Woman on the Edge of Time," in VLS, No. 70, December 20, 1988, pp. 9-10.

EVA HOFFMAN

The narrative of *Accident: A Day's News* unfolds during one day, and it centers on two main events: the protagonist, an East German writer, hears the news of the Chernobyl nuclear disaster; at the same time, her brother is undergoing an intricate brain-tumor operation.

Fictionally, this is a risky premise; the horrors and the marvels of technology are the stuff of headlines, tracts, ideological polemics and science-fiction melodrama. But in this powerful, brooding and often surprisingly lyrical novel, Christa Wolf avoids both sensationalism and pamphleteering. What interests her are not the bare events themselves—astonishing though they are—but how they register on our consciousness and imagination, how the deep intrusions of technology into our existence alter the substance of our world, our very sense of what it means to be human, of who and what we are. . . .

[In] such novels as *Cassandra, The Quest for Christa T.* and *Patterns of Childhood,* [Wolf] has probed the interaction between large historical forces—war, fascism—and the individual personality. *Accident* brings that investigation right up to the present, and takes on the courageous task of bringing our awareness into alignment with our current reality. The novel is written in the form of an associative, interior meditation, addressed by the narrator to her much-loved and now unconscious brother, in which she circles around, with an almost obsessive intensity, the two events that have suddenly transformed her world.

"Once again, so it seemed, our age had created a Before and After for itself," she says, and as she goes through the ordinary motions of her day—working in her garden, visiting neighbors in her village, talking on the telephone to her friends and daughters—she finds that in the light of Chernobyl the most familiar details of her life have undergone a quiet, terrible mutation. A beautiful blue sky becomes infused with a sense of menace. . . .

Chernobyl is clearly an example of technology at its most malignant; the brain-tumor operation—we're told early on it will be successful—might be viewed as science at its most benevolent. But the depictions of the surgery, imagined in close detail by the narrator, are actually deeply disturbing. The surgeon, she knows, may have to sacrifice her brother's sense of smell; a small, terrifying choice. If the surgical needles slip, they may impair her brother's memory. In such minute movements and decisions, not only does her brother's life hang in the balance, but the nature of his very subjectivity, and of personhood, is also brought into question. . . .

The infiltration of technology, the novel suggests, has fundamentally affected not only external nature, but also our most cherished assumptions about human nature. Who are we, when our temperament, sensations, most individual traits, can be manipulated by a nuance of a scalpel? The violation of such tamperings is felt in the novel with a kind of anguish; and occasionally, the anger turns a bit pat or righteous. The Faustian urge to know the innermost secrets of nature, and to exercise the power of such knowledge, seems to be in this novel expressly male, and too vaguely connected to authoritarianism, the hunger for profit and an assortment of other standard evils.

But paradoxically, the tone that most often prevails in this novel is tenderness—as if the author were describing a world that is all the more to be loved because it is vulnerable, fragile, already almost lost. Even as she takes in the awful news of the day, the narrator becomes excited by an anecdote of her grandson's childish accomplishment; she analyzes a problematic friendship—the personal situation, after all!—and she makes immense, moving efforts of empathy toward her brother.

And she contemplates—in some of the most provocative passages in the novel—the losses within language itself. Words that were once beautiful, she reflects, become, under the irradiation of Chernobyl, contaminated, "archaic," inadequate. "It should be interesting to see which poet would be the first to dare sing the praises of a white cloud," she muses, after remembering a verse of pastoral poetry. "An invisible cloud of a completely different substance had seized the attention of our feelings—completely different feelings."

Christa Wolf may not have found a completely new language for the "completely different feelings," but the very tenor of her voice—impassioned, intimate, variable—is an antidote to the brave new world she is describing. It is a voice that allows us poignantly to gauge how the large and abstract forces shaping our world fall upon one vulnerable, perishable entity that we still like to think of as human. It has always been the special function of the novel to give us the story of our sensibility, to show us what it is like to live, to feel and to perceive, within the circumstances of a particular time; to that history of lived experience, Christa Wolf has contributed an important update.

Eva Hoffman, "The Post-Chernobyl Blues, from an East German Perspective," in The New York Times, April 12, 1989, p. C23.

MARY GORDON

Christa Wolf has set herself nothing less than the task of exploring what it is to be a conscious human being alive in a moment of history. . . . Urgency and seriousness mark her work. There is nothing of the entertainment in anything she writes. Plot exists where it does only as a kind of inevitable vector: two of her novels [*Cassandra* and *No Place on Earth*] are reworkings of stories whose endings are predetermined so that plot is beside the point of authorial planning. . . .

Christa Wolf is East German. Her work is stripped of elements that exist merely to give pleasure, as if she has refused the corrupt blandishments of the bourgeois palate and wants to seek only the most useful, nourishing of foods. The considerable beauty of her novels emanates from their spareness. Even *Cassandra,* the busiest of them, doesn't contain diversions. But her books aren't cold, distant or judging. She isn't Beckett. Nature and domestic life are sources of great pleasure: life lived in houses, meals prepared and shared with friends, a view of a lake, the scent of herbs crushed in the palm as one walks up a mountain. The task of integrating a life, the exhausting effort of living fully and justly, shape all of Christa Wolf's fictions. Her books are difficult, like certain kinds of prayer. But finishing them, the reader is covered by a sense of completeness, of having been taken on a journey in the company of a seer who has stared, with attention, mercy and courage, into the world's heart.

Certainly *Accident: A Day's News* is a difficult book. Even the subject—nuclear disaster and surgery that can ruin, stop or prolong life—is difficult to contemplate. Ms. Wolf's prose is extremely dense; her structure is an intricately connected web of associations. I'm not sure that she has been well served by her translators, Heike Schwarzbauer and Rick Takvorian, who seem to have swallowed large lumps of German syntax whole. There is no action in the novel except that of waiting for news: the news of the extent of radioactive damage and of the results of risky surgery.

The "I" of the narrative is a woman, a writer alone in a house in the country. Before Chernobyl, many of her pleasures were simple, natural ones: tending her garden, cooking herself meals. But waiting for the news of spreading disaster, she must confront the truth that what had once been a source of pleasure and nourishment for her may now be a source of poisoning and death. She explores the nature of disaster and salvation that technology can bring. The world may be unlivable; the doctors may have saved her brother's life. Her task, as waiter-for-the-news, is to try to understand the nature of the news that she will hear, of the men (she makes the point that they are not women) whose activities will cause events to occur, the nature of the world that the events will leave in their wake. . . .

What does it mean to live a life? Christa Wolf keeps asking. To read her, we must accept a language that is aphoristically thick, to believe, for example, that a mother and a daughter have telephone conversations like this one:

> My oldest daughter sounded tired, I still pounced
> on her with the question: What do you consider our
> blind spot? Oh, Mother! I asked her whether her
> answer would include the expression 'living a lie.'
> Not necessarily, she said, she would talk about that
> region of our soul, our perception, which remained
> in the dark because it was too painful for us to face.

What makes Ms. Wolf's language and method psychologically satisfying and rescues it from lifelessness is that she roots her most abstract notions in concrete life. The telephone call with her older daughter is balanced by another with her younger daughter in which mother and daughter discuss children's behavior. A proud grandmother, the narrator is enchanted by hearing that a 1½-year-old, her grandson, puts a wingnut on his thumb and prances around the kitchen saying, "Me Punch. Me Punch." Isn't he advanced? the narrator asks her daughter. Certainly most 1½-year-olds aren't up to that. She tells her daughter that "Shakespeare and Greek tragedy wouldn't do a thing for me now compared with your children's stories. And, by the way, did she know that the radiation level at the time of the above-ground nuclear-weapons tests in the 1960s was said to have been higher than now.

"You sure know how to make a person feel good, said my youngest daughter."

This pattern of traveling from the particular to the universal, from the familial to the political, this refusal to separate realms of thought, characterizes all of *Accident: A Day's News,* and allows it both a naturalness and an enormous scope. At one point in the novel, the narrator goes from thinking about the odd details of her brother's surgery—that which determines all personality can be wrapped in foil, tied off, picked at like a piece of metal—to bicycling into the village for her day's errands. She sees a four-leaf clover; it reminds her of the war. She passes her porch, where she waves visitors off, and remembers that the man who once lived there was taken off by the Russians because he was a driver for the Gestapo. She is brought back to thinking of her brother, with whom she lived through the war, remembering that in his anesthetized condition, he has not experienced Chernobyl. She thinks of the faces of the victims on television: she will not allow these faces to become abstract to her, removed: "Now we hear that every new technology requires sacrifices at first. I tried to steel myself against the faces of people which might appear—did appear—on television, who would try to force a smile. Whose hair would have fallen out. Whose doctors would use the word 'brave.'"

When Christa Wolf tries to understand the impulses that have led the men who have devoted themselves to feeding the evergrowing monster of nuclear technology, she roots her question in the idea of desire. "Whence this desire for fission, for fire and explosions!" she once asked her brother; their relationship has taken the form of her asking questions in heated terms and his insisting that she cool down, lower the volume of her language. "You forbade me to use the word 'desire' in this connection," the narrator remembers. "Desire, desire . . . you said. That was another one of those exaggerated, partisan expressions. It was much simpler than that. Once someone had begun to invent something. Or to discover something: then he just couldn't stop anymore."

He reminds her that she has been like this in her writing, has known that words can wound and has not stopped the projectile of her wounding words. What, she wonders, is the connection between language and this taste for destruction that seems built into the species? She has read that language, agriculture and murder became part of the human experience at the same evolutionary time. Devoting her life to language as she has, is she part of the murderous complicity whose end is the China syndrome? How does her desire for purity of speech tie in with the scientist's compulsion to follow whatever lead is offered him, and the brain surgeon's confidence that

he can play with those body parts which render us recognizable to ourselves? "Is it worthwhile, brother," she asks, "staking one's life on being able to express oneself ever more precisely, discernibly, unmistakably."

These are exactly the things on which Christa Wolf stakes her life. She uses language as if her life depended upon finding the connections among the conflicting elements that make up the whole of life. *Accident: A Day's News* has the grandeur of a noble labor. The woman, the writer, the sister, the mother, the cook, the gardener, the citizen of the world must use her whole life to keep back the lie of separateness: the poison of the lie that fission is to be desired, the disease of schizophrenia with which each modern man and woman lives, forgetting that terrible forces shape our lives. Is *Accident: A Day's News* hopeful or despairing? The question is impossible to answer; the terms are wrong. What it offers is a model of passionate engagement: we are where we are, where others, not only ourselves but those who go before and after us, are, have been, will be. It is a precious place. The book ends with a final message from the woman to her brother: "How difficult it would be, brother, to take leave of this earth."

Mary Gordon, "Living with Hellish Dangers," in The New York Times Book Review, April 23, 1989, p. 3.

CELIA GILBERT

[In *Accident: A Day's News,* Christa Wolf] treats a theme of imminent retribution. What are we doing to the earth? she asks. What is it in our human brain, nature and culture, that could bring us to poison the world? What can our response be to such a transformation?

Accident takes place in one day in the life of an older East German woman, a writer, at the time of the reactor meltdown at Chernobyl. Nameless, alone in her house in a small village at springtime, as clouds of radiation are drifting westward over Europe, the woman listens to the hourly bulletins on the radio while anxiously awaiting news of her brother, who is undergoing an operation for a brain tumor.

Wolf's genius takes the small facts of this woman's life: her annoyance with her neighbor's chickens; her hopes for transplanting a japanese cherry; her delight in uprooting a nettle; a telephone conversation with a friend, to mitigate the encroaching threat. Bits of poetry, fairy stories, literature, essays, all find their way into the text as the narrator gathers all she can to construct a support for herself and us. As diligently as she goes through her refrigerator questioning what is and is not safe to eat, she tries to understand theories of science, anthropology, language, and the conflicting testimony of the "experts."

She phones her daughters for alarmed consultations. What to do when they have been told not to drink milk or eat greens? What to say when she finds her daughter agonized because she had just showered the children, only to learn that this does not remove the radioactivity, but opens the pores so it will be more absorbed? And alarm shifts to delight when she learns her grandson of one and a half has already the capacity to imagine himself as someone else.

Aging makes more urgent her quest to understand a world that seems more and more chaotic. Talking to her brother in her head, she says, "growing older means: all that one would never have thought possible comes true." Unable to write, she leaves the house. History flows around her in the village. She talks with her neighbors, old men who were at the Russian front and saw the cruelties of war. She encounters on her land a family come to search for the grave of a young child buried there, dead of typhoid in the year after the war. Despite her sympathy, she grows angry with them; they reawaken the fearful memories of that time, a time which could so easily return.

What makes us human, what is civilized, what do we know about the evolution of the brain, she asks. Images of the operation they are performing on her brother torment her, along with her fears that in "saving" him, they will destroy some vital sense, some part of his memory or personality.

In the nearby forest under ancient beeches stands a circle of stones. No one really knows their age, she thinks. For her they are the symbol of ancestors and past attempts, like ours, to become human through ceremonies and traditions.

Night falls. She learns her brother's operation appears to be a success. She cleans up the dishes, prepares for sleep by reading, and opens, for the first time, Conrad's *Heart of Darkness*.

> He set right out into the heart of the blind spot of that culture to which he also belonged . . . And he saw the light which must have led him, too, on his way like a "running blaze on a plain, like a flash of lightning in the clouds."

"We live in the flicker, may it last as long as the old earth keeps rolling," says the narrator, who sleeps, then, awakening from a nightmare, calls out to her brother, "How difficult it would be, brother, to take leave of this earth."

For years I've been hearing praises of Christa Wolf's work, and now I can't wait to read everything she has written. I will turn again and again to the beauty and richness of this seamless meditation. It gives voice to all of us, to our despair and horror; by a miracle that only a great writer can bring about, it comforts without deception.

> *Celia Gilbert, "Unnatural Disasters," in* The Women's Review of Books, *Vol. VI, Nos. 10 & 11, July, 1989, pp. 20-1.*

ELAYNE RAPPING

Accident's focus is the destructiveness of modern technology and the mysteries of the soul that impel it to invent such self-annihilating marvels. "No surgeon could penetrate through to that hectic group of neural connections in the brains of those men who thought up the procedures for the so-called peaceful utilization of nuclear energy," the narrator thinks bitterly. And yet she is helplessly awaiting news that the cold-blooded expertise of medical science has been skillful enough to heal her brother, to return him to the state of thinking, feeling "selfhood" that scientific knowledge threatens to obliterate on a global scale.

Wolf's prose is as dense and spare as poetry and similar in its method. There is no narrative imperative to the book's structure, no "events" to propel the action. There is only the narrator thinking and waiting. Thought follows thought and all connect metaphorically to the novel's theme. At one point a friend calls to "hear my voice" and ask "whether I actually knew that she liked me." This leads the narrator to ponder

what people really want and to conclude it is "to experience strong emotions and they want to be loved." From there she meditates on the possibility that the world of scientific research is really a "substitute gratification . . . a substitute life" for those who have lost their sense of what life can and should be. (p. 28)

I think it is no accident that it is a woman who has written this beautiful but painful meditation on the human implications of nuclear technology. The book is infused with a feminist sensibility; the symbiotic interdependence of private and public life—what feminists used to mean by "the personal is the political"—is a given. Nor is there any doubt that it is men who have created the circumstances of the perilous modern existence which Chernobyl and Three Mile Island most frighteningly represent; men who have been socialized to fragment themselves so as to think of the hazards of nuclear technology only as a technical problem.

The image of Faust occurs throughout the novel as do passages like these:

> A list of activities which these men of science and technology presumably do not pursue or which, if forced upon them, they would consider a waste of time: Changing a baby's diapers. Cooking, shopping with a child on one's arm or in the baby carriage. Doing the laundry, hanging it up to dry, taking it down, folding it, ironing it, darning it. Sweeping the floor, mopping it, polishing it, vacuuming it. Dusting. Sewing. Knitting. Crocheting. Embroidering. Doing the dishes. Doing the dishes. Doing the dishes. Taking care of a sick child. Thinking up stories to tell. Singing songs.

Before male readers, who more and more do these things, explode in outrage, let me reassure them that Wolf is talking about traditional male behavior in a broad historic context. In fact, as a writer and an intellectual, the narrator includes herself in that passage. "And how many of these activities," she asks herself, "do I myself consider a waste of time?" It's a question all of us have asked ourselves. But for Wolf it functions primarily as a symbol of that aspect of the modern condition that fragments us, that separates us from what traditionally has been our relationship to nature and the life cycle. The narrator sees herself standing at a crossroads, loving what is clearly a lost past and fearing an unknown and ominous future.

Near the end of the book she tells of watching a television discussion of "the accident." It is as perceptive a comment on how the media work to reassure and mystify as I've read. "That evening," she says, "they put some gentlemen in front of the cameras who, solely on account of their nicely tailored gray or bluish-gray suits, the matching ties, the matching haircuts, their prudent choice of words and the whole official capacity of their posture, radiated a soothing effect." She reflects that most people watching—herself included—"after a hard day's work and [with] their beer—wine in my case, what of it? . . . want to be presented with something that makes them happy." "It would be unjust," she adds with irony, "to reproach them for this behavior merely because it contributes to our deaths."

While there is no resolution to the book's dilemma—how could there be?—it is, in a strange way, ultimately comforting. In its necessarily futile efforts to understand and come to terms with a terrifying situation, it becomes what it mourns, an experience of wholeness and integration. The narrator's very effort to face the meaning of nuclear power, to accept its unfathomability and yet to take responsibility for whatever can be understood or done, is cathartic and healing.

Wolf's sense of personal isolation may seem politically irresponsible to some. After all, we can protest, we can organize, we can act. But that is such a narrow reading of this profound and courageous work. Wolf is recording an experience of loss, impotence and terror. To read this novel is to plunge into that abyss in the best possible company. (pp. 28-9)

> *Elayne Rapping, "Coming to Terms with Terror,"*
> *in* The Nation, *New York, Vol. 249, No. 1, July 3,*
> *1989, pp. 28-9.*

□ Contemporary
Literary Criticism
Indexes

Literary Criticism Series
    Cumulative Author Index
Cumulative Nationality Index
Title Index, Volume 58

This Index Includes References to Entries in These Gale Series

Contemporary Literary Criticism

Presents excerpts of criticism on the works of novelists, poets, dramatists, short story writers, scriptwriters, and other creative writers who are now living or who have died since 1960. Cumulative indexes to authors and nationalities are included, as well as an index to titles discussed in the individual volume.

Twentieth-Century Literary Criticism

Contains critical excerpts by the most significant commentators on poets, novelists, short story writers, dramatists, and philosophers who died between 1900 and 1960. Cumulative indexes to authors, nationalities, and titles discussed are included in each new volume.

Nineteenth-Century Literature Criticism

Offers significant passages from criticism on authors who died between 1800 and 1899. Cumulative indexes to authors, nationalities, and titles discussed are included in each new volume.

Literature Criticism from 1400 to 1800

Compiles significant passages from the most noteworthy criticism on authors of the fifteenth through eighteenth centuries. Cumulative indexes to authors, nationalities, and titles discussed are included in each new volume.

Classical and Medieval Literature Criticism

Offers excerpts of criticism on the works of world authors from classical antiquity through the fourteenth century. Cumulative indexes to authors, titles, and critics are included in each volume.

Short Story Criticism

Compiles excerpts of criticism on short fiction by writers of all eras and nationalities. Cumulative indexes to authors, nationalities, and titles discussed are included in each new volume.

Children's Literature Review

Includes excerpts from reviews, criticism, and commentary on works of authors and illustrators who create books for children. Cumulative indexes to authors, nationalities, and titles discussed are included in each new volume.

Contemporary Authors Series

Encompasses five related series. *Contemporary Authors* provides biographical and bibliographical information on more than 92,000 writers of fiction, nonfiction, poetry, journalism, drama, motion pictures, and other fields. Each new volume contains sketches on authors not previously covered in the series. *Contemporary Authors New Revision Series* provides completely updated information on active authors covered in previously published volumes of *CA*. Only entries requiring significant change are revised for *CA New Revision Series*. *Contemporary Authors Permanent Series* consists of updated listings for deceased and inactive authors removed from the original volumes 9-36 when these volumes were revised. *Contemporary Authors Autobiography Series* presents specially commissioned autobiographies by leading contemporary writers. *Contemporary Authors Bibliographical Series* contains primary and secondary bibliographies as well as analytical bibliographical essays by authorities on major modern authors.

Dictionary of Literary Biography

Encompasses three related series. *Dictionary of Literary Biography* furnishes illustrated overviews of authors' lives and works and places them in the larger perspective of literary history. *Dictionary of Literary Biography Documentary Series* illuminates the careers of major figures through a selection of literary documents, including letters, notebook and diary entries, interviews, book reviews, and photographs. *Dictionary of Literary Biography Yearbook* summarizes the past year's literary activity with articles on genres, major prizes, conferences, and other timely subjects and includes updated and new entries on individual authors. A cumulative index to authors and articles is included in each new volume.

Concise Dictionary of American Literary Biography

A six-volume series that collects revised and updated sketches on major American authors that were originally presented in *Dictionary of Literary Biography*.

Something about the Author Series

Encompasses two related series. *Something about the Author* contains heavily illustrated biographical sketches on juvenile and young adult authors and illustrators from all eras. *Something about the Author Autobiography Series* presents specially commissioned autobiographies by prominent authors and illustrators of books for children and young adults.

Yesterday's Authors of Books for Children

Contains heavily illustrated entries on children's writers who died before 1961. Complete in two volumes.

Literary Criticism Series
Cumulative Author Index

This index lists all author entries in the Gale Literary Criticism Series and includes cross-references to other Gale sources. References in the index are identified as follows:

AAYA: *Authors & Artists for Young Adults,* Volumes 1-2
CAAS: *Contemporary Authors Autobiography Series,* Volumes 1-10
CA: *Contemporary Authors* (original series), Volumes 1-129
CABS: *Contemporary Authors Bibliographical Series,* Volumes 1-3
CANR: *Contemporary Authors New Revision Series,* Volumes 1-28
CAP: *Contemporary Authors Permanent Series,* Volumes 1-2
CA-R: *Contemporary Authors* (revised editions), Volumes 1-44
CDALB: *Concise Dictionary of American Literary Biography,* Volumes 1-6
CLC: *Contemporary Literary Criticism,* Volumes 1-58
CLR: *Children's Literature Review,* Volumes 1-20
CMLC: *Classical and Medieval Literature Criticism,* Volumes 1-4
DLB: *Dictionary of Literary Biography,* Volumes 1-90
DLB-DS: *Dictionary of Literary Biography Documentary Series,* Volumes 1-7
DLB-Y: *Dictionary of Literary Biography Yearbook,* Volumes 1980-1988
LC: *Literature Criticism from 1400 to 1800,* Volumes 1-12
NCLC: *Nineteenth-Century Literature Criticism,* Volumes 1-26
SAAS: *Something about the Author Autobiography Series,* Volumes 1-9
SATA: *Something about the Author,* Volumes 1-57
SSC: *Short Story Criticism,* Volumes 1-5
TCLC: *Twentieth-Century Literary Criticism,* Volumes 1-36
YABC: *Yesterday's Authors of Books for Children,* Volumes 1-2

Author Index

Powell, Padgett 1952-............ **CLC 34**
See also CA 126

Powers, J(ames) F(arl)
1917- .... **CLC 1, 4, 8, 57; SSC 4**
See also CANR 2; CA 1-4R

Pownall, David 1938-............ **CLC 10**
See also CA 89-92; DLB 14

Powys, John Cowper
1872-1963 .... **CLC 7, 9, 15, 46**
See also CA 85-88; DLB 15

Powys, T(heodore) F(rancis)
1875-1953 .... **TCLC 9**
See also CA 106; DLB 36

Prager, Emily 1952-............. **CLC 56**

Pratt, E(dwin) J(ohn) 1883-1964.... **CLC 19**
See also obituary CA 93-96

Premchand 1880-1936 .... **TCLC 21**

Preussler, Otfried 1923-........... **CLC 17**
See also CA 77-80; SATA 24

Prevert, Jacques (Henri Marie)
1900-1977 .... **CLC 15**
See also CA 77-80; obituary CA 69-72;
obituary SATA 30

Prevost, Abbe (Antoine Francois)
1697-1763 .... **LC 1**

Price, (Edward) Reynolds
1933-............ **CLC 3, 6, 13, 43, 50**
See also CANR 1; CA 1-4R; DLB 2

Price, Richard 1949- .... **CLC 6, 12**
See also CANR 3; CA 49-52; DLB-Y 81

Prichard, Katharine Susannah
1883-1969 .... **CLC 46**
See also CAP 1; CA 11-12

Priestley, J(ohn) B(oynton)
1894-1984 .... **CLC 2, 5, 9, 34**
See also CA 9-12R; obituary CA 113;
DLB 10, 34; DLB-Y 84

Prince (Rogers Nelson) 1958?- ..... **CLC 35**

Prince, F(rank) T(empleton) 1912- .. **CLC 22**
See also CA 101; DLB 20

Prior, Matthew 1664-1721........... **LC 4**

Pritchard, William H(arrison)
1932- .... **CLC 34**
See also CANR 23; CA 65-68

Pritchett, V(ictor) S(awdon)
1900- .... **CLC 5, 13, 15, 41**
See also CA 61-64; DLB 15

Procaccino, Michael 1946-
See Cristofer, Michael

Prokosch, Frederic 1908-1989.... **CLC 4, 48**
See also CA 73-76; DLB 48

Prose, Francine 1947-............. **CLC 45**
See also CA 109, 112

Proust, Marcel 1871-1922 .. **TCLC 7, 13, 33**
See also CA 104, 120; DLB 65

Pryor, Richard 1940-............. **CLC 26**
See also CA 122

Przybyszewski, Stanislaw
1868-1927 .... **TCLC 36**
See also DLB 66

Puig, Manuel 1932- .... **CLC 3, 5, 10, 28**
See also CANR 2; CA 45-48

Purdy, A(lfred) W(ellington)
1918- .... **CLC 3, 6, 14, 50**
See also CA 81-84

Purdy, James (Amos)
1923- .... **CLC 2, 4, 10, 28, 52**
See also CAAS 1; CANR 19; CA 33-36R;
DLB 2

Pushkin, Alexander (Sergeyevich)
1799-1837 .... **NCLC 3**

P'u Sung-ling 1640-1715 .... **LC 3**

Puzo, Mario 1920-........ **CLC 1, 2, 6, 36**
See also CANR 4; CA 65-68; DLB 6

Pym, Barbara (Mary Crampton)
1913-1980 .... **CLC 13, 19, 37**
See also CANR 13; CAP 1; CA 13-14;
obituary CA 97-100; DLB 14; DLB-Y 87

Pynchon, Thomas (Ruggles, Jr.)
1937- .... **CLC 2, 3, 6, 9, 11, 18, 33**
See also CANR 22; CA 17-20R; DLB 2

Quasimodo, Salvatore 1901-1968 ... **CLC 10**
See also CAP 1; CA 15-16;
obituary CA 25-28R

Queen, Ellery 1905-1982 .... **CLC 3, 11**
See also Dannay, Frederic; Lee, Manfred
B(ennington)

Queneau, Raymond
1903-1976 .... **CLC 2, 5, 10, 42**
See also CA 77-80; obituary CA 69-72;
DLB 72

Quin, Ann (Marie) 1936-1973....... **CLC 6**
See also CA 9-12R; obituary CA 45-48;
DLB 14

Quinn, Simon 1942-
See Smith, Martin Cruz
See also CANR 6, 23; CA 85-88

Quiroga, Horacio (Sylvestre)
1878-1937 .... **TCLC 20**
See also CA 117

Quoirez, Francoise 1935-
See Sagan, Francoise
See also CANR 6; CA 49-52

Rabe, David (William) 1940-... **CLC 4, 8, 33**
See also CA 85-88; DLB 7

Rabelais, Francois 1494?-1553........ **LC 5**

Rabinovitch, Sholem 1859-1916
See Aleichem, Sholom
See also CA 104

Rachen, Kurt von 1911-1986
See Hubbard, L(afayette) Ron(ald)

Radcliffe, Ann (Ward) 1764-1823 .. **NCLC 6**
See also DLB 39

Radiguet, Raymond 1903-1923 .... **TCLC 29**

Radnoti, Miklos 1909-1944 .... **TCLC 16**
See also CA 118

Rado, James 1939-............... **CLC 17**
See also CA 105

Radomski, James 1932-
See Rado, James

Radvanyi, Netty Reiling 1900-1983
See Seghers, Anna
See also CA 85-88; obituary CA 110

Rae, Ben 1935-
See Griffiths, Trevor

Raeburn, John 1941- .... **CLC 34**
See also CA 57-60

Ragni, Gerome 1942-............. **CLC 17**
See also CA 105

Rahv, Philip 1908-1973 .... **CLC 24**
See also Greenberg, Ivan

Raine, Craig 1944-............... **CLC 32**
See also CA 108; DLB 40

Raine, Kathleen (Jessie) 1908- ... **CLC 7, 45**
See also CA 85-88; DLB 20

Rainis, Janis 1865-1929 .... **TCLC 29**

Rakosi, Carl 1903-............... **CLC 47**
See also Rawley, Callman
See also CAAS 5

Ramos, Graciliano 1892-1953 ..... **TCLC 32**

Rampersad, Arnold 19??-.......... **CLC 44**

Ramuz, Charles-Ferdinand
1878-1947 .... **TCLC 33**

Rand, Ayn 1905-1982........ **CLC 3, 30, 44**
See also CA 13-16R; obituary CA 105

Randall, Dudley (Felker) 1914-...... **CLC 1**
See also CANR 23; CA 25-28R; DLB 41

Ransom, John Crowe
1888-1974 .... **CLC 2, 4, 5, 11, 24**
See also CANR 6; CA 5-8R;
obituary CA 49-52; DLB 45, 63

Rao, Raja 1909-.............. **CLC 25, 56**
See also CA 73-76

Raphael, Frederic (Michael)
1931-.................... **CLC 2, 14**
See also CANR 1; CA 1-4R; DLB 14

Rathbone, Julian 1935- .... **CLC 41**
See also CA 101

Rattigan, Terence (Mervyn)
1911-1977 .... **CLC 7**
See also CA 85-88; obituary CA 73-76;
DLB 13

Ratushinskaya, Irina 1954-........ **CLC 54**

Raven, Simon (Arthur Noel)
1927-...................... **CLC 14**
See also CA 81-84

Rawley, Callman 1903-
See Rakosi, Carl
See also CANR 12; CA 21-24R

Rawlings, Marjorie Kinnan
1896-1953 .... **TCLC 4**
See also YABC 1; CA 104; DLB 9, 22

Ray, Satyajit 1921-............... **CLC 16**
See also CA 114

Read, Herbert (Edward) 1893-1968 .. **CLC 4**
See also CA 85-88; obituary CA 25-28R;
DLB 20

Read, Piers Paul 1941- ...... **CLC 4, 10, 25**
See also CA 21-24R; SATA 21; DLB 14

Reade, Charles 1814-1884 .... **NCLC 2**
See also DLB 21

Reade, Hamish 1936-
See Gray, Simon (James Holliday)

Reading, Peter 1946-.......... **CLC 47**
See also CA 103; DLB 40

Reaney, James 1926-............. **CLC 13**
See also CA 41-44R; SATA 43; DLB 68

Rebreanu, Liviu 1885-1944 .... **TCLC 28**

Author Index

Author Index

CLC Cumulative Nationality Index

ALBANIAN
Kadare, Ismail **52**

ALGERIAN
Camus, Albert **1, 2, 4, 9, 11, 14, 32**
Cohen-Solal, Annie **50**

AMERICAN
Abbey, Edward **36**
Abbott, Lee K., Jr. **48**
Abish, Walter **22**
Abrahams, Peter **4**
Abrams, M. H. **24**
Acker, Kathy **45**
Adams, Alice **6, 13, 46**
Addams, Charles **30**
Adler, C. S. **35**
Adler, Renata **8, 31**
Ai **4, 14**
Aiken, Conrad **1, 3, 5, 10, 52**
Albee, Edward **1, 2, 3, 5, 9, 11, 13, 25, 53**
Alexander, Lloyd **35**
Algren, Nelson **4, 10, 33**
Allen, Woody **16, 52**
Alta **19**
Alter, Robert B. **34**
Alther, Lisa **7, 41**
Altman, Robert **16**
Ammons, A. R. **2, 3, 5, 8, 9, 25, 57**
Anaya, Rudolfo A. **23**
Anderson, Jon **9**
Anderson, Poul **15**
Anderson, Robert **23**
Angell, Roger **26**
Angelou, Maya **12, 35**
Anthony, Piers **35**
Apple, Max **9, 33**
Appleman, Philip **51**
Archer, Jules **12**

Arnow, Harriette **2, 7, 18**
Arrick, Fran **30**
Ashbery, John **2, 3, 4, 6, 9, 13, 15, 25, 41**
Asimov, Isaac **1, 3, 9, 19, 26**
Auchincloss, Louis **4, 6, 9, 18, 45**
Auden, W. H. **1, 2, 3, 4, 6, 9, 11, 14, 43**
Auel, Jean M. **31**
Auster, Paul **47**
Bach, Richard **14**
Baker, Elliott **8**
Baker, Russell **31**
Bakshi, Ralph **26**
Baldwin, James **1, 2, 3, 4, 5, 8, 13, 15, 17, 42, 50**
Bambara, Toni Cade **19**
Banks, Russell **37**
Baraka, Imamu Amiri **1, 2, 3, 5, 10, 14, 33**
Barbera, Jack **44**
Barnard, Mary **48**
Barnes, Djuna **3, 4, 8, 11, 29**
Barrett, William **27**
Barth, John **1, 2, 3, 5, 7, 9, 10, 14, 27, 51**
Barthelme, Donald **1, 2, 3, 5, 6, 8, 13, 23, 46**
Barthelme, Frederick **36**
Barzun, Jacques **51**
Baumbach, Jonathan **6, 23**
Bausch, Richard **51**
Baxter, Charles **45**
Beagle, Peter S. **7**
Beattie, Ann **8, 13, 18, 40**
Becker, Walter **26**
Beecher, John **6**
Behrman, S. N. **40**
Belitt, Ben **22**
Bell, Madison Smartt **41**
Bell, Marvin **8, 31**
Bellow, Saul **1, 2, 3, 6, 8, 10, 13, 15, 25, 33, 34**

Benary-Isbert, Margot **12**
Benchley, Peter **4, 8**
Benedikt, Michael **4, 14**
Benford, Gregory **52**
Bennett, Hal **5**
Bennett, Jay **35**
Benson, Jackson J. **34**
Benson, Sally **17**
Bentley, Eric **24**
Berger, Melvin **12**
Berger, Thomas **3, 5, 8, 11, 18, 38**
Bergstein, Eleanor **4**
Berriault, Gina **54**
Berrigan, Daniel J. **4**
Berrigan, Ted **37**
Berry, Chuck **17**
Berry, Wendell **4, 6, 8, 27, 46**
Berryman, John **1, 2, 3, 4, 6, 8, 10, 13, 25**
Bessie, Alvah **23**
Betts, Doris **3, 6, 28**
Bidart, Frank **33**
Bishop, Elizabeth **1, 4, 9, 13, 15, 32**
Bishop, John **10**
Blackburn, Paul **9, 43**
Blackmur, R. P. **2, 24**
Blaise, Clark **29**
Blatty, William Peter **2**
Blessing, Lee **54**
Blish, James **14**
Bloch, Robert **33**
Bloom, Harold **24**
Blount, Roy, Jr. **38**
Blume, Judy **12, 30**
Bly, Robert **1, 2, 5, 10, 15, 38**
Bochco, Steven **35**
Bogan, Louise **4, 39, 46**
Bogosian, Eric **45**
Bograd, Larry **35**
Bonham, Frank **12**

Nationality Index

Nationality Index

Nationality Index

Nationality Index

Nationality Index

CLC-58 Title Index